MAP OF OHIO
SHOWING COUNTY SEATS

McDERMOTT'S
OHIO REAL PROPERTY
LAW AND PRACTICE

by

THOMAS J. McDERMOTT

FOURTH EDITION

by

SHERMAN S. HOLLANDER

Volume 1

THE MICHIE COMPANY
Law Publishers
CHARLOTTESVILLE, VIRGINIA

DEDICATED TO THE MEMORY
OF
SHERMAN S. HOLLANDER

Senior Partner
Salim, Hollander, Esper & Nolfi
Cleveland, Ohio

Lawyer, Scholar, Author, Lecturer, and Gentleman,

whose diligent efforts, extensive knowledge and mastery of his subject made possible this comprehensive revision of a standard text — **Ohio Real Property Law and Practice.**

During his term as President of the Ohio Title Association, as Chairman of the Ohio State Bar Association, Real Estate Section, and as a practicing lawyer, Sherman was never too busy to share his real estate expertise with anyone who sought his guidance.

He touched us all deeply and we shall miss him greatly.

Edward N. Salim
Thomas L. Esper

Cleveland, Ohio
April 1988

iii

TABLE OF CONTENTS
Volume 1

Dedication
Foreword
Citations

CHAPTER 3: BOUNDARIES AND DESCRIPTIONS

DIVISION 3-1: IN GENERAL

CHAPTER 5: COTENANCY AND JOINT OWNERSHIP

DIVISION 5-1: IN GENERAL

CHAPTER 7: CROPS AND OTHER GROWING THINGS

DIVISION 7-1: IN GENERAL

CHAPTER 8: DEEDS

DIVISION 8-1: IN GENERAL

DIVISION 8-2: ACKNOWLEDGMENT

CHAPTER 9: DESCENT AND WILLS

DIVISION 9-1: DESCENT

CHAPTER 10: EASEMENTS

DIVISION 10-1: IN GENERAL

CHAPTER 11: ESTATES AND FUTURE INTERESTS

DIVISION 11-1: IN GENERAL

CHAPTER 13: FIXTURES

DIVISION 13-1: IN GENERAL

CHAPTER 14: HUSBAND AND WIFE

DIVISION 14-1: IN GENERAL

CHAPTER 15:   INFANTS, INSANE PERSONS AND OTHER INCOMPETENTS

DIVISION 15-1:   IN GENERAL

CHAPTER 16: JUDGMENTS

DIVISION 16-1: IN GENERAL

TABLE OF CONTENTS

DIVISION 16-7: PROCESS AND ITS SERVICE

CHAPTER 17: JUDICIAL SALES

DIVISION 17-1: IN GENERAL

TABLE OF CONTENTS

DIVISION 17-2: PARTIES; PROCEDURE

DIVISION 17-3: BANKRUPTCY

TABLE OF CONTENTS

DIVISION 17-4: OTHER CLASSES OF PROCEEDINGS

FOREWORD

In 1950 Thomas J. McDermott authored the first edition of **Ohio Real Property Law and Practice.** Now in its fourth edition, it recognizes the course of development of real property law practice in Ohio and perpetuates the treatise as the standard in the field.

This edition reflects changes in the law since the last revision in 1980, preserving much of the authority provided throughout the earlier editions, and enhancing such with statutory changes and inclusion of the significant cases and important collateral references necessary to the efficient practice of real property law in Ohio.

The Publisher

CITATIONS

Citations to other works are abbreviated in this treatise as follows:

Am Jur: American Jurisprudence (Bancroft-Whitney Co., San Francisco, Calif., and The Lawyers Co-operative Pub. Co., Rochester, N.Y.)

Am Jur 2d: American Jurisprudence, Second Edition (Bancroft-Whitney Co., San Francisco, Calif., and The Lawyers Co-operative Pub. Co., Rochester, N.Y.)

Am Law of Prop: American Law of Property, Casner ed. 1954 (Little, Brown and Co., Boston, Mass.)

ALR: American Law Reports (Bancroft-Whitney Co., San Francisco, Calif., and The Lawyers Co-operative Pub. Co., Rochester, N.Y.)

ALR2d: American Law Reports, Second Series (Bancroft-Whitney Co., San Francisco, Calif., and The Lawyers Co-operative Pub. Co., Rochester, N.Y.)

ALR3d: American Law Reports, Third Series (Bancroft-Whitney Co., San Francisco, Calif., and The Lawyers Co-operative Pub. Co., Rochester, N.Y.)

ALR4th: American Law Reports, Fourth Series (Bancroft-Whitney Co., San Francisco, Calif., and The Lawyers Co-operative Pub. Co., Rochester, N.Y.)

CJS: Corpus Juris Secundum (The American Law Book Co., Brooklyn, N.Y.)

O Jur 2d: Ohio Jurisprudence, Second Series (The Lawyers Co-operative Pub. Co., Rochester, N.Y.)

O Jur 3d: Ohio Jurisprudence, Third Series (The Lawyers Co-operative Pub. Co., Rochester, N.Y.)

Powell: Powell, Real Property (Matthew Bender and Co., Inc., Albany, N.Y.)

Restatement, Property: Restatement of the Law of Property (American Law Institute Publishers, St. Paul, Minn.)

Simes and Smith: Simes and Smith, Law of Future Interests, 2d ed. 1956 (West Pub. Co., St. Paul, Minn.)

Tiffany: Tiffany, Real Property, 3d ed. 1939 (Callaghan and Co., Chicago, Ill.)

CHAPTER 1: ABSTRACTS AND RECORDS OF TITLE

DIVISION 1-1: ABSTRACTS AND OTHER EVIDENCES OF TITLE

DIVISION 1-2: RECORDS AND RECORDING LAWS

DIVISION 1-1:   ABSTRACTS AND OTHER EVIDENCES OF TITLE

SECTION 1-11: ABSTRACTS OF TITLE

1-11A   Definitions.

"An abstract of title is a memorandum or concise statement, in orderly form, of the substance of documents or facts, appearing on the public records, which affect the title to real property." State ex rel. Doria v. Ferguson, 145 OS 12, 60 NE2d 476, 478, 30 OO 241 (1945).

An abstract of title may be described as a methodically written history of the title to a specific tract of land. It consists of a summary of the material parts of all conveyances, transfers, proceedings and other facts of record which affect or may affect the title, including extinguished encumbrances. These facts, together with reference maps, are arranged in chronological order to show the origin, course and incidents of the ownership without the necessity of examining the public records or the original instruments.

A limited abstract of title is one covering only a given period of time instead of beginning with the conveyance from the government.

1-11B   Methods of Preparation.

Legal liability, see Section 1-42.
Methods of searching, see 1-41D.

An abstract of title is made by abstracting the public records, that is to say, by setting forth only the material parts or substance of the pertinent records. The indexes to be searched and the records to be abstracted are the same as those used in a title examination made directly from the public records.

Discrepancies on record should be underscored to indicate they are not errors of the abstracter. Omissions (such as no statement of marital status, missing links in the chain, and lack of service of process) should be noted in order to avoid unnecessary questions from the examiner.

3

A competent abstractor must have a thorough knowledge in order to determine which parts of the record are material to the title. He must have the skill to show and arrange the material matters for the convenience of the examiner. Accuracy and care are his indispensable qualifications. He should keep in mind that the purpose of the abstract is to enable the examiner to make a complete opinion on the record title from the abstract alone.

The diversity of practices between the counties of the state makes a detailed consideration of the methods of preparing an abstract of title impracticable for this book. However, each chapter herein treats of matters which are material to titles and which are, therefore, within the scope of the knowledge and skill required of an abstracter.

1-11C   Essentials of an Abstract of Title.

It should be kept in mind that the purpose of an abstract of title is to enable the examiner to write a complete opinion on the title without referring further to the record or to the abstracter.

The caption should contain: a full and accurate description of the subject land (also being sufficient for transfer on the tax records); a showing that the manuscript is an abstract of title; and a statement of the commencement of the period covered, unless the period is stated in the certificate.

A map of the premises follows the caption description. Reference maps, showing the various descriptions and locating the subject land with reference to the boundaries of such descriptions, are placed in the abstract wherever necessary for the information and convenience of the examiner.

The description in a conveyance may be omitted when it is verbatim with a description referred to, but a different description should not be omitted although there is a statement of the abstracter that it describes the same land.

If a deed does not show the marital status of persons who are grantors, a note should so state.

The operative words of the granting clause and of the habendum clause are frequently omitted when it is certified that a fee simple is conveyed unless otherwise noted.

An acknowledgment is ordinarily shown by a statement of the place of acknowledgment together with the number of witnesses, if any are required.

The cancellation of a mortgage should be shown in full. The authority of a fiduciary canceling a mortgage must be shown. A canceled mortgage may be abstracted briefly.

The terms of an unexpired lease should be set forth in considerable detail, especially any options to renew or to purchase. If the lease is very long it may be abstracted briefly and reference made to the record.

Involuntary liens which are dormant or expired are omitted in some communities, but if that is done the certificate should so state.

The essentials of administration of estates vary widely according to the facts in the particular case. Wills should be shown in full in all cases.

4

Showing the docket entries of a judicial proceeding is not sufficient. The return of service of summons and the jurisdictional facts for service by publication should be fully set forth. Pleadings should usually be abstracted, and decrees of confirmation and other judgments shown in full.

The certificates states what the abstracter has done and determines his liability. It should have at least a clear statement that the foregoing abstract of title contains a correct and complete abstract of all matters of record in the county which affect the title to the subject premises.

SECTION 1-12: CERTIFICATES OF TITLE

1-12A Definition.

Examination of title in general, see Division 1-4.

A certificate of title is the written opinion of a lawyer that the title to the land described therein is marketable and unencumbered as appears of record except only the defects and encumbrances set forth. It may be based upon an abstract of title or upon a direct examination of the public records.

A layman or a corporation may not make a certificate of title because doing so is practicing law. See Unauthorized Practice of Law at 1-41H.

1-12B Contents.

Standard of Title Examination

(Adopted by Ohio State Bar Association in 1952)

Problem 2.3A:
What should a report on title contain?

Standard 2.3A:
The certificate or opinion should include:
(1) The period of time of the examination.
(2) That the opinion is based on an abstract of title or is based on an examination of the public records of _____ County, Ohio, as disclosed by the public indexes relating to the premises.
(3) That the opinion or certificate does not purport to cover the following:
(a) Matters not of record,
(b) Rights of persons in possession,
(c) Questions which a correct survey or inspection of the premises would disclose,
(d) Rights to file mechanics' liens,
(e) Special taxes and assessments now shown by the county treasurer's records,
(f) Zoning and other governmental regulations.
(4) An opinion or certification that the _____ title is vested in _____ by instrument of record, recorded in _____ Records, Volume ____, Page ____.

(5) That the title is marketable and free from encumbrances except those matters set forth.

(6) Clear and concise language setting forth the defects and encumbrances.

SECTION 1-13: TITLE GUARANTEES

1-13A Generally.

A title guarantee (also known as a guaranty of title) is an indemnity contract by which the title company guarantees, not to exceed the given amount, that the title to the described land is good and unencumbered of record in the named owner except only the defects and encumbrances set forth. This kind of title evidence is distinguished from a certificate of title in that absence of negligence is not a defense against liability thereon. It is distinguished from a title insurance policy in being protection only against matters which appear of record.

SECTION 1-14: TITLE INSURANCE POLICIES

Title insurance companies, see 4-29C.

1-14A Definition.

A title insurance policy is an indemnity contract whereby the title insurance company insures the owner of an interest in the described real estate against damage as set forth in the policy. The principal forms are: an owner's policy insuring the owner of the fee simple title; a mortgagee's policy insuring the holder of a mortgage on the premises; and a lessee's policy insuring the owner of a leasehold interest in the premises. The single premium is payable when the policy is issued.

1-14B Protection.

A policy of title insurance obligates the title insurance company to pay any loss, up to a fixed amount and as provided in the policy, which is suffered by the insured because of defects in title or encumbrances thereon existing at the date of the policy and not excepted therein. The company agrees to defend against alleged defects and encumbrances, and to pay the expenses of litigation, although the adverse claims are invalid. The insured is protected after he has conveyed the property with a warranty. The protection extends to the heirs and devisees of the insured but is generally not assignable.

The policy protects against omissions of the abstracter and errors of the title examiner, and also against the many claims which may be enforceable over the rights of a bona fide purchaser although the claims are not of record. For a description of such claims, see 1-32H.

Although insuring against valid claims, some policies do not insure against loss from the title being unmarketable. Such a loss can occur, even though the adverse claim is unenforceable, as when the purchaser refuses to perform the contract on the ground of unmarketability.

LAW IN GENERAL

The fundamental rule applies, whether the insured is the owner or a mortgagee, that recovery within the policy limits is for the actual damage or loss sustained from a defect or encumbrance affecting his title which was not excepted from the policy's coverage. It has also been held that the face amount of the policy does not limit liability for negligence. 60 ALR2d 972.

A defect, lien, or encumbrance is "created, suffered, assumed, or agreed to" by the insured if it is a result of some illegal or inequitable dealings by the insured, but not if brought about by his accidental or innocent conduct. 87 ALR3d 515.

DIVISION 1-2: RECORDS AND RECORDING LAWS

SECTION 1-21: INTRODUCTION; RECORDING ACTS GENERALLY

Lis pendens, see Section 17-12.
Period of the search, see 1-31D.
Records to be searched, see 1-41D.

1-21A Theory of the Recording Acts.

Bona fide purchaser, see Section 1-32.

R.C. 5301.25 provides: "(A) All deeds, land contracts referred to in division (B)(2) of section 317.08 of the Revised Code, and instruments of writing properly executed for the conveyance or encumbrance of lands, tenements, or hereditaments, other than as provided in section 5301.23 of the Revised Code, shall be recorded in the office of the county recorder of the county in which the premises are situated, and until so recorded or filed for record, they are fraudulent, so far as relates to a subsequent bona fide purchaser having, at the time of purchase, no knowledge of the existence of such former deed or land contract or instrument.

"(B) Whenever a survey is made of lands which are being conveyed, the county recorder shall require that the name of the person who made the survey appear in the deed. Such name shall either be printed, typewritten, stamped, or signed in a legible manner. An instrument is in compliance with this section if it contains a statement in the following form:

"'A survey of this property was made by _____,
(Name)

"Division (B) of this section does not apply to any court decree, order, judgment, or writ, nor to any instrument executed or acknowledged outside of this state, or executed within this state prior to September 20, 1965." (As eff. 10-27-81.)

No substantial change has been made in this statute since 1885 except that the clause as to land contracts was added in 1961 and division (B) in 1965.

Section 5301.23 provides that mortgages take effect from the time they are delivered to the recorder for recording.

The general theory of the recording act is that a bona fide purchaser is protected against unrecorded conveyances and encumbrances if he does not have actual notice at the time of the purchase. An exception to the rule is that mortgages do not take effect until filed for record.

1-21B Effect of Recording.

See Division 1-3 for chain of title, notice, priorities, and rights of bona fide purchaser.

When not entitled to record, see 1-31E.

R.C. 5301.39 provides that the court shall make an order for record in the office of the county recorder when a lien is released or a title is changed by a judgment or decree and provides for cases where the recorder requires a separate instrument of release. (As eff. 12-17-73.)

This statutory provision is merely directory and such entry on the record is not essential to remove a mortgage as a cloud upon the title when a proper foreclosure sale has been had. Walker v. Scott, 7 App 335, 29 CC(NS) 89 (1914). No legal effect results from the recording in the office of the county recorder of any judgment or decree rendered by a court of the same county.

As between the grantor and his grantee the deed conveys valid title although not recorded. Harris v. Paul, 37 App 206, 174 NE 615, 9 Abs 201, 33 OLR 586 (1930).

Further research: O Jur 2d, Records and Recording Laws § 37.

LAW IN GENERAL

The effect of recording acts is to give constructive notice to all persons dealing with the land of properly recorded instruments in the chain of title. Constructive notice is also given of presently outstanding claims if such claims are entitled to record and recorded during the period of record ownership of the person under whom the claim is made. A stray deed or other interloping conveyance, being one from a stranger to the record chain of title, is not constructive notice and generally does not make a title unmarketable, but its recitals or the circumstances may be such as to put on inquiry a purchaser having actual notice of such conveyance. Am Law of Prop § 1878; Tiffany § 1265.

Recording is not essential to the validity of a conveyance as between the parties, unless so provided by statute. The recording of an instrument does not give it any greater effect than it has between the parties, and therefore an instrument invalid between the parties does not affect the rights of third persons. Am Jur 2d, Records and Recording Laws § 98; CJS, Records § 32; Tiffany § 1276.

Recording charges with notice only subsequent purchasers and encumbrancers; for example, a mortgagee is not charged with notice of a record subsequent to the mortgage, or a grantor does not have constructive notice of alterations made in a deed by the grantee. Tiffany § 1275.

1-21C Records as Evidence.

R.C. 2127.35, quoted at 12-14S, in part provides for confirmation of sale under the probate code and order to make a deed. "The deed shall be received in all courts as prima-facie evidence that the executor, administrator, or guardian in all respects observed the direction of the court, and complied with the requirements of the law, and shall convey the interest in the real estate directed to be sold by the court, and shall vest title to the interest in the purchaser as if conveyed by the deceased in his lifetime, or by the ward free from disability, and by the owners of the remaining interests in the real estate." (As eff. 1-1-76.)

R.C. 2329.37 provides: "The deed provided for in section 2329.36 of the Revised Code shall be prima facie evidence of the legality and regularity of the sale. All the estate and interest of the person whose property the officer so professed to sell and convey, whether it existed at the time the property became liable to satisfy the judgment, or was acquired afterward, shall be vested in the purchaser by such sale." (As eff. 10-1-53.) Section 2329.36 provides for deeds made by officers pursuant to order of the court of common pleas.

R.C. 5301.43 provides: "A copy of the record of a deed or other instrument of writing, certified by the county recorder with his official seal affixed thereto, shall be received in all courts and places within this state, as prima-facie evidence of the existence of such instrument, and as conclusive evidence of the existence of such record." (As eff. 10-1-53.)

Further research: O Jur 2d, Records and Recording Laws § 11.

LAW IN GENERAL

Records made under authority of the recording laws are generally admissible as primary evidence even in the absence of a statute so providing. The rule applies to recitals which are properly a part of the recorded instrument. Presumptions arise to support the validity of instruments properly of record. Am Law of Prop § 17.34.

1-21D Effective Date of Record.

When all the requisites have been performed which authorize a recording officer to record any instrument whatever, it is in law considered as recorded, although the manual labor of writing it in a book kept for that purpose has not been performed. King v. Kenny, 4 Ohio 79, 83 (1829).

Deed was held prior to judgments where deed was delivered to recorder on 15th but entered as of 19th and judgments were on the 18th. Hoffman, Burneston & Co. v. Mackall, 5 OS 124 (1855).

9

The presumption is that the endorsement speaks the truth, but the true time of delivery may be shown. H. B. Clafflin Co. v. Evans, 55 OS 183, 45 NE 3 (1896).

Consecutive file numbers by county recorder are not for the purpose of establishing priority. Endorsed filing time will prevail unless contrary evidence is clear and convincing. Franks v. Moore, 48 App 403, 194 NE 39, 1 OO 582, 16 Abs 585 (1933); Himelright v. Franks, 16 Abs 103 (App. 1933).

The time of filing for record, not the time of actual copying, is the operative date of the recording.

1-21E   Place and Manner of Recording.

Errors of recording officer, see also Section 1-25.

R.C. 9.01 provides that any office or officer of the state or of any political subdivision who is authorized to record or keep any record or instrument may record or copy the same by various photographic and other processes. (As eff. 7-1-85.)

R.C. 307.58 and 317.17 provide for transcribing, upon order of county commissioners, of records of county recorder and that the records so made shall have the same force as the original records. (As eff. 10-1-53.)

R.C. 317.11 provides that the recorder may refuse to receive an instrument for record if a signature is illegible unless such name is printed, typewritten or stamped thereon, or unless an affidavit thereon or attached shows correct name; it does not apply to an instrument executed or acknowledged outside Ohio. (As eff. 10-1-53.)

R.C. 317.111 provides: "No instrument by which the title to real estate or personal property, or any interest therein or lien thereon, is conveyed, created, encumbered, assigned, or otherwise disposed of, shall be received for record or filing by the county recorder unless the name of the person who, and governmental agency, if any, which, prepared such instrument appears at the conclusion of such instrument and such name is either printed, typewritten, stamped, or signed in a legible manner. An instrument is in compliance with this section if it contains a statement in the following form: 'This instrument was prepared by (name).

"This section does not apply to any instrument executed prior to October 5, 1955, nor to the following: any decree, order, judgment, or writ of any court; any will or death certificate; any instrument executed or acknowledged outside of this state." (As eff. 1-1-61.)

R.C. 317.112 requires that instruments submitted to the county recorder for recording or filing "be of a quality of paper that permits the legible reproduction of the instrument by photographic or microphotographic processes" and also that the contents be sufficiently legible to permit photographic reproduction. The recorder may require, as a condition of accepting a document which fails to meet legibility requirements, that the instrument have attached a true copy certified as such. (As eff. 1-1-81.)

R.C. 5301.37 provides: "Whenever the county recorder in making photostatic or photographic records leaves no margin suitable for the entering or recording of assignments, cancellations, or further transactions relating to the instruments so recorded, or whenever such margin is completely filled with assignments, cancellations, or further transactions relating to the instruments so recorded, such transaction shall be effected by separate instruments executed and recorded according to law." (As eff. 10-1-53.)

Entries made on the margin of the record book by the recorder are not part of the original papers and do not affect the title. Foster v. Dugan, 8 Ohio 87 (1837).

Upon division of a county, records of the former county affecting land in the new county continue to be constructive notice. Davidson v. Root, 11 Ohio 98 (1841).

A deed from Lemuel Granger, recorded by mistake as Samuel Granger, will not be notice to a subsequent purchaser without actual notice, but such purchaser will hold the land as against the title of the former purchaser. Jennings v. Wood, 20 Ohio 261 (1851).

Where the record of the first mortgage described the premises as the southeast quarter instead of the southwest quarter by a mistake of the recorder, it cannot be said that the second mortgagee was bound to take notice of the first mortgage from the record, or that the record was sufficient to put him upon inquiry. The lien is not defeated as to a subsequent encumbrancer with notice in fact. Brown v. Kirkman, 1 OS 116 (1853).

A mortgage recorded in the "record of deeds," and indexed in the general index with the letters "mtg." annexed, is operative as a mortgage against a subsequent purchaser for value without actual notice of said mortgage. Smith v. Smith, 13 OS 532 (1862).

An easement for a gas pipeline improperly recorded in the lease records is sufficient as constructive notice to subsequent purchasers of the servient estate. Roebuck v. Columbia Gas Transmission Corp., 57 App2d 217, 386 NE2d 1363, 11 OO3d 256 (1977).

The county recorder is not authorized to record a lease containing a map by pasting the map on the record. 1936 OAG 5650.

Further research: O Jur 2d, Records and Recording Laws § 31.

LAW IN GENERAL

Instruments must be recorded in the county where the land lies at the time of recordation. They remain constructive notice when the land is subsequently included within the boundaries of another county. Am Jur 2d, Records and Recording Laws § 74.

An instrument is generally notice only as it appears of record, although a subsequent purchaser is bound to take notice of an error apparent on the face of the record. Under the minority rule, the grantee is protected against errors in recording. Under the majority rule, usually followed in Ohio, the record of an instrument recorded in the wrong book or a record showing an invalid instrument is not constructive notice. Am Jur 2d, Records and Recording Laws § 130; Am Law of Prop §§ 17.31, 18.13; Tiffany § 1273.

SECTION 1-22: CURATIVE ACTS

1-22A Generally.

The several curative statutes are shown herein at their appropriate topics. All of them may be found through use of the index.

LAW IN GENERAL

Although retroactive, a curative act is binding on persons becoming purchasers subsequent to the enactment, and on parties to an instrument or proceeding which is valid between the parties, when the act cures defects in the formalities required for judicial or statutory proceedings. These acts are valid if they merely change a rule of evidence or dispense with requirements as the legislature could have done originally. However, such a statute is unconstitutional and ineffective insofar as it waives requirements essential to jurisdiction of the court, or insofar as making records constructive notice impairs vested rights of innocent third parties who paid a consideration. In order to accomplish their purpose fully, curative acts should operate both to make the instrument admissible in evidence and to make it constructive notice. Am Law of Prop §§ 12.84, 18.40, 18.94.

SECTION 1-23: CUSTODY AND USE OF RECORDS

1-23A Rights to Inspect and Use.

R.C. 149.43 provides: "(A) As used in this section:

"(1) 'Public record' means any record that is kept by any public office, including, but not limited to, state, county, city, village, township, and school district units, except medical records, records pertaining to adoption, probation, and parole proceedings, records pertaining to actions under section 2151.85 of the Revised Code and to appeals of actions arising under that section, records listed in division (A) of section 3107.42 of the Revised Code, trial preparation records, confidential law enforcement investigatory records, and records the release of which is prohibited by state or federal law.

"(2) 'Confidential law enforcement investigatory record' means any record that pertains to a law enforcement matter of a criminal, quasi-criminal, civil, or administrative nature, but only to the extent that the release of the record would create a high probability of disclosure of any of the following:

"(a) The identity of a suspect who has not been charged with the offense to which the record pertains, or of an information source or witness to whom confidentiality has been reasonably promised;

"(b) Information provided by an information source or witness to whom confidentiality has been reasonably promised, which information would reasonably tend to disclose his identity;

12

"(c) Specific confidential investigatory techniques or procedures or specific investigatory work product;

"(d) Information that would endanger the life or physical safety of law enforcement personnel, a crime victim, a witness, or a confidential information source.

"(3) 'Medical record' means any document or combination of documents, except births, deaths, and the fact of admission to or discharge from a hospital, that pertains to the medical history, diagnosis, prognosis, or medical condition of a patient and that is generated and maintained in the process of medical treatment.

"(4) 'Trial preparation record' means any record that contains information that is specifically compiled in reasonable anticipation of, or in defense of, a civil or criminal action or proceeding, including the independent thought processes and personal trial preparation of an attorney.

"(B) All public records shall be promptly prepared and made available for inspection to any person at all reasonable times during regular business hours. Upon request, a person responsible for public records shall make copies available at cost, within a reasonable period of time. In order to facilitate broader access to public records, governmental units shall maintain public records in such a manner that they can be made available for inspection in accordance with this division.

"(C) If a person allegedly is aggrieved by the failure of a governmental unit to promptly prepare a public record and to make it available to him for inspection in accordance with division (B) of this section, or if a person who has requested a copy of a public record allegedly is aggrieved by the failure of a person responsible for it to make a copy available to him in accordance with division (B) of this section, the person allegedly aggrieved may commence a mandamus action to obtain a judgment that orders the governmental unit or the person responsible for the public record to comply with division (B) of this section and that awards reasonable attorney's fees to the person that instituted the mandamus action. The mandamus action may be commenced in the court of common pleas of the county in which division (B) of this section allegedly was not complied with, in the supreme court pursuant to its original jurisdiction under Section 2 of Article IV, Ohio Constitution, or in the court of appeals for the appellate district in which division (B) of this section allegedly was not complied with pursuant to its original jurisdiction under Section 3 of Article IV, Ohio Constitution.

"(D) Chapter 1347 of the Revised Code does not limit the provisions of this section." (As eff. 10-15-87.)

The public use of a public record is subject to the limitation that it must not endanger the safety of the record, or unreasonably interfere with the discharge of the duties of the officer charged with custody of the same. And, conceding the general rule as to the right of an abstracter or insurer of titles to have access to the office of a clerk or register for the purpose of inspecting or copying the public records, the exercise of such right is, nevertheless, subject to any reasonable rules and regulations which the clerk or register may make with respect to the use and occupancy of his office. State ex rel. Louisville Title Ins. Co. v. Brewer, 147 OS 161, 70 NE2d 265, 34 OO 36 (1946).

Microfilm copies of public records must be made available for duplication by the public by a method chosen by the recorder and the costs charged shall be reasonable. Lorain County Title Co. v. Essex, 53 App2d 274, 373 NE2d 1261, 7 OO3d 330 (1976).

Further research: O Jur 2d, Records and Recording Laws § 21.

LAW IN GENERAL

Any person interested in public records may inspect or copy them, but subject to such reasonable regulations as may be prescribed by the custodian of the records. The right is limited to records which the officer is required by law to keep. An abstracter is entitled to the same general privileges as the public. It has been held that a title examiner or insurer does not have the right to copy or abstract all the records. Am Jur 2d, Abstracts of Title § 8; Am Jur 2d, Records and Recording Laws §§ 19, 189; CJS, Records § 35.

SECTION 1-24: PARTICULAR TYPES OF INSTRUMENTS AND RECORDS

Chattel records, see Section 13-12.

1-24A Entitled to Record.

When not entitled to record, see 1-31E.

R.C. 317.08 provides: "Except as provided in division (F) of this section, the county recorder shall keep five separate sets of records as follows:

"(A) A record of deeds, in which shall be recorded all deeds and other instruments of writing for the absolute and unconditional sale or conveyance of lands, tenements, and hereditaments; all notices, as provided for in sections 5301.47 to 5301.56 of the Revised Code; all judgments or decrees in actions brought under section 5303.01 of the Revised Code; all declarations and by-laws as provided for in sections 5311.01 to 5311.22 of the Revised Code; affidavits as provided for in section 5301.252 of the Revised Code; all certificates as provided for in section 5311.17 of the Revised Code; all articles dedicating archaeological preserves accepted by the director of the Ohio historical society under section 149.52 of the Revised Code; all articles dedicating nature preserves accepted by the director of natural resources under section 1517.05 of the Revised Code; all agreements for the registration of lands as archaeological or historic landmarks under section 149.51 or 149.55 of the Revised Code; and all conveyances of conservation easements under section 5301.68 of the Revised Code;

"(B) A record of mortgages, in which shall be recorded:

"(1) All mortgages, including amendments, supplements, modifications, and extensions thereof, or other instruments of writing by which lands, tenements, or hereditaments are or may be mortgaged or otherwise conditionally sold, conveyed, affected, or encumbered;

"(2) All executory installment contracts for the sale of land executed after September 29, 1961, which by the terms thereof are not required to be fully performed by one or more of the parties thereto within one year of the date of the contracts;

"(3) All options to purchase real estate, including supplements, modifications, and amendments thereof, but no such instrument shall be recorded if it does not state a specific day and year of expiration of its validity.

"(C) A record of powers of attorney;

"(D) A record of plats, in which shall be recorded all plats and maps of town lots, of the subdivision thereof, and of other divisions or surveys of lands, and any center line survey of a highway located within the county, the plat of which shall be furnished by the director of transportation or county engineer and all drawings as provided for in sections 5311.01 to 5311.22 of the Revised Code;

"(E) A record of leases, in which shall be recorded all leases, memoranda of leases, and supplements, modifications, and amendments thereof.

"All instruments or memoranda of instruments entitled to record shall be recorded in the proper record in the order in which they are presented for record. The recorder may index, keep, and record in one volume unemployment compensation liens, federal tax liens, personal tax liens, mechanics liens, notices of liens, certificates of satisfaction or partial release of estate tax liens, discharges of recognizances, excise and franchise tax liens on corporations, and liens provided for in sections 1513.33, 1513.37, 511.021, and 5311.18 of the Revised Code.

"The recording of an option to purchase real estate, including any supplement, modification, and amendment thereof, under this section shall serve as notice to any purchaser of an interest in the real estate covered by the option only during the period of the validity of the option as stated in the instrument.

"(F) In lieu of keeping the five separate sets of records required in divisions (A) to (E) of this section and the records required in division (G) of this section, a county recorder may record all the instruments required to be recorded by this section in two separate sets of record books. One set shall be called the "official records" and shall contain the instruments listed in divisions (A), (B), (C), and (E), and (G) of this section. The second set of records shall contain the instruments listed in division (D) of this section."

"(G) Except as provided in division (F) of this section, the county recorder shall keep a separate set of records containing all corrupt activity lien notices filed with the recorder pursuant to section 2923.36 of the Revised Code." (As eff. 10-20-87.)

R.C. 317.14 to 317.16 provide that when any instrument for the sale, conveyance or encumbrance of lands has been recorded in the proper records of a county of the state (whether or not the county in which such instrument is recorded ever comprised a part of the territory in which such lands are situated), a copy certified by the recorder may be recorded in the county where the lands or part thereof now lie, with full legal effect.

R.C. 2323.261 provides that a copy of the record, or part of the record, of any extracounty proceeding that affects the title to or possession of real property, when authenticated as provided in Civil Rule 44, may be filed in the office of the clerk of common pleas court. The copy shall be admitted to record and have the same effect as a similar record of a local proceeding. (As eff. 10-21-77.)

R.C. 4153.42 provides that a map of an abandoned mine shall be filed with the county recorder and the chief of division of mines. (As eff. 1-25-77.)

R.C. 5301.27 provides: "When any lands are left encumbered, by a deed, will, or other instrument of record, with the payment of money, or the performance of any acts by the grantee or devisee, such grantee or devisee or his heirs or assigns, upon the payment of the money or the performance of the acts, may present the receipt of such payment, or the proof of the performance of such acts, to the probate court of the county in which such lands are situated. The court must enter such payments and the proof of the performance of such acts on its journal, record the receipts and the proof of the performance of such acts on the margin of the will record in which such encumbrances are created, and order that this be done in like manner on the margin of the deed record by the county recorder. Such lands will then be relieved from the encumbrances except for fraud.

"No such record of receipts or orders may be made by the probate judge nor shall he enter proof of the performance of such acts until notice thereof has been given as is required by sections 2109.32 and 2109.33 of the Revised Code." (As eff. 10-1-53.) Sections 2109.32 and 2109.33 provide for notice of hearing in probate court on a fiduciary's account.

For further provisions on particular types of instruments, see the respective topics.

In the performance of his statutory duties, a county recorder may exercise some discretion and is not absolutely required to accept, record and index every instrument presented to him. He may refuse to do so if the description of the property is not definite, accurate and detailed. State ex rel. Preston v. Shaver, 172 OS 111, 173 NE2d 758, 15 OO2d 202 (1961).

The recording of a copy of a deed can have no effect. Lewis v. Baird, 2 OFD 197 (1842).

An instrument purporting to be a photographic or photostatic copy of a deed to real estate is not entitled to record and the county recorder has neither the right nor the duty to receive and record it. 1942 OAG 5369.

A water utility lien held by a private water utility corporation which purports to encumber or affect real property is recordable in the mortgage records. 1969 OAG 002.

A county recorder must accept for filing any instrument which purports to transfer an interest in real estate. 1969 OAG 139.

16

1-24B   Affidavits; Recitals.

Recitals as notice, see 1-31F.

R.C. 5301.011 provides: "A recorded grant, reservation, or agreement creating an easement or a recorded lease of any interest in real property shall contain a reference by volume and page to the record of the deed or other recorded instrument under which the grantor claims title, but the omission of such reference shall not affect the validity of the same." (As eff. 1-23-63.) A similar provision as to deeds is contained in R.C. 319.20.

R.C. 5301.252 provides: "(A) An affidavit stating facts relating to the matters set forth under division (B) of this section that may affect the title to real estate in this state, made by any person having knowledge of the facts or competent to testify concerning them in open court, may be recorded in the office of the county recorder in the county in which the real estate is situated. When so recorded, such affidavit, or a certified copy thereof, shall be evidence of the facts therein stated, insofar as such facts affect title to real estate.

"(B) The affidavits provided for under this section may relate to the following matters:

"(1) Age, sex, birth, death, capacity, relationship, family history, heirship, names, identity of parties, marriage, residence, or service in the armed forces;

"(2) possession;

"(3) the happening of any condition or event that may create or terminate an estate or interest;

"(4) the existence and location of monuments and physical boundaries, such as fences, streams, roads, and rights of way;

"(5) in an affidavit of a registered surveyor, facts reconciling conflicts and ambiguities in descriptions of land in recorded instruments.

"(C) The county recorder for the county where such affidavit is offered for record shall receive and cause the affidavit to be recorded as deeds are recorded, and collect the same fees for recording such affidavit as for recording deeds.

"(D) Every affidavit provided for under this section shall include a description of the land, title to which may be affected by facts stated in such affidavit, or a reference to an instrument of record containing such description, and shall state the name of the person appearing by the record to be the owner of such land at the time of the recording of the affidavit. The recorder shall index the affidavit in the name of such record owner.

"(E) Any person who knowingly makes any false statement in any such affidavit is guilty of perjury under Section [2921.11] of the Revised Code." (As eff. 1-13-72.)

The county recorder may not refuse to accept and to record an oil and gas lease which fails to contain the specific reference required by R.C. 5301.011. 1964 OAG 1053.

Standard of Title Examination

(Adopted by Ohio State Bar Association in 1953 and amended in 1956)

Problem 5.3B:

Should a recital as to heirship in an instrument, verified pleading or decree be accepted as proof of the facts stated in lieu of a certificate for transfer or of an affidavit for transfer?

Standard 5.3B:

Yes, provided the instrument or verified pleading has been of record for more than thirty years and is not in conflict with other instruments of record.

LAW IN GENERAL

Affidavits are not competent evidence as a rule, except as admissions against interest or as provided by statute. However, they are in common use even where not admissible in evidence, for example, to show the marital status of a grantor. They are generally accepted as reassurance on defects which do not make a title technically unmarketable. Neither are recitals conclusive, although they are likewise useful in removing clouds on the title. Am Law of Prop §§ 17.34, 18.42, 18.92.

1-24C Rerecording.

The instrument should be again witnessed and acknowledged if the change before rerecording is material. If the change is not a material alteration, the rerecorded instrument without reacknowledgment ordinarily constitutes a valid record.

A recorder has no authority to alter a record, even at the request of the parties. See 1-25B.

1-24D Indexes.

List of indexes, see 1-41D.

R.C. 317.18 in part provides: "At the beginning of each day's business the county recorder shall make and keep up general alphabetical indexes, direct and reverse, of all the names of both parties to all instruments theretofore received for record by him." Further detailed provisions are made for such indexes. (As eff. 8-19-82.)

R.C. 317.19 provides: "The county recorder shall keep a daily register of deeds and a daily register of mortgages, in which he shall note, as soon as filed, in alphabetical order according to the names of the grantors, respectively, all deeds and mortgages affecting real estate, filed in his office. He shall keep such register in his office, and it shall be open to the inspection of the public during business hours. The recorder may destroy such daily register after the expiration of a period of ten years from the date of the last entry in such register." (As eff. 9-16-57.)

R.C. 317.20 provides that the county commissioners may direct the making of sectional or location indexes. (As eff. 8-19-82.)

RECORDS AND RECORDING LAWS

R.C. 317.201 provides that the county recorder shall maintain a "Notice Index" for recording notices for preservation of claims under the Marketable Title Act. (As eff. 8-19-82.)

Indexing is not necessary in order to make the record constructive notice to a subsequent purchaser; his remedy is against the recorder. Green v. Garrington, 16 OS 548 (1866); Pattison v. Jordan, 3 CC 233, 2 CD 132 (1888).

A certificate of judgment is a lien upon lands within the county from the moment it is filed in the office of the clerk of court regardless of the time when it is docketed and indexed. The failure of the clerk to index it when it is filed constitutes negligence. Maddox v. Astro Investments, 45 App2d 203, 343 NE2d 133, 74 OO2d 312 (1975).

1-24E Contracts for Sale before August 11, 1961.

Recital in deed of land contract, see 1-31F.

"... [E]xecutory contract for the purchase and sale of land is not an instrument entitled to be recorded ... thereby giving notice to prospective purchasers of equity owned or claimed under such contract." Standard Oil Co. v. Moon, 34 App 123, 170 NE 368, 8 Abs 230, 31 OLR 239 (1930). A theory of recording in the mortgage records is submitted by an article at 33 OO 122.

An executory contract for the sale of land is not entitled to be recorded in the office of the county recorder in any of the records which the recorder is authorized and required to keep by the terms of R.C. 317.08. 1955 OAG 5064.

Possession by the purchaser is actual notice; the record of the contract may be actual notice if such notice is proved.

SECTION 1-25: ERRORS OF RECORDING OFFICER

Consecutive filing numbers, see 1-21D.
Effect of errors, see 1-21E.
Indexes, see 1-24D.

1-25A Liability of Recorder.

R.C. 317.02 provides: "Before entering upon the duties of his office, the county recorder shall give a bond, conditioned for the faithful discharge of the duties of his office, signed by a bonding or surety company authorized to do business in this state, or, at his option, by two or more freeholders having real estate in the value of double the amount of the bond over and above all encumbrances to the state in the sum of not less than ten thousand dollars, the surety company and the amount of the bond to be approved by the board of county commissioners. The expense or premium for such bond shall be paid by the board and charged to the general fund of the county. Such bond, with the oath of office required by sections 3.22 and 3.23 of the Revised Code, and by Section 7 of Article XV, Ohio Constitution, and the approval of the board indorsed thereon, shall be deposited with the county treasurer." (As eff. 3-18-69.)

R.C. 317.33 provides: "If a county recorder refuses to receive a deed or other instrument of writing presented to him for record, the legal fee for recording it being paid or tendered; or refuses to give a receipt therefor, when required; or fails to number consecutively all deeds or other instruments of writing upon receipt thereof; or fails to index a deed or other instrument of writing, by the morning of the day next after it is filed for record; or neglects, without good excuse, to record a deed or other instrument of writing within twenty days after it is received for record; or demands and receives a greater fee for his services than that allowed by law; or knowingly endorses on a deed or other instrument of writing a different date from that on which it was presented for record, or a different date from that on which it was recorded; or refuses to make out and certify a copy of any record in his office, when demanded, his legal fee therefor being paid or tendered; or purposely destroys, defaces, or injures any book, record, or seal belonging to his office, or any deed or other instrument of writing deposited therein for record, or negligently suffers it to be destroyed, defaced, or injured; or does or omits any other act, contrary to sections 317.01 to 317.33, inclusive, of the Revised Code, he shall be liable to a suit on his bond, at the instance and for the use of the party injured by such improper conduct." (As eff. 10-1-53.)

County recorders and common pleas court clerks and their deputies are liable, both personally and on their bonds, to the persons who may have been injured through their negligent errors and omissions, including those arising from indexing and filing of papers within their respective offices. The principle of sovereign immunity does not apply to protect public officers and their deputies from personal liability in the performance of ministerial duties. 1970 OAG 077.

1-25B   Correction of Records.

Nunc pro tunc entries, see 16-15B.
Rerecording, see 1-24C.

Courts of record have inherent power to make their records speak the truth. Caprita v. Caprita, 145 OS 5, 60 NE2d 483, 30 OO 238, 158 ALR 1201 (1945).

Where a first mortgage on real property is released on the record by the mistake of the recorder and thereafter the property is mortgaged to a second mortgagee and sold to purchasers, all of whom relied upon the record, the first mortgage may be foreclosed against the second mortgagee and the purchasers. Commercial Bldg. & Loan Co. v. Foley, 25 App 402, 158 NE 236, 6 Abs 11 (1927).

The description in a mortgage may be corrected in equity, but not to the prejudice of a subsequent mortgagee. An alteration by the recorder of a record, even if requested by the parties to make it, is void as to persons not having actual notice of the alteration. Youtz v. Julliard, 10 Dec Repr 298, 20 WLB 26 (C.P. 1888).

Further research: O Jur 2d, Records and Recording Laws § 14.

LAW IN GENERAL

Apparent alterations in the record are ordinarily presumed to have been made immediately after the original copying. CJS, Records § 23; Thompson § 4351.

SECTION 1-26: LOST OR DESTROYED RECORDS

1-26A Rules.

R.C. 317.30 provides that when any county records affecting real estate are destroyed, the original instrument or a certified copy of the record may be recorded and be effective as evidence. (As eff. 10-1-53.)

R.C. 711.34 to 711.38 provide for application to county commissioners to supply a lost or destroyed plat and record thereof. (As eff. 10-1-53.)

R.C. 2107.29 to 2107.32 provide for the restoration of the destroyed record of a will and its probate. (As eff. 10-1-53.)

R.C. 2729.01 provides that the probate court may order the restoration of the record of any proceeding or document required to be recorded or filed, except a will and probate thereof. (As eff. 10-1-53.)

R.C. 2729.05 and 2729.06 provide that a deed of a person appointed or authorized by the court (but not an auditor's tax deed) shall be prima facie evidence of the regularity of judicial proceedings when the record of the action has been lost or destroyed by fire, riot or civil commotion. (As eff. 10-1-53.)

R.C. 2729.07 provides for an action in probate court to establish an instrument conveying real estate, or a will and the probate thereof, which has been lost or destroyed by fire, riot or civil commotion. (As eff. 10-1-53.)

R.C. 2729.09 to 2729.13 provide for the restoration of lost or destroyed road records; and for presumption of location of road when record is not restored. (As eff. 10-1-53.)

R.C. 2729.14 to 2729.20 provide for the replacement of court records which have been lost or destroyed by fire, riot or civil commotion. (As eff. 10-1-53.)

Further research: O Jur 3d, Lost and Destroyed Instruments and Records § 5.

LAW IN GENERAL

The destruction of a public record usually does not affect its operation as constructive notice. Courts of equity have jurisdiction of proceedings to restore lost or destroyed records. Am Jur 2d, Lost and Destroyed Records § 26; CJS, Records § 42; Tiffany § 1271.

1-26B Authorized Destruction.

R.C. 149.38 creates a county records commission in each county to provide rules and regulations for retention and disposal of public records of the county. (As eff. 12-23-86.)

21

R.C. 149.39 creates a city records commission to provide rules for retention & destruction of municipal records. (As eff. 12-23-86.)

R.C. 2101.141 provides that inventories, schedules of debts, accounts, pleadings, vouchers, wills, trusts, bonds, and other papers filed in probate court by fiduciaries and entries by the court in conjunction therewith may be ordered microfilmed and destroyed after closing or termination of the administration of the estate, trust or other fiduciary relationship, and may be destroyed without microfilming after twenty-one years after the closing or termination and after compliance with R.C. 149.38. (As eff. 10-31-73.)

SECTION 1-27: NAMES; VARIANCE IN NAME

Abstracting standards, see 1-45B.

1-27A Notice.

A deed from Lemuel Granger is not constructive notice when it is recorded as from Samuel Granger. Jennings v. Wood, 20 Ohio 261 (1851).

The law does not impose upon anyone who searches the record, the duty of knowing the synonym for one's Christian or surname in foreign languages. Jezerniac v. Dunn, 2 Abs 343 (App. 1924).

Standard of Title Examination

(Adopted by Ohio State Bar Association in 1952; amended 1955 and 1967)

Problem 3.8A

When shall a variance between the name of a grantor and the name of the grantee in the next preceding deed be considered a defect of title?

Standard 3.8A:

A variance shall not be considered a defect, in the absence of other facts:

(a) when the name of the grantee agrees with the name of the grantor as the latter appears of record in the granting clause, or in the signature, or in the certificate of acknowledgment;

(b) when the variance consists of commonly recognized abbreviation or derivative;

(c) when the identity of a corporation can be inferred with reasonable certainty from the names used and other circumstances of record, even though the exact name of the corporation is not used and variations in the name exist from instrument to instrument. Among other variances, addition or omission of the word "the" preceding the name; use or nonuse of the symbol "&" for the word "and"; use or nonuse of abbreviations for "company," "limited," "corporation" or "incorporated"; and inclusion or omission of all or part of a place or location ordinarily may be ignored. Affidavits and recitals of identity may be used and relied upon to obviate variances too substantial or too significant to be ignored;

(d) when the difference is trivial or the error is apparent on the face of the instrument;

(e) when the names, although spelled differently, sound alike or when their sounds cannot be distinguished or when common usage, by corruption or abbreviation, has made their pronunciation identical, and the instruments are not of recent dates;

(f) when a middle name or initial is used in one instrument and not in another, unless the examiner is otherwise put on inquiry;

(g) when both instruments have been of record for more than 21 years.

LAW IN GENERAL

A variation may be such that there is no presumption of identity but the record operates to put a purchaser on notice; as, for example, the lien of a judgment against J. A. Jones on land in the name of John A. Jones. A presumption of identity is essential to marketability. 57 ALR 1478.

An incorrect name will not invalidate a deed as between the parties. Am Law of Prop § 12.40.

1-27B Evidence of Identity.

Title acquired as "D. Sam" and deed tendered from "Di Paola, sometimes known as D. Sam." Held, that specific performance will be refused where the contract called for a title free from clouds. Novogroder v. Di Paola, 11 App 374, 30 CC(NS) 421 (1919).

Standard of Title Examination

(Adopted by Ohio State Bar Association in 1953)

Problem 3.8C:

Should an examiner rely upon a recital purporting to cure an error in the name of a person in the chain of title?

Standard 3.8C:

Yes, unless the variance is so great or unless the other circumstances are such as to create a reasonable doubt of the truth of the recital.

LAW IN GENERAL

Similarity of a name in different instruments or in the same instrument is ordinarily sufficient evidence of identity if the difference is slight and there is no other matter raising a doubt of identity. An error apparent upon the face of a written instrument does not affect validity if the person can be identified with certainty from the whole instrument, as when a grantor signs correctly although his name is erroneously written in the deed. The correct name of a person in the certificate of acknowledgment is evidence of the identity of the person executing the instrument. Am Law of Prop §§ 18.29, 18.32; Tiffany § 3156.

1-27C   Idem Sonans.

Abstracting standards, see 1-45B.

"It is not every mistake in names which will invalidate an instrument or proceeding. This effect will follow where the person cannot be identified, or where the error is such as to describe another. But words are intended to be spoken; and where the sound is substantially preserved, bad spelling will not vitiate." A proceeding in the name of Abigail Pillsby is binding on Abigail Pillsbury. Pillsbury v. Dugan, 9 Ohio 117, 120 (1839).

The common-law rule of idem sonans is modified so as to require the Christian name and surname to retain the same initial letter. Chester C. Earnest and C. C. Ernest are idem sonans. Gleich v. Earnest, 36 App 326, 173 NE 212, 9 Abs 126 (1930).

Marketability is not impaired when title is taken as Esterly and divested as Easterly. Horton v. Matheny, 72 App 187, 51 NE2d 41, 27 OO 69 (1943).

Further research: O Jur 3d, Names § 18.

LAW IN GENERAL

Under the doctrine of idem sonans a different spelling of a name is immaterial both as to evidence of identity and as to notice if the sound is the same or only slightly different. The rule is ordinarily not applied to records operating as constructive notice when spelling is different as to the first letter of the name. Am Jur 2d, Name § 17; Am Law of Prop §§ 17.18, 18.30; CJS, Names § 14.

Courts are apparently agreed that the doctrine of idem sonans should be applied less freely in cases of constructive or substituted process than in the ordinary situation. 45 ALR2d 1090.

1-27D   Initials; Abbreviations.

See Standard of Title Examination at 1-27A.

The designation of the defendant as M. S. Daniels, although his Christian name is Morris, is sufficient if such designation is that commonly used by him and indicates who is meant thereby. Daniels v. Taylor, 13 CC(NS) 116, 21 CD 611 (1910), affd. 86 OS 307, 99 NE 1125 (1912).

Further research: O Jur 3d, Names §§ 8, 9.

LAW IN GENERAL

A middle name is generally considered material, especially when preceded by an initial. The old rule is still followed in a few jurisdictions that a middle name or initial is not recognized and that an error therein or omission thereof is immaterial. There is ordinarily no presumption that a letter or letters preceding a surname are initials and not the given name itself, although some cases hold that a judicial proceeding using initials instead of the given name is subject to objection. Constructive notice is not defeated by use of common abbreviations or derivatives. Am Jur 2d, Name § 4; Am Law of Prop § 18.30; 122 ALR 909; CJS, Names §§ 4, 6.

1-27E Prefix or Suffix; Married Women.

Service of process, see 16-75C.
Standard of Title Examination, see also 1-27A.

A transcript of a judgment against Mrs. Wm. Rogers, filed in the office of the clerk of court, does not constitute such judgment a lien on the lands of Lucy Rogers, although she may in fact be Mrs. Wm. Rogers. Uihlein v. Gladieux, 74 OS 232, 78 NE 363, 4 OLR 59 (1906).

Standard of Title Examination

(Adopted by Ohio State Bar Association in 1953; amended 1967)

Problem 3.8B:
   Should an objection be made because a grantor or a grantee is designated by her husband's given name, as "Mrs. John Doe"?

Standard 3.8B:
   Yes. Evidence as to the person intended by such designation should be required.

Further research: O Jur 3d, Names § 12.

LAW IN GENERAL

Mrs., Junior, Senior, etc., are not part of a person's name. The legal name of a married woman consists of her own Christian name and the surname of her husband. It has been held that the use of her husband's Christian name with the prefix "Mrs." is not constructive notice, as of a judgment lien on property held by her in her correct name. A prefix or suffix may raise a question of identity. Am Jur 2d, Name § 8; 35 ALR 417; CJS, Names §§ 3, 5.

1-27F Fictitious Names.

A deed to a fictitious person is void. A deed to an actual person under a fictitious name may be sustained. See also 8-32C.

1-27G Change of Name.

R.C. 1701.73 provides that an amendment or amended articles changing the name of a corporation *may* be filed with the county recorder and shall be recorded in the deed records. (As eff. 9-30-74.)
   R.C. 1701.81 provides for the filing and effect of filing of certificate of merger with the secretary of state. (As eff. 3-17-87.)
   R.C. 1701.82 provides that upon merger or consolidation all property of every description and all obligations of the constituent corporations shall

25

thereafter be deemed transferred to and vested in the surviving or new corporation without further act or deed; and title to any real estate or any interest therein shall not in any way be impaired. (As eff. 3-17-87.)

R.C. 2717.01 provides procedure in probate court for a person desiring to change his name. (As eff. 12-17-86.)

A person may adopt any name by which he is known, provided it is done in good faith and not against public policy, nor for a fraudulent purpose. State ex rel. Bucher v. Brower, 7 O Supp 51, 21 OO 208 (C.P. 1941).

Further research: O Jur 3d, Names § 13.

LAW IN GENERAL

A person may assume a new name so as to have it become his legal name provided this is not done for the purpose of defrauding another person. The designation of a person by the name under which he is commonly known is sufficient as being his name. CJS, Names § 9.

SECTION 1-28: SLANDER OF TITLE; DISPARAGEMENT OF PROPERTY

Erroneous title opinion, see Section 1-42.

1-28A   General Rules.

A false and malicious statement as to the title or interest falls within that branch of the law of libel and slander designated as slander of title, or slander of property. An action may be brought against anyone who falsely and maliciously defames the property of another, and, thereby causes him some special pecuniary damage or loss. Buehrer v. Provident Mut. Life Ins. Co., 37 App 250, 174 NE 597, 9 Abs 281 (1930), affd. 123 OS 264, 175 NE 25 (1931).

Further research: O Jur 3d, Defamation and Privacy § 152.

LAW IN GENERAL

Some authorities state that the publication must be directly to the prospective purchaser or that communication to him be authorized.

Publication made in the reasonable conduct of a person's own affairs with good faith and belief in its truth will not sustain an action for damages. Defamatory matter published in the ordinary course of a judicial proceeding is privileged. Am Jur 2d, Libel and Slander § 540; CJS, Libel and Slander § 269.

Malice is ordinarily held to be an essential element. There is considerable authority that malice is not necessary if the untrue publication could be reasonably expected to prevent a sale of the property. 129 ALR 179.

Special damages may be recovered for false words or conduct tending to cast doubt on the right or title of a person to particular property. Words or conduct disparaging property or reflecting on its value are subject to like rules.

Publication of the false statement is generally actionable if it causes special damages as a reasonable and proximate result. Execution, acceptance, or filing a false instrument purporting to affect the title may be slander of title. 39 ALR2d 840; 4 ALR 4th 532.

DIVISION 1-3: NOTICE; PRIORITIES

SECTION 1-31: CONSTRUCTIVE NOTICE AND PRIORITIES GENERALLY

1-31A Definition.

Constructive notice is that which the law regards as sufficient to give notice, and is regarded as a substitute for actual notice. Actual notice may be (1) express or direct information, or (2) implied or inferred from the fact that the person had means of knowledge. In re Fahle's Estate, 90 App 195, 105 NE2d 429, 47 OO 231 (1950).

Further research: O Jur 3d, Notice and Notices §§ 7, 8.

LAW IN GENERAL

Constructive notice is notice conclusively imputed to a person by a legal inference from established facts. It excludes actual notice. Under the doctrine of constructive notice a person is regarded as having knowledge of certain records.

Constructive notice is also said to include the knowledge imputed to a person who knows facts sufficient to put him on inquiry and to require him to make an investigation which would disclose the unrecorded rights; this form of notice is sometimes treated as actual notice. Am Law of Prop § 17.11.

1-31B Priorities Not Governed by Statute.

Equitable interests, see also 1-34B.

As between persons having equitable interests, if their equities are in other respects equal, the oldest in point of time will prevail, but this rule does not apply when the junior equity is superior in merit. Hume v. Dixon, 37 OS 66, 6 WLB 245 (1881).

LAW IN GENERAL

Except as provided by the recording laws, priority is governed by the following rules. Legal interests have priority of right between themselves strictly according to priority of time. Between a legal and an equitable interest the legal one has priority if acquired for value without notice of the equity. Between equal equitable interests the earlier will prevail, although a later but greater equity is preferred. A later equity is given precedence when the holder afterward acquires the legal title without notice of the earlier one. It is frequently held that the holder of the later equitable interest also has priority when he acquires the legal title with notice of the earlier equitable interest, provided he acquired his equitable interest without such notice. Am Law of Prop §§ 16.106B, 17.1; Tiffany § 1257.

1-31C   The Chain of Title.

Estoppel as to after-acquired title, see Section 8-34.
List of records in chain of title, see 1-41D.
Period of the search, see 1-31D.
Restrictions, see 6-33B.
Stray deeds, see also 1-21B.

A deed, out of the chain of title as recorded, is no notice to a subsequent purchaser. Leiby v. Wolf, 10 Ohio 83 (1840).

Purchaser is not chargeable with constructive notice of recitals of unauthorized deed, duly recorded, from the executors of a person through whose heirs the purchaser claims title. Blake v. Graham, 6 OS 580 (1856).

A mortgage recorded after the mortgagor had conveyed the land to a third person is ineffective to convey any interest in the land. Wood v. Smith, 50 NE2d 793, 38 Abs 556 (App. 1943).

A stray deed or purported conveyance of real estate by persons who are not shown to have an interest therein does not constitute a cloud on that title. Horton v. Matheny, 72 App 187, 51 NE2d 41, 27 OO 69 (1943).

Standard of Title Examination

(Adopted by Ohio State Bar Association in 1955)

Problem 3.13A:
   Is a cloud on the title created by a deed or encumbrance from a stranger to the record title?

Standard 3.13A:
   A stray deed or other interloping instrument does not create a cloud on the title unless its recitals or other known circumstances are sufficient to put a purchaser on inquiry.

Further research: O Jur 2d, Records and Recording Laws § 38.

LAW IN GENERAL

A record is in the chain of title if it is in the period of ownership as disclosed by the series of successive transfers. As a general rule, a bona fide purchaser does not have constructive notice of an instrument made by any person unless the instrument is duly filed for record during the period such person is the owner as shown by the chain of title. Am Law of Prop § 17.17; Tiffany § 1265.

A description giving the wrong range or block number is ordinarily said to be out of the chain of title and not constructive notice. Am Jur 2d, Records and Recording Laws § 144; Am Law of Prop § 17.23.

The cases are conflicting as to whether easements, restrictions and other covenants are in the chain of title and constructive notice where imposed upon a tract retained by the grantor when he conveys another tract. The better rule, which is supported by the greater authority, is that such servitudes are encumbrances in the chain of title. Am Jur 2d, Records and Recording Laws § 120; Am Law of Prop § 17.24.

1-31D Period of Search.

After-acquired title, see Section 8-34.
Chain of title, see 1-31C.
Commencement of the search, see 1-41D.
Marketable Title Act, see Section 1-44.

The mortgage is notice from the time it is filed for record where the grantor receives a purchase money mortgage and files it prior to the filing for record of the deed. Equitable Development Corp. v. V & L Constr. Co., 3 Misc 198, 207 NE2d 803, 32 OO2d 551 (1965).

Standard of Title Examination

(Adopted by Ohio State Bar Association in 1952; amended 1969)

Problem 2.2A:
   What period of time should be required as the basis for an opinion on title?

Standard 2.2A:
   A period of examination made pursuant to the Ohio Marketable Title Act, Section 5301.47 et seq., Ohio Revised Code, shall be sufficient.

Standard 2.2A is misleading if it is interpreted as prescribing a specific number of years as the basic period for an opinion on title. The Marketable Title Act establishes a period of time back to the root of title instrument which has been of record for more than forty years. It also defines a number of exceptions. Thus, an opinion based on the Marketable Title Act may require a search of much longer than forty years if the root of title instrument is much earlier than that period of time. The opinion, to be accurate, would have to except each of the items which are excepted or excluded from the protection of the Marketable Title Act; the exceptions include matters specifically preserved by filing of a notice, or by possession by the same owner continuously for a period of forty years or more. See 1-44A.

Standard of Title Examination 2.2B which required that the period of time of the examination be stated was eliminated by action of the Ohio State Bar Association on May 8, 1969.

A search should be made in the names of both the grantor and the grantee during the period that the conveyance is unrecorded, that is, in the name of each owner from the execution date of the deed to him until the recording date of the deed from him. This overlap arises because delivery of a deed may be at any time after execution and before recording.

Search must be made of all records during the period of ownership which may establish defects in or encumbrances on the title. Further search during a time in addition to the period of ownership must be made in some instances, as for liens or bankruptcies which attach to after-acquired property.

Under the doctrine of estoppel by deed (see 8-34B) a search must be made in the name of a common grantor prior to the date of the deed to him when an after-acquired title is involved.

Federal tax liens are an exception to the rule and an examination must be made for them in the name of a grantee for the time prior to his ownership.

LAW IN GENERAL

Under the rule above as to the chain of title, a purchaser need examine the records for conveyances from a certain grantor only from the time of execution of the conveyance to the grantor until the time of filing the conveyance from him. There may be an overlapping of the examination period between successive owners for the time conveyances are unrecorded because the records do not disclose the time of delivery. Am Law of Prop § 17.19; Tiffany § 1268.

An exception requiring examination for conveyances from each grantee prior to acquisition of title by him is made in some cases where an after-acquired title passes by estoppel under a previous conveyance by him. An exception requiring examination in the name of each grantor subsequent to his parting with title is made by some decisions where his grantee had notice of a prior unrecorded conveyance and such conveyance was afterward recorded before the transfer from said grantee. Under the latter decisions a search must be made for the recording of another deed from each grantor, during the period his grantee is in the chain of title. Am Jur 2d, Records and Recording Laws §§ 118, 121; Am Law of Prop § 17.20; Tiffany § 1234.

The doctrine of common source of title is well established where the title to or possession of real estate is involved in an action. Under the doctrine it is not necessary for the plaintiff to show his title prior to the common source. A defect in the title of the common source is immaterial. 5 ALR2d 375.

1-31E When Not Entitled to Record.

Recording acts, see Section 1-21.

The mere fact of recording a deed, without the legal requisites, gives it no validity. Johnston v. Haines, 2 Ohio 55 (1825).

If the instrument is not such as the law authorizes to be recorded, the act of recording is a nullity. Ramsey v. Riley, 13 Ohio 157, 167 (1844).

The mortgage not having been acknowledged, it was defective and was not entitled to record, and the record thereof was a nullity, and was notice to no one and bound no one. Straman v. Rechtine, 58 OS 443, 456, 51 NE 44, 39 WLB 383, 40 WLB 74 (1889).

Recording of instrument does not constitute notice thereof unless its recording is provided by statute. Stanton v. Schmidt, 45 App 203, 186 NE 851, 11 Abs 281, 39 OLR 52 (1931).

A mortgagee is not charged with constructive notice of a land contract recorded in the miscellaneous records but not entitled to record. Mellon Nat. Mortgage Co. v. Jones, 54 App2d 45, 374 NE2d 666, 8 OO3d 52 (1977).

LAW IN GENERAL

If the statutes do not provide for recording an instrument, or if it is not executed according to the formalities prescribed by law, it is not entitled to record. The record of any instrument not entitled to record is not constructive notice, although it may show an equitable right and be actual notice. Am Jur 2d, Records and Recording Laws § 7; Am Law of Prop §§ 17.27, 17.31; 3 ALR2d 577; Tiffany § 1263.

1-31F Recitals.

Grantee and all who hold his title are bound by the recitals and admissions in his deed. McChesney v. Wainwright, 5 Ohio 452 (1832).

A party tracing title through a regularly executed deed is concluded by its recitals. Scott v. Douglass, 7 Ohio (pt. 1) 227 (1835).

Reference to the agreements was sufficient to put the grantees on inquiry and had the same effect as if the agreements were set out in full in the deeds. Arnoff v. Williams, 94 OS 145, 149, 113 NE 661 (1916).

Standard of Title Examination

(Adopted by Ohio State Bar Association in 1955)

Problem 3.12A:
   When should a recital, contained in an instrument in the chain of title, of a right to purchase under a contract by a person otherwise a stranger to the title, no longer be considered a cloud?

Standard 3.12A:
   After the instrument containing the recital has been of record for 15 years, provided the land has been apparently conveyed to a bona fide purchaser since the date of such instrument.

Further research: O Jur 2d, Records and Recording Laws § 39.

LAW IN GENERAL

A purchaser is bound by statements and references properly contained in instruments in the chain of title. Actual or constructive notice of recitals obliges the purchaser to make reasonable inquiry. He is charged with knowledge he would have obtained from such inquiry. Some cases hold that a reference to another instrument is not notice unless the reference discloses an equity in a third person or unless the instrument is recorded. Recitals in records not in the chain of title, such as satisfied mortgages and dismissed court proceedings, are not notice. Am Jur 2d, Records and Recording Laws § 146; Am Law of Prop § 18.85; Tiffany § 1293.

1-31G Circuity of Lien; Circular Priority.

Priority of dower, see also 14-23F.

In determining priority where the mortgaged property is subject to prior judgment liens, the exemption in lieu of homestead will be paid to the mortgagee, then the judgment liens and the mortgage lien will be satisfied in their order of priority in time. Clemens v. Second Nat. Bank, 22 Abs 173 (App. 1936).

Where circuity of liens exists there is no method of logic or mathematics that can effectively solve the question of priorities in distribution. Distribution is made on the actual equities of the parties in the particular case. Kingsberry Mortgage Co. v. Maddox, 13 Misc 98, 233 NE2d 887, 42 OO2d 158 (C.P. 1968).

A federal tax lien once filed has priority over state and local tax liens thereafter accruing. Where the proceeds of judicial sale are insufficient to pay all liens in full, there shall be set aside a fund equal to the amount of the creditor liens preferred over the federal lien to the extent the proceeds are sufficient, out of which fund the state taxes shall first be paid, and the remainder of such fund shall be paid to creditors whose liens are so preferred over the federal lien, and the remainder of the proceeds of sale to the United States. Southern Ohio Savings Bank & Trust Co. v. Bolce, 165 OS 201, 135 NE2d 382, 59 OO 290 (1956).

LAW IN GENERAL

A difficult problem in priorities arises where there are three liens and the third lien in order of time is subsequent in priority to the second lien but has priority over the earliest lien. The situation is not uncommon where federal tax liens, dower, judgment liens or waivers of priority are concerned. Four solutions are set forth by the decisions and others are offered by text writers. Am Law of Prop § 17.33.

SECTION 1-32: BONA FIDE PURCHASER

After-acquired title, see Section 8-34.
Quitclaim deeds, see 8-15C.

1-32A Definition.

The legacies may be enforced against the land in the hands of the purchasers from the devisee, although they purchased without actual notice of the encumbrance and for good consideration paid. Nellons v. Truax, 6 OS 97 (1856).

In the absence of statute a purchaser of real estate who acquires the legal title in good faith for a valuable consideration without notice of an existing equity takes the property free from such equity. Shaker Corlett Land Co. v. Cleveland, 139 OS 536, 41 NE2d 243, 23 OO 27 (1942).

A bona fide purchaser is one who has in good faith paid a valuable consideration without notice of an adverse right in another person. The term is synonymous with innocent purchaser for value.

1-32B   Consideration.

The three essentials of a bona fide purchase are the absence of notice, the presence of a valuable consideration, and the presence of good faith. Dietsch v. Long, 72 App 349, 366, 43 NE2d 906, 27 OO 294, 301, 36 Abs 360 (1942).

LAW IN GENERAL

The grantee is a bona fide purchaser if he did not have notice of the adverse claim at the time of payment of the consideration. He is not protected as to the consideration, or part thereof, paid after notice even when he had received the conveyance before notice. Am Law of Prop § 17.10; 109 ALR 163; Powell § 916; Tiffany § 1304.

A good consideration, instead of a valuable one, does not constitute a purchase for value. Satisfaction of a preexisting debt is usually held to be a valuable consideration. The consideration is not required to be the full value but the disproportion may be so great as to show a lack of good faith. Tiffany § 1300.

1-32C   Necessity of Legal Title.

The plea of bona fide purchaser is no defense against a legal title. Larrowe v. Beam, 10 Ohio 498 (1841).

What protection will be extended to a bona fide purchaser, without notice, is a question which does not arise where neither party has the legal title. Woods v. Dille, 11 Ohio 455 (1842), revd. on other grounds 14 Ohio 122 (1846).

A party having an equitable title to real estate, and not the legal title, is not protected as a bona fide purchaser without notice of prior equities. Sause v. Ward, 7 App 446, 28 CC(NS) 33, 30 CD 1 (1917).

The principal may recover damages in his own name notwithstanding the agent may have contracted in the latter's name without disclosing his agency. Bowden v. Meade, 1 Abs 596 (App. 1923).

Further research: O Jur 2d, Vendor and Purchaser § 83.

LAW IN GENERAL

A purchaser not acquiring the legal title is held, in a majority of the cases, not entitled to protection as a bona fide purchaser. Tiffany § 1279.

1-32D   Time of Recording.

Period of the search, see 1-31D.

Under the recording statute, shown at 1-21A, the bona fide purchaser is not required to record his deed before the earlier deed from the same grantor is recorded.

1-32E   Burden of Proof.

The burden of proof as to the payment of a valuable consideration rests upon the subsequent purchaser; upon such proof, the burden of proving his bad faith, and his knowledge, at the time of his purchase, of the existence of a former unrecorded deed from the same grantor, rests upon the holder of the prior deed. Morris v. Daniels, 35 OS 406, 5 WLB 108 (1880).

LAW IN GENERAL

By the weight of authority, the subsequent purchaser has the burden of proof but, upon his proving the payment of a valuable consideration, the earlier claimant is required to introduce evidence of notice. Am Law of Prop § 17.35; Tiffany § 1310.

1-32F   Judgment Creditors; Mortgagees; Judicial Sales.

Lis pendens, see Section 17-12.
Reversal, see Section 16-14.

Purchaser at sheriff's sale takes title as bona fide purchaser although he has notice, before the sheriff's deed and after the sale, of an adverse equity. Oviatt v. Brown, 14 Ohio 285 (1846).

The rights of the judgment creditor, when he becomes the purchaser, are not different from those of other purchasers at judicial sales. Sternberger v. Ragland, 57 OS 148, 48 NE 811, 38 WLB 267, 309 (1897); McBride v. Longworth, 14 OS 349 (1863).

A purchaser without notice at judicial sale has all the rights of a bona fide purchaser for value and is within the protection of the recording statutes. Weir v. Snider Saw Mill Co., 88 OS 424, 103 NE 133, 11 OLR 266, 58 WLB 397 (1913).

A mortgagee in foreclosure action who acquires title by sheriff's deed succeeds to all the rights of all parties. Hilling v. Cincinnati, 54 App 293, 7 NE2d 1, 8 OO 17, 22 Abs 628 (1936). And retains all rights as mortgagee. Lumbermen's Mortgage Co. v. Stevens, 46 App 5, 187 NE 641, 12 Abs 553, 39 OLR 232 (1932).

LAW IN GENERAL

A mortgagee of a legal interest is ordinarily regarded as a bona fide purchaser but subject to statutory requirements such as that of recording the mortgage. Tiffany § 1459.

A purchaser in good faith at execution or judicial sale is generally entitled to the protection of the recording laws. A judgment creditor is not so entitled in some decisions to the extent the debt is credited on the purchase price. Am Jur 2d, Records and Recording Laws § 166; Tiffany §§ 1281, 1309.

The right to protection as a bona fide purchaser is ordinarily regarded as an affirmative defense which must be pleaded. 33 ALR2d 1326.

1-32G Transfer of Rights.

Where a bona fide purchaser conveys to one with notice of outstanding equities, the latter holds the title of his grantor. Card v. Patterson, 5 OS 319 (1855).

Further research: O Jur 2d, Vendor and Purchaser § 84.

LAW IN GENERAL

The rights of a person as a bona fide purchaser are not affected by the fact that he acquired title from a purchaser charged with notice of an outstanding unrecorded interest. However, the rights of a bona fide purchaser do not pass on a conveyance to a former owner who was charged with notice of a prior equity; that is, a bona fide purchaser does not transfer his rights as such to a purchaser who had previously acquired the land with notice. Tiffany § 1307.

1-32H Adverse Claims Not of Record.

Many types of claims may prevail over the rights of a bona fide purchaser even though no notice of the claims appears on the record.

Some of these are the results of: Marital status incorrectly given; after-born or other undisclosed heirs; mental incompetence; minority; recording or indexing mistakes; falsification of records; delivery of deed after death or without authority; title by adverse possession; alteration of instrument after delivery; expired power of attorney; insufficient authority of corporate officers; impersonation or similarity of names; foreign bankruptcy; mechanics' liens; erroneous description; encroachments and rights of persons in possession; fraud or false affidavits; certain liens, assessments, taxes and fines; lack of jurisdiction for judgment; governmental regulations; forgery.

The law must be applied to the facts of the case if the adverse claim has not been barred by judgment, deed, limitation of action, or estoppel. See the appropriate topic for the particular matter.

SECTION 1-33: ACTUAL NOTICE GENERALLY; POSSESSION

1-33A Rules.

If, in the investigation of a title, a purchaser, with common prudence, must have been apprised of another right, notice of that right is presumed. Reeder v. Barr, 4 Ohio 446, 458 (1831).

Further research: O Jur 2d, Vendor and Purchaser § 87.

LAW IN GENERAL

The recording acts do not protect a purchaser having actual notice of an adverse claim. The rule applies to instruments recorded but not entitled to record; therefore, when the purchaser finds the record of an interest, it is actual notice and is effective as to him as though entitled to record. The doctrine of actual notice applies equally to matters not of record and to facts which would have been disclosed by an inquiry reasonably required by the known facts. 3 ALR2d 577; Tiffany §§ 1264, 1283.

A prior unrecorded conveyance will be given effect where the notice is sufficient in equity to oblige the purchaser to make inquiry. The presumption of notice is rebutted when an investigation, which is reasonable in extent under the circumstances, fails to disclose the adverse claim. Tiffany § 1284.

1-33B Possession.

Joint occupant, see also 2-34C.

When a mother conveys title to her son but continues to reside in the premises and thereafter enters into an unrecorded life lease for the premises, the continued exclusive possession of the premises by the mother is notice of her rights, and the mortgage is subordinate thereto. Sinclair Refining Co. v. Chaney, 114 App 538, 184 NE2d 214, 20 OO2d 88 (1961).

The delivery of a deed is considered as giving possession in contemplation of law, and the grantee is presumed to have entered, unless that presumption is rebutted by facts wholly inconsistent with it, as when the premises, at the time of the grant, are in the actual seisin of a third person claiming title adversely to the grantor. Holt v. Hemphill, 3 Ohio 232, 238 (1827).

A purchaser of land in possession of a third person is chargeable with notice of the occupant's title and equities. Kelley v. Stanbery, 13 Ohio 408 (1844); McKinzie v. Perrill, 15 OS 162 (1864).

The acts of possession need not extend to the entire tract leased; in order to charge the purchaser with notice of the adverse claim, such acts as to part are regarded as sufficient to raise the duty of inquiry to the extent and source of the possessor's rights. Pure Oil Co. v. Turner, 119 OS 271, 281, 163 NE 911, 6 Abs 385, 390, 26 OLR 519 (1928).

In the case of a vendor remaining in possession, his possession will not be notice that he holds any interest in the property inconsistent with his deed, although it would be as to all rights obtained subsequent to the deed. Forsha v. Longworth, 1 CC 271, 1 CD 149 (1885).

Possession gives no notice of any rights of a third person in the property obtained previously through the possessors if those rights are not actually known or entitled to constructive notice through the public records. There is no duty to inquire of a possessor as to the rights of third parties claiming through him. Mellon Nat. Mortgage Co. v. Jones, 54 App2d 45, 374 NE2d 666, 8 OO3d 52 (1977).

The equitable interest of a purchaser under a land contract takes priority over federal tax liens against the seller which were filed after the purchaser took possession of the premises and before he recorded his land contract. State Fidelity Federal Savings & Loan Assn. v. Wehrly, 25 Misc 221, 263 NE2d 801, 54 OO2d 314 (C.P. 1970).

Further research: O Jur 3d, Notice and Notices, § 16.

LAW IN GENERAL

Possession of a third person is notice to a purchaser of the legal and equitable rights claimed under the possession to the extent that the rights may be disclosed by a reasonable investigation or by inquiry of the occupant. Actual notice of the possession is not necessary, unless by statute, but the possession must be visible. Am Law of Prop § 17.12; 17 ALR2d 331; Tiffany § 1287.

When the person in possession has an interest of record, a purchaser is not put on inquiry as to any additional rights of the possessor. By analogy, the joint possession of two persons is imputed to the record title of one of them. Am Law of Prop § 17.13; 2 ALR2d 857; Tiffany § 1289.

The possession of a grantor after his conveyance is an exception to the rule, unless its long continuance or other circumstances are sufficient to put a reasonably prudent person on inquiry. Am Law of Prop § 17.14.

Possession is generally notice of the rights of one under whom the possessor holds; for example, possession of a tenant is notice of the rights of the landlord. 1 ALR2d 322; Tiffany § 1291.

A majority of the decisions hold that possession by a tenant charges a subsequent purchaser or mortgagee with notice of the tenant's agreement with the owner-landlord to purchase the property. 37 ALR2d 1113.

1-33C Principal and Agent.

Knowledge of or notice to an agent is not binding upon his principal unless it appears that such agent had authority to deal in reference to those matters which the knowledge or notice affected, or had a duty to communicate the same to his principal. Myers v. John Hancock Mut. Life Ins. Co., 108 OS 175, 140 NE 504, 1 Abs 467, 2 Abs 7, 21 OLR 140 (1923).

LAW IN GENERAL

A principal is usually charged with actual notice to his agent if the fact is within the scope of the agency and not fraudulently concealed by the agent. The notice must be of some matter which it is the duty of the agent to communicate to his principal. A client is not charged with notice to an attorney at law who is acting as a professional advisor and not as an attorney in fact. Tiffany § 1286.

SECTION 1-34: EASEMENTS; TRUSTS; EQUITIES; OTHER INTERESTS

1-34A Easements.

See also Section 10-19.

An unrecorded easement is not enforceable against a bona fide purchaser for value who has no actual or constructive notice of such easement. Tiller v. Hinton, 19 OS3d 66, 482 NE2d 946 (1985).

The mere use of a sewer of which there is no record evidence and of which the purchaser of the servient land had no knowledge does not give others a right to continue the use. Bates v. Magennis, 19 CC(NS) 67, 32 CD 350 (1909).

LAW IN GENERAL

A purchaser takes subject to easements disclosed by the public records of his chain of title, and to easements apparent upon an ordinary inspection of the premises. A bona fide purchaser acquires the property free from the easement if he is not charged with constructive notice, unless the servitude may be discovered by a reasonable inspection. Am Jur 2d, Easements § 86; CJS, Easements § 47; Tiffany § 828.

1-34B Equitable Interests; Trusts.

See also 1-31B.

What protection will be extended to a bona fide purchaser, without notice, is a question which does not arise where neither party has the legal title. Woods v. Dille, 11 Ohio 455 (1842), revd. on other grounds 14 Ohio 122 (1846).

Where neither party has the legal title, the rule which protects a bona fide purchaser without notice does not apply; and where, in such case, the equities are equal, the oldest equity must prevail. Elstner v. Fife, 32 OS 358, 3 WLB 137 (1877).

As between lien holders having equitable interests, if one also has the legal estate, or the right to use the legal title in support of his security, his lien will be given preference. Campbell v. Sidwell, 61 OS 179, 55 NE 609, 42 WLB 350, 43 WLB 2 (1899).

Standard of Title Examination

(Adopted by Ohio State Bar Association in 1971)

Problem 3.18A:
  Should objection be made to a title dependent upon a disclosed trust not of record?

Standard 3.18A:
  Yes. All such trust agreements should be recorded.

LAW IN GENERAL

Priority of time gives priority of right between equal equitable claims. Equitable interests may be unequal because of the character of the equities, consideration paid for one of them, notice of earlier equity, or fraud or laches of one claimant. Am Jur 2d, Vendor and Purchaser § 637.

A conveyance of an equitable interest, or from a stranger to the legal title, is not constructive notice to a subsequent purchaser of the legal title. However, the grantee of such a conveyance is bound by the record of the title acquired thereunder. Am Jur 2d, Records and Recording Laws § 116.

The general rules apply to a conveyance from a trustee so that a bona fide purchaser takes the property free from the trust if he has exercised due diligence to discover the trust or to ascertain the authority of the trustee. Am Jur 2d, Trusts § 269.

1-34C Options.

LAW IN GENERAL

A purchaser having actual or constructive notice of a recently expired option may be put on inquiry as to whether the option has been exercised and an unrecorded deed is in existence. A careful examiner may require evidence in the matter. Am Law of Prop § 18.81.

1-34D Conveyance of Other Land.

Chain of title, see 1-31C.
Restrictions as to use, see 6-33B.

Easements and covenants are commonly held to be constructive notice when contained in a prior recorded conveyance of other land owned by the same grantor.

A recorded deed conveying part of a parcel of land owned by the grantor may not be notice of an easement granted in the deed over adjacent land retained by the grantor, if the description of the easement does not clearly define it as being within the retained parcel. Spring Lakes Ltd. v. OFM Co., 12 OS3d 333 (1984).

DIVISION 1-4: EXAMINATION IN GENERAL

SECTION 1-41: INTRODUCTION; METHODS

1-41A "Title."

"Title" embraces a wide field and is the concern of each chapter of this book. The most satisfactory of the definitions of the word, as to real property, is that it means ownership. Confusion arising from the different uses of the word may be avoided by using "marketable title," "record title," "equitable title," "legal title," or "title by adverse possession," when one of such meanings is intended.

Use of the expression "good title" is not recommended as it may be ambiguous in meaning a title which can be successfully defended or in meaning a marketable title of record. For example, when a person has acquired title by adverse possession without a judgment or deed, his title is good in one sense although it is not marketable.

1-41B   Title Examination Generally.

Title examination is the art of applying a knowledge of real property law to particular facts in order to determine the status of the ownership of specific land.

Examination of title primarily refers to the ownership as shown by the public title records. It is the process of determining whether the title is marketable, that is, whether the ownership is subject to outstanding encumbrances or to reasonable doubt as to its validity.

Particular matters of title are treated throughout this work. The index and the appropriate subdivisions should be consulted on problems of title arising in the course of an examination.

1-41C   Opinions on Title.

Form of certificate, see 1-12B.

The title opinion resulting from the examination may be said to be the conclusion of the examining lawyer as to what would be the judgment of the court on marketability if the matter were submitted to judicial determination. However, it is customary for the examiner to report defects which present a reasonable possibility rather than a real hazard of litigation; an example of this is the possibility of dower where a recent deed does not show that the grantor is unmarried, in which case the title has been held marketable as there is no presumption that the grantor was married.

Standard of Title Examination

(Adopted by Ohio State Bar Association in 1952)

Problem 2.1A:

When an attorney examines a title which he believes should not be approved and he knows that another has approved it, should he communicate with the other attorney?

Standard 2.1A:

Yes, if practicable an opportunity should be afforded for discussion and correction.

1-41D   Methods of Searching; Indexes.

Abstracting standards, see 1-45B.
Chain of title, see 1-31C.
Period of the search, see 1-31D.

Tract indexes are maintained by the recorder in a few counties where deeds and some other types of instruments are indexed according to the location of the land. Examination of public records of title ordinarily begins with a search of the index to deed grantees in the name of the present purported owner. The deed thus found shows the legal description of the land and the name of the grantor. A search is then made of the grantee index in the name of that grantor. The search of this index is continued in like manner until the earliest deed in the desired period is found. In addition to showing the chain of title, this also discloses corrective and curative conveyances. Links in the chain which are not found in the grantee indexes may be discovered through a search of court records and tax records or maps. Missing links may also be located by finding the government grant (which is often recorded many years after it is issued) from the grantor indexes and then tracing the chain through such indexes and the court indexes.

The list of all owners so found constitutes the chain of title. Each name on the list is searched for in the deed grantor index and in all the indexes indicated below for the period between the execution date of the conveyance to an owner and the filing date of the conveyance from him. After the records are found, the examination of them is essentially the same as when made of an abstract of title. Most of the contents of this work concern the significance of the various matters found by the search.

It is not practicable to make an exact list of indexes applicable to all counties because of the numerous variations in the customs of keeping some records. Many counties have certain separate records and indexes which are not maintained by other counties; for example, in some counties Motor Vehicle Liability Bonds are separately indexed instead of being entered in the mortgage index, and a few counties maintain a separate record and index of Sales Tax Liens.

INDEXES OF RECORDS TO BE SEARCHED

See also list adopted by Columbus Bar Association at 1-45B.

Recorder's office

Deed (grantor and grantee)
Mortgage (mortgagor), Options and Land contracts
Lease (lessor)
Mechanic's Lien
Powers of attorney
Plat
Miscellaneous

Corrupt activity lien notices
Certificate of Authority to Pay Taxes
Federal Tax Lien
Recognizance or Bail Bond
Unemployment Taxes
Personal Property Tax Lien
Notice Index Preserving Interests
Daily Registers
Certificates of Partnership

Clerk of court's office

Pending Cases and Judgments
Execution
Certificate of Judgment
Domestic Relations

Probate court

Administration of Estates
Appropriations
Assignment for Benefit of Creditors
Inheritance Taxes without Administration
Guardianships
Lunacy Cases
Land Sales and Other Civil Cases

Auditor's and treasurer's offices

Agricultural Credits
Homestead Exemptions
General Tax Duplicates
Special Assessments
Maps

Sheriff's office

Foreign Execution

Further indexes

(As indicated by the records found from the foregoing indexes)
Ordinance
County Commissioners' Records
Franchise Taxes
Partition Fence Record
Special Assessments
Adoption

Aid for Aged
Change of Name
Designation of Heir
Marriage Record
Birth and Death Record
Cancellation of Corporate Charter
Financing Statements
Power of Attorney
County Engineer's Maps and Surveys
County Engineer's Road Records
County Auditor's Tax Sales
Transfer Record
Tax Additions and Abatements
Public Utility Taxes
Tax Exemption
Court of Appeals
Municipal Court
Federal Estate Taxes
Sales Taxes
Federal Court and Marshal's Office

1-41E   Caveat Emptor; Matters Not of Record.

Bona fide purchaser, see Section 1-32.
Closing reminders, see 8-45E.

Under the doctrine of caveat emptor the purchaser takes subject to defects and encumbrances with the right to only such damages as may be afforded by the covenants. He cannot recover his actual damages arising from the title being unmarketable because of claims which may never be asserted. Breach of covenants, see 6-13F and Division 6-2.

Protection of the prospective purchaser or lien holder requires investigation of matters not of record such as (a) rights of persons in possession, including visible easements, (b) location of improvements and encroachments which may be ascertainable only by a survey, (c) claims for labor performed or materials furnished which may become liens as of a date prior to being recorded, (d) pending special assessments for public improvements, and (e) zoning or other governmental regulations. Other particular claims, see 1-32H.

1-41F   Obligation to Furnish Title Evidence.

A custom which would relieve a purchaser from the obligations imposed upon him by the doctrine of caveat emptor, which requires a vendee to protect himself by express covenants and investigation of the title which he is to acquire, is contrary to law. Thomas v. Guarantee Title & Trust Co., 81 OS 432, 91 NE 183, 7 OLR 615, 55 WLB 71 (1910).

The vendor is under no obligation, in the absence of express provisions, to furnish the vendee with an abstract of title. Spengler v. Sonnenberg, 88 OS 192, 202, 102 NE 737, 11 OLR 71, 115, 58 WLB 231, 271 (1913).

1-41G   Title Charges as Court Costs.

R.C. 2127.28, quoted at 12-14R, in part provides: "The court may allow payment for certificate or abstract of title or policy of title insurance in connection with the sale of any land by an executor, administrator, or guardian." (As eff. 1-1-76.)

R.C. 5501.18 provides that the director of highways may enter into contracts for the purpose of supplying abstracts of title, title guarantees, title insurance policies (or for certain other purposes), without advertising for bids. (As eff. 9-28-73.)

Civil Rule 54(D) (costs) provides that costs shall be allowed to the prevailing party except when provision is made in a statute or the rules and unless the court otherwise directs. (As eff. 7-1-70.)

"Taxable costs are made so either by statute, rule of court, or order of court in a specific case, or by established usage, the equivalent of a rule." Parkerson v. Borst, 256 Fed 827, 828 (1919). See also The Daniel Kern, 29 F2d 288 (1928).

The cost of an abstract or certificate of title may be taxed as court costs in tax foreclosure proceedings and paid from the county treasury. 1922 OAG 543.

Costs of title examination are allowed as court costs by rule of court or by custom in many counties.

1-41H   Unauthorized Practice of Law.

R.C. 317.111 provides: "No instrument by which the title to real estate or personal property, or any interest therein or lien thereon, is conveyed, created, encumbered, assigned, or otherwise disposed of, shall be received for record or filing by the county recorder unless the name of the person who, and governmental agency, if any, which, prepared such instrument appears at the conclusion of such instrument and such name is either printed, typewritten, stamped, or signed in a legible manner. An instrument is in compliance with this section if it contains a statement in the following form: 'This instrument was prepared by (name).'

"This section does not apply to any instrument executed prior to October 5, 1955, nor to the following: any decree, order, judgment, or writ of any court; any will or death certificate; any instrument executed or acknowledged outside of this state." (As eff. 1-10-61.)

Title guarantee and trust companies are not permitted to issue a certificate containing an opinion as to the condition or validity of titles which is not guaranteed by such companies. Land Title Abstract & Trust Co. v. Dworken, 129 OS 23, 193 NE 650, 1 OO 313 (1934).

Making a certificate of title is practice of law. A corporation cannot lawfully engage in the practice of law; nor can it do so indirectly through the employment of qualified lawyers. Judd v. City Trust & Savings Bank, 133 OS 81, 12 NE2d 288, 10 OO 95 (1937).

One who furnishes to another a certificate or memorandum containing a statement of the substance of documents or facts appearing on the public records, which affect the title to real estate, without expressing any opinion as to the legal significance of what is found or as to the validity of the title, is not engaged in the practice of law. State ex rel. Doria v. Ferguson, 145 OS 12, 60 NE2d 476, 30 OO 241 (1945).

An affidavit for a mechanic's lien is not rendered invalid by the fact that it is accepted for record without the name of the person who prepared it being noted thereon. The county recorder should have refused to accept it. But having placed it on record, the landowner is not prejudiced. The obvious purpose of R.C. 317.111 is to give the bar a ready weapon in its fight to protect the public from the unauthorized practitioner. Brown & Sons v. Honabarger, 171 OS 247, 168 NE2d 880, 12 OO2d 375 (1960).

The parties are entitled to a determination of their rights and liabilities in an action for specific performance without regard to the contract to purchase having been prepared by a person not licensed to practice law. Frank v. Moore, 1 App 2d 90, 198 NE2d 82, 30 OO2d 112, 93 Abs 225 (1963).

LAW IN GENERAL

Drafting of instruments to perfect title by others than lawyers is almost universally regarded as unauthorized practice of law. The decisions are diverse as to which title examination activities by an insurance company, title and abstract company, or bonding institution constitute illegal practice of law. Statutes exempting title companies from prohibitions against law practice by corporations are not conclusive in view of the principle that the legislature cannot constitutionally encroach upon the judiciary's right to define the practice of law. 85 ALR2d 184.

SECTION 1-42: LEGAL LIABILITY

1-42A Basis of Liability; Qualifications Required.

An action against an abstractor to recover damages for negligence must be founded on contract. Thomas v. Guarantee Title & Trust Co., 81 OS 432, 91 NE 183, 7 OLR 615, 55 WLB 71 (1910).

Where, under a title abstracter's indemnity policy, the insurer agreed to indemnify the insured title company against claims made during the subsistence of the policy for errors whenever committed, the policy did not cover an error made while the policy was in force but not discovered until after the policy had terminated. Reid v. Dayton Title Co., 31 Misc 275, 278 NE2d 384, 60 OO2d 233 (1972).

Further research: O Jur 3d, Abstracts and Land Titles § 8.

LAW IN GENERAL

An examining attorney, or an abstracter, impliedly represents that he possesses a reasonable degree of knowledge and skill. He is liable for failure to exercise such knowledge and skill with due care when his negligence is the proximate cause of injury to his client, that is, the client must have changed his position in reliance upon the report. The liability of the examiner or abstracter is determined by his contract, which is evidenced by his certificate. He does not guarantee the titles he approves and is responsible for an erroneous opinion only within the above limits. Legal liability may attach for slander of title, as against an examiner for reporting a void encumbrance to be subsisting. Accuracy and care are his indispensable qualifications. Am Jur 2d, Abstracts of Title § 12; 71 ALR 349; 28 ALR2d 891.

1-42B To Whom Liable.

The general rule is that an abstracter can be held liable for negligence only to the person who employed him. Thomas v. Guarantee Title & Trust Co., 81 OS 432, 91 NE 183, 7 OLR 615, 55 WLB 71 (1910).

Further research: O Jur 3d, Abstracts and Land Titles § 7.

LAW IN GENERAL

The general rule is that an examining attorney or an abstracter is liable only to those in privity, that is, to those having a contract relationship with him. The employment, not the opinion or abstract, is the contract. Some decisions hold that an abstracter is liable to a third person if he knew that the abstract was to be relied upon by such person. Am Jur 2d, Abstracts of Title § 15; 68 ALR 376; CJS, Abstracts of Title §§ 9, 11.

1-42C Limitation of Actions.

R.C. 2305.07 provides: "Except as provided in section 1302.98 of the Revised Code, an action upon a contract not in writing, express or implied, or upon a liability created by statute other than a forfeiture or penalty, shall be brought within six years after the cause thereof accrued." (As eff. 7-1-62.) Section 1302.98 applies to contracts for sale of goods.

R.C. 2305.11 in part provides that an action for malpractice shall be brought within one year after the cause thereof accrues. (As eff. 10-20-87.)

A cause of action in favor of a client against an attorney for malpractice accrues at the time the contract of employment is terminated. McWilliams v. Hackett, 19 App 416 (1923). The limitation of action is one year under R.C. 2305.11.

Although the action for the attorney's negligence is upon an implied contract, the one-year statute of limitation applies. Long v. Bowersox, 8 NP(NS) 249, 19 OD 494 (1909); Galloway v. Hood, 69 App 278, 43 NE2d 631, 24 OO 66 (1941).

A cause of action for malpractice accrues, at the latest, when the attorney-client relationship finally terminates. Keaton Co. v. Kolby, 27 OS2d 234, 271 NE2d 772, 56 OO2d 139 (1971).

LAW IN GENERAL

The statute of limitations on a claim against an examiner or abstracter starts to run from the time the opinion or abstract is delivered, not from the time the damage is sustained or is discovered. Am Jur 2d, Abstracts of Title § 24.

1-42D Title Plant as Subject to Execution and Taxation.

LAW IN GENERAL

By the weight of authority, privately owned title records and abstract books are subject to execution and taxation. Am Jur 2d, Abstracts of Title § 2; 52 ALR 826.

SECTION 1-43: MARKETABLE TITLE

Affidavits, see 1-24B.
Marketable Title Act, see Section 1-44.
Recitals as constructive notice, see 1-31F.
Standards of title examination, see also 1-45A.

1-43A Rules.

A marketable title is such as a reasonably prudent purchaser or title examiner would accept. Hefferson v. Wuest, 3 Abs 753 (Cin. Super. Ct. 1925).

A purchaser need not accept a doubtful title, and he is not required to show that it is bad, it being sufficient if the title is questionable. Domigan v. Domigan, 46 App 542, 189 NE 860, 16 Abs 423, 40 OLR 98 (1933).

A contract to furnish an abstract of title "showing a merchantable title *of record*" is not complied with when the abstract tendered showed a one-third interest outstanding even though the record origin thereof is eighty-five years old. Horton v. Matheny, 72 App 187, 51 NE2d 41, 27 OO 69 (1943.)

Where a vendor agrees to execute a deed of general warranty, he is bound to convey a marketable title in fee simple. Laymon v. Bennett, 75 App 233, 61 NE2d 624, 30 OO 581, 42 Abs 561 (1944).

Standard of Title Examination

(Adopted by Ohio State Bar Association in 1952;
supplemented with Comment 1.1B in 1965)

Problem 1.1A:
What is the general rule as to marketability?

Standard 1.1A:

47

A marketable title is one which a purchaser would be compelled to accept in a suit for specific performance.

Objections to a title should not be made by an attorney when the irregularities or defects do not impair the title or cannot reasonably be expected to expose the client to the hazard of adverse claims, litigation or expense in clearing the title.

Comment 1.1A:

The Supreme Court states the following in the syllabus of McCarty v. Lingham (111 OS 551, 146 NE 64): "A 'marketable title' imports such ownership as insures to the owner the peaceable enjoyment and control of the land as against all others."

Comment 1.1B:

See Revised Code Section 5301.47 et seq. (Marketable Title Act).

After delivery of the deed, the grantor is not responsible or liable for an unmarketable title, unless under his covenants. See 6-13F.

Further research: O Jur 2d, Vendor and Purchaser § 49.

LAW IN GENERAL

A marketable title is one which a court of equity will compel a purchaser to accept in a suit for specific performance. The agreement of the vendor to convey a marketable title is implied unless the contract expressly provides otherwise. A title subject to a reasonable doubt is unmarketable. Whether a particular defect supports a reasonable doubt is within the sound discretion of the court. A clear record title is not required unless by contract. However, numerous cases require a marketable record title as well as a title which is good in fact. Defects and encumbrances which are believed to be merely apparent are designated as clouds on the title. Title by adverse possession may be sufficient, but it has been held that more convincing proof of validity must be produced than would be necessary to defend the title if directly attacked by an adverse claimant. A vendee will not be compelled to accept a title which would expose him to the hazard of litigation to establish it. Rightful possession, aside from the records, is essential to marketable title. A marketable title is not the equivalent of a valid title even as to matters of record; for example, the presumptions of continuance of life and of competency may be sufficient for marketability as to a conveyance by an attorney in fact, even though no title may have been actually conveyed due to the death or incompetency of the principal. Am Jur 2d, Specific Performance §§ 118, 120; Am Law of Prop §§ 11.48, 18.7; 57 ALR 1253; CJS, Vendor and Purchaser § 189.

1-43B   Liens.

Standard of Title Examination
(Adopted by Ohio State Bar Association in 1953)

Problem 4.5A:

48

Should any record of a mortgage release in the office of the county recorder be required when the mortgaged land has been conveyed pursuant to a proper foreclosure sale?

Standard 4.5A:
No.

Standard of Title Examination

(Adopted by Ohio State Bar Association in 1957)

Problem 4.5B:
Should the title to real estate be considered unmarketable if any lien thereon has been judicially extinguished but no record of its cancellation has been noted on the record of such lien?

Standard 4.5B:
No.

Further research: O Jur 2d, Vendor and Purchaser § 53.

LAW IN GENERAL

A purchaser will not be required, as a general rule, to accept a title subject to an encumbrance unless by express agreement. However, exceptions are often made on equitable grounds, as when a mortgage may be paid and the amount deducted from the purchase price. Am Law of Prop § 11.49; CJS, Vendor and Purchaser § 201.

1-43C   Restrictions.

Ordinary building restrictions applicable to the property in the neighborhood, of which a proposed purchaser has knowledge, cannot be classed as an encumbrance unless they affect the marketable quality of the title, and the presumption is that they are a benefit rather than a detriment to the property. Egle v. Morrison, 6 CC(NS) 609, 17 CD 497 (1904).

Building restrictions will bar specific performance when contract provides for title "clear, free and unencumbered." Morgan v. Pastor, 10 Abs 691 (App. 1931).

Further research: O Jur 2d, Vendor and Purchaser § 60.

LAW IN GENERAL

Enforceable restrictions on the use of the land generally render the title unmarketable if they require anything not provided by law. They are held not to be an encumbrance nor to cause unmarketability when they increase the value of the land. The existence of zoning regulations or statutory restrictions is usually not sufficient ground for refusing specific performance to the vendor. Am Law of Prop § 11.49; 39 ALR3d 362.

1-43D   Easements.

A person who contracts for the purchase of real estate, providing a "clear title" thereto is furnished, is not obliged to perform where the real estate is burdened with easements. Frank v. Murphy, 64 App 501, 29 NE2d 41, 18 OO 221 (1940).

LAW IN GENERAL

Easements, especially if for a public use, are often found to be beneficial and not to make the title unmarketable. Easements in gross are generally not encumbrances running with the land. Am Law of Prop § 11.49.

Defects in the title to or encumbrances upon appurtenant easements have been held to make the title to the dominant land unmarketable. The lack or obstruction of a public way may also be ground for a refusal of specific performance.

Easements which encumber the land and are not beneficial to the property are frequently held to justify the purchaser in refusing to accept the title, especially when the contract provides for a conveyance free from encumbrances. However, many courts grant specific performance when the easement does not materially interfere with the enjoyment of the land or when the easement is visible or was known to the vendee. Am Jur 2d, Vendor and Purchaser § 221; 78 ALR 57; CJS, Vendor and Purchaser § 206.

1-43E   Encroachments.

Actions on account of encroachments, see 3-11A.

LAW IN GENERAL

A substantial occupancy of the land by an adjoining owner is an encroachment rendering the title unmarketable. The rule is equally applicable when the encroachment is upon the adjoining land by a structure, unless such encroachment is permitted by an easement of record or by prescription. A trivial or beneficial encroachment is usually not sufficient to invoke the rule, unless by express stipulation. Am Jur 2d, Vendor and Purchaser § 216; Am Law of Prop § 11.49; 47 ALR2d 331; CJS, Vendor and Purchaser § 208.

1-43F   Vendee in Possession.

LAW IN GENERAL

A purchaser in possession cannot defeat the vendor's right by questioning the title. The rule is based upon the right to possession and is analogous to denial of a landlord's title by a tenant. The purchaser has the right to set off against the purchase price the amount expended by him in acquiring a valid outstanding interest. When the vendee has been evicted or has surrendered possession to the vendor, he is usually held entitled to assert an adverse claim which he has acquired. When the vendor brings an action for the purchase price, equity may grant relief in particular cases on account of defects in his title. Am Jur 2d, Vendor and Purchaser § 343; Am Law of Prop § 11.52.

1-43G   Recording Acts and Notice.

Questions of marketability are often settled by reference to the recording acts and to the law of notice. See Divisions 1-2 and 1-3.

1-43H   Eliminating Objection to Title; Waiver.

A purchaser cannot be compelled to accept indemnity, security, or insurance as a substitute for a marketable title. Zinser v. Dornette, 2 Abs 346 (Cin. Super. Ct. 1924).

Unmarketable titles may become marketable in various ways. See the index on deeds, adverse possession, affidavits, curative acts, declaratory judgments, estoppel, limitation of actions, quieting title, and reformation for manner of eliminating objections to title.

LAW IN GENERAL

Waiver of the right to have a defect of title remedied may be implied from the conduct of the purchaser. Mere knowledge of the defect on the part of the purchaser at the time of making the contract is ordinarily not a waiver. Am Law of Prop § 11.52.

SECTION 1-44:   MARKETABLE TITLE ACT

1-44A   Generally.

The effect of the act is to extinguish certain interests and to cure certain title defects which arose before the root of title was recorded. The root of title is the most recent deed, will, descent, court decree, etc. furnishing a basis for title marketability which has been of record for forty years or more. The gist of the act is "marketable record title" and the key word is "record" as shown by the first paragraph of R.C. 5301.48 as follows:

"Any person having the legal capacity to own land in this state, who has an unbroken chain of title of record to any interest in land for forty years or more, has a marketable record title to such interest as defined in section 5301.47 of the Revised Code, subject to the matters stated in section 5301.49 of the Revised Code."

The limitations in section 5301.49 are (A) certain interests and defects which are a part of or referred to in the deeds, wills, inheritance records, court decrees, etc. in the chain of title, (B) interests preserved by filing of proper notice or by continuous possession of same owner for forty years or more, (C) certain rights arising from adverse possession, (D) certain interests under instruments recorded after the root of title but occurring prior thereto, (E) the exceptions stated in section 5301.53.

Said exceptions in section 5301.53 are: (A) rights of any lessor or lessee, (B) easements for a railroad or public utility purpose, (C) any easement which is clearly observable, (D) any easement if its existence is evidenced by a physical facility, (E) mineral rights, (F) railroad and public utility mortgages, (G) any right of the United States or state of Ohio, or any political subdivision or agency thereof. These exceptions often make it advisable to examine the record title prior to the root of title. Nevertheless the Act is advantageous in eliminating clouds, defects and aged interests. Extinguishment of a valuable interest can be prevented by simply filing the prescribed preserving notice.

"Mortgage" is a title transaction under R.C. 5301.47 (F). However, under R.C. 5301.47 (E), it is not a root of title unless "purporting to create the interest claimed." An ordinary mortgage does not purport to create a claimed fee simple.

The Act consists of R.C. 5301.47 to 5301.56 as follows:

R.C. 5301.47 provides: "As used in sections 5301.47 to 5301.56, inclusive, of the Revised Code:

"(A) 'Marketable record title' means a title of record, as indicated in section 5301.48 of the Revised Code, which operates to extinguish such interests and claims, existing prior to the effective date of the root of title, as are stated in section 5301.50 of the Revised Code.

"(B) 'Records' includes probate and other official public records, as well as records in the office of the recorder of the county in which all or part of the land is situated.

"(C) 'Recording,' when applied to the official public records of the probate or other court, includes filing.

"(D) 'Person dealing with land' includes a purchaser of any estate or interest therein, a mortgagee, a levying or attaching creditor, a land contract vendee, or any other person seeking to acquire an estate or interest therein, or impose a lien thereon.

"(E) 'Root of title' means that conveyance or other title transaction in the chain of title of a person, purporting to create the interest claimed by such person, upon which he relies as a basis for the marketability of his title, and which was the most recent to be recorded as of a date forty years prior to the time when marketability is being determined. The effective date of the 'root of title' is the date on which it is recorded.

"(F) 'Title transaction' means any transaction affecting title to any interest in land, including title by will or descent, title by tax deed, or by trustee's, assignee's, guardian's, executor's, administrator's, or sheriff's deed, or decree of any court, as well as warranty deed, quitclaim deed, or mortgage." (As eff. 9-29-61.)

R.C. 5301.48 provides: "Any person having the legal capacity to own land in this state, who has an unbroken chain of title of record to any interest in land for forty years or more, has a marketable record title to such interest as defined in section 5301.47 of the Revised Code, subject to the matters stated in section 5301.49 of the Revised Code.

"A person has such an unbroken chain of title when the official public records disclose a conveyance or other title transaction, of record not less than forty years at the time the marketability is to be determined, which said conveyance or other title transaction purports to create such interest, either in:

"(A) The person claiming such interest; or

"(B) Some other person from whom, by one or more conveyances or other title transactions of record, such purported interest has become vested in the person claiming such interest; with nothing appearing of record, in either case, purporting to divest such claimant of such purported interest." (As eff. 9-29-61.)

R.C. 5301.49 provides: "Such record marketable title shall be subject to:

"(A) All interests and defects which are inherent in the muniments of which such chain of record title is formed; provided that a general reference in such muniments, or any of them, to easements, use restrictions, or other interests created prior to the root of title shall not be sufficient to preserve them, unless specific identification be made therein of a recorded title transaction which creates such easement, use restriction, or other interest; and provided that possibilities of reverter, and rights of entry or powers of termination for breach of condition subsequent, which interests are inherent in the muniments of which such chain of record title is formed and which have existed for forty years or more, shall be preserved and kept effective only in the manner provided in section 5301.51 of the Revised Code;

"(B) All interests preserved by the filing of proper notice or by possession by the same owner continuously for a period of forty years or more, in accordance with section 5301.51 of the Revised Code;

"(C) The rights of any person arising from a period of adverse possession or user, which was in whole or in part subsequent to the effective date of the root of title;

"(D) Any interest arising out of a title transaction which has been recorded subsequent to the effective date of the root of title from which the unbroken chain of title or record is started; provided that such recording shall not revive or give validity to any interest which has been extinguished prior to the time of the recording by the operation of section 5301.50 of the Revised Code;

"(E) The exceptions stated in section 5301.53 of the Revised Code." (As eff. 1-23-63.)

R.C. 5301.50 provides: "Subject to the matters stated in section 5301.49 of the Revised Code, such record marketable title shall be held by its owner and shall be taken by any person dealing with the land free and clear of all interests, claims, or charges whatsoever, the existence of which depends upon any act, transaction, event, or omission that occurred prior to the effective date of the root of title. All such interests, claims, or charges, however denominated, whether legal or equitable, present or future, whether such interests, claims, or charges are asserted by a person sui juris or under a disability, whether such person is within or without the state, whether such person is natural or corporate, or is private or governmental, are hereby declared to be null and void." (As eff. 9-29-61.)

R.C. 5301.51 provides: "(A) Any person claiming an interest in land may preserve and keep effective such interest by filing for record during the forty-year period immediately following the effective date of the root of title of the person whose record title would otherwise be marketable, a notice in writing, duly verified by oath, setting forth the nature of the claim. No disability or lack of knowledge of any kind on the part of anyone shall suspend the running of said forty-year period. Such notice may be filed for record by the claimant or by any other person acting on behalf of any claimant who is:

"(1) Under a disability;

"(2) Unable to assert a claim on his own behalf; or

"(3) One of a class, but whose identity cannot be established or is uncertain at the time of filing such notice of claim for record.

"(B) If the same record owner of any possessory interest in land has been in possession of such land continuously for a period of forty years or more, during which period no title transaction with respect to such interest appears of record in his chain of title, and no notice has been filed by him on his behalf as provided in division (A) of this section, and such possession continues to the time when marketability is being determined, such period of possession is equivalent to the filing of the notice immediately preceding the termination of the forty-year period described in division (A) of this section." (As eff. 9-29-61.)

R.C. 5301.52 provides: "To be effective and to be entitled to record, the notice referred to in section 5301.51 of the Revised Code shall contain an accurate and full description of all land affected by such notice which description shall be set forth in particular terms and not by general inclusions; but if said claim is founded upon a recorded instrument, then the description in such notice may be the same as that contained in such recorded instrument. Such notice shall be filed for record in the office of the recorder of the county or counties where the land described therein is situated. The recorder of each county shall accept all such notices presented to him which describe land situated in the county in which he serves and shall enter and record the same in the deed records of said county, and each recorder shall be entitled to charge the same fees for the recording thereof as are charged for recording deeds. In indexing such notices in his office each recorder shall enter such notices under the grantee indexes of deeds under the names of the claimants appearing in such notices. Such notices shall also be indexed under the description of the real estate involved in a book set apart for that purpose to be known as the 'Notice Index.'" (As eff. 9-29-61.)

R.C. 5301.53 provides: "The provisions of sections 5301.47 to 5301.56 of the Revised Code, shall not be applied:

"(A) To bar any lessor or his successor as reversioner of his right to possession on the expiration of any lease or any lessee or his successor of his rights in and to any lease;

"(B) To bar or extinguish any easement or interest in the nature of an easement created or held for any railroad or public utility purpose;

"(C) To bar or extinguish any easement or interest in the nature of an easement, the existence of which is clearly observable by physical evidence of its use;

"(D) To bar or extinguish any easement or interest in the nature of an easement, or any rights granted, excepted, or reserved by the instrument creating such easement or interest, including any rights for future use, if the existence of such easement or interest is evidenced by the location beneath, upon, or above any part of the land described in such instrument of any pipe, valve, road, wire, cable, conduit, duct, sewer, track, pole, tower, or other physical facility and whether or not the existence of such facility is observable;

"(E) To bar or extinguish any right, title, estate, or interest in coal, and any mining or other rights pertinent thereto or exercisable in connection therewith;

"(F) To bar or extinguish any mortgage recorded in conformity with section 1701.66 of the Revised Code;

"(G) To bar or extinguish any right, title, or interest of the United States, or of the State of Ohio, or any political subdivision, body politic, or agency thereof." (As eff. 9-30-74.)

R.C. 5301.54 provides: "Nothing contained in sections 5301.47 to 5301.56, inclusive, of the Revised Code, shall be construed to extend the period for the bringing of an action or for the doing of any other required act under any statutes of limitations, nor, except as provided in sections 5301.47 to 5301.56, inclusive, of the Revised Code, to affect the operation of any statutes governing the effect of the recording or the failure to record any instrument affecting land." (As eff. 9-29-61.)

R.C. 5301.55 provides: "Sections 5301.47 to 5301.56, inclusive, of the Revised Code, shall be liberally construed to effect the legislative purpose of simplifying and facilitating land title transactions by allowing persons to rely on a record chain of title as described in section 5301.48 of the Revised Code, subject only to such limitations as appear in section 5301.49 of the Revised Code." (As eff. 9-29-61.)

R.C. 5301.56 provides: "Regardless of when the forty-year period specified in sections 5301.47 to 5301.56 of the Revised Code expires, for the purpose of filing a notice under division (A) of section 5301.51 of the Revised Code as to right, title, estate, or interest in and to minerals, with the exception of coal, such period shall not be considered to expire until after December 31, 1976." (As eff. 9-30-74.)

"Language such as 'subject to easements and restrictions of record' is inadequate to preserve these interests * * * Any interest in land such as an easement or use restriction in existence prior to a root of title is extinguished unless it is: (1) specifically stated or identified in the root of title; (2) specifically stated or identified in one of the muniments of the chain of record title within forty years after the root of title; (3) recorded pursuant to R.C. 5301.51 and 5301.52; (4) one of the other exceptions provided for in R.C. 5301.49; (5) one of the rights that cannot be barred by the Marketable Title Act provided in R.C. 5301.53." Semachko v. Hopko, 35 App2d 205, 301 NE2d 560, 64 OO2d 316 (1973).

Where A reserves the oil and gas rights in a conveyance of land to B in 1916, and under the terms of the will of A, the oil and gas rights are transferred to the devisees of A in 1957, that transfer preserves the separated oil and gas rights, and the title of the successors in title to B is not freed of the oil and gas rights, though no preserving notice was filed in the chain of title of B. Heifner v. Bradford, 4 OS3d 49, 446 NE2d 440 (1983).

Where a deed since the root of title deed specifically refers to a setback use restriction as having been created in a recorded plat, the restriction is preserved even though its true source was a deed prior to the root of title rather than the plat. Toth v. Berks Title Ins. Co., 6 OS3d 338, 453 NE2d 639 (1983). Also, see dissenting opinion.

Standard of Title Examination

(Adopted by Ohio State Bar Association in 1969)

Problem 8.1A:

Can a title instrument which otherwise qualifies as a root of title by which results from defective legal proceedings be deemed a proper root of title?

Standard 8.1A:

Yes.

Comment 8.1A:

It is unnecessary to examine the legal proceedings which form a basis for the title instrument in question.

Appendix to Standard 8.1A

(Approved by Ohio State Bar Association in 1970)

The Ohio Marketable Title Act is patterned after the Model Act which, in turn, was based on the Michigan Marketable Title Act. The Ohio Marketable Title Act, Revised Code 5301.47 et seq., became effective September 29, 1961.

The material which follows is in substance a comment on the Model Act contained in "The Improvement of Conveyancing by Legislation," by Lewis M. Simes and Clarence B. Taylor, published by the University of Michigan Law School, Ann Arbor, in 1960. The comment has been revised so that all references are to the Ohio Act rather than the Model Act * * *

Section 5301.48 of the [Ohio] Act states that a person has a marketable title to an interest in land if he has an unbroken chain of record title for a period of not less than forty years. Chain of title is then defined by two clauses, the first of which states the case where the chain of title consists only of a single instrument or transaction, and the second where it consists of two or more instruments or transactions. The obvious proposition is stated that, in order to constitute a chain of title, nothing must appear of record purporting to divest the claimant of the marketable title.

It should be noted at this point that the term marketable record title as used in the Act, and as defined in Section 5301.47, does not mean a title which a vendee under a land contract can be compelled to accept. It means simply that the forty-year title extinguishes all prior interest, subject to a very few exceptions. It is true, if these prior interests are extinguished, the title will generally be marketable in every sense of the word, but that does not necessarily follow. All the statute says is that, subject to the exceptions and qualifications stated in Section 5301.49, all interests prior to the beginning of the forty-year period are extinguished. The qualifications stated in Section 5301.49 may sometimes mean that the title is not really marketable from a commercial standpoint.

One further general observation as to the operation of the statute should be made. If at any given time there is a dealing with the title of the record owner, the chain of title which he must show, in order that it be marketable under the terms of the Act, will generally be somewhat more than forty years in length, for it will only be by an unusual coincidence that there will be a recorded title transaction exactly forty years back. Hence he will go back of forty years to the last recorded title transaction prior to forty years. That recorded title transaction is described in the Act as the root of title. Thus suppose, in 1959, A wishes to sell a certain piece of land. Assume that the instrument on record concerning the land is a conveyance from X to A in fee simple, recorded in 1900. The record of this instrument constitutes A's chain of title as defined in the Act, and the instrument is his root of title. Hence, in order to show a marketable title, he must show the record of that instrument. Of course, if we are looking at the Act, not from the standpoint of dealing with the title at any given time, but from the standpoint of its operation in extinguished ancient claims, we must conclude that such claims were extinguished exactly forty years after the effective date of the root of title. That is to say, in the example suggested, in 1940 the Act operated to extinguish interests based solely on title transactions prior to 1900, the effective date of the root of title.

The specific provisions of Section 5301.49 (A) state an idea embodied in the Michigan Act and in other marketable title acts. It simply says you cannot rely on a forty-year chain of title to extinguish defects and interests which are recognized in that same chain of title. For example, suppose a deed recorded in 1910 shows that A conveyed to B for life remainder to C. No subsequent instruments affecting the title are on record. In 1959 C wishes to sell the property in fee simple absolute, and claims that the Act has extinguished B's life estate. B's life estate has not been extinguished, because C must show the deed recorded in 1910 as his chain of title, and the life estate is an interest "inherent in the muniments of which such chain of record title is formed."

On the other hand, suppose, as before, in 1910 a deed was recorded in which A conveys to B for life remainder to C. Then assume also that in 1912

C conveys to X in fee simple absolute and X at once records. There being nothing else on the record in 1959 with respect to the tract of land involved, X has a fee simple absolute under the Act. X's root of title is the 1912 deed, which conveys in fee simple absolute. Hence, forty years thereafter, or in 1952, B's life estate was extinguished.

The proviso concerning a general reference is designed to avoid any necessity for a search of the entire record back of the forty-year period, and to eliminate the uncertainties caused by general references.

Section 5301.49 (B) refers to the filing of the notice to prevent the extinguishment of interests arising prior to the effective date of the root of title. Thus, in the example last given, if B who originally had a life estate, had filed a notice after 1912 and prior to 1952, his life estate would have been preserved. It should be noted also that the forty-year period within which the claimant must file is not forty years from the time the claimant aquired his interest. It is forty years after the effective date of the root of title of the person claiming marketable title. This is expressly stated in Section 5301.51 (A). Of course, the claimant will never have less than forty years, but he may have much more than that period after his interest was created. Thus, in the case suggested, B's life estate arose in 1910, but he has until forty years after 1912, the effective date of X's root of title, within which to file his notice of claim. This is because the Act is quieting a forty-year record title, and because it is not in any real sense a statute of limitations on adverse claims.

Section 5301.49 (B) also provides that the marketable record title is subject to interests preserved by a possession which is equivalent to the filing of a notice. This proposition is stated more fully in Section 5301.51 (B), and will be developed later.

Section 5301.49 (C) preserves, as against the holder of the marketable title, any title by adverse possession which accrued in whole or any part after the effective date of the root of title. Thus suppose A conveys land to B in fee simple and the deed is recorded in 1912, there being no other recorded instruments concerning the land except such as were recorded prior to 1912. Let us also assume that X entered into hostile possession of the land in 1892, claiming in fee simple, and remained in possession until 1915, the period of the applicable statute of limitations being twenty-one years. While B gets a marketable record title in 1952, forty years after the effective date of his root of title, it is subject to X's title by adverse possession which ripened in 1913, and therefore X has the better title. One reason why X acquires title by adverse possession in this way, counting twenty-three adverse years prior to the effective date of B's root of title, is that the statute does not modify the period of the statute of limitations for title by adverse possession. Section 5301.54 of the Act so declares. If we were to say that X could not get a title by adverse possession until twenty-one years after 1912, then we would be requiring forty-one years of adverse possession.

On the other hand, if the period of adverse possession is wholly prior to the effective date of the root of title, then the title by adverse possession is wiped out just like any other title which arises from an event occurring prior to the effective date of the root of title. Suppose, a deed is recorded in 1912, conveying a tract of land to A in fee simple. But X had entered into hostile possession in 1886, claiming in fee simple, and remained in possession for a period of twenty-one years, the period of the statute of limitations. Thus, in 1907, X acquired a title in fee simple by adverse possession. But, assuming that no other title transactions appear of record except A's deed, A has a marketable title in fee simple absolute in 1952, which cuts off X's title by adverse possession.

Section 5301.49 (D) deals with the question: What is the effect of instruments being recorded during the forty-year period after the effective date of the root of title, which are a part of or constitute an independent chain of title? Suppose a deed conveying land from A to B in fee simple is recorded in 1912. A second deed conveying the same land from B to C in fee simple is recorded in 1925. In 1915, a deed conveying the same land from X to Y in fee simple is recorded. In 1955, Y may be said to have a marketable record title under the statute, since 40 years has elapsed after the effective date of his root of title, 1915. And the 1925 conveyance from B to C cannot be said to purport to divest Y, since it is an entirely independent chain of title. Nevertheless, by the terms of this clause, Y takes subject to the interest of C arising from the deed recorded in 1925. It will be noted, therefore, that the recording of C's deed in 1925 operated in much the same way as if he had filed a notice, and prevented Y from wiping out C's title in 1955. Suppose, however, that a conveyance from A to B in fee simple is recorded in 1912 and then a conveyance from B to C in fee simple is recorded in 1957. Another chain of title consists in a conveyance in fee simple from X to Y, recorded in 1915. In 1955 Y has a marketable title under the statute; and this wipes out B's interest at that time. Therefore, in accordance with the proviso in Section 5301.49 (D), B's interest, which was once extinguished, is not revived, and Y's title is not subject to it. It is true, we can say that in a sense Y's title is subject to a conveyance from B to C, but this conveyance has merely the force of a wild deed, and does not carry any interest to C.

One qualification must be made concerning this proposition, if certain additional facts are added. Assume, again, that A conveyed to B in fee simple by a deed which was recorded in 1912, and that there is no other conveyance in this chain of title until a deed from B to C is recorded in 1957. Assume also that B took possession of the land and remained in possession continuously until the conveyance from B to C in 1957. At the same time assume a conveyance from X to Y which was recorded in 1915. Here under the exception stated in Section 5301.49 (B) and elaborated in Section 5301.51 (B), B had a good title when he conveyed to C in 1957. If B had filed a notice of his claim immediately before 1955, the date on which the deed to Y would have been on record forty years, B's interest would have been completely protected under the provisions of Section 5301.51 (A). But Section 5301.51 (B) provides that, if B has been in possession during the entire forty-year period since the deed to Y was recorded, and if, during that time, no title transaction was recorded in his chain of title, and if B was still in possession at the time when marketability was being determined (that is, in 1957), then B's title is treated as if B had recorded a notice of claim immediately before 1955. This is a situation which is very unlikely to arise, since there must be no title transaction in the chain of title of the possessory owner on record during a period of at least forty years, and the possessory owner must have been in possession during that entire period and must still be in possession. But if such a situation should arise, it would seem to be unfair to deprive B of his title as against Y (who may have been a grantee under a wild deed) merely because B failed to file a notice of claim. It is to take care of this extraordinary situation that Section 5301.51 (B) is included.

It should be noted that this is the only situation where the mere fact of possession is significant in determining marketable title under the Act. Even here, possession is considered only if a person having a record chain of title is in possession at the time marketability is being determined. Moreover, this possession has significance only if we also find a period of forty years in the record chain of title of such person, during which there are no title transactions. Otherwise, the interest or claim of the possessor would be preserved by the appearance of record of the recorded title transactions.

Section 5301.50 declares the extent to which all interests prior to the effective date of the root of title are extinguished. It is clear that this extinguishment is absolute and not relative, and that the interests are not revived. The same proposition is stated in the proviso of Section 5301.49 (D).

Sections 5301.51 and 5301.52 give the details as to the requirements for the filing of a notice of claim. It should be noted that the last sentence of Section 5301.52 provides for a "Notice Index." This is because in counties where no tract index is available, it would be difficult to find such notices in grantor-grantee indexes or in miscellaneous indexes.

[End of this Appendix]

SECTION 1-45: STANDARDS OF TITLE EXAMINATION

1-45A   Generally.

The following is the foreword, prepared by Thomas J. McDermott, for the publication of Standards of Title Examination, distributed by Ohio State Bar Association:

The primary purpose of standards of title examination is to promote uniformity of practice pertaining to marketability of titles. Several advantages accrue to both the public and to the profession through observance of the standards. The public interest is served by increasing the stability and negotiability of titles. No undue burden is placed upon clients when the standards are properly prepared. Lawyers are benefited by improved public relations, by guidance and authority on problems which may be debatable, by avoidance of unprofitable controversies between themselves, by elimination of labor and expense in curing irregularities, and by a protection against criticism and charges of negligence when the approved rules have been followed.

We are all acquainted with an evil at which these canons are aimed, to wit: — objections made only because the lawyer fears that the thoroughness of his examination may be disparaged by a subsequent examination. Objections are sometimes made not because the examiner believes that the irregularity is actually significant or makes the title unmarketable but because of the prospect that a following examiner may make the objection. This evil can be remedied when the action of the second examiner can be ascertained in advance by reference to the promulgations of our state association.

Standards of title examination have been adopted by the bar associations of seventeen other states. All reports from these states show that the bar welcomes and appreciates the benefits. As was said in a report of the Connecticut committee to the American Bar Association, "The reputable conveyancers are all following them as if they were a bible." Marketable title acts do not necessarily conflict because most questions of marketability arise during the period not affected by such enactments.

The only sanction for the standards is the attitude of the bar as a whole; their effectiveness depends upon a general observance. Enforcement through legislative action is believed not to be proper; the inflexibility resulting from incorporation in statutes is thought to be inadvisable. Infallibility is not claimed for these rules and is not necessary for their purpose. Even a decision of the Supreme Court may be overruled. We are convinced that these standards may be confidently relied upon until amendment is required by subsequent statute or judicial decision. An attorney can be justified as reasonably prudent when following the course approved by this association.

This program was initiated in the Ohio State Bar Association during 1950 and was one of the reasons for an ABA award to it this year. The project is a living one as both old and new problems will continue to call for consideration. The scope of the work has been limited by the committee's policy of proposing standards for adoption by the association only where the practice has been diverse and where no substantial doubt as to the law or as to the better practice has been found.

The benefits can be greatly extended by a widespread submission of recommendations. Suggested standards are solicited and may be presented to any member of the committee or may be sent to the association office. Some county associations have already acted by adopting the standards and it is hoped that many more will do so. Additional standards applicable to specific local situations may be found helpful in some communities.

Standard of Title Examination

(Adopted by Ohio State Bar Association in 1960)

Standard 1.2A:

An attorney drawing a contract for the sale or purchase of land should recommend that the terms of the contract provide that marketability be determined in accordance with Title Standards of the Ohio State Bar Association and that the existence of encumbrances and defects, and the effect to be given to any found to exist, be determined in accordance with such standards.

Comment 1.2A:

An attorney, drawing a contract for the sale or purchase of land, should recommend the inclusion of the following language or its equivalent in the contract:

"Marketability of title, if the owner is required to furnish marketable title, shall be determined in accordance with the Title Standards approved by the Ohio State Bar Association."

The Standards of Title Examination, as adopted and amended by Ohio State Bar Association, may be found at the subsections indicated below.

1-45B Abstracting Standards.

Six-year limitation on enforcement of particular state liens, see R.C. 2305.26 at 16-42A.

COLUMBUS BAR ASSOCIATION
REAL PROPERTY SEARCH STANDARDS*
Effective March 1, 1982

General

It is the responsibility of all persons making title searches (hereinafter referred to as "abstractors") to keep informed with respect to the time lag of indexing in all the various offices.

Generally, in searching the indexes, the rule of *idem sonans* should be followed. Names such as "A. John Doe" should be searched both under "A" and "J" in indexes using first name divisions; names such as "C(K)arl" and C(K)atherine" should be searched under "C" and "K" in such indexes. Corporate names such as "John A. Smith, Inc." should be searched both under "J" and "S". If title is acquired by nickname, the proper name should also be searched. For example, "Tony" requires a search for "Anthony". Attention is called to the fact that there are special headings used in the various indexes including "schools", "churches", "lot owners", "vacations", "annexations", etc.

Relative to corporate title holders, since the abstractor is to include the Articles of Incorporation, he should also include all pertinent amendments, mergers or consolidations. If a change of name of the corporation is disclosed, the search should be made under both the new name and the former name, from the date of the name change.

Land contract vendees must be searched as fee owners.

The abstractor's certificates should contain a representation that the work was performed in accordance with the standards of the Columbus Bar Association in effect as of the date thereof. Failure to include such a representation in

---

*Adopted by the Columbus Bar Association, Real Property Committee, on January 21, 1982. Adopted by the Board of Governors, Columbus Bar Association, on January 29, 1982.

the certificate shall be grounds for rejection of the abstract by the examining attorney.

The standards and suggested form of certification which will comply with the requirements of these Search Standards with respect to root of title abstracts are set forth on the instrument attached hereto and entitled "Additional Standards and Suggested Tail Sheet for Root of Title Abstracts."

The attached instrument entitled "Suggested Tail Sheet for Conventional Abstract" will comply with the requirements of these Search Standards.

New Indexes and Records

It is the responsibility of all abstractors to keep informed as to the creation of new indexes subsequent to the adoption of these Search Standards. To the extent that the information contained in any new indexes affects title, it is the intent of these Search Standards to require the abstractor to report said information.

County Records and Search Periods

Office	Records to be Searched	Period of Search for Each Titleholder Since Last Evidence of Title
Recorder	Grantor Index Grantee Index Mortgagor Index Lessor Index Miscellaneous Records Direct Index Miscellaneous Records Reverse Index Authority to Pay Tax Lien	From date title acquired to date title divested.
Recorder	Recognizance Lien Index Unemployment Compensation Lien Index Personal Property Tax Lien Index	From 6 years prior to the date of search to the date title divested. *NOTE:* A titleholder may be searched only for his/her period of ownership rather than searching the period indicated above.
Recorder	Federal Tax Lien Index	From beginning of Index to the date title divested.
Recorder	Excise & Franchise Tax Lien Index (as to corporations only)	From beginning of Index to the date title divested (to pick up charter cancellations as well as tax liens).
Recorder	Notice Index	From beginning of Index to date title divested.
Recorder	Liens Against Index	During the 6 years prior to the date of search, from the date title acquired to 60 days after title divested.
Recorder	Power of Attorney Index	No search necessary unless you have notice of exercise of Power of Attorney during your period of search.
Recorder	Daily Records	For period necessary to complete search to date of search.

Office	Records to be Searched	Period of Search for Each Titleholder Since Last Evidence of Title
Recorder	Partnership Index	No search necessary unless you have notice of partnership in title during period of search.
Sheriff	Foreign Executions	During the 5 years prior to the date of search from the date title acquired to date title divested.
Clerk — Civil Div.	General Index	From 10 years prior to the date of the search to the date title divested. *NOTE:* A titleholder may be searched only for his/her period of ownership rather than searching the period indicated above.
Clerk — Domestic Relations Div.	Divorce and Dissolution Index	From the date title acquired to the date title divested.
Clerk — Domestic Relations Div.	Daily Record of New Cases	For period necessary to complete search to date of certificate.
Probate Court	General Index	From the date title acquired to the date title divested.
Probate Court	Marriage Record Index	From the date title acquired to the date title divested. *NOTE:* Search necessary only for female titleholders. No search necessary if spouse disclosed in chain of title.

Office	Records to be Searched	Information Required
Auditor	Auditor's Duplicate	Name of property owner Street address Parcel No. & taxing district Valuation Brief description (lot number or number of acres)
Auditor — Agricultural Recoupment Desk	Agricultural Recoupment Valuation	May be reduction in tax valuation due to past agricultural use of property that may be recouped as a lien in the future.
Treasurer	Treasurer's Duplicate	Current taxes Delinquent taxes and penalties Special assessments Homestead exemption

Searches with Respect to Condominium Property

In addition to searching the owner's name in the records set forth above, abstractors making searches with respect to condominium property should search the following records in the name of the condominium unit owner's association:

67

Office	Records to be Searched	Information Required
Recorder	Grantor Index	Locate amendments to condominium declaration.
Clerk — Civil Div.	General Index	Determine if there are suits or judgments against the association which might affect the buyer's future assessments, easements, or the common area, right to use the common area, etc.

**Searches with Respect to
U.S. District Court and
U.S. Bankruptcy Court**

Period of Search

Recognizing that historically the Real Property Search Standards of the Columbus Bar Association have not required a search of records in the office of the Clerk of the U.S. District Court and the Clerk of the U.S. Bankruptcy Court and the fact that closed files from those courts are routinely sent to other federal government locations for retention after a period of time pursuant to federal government regulations, the abstractor shall have no responsibility, unless specifically requested otherwise, to conduct any examination of the records in either of these offices as of a date prior to the date of the last continuation or prior to the date of acquisition of title by the present fee owner, whichever date is earlier. Except when preparing an original abstract or a root of title abstract, in which case the abstractor shall search such records for the entire period covered by the abstract.

Information to be Shown

The abstractor should set forth the following information:

(a) Clerk of U.S. District Court — with respect to actions affecting real property the same information that would be disclosed if the action had been filed in the Common Pleas Court.

(b) Clerk of U.S. Bankruptcy Court — all bankruptcy proceedings involving the owner of an interest in the real property under investigation during the period of that owner's ownership, together with the applicable chapter of the Bankruptcy Act or Code under which the proceeding was filed, the date of filing, whether the real property was scheduled as an asset of the estate, all actions affecting the real property, whether the case is pending or has been closed, the date of the closing of the case, and the date of discharge, if any.

SUGGESTED TAIL SHEET FOR
CONVENTIONAL ABSTRACT

Section _____

The premises stand charged for taxation on the Duplicate of Franklin County, Ohio for the current year in the name of:

at a valuation of: Land-$ Buildings-$ Total-$

as to:

Taxing District and Parcel Number:

Street Address

Taxes for

Special assessments noted on the Treasurer's Duplicate affecting the premises are as follows:

No examination was made for assessments not indexed or otherwise shown on the County Treasurer's Duplicate. No examination was made in indexes in the Franklin County Municipal Court. No examination was made in any other indexes not required to be examined by the current search standards of the Columbus Bar Association.

An examination has been made of the indexes in the U.S. District Court and the U.S. Bankruptcy Court only from the date of the last continuation or the date on which the present fee owner acquired title to the premises, whichever date is earlier.

I hereby certify that the foregoing continuation of Abstract of Title, consisting of _____ sections, was collated by me from the records of Franklin County, Ohio, the U.S. District Court and the U.S. Bankruptcy Court situated in such county in accordance with the current standards of the Columbus Bar Association, and I further certify that the same contains either a copy or abstract of every instrument of record in said County and in said U.S. District Court and U.S. Bankruptcy Court that in any way affects said premises, as shown by the respective indexes to said County and U.S. District Court and U.S. Bankruptcy Court records.

DATED: Respectfully submitted,

_____

Name:
Address:
Phone Number:

ADDITIONAL STANDARDS AND
SUGGESTED TAIL SHEET FOR
ROOT OF TITLE ABSTRACTS

An abstract of title which commences at a root of title as defined in Ohio Revised Code Section 5301.47 (Marketable Title Act), which is otherwise collated and prepared in accordance with the Search Standards of the Columbus Bar Association, and which contains the certification hereinafter set forth, shall be deemed to be a complete abstract of title in accordance with the Search Standards of the Columbus Bar Association.

The certification shall be substantially as follows:

"I hereby certify that this Abstract of Title consisting of _____ sections was collated by me from the records of Franklin County, Ohio, and the U.S. District Court and U.S. Bankruptcy Court located in such county, in accordance with the current Search Standards of the Columbus Bar Association, and I further certify that the same contains either a copy or abstract of every instrument of record in said county, said U.S. District Court and said U.S. Bankruptcy Court that in any way affects said premises, as shown by the respective indexes to said county and court records, (1) from the date of the root of title, which is the instrument of record in Deed Book _____, page _____, filed with the Recorder of Franklin County, Ohio, on _____, and (2) from the date of the U.S. patent to the date of the root of title with respect to the following interests which are excepted from the operation of the Marketable Title Act:

(a) Any interest of a lessor or his successor as reversioner of his right to possession on the expiration of any lease or any interest of a lessee or his successor of his rights in and to any lease;

(b) Any easement or interest in the nature of an easement, or any rights granted, excepted or reserved by the instrument creating such easement or interest;

(c) Any right, title, estate or interest in coal, and any mining or other rights appurtenant thereto or exercisable in connection therewith;

(d) Any mortgage recorded in conformity with Section 1701.66 of the Revised Code (public utilities); and

(e) Any right, title or interest of the United States or of the State of Ohio, or any political subdivision, body politic or agency thereof."

The Marketable Title Act in Ohio Revised Code Section 5301.53(B), (C) & (D) specifies the types of easements which the Act does not extinguish by operation of law. In order to relieve the abstractor of the burden of determining whether a particular easement is an easement of the nature described in Ohio Revised Code Section 5301.53(B), (C) & (D), the Standards, in subparagraph (b) of the foregoing certification, require that all easements, of whatever nature, be shown.

DIVISION 1-5: REGISTRATION OF TITLES

SECTION 1-51: THE SYSTEM

1-51A In General.

R.C. 5309.01 to 5309.98 and 5310.01 to 5310.16 provide a system, known as the "Torrens System," separate and distinct from the general recording acts system. The purpose is to make the title conclusively ascertainable by reference to a certificate issued and recorded by the county recorder. The distinguishing feature is registration of the title instead of registration of the evidence of title. Adverse possession, prescription and the the general recording acts do not apply to registered land. Initial registration, in the nature of a suit to quiet title, and withdrawal from the system are optional with the landowner. The system is not in extensive use. Upon withdrawal, all deeds and mortgages theretofore conveying the registered land shall be recorded according to law.

In order to obtain a lien over a mortgage duly entered, a materialman must file an affidavit before the mortgage is filed setting forth his intention to assert a mechanic's lien. Gough Lumber Co. v. Crawford, 124 OS 46, 176 NE 677, 10 Abs 94, 34 OLR 477 (1931).

A subsequent purchaser of registered land who receives a certificate of title without good faith takes the lands subject to an outstanding equity. Shaker Corlett Land Co. v. Cleveland, 139 OS 536, 41 NE2d 243, 23 OO 27 (1942).

Although the grantee of an auditor's tax deed has obtained a decree quieting his title, the county recorder will not be required to issue a certificate of title until a court order is obtained as provided by R.C. 5309.60. State ex rel. Barnhart v. Watt, 164 OS 320, 131 NE2d 217, 58 OO 102 (1955).

Provision for vacating judgment after term, will prevail over R.C. 5309.23 and 5309.24 where one of defendants died before judgment. Cline v. Hammond, 48 App 228, 192 NE 869, 1 OO 206, 11 Abs 126 (1931).

The decision of the recorder that a certain document shall be canceled and not carried forward to a subsequent certificate does not divest any right. Pennsylvania R. Co. v. Kearns, 71 App 209, 48 NE2d 1012, 26 OO 33, 37 Abs 501 (1943).

A lien filed in accordance with the Torrens Act after filing of the petition in bankruptcy is invalid against the trustee in bankruptcy in the county in which is kept the record of the original proceedings, although no notice of the bankruptcy was filed with the county recorder. In re Kabbage, 93 F Supp 515, 43 OO 332, 59 Abs 572 (1950).

Provisions of the Torrens Act designed to protect a purchaser against liens have no application to the case of a tax sale of forfeited registered land against which there are unregistered assessments. Adams v. Nibbor Realty Co., 93 NE2d 727, 57 Abs 241 (App. 1950).

Special assessments are enforceable liens although not memorialized where they accrued as a result of petition by predecessors in title of the owners. Monroe v. Durkin, 118 NE2d 851, 72 Abs 245 (App. 1954).

The failure to memorialize the judgment of forfeiture for nonpayment of taxes invalidated the subsequent auditor's sale. Kohrman v. Rausch, 138 NE2d 22, 75 Abs 193 (App. 1956).

The grantee of a tax deed for registered land must affirmatively prove strict compliance with the statutes relative to tax sales in order to be entitled to registration of his title. Hale v. McChesney, 100 NE2d 95, 59 Abs 367 (C.P. 1951).

An action for recovery from the assurance fund may be brought within six years after the subject property is vested in the damaged party. The action may be tried by the court. Macy v. Herbert, 28 OS2d 124, 276 NE2d 645, 57 OO2d 327 (1971).

An easement that arose by implication of law subsequent to the registration of title under R.C. Chapters 5309 and 5310 (Torrens System) will not be recognized and enforced against the alleged servient estate if the implied easement is not noted or memorialized on the register of titles. Kincaid v. Yount, 9 App3d 145, 459 NE2d 235 (1983).

Further research: O Jur 3d, Abstracts and Land Titles § 11.

LAW IN GENERAL

An impartial study of the Torrens System was made in 1938 under a grant from Carnegie Corporation. The report made by Professor Richard R. Powell and published by the New York Law Society as "Registration of the Title to Land in the State of New York," contains the following: "In fact the collected evidence indicates that title registration involves difficulties, expenses and personnel problems more troublesome and irremediable than those encountered in recordation. It would be to the public interest to enact forthwith a law putting an end to further registrations in the state of New York."

The report also shows that statutes have been enacted in twenty states and repealed in eight of them. In six of the remaining states, registration was never substantial and has decreased. In the other six states (Hawaii, Illinois, Massachusetts, Minnesota, New York, and Ohio) the system has been extensively used in very few counties.

As a general rule a purchaser for value in good faith will be protected against any unregistered claims in regard to the land even though such claims are prior in time to the purchaser's title. 42 ALR2d 1389.

Additional references: Am Jur 2d, Registration of Land Titles § 1 et seq.; Am Law of Prop § 17.37 et seq.; CJS, Registration of Land Titles § 1 et seq.; Powell § 919; Tiffany § 1314.

1-51B Index to Revised Code.

Judicial sale proceedings, 5309.61 to 5309.64, 5309.66, 5309.67, 5309.81, 5309.94.

Jurisdiction of common pleas and probate courts, concurrent, 5309.02.

Land sales in probate court, 5309.45.

Law changed only as expressly provided, 5309.85, 5309.91.

Liens, 5309.47 to 5309.57.

Lis pendens, 5309.58.

Losses paid from assurance fund, 5310.05 to 5310.14.

Lost or destroyed certificates, 5309.31.

Mechanics' liens, 5309.57.

Mistakes, effect of, 5309.87.

Mistakes in certificate, 5309.76.

Notice of unregistered interest, effect of, 5309.34.

Notice to owner upon filing, 5309.82.

Original registration, 5309.08 to 5309.24, 5309.66, 5309.67.

Partition proceedings, 5309.61 to 5309.64.

Part, transfer of, 5309.41.

Penalties, 5310.16 to 5310.20, 5310.99.

Pending action, notice of, 5309.58.

Platting, 5309.27.

Powers of attorney, 5309.74, 5309.75.

Prescription, 5309.89.

Priorities, 5310.02.

Questions to be referred to court, 5309.27, 5309.29, 5309.43, 5309.45, 5309.46, 5309.52, 5309.60, 5309.69, 5309.83.

Recorder, powers of, 5309.03, 5310.04.

Records to be kept, 5309.25, 5309.30, 5309.32, 5309.33, 5309.35, 5309.38, 5309.39, 5309.41, 5309.65, 5309.86, 5309.95 to 5309.97.

Rules of court, 5309.98.

Separate certificates, 5309.27.

Service of process, 5309.81, 5309.94.

Stay of registrations for 24 hours, 5309.78.

Surrender of certificate, 5309.44, 5309.68.

Taxes, certificate of, 5309.37.

Tax sales, 5309.59, 5309.60.

Tax titles, 5309.07.

Transfer by county auditor, 5309.37.

Trust, declarations of, 5309.69.

Unregistered valid interests, 5309.28.

Variance between owner's duplicate and original, 5309.25.

What may be registered, 5309.05 to 5309.07, 5309.29.

Will, transfer under, 5309.45, 5309.46.

Withdrawal from system, 5309.68.

CHAPTER 2: ADVERSE POSSESSION

DIVISION 2-1:   IN GENERAL

SECTION 2-11:   INTRODUCTION; NATURE OF THE TITLE AND RIGHTS ACQUIRED

Limitation of actions generally, see Section 16-41.

2-11A   Statutes; Generally.

R.C. 2305.04 provides: "An action to recover the title to or possession of real property shall be brought within twenty-one years after the cause thereof accrued, but if a person entitled to bring such action, at the time the cause thereof accrues, is within the age of minority, of unsound mind, or imprisoned, such person, after the expiration of twenty-one years from the time the cause of action accrues, may bring such action within ten years after such disability is removed." (As eff. 10-1-53.)

R.C. 5309.89 provides: "No title to registered real property in derogation of that of the registered owner shall be acquired by prescription or adverse possession." (As eff. 10-1-53.)

Title by adverse possession cannot be defeated without a showing either that the use was permissive or that the presumed conveyance was impossible. Board of Education v. Nichol, 70 App 467, 46 NE2d 872, 25 OO 206 (1942).

Further research: O Jur 3d, Adverse Possession and Prescription § 97.

LAW IN GENERAL

Such statutes are a form of statutes of limitation; however, their underlying principle is not merely that enforcement of the dispossessed owner's rights is barred but that his title is extinguished when he has had a cause of action during the entire period against the adverse possessor. After the statutory period has elapsed, the adverse possessor's title can be defeated only as can the title of any owner. Title has been sustained in some cases on the presumption of a lost grant where there has not been compliance with all the requirements of adverse possession under the statutes. Am Jur 2d, Adverse Possession § 239; Am Law of Prop §§ 15.2, 15.15; CJS, Adverse Possession § 247; Tiffany § 1171.

The overwhelming majority of the cases hold that a clearly established title by adverse possession is marketable. The courts are agreed that the vendor's burden includes the production of evidence to establish convincingly all the necessary elements of sufficient possession. 46 ALR2d 547.

2-11B Extent of the Interest Acquired; Encumbrances Extinguished.

Area of actual possession, see 2-34A.

Where one remains in actual, visible, exclusive, hostile and continuous possession of land for a period of twenty-one years, he thereby acquires title to the land. Cleveland Co-op. Stove Co. v. Cleveland & Pittsburgh R.R., 23 CC(NS) 260, 34 CD 236 (1912).

One who has been in the actual, open, notorious and hostile possession of real property under claim of right continuous and exclusive for the period of twenty-one years obtains title by adverse possession. McClellan v. Broadsword, 14 Abs 274 (App. 1932).

Further research: O Jur 3d, Adverse Possession and Prescription § 101.

LAW IN GENERAL

The estate acquired is only to the extent of the adverse claim of the possessor. A fee simple is ordinarily claimed and acquired. The new title is said to vest as of the inception of the adverse possession. It may not be free of an encumbrance which is dependent upon the extinguished title of the former owner where the holder of the encumbrance had no cause of action against the adverse possessor; thus, a judgment lien has been upheld on the ground that the occupancy was not inconsistent with the lien. Easements, restrictive covenants, and other encumbrances existing before the adverse possession commenced are not affected thereby unless irreconcilable; thus, a prior easement is not extinguished by adverse possession of the servient land unless the possession is inconsistent with the right to enjoy the easement during the prescribed period. The new owner cannot compel the former owner to execute a conveyance and his only right to establish a record title is by judgment of the court. Am Law of Prop § 15.14; CJS, Adverse Possession § 64; Powell § 1025.

2-11C Possessory Rights.

LAW IN GENERAL

Prior to the expiration of the statutory period, the possession of the disseisor is good against anyone who cannot show a superior right. The title acquired relates back to the commencement of the possession; therefore, the disseisor is not liable, after the period has run, to the former owner for the wrongful possession during the period. Am Jur 2d, Adverse Possession § 237; CJS, Adverse Possession § 251.

2-11D Bona Fide Purchasers.

LAW IN GENERAL

A bona fide purchaser of the record title is not protected against a title acquired by adverse possession, even when the person who has so acquired title is not presently in actual or visible possession of the property. 9 ALR2d 850; Tiffany § 1177.

2-11E Actions for Recovery.

Ejectment, see 16-62A.
Occupying claimants, see 16-62C.
Quieting title, see Section 16-65.

Paying taxes is not enough to constitute an adverse possession. Ewing v. Burnet, 1 OFD 537, Fed Cas 4591 (1835), affd. 36 US 41, 9 L Ed 624.

Adverse possession may be proven by testimony of any person having knowledge of the usage. Witnesses are not limited to persons in the chain of title with the claimant. Lyman v. Ferrari, 66 App2d 72, 419 NE2d 1112, 20 OO3d 138 (1979).

Further research: O Jur 3d, Adverse Possession and Prescription § 107.

LAW IN GENERAL

The defense of the statute of limitations need not be pleaded when the title is title by adverse possession. All reasonable presumptions are ordinarily made in favor of the dispossessed owner, but the burden of proof is upon him who has the affirmative of the issue. However, hostility of possession is presumed in some of the cases where there is no evidence to the contrary.

Payment of taxes is not a prerequisite to recovery and is merely evidence in the case.

A difficulty sometimes arises for the adverse claimant at a trial when he admits that he did not intend to claim beyond the true line instead of saying that he did intend to claim up to the line occupied. See also Section 2-23.

Am Jur 2d, Adverse Possession §§ 246, 248, 249; CJS, Adverse Possession §§ 210, 213, 215, 216, 218, 258; Tiffany § 1143.

SECTION 2-12: PRESCRIPTION

2-12A Nature; Extent.

Where a right to use is conferred by grant, any use reasonably consistent with such grant will be referred to such grant and will not be deemed adverse. Kelley v. Armstrong, 102 OS 478, 132 NE 15, 19 OLR 116 (1921).

Prescription rests upon the presumption of a past grant inferred from and evidenced by an adverse enjoyment for a period of twenty-one years. Kimball v. Anderson, 125 OS 241, 181 NE 17, 36 OLR 307 (1932).

Prescription relates to incorporeal rights while adverse possession applies to an interest in the title to property. Nye v. Taylor, 4 Abs 221 (App. 1925).

A right acquired by adverse user is limited to the extent of the notice to the owner of the right that is in process of being acquired against him. Perrin v. Sethman, 8 Abs 723 (App. 1930).

Further research: O Jur 3d, Adverse Possession and Prescription § 10.

LAW IN GENERAL

Prescription is the acquisition of an easement by adverse user of the land of another person. The courts follow the law of adverse possession of land itself in the creation of incorporeal rights in land. It is sometimes said that a grant will be presumed after the statutory period has elapsed, but that the presumption is ordinarily not rebuttable. Am Law of Prop § 8.44; Powell § 1026; Restatement, Property § 457; Tiffany §§ 796, 1192.

The extent and duration of an easement by prescription are determined from the circumstances of the denial of the rights of the servient owner. CJS, Easements § 74; Restatement, Property § 461.

2-12B   Requirements.

An easement by prescription may be acquired by open, notorious, continuous, adverse use for a period of twenty-one years. Pennsylvania R. Co. v. Donovan, 111 OS 341, 145 NE 479, 2 Abs 738, 739, 22 Abs 599, 600 (1924).

Use of a passageway over an unenclosed, adjoining vacant lot in a city will not ripen into an easement by prescription unless such passageway is of such permanent construction as to give notice of a claim of right. Davidson v. Dunn, 16 App 263, 21 OLR 338 (1922). See also 46 ALR2d 1140.

Open, continuous and exclusive use of real property with the knowledge but not the permission of the owners and their predecessors in interest is an adverse use which ripens into a prescriptive right at the expiration of twenty-one years. No easement by prescription can be acquired where the privilege is used by the express or implied permission or license of the owner of the land. Meinke v. Schober, 12 O Supp 41, 29 OO 1, 38 Abs 467 (C.P. 1943).

As a general rule, an easement cannot be lost by mere nonuser, but it is subject to loss by adverse user. In order to result in the loss of an easement, the adverse use must be continued for the period necessary to create an easement, that is, the statutory period for the recovery of real property, or twenty-one years. Szaraz v. Consolidated R.R., 10 App3d 89, 460 NE2d 1133 (1983).

Further research: O Jur 3d, Adverse Possession and Prescription § 40. See also Division 2-3 in this chapter.

LAW IN GENERAL

The adverse use must comply with the requirements for adverse possession of land. Acts of the owner which do not actually interrupt the adverse use do not toll the running of the period. Right of possession of both tracts in the same person does stop the running of the statutory period. Continuous use can be shown without showing a constant use. To meet the requirement of exclusiveness in the claimant where the use is in common with others, his use must be with a claim of right peculiar to himself. The use must be definite and be substantially the same throughout the prescriptive period. Tiffany §§ 1199, 1202.

Adjoining owners' use in common of a strip along the boundary is held sufficient, in a majority of the cases, to sustain acquisition of an easement by prescription unless user by permission is shown. 27 ALR2d 332.

A prescriptive right cannot be acquired where the user is by the express or implied permission of the owner of the land. An offer by the claimant to purchase the right is not conclusive as to whether the use is hostile. Tiffany § 1196.

A general test of the running of the prescriptive period is whether the claimed adverse use gives the landowner a right of action; for example, rights to light, air, or percolating water cannot be acquired by prescription. Am Law of Prop § 8.53; Tiffany §§ 1194, 1201.

2-12C By and against Whom Acquired; Leases.

See also Division 2-2.

Use by tenant may ripen into easement by prescription in favor of landlord's estate. Davidson v. Dunn, 16 App 263, 21 OLR 338 (1922).

Where the encroaching co-owner of a common easement has obstructed it and subjected it to other uses for over twenty-one years and has erected considerable private improvements thereon, and where the other co-owners have made occasional use of part of the easement, the latter will be allowed damages for the permanent obstruction. Cramer v. New Philadelphia Brewery, 16 O Supp 140, 31 OO 369, 43 Abs 599 (C.P. 1945).

Further research: O Jur 3d, Adverse Possession and Prescription § 31.

LAW IN GENERAL

An easement by prescription cannot be annexed to a term of years. Adverse use of an easement by a tenant upon land of a third party inures to the benefit of the landlord. The prescriptive period will not commence to run against a landlord unless he has a right of action, but the period will continue to run if it commenced during the landlord's possession. Am Jur 2d, Easements and Licenses § 17.

2-12D Incidents.

LAW IN GENERAL

All the owners of the dominant land have the benefit of an easement created by prescription. Restatement, Property § 462.

After the prescriptive period has elapsed, the adverse user is not liable for his use during the period. Am Law of Prop § 8.62; Restatement, Property § 465.

2-12E Particular Types of Easements.

An easement in the light and air from the premises of another cannot be acquired in Ohio by use or prescription. Mullen v. Stricker, 19 OS 135 (1869).

An easement by prescription is acquired by each of owners of adjoining lots where a common driveway is constructed under an oral agreement and used adversely for the prescriptive period. Shanks v. Floom, 162 OS 479, 124 NE2d 416, 55 OO 385 (1955).

The right to maintain the projection of eaves over the land of another becomes absolute at the end of twenty-one years, equally with the right to maintain a foundation or superstructure. McCleery v. Alton, 8 CC(NS) 481, 19 CD 97 (1906).

One may not obtain by prescription, or otherwise than by purchase, the right to commit a nuisance such as to cast sewage upon the lands of another. Vian v. Sheffield Bldg. & Development Co., 85 App 191, 88 NE2d 410, 44 OO 144 (1948).

Further research: O Jur 3d, Adverse Possession and Prescription §§ 91, 92.

LAW IN GENERAL

Highways and streets may usually be established by public user under the general rules of prescription. Some cases hold that the public authorities must affirmatively consent to the establishment of a public way by prescription. Such consent is almost uniformly required in order to bind the state or municipality to maintain the way. Am Jur 2d, Highways, Streets and Bridges §§ 25, 28; Am Law of Prop § 9.50; CJS, Highways § 3; Tiffany § 1211.

A right to maintain a public nuisance cannot be acquired by prescription. This rule has been applied to obstruction of highways and to pollution of streams. Tiffany § 1192.

Additional citations for this section: Am Jur 2d, Easements and Licenses §§ 32, 33; CJS, Easements § 6; Powell § 413.

DIVISION 2-2: BY AND AGAINST WHOM INTEREST IS ACQUIRED

SECTION 2-21: GOVERNMENT; HIGHWAYS AND STREETS

Highways by prescription, see 2-12E.

2-21A State and United States.

By reason of the amendment of R.C. 5303.01 effective March 31, 1973 (see 16-65A), the state or any agency or political subdivision thereof may be made a party to an action to quiet title. No reported decision has construed this amendment, but it appears to open the door to an adverse possession claim against the sovereign.

While the legal title remains in the government, the statute of limitations does not run against one who holds a certificate of survey or of purchase. Duke v. Thompson, 16 Ohio 34 (1847).

No adverse occupation and user of land belonging to the state of Ohio, however long continued, can divest the title of the state in and to such lands. Haynes v. Jones, 91 OS 197, 110 NE 469, 12 OLR 390, 450, 451, 60 WLB 24, 39, 143 (1915).

A municipal corporation can acquire title to private property by adverse possession. State ex rel. AAA Investment v. City of Columbus, 17 OS3d 151, 478 NE2d 773 (1985).

Further research: O Jur 3d, Adverse Possession and Prescription § 54.

LAW IN GENERAL

Adverse possession does not operate against the United States or a state unless a statute so provides. An occupant may so acquire rights in public lands against all third persons, but the statutory period does not commence to run against a purchaser from the state until the patent is issued, or until he becomes entitled to it. Am Jur 2d, Adverse Possession § 205; 55 ALR2d 554; CJS, Adverse Possession § 11; Tiffany § 1170.

A presumption of a conveyance from the state may nevertheless be upheld, notwithstanding the rule that statutes of limitations do not run against the state. Powell § 1020; Tiffany § 1136.

The state may acquire title by adverse possession, at least if there is a cause of action against the agents of the state in possession. Tiffany § 1154.

It has generally been held that the United States, a state, or other governmental body, may acquire title by adverse possession. There is, however, some authority that a municipality cannot acquire title by prescription or adverse possession. 18 ALR3d 678.

2-21B Subdivisions of the State.

Statutes of limitations run against a town or city corporation. Cincinnati v. First Presbyterian Church, 8 Ohio 298 (1838).

Trustees of a township holding title to lands granted to them by the general government for school purposes, are not exempt from the operation of the statute of limitations, in an action prosecuted by them to recover possession of the premises. Oxford Tp. v. Columbia, 38 OS 87, 7 WLB 221 (1882).

No right by prescription to maintain the pipes in the street would vest in the plaintiff although used more than twenty-one years as the city had no power to make the grant. Elster v. Springfield, 49 OS 82, 30 NE 274, 27 WLB 73, 162 (1892).

All attempts to extend the exemption from the operation of the statute of limitations to others than the general and state governments have failed. Hartman v. Hunter, 56 OS 175, 180, 46 NE 577, 37 WLB 249, 254 (1897).

A board of education or school district is amenable to the statute of limitations. When a statute does not expressly exempt a subordinate political subdivision from its operation, the exemption therefrom does not exist. State ex rel. Board of Education v. Gibson, 130 OS 318, 199 NE 185, 4 OO 352 (1935).

A private person, claiming title to land which originally belonged to the public for street purposes, should base his claim on estoppel rather than the statute of limitations. Hermann v. Spitzmiller, 24 CC(NS) 20, 34 CD 453 (1914).

When the public acquires a prescriptive right to the use of land for an alley, a member of the public does not acquire a separate easement but he may maintain an action for injunctive relief. Smith v. Krites, 90 App 38, 102 NE2d 903, 46 OO 360 (1950).

A private litigant, in an action against a local board of education, can rely upon adverse possession to obtain title to land held in trust by it for school purposes. Brown v. Board of Education, 20 OS2d 68, 253 NE2d 767, 49 OO2d 347 (1969).

The decisions supporting the rule that subdivisions of the state are subject to the statute of limitations as to recovery of real property have never been directly overruled. However, they have been so criticized by the courts that it is doubtful to what extent they would now be followed. O Jur 3d, Adverse Possession and Prescription §§ 73, 79. See also 2-21C, 2-21D and 2-21E for statutory and judicial exceptions to the doctrine as to highways and streets.

Further research: O Jur 3d, Adverse Possession and Prescription § 71.

LAW IN GENERAL

The decisions are diverse where the disseised owner is a municipality or other subdivision of the state. In most states, title cannot be acquired by adverse possession against a subdivision of the state provided the land is held for a purely public purpose. The weight of authority is that title cannot be so acquired against highways and streets or dedicated property. Am Jur 2d, Adverse Possession § 206; 55 ALR2d 554; Am Law of Prop § 9.55; CJS, Adverse Possession §§ 5, 12; Tiffany §§ 929, 1170.

2-21C Unopened Streets.

R.C. 2305.05 provides: "If a street or alley, or any part thereof, laid out and shown on the recorded plat of a municipal corporation, has not been opened to the public use and occupancy of the citizens thereof, or other persons, and has been enclosed with a fence by the owners of the inlots, lots, or outlots lying on, adjacent to, or along such street or alley, or part thereof, and has remained in the open, uninterrupted use, adverse possession, and occupancy of such owners for the period of twenty-one years, and if such street, alley, inlot, or outlot is a part of the tract of land so laid out by the original proprietors, the public easement therein shall be extinguished and the right of such municipal corporation, the citizens thereof, or other persons, and the legislative authority of such municipal corporation and the legal authorities thereof, to use, control, or occupy so much of such street or alley as has been fenced, used, possessed, and occupied, shall be barred, except to the owners of such inlots or outlots lying on, adjacent to, or along such streets or alleys who have occupied them in the manner mentioned in this section." (As eff. 10-1-53.)

Adverse possession against unopened street or alley cannot be enforced against the state or any of its subdivisions other than municipalities. Beard v. Beatty, 3 App 354, 21 CC(NS) 522, 28 CD 554 (1914).

In order to obtain title to part of a duly dedicated street it is also necessary, by virtue of R.C. 2305.05, that the street has not been open for public use and has been enclosed by a fence. "Open for public use" means only that the public make some use of the street. Byerlyte Corp. v. Cleveland, 32 Abs 609 (App. 1940).

To bar the rights of the municipality in a street or alley, the statute imposes an absolute requirement that such street or alley be completely surrounded by a fence on all sides for the full period of twenty-one years. In re Application of Loose, 107 App 47, 153 NE2d 146, 7 OO2d 374, 78 Abs 399 (1958).

Further research: O Jur 3d, Adverse Possession and Prescription § 81.

2-21D   Encroachment on Highway or Street.

An adjacent landowner who encloses by a fence, however constructed, a portion of a public highway, cannot acquire title by adverse possession, however long continued. Heddleston v. Hendricks, 52 OS 460, 40 NE 408, 33 WLB 143, 217 (1895).

The maintenance of structures in a public street which interrupt public travel thereon and are public nuisances therein cannot ripen into a prescriptive right to an easement in favor of the party erecting or maintaining them. Yackee v. Napoleon, 135 OS 344, 21 NE2d 111, 14 OO 231 (1939).

Further research: O Jur 3d, Adverse Possession and Prescription § 73.

2-21E   Entire Highway or Street.

See also 2-12B.

Adverse possession operates as well against the dedicator as against the public. Stevens v. Shannon, 6 CC 142, 3 CD 386 (1892).

Grantee, for a period of more than twenty-one years, continued in the occupation and entirely excluded the public therefrom: Held, that his possession was such as to give him title to that part of the street by adverse possession against the city. Mott v. Toledo, 17 CC 472, 7 CD 216 (1897), affd. 60 OS 601, 54 NE 1100, 41 WLB 268 (1899).

The general principle that the statute of limitations will not bar public authorities from removing a street nuisance applies to a case where such authorities maintain their rights therein; but this doctrine cannot be extended to a case where one, by a fence or other structure, has entirely excluded the public from the street. Seese v. Maumee, 7 CC(NS) 497, 18 CD 768, 50 WLB 449 (1905).

Since R.C. 5589.01 and 5589.99 makes it a criminal offense to obstruct public ground, highway, street or alley of a municipality, it follows that no rights may be acquired by adverse possession thereof. Harbor Land Co. v. Fairport, 49 NE2d 194, 7 OO 405, 23 Abs 44 (App. 1936). This case follows the modern trend that neither title nor an easement can be acquired against a highway or street by adverse possession or prescription.

Caveat: The earlier cases sustaining adverse possession of the entire width of a street may not be followed. They are likely to be overruled or avoided in future litigation as was done in the Harbor Land Co. case. See also comment at 2-21B.

Further research: O Jur 3d, Adverse Possession and Prescription § 80.

SECTION 2-22: PERSONS UNDER DISABILITY

2-22A Generally.

Disability after cause of action accrues, see 16-42B.
See the terms of R.C. 2305.04 at 2-11A.

Where a person is under the saving clause, the statute begins to run at his death, and it continues to run notwithstanding the disability of his heirs. Carey v. Robinson, 13 Ohio 181, 195 (1844).

Further research: O Jur 3d, Adverse Possession and Prescription § 55.

LAW IN GENERAL

A statutory extension of the required period of adverse possession on account of personal disabilities normally applies only to disabilities existing at the time the adverse possession commenced; thus a disability occurring after the cause of action accrued does not extend the period unless by specific statutory provision. Neither can the disabilities of different persons be tacked to extend the period. That is to say, the disabilities of successive owners cannot be added although all existed at the time the adverse possession commenced. Am Jur 2d, Adverse Possession § 130; Am Law of Prop § 15.12; CJS, Adverse Possession § 127; Powell § 1022; Tiffany § 1169.

SECTION 2-23: ADJOINING OWNERS; BOUNDARIES

2-23A Generally.

The statute of limitation applies although the possession may have grown out of the mutual mistake of the parties respectively, in respect to the locality of what was originally the true line between them. Yetzer v. Thoman, 17 OS 130 (1866).

A fence maintained for more than twenty-one years on the supposed section line becomes the true line. Helbling v. Werk Realty Co., 2 App 478, 21 CC(NS) 361, 26 CD 256 (1913).

Where boundary is a straight line, adverse possession by a building, along part of line, will extend to entire length of boundary. Wilson v. Sidle, 4 NP(NS) 465, 17 OD 393 (1906); Epstein v. Kraft, 16 CC(NS) 251, 26 CD 528 (1908).

Further research: O Jur 3d, Adverse Possession and Prescription § 95.

LAW IN GENERAL

The general rule is that title may be acquired by adverse possession even though by mistake the possession is not to the true line. However, the possession is frequently held not to be adverse when the parties to an agreement erroneously fixing the boundary intend only to claim to the true line. The erection of a building encroaching on the adjoining owner generally starts the running of the statutory period. It has been held that an easement is acquired by an overhanging encroachment. Am Jur 2d, Adverse Possession § 39, Boundaries § 82; Am Law of Prop § 15.5; 97 ALR 14; CJS, Adverse Possession § 82; Tiffany § 1159.

The boundaries of land acquired by adverse possession are usually determined by actual use and occupation. When the possession is under color of title it may be effective as to the entire tract. Tiffany § 1155.

The trend of modern decisions is that exclusive possession and use are presumed to be hostile and adverse even when occupancy is due to mistake and with an intention to claim to the true line. 80 ALR2d 1171.

SECTION 2-24: REMAINDERMEN AND REVERSIONERS; OTHER FUTURE INTERESTS

Future interests generally, see 11-18C.
Quieting title, see 16-65B.

2-24A   Generally.

The statute of limitations does not begin to run against the remaindermen until after the death of the life tenant, and no possession prior to his death will bar or affect their right or estate. Holt v. Lamb, 17 OS 374 (1867); Webster v. Pittsburg, C. & T. R.R., 78 OS 87, 84 NE 592, 5 OLR 621, 53 WLB 99 (1908).

Possession is not adverse, within the meaning of the statutes of limitation, as against the remainderman until a right of entry accrues to him. Carpenter v. Denoon, 29 OS 379, 2 WLB 63 (1876).

The statute of limitations did not start to run against the issue until the death of the first donee in tail. Harris v. Maholm, 20 NP(NS) 439, 28 OD 228 (1918).

"We contend that under G.C. 11901 (R.C. 5303.01), a remainderman has the right, when it is brought home to him that the occupant is claiming adversely against not only the life tenant, but against the world, to bring an action to assert his claims, and that if he fails to do so within the statutory period, his rights should be barred. This is the holding of the Nebraska and Iowa courts, and we submit that there is nothing in the Ohio cases since 1893, the date of the revision of G.C. 11901, which binds the Ohio courts to hold other than has been held by the Iowa and Nebraska courts." Charles C. White, "Quiet Title and Adverse Possession," 24 OLR 401.

Further research: O Jur 3d, Adverse Possession and Prescription §§ 87, 88, 89.

LAW IN GENERAL

The possession of a life tenant is not adverse to the remaindermen unless he acquires an independent title or unless the remaindermen are charged with actual notice of the hostile claim. Possession by a third person prior to the death of the life tenant is generally not adverse to the remaindermen. In a few jurisdictions it is held that a statute will run against the remainderman when it is brought home to him that the occupant is claiming adversely not only against the life tenant but against the world, especially where the remainderman has a right of action such as to quiet title.

Adverse possession against a trustee may be effective against a remainder held in trust. The statute does not begin to run against the reversioner of an estate in fee tail until the failure of issue. These rules apply to vested future interests in general but do not apply when the statute commenced to run before the future interest was created. The rule must be kept in mind that the period does not commence to run against a person until he has a right of action.

Am Jur 2d, Adverse Possession § 225; Am Law of Prop § 15.8; 58 ALR2d 299; CJS, Estates § 66; Powell § 301; Simes and Smith § 1962; Tiffany §§ 1152, 1184.

SECTION 2-25:   COTENANTS

2-25A   Generally.

When a grantee enters as a tenant in common, his possession will be presumed to be not adverse to his cotenants until by unmistakable acts or declarations, of which his cotenants had or ought to have taken notice, he claims the entire ownership. Hogg v. Beerman, 41 OS 81, 11 WLB 252 (1889).

Actual notice of the ouster is not necessary, but possession of a cotenant may become adverse by acts so open and so notorious as to show that he claims exclusive title and possession. Watters v. Tucker, 6 Abs 411 (App. 1928).

Further research: O Jur 3d, Adverse Possession and Prescription § 59.

LAW IN GENERAL

The possession of one cotenant is presumed to be not adverse to the others. The statutory period will not run unless there is an ouster, that is, unless the disseisin is under such circumstances as will charge the other cotenants with notice. As a general rule, notice is not necessary of the adverse possession by a grantee or mortgagee of one cotenant. Am Law of Prop § 15.7; CJS, Adverse Possession § 96; Tiffany § 1185.

Where a stranger enters into open and exclusive possession under a conveyance from one of the cotenants, the conveyance is deemed an ouster and the period of adverse possession commences. 32 ALR2d 1214.

To acquire the entire title in himself, a tenant in common must establish that he was in actual possession, that he in fact claimed adversely, and that his cotenant or cotenants had knowledge or notice. 82 ALR2d 5.

SECTION 2-26: MINES AND MINERALS

2-26A Generally.

In quiet title action by heirs of grantor who reserved minerals in 1864, the court held in favor of plaintiffs although defendants' chain of title for sixty-four years contained no exceptions. Gill v. Fletcher, 74 OS 295, 78 NE 433, 4 OLR 149, 51 WLB 225 (1906).

Minerals that have been severed from the surface by conveyance cannot be acquired by the owner of the surface by adverse possession by force of the possession of his own estate, or by nonuse of the owner of the minerals, or by reason of the failure of taxing authorities to levy taxes separately on the minerals. Yoss v. Markley, 68 NE2d 399, 34 OO 4, 46 Abs 217 (C.P. 1946).

Oil and gas rights reserved in a deed in 1916 need not be preserved by a notice in the chain of title of the surface ownership to survive under the Marketable Title Act. Heifner v. Bradford, 4 OS3d 49, 446 NE2d 440 (1983).

Further research: O Jur 3d, Adverse Possession and Prescription § 68.

LAW IN GENERAL

Title to mines and minerals may be acquired by adverse possession. After title to the minerals has been severed from the title to the surface, the lower owner does not lose his title by nonuser or by adverse possession of the surface commenced after the severance. Nonuser of the minerals raises no presumption to support adverse possession. Am Jur 2d, Adverse Possession § 214; Am Law of Prop § 10.7; 35 ALR2d 124; CJS, Mines and Minerals § 135; Tiffany § 1158.

SECTION 2-27: TRUSTEES

2-27A Generally.

Both principle and authority clearly establish the doctrine that where the legal estate is in a trustee competent to protect it, adverse possession will become a bar against him under the same circumstances that would bar one seized in fee in his own right, and that when an action by such a trustee is barred his beneficiary is also barred. As between trustee and beneficiary, the statute will not begin to run until an unmistaken disclaimer of the trust is known to a beneficiary competent to sue. Veazie v. McGugin, 40 OS 365, 10 WLB 431 (1883).

Further research: O Jur 3d, Adverse Possession and Prescription § 53.

LAW IN GENERAL

As between persons in a fiduciary or confidential relationship, possession is presumed not to be adverse. The possession of a trustee is not adverse to the beneficiary of the trust unless the latter is charged with actual notice of the hostile nature of the possession. Adverse possession by a third party against a trustee also operates to bar recovery by the beneficiary. Am Jur 2d, Adverse Possession § 196; Am Law of Prop § 15.7; CJS, Adverse Possession § 125; Tiffany § 1179.

SECTION 2-28: OTHER PERSONS

2-28A Dower.

Right of dower may be barred after the lapse of twenty-one years from the date of death of the spouse. Ater v. Simpkins, 16 App 461 (1922).

LAW IN GENERAL

Dower may be barred by the running of the statutory period commencing at the death of the spouse holding title. Possession of the heirs is presumed to be not adverse to the surviving spouse. The same presumption is applied to the possession of the surviving spouse as against the heirs. Am Jur 2d, Adverse Possession § 235; CJS, Adverse Possession §§ 136, 140.

2-28B Third Persons.

A landlord is not regarded as a third person. See 2-33A.

LAW IN GENERAL

Adverse possession has been held to inure to the benefit of third persons, as to a remainderman when a life tenant is in possession under a devise or conveyance from one having no title. Tiffany § 1174.

2-28C Miscellaneous.

Joint occupants, see 2-34C.

Possession under a contract of purchase does not become adverse while payments are made. Woods v. Dille, 11 Ohio 455 (1842), revd. on other grounds 14 Ohio 122 (1846).

A grantor in a warranty deed is not estopped from claiming a prescriptive right to use a portion of the land conveyed where such use is adverse for more than twenty-one years after such conveyance. Kimball v. Anderson, 125 OS 241, 181 NE 17, 36 OLR 307 (1932).

Further research: O Jur 3d, Adverse Possession and Prescription § 49.

LAW IN GENERAL

A cemetery lot may be the subject of adverse possession. The same is true as to part of a building. Adverse possession does not operate against a mere lien. Am Jur 2d, Adverse Possession § 204.

Possession usually cannot be shown to be adverse by a tenant against his landlord, between mortgagor and mortgagee, by a purchaser against his vendor, nor by a grantor against his grantee until the intention to hold adversely is brought to the attention of the other. Am Jur 2d, Adverse Possession § 166; Am Law of Prop § 15.7; 39 ALR2d 353; CJS, Adverse Possession § 122; Powell § 1023; Tiffany § 1178.

The possession of the donee under a parol gift is adverse from its inception notwithstanding the gift is ineffective to convey title. 43 ALR2d 6.

DIVISION 2-3: NATURE OF THE REQUIRED POSSESSION

SECTION 2-31: PERIOD; CONTINUITY; TACKING

2-31A Period.

Statute (R.C. 2305.04) at 2-11A.

Possession of these lands by the defendant and those under whom he claims for a period of ninety-two years will not avail him as a defense, as the title to these lands was in the United States from March 1, 1784 to February 18, 1871, and the statute of limitations does not run and cannot be pleaded against the United States or the state. The tax title for fifty-four years of the defendant does not estop the plaintiff, as the grantee of the state, from claiming these lands. Ohio State University Trustees v. Satterfield, 2 CC 86, 1 CD 377 (1886).

Further research: O Jur 3d, Adverse Possession and Prescription § 11.

LAW IN GENERAL

The necessary period will not commence to run until the claimant takes possession and also not until a cause of action accrues to the dispossessed owner. CJS, Adverse Possession § 201; Powell § 1019.

2-31B Continuity.

Change in possession or use, see 2-32B.

The temporary interruption of actual residence on the land, caused by the unlawful and violent acts of strangers, will not prevent the statute from continuing to run where there is no adverse entry or offer to redeem. Clark v. Potter, 32 OS 49, 2 WLB 321 (1876).

If one person occupies property for ten years and abandons it, and another person obtains possession, not under the first occupant but independently, these facts do not establish title by possession in the last occupant. Morehouse v. Burgot, 22 CC 174, 12 CD 163 (1901); McNeely v. Langan, 22 OS 32 (1871).

LAW IN GENERAL

If the continuity of the adverse possession is interrupted, the time previous to the interruption will not be considered a part of the statutory period. Actual possession does not require actual occupancy, but acquisition of title is defeated by failure of the possession to be continuous. Such failure occurs when the acts of the disseisor show he was not claiming adversely for the entire period, or when the true owner or a third person takes actual possession adversely to the first disseisor. Am Jur 2d, Adverse Possession § 54; CJS, Adverse Possession § 149; Powell § 1014; Tiffany § 1145.

Abandonment of the property destroys the necessary continuity, but temporary and reasonable breaks in the possession do not have that effect. Seasonal possession may be sufficient. A judgment for possession against the disseisor arrests the running of the statute as of the time the suit is commenced. Entry by the true owner may be a fatal interruption. Bargaining for or offering to purchase an outstanding claim does not ordinarily interrupt continuity, although a clear acknowledgment of the true owner's title will do so. The period ceases to run when the possession ceases to be hostile. Am Jur 2d, Adverse Possession § 77; Am Law of Prop § 15.9; 24 ALR2d 632; CJS, Adverse Possession § 169; Tiffany § 1160.

2-31C Tacking.

Tacking of disabilities, see Section 2-22.

Adverse users by different persons may be united or tacked to each other to make up the prescriptive period provided there is privity between them and no interval during which the possession was not adverse. Zipf v. Dalgarn, 114 OS 291, 151 NE 174, 4 Abs 177, 182, 24 OLR 300 (1926).

Successive possessions may be tacked although the land is not included in the description in the deed to the grantee claiming by adverse possession. Sinclair Refining Co. v. Romohr, 95 App 93, 117 NE2d 489, 52 OO 456 (1953).

Further research: O Jur 3d, Adverse Possession and Prescription §§ 26, 27.

LAW IN GENERAL

Tacking is the addition of the successive actual possessions of two or more persons to make up the statutory period. It is usually upheld provided there is privity between such persons by operation of law or by transfer or contract. An intention to transfer is ordinarily sufficient to establish privity and permit tacking. The rule applies when the area is contiguous even though not included in the description. Am Jur 2d, Adverse Possession § 58; Am Law of Prop § 15.10; 17 ALR2d 1128; CJS, Adverse Possession § 154; Powell § 1021; Tiffany § 1146.

SECTION 2-32: AS HOSTILE AND UNDER CLAIM OF RIGHT; CHANGE IN USE

2-32A Rule; Permission.

Offer to purchase or acknowledgment of title, see 2-31B.

Where one uses a way over the land of another without his permission as an incident to his own land and continues to do so with the knowledge of the owner, such use is of itself adverse, and evidence of a claim of right, and where the owner of the servient estate claims that the use was permissive, he has the burden of showing it. Pavey v. Vance, 56 OS 162, 46 NE 898, 37 WLB 254, 296 (1897).

A use never ripens into a prescriptive right unless it is adverse and not merely permissive. Pennsylvania R.R. v. Donovan, 111 OS 341, 145 NE 479, 2 Abs 675, 676, 22 OLR 599, 600 (1924).

Adverse possession of real estate loses its adverse character when the holder thereof, for a sufficient consideration, agrees with the true owner that suit to recover such possession shall not be brought during the lifetime of each of them. Dietrick v. Noel, 42 OS 18, 11 WLB 134 (1884).

Neither a mere offer to buy within the twenty-one years, nor an acknowledgment by the claimant within that time that the title is in another will have the effect of arresting the running of the statute unless such act creates an estoppel. McAllister v. Hartzell, 60 OS 69, 53 NE 715, 41 WLB 236, 303 (1899).

It is error for the court to charge that adverse possession sufficient to establish title must be undisputed. Heller v. Hawley, 8 CC(NS) 265, 18 CD 678, 51 WLB 278 (1905).

An agreement to submit a question of boundary to arbitration defeats the operation of the statute of limitations. Hunt v. Guilford, 4 Ohio 310 (1831); Gustafson v. Ursales, 3 App 136, 20 CC(NS) 275 (1914).

Notification to adverse possessor, followed by no overt act to oust possessor, would not prevent running of statute of limitations. Sowa v. Schaefer, 38 App 522, 175 NE 745, 10 Abs 457 (1931).

The continued and uninterrupted use of land of another for twenty-one years by the owner of the adjoining land, not having been authorized by express permission or license by the owner of the servient estate but merely acquiesced in by him, ripens into a prescriptive right to its use as an easement. Sting v. Rothacker, 82 App 107, 80 NE2d 819, 37 OO 454 (1947).

The building of a permanent structure on the property of another is an adverse possession, unless the possession is under a contract or license. Wilberforce University v. College of Education & Industrial Arts, 86 App 121, 90 NE2d 172, 40 OO 521 (1948).

Where a party establishes adverse possession for twenty-one years, he thereby, except as to persons under disability, acquires a title to the land, irrespective of any question of motive or mistake. Fulton v. Rapp, 98 NE2d 430, 45 OO 494, 59 Abs 105 (App. 1950).

While acts of the adverse claimant of an easement admitting the right of the titleholder would militate against the acquisition of such easement by prescription, no act by an adverse claimant who has exclusive occupancy by a disseisin will prevent acquisition of title to the fee unless the act estops the claimant or suspends the right of the titleholder to recover possession. Manos v. Day Cleaners & Dyers, Inc., 91 App 361, 108 NE2d 347, 48 OO 455 (1952).

Where a drain line has been constructed with the consent and cooperation of the servient owner, it must be concluded that original use was permissive. Grau v. Kramer, 91 NE2d 905, 41 OO 332, 57 Abs 402 (C.P. 1950).

The existence of a family relationship between the parties imposes upon the claimant the burden of proving his claim of adverse possession by clear and convincing evidence, rather than by a preponderance of the evidence. Demmitt v. McMillan, 16 App3d 138, 474 NE2d 1212 (1984).

Further research: O Jur 3d, Adverse Possession and Prescription § 17.

LAW IN GENERAL

The possession must be hostile to the true owner with an intention to hold under a claim of right; this means only that the adverse possessor must claim the entire right of possession and intend to exclude the true owner from exercising any rights of ownership. Am Jur 2d, Adverse Possession § 32; CJS, Adverse Possession §§ 26, 59; Powell § 1015; Tiffany § 1146.

Possession is never adverse when it is by the express or implied permission of the owner or when it is admitted to be subordinate to the superior title. Am Jur 2d, Adverse Possession § 82; Am Law of Prop § 15.4; CJS, Adverse Possession § 77.

2-32B Change in Possession or Use.

Permissible uses, see Section 10-13.

A use of premises permissive in the beginning can be changed to one which is hostile and adverse only by the most unequivocal conduct on the part of the user, and evidence of adverse possession must be positive and must be strictly construed against the person claiming a prescriptive right to an easement. Hinman v. Barnes, 146 OS 497, 66 NE2d 911, 32 OO 564 (1946); Pierce v. Cherry Valley Farms, 146 OS 400, 66 NE2d 639, 32 OO 448 (1946).

To acquire a prescriptive right the user must be continued, without substantial interruption or change, for the period of the statutory limitation pertaining to actions for the recovery of real property. Smith v. Krites, 90 App 38, 102 NE2d 903, 46 OO 360 (1950).

Further research: O Jur 3d, Adverse Possession and Prescription § 21.

LAW IN GENERAL

A change in the character of the possession or a change in the nature of the use will not cause the statutory period to commence as to such change until the owner is charged with notice of the new claim. This rule applies to enlargement of an easement. Am Law of Prop § 15.6; 110 ALR 915; CJS, Adverse Possession §§ 84-87; Tiffany § 1142.

A prescriptive right-of-way cannot be acquired to pass over a tract of land generally: the adverse use must have been over a uniform route. 80 ALR2d 1095.

SECTION 2-33: AS ACTUAL, VISIBLE, AND EXCLUSIVE; OCCUPANCY

2-33A   As Actual; Occupancy.

Adverse possession may be made or continued by a landlord or by his tenant for him. Powers v. Malavazos, 25 App 450, 158 NE 654, 6 Abs 62 (1927).

Neither actual occupation, cultivation, nor residence are necessary to constitute actual possession when the property is so situated as not to admit of any permanent useful improvement, and the continued claim of the party has been evidenced by public acts of ownership. McClellan v. Broadsword, 14 Abs 274 (App. 1932).

When the owner of rural land had it surveyed and had it graded, he interrupted the adverse possession of the occupant even though the occupant continued to use part of it as a garden. Montieth v. Twin Falls United Methodist Church, Inc., 68 App2d 219, 428 NE2d 870, 23 OO3d 346 (1980).

Further research: O Jur 3d, Adverse Possession and Prescription § 13.

LAW IN GENERAL

To be adverse under the statute, the possession must be actual, visible, and exclusive. Actual possession does not necessarily mean actual occupancy as the possession by a tenant or agent is the possession of the landlord or principal. It is required that acts of ownership be clearly exercised over the land by the claimant so that the owner would have actual notice of the adverse claim if he had made proper inquiry. Fences or other marking of the limits of possession are not essential but are very important as evidence. The general criterion is the degree of control that would be exercised by an ordinary owner. The principal question here as in other aspects of adverse possession is whether the owner had a right of action against the adverse possessor during all the required period. Am Jur 2d, Adverse Possession § 13; Am Law of Prop § 15.3; CJS, Adverse Possession § 30; Tiffany § 1137.

2-33B   As Visible.

To recover upon prior possession alone, that possession must have been open and notorious. Abram v. Will, 6 Ohio 164 (1833).

The possession must be so open, visible, and notorious as to raise the presumption of notice to the world or so patent that if the owner remains in ignorance it is his own fault. Fulton v. Rapp, 98 NE2d 430, 45 OO 494, 59 Abs 105 (App. 1950).

Further research: O Jur 3d, Adverse Possession and Prescription § 23.

LAW IN GENERAL

The possession must be to the actual notice of the owner or must be so open, notorious and visible as to warrant the inference that the owner would, in the exercise of ordinary prudence, have known of it. Am Jur 2d, Adverse Possession § 47; Am Law of Prop § 15.3; CJS, Adverse Possession § 48; Powell § 1013.

2-33C As Exclusive.

A party relying on the statute of limitations for his title must show that he has had exclusive possession for twenty-one years. To establish a right-of-way by prescription the use need not be so exclusive as it must be to acquire title to the property. Haimeyer v. Tietig, 9 Dec Repr 438, 13 WLB 540 (Cin. Super. Ct. 1885).

Common use of a driveway is insufficient to prevent the operation of the doctrine of prescriptive right to an easement when all of the elements thereof are present. Glander v. Mendenhall, 68 NE2d 105, 39 Abs 104 (App. 1943).

Further research: O Jur 3d, Adverse Possession and Prescription § 39.

LAW IN GENERAL

The possession does not comply with the requirement of being exclusive if the owner is also in possession or if persons other than the claimant exercise like acts of ownership. Permissive use by the public or others does not defeat the right. Ouster or disseisin may be shown by actual possession or by acts of ownership. Am Jur 2d, Adverse Possession § 53; CJS, Adverse Possession § 54; Tiffany § 1141.

SECTION 2-34: COLOR OF TITLE

2-34A Rule.

The statute of limitations is available to protect the possession of a party who enters without color of title. Paine v. Skinner, 8 Ohio 159 (1837).

One who enters upon land under color of title, intending to take possession of the entire tract, no part of which is held adversely at the time of his entry, is deemed to be in possession to the extent of his claim. Clark v. Potter, 32 OS 49, 2 WLB 321 (1876).

Where the entry is without color of title or with insufficient description, the adverse possession extends only to that part of the land actually occupied and improved. Humphries v. Huffman, 33 OS 395, 3 WLB 1015 (1878).

Deed purporting to grant land to which the grantor had no title, held to give the grantee "color of title" for purpose of securing adverse possession of entire tract by actual possession of part. Powers v. Malavazos, 25 App 450, 158 NE 654, 6 Abs 62 (1927).

Acquisition of title will not be defeated because plaintiff's deed did not particularly describe the strip of land in controversy. Paulken v. Rose, 16 O Supp 149, 31 OO 260 (C.P. 1945).

Further research: O Jur 3d, Adverse Possession and Prescription § 44.

LAW IN GENERAL

Possession under color of title means that the possessor claims under what purports to be a valid conveyance, decree or contract. The possession may be adverse as to the entire tract which is sufficiently described although the actual occupancy is of a part only. Such constructive possession does not operate against a person in actual occupancy or against a third person upon whose land the description encroaches. Am Law of Prop §§ 15.4, 15.11; CJS, Adverse Possession § 226; Powell § 1017; Tiffany § 1155.

2-34B Statutes.

Ohio has no statute regarding color of title.

LAW IN GENERAL

Color of title is not essential unless so provided by statute. In any case, it may be very helpful in establishing the nature and extent of the possession. Am Jur 2d, Adverse Possession § 96; CJS, Adverse Possession § 67.

2-34C Joint Occupants.

See also 1-33B.

The statute of limitations did not operate in favor of a parent who purchased property in his own name with money belonging to himself and his children who also occupied the property. Paschall v. Hinderer, 28 OS 568, 2 WLB 50 (1876).

Where the premises are jointly occupied by two persons the possession is presumed to be in accord with the record title. Farmers' & Merchants' Nat. Bank v. Wallace, 45 OS 152, 12 NE 439, 17 WLB 326, 18 WLB 3 (1887).

Where the husband's name was added by mistake to his wife's name as grantee upon amicable partition and the wife was an heir, his possession was not adverse during her lifetime. Waterman v. Waterman, 10 CC(NS) 605, 12 CD 798 (1895).

LAW IN GENERAL

Possession is said to be in accord with the color of title; joint possession of two persons is referable to the record title of one of them, as when husband

and wife are the occupants and the conveyance is to the wife alone. Tiffany § 1176.

Neither husband nor wife living together can ordinarily hold adversely to the other, but it is sometimes held that one can do so if under color of title. Am Jur 2d, Adverse Possession § 184; Tiffany § 1190.

CHAPTER 3: BOUNDARIES AND DESCRIPTIONS

DIVISION 3-1: IN GENERAL

DIVISION 3-2: CONSTRUCTION OF DESCRIPTIONS

DIVISION 3-1:   IN GENERAL

SECTION 3-11:   INTRODUCTION; ENCROACHMENTS

3-11A   Actions; Encroachments Generally.

Marketability of title, see 1-43E.
Reformation, see Section 16-66.

Although plaintiff was not in possession of the land, he was entitled to maintain action to quiet title under equity jurisdiction of the court where there was confusion of boundaries caused by improper conduct of parties. Pattison v. Jordan, 3 CC 233, 2 CD 132 (1888).

Injunction is proper remedy in boundary dispute where defendant is not in possession of land. Kirk v. Weldy, 1 Abs 782 (App. 1923).

Vendors held liable without proof of fraud or intentional misrepresentation where the contract was to sell a two-story house and one foot of the roof was not on the lot conveyed but extended over the adjoining lot. Leppert v. Bosserman, 21 App 366, 153 NE 114, 4 Abs 562 (1926).

Where A has, through his mistake, erected a building encroaching two feet upon plaintiff's land, plaintiff will be required, as a condition precedent to a decree of equitable relief, to make a conveyance to A at a price fixed by the court. Orvetz v. Iroquois Realty Co., 5 Abs 534 (App. 1926). Note, occupying claimants, see Section 16-62.

A mandatory injunction is the proper remedy where one landowner has built structures encroaching on adjoining land without right or acquiescence. McGee v. Randolph, 90 NE2d 599, 56 Abs 24 (App. 1949).

Further research: O Jur 3d, Adjoining Landowners § 7.

LAW IN GENERAL

Problems of boundaries and descriptions commonly concern encroachments by adjoining owners. An encroachment may constitute a nuisance or a continuing trespass. Statutes of limitations as to trespass upon or injury to real property have been applied to actions for encroachment. 24 ALR2d 903; CJS, Adjoining Landowners §§ 40, 41.

A mandatory injunction will ordinarily issue to compel the removal of encroaching structures. An injunction is occasionally refused because the issuance would be inequitable under the circumstances, such as laches or a slight encroachment innocently made. In such case the plaintiff is limited to his action at law for damages. The courts are not in agreement as to when ejectment may be maintained. The owner may generally abate or personally remove the encroachment if the resulting damage is not excessive. Am Jur 2d, Adjoining Landowners § 128; 28 ALR2d 679; CJS, Adjoining Landowners § 43.

Encroachment by a structure onto the land conveyed has been held not to breach covenants for title unless a right to the encroachment has been acquired by prescription or adverse possession. When improvements on the land conveyed extend across the boundary line, covenants for title are usually held not to be breached, although the vendee may have an action for breach of the contract for sale. Am Law of Prop § 12.128.

3-11B Estoppel.

See also Section 16-69.

The presence of a house on a lot conveyed indicated that the grantor intended to convey all of the ground occupied by the house. A deed describing the boundary in such manner as to exclude four feet of the house, and all later conveyances in the chain of title, was subject to reformation on the petition of a subsequent grantee. Deubel v. Dearwester, 36 App 60, 172 NE 640, 8 Abs 432, 32 OLR 194 (1930).

The first purchaser from a common grantor has no valid claim of title to unimproved land as against the subsequent purchaser of the adjoining lot where the claim is based upon misrepresentation of the lot line location by the common grantor. Thornburg v. Burden, 93 App 363, 113 NE2d 683, 51 OO 154 (1952).

Where a builder owns adjoining properties and sells a house and driveway, the location of which is apparent to the purchaser, it is a sufficient representation that the house and driveway are on the lot sold by the builder. Morski v. Cedarcrest Homes, Inc., 7 App2d 45, 218 NE2d 640, 36 OO2d 123 (1966). Note, on contract to sell houses, see 3-11A.

LAW IN GENERAL

An adjoining owner may be estopped to assert his title by apparent acquiescence in or silence concerning improvement of the property. 76 ALR 312.

3-11C Easements for Encroachments.

Easements by implication, see Section 10-12.

Where A has, through a mutual mistake with adjoining owner in attempting to fix the true boundary line, built upon land of adjoining owner, A was entitled to occupy the building on condition that he pay adjoining owner damages and rental, but was not entitled to a conveyance in fee. Francis v. Micklethwait, 12 Abs 288 (App. 1932).

LAW IN GENERAL

An easement by implication has been held to be created upon severance of adjoining parcels by the common owner when there is encroachment by a structure on one of the parcels. 53 ALR 910.

SECTION 3-12: LATERAL SUPPORT

3-12A Rules.

A deed of general warranty does not carry with it, by way of implied easement on grantor's adjoining land, a right of lateral support sufficient to maintain the building on the lot so conveyed. Heimerdinger v. Schneider, 22 CC(NS) 415, 33 CD 652 (1914).

The right of lateral support does not extend to buildings or improvements upon adjoining land which increase the downward and lateral pressure. Davis v. Sap, 20 App 180, 152 NE 758, 4 Abs 533 (1922).

The right of lateral support is a property right which attaches to and passes with the grant of an easement for pipelines. East Ohio Gas Co. v. James Bros. Coal Co., 85 NE2d 816, 40 OO 440, 53 Abs 438 (C.P. 1948).

Further research: O Jur 3d, Adjoining Landowners § 11.

LAW IN GENERAL

An owner of land has the right to lateral support in that adjacent land may not be removed so as to cause a sinking of his land. This right does not extend, unless by statute, to support for the increased burden caused by structures on the land. A right to support of buildings cannot be acquired by prescription, but may be acquired by implied grant under the principles of implied easements. Am Jur 2d, Adjoining Landowners § 37; Am Law of Prop § 28.36; CJS, Adjoining Landowners §§ 9, 11; Powell § 699; Tiffany § 752.

An owner is liable for all damages where he raises his land above the level of the adjacent land. Powell § 697.

No recovery can ordinarily be had for injury to nonadjoining land unless it and the adjoining land are owned by the same person or unless the removal is negligent. 87 ALR2d 710.

3-12B Negligence.

"Although a recovery may be had for damages to land by reason of the removal of lateral support without proof of negligence, negligence must be pleaded and proved in order to recover for damages to buildings upon the land from which lateral support has been removed." Cincinnati v. Trinkle, 17 Abs 223, 40 OLR 102 (App. 1934).

An owner who uses reasonable care in removing lateral support owes no duty to protect adjoining buildings by underpinning or shoring. Coward v. Fleming, 89 App 485, 102 NE2d 850, 46 OO 289 (1951).

LAW IN GENERAL

An excavator is liable for a falling of soil in its natural condition, irrespective of whether he was negligent. He is liable for injuries to buildings on the adjoining land if he failed to give notice and exercise reasonable care in making the excavation. Am Jur 2d, Adjoining Landowners § 43; Am Law of Prop § 28.39; CJS, Adjoining Landowners §§ 3, 15; Powell § 700; Tiffany § 753.

The landowner is not liable for damage to structures on adjoining land resulting from excavation work by an independent contractor unless he is negligent, owes a duty, authorized the damaging acts, or should have taken precautions. 33 ALR2d 111.

3-12C Removal of Buildings.

LAW IN GENERAL

The owner of a building is not obliged to continue the support of his neighbor's building on account of the mere fact of such support. The right of removal does not extend to owners of distinct parts of a building. CJS, Adjoining Landowners § 8.

3-12D Remedies.

The measure of damages is usually the difference in value of the property before and after the injury. Ohio Collieries Co. v. Cocke, 107 OS 238, 140 NE 356, 1 Abs 276, 20 OLR 631, 632 (1923).

A municipal corporation is liable for damages to buildings as well as to land resulting from its negligent removal of lateral support. Keating v. Cincinnati, 38 OS 141, 7 WLB 263 (1882). Or when it is liable for a change of grade or the establishment of an unreasonable grade. Cloyd v. Cuyahoga Falls, 41 App 283, 179 NE 516, 11 Abs 76 (1931).

LAW IN GENERAL

The usual remedy for removal of lateral support is an action for damages. An injunction will be granted if the necessary equitable grounds exist. Am Jur 2d, Adjoining Landowners § 67; Am Law of Prop § 28.47; CJS, Adjoining Landowners § 30; Powell § 701.

The measure of damages is primarily the diminution in the market value of the plaintiff's premises by reason of the excavation. Costs of repairs are not uncommonly allowed together with the remaining depreciation in value, if any. 36 ALR2d 1253.

3-12E Statute in Municipalities.

R.C. 723.49 provides that if owner of land digs farther than nine feet below the curb of street (if there be no curb, then below established grade of street, or, if no established grade, then below the surface of adjoining lots), he shall be liable for damages to buildings on adjoining lots. (As eff. 10-1-53.)

R.C. 723.50 provides: "The owner or possessor of any lot or land in any municipal corporation may dig, or cause to be dug, any cellar, pit, or excavation, to the full depth of the foundation wall of any building upon adjoining lots, or to the full depth of nine feet below the established grade of the street or streets on which such lot abuts, without reference to the depth of adjoining foundation walls, without incurring the liability prescribed in section 723.49 of the Revised Code, and may, on thirty days' notice to adjoining owners, grade and improve the surface of any lot to correspond with the established grade of the street, streets, or alleys upon which such lot or land abuts, without incurring liability." (As eff. 10-1-53.)

The statute does not modify the common-law rule as to the lateral support of the soil itself. Belden v. Franklin, 8 CC(NS) 159, 18 CD 373, 51 WLB 123 (1906).

Further research: O Jur 3d, Adjoining Landowners § 14.

SECTION 3-13: PARTY WALLS

3-13A Definition.

Each of the owners of a party wall owns in severalty so much thereof as stands upon his land, subject to the easement of the other, and has a right to use that wall for any purpose not inconsistent with its use as a party wall. Mitchell Store Bldg. Co. v. Starr Piano Co., 18 NP(NS) 547, 27 OD 278 (1916).

Further research: O Jur 3d, Adjoining Landowners §§ 18, 19.

LAW IN GENERAL

A party wall is usually a wall upon both sides of a boundary line with each of the adjoining owners having an easement in the part of the wall on the contiguous land. The term may refer to a division wall entirely upon land of one owner with an easement in the adjoining owner; or to a division wall which, together with the land thereunder, is owned in common. CJS, Party Walls § 1; Powell § 688; Tiffany § 770.

3-13B Creation.

A parol agreement, where the joint wall has been erected, may be validated on the theory of estoppel or part performance. Miller v. Brown, 33 OS 547, 3 WLB 1149 (1878).

Further research: O Jur 3d, Adjoining Landowners § 20.

LAW IN GENERAL

A party wall is said to exist only by statute, by prescription, or by express or implied contract. A party wall is created by implied reservation and grant when separate grantees, with actual or constructive notice of the use of a division wall, purchase contiguous parcels from a common grantor. CJS, Party Walls § 5; Powell § 689.

When a division wall between two buildings belonging to different owners is partly upon the land of each, a presumption arises that it is a party wall. CJS, Party Walls § 3.

3-13C Permissible Uses; Repairs and Improvements.

Though the right be acquired by prescription, it may be said to have been created by contract. Defendant may be enjoined from cutting away portion of wall which would mar appearance and diminish strength of plaintiff's building. Brucks v. Weinig, 34 App 1, 169 NE 827, 8 Abs 94, 31 OLR 203 (1929).

Changing conditions in the neighborhood may, in the absence of an express agreement, alter one's right in a party wall. McCormick v. McCann, 94 NE2d 55, 57 Abs 203 (C.P. 1950).

Further research: O Jur 3d, Adjoining Landowners § 26.

LAW IN GENERAL

The use of party walls is controlled by the general rules as to easements. Ordinarily, neither party may extend beams beyond the center or maintain openings in the wall. Either owner may, as a general rule, add to or improve the wall provided he does not injure the adjoining building. Either owner of a party wall generally has the right to increase its height if he can do so without injury to the other owner. 2 ALR2d 1135; 24 ALR2d 1053; CJS, Party Walls §§ 15, 17; Powell § 690; Tiffany § 807.

3-13D   Termination; Transfer.

Rights in a party wall pass with a conveyance of the land to which they are appurtenant. Platt v. Eggleston, 20 OS 414 (1870).

Further research: O Jur 3d, Adjoining Landowners § 30.

LAW IN GENERAL

The right to use a party wall passes as an appurtenant easement. Rights to a party wall are terminated, under the majority rule, upon the destruction of the wall or of the supported building, especially when the wall is entirely upon the land of the adjoining owner. Some cases hold that a change of conditions in the neighborhood may be sufficient to extinguish the easement. 85 ALR 291; CJS, Party Walls § 11; Powell § 691; Tiffany § 818.

3-13E   Remedies; Running with the Land.

We have not in this state any act regulating party walls, and consequently the rights and liabilities of the parties must depend upon the provisions of the contract between them, and the principles of law applicable to those provisions. Hieatt v. Morris, 10 OS 523, 526 (1860).

The covenants of party wall agreements run with the land. Hall v. Geyer, 14 CC 229, 7 CD 436 (1896).

The damage recoverable for injury to a building by destruction of an adjoining building is the reasonable cost of restoration or repair, which damage may not exceed the difference in the market value of the property before and after the injury. Zaras v. Findlay, 112 App 367, 176 NE2d 451, 16 OO2d 306 (1960).

Further research: O Jur 3d, Adjoining Landowners § 37.

LAW IN GENERAL

The existence of a party wall has been held not to make a title unmarketable. However, covenants running with the land which impose additional burdens usually entitle an intending purchaser to reject the title. 81 ALR2d 1020.

SECTION 3-14: LIGHT, AIR AND VIEW

3-14A Rule.

Prescription, see 2-12E.

LAW IN GENERAL

A landowner has no right, unless by an easement, to the view or to unobstructed light and air from the adjoining land. Such easements are normally not created by implication or by prescription. Am Jur 2d, Adjoining Landowners § 89; CJS, Adjoining Landowners § 68.

3-14B Spite Fences.

The owner has the legal right to erect and maintain a high fence for the purpose of shutting off light and air from his neighbor. Letts v. Kessler, 54 OS 73, 42 NE 765, 35 WLB 33, 42, 62 (1896).
Further research: O Jur 3d, Adjoining Landowners §§ 8, 9.

LAW IN GENERAL

A majority of the cases hold that a person may erect a building or fence on his own land with the sole purpose to spite his neighbor. However, the modern trend is to allow the aggrieved party an action for damages and abatement. Some courts regard such a structure as a nuisance. Am Jur 2d, Adjoining Landowners §§ 106-117; Powell § 696; Tiffany § 716.

3-14C Right of Privacy.

LAW IN GENERAL

The right of privacy cannot be enforced against windows or openings on the adjoining property. CJS, Adjoining Landowners § 70.

SECTION 3-15: FENCES

Spite fences, see 3-14B.

3-15A Duty and Right to Fence.

Easements, see 10-13D.

R.C. 951.02 provides that horses, mules, cattle, sheep, goats, swine, or geese shall not be permitted to run at large in the public thoroughfare or upon enclosed land. (As eff. 11-3-78.)
The rule of the common law of England requiring the owner of cattle, horses, hogs, etc., to keep them on his own land, or within enclosure, has

never been in force in Ohio. Kerwhacker v. Cleveland C. & C. R.R., 3 OS 172 (1854).

Further research: O Jur 3d, Animals § 36.

3-15B Partition Fences.

R.C. 971.02 provides: "The owners of adjoining lands shall build, keep up, and maintain in good repair, in equal shares, all partition fences between them, unless otherwise agreed upon by them in writing and witnessed by two persons. The fact that any land or tract of land is wholly unenclosed or is not used, adapted, or intended by its owner for use for agricultural purposes shall not excuse the owner thereof from the obligations imposed by sections 971.01 to 971.37 of the Revised Code on him as an adjoining owner. Sections 971.01 to 971.37 of the Revised Code do not apply to the enclosure of lots in municipal corporations, or of adjoining lands both of which are laid out into lots outside municipal corporations, or affect sections 4959.02 to 4959.06 of the Revised Code, relating to fences required to be constructed by persons or corporations owning, controlling, or managing a railroad." (As eff. 3-8-79.)

R.C. 971.04 to 971.10 provide that the township trustees may assign to each owner his equal share of such fence to be constructed or kept in repair; that the trustees may construct such fence; that the cost of such proceeding and any fences constructed by the trustees shall be placed on the tax duplicate and become a lien; and that all divisions shall be recorded by the county recorder in "Partition Fence Record," and shall be final between the parties and successive owners thereafter until such divisions become unequal by a sale or division of land.

Similar provisions have been effective since 1906, except that prior to July 7, 1955, R.C. 971.02 did not contain the sentence imposing the statutory obligations on land wholly unenclosed or on land not used or intended for agricultural purposes.

The provisions of these sections may not be applied in any case where the construction or maintenance of a partition fence is for the sole benefit of one of the adjoining owners. 1955 OAG 5018.

Where the owner of a private right-of-way, which passes through farm lands owned by others, uses it as a farm outlet to a public highway, he is required by R.C. 971.01 and 971.02 to build and keep up one half of the fence on each side of his right-of-way. Zarbaugh v. Ellinger, 99 OS 133, 124 NE 68, 6 ALR 208, 16 OLR 437, 465, 64 WLB 16, 32 (1918).

A landowner will not be relieved from sharing in the construction of a partition line fence on the ground of no benefit to his land, without adducing proof, if the allegation of no benefit is challenged, that the cost will exceed the difference between the land value before and after the installation. "Laid out in lots" contemplates subdivision or platting in compliance with R.C. 711.001 et seq. Glass v. Dryden, 18 OS2d 149, 248 NE2d 54, 47 OO2d 313 (1969).

Further research: CJS, Fences § 5; Powell § 693; Tiffany § 771.

SECTION 3-16: TREES AT BOUNDARIES

3-16A Trees Near the Boundary.

An owner of land has the right to cut off or eliminate any portion of a tree which protrudes in or overhangs upon his property. Murray v. Heabron, 74 NE2d 648, 35 OO 135 (C.P. 1947).

Further research: O Jur 3d, Adjoining Landowners § 10.

LAW IN GENERAL

The overhanging branches and encroaching roots of a tree on the adjoining land may be removed as a nuisance. The location of the trunk determines the ownership of a tree; the branches, roots, and fruit remain the property of the same owner after removal. The owner of a tree has a license imposed by law to enter the adjacent land to remove fruit from overhanging branches. The same rules apply to bushes and hedge fences. A tree likely to fall across the boundary is a nuisance, and the owner is liable for damages if he is negligent in its maintenance. Am Jur 2d, Adjoining Landowners § 25; Am Law of Prop § 19.15; CJS, Adjoining Landowners § 50; Tiffany § 603.

3-16B Trees on the Boundary.

LAW IN GENERAL

When the trunk of the tree extends over the boundary, the adjoining landowners are tenants in common. If one co-owner injures a tree by removing the branches overhanging his land, he is liable to the other owner for half the damages. Am Jur 2d, Adjoining Landowners §§ 35, 36; Am Law of Prop § 19.15; CJS, Adjoining Landowners § 55.

Trees, shrubs, hedges and other similar growths standing on the boundary line have been generally considered to be property owned in common by the adjoining landowners. However, the right to cut branches of a line growth has been upheld under certain circumstances, but a right to cut roots is not clear. 26 ALR3d 1372.

SECTION 3-17: DAMAGES

3-17A Generally.

Trespass and nuisance, see Section 16-68.

LAW IN GENERAL

A person is liable for the discharge or percolation of offensive substances on the adjoining land as for a nuisance. Am Jur 2d, Adjoining Landowners § 33; CJS, Adjoining Landowners § 62.

3-17B Negligence.

Where the injury was not the natural, necessary or probable consequence of the act and could not have been foreseen, no recovery can be had unless there be an actual or constructive trespass or negligence in doing the work. Louden v. Cincinnati, 90 OS 144, 106 NE 970, 11 OLR 518, 59 WLB 102 (1914).

LAW IN GENERAL

There is liability between adjoining owners for negligence in general. When a person fails to use reasonable care in the construction and maintenance of his buildings, the adjoining owner can recover damages. This rule does not apply to support of buildings nor require the owner of part of a building to keep his part in good repair. Am Jur 2d, Adjoining Landowners § 10; CJS, Adjoining Landowners § 60.

SECTION 3-18: LAND MEASURE

3-18A Equivalents.

Mile — 8 furlongs — 80 chains — 320 rods — 1,760 yards — 5,280 feet.
Rod — pole — perch — 16.5 feet — 5.5 yards — 25 links — $1/4$ chain.
Chain — 66 feet — 4 rods — 100 links.
Link — $1/100$ chain — 7.92 inches — $66/100$ foot — $4/100$ rod.
Inch — 0.1262 link — 0.0833 foot — 0.0277 yard — 0.005 rod — 0.0012 chain.
Foot — 12 inches — 1.5151 links — 0.3333 yard — 0.0606 rod — 0.0151 chain.
Yard — 36 inches — 3 feet — 4.5454 links — 0.1818 rod — 0.0454 chain.
Arpent — 192.24 feet.
Vara — 2.7806 feet — 33.3672 inches.
Meter — 39.3685 inches — 3.2807 feet.
Township — 36 sections.
Section — 640 acres — one mile square.
Acre — 4 roods — 160 sq. rods — 10 sq. chains — 43,560 sq. feet — 208.71 feet square — 5645.373 sq. varas — 1.834 sq. arpents.
Square rod — 272.25 square feet.
Square two acres is 295.16 feet on each side.
An acre 50 feet wide is 871.2 feet long.
A square acre is 208.71 feet on each side.
A square half acre is 147.58 feet on each side.
A square third acre is 120.50 feet on each side.
A square quarter acre is 104.36 feet on each side.
A square eighth acre is 73.79 feet on each side.
A circular acre is 235.50 feet in diameter.
A circular quarter acre is 117.75 feet in diameter.
To find a true bearing from a given magnetic bearing, add the magnetic declination if the given bearing is NE or SW, or subtract the magnetic declination if the given bearing is NW or SE. In Ohio, the current magnetic declination varies from approximately zero in the Cincinnati area to approxi-

mately five degrees in the northeast corner of the state; it changes slightly from year to year.

A curve that changes in direction by one degree in 100 feet is called a one-degree curve. The radius of a one-degree curve is approximately 5,730 feet. To find the radius of any curve, divide this number by the number of degrees in the particular curve.

3-18B To Compute Area of.

A parcel of four sides with right angles (a rectangle): multiply the length by the breadth.

A parcel of four sides with parallel lines but not necessarily right angles (a parallelogram): multiply the base by the perpendicular height.

A parcel of three sides (a triangle): multiply the base by half the perpendicular height.

A parcel of four sides with two of them parallel (a trapezoid): multiply half the sum of the two parallel sides by the perpendicular distance between them.

A parcel with a side not a straight line: find the average breadth, or divide the parcel in order to proceed as above.

To ascertain acreage: divide square feet by 43,560, or multiply square feet by .000023.

3-18C Conversion of Rods to Feet.

	0	1	2	3	4	5	6	7	8	9
0	0	16.5	33.0	49.5	66.0	82.5	99.0	115.5	132.0	148.5
10	165.0	181.5	198.0	214.5	231.0	247.5	264.0	280.5	297.0	313.5
20	330.0	346.5	363.0	379.5	396.0	412.5	429.0	445.5	462.0	478.5
30	495.0	511.5	528.0	544.5	561.0	577.5	594.0	610.5	627.0	643.5
40	660.0	676.5	693.0	709.5	726.0	742.5	759.0	775.5	792.0	808.5
50	825.0	841.5	858.0	874.5	891.0	907.5	924.0	940.5	957.0	973.5
60	990.0	1006.5	1023.0	1039.5	1056.0	1072.5	1089.0	1105.5	1122.0	1138.5
70	1155.0	1171.5	1188.0	1204.5	1221.0	1237.5	1254.0	1270.5	1287.0	1303.5
80	1320.0	1336.5	1353.0	1369.5	1386.0	1402.5	1419.0	1435.5	1452.0	1468.5
90	1485.0	1501.5	1518.0	1534.5	1551.0	1567.5	1584.0	1600.5	1617.0	1633.5
100	1650.0	1666.5	1683.0	1699.5	1716.0	1732.5	1749.0	1765.5	1782.0	1798.5
110	1815.0	1831.5	1848.0	1864.5	1881.0	1897.5	1914.0	1930.5	1947.0	1963.5
120	1980.0	1996.5	2013.0	2029.5	2046.0	2062.5	2079.0	2095.5	2112.0	2128.5
130	2145.0	2161.5	2178.0	2194.5	2211.0	2227.5	2244.0	2260.5	2277.0	2293.5
140	2310.0	2326.5	2343.0	2359.5	2376.0	2392.5	2409.0	2425.5	2442.0	2458.5
150	2475.0	2491.5	2508.0	2524.5	2541.0	2557.5	2574.0	2590.5	2607.0	2623.5
160	2640.0	2656.5	2673.0	2689.5	2706.0	2722.5	2739.0	2755.5	2772.0	2788.5

DIVISION 3-2: CONSTRUCTION OF DESCRIPTIONS

SECTION 3-21: GENERALLY

Construction of deeds generally, see Section 8-31.
Effect of error, see 1-21E.

3-21A Primary Rule.

The object of construction is to ascertain the intent of the parties and this intent governs unless the language employed renders it impossible to give it effect. Wolfe v. Scarborough, 2 OS 361 (1853).

Where lands are granted by metes and bounds, all the area within those bounds, and no more, passes. The intention of the parties cannot be to contradict the description. McAfferty v. Conover, 7 OS 99 (1857); Lockwood v. Wildman, 13 Ohio 430 (1844).

Further research: O Jur 3d, Adjoining Landowners § 41.

LAW IN GENERAL

A description must be certain or capable of being made certain. It is sufficient for an effective conveyance if the land can thereby be identified. The intention of the parties controls the construction but the intention cannot contradict the terms of the description. The rules of interpretation are merely aids in ascertaining the intention. However, the intention does not enlarge the grant; thus, a recital of intent to convey a larger tract than described is not an effective conveyance of the part not included in the description. Am Jur 2d, Boundaries § 2; Am Jur 2d, Deeds § 228; Am Law of Prop §§ 12.110, 12.122; CJS, Boundaries § 3.

3-21B Reformation.

Reformation generally, see Section 16-66.

Where one tract of land was described by mistake instead of another, the mistake cannot be corrected at law by proof of the intention of the parties. McAfferty v. Conover, 7 OS 99 (1857).

3-21C Marketability.

See also Section 1-43.

Standard of Title Examination

(As amended by Ohio State Bar Association in 1960)

Problem 3.2B:

Should objection be made on account of minor typographical errors, irregularities or deficiencies in a description of land?

Standard 3.2B:

Such an objection should not be made when a subsequent conveyance contains a correct description.

Comment:

Errors, irregularities and deficiencies in property descriptions in the chain of title do not impair marketability unless, after all circumstances of record are taken into account, a substantial uncertainty exists as to the land which was conveyed or intended to be conveyed, or the description falls beneath the minimal requirement of sufficiency and definiteness which is essential to an effective conveyance. Lapse of time, subsequent conveyances, the manifest or typographical nature of errors or omissions, accepted rules of construction and other considerations should be relied upon to approve marginal, sufficient or questionable descriptions.

LAW IN GENERAL

The general rules as to marketable title are applied when there are defects or variations in description. Indefiniteness may make a title unmarketable while the conveyance itself is valid by virtue of facts not of record. 15 ALR 1483.

3-21D Certainty Required; Notice.

If the description is so imperfect that it cannot be known what land was intended to be conveyed, the deed is void. McChesney v. Wainwright, 5 Ohio 452 (1832).

If a deed refers to another deed and the land can be ascertained by such reference, the description is sufficiently certain. McChesney v. Wainwright, 5 Ohio 452 (1832).

If the property cannot be identified from the description in the tax deed, the deed is void for uncertainty. Chalfant v. Birney, 126 NE2d 359, 71 Abs 158 (C.P. 1954).

Further research: O Jur 3d, Deeds § 149.

LAW IN GENERAL

In some cases, a description insufficient for a conveyance is held to put a subsequent purchaser on inquiry and to constitute constructive notice; while other cases hold that a deed containing a description requiring reformation is not such notice. Of course, actual notice of the record may be sufficient to protect the rights of the grantee under the defective instrument. Am Jur 2d, Boundaries § 6; Am Law of Prop § 18.34.

The requirement of certainty is complied with if the description can be made certain, as by reference to another deed. However, although good between the parties, the description may be too indefinite to be notice; or the description may not be sufficient for a marketable title, as a reference to an unrecorded instrument. Extrinsic evidence is inadmissible if the description is clear and unambiguous. The boundaries of a description by lot number are ascertained from the actual survey referred to, or by a new survey according to the plan when the original survey is insufficient. When the general description is certain (as by lot number) the addition of dimensions, courses or other details will not affect the grant, subject to the rule as to the intention manifested. A conveyance is void when the description is equally applicable to two or more parcels owned by the grantor. Am Jur 2d, Boundaries § 76; CJS, Boundaries § 20.

3-21E Conflicting Clauses.

Where land can be identified by the description, it will pass by the deed although some of the terms are false. Eggleston v. Bradford, 10 Ohio 312 (1840).

A metes-and-bounds description fully describing certain premises is not modified in any respect by the addition thereto of words which refer to the source of grantor's title. Burks v. Louisville Title Ins. Co., 95 App 509, 121 NE2d 94, 54 OO 128 (1953).

A misdescription in one or more particulars is of no consequence if the residue of the description enables the court to correct the error and ascertain the land. Betzing v. Beckman, 193 NE2d 741, 24 OO2d 398, 92 Abs 301 (C.P. 1963).

In construction of a will, after discarding the erroneous description of property, the slightest means of identification of the property claimed to have been the intended subject of the devise may be seized upon to avoid intestacy. Mastics v. Kiraly, 196 NE2d 172, 26 OO2d 266, 93 Abs 193 (Prob. 1964).

Further research: O Jur 3d, Adjoining Landowners § 62.

LAW IN GENERAL

All parts of the description should be given effect if possible. When the calls are irreconcilable, the call which is least certain and most likely to be mistaken may be disregarded. If the inconsistencies are of equal certainty, actual possession will be considered. Am Jur 2d, Boundaries §§ 64, 66; CJS, Boundaries § 47.

A grant is construed favorably to the grantee. This is a rule of last resort. It does not apply to deeds from the government which are construed in favor of the grantor. Tiffany § 978.

3-21F Omissions; Part of Tract.

"Description in a deed, seventy acres in southwest corner, good, and includes the land in an equal square." Walsh v. Ringer, 2 Ohio 327 (1826).

We find no difficulty in discovering a description certain enough, neglecting the mistaken number. Eggleston v. Bradford, 10 Ohio 312, 316 (1840).

Further research: O Jur 3d, Deeds § 155.

LAW IN GENERAL

Courts are liberal in construing descriptions when necessary to avoid invalidity for lack of certainty. For such purpose, incorrect parts may be ignored if a sufficient description remains. A grant of a certain number of acres in a given corner of a tract will convey a parcel in a square form or, if that is not possible, in a rectangular form. If no attempt is made to locate the acreage or part of a larger tract, it is generally held that the grantee acquires the proportionate undivided interest in the whole. In such circumstances some decisions permit the grantee to select the location. Am Jur 2d, Deeds § 159; CJS, Boundaries § 23; CJS, Deeds § 30.

3-21G Precedence of Calls.

An order of precedence has been established among different calls for the location of boundaries of land, and other things being equal, resort is to be had first to natural objects or landmarks, next to artificial monuments, then to adjacent boundaries, then to courses and distances, and lastly to quantity. Haverstick v. Beaver, 37 NE2d 650, 34 Abs 363 (App. 1941).

Further research: O Jur 3d, Adjoining Landowners §§ 63, 64, 67.

LAW IN GENERAL

The precedence among conflicting calls, unless a contrary intention is expressed, is: first, to natural objects or landmarks; next, to artificial monuments; then, to adjacent boundaries; then, to courses; then, to distances; and lastly, to quantity. Am Jur 2d, Boundaries §§ 3, 65; Am Law of Prop § 12.117; CJS, Boundaries § 49.

3-21H Monuments; Adjoiners.

Monuments control course and distance provided the variance is not too great but if the monument cannot be found this rule has no application. McCoy v. Galloway, 3 Ohio 282 (1827).

Where there is a discrepancy in the calls, the line actually run is to be found by having recourse to the more certain, fixed and natural objects called for in the boundary. Wyckoff v. Stephenson, 14 Ohio 13 (1846). The rule cannot pervert the manifest intention. Spiller v. Nye, 16 Ohio 16 (1847).

Where a description designates a line along the tract of an adjoining owner, the call for a distance must be rejected. The adjoining land is construed as a monument. Calhoun v. Price, 17 OS 96 (1866).

A deed conveying "all the land lying between the strip one hundred feet wide, hereinabove described, and the Pennsylvania and Ohio canal," conveying a supposed locality between two points, excludes the termini and does not, therefore, convey to the center of the canal. New York, P. & O. R.R. v. Stubbings, 12 CD 699 (1888).

A call for a street, river or other monument as a boundary is presumed to mean to the center line, instead of to the edge, of such monument. Paine v. Consumers' Forwarding & Storage Co., 8 OFD 580, 19 CCA 99, 71 Fed 626, 37 WLB 102, 42 WLB 175 (1895).

Further research: O Jur 3d, Adjoining Landowners § 43.

LAW IN GENERAL

The center of a monument, except when it is a building or other land, is the boundary unless a contrary intention is manifested. Calls for adjacent owners, trees, fences, stakes, buildings, marked lines, and established corners are regarded as monuments. A reference to adjoining land refers to the true boundary line. Am Jur 2d, Boundaries §§ 5, 69; CJS, Boundaries § 20; Powell § 891.

3-21I Plats.

Surveys, generally, see Section 3-26.

Calls for course and distance may be controlled by a plat, which is made part of a contract or deed. Wolfe v. Scarborough, 2 OS 361 (1853).

Course and distance must give way to monuments in description of lands. Lines on plat held monuments to which figures in notes on plat must yield. Cardosi v. Wise, 44 App 205, 184 NE 863, 14 Abs 698, 38 OLR 5 (1933).

Where the owner of platted Lots 5 and 6 conveys Lot 5 but, by metes-and-bounds description, includes part of Lot 6 without mentioning such lot, and later conveys Lot 6, the second grantee has title to the full lot. Baker v. Koch, 114 App 519, 183 NE2d 434, 20 OO2d 8 (1960).

Wooden stakes or other monuments placed on the land by the original surveyor of the lots are monuments and the boundary lines of lots so established are primary. The plat is derivative and secondary. "As set forth by McDermott and as is inherent in the relationship between the survey on the land and the plat, the survey as actually made on the land must govern." Sellman v. Schaaf, 26 App2d 35, 269 NE2d 60, 55 OO2d 69 (1971).

Standard of Title Examination

(Adopted by Ohio State Bar Association in 1952)

Problem 3.2A:

Should an objection to the title be raised because one or more deeds in the chain of title contains an error with respect to the reference to the proper plat book and plat book page of platted land?

Standard 3.2A:

If the deed refers to a subdivision by an exclusive descriptive name, an objection should not be raised because of an error in the reference to the plat book and the plat book page where said subdivision is recorded.

Further research: O Jur 3d, Adjoining Landowners § 68.

LAW IN GENERAL

A reference in a deed to a plat incorporates the plat and constitutes an adoption of the survey as a part of the description. A conveyance by lot number assigned by a plat incorporates the plat as part of the description. The survey as actually made controls the representation of it on the plat. A conveyance is not affected by the fact that the plat referred to is invalid, is insufficient as a dedication, or is not recorded. Marked lines on a plat may be treated as monuments. Am Law of Prop § 12.103.

3-21J Quantity.

See also Section 3-22.

LAW IN GENERAL

Quantity is usually the most uncertain part of a description but it may control course and distance, as when an intention is disclosed to convey one half of a tract. Am Jur 2d, Boundaries § 75; Am Law of Prop § 12.107; CJS, Boundaries § 57.

3-21K Reversing Lines.

When there is an error in one particular of the description, the other particulars may be amply sufficient to correct the mistake and identify the land. A misdescription in one or more particulars is of no consequence if the residue of the description enables us to correct the error and ascertain the land meant to be conveyed. It is obvious that the legal title passed. Thomas v. White, 2 OS 540, 548, 550 (1853).

LAW IN GENERAL

Descriptions are presumed to be according to actual surveys. Lines which are actually run and marked on the ground will control. Whether a survey was actually made or was presumed, lines may be run in the reverse direction if known calls can be thereby harmonized or if a mistake in an earlier survey can be shown. Under this rule, an indefinite point of beginning may be ascertained from an undisputed corner, or ascertained by running back for the designated distance from the monument at the end of the first line. Am Jur 2d, Boundaries § 60; Am Law of Prop § 12.105; CJS, Boundaries §§ 9, 12, 14.

SECTION 3-22: DEFICIENCY OR SURPLUS; MORE OR LESS

3-22A More or Less.

A description, in a deed, by metes and bounds and as containing a certain number of acres, does not constitute a covenant as to acreage although "more or less" be omitted. After acceptance of a deed by the vendee as performance of the stipulation to sell and convey the land described in the agreement, in the absence of fraud or mistake, no recovery can be had by the vendee for a deficiency in the land conveyed. Brumbaugh v. Chapman, 45 OS 368, 13 NE 584, 18 WLB 345, 397 (1887).

Further research: O Jur 2d, Vendor and Purchaser § 38.

LAW IN GENERAL

The addition of the words "more or less" to distance or quantity does not modify the designation if no other calls are given. "More or less" or "about" covers only an inaccuracy or reasonable variation from the specified amount. The words do not justify a misrepresentation nor preclude relief for fraud or lack of good faith. The qualifying words will relieve the grantor or the grantee from making compensation when the shortage or excess is not material. 70 ALR 368; Tiffany § 994.

3-22B Allocation of Deficiency or Surplus.

Adverse possession, see 2-23A.

Where the plat shows the lots were intended to meet, the surplus ground ascertained to exist will be divided between the grantees in proportion to the lengths of their respective lines, as shown by the plat and stated in their deeds. Marsh v. Stephenson, 7 OS 264 (1857); Epstein v. Kraft, 16 CC(NS) 251, 26 CD 528 (1908).

If there is a shortage on a plat in which the owner intended to plat all his property, it is a well settled rule in this state that such shortage will be divided as near as possible pro rata between the owners of the whole. Columbus S. & C. R.R. v. Tuttle, 18 CC 630, 7 CD 63 (1896).

Where there is a shortage in the actual land platted into lots and blocks with intervening alleys and streets, each block where possible must be treated as separate and distinct. Labus v. Jones, 197 NE2d 244, 26 OO2d 189, 93 Abs 161 (C.P. 1963).

Further research: O Jur 3d, Adjoining Landowners § 49.

LAW IN GENERAL

A deficiency or surplus in the quantity of land, appearing after a tract has been subdivided and the parts separately owned, will be divided proportionately among the subdivisions, as a rule. The rule has been applied even when the tract has not been platted, although ordinarily the last purchaser bears the deficiency and the original owners retain the surplus in such a case if the transfers are not simultaneous. An exception to the rule occurs when the boundaries of the subdivisions have been fixed by adverse possession or when monuments fix the original corners of a lot. Where lots are in separate blocks, the shortage or excess in any block will ordinarily be apportioned among the lots in such block. Am Jur 2d, Boundaries § 63; Am Law of Prop § 12.123; 97 ALR 1227; CJS, Boundaries § 124.

3-22C Remedies.

Specific performance was granted with diminution of the purchase price upon petition of vendor where shortage was 16.5 acres from 150 acres. Harris v. Schuholz, 129 OS 449, 195 NE 868, 2 OO 435 (1935).

Grantee was denied rescission and a money judgment where shortage was 25 acres from farm supposed to contain 88 acres. Fillegar v. Walker, 54 App 262, 6 NE2d 1010, 7 OO 416, 23 Abs 20 (1936).

A purchaser cannot maintain an action as to area of land purchased where, before the transfer of title, he learned the facts as to the quantity or facts putting him under a duty to investigate. Ralston v. Grinder, 8 App2d 208, 221 NE2d 602, 37 OO2d 213 (1966).

LAW IN GENERAL

Irrespective of the use of qualifying words, when there is a mistake as to quantity, equity may grant relief by way of rescission, of fixing compensation, or of abatement of the purchase price. Sufficient equitable ground for relief exists when the quantity directly influenced the price or was a controlling motive for entering into the contract. The amount of the deficiency or excess in particular cases is of little value as a guide because equities vary according to the particular circumstances and according to the conscience of the chancellor. 1 ALR2d 9.

SECTION 3-23: WATERS AND WATERCOURSES

3-23A As Being All Grantor Owns.

A conveyance, except a governmental grant, is generally presumed to convey all the land of the grantor. Busch v. Wilgus, 24 NP(NS) 209, 1 Abs 20 (1922).

LAW IN GENERAL

When the grantor owns land bounded by a stream or other body of water, a conveyance is generally presumed to pass the land under water which the grantor owns, unless excluded by the terms of the description, but subject to the public easement in navigable waters. Public grants are an exception to the rule and are construed against the grantee. Am Law of Prop § 12.113; CJS, Navigable Waters § 120; CJS, Waters § 84.

3-23B Low or High Watermark.

When land under water is excluded by the description, the water edge at low watermark is the boundary. McCullock v. Aten, 2 Ohio 307 (1826).

LAW IN GENERAL

When land under water is not included, the low watermark is usually the boundary, except that high watermark is presumed as to navigable waters where the bed is owned by the state. Am Law of Prop § 12.27; CJS, Boundaries § 27.

3-23C Thread of Stream.

The thread of the stream, notwithstanding it may have changed in location by attrition and accretion, will control the courses and distances named in a conveyance, and will continue to be the boundary line. Niehaus v. Shepherd, 26 OS 40 (1875).

Further research: O Jur 3d, Adjoining Landowners §§ 51, 52.

LAW IN GENERAL

The thread of a stream is the line midway between the shores irrespective of the depth of the channel. This is ordinarily the boundary line. Am Jur 2d, Boundaries § 28; CJS, Waters § 71.

3-23D Bounded by; To; Along.

A call in a survey, for a stream not navigable, is a call for the main branch of such stream, and the boundary is the middle of the stream. Benner v. Platter, 6 Ohio 504 (1834).

Where description is "to the south bank" and "with the courses of the south bank," the stream, at low watermark, is the boundary. Lamb v. Rickets, 11 Ohio 311 (1842).

LAW IN GENERAL

Title to the center of the watercourse, when the grantor owns so far, is usually presumed to be conveyed when land is described as bounded by, to, or along the stream. An intention not to convey land under water is usually found when the description is to and along the bank, shore, margin or edge of a body of water. Naming an object on the bank as a monument is not sufficient to except the bed of the stream. Am Jur 2d, Boundaries § 24; 74 ALR 597; CJS, Boundaries § 31.

3-23E Watercourse Between States.

The territorial limits of the State of Ohio extend on the southeast to the low watermark at the time of the grant of the Northwest Territory. Booth v. Shepherd, 8 OS 243 (1858); Greene v. Wilson Sand & Supply Co., 6 Abs 294 (App. 1928).

The boundary line between the United States and Canada through Lake Erie is the northern boundary of this state. Edson v. Crangle, 62 OS 49, 56 NE 647, 43 WLB 103, 227 (1900). See also 43 U.S.C. § 1312.

Further research: O Jur 2d, State of Ohio § 6.

3-23F Meander Lines; Apportionment.

Meander lines which are run as near the water line as convenient are not intended as the boundary, and the center of the stream continues as the boundary. Chesbrough v. Head, 3 CC(NS) 516, 13 CD 427 (1902).

The deeds of adjoining owners of land which extends to certain fixed monuments upon opposite banks of a small nonnavigable stream and thence along such banks respectively, carry title in each proprietor to the middle thread of the stream at low water. Limle v. Robison, 4 App 236, 21 CC(NS) 428, 25 CD 313 (1915).

Further research: O Jur 3d, Adjoining Landowners § 53.

LAW IN GENERAL

Meander lines are the straight lines of a survey along the approximate course of the stream and a short distance back from the water's edge. The presumption obtains that the thread of the stream is intended notwithstanding such a survey. This rule applies to a lake which is of regular shape and much longer than wide. Various rules have been adopted in determining the division of beds of waters having a curved or irregular shore line. Am Jur 2d, Boundaries § 29; Am Law of Prop §§ 12.27, 12.114; CJS, Boundaries § 30; Tiffany § 664.

The common basis for apportionment of the area of a river is the extent of the individual tract's frontage on the shore. Judicial rules or methods for division of the area between two or more riparian owners on the same bank are subject to variation or exception where necessary to avoid an inequitable result. 65 ALR2d 143.

3-23G   Dedication; Lot Description.

Where lake level was afterwards lowered by artificial means, a presumption of intention of the parties arose that margin of lake described in deed as boundary of lot conveyed was where stakes were set. Clayton v. Chippewa Lake Park Co., 3 Abs 573 (App. 1925).

Where a water line is a boundary of a given lot, a deed describing the lot by its number conveys the land up to the shifting water line. Lake Front-East Fifty-Fifth St. Corp. v. Cleveland, 7 O Supp 17, 21 OO 1 (C.P. 1939).

SECTION 3-24: HIGHWAYS AND STREETS

3-24A   When Fee in Government.

When the title to a thoroughfare is in the government, a conveyance of the adjoining land does not extend beyond the edge of the thoroughfare. A duly recorded plat vests in the municipality or county the fee simple title to land designated or intended for streets, alleys, or other public purposes.

3-24B   As Including Thoroughfare.

Upon vacation of alley by city, abutting lot owners, as to that portion of alley abutting their properties, were vested with fee simple interest in one-half of width of strip of land which formerly comprised alley, irrespective of fact that original owner and dedicator of land was not predecessor in title to all such abutting lot owners, subject, however, to those rights which other owners might have in alley as necessary means of access to their properties. R.C. § 723.08. Taylor v. Carpenter, 45 OS2d 137, 341 NE2d 843 (1976).

Previous Ohio decisions had held that the owner of adjoining land is presumed to own to the center of the highway because it is presumed the land was taken from him. But the title may show that he did not own the land covered by the highway. Bingham v. Doane, 9 Ohio 165 (1839). Also see Middle States Securities Co. v. Smith, 5 Abs 566 (App. 1926).

LAW IN GENERAL

A description running along or bounded by a highway is presumed to convey to the center or so far as is owned by the grantor. Some cases hold that a description of land bounded by the side or edge of the road is sufficient for a conveyance of grantor's land in the highway. The presumption that the grantee takes to the center of the highway may be rebutted by a clear expression in the deed. It has been held not to be rebutted by the expressions "bounded by," "to," "along," "on," "abutting" and "fronting." Decisions as to land bounded by water may be applied by analogy. By the weight of authority, a deed by lot number with reference to a plat conveys the interest of the grantor in the street or vacated street. Am Jur 2d, Boundaries § 38; Am Law of Prop § 12.112; 49 ALR2d 982; CJS, Boundaries § 35; Tiffany § 996.

3-24C Measuring from Center Line.

LAW IN GENERAL

A call for a certain distance from a highway is presumed to mean from the center line. However, the contrary presumption may be held to exist in certain communities where it is a local custom to measure from the side line. Tiffany § 996.

3-24D Practical Location.

LAW IN GENERAL

A highway is a monument as actually used. The practical location of a thoroughfare is presumed to be the boundary, even though it was a proposed street at the time of the grant. Tiffany § 996.

3-24E Railroads; Private Ways.

LAW IN GENERAL

The rule is that the grantee presumably takes title to the adjoining servient land. It is generally regarded as applying to conveyances of land abutting on railroad rights-of-way. Am Jur 2d, Boundaries § 54; CJS, Boundaries § 45.

SECTION 3-25: PARTICULAR WORDS

3-25A House or Other Structure.

A grant or devise of a dwelling house conveys also any buildings belonging to it and the land on which it is built. In re Niesen's Estate, 103 NE2d 24, 46 OO 164, 64 Abs 485 (Prob. 1951).

LAW IN GENERAL

A conveyance or exception of a house or other structure ordinarily includes the land essential to its use for the purpose indicated. Am Law of Prop § 12.128.

3-25B Half.

Extrinsic testimony is admissible to identify land conveyed as "a tract of land known as the east half of the southwest division of Section 17," and to show that the land conveyed is less than the mathematical half of the division. Schlief v. Hart, 29 OS 150 (1876).

LAW IN GENERAL

"Half" means half in quantity unless other words or circumstances show a different intent. The expression "west half" is presumed to require the dividing line to run north and south, or parallel with a straight boundary line, and not to require equal division of the north or south boundary line. Government surveys are an exception, by statute, to the rule. A deed for half of a section or tract according to government surveys conveys to a line equally distant from the boundaries of the parcel. Am Jur 2d, Deeds § 246; Am Law of Prop § 12.106.

3-25C All My Land.

A deed conveying "all right, title, interest or claim to any land descended to me from A or B" is sufficiently descriptive to pass title to any legal or equitable estate which the grantor inherited from A or B. Barton v. Morris, 15 Ohio 408 (1846).

LAW IN GENERAL

A deed having a description such as "all my land" may be an effective conveyance, although it does not have priority over a previous unrecorded conveyance of a specific part. CJS, Deeds § 104.

3-25D North, East, South, West.

The word "northerly" used in a deed does not necessarily mean due north, but when not controlled by position of monuments, or by lines described with reasonable certainty, may be construed to mean due north, particularly when it is necessary to so hold in order to prevent uncertainty. New York P. & O. R.R. v. Stubbings, 12 CD 699 (1888).

LAW IN GENERAL

"North," "east," "south" or "west" are construed to mean due north, east, south or west when not controlled by other definite description. When there are monuments or definite courses the terms have their ordinary meaning of inclining either way but toward the given direction. The implication of intending a general direction is greater when the suffix "erly" is used, but the word will be construed as meaning one of the cardinal compass points unless a different intention is otherwise indicated. North, south, east and west are commonly construed to mean parallel with the lines of the tract or lot being subdivided instead of running to the points of the compass. Am Jur 2d, Deeds § 248; Am Law of Prop § 12.105.

3-25E Miscellaneous Words.

"North with the half section line" denotes direction and not necessarily that the line intended is identical with the half section line. Puntt v. Zimmer, 8 CC(NS) 455, 19 CD 721 (1906).

Where the conveyance to the board of education is unrecorded, a deed, including the school lot in the description with a provision "except the right owned by the board of education," excepts the fee simple title to the school lot. Shewell v. Board of Education, 88 App 1, 96 NE2d 323, 43 OO 375 (1950).

Description in a deed "being 60 feet front and rear off of the entire east side" of a tract was construed in this case to mean more than 60 feet front (or in effect as the easterly 60 feet) where the rear line was perpendicular to the east line but the front line was not perpendicular to the east line. Boron v. Lemmon, 6 O Supp 203, 21 OO 506 (C.P. 1941).

SECTION 3-26: SURVEYS

3-26A Rules.

R.C. 315.28 to 315.34 provide for survey by county engineer of any land of which any corner or line is lost or uncertain.

In locating a deed upon the land the rule is, first to find the original lines as actually run; second, to run lines from acknowledged corners or calls; third, to run lines according to the courses and distances called for in the deed. Avery v. Baum, Wright 576 (1834).

In the Virginia Military Tract the original surveys were made by the magnetic meridian. Most of the Congress lands were surveyed by the true meridian. In contracts and private surveys the magnetic meridian has been generally adopted. McKinney v. McKinney, 8 OS 423, 427 (1858).

County engineers may be required to run lot lines and the fees paid into the county treasury. 1917 OAG 1264.

LAW IN GENERAL

In locating a description upon land the rule is: first, to find the original lines as actually run; second, to run lines from acknowledged corners, or calls; third, to run lines according to calls for courses and distances. Conveyances are presumed to be made according to a prior actual survey. It is said that the primary purpose of construction is to follow the footsteps of the surveyor on the ground. Am Jur 2d, Boundaries § 55; Am Law of Prop § 12.116; CJS, Boundaries §§ 14, 49.

3-26B Effect of Surveys.

LAW IN GENERAL

A map is the usual and proper method of recording a survey. It is incorporated in a deed by reference. A survey does not vary a deed which does not refer to the survey nor to any of the monuments. Am Jur 2d, Boundaries § 111; CJS, Boundaries § 24.

3-26C Resurveys.

Original government surveys, see Section 3-27.

R.C. 315.20, repealed effective 4-4-85, provided that "No resurvey made after June 1, 1831, by any person except the county engineer or his deputy shall be considered as legal testimony in any court, unless it is made by mutual consent, reduced to writing, and signed by the parties, or is made by order of court." (G.C. 2797 as eff. 1831.)

Further research: O Jur 3d, Adjoining Landowners § 61.

LAW IN GENERAL

The older survey will prevail, as a general rule, when a conflict exists between the lines of different surveys. The purpose of a resurvey is to ascertain the lines of the original survey of the premises. Am Jur 2d, Boundaries § 61; Am Law of Prop § 12.111.

3-26D Ohio Coordinate System.

R.C. 157.01 to 157.08 provide a system of surveying based upon reference to triangulation stations and plane rectangular coordinates established by United States Coast and Geodetic Survey. The state is divided into a North Zone and a South Zone having grids of parallel lines with x lines running generally north and south, and y lines running generally east and west. A description by this system is subordinate to United States public land surveys. It is added to the ordinary description. A purchaser or mortgagee is not required to rely upon such a description. A survey made under the system will enable a parcel to be accurately relocated although some or all of the ordinary landmarks are later altered or destroyed. (As eff. 10-1-85.)

Further research: O Jur 3d, Adjoining Landowners § 60; Am Law of Prop § 12.109.

3-26E   How to Read Courses in Surveyor's Description.

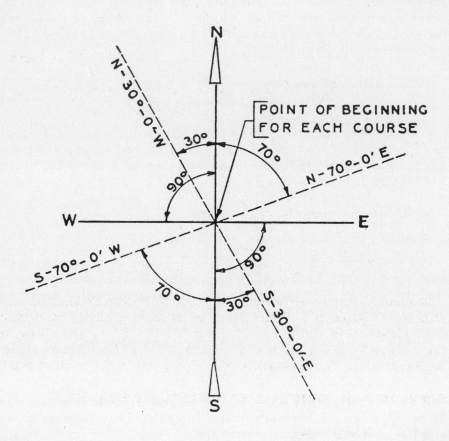

Bearings are read in degrees and minutes from the north or from the south.

126

3-26F   Illustration of Surveyor's Plat and Description.

Beginning at A; thence North (at an angle of) 50 degrees (toward the) East a distance of 200 feet to B; thence South (at an angle of) 40 degrees (toward the) East a distance of 100 feet to C; thence South (at an angle of) 50 degrees (toward the) West a distance of 200 feet to D; thence North (at an angle of) 40 degrees (toward the) West a distance of 100 feet to the place of beginning.

SECTION 3-27:   ORIGINAL GOVERNMENT SURVEYS

3-27A   The System.

All the original surveys, except in the Virginia Military Tract, were made under the rectangular plan. This innovation in surveying is a great boon in contributing to the certainty and stability of titles, and was first used in Ohio.

Congress lands were sold under general federal laws. Most were surveyed by the true meridian. The original surveys in the Virginia Military Tract were made by the magnetic bearing.

LAW IN GENERAL

Under the system, Congress lands are divided into townships, each six miles square. A township consists of thirty-six sections, each one mile square.

127

Quarter sections of one hundred and sixty acres each are recognized in describing the land although the lines are not actually run. A variance in the area of the divisions is caused in some instances by the convergence of the meridians running north and by irregularities in the land. Each tier of townships running north and south, known as a range, is numbered east or west from a certain meridian, known as a principal meridian. Each tier of townships running east and west is numbered north and south from a certain parallel of latitude, known as principal base line. A few variations exist in the earliest surveys; for example, townships in the Ohio River Survey are numbered north from the Ohio River. Am Jur 2d, Public Lands §§ 39, 41, 42; Am Law of Prop § 12.100; CJS, Public Lands § 28; Tiffany § 991.

3-27B Apportionment of Surplus or Deficiency.

LAW IN GENERAL

Any surplus, deficiency or irregularity in the survey of a township or of a section is applied to the north and west sides. This rule may not be followed when the monuments are lots. Am Jur 2d, Boundaries § 62; CJS, Boundaries § 125.

3-27C Proof of Survey.

LAW IN GENERAL

The location of corners as originally established by government surveyors is conclusive. If the actual corner cannot be found nor its location proven, the government field notes are used as evidence of the location. CJS, Boundaries § 12; Tiffany § 991.

DIVISION 3-3: ESTABLISHMENT OF BOUNDARIES

SECTION 3-31: AGREEMENT OF PARTIES

3-31A Rules.

Adverse possession, see Section 2-23.

R.C. 2711.01 provides: "A provision in any written contract, except as hereinafter provided, to settle by arbitration a controversy thereafter arising out of such contract, or out of the refusal to perform the whole or any part thereof, or any agreement in writing between two or more persons to submit to arbitration any controversy existing between them at the time of the agreement to submit, or thereafter arising, from a relationship then existing between them or which they simultaneously create, shall be valid, irrevocable, and enforceable, save upon such grounds as exist at law or in equity for the revocation of any contract.

"Sections 2711.01 to 2711.15 of the Revised Code shall not apply to controversies involving the title to or the possession of real estate, with the following exceptions:

"(A) Controversies involving the amount of increased or decreased valuation of the property at the termination of certain periods, as provided in a lease;

"(B) Controversies involving the amount of rentals due under any lease;

"(C) Controversies involving the determination of the value of improvements at the termination of any lease;

"(D) Controversies involving the appraisal of property values in connection with making or renewing any lease;

"(E) Controversies involving the boundaries of real estate." (As eff. 7-28-75.)

R.C. 5301.21 and 5301.22 provide that when the owners of adjoining tracts agree upon a corner or line in a written instrument executed as prescribed for deeds, such corner or line shall thenceforth be deemed established. Such instrument may be executed by a guardian and must be recorded by the recorder in the book in which surveys are recorded. When a tract of land is owned by the state, the officer or board having administrative control thereof, with the approval of the attorney general, may execute such an instrument.

The fixing of a boundary line by parol is not within the operation of the statute of frauds — no estate is thereby created; but where the boundary line is fixed by the parties, in settlement of the dispute, they hold up to it by virtue of their title deeds, and not by virtue of the parol transfer. Bobo v. Richmond, 25 OS 115 (1874); Engle v. Beatty, 41 App 477, 180 NE 269, 11 Abs 597 (1931).

Where adjoining owners settle a disputed boundary the agreement need not be such as would of itself transfer title or right of possession. This view is consistent with the principle that when adjoining owners, in attempting to find the true line, by mistake fix upon an incorrect one, they may on discovering the true line, occupy it at any time before the statute of limitations has run. Hills v. Ludwig, 46 OS 373, 24 NE 596, 21 WLB 203 (1889); Smith v. McKay, 30 OS 409, 2 WLB 4 (1876).

Where abutting owners attempted to fix their true boundary line, but this line was not correctly located, and nothing had occurred which would work an estoppel, plaintiff was entitled to have the true line established by a proper survey. Brown v. Smith, 12 Abs 497 (App. 1932).

Further research: O Jur 3d, Adjoining Landowners § 69.

LAW IN GENERAL

Adjacent owners cannot change a known boundary between their lands except by a conveyance. When the line is uncertain or disputed, it may be fixed by parol agreement. Many courts require actual or constructive possession for some period in order to make the agreement conclusive. The agreement does not violate the statute of frauds nor the parol evidence rule because it does not operate as a conveyance but rather as the determination of indefinite or uncertain facts. This rule does not conflict with the further rule that a parole agreement fixing the line is not binding, in the absence of estoppel or rights of third parties, when the parties act in the erroneous belief they are fixing the true line and afterward discover the mistake. Acquiescence or action based on the agreement, under the latter rule, has been held in a few states to bind the parties. 113 ALR 423; CJS, Boundaries § 63; Tiffany § 653.

SECTION 3-32: CONDUCT OF PARTIES

3-32A Rules; Practical Location.

Adverse possession, see Section 2-23.

Where boundary line between parcels of real estate is uncertain in language of will, it may be made definite and certain by conduct of interested parties. Taylor v. Kemple, 5 Abs 593 (App. 1927).

LAW IN GENERAL

Where the description of a boundary is ambiguous or disputed, the conduct of the parties in holding possession to a certain line may be sufficient to show the intention of the parties and the effect of the conveyance. An agreement fixing the line may be implied from a practical location, such as a fence, or from acquiescence. Acquiescence, in itself, is strong evidence that the claimed line is the true line. An adjoining owner may be estopped from claiming to the true line when it would be inequitable for him to do so under the circumstances of a particular case. CJS, Boundaries § 72; Tiffany § 654.

SECTION 3-33: JUDICIAL OR OFFICIAL ACTION

3-33A Form of Action.

Reformation, see Section 16-66.

In determining the true line between lots, the court may consider adverse possession, estoppel, fixed lines by agreement, and other considerations. The actual improvement of lots and occupancy with residences is irrelevant in the absence of any claim of adverse possession. Overmyer v. Fullerton, 21 Abs 334 (App. 1936).

Further research: O Jur 3d, Adjoining Landowners § 83.

LAW IN GENERAL

Disputed boundaries may be determined by an action in ejectment when the title is in question, or in trespass when the claimant has not been dispossessed. A dispute as to title is not a ground of equity jurisdiction. True lines will be found and fixed by courts of equity when authorized by statute or when grounds of equitable jurisdiction exist. Am Jur 2d, Boundaries § 91; CJS, Boundaries § 87; Tiffany § 653.

3-33B Procedure.

Where evidence is complete and unambiguous, question of location of lot line is generally question for the court. Cardosi v. Wise, 44 App 205, 184 NE 863, 14 Abs 698, 38 OLR 5 (1933).

Further research: O Jur 3d, Adjoining Landowners § 96.

LAW IN GENERAL

Extrinsic evidence may not be introduced, in the absence of equitable considerations, to explain the calls nor to show a different intention of the grantor when the description is definite and unambiguous. Am Jur 2d, Boundaries § 103; CJS, Boundaries § 100.

CHAPTER 4: CORPORATIONS AND ASSOCIATIONS

DIVISION 4-1: IN GENERAL

SECTION 4-11: INTRODUCTION
4-11A   Franchises
4-11B   Service of Process

SECTION 4-12: CORPORATE POWER TO ACQUIRE AND HOLD
4-12A   Generally

SECTION 4-13: CORPORATE POWER TO SELL, CONVEY AND ENCUMBER
4-13A   Limitations on the Power; Capacity
4-13B   Authority to Exercise Power
4-13C   Form
4-13D   Seal
4-13E   Purchase by Officer

DIVISION 4-2: PARTICULAR TYPES OF ORGANIZATIONS

SECTION 4-21: NONPROFIT CORPORATIONS
4-21A   Statutory Regulations
4-21B   Religious Corporations

SECTION 4-22: DISSOLVED CORPORATIONS
4-22A   Rules
4-22B   Statutory Liquidation; Banks
4-22C   Service of Process

SECTION 4-23: FOREIGN CORPORATIONS
4-23A   Rules
4-23B   Failure to Obtain License
4-23C   Service of Process

SECTION 4-24: CEMETERIES
4-24A   Establishment and Regulation
4-24B   Title and Rights of Lot Owners
4-24C   Sale or Transfer

SECTION 4-25: BANKS AND LOAN ASSOCIATIONS
4-25A   Generally
4-25B   As Mortgagees

SECTION 4-26: RELIGIOUS SOCIETIES; BENEVOLENT ASSOCIATIONS
4-26A   Rules
4-26B   Sale or Encumbrance

SECTION 4-27: REAL ESTATE INVESTMENT TRUSTS; JOINT STOCK COMPANIES
4-27A   Real Estate Investment Trusts
4-27B   Joint Stock Companies

SECTION 4-28: PARTNERSHIPS
4-28A   Generally
4-28B   Uniform Partnership Act

SECTION 4-29: OTHER ORGANIZATIONS
4-29A   Unincorporated Bodies Generally
4-29B   Railroads
4-29C   Title Insurance Companies

133

DIVISION 4-1:   IN GENERAL

SECTION 4-11:   INTRODUCTION

4-11A   Franchises.

R.C. 2733.26 provides that the trustees, appointed by the court in quo warranto proceedings to oust a corporation from the exercise of its franchise, shall be vested with the title to all the property, real and personal, of the corporation from the date of their appointments. (As eff. 10-1-53.)

Further research: O Jur 3d, Business Relationships §§ 775, 779, 782.

LAW IN GENERAL

A franchise is a special privilege conferred by the government, the most important now being the right to exist as a corporation, which may include the power to appropriate land. A franchise is considered in the nature of real property when it relates directly to particular land; an example is an interest resembling an easement created by a municipal franchise for construction under streets owned in fee by the city. Quo warranto is a proceeding to determine the right to exercise a franchise or office, and may be instituted in behalf of the state to forfeit the charter of a corporation and oust it from exercise of its powers. Title to the real property necessary to the exercise of the franchise of a public service corporation is regulated by public policy. CJS, Quo Warranto § 30; Powell § 431.

4-11B   Service of Process.

Dissolved corporations, see 4-22C.
Foreign corporations, see 4-23C.

See Civil Rule 4.2 (who may be served) shown at 16-74A.
R.C. 1701.07 provides:

"(A) Every corporation shall have and maintain an agent, sometimes referred to as the "statutory agent," upon whom any process, notice, or demand required or permitted by statute to be served upon a corporation may be served. The agent may be a natural person who is a resident of this state, or may be a domestic corporation or a foreign corporation holding a license as such under the laws of this state that is authorized by its articles of incorporation to act as such agent and that has a business address in this state.

"(B) The secretary of state shall not accept original articles for filing unless there is filed with the articles a written appointment of an agent, signed by the incorporators or a majority of them. In all other cases, the corporation shall appoint the agent and shall file in the office of the secretary of state a written appointment of such agent.

"(C) The written appointment of an agent shall set forth the name and address in this state of the agent, including the street and number or other particular description, and shall otherwise be in such form as the secretary of state prescribes. The secretary of state shall keep a record of the names of corporations, and the names and addresses of their respective agents.

"(D) If any agent dies, removes from the state, or resigns, the corporation shall forthwith appoint another agent and file with the secretary of state a written appointment of the agent.

"(E) If the agent changes his or its address from that appearing upon the record in the office of the secretary of state, the corporation shall forthwith file with the secretary of state a written statement setting forth the new address.

"(F) An agent may resign by filing with the secretary of state a signed statement to that effect. The secretary of state shall forthwith mail a copy of the statement to the corporation at its principal office. Upon the expiration of sixty days after the filing, the authority of the agent shall terminate.

"(G) A corporation may revoke the appointment of an agent by filing with the secretary of state a written appointment of another agent and a statement that the appointment of the former agent is revoked.

"(H) Any process, notice, or demand required or permitted by statute to be served upon a corporation may be served upon the corporation by delivering a copy of it to its agent, if a natural person, or by delivering a copy of it at the address of its agent in this state, as such address appears upon the record in the office of the secretary of state. If (1) the agent cannot be found, or (2) the agent no longer has that address, or (3) the corporation has failed to maintain an agent as required by this section, and if in any such case the party desiring that such process, notice, or demand be served, or the agent or representative of the party, shall have filed with the secretary of state an affidavit stating that one of the foregoing conditions exists and stating the most recent address of the corporation which the party after diligent search has been able to ascertain, then service of process, notice, or demand upon the secretary of state, as the agent of the corporation, may be initiated by delivering to him or at his office quadruplicate copies of such process, notice, or demand and by paying to him a fee of five dollars. The secretary of state shall forthwith give notice of the delivery to the corporation at its principal office as shown upon the record in his office and at any different address shown on its last franchise tax report filed in this state, or to the corporation at any different address set forth in the above mentioned affidavit, and shall forward to the corporation at said addresses, by certified mail, with request for return receipt, a copy of the process, notice, or demand; and thereupon service upon the corporation shall be deemed to have been made.

"(I) The secretary of state shall keep a record of each process, notice, and demand delivered to him or at his office under this section or any other law of this state which authorizes service upon him, and shall record the time of such delivery and his action thereafter with respect thereto.

"(J) This section does not limit or affect the right to serve any process, notice, or demand upon a corporation in any other manner permitted by law.

135

"(K) Every corporation shall state in each annual report filed by it with the department of taxation the name and address of its statutory agent.

"(L) Except when an original appointment of an agent is filed with the original articles, a written appointment of an agent or a written statement filed by a corporation with the secretary of state shall be signed by the chairman of the board, the president, a vice-president, the secretary, or an assistant secretary.

"(M) For filing a written appointment of an agent other than one filed with original articles, and for filing a statement of change of address of an agent, the secretary of state shall charge and collect a fee of three dollars.

"(N) Upon the failure of any corporation to appoint another agent or to file a statement of change of address of an agent, the secretary of state shall give notice thereof by certified mail to such corporation and unless such default is cured within thirty days after the mailing of such notice or within such further period as the secretary of state grants, the secretary of state may, upon the expiration of such period, cancel the articles of such corporation, give notice of such cancellation to the corporation by certified mail, and make a notation of such cancellation on his records.

"A corporation whose articles have been cancelled may be reinstated by filing an application for reinstatement and the required appointment of agent or required statement, and by paying a filing fee of ten dollars. The secretary of state shall furnish the tax commissioner a monthly list of all corporations cancelled and reinstated under this division.

"(O) This section does not apply to banks, trust companies, insurance companies, or any corporation defined under the laws of this state as a public utility for taxation purposes." (As eff. 10-20-78.)

Civil Rule 4.2 provides that, "Service of process, except service by publication as provided in Rule 4.4(A) ... shall be made as follows:"

"(6) Upon a corporation either domestic or foreign: by serving the agent authorized by appointment or by law to receive service of process; or by serving the corporation by certified mail at any of its usual places of business; or by serving an officer or a managing or general agent of the corporation; ..."

"Summons may be served upon a corporation by delivering the copy to "the person in charge" of an office occupied by the corporation whether or not such person is an employee of the corporation. Such service should not be quashed, although the sheriff made no reasonable effort to find the officers named in the statute, if "the person in charge" did bring the summons promptly to the attention of the chief officer. Moriarty v. Westgate Center, Inc., 172 OS 402, 176 NE2d 410, 16 OO2d 252 (1961).

Service by publication on a domestic corporation cannot be had unless the affidavit shows that it has failed to elect officers or appoint an agent upon whom service of summons can be made, and has no place of doing business in this state. Morton v. Davezac, 20 App 427, 152 NE 679, 3 Abs 637 (1925).

Service will be quashed when it is upon the "director" of a nonprofit corporation and there is no showing that service was attempted on the president or other chief officer. Center v. St. Peter's Episcopal Church, 11 OS2d 64, 227 NE2d 599, 40 OO2d 68 (1967).

Service upon the statutory agent under R.C. 1701.07 provides an alternative manner in which a domestic corporation may be served. Where the summons commands the sheriff to serve the statutory agent, but not the corporation, notice is sufficient if a copy of the complaint is also served. Baldine v. Klee, 10 Misc 203, 224 NE2d 544, 39 OO2d 295 (C.P. 1965), revd. on other grounds 14 App2d 181, 237 NE2d 905, 43 OO2d 391 (1968).

Certified mail service on a corporation is effective if addressed and delivered to its usual place of business. No person or officer need be specified or served under Civil Rules 4.1 and 4.2. Samson-Sales, Inc. v. Honeywell, Inc., 66 OS2d 290, 421 NE2d 522, 20 OO3d 277 (1981).

SECTION 4-12: CORPORATE POWER TO ACQUIRE AND HOLD

4-12A Generally.

R.C. 1701.13 in part provides: "(F) In carrying out the purposes stated in its articles and subject to limitations prescribed by law or in its articles, a corporation may:

"(1) Purchase or otherwise acquire, lease as lessee, invest in, hold, use, lease as lessor, encumber, sell, exchange, transfer, and dispose of property of any description or any interest in such property." (As eff. 11-22-86.)

Further research: O Jur 3d, Business Relationships § 242.

LAW IN GENERAL

A corporation may acquire any estate in land except as limited by constitution, statute, or its articles of incorporation. It cannot hold land for an unauthorized use but the problem does not often arise because only the state or a stockholder may object. De facto corporations are entitled to take title, and it is also held that title may be acquired under a deed made a short time before the grantee was incorporated. Am Jur 2d, Corporations § 985; Am Law of Prop § 18.47; CJS, Corporations § 1088; Powell § 145.

SECTION 4-13: CORPORATE POWER TO SELL, CONVEY AND ENCUMBER

Merger or change of name, see 1-27G.

4-13A Limitations on the Power; Capacity.

R.C. 1701.13 in part provides: "(H) No lack of, or limitation upon, the authority of a corporation shall be asserted in any action except (1) by the state in an action by it against the corporation, (2) by or on behalf of the corporation against a director, an officer, or any shareholder as such, (3) by a shareholder as such or by or on behalf of the holders of shares of any class against the corporation, a director, an officer, or any shareholder as such, or (4) in an action involving an alleged overissue of shares. This division shall apply to any action brought in this state upon any contract made in this state by a foreign corporation." (As eff. 11-22-86.)

R.C. 1701.76 provides that a corporation may dispose of all or substantially all of its assets if not sold in the usual course of its business, when and as authorized by the board of directors and by vote of shareholders who have at least two-thirds of voting power or by vote as the articles may require (but not less than a majority of such voting power) and as required by the articles, at a meeting called for that purpose; notice to be given to all shareholders; an action to set aside such disposition on the ground that the provisions of the Revised Code have not been complied with shall be brought within ninety days after such transaction or be forever barred. If a resolution is adopted pursuant to R.C. 1701.86, the directors may dispose of assets without the necessity of shareholders' authorization. (As eff. 2-26-87.)

R.C. 1701.85 provides for relief of a dissenting shareholder of a domestic corporation. (As eff. 12-23-86.)

A public service corporation has no power to alienate its franchise nor any interest in real estate acquired and held solely for the purpose of the execution of such franchise. Coe v. Columbus, P. & I. R.R., 10 OS 372 (1859).

A de facto corporation has capacity to hold, encumber and convey the legal title to real estate. A judgment of ouster in quo warranto is not retroactive and will not divest or defeat rights acquired or liabilities incurred previously by or against it in good faith. Society Perun v. Cleveland, 43 OS 481, 3 NE 357, 14 WLB 304, 15 WLB 12 (1885).

It is the duty of a purchaser of the entire assets of a corporation to ascertain, before making such purchase, whether the corporation has fully complied with the statutes authorizing it to make such sale; otherwise the purchaser takes the property subject to the rights of the stockholders not consenting thereto. Cyclone Drill Co. v. Zeigler, 99 OS 151, 124 NE 131, 16 OLR 364, 63 WLB 473 (1918).

These statutes do not apply to sale of all of a corporation's tangible property or all its real estate, but apply only when corporation undertakes to sell its entire property and assets. Painter v. Brainard-Cedar Realty Co., 29 App 123, 163 NE 57, 6 Abs 723 (1928).

Dissenting shareholder must object in writing and demand the appraised value within the statutory period, in the absence of fraud. Klein v. United Theaters Co., 80 App 173, 75 NE2d 67, 35 OO 507, 48 Abs 362 (1947).

Further research: O Jur 3d, Business Relationships § 245.

LAW IN GENERAL

The power of a corporation to alienate its property is limited only by provisions of its charter, by statute or constitution, or by public policy. The power to alienate includes the power to mortgage. Am Law of Prop §§ 12.76, 14.47; Tiffany § 1376.

Enforcement of liens against a public service corporation is usually denied when a sale would prevent exercise of its functions. Quasi-public corporations are prohibited by public policy from selling property which would make them unable to perform their duties to the public. CJS, Corporations § 1103.

Problems as to the capacity of corporations are infrequent because a bona fide purchaser ordinarily acquires an indefeasible title unless the state commences proceedings before the conveyance by the corporation. Am Law of Prop §§ 12.76, 18.47; CJS, Corporations § 1095; Powell § 145.

4-13B Authority to Exercise Power.

R.C. 1701.59 provides: "(A) Except as authorized by section 1701.59 of the Revised Code, and except where the law, the articles, or the regulations require action to be authorized or taken by shareholders, all of the authority of a corporation shall be exercised by or under the direction of its directors. For their own government, the directors may adopt bylaws that are not inconsistent with the articles or the regulations.

"(B) A director shall perform his duties as a director, including his duties as a member of any committee of the directors upon which he may serve, in good faith, in a manner he reasonably believes to be in or not opposed to the best interests of the corporation, and with the care that an ordinarily prudent person in a like position would use under similar circumstances. In performing his duties, a director is entitled to rely on information, opinions, reports, or statements, including financial statements and other financial data, that are prepared or presented by:

"(1) One or more directors, officers, or employees of the corporation who the director reasonably believes are reliable and competent in the matters prepared or presented;

"(2) Counsel, public accountants, or other persons as to matters that the director reasonably believes are within the person's professional or expert competence;

"(3) A committee of the directors upon which he does not serve, duly established in accordance with a provision of the articles or the regulations, as to matters within its designated authority, which committee the director reasonably believes to merit confidence.

"(C) For purposes of division (B) of this section:

"(1) A director shall not be found to have violated his duties under division (B) of this section unless it is proved by clear and convincing evidence that the director has not acted in good faith, in a manner he reasonably believes to be in or not opposed to the best interests of the corporation, or with the care that an ordinarily prudent person in a like position would use under similar circumstances, in any action brought against a director, including actions involving or affecting any of the following:

"(a) A change or potential change in control of the corporation;

"(b) A termination or potential termination of his service to the corporation as a director;

139

"(c) His service in any other position or relationship with the corporation.

"(2) A director shall not be considered to be acting in good faith if he has knowledge concerning the matter in question that would cause reliance on information, opinions, reports, or statements that are prepared or presented by the persons described in divisions (B)(1) to (3) of this section to be unwarranted.

"(3) Nothing contained in this division limits relief available under section 1701.60 of the Revised Code.

"(D) A director shall be liable in damages for any action he takes or fails to take as a director only if it is proved by clear and convincing evidence in a court of competent jurisdiction that his action or failure to act involved an act or omission undertaken with deliberate intent to cause injury to the corporation or undertaken with reckless disregard for the best interests of the corporation. Nothing contained in this division affects the liability of directors under section 1701.95 of the Revised Code or limits relief available under section 1701.60 of the Revised Code. This division does not apply if, and only to the extent that, at the time of a director's act or omission that is the subject of complaint, the articles or the regulations of the corporation state by specific reference to this division that the provisions of this division do not apply to the corporation.

"(E) For purposes of this section, a director, in determining what he reasonably believes to be in the best interests of the corporation, shall consider the interests of the corporation's shareholders and, in his discretion, may consider any of the following:

"(1) The interests of the corporation's employees, suppliers, creditors, and customers;

"(2) The economy of the state and nation;

"(3) Community and societal considerations;

"(4) The long-term as well as short-term interests of the corporation and its shareholders, including the possibility that these interests may be best served by the continued independence of the corporation.

"(F) Nothing contained in division (C) or (D) of this section affects the duties of either of the following:

"(1) A director who acts in any capacity other than his capacity as a director;

"(2) A director of a corporation that does not have issued and outstanding shares that are listed on a national securities exchange or are regularly quoted in an over-the-counter market by one or more members of a national or affiliated securities association, who votes for or assents to any action taken by the directors of the corporation that, in connection with a change in control of the corporation, directly results in the holder or holders of a majority of the outstanding shares of the corporation receiving a greater consideration for their shares than other shareholders." (As eff. 12-23-86.)

R.C. 1701.64 in part provides: "(A) *** Any two or more offices may be held by the same person, but no officer shall execute, acknowledge, or verify any instrument in more than one capacity if such instrument is required by law or by the articles, the regulations, or the bylaws to be executed, acknowledged, or verified by two or more officers." (As eff. 10-31-67.)

Standard of Title Examination

(Adopted by Ohio State Bar Association in 1952; amended in 1964 and 1972)

Problem 3.11A:

When should the authority and identity of officers of a corporation to execute a corporate deed not be questioned?

Standard 3.11A:

The authority and identity should not be questioned when the deed is executed by an officer, in the absence of known facts creating a doubt. This standard is not intended to apply to the requirements of an attorney for the purchaser from a corporation or an attorney for such a purchaser's mortgage lender at the time of the closing of the purchase or the loan.

Standard of Title Examination

(Adopted by Ohio State Bar Association in 1967)

Problem 3.11C:

When should corporate existence (either foreign or domestic) not be questioned?

Standard 3.11C:

Where an instrument of a private corporation appears in the title and has been of record for a period of at least seven years, and the instrument is executed in proper form, the examiner may assume that the corporation was legally in existence at the time the instrument took effect.

Further research: O Jur 3d, Business Relationships § 344.

LAW IN GENERAL

The authority of a corporation to sell, convey or encumber its property is vested in the board of directors in the absence of contrary provisions of its charter or bylaws or of statute. Executive officers or agents have no such authority by virtue of their office, but a power may be implied from the ordinary conduct of the corporate business; authority of the president and secretary to sell, convey or mortgage is generally presumed, especially when sufficient time has elapsed to show acquiescence by the corporation. A corporate conveyance to the officer executing it is not void. In any case, a corporation may be estopped to deny the validity of an instrument. Am Jur 2d, Corporations § 1227; Am Law of Prop § 18.47; CJS, Corporations § 1100.

4-13C Form.

A deed from a corporation must name it as the grantor. Hatch v. Barr, 1 Ohio 390 (1824).

A deed from a corporation is sufficient where it is signed by the officers without the corporate name and with the corporate seal. Sheehan v. Davis, 17 OS 571 (1867).

A deed executed in due form and delivered will be presumed to have been authorized by the directors; and the mere fact that such authority is not found in their minutes is not sufficient to rebut the presumption. Cincinnati, H. & D. R.R. v. Harter, 26 OS 426 (1875); Kiebler Realty Co. v. Miller, 29 App 130, 163 NE 51, 6 Abs 724 (1927).

Standard of Title Examination

(Adopted by Ohio State Bar Association in 1955)

Problem 3.11B:

Is a corporate deed sufficiently executed where the name of the corporation does not appear in the signature or certificate of acknowledgment?

Standard 3.11B:

The title is not unmarketable where the deed appears to be signed and acknowledged by the corporate officers if the deed as a whole purports to be that of the corporation.

Further research: O Jur 3d, Business Relationships §§ 256, 259.

LAW IN GENERAL

All parts of a conveyance in behalf of a corporation should name it as the grantor. A deed from an officer of a corporation may be upheld as the deed of the corporation if that appears from the face of the instrument to be the intention. Tiffany § 1065.

4-13D   Seal.

R.C. 1701.13 in part provides: "(B) A corporation may adopt and alter a corporate seal and use the same or a facsimile of the corporate seal, but failure to affix the corporate seal shall not affect the validity of any instrument." (As eff. 11-22-86.)

Since 1883 the seal of a corporation is not necessary to the execution of a valid deed of its lands in this state. East End Bldg. & Loan Co. v. Hughey, 16 CC 19, 8 CD 724 (1898).

4-13E   Purchase by Officer.

LAW IN GENERAL

Purchase of corporate property from the corporation by a corporate officer or director is merely voidable, not void. Such a purchase will be set aside as to the officer if it is unfair to the stockholders. A conveyance pursuant to the contract is valid as to bona fide purchasers from the officer. 24 ALR2d 71.

DIVISION 4-2: PARTICULAR TYPES OF ORGANIZATIONS

SECTION 4-21: NONPROFIT CORPORATIONS

4-21A Statutory Regulations.

R.C. 1702.06 requires a nonprofit corporation to have a statutory agent as is required of a corporation for profit by R.C. 1701.07 as shown at 4-11B. (As eff. 10-20-78.)

R.C. 1702.08 provides that when an unincorporated society or association becomes a corporation all its property and obligations shall pass to and vest in the corporation. (As eff. 1-10-61.)

R.C. 1702.30 in part provides: "(A) Except where the law, the articles, or the regulations require that action be otherwise authorized or taken, all of the authority of a corporation shall be exercised by or under the direction of its trustees. For their own government the trustees may adopt bylaws that are not inconsistent with the articles or the regulations." (As eff. 8-7-80.)

See also R.C. 1701.59 quoted at 4-13B.

R.C. 1702.36 provides: "The trustees may authorize any mortgage, pledge, or deed of trust of all or any of the property of the corporation of any description, or any interest therein, for the purpose of securing the payment or performance of any obligation or contract. Unless the articles or the regulations, or the terms of any trust on which the corporation holds any particular property, otherwise provide, no vote or consent of members or authorization from the court under section 1715.39 of the Revised Code is necessary for such action." (As eff. 10-11-55.)

R.C. 1702.39 provides: "(A) Unless the articles or the regulations, or the terms of any trust on which the corporation holds any particular property, otherwise provide, a lease, sale, exchange, transfer, or other disposition of any assets of a corporation may be made without the necessity of procuring authorization from the court under section 1715.39 of the Revised Code, upon such terms and for such consideration, which may consist, in whole or in part, of money or other property, including shares or other securities or promissory obligations of any corporation for profit, domestic or foreign, as may be authorized by the trustees; provided that a lease, sale, exchange, transfer, or other disposition of all, or substantially all, the assets may be made only when such transaction is also authorized (either before or after authorization by the trustees) by the voting members at a meeting held for such purpose, by the affirmative vote of a majority of the voting members present if a quorum is present, or, if the articles or the regulations provide or permit, by the affirmative vote of a greater or lesser proportion or number of the voting members, and by such affirmative vote of the voting members of any particular class as is required by the articles or the regulations. Notice of the meeting of the members shall be given to all members whether or not entitled to vote

143

thereat. Such notice shall be accompanied by a copy or summary of the terms of such transaction.

"(B) The corporation by its trustees may abandon the proposed lease, sale, exchange, transfer, or other disposition of all or substantially all of the assets of the corporation, subject to the contract rights of other persons, if such power of abandonment is conferred upon the trustees either by the terms of the transaction or by the same vote of voting members and at the same meeting of members as that referred to in division (A) of this section or at any subsequent meeting.

"(C) An action to set aside a conveyance by a corporation, on the ground that any section of the Revised Code applicable to the lease, sale, exchange, transfer, or other disposition of all or substantially all the assets of such corporation has not been complied with, shall be brought within ninety days after such transaction, or such action shall be forever barred." (As eff. 10-11-55.)

R.C. 1702.59 provides for cancellation of the articles of a nonprofit corporation for failure to file every five years a statement of its continued existence. (As eff. 10-20-78.)

Chapter 1702 of the Revised Code (nonprofit corporation law) contains other statutes similar to those in Chapter 1701 (general corporation law).

Further research: O Jur 3d, Associations and Corporations Not for Profit § 20.

4-21B   Religious Corporations.

See also Section 4-26.

R.C. 1702.09 provides: "The fact that a religious society, ecclesiastical society, or church has been continuously in existence since January 1, 1925, claiming to have been legally incorporated as such, and exercising authority and performing duties as such during such time, shall be prima-facie evidence of the due incorporation as claimed by such organization." (As eff. 10-11-55.)

The civil court's role as a tribunal to bring order to church controversies is narrowly limited. The control of the name and property of the particular church must be determined only by reference to the provisions of the Code of Regulations and By-Laws of the not for profit corporation holding title, the corporate laws of this state, and any other secular instruments not requiring the resolution of religious tenets or doctrine. Serbian Orthodox Church Congregation of St. Demetrius v. Kelemen, 21 OS2d 154, 256 NE2d 212, 50 OO2d 367 (1970).

LAW IN GENERAL

The tendency of the decisions and statutes concerning the capacity and authority of religious corporations to hold and transfer land is to uphold the centralized or hierarchal control of the denomination. Powell § 141.

SECTION 4-22: DISSOLVED CORPORATIONS

Receivers, see Section 17-44.

4-22A Rules.

R.C. 1701.88 in part provides: "(A) When a corporation is dissolved voluntarily or when the articles of a corporation have been canceled or when the period of existence of the corporation specified in its articles has expired, the corporation shall cease to carry on business and shall do only such acts as are required to wind up its affairs, but for such purpose it shall continue as a corporation." (As eff. 10-10-84.)

Under the provisions of subsection (F) of Section 1701.88, quoted at 4-22B, all deeds and other instruments of the dissolved corporation shall be executed, acknowledged and delivered by the officers appointed by the directors. The officers so empowered are normally those last qualified and acting.

R.C. 5727.54 provides for cancellation of charter of a public utility company for failure to report or pay any tax. (As eff. 10-11-55.)

R.C. 5733.20 provides that the secretary of state shall cancel the articles of incorporation of any corporation which fails to make any report or pay any tax. A certificate of the action so taken shall be forwarded to the county recorder of the county of the principal place of business for filing. (As eff. 10-11-55.)

R.C. 5733.22 provides that upon reinstatement a certificate thereof may be filed in the recorder's office of any county. (As eff. 9-30-74.)

Mortgages upon real estate executed by a corporation after its articles of incorporation had been canceled for default in payment of franchise tax, are valid liens and entitled to payment prior to claims of general creditors. Eversman v. Ray Shipman Co., 115 OS 269, 152 NE 643, 4 Abs 394, 395, 24 OLR 479 (1926).

A corporation continues to exist after dissolution, for the purpose of winding up its affairs, and during such period it may sue and be sued on existing contracts. Diversified Property Corp. v. Winters Nat. Bank & Trust Co., 13 App2d 190, 234 NE2d 608, 42 OO2d 307 (1967).

Under R.C. 1701.88(A) of the General Corporation Act, when articles of a corporation are cancelled, whether by the Secretary of State or otherwise, the authority of the corporation to do business ceases, and after such termination officers who carry on new business do so as individuals, lose the protection of the Corporation Act and are personally responsible for such obligations as they incur. Chatman v. Day, 7 App3d 281, 455 NE2d 672 (1982).

Further research: O Jur 3d, Business Relationships § 766.

4-22B Statutory Liquidation; Banks.

R.C. 1701.88 in part provides: "(D) The directors of the corporation and their survivors or successors shall act as a board of directors in accordance with the regulations and bylaws until the affairs of the corporation are completely wound up. Subject to the orders of courts of this state having jurisdiction over the corporation, the directors shall proceed as speedily as is practicable to a complete winding up of the affairs of the corporation and, to the extent necessary or expedient to that end, shall exercise all the authority of the corporation. Without limiting the generality of such authority, they may fill vacancies, elect officers, carry out contracts of the corporation, make new contracts, borrow money, mortgage or pledge the property of the corporation as security, sell its assets at public or private sale, make conveyances in the corporate name, lease real estate for any term, including ninety-nine years renewable forever, settle or compromise claims in favor of or against the corporation, employ one or more persons as liquidators to wind up the affairs of the corporation with such authority as the directors see fit to grant, cause the title to any of the assets of the corporation to be conveyed to such liquidators for that purpose, apply assets to the payment of obligations, and, after paying or adequately providing for the payment of all known obligations of the corporation, distribute the remainder of the assets either in cash or in kind among the shareholders according to their respective rights and interests. In addition, they may perform all other acts necessary or expedient to the winding up of the affairs of the corporation.

"Division (E) of section 1701.76 of the Revised Code applies to the disposition of a voluntarily dissolved corporation's assets by its directors.

"(E) Without limiting the authority of the directors and subject to division (E) of section 1701.76 of the Revised Code, any action within the purview of this section which is authorized or approved at a meeting held for such purpose by the holders of shares entitling them to receive two-thirds of the value of the remaining assets shall be conclusive for all purposes upon all shareholders of the corporation.

"(F) All deeds and other instruments of the corporation shall be in the name of the corporation and shall be executed, acknowledged, and delivered by the officers appointed by the directors."

"(G) At any time during the winding up of its affairs, the corporation by its directors may make application to the court of common pleas of the county in this state in which the principal office of the corporation is located to have the winding up continued under supervision of the court, as provided in section 1701.89 of the Revised Code." (As eff. 10-10-84.)

R.C. 1701.91 provides for judicial dissolution of a corporation. (As eff. 3-17-87.)

Trustees, receivers or other officials appointed to wind up the affairs of a corporate trustee have no authority to execute the trust. State ex rel. Squire v. Cleveland Trust Co., 58 App 16, 15 NE2d 640, 11 OO 420, 26 Abs 340 (1937).

LAW IN GENERAL

Although a conveyance by a judicial liquidator in another state is ordinarily not recognized, a statutory liquidator succeeding to the title of the corporation has the same power to convey land in a foreign state as the corporation would have if not in liquidation. A receiver of a national bank is a statutory liquidator and succeeds to the title of the bank. It is generally held that title passes to a liquidator although not expressly so provided in the statute. A court of general jurisdiction has the power to order a sale in such case. Am Law of Prop § 13.19.

4-22C Service of Process.

See also R.C. 1701.07 at 4-11B.

R.C. 1701.88 in part provides: "(C) Any process, notice, or demand against the corporation may be served by delivering a copy to an officer, director, liquidator, or person having charge of its assets or, if no such person can be found, to the statutory agent." (As eff. 10-10-84.)

SECTION 4-23: FOREIGN CORPORATIONS

4-23A Rules.

Jurisdiction of nonresidents, see 16-77B.

The amount and kind of activities which must be carried on by the foreign corporation in the state of the forum so as to make it reasonable and just to subject the corporation to the jurisdiction of that state are to be determined in each case. The requirement of obtaining license is a helpful but not a conclusive test. Perkins v. Benguet Consolidated Mining Co., 342 US 437, 96 L Ed 485, 72 Sup Ct 413, 47 OO 216, 63 Abs 146 (1952).

The fundamental principle underlying the "doing business" concept seems to be the maintenance within the jurisdiction of a regular continuous course of business activities, whether or not inclusive of the final stage of contracting. Bach v. Friden Calculating Mach. Co., 167 F2d 679, 38 OO 46 (1948).

A foreign corporation may be said to be doing business in Ohio when it purchases or deals in real estate within the state, when the transaction is in fulfillment of its corporate purposes and is a part of its ordinary business. 1949 OAG 594.

Further research: O Jur 3d, Business Relationships § 814.

LAW IN GENERAL

A foreign corporation has only the powers conferred by the law of the state of its creation. Subject to the law of its domicile, a corporation can acquire and convey land in another state unless prohibited by the statutes or public policy of the state where the land is located. The right of a foreign corporation to acquire and hold real estate can be attacked only by the state. Am Jur 2d, Foreign Corporations §§ 134, 137; CJS, Corporations § 1868.

4-23B Failure to Obtain License.

R.C. 1703.29 provides that the failure of any (foreign) corporation to obtain a license under the provisions of that act shall not impair or affect the validity of any contract with such corporation, but no foreign corporation which should have obtained such license shall maintain any action in any of the courts of this state until it shall have obtained such license. (As eff. 10-1-53.)

4-23C Service of Process.

Long-arm statute, see 16-77B.

R.C. 1703.041 in part provides: "(H) Process may be served upon a foreign corporation by delivering a copy of it to its designated agent, if a natural person, or by delivering a copy of it at the address of its agent in this state, as such address appears upon the record in the office of the secretary of state." (As eff. 10-20-78.)

R.C. 1703.19 provides: "The secretary of state shall be the agent of any foreign corporation licensed to do business in this state, upon whom process against it from any court in this state or from any public authorities may be served within this state if the designated agent cannot be found, if the corporation has failed to designate another agent when required to do so under Sections 1703.01 to 1703.31 of the Revised Code, or if the license of a corporation to do business in this state has expired or has been canceled. Pursuant to such service, suit may be brought in the county where the principal office of the corporation in this state is or was located, or in any county in which the cause of action arose. Such service shall be made upon the secretary of state by leaving with him, or with an assistant secretary of state, triplicate copies of such process and a fee of five dollars which shall be included as taxable costs in case of judicial proceedings. Upon receipt of such process and fee the secretary of state shall forthwith give notice to the corporation, both at its principal office and at its principal office in this state, of the service of such process, shall forward to each of such offices by certified mail, with request for return receipt, a copy of such process, and shall retain a copy of such process in his files.

"The secretary of state shall keep a record of any such process served upon him and shall record therein the time of such service and his action thereafter with respect to it.

"This section does not affect any right to serve process upon a foreign corporation in any other manner permitted by law." (As eff. 10-20-78.)

R.C. 1703.191 provides: "Any foreign corporation required to be licensed under Sections 1703.01 to 1703.31 of the Revised Code, which transacts business in this state without being so licensed, shall be conclusively presumed to have designated the secretary of state as its agent for the service of process in any action against such corporation arising out of acts or omissions of such corporation within this state, including, without limitation, any action to recover the statutory forfeiture for failure to be so licensed. Pursuant to such service, suit may be brought in Franklin county, or in any county in which such corporation did any act or transacted any business. Such service shall be made upon the secretary of state by leaving with him, or with an assistant secretary of state, duplicate copies of such process, together with an affidavit of the plaintiff or one of the plaintiff's attorneys, showing the last known address of such corporation, and a fee of five dollars which shall be included as taxable costs in case of judicial proceedings. Upon receipt of such process, affidavit, and fee the secretary of state shall forthwith give notice to the corporation at the address specified in the affidavit and forward to such address by certified mail, with a request for return receipt, a copy of such process.

"The secretary of state shall retain a copy of such process in his files, keep a record of any such process served upon him, and record therein the time of such service and his action thereafter with respect thereto.

"This section does not affect any right to serve process upon a foreign corporation in any other manner permitted by law." (As eff. 10-20-78.)

R.C. 3909.05 and 3909.15 provide for service upon or waiver of service by foreign life insurance companies. (As eff. 10-1-53.)

See Civil Rule 4.2 (who may be served) shown at 16-74A.

Service of summons upon the designated statutory agent of a foreign corporation after cancellation of its license to do business in Ohio is not effectual to give jurisdiction. Tank Car Stations v. Harsany, 148 OS 459, 76 NE2d 716, 36 OO 106 (1947).

Service by publication on a foreign corporation is valid if the case is one of those mentioned in R.C. 2703.14. Vallette v. Kentucky Trust Co. Bank, 12 Dec Repr 299 (1855).

Further research: O Jur 3d, Business Relationships § 907.

SECTION 4-24: CEMETERIES

4-24A Establishment and Regulation.

R.C. 517.01 provides that township trustees may acquire land for cemetery purposes; not to exceed ten acres may be appropriated. (As eff. 1-1-66.)

R.C. 517.09 provides: "No lot held by any individual in a cemetery, shall, in any case, be levied on or sold on execution." (As eff. 10-1-53.)

R.C. 517.10 provides that the title to and control of public cemeteries outside a municipal corporation shall be vested in the board of township trustees, except such as are owned or under the care of a religious or benevolent society, or an incorporated company or association, or under the control of any municipality. (As eff. 10-1-53.)

R.C. 517.27 provides that title and control of public burying ground may be conveyed by an association or society, or trustees thereof, to township trustees. (As eff. 10-1-53.) This section, requiring township trustees to take over burial grounds, is mandatory. 1937 OAG 13.

R.C. 759.08 provides that the title to public burial grounds located within a municipal corporation (except those owned or under the care of a religious or benevolent society, or an incorporated company or association) is vested in such municipal corporation. (As eff. 10-1-53.)

R.C. 1721.01 provides for the acquisition and sale of land by and from cemetery associations. (As eff. 11-26-75.)

R.C. 1721.10 provides when burial grounds shall be exempt from execution, taxation, dower and partition. (As eff. 10-1-53.)

While cemetery lands cannot be sold by any legal process, an assessment for street improvement may be enforced by the appointment of a receiver, by sequestration, or by such other remedy as courts of equity afford. Lima v. Cemetery Assn., 42 OS 128, 11 WLB 167 (1884).

All of the land of a city cemetery, including the house of the caretaker in which the cemetery records are maintained, is entitled to exemption from taxation under R.C. 5709.08 and R.C. 5709.121. City of Wellsville v. Kinney, 66 OS 2d 136, 420 NE2d 123, 20 OO3d 156 (1981).

Further research: O Jur 3d, Cemeteries and Dead Bodies § 4.

4-24B Title and Rights of Lot Owners.

A document, in order to transfer burial rights in a lot effectually, need not take the form of a real estate deed. Fraser v. Lee, 8 App 235 (1917).

Adverse possession applies to burial lots in cemeteries. Corkill v. Calvary Cemetery Assn., 15 O Supp 64, 29 OO 554 (C.P. 1944).

Although a deed for a burial lot may run to the grantee, his heirs and assigns, he takes only an easement or a right of burial, rather than an absolute title. Persinger v. Persinger, 86 NE2d 335, 39 OO 315, 54 Abs 295 (C.P. 1949).

A burial lot does not pass under a general residuary clause in a will, but descends to the heirs as intestate property. Persinger v. Persinger, 86 NE2d 335, 39 OO 315, 54 Abs 295 (C.P. 1949).

Further research: O Jur 3d, Cemeteries and Dead Bodies § 48.

LAW IN GENERAL

The purchaser of a lot in a cemetery ordinarily does not require a fee even though a deed is delivered to him. He acquires a right of burial which is unique among property interests, although it is sometimes designated as an easement or a license. The right passes by inheritance, but courts frequently hold that it does not pass by devise. Alienation is often restricted by terms of the original conveyance or by rules of the cemetery owner. The interest is generally not subject to partition, execution or liens. Am Jur 2d, Cemeteries § 25; CJS, Cemeteries § 23; Powell § 262; Tiffany § 774.

In the absence of a specific devise or statutory restriction, the common-law rule is that a burial lot passes to the heirs at law of the testator, as if he had died intestate. 26 ALR3d 1425.

4-24C Sale or Transfer.

R.C. 517.22 provides: "The board of township trustees, or the trustees or directors of cemetery associations, may, after notice has first been given in two newspapers of the county, of general circulation, dispose of, at public sale, and make conveyance of any cemeteries under their control that they have determined to discontinue as burial grounds, but possession thereof shall not be given to a grantee until after the dead therein buried, together with stones and monuments, have been removed as provided by section 517.21 of the Revised Code." (As eff. 10-1-53.)

R.C. 517.21 and 517.28 provide the manner of abandonment of a public or private cemetery. (As eff. 10-1-53.)

R.C. 517.29 provides that probate court may order the sale of an abandoned cemetery owned by a municipal corporation and located outside its limits. (As eff. 10-1-53.)

R.C. 759.04 and 759.07 provide for the sale or mortgage by the legislative authority of a municipal corporation of cemetery grounds owned by it and not used for burial purposes. (As eff. 10-1-53.)

R.C. 759.42 provides for the transfer to an incorporated cemetery association of cemetery lands owned and controlled by a municipal corporation or township. (As eff. 10-1-53.)

R.C. 1715.02 to 1715.04 provide for sale of cemetery land held by a religious or educational corporation or society; for transfer of burial grounds owned by a religious or benevolent society to an incorporated cemetery association or to the trustees of two or more townships.

R.C. 1721.15 provides procedure in common pleas court for sale by trustees of a cemetery association. (As eff. 10-1-53.)

It appearing that many bodies still remain, there has not been a complete abandonment of said premises inconsistent with its preservation as a graveyard. Newark v. Burnette, 92 OS 539, 112 NE 1082, 13 OLR 107, 135, 60 WLB 271, 283 (1915).

A church may be permitted to vacate part of an ancient cemetery for the purpose of erecting a building without removal and reinterment of the bodies. Schaeffer v. Unknown Heirs, etc. of Fletcher, 175 NE2d 776, 16 OO2d 301, 86 Abs 425 (C.P. 1961).

SECTION 4-25: BANKS AND LOAN ASSOCIATIONS

Receivers, see Section 17-44.
Statutory liquidation, see 4-22B.

4-25A Generally.

R.C. 1151.27 provides limitations upon the holding of real estate by building and loan associations. (As eff. 12-13-84.)

LAW IN GENERAL

Banks are restricted by statute or by charter from acquiring and conveying real estate except as incidental to their ordinary business. The unauthorized acquisition of real property by a national bank does not affect the vesting of title. The power of a banking corporation to convey is incidental to its power to hold realty. A national bank has the authority to warrant the title conveyed. It is prohibited from holding for more than five years any real estate acquired to secure a debt due it. Am Jur 2d, Banks §§ 279 to 281; CJS, Banks and Banking § 689; Powell § 147.

4-25B   As Mortgagees.

R.C. 1151.29 to 1151.32 provide limitations upon real estate loans made by building and loan associations.

R.C. 1321.52 provides that no person shall engage in the business of lending and taking as security other than a first lien on borrower's property without having obtained a certificate of registration from the division of consumer finance. (As eff. 6-20-85.)

SECTION 4-26:   RELIGIOUS SOCIETIES; BENEVOLENT ASSOCIATIONS

Religious corporations, see 4-21B.
Unincorporated bodies generally, see 4-29A.

4-26A   Rules.

R.C. 1715.07 and 1715.09 provide for the transfer of property from an ecclesiastical corporation to the church with which it is connected or to a consolidated organization. (As eff. 10-1-53.)

R.C. 1715.16 provides for the appointment of and descent from the trustees of a religious society. (As eff. 10-1-53.)

R.C. 1715.17 provides: "Property conveyed in trust for the use of a religious society, church, or association, whether incorporated or not, shall be held by the trustees and their successors, appointed as provided in the instrument creating the trust, or in case no provision for successor trustees is made in such instrument, then by such successor trustees as are appointed by a competent court. No person shall be elected or appointed by such society, church, or association to act as trustee to the exclusion of any trustee appointed as provided in this section.

"Title to property conveyed after October 30, 1965 to and in the name of a religious society, church, or association; charitable or other eleemosynary organization; labor union, national, state, district, regional, or other unit; whether incorporated or not, may be held in the name of such group or organization. Any right, title, or interest in property in the name of any such group or organization on October 30, 1965 is hereby confirmed in that name as if the conveyance or grant thereof had been made after such date." (As eff. 2-21-67.)

R.C. 1715.37 provides for conveyance upon the consolidation of charitable, benevolent, or educational organizations. (As eff. 10-1-53.)

R.C. 5307.22 to 5307.24 provide for partition of real estate between religious corporations or societies. (As eff. 10-1-53.)

In resolving a dispute between a local church and the national church with which it is affiliated, a court looks to the lines of church authority in determining whether the church is hierarchical or congregational. State ex rel. Morrow v. Hill, 51 OS2d 74, 364 NE2d 1156, 5 OO3d 45 (1977).

A dispute over disposition of the property of a congregationally autonomous church, when not involving any ecclesiastical questions, is subject to the jurisdiction of the courts. Mack v. Huston, 23 Misc 121, 256 NE2d 271, 51 OO2d 407 (C.P. 1970).

Further research: O Jur 2d, Religious Societies § 38.

LAW IN GENERAL

When the property rights of a subordinate body of a church organization are in controversy, the civil courts will ordinarily follow the rules and judgments of the superior church tribunals. Local units of fraternal and benevolent associations are subjected to this rule in a lesser degree than are religious societies. When a local congregation joins a general religious organization, it becomes bound by the rules of the latter, which prevail over inconsistent local regulations. However, in some denominational systems the general organization has no authority over the local churches. Am Jur 2d, Religious Societies §§ 36, 46, 52; CJS, Religious Societies § 35; Powell § 130.

4-26B Sale or Encumbrance.

Incorporated religious societies, see statutes at 4-21A.

R.C. 1715.05 provides that the common pleas court may order the disposition of real estate held by church trustees, upon their petition, when for twenty years such real estate has not been claimed by or appropriated to the use of churches or congregations as ordinarily contemplated. (As eff. 10-7-77.)

R.C. 1715.12 provides that a board consisting of five or more trustees elected by an ecclesiastical body, with the prescribed statement filed in the office of the secretary of state, may dispose of real estate without complying with R.C. 1715.39. (As eff. 10-1-53.)

R.C. 1715.14 provides for the disposition of the real property of a congregation or society which becomes extinct. (As eff. 10-1-53.)

The local conference of the merged denominations has the right to file a petition for the sale of land of a local church which was merged and has ceased to exist. Beauchamp v. Trustees, 110 App 109, 160 NE2d 343, 12 OO2d 346 (1959).

R.C. 1715.39 in part provides: "When a charitable or religious society or association desires to sell, lease, exchange, or encumber by mortgage or otherwise any real estate owned by it, held in trust by it for a specified religious or charitable purpose, or held for its use or benefit by trustees chosen by it or otherwise constituted, for any such purpose, except grounds used as burial places for the dead, then the trustees, wardens, and vestry, or other officers entrusted with the management of the affairs of such society or association or holding the title to such property, or such society or association itself if it is incorporated in this state, may file, in the court of common pleas of the county in which the real estate is situated, a petition stating how and by whom the title to such real estate is held, the desire of such society or association to make the sale, lease, exchange, or encumbrance, and the object thereof. If upon the hearing of the case it appears that such sale, exchange, lease, or encumbrance is desired by the members of the society or association and that it is proper that authority should be given to accomplish it, the court may authorize the trustees or other officers of the society or association, or, if it is incorporated, the society or association itself, to sell, lease, exchange, or encumber such real estate in accordance with the prayer of the petition and upon such terms as the court deems reasonable.

* * *

"The petitioner shall cause notice of the pendency and prayer of the petition to be published, in some newspaper of general circulation in the county where the real estate proposed to be sold, leased, exchanged, or encumbered is situated, for four consecutive weeks before the application is heard." (As eff. 10-1-53.)

The trustees or other designated officers of an unincorporated church society and not the church itself are authorized to file the petition under R.C. 1715.39. In re Pettisville Union Church Society, 17 O Supp 103, 32 OO 443 (C.P. 1946).

Authorization from the court under R.C. 1715.39 may not be necessary when the property is owned by a corporation as provided by R.C. 1702.36 and 1702.39 at 4-21A.

When the legal title is in trustees, appointed as provided in R.C. 1715.17 at 4-26A, they may have the authority under the trust instrument to dispose of the society's real estate without recourse to R.C. 1715.39. The statute is permissive in such a case.

R.C. 1715.40 provides for alienation to other boards of trustees of the same denomination. (As eff. 10-1-53.)

R.C. 1715.41 provides: "The trustees or other officers of a charitable or religious society or association who are authorized to make a sale, lease, exchange, or encumbrance in accordance with sections 1715.39 to 1715.41, inclusive, of the Revised Code, shall make return thereof to the court of common pleas ordering it, at such time as such court orders. Thereupon, if satisfied that the sale, lease, exchange, or encumbrance was made according to its order, the court shall approve it and order that the proceeds be invested in other real estate for the use of such society or association and used in payments of its debts or otherwise invested or disposed of according to the prayer of the petition." (As eff. 10-1-53.)

R.C. 1715.411 provides: "When the trustees or other officers mentioned in sections 1715.37 to 1715.41, inclusive, of the Revised Code, have sold and conveyed by deed in fee simple or mortgaged any real estate therein mentioned, without proceeding as required by those sections, and the deed of conveyance or mortgage has been of record for five years without legal action to set aside said deed or mortgage, such sale and conveyance or mortgage shall have the same validity and effect as if it had been made by proceedings as required by those sections. This section is effective as to both past and future transactions." (As eff. 8-15-72.)

R.C. 5303.32 and 5303.33 provide that when real estate, except burial grounds, is held by any person or trustee for public religious use or when held by a particular religious society or denomination and abandoned for such use, the common pleas court, upon petition of a citizen of the vicinity, may make an order for the sale of such property. (As eff. 10-1-53.)

G.C. 10055, which was omitted from the Revised Code, provided: "When the trustees or other officers mentioned in the preceding sections heretofore have sold and conveyed by deed in fee simple or mortgaged any real estate therein mentioned, without proceeding as required by such sections, and the grantees thereof, and their successors in line of title, for five years since the date of such conveyance, held continued, exclusive, notorious and adverse possession of the real estate so conveyed, such sales, conveyances and mortgages shall have the same validity and effect as if they had been made by proceedings instituted under such sections and duly confirmed by the court of common pleas." (As eff. 1898.) (As provided by R.C. 1.24, in enacting the Revised Code, "it is the intent of the General Assembly not to change the law as heretofore expressed by the section or sections of the General Code in effect on the date of the enactment of this act.")

Further research: O Jur 2d, Religious Societies § 44.

SECTION 4-27: REAL ESTATE INVESTMENT TRUSTS; JOINT STOCK COMPANIES

4-27A Real Estate Investment Trusts.

R.C. Chapter 1747, effective 7-17-78, provides procedures under which a real estate investment trust may do business in Ohio.

R.C. 1747.01 contains definitions applicable to the chapter.

R.C. 1747.02 requires compliance with the chapter as a condition of a real estate investment trust doing business in the state and allows continuance of existing trusts provided they comply with the requirements of R.C. 1747.03 within one year.

R.C. 1747.03 provides: "(A) Before transacting real estate business in this state, a real estate investment trust shall file the following report in the office of the secretary of state, on forms prescribed by the secretary of state:

"(1) An executed copy of the trust instrument or a true and correct copy of it, certified to be such by a trustee before an official authorized to administer oaths or by a public official in another state in whose office an executed copy is on file;

"(2) A list of the names and addresses of its trustees;

"(3) The address of its principal office;

155

"(4) In the case of a foreign real estate investment trust, the address of its principal office within this state, if any;

"(5) The business name of the trust;

"(6) The name and address within this state of a designated agent upon whom process against the trust may be served;

"(7) The irrevocable consent of the trust to service of process on its designated agent and to service of process upon the secretary of state if, without the registration of another agent with the secretary of state, its designated agent has died, resigned, lost authority, dissolved, become disqualified, or has removed from this state, or if its designated agent cannot, with due diligence, be found;

"(8) Not more than ninety days after the occurrence of any event causing any filing made pursuant to divisions (A)(2) to (6) of this section, or any previous filing made pursuant to this division, to be inaccurate or incomplete, all information necessary to maintain the accuracy and completeness of such filing.

"(B) For filing under this section, the secretary of state shall charge and collect a fee of fifty dollars, except that for filing under division (A)(8) of this section, the secretary of state shall charge and collect a fee of ten dollars.

"(C) All persons shall be given the opportunity to acquire knowledge of the contents of the trust instrument and other information filed in the office of the secretary of state, but no person dealing with a real estate investment trust shall be charged with constructive notice of the contents of any such instrument or information by reason of such filing.

"(D) A copy of a trust instrument or other information filed in the office of the secretary of state shall be prima-facie evidence of the existence of the instrument or other information and of its contents, and as conclusive evidence of the existence of such record." (As eff. 7-17-78.)

R.C. 1747.04 provides: "A trust instrument may be amended in the manner specified in it or in any manner that is valid under the common or statutory law applicable to the trust created thereunder. However, no amendment adopted subsequent to the initial filings required by section 1747.03 of the Revised Code is legally effective in this state until an executed or certified true and correct copy of the amendment has been filed in the office of the secretary of state accompanied by a fee of twenty-five dollars." (As eff. 7-17-78.)

R.C. 1747.05 provides: "(A) Subject to the limitations of division (C) of this section, every real estate investment trust authorized to transact real estate business in this state has the following general powers:

"(1) To take, hold, and dispose of any estate or interest in real or personal property;

"(2) To sue and be sued, complain and defend, in all courts;

"(3) To transact its business, carry on its operations, and exercise the powers granted by this chapter in any state;

"(4) To make contracts, incur liabilities, lend or borrow money and to receive or give security therefor; to sell, mortgage, lease, pledge, exchange, convey, transfer, and otherwise dispose of all or any part of its property and assets; to issue bonds, notes, and other obligations and secure them by mortgage or deed of trust of all or any part of its property, franchises, or income;

"(5) To acquire by purchase or in any other manner and to take, receive, own, hold, use, employ, improve, encumber, and otherwise deal in or with real or personal property or any interests in the property, wherever situated;

"(6) To purchase, take, receive, subscribe for, or otherwise acquire, own, hold, vote, use, employ, sell, mortgage, loan, pledge, or otherwise dispose of, and otherwise use and deal in and with, securities, shares, or other interests in or obligations of domestic or foreign corporations, other real estate investment trusts, associations, partnerships, and individuals, or direct or indirect obligations of any state or municipal corporation, or any instrumentality thereof;

"(7) To elect or appoint trustees, officers, and agents of the trust for the period of time the trust instrument or bylaws provides, to define the authority and duties of such trustees, officers, and agents, and to adopt and operate employee and officer benefit plans;

"(8) To make and alter bylaws not inconsistent with law or with its trust instrument for regulating the government of the trust and for the administration of its affairs;

"(9) To curtail or cease its trust activities by a partial or complete distribution of its assets and to terminate its existence by voluntary dissolutions;

"(10) To exercise the foregoing powers in the business name of the trust or in the name of one or more of its trustees or nominees;

"(11) To exercise the foregoing powers by acting through one or more of its duly authorized trustees, officers, or agents;

"(12) Generally, to exercise the powers set forth in its trust instrument and those granted by law and to do every other act or thing not inconsistent with law, which may be appropriate to promote and attain the purposes set forth in its trust instrument.

"(B) The original or a copy of the record of the proceedings or meetings of holders of certificates of beneficial interest in the trust estate of a real estate investment trust authorized to transact real estate business in this state or of the trustees shall be prima-facie evidence of the facts stated therein when certified to be true by a trustee, secretary, or assistant secretary of the real estate investment trust. Every meeting referred to in such certified original or copy shall be deemed duly called and held, all motions and resolutions adopted and proceedings had at such meeting shall be deemed duly adopted and had, and all elections or appointments of trustees, officers, or agents chosen at such meeting shall be deemed valid, until the contrary is proven. If a person who is not a holder of a certificate of beneficial interest in the trust estate has acted in good faith in reliance upon any such certified original or copy of such record, it is conclusive in his favor.

"(C) Nothing in this section grants a real estate investment trust any power that would violate the public policy of this state, nor shall any such trust be authorized to engage in any business that a private corporation for profit organized under the laws of this state may not legally transact, nor does anything in this section grant to any such trust any power or authorize any action specifically denied by the terms or operation of its trust instrument." (As eff. 7-17-78.)

R.C. 1747.06 provides: "(A) A real estate investment trust may take, hold, and dispose of any estate or interest in real property in its business name, or in the name of one or more of its trustees, or in the name of one or more of its nominees. A conveyance to a real estate investment trust in its business name shall recite that the grantee is a real estate investment trust, and the estate or interest so acquired can be conveyed by the trust only in its business name. Any estate or interest in real property taken, held, or disposed of by a real estate investment trust in its business name prior to the effective date of this section is hereby confirmed as if the conveyance thereof had been made pursuant to the authority of this section.

"(B) The fact that a recorded deed, mortgage, or other conveyance of an estate or interest in real property designates a real estate investment trust or one or more trustees or nominees of a real estate investment trust as the grantee does not give notice to or put upon inquiry any person dealing with the property that there are any limitations on the power of such trust, trustees, or nominees to dispose of or encumber the estate or interest specified in such conveyance, unless such conveyance specifically contains such limitations or incorporates by reference another instrument of record in the same county which specifically contains such limitations. As to all bona fide purchasers and encumbrancers of the property, a conveyance, release, or encumbrance by such trust, trustees, or nominees transfers or releases the estate or interest in the property specified free from the claims of the holders of certificates of beneficial interest in the trust estate and free from any obligation on the part of such purchaser or encumbrancer to see to the application of any purchase money or other consideration." (As eff. 7-17-78.)

R.C. 1747.07 provides: "Real estate investment trusts are subject to all applicable provisions of law, rules of procedure, and rules of court, now in effect or hereafter enacted, relating to domestic or foreign corporations, with regard to service of process." (As eff. 7-17-78.)

R.C. 1747.08 provides: "A certificate of beneficial interest is a security subject to Chapter 1707 of the Revised Code." (As eff. 7-17-78.)

R.C. 1747.09 provides: "Unless otherwise stated in the trust instrument, a real estate investment trust authorized to transact real estate business in this state has a perpetual period of existence and is not affected by any rule against perpetuities. Nothing contained in this section shall be construed or interpreted to limit, prohibit, or invalidate any provision of a trust instrument providing that such real estate investment trust may be terminated at any time by action of the trustees or by the vote of a specified percentage in interest of the beneficial owners thereof." (As eff. 7-17-78.)

R.C. 1747.10 provides: "Any domestic or foreign real estate investment trust authorized to transact real estate business in this state may surrender its authority at any time by filing in the office of the secretary of state a verified copy of a resolution duly adopted by its trustees declaring its intention to withdraw, accompanied by a fee of ten dollars. Such real estate investment trust then ceases and is without authority to transact real estate business in this state, except as necessary for the concluding thereof." (As eff. 7-17-78.)

R.C. 1747.11 provides generally that a real estate investment trust which conducts business in this state without authority shall forfeit one thousand to ten thousand dollars in an action brought by the attorney general or the prosecuting attorney, and the trust shall be required to pay the filing fees required by R.C. 1747.03(B) plus interest. The recovery action shall be brought within five years after the trust ceased doing business in Ohio. (As eff. 7-17-78.)

R.C. 1747.12 provides: "(A) The failure of any real estate investment trust to be authorized to transact real estate business in this state does not affect the validity of any contract with such trust, or the validity of the title to any estate or interest in real property taken, held, or disposed of by such trust. No real estate investment trust that should have been so authorized, nor any persons on its behalf shall maintain any action in any court of this state until it has obtained such authority by filing with the secretary of state as required by division (B) or (C) of this section, paying the fee associated with the filing, and further paying to the secretary of state a forfeiture of one thousand dollars.

"(B) If such real estate investment trust has not been previously authorized to transact real estate business in this state or if its authority has been surrendered, it shall make the filings specified in divisions (A)(1) to (7) of section 1747.03 of the Revised Code and pay the specified fee for the filing.

"(C) If such real estate investment trust has been previously authorized to transact real estate business in this state and its authority has expired for failure to make the filings required by division (A)(8) of section 1747.03 of the Revised Code, it shall make such filings, and pay the specified fee for the filings.

"(D) Full compliance with this section prior to the bringing of an action to recover a forfeiture under section 1747.11 of the Revised Code constitutes a bar to such action." (As eff. 7-17-78.)

R.C. 1747.13 provides: "No person knowingly shall prepare, make, assist in preparing or making, or procure or advise the preparing or making of any false or fraudulent filings required or permitted by sections 1747.01 to 1747.13 of the Revised Code." (As eff. 7-17-78.)

R.C. 1747.99 provides: "Whoever violates section 1747.13 of the Revised Code shall be fined not more than ten thousand dollars." (As eff. 7-17-78.)

Prior to the enactment of R.C. Chapter 1747 a business trust in Ohio was not authorized to hold title to land in the name of the trust, and the title was required to be held in the names of the trustees. To avoid the possibility of being construed as a partnership, the trust had to meet the prerequisites of a valid private trust. Berry v. McCourt, 1 App2d 172, 204 NE2d 235, 30 OO2d 203 (1965).

LAW IN GENERAL

A business trust, also known as a Massachusetts trust, is an adaptation to business purposes of the law of trusts, the shareholders having only an equitable interest. The trustee takes title and administers the property according to the declaration of trust. Powell § 137.

4-27B Joint Stock Companies.

LAW IN GENERAL

A joint stock company is a specialized form of partnership in which the title to land is in the name of a certain officer who operates in the manner of a trustee and who is governed by the association agreement. The interests of the shareholders are transferable and are treated as personalty. Am Law of Prop § 18.50; Powell § 136.

SECTION 4-28: PARTNERSHIPS

Service of process, see also Civil Rule 4.2 at 16-74A.

4-28A Generally.

R.C. 1336.08 of Uniform Fraudulent Conveyance Act provides: "Every conveyance of partnership property and any partnership obligation incurred, when the partnership is or will be thereby rendered insolvent, is fraudulent as to partnership creditors, if the conveyance is made or obligation is incurred:

"(A) To a partner, whether with or without a promise by him to pay partnership debts; or

"(B) To a person not a partner without fair consideration to the partnership as distinguished from consideration to the individual partners." (As eff. 10-23-61.)

R.C. 1777.02 provides: "Except as provided in this section, every partnership transacting business in this state under a fictitious name, or under a designation not showing the names of the persons interested as partners in the partnership, shall file for record, with the county recorder of the county in which its principal office or place of business is situated and of each county in which it owns real property, a certificate to be recorded and indexed by the recorder, stating the names in full of all the members of the partnership and their places of residence. The county auditor shall not transfer, and the county recorder shall not record, any conveyance of real property to or from any such partnership, unless the instrument is endorsed by the county recorder, showing that the partnership has filed and the county recorder has recorded the certificate required by this section. For the recording and indexing of each certificate required by this section, the recorder shall charge the partnership filing the certificate the fee indicated by section 317.32 of the Revised Code.

"The certificate shall be signed by the partners and acknowledged by some officer authorized to take acknowledgments of deeds, except that in the case of a joint stock company or a commercial partnership, whose capital stock is represented by shares or certificates of stock transferable on the books of the concern and whose business is conducted by a board of directors and by officers, the president, secretary, or cashier of such company or partnership may sign and acknowledge the certificate, giving in it the names of all the persons interested as partners or shareholders in such company or partnership, and except that in the case of a domestic or foreign limited partnership that is formed under or subject to Chapter 1782 of the Revised Code, there may be filed, in lieu of such certificate, a manually signed or certified copy of the certificate of limited partnership specified in section 1782.08 of the Revised Code or the application for registration as a foreign limited partnership specified in section 1782.49 of the Revised Code.

"A commercial partnership established and transacting business without the United States, without filing the certificate prescribed in this section, may use in this state the partnership name used by it there, although such name is fictitious or does not show the names of the persons interested as partners in the business." (As eff. 4-1-85.)

R.C. 1779.01 to 1779.08 provides for filing in probate court of inventory and appraisement of partnership assets and for purchase of deceased partner's interest by surviving partners.

The Uniform Partnership Act specifically retains the availability of R.C. 1779.01 to 1779.08, providing procedure in probate court for the purchase of a deceased partner's interest in the partnership by the surviving partner or partners.

R.C. 1782.24 and 1782.21 provide the rights and powers of partners in a limited partnership. (As eff. 4-1-85.)

R.C. 1783.06 provides that a limited partnership association may own and convey real estate. (As eff. 10-1-53.)

Prior to September 14, 1949 a partnership was incapable of taking the legal title to real estate, although it could acquire the equitable title. Rammelsberg v. Mitchell, 29 OS 22, 1 WLB 298 (1875).

Partnership property, though the legal title is in the names of the individual partners, is liable for the payment of the firm's liabilities, in preference to claims of separate creditors except those of bona fide purchasers for value, without notice that the same was partnership property. Page v. Thomas, 43 OS 38, 1 NE 79, 13 WLB 269, 372 (1885).

Parol evidence is admissible to show that land is partnership property although the contract is in the names of the partners instead of the partnership name. Teare v. Cain, 7 CC 375, 4 CD 643 (1893).

Since July 1, 1971, service of process is accomplished upon a partnership, a limited partnership, or a limited partnership association by serving the entity by certified mail at any of its usual places of business, or by serving a partner, limited partner, or manager or member. Civil Rule 4.2(7).

Subject to the rights of partnership creditors, an agreement between partners that the survivor shall become the sole and absolute owner of the partnership property may be enforced in common pleas court. Steigert v. Steigert, 57 App 255, 13 NE2d 583, 10 OO 446, 21 Abs 683 (1936).

Service of summons is not valid where a copy of summons is left at a partnership office established in Ohio solely for the purpose of supervising a construction project in Kentucky, since the partnership does not have a "usual place of doing business" within the meaning of R.C. 2703.08. "This court questions whether the decision of Smith v. Pinkerton (supra) should apply if the partnership had been 'doing business' in this state." Modern Contract Furnishings, Inc. v. Bishop International Engineering Co., 165 NE2d 703, 704, 14 OO2d 350, 83 Abs 473 (C.P. 1960).

The provisions of R.C. 1777.02 apply to mortgages, 99-year leases and generally to all conveyances which require transfer by the county auditor or record by the county recorder. 1972 OAG 075.

Further research: O Jur 3d, Business Relationships § 925.

4-28B   Uniform Partnership Act.

R.C. 1701.13 (F) (4) provides that a corporation may "Be a partner, member, associate, or participant in other enterprises or ventures, whether profit or nonprofit." (As eff. 11-22-86.)

R.C. 1775.07 provides: "(A) All property originally brought into the partnership stock or subsequently acquired by purchase or otherwise, on account of the partnership, is partnership property.

"(B) Unless the contrary intention appears, property acquired with partnership funds is partnership property.

"(C) Any estate in real property may be acquired in the partnership name. A conveyance to a partnership in the partnership name shall recite that the grantee is a partnership. Title so acquired can be conveyed only in the partnership name.

"(D) A conveyance to a partnership in the partnership name, though without words of inheritance, passes the entire estate of the grantor unless a contrary intent appears." (As eff. 10-1-53.)

R.C. 1775.08 in part provides: "(A) Every partner is an agent of the partnership for the purpose of its business, and the act of every partner, including the execution in the partnership name of any instrument, for apparently carrying on in the usual way the business of the partnership of which he is a member binds the partnership, unless the partner so acting has in fact no authority to act for the partnership in the particular matter, and the person with whom he is dealing has knowledge of the fact that he has no such authority.

"(B) An act of a partner which is not apparently for the carrying on of the business of the partnership in the usual way does not bind the partnership unless authorized by the other partners." (As eff. 10-1-53.)

R.C. 1775.09 provides: "(A) Where title to real property is in the partnership name, any partner may convey title to such property by a conveyance executed in the partnership name; but the partnership may recover such property unless the partner's act binds the partnership under division (A) of section

1775.08 of the Revised Code, or unless such property has been conveyed by the grantee or a person claiming through such grantee to a holder for value without knowledge that the partner, in making the conveyance, has exceeded his authority.

"(B) Where title to real property is in the name of the partnership, a conveyance executed by a partner, in his own name, passes the equitable interest of the partnership, provided the act is one within the authority of the partner under division (A) of section 1775.08 of the Revised Code.

"(C) Where title to real property is in the name of one or more but not all the partners, and the record does not disclose the right of the partnership, the partners in whose name the title stands may convey title to such property, but the partnership may recover such property if the partners' act does not bind the partnership under division (A) of section 1775.08 of the Revised Code, unless the purchaser, or his assignee, is a holder for value, without knowledge.

"(D) Where the title to real property is in the name of one or more or all of the partners, or in a third person in trust for the partnership, a conveyance executed by a partner in the partnership name, or in his own name, passes the equitable interest of the partnership, provided the act is one within the authority of the partner under division (A) of section 1775.08 of the Revised Code.

"(E) Where the title to real property is in the names of all the partners, a conveyance executed by all the partners passes all their rights in such property." (As eff. 10-1-53.)

R.C. 1775.24 provides: "(A) A partner is coowner with his partners of specific partnership property holding as a tenant in partnership.

"(B) The incidents of this tenancy are such that:

"(1) A partner, subject to sections 1775.01 to 1775.42 of the Revised Code, and to any agreement between the partners, has an equal right with his partners to possess specific partnership property for partnership purposes; but he has no right to possess the property for any other purpose without the consent of his partners.

"(2) A partner's right in specific partnership property is not assignable except in connection with the assignment of rights of all the partners in the same property.

"(3) A partner's right in specific partnership property is not subject to attachment or execution, except on a claim against the partnership. When partnership property is attached for a partnership debt, the partners, or any of them, or the representatives of a deceased partner, cannot claim any right under exemption laws.

"(4) On the death of a partner his right in specific partnership property vests in the surviving partners, unless he was the last surviving partner, in which case his right in the property vests in his legal representative. The surviving partners have, or the legal representative of the last surviving partner has, no right to possess the partnership property for any but a part-

163

nership purpose. This division is subject to the procedures set forth in sections 1779.01 to 1779.08 of the Revised Code.

"(5) A partner's right in specific partnership property is not subject to dower, statutory interest of a surviving spouse, heirs, or next of kin, or allowance to a surviving spouse or minor children." (As eff. 9-28-79.)

R.C. 1775.25 provides: "A partner's interest in the partnership is his share of the profits and surplus, and the same is personal property." (As eff. 10-1-53.)

R.C. 1775.29 provides: "On dissolution the partnership is not terminated, but continues until the winding up of partnership affairs is completed." (As eff. 10-1-53.)

R.C. 1775.36 provides: "Unless otherwise agreed, the partners who have not wrongfully dissolved the partnership or the legal representatives of the last surviving partner, not bankrupt, has [sic] the right to wind up the partnership affairs. Any partner, his legal representative, or his assignee, upon cause shown, may obtain winding up by the court. In case of the death of a partner, the right of the survivors to wind up is subject to sections 1779.01 to 1779.08, inclusive, of the Revised Code." (As eff. 10-1-53.)

The Uniform Partnership Act does not make a legal partnership an independent juristic entity, and whatever recognition is given therein to the entity theory is solely for procedural or conveyancing purposes. Church Budget Envelope Co. v. Cornell, 136 NE2d 101, 2 OO2d 158, 72 Abs 504 (App. 1955).

After dissolution, a partnership may continue for the purpose of doing all acts necessary to complete a leasehold contract previously entered into. Lebanon Trotting Assn. v. Battista, 37 App2d 61, 306 NE2d 769, 66 OO2d 108 (1972).

Creditors of individual debtor-partners may satisfy their claims from the individual partner's interest (as defined in R.C. 1775.25) by subjecting it to a charging order under circumstances that fall within the statutory design of R.C. 1775.27. Buckman v. Goldblatt, 39 App2d 1, 314 NE2d 188, 68 OO2d 69 (1974).

"The nature of this tenancy [tenancy in partnership] is such that the partner has only an equal right with his partners to possess the specific partnership property, his right is not assignable, is not subject to attachment or execution, and on his death it vests in the surviving partner and is not subject to dower." Robert E. Matthews and Justin H. Folkerth, "Ohio Partnership Law and the Uniform Partnership Act," 9 OSLJ 616, 635 (1948).

"How will the title examiner know that the partner who executed the conveyance was in fact a partner or had authority to convey? ... If the grantee wishes to relieve all uncertainty, he may get a certified statement from the other partner, just as a person taking title from a corporation may make certain by obtaining a certified copy of a resolution of the board of directors authorizing the conveyance and of the appointment of the officers executing the conveyance." 9 OSLJ 616, 636. See also 40 OO 268.

Standard of Title Examination

(Adopted by Ohio State Bar Association in 1952 and 1955)

Problem 3.5A:

What should be required to show the authority of partners to execute conveyances in behalf of the partnership?

Standard 3.5A:

A conveyance from a partnership holding the title is sufficient if it recites that the partners executing it are all the partners, in the absence of information to the contrary. When it does not appear that all the partners executed the conveyance, satisfactory evidence of authority should be required.

Authority of the partner or partners executing the conveyance should be presumed after it has been of record for five years.

Standard of Title Examination

(Adopted by Ohio State Bar Association in 1952)

Problem 3.5B:

Should an objection be made to the title because a deed to a partnership does not disclose that the grantee is a partnership?

Standard 3.5B:

No, the requirement should be considered directory, and the defect not such as will prevent the title from passing to the partnership.

LAW IN GENERAL

The common law has been supplanted by adoption of the Uniform Partnership Act and a statutory "tenancy in partnership" established under provisions of the act: a partnership can acquire, convey and deal with land in its own name; property acquired with partnership funds is partnership property unless a contrary intention appears; title to partnership property taken in the name of a partner may be acquired by a bona fide purchaser free of the trust, but otherwise it is the naked legal title; a partner's right in specific partnership property is assignable only in connection with an assignment of the rights of all the partners in the same property; spouses, heirs and creditors of individual partners cannot assert claims directly against the partnership lands; upon the death of a partner his right in specific partnership property vests, for partnership purposes, in the surviving partner or partners, or in the personal representative of the last surviving partner.

The Act affects a conversion by law to personal property of all real property belonging to the partnership. Creditors are protected by a continuance of the partnership until the winding up is completed (although a technical dissolution has occurred) and by freedom of the property from exemption and homestead claims of the partners. The firm and its members are protected by a device known as the "charging order" which restrains disruption of the business. Unless otherwise agreed, the partners who have not wrongfully dissolved the partnership or the legal representatives of the last surviving partner, not bankrupt, have the right to wind up the partnership affairs; provided, however, that any partner, his representative or his assignee may, upon cause shown, obtain winding up by the court.

Even though partnership realty is given many of the incidents of corporate realty, the Act is not based upon the legal entity theory. Therefore, although most questions of title are answered by the terms of the Act, the solution of the inevitable problems not covered by the Act will be found by considering the common law and its aggregate theory of a partnership. The question whether less than all the partners may act for the partnership in conveying or encumbering the land depends upon their actual authority. When title is in a grantee of the partnership, title examiners generally require evidence of authority if the conveyance is executed by less than all the partners. Bona fide purchasers from a grantee of a partnership are protected by the terms of the Act. Am Law of Prop § 6.9; Powell § 139.

Under the Uniform Partnership Act all real estate owned by the partnership is converted to personalty for all purposes including descent and distribution. 80 ALR2d 1107.

SECTION 4-29: OTHER ORGANIZATIONS

Religious societies, see also Section 4-26.

4-29A Unincorporated Bodies Generally.

R.C. 1715.17 in part provides: "Title to property conveyed after October 30, 1965 to and in the name of a religious society, church, or association; charitable or other eleemosynary organization; labor union, national, state, district, regional, or other unit; whether incorporated or not, may be held in the name of such group or organization. Any right, title, or interest in property in the name of any such group or organization on October 30, 1965 is hereby confirmed in that name as if the conveyance or grant thereof had been made after such date." (As eff. 2-21-67.)

The capacity of certain organizations to hold title to real estate, conferred by R.C. 1715.17 above, does not include or imply the power to convey or to encumber the same in the manner of a corporation or partnership.

R.C. 1715.43 provides: "Any unincorporated lodge or other subordinate body of any society or order, which is chartered by its grand lodge or body, may take and hold real estate for its own use and benefit, by lease, purchase, grant, devise, gift, or otherwise; may loan its funds and secure such loans, or any unpaid purchase money, by mortgage on otherwise unencumbered real estate; and may borrow money, and execute and deliver notes or bonds, and mortgages on real property of the lodge to secure such notes or bonds, in the name and by the number of said lodge or other subordinate body according to the register of its grand lodge or body.

"The presiding officer of such lodge or other such lodge or other subordinate body, together with the secretary or officer keeping its records, may make conveyances, leases, or mortgages of any real estate belonging to such lodge or other subordinate body, when authorized to do so by a vote of the members present at a regular meeting held by said lodge or other subordinate body, after at least ten days' notice has been given to all members thereof by mailing a written notice of said proposed action to the last known post-office address of each such member, under the regulations of such lodge or other subordinate body, and not in conflict with the regulations prescribed by the respective grand lodge or body.

"All such conveyances, leases, or mortgages shall be in the name of the lodge, shall be attested by the presiding officer and the secretary or other officer in charge of its records, and shall have affixed the seal of such lodge or other subordinate body. Any mortgage taken by such a lodge or other subordinate body in its name and number may, when paid and satisfied, be released by the presiding officer and the secretary or officer keeping its records, and such release shall be attested by the seal of the lodge or other subordinate body." (As eff. 10-1-53.)

A sale or encumbrance by an unincorporated body must be in accordance with its constitution, bylaws and regulations. If it is not subject to a superior body and the statutes as to religious societies do not apply, authority to dispose of property may be given by the organization members. It can dispose of only the equitable title unless authorized to hold legal title by statute. A record should be recorded with the conveyance showing the applicable provisions of the constitution(s) and bylaws, due notice to all members of a meeting called for the purpose, and authority to named persons to execute the conveyance.

R.C. 1745.01 provides: "Any unincorporated association may contract or sue in behalf of those who are members and, in its own behalf, be sued as an entity under the name by which it is commonly known and called." (As eff. 9-30-55.)

R.C. 1745.02 provides: "All assets, property, funds, and any right or interest, at law or in equity, of such unincorporated association shall be subject to judgment, execution and other process. A money judgment against such unincorporated association shall be enforced only against the association as an entity and shall not be enforceable against the property of an individual member of such association." (As eff. 9-30-55.)

See Civil Rule 4.2 (who may be served) shown at 16-74A.

A suitor may at his election pursue the remedy provided by R.C. 1745.01 et seq. or he may maintain his action against the individual members of the unincorporated association. Lyons v. American Legion Post No. 650 Realty Co., 172 OS 331, 175 NE2d 733, 16 OO2d 113 (1961).

LAW IN GENERAL

Unincorporated societies and associations are without capacity, as a general rule, to acquire and hold the legal title to real property. This situation is often met by taking title in the name of trustees. If a gift is to a charitable group the court will appoint a trustee. Transactions concerning the equitable interests of an unincorporated nonprofit association are not invalid when in accordance with an agreement between the members or with its constitution and bylaws; however, a great departure from the uses for which the property was acquired may be judicially restrained. Recitals of corporate existence have been held to make deeds of unincorporated organizations effective. However, it is usually held that the legal title remains in the grantor upon an attempted conveyance to an unincorporated association and that the latter cannot convey a title which it does not have. Am Law of Prop §§ 12.78, 18.50; 15 ALR2d 1451; Powell § 134.

4-29B   Railroads.

R.C. 4955.27 provides that when a person owns fifteen or more acres of land through which a railroad passes, the railroad may be required to construct a private crossing. (As eff. 10-1-53.)

From 1882 to October 1, 1953 it was required by G.C. 8761 (now R.C. 4961.15) that a conveyance by a railroad be signed by the president under the corporate seal. Such conveyances signed otherwise were validated by R.C. 4961.151.

4-29C   Title Insurance Companies.

R.C. 1109.28 to 1109.31 provide for bank and trust company powers of title guaranty and trust companies which were organized before July 12, 1919.

R.C. 1109.31 transfers supervision of title guaranty and trust companies and title guaranty companies, engaged in the title insurance business, from the auditor of state to the superintendent of insurance and, to the extent they are not engaged in such business, to the superintendent of banks. (As eff. 1-2-68.) Examination by the superintendent of insurance or his appointee is provided by R.C. 3901.07.

R.C. 1735.01 to 1735.04 provide the powers of a title guaranty and trust company; and that no such company shall do business until its capital stock amounts to at least $100,000 and until $50,000 in securities, has been deposited with the treasurer of state.

R.C. 3929.01 and 3929.07 provide that a company may be organized or admitted to insure titles to property in this state and shall deposit with the superintendent of insurance $50,000 in certain bonds, or deposit in another state $100,000 in securities. A company organized and engaged in business in this state under R.C. 1735.01 to 1735.04 on August 6, 1961 may write title insurance without an additional deposit therefor.

R.C. 3935.02 makes title insurance companies subject to R.C. 3935.01 to 3935.17. (As eff. 1-14-72.) The sections referred to provide for rating bureaus, filing of rates, and regulation by the superintendent of insurance.

R.C. 3953.04 requires title insurance companies to comply with R.C. 3929.30. (As eff. 1-14-72.) The section referred to provides for an annual report to the superintendent of insurance.

R.C. 3953.01 to 3953.28 provide detailed requirements concerning title insurance and apply to title insurance companies, including title guaranty and trust companies. Nonsubstantive amendments have been made to some of the sections.

Further research: O Jur 3d, Abstracts and Land Titles § 1.

4-29D Agricultural Societies.

R.C. 1711.14 provides for appropriation procedure. (As eff. 1-1-66.)

R.C. 1711.23, 1711.25, 1711.26, 1711.32, 1711.33 provide for alienation and other disposition of land of a county agricultural society. (As eff. 10-1-53.)

R.C. 1729.02 and 1729.03 provide that incorporated cooperative agricultural associations shall have the power to exercise all privileges of ownership over such real or personal property as may be necessary or convenient to its business. (As eff. 10-1-53.)

4-29E Miscellaneous Organizations.

R.C. 1713.24 provides procedure for sale by trustees of a university, college, or other institution of learning, incorporated by authority of this state under special charter and owned in shares or stock subscribed and taken. (As eff. 10-1-53.)

R.C. 1715.25 concerning Young Men's Christian Association in part provides: "The association may acquire, hold, convey, lease, encumber by mortgage, improve, and otherwise handle any real or personal property necessary or convenient to carry out its objects." (As eff. 10-1-53.)

R.C. 1717.02 referring to a humane society in part provides: "All property acquired by such a society, by gift, devise, or bequest, for special purposes, shall be vested in its board of trustees, which shall consist of three members elected by the society. The board shall manage such property and apply it in accordance with the terms of the gift, devise, or bequest, and may sell it and reinvest the proceeds." (As eff. 10-1-53.)

R.C. 1725.05 provides that an incorporated commercial association may sell and convey its real estate by a two-thirds vote of its board of directors. (As eff. 10-1-53.)

R.C. 3337.02 and 3337.03 provide for the sale and conveyance of land held under leases from Ohio University. (As eff. 10-1-53.)

R.C. 3345.18 provides for grants for highway purposes by colleges and universities created by the general assembly. (As eff. 9-28-73.)

R.C. 3735.62 provides that five or more veterans may form a corporation not for profit for the purpose of purchasing real property and constructing thereon residences for sale to members of such corporation. (As eff. 10-11-55.)

CHAPTER 5: COTENANCY AND JOINT OWNERSHIP

DIVISION 5-1: IN GENERAL

SECTION 5-11: INTRODUCTION; POSSESSION AND OUSTER
5-11A   Rules
5-11B   Adverse Possession

SECTION 5-12: ACQUISITION OF OUTSTANDING INTEREST
5-12A   Rules

SECTION 5-13: TRANSACTIONS WITH THIRD PERSONS
5-13A   Acts of One Cotenant as Binding Another
5-13B   Effect of Grant by One Cotenant

SECTION 5-14: CONTRIBUTION
5-14A   Improvements
5-14B   Repairs
5-14C   Current Charges
5-14D   Encumbrances

SECTION 5-15: ACCOUNTING
5-15A   Rents from Third Persons
5-15B   Profits from Possession
5-15C   Management

SECTION 5-16: MINERALS; TIMBER
5-16A   Generally

DIVISION 5-2: PARTICULAR CLASSES OF INTERESTS

SECTION 5-21: TENANCY IN COMMON
5-21A   Characteristics
5-21B   Creation

SECTION 5-22: JOINT TENANCY
5-22A   Characteristics and Creation
5-22B   Conveyance by One Tenant

SECTION 5-23: COMMUNITY PROPERTY
5-23A   Generally

SECTION 5-24: OTHER INTERESTS
5-24A   Tenancy by the Entirety
5-24B   Coparceners
5-24C   Conveyance to Grantor and Another Person
5-24D   Condominiums and Cooperatives

DIVISION 5-3: PARTITION

SECTION 5-31: GENERALLY
5-31A   Definition; Waiver of Right
5-31B   Restraints on the Right
5-31C   Effect on Title

SECTION 5-32: VOLUNTARY PARTITION
5-32A   Generally

SECTION 5-33: PERSONS ENTITLED AND PROPERTY SUBJECT
5-33A   Life Estates; Remainders and Other Future Interests

171

DIVISION 5-1:   IN GENERAL

SECTION 5-11:   INTRODUCTION; POSSESSION AND OUSTER

5-11A   Rules.

"As a general rule, the possession of one tenant in common is the possession of all. But if one tenant is actually put out or kept out of possession by another, he may have ejectment to recover possession." Penrod v. Danner, 19 Ohio 218, 221 (1850).

Further research: O Jur 3d, Cotenancy and Partition § 5.

LAW IN GENERAL

A person is not entitled to exclude his cotenant from the possession of any part of the land. Each co-owner has the right to possession of the entire property, subject to the equal right of the others. A violation of this right is an ouster. Under this rule a cotenant may use and enjoy the whole common estate, being liable only for a failure to exercise ordinary care, so long as he does not deny the ownership and rights of the other cotenants. However, occupancy by one constitutes exclusion of the others when the property can be occupied by only one person. The usual remedy of the ousted co-owner is ejectment and recovery of the reasonable value of the use and occupation. Am Jur 2d, Cotenancy and Joint Ownership § 33; Am Law of Prop § 6.13; Powell § 603; Tiffany § 449.

5-11B   Adverse Possession.

See also Section 2-25.

"The statute of limitations does not run in favor of a tenant in common in occupancy of the premises, against his cotenant, until some overt act of an unequivocal character, clearly indicating an assertion of ownership of the entire premises, to the exclusion of the right of the cotenant." Youngs v. Heffner, 36 OS 232 (1880).

SECTION 5-12: ACQUISITION OF OUTSTANDING INTEREST

5-12A   Rules.

If one of several cotenants of the remainder in fee purchases lands at the tax sale, the purchase will be held to inure to the benefit of all the cotenants in remainder. Clark v. Lindsey, 47 OS 437, 25 NE 422, 23 WLB 468, 24 WLB 354 (1890).

Further research: O Jur 3d, Cotenancy and Partition § 18.

LAW IN GENERAL

The acquisition by one tenant of an adverse interest or outstanding claim generally inures to the benefit of all, with a right to contribution in the one so acquiring. The other cotenants lose their right to claim the benefit if they fail to pay their share of the cost within a reasonable time after notice. The doctrine is an equitable one and is not applied in some cases where there is no confidential relationship between the parties. In most jurisdictions, the rule applies to purchases at tax sales and at foreclosure sales, but not at partition sales nor at probate land sales. Acquisition of title not adverse is excluded from operation of the rule. An action to enforce contribution may be maintained by the purchaser if he is not compensated by his cotenants within a reasonable time. Am Jur 2d, Cotenancy and Joint Ownership § 68; Am Law of Prop § 6.16; Powell § 605; Tiffany § 463.

SECTION 5-13: TRANSACTIONS WITH THIRD PERSONS

5-13A   Acts of One Cotenant as Binding Another.

One cannot bind his cotenant, except for necessary repairs, taxes, etc. Gleason v. Squires, 39 App 88, 176 NE 593, 9 Abs 729, 34 OLR 432 (1931).

LAW IN GENERAL

A cotenant has no implied authority to bind his cotenants. They may be bound by ratification or estoppel. Am Jur 2d, Cotenancy and Joint Ownership § 90; Tiffany § 451.

5-13B   Effect of Grant by One Cotenant.

A deed by a tenant in common, purporting to convey in severalty, is a good conveyance of the grantor's undivided interest in the land described. White v. Sayre, 2 Ohio 110 (1825).

The effect of a deed by one tenant, describing part of the land owned in common, is to pass to the purchaser the grantor's proportional interest in the land described in the deed. Dennison v. Foster, 9 Ohio 126 (1839).

An examination of the cases will show that conveyances of easements by one owner of an undivided interest are upheld only so far as they do not injuriously affect the rights of the holders of the other undivided shares. Thomason v. Dayton, 40 OS 63, 69, 9 WLB 280 (1883).

Further research: O Jur 3d, Cotenancy and Partition § 21.

LAW IN GENERAL

A conveyance of a specific part of the land by one cotenant cannot affect the rights of the others. It generally operates to estop the grantor from claiming the particular part against his grantee. Such a conveyance has been held to convey the undivided interest of the grantor in the portion granted or, under special circumstances, to transfer the grantor's interest in the entire tract. Am Law of Prop § 6.10; Powell § 608; Tiffany § 454.

An undivided interest may be validly leased or mortgaged. A dedication or a grant of an easement by one cotenant does not bind the others nor estop a subsequent grantee of all the cotenants. An individual cotenant may give a third party a license to use the property as the tenant himself may do, provided an ouster of his cotenants is not involved. An easement from one cotenant becomes effective on the land subsequently allotted to him in partition. Am Law of Prop § 6.11; 49 ALR2d 797; Powell § 407; Tiffany § 456.

SECTION 5-14:   CONTRIBUTION

5-14A   Improvements.

Partition proceedings, see 5-34B.

LAW IN GENERAL

One cotenant is not entitled, as a general rule, to maintain an action for contribution, accounting or other remedy against the others for improvements made by him. He will be compensated for the increased selling price on partition. He has a lien if the improvements were made with the consent of the other cotenants. Am Jur 2d, Cotenancy and Joint Ownership § 63; Am Law of Prop § 6.18; Tiffany § 462.

5-14B   Repairs.

Partition proceedings, see 5-34B.

One owner of a right-of-way in common cannot compel contribution from the other by himself making the repairs. Lyon v. Fels, 8 NP 450, 11 OD 706 (1901).

Further research: O Jur 3d, Cotenancy and Partition §§ 13, 15.

LAW IN GENERAL

One co-owner cannot recover the cost of repairs made by him, in the absence of a contract with the other owners, except as a deduction from rents and profits. Some authorities assert that recovery may be had for necessary repairs if notice was given to the other cotenants. Am Jur 2d, Cotenancy and Joint Ownership § 62; Am Law of Prop § 6.18; Powell § 604; Tiffany § 461.

5-14C   Current Charges.

If one of several tenants in common of the remainder purchases the land at tax sale, the purchase will be held to inure to the benefit of all the cotenants in remainder, and he will be entitled to contribution toward the cost and expense. Clark v. Lindsey, 47 OS 437, 25 NE 422, 23 WLB 468, 24 WLB 354 (1890).

Further research: O Jur 3d, Cotenancy and Partition §§ 14, 17.

LAW IN GENERAL

A cotenant is usually entitled to contribution for payment of taxes, interest, maintenance costs, and other ordinary current expenses except when he has been the sole occupant. Am Law of Prop § 6.17; 136 ALR 1022; Tiffany § 459.

5-14D   Encumbrances.

When the joint obligation of all the tenants in common is performed by part of them, the ones performing are entitled to contribution from the cotenants who failed to perform, and they have an equitable lien for the amount due. Westrick v. Unterbrink, 90 App 283, 105 NE2d 885, 47 OO 340 (1950).

Further research: O Jur 3d, Cotenancy and Partition § 18.

LAW IN GENERAL

When one cotenant pays off an encumbrance on the whole interest, he usually has a right of contribution or of subrogation. However, contribution is not allowed unless the other cotenant was personally liable on the debt, or unless the payment was ratified as by a common possession. Am Jur 2d, Cotenancy and Joint Ownership § 67; Am Law of Prop § 6.17; 48 ALR2d 1305.

SECTION 5-15:   ACCOUNTING

Partition, see 5-34A.

5-15A   Rents from Third Persons.

R.C. 5307.21 in part provides: "One tenant in common, or coparcener, may recover from another tenant in common, or coparcener his share of rents and profits received by such tenant in common or coparcener from the estate, according to the justice and equity of the case." (As eff. 10-1-53.)

The right of action for a share of the rents and profits is not restricted to an action in equity, but may be an action at law. Warner v. Matthews, 79 App 111, 69 NE2d 59, 34 OO 482, 46 Abs 568 (1946).

A tenant in common may deduct expenditures for necessary improvements, repairs and taxes in accounting for rents collected. Magee v. Kiesewetter, 98 App 539, 130 NE2d 704, 58 OO 77 (1955).

Further research: O Jur 3d, Cotenancy and Partition § 10; 51 ALR2d 388; Powell § 604.

5-15B   Profits from Possession.

By virtue of R.C. 5307.21, a tenant in common of a residence, who occupies and has sole possession of the premises, is liable to account to his cotenants for their share of the reasonable rental value of such occupancy and possession. Cohen v. Cohen, 157 OS 503, 106 NE2d 77, 47 OO 363 (1952).

Further research: O Jur 3d, Cotenancy and Partition § 11.

LAW IN GENERAL

A cotenant is, by the weight of authority, entitled to retain the crops and profits accruing from his own occupancy and use of the premises unless he has ousted or excluded the other owners. However, the prevailing view is otherwise as to profits from a use which reduces the value of the land. Am Jur 2d, Cotenancy and Joint Ownership § 45; Am Law of Prop § 6.14; 51 ALR2d 388; Tiffany § 450.

5-15C   Management.

LAW IN GENERAL

A cotenant is ordinarily not entitled to compensation for managing, selling or caring for the common property unless under an express or implied contract with the others. Am Law of Prop § 6.18; Tiffany § 450.

SECTION 5-16:   MINERALS; TIMBER

5-16A   Generally.

Waste generally, see Section 11-19.

R.C. 5307.21 in part provides: "One coparcener may maintain an action of waste against another coparcener." (As eff. 10-1-53.)

A receiver will be appointed to take possession of mining property where there are a number of joint proprietors who cannot agree as to the working of the mines. Barbour v. Lockard, 9 Dec Repr 254, 11 WLB 319 (Cin. Super. Ct. 1884).

LAW IN GENERAL

A cotenant may work an existing mine or well and, in most states, may open mines or wells; where he makes a valid lease, the lessee becomes a cotenant to the extent of the rights granted. One owner is not entitled to contribution for expenses, and he must ordinarily account for profits to his co-owners. Am Jur 2d, Mines and Minerals § 161; Am Law of Prop § 10.19.

One of the tenants may cut timber so long as waste is not committed. It has been held that he must account for the value of growing trees. The same standard as to what constitutes waste by a tenant for life or for years is not applied to cotenants, as a rule, since a cotenant in fee may make reasonable use of the property as an owner in fee. A cotenant is liable for waste when his use exceeds a reasonable enjoyment and results in permanent injury to the property. Am Law of Prop § 6.15; 5 ALR2d 1368.

DIVISION 5-2: PARTICULAR CLASSES OF INTERESTS

SECTION 5-21: TENANCY IN COMMON

5-21A Characteristics.

LAW IN GENERAL

A tenant in common owns some undivided part of an interest in land and has the same rights to possession as an owner of an entire interest except for the right of exclusive possession. Tenancy in common is characterized by the single unity of possession, each tenant being entitled to possession without the right to exclude the others. Am Law of Prop § 6.5; CJS, Tenancy in Common § 4; Powell § 601; Tiffany § 426.

5-21B Creation.

Where two persons take property as tenants in common under a deed which is silent in regard to their respective shares, there is a presumption that their shares are equal. Huls v. Huls, 98 App 509, 130 NE2d 412, 58 OO 46 (1954).

A tenancy in common is created when two or more persons become the owners of undivided interests in a parcel of land without any effective provisions regarding the nature of the estate.

SECTION 5-22: JOINT TENANCY

Survivorship deeds, see Section 8-16.

5-22A Characteristics and Creation.

It may be broadly stated that title to either real or personal property by technical joint tenancy is not recognized in this state; that is to say, joint tenancy, with the necessary attributes of unity of interest, title, time, and possession, and the equally necessary concomitant of jus accrescendi, is no longer recognized, and whenever the expression "joint tenancy" is found, without any effort to provide expressly for survivorship, it is uniformly construed as a tenancy in common. In re Hutchison's Estate, 120 OS 542, 550, 166 NE 687, 7 Abs 333, 335, 29 OLR 257 (1929).

5-22B   Conveyance by One Tenant.

If joint tenancy is expressed without words of survivorship, it will be considered as tenancy in common. Foraker v. Kocks, 41 App 210, 180 NE 743, 11 Abs 545, 36 OLR 156 (1931).

SECTION 5-23:   COMMUNITY PROPERTY

5-23A   Generally.

In the community property states it is provided by statute that property acquired during the marriage by a husband or wife is presumed to be community property, each spouse having an equal interest. The community is somewhat in the nature of a partnership with equal division of the acquisitions. Separate property is that owned by either spouse before the marriage or afterward acquired by gift, devise, bequest or descent, or by exchange for separate property. Community property may be converted into separate property by agreement of the spouses. This kind of tenancy does not exist in Ohio.

SECTION 5-24:   OTHER INTERESTS

5-24A   Tenancy by the Entirety.

Statutory disclaimer of beneficial interest, see 9-11G.
Survivorship deeds, see 8-16A.

Tenancy by the entirety did not exist in Ohio prior to the enactment of R.C. 5302.17. The right to create such an estate was terminated by amendment effective April 4, 1985.

5-24B   Coparceners.

The estate in coparcenary was created at common law when two or more heirs acquired the fee as though they were one heir. It is not recognized in Ohio law.

5-24C   Conveyance to Grantor and Another Person.

See also 8-32E.

The modern cases in appellate courts concerning deeds from a person to himself and another person are from other states and involve joint tenancy. The cases are about equally divided as to the effectiveness of such deeds. A multitude of cases hold that a deed is ineffective insofar as it is a conveyance to the grantor. It is submitted that the resulting uncertainty in Ohio should be resolved by statute, as has been done in several states, in favor of the grantor's intention, as in creating the right of survivorship without the intervention of a straw man.

5-24D Condominiums and Cooperatives.

R.C. 5311.01 to 5311.27 extensively revise the condominium law. The revision imposes consumer protection-type disclosure requirements on the sale of residential condominiums and authorizes civil actions for violations, including actions by the Attorney General; expressly authorizes and prescribes special requirements for expandable and conversion condominiums, permits non-residential condominium units to be subdivided and combined with other units, and permits allocation of interests in common areas and facilities on the basis of par value; requires additional information in declarations submitting the condominium to the condominium law, especially in the case of expandable and leasehold condominiums; requires certain warranties on residential condominiums; provides a specific timetable for assumption of control of the unit owners association by unit owners other than the developer in residential condominiums; and restricts the applicability of the mechanics' lien law against condominium property conveyed to purchasers for value in good faith.

No separate index is provided for liens under R.C. 5311.18 on condominium units for their unpaid portions of common expenses. Some recorders record these certificates and other liens in the mortgage records.

The Columbus Bar Association-Search Standards (printed at 1-45B) show the method of searches as to condominium property.

Fencing or other construction on the common areas of a condominium is not authorized by an amendment to the declaration unless the amendment is approved by all unit owners. Grimes v. Moreland, 41 Misc 69, 322 NE2d 699, 75 OO2d 134 (C.P. 1974).

Every owner of a condominium unit has an interest in the entire common area. The proper party to an action to recover damages for defects in the common area is the unit owner's association, in accordance with R.C. 5311.20. A misrepresentation as to the life of a roof may be a basis for such an action against the developer. The release of the developer in the declaration and bylaws is ineffective against such a claim and not binding on the owner's association or the owners. Stony Ridge Hill Condominium Owners Ass'n v. Auerbach, 64 App2d 40, 410 NE2d 782, 18 OO3d 26 (1979).

A municipal ordinance which permits tenants, upon conversion of their building to a condominium, to terminate their leases without penalty, is not unconstitutional, does not impair the obligation of contracts and does not violate the condominium statutes. Professional Investments of America, Inc. v. McCormick, 14 Misc 2d 1, 469 NE2d 1357 (1984).

A provision for expanding a condominium without the consent of every unit owner to the change of percentage interest in the common area of a condominium whose declaration was filed prior to October 1, 1978 is void. CDM Assocs. v. Coronado Woods Ass'n, 8 App3d 48, 455 NE2d 1335 (1982).

Standards of Title Examination

(Adopted by Ohio State Bar Association in 1976)

10.1 — CONDOMINIUMS — BYLAWS

Problem A:
If the bylaws of a condominium are amended must the declaration be amended?

Standard A:
Yes.

Comment A:
The bylaws are attached to the declaration and for the bylaws to be amended, it is necessary to amend the declaration in the manner provided for in the declaration which shall be by not less than 75% of the voting powers. (R.C. 5311.05 (B) (9), 5311.06 (A) and 5311.08 (A).)

Problem B:
Must the bylaws be signed, witnessed and acknowledged by the owner?

Standard B:
No.

Comment B:
A true copy of the bylaws must be attached to the declaration. Chapter 5311 makes no requirement as to the execution of the bylaws. However see R.C. 5311.05 (A) as to the requirements for execution of the declaration.

10.2 — CONDOMINIUMS — DRAWINGS

Problem A:
R.C. 5311.07 provides that the drawings shall bear the certified statement of a registered surveyor and registered architect or registered surveyor and licensed professional engineer. May the certified statement be made by one person acting in both of these capacities, if he is so qualified?

Standard A:
Yes.

Comment A:
If one individual does perform both functions his certification should clearly show that he is making the statement in both capacities.

Problem B:
Must the drawings show that the building or buildings are completed when the declaration is filed?

Standard B:
Yes.

Comment B:

R.C. 5311.05 and 5311.07 provide that the declaration shall state the principal materials of which the building or buildings are constructed and that the drawings shall show them as constructed. They must be finished to such an extent that the drawings and certification required by R.C. 5311.07 may be made. Some improvements may be deferred, however, until the sale to satisfy the requirements and wishes of the purchaser.

Problem C:

Should the drawings show the building or buildings in such detail that the boundaries of the cubicles in space comprising the units can be located and reconstructed therefrom?

Standard C:

Yes.

Comment C:

The detail so required is no more than that required for a proper plat of a boundary survey. A plat of a boundary survey is sufficiently detailed if it can be used to locate and reconstruct the boundaries of the land in the field. Similarly, the drawings of the building or buildings are sufficiently detailed in this respect if the three dimensional boundaries of the cubicles in space comprising the units can be located and reconstructed in the field.

10.3 — CONDOMINIUMS — DECLARATION

Problem A:

Must the percentages of interest in the common area and facilities appertaining to each unit that are set forth in the declaration total one hundred per cent?

Standard A:

Yes.

Comment A:

R.C. 5311.04 provides that the common areas and facilities shall be owned by the unit owners as tenants in common and shall remain undivided, that the percentages of interest of the units in the common areas and facilities shall be those percentages set forth in the declaration, and that such percentages shall not be altered except by an amendment to the declaration approved by all of the unit owners affected. If such percentages total less than one hundred per cent, an interest in the common area and facilities would remain in the declarant after he no longer owned any of the units. If such percentages total more than one hundred per cent, it would be impossible to determine the respective interests of the unit owners in the common areas and facilities in the absence of a corrective amendment unanimously approved by the unit owners.

LAW IN GENERAL

"Cooperative" usually indicates a corporate or business trust holding title to all the premises and granting rights of occupancy. Powell § 631.

181

In the ordinary cooperative, an apartment building and the land are owned by a corporation. Each of the stockholders is entitled to a "proprietary lease" of an apartment. Each proprietary lessee is assessed a proportionate part of the common expenses which include operation and maintenance of the property, taxes, and mortgage costs. Mortgage financing is generally not feasible for the individual lessee.

A condominium establishes a system of separate ownership for parts of a building, or for definite cubes of space, with ownership in common of certain facilities and parts of the property. Each owner receives a deed and makes his individual tax and mortgage payments. Holding title to part of a building has long been possible under the common law. However, legislation is necessary for satisfactory operation and maintenance of property owned in common, such as the roof and foundation. Under these statutes the common ownership cannot be partitioned or be separated from the unit ownership. The basic documents are the recorded declaration, the bylaws and the house regulations which govern the proportionate co-ownership, administration, and use of the entire property.

DIVISION 5-3: PARTITION

SECTION 5-31: GENERALLY

5-31A Definition; Waiver of Right.

A waiver of the right to partition is required by the statute of frauds to be in writing. Jacob v. Fisher, 5 NP 419, 7 OD 423 (1898).

A covenant not to partition is valid so long as a reasonable time limitation is stated therein, or may be derived therefrom. Raisch v. Schuster, 47 App2d 98, 352 NE2d 657, 1 OO3d 202 (1975).

Further research: O Jur 3d, Cotenancy and Partition § 31.

LAW IN GENERAL

Partition is the division of property between co-owners by their agreement or by a legal proceeding through which the property may either be physically divided or be sold and the proceeds distributed. The right to compel partition can be limited by contract. Many cases hold that the right can be waived for a reasonable time only. CJS, Partition §§ 1, 44.

5-31B Restraints on the Right.

A testamentary provision that division of real estate be postponed for two years after the death of the life tenant is valid, and suit for partition cannot be maintained before the expiration of such time. Steinman v. Steinman, 5 CC(NS) 600, 17 CD 460 (1905). See Davison v. Wolf, 9 Ohio 73 (1839).

A provision in a will, that the property devised shall not be partitioned or sold until after the decease of testator's children, is void. Murdock v. Lord, 14

NP(NS) 156, 31 OD 593 (1913). See Wuest v. Wuest, 8 NP 298, 11 OD 147 (1901).

Further research: O Jur 3d, Cotenancy and Partition § 44.

LAW IN GENERAL

A testamentary restriction or other restraint on the right to have partition is generally valid provided it is for a reasonable time. Some cases uphold restraints upon partition when limited to a period not exceeding lives in being plus twenty-one years. A restraint does not prevent voluntary partition, nor does it apply when all the undivided shares are conveyed to one person. Am Law of Prop § 26.72; CJS, Partition § 43; Powell § 846; Restatement Second, Property (Donative Transfers) § 4.5; Tiffany § 468.

5-31C Effect on Title.

Upon partition, whether by election, by purchase or amicable, title is held by purchase only as to those interests for which consideration is actually paid. The interest of the former cotenant remains an estate of inheritance when he becomes the sole owner. Lawson v. Townley, 90 OS 67, 106 NE 780, 11 OLR 463, 59 WLB 77 (1914); Lee v. Fike, 28 App 283, 162 NE 682, 6 Abs 151 (1928); Huseman v. Fingermeyer, 106 OS 113, 139 NE 862, 1 Abs 38, 39, 20 OLR 455, 457 (1922).

Further research: O Jur 3d, Cotenancy and Partition §§ 170, 171.

SECTION 5-32: VOLUNTARY PARTITION

5-32A Generally.

Dower, see 14-22A.

In Ohio parol partition, consummated by possession and acquiescence for any period less than that which creates the bar of the statute of limitations, does not vest the legal title in severalty to the allotted shares; but such a partition acquiesced in for any considerable length of time, will estop any person joining in it and accepting exclusive possession under it from asserting title or right to possession in violation of its terms. Berry v. Seawall, 13 CCA 101, 65 Fed 742 (1895); Piatt v. Hubbell, 5 Ohio 243 (1831).

Further research: O Jur 3d, Cotenancy and Partition § 33.

LAW IN GENERAL

Voluntary partition may be effected by mutual conveyances or releases. A covenant of warranty is not implied according to the prevailing rule. An agreement for partition is not binding on any of the cotenants unless all are bound. Parol partition may be enforced in equity on the ground of part performance or other equitable principle. Am Jur 2d, Partition §§ 17, 29; Am Law of Prop § 6.19; CJS, Partition § 2; Powell § 610; Tiffany § 469.

SECTION 5-33: PERSONS ENTITLED AND PROPERTY SUBJECT

Equitable conversion, see 16-63F.
Judicial sale and reinvestment, see Section 17-42.
Testamentary direction to sell, see 16-63B.

5-33A Life Estates; Remainders and Other Future Interests.

Neither life tenants nor remaindermen can compel the other to suffer partition of their interests. Embleton v. McMechen, 110 OS 18, 143 NE 177, 34 ALR 689, 2 Abs 244, 245, 22 OLR 29 (1924). Remaindermen cannot have partition subject to the life estate. Eberle v. Gaier, 89 OS 118, 105 NE 282, 11 OLR 327, 338, 58 WLB 464, 474 (1913).

A tenant for life of one undivided half is not entitled to have the value of his life estate paid to him in money over the objection of the remaindermen, but one-half the proceeds should be invested according to law and the income paid to the life tenant, and upon his death the principal paid to the remaindermen. Wyman v. Newberry, 31 App 317, 167 NE 414, 7 Abs 295 (1929).

One of the life tenants in common may maintain an action in partition against the other life tenants. Bachscheider v. Bachscheider, 23 NP(NS) 521 (C.P. 1921).

A reversion alone is not subject to partition. Only those persons having possession or an immediate right to possession, including lessors, are entitled to partition. Forest Park Properties, Inc. v. Pine, 9 App2d 348, 224 NE2d 763, 38 OO2d 427 (1966).

Further research: O Jur 3d, Cotenancy and Partition §§ 66, 68.

LAW IN GENERAL

A tenant in common of a life estate may compel partition of such estate. When an undivided share is owned in fee simple, partition of the life estate may be compelled either by the fee owner or by the tenant in common of the life estate according to the prevailing rule. A person or persons entitled to the entire possession and not owning a share in the remainder cannot enforce partition against the remainderman or remaindermen. Am Law of Prop §§ 4.92, 6.22; CJS, Partition § 57; Restatement, Property § 125; Simes and Smith § 1766; Tiffany § 476.

Partition cannot be compelled by a remainderman nor by any other owner of a future interest who does not also have a possessory interest. The owner of a future interest and the owner of a present interest, acting together, have the same right to partition as would the grantee of both interests. The owners of future interests may be subjected to partition although they do not have the right to compel partition as when another person owns an undivided interest in fee simple. Am Law of Prop §§ 4.95, 6.23; Powell § 289; Restatement, Property § 170; Simes and Smith § 1765; Tiffany § 496.

5-33B   Leaseholds.

A leasehold interest for oil and gas with appurtenances is partitionable, either under the statute or in equity. Black v. Sylvania Producing Co., 105 OS 346, 137 NE 904, 1 Abs 214, 20 OLR 166, 176 (1922).

The existence of a lease, granting an option to the lessee to purchase the land, is no obstacle to partition. Crowe v. Crowe, 12 App 43, 31 CC(NS) 492 (1919).

Further research: O Jur 3d, Cotenancy and Partition § 58.

LAW IN GENERAL

The existence of a lease will not prevent partition of the land subject to the lease. Am Law of Prop § 4.94; Restatement, Property § 174; Simes and Smith § 1764.

A cotenant for years may generally maintain partition of the leasehold. CJS, Partition § 57.

5-33C   Ownership in Severalty.

The owner of a moiety in real estate in fee simple who is also the owner of a life estate in the other moiety is entitled to partition. Heiden v. Howes, 77 App 525, 67 NE2d 641, 33 OO 353, 45 Abs 289 (1945); Morgan v. Staley, 11 Ohio 389 (1842).

LAW IN GENERAL

Partition does not lie when parts of property are owned in severalty. Tiffany § 475.

5-33D   Husband and Wife.

A husband or wife may bring an action in partition against his or her spouse as to real estate owned jointly. Shafer v. Shafer, 30 App 298, 163 NE 507, 6 Abs 481 (1928).

Such action is not ousted by a subsequent divorce and alimony action. Shively v. Shively, 88 App 7, 95 NE2d 276, 43 OO 385, 58 Abs 19 (1950).

The interest of the wife, having by virtue of the separation agreement been converted in equity into personal property, cannot, without the consent of her husband, be reconverted by her into real property so as to sustain an action for partition of the property. Bonadio v. Bonadio, 30 NP(NS) 470 (C.P. 1933).

Further research: O Jur 3d, Cotenancy and Partition §§ 69, 75.

5-33E   Trusts; Equitable Interests.

An owner of an undivided legal or equitable interest in land is not entitled to partition unless he is in possession or has a right to immediate possession. Knecht v. George, 69 NE2d 228, 45 Abs 574 (App. 1943); Lauer v. Green, 99 OS 20, 121 NE 821, 16 OLR 363, 364, 63 WLB 473, 64 WLB 32 (1918).

LAW IN GENERAL

The owner of an equitable interest is ordinarily not entitled to partition unless he has a right to a conveyance of the legal title. A trustee may generally maintain the action. CJS, Partition § 32; Tiffany § 477.

5-33F Dower.

Judicial sales, see 5-34H.

Dower does not prevent partition unless it has been assigned in the entire land sought to be partitioned. Lape v. Lape, 22 NP(NS) 392, 31 OD 188 (1920). Further research: O Jur 3d, Cotenancy and Partition § 59.

LAW IN GENERAL

Dower does not prevent partition, but land assigned as dower cannot be partitioned so as to affect the dower right. CJS, Partition § 59.

5-33G Partnerships.

Where all the partners ask for a termination of the partnership, or where it has ceased to exist, the court will treat the residuum of real estate, after paying all partnership debts, as held by the partners in cotenancy and decree a partition. Moody v. Powers, 16 CC(NS) 586, 27 CD 614 (1907).

The Uniform Partnership Act does not appear to prevent a decree of partition if the partnership affairs have been wound up except for disposition of the real estate.

Further research: O Jur 3d, Cotenancy and Partition § 72.

5-33H Other Possessory Interests.

If the tenant is not prevented by some intervening estate from recovering the possession in an action at law, he will not be disabled to prosecute his writ of partition. Tabler v. Wiseman, 2 OS 207 (1853).

The heirs and devisees of a lessor who are entitled to rents accruing from time to time under a lease for ninety-nine years renewable forever, are entitled to partition. Rawson v. Brown, 104 OS 537, 136 NE 209, 20 OLR 44, 45 (1922).

SECTION 5-34: JUDICIAL PROCEDURE

5-34A Equity Jurisdiction; Statutes.

Accounting, see also Section 5-15.
Conflict of jurisdiction, see 16-22B.

R.C. 5307.02 provides (place of partition proceedings): "When the estate is situated in one county, the proceedings for partition shall be had in that county. When the estate is situated in two or more counties, such proceedings may be had in any county in which a part of such estate is situated." (As eff. 10-1-53.)

R.C. 5307.03 provides (filing of petition; contents): "A person entitled to partition of an estate may file his petition therefor in the court of common pleas, setting forth the nature of his title, a pertinent description of the lands, tenements, or hereditaments of which partition is demanded, and naming each tenant in common, coparcener, or other person interested therein, as defendant. When the title to such estate came to such person by descent or devise upon the death of an inhabitant of this state, a partition thereof shall not be ordered by the court within one year from the date of the death of such decedent, unless the petition sets forth and it is proved that all claims against the estate of such decedent have been paid, or secured to be paid, or that the personal property of the deceased is sufficient to pay them." (As eff. 10-1-53.)

R.C. 5307.04 provides (order of partition): "If the court of common pleas finds that the plaintiff in an action for partition has a legal right to any part of the estate, it shall order partition thereof in favor of the plaintiff or all parties in interest, appoint three disinterested and judicious freeholders of the vicinity to be commissioners to make the partition, and order a writ of partition to issue." (As eff. 10-1-53.)

R.C. 5307.06, 5307.07 and 5307.08 provide for platting the property if the commissioners divide any tract. (As eff. 7-4-84.)

R.C. 5307.09 provides (commissioners to appraise land when they cannot divide it): "When the commissioners provided for in section 5307.04 of the Revised Code are of opinion that the estate cannot be divided according to the demand of the writ of partition without manifest injury to its value, they shall return that fact to the court of common pleas with a just valuation of the estate. If such court approves the return, and one or more of the parties elects to take the estate at such appraised value, it shall be adjudged to them, upon their paying to the other parties their proportion of its appraised value, according to their respective rights, or securing it as provided in section 5307.10 of the Revised Code." (As eff. 10-1-53.)

R.C. 5307.10 provides (terms of payment when estate taken by party; execution of conveyance): "If one or more of the parties in the action for partition elects to take the estate at the appraised value, unless on good cause shown by special order the court of common pleas directs the entire payment to be made in cash, or all the parties in interest agree thereon, the terms of payment shall be one third cash, one third in one year, and one third in two years, with interest, the deferred payments to be secured to the satisfaction of the court. On payment being made in full, or in part, with sufficient security for the remainder, as provided in this section, according to the order of the court the sheriff shall make and execute a conveyance to the parties electing to take it." (As eff. 10-1-53.)

R.C. 5307.11 provides (sale of estate when no election made): "If no election to take the estate is made, at the instance of a party, the court of common pleas may order a sale of the estate at public auction, by the sheriff who executed the writ of partition, or his successor in office." (As eff. 10-1-53.)

R.C. 5307.12 provides (conduct of sale; terms): "A sale of an estate under section 5307.11 of the Revised Code shall be made at the door of the courthouse, unless for good cause the court of common pleas directs it to be made on the premises. The sale shall be conducted as upon execution, except that [it] is unnecessary to appraise the estate; but it shall not be sold for less than two thirds of the value returned by the commissioners provided for in section 5307.04 of the Revised Code. Unless by special order, on good cause shown, the court directs the entire payment to be made in cash, the purchase money shall be payable one third on the day of sale, one third in one year, and one third in two years thereafter, with interest." (As eff. 10-1-53.)

R.C. 5307.13 provides (confirmation of sale and execution of conveyance): "On the sheriff's return of his proceedings to sell the estate, the court of common pleas shall examine them. If a sale has been made, and the court approves it, the sheriff shall execute and deliver a deed to the purchaser on receiving payment of the consideration money, or taking sufficient security therefor, to the satisfaction of the court." (As eff. 10-1-53.)

R.C. 5307.15 provides (proceedings when estate has been once offered and not sold): "When the estate has been offered once and not sold, alias writs for its sale may issue as often as need be. The court of common pleas may order a revaluation by three disinterested freeholders of the vicinity and direct a sale of the estate at not less than two thirds of such revaluation, or, if deemed for the interest of the parties, the court may order a sale without such revaluation, at not less than a sum it fixes." (As eff. 10-1-53.)

All partition cases must still be regarded as chancery cases and therefore appealable. Wagner v. Armstrong, 93 OS 443, 113 NE 397, 14 OLR 21, 42, 61 WLB 83, 93 (1916).

Equitable partition, or partition under the equity jurisdiction of the court, is an additional remedy to statutory partition. In re Parrett, 86 App 162, 90 NE2d 425, 41 OO 20 (1949).

Where two or more cotenants in a partition proceeding individually elect to take the property at its appraised value, a public sale is required. Rankin v. Coffer, 174 NE2d 631, 85 Abs 391 (App. 1960).

Further research: O Jur 3d, Cotenancy and Partition § 36.

5-34B Improvements.

A court of equity has power to make allowance to cotenant for moneys invested or expended for the benefit of the property. Such claim does not stand in the position of a lien, but rather in the nature of an investment out of which claimant is to have a share of the rents and profits, and an allowance with reference to the amount invested and the deterioration of the property or loss by fire. Wachenheimer v. Standart, 19 CC 693, 8 CD 328 (1895).

Further research: O Jur 3d, Cotenancy and Partition §§ 151, 152.

LAW IN GENERAL

In decreeing partition the court will make an allowance to a cotenant who has made permanent improvements increasing the value of the premises if such an order appears equitable. Consent by the other owners to the improvement is not necessary, the allowance and its amount being governed by equitable considerations. Compensation may be made to the claimant by assigning him the improved portion or an increased quantity, or by an additional allowance out of the proceeds of sale. Regard will be given to the rents and profits received by the cotenant making the improvement. CJS, Partition § 139.

5-34C Owelty; Equalization of Shares.

The doctrine of owelty (equality) of partition is applied where it is impossible or impracticable to divide the estate physically in equal shares, and unequal allotments are therefore made subject to a charge upon the greater. Owelty of partition does not exist in this state as a statutory right but is recognized where the unequal division is made by consent. Fleming v. Morningstar, 4 NP(NS) 405, 17 OD 430 (1904).

In a partition action, it is proper for a court to determine that the interests of the co-owners are proportional to the amount of money each invested in purchasing the premises. Spector v. Giunta, 62 App2d 137, 405 NE2d 327, 16 OO3d 299 (1978).

Further research: O Jur 3d, Cotenancy and Partition § 32.

5-34D Warranty of Title.

Judicial sales, see 17-15C.

LAW IN GENERAL

A warranty of the title received by each cotenant on compulsory partition is implied. It does not extend to subsequent purchasers from them nor to purchasers at partition sale. CJS, Partition § 125.

5-34E Questions of Title.

An answer in partition denying that plaintiffs have any title to or interest in the premises does not oust the court of jurisdiction. Perry v. Richardson, 27 OS 110, 1 WLB 58 (1875).

5-34F Fiduciaries as Parties.

Conflict of jurisdiction, see also 16-22B.

R.C. 2127.41 provides for filing certificate in partition proceedings of amount necessary to pay debts, expenses and legacies by executor or administrator. (As eff. 1-1-76.)

R.C. 5307.19 provides: "The guardian of a minor, idiot, imbecile, or insane person, on behalf of his ward, may perform any act, matter, or thing respecting the partition of an estate which such ward could do under sections 5307.01 to 5307.25, inclusive, of the Revised Code, if he were of age and of sound mind. On behalf of such ward, the guardian may elect to take the estate, when it cannot be divided without injury, and make payments therefor on the ward's behalf." (As eff. 10-1-53.)

R.C. 5307.20 provides: "A person appointed according to the laws of any other state or country, to take charge of the estate of an idiot or insane person not a resident of this state, upon being authorized in this state to take charge of such estate situated therein, may act in the partition of the estate the same as the guardian of an idiot or insane person is authorized to do by section 5307.19 of the Revised Code." (As eff. 10-1-53.)

A guardian may institute proceeding for partition or consent to the same. Merritt v. Horne, 5 OS 307 (1855).

An infant co-owner must be made a party in partition proceedings. Weiland v. Muntz, 2 CC(NS) 71, 15 CD 185, 48 WLB 890 (1903).

A guardian appointed by the probate court of another state was fully authorized to plead on behalf of his minor ward in a partition action, and by so doing entered the appearance of both and thereby conferred jurisdiction upon the court, and the same was not subject to collateral attack. Kunzelmann v. Duval, 61 App 360, 22 NE2d 632, 14 OO 519, 29 Abs 200 (1939).

Where the personal property of a deceased person is insufficient to pay debts of the estate and partition proceedings are instituted, the executor or administrator may elect to bring an action to sell real property to pay debts, or may elect to file a certificate in the partition proceeding of the amount necessary to pay debts. Burrier v. Kiefer, 90 App 571, 107 NE2d 565, 48 OO 210 (1951).

The fact that the guardians of the minor owners are parties is not sufficient, but the minors themselves must also be made defendants and served with summons. Burns v. Burns, 20 NP(NS) 116, 27 OD 510 (1917).

Further research: O Jur 3d, Cotenancy and Partition § 100.

5-34G   Liens.

R.C. 323.46 (as eff. 4-4-85) and 5721.26 (as eff. 4-4-85) provide that when a cotenant has paid his portion of the taxes and partition is made, his payment shall be deemed to have been made on the portion set off to him. The county auditor may make a certificate releasing such portion of the land.

Mortgagees and other encumbrancers are proper parties but not necessary parties in an action for partition. A lien holder has no right to elect to purchase the property at its appraised value. Malone v. Malone, 119 App 503, 199 NE2d 405, 28 OO2d 127, 93 Abs 481 (1963).

Further research: O Jur 3d, Cotenancy and Partition §§ 92, 138.

LAW IN GENERAL

A lien against the undivided interest of a cotenant is transferred to the portion set off to him even though the lien holder is not a party. Lien holders are not necessary parties, but their liens are unaffected if they are not parties. When the property is sold in partition, the rule is that a lien on an undivided interest is transferred to the debtor's share of the proceeds and the land is free of the liens of the parties. Am Law of Prop § 6.24; CJS, Partition § 56; Tiffany §§ 471, 482.

5-34H   Dower.

Voluntary partition, see 14-22A.

R.C. 5307.17 and 5307.18 provide procedure for assignment of dower in an estate of which partition is sought. (As eff. 10-1-53.)

Partition divests the wife of a cotenant in fee of her inchoate right of dower and passes the entire estate to the purchaser. Weaver v. Gregg, 6 OS 547 (1856).

The spouses of the coparceners were not necessary parties to the action in partition. Snodgrass v. Bedell, 134 OS 311, 320, 16 NE2d 463, 12 OO 103, 107 (1938).

In an action for partition the wife of a bankrupt cotenant is a proper party and the common pleas court has jurisdiction to adjudicate her claim for an allowance in lieu of dower. Russell v. Russell, 137 OS 153, 28 NE2d 551, 17 OO 506 (1940).

The spouse of a cotenant is neither a necessary nor a proper party in an action in partition between cotenants. Dunkle v. Dunkle, 137 NE2d 170, 2 OO2d 399, 73 Abs 477 (C.P. 1956).

Further research: O Jur 3d, Cotenancy and Partition §§ 70, 99.

5-34I   Costs; Attorney Fees.

R.C. 5307.25 provides that having regard to the interest of the parties, the benefit each may derive from a partition, and according to equity, the court shall tax the costs and expenses which accrue in the action, including reasonable counsel fees, which must be paid to plaintiff's counsel unless the court awards some part thereof to other counsel for services in the case for the common benefit of all parties; and that execution may issue therefor as in other cases. (As eff. 10-1-53.)

Where mortgagee files a cross-petition requesting foreclosure and acquiescing in partition proceeding, fees may be awarded the attorney for the plaintiff out of the proceeds of the sale, even though the property is sold for less than the mortgage indebtedness. Klosterman v. Klosterman, 58 App 511, 16 NE2d 826, 12 OO 303, 27 Abs 189 (1938).

When a cause in partition is dismissed before partition is completed, compensation may be awarded for value of attorney's services rendered for the common benefit of all parties. Hudson v. Hoster, 47 NE2d 895, 39 Abs 9 (App. 1943).

In a partition proceeding, in determining whether counsel for the defendant rendered service for the common benefit of all parties, the trial court is required to exercise a sound discretion. Foureman v. Foureman, 82 App 380, 80 NE2d 266, 38 OO 53, 50 Abs 539 (1947).

Where the plaintiff in a partition action was the successful bidder at the judicial sale and the plaintiff thereafter fails to complete the purchase, the court did not abuse its discretion by dismissing the action and ordering the plaintiff to pay all costs of the suit. Schneider v. Schneider, 8 App3d 134, 456 NE2d 509 (1982).

In an action for partition of real property, no counsel fee, whether to the plaintiff's counsel or otherwise, can be allowed by the court and taxed as costs in the case, under R.C. 5307.25, unless the services were rendered for the common benefit of all the parties. The time expended by plaintiff's attorney in having property partitioned is clearly for the benefit of both parties and is reimbursable; however, time spent in controversy over the amount of equities, rents and setoffs is for the benefit of a particular client and therefore is not reimbursable. Hawkins v. Hawkins, 11 Misc2d 18, 464 NE2d 199 (1984).

Further research: O Jur 3d, Cotenancy and Partition § 160.

CHAPTER 6:   COVENANTS AND RESTRICTIONS

DIVISION 6-1:   IN GENERAL

SECTION 6-11:   INTRODUCTION; CREATION AND CONSTRUCTION

SECTION 6-12:   RUNNING WITH THE LAND

SECTION 6-13:   DAMAGES

DIVISION 6-2:   COVENANTS FOR TITLE

SECTION 6-21:   GENERALLY

SECTION 6-22:   COVENANTS OF WARRANTY AND FOR QUIET ENJOYMENT

SECTION 6-23:   COVENANTS FOR SEISIN AND OF RIGHT TO CONVEY

SECTION 6-24:   COVENANT AGAINST ENCUMBRANCES

DIVISION 6-3:   RESTRICTIONS AS TO USE

SECTION 6-31:   GENERALLY; CREATION AND CONSTRUCTION

DIVISION 6-1: IN GENERAL

SECTION 6-11: INTRODUCTION; CREATION AND CONSTRUCTION

6-11A Definition.

"Covenant" denotes a contract. The common use of the word refers to promises concerning real property as contained in conveyances or other instruments.

6-11B Terms of Creation.

Implied covenants, see 6-21D.

In the construction of covenants the intention of the parties is to govern, and that intention must be collected from the whole instrument taken together. Courcier v. Graham, 1 Ohio 330 (1824).

Notwithstanding the words "said premises shall revert to the said grantors," we find sufficient reason to construe said provision not as a condi-

194

tion subsequent but as a restrictive covenant. Second Church of Christ, Scientist v. Le Prevost, 67 App 101, 35 NE2d 1015, 21 OO 122 (1941).

Where land is conveyed "so long as" used for a specific purpose and provision is made for forfeiture or reversion, the title conveyed is a fee simple determinable and the reversion may be enforced. Board of Van Wert County Commissioners v. Consolidated Rail Corp., 14 Misc2d 4 (1983).

Where the words "to construct a Rail Road and for no other purpose" appear in a prefatory clause in a deed and no forfeiture or reverter or right of reentry is expressed, the deed conveys an indefeasible fee simple interest. Little Miami, Inc. v. Wisecup, 13 App3d 239 (1984).

Further research: O Jur 3d, Deeds §§ 101, 133, 189.

LAW IN GENERAL

The cardinal rule in the interpretation of covenants is to follow the intention of the parties as expressed by the whole instrument and, if it is ambiguous, as shown by the circumstances attending its execution. Am Jur 2d, Covenants, etc. § 5; CJS, Covenants § 20.

Implied covenants are not favored in the law and will not be recognized unless they can be said to be express covenants as being inferred from express words. No particular words are essential to an express covenant. Am Jur 2d, Covenants, etc. § 12; CJS, Covenants § 12.

6-11C Law of Situs.

LAW IN GENERAL

The construction of covenants running with the land is governed by the law of the state where the land is located. Am Jur 2d, Covenants, etc. § 46; CJS, Covenants § 55.

6-11D Invalid Conveyances.

A deed not attested by two witnesses cannot contain an effective covenant, and the warranty therein does not work an estoppel against the maker. Patterson v. Pease, 5 Ohio 190 (1831).

LAW IN GENERAL

A covenant is unenforceable if contained in an invalid deed, unless the covenant is personal or entirely independent. CJS, Covenants § 4.

6-11E Conditions; Specified Uses.

See also 11-42A.

When value is paid, a stipulation in a deed that the estate is to be used only for certain purposes is construed to be a covenant running with the land. To reinvest the title in the grantor, his heirs or assigns, there must be words of forfeiture or re-entry in the deed. Ashland v. Greiner, 58 OS 67, 75, 50 NE 99, 39 WLB 171, 296 (1898).

A conveyance for a certain purpose does not constitute a condition subsequent or engraft a limitation on the title. Larwill v. Farrelly, 8 App 356, 28 CC(NS) 305, 30 CD 196 (1918).

LAW IN GENERAL

A conveyance for specified uses without words of forfeiture creates a covenant, as courts favor construction of particular provisions to be covenants rather than conditions subsequent. The absence of consideration is a factor in ascertaining the intention in a number of cases. Am Jur 2d, Estates §§ 143, 147; 116 ALR 76.

6-11F   As Binding Grantee.

A grantee is bound by his covenants without signing the deed. A covenant inserted in a deed poll binds the grantee, his heirs and assigns, when it relates to the premises conveyed. Northern Ohio Traction & Light Co. v. Quaker Oats Co., 114 OS 685, 152 NE 5, 4 Abs 256, 24 OLR 365 (1926).

LAW IN GENERAL

Covenants in a deed poll are generally held to bind the grantee as effectively as though he had executed the instrument. Am Jur 2d, Covenants, etc. § 2; CJS, Covenants § 8.

6-11G   Fiduciaries; Agents.

Unless the executor be specially thereunto authorized by the will, no warranty by an executor or administrator, on a sale of property of an estate, can bind the estate. Westfall v. Dungan, 14 OS 276 (1863).

LAW IN GENERAL

A person acting in a fiduciary or representative capacity does not bind the estate or his principal by making a covenant unless he is required or authorized to do so. He is generally held to be personally bound by an unrestricted covenant made beyond his duty. CJS, Covenants § 26.

SECTION 6-12:   RUNNING WITH THE LAND

Running with the land in equity, see restrictions at Division 6-3.

6-12A   Nature of Operation.

A covenant running with the land, which imposes a financial burden on land, creates an interest in property and is valid in appropriation proceedings. Hughes v. Cincinnati, 175 OS 381, 195 NE2d 552, 25 OO2d 378 (1964).

The word "assigns" is relatively unimportant as to whether a covenant runs with the land; the important fact is the intention of the parties. Maher v. Cleveland Union Stockyards Co., 55 App 412, 9 NE2d 995, 9 OO 112, 22 Abs 199 (1936).

Further research: O Jur 3d, Deeds § 113.

LAW IN GENERAL

Covenants operate in personam but are said to "run with the land" when the benefits or the burdens may pass to subsequent owners of the land. The grantee of a deed poll (that is, a deed executed by the grantor only) is, in the prevailing view, bound by a covenant therein by reason of his acceptance of the conveyance. Tiffany § 848.

6-12B   Rule of Construction; "Touch and Concern."

A covenant will not run with the land if an intention to the contrary appears. But an intention to make it run will not make it run, if it does not touch or concern the land. Masury v. Southworth, 9 OS 340, 348 (1859).

Further research: O Jur 3d, Deeds § 112.

LAW IN GENERAL

By the weight of modern authority, the intention of the parties is the primary rule for determining whether a covenant runs with the land. A covenant will not run with the land if an intention to the contrary appears; but an intention to make it run is not effectual if it does not touch or concern the land. The intention may be ascertained from the whole instrument and the circumstances attending the transaction. When a fee is conveyed, the covenant must touch and concern the land conveyed in order to run either with the land of the grantee or with the retained land of the grantor. The benefit of a covenant runs with the land conveyed to the grantee even when it is personal or in gross as to the grantor. Some authorities hold that the burden of a covenant does not run unless there is a corresponding benefit to other land. Am Law of Prop §§ 9.4, 9.13; CJS, Covenants § 54; Powell § 673; Tiffany § 854.

6-12C   Affirmative Covenants.

Where a deed poll contains a covenant running with the land to maintain fences, the grantee, by accepting the deed, will be deemed to have entered into an express undertaking to perform, and such undertaking will become obligatory upon a subsequent owner. Hickey v. Lake Shore & M. S. Ry. Co., 51 OS 40, 36 NE 672, 31 WLB 68, 166 (1894).

Further research: O Jur 3d, Deeds § 117.

LAW IN GENERAL

A covenant normally runs with the land and is enforceable by subsequent owners if it benefits the land of one of the parties to the covenant. The statute of limitations generally does not start to run against such covenants until demand of performance. By the weight of authority, equity will enforce affirmative agreements against purchasers with notice as equitable servitudes. Am Law of Prop §§ 9.16, 9.36; 17 ALR2d 1251; Powell § 680; Tiffany § 859.

Covenants which otherwise satisfy the requirements of necessary intention, privity and "touch and concern" generally run with the land, both at law and in equity, both as to benefit and burden, and may also be enforceable as an equitable charge. 68 ALR2d 1027.

6-12D Technical Requirements; Liens.

Covenants in inoperative deeds do not run with the land. Wallace v. Miner, 6 Ohio 367 (1834).

LAW IN GENERAL

Equity will enforce personal agreements in the nature of covenants running with the land, although the technical requirements for such covenants are not fulfilled, if the actual or constructive notice is sufficient. In some circumstances the court may find that the burden is enforceable as a lien. Am Jur 2d, Covenants, etc. § 26; Am Law of Prop § 9.17; 23 ALR2d 520.

6-12E Formalities; "Assigns"; Spencer's Case.

The use of the words "assigns" or "heirs and assigns," as required by the rule in Spencer's Case, is not necessary to create a covenant running with the land; the material inquiries are whether the parties intended to impose such burden on the land, and whether it is one that may be imposed consistently with principle and equity. Johnson v. American Gas Co., 8 App 124, 28 CC(NS) 513, 30 CD 404 (1917).

Further research: O Jur 3d, Deeds § 111.

LAW IN GENERAL

The formalities necessary are determined by the requirements for the transaction; for example, oral agreements are enforceable as running with the land if they are part of a valid oral lease.

In order for the covenant to run with the land, the rule in Spencer's Case requires the successors of the covenantor to be expressly bound when the covenant relates to something not in being, such as a wall to be constructed. But the modern cases generally hold that the use of the word "assigns" is not necessary if the intent to bind them otherwise appears, regardless of whether the promise relates to a thing in being. Am Jur 2d, Covenants, etc. § 32; Am Law of Prop §§ 9.2, 9.9.

6-12F Privity of Estate.

If the entire interest of separate parts of land pass to different individuals, a right of action accrues to each party. But a plain distinction is made between the holder of a part of the land and the holder of a part of the estate (a life estate). The latter cannot sustain an action of covenant. St. Clair v. Williams, 7 Ohio (pt. 2) 110 (1836).

Further research: O Jur 3d, Deeds § 115.

LAW IN GENERAL

The term "privity of estate" refers to the existence of a mutual or a successive relationship in the same land between different persons; thus, the privity of estate between tenants in common is a mutual relationship, between grantor and grantee is successive, and between landlord and tenant is both mutual and successive. As a general rule, a covenant attaches only to the legal estate.

Privity of estate between covenantor and covenantee is necessary for the burden of a covenant to run with the land. The heirs and assigns of the covenantor are not bound unless there is such privity.

A majority of the cases hold that privity of estate is essential for the benefit of a covenant to run with the land. However, the Restatement of the Law of Property takes the position that the successor in interst of the covenantee can enforce the covenant against the covenantor under the law of third-party beneficiary contracts when there was no privity of estate between the covenantor and covenantee.

A covenant will generally run with the land if contained in a conveyance of the fee. In order for it to run it is necessary that the covenant be a part of the same transaction as the conveyance, unless an easement furnishes the privity for a later covenant.

Am Jur 2d, Covenants, etc. § 34; Am Law of Prop §§ 9.5, 9.11, 9.14; Powell § 674; Tiffany § 849.

6-12G Breaches Not During Ownership.

A covenant broken before the conveyance does not enable the grantee to sue unless there is an express assignment. Hall v. Plaine, 14 OS 417 (1863).

A grantee is not liable for breach of a covenant running with the land where the breach occurred after he conveyed the land. Hickey v. Lake Shore & M. S. Ry., 51 OS 40, 36 NE 672, 31 WLB 68, 166 (1894).

A subsequent owner is not liable for the lessor's breach of a covenant in the lease requiring the performance of a single act or a series of contemporaneous acts. Berner v. Gelman, 102 App 319, 143 NE2d 605, 2 OO2d 354 (1956).

The original covenantor, in a covenant running with the land, is liable only for breaches before he conveys the burdened land. The grantee of the covenantor stands in his place as to liability arising after the conveyance. Peto v. Korach, 17 App2d 20, 244 NE2d 502, 46 OO2d 29 (1969).

Further research: O Jur 3d, Deeds § 130.

LAW IN GENERAL

A subsequent grantee of the covenantee may obtain relief for breaches of covenants running with the land occurring only during his ownership and without regard to equities between the original parties. A subsequent grantee of the original covenantor is liable only for breaches occurring during his ownership; an original covenantor is generally not liable for damages occurring after he parts with the title, except under covenants for title, unless it appears that a personal obligation was intended. An original covenantee may sue on causes of action arising while he owned the estate but not on those arising thereafter. Am Jur 2d, Covenants, etc. §§ 21, 25; Am Law of Prop § 9.18; Powell § 681.

SECTION 6-13: DAMAGES

6-13A   Venue; Limitation of Actions.

The remedy for breach of covenants is at law for damages as equity usually refuses to exercise its jurisdiction. Hill v. Butler, 6 OS 207 (1856).

Further research: O Jur 3d, Deeds § 167.

LAW IN GENERAL

Equity will ordinarily not exercise its jurisdiction in actions for breach of covenants, the covenantee being usually limited to his remedy at law for damages. An action by a subsequent grantee generally must be brought in the state where the land is situated. Liability is governed by the law at the time of making the covenant. The right of action usually accrues at the time of the breach and must be exercised within fifteen years. However, some courts hold that the statute of limitation does not begin to run against actions for breach of the covenant for seisin or for breach of the covenant against encumbrances until substantial damages have been sustained. Am Jur 2d, Covenants, etc. § 110.

Where the grantee takes possession, most courts hold that the statute of limitation does not start to run against an action for breach of a covenant of warranty until he is actually or constructively evicted. 95 ALR2d 913.

6-13B   Recovery from Whom.

The grantee in possession may maintain an action, until satisfaction, against all the previous covenantors for breach of a covenant for title which runs with the land. Backus v. McCoy, 3 Ohio 211 (1827). See also 6-22A.

The usual covenant of warranty is joint and several. The fact that each owned an undivided half interest does not limit liability. Sauner v. Dragoo, 6 Abs 134 (App. 1928).

LAW IN GENERAL

A subsequent grantee may maintain actions for damages under a covenant for title against all the previous covenantors, but the satisfaction of one judgment will bar his recovery on another. Am Jur 2d, Covenants, etc. § 119.

6-13C Complete Failure of Title.

On a covenant of warranty of title, where plaintiff has been evicted by title paramount, and the whole premises lost, the rule of damages is the consideration paid, with interest. But, when the plaintiff has enjoyed the rents and profits, he can recover interest for only a period of four years. Clark v. Parr, 14 Ohio 118 (1846).

LAW IN GENERAL

The general rule as to the measure of damages for breach of a covenant for title when there is complete failure of title is the consideration paid with interest plus reasonable expenses of defending the title. The covenantee may recover more than the general rule when liquidated damages, not amounting to a penalty, are stipulated or when the action is for fraud. Am Jur 2d, Covenants, etc. § 132.

6-13D Partial Breach.

The recovery for partial breach is proportionate to the value of the interest which fails. The rule of damages is the depreciation of the value of the entire interest, estimating such value according to the consideration money paid to the covenantor. Johnson v. Nyce, 17 Ohio 66 (1848).

Further research: O Jur 3d, Deeds § 168.

LAW IN GENERAL

In cases of partial breach under the general rule, in addition to the limitation of the amount of recovery to the consideration paid, the covenantee is limited to the amount of his actual loss. When the failure of title is to part of the land, the measure of damages is the proportion of the consideration which the value of the land lost bears to the land conveyed, as of the time of conveyance. The value received will be credited when the deficiency is in the estate; for instance, when the life estate is owned and a fee warranted, the value of the life estate will be deducted. CJS, Covenants § 114.

6-13E Defects; Encumbrances.

In an action for the breach of a covenant against encumbrances, the rule of damages is the amount paid to extinguish the encumbrance, provided the same does not exceed the consideration money and interest. Foote v. Burnet, 10 Ohio 317 (1840).

LAW IN GENERAL

If the defect or encumbrance does not go to the validity of the title, as an easement, the rule of damages is the diminished value of the land conveyed. Similarly, when the grantee purchases a valid outstanding lien or title, the measure of damages is the amount fairly paid for it with reasonable costs, but not to exceed the original consideration with interest. Am Jur 2d, Covenants, etc. § 144.

6-13F Expenses; Interest.

Expenses, including attorney fees, may be recovered where the covenantee has been evicted and the expenses were necessarily incurred in obtaining the paramount title. Lane v. Fury, 31 OS 574 (1877); McAlpin v. Woodruff, 11 OS 120 (1860).

Recovery cannot be had for breach of a covenant of warranty until there has been an eviction or the equivalent. Millison v. Drake, 123 OS 249, 174 NE 776, 9 Abs 446, 34 OLR 97 (1931).

Grantee cannot maintain action against his grantor for expenses incurred in bringing proceedings to quiet the title. Swaninger v. Gerstner, 9 Abs 620 (App. 1931).

LAW IN GENERAL

Interest is generally computed from the time the consideration was paid but the amount may be limited where the covenantee has enjoyed the rents and profits. Reasonable costs of an unsuccessful defense of the title are recoverable. Expenses of successful litigation or of a suit instituted by the covenantee ordinarily cannot be recovered when the adverse claim is unfounded nor when the adverse claim is not presently asserted. Am Jur 2d, Covenants, etc. §§ 148, 150; CJS, Covenants § 149; Tiffany § 1019.

6-13G Limitations on Recovery.

Damages cannot be awarded either for the increased value of the land or the improvements made. Backus v. McCoy, 3 Ohio 211 (1827).

The rule of damages, where the eviction goes to the entire estate, is the amount of the debt with interest discharged by the foreclosure. Lloyd v. Quimby, 5 OS 262 (1855).

LAW IN GENERAL

The value of the land at the time of conveyance by the covenantor, as measured by the consideration paid, is said to be the basis of recovery. When the action is brought by a subsequent grantee, the recovery may be further limited to the consideration paid by such grantee. It may be said in general that a covenantee cannot recover more than his actual loss under a valid claim which was asserted. Am Jur 2d, Covenants, etc. § 133; Tiffany §§ 1016, 1021.

DIVISION 6-2: COVENANTS FOR TITLE

SECTION 6-21: GENERALLY

Statutory covenants, see 8-11D.

6-21A Classification.

The usual covenants for title are (1) that the grantor will warrant and defend, (2) that the grantee shall quietly enjoy, (3) that the grantor is lawfully seized and has good right to convey, and (4) that the land is free from encumbrances.

Further research: O Jur 3d, Deeds § 135.

6-21B Running with the Land.

See also Section 6-12 and the particular covenants.

LAW IN GENERAL

A covenant of warranty runs with the land until breached; that is, suit may be maintained against the covenantor by the owner of the land at the time of the breach. After breach of a covenant the right is a cause of action and does not pass by deed nor by descent. A release of a covenant is not binding on a subsequent owner without notice. Am Law of Prop § 12.131; CJS, Covenants § 74; Tiffany § 1022.

6-21C Breaches.

See also 6-13F.
Breaches not during ownership, see also 6-12G.

To sustain an action on the warranty, it is not necessary to give notice to the warrantor of the commencement of the action upon which the eviction was had. King v. Kerr, 5 Ohio 155 (1831).

An action for the breach of the covenant of warranty in a deed cannot be sustained until there has been an eviction or something equivalent. Johnson v. Nyce, 17 Ohio 66 (1848).

If the right to projection of eaves over adjoining owner did not belong to grantor, the projection not being within the description of the premises contained in the deed, the same did not pass, and hence he did not covenant to warrant and defend it. Meek v. Breckenridge, 29 OS 642 (1876).

Upon suit being brought upon a paramount claim against one who is entitled to the benefit of any of the covenants for title, he can, by giving proper notice of the action to the party bound by the covenants, and requiring him to defend it, relieve himself of the burden of being obliged afterwards, in an action on the covenants against the covenantor so notified, to prove the validity of the title of the adverse claimant. Weyer v. Sager, 21 CC 710, 12 CD 193 (1901).

Further research: O Jur 3d, Deeds §§ 148, 155.

LAW IN GENERAL

Covenants are not breached by an interest previously in the grantee. The covenantee is not obliged to purchase an outstanding claim; in order to recover where he does so, it is necessary that the claim be valid and be actually existing, that is, not an inchoate interest. Am Jur 2d, Covenants, etc. § 45; Am Law of Prop § 12.131; CJS, Covenants § 87; Tiffany § 1014.

6-21D Implied Covenants; Merger of Contract for Sale.

Statutory covenants, see 8-11D.

LAW IN GENERAL

Covenants for title are not implied in a conveyance unless by statute. The obligation under the covenant for title which is implied in a contract for sale is discharged by acceptance of a deed without covenants. Am Law of Prop § 12.124.

6-21E After-acquired Title.

See Section 8-34.

Covenants for title commonly operate to transfer an after-acquired title by estoppel.

6-21F Knowledge of Grantee.

The obligations of covenants of warranty cannot depend on the knowledge or want of knowledge of the parties to the covenant. Lloyd v. Quimby, 5 OS 262, 265 (1855).

Parol evidence is not admissible to show an understanding of the parties that known encumbrances were excluded from the operation of the covenant against encumbrances. Long v. Moler, 5 OS 272 (1855).

A promise to assume a lien is in effect a discharge of the grantor from liability on the covenant of warranty so far as said lien is concerned. McKenzie v. Buchamann, 5 App 270, 25 CC(NS) 529, 27 CD 303 (1916).

LAW IN GENERAL

Knowledge on the part of the covenantee of an encumbrance or defect in title will not of itself prevent enforcement of the covenant. CJS, Covenants § 38.

SECTION 6-22: COVENANTS OF WARRANTY AND FOR QUIET ENJOYMENT

6-22A Definition; Running with the Land.

Statutory forms, see 8-11D.

The holder of a covenant of warranty, at the time of eviction, may maintain a separate action against every intermediate warrantor. King v. Kerr, 5 Ohio 155 (1831).

Covenant of warranty, until eviction, attends the land and passes to heir or assignee. King v. Kerr, 5 Ohio 155 (1831).

A covenant of warranty in a deed binds the grantor to make compensation when the grantee is damaged by the lawful claims of third persons. It has practically the same effect as the covenant for quiet enjoyment but does not always include a covenant against encumbrances. Peoples' Savings Bank v. Parisette, 68 OS 450, 67 NE 896, 1 OLR 88, 48 WLB 536, 667 (1903).

Further research: O Jur 3d, Deeds § 138.

LAW IN GENERAL

By a covenant of warranty the grantor covenants to warrant and defend the premises against all lawful claims of third persons. It operates to give the grantee a right to compensation when his possession is disturbed by a valid claim existing at the date of the conveyance. A covenant for quiet enjoyment is to the same practical effect. These covenants run with the land; they pass on a transfer of the land notwithstanding that subsequent conveyances do not contain covenants. Am Jur 2d, Covenants, etc. § 50; Am Law of Prop § 12.129; Powell § 908; Tiffany § 1010.

6-22B Limited or Special Warranty.

Text on statutory form, see 8-11D.

A covenant of warranty is special or limited when it is restricted to operate against certain claims only, usually against the right of persons claiming under the grantor.

6-22C Breaches Generally.

See also Section 6-13 and 6-21C.

LAW IN GENERAL

The covenant is not breached unless there is an eviction from all or part of the premises under a lawful claim. The eviction may be constructive, not actual, as when the covenantee buys a superior title instead of giving up possession. He is entitled to recover on the covenant if the adverse claim is valid and if it has been asserted to his damage. An eviction may consist of the payment of a mortgage or other lien when the payment is necessary to prevent actual eviction. Inability to obtain possession is equivalent to an eviction if the adverse occupancy is under a rightful and paramount title. Easements are a breach of the covenant when the grantee is not charged with notice. Some courts hold servitudes to be a breach notwithstanding they are visible or apparent. Dower consummate, but not dower inchoate, is within the covenant. Am Jur 2d, Covenants, etc. § 54; CJS, Covenants §§ 45, 66, 108; Tiffany § 1011.

SECTION 6-23: COVENANTS FOR SEISIN AND OF RIGHT TO CONVEY

6-23A Nature of the Covenants.

A covenant of seisin is an assurance to the purchaser that the grantor has the very estate in quantity and quality which he purports to convey. A covenant of right to convey is practically equivalent. The covenantee does not have a right of action under a covenant of seisin until eviction if the covenantor had the actual possession, though not the legal title, and puts him in possession. Wetzell v. Richcreek, 53 OS 62, 40 NE 1004, 33 WLB 271, 319 (1895).

Further research: O Jur 3d, Deeds § 150; Am Law of Prop § 12.127; CJS, Covenants §§ 40, 63; Powell § 905; Tiffany § 1000.

6-23B Breaches Generally.

See also Section 6-13 and 6-21C.

When the covenantor is in possession claiming title, a covenant of seisin is a real covenant running with the land. Backus v. McCoy, 3 Ohio 211 (1827).

In an action to recover damages for a breach of a covenant of seisin and of good right to convey, the measure of damages is the consideration, with interest from the time of the conveyance. Conklin v. Hancock, 67 OS 455, 66 NE 518, 48 WLB 133, 275 (1902).

Where the covenantor of seisin was not in possession at the time of conveyance, there was an immediate eviction and the covenant did not run with the land. Action must be commenced within fifteen years. Baughman v. Hower, 56 App 162, 10 NE2d 176, 9 OO 98, 24 Abs 371 (1937).

Further research: CJS, Covenants § 96.

SECTION 6-24: COVENANT AGAINST ENCUMBRANCES

6-24A Definition; Running with the Land.

A covenant against encumbrances is a covenant running with the land until the encumbrances are removed. Foote v. Burnet, 10 Ohio 317, 333 (1840).

Encumbrance, which is a broader term than lien, is any right or interest in land subsisting in another than owner, to diminution of value of estate, though consistent with conveyance of fee. Condorodis v. Kling, 33 App 452, 169 NE 836 (1928).

Each subsequent covenantor under covenant against encumbrances is liable to all subsequent covenantees and on paying damages will have claim for indemnity against prior covenantor. Lyons v. Chapman, 40 App 1, 178 NE 24, 11 Abs 192 (1931).

Further research: O Jur 3d, Deeds § 157; Am Law of Prop § 12.128; CJS, Covenants §§ 42, 65; Powell § 907; Tiffany § 1002.

6-24B   Breaches Generally.

Taxes and assessments are within the scope of a covenant against encumbrances where the deed is executed subsequent to the time the lien attached, as fixed by statute. Long v. Moler, 5 OS 272 (1855); Craig v. Heis, 30 OS 550, 2 WLB 4 (1876).

In an action on a covenant against encumbrances, it is not necessary to aver or prove an eviction. Stambaugh v. Smith, 23 OS 584 (1873). A covenant against encumbrances is not broken unless there is at the time of the conveyance a valid, legal and subsisting lien. Price v. Foster, 36 App 526, 173 NE 618, 5 Abs 293 (1927); Rabel v. Downs, 23 App 352, 155 NE 403, 5 Abs 36 (1926).

A gas pipeline is a breach of the covenant against encumbrances although grantee had knowledge of it, it was visible, and deduction was made from the purchase price. Kunkle v. Beck, 1 App 70, 18 CC(NS) 565, 26 CD 418 (1913).

Grantor covenanting that title is unencumbered, held liable in damages to grantee for breach of covenant by existence of easement over land. Fassnacht v. Bessinger, 35 App 509, 172 NE 636, 8 Abs 202 (1930).

An inchoate right of dower is within the operation of the ordinary covenant against encumbrances. Deibel v. Kinnear, 17 Abs 684 (App. 1934).

A covenant against encumbrances is breached as soon as made if an encumbrance in fact exists. In an action based on such a breach, only nominal damages can be recovered unless the covenantee has removed the encumbrance, had his possession disturbed, or had his use or enjoyment of the land interfered with by reason of the encumbrance. Stockman v. Yanesh, 68 OS2d 63, 428 NE2d 417, 22 OO3d 265 (1981), follows and approves Stambaugh v. Smith, 23 OS 584 (1873).

Further research: O Jur 3d, Deeds § 156; O Jur 3d, Buildings, Zoning and Land Controls § 53.

LAW IN GENERAL

This covenant is broken, if at all, at the time it is made. Only nominal damages are recoverable before eviction. Liens, easements, burdensome covenants or restrictions, dower, and leases are usually within the covenant. Some courts hold that easements are not a breach if their existence was known to the grantee. Knowledge of the grantee, in itself, is usually not a defense but notice may be sufficient basis for defense, as where he agrees to assume a mortgage or accepts an existing lease. Parol evidence is sometimes held inadmissible, except in reformation, to show an understanding that no encumbrances were excepted from the operation of the covenant. Am Jur 2d, Covenants, etc. § 83; CJS, Covenants § 98; Tiffany § 1003.

DIVISION 6-3: RESTRICTIONS AS TO USE

SECTION 6-31: GENERALLY; CREATION AND CONSTRUCTION

6-31A Validity.

See also Section 6-35.

In order that restrictive agreements in a deed may be declared void as against public policy, the same must violate some statute, or be contrary to judicial decision, or be against public health, morals, safety or welfare, or in some form be injurious to the public good. Dixon v. Van Sweringen Co., 121 OS 56, 166 NE 887, 7 Abs 351, 29 OLR 280 (1929).

A restriction requiring future homes to be comparable with other structures on lots in the immediate vicinity is void as being vague and indefinite. Hollyhock Farms, Inc. v. Schoenlaub, 167 NE2d 128, 11 OO2d 317, 83 Abs 406 (C.P. 1959).

Further research: O Jur 3d, Buildings, Zoning and Land Controls § 60.

6-31B Statute of Frauds.

LAW IN GENERAL

Covenants are subject to the statute of frauds, except that covenants in a deed poll are binding on the grantee without being signed by him. Oral promises may be enforceable under the doctrines of estoppel or part performance. Am Jur 2d, Covenants, etc. § 172; Am Law of Prop § 9.25; 5 ALR2d 1316; Restatement, Property § 522; Tiffany § 860.

6-31C Form of Creation.

Constructional preferences, see also Section 11-42.

Contract for restrictions is not entitled to record in deed records and record is not constructive notice. Query whether it is entitled to record in mortgage record. Stanton v. Schmidt, 45 App 203, 186 NE 851, 11 Abs 281, 39 OLR 52 (1931). Should be recorded in mortgage record. 1934 OAG 2633.

Restrictions can be enforced in equity though not in the form of covenants nor, technically speaking, of covenants running with the land of the defendant, where he has actual or constructive notice of the restrictions. Arthur v. Bender, 90 App 187, 101 NE2d 140, 47 OO 205, 60 Abs 261 (1951).

A grantee is deemed to have notice of restrictions contained in a recorded declaration where the conveyance is "subject to restrictions of record" and there is substantially uniform compliance with such restrictions. Carranor Woods Property Owners' Ass'n v. Driscoll, 106 App 95, 153 NE2d 681, 6 OO2d 361 (1957).

In order to establish the existence of a general plan or scheme in a subdivision, it is not necessary that identical restrictions be found in every deed, so long as the general plan or scheme is apparent and the purchaser has actual or constructive notice. Bailey Development Corp. v. MacKinnon-Parker, Inc., 60 App2d 307, 397 NE2d 405, 14 OO3d 277 (1977).

Constructive notice of use restrictions on an allotment may be given, without inserting them in each deed, by setting them forth on the recorded plat, or by a conveyance to a straw man and including the restrictions in the deed from the straw man back to the allotter.

LAW IN GENERAL

Although normally created by a technical covenant, restrictions as to use of property may also be imposed by reservation in a deed or by a condition annexed to the grant. Even when apt words of condition or reservation are used, the courts tend to favor construction and operation as covenants. CJS, Deeds § 162.

The fact that the conveyance or the warranty is made "subject to" restrictions set forth in a certain instrument referred to will not subject the conveyed lands to restrictions which do not otherwise apply to such lands. 84 ALR2d 780.

6-31D Rule of Interpretation.

A restrictive covenant that no dwelling shall be erected less than twenty-four feet from street line, etc., does not apply to a business block. Kiley v. Hall, 96 OS 374, 117 NE 359, 15 OLR 175, 62 WLB 247 (1917).

Where a doubt exists as to the meaning of the language used in a restrictive covenant, such doubt will be resolved against the restriction and in favor of the free use of the real estate. Hitz v. Flower, 104 OS 47, 135 NE 450, 19 OLR 550 (1922); Lebo v. Fitton, 71 App 192, 41 NE2d 402, 26 OO 13, 35 Abs 479 (1942); Exchange Realty Co. v. Bird, 16 Abs 391 (App. 1933).

Circumstances may justify a court of equity in finding that the parties did not intend a forfeiture, even though apt words are used. Second Church of Christ, Scientist v. Le Prevost, 67 App 101, 35 NE2d 1015, 21 OO 122 (1941).

Further research: O Jur 3d, Buildings, Zoning and Land Controls § 68.

LAW IN GENERAL

The circumstances of the transaction will be considered in construing a covenant. The primary rule in construction of restrictions is to ascertain the intention, with the further principle that they are strictly construed and all doubts resolved in favor of the free use of the property. By the weight of authority, restrictions as to use will be treated as equitable servitudes in the nature of incorporeal property interests in the burdened land rather than as contracts. Under this theory, an agreement runs with the land without privity of estate under a conveyance. Am Jur 2d, Covenants, etc. § 185; Am Law of Prop §§ 9.24, 9.26; CJS, Deeds § 163; Restatement, Property § 526.

SECTION 6-32: PARTICULAR APPLICATIONS

6-32A Plats.

Where plat is made of land with restrictions, showing restrictions to be for the benefit of all land, and plat is recorded, restrictive rights and liabilities pass to successors in title of original landowners. Solar v. Ruehlman, 33 App 224, 168 NE 861 (1929).

LAW IN GENERAL

The plat and the deed must be construed together to ascertain the restrictions imposed. Covenants on a plat do not create any rights until a lot has been sold with reference thereto. The plat provisions are usually constructive notice. Merely marking restrictions on a plat, without reference to them in the plat acknowledgment or in a deed, does not necessarily make them effective by implication. Am Jur 2d, Covenants, etc. § 179.

6-32B Racial Restrictions; Discrimination.

R.C. 4112.02 prohibits discrimination in selling, leasing, financing, or otherwise denying commercial housing, or in loaning money for a personal residence, because of race, color, religion, sex, ancestry, handicap, age, or national origin; preference may be given by any religious, denominational, private, or fraternal organization to its members. (As eff. 9-28-87.) Proceedings before the Ohio civil rights commission and judicial review are provided.

Restrictive covenants based on race or color do not violate any rights guaranteed by the Fourteenth Amendment so long as there has been no action by a state. Action of a state court in enforcement of restrictive covenants, having for their purpose exclusion of persons of designated race or color from ownership or occupancy of real property, constitutes an act of the state within the Fourteenth Amendment. In granting judicial enforcement of such covenants, the state denies purchasers equal protection of the laws. Shelley v. Kraemer, 334 US 1, 92 L Ed 1161, 68 Sup Ct 836, 3 ALR2d 441 (1948).

A state court's award of damages against a co-covenantor for breach of a covenant restricting the use and occupancy of real property to persons of the Caucasian race is invalid as a state action prohibited by the Fourteenth Amendment. Barrows v. Jackson, 346 US 249, 97 L Ed 1586, 73 Sup Ct 1031 (1953).

When a person is denied his right to rent property solely on the grounds of his race, a cause of action exists by reason of the provisions of 42 U.S.C. 1982, which bar all racial discriminations. Bush v. Kaim, 17 Misc 259, 44 OO2d 329 (U.S. Dist. Ct. 1969).

A person who files a frivolous suit alleging racial discrimination may be liable for attorney's fees of defendant. Smith v. Smythe-Cramer Co., 6 OBR 279 (1983).

6-32C Building Lines.

A porch built upon a brick foundation, roofed and permanently attached to the whole width of the front of the house, is an integral part of the building within the meaning of the building restriction in a deed providing that all buildings shall be erected not less than a certain distance back from the line of the street. Haas v. Strauss, 23 CC(NS) 547, 34 CD 377 (1912).

6-32D Fences.

LAW IN GENERAL

Fences, or hedges or walls similar thereto, have been held to be forbidden or regulated by restrictive covenants not expressly referring to them. Fences may be prohibited by a particular restriction against a building or structure, while a wall may not be included in the purpose of a restriction against fences. 23 ALR2d 937.

6-32E Residential Purposes.

A clause in a conveyance restricting the use of the property conveyed "for residence purposes only" does not prohibit the erection of a double or two-family house on the premises. Hunt v. Held, 90 OS 280, 107 NE 765, 12 OLR 78, 59 WLB 244 (1914); Thomas v. Harris, 13 O Supp 32, 27 OO 229 (C.P. 1943). "No more than one residence building," etc., held not to prevent the erection of a four-suite apartment house. Arnoff v. Williams, 94 OS 145, 113 NE 661, 14 OLR 132, 61 WLB 147 (1916). Restriction reading "not more than one residence or building" held to prevent erection of such apartment. Freeburg v. Backs, 58 App 551, 16 NE2d 959, 12 OO 327, 27 Abs 387 (1938).

The words "one house only on each lot" have acquired, by common understanding long observed, a special significance in the particular vicinity. The erection of an apartment may be enjoined. Arnoff v. Chase, 101 OS 331, 128 NE 319, 18 OLR 109, 65 WLB 274 (1920).

The words "not more than one dwelling shall be erected on said lot" do not prevent the erection of a building for more than one family. Frederick v. Hay, 104 OS 292, 135 NE 535, 19 OLR 712, 738 (1922).

The owners of a lot in a subdivision, which lot is restricted to use "for residence purposes only," may use such lot as a means of ingress to and egress from adjoining land that they own outside the subdivision if they impose upon such outside land the same restrictions that are applicable to lots within the subdivision. Bove v. Giebel, 169 OS 325, 159 NE2d 425, 8 OO2d 341 (1959).

A provision in a deed that "no more than one residence shall be built on each lot" clearly constitutes a prohibition of the erection thereon of a building containing four apartments. Dillon v. Gaker, 6 OO 524, 22 Abs 219 (C.P. 1936).

Where the use of all of the lots in an addition to a city is limited to "residence purposes only," a room of a residence on such a lot may be used for the casual transaction of some classes of business, or the limited following of some professional pursuits including cosmetology; provided the operation does not result in appreciable damage to other owners, creates no inconvenience or annoyance to other residents, is conducted in a residence where no feature of the construction could have been prohibited by invoking the restriction, and where no alterations have been made which would destroy its character or appearance as a residence, and does not involve the employment of other operators. Swineford v. Nichols, 177 NE2d 304, 16 OO2d 432, 87 Abs 493 (C.P. 1961).

Religious organizations owning land in a subdivision subject to restrictive covenants purporting to prohibit construction of houses of worship thereon are entitled to a declaratory judgment that such covenants are not enforceable so as to prevent such construction. West Hill Baptist Church v. Abbate, 24 Misc 66, 261 NE2d 196, 53 OO2d 107 (C.P. 1969).

Restrictive covenants "that not more than one residence shall be built upon any of said tracts" and "that the said premises shall be used for residence purposes only" do not prohibit the construction of a multiple-family dwelling or residence. Houk v. Ross, 34 OS2d 77, 296 NE2d 266, 63 OO2d 119 (1973).

A restriction for use as a private residence is not violated by use as a residential care facility for six mentally retarded adults unrelated by consanguinity. Beres v. Hope Homes, Inc., 6 App3d 71, 6 OBR 539 (1982).

Further research: O Jur 3d, Buildings, Zoning and Land Controls § 75.

LAW IN GENERAL

The general view is that incidental use of a dwelling for business or professional use does not necessarily violate a restriction to residential use, but that violation depends upon the extent or manner of such incidental use. 21 ALR3d 641.

6-32F   Consent to Construction.

Injunction to compel approval of building plans was denied as plaintiffs had an adequate remedy at law to determine whether the building they proposed to erect could be built upon their lots and comply with the restrictions. Meyer v. Reed, 89 App 527, 101 NE2d 168, 46 OO 303, 60 Abs 207 (1950).

A requirement that plans for the construction of a house be submitted and approved is so indefinite as to be unenforceable in a court of equity. Kline v. Colbert, 91 NE2d 299, 41 OO 172, 56 Abs 295 (C.P. 1949).

Such a covenant must be used in connection with some general plan or the covenant must regulate the scope of the approval. Exchange Realty Co. v. Bird, 16 Abs 391 (App. 1933); Fairfax Community Ass'n v. Boughton, 127 NE2d 641, 70 Abs 178 (C.P. 1955).

In West Hill Colony, Inc. v. Sauerwein, 138 NE2d 403, 78 Abs 340 (App. 1956) the general development plan was sufficiently definite and reasonable to make enforceable a deed provision for approval by the grantor of construction plans. 40 ALR3d 878.

Further research: 40 ALR3d 864.

6-32G Specified Business.

LAW IN GENERAL

A covenant that a certain business shall not be conducted on the premises is generally enforceable in equity if limited to a reasonable time. Am Law of Prop § 9.28.

6-32H Other Applications.

The words "temporary structure" in deed restrictions include a house trailer or mobile home. The controlling factor is the intention of the parties at the time the restrictions originate. McBride v. Behrman, 28 Misc 47, 272 NE2d 181, 57 OO2d 77 (C.P. 1971).

LAW IN GENERAL

A garage attached to a dwelling is usually considered not to be a violation of a restriction against outbuildings. 7 ALR2d 593.

There is a strong tendency of the courts to construe the term "building," as used in restrictive covenants, to give effect to the manifest intent and purposes of the parties, and they may extend the term to cover some structures not within the strict definition of the word. 18 ALR3d 850.

SECTION 6-33: RUNNING OF BURDENS; OBLIGATIONS OF PURCHASER

6-33A Subsequent Owners.

A lot owner cannot enforce restrictions contained in the deed of another lot owner where it does not appear that the latter purchased his lot with notice of a general plan for the improvement of the lots in the allotment, or with notice that such restrictions were inserted in his deed for the benefit of the owners of the other lots in the allotment. Kiley v. Hall, 96 OS 374, 117 NE 359, 15 OLR 175, 245, 62 WLB 247 (1917); Snow v. Socony Vacuum Oil Co., 69 NE2d 200, 46 Abs 317 (App. 1946).

Building restrictions will not be enforced in a suit by owners of restricted lots against the purchaser of lots without restrictions, notwithstanding the fact that in the deeds to eleven lots out of sixty-six in the allotment, the original owners of the allotment and the purchasers covenanted that in the conveyance of other lots in the allotment the deeds shall contain like restrictions. Edwards v. Ohio State Students' Trailer Park Co-op., 84 App 518, 88 NE2d 187, 40 OO 13 (1949).

The failure to include the restriction for three out of 287 lots cannot be said to destroy the general plan of the subdivision. Blum v. Hodapp, 87 App 45, 86 NE2d 807, 42 OO 282, 55 Abs 203 (1949).

A covenant in a lease restricting the use of lessor's adjoining property is a personal covenant rather than one running with the land, and as such is enforceable in equity against a lessee of the adjoining property if he has actual notice of the covenant. Gillen-Crow Pharmacies, Inc. v. Mandzak, 8 Misc 47, 220 NE2d 852, 37 OO2d 60 (C.P. 1964).

Further research: O Jur 3d, Buildings, Zoning and Land Controls § 81.

LAW IN GENERAL

Restrictions run with the land so as to bind subsequent owners, provided (a) they were so intended by the original parties, (b) they were binding on the original covenantor, (c) as to a bona fide purchaser, they are enforceable under the recording act, (d) they are created in connection with a transfer of an interest in the burdened or the benefited land, or in connection with the modification of an easement, and (e) they will presently benefit the land of either of the parties and not unreasonably burden the land of the other party. A few cases hold that, contrary to the rule, the burden of a covenant will run with the land even though the benefit is in gross, that is to say, a subsequent owner is bound although no land of the covenantee is injured by the violation. A purchaser with notice of the covenants is bound. The record of an agreement not entitled to record is not constructive notice. No owner is liable for the defaults of his predecessor or successor in interest unless such intention is shown. The owner of a part of the premises may, in particular cases, be liable for damages arising from any default. When a burdened parcel is resubdivided, the original restrictions are not enforceable between owners of parts of such parcel unless the original subdivision was made according to a uniform scheme. Am Jur 2d, Covenants, etc. § 304; Am Law of Prop § 9.31; CJS, Deeds § 167; Restatement, Property § 530; Tiffany § 862.

6-33B Technical Requirements; Implied Reciprocal Covenants.

Chain of title, see 1-31C.

The doctrine of reciprocal negative easement does not obtain in Ohio, that is, a covenant to restrict the remaining land of the common owner is not implied. Where restrictions are not mentioned in the chain of title, the restrictions contained in deeds of adjacent property cannot be enforced against land not described in such deeds unless there exists a general plan of which the grantee had notice. King v. James, 88 App 213, 97 NE2d 235, 44 OO 352, 58 Abs 417 (1950).

LAW IN GENERAL

When the covenants as to use do not technically run with the land, they may be enforced as an equitable interest except as they are invalid under the recording acts or invalid as to bona fide purchasers. Restrictions not in the chain of title have been enforced in several cases as implied reciprocal servitudes when the common grantor agreed to restrict his remaining lots, or when the earlier conveyances from the common grantor gave evidence of a general plan of which the subsequent grantee had notice; this implied restriction of the grantor's remaining land has been treated as in the nature of a negative easement. Am Law of Prop § 9.33; 144 ALR 916; Restatement, Property § 539; Tiffany §§ 858, 861.

6-33C Covenant for a Lien.

Covenants enforceable as liens, see 6-12D.

LAW IN GENERAL

Subsequent owners of the land with notice of a covenant for a lien hold the land subject to the lien, as under a party wall agreement. Restatement, Property § 540.

SECTION 6-34: RUNNING OF BENEFITS; ENFORCEMENT BY PURCHASER

6-34A Enforcement by Subsequent Owners.

The variances in the restrictions are so substantial and numerous that uniformity is not sufficient to create rights in favor of the owners of the several lots which may be enforced in equity. Shubert v. Eastman Realty Co., 1 CC(NS) 585, 15 CD 336 (1903).

One purchaser cannot enforce restrictions against another purchaser unless the latter has notice of a general plan and purchases his lot with reference thereto. Lopartkovich v. Rieger, 66 App 332, 33 NE2d 1014, 20 OO 167, 34 Abs 68 (1940).

One or more lot owners cannot enforce observance of building restrictions against another lot owner in the same allotment unless it appears that the restrictive covenants were designed and adopted for the protection of all lot owners pursuant to a uniform plan, or unless such covenants were inserted in the deed for the benefit of the lot owner seeking injunctive relief. Grant v. Hickok Oil Co., 84 App 509, 87 NE2d 708, 40 OO 9 (1948).

A restrictive covenant in a deed to the original purchaser of a lot, made expressly for the benefit of the grantor, cannot be enforced by a subsequent purchaser of part of the lot against a purchaser of another part. Rehard v. Rini, 128 NE2d 451, 72 Abs 115 (App. 1955).

The owners of unplatted land, who are intended beneficiaries of restrictive covenants, may maintain an action for the enforcement of such restrictions. Berger v. Van Sweringen Co., 6 OS2d 100, 216 NE2d 54, 35 OO2d 127 (1966).

Further research: O Jur 3d, Buildings, Zoning and Land Controls §§ 84, 85.

LAW IN GENERAL

The benefits of restrictions run with the land and may be enforced by subsequent owners of the benefited land provided (a) such owners are initial beneficiaries of the covenants, as earlier purchasers under a general plan of development, (b) such owners are intended beneficiaries of the original covenant, (c) a conveyance from a prior beneficiary does not show an intention to terminate the right, and (d) the benefits were enforceable by the original parties. Am Jur 2d, Covenants, etc. § 301; Am Law of Prop § 9.27; CJS, Deeds § 167; Restatement, Property § 541; Tiffany § 865.

The benefit of a restrictive covenant may generally be enforced by the owner of a part of the benefited land, or be assigned. An intention that restrictions are enforceable by the grantor alone may be shown. Restatement, Property § 551.

6-34B Notice.

See also 6-31C.

Notice of restrictions on lots purchased does not charge the purchaser with knowledge that like restrictions are contained in deeds to purchasers of other lots on the plat but equity will grant injunctive relief where defendant purchased with actual notice of a general building plan. Smith v. Volk, 85 App 347, 86 NE2d 30, 40 OO 231, 53 Abs 432 (1948).

When restrictions according to a general plan are inserted in each deed of an allotment, other lot owners cannot enforce the restrictions against a certain purchaser unless the restrictions set forth such right to enforce, or unless such purchaser has notice of the general plan at the time he purchases. Blum v. Hodapp, 87 App 45, 86 NE2d 807, 42 OO 282, 55 Abs 203 (1949).

Common knowledge of a community plan or purpose with a wide scope is not sufficient to put an owner on notice. Copelin v. Morris, 101 NE2d 18, 45 OO 290, 63 Abs 193 (C.P. 1951).

LAW IN GENERAL

A purchaser of one lot may enforce restrictions against a purchaser of another lot, provided he can show that such other purchaser had actual or constructive notice of a general plan or had notice that the restrictions were intended so to operate. 4 ALR2d 1364; Tiffany § 867.

SECTION 6-35: REMEDIES; MODIFICATION; EXTINGUISHMENT

6-35A Matters Terminating Right to Enforcement.

Extinguishment by Marketable Title Act, see 1-44A.

Mere acquiescence in trivial breaches of the restrictions, which are not such as to defeat the object of the general scheme substantially or indicate an intention to abandon it, will not defeat the owner's right to enforce such restrictions. Hills v. Graves, 26 App 1, 159 NE 482, 5 Abs 744 (1927); McGuire v. Caskey, 62 OS 419, 57 NE 53, 43 WLB 281 (1900).

Where covenant or restriction is still of substantial value to the dominant lot notwithstanding the changed condition of the neighborhood, a court of equity will restrain its violation. Brown v. Huber, 80 OS 183, 88 NE 322, 6 OLR 691, 54 WLB 129 (1909).

Restrictions cannot apply to the state or any of its agencies vested with the right of eminent domain in the use of lots for public purposes. Doan v. Cleveland Short Line Ry., 92 OS 461, 112 NE 505, 13 OLR 173, 60 WLB 305, 61 WLB 43 (1915).

Plaintiff is not estopped from enforcing restriction because of breaches in another section where it did not appear that such breaches were detrimental to property owners of this particular section. Guarantee Title & Trust Co. v. Offenbacher, 6 Abs 246 (App. 1927); Whitmore v. Stern, 25 App 344, 158 NE 203, 5 Abs 393 (1927).

Restrictions are ineffective where changed conditions of neighborhood substantially destroyed value of restrictions. Hayslett v. Shell Petroleum Corp., 38 App 164, 175 NE 888, 8 Abs 649, 33 OLR 331 (1930).

Where the character of the neighborhood has so changed as to render the restriction inapplicable according to its true intent and spirit, equity will not interpose by injunction, but will leave the party aggrieved to his remedy at law. Olberding v. Smith, 34 NE2d 296, 34 Abs 84 (App. 1934).

The waiver of the restriction with respect to the rear lot line fences and the failure to object to the erection of a few side line fences do not operate as a waiver to the erection of a side line fence. The test is whether there is still a substantial value in the restriction, which is to be protected. Romig v. Modest, 102 App 225, 142 NE2d 555, 2 OO2d 242 (1956).

Further research: O Jur 3d, Buildings, Zoning and Land Controls § 92.

LAW IN GENERAL

Restrictive covenants may be terminated (a) by impossibility of fulfillment of the purpose, for example, such as caused by change in the neighborhood, (b) by merger, (c) by release, (d) by mutual agreement, (e) by abandonment, (f) by estoppel, for example, such as may arise from violation or acquiescence in violation, (g) by appropriation under eminent domain, (h) by terms or provisions of their creation, or (i) expiration of a reasonable time when no duration is specified. Am Jur 2d, Covenants, etc. § 270; Am Law of Prop § 9.37; CJS, Deeds § 168; Powell § 682; Restatement, Property § 554; Tiffany § 870.

6-35B Necessity of Present Interest.

A court of equity will not intervene with injunctive power to limit the full use of property where a restrictive covenant becomes a purely personal one with the grantor, no general plan of restriction exists, the grantor has conveyed all his interest in the tract affected, and no benefit is shown accruing to him by the enforcement of the restriction. Taylor v. Summit Post No. 19,

American Legion, 60 App 201, 20 NE2d 267, 13 OO 472, 27 Abs 582 (1938); Jones v. Van Deboe Hager Co., 29 Abs 385 (App. 1939). Contra: Great Northern Bldg. & Loan Co. v. Holik, 15 O Supp 34, 33 OO 56 (C.P. 1944).

The authorities differ on the question whether a restriction can be enforced by the grantor if he should at the time not own adjacent property to be benefited thereby. This defense seems more like an excuse for violating a covenant than a sound reason for setting aside such an obligation. There is no reason why this covenant should not be enforced. Huber v. Guglielmi, 29 App 290, 163 NE 571 (1928).

A former owner of real property cannot maintain an action to enforce a restrictive covenant contained in the deeds transferring such property to and from him, where he has no present interest affected by noncompliance with the restriction. Rupel v. General Motors Corp., 120 App 152, 201 NE2d 355, 28 OO2d 388 (1963).

Further research: O Jur 3d, Buildings, Zoning and Land Controls § 86.

LAW IN GENERAL

According to the prevailing rule, a person loses his right to enforce the restrictions when he no longer has an interest in the benefited land, except when he is legally obliged to see that the covenant is performed. Am Jur 2d, Covenants, etc. § 290; Restatement, Property § 549; Tiffany § 864.

6-35C   Equitable Relief.

Where a declaratory judgment is sought on a restriction in a deed, the decision, if favorable, would determine the right to a mandatory injunction. Dillon v. Gaker, 57 App 90, 12 NE2d 150, 10 OO 130, 25 Abs 282 (1937).

Proof of actual damage is not essential to granting of injunction enforcing restrictive covenants in favor of one lot owner against another lot owner. Arthur v. Bender, 90 App 187, 101 NE2d 140, 47 OO 205, 60 Abs 261 (1951).

LAW IN GENERAL

Equitable relief may be denied when (a) the complainant has been guilty of like violations, (b) the complainant has acquiesced in like violations by another, (c) the complainant has been guilty of laches, (d) disproportionate hardship would be caused, or (e) conditions have so changed that the purpose of the covenants cannot be substantially fulfilled. A mandatory injunction requiring the removal of a structure will usually be refused unless the violation was willful or in bad faith. Damages may be awarded when equitable relief is refused, as when the change in the neighborhood prevents the granting of an injunction. Am Jur 2d, Covenants, etc. §§ 312, 328, 330; Am Law of Prop § 9.38; 4 ALR2d 1111; Restatement, Property § 560.

6-35D   Damages.

So long as he retains any of the lands to be benefited by the covenant, the grantor may enforce the same without proving that a violation of the covenant would result in actual damage to him. Hills v. Graves, 26 App 1, 159 NE 482, 5 Abs 744 (1927).

LAW IN GENERAL

In addition to the ordinary remedy of injunction, a breach of the covenant gives rise to a right of action for damages to the original owner and to a subsequent owner who is a beneficiary of the promise. Am Jur 2d, Covenants, etc. § 317; Restatement, Property § 528.

6-35E   Delay; Laches.

Equity requires diligence in the enforcement of building restrictions. H. F. Realty Co. v. Brown, 16 Abs 424 (App. 1933).

Covenants in deed prohibiting the sale of intoxicating liquors will not be enforced when the grantees or their successors in title have acquiesced in such traffic for a period of years. To obtain relief in a court of equity, the one claiming injury must apply promptly for such relief. Barclay v. Akenhead, 64 App 461, 28 NE2d 952, 18 OO 199 (1940).

Plaintiff was guilty of laches and not entitled to injunction for violation of setback line where he could have determined the violation at least six weeks before taking action. Connelly v. Morris, 102 App 544, 130 NE2d 251, 3 OO2d 84, 72 Abs 350 (1955).

A plaintiff who did not live on the lot which he owned adjacent to the defendant's lot was under no legal obligation to visit his lot to determine if defendant was erecting a building in violation of the setback restrictions in his deed, and plaintiff cannot be charged with laches where he was diligent, as soon as he had knowledge of the violation, in asserting his rights. McGrath v. Kneisley, 142 NE2d 530, 75 Abs 52 (App. 1956).

Standard of Title Examination

(Adopted by Ohio State Bar Association in 1960)

Problem 4.7A:

After what period of time should a breach of building and use conditions which entail a forfeiture of title be disregarded?

Standard 4.7A:

A title should not be considered unmarketable because of a breach of a condition or conditions as to building and use which entail a forfeiture of title if satisfactory proof is furnished that such breach has existed for more than thirty years.

Comment:

Satisfactory proof may be affidavits as to the facts of breach; recorded instruments in the chain of title; certificate of registered surveyor.

Further research: O Jur 3d, Buildings, Zoning and Land Controls § 94.

LAW IN GENERAL

Whether a delay in commencing suit amounts to laches barring plaintiff from obtaining an injunction and relegating him to a recovery of damages, depends upon the equities of the particular case. Some of the factors in the decided cases are: the degree of harm to the defendant; the expiration date of the covenants; and the good faith of the defendant. It has been said that estoppel of the plaintiff must be based on knowledge of the violation or a duty to know of it. 12 ALR2d 394.

6-35F Modification; Release.

Notice of release, see 6-21B and 6-34A.

A change in restrictions to permit construction of a shopping center is not warranted where single-family homes have been erected in reliance upon the restrictions, although the subdivider reserved the right to waive, change or cancel any and all of the restrictions "if, in its judgment, the development or lack of development warrants the same." Berger v. Van Sweringen Co., 200 NE2d 489, 32 OO2d 447, 95 Abs 325 (App. 1964).

Where property owners signed a waiver of compliance with residential restrictions on one lot, there was no waiver as to the other lots in the same subdivision. Kokenge v. Whetstone, 4 O Supp 207, 11 OO 213, 26 Abs 398 (C.P. 1938), affd. 60 App 302, 20 NE2d 965 (1938).

LAW IN GENERAL

Restrictions may be modified or released by action of all persons having a right to enforce them. Am Law of Prop § 9.23.

A reservation to the original property owner of the right to amend or revoke restrictive covenants is usually a personal covenant and enforceable only by the original covenantor and sometimes by his successor. On the other hand, where the owners are entitled under the original instrument to participate in the amendment or revocation, the covenants are termed mutual or reciprocal and the covenants run with the land. 4 ALR3d 570.

6-35G Tax Sales.

R.C. 5721.19 provides that titles acquired through tax foreclosures, upon confirmation of sale, "shall be incontestable in the purchaser and shall be free and clear of all liens and encumbrances, except a federal tax lien notice of which is properly filed *** prior to the date that foreclosure proceedings are instituted *** and the easements and covenants of record running with the land that were created prior to the time the taxes or assessments, for the nonpayment of which the land is sold at foreclosure, became due and payable." (As eff. 3-25-87.)

R.C. 5723.12 contains a similar provision which applies to land sold by the county auditor at a forfeited land sale. Thus, restrictions which were created of record after the tax delinquency arose are extinguished by the sale for delinquent taxes, while restrictions older than the delinquency survive the sale. (As eff. 4-9-81.)

6-35H   Zoning.

Constitutionality of a zoning ordinance and validity of deed restrictions are independent matters and should be decided in two separate proceedings. Deed restrictions have no effect on zoning. Central Motors Corp. v. City of Pepper Pike, 63 App2d 34, 409 NE2d 258, 13 OO3d 347 (1979).

LAW IN GENERAL

Zoning regulations do not affect the enforceability of covenants as to use except when a covenant requires a particular use which becomes unlawful. Both the zoning regulations and the deed restrictions are enforceable unless there is a direct conflict, as where the regulation requires uses for commercial purposes only and the restriction requires uses for residential purposes only. In such a case it has been held that the zoning ordinance was unreasonable and invalid. However, if the ordinance is upheld under such circumstances, the restriction is extinguished. Restatement, Property § 568.

CHAPTER 7: CROPS AND OTHER GROWING THINGS

DIVISION 7-1: IN GENERAL

DIVISION 7-1: IN GENERAL

SECTION 7-11: INTRODUCTION

7-11A   Classification.

Crops and other growing things are considered as (1) permanent natural growths, known as fructus naturales, and (2) annual crops requiring cultivation, known as fructus industriales or emblements.

Further research: Powell § 663; Tiffany § 590.

SECTION 7-12: PERMANENT GROWTHS; TREES

Cotenancy, see Section 5-16.
Trees at boundaries, see Section 3-16.
Waste, see Section 11-19.

7-12A   As Real or Personal Property.

Trees are considered as land and may not be reserved by parol from the operation of the deed. Jones v. Timmons, 21 OS 596 (1871).

Timber not taken off within the time limited, adhered to the land and lapsed into the fee. Clark v. Guest, 54 OS 298, 43 NE 862, 35 WLB 146 (1896).

Further research: O Jur 3d, Logs and Timber § 2.

LAW IN GENERAL

Permanent natural growths, such as trees or perennial bushes and grasses, are regarded as land. Upon the death of the owner, they pass to the heir or devisee. When severed unlawfully, they belong to the owner of the land. Their fruits are generally of the same classification, although the modern tendency is to consider the product as personalty when the production is largely dependent upon annual cultivation. Am Jur 2d, Crops § 4.

7-12B   Severance; Damages.

Contract for sale, see R.C. 1302.03 of Uniform Commercial Code at 13-11G.

A sale of standing timber, whether or not the parties contemplate its immediate removal by the vendee, is a contract concerning an interest in lands, within the meaning of the statute of frauds, and is voidable by either party if not in writing. Crops planted and raised annually are practically withdrawn from the operation of the statute. Hirth v. Graham, 50 OS 57, 63, 33 NE 90, 29 WLB 83, 102 (1893).

If the timber has been cut within the time limited, the grantor's reservation of right to the timber is not lost because of his failure to remove within such time. Walcutt v. Treisch, 82 OS 263, 92 NE 423, 8 OLR 102, 55 WLB 198 (1910).

The measure of damages for injury to a tree is the difference in the value of estate before such injury and value of estate thereafter. Cleveland Elec. Illum. Co. v. Merryweather, 6 Abs 528 (App. 1928).

Further research: O Jur 3d, Logs and Timber §§ 23, 24; Kapcos v. Hammond, 13 App 3d 140, 13 OBR 173 (1982).

LAW IN GENERAL

A sale or mortgage of permanent growths is within the statute of frauds, and must be in writing as required for the transfer of interests in land. A subsequent bona fide purchaser of the land takes title free from the claims of the purchaser of the timber. Am Jur 2d, Crops § 49; 7 ALR2d 517; 18 ALR2d 1150; CJS, Logs and Logging § 9; Tiffany §§ 596, 598.

A deed conveying timber without stipulating the time within which it must be removed is usually construed as requiring removal within a reasonable time, although the intention of the parties controls and such a deed may be construed as a grant in perpetuity. When timber is not removed within the stated time or within the required reasonable time, it is usually held that the purchaser thereof loses all rights in the trees and the right to enter the land. In a majority of such cases, the title to the timber reverts to the current owner of the land. The same rules are applied when standing timber is reserved or excepted from a conveyance of the land. Am Jur 2d, Logs and Timber § 34; Am Law of Prop § 19.15; 164 ALR 423; CJS, Logs and Logging § 19; Tiffany § 597.

A number of cases adhere to the common-law rule that actions to recover for injuries to real property are local, and hold that the venue of actions for damage to standing trees or timber is in the county where they were standing. 65 ALR2d 1268.

Damages for trees wrongfully cut are measured in most of the cases by the difference in the value of the land just prior to and just after the cutting. However, where the gist of the action was for the value of timber trees innocently cut, most courts have held that the proper measure was the value of the timber before the cutting. 69 ALR2d 1335.

7-12C Right to Enter Land.

License coupled with an interest, see also 10-17E.

LAW IN GENERAL

The right to enter the land and cut timber is generally regarded as incidental to the title to the timber. The licensee does not lose his right to timber which has been cut upon revocation of the license. The right is a license unless there is a compliance with the requirements for a conveyance of an interest in land. Am Jur 2d, Logs and Timber § 55; 26 ALR2d 1194; CJS, Logs and Logging § 29.

SECTION 7-13: EMBLEMENTS; ANNUAL CROPS

7-13A As Real or Personal Property.

R.C. 2115.10 provides: "The emblements raised by labor, whether severed or not from the land of the deceased at the time of his death, are assets in the hands of the executor or administrator and shall be included in the inventory required by section 2115.02 of the Revised Code."

"The executor or administrator, or the person to whom he sells such emblements, at all reasonable times may enter upon the lands to cultivate, sever, and gather them." (As eff. 10-1-53.)

Parol evidence is admissible to show a reservation of growing crops when the deed conveys certain land together with the "rents, issues and profits thereof." Crabtree v. Smith, 31 CC (NS) 593, 35 CD 477 (1919).

Emblements, except as between grantor and grantee in a deed making no reservation of crops, are "personal property." Connecticut Mut. Life Ins. Co. v. Shelly Seed Corp., 46 App 548, 189 NE 654, 16 Abs 558, 40 OLR 67 (1933).

Further research: O Jur 3d, Agriculture and Crops § 2; O Jur 3d, Deeds § 186.

LAW IN GENERAL

"Fructus industriales" or emblements are annual crops for which the industry of the cultivator is the predominating factor in production, such as grain and garden vegetables. For most purposes, including the levy of execution and transfer separately from the land, they are treated as personal property. They are considered real property for purposes of venue and jurisdiction in actions for damages to them. Principles of the law of fixtures are applicable in general in the law of crops. Am Jur 2d, Crops § 47; Am Law of Prop § 19.16.

7-13B   Growing Crops; Severance.

Contracts for sale, see R.C. 1302.03 of Uniform Commercial Code at 13-11G.

Crops rightfully severed from the land are always personalty. Growing crops may be realty or personalty. See also 7-13A.

LAW IN GENERAL

Severed emblements are personalty. Whether growing crops are realty or personalty may depend upon the particular facts; a certain crop may be treated as personal property or as real property under different circumstances in the same jurisdiction. The intention of the parties is often the determining factor. Some courts hold that a matured unharvested crop is not a growing crop but is regarded as constructively severed. Am Jur 2d, Crops § 33; CJS, Crops § 1; Powell § 663; Tiffany § 595.

7-13C   Nature of Cultivator's Interest.

Parties are tenants in common in crops produced or being produced by their joint contributions. Second Nat. Bank v. Hyde, 29 App 357, 163 NE 587 (1928).

An agreement between a tenant, who remains in possession, and a cultivator to share the crop does not constitute a subletting, but gives rise to a relationship of employer and employee. A cropping agreement does create the relation of landlord and tenant. Stoner v. Markey, 63 App 459, 27 NE2d 176, 17 OO 197, 31 Abs 351 (1940).

Further research: O Jur 3d, Landlord and Tenant §§ 84, 85.

LAW IN GENERAL

Crops planted and cultivated without a right to do so belong to the owner of the land before severance. However, even a trespasser is entitled to such crops if he also harvests them while still in possession; the measure of damages for the trespass is not the value of the crop. Am Law of Prop § 19.16.

As between landlord and tenant, the right to growing crops is generally in the tenant, although it is frequently held that a tenancy in common exists in the crops. An agreement to farm on shares may create the relationship of landlord and tenant, landowner and cropper, participants in a common venture, or partners, depending upon the construction of the agreement. A cropper's status is in the nature of an employee's; he has no estate in the land and only an equitable interest in the crops. Whether the cultivator is a cropper or a tenant is determined by whether the effect of the agreement is to give him the exclusive right to possession. Am Jur 2d, Crops § 35; Am Law of Prop § 3.6; CJS, Landlord and Tenant § 793; Powell § 261; Tiffany §§ 78, 604.

SECTION 7-14: AFTER TERMINATION OF TENANCY; AWAY-GOING CROPS

7-14A Time of Termination Uncertain.

Life estates, see also 11-63C.

One whose estate may be terminated by an event, the time whereof is uncertain, has the right to reap what he has sown. Noble v. Tyler, 61 OS 432, 438, 56 NE 191, 43 WLB 28, 127 (1900).

Where lease from April to April is silent regarding tenant's right to away-going crops (crops planted but not harvested before the tenancy is to terminate), custom in the vicinity giving tenant right to such crops annexes such right to the lease. Prysi v. Kinsey, 38 App 92, 175 NE 707, 10 Abs 157 (1930); Foster v. Robinson, 6 OS 90 (1856). Custom does give such right to the tenant in some counties but does not do so in most communities of this state.

Upon the death of life tenant, the annual tenant was entitled to cultivate and harvest the growing crops. But the owners of the fee were entitled to possession of the portion of the farm not planted in crops and to the rental. Lifer v. Cotton, 5 Abs 35 (App. 1926).

LAW IN GENERAL

Away-going crops are the emblements which a tenant may cultivate and harvest after the termination of his tenancy. Such rights exist as to crops planted during the tenancy but not harvested before the tenancy is terminated by some event not the act of the tenant, the time of happening of the event being uncertain. The rights do not extend to the fruit of trees nor to other perennial crops. A tenant for life, from period to period, or at will has such rights. In some communities a tenant is entitled, by virtue of the local custom, to away-going crops after termination of the tenancy, even when the tenancy is for a fixed duration. Am Jur 2d, Crops § 23; Am Law of Prop § 19.16; Powell § 66; Tiffany §§ 67, 599.

7-14B Forfeiture; Title Paramount.

A subtenant or sharecropper of a tenant is entitled to hold his interest in the crop on the surrender or forfeiture of lease by the tenant under whom he claims. The principle that he who sows ought to reap is applicable. Stoner v. Markey, 63 App 459, 27 NE2d 176, 17 OO 197, 31 Abs 351 (1940).

LAW IN GENERAL

In most of the cases, growing crops adhere to the land on forfeiture or on termination of the tenancy by act of the tenant. The same result occurs when a third person enters under a title paramount to the landlord's title. The vendee of a land contract is normally entitled to crops severed during his possession. Tiffany § 602.

SECTION 7-15: CONVEYANCE AND ENCUMBRANCE OF CROPS

7-15A Conveyances.

Contracts for sale, see R.C. 1302.03 of Uniform Commercial Code at 13-11G.

If the parties to a deed, either by words or in their behavior, signify their understanding that, as between them, the crop is personalty, the law will so regard it. Baker v. Jordan, 3 OS 438 (1854). See also 7-13A.

Parol evidence may be introduced to show that the growing crop was not intended to be conveyed by the lease. Youmans v. Caldwell, 4 OS 71 (1854).

The interest of a tenant in growing annual crops does not pass by the landlord's conveyance of the realty. First Security Co. v. Huddle, 16 Abs 241 (App. 1934).

LAW IN GENERAL

Growing crops pass with the land, as between grantor and grantee, unless reserved. Between vendor and purchaser of land, the transfer of unmatured crops goes with the right of possession. Am Jur 2d, Crops § 11; CJS, Crops § 6; Tiffany § 593.

7-15B Encumbrances; Judicial Sales.

See also Uniform Commercial Code at 13-12B.
Venue, see 17-11B.

R.C. 1309.15 provides that a security agreement may be secured by after-acquired collateral (including crops grown more than one year in the future). (As eff. 1-1-79.)

R.C. 1309.38 provides that the proper place of filing to perfect a security interest in crops is in the office of the county recorder in the county where the land on which they are growing or to be grown is located. (As eff. 1-1-84.)

R.C. 1309.40(D) provides that, in addition to other required indexing, financing statements covering crops growing or to be grown or timber to be cut shall also be indexed in the real estate mortgage records according to the name of the debtor or, if the financing statement shows the record owner or record lessee to be other than the debtor, then according to the name of the record owner or record lessee given in the statement. (As eff. 1-1-85.) (An examination of the index to real estate mortgagors should be made in the name of a record land contract vendee in addition to record owners and record lessees.) Other statutory provisions on security interests are shown at 13-12B.

R.C. 1917.34, which was repealed effective March 1, 1987, provided that when lands have been let, reserving rent in kind, and the crops are levied on, the interest of the landlord or tenant against whom process was not issued shall not be affected.

Growing crops do not pass with the land upon judicial sale of the latter. Cassilly v. Rhodes, 12 Ohio 88 (1843); Houts v. Showalter, 10 OS 124 (1859).

A growing crop passes by a decree which gives the land to the wife as alimony. Herron v. Herron, 47 OS 544, 25 NE 420, 24 WLB 359, 370 (1890).

Real estate mortgage pledging rents and profits does not entitle mortgagee to lien on crops afterward planted, so long as mortgagor retains possession. Norwood Savings Bank v. Romer, 43 App 224, 183 NE 45, 12 Abs 472, 36 OLR 589 (1932).

Annual crops, from the date of planting, are subject to levy of execution as personal property. First Security Co. v. Huddle, 16 Abs 241 (App. 1934).

A wheat crop planted by the mortgagor in possession prior to confirmation of foreclosure sale, does not pass to a purchaser at the judicial sale. Fourman v. Anderson, 21 Abs 222 (App. 1935).

Further research: O Jur 3d, Agriculture and Crops § 5.

LAW IN GENERAL

A mortgage of the land does not affect the right of the mortgagor in the growing crops. However, his right to dispose of them may be terminated by appointment of a receiver in foreclosure proceedings. It is frequently held that a sale or encumbrance of crops constitutes a constructive severance so that a subsequent foreclosure sale of the land does not affect the prior interest. Am Jur 2d, Crops § 17; Tiffany §§ 1418, 1420.

Crops although not severed, are subject to levy of execution and to the incidental rights of cultivation and removal by the execution purchaser. Tiffany § 594.

CHAPTER 8: DEEDS

DIVISION 8-1: IN GENERAL

SECTION 8-11: INTRODUCTION; FORM AND EXECUTION
- 8-11A   Law of Situs
- 8-11B   Effect of Defects
- 8-11C   The Parts of a Deed
- 8-11D   Statutory Deed Forms

SECTION 8-12: GRANTING CLAUSE; CONSIDERATION; HABENDUM
- 8-12A   Premises; Granting Clause
- 8-12B   Consideration
- 8-12C   Habendum

SECTION 8-13: EXCEPTION AND RESERVATION; DATE; SIGNATURE
- 8-13A   Exception and Reservation Generally
- 8-13B   Reservation or Exception to Third Party
- 8-13C   Date
- 8-13D   Signature

SECTION 8-14: SEAL; WITNESSES
- 8-14A   Seal
- 8-14B   Witnesses

SECTION 8-15: QUITCLAIM DEEDS
- 8-15A   Nature
- 8-15B   As Effective Conveyances
- 8-15C   Bona Fide Purchasers

SECTION 8-16: SURVIVORSHIP DEEDS; "OR"
- 8-16A   Nature
- 8-16B   Form
- 8-16C   "Or"
- 8-16D   Simultaneous Deaths
- 8-16E   Estates by Entireties

SECTION 8-17: ANCIENT DOCUMENTS
- 8-17A   Rule
- 8-17B   Deeds
- 8-17C   Recitals
- 8-17D   Surveys

SECTION 8-18: EXECUTION REQUIREMENTS IN EACH STATE
- 8-18A   Foreign Execution
- 8-18B   Requirements for Foreign Conformity

DIVISION 8-2: ACKNOWLEDGMENT

SECTION 8-21: GENERALLY
- 8-21A   Definition; Statute
- 8-21B   Necessity
- 8-21C   Effect of Defect
- 8-21D   Construction
- 8-21E   Proof by Witnesses
- 8-21F   Certificates of Authority and Conformity

SECTION 8-22: FORM OF CERTIFICATE; MANNER OF TAKING
- 8-22A   Contents of the Certificate

DIVISION 8-3:   CONSTRUCTION AND EFFECT

DIVISION 8-1: IN GENERAL

SECTION 8-11: INTRODUCTION; FORM AND EXECUTION

8-11A Law of Situs.

Foreign conformity, see Section 8-18.
Statute as to name of preparer, see 1-41H.

It is a principle which cannot be controverted, that the transfer of land, whether by deed or by last will and testament, must be regulated by the laws of the country where those lands are situated. Bailey v. Bailey, 8 Ohio 239, 240 (1837).

Capacity to execute a mortgage is governed by the law of the situs and not by the law of the domicile. Sell v. Miller, 11 OS 331 (1860).

Further research: O Jur 3d, Conflict of Laws § 22.

LAW IN GENERAL

The legal effect of a conveyance is governed by the law of the state where the land is situated. This rule extends to the capacity of the parties, to the validity of conveyances, to covenants running with the land, and to the requisite formalities. However, Ohio and many states have statutes validating deeds executed in another state or country in conformity with the laws of such other state or country. Am Jur 2d, Conflict of Laws § 16; Am Law of Prop § 18.27; CJS, Deeds § 11.

8-11B Effect of Defects.

Curative acts, see Section 1-22 and 8-31R.
Ratification and estoppel, see Section 16-69.
Record as notice and evidence, see Section 1-21.
Void or voidable, see 8-31L.

A deed not attested by two witnesses does not operate to pass the legal estate in lands, and it cannot contain a covenant of warranty that works an estoppel against the maker in asserting the legal title remaining in himself. Patterson v. Pease, 5 Ohio 190 (1831).

The deed of the administrator has but the attestation of one witness. The deed, therefore, conveyed no legal title. Miami Exporting Co. v. Halley, 7 Ohio (pt. 1) 11 (1835).

An imperfectly executed deed may operate as a contract of sale from the grantor so as to create an equitable estate in the purchaser, if it be plainly shown that the instrument was intended as a conveyance of the land and was accepted and treated as such by the vendee. Williams v. Sprigg, 6 OS 585 (1856); Barr v. Hatch, 3 Ohio 527 (1828). If made for a valuable consideration, Hout v. Hout, 20 OS 119 (1870).

The attestation of two subscribing witnesses is essential to the conveyance of any legal interest. Langmede v. Weaver, 65 OS 17, 60 NE 992, 45 WLB 377, 46 WLB 40 (1901).

The defectively executed deed passed an equitable right in the property to the grantees, it being shown that it was intended as a conveyance. Hollman v. Smith, 102 NE2d 483, 46 OO 314, 60 Abs 570 (App. 1951).

Standard of Title Examination

(Adopted by Ohio State Bar Association in 1953)

Problem 3.10B:
  Is a conveyance defective because a fiduciary signs and acknowledges as an individual?

Standard 3.10B:
  No, provided the conveyance otherwise clearly shows an intention to convey as fiduciary.

8-11C The Parts of a Deed.

The formal parts of a deed are the premises (the part preceding the habendum), the habendum, the reddendum containing the exception or reservation, the conditions, the covenants, and the conclusion (consisting of the testimonium and the signatures).

Aside from statutory requirements, the only essential components of a deed are grantor, grantee, words of grant, description of the land, and signature of the grantor.

Further research: Am Law of Prop § 12.38; Tiffany § 966.

8-11D Statutory Deed Forms.

R.C. 5302.01 (Creation of statutory forms; alteration.) provides: "The forms set forth in sections 5302.05, 5302.07, 5302.09, 5302.11, 5302.12, and 5302.14 of the Revised Code may be used and shall be sufficient for their respective purposes. They shall be known as 'Statutory Forms' and may be referred to as such. They may be altered as circumstances require, and the authorization of such forms shall not prevent the use of other forms. Wherever the phrases defined in sections 5302.06, 5302.08, 5302.10, and 5302.13 of the Revised Code are to be incorporated in instruments by reference, the method of incorporation as indicated in the statutory forms shall be sufficient, but shall not preclude other methods." (As eff. 10-30-65.)

R.C. 5302.02 (Rules and definitions to apply to all instruments relating to real estate.) provides: "The rules and definitions contained in sections 5302.03, 5302.04, 5302.06, 5302.08, 5302.10, and 5302.13 of the Revised Code apply to all deeds or other instruments relating to real estate, whether the statutory forms or other forms are used, where the instruments are executed on or after October 1, 1965." (As eff. 10-30-65.)

R.C. 5302.03 (Grant is sufficient word of conveyance; no covenant to be implied.) provides: "In a conveyance of real estate or any interest therein, the word 'grant' is a sufficient word of conveyance without the use of more words. No covenant shall be implied from the use of the word 'grant.'" (As eff. 10-30-65.)

R.C. 5302.04 (All interest conveyed unless otherwise stated.) provides: "In a conveyance of real estate or any interest therein, all rights, easements, privileges, and appurtenances belonging to the granted estate shall be included in the conveyance, unless the contrary is stated in the deed, and it is unnecessary to enumerate or mention them either generally or specifically." (As eff. 10-30-65.) See also R.C. 5301.02 at 8-31A.

R.C. 5302.05 (General warranty deed.) in part provides: "A deed in substance following the form set forth in this section, when duly executed in accordance with Chapter 5301. of the Revised Code, has the force and effect of a deed in fee simple to the grantee, his heirs, assigns, and successors, to his and their own use, with covenants on the part of the grantor with the grantee, his heirs, assigns, and successors, that, at the time of the delivery of such deed he was lawfully seized in fee simple of the granted premises, that the granted premises were free from all encumbrances, that he had good right to sell and convey the same to the grantee and his heirs, assigns, and successors, and that he does warrant and will defend the same to the grantee and his heirs, assigns, and successors, forever, against the lawful claims and demands of all persons." (As eff. 10-30-65.)

R.C. 5302.06 (General warranty covenants.) provides: "In a conveyance of real estate, or any interest therein, the words 'general warranty covenants' have the full force, meaning, and effect of the following words: 'The grantor covenants with the grantee, his heirs, assigns, and successors, that he is lawfully seized in fee simple of the granted premises; that they are free from

236

all encumbrances; that he has good right to sell and convey the same, and that he does warrant and will defend the same to the grantee and his heirs, assigns, and successors, forever, against the lawful claims and demands of all persons.'" (As eff. 10-30-65.)

R.C. 5302.07 (Limited warranty deed.) in part provides: "A deed in substance following the form set forth in this section, when duly executed in accordance with Chapter 5301. of the Revised Code, has the force and effect of a deed in fee simple to the grantee, his heirs, assigns, and successors, to his and their own use, with covenants on the part of the grantor with the grantee, his heirs, assigns, and successors, that, at the time of the delivery of such deed the premises were free from all encumbrances made by him, and that he does warrant and will defend the same to the grantee and his heirs, assigns, and successors, forever, against the lawful claims and demands of all persons claiming by, through, or under the grantor, but against none other." (As eff. 10-30-65.)

R.C. 5302.08 (Limited warranty covenants.) provides: "In a conveyance of real estate, or any interest therein, the words 'limited warranty covenants' have the full force, meaning, and effect of the following words: 'The grantor covenants with the grantee, his heirs, assigns and successors, that the granted premises are free from all encumbrances made by the grantor, and that he does warrant and will defend the same to the grantee and his heirs, assigns, and successors, forever, against the lawful claims and demands of all persons claiming by, through, or under the grantor, but against none other.'" (As eff. 10-30-65.)

R.C. 5302.09 (Deed of executor, administrator, trustee, guardian, receiver, or commissioner; effect of.) in part provides: "A deed in substance following the form set forth in this section, when duly executed in accordance with Chapter 5301. of the Revised Code, has the force and effect of a deed in fee simple to the grantee, his heirs, assigns, and successors, to his and their own use, with covenants on the part of the grantor with the grantee, his heirs, assigns, and successors, that, at the time of the delivery of such deed, he was duly appointed, qualified, and acting in the fiduciary capacity described in such deed, and was duly authorized to make the sale and conveyance of the premises; that in all of his proceedings in the sale thereof he has complied with the requirements of the statutes in such case provided." (As eff. 10-30-65.)

R.C. 5302.10 (Fiduciary covenants.) provides: "In a conveyance of real estate, or any interest therein, the words 'fiduciary covenants' have the full force, meaning, and effect of the following words: 'The grantor covenants with the grantee, his heirs, assigns, and successors, that he is duly appointed, qualified, and acting in the fiduciary capacity described in such deed, and is duly authorized to make the sale and conveyance of the granted premises, and that in all of his proceedings in the sale thereof he has complied with the requirements of the statutes in such case provided.'" (As eff. 10-30-65.)

R.C. 5302.11 (Quitclaim deed) in part provides: "A deed in substance following the form set forth in this section, when duly executed in accordance with

Chapter 5301. of the Revised Code, has the force and effect of a deed in fee simple to the grantee, his heirs, assigns, and successors, and to his and their own use, but without covenants of any kind on the part of the grantor." (As eff. 10-30-65.)

R.C. 5302.17 (Survivorship deed). See 8-16B.

R.C. 5302.18 provides: "A deed in which a grantor is also a grantee is effective to convey the interest in the title of the grantor or grantors to all of the grantees in the proportion and manner indicated in the deed." (As eff. 4-4-85.)

R.C. 5302.20 provides: "(A) Except as provided in section 5302.21 of the Revised Code, if any interest in real property is conveyed or devised to two or more persons for their joint lives and then to the survivor or survivors of them, such persons hold title as survivorship tenants and the joint interest created is a survivorship tenancy. Any deed or will containing language that shows a clear intent to create a survivorship shall be liberally construed to do so. The use of the word "or" between the names of two or more grantees or devisees does not by itself create a survivorship tenancy, but shall be construed and interpreted as if the word "and" had been used between the names.

(B) If two or more persons hold an interest in the title to real property as survivorship tenants, each survivorship tenant holds an equal share of the title during their joint lives, and, upon the death of any of them, the title vests in the surviving tenants as survivorship tenants. This is the case until only one survivorship tenant remains alive, at which time the survivor is fully vested with title to the real property as the sole title holder. If the last two or more survivorship tenants die under such circumstances that the survivor cannot be determined, title passes as if such last survivors had been tenants in common.

(C) A survivorship tenancy has the following characteristics or ramifications:

(1) Each of the survivorship tenants has an equal right to share in the use, occupancy, and profits, and each is subject to a proportionate share of the costs related to the ownership and use of the real property subject to the survivorship tenancy;

(2) A conveyance from all of the survivorship tenants to any other person, or from all but one of the survivorship tenants to the remaining survivorship tenant, terminates the survivorship tenancy and vests title in the grantee. A conveyance from any survivorship tenant, or from any number of survivorship tenants that is from less than all of them, to a person who is not a survivorship tenant vests the title of the grantor or grantors in the grantee, conditioned on the survivorship of the grantor or grantors of the conveyance, and does not alter the interest in the title of any of the other survivorship tenants who do not join in the conveyance.

(3) A fee simple title, leasehold interest, or land contract vendee's interest in real property, or any fractional interest in any of these interests, may be subjected to a survivorship tenancy.

238

(4) A creditor of a survivorship tenant may enforce a lien against the interest of one or more survivorship tenants by an action to marshall liens against the interest of such debtor or debtors shall be made a party to the action. Upon a determination by the court that a party or cross-claimant has a valid lien against the interest of a survivorship tenant, the title to the real property ceases to be a survivorship tenancy and becomes a tenancy in common. Each such tenant in common then holds an equal undivided share in the title. The court then may order the sale of the fractional interest of the lien debtor or debtors as on execution, and the proceeds of the sale shall be applied to pay the lien creditors in the order of their priority.

(5) If the entire title to a parcel of real property is held by two survivorship tenants who are married to each other and the marriage is terminated by divorce, annulment, or dissolution, the title, except as provided in this division, immediately ceases to be a survivorship tenancy and becomes a tenancy in common. Each such tenant in common holds an equal undivided half interest in common in the title to the real property, unless the judgment of divorce, annulment, or dissolution expressly states that the survivorship tenancy shall continue after termination of the marriage.

If a survivorship tenancy includes one or more survivorship tenants in addition to a husband or wife whose marriage is terminated by divorce, annulment, or dissolution, the survivorship tenancy is not affected by the divorce, annulment, or dissolution unless the court alters the interest of the survivorship tenants whose marriage has been terminated. (As eff. 4-4-85.)

Note: The statutory deed forms, particularly the warranty deed, must be used carefully. Since the words "General Warranty Covenants" appear in the first part of the instrument immediately following the grant of title, it is not uncommon to find that the draftsman has failed to include the exceptions to the warranties which must be inserted in the space allocated to the legal description. This failure will cause an immediate breach of warranty because the title is at least encumbered by real estate taxes which are not yet due and payable, if not also by restrictive covenants or other encumbrances.

SECTION 8-12: GRANTING CLAUSE; CONSIDERATION; HABENDUM

Description of premises, see Section 3-21.
Designation of parties, see Section 8-32.

8-12A Premises; Granting Clause.

A wife, owner of the fee of land, does not pass her title by a deed executed by her husband, unless she joins her husband in the granting part of the deed. Purcell v. Goshorn, 17 Ohio 105 (1848).

LAW IN GENERAL

The premises, sometimes called the granting clause, consist of what usually precedes the habendum and are the only essential part of a conveyance except the signature and statutory requirements. The premises include the designation of the parties, the statement of the consideration, the words of grant, the description of the property and the recitals, if any. The words of grant must show a clear intention to convey in the present. Formal or technical terms are not necessary as a rule. Am Law of Prop § 12.44; Thompson § 3130; Tiffany § 971.

8-12B   Consideration.

Bona fide purchaser, see 1-32B.
Failure of consideration, see Section 8-51.

The rule that it is necessary to express some consideration in a conveyance of real estate applies only as to executory contracts. Vale v. Stephens, 25 App 523, 159 NE 114, 5 Abs 578 (1927); Thompson v. Thompson, 17 OS 649, 655 (1867).

The recital in the deed of the consideration paid is not conclusive. The deed is prima facie evidence of the consideration, and the actual consideration as may be shown by evidence dehors the deed. Conklin v. Hancock, 67 OS 455, 66 NE 518, 48 WLB 133, 275 (1903); Detroit & I. R.R. v. Murry, 25 App 409, 158 NE 205, 5 Abs 259 (1927).

Failure of grantee to perform a promise which formed the whole or part of the consideration for the execution of a conveyance gives rise to no right of rescission in the grantor, where such failure was not expressly made a ground of forfeiture. Cleveland v. Herron, 102 OS 218, 131 NE 489, 66 WLB 218, 220 (1921); Black v. Hoyt, 33 OS 203, 212, 3 WLB 826 (1877).

Actual consideration is not necessary to validate a deed as between the parties and their privies. Validity may be challenged by creditors under the law of fraudulent conveyances. Vesy v. Giles, 108 NE2d 300, 48 OO 385, 65 Abs 522 (C.P. 1952).

Further research: O Jur 3d, Deeds § 50.

LAW IN GENERAL

A consideration is not necessary for a deed. Covenants and executory provisions may be unenforceable for lack of consideration. The consideration may also be important in fraudulent conveyances, rescission, reformation, and the rights of innocent grantees. Recital of consideration or payment is not conclusive as to the amount nor as to the payment. The grantee may show a consideration when none is recited. A recital of consideration cannot be controverted to change the legal effect of the conveyance. Recital of consideration may be decisive as giving constructive notice of encumbrances such as a vendor's lien, a resulting trust arising from payment by a third party, or an agreement to support grantor. Am Jur 2d, Deeds § 61; Am Law of Prop §§ 12.43, 18.41; CJS, Deeds § 16; Powell § 893; Tiffany § 984.

8-12C   Habendum.

Conceding the usual effect of this clause in a deed to be to define the extent of the ownership in the thing granted, to be held and enjoyed by the grantee, yet it is not an essential part of a deed, and its effect may not only be qualified and restrained by other parts of the deed, but where it is repugnant to the grant, it has no validity or effect whatever. Ball v. Foreman, 37 OS 132, 6 WLB 343 (1881).

The habendum clause should be read with the granting clause, as explanatory and modifying, if the same can be done without raising some irreconcilable repugnancy to the granting clause. The purpose of the comparison is to determine the grantor's intent. Ferris v. Schuholz, 107 App 63, 152 NE2d 285, 7 OO2d 397 (1957).

LAW IN GENERAL

The habendum, which sets forth the estate to be held by the grantee, and the granting clause will be construed so as to give effect to both if possible. Where the conflict cannot be reconciled, the rule is that the habendum cannot diminish the estate conveyed by the granting clause. It has been held, however, that the habendum may enlarge the estate theretofore described when it does not directly contradict the granting clause. Am Law of Prop § 12.47; 58 ALR2d 1374; Tiffany § 980.

The modern cases show a strong and increasing tendency to give effect to the real intention of the parties, if ascertainable from the deed as a whole, whether with or without resort to the attending circumstances, with regard to the estate conveyed despite conflicts between the granting and habendum clauses. 58 ALR2d 1374.

SECTION 8-13:   EXCEPTION AND RESERVATION; DATE; SIGNATURE

8-13A Exception and Reservation Generally.

Words of inheritance, see Section 11-12.

Parol evidence is not admissible to show that at the time of the delivery of the deed the grantor reserved the right of possession. Jones v. Timmons, 21 OS 596 (1871).

An exception removes a part of the thing described from the operation of the grant and leaves the title in the grantor. A reservation is something newly created, out of the granted premises, by force of the reservation itself; the effect is of something taken back from that which is granted. Manley v. Carl, 20 CC 161, 11 CD 1 (1900).

Whether the language used in a deed creates a reservation or exception from the grant depends upon the intention of the parties as evinced by a construction of the whole instrument in the light of the circumstances of each case. Gill v. Fletcher, 74 OS 295, 78 NE 433, 4 OLR 149, 51 WLB 225 (1906).

If an easement is being created the words will be construed as a reservation, and if ownership is retained, as an exception. Held that subsequent conveyance of the estate in question shows the intention to have been to except the estate. Akron Cold Spring Co. v. Ely, 18 App 74, 1 Abs 614 (1923).

Further research: O Jur 3d, Deeds § 92.

LAW IN GENERAL

An exception excludes a part of the described property from the operation of the deed. By a reservation the grantor takes back, out of the property conveyed, an interest not previously existing separately. The reddendum, containing the exception or reservation, is of equal force to the premises or granting clause. An exception is generally given effect regardless of its location in the deed. Several courts have upheld a reservation of a life estate to both spouses who were grantors when the title was in one of them only. Am Jur 2d, Deeds § 262; Am Law of Prop § 12.95; CJS, Deeds § 137; Tiffany § 972.

Although an interest may be called a reservation, it will be construed as an exception, and vice versa, according to the intention of the parties. Tiffany § 973.

Parol evidence is ordinarily inadmissible to show reservations or exceptions upon conveyance of real property because of the statute of frauds or because a written instrument cannot be varied or contradicted by evidence of prior or contemporaneous oral agreements. However, many cases have made exceptions to the rule, such as (a) to aid in construing doubtful or ambiguous provisions, (b) that the agreement was collateral to the conveyance, (c) that the deed did not purport to embrace all the subject matter or provisions of the oral agreement, or (d) that the agreement converted the subject matter of the reservation into personalty. 61 ALR2d 1390.

8-13B Reservation or Exception to Third Party.

Easements to third persons, see 10-11G.

Reservation in a deed, in favor of a third party not a party to the deed, is void. Kirk v. Conrad, 9 Abs 717 (App. 1931).

The Restatement of the Law of Property is authority for the proposition that a single instrument of conveyance may transfer a fee to one person and create an easement in another person, even though the conveyance of the easement is, in terms, a reservation to the person to whom it is conveyed. Hollosy v. Gershkowitz, 88 App 198, 98 NE2d 314, 44 OO 221 (1950).

LAW IN GENERAL

A reservation or exception in favor of a third party does not transfer any title to him unless the language be construed as words of grant. An exception in favor of a stranger may prevent the excepted title from passing to the grantee. Where a reservation in favor of a third party does not estop the grantee from asserting its invalidity, it may nevertheless operate to qualify the covenants or to give notice of a claim. Some cases hold that life estates and other interests in favor of third persons may be created by the form of reservations. 88 ALR2d 1199; Restatement, Property § 472; Tiffany § 974.

8-13C Date.

Where the deed is dated subsequent to the acknowledgment, the deed is not invalid if it appears to be a mere clerical error. Fisher v. Butcher, 19 Ohio 406 (1850).

If there are acknowledgments on different dates, the deed should be dated not later than the first acknowledgment.

Standard of Title Examination

(As amended by Ohio State Bar Association in 1960)

Problem 3.7A:
  Shall errors or omissions in the dates of a conveyance or other instrument affecting title, in itself, impair marketability?

Standard 3.7A:
  No.

Comment:
  Even if the date of execution is of peculiar significance, an undated instrument will be presumed to have been timely executed if the dates of acknowledgment and recordation, and other circumstances of record, support that presumption.

  Inconsistencies in recitals or indications of dates, as between dates of execution, attestation, acknowledgment, or recordation, do not, in themselves, impair marketability. Absent a peculiar significance of one of the dates, a proper sequence of formalities will be presumed notwithstanding such inconsistencies.

LAW IN GENERAL

The date of a deed is generally prima facie evidence of the time of execution and delivery. It may be omitted or be erroneous without affecting the validity of the deed. Under some decisions the date of the acknowledgment is presumed to be the date of delivery, especially when earlier than the date of the deed. Am Law of Prop §§ 12.52, 18.41; CJS, Deeds § 22.

8-13D Signature.

Fiduciary signing as individual, see 8-11B.
Variance in name, see 1-27B.

The grantor's adoption of a signature by affixing his mark thereto, the deed being in other respects regular, is as effective to transfer the estate as if his name had been written thereon in full by himself. Truman v. Lore, 14 OS 144, 154 (1862).

The fact that one of the grantors signed on an opposite page from the place for the signature does not render a deed invalid. Graham v. Burggraf, 10 CC(NS) 594, 12 CD 747 (1897).

Further research: O Jur 3d, Deeds § 25.

LAW IN GENERAL

The signature may be located in any part of the deed, except as the rule is limited by a statute requiring the deed to be "subscribed." The signature may be by mark. It may be made by another person if the grantor adopts it by being present, by delivering the deed, or by other conduct. Forgery cannot be ratified but estoppel may operate against the grantor. For marketability the signature must substantially conform to the name of the record owner or be identified, as by the certificate of acknowledgment. Am Jur 2d, Deeds § 23; Am Law of Prop §§ 12.58, 18.28; CJS, Signatures § 1; Tiffany § 1023.

SECTION 8-14: SEAL; WITNESSES

8-14A Seal.

R.C. 5.11 in part provides: "Private seals are abolished, and the affixing of what has been known as a private seal to an instrument shall not give such instrument additional force or effect, or change the construction thereof." (As eff. 10-1-53.)

Further research: O Jur 3d, Deeds § 27.

8-14B Witnesses.

Effect of defects, see 8-11B.
Foreign execution, see Section 8-18.

R.C. 5301.01 provides: "A deed, mortgage, land contract as referred to in division (B) (2) of section 317.08 of the Revised Code, or lease of any interest in real property must be signed by the grantor, mortgagor, vendor, or lessor, and such signing must be acknowledged by the grantor, mortgagor, vendor, or lessor in the presence of two witnesses, who shall attest the signing and subscribe their names to the attestation. Such signing must be acknowledged by the grantor, mortgagor, vendor, or lessor before a judge of a court of record in this state or a clerk thereof, a county auditor, county engineer, notary public, mayor, or county court judge, who shall certify the acknowledgment and subscribe his name to the certificate of such acknowledgment." (As eff. 8-11-61.) This statute has been substantially the same since 1887 except that (a) until August 18, 1943 it provided that acknowledgment should be on the same sheet as the instrument and (b) the provisions regarding land contracts were added on August 11, 1961.

A deed conveying land is not to be impeached by showing that one of the subscribing witnesses is incompetent to testify. Johnson v. Turner, 7 Ohio (pt. 2) 216 (1836).

The signature of the notary to his certificate of acknowledgment will not supply the deficiency where but one name is subscribed to the attestation clause. White v. Denman, 1 OS 110 (1853).

A grantee of an instrument for the conveyance or encumbrance of real property is disqualified, on grounds of public policy, to be an attesting witness to its execution or to certifying the acknowledgment of the grantor. Amick v. Woodworth, 58 OS 86, 50 NE 437, 39 WLB 172, 338 (1898).

A conveyance cannot be impeached merely because the witnesses are stockholders of the grantee. Read v. Toledo Loan Co., 68 OS 280, 67 NE 729, 1 OLR 42, 357, 48 WLB 502, 609 (1903).

A wife's inchoate right of dower in the property of her husband is not such as to disqualify her from witnessing or notarizing the deed conveying such property. Green v. Henderson, 52 NE2d 532, 39 Abs 213 (App. 1943).

Further research: O Jur 3d, Deeds § 28.

LAW IN GENERAL

Witnesses may sign by mark. They are not required to be present at the signing by the grantor if he acknowledges his signature to them and requests attestation by them.

Competence of witnesses is usually required to the extent that they be able to testify in the event of litigation.

A party is disqualified to act as a witness. A stockholder, employee, or attorney of a party is not disqualified. A common test is whether the person attesting would be permitted to testify as to the transaction. A disqualification is usually required to be of record.

Am Law of Prop §§ 12.59, 18.38; CJS, Deeds § 35; Tiffany § 1026.

SECTION 8-15: QUITCLAIM DEEDS

Text on statutory forms, see 8-11D.

8-15A Nature.

A quitclaim deed which conveys the real estate itself as distinguished from all of the right, title and interest of the grantor in the real estate, passes grantor's title as effectively as a deed of warranty containing full covenants and does not charge the grantee with notice of any infirmities in the title, other than those of which the grantee would have constructive notice under a warranty deed containing full covenants. Dietsch v. Long, 72 App 349, 43 NE2d 906, 27 OO 294, 36 Abs 360 (1942).

Standard of Title Examination

(Adopted by Ohio State Bar Association in 1960)

Problem 3.15A:

Does the fact that a conveyance necessary to the chain of title, including the conveyance to the proposed grantor, is a quitclaim deed impair marketability or necessitate inquiry or corrective action?

Standard 3.15A:
No.

LAW IN GENERAL

Quitclaim deeds convey whatever title the grantor has but do not imply that he has any title. The term is sometimes restricted to an instrument transferring the interest of the grantor as distinguished from a conveyance of the land itself. A distinction in legal effect may be made when the deed does not purport to convey the land but to transfer only the grantor's interest therein. Am Jur 2d, Deeds § 191; Tiffany § 959.

8-15B As Effective Conveyances.

After-acquired title, see Section 8-34.

A quitclaim deed passes all existing equities beneficial to the estate conveyed which the grantor might have enforced. Maher v. Cleveland Union Stockyards Co., 55 App 412, 9 NE2d 995, 9 OO 112, 22 Abs 199 (1936).

A quitclaim deed purporting to convey the land itself is as effective as any other form of conveyance to transfer or release any interest which the grantor presently has in the property.

8-15C Bona Fide Purchasers.

A subsequent purchaser, who holds under a quitclaim deed which purports to convey the corpus of lands, may be protected under the statute as a bona fide purchaser. When proof is made of payment of a valuable consideration, the presumption arises that the purchasers were bona fide purchasers. Morris v. Daniels, 35 OS 406, 5 WLB 108 (1880).

LAW IN GENERAL

Some decisions hold that notice of possible defects is given and that the standing of a grantee as an innocent purchaser is affected when the whole deed purports to convey only the interest of the grantor. Tiffany § 1277. See also 8-15A.

SECTION 8-16: SURVIVORSHIP DEEDS; "OR"

8-16A Nature.

Cross remainders, see 11-73A.
Deed from grantor to himself, see 8-32E.
Joint tenancy, see Section 5-22.
Statutory disclaimer of beneficial interest, see 9-11G.

A conveyance to A and B "jointly, their heirs and assigns, and to the survivor of them, his or her separate heirs and assigns" vests an estate in fee in the survivor. Lewis v. Baldwin, 11 Ohio 352 (1842).

While joint tenancy with the incidental right of survivorship does not exist in Ohio, parties may nevertheless contract for a joint ownership with the right of survivorship and at the death of one of the joint owners the survivor succeeds to the title to the entire interest. (In question was a stock certificate to James Hutchison and Letitia Hutchison, "as tenants in common of undivided equal interest for their respective lives, remainder in the whole to their survivor.") In re Hutchison's Estate, 120 OS 542, 166 NE 687, 7 Abs 288, 29 OLR 136 (1929).

If joint tenancy is expressed without words of survivorship, it will be considered as tenancy in common. Foraker v. Kocks, 41 App 210, 180 NE 743, 11 Abs 545, 36 OLR 156 (1931); In re Hutchison's Estate, 120 OS 542, 550, 166 NE 687, 7 Abs 288, 29 OLR 136 (1929).

Where a husband and wife have each deposited money in a survivorship account, such funds pass to the surviving wife by virtue of the contract and not by deed of gift, and distribution is not governed by the half-and-half statute. Berberick v. Courtade, 137 OS 297, 28 NE2d 636, 18 OO 50 (1940).

A joint bank account with right of survivorship may be properly excluded from the inventory and appraisement of a decedent's estate. In re Hatch's Estate, 154 OS 149, 93 NE2d 585, 42 OO 218 (1950).

When by deed a lot is conveyed to A and F with words "unto said grantees and the survivor of either, their heirs and assigns," an estate in fee simple is created in F at death of A. In re Dennis' Estate, 30 NP(NS) 118 (C.P. 1928).

A survivorship deed is a valid and effective means of transferring the full fee simple title to the surviving grantee, provided the language used is sufficiently clear to indicate the intention of the grantor and grantees (to said Helen Ross and Lonsy Ross and the survivor of them, her or his heirs and assigns). Ross v. Bowman, 170 O Supp 59, 32 OO 27 (C.P. 1945).

Where a valid joint and survivorship bank account is created by the decedent, the fact that she was thereafter declared incompetent and a guardian appointed does not, as a matter of law, terminate the joint and survivorship nature of the account. Miller v. Yocum, 21 OS2d 162, 256 NE2d 208, 50 OO2d 372 (1970).

A surviving spouse, who owned real property with her husband with right of survivorship, is entitled to receive contribution from the deceased spouse's estate for half of the debt discharged by her on a joint and several mortgage note. Pietro v. Leonetti, 30 OS2d 178, 283 NE2d 172, 59 OO2d 186 (1972).

The renunciation of a joint survivorship bank account by the surviving co-owner is ineffective if the account was created with his knowledge and consent. Krakoff v. United States, 313 F Supp 1089, 28 Misc 22, 55 OO2d 228 (1970), affd. 439 F2d 1023, 58 OO2d 381 (1971).

Estate taxes cannot be avoided through use of a survivorship deed, although the property is not otherwise involved in the administration proceedings.

Standard of Title Examination

(Adopted by Ohio State Bar Association in 1969)

Problem 3.4C:
Does subsequent incompetency of one or more of such (survivorship) owners alter the interests so created?

Standard 3.4C:
No.

Comment 3.4C:
The incident of survivorship is not destroyed.

Effective April 4, 1985, R.C. 5302.17 was amended to create a statutory form of survivorship deed. The newly enacted R.C. 5302.20 (see 8-11D), eff. April 4, 1985, defines the characteristics of survivorship tenancy, including the effect of a conveyance by one survivorship tenant, the right of the holder of a lien against one survivorship and the effect of divorce on survivorship tenancy.

8-16B Form.

See also 8-16C.

R.C. 5302.17, as revised eff. April 4, 1985, provides:

"A deed conveying any interest in real property to two or more persons, and in substance following the form set forth in this section, when duly executed in accordance with Chapter 5301. of the Revised Code, creates a survivorship tenancy in the grantees, and upon the death of any such person, vests the interest of the decedent in the survivor, survivors, or his or their separate heirs and assigns.

'SURVIVORSHIP DEED

_____ (marital status), of _____ County, _____ for valuable consideration paid, grant(s), (covenants, if any), to _____ (marital status) and _____ (marital status) for their joint lives, remainder to the survivor of them, whose tax-mailing addresses are _____, the following real property

———— (Description of land or interest therein and encumbrances, reservations, and exceptions, if any)

Prior Instrument Reference: ————, wife (husband) of the grantor, releases all rights of dower therein.

Witness ———— hand this ———— day of ————,

(Execution in accordance with Chapter 5301. of the Revised Code)

Any persons who are the sole owners of real property, prior to the effective date of this amendment, as tenants with a right of survivorship under the common or statutory law of this state or as tenants in common, may create in themselves and in any other person or persons a survivorship tenancy in such real property, by executing a deed as provided in this section conveying their entire, separate interests in such property to themselves and to such other person or persons.

Except as otherwise provided in this section, when a person holding property as a survivorship tenant dies, the transfer of the interest of the decedent may be recorded by presenting to the county auditor, and filing with the county recorder either a certificate of transfer as provided in section 2113.61 of the Revised Code, or an affidavit accompanied by a certificate of death. The affidavit shall recited the names of the other survivorship tenant or tenants, the address of such other tenant or tenants, the date of death of the decedent, and a description of the property. The county recorder shall make index reference to any certificate or affidavit so filed in the record of deeds. When a person holding real property as a survivorship tenant dies and the title to the property is registered pursuant to Chapter 5309. of the Revised Code, the procedure for the transfer of the interest of the decedent shall be pursuant to section 5309.081 of the Revised Code."

The wording in a granting clause and in the habendum clause reading "grant, bargain, sell and convey to the said Cloie Smith and Edna Pursley, or the survivor of them, their heirs and assigns forever" creates a joint and survivorship title and upon the death of either, the fee simple title is vested in the survivor. Curlis v. Pursley, 10 Misc 266, 227 NE2d 276, 39 OO2d 399 (C.P. 1967). See also Ready v. Kearsley at 8-16C. The case digested above and cited in Comment 3.4A below adds to the uncertainty of the effectiveness of "to A *and* B, *or* the survivor" in view of the many older cases in other jurisdictions which disapprove of such use of the word "or."

The words of survivorship should appear in the granting and habendum clauses, and not in the consideration clause alone.

Standard of Title Examination

(Adopted by Ohio State Bar Association in 1969)

Problem 3.4A:

What language creates an estate with right of survivorship?

Standard 3.4A:

Where the operative words of a deed clearly express an intention to create the right of survivorship, such expressed intention will be given effect and the survivor will take by force of the terms of the grant. Upon the death of the other grantee or grantees, the survivor acquires the entire estate, subject to the charge of death taxes.

A conveyance is sufficient to create an estate with right of survivorship when "to A and B for their joint lives, remainder to the survivor of them, his or her heirs and assigns," or the like.

A conveyance is not sufficient to create an estate with right of survivorship when "to A or B"; "to A or B, their heirs and assigns"; "to A or B, his or her heirs and assigns"; "to A and B or the survivor"; or the like.

Comment 3.4A:

The use of the disjunctive word "or" in the immediately preceding paragraph creates uncertainty as to whether the estate passes to A or B, passes to A and B with right of survivorship, or passes to A and B as tenants in common. Many decisions require deeds to be definite and grantees to be ascertainable. The courts should determine the intention and effect under the facts in a particular case. In all instances where it is desired to create an estate with the right of survivorship, the disjunctive should be scrupulously avoided. (This is true even though in hard cases a court may find a joint and survivorship estate to be created by such language as "to A and B, or the survivor of them, their heirs and assigns forever" (Curlis v. Purlsey, 10 Ohio Misc 266)).

Standard of Title Examination

(Adopted by Ohio State Bar Association in 1952)

Problem 3.4B:

What shall be sufficient proof of the first death of a grantee of a survivorship deed?

Standard 3.4B:

Showing death by the following shall be considered sufficient for a marketable title (subject to payment of inheritance tax, if any):

(a) an affidavit recorded in the office of the county recorder;

(b) a recital in a deed remaining unquestioned of record for more than ten years;

(c) a recital in a deed referring to an official death record; or

(d) a copy of an official death record recorded in the office of the county recorder.

Requirements of the county auditor or county recorder must be considered in some counties.

Note: This 1952 title standard became obsolete upon the enactment of R.C. 5302.17, as effective April 4, 1985. Upon death of a survivorship tenant after that date, see R.C. 5302.17.

8-16C "Or."

See Standard of Title Examination at 8-16B.
Construction as to vesting, see Section 11-81.
Designation of parties generally, see Section 8-32.
Lapsed gifts, see 9-26B.
Survivorship by deed to grantees from themselves, see 8-32E.

Since the effective date of R.C. 5302.20 on April 4, 1985, "The use of the word 'or' between the names of two or more grantees or devisees does not by itself create a survivorship tenancy, but shall be construed and interpreted as if the word 'and' had been used between the names." Prior to that date a deed in the disjunctive "to A or B" (as in government bonds) did not comply with the requirement of definiteness in deeds and consequently was not fully effective as a conveyance. It did not vest the title in either for uncertainty arising from the manifest impossibility of ascertaining at law who shall take where the grantor has failed to express his intent. Its effect could be judicially ascertained in equity. Under the statute providing that the entire interest of the grantor shall be conveyed in the absence of a clear intent to convey a lesser interest, it could be held that a deed from both grantees conveyed a marketable title, even though a deed from the survivor would not do so. If one of the grantees in such a case has died without making a conveyance, a decree of court was necessary to determine whether the intent was to create the right of survivorship or to convey in the alternative upon an unexpressed contingency.

It was held in Ready v. Kearsley, 14 Mich 215 (1865) (citing decision of United States Supreme Court in Hogan v. Page, 2 Wallace 605, 17 L Ed 854 (1864)) that the rule does not apply to invalidate a deed "to A or his heirs," such a deed being a valid conveyance to A if he is living, or to his heirs if he is dead. Under this pronouncement, a deed "to A and B or the survivor" is a valid conveyance to A and B in fee simple without right of survivorship if both A and B are living at the effective date of the deed.

8-16D Simultaneous Deaths.

Statute on presumed order of death, see R.C. 2105.21 at 9-11L.

A husband and wife being killed in a common accident, and it being impossible to determine that either one survived the other, the presumption must be that neither one survived the other. The joint ownership provisions of bank accounts are effective and the survivorship accounts will be equally divided between the two estates. In re Markiewicz's Estate, 129 NE2d 328, 71 Abs 143 (Prob. 1955).

"Our contention is that this statute [now R.C. 2105.21] can have no effect upon the so-called survivorship deeds.... In the case of survivorship deeds there is no estate to pass.

"There can no longer be any argument as to the validity of the so-called survivorship deeds.... The fact that it may be difficult to determine which of the two (or more) survived cannot affect the validity of the deed.... It is practically impossible for two persons to die at the same hour, minute, and second. One of the two was the survivor and the survivor takes the property by the terms of the deed. The question as to which one survived is a question for the court." Charles C. White, "Notes on Survivorship Deed—So-called," 24 OO 119.

LAW IN GENERAL

There is no presumption of survival between persons who perish in a common disaster. When property is owned jointly and there is no evidence as to survivorship, it has been held that the property descends as though owned in common. Am Jur 2d, Descent and Distribution § 103; 39 ALR3d 1332; CJS, Death § 6.

8-16E   Estates by Entireties.

Statutory disclaimer of beneficial interest, see 9-11G.

Between February 9, 1972 and April 4, 1985, R.C. 5302.17 prescribed a statutory deed form for conveying land to a husband and wife to create an "estate by the entireties." After conflicting decisions from several lower courts the Ohio Supreme Court determined that the statutory form resulted in a common law tenancy by the entirety, that such an estate was not alienable by either spouse and that the judgment lien creditor of only one spouse could not foreclose his lien. Central Nat. Bank of Cleveland v. Fitzwilliam, 12 OS3d 51, 465 NE2d 408 (1984).

The Ohio Department of Taxation treats an estate by entireties the same as other survivorship property as between husband and wife, that is, one-half of the value is taxable.

SECTION 8-17: ANCIENT DOCUMENTS

8-17A   Rule.

A paper is not admissible as an ancient document proving itself, but must be accompanied by evidence that it came from the proper custody and by evidence of its antiquity, although it may purport to be more than thirty years old. Wright v. Hull, 83 OS 385, 94 NE 813, 8 OLR 609, 56 WLB 91 (1911).

LAW IN GENERAL

Documents purporting to be thirty years or more old are, as a rule, presumed to be authentic without the ordinarily required proof of execution if produced from the proper custody and free from suspicion on the face. The presumption is rebuttable. The rule has been held to apply to public records. Am Jur 2d, Evidence §§ 856, 857, 866; CJS, Evidence § 744.

8-17B Deeds.

Writings appearing to be more than thirty years old, after preliminary proof that they were produced from proper depositories, are ancient documents and are ordinarily admitted in evidence and prove themselves. Trustees of German Township v. Farmers & Citizens Savings Bank Co., 113 NE2d 409, 51 OO 346, 66 Abs 332 (C.P. 1953).

LAW IN GENERAL

Deeds are within the rule. It has also been applied where a power of attorney for execution of a deed is not produced and where there are irregularities in the execution. Some cases hold that a deed will not be admitted in evidence under the rule without corroborative proof of possession, or of claim of right to possession, of the land. Am Jur 2d, Evidence § 863.

8-17C Recitals.

See Standard of Title Examination at 1-24B.

LAW IN GENERAL

Recitals in ancient deeds are held to be competent evidence even against strangers. It has been so decided in the determination of heirship, establishment of identity, location of disputed boundary lines, and other cases. Am Jur 2d, Evidence § 865; Am Law of Prop § 17.34.

8-17D Surveys.

One well recognized rule is that an ancient map made by a private person, or as to which no official authorization or recognition appears, is inadmissible. Broadsword v. Kauer, 161 OS 524, 120 NE2d 111, 53 OO 395, 46 ALR2d 1309 (1954).

LAW IN GENERAL

The rule applies to official maps and government surveys. It does not apply to private surveys unless accepted as public documents. Am Jur 2d, Evidence §§ 905-907; 46 ALR2d 1318.

SECTION 8-18: EXECUTION REQUIREMENTS IN EACH STATE

8-18A Foreign Execution.

Armed forces, see 8-23H.
Certificates of authority and conformity, see 8-21F.
Law of situs, see 8-11A.
Uniform Recognition of Acknowledgments Act, see 8-26A.

R.C. 5301.05 provides: "The acknowledgment of an instrument for the conveyance or encumbrance of lands, tenements, or hereditaments situated, within this state, may be made outside this state before a commissioner appointed by the governor of this state for that purpose, a consul general, vice-consul general, deputy consul general, consul, vice-consul, deputy consul, commercial agent, or consular agent of the United States resident in any foreign country." (G.C. 8515 as eff. 10-1-53.)

R.C. 5301.06 provides: "All deeds, mortgages, powers of attorney, and other instruments of writing for the conveyance or encumbrance of lands, tenements, or hereditaments situated within this state, executed and acknowledged, or proved, in any other state, territory, or country in conformity with the laws of such state, territory, or country, or in conformity with the laws of this state, are as valid as if executed within this state, in conformity with sections 1337.01 to 1337.03, inclusive, and 5301.01 to 5301.04, inclusive, of the Revised Code." (As eff. 10-1-53.)

A deed for Ohio land executed in another state must fully conform to the law of Ohio as to the form and method of execution or must fully conform to the law of the state where executed. Thus a deed for Ohio land executed without witnesses in a state which does not require witnesses, but executed on an Ohio form not valid in the state where executed is not effective in Ohio.

8-18B Requirements for Foreign Conformity.

Uniform Recognition of Acknowledgment Act, see 8-26A.

Uniform Act. Article 1 of Uniform Acknowledgment Act provides: "Any instrument may be acknowledged in the manner and form now provided by the law of this State or as provided by this Act." The Act was adopted by Ohio effective January 1, 1974.

Alabama. Witnesses: none if acknowledged, otherwise one but two if by mark. Acknowledgment: (or proven by one of two witnesses) before notary, justice of the peace, judge or clerk of Supreme Court, judge or clerk of court of appeals, judge or clerk or register of circuit court, judge of probate court; seal; separate of wife to release dower; identity known.

Alaska. Witnesses: none. Acknowledgment: (or proven by one witness) before judge or clerk of district court, notary, commissioner; identity known or proven.

Arizona. Witnesses: none. Corporate seal. Acknowledgment: before clerk or deputy clerk of court having seal, notary, recorder, justice of the peace, master, judge of a court of record; seal; expiration of commission.

Arkansas. Witnesses: none if acknowledged. Acknowledgment: (or proven by one of two witnesses) before judge of court of record, clerk of court of record, commissioner or register or recorder of deeds, notary, justice of the peace, master.

California. Witnesses: none if acknowledged, but two if by mark. Corporate seal. Acknowledgment: (or proven by one witness) before judge of Supreme Court or superior court, clerk of court of record, recorder, county clerk, court commissioner, notary, justice of the peace, deputy in name of principal; identity known or proven; seal.

Canal Zone. Witnesses: none if acknowledged. Acknowledgment: (or proven by two witnesses) before district judge or clerk, magistrate, notary; authentication; identity known or proven.

Colorado. Witnesses: none if acknowledged. Acknowledgment: (or proven by a witness) before judge, clerk or deputy clerk of a court of record, county clerk or recorder or deputy, notary, justice of the peace; expiration of commission; seal; identity known or proven.

Connecticut. Witnesses: two. Seal. Corporate seal. Acknowledgment: before judge of court of record, clerk of superior or district or common pleas court, justice of the peace, commissioner, town clerk or assistant, notary.

Delaware. Witnesses: none required but one or two are customary. Seal. Corporate seal. Acknowledgment: (or proven in court by one witness except by wife) before chancellor, judge of superior court or municipal court, notary, two justices of the peace, mayor of Wilmington; identity known; seal.

District of Columbia. Witnesses: none. Seal. Acknowledgment: before a judge, clerk of district court, notary, recorder of deeds; identity known or proven; seal.

Florida. Witnesses: two. Corporate seal. Acknowledgment: (or proven by witness except for homestead or by wife) before judge or clerk or deputy of court of record, United States commissioner, notary, justice of the peace; identity known or proven; seal; expiration of commission.

Georgia. Witnesses: two. Acknowledgment: (not necessary if one of witnesses is notary or justice of the peace or county judge and appends a statement of his official position) (or proven by one of two witnesses) before judge of state court of record, justice of the peace, notary, clerk of superior court.

Hawaii. Witnesses: none. Acknowledgment: before notary; expiration of commission; seal; identity known or proven.

Idaho. Witnesses: none. Acknowledgment: before judge or clerk of court of record, Secretary of State, United States commissioner, recorder, notary, justice of the peace, deputy in name of principal; seal if required to have one; residence of notary; identity known or proven.

Illinois. Witnesses: none if acknowledged. Acknowledgment: (or proven by one witness) before notary (seal), master, United States commissioner (seal), county clerk, justice of the peace, judge or clerk or deputy of court of record (seal of court); identity known or proven.

Indiana. Witnesses: none if acknowledged. Corporate seal. Acknowledgment: (or proven by one witness) before judge or clerk of a court of record,

255

justice of the peace, auditor, recorder, notary, mayor of a city, member of general assembly (seal), magistrate, prosecuting attorney, probate commissioner, attorney general or deputy, court reporter; authentication if without seal.

Iowa. Witnesses: none. Acknowledgment: (or proven by one witness) before judge or clerk of court having a seal, county auditor, justice of the peace, notary; identity known.

Kansas. Witnesses: none. Corporate seal. Acknowledgment: (or proven) before judge or clerk of court having seal, justice of the peace, notary, county clerk, register of deeds, mayor or clerk of city; seal; expiration of commission; identity known.

Kentucky. Witnesses: none if acknowledged. Corporate seal. Acknowledgment: (or proven by two witnesses) before county clerk, notary.

Louisiana. Witnesses: two. Acknowledgment: (or proven by affidavit of witness or of grantor) before notary, judge of a court of record, clerk or deputy of court having a seal, commissioner or register of deeds, master, justice of the peace. Signatures: to be typed or printed.

Maine. Witnesses: none. Seal. Acknowledgment: (or proven by one witness for at least one of grantors) before justice of the peace, notary, seal if he has one.

Maryland. Witnesses: one. Seal. Acknowledgment: before judge of a court of record, clerk or deputy of court having a seal, recorder, notary, justice of the peace, master.

Massachusetts. Witnesses: none. Seal or recital. Acknowledgment: (or proven by one witness for one or more of grantors) before justice of the peace, notary.

Michigan. Witnesses: two. Acknowledgment: (or proven) before judge or clerk or commissioner of court of record, clerk or deputy of court having a seal, master, justice of peace, recorder, notary; expiration of commission.

Minnesota. Witnesses: two. Corporate seal. Acknowledgment: before a member of legislature, judge or clerk or deputy of court of record, United States commissioner, notary, justice of the peace, clerk or recorder of municipality, court or county commissioners, register of deed, and county auditors and their deputies; print or stamp name of notary; expiration of commission; spouse so described; identity known.

Mississippi. Witnesses: none if acknowledged. Corporate seal. Acknowledgment: (or proven by one witness) before judge, clerk of court of record, notary (seal), justice of the peace, police justice, mayor, members of board of supervisors.

Missouri. Witnesses: none if acknowledged. Corporate seal. Acknowledgment: (or proven by one witness) before judge or clerk of court having a seal, notary, justice of the peace; wife so described; expiration of commission; seal; identity known.

Montana. Witnesses: none if acknowledged. Corporate seal. Acknowledgment: (or proven by one witness) before judge of Supreme Court or district court, clerk of court of record, notary, county clerk, justice of the peace (authentication), United States commissioner; identity known or proven; seal; expiration of commission; residence of officer.

Nebraska. Witnesses: none. Corporate seal. Acknowledgment: before judge or clerk of a court, justice of the peace, United States commissioner, notary, deputy clerk of district or county court, Secretary of State, register of deeds or deputy, county clerk or deputy (seal); identity known or proven; seal; expiration of commission.

Nevada. Witnesses: none if acknowledged. Corporate seal. Acknowledgment: (or proven by one witness except by married woman) before judge or clerk of court having seal, notary, recorder, justice of the peace (authentication); seal; identity known or proven.

New Hampshire. Witnesses: one. Seal. Acknowledgment: (or proven) before justice of the peace, notary, commissioner, judge of a court of record, clerk or deputy of court having seal, recorder, master.

New Jersey. Witnesses: none. Seal or recital of seal by natural person. Acknowledgment: (or proven by one witness) before chancellor, attorney at law, judge, master, notary, commissioner of deeds, county clerk, deputy county clerk, surrogate or deputy, register of deeds or deputy; statement as to identity.

New Mexico. Witnesses: none, but two if by mark. Corporate seal. Acknowledgment: before clerk of district court, judge or clerk of probate court (seal), notary (seal), justice of the peace, county clerk (seal); wife so described; identity known; expiration of commission.

New York. Witnesses: none if acknowledged. Acknowledgment: (or proven by one witness) before justice of the peace, official examiner of titles, referee, judge or clerk of court of record, county clerk or recorder, notary, mayor or recorder of city, surrogate, commissioner of deeds, councilman, village police justice, deputies; authentication; identity known or proven.

North Carolina. Witnesses: none. Seal. Acknowledgment: (or proven by one witness) before judge or clerk of Supreme Court or superior court, commissioner of affidavits, clerks of criminal courts, notary, justice of the peace (authentication); seal if officer has one.

North Dakota. Witnesses: none. Acknowledgment: (or proven) before judge or clerk of a court of record, notary, mayor or auditor of a city, register, justice of the peace, United States commissioner, county or city auditor, township or village clerk, deputies; identity known or proven.

Ohio. Witnesses: two. Acknowledgment: before notary, county court judge, county engineer, county auditor, mayor, judge or clerk of a court of record.

Oklahoma. Witnesses: none, but two if by mark. Corporate seal. Acknowledgment: before notary, county clerk, court clerk or county judge; spouse so described; seal; expiration of commission; identity known.

Oregon. Witnesses: none if acknowledged. Acknowledgment: (or proven by one witness) before judge or clerk of Supreme Court, circuit judge, county judge or clerk, justice of the peace, notary; expiration of commission; identity known.

Pennsylvania. Witnesses: none. Corporate seal. Acknowledgment: (or proven by two witnesses) before judge of a court of record, clerk or deputy of court having a seal, recorder, notary, justice of the peace, master, mayor, ward justice, magistrate, alderman, deputy recorder, prothonotary of Supreme Court, United States commissioner; seal; expiration of commission, identity known or proven.

Rhode Island. Witnesses: none. Acknowledgment: before state senator or representative, judge, justice of the peace, mayor, notary, town clerk, recorder.

South Carolina. Witnesses: two. Seal or recital. Acknowledgment: (or proven by one witness except to release dower) before judge, magistrate, clerk of court, notary; identity known; separate of wife to release dower.

South Dakota. Witnesses: none, if acknowledged. Acknowledgment: (or proven by one witness) before judge of court of record, clerk or deputy of court having seal, notary, justice of the peace, commissioner, register, county auditor, mayor of city; seal if officer has one; identity known or proven.

Tennessee. Witnesses: none if acknowledged. Acknowledgment: (or proven by two witnesses) before judge of a court of record, clerk or deputy of county court, or of court having a seal, recorder, justice of the peace, clerk and master of chancery court, notary; seal.

Texas. Witnesses: none. Acknowledgment: (or proven by one of two witnesses) before clerk of district court, judge or clerk of county court, notary; separate of wife; identity known or proven; seal.

Utah. Witnesses: none if acknowledged. Acknowledgment: (or proven by one witness) before judge or clerk of court having seal, notary, county clerk, recorder; identity known or proven; seal; expiration of commission.

Vermont. Witnesses: two. Seal. Acknowledgment: before justice of the peace, town clerk, notary, master, county clerk, judge or register of probate.

Virginia. Witnesses: none if acknowledged. Acknowledgment: (or proven by two witnesses) before justice, commissioner in chancery, clerk or deputy of court of record, notary; expiration of commission.

Washington. Witnesses: none. Corporate seal. Acknowledgment: before judge or commissioner of Supreme Court or superior court, clerk or deputy thereof, justice of the peace, county auditor or deputy, notary, United States commissioner; identity known; seal and residence of notary.

West Virginia. Witnesses: none if acknowledged. Acknowledgment: (or proven by two witnesses) before president of county court, justice of the peace, notary, recorder or clerk of any court; expiration of commission; identity known but officer not required so to state.

Wisconsin. Witnesses: two. Seal. Acknowledgment: before judge of a court of record, clerk or deputy of court having seal, recorder, notary, justice of the peace, master or commissioner, county clerk, police justice, United States court commissioner; seal; expiration of commission; identity known or proven.

Wyoming. Witnesses: none. Corporate seal. Acknowledgment: before judge or clerk of court of record, United States commissioner, county clerk, justice of the peace, notary; seal; expiration of commission; identity known.

DIVISION 8-2: ACKNOWLEDGMENT

SECTION 8-21: GENERALLY

Foreign execution requirements, see Section 8-18.

8-21A Definition; Statute.

R.C. 5301.01 provides: "A deed, mortgage, land contract as referred to in division (B) (2) of section 317.08 of the Revised Code, or lease of any interest in real property must be signed by the grantor, mortgagor, vendor, or lessor, and such signing must be acknowledged by the grantor, mortgagor, vendor or lessor in the presence of two witnesses, who shall attest the signing and subscribe their names to the attestation. Such signing must be acknowledged by the grantor, mortgagor, vendor, or lessor before a judge of a court of record in this state or a clerk thereof, a county auditor, county engineer, notary public, mayor, or county court judge, who shall certify the acknowledgment and subscribe his name to the certificate of such acknowledgment." (As eff. 8-11-61.) This statute has been substantially the same since 1887 except that (a) until August 18, 1943 it provided that acknowledgment should be on the same sheet as the instrument and (b) the provisions regarding land contracts were added on August 11, 1961.

An acknowledgment is a declaration before an authorized officer by the person executing an instrument that such instrument is his act and deed. It is a form of authenticating instruments provided by statutes. The term is also commonly used to designate the certificate by the officer.

259

8-21B Necessity.

There is no conveyance of a legal interest where certificate is as follows: "Personally appeared _____ who acknowledged that he did sign and seal the foregoing instrument, and that the same is his free act and deed." Smith v. Hunt, 13 Ohio 260 (1844).

Where an instrument purporting to convey real estate is acknowledged before a proper officer, but the certificate of acknowledgment is not subscribed by such officer, the instrument is not a valid conveyance, and is inoperative to pass the legal title to the grantees named therein, and may not be upheld in equity. Hout v. Hout, 20 OS 119 (1870).

LAW IN GENERAL

An acknowledgment is not essential to, nor strictly a part of, a deed unless made so by statute. However, the requirement by statute of acknowledgment or a substitute therefor is universal, at least as to the record title. Where the statute requires acknowledgment for validity of an instrument, an omission or substantial defect is fatal and an unacknowledged deed does not pass the legal title. Am Jur 2d, Acknowledgments § 4; Am Law of Prop § 12.60; CJS, Acknowledgments §§ 6, 17; Powell § 895; Tiffany § 1027.

8-21C Effect of Defect.

See also 8-11B.

While acknowledgment of a deed is necessary to entitle it to record, yet as between the parties thereto an unacknowledged deed is effective to pass whatever interest the grantor has to his grantee. Walker v. Detwiler, 110 F2d 154, 17 OO 452 (1940).

Further research: O Jur 3d, Acknowledgments, Affidavits, Oaths, and Notaries § 30.

8-21D Construction.

A mortgage is not invalid where the certificate of acknowledgment does not name the county or state but recites "within and for said county" and grantor and grantee were both described as of a particular county and no other county was named therein. Beckel v. Petticrew, 6 OS 247 (1856).

A certificate describing the officer taking as a notary public, when he was a justice of the peace and signed as such, does not invalidate the acknowledgment. Atlantic Refining Co. v. Wagner, 24 CC(NS) 275, 34 CD 587 (1901).

Standard of Title Examination

(Adopted by Ohio State Bar Association in 1953)

Problem 3.1B:

Should an objection be raised because a deed bears the signatures of only two witnesses and has certificates of acknowledgment in more than one county of the state?

Standard 3.1B:
Yes. Proof should be required that the two witnesses were present at the execution in each county.

8-21E Proof by Witnesses.

The Ohio law makes no provision for proof by witnesses as a substitute for acknowledgment. This is provided for by statutes of some states but seldom used.

8-21F Certificates of Authority and Conformity.

Standard of Title Examination

(Adopted by Ohio State Bar Association in 1952)

Problem 3.1A:
A deed is executed outside of Ohio without an attached certificate showing authority of the notary public. Should objection be made to the title?

Standard 3.1A:
No.

LAW IN GENERAL

The statute of some states require certificates, as to acknowledgments taken outside the state or county, authenticating the official character of the certifying officer or stating that the instrument is executed and acknowledged in conformity with law. Such additional certificates are not necessary in conveyance of Ohio lands. Am Jur 2d, Acknowledgments § 78; 25 ALR2d 1149; CJS, Acknowledgments § 125.

SECTION 8-22: FORM OF CERTIFICATE; MANNER OF TAKING

8-22A Contents of the Certificate.

Curative acts, see 8-31R.

R.C. 147.04 provides: "Before entering upon the discharge of his duties, a notary public shall provide himself with the seal of a notary public. The seal shall consist of the coat of arms of the state within a circle one inch in diameter and shall be surrounded by the words 'notary public,' 'notarial seal,' or words to that effect, the name of the notary public and the words 'State of Ohio.' The seal may be of either a type that will stamp ink onto a document or one that will emboss it. The name of the notary public may, instead of appearing on the seal, be printed, type-written, or stamped in legible, printed letters near his signature on each document signed by him. A notary public shall also provide himself with an official register in which shall be recorded a copy of every certificate of protest and copy of note, which seal and record shall be exempt from execution. Upon the death, expiration of term without reappointment, or removal from office of any notary public, his official register shall be deposited in the office of the county recorder of the county in which he resides." (As eff. 8-23-77.)

Where the person taking acknowledgment of a deed gives himself no official character in his certificate or subscription, the acknowledgment is insufficient and the record of the deed irregular. Johnston v. Haines, 2 Ohio 55 (1825).

In certifying acknowledgment of a deed nothing further is necessary than that the officer "shall subscribe his name" to the certificate. Fund Commissioners of Muskingum v. Glass, 17 Ohio 542 (1848). Authentication by seal is not required by statute, nor is it necessary to the validity of the mortgage. Ashley v. Wright, 19 OS 291 (1869).

Standard of Title Examination

(Adopted by Ohio State Bar Association in 1953)

Problem 3.1C:

Is a deed defective because the seal of the officer taking the acknowledgment is omitted or because his term of office has expired?

Standard 3.1C:

No.

Standard of Title Examination

(Adopted by Ohio State Bar Association in 1955)

Problem 3.1D:

Should a certificate of acknowledgment be deemed sufficient where the acknowledger is described but not named as (a) "John Doe and his wife" or (b) "Personally came the above named grantors?"

Standard 3.1D:

Yes.

Standard of Title Examination

(Adopted by Ohio State Bar Association in 1955 and amended in 1964)

Problem 3.1E:

Should omission of venue from a certificate of acknowledgment render a title unmarketable?

Standard 3.1E:

Omission of venue from the certificate does not render the title unmarketable when the authority of the certifying officer can be established by other records.

Further research: O Jur 3d, Acknowledgments, Affidavits, Oaths, and Notaries § 22.

LAW IN GENERAL

The form of the certificate must substantially comply with the requirements of the statute. Am Jur 2d, Acknowledgments § 40; CJS, Acknowledgments §§ 68, 91; Tiffany § 1030.

The omission of or variance in the name of the acknowledger can sometimes be supplied or overcome by reference to and construction with the body of the instrument. Am Jur 2d, Acknowledgments §§ 61, 66; 25 ALR2d 1124; CJS, Acknowledgments § 92.

The decisions are generally liberal as to the manner of showing the required official position and authority of the certifying officer. Am Jur 2d, Acknowledgments § 53; CJS, Acknowledgments § 87.

Omission of the officer's seal does not render his certificate ineffective unless use of the seal is clearly made mandatory by statute. A statutory requirement of statement of expiration date of notary's commission is ordinarily not mandatory, and its omission does not make the certificate insufficient. Compliance with requirement of showing that the identity of the acknowledger was known or proven is essential to validity. 25 ALR2d 1124.

8-22B Manner of Taking.

If it appeared that there was any fraud or imposition exercised upon the lessor in the acknowledgment taken by telephone or that he had in some way been misled or deceived to his injury, he might in that event rely upon full compliance with the statute requiring acknowledgment to be taken in his presence. Logan Gas Co. v. Keith, 117 OS 206, 158 NE 184, 5 Abs 418, 422, 25 OLR 386, 58 ALR 600 (1927).

Where a notary public witnesses a signing by a mortgagor, there has been an acknowledgment before such notary public. Wayne Bldg. & Loan Co. v. Hoover, 12 OS2d 62, 231 NE2d 873, 41 OO2d 279 (1967).

LAW IN GENERAL

The certificate must show that the acknowledger personally appeared before the officer and that the required acts were performed. The words used are not material. Taking an acknowledgment by use of a telephone does not comply with a statutory requirement of personal appearance before the officer. However, it is often held that the grantor is estopped and that the certificate cannot be impeached except for fraud, mistake, or other equitable ground. A certificate that the instrument was sworn to is not sufficient. Am Jur 2d, Acknowledgments §§ 31, 36; CJS, Acknowledgments §§ 122, 124.

8-22C Acknowledgment in Representative Capacity.

Acknowledgment as individual, see 8-11B.

Where there is a corporate mortgagor and the mortgage has been executed on behalf of the corporation by its president and by its secretary-treasurer, and the certificate of acknowledgment executed by the notary public states that the corporation itself is the mortgagor, and the names of the president and secretary-treasurer do not appear therein, the acknowledgment is not defective because it fails to state the names of the officers of the corporation who signed the mortgage. Mid-American National Bank & Trust Co. v. Gymnastics International, Inc., 6 App3d 11, 451 NE2d 1243 (1982).

Where the language of a lease discloses that it is the lease of a corporation, an acknowledgment by the officers of the lessor, individually and not as officers of the corporation, is sufficient. Anthony Carlin Co. v. Burrows Bros. Co., 54 App 202, 6 NE2d 761, 7 OO 180, 22 Abs 495 (1936).

LAW IN GENERAL

The certificate of an acknowledgment by a person in a representative capacity should show the identity of the principal and the character in which the agent, officer or member acts. The capacity in which the acknowledgment is made may be shown by reference to the instrument; certificates bearing the personal acknowledgment of a corporate officer have been held sufficient to validity. A deed is not sufficient which purports to be executed by an attorney in fact and acknowledged by the principal, as a deed can be acknowledged only by the person who actually signed it. Am Jur 2d, Acknowledgments § 62; 25 ALR2d 1124; CJS, Acknowledgments § 92; Tiffany § 1066.

8-22D Married Women.

There have been no special requirements in Ohio as to acknowledgments by married women since 1887.

8-22E Correction or Addition.

LAW IN GENERAL

The cases are conflicting as to whether the officer who took the acknowledgment may afterward correct or supply the certificate. However, he generally may supply it if the acknowledgment was in fact properly taken and he is still in office. A defect may always be corrected by reacknowledgment and rerecording. In any event, intervening rights may not be prejudicially affected. Am Jur 2d, Acknowledgments § 108; CJS, Acknowledgments §§ 84, 116.

8-22F Curative Acts.

See also the statutes at 8-31R.
Expiration of office, see 8-24A.
Standards of Title Examination, see 8-22A.

Curative acts are given liberal interpretation and are generally effective except that they cannot affect intervening rights which are vested. See 1-22A.

SECTION 8-23: WHO MAY TAKE

8-23A Statutes.

See also Uniform Recognition of Acknowledgments Act, 8-26A.
Foreign execution, see Section 8-18.

R.C. 147.01 provides: "The governor may appoint and commission as notaries public as many persons as he considers necessary, who are citizens of this state and are of the age of eighteen or over. A notary public shall be appointed and commissioned as a notary public for the state. The governor may revoke a commission issued to a notary public upon presentation of satisfactory evidence of official misconduct or incapacity." (As eff. 8-23-77.)

R.C. 317.28 provides: "No county recorder, deputy, or employee of such recorder, shall take the acknowledgment of any instrument required to be filed or recorded in his office." (At eff. 10-1-53.)

R.C. 5301.01 provides that acknowledgments may be taken by a judge of a court of record in this state or clerk thereof, county auditor, county engineer, notary public, mayor, or county court judge. (As eff. 8-11-61.) (These officers have been authorized since 1887.) Authority is also conferred on notary public by R.C. 147.07 (as eff. 8-23-77), county engineer by R.C. 315.23 (as eff. 2-14-67), clerk of a court of record by R.C. 2303.07 (as eff. 10-1-53) and a probate judge by R.C. 2101.05 (as eff. 10-1-53).

From 1893 to 1949, it was provided by G.C. 121, that no person holding an official position to a bank, banker or broker, shall be competent to act as notary public in any matter in which such bank, banker or broker is interested.

8-23B Sufficiency of Authority.

Acts after expiration of commission, see 8-24A.

LAW IN GENERAL

An acknowledgment is ordinarily valid when taken by a de facto officer, or by an official whose term has expired or who has resigned. Am Jur 2d, Acknowledgments § 15; CJS, Acknowledgments § 46.

8-23C Deputies.

LAW IN GENERAL

A deputy of a public officer may generally take an acknowledgment when his principal is authorized to do so. Some decisions are on the ground that ministerial acts may be performed by a deputy if the principal has the power to appoint one. The proper form is for the deputy to act in the name of his principal. Am Jur 2d, Acknowledgments, § 14; 25 ALR2d 1144; CJS, Acknowledgments § 48.

8-23D   Disqualifications.

A grantee of an instrument for the conveyance or encumbrance of real property is disqualified, on the ground of public policy, to certify the acknowledgment of the grantor. Amick v. Woodworth, 58 OS 86, 50 NE 437, 39 WLB 172, 338 (1898).

LAW IN GENERAL

A party to the instrument is disqualified to take the acknowledgment of its execution. An acknowledgment is sometimes held invalid, as to persons with notice, when taken by a person acquiring a beneficial interest under the instrument although he is not a party to it. Am Jur 2d, Acknowledgments § 16; CJS, Acknowledgments § 53; Tiffany § 1028.

A disqualification to take the acknowledgment, because of an interest which does not appear of record, is held not to affect the validity of the instrument as to bona fide purchasers nor to affect constructive notice. Conversely, constructive notice is not imparted when the disqualification appears of record. Am Jur 2d, Acknowledgments § 90; Am Law of Prop § 18.39; CJS, Acknowledgments § 57.

8-23E   Relationship; Spouse.

A wife's inchoate right of dower in the property of her husband is not such as to disqualify her from notarizing the deed conveying such property. Green v. Henderson, 52 NE2d 532, 39 Abs 213 (App. 1943).

LAW IN GENERAL

Relationship, either by blood or marriage, does not disqualify an officer to take the acknowledgment of a party, but it may give support to a claim of fraud. Am Jur 2d, Acknowledgments § 17; CJS, Acknowledgments § 56.

8-23F   Agents and Attorneys.

An officer is not disqualified to take an acknowledgment by reason of being an agent or attorney at law for one of the parties.

Further research: Am Jur 2d, Acknowledgments § 18; CJS, Acknowledgments § 54.

8-23G   Stockholders and Corporate Officers.

A mortgage cannot be impeached merely because the notary public is a stockholder of the mortgagee. Read v. Toledo Loan Co., 68 OS 280, 67 NE 729, 1 OLR 42, 357, 48 WLB 502 (1903).

LAW IN GENERAL

Being a corporate officer or director does not disqualify a person from taking an acknowledgment of an instrument to which the corporation is a party. Am Jur 2d, Acknowledgments § 20; CJS, Acknowledgments § 85.

8-23H   Armed Forces.

R.C. 147.38 provides: "Any commissioned officer of the armed forces of the United States may administer oaths, take depositions, affidavits, and acknowledgments of deeds, mortgages, leases, and other conveyances of lands, and all powers of attorney of any person, or the dependent of any person, who for the time being is in the armed forces of the United States, wherever they may be, and of persons, and dependents thereof, serving with, employed by, or accompanying the armed forces outside the United States, in the same manner as a judge of a county court, commissioner of this state, or notary public might do.

"Any oath administered and deposition or affidavit taken, or acknowledgment certified by such officer if otherwise in accordance with law, shall be as effectual for all purposes, as if administered, taken, or certified by any judge of a county court, commissioner of this state, or notary public." (As eff. 8-19-63.)

This section did not provide for dependents from July 7, 1943 to the above amendment.

After January 1, 1974, a parallel provision has been effective in Ohio as part of the Uniform Recognition of Acknowledgments Act. See 8-26A.

R.C. 147.39 provides: "All instruments referred to in section 147.38 of the Revised Code which have been executed subsequent to January 1, 1941, and which are in conformity with such section as amended July 7, 1943 are valid." (As eff. 10-1-53.)

SECTION 8-24:   TIME AND PLACE OF TAKING

8-24A   Date.

Outside state, see 8-18A.
Standard of Title Examination, see 8-22A.

R.C. 147.12 provides: "An official act done by a notary public after the expiration of his term of office is as valid as if done during his term of office." (As eff. 10-1-53.)

The subsequent acknowledgment by the sheriff, although after his term has expired, is carried back, by relation, to the time of execution of the deed. Doe v. Dugan, 8 Ohio 87, 108 (1837).

Acknowledgment is sufficient although dated prior to the deed if it appears to be a mere clerical error. Fisher v. Butcher, 19 Ohio 406 (1850).

A certificate of acknowledgment should bear its true date. It may be entirely regular and proper for such date to be subsequent to the date of the deed.

A certificate customarily states the expiration date of the officer's commission or that it has no expiration date. Such a statement is not required by statute.

Further research: O Jur 3d, Acknowledgments, Affidavits, Oaths, and Notaries §§ 16, 18.

LAW IN GENERAL

An error in or omission of the date of the certificate does not invalidate the acknowledgment. Am Jur 2d, Acknowledgments § 47; 25 ALR2d 1141; CJS, Acknowledgments § 85.

8-24B Reacknowledgments; Later Acts.

See also 8-22E.

A later corrected acknowledgment takes effect from the date of the instrument as between the parties.

Further research: Am Jur 2d, Acknowledgments § 110; CJS, Acknowledgments §§ 37, 66.

8-24C Venue.

Standard of Title Examination, see 8-22A.

R.C. 1907.18 provides that county court judges, within and coextensive with their counties, have jurisdiction and authority to take acknowledgments of instruments in writing. (As eff. 3-1-87.)

A justice of the peace may take acknowledgments outside his county of deeds for the conveyance of lands within his county. The decisions supporting similar acknowledgments have stood as the law of this state for many years and until the doctrine has become a rule of property which ought not to be disturbed. Crumbaugh v. Kugler, 2 OS 373 (1853).

An acknowledgment taken by a notary public or justice of the peace outside the county for which commissioned, for lands located outside such county, is null and void. Empire Gas & Fuel Co. v. Coolahan, 112 OS 30, 146 NE 389, 3 Abs 98, 99, 23 OLR 36, 37 (1925).

LAW IN GENERAL

As a general rule, an officer may take acknowledgments only in the district for which he is appointed. The tendency of modern law is to limit invalidity on account of the place where taken. The venue must be shown, but the omission of the state or county in which the officer acted is frequently held to be supplied by reference to the instrument or to other parts of the certificate. Am Jur 2d, Acknowledgments §§ 27, 28; CJS, Acknowledgments § 42.

SECTION 8-25: CONCLUSIVENESS OF CERTIFICATE

8-25A When Impeached.

A certificate of acknowledgment is conclusive of the facts therein stated in the absence of fraud, where the grantee is not put upon inquiry and has acted on the faith of the conveyance. Baldwin v. Snowden, 11 OS 203 (1860).

Where fraud is clearly shown, the acknowledgment may be declared invalid, and it is not necessary to show that the mortgagee had notice of such fraud. Williamson v. Carskadden, 36 OS 664 (1881).

A mere preponderance of the evidence is not sufficient to support a finding contrary to the certificate of acknowledgment. Ford v. Osborne, 45 OS 1, 12 NE 526, 17 WLB 207 (1887).

The certificate of a notary, while not conclusive where fraud or forgery is shown, should be given such weight that to overcome it the evidence must be clear and convincing. In re Lion Brewery, Inc., 3 OO 260 (Fed. 1935).

Positive statement by notary or witnesses of inflexible rule never to sign instrument, unless parties signed in their presence, carries great weight. Coshocton Nat. Bank v. Hagans, 40 App 190, 178 NE 330, 10 Abs 203 (1931).

A mortgage regular on its face but not in fact acknowledged before a notary public and in the presence of two witnesses is not entitled to record, and does not have priority over a properly executed mortgage which is recorded subsequently. Citizens Nat. Bank v. Denison, 165 OS 89, 133 NE2d 329, 59 OO 96 (1956).

Though the note was fully discharged by the mortgagor's bankruptcy, the mortgage remained valid as a lien, and even though the acknowledgment was defective, it remained valid as between the mortgagor and the mortgagee's assignee. Seabrooke v. Garcia, 7 App3d 167, 654 NE2d 961 (1982).

LAW IN GENERAL

A certificate is generally conclusive as to all statements required to be recited therein. It ordinarily may not be impeached by merely disproving the truth of the recitals, in the absence of fraud, if the officer had jurisdiction. Bona fide purchasers are protected in some of the cases against invalidity on the ground of fraud, mistake and the like. However, the certificate may be set aside in the absence of estoppel, even as to innocent parties, when it is shown that there was in fact no acknowledgment at all before an officer having jurisdiction. Am Jur 2d, Acknowledgments § 92; CJS, Acknowledgments § 121; Tiffany § 1030.

SECTION 8-26: UNIFORM RECOGNITION OF ACKNOWLEDG-MENTS ACT

8-26A Generally.

R.C. 147.51 provides that notarial acts may be performed outside this state for use in this state by the following persons authorized by other governments in addition to any other persons authorized by the laws and regulations of this state:

(A) A notary public authorized to perform notarial acts in the place in which the act is performed; (B) A judge, clerk, or deputy clerk of any court of record in the place in which the notarial act is performed; (C) An officer of the foreign service of the United States, a consular agent, or any other person authorized by regulation of the United States Department of State to perform notarial acts in the place in which the act is performed; (D) A commissioned officer in active service with the armed forces of the United States and any other person authorized by regulation of the armed forces to perform notarial acts if the notarial act is performed for one of the following or his dependents: (1) A merchant seaman of the United States; (2) A member of the armed forces of the United States; (3) Any other person serving with or accompanying the armed forces of the United States; (E) Any other person authorized to perform notarial acts in the place in which the act is performed. (As eff. 1-1-74.)

R.C. 147.52 provides for proof of authority when required. (As eff. 6-13-75.)

R.C. 147.53, 147.54 and 147.541 provide for the contents of the certificate and that "acknowledged before me" means, among other things, that "the person taking the acknowledgment either knew or had satisfactory evidence that the person acknowledging was the person named in the instrument or certificate."

R.C. 147.55 provides: "The forms of acknowledgment set forth in this section may be used and are sufficient for their respective purposes under any section of the Revised Code. The forms shall be known as 'Statutory short forms of acknowledgment' and may be referred to by that name. The authorization of the forms in this section does not preclude the use of other forms." (As eff. 1-1-74.)

R.C. 147.56 provides that this act does not diminish nor invalidate the recognition accorded to notarial acts by other laws or regulations of this state. (As eff. 1-1-74.)

R.C. 147.57 and 147.58 provide for uniform interpretation and for the title to this act. (As eff. 1-1-74.)

DIVISION 8-3: CONSTRUCTION AND EFFECT

SECTION 8-31: GENERALLY; CAPACITY

Bona fide purchasers, see Section 1-32.
Class gifts, see Division 11-9.
Construction generally, see also 11-11D.
Corporations and associations, see Chapter 4.
Covenants and restrictions, see Chapter 6.
Effect of defects, see 8-11B.
Estates and future interests, see Chapter 11.
Records and recording laws, see Division 1-2.

8-31A   Rule of Interpretation.

Law of situs, see 8-11A.

R.C. 5301.02 provides: "The use of terms of inheritance or succession are not necessary to create a fee simple estate, and every grant, conveyance, or mortgage of lands, tenements, or hereditaments shall convey or mortgage the entire interest which the grantor could lawfully grant, convey, or mortgage, unless it clearly appears by the deed, mortgage, or instrument that the grantor intended to convey or mortgage a less estate." (As eff. 10-1-53.) See also R.C. 5302.04 at 8-11D.

"Courts, in construing deeds and like written instruments, must be guided by the intention of the parties to them, and this must be determined by the language used in the instrument, the question being not what the parties meant to say, but the meaning of what they did say, as courts cannot put words into an instrument which the parties themselves failed to do." Larwill v. Farrelly, 8 App 356, 360, 28 CC(NS) 305, 30 CD 196 (1918).

Further research: O Jur 3d, Deeds § 82.

LAW IN GENERAL

Deeds are construed according to the law at the time of execution in the state where the land is situated. Rules of construction are applied to ascertain the intention of the parties from the language used. They will not be applied when the language is unambiguous nor when the effect of certain words is a rule of property. Am Jur 2d, Deeds § 159; CJS, Deeds § 80.

8-31B Construing Whole Instrument.

There is no reason why the term "heirs" in the granting clause might not be explained or qualified in the clauses which follow, so as to limit the grant to the issue of the grantee, and to show that the grantee was only to take a life estate or a qualified fee. Smith v. Hankins, 27 OS 371, 1 WLB 114 (1875).

It is a well settled rule that the plain purport and purpose of an instrument, as a whole, should control the ordinary meaning of particular words, so far as to make them conform to that purport and purpose. Newark Coal Co. v. Upson, 40 OS 17, 24 (1883).

In construing a written instrument, effect should be given to all of its words, if this can be done by any reasonable interpretation. Wadsworth Coal Co. v. Silver Creek Mining & Ry., 40 OS 559, 11 WLB 155 (1884).

The intention of the parties to a deed should be gathered, if possible, from the whole instrument; and no part of the deed should be rejected as repugnant to the granting clause, unless the repugnancy is irreconcilable. Martin v. Jones, 62 OS 519, 57 NE 238, 43 WLB 342 (1900).

Further research: O Jur 3d, Deeds § 84.

LAW IN GENERAL

The intention as expressed by the whole instrument is given effect if possible. Written parts will prevail over printed parts if they are irreconcilable. Courts will not disregard one clause as repugnant unless that is necessary in order to give effect to the deed. Am Jur 2d, Deeds §§ 162, 163; CJS, Deeds § 84; Powell § 902; Tiffany § 981.

The rule giving greater weight to written or typewritten words than to printed ones has been applied even where contrary to the old rules of preference for the granting clause or for earlier words over later ones. 37 ALR2d 820.

8-31C Operation Favored.

The modern controlling principle requires everything in the deed to be given effect if possible. Metzger v. Joyce, 70 App 94, 41 NE2d 261, 23 OO 176, 35 Abs 338 (1941).

LAW IN GENERAL

If one of two constructions would make the conveyance effective and the other ineffective, the former is preferred. Am Jur 2d, Deeds § 164; Tiffany § 964.

8-31D Technical Words.

Words of inheritance, see Section 11-12.

If the intention of the parties is apparent from an examination of the deed "from its four corners," it will be given effect regardless of technical rules of construction. Hinman v. Barnes, 146 OS 497, 66 NE2d 911, 32 OO 564 (1946). Further research: O Jur 3d, Deeds § 84.

LAW IN GENERAL

Technical words will be given their technical meaning unless a contrary intention is expressed. Am Jur 2d, Deeds § 211.

8-31E Preference for Granting Clause.

See also habendum at 8-12C.

A recital, in the consideration clause of a deed of a reservation by the grantor of a use of the land, without a forfeiture provision or right of re-entry, is a mere revocable license and does not run with the land. Licking County Agricultural Society v. Board of County Commissioners, 48 App 528, 194 NE 606, 2 OO 119, 17 Abs 235, 40 OLR 193 (1934). Further research: O Jur 3d, Deeds § 168.

LAW IN GENERAL

The granting clause prevails when its conflict with other clauses is irreconcilable. This rule is frequently applied to provisions of the habendum, especially when such provisions diminish the estate conveyed by the granting clause. However, many cases hold that the conflicting provisions are reconcilable under the rule that the intention should be gathered from the whole instrument. Am Jur 2d, Deeds § 194; CJS, Deeds § 90; Tiffany § 980.

8-31F   Order of Clauses.

LAW IN GENERAL

When conflict between clauses of a deed cannot be reconciled, a preference is given to the earlier clause if other considerations are equal. The later clause is preferred in construing a will. CJS, Deeds § 90; Restatement, Property § 246; Tiffany § 979.

8-31G   Recitals.

Constructive notice, see 1-31F.
Recitals as evidence, see 1-21C.

LAW IN GENERAL

Recitals yield to clear operative words of a deed when the two parts are repugnant and cannot be reconciled. Recitals are generally not essential to official deeds but, when made, are prima facie evidence of the facts stated.

"The same being one-half undivided interest" has been held not to limit the previous terms conveying all the interest of the grantor. However, equity will enforce the actual intention in such a case. Am Jur 2d, Deeds § 197.

8-31H   Practical and Contemporaneous Construction.

Where the meaning of a deed is uncertain, it may be found and formed in the construction placed upon it, at the time of execution and for many years afterwards, by the parties to it. Creed v. Henkel, 18 CC 883, 9 CD 861 (1898).

In construing a written instrument which is open to more than one interpretation such effect will be given to it as the conduct of the parties at the time of its execution indicates they intended it should have. Boynton v. Strauss, 18 CC(NS) 229, 33 CD 1 (1908).

LAW IN GENERAL

The practical construction by the conduct of the parties, or the surrounding circumstances, will be considered when the intention of the parties cannot be ascertained from the language used. Separate instruments executed in one transaction will be considered in particular cases. Am Jur 2d, Deeds §§ 171, 172; Tiffany § 983.

8-31I   In Favor of Grantee.

The language of a deed is the language of the grantor and will be construed most strongly against him, the effort being made to harmonize all the provisions thereof. Anderson v. Pryor, 51 App 35, 199 NE 364, 2 OO 446, 19 Abs 237 (1935); Goebel v. Cincinnati Postal Terminal & Realty Co., 120 OS 19, 165 NE 350, 7 Abs 127, 28 OLR 425 (1929).

This rule is only called into use as a last resort to resolve ambiguity. Metzger v. Joyce, 70 App 94, 41 NE2d 261, 23 OO 176, 35 Abs 338 (1941).

Further research: O Jur 3d, Deeds § 90.

LAW IN GENERAL

Construction in favor of the grantee is a rule of last resort and will be adopted only when all other rules fail. Government grants are an exception to the rule and interpretation is in favor of the government. Am Jur 2d, Deeds § 165; Tiffany § 978.

8-31J As Deed or Will.

Delivery on grantor's death, see Section 8-43.

A trust conveyance is not rendered testamentary by the reservation of a life estate and a power of revocation or modification. Cleveland Trust Co. v. White, 58 App 339, 16 NE2d 588, 9 OO 239, 24 Abs 629 (1937), affd. 134 OS 1, 15 NE2d 627, 11 OO 377 (1938).

LAW IN GENERAL

An instrument is a deed, as distinguished from a will, if it conveys a present interest, even though the interest is contingent or possession is deferred until grantor's death. An instrument is not a deed if it has no present effect and is therefore revocable. A provision that the property is conveyed "after my decease" is usually construed as merely postponing the grantee's right to possession. When an instrument cannot be given effect as a deed, it may be construed as a will if sufficiently executed and if the provisions thereof will permit such interpretation. Am Jur 2d, Deeds § 176; 31 ALR2d 538; CJS, Wills § 137.

8-31K Correction Deeds.

Acknowledgments, see 8-22E.
Ratification, see 16-69C.
Re-recording, see 1-24C.

LAW IN GENERAL

A deed of correction accepted by the grantee relates back to the date of the original instrument, except as to intervening rights, and operates as a reformation in equity. The two deeds are construed together. They are generally held to effectuate the intention of the parties, so that a deed correcting an error nullifies the prior deed to the extent of the mistake. Am Jur 2d, Deeds § 287; CJS, Deeds § 31.

8-31L Void or Voidable.

Infants, see 15-11E.
Insane persons, see 15-12E.

LAW IN GENERAL

A void deed conveys no title. It is said that ratification or estoppel cannot validate a void deed. Title is conveyed by a voidable deed, but the deed may be set aside before title is acquired by an innocent purchaser for value. CJS, Deeds § 66.

8-31M Appurtenant Rights.

See also 10-18A.

A claim for damages for a portion of property taken for a street will not pass under a deed of the portion not taken. Hatcher v. Brown, 29 NP(NS) 567 (C.P. 1932).

LAW IN GENERAL

Rights which are appurtenant to the land conveyed will pass without specific or general mention. A right of action for previous damage to the realty is not included in this rule. Am Jur 2d, Deeds § 256; CJS, Deeds § 106.

8-31N Greater Interest than Grantor Owns.

A deed by a tenant for life purporting to convey the title in fee, passes the life estate, but does not forfeit it to the reversioner or remainderman. Carpenter v. Denoon, 29 OS 379, 2 WLB 63 (1876).

By the terms of R.C. 5301.02, every grant now conveys or mortgages the grantor's entire interest unless a different intention clearly appears by the instrument.

LAW IN GENERAL

Where the granting clause includes a greater estate or larger fractional interest than the grantor owned, the deed operates to convey the interest which the grantor had. Am Jur 2d, Deeds § 289; CJS, Deeds § 104.

8-31O To Grantor's Heirs; Worthier Title.

Gifts to heirs generally, see Section 11-93.

The use of the words "heirs of the grantor" to designate the parties as grantees of the remainder is ineffectual. Kuhn v. Jackman, 32 App 164, 166 NE 247, 7 Abs 186 (1929).

LAW IN GENERAL

"Worthier title" is the doctrine that a conveyance of a remainder, or other interest, from a person to his heirs is not effective to designate either the transferees or the kind of interest the heirs may receive. This rule of the common law may obtain as to deeds even where it has been repudiated as to wills. The modern tendency is to regard it as a rule of construction rather than as a rule of law. The words "to the heirs of the grantor" or their equivalent are required for the application of the rule. Under this doctrine, a deed from A "to B for life, remainder to the heirs of A" leaves the reversion in A which he may subsequently convey or devise. The rule is independent of the rule in Shelley's Case and is sometimes known as the rule in Bingham's Case. Am Law of Prop § 4.19; 16 ALR2d 691; Powell § 381; Restatement, Property § 314; Simes and Smith § 1601; Tiffany § 312.

8-31P   Capacity.

Corporations and associations, see Chapter 4.
Incompetent persons, see Chapter 15.

Where the grantor has sufficient intellect to understand in a general way the nature, effect and immediate consequences of the transaction, and he consents to it, it is valid and binding, and cannot be set aside for lack of mentality. Monroe v. Shrivers, 29 App 109, 162 NE 780, 6 Abs 709 (1927).

LAW IN GENERAL

A person who is able to understand the nature of the act and to apprehend its consequences has the mental capacity to execute a valid deed. A greater degree of competence is often required for the execution of a deed than of a will. Am Law of Prop § 12.69; CJS, Deeds § 54.

8-31Q   Official Deeds.

Record as evidence, see 1-21C.

R.C. 3.06 in part provides: "(A) A deputy, when duly qualified, may perform any duties of his principal." (As eff. 1-10-61.)

R.C. 2329.34 and 2329.35 provide for conveyance of real estate by a master commissioner. (As eff. 10-1-53.)

R.C. 2329.36 provides for official deeds and that they contain "the names of the owners of the property sold, a reference to the volume and page of the recording of the next preceding recorded instrument by or through which the owners claim title." (As eff. 9-9-57.)

R.C. 2329.43 provides for execution of deed by successor of officer who made the sale, upon certificate from clerk of court. (As eff. 10-1-53.)

Acknowledgment of sheriff's deed is indispensable. Roads v. Symmes, 1 Ohio 281 (1824).

Deputy sheriff may execute a valid deed for lands sold on execution by himself or principal. Haines v. Lindsey, 4 Ohio 88 (1829).

A deed of deputy sheriff is void unless executed in the name of his principal. The acknowledgment of such a deed is void if made after the death of the principal. Anderson v. Brown, 9 Ohio 151 (1839).

If sheriff's deed recites enough to show his authority, it is good, though it does not recite all the statute requires. Perkins v. Dibble, 10 Ohio 433 (1841).

8-31R Curative Acts.

R.C. 5301.07 provides: "When any instrument conveying real estate, or any interest therein, is of record for more than twenty-one years in the office of the county recorder of the county within this state in which such real estate is situated, and the record shows that there is a defect in such instrument, such instrument and the record thereof shall be cured of such defect and be effective in all respects as if such instrument had been legally made, executed, and acknowledged, if such defect is due to any one or more of the following:

"(A) Such instrument was not properly witnessed.

"(B) Such instrument contained no certificate of acknowledgment.

"(C) The certificate of acknowledgment was defective in any respect.

"Any person claiming adversely to such instrument, if not already barred by limitation or otherwise, may, at any time within twenty-one years after the time of recording such instrument, bring proceedings to contest the effect of such instrument.

"This section does not affect any suit brought prior to November 9, 1959, in which the validity of the acknowledgment of any such instrument is drawn in question." (As eff. 1-10-61.)

R.C. 5301.071 provides: "No instrument conveying real estate, or any interest therein, and of record in the office of the county recorder of the county within this state in which such real estate is situated shall be deemed defective nor shall the validity of such conveyance be affected because:

"(A) The dower interest of the spouse of any grantor was not specifically released but such spouse executed said instrument in the manner provided in section 5301.01 of the Revised Code.

"(B) The officer taking the acknowledgment of such instrument having an official seal did not affix such seal to the certificate of acknowledgment.

"(C) The certificate of acknowledgment is not on the same sheet of paper as the instrument.

"(D) The executor, administrator, guardian, assignee, or trustee making such instrument signed or acknowledged the same individually instead of in his representative or official capacity." (As eff. 11-9-59.) Similar statutory provisions have been effective since June 22, 1925.

SECTION 8-32: DESIGNATION OF PARTIES

Particular types of organizations, see Division 4-2.

8-32A Certainty of Designation; Heirs.

Conveyances to heirs or a class generally, see Division 11-9.
Variance in name, see Section 1-27.

A conveyance is good where the grantee is described in sufficient terms to designate who is intended, though neither his Christian nor surname is used. Irwin v. Longworth, 20 Ohio 581 (1851).

Where an error occurs in a written instrument, apparent on its face, and from its contents, susceptible of correction, so as to identify the party with certainty, such error does not affect the validity of the instrument. Dodd v. Bartholomew, 44 OS 171, 5 NE 866, 15 WLB 223, 276 (1886).

LAW IN GENERAL

If the designation of the grantor and grantee furnishes the means of their identification, it is sufficient for the validity of the conveyance. Thus, a deed to "heirs" of a deceased person is sufficient, but not a deed to "heirs" of a living person unless by way of a future interest after a particular estate or unless the deed is construed to intend a grant to the prospective heirs now in being. Am Jur 2d, Deeds §§ 48, 53; Am Law of Prop § 12.93; CJS, Deeds § 13.

8-32B Omission from Body of Deed.

Dower release since 1925, see 8-31R.

LAW IN GENERAL

When a person executes a deed but is not named in the body thereof, he is generally held not to be a party unless he is the sole grantor. The grantee is not required to be named in the granting clause if he is clearly identified as such in the body of the deed. Am Law of Prop § 18.28.

8-32C Existence of Grantee.

"It contains none of the formalities which the wisdom of ages has settled as necessary to convey real estate.... It is indispensable to the validity of a grant, that the grantee be capable of receiving it; that is, that he be a person in being at the time of the grant made." Sloane v. McConahy, 4 Ohio 157, 169 (1829).

A transfer to a fictitious person is a mere nullity. Muskingum Valley Turnpike Co. v. Ward, 13 Ohio 120 (1844).

The grantee must be in esse except where the deed operates as a creation of a future interest, as, for example, a remainder. Britsch v. Roth, 17 O Supp 46, 31 OO 534 (C.P. 1945).

A quitclaim deed, in which the grantee is named as "Estate of _____, Ward," is an effective and valid instrument of conveyance to the ward where such intention is judicially ascertained. Alston v. Alston, 4 App2d 270, 212 NE2d 65, 33 OO2d 311 (1964).

Further research: O Jur 3d, Deeds § 38.

LAW IN GENERAL

A conveyance is not effective if a grantee is not in existence and capable of taking at the time of the deed, nor if he cannot be ascertained. An unborn child cannot be the sole grantee, even though en ventre sa mere. A deed is valid between the parties when from or to a person under an assumed or fictitious name, but not when to a fictitious person. Although it is not effective as a conveyance, an instrument may create an equitable interest, as in the representatives of a decedent when the deed is to the "estate" of the decedent. Am Jur 2d, Deeds §§ 43, 52; Am Law of Prop § 12.40; Restatement, Property § 46n.

8-32D   To A "or" B.

See also 8-16C.
Standard of Title Examination, see 8-16B.

Where a husband makes a loan from his individual funds and causes the note received in return to be made payable to himself "or" his wife, in the absence of competent evidence concerning his intention, it will be presumed he intended to transfer to his wife an undivided one-half interest in the proceeds. Parker v. Parker, 2 Misc 93, 203 NE2d 513, 30 OO2d 551 (1965).

LAW IN GENERAL

A deed to two or more persons in the disjunctive, as "to A or B," is usually invalid because of uncertainty as to the grantee. Tiffany § 967.

8-32E   From Grantor to Himself.

Conveyance to grantor and another person, see also 5-24C.
Survivorship deeds, see also Section 8-16.

R.C. 5302.18 provides: "A deed in which a grantor is also a grantee is effective to convey the interest in the title of the grantor or grantors to all of the grantees in the proportion and manner indicated in the deed." (As eff. 4-4-85.)

Where the grantor is named as grantee, the deed is a nullity; and the same rule applies as if no grantee were named in the premises. Irwin v. Longworth, 20 Ohio 581 (1851).

A deed where the grantors and grantees are the same persons which clearly shows an intention to create the right of survivorship is effective and upon the death of either of them the real estate became the property in fee simple of the survivor. Cleaver v. Long, 126 NE2d 479, 69 Abs 488 (C.P. 1955).

Further research: Am Law of Prop §§ 12.93, 18.44.

LAW IN GENERAL

The decisions are in conflict on whether it is possible for one by means of a conveyance to himself and another to transform his ownership into an ownership in joint tenancy or by the entirety. The trend of the decisions, and of legislation as well, is toward allowing the tenancies in question to be created by one conveyance. 44 ALR2d 595.

SECTION 8-33: FILLING BLANK; ALTERATION

8-33A Alterations.

The alteration, to vitiate a deed or contract in writing, must be such as to effect some change in the meaning or legal operation of the instrument. Huntington v. W. M. Finch & Co., 3 OS 445 (1854).

Erasure of grantee's name in deed and insertion of name of another held not conveyance to latter. Iciofano v. Spero, 3 Abs 263 (App. 1925).

If the deed, when delivered, is a complete deed and alterations and additions made therein have been with the knowledge of the grantors and with their consent, even after they have signed the deed and before it is delivered, it is a good deed. Sommer v. Wade, 6 Abs 118 (App. 1928).

After title has passed by the due execution of a deed, transfer cannot be effected by erasing the name of the grantee and inserting the name of another to whom the parties intend that title shall pass. McNair v. Bright, 18 Abs 92 (App. 1934).

The contract of warranty is enforceable as to the land description amended by interlineation after execution of the deed and before delivery, provided it was authorized, consented to or ratified by the grantors or if they are estopped to deny its validity. Naso v. Daniels, 8 App2d 42, 220 NE2d 829, 37 OO2d 48 (1964).

Further research: O Jur 3d, Alteration of Instruments § 12.

LAW IN GENERAL

A material alteration made after delivery, concerning the operation of a deed as a grant, does not generally change the effect of the deed as to the estate conveyed. However, substitution of the name of the grantee has been held to render the deed inoperative. A material alteration, after delivery, of executory provisions or of covenants makes them unenforceable by the person making the alteration. Alterations made before delivery are effective if authorized by all the parties. In any case the grantor may be estopped by the particular facts from denying the validity of the deed. A bona fide purchaser is often protected under the principle that the loss must fall on the one of two innocent parties who made the loss possible. Am Jur 2d, Deeds § 142; Am Law of Prop § 12.85; Tiffany §§ 970, 989.

8-33B Presumptions.

Where it is claimed by a defendant in a suit upon a promissory note, or similar instrument, that it has been altered since its execution, the burden is upon him to prove that it was so altered; the presumption being that any alteration appearing on the face of the paper, was made at or before the time of its execution. Franklin v. Baker, 48 OS 296, 27 NE 550, 25 WLB 314 (1891); Fensler v. Sterling, 132 OS 498, 9 NE2d 283, 8 OO 489 (1937).

Further research: O Jur 3d, Alteration of Instruments § 51.

8-33C Filling Blanks.

The ancient law was well settled that a valid deed could not be made by writing it over a signature and seal, made upon a blank or an empty sheet of paper. We know of no decision by which this ancient doctrine is overruled. An authority to fill one particular blank falls far short of an authority to make an entire deed. Ayres v. Harness, 1 Ohio 368, 372 (1824); Conover v. Porter, 14 OS 450 (1863); Schueler v. Lynam, 80 App 325, 75 NE2d 464, 36 OO 32, 49 Abs 225 (1947).

Grantor may be estopped to ask that invalid deed be set aside. Becker v. Shade, 17 CC(NS) 83, 32 CD 29 (1910).

Further research: O Jur 3d, Alteration of Instruments § 39.

LAW IN GENERAL

When blanks are filled in by authority of the grantor before delivery, the deed is effective. Even when filled in without authority before delivery, the grantor is usually estopped to deny the validity of the deed. When the grantor executes a blank paper which is later filled without his authority, he is frequently held not to be estopped as to the grantee. Filling a blank is equivalent to making an alteration and likewise may avoid the deed as between the parties or may raise an estoppel against the grantor. Am Jur 2d, Deeds § 138; 11 ALR2d 1372; CJS, Deeds § 33.

8-33D Blank for Name of Grantee.

The deed, if defective and ineffectual to pass the legal title because no grantee was named therein, must nevertheless be held valid in equity as a contract to convey. There is no defect apparent on the face of the conveyance and, under the circumstances, the grantor would be estopped to claim that the name of the grantee was not inserted prior to its execution. Holden v. Belmont, 32 OS 585, 589, 3 WLB 355 (1877).

Further research: O Jur 3d, Deeds § 38.

LAW IN GENERAL

Where a deed is executed with a blank for the name of the grantee, the grantor's agent acting within his authority may fill in the name before delivery. It is generally held that, during the lifetime of the grantor and with his authority, the blank may be filled in, even by the grantee. Some courts hold that the authority must be in writing. When the insertion is unauthorized, a bona fide purchaser is generally protected on the basis of estoppel. The conveyance is not effective if the purchaser knew that the name inserted was not the one intended by the grantor. Am Law of Prop § 12.42; 175 ALR 1294; CJS, Deeds § 25; Tiffany § 969.

SECTION 8-34:   ESTOPPEL BY DEED; AFTER-ACQUIRED TITLE AND PROPERTY

Equitable estoppel, see Section 16-69.

8-34A   Definition.

The general rule is that if a grantor having no title, a defective title, or an estate less than that which he assumes to grant, conveys with warranty or covenants of like import, and subsequently acquires the title or estate which he purported to convey, or perfects his title, such after-acquired or perfected title will inure to the grantee or to his benefit by way of estoppel. Ernst v. Keller, 20 App 171, 177, 151 NE 790, 4 Abs 221 (1925).

Further research: O Jur 3d, Estoppel and Waiver § 12.

LAW IN GENERAL

Estoppel by deed is a bar which precludes a party from denying any material assertion in the deed or from asserting any right inconsistent with his deed. A grantee claiming under a deed may be estopped to deny its validity or to reject its burdens. Am Law of Prop § 15.18; CJS, Estoppel § 10.

8-34B   Nature of Operation.

Period of the search, see 1-31D.

The estoppel extends to all persons subsequently acquiring the title. Douglass v. Scott, 5 Ohio 194 (1831).

Where A received a deed of conveyance in fee from B in 1851, A having executed a deed of mortgage to C in 1849 and one to D in 1854, held: "That the deed to C, being recorded prior to the execution and record of the deed to D, was entitled to the same respect in law and equity as against D that it was entitled to against B, his grantor." Philly v. Sanders, 11 OS 490 (1860).

Where one has sold with warranty what he does not own but subsequently acquires, the grantee takes the title by estoppel. Broadwell v. Phillips, 30 OS 255, 2 WLB 150 (1876).

LAW IN GENERAL

Where it appears from the recitals, covenants or other parts of a deed that the grantor intended to convey a certain interest, he is generally estopped to deny such a conveyance or to claim an after-acquired title to such interest adversely to the grantee. The grantee may compel his grantor to execute an additional deed. The rule operates in favor of the successors in interest of the grantee. Subsequent claimants under the grantor are bound under some of the decisions even though they are purchasers for value without notice. It is frequently held that an after-acquired title of the grantor actually passes to the grantee by estoppel. Some courts hold that an express or implied covenant is required for the operation of the doctrine. Am Jur 2d, Deeds § 294; Am Jur

2d, Estoppel and Waiver § 4; Am Law of Prop § 15.19; CJS, Estoppel § 21; Tiffany § 1230.

The rule as to title afterward acquired by the grantor has been applied to defeat an action for damages on the covenants of title. However, the grantee may elect to accept the after-acquired title or to pursue his claim for damages where he asserted the claim before the grantor acquired the title. Am Law of Prop § 15.23; Tiffany § 999.

8-34C   Invalid Deeds.

A covenant of warranty in a defectively executed deed does not operate as an estoppel. Patterson v. Pease, 5 Ohio 190 (1831).
Further research: Am Law of Prop § 15.24; CJS, Estoppel § 41.

8-34D   Recitals.

Recitals are not estoppels where the deeds containing them are not operative. Wallace v. Miner, 6 Ohio 367 (1834).
Further research: O Jur 3d, Estoppel and Waiver § 19.

LAW IN GENERAL

Material recitals in a deed are binding upon the parties and their privies in accord with the intention of the parties. Strangers are not bound, unless in the case of ancient deeds, and have no right to claim that recitals are estoppels. CJS, Estoppel § 36.

8-34E   Quitclaim Deeds.

If conveyance contains no covenants of warranty, or recitals, and there are no acts of the grantor amounting to an equitable estoppel, he is not estopped from asserting an after-acquired title. Hart v. Gregg, 32 OS 502, 3 WLB 281 (1877); Kinsman v. Loomis, 11 Ohio 475 (1842).

A quitclaim deed containing the clause "the said grantor, nor its successors and assigns, nor any other person claiming title through or under it, shall or will hereafter claim or demand any right or title to the premises herein conveyed" will effect an estoppel. Garlick v. Pittsburgh & Western Ry., 67 OS 223, 65 NE 896, 47 WLB 769, 48 WLB 94 (1902).

LAW IN GENERAL

Quitclaim deeds generally do not operate to transfer an after-acquired title. However, when the grantor has an equitable or inchoate interest, the subsequent acquisition by him of the legal title will inure to his grantee. The grantor may be estopped when the deed recites that a definite estate is conveyed. Contingent interests may be conveyed by a quitclaim deed. Am Jur 2d, Deeds § 303; 162 ALR 656; CJS, Estoppel § 22.

8-34F   Particular Interests; After-acquired Property.

An after-acquired legal title will not pass under a warranty as against an anterior and paramount equitable title. Buckingham v. Hanna, 2 OS 551 (1853).

The force and effect of the estoppel in favor of the first grantee is, in law, just as binding upon a subsequent grantee as it is upon the grantor of both grantees. The innocent purchaser or mortgagee who acquired his title or lien prior to acquisition of the after-acquired title by the common grantor is preferred to the subsequent purchaser or mortgagee. Philly v. Sanders, 11 OS 490 (1860).

A grantor of a warranty deed is not estopped from claiming a prescriptive right to use a portion of the land conveyed where such right is acquired by adverse possession after such deed. Kimball v. Anderson, 125 OS 241, 181 NE 17, 36 OLR 307 (1932).

A lease will operate to pass an after-acquired title. The basis of the doctrine is estoppel and the rule operates both ways. The lessor is estopped by the demise of the leasehold interest with covenant for quiet enjoyment, express or implied. The lessee is estopped because, being in undisturbed possession, he is not permitted to deny lessor's title. Liberal Savings & Loan Co. v. Frankel Realty Co., 137 OS 489, 497, 30 NE2d 1012, 19 OO 170, 173 (1940).

An unencumbered title acquired by the mortgagor subsequently to plaintiff's mortgage inured as against the mortgagor and those claiming under him. A later grantee of the mortgagor is estopped by the covenants in the mortgage from setting up an adverse claim. Laughlin v. Vogelsong, 5 CC 407, 3 CD 200 (1891), revd. on other grounds 51 OS 421, 38 NE 111 (1894).

LAW IN GENERAL

Mortgages and leases usually operate in equity on after-acquired property and titles, when they so provide, as between the parties and as to persons with actual notice. Provisions encumbering after-acquired property of public utility corporations are generally made effective by statutes or by decisions. A provision as to after-acquired property does not ordinarily prevail against bona fide purchasers. In some cases only an equitable lien is created which is subordinate to the claims of judgment creditors and others. Am Jur 2d, Mortgages § 242; Am Law of Prop § 16.34; CJS, Mortgages § 73; Powell § 443; Tiffany § 1231.

8-34G   Heirs of Grantor.

Heirs of the warrantor, standing in his place, are estopped by the warranty. Bond v. Swearingen, 1 Ohio 395, 412 (1824).

LAW IN GENERAL

Heirs are not estopped from asserting a title acquired otherwise than from the ancestor bound by the doctrine. Tiffany § 1234.

8-34H Expectancies.

See also 11-14B.

After-acquired property did not pass under a grant of "our right, title and interest" although with covenants of warranty. Burkey v. Canal Winchester Bank, 20 Abs 656 (App. 1935); White v. Brocaw, 14 OS 339 (1863). Unless the contingent remainder is specifically included. Pollock v. Brayton, 29 App 296, 163 NE 573, 6 Abs 614 (1928).

LAW IN GENERAL

A warranty deed by a prospective heir is generally held to estop him from denying its validity on the death of an ancestor. The rule does not extend to a quitclaim deed. Considerable conflict on the conveyance of expectancies exists in the cases, which are usually decided on the equities under the particular circumstances. Am Jur 2d, Assignments §§ 56, 57; 121 ALR 450.

8-34I Fiduciaries and Agents.

The doctrine of estoppel does not operate to defeat the trust estate where a person without title conveys with warranty and afterward receives title as trustee. Burchard v. Hubbard, 11 Ohio 316 (1842).

LAW IN GENERAL

The estoppel is binding only upon and operates only in favor of the parties and those claiming under them. A deed made by a person in an individual capacity does not bind him in a representative capacity. A person is not estopped individually by accepting a deed in a representative capacity. As a general rule, a grantor acting in a representative capacity is estopped to assert an individual right inconsistent with the deed. 64 ALR 1556; CJS, Estoppel § 46.

SECTION 8-35: DELIVERY

Conditions precedent, see 8-41C.
Delivery on grantor's death, see Section 8-43.
Escrow, see Division 8-4.

8-35A Necessity.

It is the delivery which gives the instrument force and effect. Kemp v. Walker, 16 Ohio 118, 121 (1847).

The title to real estate is conveyed and transferred by delivery of a deed. Kern v. Gardner, 26 App 48, 159 NE 840, 3 Abs 589 (1925).

Further research: O Jur 3d, Deeds § 57.

LAW IN GENERAL

A deed is not operative until it is delivered. Delivery is essential to any effect even in equity except, in unusual cases, a deed may be construed as a contract to convey. An undelivered deed is ineffective even as to bona fide purchasers, in the absence of ratification or estoppel; for example, rights are not ordinarily acquired under a deed if possession of it was obtained by force, theft or fraud. Am Jur 2d, Deeds § 79; Tiffany § 1035.

8-35B   Sufficiency; Revocation.

Conditional delivery, see also 8-41C.
Construction as a will, see 8-31J.
Unrecorded deed between spouses, see 8-35D.

Although there may have been no manual delivery of the deed, nor anything said, in terms, about its delivery, yet the fact of delivery may be found from the acts of the parties preceding, attending and subsequent to the execution. Dukes v. Spangler, 35 OS 119, 4 WLB 802 (1878).

Where a deed conveying real estate is executed and delivered, the destruction of the unrecorded instrument will not stop the grantee to claim the land under such conveyance, unless such claim would operate as a fraud on his part. Jeffers v. Philo, 35 OS 173, 4 WLB 858 (1878).

A delivery which will pass title occurs only when the grantor parts with his dominion over the deed with the intention to pass title. Hale v. Hale, 31 Abs 299 (App. 1938).

No particular form or ceremony is essential in the delivery of a deed; delivery may be made by words and acts or either, if accompanied with the intention that they shall have that effect. A deed is not rendered inoperative because the grantor retains possession of the property and the deed during his life where a life estate is reserved in the deed. In re McKitterick's Estate, 94 App 373, 115 NE2d 163, 52 OO 35 (1953).

The mere manual transfer of a deed does not constitute delivery unless it is coupled with an intent to make a present, immediate and unconditional conveyance of title. Tucker v. Morey, 102 App 328, 143 NE2d 627, 2 OO2d 359 (1956).

Further research: O Jur 3d, Deeds § 63.

LAW IN GENERAL

Whether or not there is a delivery is primarily a question of the intention of the grantor as to the deed being presently operative to pass title. There is no delivery when the grantor retains the right to control, to revoke, or to regain possession of the deed. The grantor must relinquish control during his lifetime in order for the delivery to be effective. A manual delivery is not essential but some act of the grantor showing an intent to make the deed presently operative is required. Neither a retaining of possession by the grantor, unless with a right to do so, nor a filing for record is conclusive. The presumption arising from the grantee's possession of the deed is rebuttable. Am Law of Prop §§ 12.64, 12.66; 141 ALR 305; 87 ALR2d 787; CJS, Deeds § 40; Powell § 896; Tiffany §§ 1034, 1036.

When the grantor gives the custody of the deed to his agent or, in some cases, to the grantee with the intention that it shall be operative if he does not cancel it or otherwise dispose of the property, then there is no delivery and the instrument can be effective only as a will. Am Jur 2d, Deeds §§ 92, 96; CJS, Deeds §§ 42, 46.

8-35C As Contract to Convey.

Defective deeds, see 8-11B.

An instrument in the form of a deed but not delivered as such may nevertheless be delivered as an executory contract so as to take the case out of the statute of frauds. Thayer v. Luce, 22 OS 62 (1871).

8-35D Presumptions; Dates.

The record of a deed is prima facie evidence of its delivery. Such prima facie case may be rebutted by proof. Mitchell v. Ryan, 3 OS 377 (1854); Frank v. Barnes, 40 App 328, 178 NE 419, 10 Abs 460 (1931).

Where deed from husband to wife was not delivered personally by him to her, but was placed on record, date of delivery thereof was date when it was filed for record. State Exchange Bank v. Royce, 26 App 508, 160 NE 526, 5 Abs 560 (1927).

A deed is presumed to have been executed and delivered as of the date it bears, but this presumption is rebuttable, and it is well settled that the true date may be established by parol testimony. Walser v. Farmers Trust Co., 126 OS 367, 185 NE 535, 37 OLR 561 (1933).

Where a husband and wife simultaneously execute mutual deeds to each other for real property which they own as tenants in common and place them unrecorded in a box in their home, to which both have access, with the understanding that upon the death of one the survivor will take all the property by the deeds of the one first dying and that the deeds of the survivor will not take effect, the transaction is ineffective to pass title to the wife after the husband's death. Kniebbe v. Wade, 161 OS 294, 118 NE2d 833, 53 OO 175 (1954).

Delivery is not shown of an unrecorded deed from husband to wife found in a joint access safety deposit box although contained, with another deed undeniably belonging to the grantee, in an envelope bearing an endorsement by the grantor that the deeds belong to the grantee. In re Ketterer's Estate, 152 NE2d 178, 78 Abs 204 (Prob. 1956).

Under former bankruptcy law (11 U.S.C. § 96(a)), a transfer of real estate is not "deemed to have been made" until the deed is recorded under Ohio law. Murphy v. Haynes, 168 NE2d 888, 83 Abs 307 (App. 1959). For current bankruptcy law, see 11 U.S.C. § 547(e). (As eff. 10-1-79.)

Standard of Title Examination

(Adopted by Ohio State Bar Association in 1952 and supplemented by Comment 3.3A in 1964)

Problem 3.3A:

Should a title be considered unmarketable when it appears from the county records that the grantor died before the deed was filed for record?

Standard 3.3A:

Yes, unless waived for lapse of time or unless there is satisfactory proof of delivery before death.

An affidavit of the notary public or the witnesses, of an attorney at law for a party in the transaction, or of other responsible persons who were present at the time of delivery, should be deemed satisfactory proof if setting forth sufficient facts.

Delivery should be presumed after the deed has been of record for twenty-one years, in the absence of other facts raising a doubt.

Comment 3.3A:

See Kniebbe v. Wade, 161 OS 294, 118 NE2d 833 (1954). This case was decided after the above standard was adopted. [See the case digest above.]

LAW IN GENERAL

Delivery is presumed, although not conclusively, from the grantee's possession of the deed or of the land. The presumption is not applied where a husband and wife execute deeds to each other with the intent that the deed of the one dying first shall be operative. Recording raises a presumption of delivery, the presumption being stronger where the conveyance is to wife or child. The date of the deed is presumed to be the time of delivery but the true time of delivery may be shown. When the date of acknowledgment is later than the date of execution, the presumption of delivery is usually held to be on such later date. Am Jur 2d, Deeds §§ 109, 115; CJS, Deeds § 184; Powell § 899; Tiffany § 1040.

8-35E To One of Grantees; by One of Grantors.

Where a regularly executed deed is delivered by the husband without the knowledge of the wife and is accepted by the grantee, acting in good faith and without knowledge of her dissent, she will be bound by such delivery. Baldwin v. Snowden, 11 OS 203 (1860).

LAW IN GENERAL

Delivery to one of the cograntees is sufficient, as a rule. Delivery by one of cograntors is not sufficient in the absence of express or implied authority from the other grantors. 162 ALR 892; CJS, Deeds § 49.

8-35F Subsequent Acts; Revesting in Grantor.

Alteration, see 8-33A.

Where a deed was delivered by grantor to grantee or his agent, and later handed back to the grantor, the title passed to the grantee, and was not reconveyed by the mere return of the deed. Baldwin v. Bank of Massillon, 1 OS 141 (1853).

Destruction by mutual consent of a deed after delivery and before recording with the intention of revesting the title will not have that effect. Spangler v. Dukes, 39 OS 642, 11 WLB 58 (1884).

Further research: O Jur 3d, Deeds § 176.

LAW IN GENERAL

Since title vests at delivery it is not divested by alteration, destruction, endorsement, loss or surrender of the deed after delivery. Redelivery of the deed by the grantee with the intention of revesting title in the grantor does not have that effect. However, courts of equity frequently give effect under the rules of ratification or estoppel to the intention of the parties in the alteration, destruction or surrender but subject to intervening rights of third persons. Am Jur 2d, Deeds § 310; CJS, Deeds § 173; Tiffany § 1067.

SECTION 8-36: ACCEPTANCE

8-36A Generally; Effective Date.

It is a general rule that acceptance by the grantee is necessary to constitute a good delivery. But where a grant is beneficial to the grantee his acceptance is presumed in the absence of proof to the contrary. Mitchell v. Ryan, 3 OS 377 (1854).

Title to real estate is not vested in the grantee of a deed until he accepts the same, notwithstanding the recording. Lemley v. Shafer, 14 App 362, 32 CC(NS) 177 (1921).

Further research: O Jur 3d, Deeds § 58.

LAW IN GENERAL

A grantee may refuse to accept a deed and, in such case, it will not operate as a conveyance. Acceptance is generally implied on delivery but actual acceptance may be at a subsequent time. A deed becomes operative at the time of delivery, which is prima facie the date of execution. Acceptance relates back to the time of delivery except that it does not do so to the prejudice of third persons. Am Law of Prop § 12.70; CJS, Deeds § 51; Tiffany § 1055.

8-36B Effect.

Covenants, see 6-11F.

Acceptance is essential to liability of the grantee on his covenants.

8-36C Manner of Acceptance.

Acceptance may be shown under the same rules as delivery is shown. See Section 8-35.

The grantee may be bound as having accepted by ratification, estoppel or any other conduct showing an intention to accept.

Further research: Am Jur 2d, Deeds § 128.

LAW IN GENERAL

An intention to take title must be manifested. As sometimes stated, there must be an intelligent assent to the conveyance and an intention that it is to become immediately effective. 74 ALR2d 992.

8-36D Presumptions.

LAW IN GENERAL

Acceptance is presumed when the conveyance is beneficial to the grantee, especially if he is incompetent. Acceptance of a conveyance in trust is likewise presumed. Recording is prima facie evidence of acceptance. The requirement of acceptance is very rarely of significance in the decision of a case. Am Jur 2d, Deeds § 132; Powell § 900.

DIVISION 8-4: ESCROW

SECTION 8-41: GENERALLY

8-41A Definition.

"An escrow in Ohio, as between grantor and grantee of real estate, is witnessed by a written instrument known as an escrow agreement, delivered by mutual consent of both parties to a third party denominated the depositary or escrow agent, in which instrument certain conditions are imposed by both grantor and grantee, which conditions the depositary or escrow agent, by the acceptance and retention of the escrow agreement, agrees to observe and obey." Squire v. Branciforti, 131 OS 344, 2 NE2d 878, 6 OO 59 (1936).

An escrow is a written instrument deposited by the grantor with a third party, beyond the further control of such grantor, until the performance of a condition or the happening of a certain event, and then to be delivered to the grantee. McGriff v. McGriff, 74 NE2d 619, 48 Abs 218 (App. 1947).

LAW IN GENERAL

An escrow is a deed, bond, money or other property deposited by one party to a contract with a third party to be held until the performance of a condition or until the happening of a specified event, and then to be delivered according to the depositor's instructions.

The term "escrow" is also commonly used to mean the transaction in which the grantor and grantee of a deed deliver to the depositary or escrowee a written agreement or instructions by which both the grantor and grantee impose certain conditions and instructions to be observed and obeyed by the depositary. CJS, Escrows § 1; Tiffany § 1048.

8-41B Unauthorized Delivery; Bona Fide Purchasers.

Deposit of deed in escrow is at grantor's risk as to innocent purchasers for value without notice and as to subsequent judgment creditors of grantee who have extended credit in reliance upon the record title. Micklethwait v. Fulton, 129 OS 488, 196 NE 166, 2 OO 484 (1935).

Further research: O Jur 3d, Escrows § 9.

LAW IN GENERAL

The delivery of a deposit without authority or without full performance of the condition is not effective between the parties unless it has been ratified. 48 ALR 405; 54 ALR 1246.

By the weight of authority, when the grantee has wrongfully obtained possession of a deed deposited in escrow, a purchaser from him for value and in good faith acquires a good title, and creditors extending credit in reliance on the record title are protected, even though the grantor of the escrow was not negligent. 54 ALR 1246.

8-41C Delivery to Grantee; Condition Precedent.

Permissible depositaries, see also 8-45A.

LAW IN GENERAL

In a considerable number of modern cases it has been held that manual delivery to the grantee is not conclusive of legal delivery in the special circumstances, and that the effective delivery may be subject to a condition precedent. A majority of the decisions are that delivery to the grantee is sufficient to pass title although made subject to a parol condition; that is, the promise of the grantee does not invalidate the deed if the grantor does not reserve any control over the deed. Am Law of Prop § 12.66; Tiffany § 1049.

SECTION 8-42: CREATION

8-42A Necessity of a Writing.

Where a duly executed deed is placed in escrow, a preliminary enforceable contract is not essential to the validity of the escrow. Farley v. Palmer, 20 OS 223 (1870).

An undelivered deed may be partial evidence of a contract to sell and be sufficient to take the case out of the operation of the statute of frauds. Thayer v. Luce, 22 OS 62 (1871).

Where an agreement for the purchase of real estate provided that the seller was to furnish an occupancy prmit, but the subsequently executed escrow agreement contained no such stipulation, the escrow agent has no duty to

291

ensure that an occupancy permit is obtained absent express incorporation of the purchase agreement into the escrow agreement. Janca v. First Federal Savings & Loan Ass'n of Cleveland, 21 App3d 211, 486 NE2d 1216 (1985).

LAW IN GENERAL

Many cases hold that the instrument or deposit may be recalled in the absence of a valid contract. By the weight of authority, a preliminary contract is not necessary, and escrow instructions signed by the party to be charged are alone a sufficient compliance with the statute of frauds. Am Jur 2d, Escrow §§ 3, 8; CJS, Escrows § 2; Tiffany § 1052.

The condition upon which the conveyance is to become effective must be agreed upon by the parties unless acceptance is presumed. The condition may be in writing or oral, or partly in writing and partly oral. Am Jur 2d, Escrow § 5.

8-42B   Revocation; Control by Grantor.

Delivery upon death, see 8-43A.
Permissible depositaries, see 8-45A.

Where a grantor delivers his duly executed deed to a third person, to be delivered by him to the grantees named therein at the grantor's death, and the grantor then and there intends to part with all right to withdraw, revoke or control the instrument, and such deed is delivered accordingly and recorded, the title to the property passes to the grantees. Oberholtz v. Oberholtz, 79 App 540, 74 NE2d 574, 35 OO 381 (1947); Crooks v. Crooks, 34 OS 610, 4 WLB 237 (1878).

A vendor had no right, without notice to his vendee, to cancel the contract for delay in payment or to withdraw the escrow. O'Brien v. Bradulov, 80 NE2d 685, 51 Abs 343 (App. 1948).

Where the grantor had access to the deed, that fact will be considered in determining whether or not the grantor had delivered the deed with the intent to convey his interest and with an acceptance by the grantee. McDevitt v. Morrow, 94 NE2d 2, 57 Abs 281 (App. 1950).

LAW IN GENERAL

To constitute an escrow the grantor must surrender all control over the instrument, and the deposit must be irrevocable, except when the condition is not performed or the event does not happen. Am Jur 2d, Escrow § 8; Am Law of Prop § 12.67; CJS, Escrows § 5; Tiffany § 1050.

8-42C   Interest as Vested or Contingent.

See also 8-44B.

"Upon delivery to the third party, or escrow agent, the escrow-grantee has either a contingent, or vested future interest, contingent when the deed is delivered subject to the performance of conditions by the grantee, vested when the deed is deposited to await the happening of a certain future event." Charles C. White, "Escrows and Conditional Delivery of Deeds in Ohio," 2 Cin. L. R. 28 (1928).

LAW IN GENERAL

After delivery as an escrow is made, if possession of the grantee is to await an event which is certain to happen, the grantee has a vested future interest. Some authorities distinguish such a conditional delivery from a delivery in escrow subject to performance of a condition, but no difference in effect is observed except that in the latter case the grantee's interest is contingent until performance. The interest of the grantee does not vest while a condition may not be performed nor while the event may not occur. Am Jur 2d, Escrow §§ 10, 20.

SECTION 8-43: DELIVERY ON GRANTOR'S DEATH

Conditional delivery, see also 8-41C.
Control by grantor, see also 8-42B.
Presumption of delivery to spouse, 8-35D.

8-43A   Rules.

"The instrument was not only revocable by the grantor at any time before his death, but not having parted with all dominion over it during life, it became, on his death, a mere nullity." Williams v. Schatz, 42 OS 47, 50, 11 WLB 146 (1884).

A deed, placed in escrow by the grantor, is not inoperative because it contains a clause that the conveyance "is not intended to be of any force or effect in the lifetime of the said grantor." Johnson v. Darling, 32 CC(NS) 113, 35 CD 699 (1921).

Where the grantor directs the depositary that in the event of the death of the grantee before the death of the grantor to return the deed to the grantor, the delivery is ineffective, and no title passes. Leatherman v. Abrams, 86 App 149, 90 NE2d 402, 41 OO 15 (1949).

Further research: O Jur 3d, Deeds § 73.

LAW IN GENERAL

The giving of a deed into the custody of a third person with instructions to deliver it to the grantee after the grantor's death is a common form of delivery. It is valid, and acceptance by the depositary is sufficient as acceptance by the grantee. The grantor must not retain control of the deed and must intend the deed to be presently effective subject to the happening of the event. Am Jur 2d, Deeds § 101; 52 ALR 1222; CJS, Deeds § 45; Tiffany § 1054.

SECTION 8-44: TIME DELIVERY BECOMES EFFECTIVE

8-44A Rule.

"Where the grantor delivers his deed to a third person to be delivered by him to the grantee at the death of the grantor, without reserving to himself any control over the instrument, and such deed is delivered accordingly to the grantee, the title passes to the grantee upon such last delivery, and, by relation, the deed takes effect as of the date of the first delivery." Crooks v. Crooks, 34 OS 610, 4 WLB 237 (1878); Ball v. Foreman, 37 OS 132, 6 WLB 343 (1881); Patrick v. Parrott, 92 OS 184, 110 NE 725, 13 OLR 75, 60 WLB 216 (1915).

Further research: O Jur 3d, Deeds § 70.

LAW IN GENERAL

The delivery into escrow generally fixes the operative date of the deed between the parties and all those claiming under them excepting intervening bona fide purchasers. The deed is effective, subject to the conditions, from the time of delivery to the escrow agent so that the death or incapacity of either or both the parties occurring before the performance of the condition does not affect the escrow. Ownership in possession passes when the condition is satisfied. Am Jur 2d, Escrow §§ 11, 28; 117 ALR 69; CJS, Escrows § 13.

8-44B Time Title Passes; "Second Delivery"; "Relation Back."

It is not essential to the validity of a deed that it be actually delivered to, or ever pass into the hands of, the grantee. If delivered to a third person as an escrow, it will take effect immediately on the performance of the condition, and if necessary for the purpose of protecting the grantee against intervening rights, will be held to take effect from the time of its first delivery. Shirley v. Ayres, 14 Ohio 307 (1846).

It is not essential to the validity of a deed left by one person with another, to be delivered to a third person on the happening of an event, certain to happen, as on the death of the grantor, that the grantee should survive the grantor. Pence v. Blackford, 11 CC 204, 5 CD 320 (1895).

Where an owner of real property executes a deed thereto and deposits it in escrow, until the escrow conditions are performed and the deed is delivered by the depositary to the grantee the legal title remains in the grantor. Caine v. Lakewood, 194 NE2d 471, 28 OO2d 355, 92 Abs 129 (C.P. 1961).

"As a result of the Ohio cases discussed or cited herein, the following affirmations may be made: An escrow deed cannot be set up as a defense in ejectment proceedings to prove an outstanding title in a third person; the grantee cannot be the depositary; the depositary must be a disinterested party; the grantee's agent is not precluded from acting as depositary; delivery by the depositary before satisfaction of conditions, passes no title as against grantor, but whether or not an innocent purchaser is protected is an open question; no actual 'second delivery' is necessary, since title passes upon performance of conditions; no title passes unless conditions be performed; to constitute a valid escrow the grantor must have relinquished all control over the deed; the depositary is a trustee rather than an agent; a preliminary enforceable contract is not essential to the validity of an escrow; the escrow instructions alone may be used to show compliance with the statute of frauds.

"The theory of escrows that we adopted for this discussion is briefly this: That there is only one delivery and that the first one; that there is only one passing of title, the time of absolute vesting being the time when the conditions are performed, or the stated period has elapsed; that upon delivery to the third party, or escrow agent, the escrow-grantee has either a contingent, or vested future interest, contingent when the deed is delivered subject to the performance of conditions by the grantee, vested when the deed is deposited to await the happening of a certain future event; that from its delivery to the third party, or escrow agent, the deed is operative against the grantor, and against all persons claiming through or under the grantor, except purchasers for value without notice; that there is no necessity for the attempted distinction, in the cases, between the typical escrow situation, and the deposit of a deed to await the happening of a certain future event; that the talk about 'first and second delivery' and 'relation back' is always confusing and never necessary.

"We submit that this theory fits the actual decision in all the Ohio cases with the possible exception of Rathmell v. Shirey, and that case can be brought within the theory, if it be conceded that general creditors of a decedent are entitled to the privileges of a purchaser for value without notice. And practically, that was what the court decided." Charles C. White, "Escrows and Conditional Delivery of Deeds in Ohio," 2 Cin. L. R. 28 (1928).

Further research: O Jur 3d, Escrows § 11; Tiffany §§ 1051, 1053.

SECTION 8-45: STATUS AND LIABILITIES OF DEPOSITARY

8-45A   Rule; Permissible Depositaries.

Delivery to grantee, see 8-41C.

There is no such personal identity between the grantee and his agent to preclude the latter from becoming the depositary of an escrow for the grantor. Cincinnati, W. & Z. R.R. v. Iliff, 13 OS 235 (1862).

The depositary occupies a dual capacity as agent insofar as the manual duties are concerned, and as a paid trustee insofar as the purchase money is concerned. Squire v. Branciforti, 131 OS 344, 2 NE2d 878, 6 OO 59 (1936).

Deeds do not operate to convey when they are delivered by grantor to his wife in escrow and he has access to them. Gross v. List, 15 CC(NS) 113, 23 CD 579 (1912).

An attorney at law may become a trustee in escrow for his client. McGriff v. McGriff, 74 NE2d 619, 48 Abs 218 (App. 1947); McGrew v. Hawker, 3 Abs 324 (App. 1925).

Further research: O Jur 3d, Escrows § 5.

LAW IN GENERAL

The depositary is a trustee in the principal aspects of an escrow. He may also act as the agent of either or both the parties in the performance of duties incidental to the transaction. In particular cases, he has been held to be a mere stakeholder. Am Jur 2d, Escrow §§ 11, 17, 23, 40; CJS, Escrows § 6.

As a general rule, a deposit with the agent of the grantor is a retention of the instrument, and a deposit with the agent of the grantee is a presently effective delivery. However, according to modern authority, the attorney or general agent of the grantee is qualified to be the escrow agent of both parties if his acceptance involves no violation of duty to his client or principal. It has been held possible for the attorney or agent of the grantor to be the depositary of an escrow. Tiffany § 1049.

8-45B   Conflict with Agreement.

The depositary under an escrow agreement has a duty to carry out the terms of the agreement as intended by the parties and may not perform any acts with reference to handling the deposit, or its disposal, which are not authorized by the escrow agreement. Escrow is controlled by the escrow agreement, placing the deposit beyond the control of the depositor and earmarking the funds to be held in a trust-like arrangement. Pippin v. Kern-Ward Bldg. Co., 8 App3d 196, 456 NE2d 1235.

8-45C   Recovery from Depositary.

Failure of escrow agent to follow instructions rendered such agent liable in damages. Union Trust Co. v. Broadway House Wrecking Co., 9 Abs 318 (App. 1931).

Further research: O Jur 3d, Escrows § 7.

LAW IN GENERAL

The depositary is charged with strict execution of his duties and is liable in damages if he parts with the deposit in a manner not authorized by the instructions. Substantial compliance is not sufficient to escape liability. CJS, Escrows § 8.

8-45D   Recovery Between the Parties.

A condition in the deposit of a deed in escrow for the sole benefit of one of the parties may be waived by such party and a delivery enforced notwithstanding such condition. Kaminski v. Lawyers Title Ins. Corp., 113 NE2d 921, 65 Abs 225 (App. 1952).

If the principal does not take all steps reasonably within his power to disaffirm promptly and effectively the unauthorized acts of the escrow agent, such principal will be deemed thereby to have ratified such acts. The principal cannot ratify beneficial portions and repudiate those which are detrimental. Ward v. National Bank of Paulding, 5 Misc 140, 212 NE2d 191, 34 OO2d 321 (C.P. 1965).

LAW IN GENERAL

Losses resulting from defaults of the depositary fall upon the party to the escrow who was entitled to the property or right at the time the loss occurred. 15 ALR2d 870.

8-45E   Closing Reminders.

AGREEMENTS AND PARTIES

Carefully read the instructions of all parties and their agreements.

Consider identification, age, competency and marital status of the parties.

If a corporation, inquire as to corporate existence, franchise tax, special provisions for this kind of corporation, whether for entire assets, and authority of the officers acting. Is this a foreign corporation needing a certificate of authority?

Is time of the essence? Is there agreement as to extension of time? When are instruments and funds to be returned if not closed? Are prorations to be as of a definite date or as of the adjourned closing? Is place of closing agreed? Date of possession and adjustment for delay? Rights upon impossibility of closing?

TITLE

What form of title evidence is required and who to pay therefor? Are contents of title report, including terms of leases, etc., acceptable to all parties? Does purchaser know of other claims?

Examine all instruments for variations in names or description, for defects and for new provisions. Is power of attorney revoked? Is good title conveyed?

File instruments and cancellations and obtain final title report.

Examination of title must be made to the time of filing the instruments for record. Where it is not possible to close in escrow and make disbursements after filing, the closing is sometimes done by reliance upon a closing affidavit of the grantor.

Plat required for recording deed?

SURVEY AND INSPECTION

Necessity of survey?

Identity of buildings on this legal description?

Location of buildings and driveway on this description?

Encroachments by adjoining owners?

Violations of restrictions and zoning ordinances?
Rights to and location of signs?
Implied easements for way of necessity, drain, etc.?
Mechanics' liens not of record?
Questioning of parties in possession?
Building condition, safety, termites, etc.?
Assessments not shown by treasurer's records?
Variation in quantity of land?
Fixtures or growing crops to be transferred?
Damage to property since contract?

LIENS OLD AND NEW

Have commitment of balance due to time to payment. Will payment be accepted? Is penalty for prepayment required? If lien holder is an individual, have the cancellation in hand.

If assumed, are any payments past due and is consent of mortgagee required? Is first mortgage due before the second mortgage?

Are there federal estate and gift taxes?

If any personal property, is it subject to mortgage, conditional sale contract, taxes, levy of execution or bulk sales law? Is bill of sale required?

Are taxes adjusted per deed or prorated per current rate?

INSURANCE, RENT, AND UTILITIES

Have insurance assigned or obtain new policy. Should amount be increased? Is it transferable and paid? Who takes risk of loss before closing?

Present assigned insurance immediately to agent for endorsement or notify him.

Is water rent or other utility delinquent?

Are rents prepaid or delinquent? To be prorated?

Arrange for transfer of utility services.

DISBURSEMENTS

Are all documents properly executed and checks endorsed?

Has down payment been disposed of and are all deposits collectible?

If exchange, treat each part as a separate transaction.

Pay vendor; taxes now payable; other liens; proration of taxes; insurance now due; insurance proration; rents adjusted or prorated; F.H.A. premium; deposits to mortgagee for future taxes, insurances, F.H.A. premium, or interest to time of first payment.

Pay fees for title evidence, attorney, closing, real estate commission, survey, recording, and of mortgagee or broker.

Obtain signatures to closing statement and receipts between the parties.

Get instructions for delivery or mailing of instruments.

DIVISION 8-5: CANCELLATION OR RESCISSION

SECTION 8-51: GENERALLY

8-51A Jurisdiction.

LAW IN GENERAL

Courts of equity have general jurisdiction to order cancellation or rescission of instruments of conveyance. The remedy is applied in accord with ordinary equitable principles. Placing the parties in status quo is usually a condition precedent to granting relief.

Further research: Am Jur 2d, Cancellation of Instruments; CJS, Cancellation of Instruments §§ 7-15.

8-51B Grounds.

The presumption of validity attaching to a deed which appears upon its face to have been executed in due form can only be overcome by clear and convincing proof. Weaver v. Crommes, 109 App 470, 167 NE2d 661, 120 OO2d 15 (1959).

Further research: O Jur 3d, Cancellation and Reformation of Instruments §§ 1, 2, 4, 10.

LAW IN GENERAL

The principal grounds for rescission are fraud; duress; undue influence; mistake; want or failure of consideration together with bad faith. Failure of consideration, such as nonpayment of the purchase price, or lack of consideration, is not ground for cancellation unless there was inequitable conduct at the time of the conveyance. Relief will be granted when the invalidity does not appear on the face and the instrument is a cloud on the title.

8-51C Notice.

When rescission is by act of a party, notice of election to rescind is necessary. Notice of action for judicial rescission is not essential unless for the protection of a party who has acted in good faith.

Further research: O Jur 3d, Cancellation and Reformation of Instruments § 31.

8-51D By Act of Parties.

See also 8-35F.

When a deed has been delivered, title cannot be revested in the grantor by a return to him or by surrender or destruction of the instrument. In particular cases of unrecorded deeds the practical effect of revesting in the grantor may be accomplished by operation of the doctrine of estoppel.

8-51E Survival of Right of Action.

The right to cancel a deed obtained from a grantor by mistake, fraud, duress or undue influence descends to his heirs if it existed in the ancestor unimpaired at the time of his death. Czako v. Orban, 133 OS 248, 13 NE2d 121, 10 OO 321 (1938).

8-51F Void or Voidable Deeds.

Collateral attack, see Section 16-13.

LAW IN GENERAL

A void deed is subject to collateral attack. As a general rule, a voidable deed may be attacked only by the person directly injured thereby. CJS, Deeds § 69.

8-51G Deed for Support of Grantor.

Where father conveyed premises to his son in consideration that son would support him during life, and the son abandoned the contract and sold his interest: Held that the father is entitled to a reconveyance against the purchaser from the son, as the purchase was under circumstances reasonably sufficient to apprise him of the father's equities. Reid v. Burns, 13 OS 49 (1861).

Notwithstanding that father's deed of property in consideration of support contained no forfeiture clause, he is entitled to decree canceling deed for fraud. Widen v. Widen, 33 App 37, 168 NE 477, 7 Abs 446 (1929).

A deed from father to son executed in consideration of son's promise to support father may be canceled for nonperformance on the ground of hardship and inadequacy of legal remedy of damages. Ford v. Ford, 71 App 396, 43 NE2d 756, 26 OO 326, 36 Abs 355 (1942).

Further research: O Jur 3d, Cancellation and Reformation of Instruments § 23.

LAW IN GENERAL

Conveyances made in consideration of the grantee's promise to support the grantor are usually canceled in equity when the grantee fails to perform the promise. Such a conveyance is frequently held to create an estate on condition subsequent or on special limitation rather than a mere covenant. Am Law of Prop § 4.7; 76 ALR 742; CJS, Cancellation of Instruments § 29; Tiffany § 216.

SECTION 8-52: MISTAKE

8-52A Rules.

Reformation, see Section 16-66.

A mistake as to the effect of a statute of descent of another state is a question of fact and equity may grant relief in such case. Miller v. Bieghler, 123 OS 227, 174 NE 774, 9 Abs 190, 34 OLR 7, 73 ALR 1257 (1931).

It is a settled rule of equity that a mistake which results from the negligence of the party complaining furnishes no ground for rescission. Hannah v. Pixley, 9 Abs 526 (App. 1930).

Where no adequate remedy at law can be had, a court of equity will grant relief from the consequences of any mistake of fact which is a material element of the transaction and which is not the result of the mistaken party's own violation of some legal duty. Alliance First Nat. Bank v. Maus, 100 App 433, 137 NE2d 305, 60 OO 350 (1955).

Further research: O Jur 3d, Cancellation and Reformation of Instruments § 24.

LAW IN GENERAL

When the mistake is unilateral, the proper remedy is rescission. Reformation will not be granted unless the mistake is mutual, except when the conveyance represents a gift. A deed will usually not be rescinded for a mistake of the grantor alone, unless he exercised ordinary diligence and the grantee obtained an unconscionable benefit.

It is said that equitable relief will not be granted for a mistake of law. However, either rescission or reformation will be granted when any material mistake is coupled with misrepresentations, misplaced confidence or other sufficient equitable ground. A mistake as to the ownership or title to the land, or as to the law of a foreign state or country, is usually considered to be a mistake of fact.

A deed may be rescinded if there was no meeting of the minds, or be reformed if it does not carry out the agreement of the parties.

Mistake does not render a deed void, and bona fide purchasers from the grantee are protected.

Am Jur 2d, Deeds § 155; CJS, Deeds § 55; Tiffany § 985.

SECTION 8-53: FRAUD; DURESS AND UNDUE INFLUENCE

8-53A Fraud.

Courts will not grant relief on the ground of defect of title when there was no fraud and no eviction. Hill v. Butler, 6 OS 207 (1856).

In the absence of fraud, parol evidence may not be accepted to vary the terms of a written contract for the sale of real estate. Dover Bay Homes, Inc. v. Quinn, 116 App 448, 184 NE2d 480, 22 OO2d 269, 90 Abs 100 (1962).

A signer of a mortgage, who is of ordinary mind and can read and is not prevented from reading what he signs, is negligent in signing without reading it and does not have a defense thereto on the ground of fraud. Leedy v. Ellsworth Constr. Co., 9 App2d 1, 222 NE2d 653, 38 OO2d 18 (1966).

Further research: O Jur 3d, Cancellation and Reformation of Instruments §§ 9-11, 16.

LAW IN GENERAL

Fraud may render a deed void in law, but usually makes it only voidable in equity. A deed is void in law if it can be said that it is not the act of the grantor, as when the instrument is materially different from what he intended to sign and he was not guilty of negligence in signing without knowing the contents. Fraudulent misrepresentations in the inducement do not make the deed void. However, misrepresentation of a fact, as of a present intention, may support equitable relief. Equity will carefully scrutinize a transaction between persons in a confidential relationship.

As between the grantor and grantee, equity will set aside a deed for fraud when the grantor has not affirmed the transaction and has restored the consideration received. A deed valid when made is not affected by subsequent acts or omissions of the grantee, as by failure to pay the consideration without fraudulent intent at the delivery of the deed. Inadequacy of consideration, standing alone, does not show fraud.

A deed will not be held void if the rights of bona fide purchasers would be affected, except under extreme circumstances, such as misrepresenting the character of the instrument to an illiterate person.

Am Jur 2d, Deeds § 142; CJS, Deeds §§ 56, 200; Tiffany § 986.

8-53B   Duress; Undue Influence.

A deed executed during the duress of the grantor is not void, but voidable only. Duress is but the extreme of undue influence. Commercial Nat. Bank v. Wheelock, 52 OS 534, 40 NE 636, 33 WLB 222 (1895).

Undue influence such as will invalidate a deed must be such as to control the mental operations of the grantor, overcome his power of resistance, and oblige him to adopt the will of another, thus producing a disposition of property which he would not have made if left freely to act according to his own pleasure. Finney v. Morehouse, 27 App 499, 161 NE 293, 6 Abs 419 (1927).

In deeds of gift from parent to child undue influence will not, because of that relation, be presumed as it sometimes is in deeds of gift from child to parent, but must be proved like other issues of fact. Taphorn v. Taphorn, 12 CC(NS) 180, 22 CD 96 (1909); Simmons v. Becker, 63 App 374, 26 NE2d 939, 17 OO 122, 30 Abs 622 (1939).

Further research: O Jur 3d, Cancellation and Reformation of Instruments § 7.

LAW IN GENERAL

Duress or undue influence makes a deed voidable, but innocent purchasers for value from the guilty grantee will be protected. This ground for rescission consists of such wrongful control of or influence over the grantor as to overcome his will and substitute the will of another person. CJS, Deeds § 61; Tiffany § 986.

SECTION 8-54: FRAUDULENT CONVEYANCES

8-54A Rules.

R.C. 1313.56 provides: "A sale, conveyance, transfer, mortgage, or assignment, made in trust or otherwise by a debtor, and every judgment suffered by him against himself in contemplation of insolvency and with a design to prefer one or more creditors to the exclusion in whole or in part of others, and a sale, conveyance, transfer, mortgage, or assignment made, or judgment procured by him to be rendered, in any manner, with intent to hinder, delay, or defraud creditors, is void as to creditors of such debtor at the suit of any creditor. In a suit brought by a creditor of such debtor for the purpose of declaring such sale void, a receiver may be appointed who shall take charge of all the assets of such debtor, including the property so sold, conveyed, transferred, mortgaged, or assigned, and also administer all the assets of the debtor for the equal benefit of the creditors of the debtor in proportion to the amount of their respective demands, including those which are unmatured." (As eff. 10-1-53.)

R.C. 1313.57 provides: "Section 1313.56 of the Revised Code does not apply unless the person to whom such sale, conveyance, transfer, mortgage, or assignment is made, knew of such fraudulent intent on the part of such debtor. Said section does not vitiate or affect any mortgage made in good faith to secure any debt or liability created simultaneously with such mortgage, if such mortgage is filed for record in the county wherein the property is situated, or as otherwise provided by law, within three days after its execution, and when, upon foreclosure or taking possession of such property, the mortgagee fully accounts for the proceeds thereof." (As eff. 10-1-53.)

R.C. 1313.58 provides for a suit by a creditor to recover possession of property to be administered as an assignment for the benefit of creditors. (As eff. 7-1-62.)

R.C. 1336.01 to 1336.12 enact the Uniform Fraudulent Conveyance Act providing, among other things, that a conveyance or an obligation without fair consideration is fraudulent as to creditors, without regard to his actual intent, when made by a person who is or will thereby be rendered insolvent, or by a person who will then have an unreasonably small capital; that a conveyance or obligation without fair consideration is fraudulent as to present and future creditors when made by a person who believes that he will incur debts beyond his ability to pay as they mature; that a conveyance or obligation is fraudulent as to present and future creditors when made to hinder, delay or defraud them; that certain partnership conveyances and obligations are fraudulent as to creditors. Remedies are provided against any person except a purchaser for fair consideration without knowledge of the fraud at the time of the purchase or one who has derived title from such purchaser. A creditor whose claim has matured may have the conveyance set aside or obligation annulled to the extent necessary to satisfy his claim, or may disregard the conveyance and attach or levy execution. A purchaser who, without actual fraudulent intent, has given less than a fair consideration may retain the property as security for repayment. When the claim has not matured, the court may make any order which the circumstances require.

R.C. 2109.56 provides that conveyances made or obtained with intent to avoid proceedings in probate court to obtain assets shall be void. (As eff. 10-1-53.)

R.C. 2127.40 provides that an action by an executor or administrator to sell real estate, conveyed by decedent with intent to defraud his creditors, and for recovery of possession shall be brought in common pleas court within four years after decease of grantor. (As eff. 1-1-76.)

R.C. 5301.61 provides: "No person having an interest in real property, buyer, lessee, tenant, or occupant of real property, knowing that such real property is mortgaged or the subject of a land contract, shall remove, or cause or permit the removal of any improvement or fixture from such real property without the consent of the mortgagee, vendor under the land contract, or other person authorized to give such consent." (As eff. 1-1-74.)

Note. Theft of real property is within the purview of R.C. 2913.02.

An action to set aside a fraudulent conveyance is barred four years after the discovery of the fraud. Combs v. Watson, 32 OS 228, 3 WLB 18 (1877).

An action may be maintained against a fraudulent grantee to recover the value of the lands, if the latter has conveyed them to an innocent purchaser. Doney v. Clark, 55 OS 294, 45 NE 316, 36 WLB 311 (1896).

The language of the statute stating in substance that conveyances made with intent to defraud are void is not for the benefit of strangers, nor of grantor or his heirs. Reck v. Reck, 46 NE2d 429, 37 Abs 217 (App. 1942).

Where a transfer of property from a husband to his wife has been attacked on the ground that the conveyance was made to defraud creditors, the burden of proof is upon the one attacking such transfer. Conrad v. Sample, 107 App 66, 156 NE2d 748, 7 OO2d 399 (1958).

"We are of the opinion that a mortgage made by a debtor with intent to hinder or delay one or more of his creditors, may not be set aside under the provisions of Section 1313.56 et seq. of the Revised Code unless such intent to hinder or delay is coupled with an intent to defraud, as demonstrated either by the extent of the hindrance or delay intended or by the circumstances surrounding the making of the mortgage." Parker v. Clary, 106 App 295, 154 NE2d 641, 645, 7 OO2d 59 (1958).

Further research: O Jur 3d, Creditors' Rights and Remedies § 742.

LAW IN GENERAL

A conveyance made to hinder, delay or defraud creditors is voidable at the instance of the creditors unless the conveyance is to a purchaser for value without notice of the fraudulent intent. This is the rule of the common law and under statutes providing that such conveyances are "void." Tiffany §§ 1323, 1328.

8-54B Consideration.

A preexisting debt is a valuable consideration when the debt is extinguished in whole or in part by the transfer. Harbine v. Harper, 21 Abs 226 (App. 1936).

When there is no consideration for a conveyance, it cannot be sustained as against existing creditors unless the debtor retains sufficient property to pay all of his then subsisting obligations. Kimble v. Doerr, 20 OO 191 (C.P. 1936); Squire v. Cramer, 64 App 169, 28 NE2d 516, 17 OO 499 (1940).

Further research: O Jur 3d, Creditors' Rights and Remedies § 753.

LAW IN GENERAL

Voluntary conveyances, being those without a substantial consideration, are usually held to be presumptively fraudulent as to existing creditors. The presumption is generally conclusive when such conveyance is made by an insolvent debtor. The grantee's knowledge of the actual or constructive fraud by the grantor is immaterial where a fair and adequate consideration was not paid. Tiffany § 1325.

8-54C Knowledge of Grantee.

Bona fide purchasers generally, see Section 1-32.

In order to establish a fraudulent conveyance under either R.C. 1336.04 or 1336.05, a creditor must prove that the debtor was insolvent or would be made so by the transfer and that the transfer was made without fair consideration. Neither the intent of the debtor or the knowledge of the transferee need be proven. In order to establish a fraudulent conveyance under R.C. 1313.56, a creditor must prove both that the debtor made the transfer with the intent to hinder, delay or defraud the creditor and that the transferee knew of the debtor's fraudulent intent. In addition, it must be shown that the debtor was insolvent or contemplating insolvency at the time of the transfer. Sease v. John Smith Grain Co., 17 App3d 223, 479 NE2d 284 (1984).

A bona fide purchaser for a valuable consideration without notice will be protected against the claims of general creditors. Holmes v. Gardner, 50 OS 167, 33 NE 644, 29 WLB 167 (1893).

A conveyance by an insolvent debtor, made with the design to prefer one creditor, or made with intent to defraud creditors, the purchaser not knowing of such design or intent, is valid. Carruthers v. Kennedy, 121 OS 8, 166 NE 801, 7 Abs 350, 29 OLR 279 (1929).

Where a husband conveys to his wife in payment of a debt owing to the wife, no presumption of fraud will be inferred on account of the relationship. Gould v. Cooper, 15 App 223, 32 CC(NS) 241 (1919). Such conveyance is valid if the wife has no knowledge of fraudulent intent. Bales v. Robinson, 3 Abs 460 (App. 1925).

It is necessary to an action under R.C. 1313.56 that the grantee have knowledge of grantor's fraudulent intent. City Trust & Savings Bank v. Weaver, 68 App 323, 40 NE2d 953, 22 OO 529 (1941).

A conveyance made without fair consideration by a debtor is fraudulent under R.C. 1336.04 if the grantor is or will be thereby rendered insolvent and neither intent of the grantor nor knowledge of the grantee is required. An antecedent debt is not "fair consideration" if the parties treat the debt as still subsisting. Cellar Lumber Co. v. Holley, 9 App2d 288, 224 NE2d 360, 38 OO2d 341 (1967).

Further research: O Jur 3d, Creditors' Rights and Remedies §§ 750, 751.

LAW IN GENERAL

Participation or acquiescence by the purchaser in the seller's fraudulent intent is essential to the invalidity of the conveyance where a fair and adequate consideration was paid. Knowledge of the grantee of the grantor's fraudulent intent is generally sufficient to invalidate the transaction except where the transfer is by way of preference in satisfaction of a preexisting debt. Preferences by an insolvent debtor of one or more of his creditors are usually sustained if the grantee did not actively participate in the debtor's intent to hinder, delay or defraud his other creditors. Fraud is presumed when there is a secret trust in favor of the grantor. Tiffany § 1326.

8-54D Dower.

Where wife releases dower in a fraudulent conveyance which is later set aside, the property is subject to her dower. Ridgway v. Masting, 23 OS 294 (1872).

LAW IN GENERAL

Dower is generally held to be restored when a fraudulent conveyance is set aside. The right of dower is protected, under the rule, against conveyance made in contemplation of marriage if fraudulent as to the wife. Am Jur 2d, Dower and Curtesy §§ 69, 70, 182.

8-54E Mortgages.

A mortgage is a conveyance within the statute. Webb v. Roff, 9 OS 430 (1859).

Where a mortgage was given to secure double the amount of the money loaned, a court of equity will not aid in its foreclosure. McQuade v. Rosecrans, 36 OS 442, 6 WLB 52 (1881).

A bona fide mortgagee will be protected as a bona fide purchaser. Shorten v. Drake, 38 OS 76, 7 WLB 220 (1882).

8-54F Relief to Fraudulent Grantor.

A deed made for the purpose of defrauding creditors is good as between the parties thereto and those claiming under them. Tremper v. Barton, 18 Ohio 418 (1849).

Where an owner conveys with intent to defraud a creditor, he cannot have the aid of a court of equity to compel the grantee to reconvey to him. Pride v. Andrew, 51 OS 405, 38 NE 84, 31 WLB 300, 32 WLB 248 (1894).

LAW IN GENERAL

Courts of equity do not aid the grantor of a fraudulent conveyance in recovery of the property. Exceptions to this rule have been made in some cases where its application was found to work an injustice. 21 ALR2d 589.

8-54G   Subsequent Creditors.

Conveyance by one who is solvent will not be set aside as to subsequent creditors without proof of actual intent to defraud such creditors. Schofield v. Cleveland Trust Co., 135 OS 328, 21 NE2d 119, 14 OO 224 (1939); Edwards v. Monning, 137 OS 268, 28 NE2d 627, 18 OO 37 (1940); Evans v. Lewis, 30 OS 11, 2 WLB 64 (1876). This was the law prior to the Uniform Fraudulent Conveyance Act which became effective 10-23-61.

One who has a tort claim against the operator of an automobile for bodily injuries is a "creditor" of such operator within the meaning of R.C. 1336.01 (C), and entitled to maintain an action to set aside a claimed fraudulent conveyance of real property, notwithstanding that his tort claim has not been reduced to judgment. Foster v. Gibson, 120 App 235, 202 NE2d 202, 29 OO2d 40 (1964).

Further research: O Jur 3d, Creditors' Rights and Remedies § 837.

LAW IN GENERAL

Creditors of the grantor, who become such subsequent to the time of the conveyance, may have it set aside if it was made with intent to defraud them. The usual rules apply as to solvency, knowledge of the grantee, and consideration. An intent to defraud existing creditors is sufficient to maintenance of the action by subsequent creditors who did not have notice of fraud in the conveyance. Tiffany § 1325.

8-54H   Subsequent Purchasers from the Grantor.

LAW IN GENERAL

A conveyance made with the grantee's knowledge of intent to defraud a subsequent purchaser from the same grantor is invalid as against such subsequent purchaser. Actual fraud is generally required, even when the first conveyance was without consideration. This rule is infrequently applied because the subsequent purchaser is protected against an unrecorded deed under the recording laws, while he is usually denied relief if he had actual or constructive notice of the first deed. Tiffany § 1329.

8-54I   Purchasers from the Grantee.

A bona fide purchaser from a fraudulent grantee takes a good title. Schultz v. Brown, 3 CC 609, 2 CD 353 (1889); Burgett v. Burgett, 1 Ohio 469 (1824).

Further research: O Jur 3d, Creditors' Rights and Remedies § 851.

LAW IN GENERAL

Purchasers for value from the grantees of fraudulent conveyances are held to take title discharged from the fraud, provided they were not charged with notice prior to the time they paid, or became irrevocably bound to pay, the purchase price. Tiffany § 1328.

8-54J   Necessary Parties Defendant.

A full determination of the rights of the grantee of an alleged fraudulent conveyance may be made without the presence of his grantor in the suit. Akron Bldg. & Loan Ass'n v. Foltz, 16 CC(NS) 299, 26 CD 572 (1908).

LAW IN GENERAL

The person holding the legal title or the beneficiaries of a trust deed, and assignees in bankruptcy or assignees for the benefit of creditors are necessary parties. Lien holders and other persons whose interests are not directly affected need not be named defendants. 24 ALR2d 395.

CHAPTER 9: DESCENT AND WILLS

DIVISION 9-1: DESCENT

DIVISION 9-2: WILLS

310

DIVISION 9-1: DESCENT

SECTION 9-11: GENERALLY

Administration of estates, see Chapter 12.
Estates and future interests, see Chapter 11.

9-11A Definition.

If a testator failed to dispose of certain property, he is as certainly intestate as to such property, as he could have been if he died intestate as to all his property. Gardner v. Gardner, 13 OS 426 (1862).

The primary meaning of the phrase "legal representatives" is "executors" or "administrators." In the statutes of descent and distribution in this state the phrase is generally construed to mean "lineal descendants" but in the half-and-half statute the phrase has the meaning of "heirs at law" or "next of kin." Larkins v. Routson, 115 OS 639, 155 NE 227, 5 Abs 44, 25 OLR 164 (1927).

Descent means the transfer on the death of a person to his heirs of title to his property not disposed of by will.

Further research: O Jur 3d, Decedents' Estates § 10.

9-11B Statute.

See charts and comments at 9-11M.
Descendants of grandparents, see 9-11F.
Law of situs, see 9-21B.

R.C. 2105.06 provides: "When a person dies intestate having title or right to any personal property, or to any real estate or inheritance, in this state, the personal property shall be distributed, and the real estate or inheritance shall descend and pass in parcenary, except as otherwise provided by law, in the following course:

"(A) If there is no surviving spouse, to the children of the intestate or their lineal descendants, per stirpes;

"(B) If there is a spouse and one child or its lineal descendants surviving, the first sixty thousand dollars if the spouse is the natural or adoptive parent of the child, or the first twenty thousand dollars if the spouse is not the natural or adoptive parent of the child, plus one-half of the balance of the intestate estate to the spouse and the remainder to the child or his lineal descendants, per stirpes;

311

"(C) If there is a spouse and more than one child or their lineal descendants surviving, the first sixty thousand dollars if the spouse is the natural or adoptive parent of one of the children, or the first twenty thousand dollars if the spouse is the natural or adoptive parent of none of the children, plus one-third of the balance of the intestate estate to the spouse and the remainder to the children equally, or to the lineal descendants of any deceased child, per stirpes;

"(D) If there are no children or their lineal descendants, then the whole to the surviving spouse;

"(E) If there is no spouse and no children or their lineal descendants, to the parents of the intestate equally, or to the surviving parent;

"(F) If there is no spouse, no children or their lineal descendants, and no parent surviving, to the brothers and sisters. whether of the whole or of the half blood of the intestate, or their lineal descendants, per stirpes;

"(G) If there are no brothers or sisters or their lineal descendants, one-half to the paternal grandparents of the intestate equally, or to the survivor of them, and one-half to the maternal grandparents of the intestate equally, or to the survivor of them;

"(H) If there is no paternal grandparent or no maternal grandparent, one-half to the lineal descendants of the deceased grandparents, per stirpes; if there are no such lineal descendants, then to the surviving grandparents or their lineal descendants, per stirpes; if there are no surviving grandparents or their lineal descendants, then to the next of kin of the intestate, provided there shall be no representation among such next of kin;

"(I) If there are no next of kin, to stepchildren or their lineal descendants, per stirpes;

"(J) If there are no stepchildren or their lineal descendants, escheat to the state." (As eff. 12-17-86.)

R.C. 2105.063 provides: "Subject to the right of the surviving spouse to elect to receive the decedent's interest in the mansion house pursuant to section 2105.062 of the Revised Code, the specific monetary share payable to a surviving spouse under division (B) or (C) of section 2105.06 of the Revised Code shall be paid out of the tangible and intangible personal property in the estate to the extent that the personal property is available for distribution. The personal property distributed to the surviving spouse, other than cash, shall be valued at the appraised value.

"Before tangible and intangible personal property is transferred to the surviving spouse in payment or part payment of the specific monetary share, the administrator or executor shall file an application that includes an inventory of the personal property intended to be distributed in kind to the surviving spouse, together with a statement of the appraised value of each item of personal property included. The court shall examine the application and make a finding of the amount of personal property to be distributed to the surviving spouse, and shall order that the personal property be distributed to the surviving spouse. The court concurrently shall make a finding of the amount of money that remains due and payable to the surviving spouse in satisfaction of the specific monetary share to which the surviving spouse is entitled under division (B) or (C) of section 2105.06 of the Revised Code. Any amount that remains due and payable shall be a charge on the title to any real property in the estate but the charge does not bear interest. This charge may be conveyed or released in the same manner as any other interest in real estate and may be enforced by foreclosure or any other appropriate remedy.

"Except any real property the surviving spouse elects to receive under section 2105.062 of the Revised Code, the title to real property in the estate shall descend and pass in parcenary to those persons entitled to it under division (B) or (C) of section 2105.06 of the Revised Code, subject to the monetary charge of the surviving spouse. The administrator or executor shall file an application for a certificate of transfer as provided in section 2113.61 of the Revised Code. The application shall include a statement of the amount in money that remains due and payable to the surviving spouse as found by the court. The certificate of transfer ordered by the court shall recite that the title to the real property described in the certificate is subject to the charge in favor of the surviving spouse, and shall recite the value in dollars of the charge on the title to the real property included in the certificate of transfer." (As eff. 12-17-86.)

Double cousins of the intestate will inherit in two capacities, both as descendants of their paternal grandparents and as descendants of their maternal grandparents. Shearer v. Gasstman, 31 NP(NS) 219, 15 Abs 103 (Prob. 1933).

9-11C Effective Date of Statute; Vested Rights.

The legal rights of a decedent's heirs or devisees become vested at the time of decedent's death and no subsequent legislative act could constitutionally divest such heirs or devisees of their rights. Scamman v. Scamman, 90 NE2d 617, 56 Abs 272 (C.P. 1950).

Further research: O Jur 3d, Decedents' Estates § 41.

9-11D Ancestral Lands; Half Blood.

See charts and comments at 9-11M.

R.C. 2105.01 provides: "In intestate succession, there shall be no difference between ancestral and nonancestral property or between real and personal property." (As eff. 10-1-53.)

Half brothers and half sisters are included in the words "brothers and sisters" in the statute. Stockton v. Frazier, 81 OS 227, 90 NE 168, 7 OLR 507, 54 WLB 488 (1909).

Recital in a deed of the consideration is conclusive for the purpose of determining the course of descent. Thiessen v. Moore, 105 OS 401, 137 NE 906, 1 Abs 245, 20 OLR 166 (1922).

Upon partition whether by election, by purchase, or amicable, title is held by purchase only as to those interests for which consideration is actually paid. Unless there is a sale of all interests, the estate of the former cotenant remains an estate of inheritance. Lee v. Fike, 28 App 283, 162 NE 682, 6 Abs 151 (1928); Lawson v. Townley, 90 OS 67, 106 NE 780, 11 OLR 463, 59 WLB 77 (1914); Huseman v. Fingermeyer, 106 OS 113, 139 NE 862, 1 Abs 38, 20 OLR 455 (1922).

Under G.C. 8573 as it existed in 1912, the estate did not vest in brothers and sisters until termination of the life estate of decedent's relict. Green v. Shough, 158 NE2d 736, 80 Abs 248 (App. 1958).

Further research: O Jur 3d, Decedents' Estates § 92.

9-11E Degrees of Kindred.

R.C. 2105.03 provides: "In the determination of intestate succession, next of kin shall be determined by degrees of relationship computed by the rules of civil law." (As eff. 10-1-53.)

The words "next of kin" in the statute of descent are descriptive of a particular person or class of persons, related to the intestate in an equal degree of consanguinity. Clayton v. Drake, 17 OS 367 (1867).

Each paragraph of the statute must be read in connection with all the other paragraphs for the purpose of determining who are the next of kin. Schroth v. Noble, 91 OS 438, 110 NE 1067, 12 OLR 510, 60 WLB 56 (1915); Weisflock v. Sigling, 116 OS 435, 156 NE 905, 5 Abs 315, 25 OLR 331 (1927).

Further research: O Jur 3d, Decedents' Estates § 84.

LAW IN GENERAL

Under the civil-law rule of computing degrees of kindred, the relationship is ascertained by counting the degrees or generations from the intestate to the common ancestor plus the degrees from the common ancestor to the claiming heir; for example, a grandchild and a great-grandchild (who are not parent and child) of a common ancestor are related to each other in the fifth degree. By the common-law rule, only the degrees from the common ancestor to his most distant heir are counted; for example, such grandchild and great-grandchild of a common ancestor are related to each other in the third degree. Tiffany § 1122.

9-11F Per Capita or Per Stirpes?

See also Section 11-94.

R.C. 2105.11 provides: "When a person dies intestate leaving children and none of the children of such intestate have died leaving children or their lineal descendants, such estate shall descend to the children of such intestate, living at the time of his death, in equal proportions." (As eff. 10-1-53.)

R.C. 2105.12 provides: "When all the descendants of an intestate, in a direct line of descent, are on an equal degree of consanguinity to the intestate, the estate shall pass to such persons in equal parts, however remote from the intestate such equal and common degree of consanguinity may be." (As eff. 10-1-53.)

We are unable to conclude that any construction limiting the application of R.C. 2105.12 to lineal descendants could be made without expressly overruling a long line of decisions of this court. Snodgrass v. Bedell, 134 OS 311, 16 NE2d 463, 12 OO 103 (1938).

R.C. 2105.13 provides: "If some of the children of an intestate are living and others are dead, the estate shall descend to the children who are living and to the lineal descendants of such children as are dead, so that each child who is living will inherit the share to which he would have been entitled if all the children of the intestate were living, and the lineal descendants of the deceased child will inherit equal parts of that portion of the estate to which such deceased child would be entitled if he were living.

"This section shall apply in all cases in which the descendants of the intestate, not more remote than lineal descendants of grandparents, entitled to share in the estate, are of unequal degree of consanguinity to the intestate, so that those who are of the nearest degree of consanguinity will take the share to which they would have been entitled, had all the descendants in the same degree of consanguinity with them who died leaving issue, been living." (As eff. 10-1-53.) From January 1, 1932 to September 1, 1935 this statute did not contain the words "not more remote than lineal descendants of grandparents."

"After the estate is equally divided in halves, descent depends upon the particular circumstances existing in the particular branch of the family, and apportionment is made as if there were two estates instead of one.... On the paternal side the one-half share is to be divided into fourteen parts. Florence G. Bedell, a first cousin, as the nearest in consanguinity, would receive one twenty-eighth portion of the real estate. The remainder would be divided among the lineal descendants of the thirteen first cousins who are deceased, per stirpes, with the roots or stirpes being first cousins." Snodgrass v. Bedell, 134 OS 311, 16 NE2d 463, 12 OO 103 (1938).

Where there are no grandparents or their lineal descendants on the paternal side, the entire estate should go to the surviving grandparents or their lineal descendants on the maternal side; and the next of kin should inherit only where there were no surviving grandparents of their lineal descendants on either side. In re Kelly's Estate, 165 OS 259, 135 NE2d 378, 59 OO 354 (1956).

As effective from January 1, 1932 to September 1, 1935, the statute did not indicate an intention to divide the estate equally between the paternal and maternal branches. Oakley v. Davey, 49 App. 113, 195 NE 406, 1 OO 144, 18 Abs 524 (1934).

No distinction is made between those of the half blood and those of the whole blood in descent to lineal descendants of grandparents under R.C. 2105.06. Sheeler v. Burkhart, 101 NE2d 401, 45 OO 415, 62 Abs 356 (Prob. 1951); Shepard v. Wilson, 61 App 191, 22 NE2d 568, 14 OO 282, 28 Abs 448 (1938).

Where the heirs of the intestate consist of lineal descendants of both the paternal and the maternal grandparents, even though such heirs are on an equal degree of consanguinity to the intestate, the estate will be divided in halves. Reimer v. Finnegan, 17 O Supp 174, 32 OO 391 (Prob. 1945).

Nieces and nephews of an intestate decedent are subject to having a debt of their father, who predeceased the decedent, set off against their distributive share, when decedent has a brother and sister still living. Gruhler v. Hossapaus, 195 NE2d 387, 28 OO2d 477, 93 Abs 71 (Prob. 1963).

LAW IN GENERAL

As a general rule, heirs will take per capita when they are all related to the intestate in the same degree. The question is primarily a matter of construction of the statutes of descent. Where representation is limited to certain degrees of kindred, the limitation is not applicable to prevent descent to persons equally related to the decedent. When the heirs are unequally related to the decedent, they usually take per stirpes; that is, the primary shares are ascertained from the number of nearest living relatives plus the number of shares descended from deceased relatives in the same degree of kindred. 19 ALR2d 191; Tiffany §§ 1119, 1124.

9-11G   Renunciation.

R.C. 1339.60 permits a person, his guardian or personal representative to renounce a right of succession to real or personal property to which that person would be entitled upon the death of a person or upon the occurrence of any other event. The disclaimer instrument must be filed with the county recorder where the disclaimed interest is in real property. If the interest is testamentary, a disclaimer must also be filed in the Probate Division of the Court of Common Pleas. The disclaimer instrument must contain a description of the real estate sufficient to identify it and a reference to the record of the instrument that created the interest disclaimed. If the land is registered, a disclaimer is entered as a memorial on the last certificate of title. The spouse of the disclaimant has no right of dower in the title to the interest disclaimed. This statute, first effective in 1976 was amended in 1980 and 1984 and the most recent amendment became effective December 17, 1986.

From October 6, 1961 until it was repealed effective March 23, 1981 R.C. 2105.061 permitted a competent adult to renounce an interest in property received by intestate succession by filing a written renunciation in Probate Court within 60 days after notice of the hearing on the inventory. Prior to October 6, 1961, an heir did not have the right to renounce benefits accruing under the statutes of descent and distribution.

Until repealed effective March 23, 1981, R.C. 2113.60 provided that a bequest or legacy which has been refused would go into the residue, if there is a residuary clause, and if not, would descend as intestate property.

9-11H   Disinheritance.

Expectancies generally, see Section 11-14.

Mere words of exclusion or disinheritance in a will will not prevent those whom the testator sought to disinherit from sharing in any property undisposed of by the will. Gorsuch v. Culbertson, 90 NE2d 627, 40 OO 529, 56 Abs 153 (C.P. 1949).

The part of a bequest invalid under the mortmain statute, and not otherwise disposed of by the will, passes to the sole issue of testator notwithstanding she is specifically disinherited by the will. Balyeat v. Morris, 28 App2d 191, 276 NE2d 258, 57 OO2d 301 (1971).

LAW IN GENERAL

An heir or distributee is not disinherited by a testamentary provision to that effect unless an effective disposition is otherwise made of the estate. 100 ALR2d 329; CJS, Descent, etc. § 46; Tiffany § 1130.

9-11I Devise to Heir; Worthier Title.

LAW IN GENERAL

At common law, a devise to an heir of exactly the same interest he would inherit is ineffective. This rule, known as the doctrine of worthier title, has been generally repudiated as to wills although it may still apply to deeds. CJS, Descent, etc. § 44; Tiffany § 1118.

9-11J Necessity of Administration.

Claims as liens, see 12-12B.
Determination of heirship, see 12-11E.
Relieving estate from administration, see 12-11H.
Standard of title examination, see 9-28B.

LAW IN GENERAL

Administration is not essential to vesting of title to realty in the heirs. It may be necessary, within the period of the statute of limitations, to establish the payment of succession taxes and of the claims of creditors. The names of the heirs and the facts of inheritance are ordinarily ascertained from administration proceedings but may be shown by an affidavit or certificate of transfer.

9-11K Presumption of Death.

Estates of absentees and presumed decedents, see 12-11D.
Presumption of order of death, see statute at 9-11L.

Where an individual leaves his family and usual place of residence and goes to parts unknown or a distant state and is not heard from for a period of seven or more years, a presumption arises that he is dead. Such presumption may be rebutted. Brunny v. Prudential Ins. Co., 151 OS 86, 84 NE2d 504, 38 OO 533 (1949).

The common-law presumption is, in the absence of definite evidence to the contrary, that such person is dead at the end of seven years. Thompson v. Parrett, 82 App 366, 78 NE2d 419, 38 OO 42, 52 Abs 16 (1948).

The Ohio cases support the general proposition of law that when it can be proven that a missing person died on a certain date, either within seven years or after more than seven years absence from the place of his last domicile, his date of death shall be regarded as having arisen on such proven date, rather than on the date of the decree when he is merely presumed to be dead under the provisions of R.C. 2121.01 et seq. providing for the administration of the known estate of a presumed decedent. The common-law rule as to presumption of death has not been abrogated by those sections. Freiberg v. Schloss, 112 NE2d 352, 50 OO 156, 65 Abs 331 (Prob. 1953).

Further research: O Jur 3d, Death § 1.

9-11L Death within Thirty Days; Presumed Order of Death.

Survivorship deeds, see 8-16D.

R.C. 2105.21 provides: "When there is no evidence of the order in which the death of two or more persons occurred, no one of such persons shall be presumed to have died first and the estate of each shall pass and descend as though he had survived the others. When the surviving spouse or other heir at law, legatee or devisee dies within thirty days after the death of the decedent, the estate of such first decedent shall pass and descend as though he had survived such surviving spouse, or other heir at law, legatee or devisee. A beneficiary of a testamentary trust shall not be deemed to be a legatee or devisee within the meaning of this section. This section shall prevail over the right of election of a surviving spouse.

"This section shall not apply in the case of wills wherein provision has been made for distribution of property different from the provisions of this section. In such case such provision of the will shall not prevail over the right of election of a surviving spouse." (As eff. 10-16-53.)

From January 1, 1932 to October 15, 1953 this statute was effective as follows: "When there is no evidence of the order in which the death of two or more persons occurred, no one of such persons shall be presumed to have died first, and the estate of each shall pass and descend as though he had survived the other or others. When the surviving spouse or other heir at law or legatee dies within three days after the date of death of the decedent, or within thirty days after the date of death of such decedent if such death resulted from a common accident, the estate of such first decedent shall pass and descend as though he had survived such heir at law or legatee. The provisions of this section shall prevail over the right of election of a surviving spouse."

This statute does not establish a presumption of the order of death, but merely defines the right of inheritance to property of those who die within the time and under the circumstances therein described. Ostrander v. Preece, 129 OS 625, 196 NE 670, 3 OO 24, 103 ALR 218 (1935).

There is no widow within the meaning and intent of the statute, and no year's allowance, and no property not treated as assets may be claimed by her personal representative. In re Metzger's Estate, 140 OS 50, 42 NE2d 443, 23 OO 257 (1942).

This statute has no application to joint survivorship accounts or other rights vested under contract law. In re Kessler's Estate, 85 App 240, 85 NE2d 609, 40 OO 167, 54 Abs 366 (1949).

The heirs at law of the deceased surviving spouse cannot inherit the property given to him by the will of the spouse who died within thirty days prior to his death, unless such will clearly indicates a desire that R.C. 2105.21 shall not be effective with respect to such property. Barrick v. Fligle, 103 App 507, 146 NE2d 330, 4 OO2d 15 (1957).

For the last two sentences of R.C. 2105.21 to come into operation, the will must say specifically or in unmistakable language that the devisee or legatee shall take under the will even though he or she does not survive the testator for thirty days. The word "wills" does not apply to the will of the surviving spouse. Alten v. Barnecut, 109 App 497, 168 NE2d 9, 12 OO2d 68 (1959).

The property exempt from administration and the year's support are not intestate successions but are debts and preferred claims and therefore not affected by R.C. 2105.21. The statute does not affect a widow as beneficiary of a testamentary trust. In re Priest's Estate, 156 NE2d 206, 79 Abs 444 (Prob. 1958).

The provisions of the order of death statute apply to the estate of the first decedent. The statute did not preclude application of the half-and-half statute to the estate of the second decedent. Battista v. Feihl, 191 NE2d 597, 23 OO2d 252, 91 Abs 391 (Prob. 1963).

When a relative devisee or legatee dies within thirty days after death of decedent, leaving a widow and one child, the child takes the share of decedent's estate that her father would have received by virtue of R.C. 2105.21 and 2107.52. Ruble v. Waites, 72 OO2d 389 (Prob. 1975).

LAW IN GENERAL

There is no presumption of survivorship between persons who perish in a common disaster. When property is owned jointly and there is no evidence as to survivorship, it has been held that the property descends as though owned in common. Am Jur 2d, Descent and Distribution § 103; 39 ALR3d 1332; CJS, Death § 6.

9-11M Charts of Descent.

Death within thirty days, see 9-11L.

DESCENT UNDER R.C. 2105.06 OF PERSONS DYING JANUARY 1, 1976 TO DATE

In each of the following items it is assumed that none of the items preceding it apply to the particular facts at the death of the intestate. R.C. 2105.06 quoted at 9-11B.

A. If no surviving spouse, to children or their lineal descendants, per stirpes.

B. If one child or his lineal descendants: (1) to the surviving spouse the first $60,000 if the natural or adoptive parent of the child, or the first $20,000 if not such parent, plus half of the balance of the intestate estate and (2) the remainder to the child or his lineal descendants, per stirpes.

C. If more than one child or their lineal descendants: (1) to the surviving spouse the first $60,000 if the natural or adoptive parent of one of the children, or the first $20,000 if the parent of none, plus one-third of the balance of the intestate estate and (2) the remainder to the children equally, or to the lineal descendants of any deceased child, per stirpes.

D. To surviving spouse.

E. To surviving parents or parent.

F. To brothers and sisters, whether of the whole or half blood, or their lineal descendants, per stirpes.

G and H. (1) One-half to surviving paternal grandparents or grandparent. If none, to their lineal descendants, per stirpes. If none, to same as other half by (2).

(2) One-half to surviving maternal grandparents or grandparent. If none, to their lineal descendants, per stirpes. If none, to same as other half by (1).

(3) If no grandparents or their lineal descendants to next of kin of intestate without representation of deceased next of kin.

I. To stepchildren or their lineal descendants, per stirpes.

J. To State of Ohio.

Modifications (shown in this chapter) of the basic statute may occur: (a) when an advancement has been made to an heir, (b) when a child is posthumous, (c) when an heir has been designated, (d) when an illegitimate child has become legitimate, (e) when intestate was murdered, (f) when an heir dies within thirty days of intestate, (g) when heir renounces or disclaims his interest, (h) when the heirs are equally related to the intestate, they take equally, or (i) when the heirs (not more remote than descendants of grandparents) are unequally related to the intestate, they take with representation, that is, with the primary share being ascertained from the number of living relatives plus the number of the same degree of kindred who died before the intestate leaving lineal descendants.

GRAPHIC CHART OF DESCENT (under R.C. 2105.06)
from persons dying after December 31, 1975

DECEDENT WITH SURVIVING SPOUSE

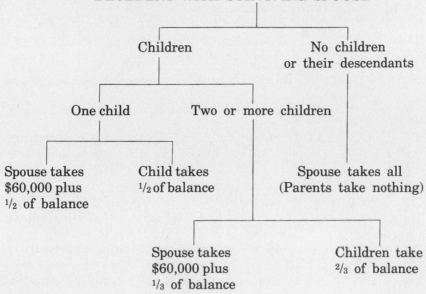

NOTES:

Descendants of a deceased child take his share.

A surviving spouse not the natural or adoptive parent of one of the children takes $20,000 instead of the $60,000 above.

For possible modifications of the above basic chart, see the paragraph above the chart.

The $60,000 or $20,000 inherited by the surviving spouse is in the nature of a lien attaching on the date of death but subordinate to all debts and obligations of the intestate and of the estate in administration. Payment of the charge and recital in a certificate of transfer are provided for by R.C. 2105.063 shown at 9-11B. A surviving spouse electing to take against the will does not take the $60,000 or $20,000.

In each item of the following charts, it is assumed that none of the preceding items in that chart can be complied with at the death of the intestate.

CHART 1931 TO 1976 GENERALLY

January 1, 1932 through September 1, 1935.

1. If no surviving spouse, to children or their lineal descendants, per stirpes.

321

2. If one child or its lineal descendants, one-half to surviving spouse and one-half to the child or its lineal descendants, per stirpes.

3. If more than one child or their lineal descendants, one-third to the surviving spouse and two-thirds to children or their lineal descendants, per stirpes.

4. Three-fourths to surviving spouse and one-fourth to surviving parents or parent.

5. To surviving spouse.

6. To surviving parents or parent.

7. To brothers and sisters, whether of the whole or half blood, or their lineal descendants, per stirpes.

8. To surviving grandparents or grandparent.

9. To lineal descendants of grandparents, per stirpes.

10. To next of kin of the intestate, per stirpes. No representation.

11. To stepchildren or their lineal descendants, per stirpes.

12. To State of Ohio.

G.C. 10503-4.

September 2, 1935 through December 31, 1975.

1. If no surviving spouse, to children or their lineal descendants, per stirpes.

2. If one child or its lineal descendants, one-half to surviving spouse and one-half to the child or its lineal descendants, per stirpes.

3. If more than one child or their lineal descendants, one-third to the surviving spouse and two-thirds to children or their lineal descendants, per stirpes.

4. (a) Three-fourths to surviving spouse and one-fourth to surviving parents or parent. (b) To surviving spouse if no surviving parent.

5. To surviving parents or parent.

6. To brothers and sisters, whether of the whole or half blood, or their lineal descendants, per stirpes.

7 and 8. (a) One-half to surviving paternal grandparents or grandparent. If none, to their lineal descendants, per stirpes. If none, to same as other half by (b).

(b) One-half to surviving maternal grandparents or grandparent. If none, to their lineal descendants, per stirpes. If none, to same as other half by (a).

(c) If no grandparents or their lineal descendants to next of kin of intestate without representation.

9. To stepchildren or their lineal descendants, per stirpes.

10. To State of Ohio.

G.C. 10503-4; R.C. 2105.06.

CHART FOR ANCESTRAL REAL ESTATE

March 4, 1865 through July 3, 1923.

1. To children or their legal representatives.

2. To surviving spouse for life.

3. To brothers and sisters, of the blood of the ancestor from whom the estate came, or their legal representatives.

4. To such ancestor.

5. To children of such ancestor, or their legal representatives.

6. To surviving spouse of such ancestor for life, if a parent of the intestate.

7. To brothers and sisters of such ancestor, or their legal representatives.

8. To brothers and sisters of intestate, or their legal representatives.

9. To next of kin, of the blood of such ancestor, or their legal representatives.

10. To surviving spouse.

11. To next of kin of intestate.

12. To children of deceased spouse or spouses, whose marriage was not annulled prior to death, or their legal representatives.

13. To brothers and sisters of such spouse, or their legal representatives.

14. To State of Ohio.

R.S. 4158, 4160, 4161; G.C. 8573, 8575, 8576.

July 4, 1923 through December 31, 1931.

1. To children, or their legal representatives.

2. To surviving spouse for life.

3. To surviving parents or parent for life.

4. To brothers and sisters, of the blood of the ancestor from whom the estate came, or their legal representatives.

5. To such ancestor.

6. To children of such ancestor, or their legal representatives.

7. To surviving spouse of such ancestor, if a parent of the intestate.

8. To brothers and sisters of such ancestor, or their legal representatives.

9. To brothers and sisters of intestate, or their legal representatives.

10. To next of kin, of the blood of such ancestor, or their legal representatives.

11. To surviving spouse.

12. To next of kin of intestate.

13. To children of any deceased spouse or spouses, whose marriage was not annulled prior to death, or their legal representatives.

14. To brothers and sisters of such spouse, or their legal representatives.

15. To State of Ohio.

G.C. 8573, 8575, 8576.

CHART FOR NONANCESTRAL REAL ESTATE

March 4, 1865 through July 9, 1919.

1. To children and their legal representatives.

2. To surviving spouse.

323

3. To brothers and sisters of the whole blood and their legal representatives.

4. To brothers and sisters of the half blood and their legal representatives.

5. To father.

6. To mother.

7. To next of kin and their legal representatives.

8. To children of any deceased spouse or spouses, whose marriage was not annulled prior to death, or their legal representatives.

9. To brothers and sisters of such spouse, or their legal representatives.

10. To State of Ohio.

R.S. 4159, 4161; G.C. 8574, 8576.

July 10, 1919 through July 3, 1923.

1. To children and their legal representatives.

2. To surviving spouse.

3. To brothers and sisters of the whole blood and their legal representatives.

4. To brothers and sisters of the half blood and their legal representatives.

5. To surviving parents or parent.

6. To next of kin and their legal representatives.

7. To children of any deceased spouse or spouses, whose marriage was not annulled prior to death, or their legal representatives.

8. To brothers and sisters of such spouse, or their legal representatives.

9. To State of Ohio.

G.C. 8574, 8576.

July 4, 1923 through December 31, 1931.

1. To children and their legal representatives.

2. To surviving spouse.

3. To surviving parents or parent for life.

4. To brothers and sisters of the whole blood and their legal representatives.

5. To brothers and sisters of the half blood and their legal representatives.

6. To surviving parents or parent.

7. To next of kin and their legal representatives.

8. To children of any deceased spouse or spouses, whose marriage was not annulled prior to death, or their legal representatives.

9. To brothers and sisters of such spouse or their legal representatives.

10. To State of Ohio.

G.C. 8574, 8576.

SECTION 9-12: ADVANCEMENTS

9-12A   Definition.

R.C. 2105.051 provides: "When a person dies, property that he gave during his lifetime to an heir shall be treated as an advancement against the heir's share of the estate only if declared in a contemporaneous writing by the decedent, or acknowledged in writing by the heir to be an advancement. For this purpose, property advanced is valued as of the time the heir came into possession or enjoyment of the property, or as of the time of death of the decedent, whichever occurs first. If the heir does not survive the decedent, the property shall not be taken into account in computing the intestate share to be received by the heir's issue, unless the declaration or acknowledgment provides otherwise." (As eff. 1-1-76.)

R.C. 2105.052 provides: "Any debt owed to a decedent shall not be charged against the intestate share of any person except the debtor. If the debtor fails to survive decedent, the debt shall not be taken into account in computing the intestate share of the debtor's issue." (As eff. 1-1-76.)

An advancement is simply an anticipation of the distribution which the law would make at the death of the donor and is limited to children, or their descendants, of an intestate. The parent's intention is the controlling principle in the application of the doctrine of advancements. In re Morton's Estate, 2 O Supp 361, 6 OO 343, 21 Abs 438 (Prob. 1936).

Further research: O Jur 3d, Decedents' Estates § 183.

LAW IN GENERAL

An advancement is an inter vivos gift to a child from the parent with the intention of the latter that the gift shall represent part or all of the share in the parent's estate which the child would inherit on the subsequent death of the parent intestate. Am Jur 2d, Advancements § 1; Am Law of Prop § 14.10; CJS, Descent, etc. § 91; Powell § 1009; Tiffany § 1129.

9-12B Grandchild; Spouse of Child.

A gift to a son-in-law, intended by the ancestor to be charged as an advancement against his daughter, will be so charged if she, knowing the fact and intention of the gift, acquiesced therein. Dittoe v. Cluney, 22 OS 436 (1872).

In the partition of the lands of an intestate among his children and the children of a deceased son, the portion which the latter inherit should be charged with an advancement made to their father by such intestate. Parsons v. Parsons, 52 OS 470, 40 NE 165, 33 WLB 166 (1895).

LAW IN GENERAL

By the weight of authority, an advancement may be made to a grandchild or to the spouse of a child. Am Jur 2d, Advancements §§ 23, 25; CJS, Descent, etc. § 95.

9-12C Partial Intestacy.

The partial disposition of an estate by will does not exclude the operation of the statute regulating advancements in the distribution of the intestate residuum. Dittoe v. Cluney, 22 OS 436 (1872).

9-12D Hotchpot.

Under the doctrine of hotchpot, debts of the heirs to the intestate, or advancements whether of personal or real property are considered part of the property to be divided, so that the shares of the heirs can be equalized. Tobias v. Richardson, 5 CC(NS) 74, 16 CD 81 (1904); Dow v. Dow, 3 NP(NS) 125, 15 OD 576, 50 WLB 98 (1905).

Further research: O Jur 3d, Decedents' Estates § 203.

LAW IN GENERAL

Hotchpot is the doctrine under which the recipient of an advancement may bring in the value of his gift for the purpose of division. An heir may thereby show that he has not received his full share of the estate. Am Jur 2d, Advancements § 54; CJS, Descent, etc. § 106.

9-12E Time of Valuation.

See 9-12A.

9-12F Presumptions.

As between parent and child, a deed of gift from the former is presumed to be made by way of an advancement and the burden is upon the latter to show the contrary. Cowden v. Cowden, 7 CC(NS) 277, 18 CD 71, 51 WLB 27 (1905).

The real consideration may always be shown to determine whether a deed was given as an advancement. Stump v. Boyd, 8 Abs 59 (App. 1929).

LAW IN GENERAL

A gift from parent to child is generally presumed to be an advancement. The rule is not changed by recital of a nominal consideration. The presumption does not obtain where the child gave a substantial consideration, although some cases hold that the excess value of the gift over the consideration is an advancement. Am Law of Prop § 14.10; Powell § 1009; Tiffany § 1129.

SECTION 9-13: ADOPTED CHILDREN

9-13A Inheritance by Adopted Children.

Statute and chart, see 9-13G.

Prior to August 28, 1951 an adopted child inherited from his natural father and also from his adoptive father. Knese v. Hake, 16 OD 466, 3 OLR 610 (1906). For present statute, see 9-13G.

The right to inherit is not defeated by the absence from the proceedings of adoption of assent thereto on the part of both of the natural parents. Taylor v. Bushnell, 29 CC(NS) 497, 35 CD 642 (1919).

Where probate court was without jurisdiction in first instance in adoption, proceedings were not voidable but void. McClain v. Lyon, 24 App 279, 156 NE 529, 6 Abs 60 (1926).

A presumption of law arises from a decree of adoption that all the provisions of law relating thereto have been legally complied with, and subsists until overcome by proof to the contrary. Martin v. Fisher, 25 App 372, 158 NE 287, 5 Abs 596 (1927).

A declaration or finding that adoption is void for feeblemindedness of child does not cut off rights acquired by descent by the adopted child prior to such declaration. Steiner v. Rainer, 69 App 6, 42 NE2d 684, 23 OO 306 (1941).

In a proceeding to determine heirship, an attack on a judgment of adoption on the ground that the court rendering it had no jurisdiction is a collateral attack. In re Dickman's Estate, 81 App 281, 79 NE2d 172, 37 OO 125 (1946).

A testamentary provision for "lineal descendants of my blood" furnishes "other clear identification" so as to enable them to succeed to a designated portion of testator's estate, although such children were previously adopted by nonrelatives. Saintington v. Saintington, 5 App2d 133, 214 NE2d 124, 34 OO2d 243 (1966).

A child who was adopted by his stepfather before his natural father's death may inherit through his natural father from the latter's mother. First Nat. Bank of East Liverpool v. Collar, 27 Misc. 88, 272 NE2d 916, 56 OO2d 302 (C.P. 1971).

Further research: O Jur 3d, Family Law § 238.

9-13B Inheritance through Adoptive Parent.

Statute on words which include adopted children, see 9-13G.

A child adopted after the death of the testator by the devisee of a life estate will take under a devise of the remainder "to the heirs at law" of the life tenant. Smith v. Hunter, 86 OS 106, 99 NE 91, 10 OLR 72, 57 WLB 203 (1912).

Where the context of a will seems to confine the benefits to blood relatives, "children" or "issue" will not be construed to include adopted children; and otherwise they will be so construed. Albright v. Albright, 116 OS 668, 157 NE 760, 5 Abs 345, 25 OLR 343 (1927).

Since 1931 an adopted child is enabled to take through his adoptive parent from the latter's ancestors whether the property passes by will or by operation of law. Flynn v. Bredbeck, 147 OS 49, 68 NE2d 75, 33 OO 243 (1946). Prior to 1932, see chart at 9-13G.

Where, in providing for his "heirs at law" after a life interest, a testator indicates his intention that such heirs should be determined at the date of the expiration of such life interest, then a child adopted long after testator's death will take under the statutory law existing on such date of expiration, even though such adopted child would not have taken under the statutory law as existing at testator's death. Tiedtke v. Tiedtke, 157 OS 554, 106 NE2d 637, 47 OO 411 (1952).

"Where a testator bequeathed property to 'each of my then living grandchildren, whether born prior or subsequent to my decease,' there is a presumption, in the absence of any language in the will to the contrary, that the testator intended only the blood children of his children to partake of his bounty." The use of the word "born" was the controlling factor in this decision. Third Nat. Bank & Trust Co. v. Davidson, 157 OS 355, 105 NE2d 573, 47 OO 257 (1952).

A child adopted after death of testator by the devisee of life estate held not to come within the testamentary intent in either of these wills which provided "in case (life tenant) should die without leaving issue" and "if (life tenant) should die leaving a child or children." Central Trust Co. v. Hart, 82 App 450, 80 NE2d 920, 38 OO 88, 51 Abs 270 (1948).

"Lawful issue" in this will is construed to exclude the adopted children of settlor's son. An adopted child is deemed to be excluded from a class of beneficiaries under a trust where the settlor was a stranger to the adoption and had not otherwise manifested an intent to include adopted children. National City Bank of Cleveland v. Mitchell, 13 App2d 141, 234 NE2d 916, 42 OO2d 262 (1968).

A bequest to grandchildren of the testatrix should be construed to include the adopted children of a child of the testatrix where the adoptions occurred between the execution of the will and the death of testatrix, she knew and approved of the adoptions, and she failed to change the will. Weitzel v. Weitzel, 16 Misc. 105, 239 NE2d 263, 45 OO2d 55 (Prob. 1968).

Children adopted by children of the testator are included in a class gift to his "grandchildren" in the absence of other language to the contrary in instruments executed after August 28, 1951. Conkle v. Conkle, 31 App2d 44, 285 NE2d 883, 60 OO2d 144 (1972).

Further research: O Jur 3d, Family Law § 240.

9-13C Inheritance from Adopted Children.

Where prior to August 28, 1951, an adopted child died intestate leaving no spouse or issue, his property passed to his blood kin and not to his kin by adoption, even though such property was inherited by the adopted child from his adopting mother and his brother by adoption and was identifiable as identical. The statute in force at the decease of the adopted child determines succession and inheritance. National Bank of Lima v. Hancock, 85 App 1, 88 NE2d 67, 40 OO 30 (1948).

William R. Kinney, in a circular letter, dated January 23, 1950, referring to the above decision stated: "It is fairly clear from the opinion itself that if there are relatives by adoption as close as brothers or sisters, or lineal descendants of such adoptive brothers and sisters, the broad rule of law as laid down in the syllabus would not apply. It is also clear that had the adopted child in this case died before January 1, 1944, such rule of law would not have applied to the property which such adopted child had inherited from her adopting mother."

Prior to January 1, 1944, the statute provided that if the death of the adopted child occur subsequently to the death of the adopting parents, and such adopted child be without issue, then the property of the deceased adopting parent shall descend to the next of kin of such parent. Kroff v. Amrhein, 94 OS 282, 114 NE 267, 14 OLR 204, 61 WLB 190 (1916). This clause does not apply to property which the adopted child may have conveyed prior to his death. Spangenberg v. Guiney, 2 NP 39, 3 OD 163 (1895).

Since August 27, 1951 the kin by adoption inherit as provided by R.C. 3107.15, shown at 9-13G.

Further research: O Jur 3d, Family Law § 242.

9-13D Inheritance through Adopted Children.

Lapse statute, see 9-26A.

If an adopted child dies during the lifetime of the adopting parents, leaving a child as survivor, such surviving child inherits by representation from the adopting parents. Kroff v. Amrhein, 94 OS 282, 114 NE 267 (1916).

Inheritance through an adopted child since August 27, 1951 is expressly provided by R.C. 3107.15, shown at 9-13G.

9-13E Amendment of Statute.

The right of an adopted child to inherit from adopting parents is governed by the rights of inheritance in force at the time of decedent's death. Staley v. Honeyman, 98 NE2d 429, 59 Abs 203 (App. 1950), affd. 157 OS 61, 104 NE2d 172, 47 OO 67 (1952); In re Todhunter's Adoption, 35 NE2d 992, 33 Abs 567 (App. 1941).

The status as an adopted child is determined by the law in effect at the time of the alleged adoption. See also 9-13F.

9-13F Foreign Adoption.

The status of any person, with its inherent capacity of succession or inheritance, is to be ascertained by the law of the domicile which creates the status. A person adopted in another state inherits as though adopted in Ohio. Barrett v. Delmore, 143 OS 203, 54 NE2d 789, 28 OO 133, 153 ALR 192 (1944).

The status of one claiming to be an heir as a result of adoption is to be determined by the adoption laws in effect at the time when and in the state where the alleged adoption took place. Belden v. Armstrong, 93 App 307, 113 NE2d 693, 51 OO 62 (1951).

Under comity between nations, an adoption decree of a foreign country will be given effect in this state, if the foreign court had jurisdiction to fix the status of the child with respect to the adoptive parents, and if such decree is not repugnant to the laws of Ohio. National City Bank of Cleveland v. Judkins, 8 Misc 119, 219 NE2d 456, 37 OO2d 200 (C.P. 1964).

Further research: 87 ALR2d 1240.

9-13G   Statute and Chart.

R.C. 3107.01 to 3107.19 provide procedure in adoptions.

R.C. 3107.15 provides that except as to the spouse and relatives of the spouse of a petitioner, a final decree of adoption, or an interlocutory order of adoption which is not later vacated, terminates all legal relationships between the adopted person and his former relatives for all purposes including inheritance and the interpretation of statutes and instruments, whether executed before or after the adoption, which do not expressly include the person by name or by some designation not based on a parent and child or blood relationship. Such a decree or order creates the relationship of parent and child between the petitioner and the person adopted for all purposes including instruments which do not expressly exclude an adopted person from their operation. Notwithstanding the foregoing provisions, if the parent of a child dies and a spouse of the living parent adopts the child, the child's rights from and through the deceased parent are not restricted or curtailed by the adoption. (As eff. 1-1-77.)

CHART OF INHERITANCE

1859 through December 31, 1931.

Adopted child inherited from but not through adopting parents. Upon the death of adopted child without issue, property of previously deceased adopting parent shall descend to the next of kin of such parent and not of such child. G.C. 8030; Quigley v. Mitchell, 41 OS 375, 12 WLB 276 (1884). An adopted child is enabled to inherit from the adopter, but not through him, from his ancestors. Phillips v. McConica, 59 OS 1, 51 NE 445, 40 WLB 260 (1898).

January 1, 1932 through December 31, 1943.

Adopted child inherited from and through adopting parents all property except that expressly limited to the heirs of the body of the adopting parents. Upon the death of adopted child without issue, property of previously deceased adopting parent shall descend to the next of kin of such parent and not of such child. (G.C. 10512-19.)

January 1, 1944 through August 27, 1951.

Adopted child inherited from and through adopting parents all property except that expressly limited to the heirs of the body of the adopting parents. (G.C. 10512-23.)

August 28, 1951 to date.

For the purpose of inheritance to, through, and from a legally adopted child, such child shall be treated the same as if it were the natural child of its adopting parents except as to property expressly limited to heirs of the body of the adopting parents, and shall cease to be treated as the child of his natural parents for the purposes of intestate succession except in the case of adoption by a stepfather or stepmother. See R.C. 3107.15, supra.

SECTION 9-14: ILLEGITIMATE CHILDREN

9-14A Rule.

See also 11-92B.

R.C. 2105.17 provides: "Children born out of wedlock shall be capable of inheriting or transmitting inheritance from and to their mother, and from and to those from whom she may inherit, or to whom she may transmit inheritance, as if born in lawful wedlock." (As eff. 1-1-76.)

R.C. 2105.18 provides: "The natural father of a child may file an application in the probate court of the county in which he resides, in the county in which the child resides, or the county in which the child was born, acknowledging that the child is his. If such an application is filed, upon consent of the mother, or if she is deceased, incompetent, or has surrendered custody, upon consent of the person or agency having custody of the child or of a court having jurisdiction over the child's custody, the probate court, if satisfied that the applicant is the natural father, and that establishment of the relationship is for the best interest of the child, shall enter the finding of fact upon its journal. Thereafter, the child is the child of the applicant, as though born to him in lawful wedlock." (As eff. 6-29-82.)

A mere acknowledgment by the natural father, without marriage to the mother, does not enable the child to inherit either from or through the natural father. Blackwell v. Bowman, 150 OS 34, 80 NE2d 493, 37 OO 323 (1948).

The status of legitimacy conferred by the law of another state places the child in the same situation with regard to the inheritance of Ohio land as though he had acquired such status in Ohio. Howells v. Limbeck, 172 OS 297, 175 NE2d 517, 16 OO2d 68, 87 ALR2d 1269 (1961).

A man who marries a woman while she is pregnant is presumed in law to be the father of the child, and no formal acknowledgment under R.C. 2105.18 is required for such child to inherit. The evidence of actual paternity was not refuted. Romweber v. Martin, 30 OS2d 25, 282 NE2d 36, 59 OO2d 58 (1972).

The word "children" in the statute of descent and distribution (R.C. 2105.06) and the half-and-half statute (R.C. 2105.10 repealed eff. 1-1-76) includes one who is in fact the illegitimate child of his deceased father. However, in this case the claimant was found not to be the illegitimate child of the decedent. Green v. Woodard, 40 App2d 101, 318 NE2d 397, 69 OO2d 130 (1974). Contra: Moore v. Dague, 46 App2d 75, 345 NE2d 449, 75 OO2d 68 (1975).

LAW IN GENERAL

At common law, there is no right of inheritance by, from or through an illegitimate child except for descent from him to his lineal descendants. Am

331

Jur 2d, Bastards § 146; 83 ALR 1330; 48 ALR2d 759; 60 ALR2d 1182; CJS, Bastards § 24; Powell § 1003; Tiffany § 1126.

By the weight of authority, a devise to "children," "heirs," or "issue" does not include illegitimates unless the context or circumstances show such an intention of the testator. Evidence extrinsic to the will is generally held to be inadmissible to show an intention that "children" is to include illegitimate children, if there are legitimate children. Am Jur 2d, Bastards §§ 135, 136.

The acquisition of legitimate status by a child in another state is generally given effect in the state of the situs of the property. 87 ALR2d 1274.

SECTION 9-15: HUSBAND AND WIFE

9-15A Rule.

Election by surviving spouse, see Section 9-27.

In its technical sense the term "heirs" embraces those who take estate of intestate under statute of descent and distribution, and in the event such statute designates widow, she takes as heir. Holt v. Miller, 133 OS 418, 14 NE2d 409, 11 OO 85 (1938).

The term next of kin does not include husband or wife. Russell v. Roberts, 54 App 441, 7 NE2d 811, 8 OO 196, 23 Abs 435 (1936).

The surviving spouse, standing in the relation of an heir at law with those who take under the statutes of descent and distribution, takes subject to decedent's debts. Disher v. Disher, 35 NE2d 582, 8 OO 203, 21 Abs 610 (App. 1936).

SECTION 9-16: OTHER CLASSES OF HEIRS

9-16A After-born Heirs.

R.C. 2105.14 provides: "Descendants of an intestate begotten before his death, but born thereafter, in all cases will inherit as if born in the lifetime of the intestate and surviving him; but in no other case can a person inherit unless living at the time of the death of the intestate." (As eff. 10-1-53.)

9-16B Murderer; Civil Death.

R.C. 2105.19 provides: "(A) Except as provided in division (C) of this section, no person who is convicted of, pleads guilty to, or is found not guilty by reason of insanity of a violation of or complicity in the violation of section 2903.01, 2903.02, or 2903.03 of the Revised Code or of an existing or former law of any other state, the United States, or a foreign nation, substantially equivalent to a violation of or complicity in the violation of any of these sections, no person who is indicted for a violation of or complicity in the violation of any of those sections or laws and subsequently is adjudicated incompetent to stand trial on that charge, and no juvenile who is found to be a delinquent child by reason of committing an act that, if committed by an adult, would be a violation of or complicity in the violation of any of those sections or laws, shall in any way benefit by the death. All property of the decedent, and all money, insurance proceeds, or other property or benefits payable or distributable in respect of the decedent's death, shall pass or be paid or distributed as if the person who caused the death of the decedent had predeceased the decedent.

"(B) A person prohibited by division (A) of this section from benefiting by the death of another is a constructive trustee for the benefit of those entitled to any property or benefit that the person has obtained, or over which he has exerted control, because of the decedent's death. A person who purchases any such property or benefit from the constructive trustee, for value, in good faith, and without notice of the constructive trustee's disability under division (A) of this section, acquires good title, but the constructive trustee is accountable to the beneficiaries for the proceeds or value of the property or benefit."

"(C) A person who is prohibited from benefiting from a death pursuant to division (A) of this section either because he was adjudicated incompetent to stand trial or was found not guilty by reason of insanity, or his guardian appointed pursuant to Chapter 2111, of the Revised Code or other legal representative, may file a complaint to declare his right to benefit from the death in the probate court in which the decedent's estate is being administered or which released the estate from administration. The complaint shall be filed no later than sixty days after the person is adjudicated incompetent to stand trial or found not guilty by reason of insanity. The court shall notify each person who is a devisee or legatee under the decedent's will, or if there is no will, each person who is an heir of the decedent pursuant to section 2105.06 of the Revised Code that such a complaint has been filed within ten days after the filing of such a complaint. The person who files the motion, and each person who is required to be notified of the filing of the motion under this division is entitled to a jury trial in the action. To assert the right, the person desiring a jury trial shall demand a jury in the manner prescribed in the civil rules.

"A person who files a complaint pursuant to this division shall be restored to his right to benefit from the death unless the court determines, by a preponderance of the evidence, that the person would have been convicted of a violation of, or complicity in the violation of, section 2903.01, 2903.02, or 2903.03 of the Revised Code, or of a law of another state, the United States, or a foreign nation that is substantially similar to any of those sections, if he had been brought to trial in the case in which he was adjudicated incompetent or if he were not insane at the time of the commission of the offense." (As eff. 10-17-85.)

The three sections mentioned in (A) above refer to aggravated murder, murder, and voluntary manslaughter.

A husband who has been finally adjudged guilty of murdering his wife does not take anything as exempt from administration from the estate of his victim. Bauman v. Hogue, 160 OS 296, 116 NE2d 439, 52 OO 183 (1953).

This section has no effect upon one never brought to trial or convicted. Demos v. Freemas, 26 Abs 601 (App. 1938). It is not applicable unless there is a conviction by a court of competent jurisdiction. Winters Nat. Bank & Trust

Co. v. Shields, 3 O Supp 134, 14 OO 438, 29 Abs 193 (Prob. 1939); Harrison v. Hillegas, 1 O Supp 160, 13 OO 523, 28 Abs 404 (Prob. 1939).

Where a conviction has not been shown, the widow is entitled to her statutory allowances and her intestate share in the net estate of her husband, notwithstanding the fact that she has feloniously taken his life. Winters Nat. Bank & Trust Co. v. Shields, 3 O Supp 134, 14 OO 438, 29 Abs 193 (Prob. 1939).

Section 2105.19 does not provide that one shall be divested of property which he has inherited, but simply prevents an inheritance. Egelhoff v. Presler, 16 O Supp 195, 32 OO 252, 44 Abs 376 (Prob. 1945).

A husband who has been adjudged guilty of first degree manslaughter in the death of his wife is entitled to the statutory share of a surviving spouse. Wadsworth v. Siek, 23 Misc 112, 254 NE2d 738, 50 OO2d 507 (C.P. 1970).

The Ohio statute does not apply to title to an estate by entireties or to other survivorship property although it does indicate the public policy. The American decisions are in marked conflict on whether any interest accrues to the survivor who murdered his cotenant. 42 ALR3d 1119.

Ohio has no "civil death" statute.

Further research: O Jur 3d, Decedents' Estates § 153.

9-16C By Affinity.

An illegitimate child, whose mother subsequently marries a man, not the child's father, is the stepchild of such man under the statute of descent and distribution. Kest v. Lewis, 169 OS 317, 159 NE2d 449, 8 OO2d 317 (1959).

Stepchildren inherit irrespective of the dissolution of the marriage by divorce. In re McGraff's Estate, 83 NE2d 427, 38 OO 187, 54 Abs 336 (Prob. 1948).

9-16D Designated Heirs.

Lapse statute, see 9-26A.

R.C. 2105.15 provides: "A person of sound mind and memory may appear before the probate judge of his county and in the presence of such judge and two disinterested persons of such person's acquaintance, file a written declaration declaring that, as his free and voluntary act, he did designate and appoint another, stating the name and place of residence of such person specifically, to stand toward him in the relation of an heir at law in the event of his death. Such declaration must be attested by the two disinterested persons and subscribed by the declarant. If satisfied that such declarant is of sound mind and memory and free from restraint, the judge thereupon shall enter that fact upon his journal and make a complete record of such proceedings. Thenceforward the person designated will stand in the same relation, for all purposes, to such declarant as he could if a child born in lawful wedlock. The rules of inheritance will be the same between him and the relations by blood of the declarant, as if so born. A certified copy of such record will be prima facie evidence of the fact stated therein, and conclusive evidence, unless impeached for actual fraud or undue influence. After a lapse of one year from the date of such designation, such declarant may have such designation vacated or changed by filing in said probate court an application to vacate or change such designation of heir; provided, that there is compliance with the procedure, conditions, and prerequisites required in the making of the original declaration." (As eff. 10-1-53.)

From January 1, 1932 to August 27, 1939 no provision was made for vacation or change of designation.

From 1854 to December 31, 1931, former G.C. 8598 provided that a person may designate an heir at law by declaration filed in probate court, and that the rules of inheritance shall be the same between them as if born in lawful wedlock.

A designated heir is not "issue of the body, or an adopted child" under the statute voiding charitable gifts made within one year. Theobald v. Fugman, 64 OS 473, 60 NE 606, 45 WLB 318, 382 (1901).

A person who has been designated and appointed by another as an heir at law inherits from but not through his designator. Blackwell v. Bowman, 150 OS 34, 80 NE2d 493, 37 OO 323 (1948).

Devise to daughter for life and at her death to her heirs at law in fee, held not to exclude designated heir although designation was after death of testator. Laws v. Davis, 34 App 157, 170 NE 601, 31 OLR 419 (1929).

Probate court may, sua sponte, set aside its previous decree of such designation. Horine v. Horine, 16 Abs 155 (App. 1934).

The only benefits conferred by R.C. 2105.15 are rights of inheritance and no additional legal relationships are created. A designated heir is not entitled to a child's exemption under the Ohio Estate Tax law. In re Howell, 278 NE2d 926, 57 OO2d 364 (Prob. 1971).

SECTION 9-17: ESCHEAT

9-17A Generally.

Aliens, see also Section 15-15.

R.C. 2105.09 provides for the use or disposition of lands escheated to the state. (As eff. 9-8-86.)

An enactment, after the death of the intestate and before proceedings to declare the escheat, providing additional heirs, prevents the escheat to the state and entitles such heirs to the estate. Lewis v. Eutsler, 4 OS 354 (1854).

There is no authority for escheating property to the state where there is no finding by the court of an absence of heirs. Maurer v. Mihalyne, 105 App 83, 151 NE2d 383, 5 OO2d 367 (1957).

To "escheat" means to revert to the government because of the nonexistence of legal heirs. State ex rel. Rich v. Page, 6 O Supp 104, 20 OO 155, 33 Abs 647 (C.P. 1941).

Further research: O Jur 3d, Abandoned, Lost, and Escheated Property § 21.

LAW IN GENERAL

Escheat is not technically a devolution of property by descent but is a devolution of property of an intestate. Property is said to escheat to the state when no person is lawfully entitled to take or hold it. The state acquires ownership by escheat of the property of a person who dies intestate and without heirs. Title is so acquired in the nature of forfeiture where statutes prohibit inheritance by or through aliens.

The state acquires all the rights of the former owner and ordinarily takes subject to all valid encumbrances on the property at the time of the escheat.

The right of the state may be released or abandoned. Adverse possession has been held to defeat an escheat on the theory of a presumed grant. A conveyance prior to the time of forfeiture may prevent escheat even though the conveyance is voidable.

Procedure to establish the escheat was necessary at common law, except as to aliens. Judicial proceedings are often held necessary to vest the title in the state. Title has been held to vest in the state immediately upon the death of a person intestate and without heirs.

Where a lawful heir appears after the escheat has been declared, he can recover the property in the absence of a statute barring him.

79 ALR 1364; Powell §§ 158, 989; Tiffany § 1237.

SECTION 9-18: HALF-AND-HALF STATUTE

9-18A Statute.

R.C. 2105.10 repealed effective January 1, 1976, provided: "When a relict of a deceased husband or wife dies intestate and without issue, possessed of identical real estate or personal property which came to such relict from any deceased spouse by deed of gift, devise, bequest, descent, or by an election to take under section 2105.06 of the Revised Code, such estate, real and personal, except one half thereof which shall pass to and vest in the surviving spouse of such relict, shall pass to and vest in the children of the deceased spouse from whom such real estate or personal property came, or their lineal descendants, per stirpes. If there are no children or their lineal descendants, such estate, except for the one-half passing to the surviving spouse of such relict, shall pass and descend as follows:

"(A) One half to the other heirs of such relict as provided by sections 2105.01 to 2105.09, inclusive, and 2105.11 to 2105.21, inclusive, of the Revised Code, and in the same manner and proportions as if the relict had left no surviving spouse;

"(B) One half to the parents of the deceased spouse from whom such real estate or personal property came, equally, or the survivor of such parents;

"(C) If there is no parent surviving, to the brothers and sisters, whether of the whole or of the half blood of such deceased spouse, or their lineal descendants, per stirpes;

"(D) If there are no children of the deceased spouse from whom such real estate or personal property came, or their lineal descendants, no parent and no brothers or sisters, whether of the whole or of the half blood, or their lineal descendants, who survive such relict, then this section shall not apply and all such real estate and personal property shall pass and descend as provided by sections 2105.01 to 2105.09, inclusive, and 2105.11 to 2105.21, inclusive, of the Revised Code." (G.C. 10503-5 as eff. 8-22-41.)

9-18B Chart.

April 11, 1877 (original) through April 5, 1881 (74 O.L. 81).

When relict of deceased spouse dies intestate and without issue, nonancestral property which came to such relict from a deceased spouse shall pass one-half to the brothers and sisters of such relict or their legal representatives and one-half to the brothers and sisters of such deceased spouse or their personal representatives.

April 6, 1881 through July 3, 1923 (Sec. 4162, 78 O.L. 107).

When relict of deceased spouse dies intestate and without issue, property which came to such intestate by deed of gift, devise or bequest from a deceased spouse shall pass to the children, or their legal representatives, of such deceased spouse. If no such children then one-half to the brothers and sisters, or their legal representatives, of such relict and one-half to the brothers and sisters, or their legal representatives, of such deceased spouse.

July 4, 1923 through December 31, 1931 (G.C. 8577, 110 O.L. 13).

When relict of deceased spouse dies intestate and without issue, property acquired by 7 of ancestral chart July 4, 1923 through December 31, 1931 and also property which came to such intestate by deed of gift, devise or bequest from a deceased spouse shall pass to children, or their legal representatives, of such deceased spouse. If no such children or their legal representatives then one-half to the brothers and sisters, or their legal representatives, of such relict and one-half to the brothers and sisters, or their legal representatives, of such deceased spouse.

January 1, 1932 through September 1, 1935 (G.C. 10503-5, 114 O.L. 320).

When the relict of a deceased spouse dies intestate and without issue, the property which came to such intestate by deed of gift, devise, bequest or descent from a deceased spouse (except for the intestate share of the surviving spouse if any, of such relict) shall pass to the children (or the next of kin of deceased children) of such deceased spouse. If no such children or their next of kin, then (except for the intestate share of the surviving spouse, if any of such relict) one-half to the brothers and sisters (or their next of kin) of such relict

337

and one-half to the brothers and sisters (or their next of kin) of such deceased spouse.

September 2, 1935 through August 21, 1941 (G.C. 10503-5, 116 O.L. 385).

When the relict of a deceased spouse dies intestate and without issue, the property which came by deed of gift, devise, bequest or descent from a deceased spouse to such relict shall pass:
1. (a) One-half to the surviving spouse of relict;
   (b) One-half (or all if no surviving spouse of relict) to the children, or next of kin of deceased children, of the deceased spouse from whom the property came.
2. If there are no children (or their next of kin) of the deceased spouse from whom the property came, then such property shall pass:
   (a) One-half to the surviving spouse of relict;
   (b) One-fourth (or one-half if no surviving spouse of relict) to the brothers and sisters, or their next of kin, of relict;
   (c) One-fourth (or one-half if no surviving spouse of relict) to the brothers and sisters, or their next of kin, of the deceased spouse from whom the property came.

August 22, 1941 to January 1, 1976 (G.C. 10503-5, R.C. 2105.10).

When the relict of a deceased spouse dies intestate and without issue, the identical property which came to such relict by deed of gift, devise, bequest, descent, or election to take under the law, from a deceased spouse, shall pass:
1. (a) One-half to the surviving spouse of relict;
   (b) One-half (or all if no surviving spouse of relict) to the lineal descendants of the deceased spouse from whom the property came, per stirpes.
2. If there are no lineal descendants of the deceased spouse from whom the property came, then
   (a) One-half to surviving spouse of relict;
   (b) One-fourth (or one-half if no surviving spouse of relict) to the heirs of relict under paragraphs F to J, inclusive, of R.C. 2105.06;
   (c) One-fourth (or one-half if no surviving spouse of relict) to the surviving parent or parents of the deceased spouse from whom the property came; if no such parent, to the brothers and sisters (whether of the whole or half blood) of such deceased spouse or their lineal descendants, per stirpes.
3. If there are no such lineal descendants, parents, brothers, sisters or lineal descendants of brothers or sisters of the deceased spouse from whom the property came, then to the heirs of relict under R.C. 2105.06.

DIVISION 9-2: WILLS

SECTION 9-21: GENERALLY; RULES OF INTERPRETATION

Adopted children, see Section 9-13.
Class gifts, see Division 11-9.
Construction as to vesting, see Section 11-81.
Construction generally, see also 11-11D.
Equitable conversion, see Section 16-63.
Estates and future interests, see Chapter 11.
Executors and administrators, see Chapter 12.
Illegitimate children, see Section 9-14.

9-21A Definition.

Construction as deed or will, see 8-31J.

R.C. 2107.01 provides: "In Chapters 2101. to 2131., inclusive, of the Revised Code, 'will' includes codicils and lost, spoliated, or destroyed wills." (As eff. 10-1-53.)

A will is commonly defined as any instrument executed with the formalities of law whereby a person makes a disposition of his property to take effect after his death. Tax Commission v. Parker, 117 OS 215, 158 NE 89, 5 Abs 419, 25 OLR 387 (1927).

An instrument may be probated as a valid will even though it does not dispose of property. In re Crowe's Will, 4 O Supp 370, 17 OO 8, 31 Abs 35 (Prob. 1940).

A will is the legal declaration of a person's wishes as to the disposition of his property, or as to the appointment of an executor, to take effect at his death.

9-21B Law of Situs; Conflict of Laws.

It is a well settled principle of public law, that the acquisition of real property, whether by descent or by devise, is governed by the lex rei sitae. Jones v. Robinson, 17 OS 171 (1867).

The laws of Ohio govern in the construction of wills disposing of lands situated in this state. Jennings v. Jennings, 21 OS 56 (1871).

Under Ohio law, the law of the situs applies in construing testamentary language purporting to devise real estate located in a sister state. Nolan v. Borger, 203 NE2d 274, 32 OO2d 255, 95 Abs 225 (Prob. 1963).

Intestate succession to personal property is governed by the law of the deceased owner's domicile. However, the law of the situs may require administration in that state for the protection of resident creditors and the law of the domicile will not be applied if the result is contrary to the public policy of the state of the situs. Howard v. Reynolds, 30 OS2d 214, 283 NE2d 629, 59 OO2d 228 (1972).

Further research: O Jur 3d, Conflict of Laws §§ 29, 33.

LAW IN GENERAL

The validity, construction and effect of a devise are determined by the laws of the state in which the land is located. In ascertaining testator's actual intent from words which do not invoke a rule of property, some courts consider the law and usage of his domicile. Am Law of Prop § 14.25; CJS, Wills § 587; Powell § 980.

9-21C Intention of the Testator.

Construction generally, see also 11-11D.

In the construction of wills the intention of the testator must govern if it be not inconsistent with the rules of law. Such intention, if clearly manifested, will be carried into effect if it be not unlawful and does not create an estate forbidden by law. King v. Beck, 15 Ohio 559 (1846).

Further research: O Jur 3d, Decedents' Estates § 541.

LAW IN GENERAL

The primary rule in the construction of a will is to ascertain the intention of the testator as expressed in the will. The testator's intention does not overcome positive law, but all principles of interpretation are subject to this primary rule. A judicial ascertainment of the intention prevails over all general rules. The intention of the testator may be so uncertain that part or all of the will is ineffective. CJS, Wills § 590.

Parts of a will may be ineffective to such an extent that the general scheme of the testator cannot be fulfilled and the entire will fails. On the other hand, if the general plan of an incomplete will is apparent, provisions by implication may be found to make the plan effective. CJS, Wills § 151; Powell § 325.

9-21D Conflicting Clauses; Whole Instrument Construed.

Conflicting provisions in a will should be reconciled so as to conform to the manifest general intent, and it is only in cases where such provisions are wholly and absolutely repugnant that either of them should be rejected. Baxter v. Bowyer, 19 OS 490 (1869).

"Now, it is rudimentary in the construction of wills that the intention of the testator is to be ascertained, and the whole will given force and effect, if such a construction can be reached consistent with the application of legal principles, and that, when an instrument is open to two constructions, one of which will give effect to the whole instrument and the other will destroy a part of it, the former must always be adopted." Tax Commission v. Oswald, 109 OS 36, 141 NE 678, 1 Abs 859, 21 OLR 329 (1923).

The law is that a devise by unequivocal terms cannot be cut down by language not equally clear and certain. Clark v. Clark, 13 App 164, 31 CC(NS) 472 (1920); Riley v. Riley, 30 App 73, 163 NE 922 (1928).

The intention of a testator as expressed in the items of his will cannot be changed by the numbering of the various items or the order in which they are arranged. Huffman v. Berry, 15 App 372 (1921).

The intention of the testator must be gathered from the language of the whole will. Rugg v. Smith, 40 App 101, 177 NE 784, 9 Abs 718, 34 OLR 513 (1931).

Where a fee simple estate is clearly given, a remainder given in language not equally clear is void. The court is required to reconcile, if possible, the devise to the first taker with the devise of a remainder, and if the language is susceptible of a construction which will give effect to both provisions the will must be so construed. Where, by one clause in a will property is devised or bequeathed, by words prima facie importing an absolute estate, and by subsequent clause is given in remainder to another person, the first devisee or legatee takes only a life estate, and the limitation over is valid. DeWolf v. Frazier, 80 App 150, 73 NE2d 212, 35 OO 485, 49 Abs 244 (1947).

When, under the provisions of a will, an estate in fee is given the first taker in unequivocal terms, an attempt to give to others "all ... that shall remain unused" at the time of the death of the first taker, does not cut down, to a life estate, the fee first given. Gill v. Leach, 81 App 480, 80 NE2d 256, 37 OO 311 (1947). The will does not contain words giving a power to sell.

A will and codicil are to be construed together as parts of the same instrument, and the intent of the testator is to be gathered from the whole. First Troy Nat. Bank & Trust Co. v. Holder, 109 App 445, 167 NE2d 370, 11 OO2d 450 (1959).

The husband acquired an absolute fee simple under the devise: "I direct that all of the property and possessions listed below go to my husband ... and after that to my children...." It does not "clearly appear," as required by R.C. 2107.51, that the devisor intended to convey a less estate to the husband. Kohout v. Kohout, 4 Misc. 38, 203 NE2d 869, 31 OO2d 180 (1965).

Further research: O Jur 3d, Decedents' Estates §§ 528, 529, 566, 567.

LAW IN GENERAL

The intention of the testator is ascertained from a consideration of all the provisions of the will. It is frequently held that all words and provisions will be given effect if possible.

When the conflict between parts of a will cannot be reconciled, a preference is given to the latter part, although the earlier clause is preferred in construction of a deed. The provisions of the later of two wills or codicils control.

A subsequent clause does not cut down nor defeat a gift unless by language at least as clear and certain as the prior clause.

17 ALR2d 7; CJS, Wills § 620; Restatement, Property § 246.

9-21E Consideration of the Circumstances.

When the court is in doubt as to the true intention of the testatrix, as expressed by the language of the will, evidence as to conditions and surrounding circumstances at the time of execution of the will is admissible. Craft v. Shroyer, 81 App 253, 74 NE2d 589, 37 OO 77, 49 Abs 385 (1947).

When a devise or bequest in a will is expressed in unequivocal terms, an interpretation by interested parties contrary to the legal meaning is of no effect, provided the elements of estoppel or contract are not present. Gill v. Leach, 81 App 480, 80 NE2d 256, 37 OO 311 (1947).

Before any testimony may be received bearing upon a latent ambiguity in a will, the language must be susceptible to proof that it will apply equally to two or more subjects or things. In re Marker's Estate, 104 NE2d 592, 61 Abs 251 (App. 1951).

A latent ambiguity is one where language employed is clear and intelligible and suggests but a single meaning, but some extrinsic fact or some extraneous evidence creates a necessity for interpretation of a choice among two or more possible meanings. Fifth Third Union Trust Co. v. Athenaeum of Ohio, 169 NE2d 707, 12 OO2d 188, 84 Abs 208 (Prob. 1959).

Further research: O Jur 3d, Decedents' Estates § 554.

LAW IN GENERAL

Extrinsic evidence is admissible to aid in the interpretation of an ambiguous will, but is not admissible to vary the terms of the will nor to show an intention of the testator different from that disclosed by the language of the will. Am Jur 2d, Wills § 1279.

9-21F   Against Intestacy.

R.C. 2107.51 provides: "Every devise of lands, tenements, or hereditaments in a will shall convey all the estate of the devisor therein, unless it clearly appears by the will that the devisor intended to convey a less estate." (As eff. 10-1-53.)

Courts will construe a will to avoid intestacy, if possible, but cannot prevent a lapse where words constituting testate disposition are lacking. Nelson v. Minton, 46 App 39, 187 NE 576, 14 Abs 679, 38 OLR 287 (1933); Gilpin v. Williams, 17 OS 396 (1867).

A testator is never presumed to die intestate as to any part of his estate and a court of equity will put such a construction upon equivocal words as will prevent such result. Fifth Third Union Trust Co. v. Wilensky, 79 App 73, 70 NE2d 920, 34 OO 458, 46 Abs 620 (1946).

The fact that a construction of the will which will render the remainder contingent may produce an intestacy as to the share of any of the designated remaindermen, who may die during the continuance of the precedent estate without leaving children, is a consideration which will influence the court to regard the remainder as vested. Cleveland Trust Co. v. Andrus, 95 App 503, 121 NE2d 68, 54 OO 125 (1953).

Further research: O Jur 3d, Decedents' Estates §§ 566, 567; CJS, Wills § 614.

9-21G Preference as to Heirs.

Gifts to children and the like, see Section 11-92.
Per capita or per stirpes, see Section 11-94.

When the language used in the residuary clause admits of two constructions, that construction will be given which will be more favorable to the heirs at law. City Trust & Savings Bank v. Hanley, 17 App 467 (1923).
Further research: O Jur 3d, Decedents' Estates § 570.

LAW IN GENERAL

A preference for equal distribution among persons similarly related to the testator or for persons of the blood of the testator is not infrequently a basis for resolving an ambiguity. CJS, Wills § 698.
A testamentary gift to a class or group of relatives has usually been held to include those of half blood. 49 ALR2d 1362.

9-21H Title of Devisee.

Claims against estate, see Section 12-14.

When will directs executor to sell and bequeaths proceeds to his children, the children have the naked legal title subject to be divested by exercise of the power by the executor. Hoffman v. Hoffman, 61 App 371, 22 NE2d 652, 15 OO 255, 29 Abs 345 (1939).
An heir to inherited property holds such property subject to the conditions and equities attached to it and encumbered with all the liens existing thereon during the lifetime of the ancestor. Wittkamp v. Wittkamp, 126 NE2d 473, 69 Abs 605 (C.P. 1954).
A devisee takes the title of the testator, that is, he is not a bona fide purchaser under the recording acts.

9-21I Time Becoming Effective; After-acquired Property.

R.C. 2107.50 provides: "Any estate, right, or interest in any property of which a decedent was possessed at his decease shall pass under his will unless such will manifests a different intention." (As eff. 10-1-53.)
The will speaks, not from the time of execution, but from the time of the death of the testator. Judy v. Trollinger, 110 OS 576, 144 NE 44, 2 Abs 372, 22 OLR 160 (1924); Ohio Nat. Bank v. Boone, 139 OS 361, 40 NE2d 149, 22 OO 414, 144 ALR 1150 (1942).

LAW IN GENERAL

A will is intended to be operative only upon the death of the maker. It generally speaks from the time of the testator's death. The law as it existed at that time is usually applied.

Events or facts occurring after the execution of the will and before the death of the testator are usually not considered in ascertaining his intention, unless he so indicated as by a gift to a class or by a devise "to C if B dies."

Property acquired by the testator after the execution of the will ordinarily passes by the will. The phrase "all my property" sufficiently shows an intention to pass after-acquired property.

Am Law of Prop § 14.9; CJS, Wills § 78; Powell § 319; Tiffany § 1069.

9-21J Renunciation; Election to Accept Burdens.

Acceleration, see 11-16C.
Statutory disclaimer of beneficial interest, see 9-11G.

If a testator has attempted to dispose of property which is not his own, and has given a benefit to the person to whom that property belongs, the devisee accepting the benefit so given to him must make good the testator's attempted disposition. Johnston v. Swickard, 71 NE2d 720, 34 OO 512, 48 Abs 77 (Prob. 1932); Huston v. Cone, 24 OS 11 (1873); White v. Brocaw, 14 OS 339 (1863).

A beneficiary is not bound to accept a legacy or devise but may disclaim or renounce his right under the will even where the gift is beneficial provided he has not already accepted it. Ohio Nat. Bank v. Miller, 25 OO2d 465 (App. 1943).

Title passes upon the death of the testator to the devisee or legatee but subject to being divested by renunciation, which must be within a reasonable time. In re Hartman's Estate, 14 O Supp 112, 29 OO 256 (Prob. 1944).

The doctrine of equitable election — that a person who, by electing to take under a will, accepts the benefits accruing to him therefrom cannot assert rights inconsistent therewith — may not be applied to the prejudice of third persons. Luttrell v. Luttrell, 4 App2d 305, 212 NE2d 641, 33 OO2d 351 (1965).

LAW IN GENERAL

A devisee may renounce the gift for any reason if he does so within a reasonable time, as a rule. A renunciation relates back to the death of the testator so as to prevent the vesting. Neither an acceptance nor a renunciation may be retracted. Am Law of Prop § 14.15.

A person given a benefit under a will (or other document) must elect between that benefit and any other right inconsistent with the will, even though he already owns part of the benefit. 60 ALR2d 789.

Renunciation, to be effective, must be express or be by unequivocal act. The burden of proving acceptance of a beneficial gift is upon the beneficiary or of an onerous devise is upon those who allege acceptance. 93 ALR2d 8.

9-21K Devise to Testator's Heir; Worthier Title.

LAW IN GENERAL

Under the doctrine of worthier title an heir takes by descent and the devise is void when it is of the same estate he would take as heir. The rule has been said to be obsolete as to wills even though in effect as to deeds. The application of the doctrine to lapse statutes has been refused in some cases. Am Jur 2d, Wills § 1516; 3 ALR2d 1419.

9-21L Incorporation of Separate Instrument.

Pour over to a trust, see 9-26A.

R.C. 2107.05 provides: "An existing document, book, record, or memorandum may be incorporated in a will by reference, if referred to as being in existence at the time the will is executed. Such document, book, record, or memorandum shall be deposited in the probate court when the will is probated or within thirty days thereafter, unless the court grants an extension of time for good cause shown. A copy may be substituted for the original document, book, record, or memorandum if such copy is certified to be correct by a person authorized to take acknowledgments on deeds." (As eff. 10-1-53.)

Further research: O Jur 3d, Decedents' Estates §§ 341, 342; 3 ALR2d 682; CJS, Wills § 163.

9-21M Abatement of Devises and Legacies; Contribution.

Primary liability of personalty, see 12-12A.

R.C. 2107.54 provides: "(A) When real or personal property, devised or bequeathed, is taken from the devisee or legatee for the payment of a debt of the testator, the other devisees and legatees shall contribute their respective proportions of the loss to the person from whom such payment was taken so that the loss will fall equally on all the devisees and legatees according to the value of the property received by each of them.

"If, by making a specific devise or bequest, the testator has exempted a devisee or legatee from liability to contribute to the payment of debts, or if the will makes a different provision for the payment of debts than the one prescribed in this section, the estate shall be applied in conformity with the will.

"(B) A devisee or legatee shall not be prejudiced by the fact that the holder of a claim secured by lien on the property devised or bequeathed failed to present such claim to the executor or administrator for allowance within the time allowed by sections 2117.06 and 2117.07 of the Revised Code, and the devisee or legatee shall be restored by right of contribution, exoneration, or subrogation, to the position he would have occupied if such claim had been presented and allowed for such sum as is justly owing on it.

"(C) A devisee of real estate that is subject to a mortgage lien that exists on the date of the testator's death, who does not have a right of exoneration that extends to that lien because of the operation of division (B) of section 2113.52 of the Revised Code, has a duty to contribute under this section to devisees and legatees who are burdened if the claim secured by the lien is presented and allowed pursuant to Chapter 2117. of the Revised Code.

"(D) This section does not affect the liability of the whole estate of the testator for the payment of his debts. This section applies only to the marshaling of the assets as between those who hold or claim under the will." (As eff. 10-14-83.)

R.C. 2107.55 provides: "When a part of the estate of a testator descends to a child born or adopted, or to an heir designated, after the execution of the will, or to a child absent and reported to be dead at the time of execution of the will but later found to be alive, or to a witness to a will who is a devisee or legatee, such estate and the advancement made to such child, heir, or witness for all the purposes mentioned in section 2107.54 of the Revised Code shall be considered as if it had been devised to such child, heir, or witness and he shall be bound to contribute with the devisees and legatees, as provided by such section, and may claim contribution from them accordingly." (As eff. 10-1-53.)

R.C. 2107.56 provides: "When any of the persons liable to contribute toward the discharge of a testator's debt according to sections 2107.54 and 2107.55 of the Revised Code, is insolvent, the others shall be severally liable to each other for the loss occasioned by such insolvency, each being liable in proportion to the value of the property received by him from the estate of the deceased. If any one of the persons liable dies without paying his proportion of such debt, his executors and administrators shall be liable therefor to the extent to which he would have been liable if living." (As eff. 10-1-53.)

R.C. 2107.58 provides: "When a sale of lands aliened or unaliened by a devisee or heir is ordered for the payment of the debts of an estate, sections 2107.53 to 2107.57, inclusive, of the Revised Code do not prevent the probate court from making such order and decree for the sale of any portion of the aliened or unaliened land as is equitable between the several parties, and making an order of contribution and further order and decree to settle and adjust the various rights and liabilities of the parties." (As eff. 10-1-53.)

The testator specifically devised his real estate to a son and bequeathed a general pecuniary legacy to another son. Held that the real estate could not be charged with payment of the legacy even though no personal property was available for the payment. Geiger v. Worth, 17 OS 564 (1867).

Both specific legatees and specific devisees must contribute pro rata to the payment of testator's debts in case the residuary and general legacies and devises are insufficient for such payment. McArther v. McArther, 29 OO2d 137, 93 Abs 367 (Prob. 1961).

General legatees and devisees must first contribute to the payment of debts; but if that is insufficient, specific legatees and devisees must contribute. Gionfriddo v. Palatrone, 196 NE2d 162, 26 OO2d 158, 93 Abs 257 (Prob. 1964).

A devise of "All my real property, of every kind and description" to testatrix's husband for life with remainder to her nephew is, in the absence of a clear intent to make a specific devise, to be interpreted as a general legacy. The husband may elect to purchase the residence. In re Witteman's Estate, 15 App 2d 126, 239 NE2d 107, 44 OO2d 255 (1968).

Further research: O Jur 3d, Decedents' Estates §§ 934-937.

LAW IN GENERAL

Devises between themselves and legacies between themselves generally abate in the following order: (1) residuary; (2) general (or pecuniary legacies); (3) specific or demonstrative. When the question is between specific devises and specific legacies, most courts hold that they abate together. Land devised by the residuary clause is subjected to payment of debts before recourse is had to pecuniary legacies. However, as a rule, testator's realty is not taken to pay legacies, when the personalty before payment of debts is insufficient to pay pecuniary legacies, unless expressly or by implication made a charge on the realty. An exception to this rule is usually made and the pecuniary legacy is preferred when the residuary clause blends personalty and realty. Am Law of Prop § 14.23; CJS, Wills § 1153.

9-21N Lien of Legacies and Charges.

Express words are not necessary to charge pecuniary legacies upon the real estate. Clyde v. Simpson, 4 OS 445 (1854).

Where special bequests are followed by an item leaving all the rest, residue and remainder of the estate to others, the language expresses the manifest intent of the testator that the bequests should be a charge on the real estate if the personal estate is insufficient. White Cross Hospital Ass'n v. Sater, 20 Abs 5 (App. 1935); Moore v. Beckwith, 14 OS 129 (1862).

A general legacy cannot be charged upon a specific devise unless such intention appears clearly from the will. Geiger v. Worth, 17 OS 564 (1867); Knepper v. Knepper, 103 OS 529, 134 NE 476, 19 OLR 462 (1921).

A testator devised all his real estate to his son; he, however, to pay the testator's daughter a legacy, in annual installments. Held, that the legacy was an equitable charge upon the estate devised; and that an action by the daughter to recover the unpaid installments was barred after the lapse of six years from the time the right of action accrued on said installments respectively. Yearly v. Long, 40 OS 27, 9 WLB 302 (1883).

An action to recover a general pecuniary legacy is not exempt from the operation of the statute of limitations. The cause of action accrues when, by the terms of the will or rules of law, it becomes due and payable, and the executor has sufficient assets applicable thereto. Webster v. American Bible Society, 50 OS 1, 33 NE 297, 29 WLB 82, 141 (1893).

The rule charging legacies on the residuary estate is applied only when the testator must have realized that satisfaction out of the residuary estate is necessary. Koontz v. Hubley, 111 OS 414, 145 NE 590, 2 Abs 770, 22 OLR 636 (1924).

Statute of limitations does not bar a suit to enforce a lien upon lands for installments of an annuity which have been in arrears for more than six years, where the will by which the lands were devised expressly provides that the annuity "shall be and remain a charge and lien" thereon. Waterfield v. Rice, 49 CCA 504, 111 Fed 625 (1901).

A devise to sons of testator provided they pay certain legacies, held not to convey estate subject to be defeated on condition, but merely to create charge upon estate. Beck v. Bailey, 32 App 423, 168 NE 220, 7 Abs 275, 29 OLR 361 (1929).

A specific devisee is exempt from the liability to contribute to the payment of debts when there is a residuary estate out of which the debts may be paid. In re Dickey's Estate, 87 App 255, 94 NE2d 223, 42 OO 474, 57 Abs 346, 20 ALR2d 1220 (1949).

Where the testator was possessed of personal property sufficient to satisfy the cash bequests, he did not intend to charge his real estate with the payment of the legacies. Bauman v. Bauman, 88 NE2d 196, 41 OO 139, 55 Abs 398 (Prob. 1937).

Further research: O Jur 3d, Decedents' Estates § 918.

LAW IN GENERAL

The will may impose liens on devised real estate for legacies and other charges. Legacies are prima facie payable out of the personal estate, but become charges on realty by express provision or necessary implication of the will. Courts favor construction of a direction to the devisee to pay a sum of money as a charge and not as a condition defeating the devise. Land devised by general residuary clause is usually charged by implication with the lien of a legacy. Probate of the will is notice although the lien is an equitable one. When the devisee accepts the testamentary gift, he becomes personally liable for the entire charge even though the charge exceeds the value of the land. The statute of limitations on the personal liability has been applied to the lien in some cases; while the lien exists, under other decisions, for the longer period of limitations with respect to interests in land. Am Law of Prop § 12.24; CJS, Wills § 1297; Powell § 475.

9-210   "After Payment of my Debts."

LAW IN GENERAL

When a devise is "after payment of my debts," a majority of the decisions find that exoneration of other property was intended. The cases on construction of the phrase "subject to payment of debts" are about equally divided. 2 ALR2d 1310.

9-21P   Restraints; Forfeiture.

Behavior requirements, see 11-81N.
Burdens accepted with benefits, see 9-21J.
Illegal conditions, see 11-81O.
Restraints on marriage, see Section 14-16.

A condition in a will whereby the testator excludes any one of his heirs who "goes to law to break the will" from any part or share of his estate, is valid and binding. Bradford v. Bradford, 19 OS 546 (1869); Bender v. Bateman, 33 App 66, 168 NE 574, 29 OLR 340 (1929).

An in terrorem clause providing for disinheritance of testator's children is not violated by their procedure in court to have declared invalid a bequest to charities under a will executed within one year of testator's death. Kirkbride v. Hickok, 155 OS 293, 98 NE2d 815, 44 OO 297 (1951).

Courts of law and equity will, if possible, construe provisions in wills and deeds in such a way as to avoid forfeiture. Beck v. Bailey, 32 App 423, 168 NE 220, 7 Abs 275, 29 OLR 361 (1929).

Where beneficiary denies, in an action for declaratory judgment, the validity of part of a will containing an "in terrorem" clause, he will not thereby be precluded from taking. Moskowitz v. Federman, 72 App 149, 51 NE2d 48, 27 OO 53 (1943).

Further research: O Jur 3d, Decedents' Estates § 793.

LAW IN GENERAL

A provision making a devise contingent upon not contesting the will is valid except when there is probable cause for the contest; at least the provision is not enforced if such cause is on the ground of forgery or of revocation by a later will or codicil. An attack on part of the will does not cause forfeiture of the devise if it is successful; nor is the devise forfeited if the attack is upon probable cause on the ground that such part of the will is an invalid restraint, or violates a statute limiting charitable ownership, or does not comply with the rule against perpetuities, or sometimes on other grounds. A condition against claims against the estate is enforced. A condition against interfering with the administration is not enforced provided the devisee acts with probable cause. A provision is valid which requires the devisee to renounce other claims against the estate as a condition precedent to accepting the devise. Am Law of Prop § 27.3; 49 ALR2d 198; CJS, Wills § 977; Powell § 856; Restatement Second, Property (Donative Transfers) § 9.1; Simes and Smith § 1518.

The "in terrorem" doctrine is that a condition subsequent is void if no gift over on breach is provided, it being presumed that the condition was intended only to frighten the beneficiary. It is applied only to bequests of personal property and its application in any case has been severely criticized. Am Law of Prop § 27.2; CJS, Wills § 992.

A provision for forfeiture of a gift is invalid if made for the purpose of causing or continuing separation of a parent and infant child. A provision requiring certain religious beliefs or affiliation is valid, except as encouraging the separation of parent and infant child, at least if the recipient is a member of the family of the grantor or testator. Restraints against bad habits are enforceable. Restraints which require a certain education or occupation are valid, unless made for the purpose of separating a parent and infant child. Am Law of Prop § 27.19; Restatement Second, Property (Donative Transfers) § 7.2; Simes and Smith § 1517.

Whether performance of the condition is excused by impossibility of performance depends upon the intention of the grantor or testator. Restraints are generally valid unless the provisions are contrary to law or to public policy, CJS, Wills § 1000; Powell § 858; Restatement Second, Property (Donative Transfers) § 5.1.

9-21Q   Suits to Construe Wills.

Declaratory judgments, see Section 16-61.

R.C. 2107.40 provides: "At any time before the period of the election provided by section 2107.39 of the Revised Code has expired, the surviving spouse may file a complaint in the probate court making all persons interested in the will defendants, asking a construction of the will in favor of the spouse, and for the judgment of the court." (As eff. 1-1-76.)

R.C. 2107.46 provides: "Any fiduciary may maintain an action in the probate court against creditors, legatees, distributees, or other parties and ask the direction or judgment of the court in any matter respecting the trust, estate, or property to be administered and the rights of the parties in interest.

"If any fiduciary fails for thirty days to bring such action after a written request from a party in interest, the party making such request may institute the suit." (As eff. 1-1-76.)

Where the above statute does not apply, the estate having been closed, the probate court has exclusive jurisdiction to construe wills. Van Stone v. Van Stone, 95 App 406, 120 NE2d 154, 53 OO 438 (1952).

Further research: O Jur 3d, Decedents' Estates § 738.

9-21R   Other Particular Words Construed.

A devise of the "proceeds of my real estate" vests fee simple title in devisee. Isherwood v. Isherwood, 16 CC 279, 8 CD 409 (1896); Minor v. Shippley, 21 App 236, 152 NE 768, 23 OLR 551 (1923).

"It is my wish that if at the death of my wife, our son be living, all our property go to him" places no limitation upon the fee simple granted to the wife. Powell v. Layton, 79 App 279, 69 NE2d 444, 35 OO 44, 47 Abs 41 (1946).

A will providing "I give, devise and bequeath all my property, both real and personal, to my wife, ... At her demise, I request that each of our children ... be given his or her proportionate share of the estate due consideration being given to those children and persons working and caring for the farm property," gives a fee simple title to testator's wife. Perdue v. Morris, 93 App 538, 114 NE2d 286, 51 OO 232 (1952). See also 9-21D.

A devise of a house carried with it the land on which the house stands and that appurtenant thereto. Loose v. Loose, 16 O Supp 29, 30 OO 333 (Prob. 1945).

SECTION 9-22: EXECUTION

9-22A Statute.

R.C. 2107.03 provides: "Except oral wills, every last will and testament shall be in writing, but may be handwritten or typewritten. Such will shall be signed at the end by the party making it, or by some other person in such party's presence and at his express direction, and be attested and subscribed in the presence of such party, by two or more competent witnesses, who saw the testator subscribe, or heard him acknowledge his signature." (As eff. 10-1-53.)

Further research: O Jur 3d, Decedents' Estates §§ 334, 340.

9-22B Signature.

Where an instrument is not signed at the end thereof (the maker's signature appearing only in the attestation clause) an order of a probate court admitting it to probate as a will is a nullity. In re Eakins' Will, 63 App 265, 26 NE2d 219, 16 OO 583 (1939).

A will may be admitted to probate where there is a mark made by testatrix although her name does not appear in the body of the will or at the end thereof. In re Ryan's Will, 9 O Supp 29, 23 OO 356, 36 Abs 341 (Prob. 1942).

An instrument cannot be admitted to probate if there is a dispositive provision below the signature as an essential part of the instrument as a will. In re MacNealy's Will, 14 O Supp 28, 29 OO 48, 40 Abs 565 (Prob. 1944).

Further research: O Jur 3d, Decedents' Estates § 349.

9-22C Witnesses; Publication.

Republication, see also 9-24E.
See also statute at 9-22A.

R.C. 2107.15 provides: "If a devise or bequest is made to a person who is one of only two witnesses to a will, the devise or bequest is void. The witness shall then be competent to testify to the execution of the will as if such devise or bequest had not been made. If such witness would have been entitled to a share of the testator's estate in case the will was not established, he shall have so much of such share which does not exceed the bequest or devise to him. The devisees and legatees must contribute for that purpose as for an absent or after-born child under section 2107.34 of the Revised Code." (As eff. 1-1-76.)

Formal defects in the execution of a will are cured by its republication in a valid codicil. Robinson v. Harmon, 107 App 206, 157 NE2d 749, 8 OO2d 96 (1958).

In Ohio a witness-executor or witness-trustee is not an incompetent subscribing witness to a will by reason of such fact. Fazekas v. Gobozy, 150 NE2d 319, 78 Abs 258 (App. 1958).

Further research: O Jur 3d, Decedents' Estates § 365.

9-22D Holographic Wills; Nuncupative Wills.

R.C. 2107.60 provides for oral wills as to personal estate only. (As eff. 10-1-53.)

Ohio has no special statute as to holographic wills, that is, wills entirely in the handwriting of the testator. Nuncupative wills are oral declarations, made at the time of last illness, disposing only of personal property.

SECTION 9-23: TESTAMENTARY CAPACITY; UNDUE INFLU-ENCE

9-23A Testamentary Capacity.

R.C. 2107.02 provides: "A person of the age of eighteen years, or over, of sound mind and memory, and not under restraint may make a will." (As eff. 8-10-65.) Prior to August 10, 1965, the statute read "of full age" instead of "of the age of eighteen years, or over."

Testamentary capacity exists when the testator has sufficient mind and memory to understand the nature of the business in which he is engaged, to comprehend generally the nature and extent of his property, to hold in his mind the names and identity of those who have natural claims upon his bounty, and to be able to appreciate his relation to the members of his family. Niemes v. Niemes, 97 OS 145, 119 NE 503, 15 OLR 484, 565, 62 WLB 527, 63 WLB 47 (1917).

An adjudication of insanity or imbecility does not make a prima facie case of testamentary incapacity, but in view of the presumption of the continuance of such mental condition, it will of course be considered in determining the ultimate fact as to whether such person possessed sufficient testamentary capacity. Potts v. First-Central Trust Co., 47 NE2d 823, 37 Abs 382 (App. 1940).

A person under guardianship for mental incompetency is presumed to be insane; however, a last will and testament executed by such person while under legal guardianship and admitted to probate is not presumed to be invalid. To the contrary, the order of probate is prima facie evidence of the attestation, execution, and validity of the will. Hermann v. Crossen, 160 NE2d 404, 81 Abs 322 (App. 1959).

Evidence of testator's mental and physical condition within a reasonable time before and after the making of the will is admissible as throwing light on his mental condition at the time of the execution of the will in question. There is no agreed definition of the phrase "reasonable time." Oehlke v. Marks, 2 App2d 264, 207 NE2d 676, 31 OO2d 381 (1964).

Further research: O Jur 3d, Decedents' Estates § 281.

LAW IN GENERAL

As a general rule, a person capable of transacting ordinary business has capacity to make a will. A person is said to have the mental capacity necessary for making a will if he comprehends the nature and extent of his property in a general way, and knows those who would ordinarily be the objects of his bounty. CJS, Wills § 15; Powell § 947.

A person under full legal age does not have capacity to dispose of real estate by will. The appointment of a guardian for an incompetent does not of itself invalidate either a previously or subsequently executed will, although it may raise a presumption of mental incapacity. Am Jur 2d, Wills § 56; 89 ALR2d 1120.

Testamentary capacity as to real property is governed by the law of the state where the property is located and as to personal property by the law of the state of the testator's domicile. CJS, Wills § 4.

9-23B Undue Influence.

A will cannot be impeached for undue influence unless some restraint is imposed upon the testator in the disposition of his property in accordance with his own independent wishes and judgment. Monroe v. Barclay, 17 OS 302 (1867).

Further research: O Jur 3d, Decedents' Estates §§ 396, 397, 400.

LAW IN GENERAL

Undue influence which will invalidate a will is such persuasion or importunity as to overpower the will of testator without convincing his judgment, and involves the substitution of another's wishes for those of the testator. CJS, Wills § 224; Powell § 948; Tiffany § 1081.

SECTION 9-24: REVOCATION; ALTERATION; ADEMPTION

After-born and pretermitted children, see 9-25A.

9-24A Revocation Generally.

R.C. 2107.33 provides:

"(A) A will shall be revoked by the testator by tearing, canceling, obliterating, or destroying it with the intention of revoking it, or by some person in the testator's presence, or by the testator's express written direction, or by some other written will or codicil, executed as prescribed by sections 2107.01 to 2107.62 of the Revised Code, or by some other writing that is signed, attested, and subscribed in the manner provided by those sections. A will that has been declared valid and is in the possession of a probate judge may also be revoked according to division (C) of section 2107.084 of the Revised Code.

"(B) If a testator removes a will that has been declared valid and is in the possession of a probate judge pursuant to section 2107.084 of the Revised Code from the possession of the judge, the declaration of validity that was rendered no longer has any effect.

"(C) If after executing a will, a testator is divorced, obtains a dissolution of marriage, has his marriage annulled, or, upon actual separation from his spouse, enters into a separation agreement pursuant to which the parties intend to fully and finally settle their prospective property rights in the property of the other, whether by expected inheritance or otherwise, any disposition or appointment of property made by the will to the former spouse or to a trust with powers created by or available to the former spouse, any provision in the will conferring a general or special power of appointment on the former spouse, and any nomination in the will of the former spouse as executor, trustee, or guardian, shall be revoked unless the will expressly provides otherwise.

"(D) Property prevented from passing to a former spouse or to a trust with powers created by or available to the former spouse because of revocation by this section shall pass as if the former spouse failed to survive the decedent, and other provisions conferring some power or office on the former spouse shall be interpreted as if the spouse failed to survive the decedent. If provisions are revoked solely by this section, they shall be deemed to be revived by the testator's remarriage with the former spouse or upon the termination of a separation agreement executed by them.

"(E) A bond, agreement, or covenant made by a testator, for a valuable consideration, to convey property previously devised or bequeathed in a will, does not revoke the devise or bequest. The property passes by the devise or bequest, subject to the remedies on the bond, agreement, or covenant, for a specific performance or otherwise, against the devisees or legatees, that might be had by law against the heirs of the testator, or his next of kin, if the property had descended to them.

"(F) As used in this section:

"(1) 'Trust with powers created by or available to the former spouse' means a trust that is revocable by the former spouse, with respect to which the former spouse has a power of withdrawal, or with respect to which the former spouse may take a distribution that is not subject to an ascertainable standard but does not mean a trust in which those powers of the former spouse are revoked by section 1339.62 of the Revised Code or similar provisions in the law of another state.

"(2) 'Ascertainable standard' means a standard that is related to a trust beneficiary's health, maintenance, support, or education." (As eff. 12-17-86.)

A joint, mutual or reciprocal will, which is made in performance of a contract to make a will, is revocable. Even though the will contains a covenant not to revoke or a declaration it is irrevocable, it may still be revoked. In re Piasecki's Estate, 201 NE2d 840, 30 OO2d 169, 95 Abs 257 (Prob. 1964).

Since R.C. 2107.33 permits revocation of a will only in its entirety, no partial revocation will be recognized. In re Downie's Estate, 6 Misc 36, 213 NE2d 833, 35 OO2d 31 (Prob. 1966).

Further research: O Jur 3d, Decedents' Estates §§ 419, 421.

LAW IN GENERAL

A testator may revoke his will by a later will or codicil, or by destroying, canceling or mutilating it with the intention to revoke. 59 ALR2d 11; CJS, Wills § 266; Powell § 974; Tiffany § 1085.

A failure to find the will of a decedent gives rise to a presumption that it was revoked. The presumption is not conclusive. 3 ALR2d 949.

A devise of land is not extinguished, according to the majority rule, by a gift of other property to the devisee by the testator during the lifetime of the latter. A legacy may be satisfied in that manner, by the weight of authority. Am Law of Prop § 14.11; CJS, Wills § 294.

9-24B   Marriage.

R.C. 2107.37 provides: "A will executed by an unmarried person is not revoked by a subsequent marriage." (As eff. 1-1-76.)

The common-law rule that marriage alone does not revoke a will of the husband made before marriage is not abrogated in this state. Munday v. Munday, 15 CC 155, 8 CD 44 (1897).

Further research: CJS, Wills § 291; Powell § 975; Tiffany § 1089.

9-24C   Divorce.

For revocation by divorce, etc. see R.C. 2107.33 quoted at 9-24A.

A revocation of a will is not implied by law from a written property settlement and divorce when the circumstances were that the testatrix married the sole beneficiary more than a year after execution of the will, that the will contained no mention of the prospective marital relationship as the motive for the disposition, and that the testatrix lived for several months after the divorce. The court stresses that "other factors unrelated to matrimony may have motivated such disposition" by testatrix. Codner v. Caldwell, 156 OS 197, 101 NE2d 901, 46 OO 89 (1951).

A court is warranted in finding an implied revocation of legacies and devises to the divorced spouse under a will executed during the marriage where the divorce was coupled with a full settlement of property rights. Younker v. Johnson, 160 OS 409, 116 NE2d 715, 52 OO 320 (1954).

Determination that a will, naming the wife as beneficiary, was revoked by her divorce from testator may be made only by common pleas court in an action to contest the will. In re Lester's Estate, 76 App 263, 64 NE2d 71, 31 OO 579 (1945).

A divorce decree, not coupled with a voluntary separation agreement contemplating a full settlement of property rights, does not warrant a court finding an implied revocation of a will executed during marriage. Lang v. Leiter, 103 App 119, 144 NE2d 332, 3 OO2d 184 (1956).

Further research: O Jur 3d, Decedents' Estates § 456; 71 ALR3d 1297; CJS, Wills § 293; Powell § 976; Tiffany § 1091.

9-24D   Revocation by Invalid Disposition.

A will may be valid in part, and void in part, as to its provisions. Mears v. Mears, 15 OS 90 (1864); Johnson v. Ramsey, 18 App 321 (1923).

LAW IN GENERAL

An express revocation is given effect, in a majority of the cases, although contained in a will or codicil making an invalid disposition, unless a contrary testamentary intention is found. When no express revocation is contained in the subsequent instrument making the invalid disposition, the gift in the original will is effective unless the testator manifested an intention to revoke notwithstanding the failure of the substitutional gift. 28 ALR2d 526; Powell § 320.

9-24E   Revival; Republication.

R.C. 2107.38 provides: "If a testator executes a second will, the destruction, cancellation, or revocation of the second will shall not revive the first will unless the terms of such revocation show that it was such testator's intention to revive and give effect to his first will or unless, after such destruction, cancellation, or revocation, such testator republishes his first will." (As eff. 10-1-53.)

The intention of the testator to revive the earlier will must be gathered from an instrument executed as a will. Republication is accomplished only by compliance with all the statutory formalities of original execution. Shinn v. Phillips, 197 NE2d 564, 31 OO2d 537, 94 Abs 153 (App. 1964).

Further research: O Jur 3d, Decedents' Estates § 460.

LAW IN GENERAL

A revoked will or one originally invalid may be made effective, as modified by its codicils, by republication. The republication may consist of re-executing the will or of executing a codicil. CJS, Wills § 299; Tiffany § 1096.

9-24F   Alteration.

A clause in a will cannot be revoked by the testator drawing ink lines through the words thereof without an intent to revoke the whole will. When the words of such clause remain legible, the whole will should be admitted to probate including such erased clause as a valid part of such will. Giffin v. Brooks, 48 OS 211, 31 NE 743, 25 WLB 153 (1891); Cummings v. Nichols, 53 App 520, 5 NE2d 923, 6 OO 414, 22 Abs 12 (1936).

Further research: O Jur 3d, Decedents' Estates §§ 411-414.

LAW IN GENERAL

Clauses substituted or added by the testator after execution of the will are not effective unless the will is again executed. Testator's attempted physical alteration of a will after execution usually does not revoke the will nor a part thereof unless an intent to revoke the entire will is shown. The onus is generally on the will proponent to show that material alterations were made before the execution. 34 ALR2d 619.

9-24G Ademption.

Contracts for sale, see 16-63G.

R.C. 2107.35 provides: "An encumbrance upon real or personal estate for the purpose of securing the payment of money or the performance of a covenant shall not revoke a will previously executed and relating to such estate." (As eff. 9-4-57.)

R.C. 2107.36 provides: "An act of a testator which alters but does not wholly divest such testator's interest in property previously devised or bequeathed by him does not revoke the devise or bequest of such property, but such devise or bequest shall pass to the devisee or legatee the actual interest of the testator, which would otherwise descend to his heirs or pass to his next of kin; unless, in the instrument by which such alteration is made, the intention is declared that it shall operate as a revocation of such previous devise or bequest.

"If the instrument by which such alteration is made is wholly inconsistent with the previous devise or bequest, such instrument will operate as a revocation thereof, unless such instrument depends on a condition or contingency, and such condition is not performed or such contingency does not happen." (As eff. 10-1-53.)

R.C. 2107.501 enacted to provide compensation to a devisee or legatee of specifically devised or bequeathed property if sold by the testator's guardian or if insurance proceeds, condemnation award, or foreclosure proceeds have been paid or are payable. (As eff. 12-17-86.)

Where a testator, subsequent to making his will, conveyed his entire estate in property specifically devised, such conveyance constitutes a complete revocation of the devise, even though a mortgage to the testator had been executed to secure the unpaid balance of the purchase price. Lewis v. Thompson, 142 OS 338, 52 NE2d 331, 27 OO 262 (1943).

Where the testator, subsequent to the execution of a will specifically devising lands, voluntarily conveys the land, the will is revoked pro tanto. Gordon v. Bartlett, 62 App 295, 23 NE2d 964, 16 OO 13, 28 Abs 161 (1938).

If the testator, because of mental incompetency, did not have capacity to make a new will from the time the real estate was sold by his guardian until his death, then the devise of such real estate was not adeemed. Bishop v. Fullmer, 112 App 140, 175 NE2d 209, 16 OO2d 60 (1960).

Further research: O Jur 3d, Decedents' Estates §§ 448, 896, 897.

LAW IN GENERAL

Ademption is the revocation of testamentary gifts by alienation or destruction of the subject matter during the testator's lifetime. Conveyance by the testator of land devised under a previous will cancels or adeems the devise. Am Law of Prop § 14.13; CJS, Wills § 1172; Powell § 978; Tiffany § 1092.

SECTION 9-25: OMITTED AND AFTER-ACQUIRED HEIRS

9-25A After-born and Pretermitted Children.

Death within thirty days, see 9-11L.

R.C. 2107.34 provides: "If, after making a last will and testament, a testator has a child born alive, or adopts a child, or designates an heir in the manner provided by section 2105.15 of the Revised Code, or if a child or designated heir who is absent and reported to be dead proves to be alive, and no provision has been made in such will or by settlement for such pretermitted child or heir, or for the issue thereof, the will shall not be revoked; but unless it appears by such will that it was the intention of the testator to disinherit such pretermitted child or heir, the devises and legacies granted by such will, except those to a surviving spouse, shall be abated proportionately, or in such other manner as is necessary to give effect to the intention of the testator as shown by the will, so that such pretermitted child or heir will receive a share equal to that which such person would have been entitled to receive out of the estate if such testator had died intestate with no surviving spouse, owning only that portion of his estate not devised or bequeathed to or for the use and benefit of a surviving spouse. If such child or heir dies prior to the death of the testator, the issue of such deceased child or heir shall receive the share the parent would have received if living.

"If such pretermitted child or heir supposed to be dead at the time of executing the will has lineal descendants, provision for whom is made by the testator, the other legatees and devisees need not contribute, but such pretermitted child or heir shall take the provision made for his lineal descendants or such part of it as, in the opinion of the probate judge, may be equitable. In settling the claim of a pretermitted child or heir, any portion of the testator's estate received by a party interested, by way of advancement, is a portion of the estate and shall be charged to the party who has received it.

"Though measured by sections 2105.01 to 2105.21, inclusive, of the Revised Code, the share taken by a pretermitted child or heir shall be considered as a testate succession. This section does not prejudice the right of any fiduciary to act under any power given by the will, nor shall the title of innocent purchasers for value of any of the property of the testator's estate be affected by any right given by this section to a pretermitted child or heir." (As eff. 10-5-61.)

Prior to October 5, 1961, the devises and legacies to a surviving spouse were abated, together with the others, in favor of after-born or pretermitted heirs.

Where a testatrix executed a will devising her entire estate to her husband and providing that if he predecease her, such entire estate shall be placed in trust "for the use and benefit of my children," there is no pretermission of after-born children. Provident Savings Bank & Trust Co. v. Nash, 75 App 493, 62 NE2d 736, 31 OO 290 (1945).

A "settlement" is a provision extraneous to the will with intention to preclude such child from taking any other part of testator's estate. City Nat. Bank & Trust Co. v. Kelly, 1 O Supp 311, 19 OO 231, 32 Abs 559 (Prob. 1940).

Where a testator executes his will devising his entire estate to his wife who is six months pregnant with a seventh child, an intention to disinherit said after-born child may be implied so that such child has no interest in the estate. Spieldenner v. Spieldenner, 122 NE2d 33, 54 OO 290, 69 Abs 142 (Prob. 1954).

Further research: O Jur 3d, Decedents' Estates § 272.

9-25B After-adopted Children.

See statute at 9-25A.

Adoption of child after making of will has the same effect in revoking will as existence of after-born children. Surman v. Surman, 114 OS 579, 151 NE 708, 4 Abs 275, 24 OLR 374 (1926).

SECTION 9-26: LAPSED AND VOID GIFTS

Class gifts, see Division 11-9.
Survival requirement generally, see Section 11-81.

9-26A Generally.

Death of devisee within thirty days, see 9-11L.

R.C. 2107.52 provides: "When a devise of real or personal estate is made to a relative of a testator and such relative was dead at the time the will was made, or dies thereafter, leaving issue surviving the testator, such issue shall take the estate devised as the devisee would have done if he had survived the testator. If the testator devised a residuary estate or the entire estate after debts, other legacies and devises, general or specific, or an interest less than a fee or absolute ownership to such devisee and relatives of the testator and such devisee leaves no issue, the estate devised shall vest in such other devisees surviving the testator in such proportions as the testamentary share of each devisee in the devised property bears to the total of the shares of all of the surviving devisees, unless a different disposition is made or required by the will." (As eff. 10-1-53.)

R.C. 2107.63 provides that a testator may devise, bequeath, or appoint any interest in real or personal property to a trustee of a trust evidenced by an instrument executed before or on the same date as the will, and to be subject to all amendments to the trust. This section not to affect the right of election by a surviving spouse. (As eff. 1-23-63.) Such testamentary provision is said to "pour over" to a trust.

The phrase "relative of a testator" in R.C. 2107.52 is restricted to relationships which are consanguineous, and excludes relationships which are affinitive, to the testator. Schuck v. Schuck, 156 NE2d 351, 7 OO2d 198, 80 Abs 394 (Prob. 1958).

The word "issue" as used in the antilapse statute means "descendant," adopted as well as natural; and a grandchild of a relative of testator is within the term. Third Nat. Bank & Trust Co. v. Glendening, 175 NE2d 239, 17 OO2d 337, 86 Abs 340 (Prob. 1960).

Where the gift is construed as being to individuals and not to a class, the share of a nonrelative who predeceased the testator lapses. Kovar v. Kortan, 3 Misc 63, 32 OO2d 302 (1965).

A bequest conditioned by "who shall be living at the time of my decease" will prevent operation of the antilapse statute and will cause the bequest to lapse. Day v. Brooks, 10 Misc 273, 224 NE2d 557, 39 OO2d 441 (Prob. 1967). Contra: Detzel v. Nieberding, 7 Misc 262, 219 NE2d 327, 36 OO2d 358 (Prob. 1966.)

A limitation to those of a group named who survive the testator is not subject to the antilapse statute. Detzel v. Nieberding is clearly and completely erroneous. Shalkhauser v. Beach, 14 Misc 1, 233 NE2d 527, 43 OO2d 20 (Prob. 1968).

Further research: O Jur 3d, Decedents' Estates § 870.

LAW IN GENERAL

In the absence of statute, a gift will lapse on the death of the devisee or legatee during the testator's lifetime or before the gift vests. Am Law of Prop § 14.14; CJS, Wills § 1199; Tiffany § 1083.

Lapse statutes generally have no application when the gift vests during the lifetime of devisee or legatee; for example, a legacy charged on a remainder usually survives when the legatee dies during the existence of the preceding life estate. 6 ALR2d 363.

A lapse statute does not apply where the testator has manifested such intention. If the statute does apply, the substituted person takes directly from the testator. Am Law of Prop § 21.28.

Ohio follows the general rule that antilapse statutes are applicable to gifts to a class, 56 ALR2d 950.

9-26B "Or"; "And."

See also 8-16C and 11-81F.

"Devise to another and his heirs lapsed on devisee predeceasing testator." Evers v. Williams, 43 App 555, 184 NE 19, 12 Abs 726, 37 OLR 291 (1932).

The words "or her heirs" following a devise or bequest prevent a lapse in case the named devisee or legatee predeceases the testatrix. Hewes v. Mead, 81 App 489, 80 NE2d 212, 37 OO 328 (1947).

"Survivors" relates to the survivors of the class where the devise is to testator's three children "or their survivors," so that the son of a child who predeceased the testator does not share in the estate. Hamilton v. Pettifor, 165 OS 361, 135 NE2d 264, 59 OO 470 (1956).

Further research: O Jur 3d, Decedents' Estates § 561.

LAW IN GENERAL

A gift to one "and his heirs" ordinarily does not show an intention to substitute the heirs. A gift to a person "or his heirs" usually does show such intention, so that the heirs take if the ancestor is dead at the time of testator's death. This rule has been applied to gifts to a person "or his children." 11 ALR2d 1387; Tiffany § 1082.

9-26C Residuary Clause.

Antilapse statute, see 9-26A.

Where the residuary clause is limited to "the balance" that remains from a fund, the amount of void or lapsed legacies does not pass under such clause. Davis v. Davis, 62 OS 411, 57 NE 317, 43 WLB 280 (1900); Bane v. Wick, 19 Ohio 328 (1850).

If a bequest or devise of a part of the residue lapses or is otherwise ineffective, that part will ordinarily pass to the other persons entitled to portions of the residue, except as provided by statute when a deceased devisee leaves issue and except when a different intention is manifested by the testator. Commerce Nat. Bank v. Browning, 158 OS 54, 107 NE2d 120, 48 OO 28 (1952).

Where trust, created by will, of interest in land was void, the interest in realty became part of the general estate, subject to the payment of legacies, in view of provision for sale of all realty to pay legacies, and did not pass to residuary beneficiary. Ward v. Worthington, 28 App 325, 162 NE 714, 6 Abs 646 (1928).

The rule that general residuary clause carried whatever is not legally disposed of does not apply to a residuary clause limited by its terms to what remains after the payment of specific legacies; in such a case there is another residuum undisposed of. In re Stewart, 45 NE2d 792, 37 Abs 105 (App. 1942).

Under the second part of the lapse statute, the share, in the residuary devise to relatives, given to a primary devisee who dies without issue before the death of the testator, passes to the issue of another predeceased primary devisee as well as to surviving primary devisees. Kammer v. Raver, 96 NE2d 439, 43 OO 302, 59 Abs 138 (Prob. 1950).

A bequest of "all the rest and residue of property" which testatrix owns is sufficient to include a lapsed legacy. Kellogg v. Campbell, 3 Misc. 27, 209 NE2d 645, 32 OO2d 252 (1965).

LAW IN GENERAL

A lapsed or void gift ordinarily passes under a general residuary clause, except that under the prevailing rule the lapsed portion of a residuary gift passes as intestate property. Under the Ohio and some other statutes, the residuary portion of a blood relative of the testator may pass to the other residuary devisees. Am Law of Prop § 21.30; CJS, Wills § 1226; Tiffany § 1084.

9-26D Adopted Children; Other Particular Classes.

Adopted children, see also Section 9-13.

A designated heir is included within the meaning of "child or other relative" in the lapse statute. White v. Agnew, 38 WLB 47, affd. 56 OS 796, 49 NE 1119, OSU 644 (1897).

361

The lapse statute applies to a devise to children as a class even though a child had died before the execution of the will. Woolley v. Paxson, 46 OS 307, 24 NE 599, 21 WLB 130, 303 (1889); Shumaker v. Pearson, 67 OS 330, 65 NE 1005, 47 WLB 901, 48 WLB 147 (1902).

The issue will take although the testator directed "I have decided to exclude from any participation in my estate any and all persons not mentioned in this my will and codicil." Larwill v. Ewing, 73 OS 177, 76 NE 503, 3 OLR 494, 51 WLB 7 (1905).

A devise of real estate by a wife to her husband will lapse if his death precedes hers, although he leaves issue of a former marriage surviving testatrix. Schaefer v. Bernhardt, 76 OS 443, 81 NE 640, 5 OLR 112, 52 WLB 303 (1907).

A designated heir is to be regarded the same as "issue" insofar as it involves his right to inherit from the person so designating under the statutes of descent and distribution. Cochrel v. Robinson, 113 OS 526, 149 NE 871, 3 Abs 738, 23 OLR 607 (1925).

Under the lapse statute, since 1931 the word "issue" embraces an adopted child of the original devisee. Flynn v. Bredbeck, 147 OS 49, 68 NE2d 75, 33 OO 243 (1946). Under the statute as it existed from 1859 through 1931, a devise or legacy lapsed although the original devisee or legatee left an adopted child surviving the testator. Phillips v. McConica, 59 OS 1, 51 NE 445, 40 WLB 260, 293 (1898).

The surviving children of a designated heir who predeceases his designator do not have any right of inheritance in the estate of such designator, unless the designation of the heir occurs after the execution of a will of the designator. Kirsheman v. Paulin, 155 OS 137, 98 NE2d 26, 44 OO 134 (1951).

A devise to an illegitimate child, whose decease occurs prior to that of the testator, lapses and does not pass to the children of said illegitimate child. Owens v. Humbert, 5 App 312, 25 CC(NS) 522, 27 CD 307, 61 WLB 259 (1916).

A stepchild is not a child or other relative within the meaning of the statute on lapsed devises. Kegler v. Kempter, 74 App 279, 58 NE2d 701, 29 OO 418 (1942).

Further research: O Jur 3d, Family Law § 238.

9-26E Charitable Gifts within Six Months.

R.C. 2107.06, repealed effective August 1, 1985, provided that "(A) If a testator dies leaving issue and by his will devises or bequeaths his estate, or any part thereof, in trust or otherwise to any municipal corporation, county, state, country, or subdivision thereof, for any purpose whatsoever, or to any person, association, or corporation for the use or benefit of one or more benevolent, religious, educational, or charitable purposes, such devises and bequests shall be valid in their entirety only if the testator's will was executed more than six months prior to the death of the testator. If such will was executed within six months of the testator's death, such devises and bequests shall be valid to the extent they do not in the aggregate exceed twenty-five percent of the value of the testator's net probate estate, and in the event the aggregate of the devises and bequests exceeds twenty-five percent thereof, such devises and bequests shall be abated proportionately so that the aggregate thereof equals twenty-five percent of the value of the testator's net probate estate.

"(B) The execution of a codicil to the testator's will within six months of his death shall not affect the validity of any such devises and bequests made by will or codicil executed more than six months prior to his death, except as the same are revoked or modified by the codicil. If a codicil executed within such period increases the aggregate of such devises and bequests to more than twenty-five percent of the value of the testator's net probate estate, such increase by codicil is invalidated to the extent that such increases, plus the aggregate contained in the will and not revoked by the codicil, exceeds twenty-five percent of the value of the testator's net probate estate; and the amount of the codicil's increase of each such devise and bequest in the will and each such devise and bequest contained in the codicil which was not contained in the will shall be abated proportionately.

"(C) The portion of any such devises and bequests which is invalid under this section shall be distributed per stirpes among such testator's issue unless expressly otherwise provided in the will or codicil.

"(D) As used in this section, 'the value of the testator's net probate estate' means the probate inventory value of all the testator's assets which are subject to the jurisdiction of the probate court, less all debts and costs and expenses of administration, but prior to the payment of an estate or inheritance taxes, and 'issue' means a child or children, including an adopted child or adopted children, and their lineal descendants." (As eff. 10-6-65.)

Prior to October 6, 1965, R.C. 2107.06 provided: "If a testator dies leaving issue, or an adopted child, or the lineal descendants of either, and the will of such testator gives, devises, or bequeaths such testator's estate, or any part thereof, to a benevolent, religious, educational, or charitable purpose, or to any state or country, or to a county, municipal corporation, or other corporation, or to an association in any state or country, or to persons, municipal corporations, corporations, or associations in trust for such purposes, whether such trust appears on the face of the instrument making such gift, devise, or bequest or not, such will as to such gift, devise, or bequest, shall be invalid unless it was executed at least one year prior to the death of the testator."

A power to appoint to an educational institution is not rendered invalid by the death of the testator within one year after the execution of the will. Thomas v. Trustees of Ohio State University, 70 OS 92, 70 NE 896, 2 OLR 4, 49 WLB 190 (1904); Ohio State University Trustees v. Folsom, 56 OS 701, 47 NE 581, 37 WLB 433 (1897).

Such bequests are not rendered invalid as respects a designated heir. Theobald v. Fugman, 64 OS 473, 60 NE 606, 45 WLB 318, 382 (1901).

Such gifts are invalid if the testator died leaving an adopted child living, or its lineal descendants. Barrett v. Delmore, 143 OS 203, 54 NE2d 789, 28 OO 133, 153 ALR 192 (1944).

A gift to a charity is void if the testator dies within one year after the execution of his will, leaving issue of his body. Children of the testator do not waive their rights by acceptance of benefits under the will. Kirkbride v. Hickok, 155 OS 293, 98 NE2d 815, 44 OO 297 (1951).

An otherwise valid exercise of a general testamentary power of appointment in favor of a charitable corporation is not rendered invalid by the fact that the donor of the power died within a year of the execution of his will leaving a son. In re Lowe's Estate, 119 App 303, 27 OO2d 319, 92 Abs 369 (1963).

When the persons named in the statute are not benefited by the invalidity of the gift, the gift to the benevolent, religious, educational or charitable institution is valid. Deeds v. Deeds, 94 NE2d 232, 42 OO 384, 58 Abs 129 (Prob. 1950).

A testator, whose grandchild was adopted by another before testator's death, dies without issue or the lineal descendant of issue under the statute regarding charitable devises within one year of death. Campbell v. Musart Society of the Cleveland Museum of Art, 131 NE2d 279, 2 OO2d 517, 72 Abs 46 (Prob. 1956).

Waiver of the benefits thereby created with the consequent validation of the testamentary devises or bequests of a charitable nature are permitted and validated by R.C. 2107.06. Ireland v. Cleveland Trust Co., 157 NE2d 396, 11 OO2d 237, 80 Abs 94 (Prob. 1958).

A codicil, executed within a year of testator's death, substituting an item in the will, reducing bequests to relatives and consequently increasing bequests to charities, unconditionally revokes the bequests in the substituted item of the will to the same charities. Newman v. Newman, 199 NE2d 904, 28 OO2d 154, 94 Abs 321 (Prob. 1964).

Grandchildren are not heirs at law where all the testator's children survive him, and do not come within the protection of R.C. 2107.06. The statute does not apply when those whom the statute is designed to protect have, in fact, no interest to protect. Central Nat. Bank v. Morris, 10 App2d 225, 227 NE2d 418, 39 OO2d 433 (1967).

Further research: O Jur 3d, Decedents' Estates §§ 312, 313, 315, 319, 320.

9-26F Withholding Will from Probate.

R.C. 2107.10 provides: "(A) No property or right, testate or intestate, shall pass to a beneficiary named in a will who knows of the existence of the will for three years and has the power to control it, and, without reasonable cause, intentionally conceals or withholds it or neglects or refuses within the three years to cause it to be offered for or admitted to probate. The estate devised to such devisee shall descend to the heirs of the testator, not including any heir who has concealed or withheld the will.

"(B) No property or right, testate or intestate, passes to a beneficiary named in a will when the will was declared valid and filed with a probate judge pursuant to section 2107.084 of the Revised Code, the declaration and filing took place in a county different from the county in which the will of the testator would be probated under section 2107.11 of the Revised Code, and the named beneficiary knew of the declaration and filing and of the death of the testator and did not notify the probate judge with whom the will was filed. This division does not preclude a named beneficiary from acquiring property or rights from the estate of the testator for failing to notify a probate judge if it is his reasonable belief that the judge has previously been notified of the testator's death." (As eff. 1-1-79.)

The divesting of a beneficiary is a forfeiture and action must be brought within one year from the time the cause of action arose. Stillwell v. Tudor, 80 App 190, 75 NE2d 94, 35 OO 514 (1946). Contra: that the statute does not provide for forfeiture, but prevents any estate from passing to the negligent devisee. Barron v. McCann, 25 App 520, 159 NE 104, 6 Abs 127 (1927).

A beneficiary is not barred unless he has the purpose of delaying administration or defeating some rights or benefits given by the terms of the will. Hoskins v. Lentz, 7 O Supp 132, 7 OO 214, 23 Abs 5 (Prob. 1936). Contra: that the sole devisee neglecting to submit the will to probate for more than three years after testator's death is thereby barred as a devisee thereunder. Lawson v. Thomas, 48 App 311, 193 NE 655, 1 OO 483, 16 Abs 503 (1934).

The failure of a remainderman to have a will probated during the life tenant's life, where the remainderman had access to it, amounted to an intentional withholding of and neglect to probate the will, and he takes none of the estate. In re Varley's Will, 10 O Supp 109, 27 OO 162, 37 Abs 275 (Prob. 1938).

Further research: O Jur 3d, Decedents' Estates § 325.

SECTION 9-27: ELECTION BY SURVIVING SPOUSE

Charts, see 9-27F.
Death within thirty days, see 9-11L.

9-27A Statutes.

R.C. 2107.39 provides: "(A) After the probate of a will and the filing of the inventory and the appraisement, the probate court shall issue a citation to the surviving spouse, if any is living at the time of the issuance of the citation, to elect whether to take under the will or under section 2105.06 of the Revised Code.

"(B) If the surviving spouse elects to take under section 2105.06 of the Revised Code and if the value of the property that the surviving spouse is entitled to receive is equal to or greater than the value of the decedent's interest in the mansion house as determined under section 2105.062 of the Revised Code, the surviving spouse is also entitled to make an election pursuant to division (A) of section 2105.062 of the Revised Code.

"(C) If the surviving spouse elects to take under section 2105.06 of the Revised Code, the spouse shall take not to exceed one half of the net estate unless two or more of the decedent's children or their lineal descendants survive, in which case the spouse shall take not to exceed one-third of the net estate.

"For purposes of this division, the net estate shall be determined before payment of federal estate tax, estate taxes under Chapter 5731, of the Revised Code, or any other tax that is subject to apportionment under section 2113.86 or 2113.861 of the Revised Code.

"(D) Unless the will expressly provides that in case of an election under division (A) of this section there shall be no acceleration of remainder or other interests bequeathed or devised by the will, the balance of the net estate shall be disposed of as though the spouse had predeceased the testator.

"(E) The election under division (A) of this section shall be made at any time after the probate of the will, but not later than one month after the service of the citation to elect. On a motion filed before the expiration of the one-month period, and for good cause shown, the court may allow further time for the making of the election. If no action is taken by the surviving spouse within the one-month period, it is conclusively presumed that the surviving spouse elects to take under the will. The election shall be entered on the journal of the court.

"When proceedings for advice or to contest the validity of a will are begun within the time allowed by this division for making the election, the election may be made within three months after the final disposition of the proceedings, if the will is not set aside.

"(F) When a surviving spouse succeeds to the entire estate of the testator, having been named the sole devisee and legatee, it shall be presumed that the spouse elects to take under the will of the testator. No citation shall be issued to the surviving spouse as provided in division (A) of this section, and no election shall be required, unless the surviving spouse manifests a contrary intention." (As eff. 12-17-86.)

R.C. 2107.41 provides: "If the surviving spouse dies before probate of the will, or, having survived such probate, thereafter either fails to make the election provided by section 2107.39 of the Revised Code or dies before the expiration of the time set forth by such section without having made such election, such spouse shall be conclusively presumed to have elected to take under the will and such spouse and the heirs, devisees, and legatees of such spouse who dies either before or after probate of the will without having elected, and those claiming through or under them shall be bound thereby, and persons may deal with the property of the decedent accordingly; provided that where applicable the provisions of section 2105.21 of the Revised Code shall prevail over the provisions relating to the right of election of a surviving spouse." (As eff. 10-16-53.)

R.C. 2107.42 provides: "If a surviving spouse elects to take under the will, the spouse shall be barred of all right to an intestate share of the property passing under the will and shall take under the will alone, unless it plainly appears from the will that the provision for the spouse was intended to be in addition to an intestate share. An election to take under the will does not bar the right of the surviving spouse to an intestate share of that portion of the

estate as to which the decedent dies intestate. Unless the will expressly otherwise directs, an election to take under the will does not bar the right of the
surviving spouse to remain in the mansion of the deceased consort, nor the
right of the surviving spouse to receive the allowance for the support provided
by section 2117.20 of the Revised Code." (As eff. 1-1-76.)

R.C. 2107.43 provides: "The election of a surviving spouse to take under
section 2105.06 of the Revised Code and thereby refusing to take under the
will shall be made in person before the probate judge, or a deputy clerk who
has been appointed to act as a referee under the provisions of section 2315.37
of the Revised Code, except as provided in sections 2107.44 and 2107.45 of the
Revised Code.

"When the election is made in person before such judge or referee, the judge
or referee shall explain the will, the rights under such will, and by law, in the
event of a refusal to take under the will." (As eff. 5-26-76.)

R.C. 2129.07 provides that when a copy of a will probated in a foreign
country has been duly admitted to record in an Ohio county in which there is
any estate upon which the will may operate, "and when no ancillary administration proceedings have been had or are being had in Ohio, Sections 2107.39
to 2107.45 of the Revised Code, relating to election shall be the same as in the
case of resident decedents, except that such election shall be made not later
than six months after the record of such copy." (As eff. 10-7-77.)

In order to prevent, pursuant to R.C. 2107.39, acceleration of the remainder
or other interest, the testator must use words which anticipate an election to
take against the will or at least must use words which prohibit the acceleration in any event. In the absence of such words, the statute constitutes an
election to take against the will as a constructive death of the surviving
spouse. Funkhouser v. Dorfmeier, 202 NE2d 226, 31 OO2d 42, 95 Abs 140
(Prob. 1963).

Where a will probated in another state has been duly admitted to record in
this state, and where it is not established that the widow had claimed anything under that will, such widow has the right with respect to Ohio real
estate owned by the testator at his death to elect to take the property under
the Ohio statute of descent and distribution, even though no such election is
permitted by the law of the state of the testator's domicile. Pfau v. Moseley, 9
OS2d 13, 222 NE2d 639, 38 OO2d 8 (1966).

The right to elect against the will is personal and does not survive the death
of the surviving spouse. Death is not a legal disability which permits the court
to make such election. In re Estate of LaSpina, 60 OS2d 101, 397 NE2d 1196,
14 OO3d 336 (1979).

Further research: O Jur 3d, Decedents' Estates § 834.

9-27B   Dower.

Since December 31, 1931, the statutes have contained no provision regarding dower upon an election to take under the will. No decisions have been
found under the 1932 Probate Code on whether such election bars dower to

which the surviving spouse would otherwise be entitled in lands conveyed or encumbered by the deceased spouse alone.

Further research: O Jur 3d, Decedents' Estates § 857.

9-27C Equitable Conversion.

The doctrine can have no application in ascertaining the share of a widow electing to take under the law. Geiger v. Bitzer, 80 OS 65, 88 NE 134, 6 OLR 661, 54 WLB 105 (1909).

LAW IN GENERAL

The surviving spouse is denied the benefit of a conversion directed by the will when the will is renounced. Am Jur 2d, Equitable Conversion § 13.

9-27D Manner and Presumption of Election.

See also charts at 9-27F.

The statutory provision that the surviving spouse shall take under the will, unless an election is filed in the time specified, has no application where such spouse is incompetent. Ambrose v. Rugg, 123 OS 433, 175 NE 691, 9 Abs 477, 34 OLR 226, 74 ALR 449 (1931).

If the surviving spouse remains alive and competent and fails to elect within nine months after appointment of the first administrator or executor, he will be conclusively presumed to have elected to take under the will. In re Witteman's Estate, 3 OS2d 66, 209 NE2d 427, 32 OO2d 49 (1965).

Under the facts and equities in this case, the election to take under the law should not be stricken from the files although filed more than nine months after the appointment of an executor. Third persons may rely upon the statutory presumption that the surviving spouse has elected to take under the will, and that having relied upon such presumption, the presumption as to them cannot be rebutted. In re Bersin's Estate, 98 App 432, 129 NE2d 868, 57 OO 475 (1955).

Further research: O Jur 3d, Decedents' Estates § 837.

9-27E Effects of Election.

Charts, see 9-27F.
Statutes, see 9-27A.

If an estate of deceased husband consists wholly or in part of real estate, and his widow, as relict, elects not to take under his will but under the statute of descent and distribution, she takes her quantitative share in such real estate as an estate of inheritance, subject to sale, if necessary, to pay debts of the estate of her deceased husband. Barlow v. Winters Nat. Bank & Trust Co., 145 OS 270, 61 NE2d 603, 30 OO 484, 160 ALR 423 (1945).

Where a widow elects to take under the statute of descent and distribution, the amount of the federal estate tax on decedent's estate should be deducted therefrom before computing the widow's share thereof. Campbell v. Lloyd, 162 OS 203, 122 NE2d 695, 55 OO 102 (1954).

We reject the rule of the Bolles and Harris cases, to the effect that, if a settlor reserves to himself the income during life, with the right to amend or revoke the trust or any part thereof, such reserved rights and powers defeat the parting of dominion over the trust property and thereby create a right in the widow to assert her right to distributive share of the property in such trust at settlor's death. Smyth v. Cleveland Trust Co., 172 OS 489, 179 NE2d 60, 18 OO2d 42 (1961).

The widow has no interest or title to specifically devised personal property where the remaining estate is sufficient to make her total share of the net estate that amount to which she is entitled under the provisions of the statute. Winters Nat. Bank & Trust Co. v. Riffe, 2 OS2d 72, 206 NE2d 212, 31 OO2d 56 (1965).

Specific devisees, whose devises are diminished by election not to take under the will, have an equitable lien enforceable against the real estate of the residuary estate. Wyer v. King, 67 App 321, 36 NE2d 897, 21 OO 290, 32 Abs 399 (1940). See also 11-16C.

Upon election to take under a will giving surviving husband "the amount that he is allowed under the laws of Ohio" and giving the residue to sisters and nieces, he takes only twenty percent of the estate (not less than $500 nor more than $2500) and right to reside in mansion house for one year; but should he elect to take under the law he would also take one-half of the net estate. Schardt v. Prexler, 67 NE2d 549, 45 Abs 119 (App. 1946).

The share of the surviving spouse electing to take under the law is a charge not only against the residuary estate but also proportionately against specific bequests. Such spouse is vested, as of the time of testator's death, with an undivided one-third interest in all the real and personal property owned by the testator at his death. Blackford v. Vermillion, 107 App 26, 156 NE2d 339, 7 OO2d 350 (1958).

"This court is of the opinion and so finds that while the Supreme Court reversed itself as on record in the Bolles and Harris cases, by its decision in the Smyth case, that as quickly as possible thereafter, the Legislature for all practical purposes reversed the Supreme Court" by enacting R.C. 2107.63, the pourover statute, reserving the right to elect against the will. Purcell v. Cleveland Trust Co., 200 NE2d 602, 28 OO2d 262, 94 Abs 455 (Prob. 1964). Caveat: This is a probate court opinion.

The executor nominated by the will is both an administrator as to the electing surviving spouse, who takes by way of inheritance, and an executor as to the other beneficiaries named in the will and the creditors. The election is not a debt covered by the statute on contribution. Winters Nat. Bank & Trust Co. v. Riffe, 194 NE2d 921, 27 OO2d 261, 93 Abs 171 (Prob. 1963), revd. on other grounds 2 OS2d 72, 206 NE2d 212, 31 OO2d 56 (1965).

"It is our holding that this case is controlled by Smyth v. Cleveland Trust Co., 172 OS 489, 179 NE2d 60, and the doctrine clearly enunciated therein bars the husband's invasion of the inter vivos trust established by his wife in this case, and the only rights he has are those specifically given to him by the trust agreement." Purcell v. Cleveland Trust Co., 6 App2d 235, 217 NE2d 876, 35 OO2d 426 (1965).

The statutory share of a surviving spouse electing to take against the will is not altered by testamentary provision for payment of succession taxes. Weeks v. Vandeveer, 13 OS2d 15, 233 NE2d 502, 42 OO2d 25 (1968).

Further research: O Jur 3d, Decedents' Estates § 855.

LAW IN GENERAL

The part of an estate which passes to the surviving spouse upon election to take under a will giving the spouse such share as the law allows, or similar provision, depends on the intention of the testator which is to be ascertained in accordance with the usual rules for construction. 36 ALR2d 147.

9-27F Charts.

See statutes at 9-27A.

May 8, 1894 through July 28, 1925.

Upon election to take under the will, the surviving spouse is barred of dower and distributive share but not of right to mansion or year's allowance, unless it plainly appears to the contrary by the will.

Upon election to take under the law, surviving spouse retains dower and distributive share.

Upon failure to elect, surviving spouse takes as though consort died intestate leaving children.

July 29, 1925 through December 31, 1931.

Upon election to take under the will, the surviving spouse is barred of dower and distributive share but not of right to mansion or year's allowance, unless it plainly appears to the contrary by the will.

Upon election to take under the law, surviving spouse takes as though consort died intestate leaving children.

Upon failure to elect, surviving spouse takes under the will.

January 1, 1932 through September 1, 1935.

Upon election to take under the will, surviving spouse is barred of all right to an intestate share but not of right to (a) mansion or (b) year's allowance, unless it plainly appears otherwise from the will.

Upon election to take under the law, surviving spouse takes as though consort died intestate, but not to exceed one-half of the estate.

Upon failure to elect, surviving spouse (a) takes under the will if living one month after service of citation, (b) takes under the statute of descent and distribution and not to exceed one-half of the estate if not living one month after service of citation, (c) takes under the statute of descent and distribution and not to exceed one-half of the estate if citation is not issued and he or she dies without electing. Query: If citation was not issued and surviving spouse was still alive and had not elected?

September 2, 1935 through August 21, 1941.

Upon election to take under the will, surviving spouse is barred of all right to an intestate share but not of right to (a) mansion, (b) year's allowance, nor (c) property not deemed assets of the estate for administration unless it plainly appears otherwise from the will.

Upon election to take under the law, surviving spouse takes as though consort died intestate, but not to exceed one-half of the net estate.

Upon failure to elect, surviving spouse takes under the will.

August 22, 1941 through October 15, 1953.

Upon election to take under the will, surviving spouse is barred of the right to an intestate share of the property passing under the will but not (a) of right to intestate share of property which does not pass under the will, (b) of right to mansion, (c) of right to property not deemed assets of the estate for administration, nor (d) of right to year's allowance, unless it plainly appears otherwise from the will.

Upon election to take under the law, surviving spouse takes as though consort died intestate, but not to exceed one-half of the net estate.

Upon failure to elect, surviving spouse takes under the will.

October 16, 1953 to date.

Upon election to take under the will, surviving spouse is barred of the right to an intestate share of the property passing under the will but not (a) of right to intestate share of property which does not pass under the will, (b) of right to mansion, (c) of right to property not deemed assets of the estate for administration, nor (d) of right to year's allowance, unless it plainly appears otherwise from the will.

Upon election to take under the law, surviving spouse takes as though consort died intestate, but not to exceed one-half of the net estate. The balance of the net estate shall be disposed of as though the spouse had predeceased the testator, unless the will provides there shall be no acceleration.

Upon failure to elect, surviving spouse takes under the will whether such spouse dies before the probate of the will or dies thereafter.

Note: If both spouses die within a thirty-day period, the survivor (or representative) has no right of election. See 9-11L.

SECTION 9-28: PROBATE; CONTEST

9-28A Probate Generally.

R.C. 2107.11 provides: "A will shall be admitted to probate:

"(A) In the county in which the testator was domiciled if, at the time of his death, he was domiciled in this state;

"(B) In any county of this state where any real or personal property of such testator is located if, at the time of his death, he was not domiciled in this state, and provided that such will has not previously been admitted to probate in this state or in the state of such testator's domicile;

"(C) In the county of this state in which a probate court rendered a judgment declaring that the will was valid and where the will was filed with the probate court.

"For the purpose of this section, intangible personal property is located in the place where the instrument evidencing a debt, obligation, stock, or chose in action is located or if there is no such instrument where the debtor resides." (As eff. 1-1-79.)

R.C. 2107.18 provides: "The probate court shall admit a will to probate if it appears from the face of the will, or if demanded under section 2107.14 of the Revised Code, from the testimony of the witnesses that its execution complies with the law in force at the time of execution in the jurisdiction where executed, or with the law in force in this state at the time of death, or with the law in force in the jurisdiction where the testator was domiciled at the time of his death.

"The probate court shall admit a will to probate when there has been a prior judgment by a probate court declaring that the will is valid, rendered pursuant to section 2107.084 of the Revised Code, if the will has not been removed from the possession of the probate judge and has not been modified or revoked under division (C) or (D) of section 2107.084 of the Revised Code." (As eff. 1-1-79.)

R.C. 2107.26 provides for the admission to probate of lost or spoliated wills. (As eff. 10-1-53.)

Where the will treats the separate property of each as a joint fund, and is in the nature of a compact, it cannot be admitted to probate as a joint will, nor as the separate will of either. Walker v. Walker, 14 OS 157 (1862).

A prima facie case is all that is required for admission to probate. In re Elvin's Will, 146 OS 448, 66 NE2d 629, 32 OO 534 (1946).

"Resident" is not synonymous with "domiciled." The appointment of an administrator in the county where decedent was resident is suspended by the probate of the will of such decedent in the county where he was domiciled. State ex rel. Overlander v. Brewer, 147 OS 386, 72 NE2d 84, 34 OO 338 (1947).

"Domicile" and "residence" are frequently used synonymously, especially in statutes, as meaning "domicile." State ex rel. Overlander v. Brewer, 147 OS 386, 72 NE2d 84, 34 OO 338 (1947). When precisely used, domicile means the place where one has voluntarily fixed his habitation, not for a special or temporary purpose, but with the intention of making it his permanent home, and to which when he is absent, he intends to return. Residence and intention taken together constitute domicile. An established domicile is presumed to continue until another has been proven to have been acquired in its stead. In re Stephan's Estate, 5 O Supp 21, 17 OO 361, 31 Abs 457 (Prob. 1940).

Both intention and actual residence must be present in order to establish a new domicile. Indian Hill v. Atkins, 90 NE2d 161, 57 Abs 210 (App. 1949).

"Tenants in common of real estate who are also owners, severally, of personal property, may dispose of the same by will by uniting in a single instrument, where the bequests are severable and the instrument is not in the nature of a compact, but is, in effect, the will of each, revocable by him, and subject to probate as such several will." Betts v. Harper, 39 OS 639, 11 WLB 58 (1884); Ballard v. Ballard, 5 App 469, 26 CC(NS) 490, 27 CD 562, 62 WLB 9 (1916).

The domicile of a person entering the armed forces is not changed by the mere fact that he changes his place of abode, but such domicile is changed where he intends to make such change. Draper v. Draper, 107 App 379, 151 NE2d 379, 7 OO2d 354, 78 Abs 5 (1958).

One of the subscribing witnesses may prove the execution of the will and its due attestation. In re Halterman's Will, 12 O Supp 150, 27 OO 521, 39 Abs 43 (Prob. 1943).

Where the signatures of witnesses cannot be proven, the will may be admitted to probate if two or more witnesses testify that the signature of the testator is genuine. In re Blickensderfer's Will, 13 O Supp 93, 28 OO 42, 40 Abs 217 (C.P. 1944).

A will must be admitted to probate when the proponents introduce substantial evidence tending to prove the validity of the will. The proponents have established a prima facie case and the will should have been admitted to probate. In re Young, 60 App 2d 390, 397 NE2d 1223, 14 OO3d 359 (1978).

A "spoliated will," such as is contemplated in R.C. 2107.26, refers only to one which has been affected by some act of one other than the testator. In re Downie's Estate, 6 Misc 36, 213 NE2d 833, 35 OO2d 31 (Prob. 1966). Revocation or alteration, see Section 9-24.

Further research: O Jur 3d, Decedents' Estates § 954.

LAW IN GENERAL

Probate of a will is the official proof of an instrument as a valid will. It establishes the prima facie validity as to execution and as to testator's capacity. It does not determine the validity or construction of a devise. A will is not effective and cannot be used in evidence to establish the title until it has been admitted to probate. Whenever probated a will takes effect from the date of testator's death. Am Law of Prop § 14.35; CJS, Wills § 310; Powell § 964.

9-28B Necessity of Administration.

Administration generally, see Chapter 12.

R.C. 2107.61 provides: "Unless it has been admitted to probate or record, as provided in sections 2107.01 to 2107.62, inclusive, and 2129.05 to 2129.07, inclusive, of the Revised Code, no will is effectual to pass real or personal estate." (As eff. 10-1-53.)

Title does not depend upon the appointment of an executor or administrator. Administration may be necessary, during the period claims are not barred by limitation, to show the payment of legacies, taxes and other claims against the estate.

Standard of Title Examination

(Originally adopted by Ohio State Bar Association in 1967
and revised for clarification in 1975)

Problem 3.17A:

Does the fact that a decedent's estate has not been closed prevent his heirs or devisees from conveying good title?

Standard 3.17A:

No, provided any estate or inheritance tax liens to which the estate is subject are either discharged or the real property in question released therefrom, and provided one or more partial accounts of the fiduciary have been approved which appear to show payment of all claims against the estate.

Comment 3.17A:

If decedent has been dead more than ten years, any estate or inheritance tax liens will have expired. Sec. 5731.171, R.C. (Ohio Inheritance Tax), Sec. 5731.38 R.C. (Ohio Estate Tax) and Sec. 6324(a) (1), Int. Rev. Code (Federal Estate Tax). If administration proceedings have been pending four years or more, consideration should be given to the effect of Sec. 2117.36, R.C. with respect to claims against the estate.

Depending on the circumstances of the particular case, other things may sometimes prevent the heirs or devisees from conveying good title, such as a pending or possible will contest, a statutory bar to taking an inheritance or devise, an unresolved question concerning the identity of the heirs or devisees, one or more competing rights of the surviving spouse, unpaid legacies which are a charge against the real property in question, etc.

9-28C Foreign Wills.

See also Section 12-15.
Admitting to probate in this state, see 9-28A.

R.C. 2107.21 provides: "If real estate devised by will is situated in any county other than that in which the will is proved, declared valid, or admitted to probate, an authenticated copy of the will and the order of probate or the judgment of validity shall be admitted to the record in the office of the probate judge of each county in which such real estate is situated upon the order of such judge. The authenticated copy shall have the same validity therein as if probate had been had in such county." (As eff. 1-1-79.) In such case title is unmarketable unless there is compliance with this statute.

R.C. 2107.48 provides: "There shall be no proceeding in this state to contest a will executed and proved according to the law of another state or of a foreign country, relative to property in this state; but if such will is set aside in the state or country in which it is executed and proved, it shall be invalid in this state as to persons claiming under it who have notice of its being set aside, and invalid as to all other persons from the time and authenticated copy of the final order or decree setting it aside is filed in the office of the probate judge of the county in which the will is recorded." (As eff. 1-1-79.)

R.C. 2129.05 provides: "Authenticated copies of wills, executed and proved according to the laws of any state or territory of the United States, relative to property in this state, may be admitted to record in the probate court of a county where a part of such property is situated. Such authenticated copies, so recorded, shall be as valid as wills made in this state.

"When such a will, or authenticated copy, is admitted to record, a copy thereof, with the copy of the order to record it annexed thereto, certified by the probate judge under the seal of his court, may be filed and recorded in the office of the probate judge of any other county where a part of such property is situated, and it shall be as effectual as the authenticated copy of such will would be if approved and admitted to record by the court." (As eff. 10-1-53.)

R.C. 2129.06 provides: "A will executed, proved, and allowed in a country other than the United States and territories thereof, according to the laws of such foreign state or country, may be allowed and admitted to record in this state in the manner and for the purpose mentioned in sections 2129.07 to 2129.30, inclusive, of the Revised Code." (As eff. 10-1-53.)

R.C. 2129.07 provides procedure for admission to record of will allowed in a foreign country. (As eff. 10-7-77.)

Further research: O Jur 3d, Decedents' Estates § 1160.

9-28D After-discovered Wills; Bona Fide Purchasers.

R.C. 2107.22 provides for probate of a later will and for revocation of the earlier one upon giving notice to persons interested in the earlier will and to those persons required to be notified under R.C. 2107.13. (As eff. 1-1-79.) See R.C. 2107.13 at 9-28F.

R.C. 2107.47 provides: "(A) The title, estate, or interest of a bona fide purchaser, lessee, or encumbrancer, for value, in land situated in this state, that is derived from an heir of a decedent and acquired without knowledge of a will of the decedent that effectively disposes of it to another person, shall not be defeated by the production of a will of the decedent, unless, in the case of a resident decedent, the will is offered for probate within three months after the date of the appointment of the executor or administrator, or unless, in the case of a nonresident decedent, the will is offered for record in this state within three months after the date of the appointment of the executor or administrator.

"(B) The title, estate, or interest of a bona fide purchaser, lessee, or encumbrancer, for value, in land situated in this state, that is derived from a beneficiary under a will of a decedent and acquired without knowledge of a later will of the decedent that effectively disposes of it to another person, shall not be defeated by the production of a later will of the decedent, unless, in the case of a resident decedent, the later will is offered for probate within three months after the date of the appointment of the executor or administrator, or unless, in the case of a nonresident decedent, the later will is offered for record in this state within three months after the date of the appointment of the executor or administrator." (As eff. 2-2-82.)

LAW IN GENERAL

A will or codicil may be admitted to probate when discovered even though the period has expired for contest of a prior probated will. There is very little dissent from the rule that a will may be probated even though it is discovered after intestate administration has been completed.

Where there has been no administration of the estate, the purchaser of decedent's land from the heirs generally acquires no title as against the devisees under a will thereafter admitted to probate. The devisees may be barred in some instances by estoppel.

Where the estate had been administered as intestate, title has been upheld, by most of the decisions, in the purchaser from the heirs as against the devisees under an after-discovered will by virtue of such purchaser's reliance on the judicial procedure. The rights of bona fide purchasers from the devisee under a prior will have been protected in a majority of the cases when a later will is afterward admitted to probate.

Am Law of Prop § 14.39; 22 ALR2d 1107.

9-28E Contest.

Restraints upon contest, see 9-21P.

R.C. 2107.081 to 2107.085 provide procedure by the testator for judgment during his lifetime declaring the validity of his will. (As eff. 1-1-79.)

R.C. 2107.71 to 2107.75 provide that an action to contest a will shall be brought in the probate court where admitted; that the Civil Rules shall govern except as otherwise provided in these sections; who are necessary parties; that the order of probate is prima facie evidence of validity; and that when the will is set aside the court shall allow reasonable compensation to the fiduciary and the defending attorneys. Contest is restricted if the will was declared valid during the testator's lifetime.

R.C. 2107.76 provides: "If within four months after a will is admitted to probate, no person files an action permitted by section 2107.71 of the Revised Code to contest the validity of the will, the probate shall be forever binding, except as to persons under any legal disability, or to such persons for four months after such disability is removed. The rights saved shall not affect the rights of a purchaser, lessee, or encumbrancer for value in good faith, nor impose any liability upon a fiduciary who has acted in good faith, or upon a person delivering or transferring property to any other person under authority of a will, whether or not the purchaser, lessee, encumbrancer, fiduciary, or other person had notice, actual or constructive, of the legal disability." (As eff. 1-1-79.)

No right exists to maintain an action to contest the validity of a will except as it is specifically provided by statute. Case v. Smith, 142 OS 95, 50 NE2d 142, 26 OO 282 (1943); In re Frey's Estate, 139 OS 354, 40 NE2d 145, 22 OO 411 (1942).

It is mandatory and jurisdictional that the executor be made a party and a summons, duly followed by service, be issued within six months after the will was admitted to probate; making him a party in his individual capacity as heir or devisee is not sufficient. Peters v. Moore, 154 OS 177, 93 NE2d 683, 42 OO 254 (1950); Bynner v. Jones, 154 OS 184, 93 NE2d 687, 42 OO 257 (1950).

All the devisees, legatees and heirs at law of the testator must be made parties to an action to contest a will during the six-month period as prescribed by statute. Gravier v. Gluth, 163 OS 232, 126 NE2d 332, 56 OO 228 (1955).

A will contest may not be commenced as a cross claim or counterclaim in an action commenced by an executor for construction of a will. Hess v. Sommers, 4 App 3d 281, 448 NE2d 494 (1982).

The statute, R.C. 2305.17, providing that an attempt to commence an action is equivalent to its commencement if service is made within sixty days, did not apply to an action to contest a will where the only parties served within the prescribed period were interested in having the will set aside. Sours v. Shuler, 42 App 393, 181 NE 908, 12 Abs 108, 36 OLR 544 (1932).

Vacation of judgment as to one party in a will contest proceeding vacates it as to all parties. Beachler v. Ford, 77 App 41, 60 NE2d 330, 32 OO 317, 42 Abs 609 (1945).

The savings clause of R.C. 2305.19, for commencing a new action when a suit has failed otherwise than on the merits, is not available in regard to a will contest action. Alakiotis v. Lancione, 12 Misc 257, 232 NE2d 663, 41 OO2d 381 (C.P. 1966).

The attorney general is a necessary party to a will contest where the will creates a charitable trust under the terms of R.C. 109.25, but not where the will contains an unconditional bequest to a trustee of an existing charitable trust. O'Neal v. Buckley, 67 App2d 45, 425 NE2d 924, 21 OO3d 354 (1979).

A party to a will contest has no right to a jury trial. The probate court may, in its discretion, impanel a jury or try the facts itself. State ex rel. Kear v. Court, 67 OS2d 189, 423 NE2d 427, 21 OO3d 118 (1981).

Further research: O Jur 3d, Decedents' Estates § 1174.

9-28F Notice of Application to Probate.

R.C. 2107.13 provides: "No will shall be admitted to probate without notice to the surviving spouse known to the applicant, and to the persons known to the applicant to be residents of the state who would be entitled to inherit from the testator under sections 2105.01 to 2105.21 of the Revised Code, if he had died intestate." (As eff. 5-26-76.)

An order of probate without notice to the persons entitled thereto is void. Mere knowledge of the order to probate will not estop next of kin from attacking such order where it is not shown that the proponents of the will were misled by silence or delay, or that they were prejudiced thereby. Scholl v. Scholl, 123 OS 1, 173 NE 305, 8 Abs 693, 33 OLR 219 (1930).

The knowledge of the persons to receive notice must be had by either the proponent of the will or the court. By joining as plaintiff in the will contest case, an heir of testator is barred from attacking the regularity of the order of probate or the jurisdiction of the court that made it. In re Hammer's Estate, 99 App 1, 130 NE2d 437, 58 OO 104 (1955).

Notice of the application to probate a will is not required to the surviving spouse who is a nonresident of the state of Ohio. Armstrong v. Brufach, 136 NE2d 463, 59 OO 352, 74 Abs 370 (C.P. 1950).

Notice may be served upon a minor who is in the military service and is entitled to notice of the probate of decedent's will by leaving such notice at his usual place of residence in Ohio or by sending it to such residence by registered mail. The Soldiers' and Sailors' Civil Relief Act has no application. Case v. Case, 124 NE2d 856, 55 OO 317, 70 Abs 2 (Prob. 1955).

9-28G Refusal to Probate.

R.C. 2107.181 provides: "If it appears that the instrument purporting to be a will is not entitled to admission to probate, the court shall enter an interlocutory order denying probate of the instrument, and shall continue the matter for further hearing. The court shall order that not less than ten days' notice of the further hearing be given by the applicant, the executor named in the instrument, the persons holding a power to nominate an executor as described in section 2107.65 of the Revised Code, or a commissioner appointed by the court, to all persons named in the instrument as legatees, devisees, beneficiaries of a trust, trustees, executors, or persons holding a power to nominate an executor, coexecutor, successor executor, or successor coexecutor as described in section 2107.65 of the Revised Code. Upon further hearing, witnesses may be called, subpoenaed, examined, and cross-examined in open court or by deposition, and their testimony reduced to writing and filed in the same manner as in hearings for the admission of wills to probate. Thereupon, the court shall revoke its interlocutory order denying probate to the instrument, and admit it to probate, or enter a final order refusing to probate it. A final order refusing to probate the instrument may be reviewed on appeal." (As eff. 10-14-83.)

CHAPTER 10: EASEMENTS

DIVISION 10-1: IN GENERAL

DIVISION 10-1: IN GENERAL

SECTION 10-11: INTRODUCTION; CREATION GENERALLY

Party walls, see Section 3-13.
Prescription, see Section 2-12.

10-11A   Definition.

An easement is a right without profit, created by grant or prescription, which the owner of one estate may exercise in or over the estate of another for the benefit of the former. Yeager v. Tuning, 79 OS 121, 86 NE 657, 6 OLR 554, 53 WLB 447 (1908).

An easement may be defined as a right of a person to a limited use or enjoyment of the land of another person, such right not being terminable at the will of the landowner.

Further research: O Jur 3d, Easements § 1.

10-11B   Classification.

Easements are primarily classified as appurtenant easements and easements in gross. Easements in gross are treated in Section 10-16.

Further research: O Jur 3d, Easements § 11.

LAW IN GENERAL

An easement is appurtenant to specific land when it is incidental to the possession of that land and benefits the possessor in the physical use or enjoyment of the dominant land. Its character is dependent upon the nature of the dominant tenement; thus, if appurtenant to a leasehold it is personal property, and if appurtenant to a fee it is a fee interest. Am Law of Prop § 8.6.

10-11C   Negative and Affirmative Easements; Covenants.

Restrictions as to use, see Division 6-3.

LAW IN GENERAL

When an agreement restrains an owner from doing certain acts on his land, the right created is sometimes called a negative easement as distinguished from a right to an active use of the land, called an affirmative easement. A negative easement is always an appurtenant easement. The doctrine of negative easements ordinarily applies to easements for light, air, support of buildings, and the flow of an artificial stream. An active duty in the nature of an easement is occasionally imposed by covenant on the owner of the land, as an agreement to maintain a fence. Promises made with respect to the use of land are somewhat in the nature of easements but are created by covenants. Am Jur 2d, Easements and Licenses §§ 8, 22, 23; Am Law of Prop § 8.11; Tiffany § 756.

10-11D Reciprocal Easements.

LAW IN GENERAL

The cases are conflicting with respect to reciprocal easements; for example, the doctrine has been both applied and rejected when the upper riparian owner has acquired a prescriptive right to divert water, and the lower owner claims a reciprocal right to the maintenance of the artificial condition. No Ohio law has been found on this subject. Tiffany § 1210.

10-11E Cotenants.

An easement from one cotenant is not effective as to the shares of the other cotenants. See Section 5-13.

10-11F Manner of Creation.

Easements by implication, see Section 10-12.

An easement can be created only by deed or prescription. A parol agreement by several adjoining landowners does not create an easement but is merely a parol license and is revocable by any one of such owners, although in reliance thereon poles have been erected and a telephone line constructed. Yeager v. Tuning, 79 OS 121, 86 NE 657, 6 OLR 554, 53 WLB 447 (1908).

No particular words are necessary to grant an easement, and if words are used which clearly show an intention to give such easement, such intent will be carried into effect. Mansfield v. Richardson, 4 Abs 319 (App. 1926).

The fact that a deed does not contain the word "assigns" or that the covenant relates to a thing not "in esse" at the time the conveyance is made, is relatively unimportant as to whether a covenant is personal or runs with the land; the important fact being the intention of the parties. Maher v. Cleveland Union Stockyards Co., 55 App 412, 9 NE2d 995, 9 OO 112, 22 Abs 199 (1936).

Words of inheritance are necessary, in instruments effective prior to the year 1925, to create an easement for a duration longer than the life of the grantee. Warren v. Brenner, 89 App 188, 101 NE2d 157, 45 OO 437 (1950).

One easement cannot be imposed upon another easement. A reservation of the free right to pass, in granting a right-of-way for a toll road, does not run with the land. Turpin v. Batavia Pike & Miami Bridge Co., 7 NP 12, 9 OD 668, 47 WLB 438 (1899).

Whether an easement is an appurtenance running with the land must be determined from the language used in the deed, in the surrounding circumstances at the time the right is created, and the intention of the parties at the time the deed was executed. Siferd v. Stambor, 5 App2d 79, 214 NE2d 106, 34 OO2d 189 (1966).

Where an owner of land, without objection, permits another to expend money in reliance upon a supposed easement when in justice and equity the former ought to have disclaimed his conflicting rights, such owner is estopped to deny the easement. Monroe Bowling Lanes v. Woodsfield Livestock Sales, 17 App2d 146, 244 NE2d 762, 46 OO2d 208 (1969).

A grant, reservation or agreement creating an easement should contain a reference to the recorded source of grantor's title but omission of the reference does not affect validity of the same. For the statute, see 1-24B.

Further research: O Jur 3d, Easements § 18.

LAW IN GENERAL

Easements may be created by prescription, implication, deed or will. Easements may become effective by refusal of an injunction, by estoppel, or by eminent domain. Powell § 411.

An easement may be granted to take effect or to be enjoyed in the future. CJS, Easements § 51.

When created by deed or will the same formalities are required for an easement as for the grant or devise of an estate in land. Am Law of Prop § 8.17; CJS, Easements § 5; Powell § 406; Restatement, Property § 467.

10-11G   Reservations; Exceptions.

Deeds to third parties, see also 8-13B.

Easements may be created by reservation or exception. A reservation to a third person who is not a party to the deed is not sufficient to create an easement. Kirk v. Conrad, 9 Abs 717 (App. 1931).

Further research: O Jur 3d, Easements § 27.

LAW IN GENERAL

Easements may be created by reservation and usually also by exception in accordance with the intention of the parties. A reservation cannot create an easement in a stranger to the deed; however, the intention of the parties may be, and the deed accordingly construed, to grant the fee to one person and to grant an easement to another person, although the latter grant is in the form of a reservation. Am Law of Prop § 8.24; Powell § 407; Restatement, Property § 472.

SECTION 10-12: EASEMENTS BY IMPLICATION; WAYS OF NE-CESSITY

Lateral support, see Section 3-12.
Light, air and view, see Section 3-14.

10-12A Transactions in Which Created.

When the owner of an entire estate makes one part of it visibly dependent for the means of access upon another part, and creates a way for its benefit over the other, and then grants the dependent part, the way constitutes an easement appurtenant to the estate granted. National Exchange Bank v. Cunningham, 46 OS 575, 22 NE 924, 22 WLB 353, 439 (1889); Baker v. Rice, 56 OS 463, 47 NE 653, 37 WLB 402, 38 WLB 4 (1897). A common driveway may be established in this manner. Frate v. Rimenik, 115 OS 11, 152 NE 14, 4 Abs 303, 24 OLR 412 (1926).

Further research: O Jur 3d, Easements § 30.

LAW IN GENERAL

Implied easements arise upon severance of common ownership, transfer of part of grantor's land, simultaneous grants, partition, devise, or judicial sale. Am Jur 2d, Easements and Licenses § 24; 58 ALR 824; Powell § 411.

10-12B Requirements.

"While implied grants of easements are not favored, being in derogation of the rule that written instruments shall speak for themselves, the same may arise when the following elements appear: (1) A severance of the unity of ownership in an estate; (2) that before the separation takes place, the use which gives rise to the easement shall have been so long continued and obvious or manifest as to show that it was meant to be permanent; (3) that the easement shall be reasonably necessary to the beneficial enjoyment of the land granted or retained; (4) that the servitude shall be continuous as distinguished from a temporary or occasional use only." Ciski v. Wentworth, 122 OS 487, 172 NE 276, 8 Abs 387, 32 OLR 181 (1930); Trattar v. Rausch, 154 OS 286, 95 NE2d 685, 43 OO 186 (1950); Deyling v. Flowers, 10 App3d 19, 460 NE2d 280 (1983).

The implied easement is not enforceable against a subsequent bona fide purchaser for value of the servient parcel who has no actual or constructive notice of such easement. Renner v. Johnson, 2 OS2d 195, 207 NE2d 751, 31 OO2d 406 (1965).

An equitable easement is not enforceable against a bona fide purchaser for value who has no actual or constructive notice of the easement. The burden of proof is upon the party claiming the implied easement to establish that such easement was apparent to the party sought to be charged with the knowledge of it. Campbell v. Great Miami Aerie No. 2309, Fraternal Order of Eagles, 15 OS3d 79, 472 NE2d 711 (1984).

383

Further research: O Jur 3d, Easements § 35.

LAW IN GENERAL

Implied easements must be reasonably necessary, permanent and apparent. They are not created unless they can be discovered by a reasonable investigation of the visible facts. The circumstances of the transaction may determine whether an easement is created. If a conveyance is involved, it must comply with the formal requirements for a conveyance of land. Am Law of Prop § 8.31; CJS, Easements § 31; Restatement, Property § 474; Tiffany § 781.

10-12C Particular Applications.

The moving of poles to a strip of ground over which the state has been given an easement for widening or improving the highway, is not an additional burden. Ohio Postal Telegraph-Cable Co. v. Smith, 128 OS 400, 191 NE 698, 40 OLR 649 (1934).

To imply grant of private way in favor of part of tract partitioned, not covered by way, it need be only reasonably necessary to such part. Jones v. Bethel, 20 App. 442, 152 NE 734, 4 Abs 610 (1925).

LAW IN GENERAL

An easement by implication passes to the purchaser when the owner of two parcels conveys the one of them to which a beneficial use of the other is appurtenant; for example, a sale by the common owner of the parcel using a drain, water pipe or driveway located on the other parcel. Encroachment of a building may also create an implied easement. The rules of implied easements are commonly applied to halls, stairways, private sewers and pipes. Am Jur 2d, Easements and Licenses § 27; CJS, Easements § 43.

10-12D Reference to Map or Boundary; Representation.

Where a deed describes a lot by reference to an undedicated plat, the grantor is estopped to deny the right of the grantee to use, for street purposes, the whole street shown. A deed describing land as bounding upon a street conveys the interest of the grantor to the center of the street. Finlaw v. Hunter, 87 App 543, 96 NE2d 319, 43 OO 355 (1949).

Further research: O Jur 3d, Easements § 31.

LAW IN GENERAL

Conveyances referring to streets or ways owned by the grantor as boundaries are sufficient to create easements by implication. Representation by the grantor has been held to estop him from denying the existence of the easement. A deed made with reference to a map always conveys a right to use the streets and ways shown thereon, even though not abutting, for access to the public highway; some of the cases confine the uses to the extent reasonably beneficial to the grantee. 7 ALR2d 607; 45 ALR2d 462; CJS, Easements § 39; Powell §§ 409, 415; Tiffany § 799.

10-12E   Removal of Chattels or Minerals.

License coupled with an interest, see 10-17E.

On abandonment of its right-of-way, the railroad company may remove fixtures as personal property. Wagner v. Cleveland & T. R.R., 22 OS 563 (1872).

In a conveyance severing the estate in the surface from the estate in the underlying minerals, there is an implied grant or reservation of right to access to the estate below. Chartiers Oil Co. v. Curtiss, 14 CC(NS) 593, 24 CD 106 (1911).

LAW IN GENERAL

A grant of minerals or other things on the land creates an implied way for their removal. CJS, Easements § 38; Powell § 410.

10-12F   Prior Severance of Servient Parcel.

See also 1-34A.

Where drain is constructed by the common owner, who makes prior conveyance of servient lot without a reservation of the easement to a grantee with actual notice thereof, the subsequent grantee of the dominant lot has a right to the continued use of the drain, provided the drain is reasonably necessary. Weber v. Miller, 9 CC 674, 4 CD 483, 1 OD 520 (1893).

Further research: CJS, Easements § 34; Tiffany §§ 780, 791.

10-12G   Easements of Necessity.

When the owner of a house equipped with a private underground drain sells the lot upon which the house is located and retains the land upon which the drain is located, the purchaser has an implied easement to the continued use of the drain to its outlet as against the common owner. Blanchet v. Ottawa Hills Co., 63 App. 177, 25 NE2d 861, 16 OO 470 (1939).

Further research: O Jur 3d, Easements § 47.

LAW IN GENERAL

An easement of necessity upon adjoining land of the grantor arises when he sells a parcel to be used for a certain purpose requiring the right. It continues only so long as the necessity exists. Such an easement is created at the time of the original severance, whether the severance is voluntary or involuntary. The creation has been said to be by operation of law, although "implied intent" is the more favored basis. Am Jur 2d, Easements and Licenses § 29; CJS, Easements § 35; Powell § 410; Tiffany § 792.

10-12H   Ways of Necessity.

To warrant the inference of a way reserved by implication, it must be of strict necessity to the remaining land of the grantor; if he has another mode of access to his land, however inconvenient, he cannot claim a way by implication in the lands conveyed. Meredith v. Frank, 56 OS 479, 47 NE 656, 37 WLB 402, 38 WLB 9 (1897); Trattar v. Rausch, 154 OS 286, 95 NE2d 685, 43 OO 186 (1950).

A grantor who conveys land in fee simple to a railroad company for a right-of-way, and does not have access to his remaining land except over said right-of-way, has reserved to himself by operation of law a way of necessity over the land conveyed. Baltimore & O. R.R. v. Gilmore, 19 App 489, 3 Abs 702 (1925).

Ways of necessity cannot exist where there is no unity of ownership of the alleged dominant and servient estate, for no one can have a way of necessity over the land of a stranger. Hillery v. Jackson, 56 NE2d 921, 40 Abs 202 (App. 1931).

LAW IN GENERAL

A way of necessity upon land of the grantor is created by implication in favor of the grantee when access to the land conveyed can be had only across remaining land of the grantor or across land of third persons. Such a right-of-way also arises in favor of the grantor when his remaining land can be reached only through the land of his grantee or third persons. CJS, Easements § 36; Tiffany § 793.

A way of necessity will not be implied if there is another, though very inconvenient, way. The necessity is determined as of the time of the severance of ownership of the parcels. Tiffany § 794.

The acquisition of another right-of-way usually extinguishes a way of necessity. Tiffany § 819.

SECTION 10-13:   PERMISSIBLE USES; OBSTRUCTION

10-13A   Rules.

The owner of the fee may use the property as he sees fit so long as such use does not interfere with the right to use acquired by the owner of the easement. Wolf v. Roberts, 15 O Supp 116, 30 OO 499, 42 Abs 449 (C.P. 1945); Clement v. Fishler, 28 App. 392, 162 NE 706, 5 Abs 663 (1927).

The right of an easement owner to park on an easement depends upon the circumstances of each case, with the gist being that the right is present so long as there is no unreasonable interference with the rights of the servient state. State v. Larason, 143 NE2d 502, 75 Abs 211 (C.P. 1956).

Where a pipeline easement does not specify its dimensions, they shall be determined by what is reasonably necessary and convenient for the purpose for which the easement was granted. Roebuck v. Columbia Gas Transmission Corp., 57 App2d 217, 386 NE2d 1363, 11 OO3d 256 (1977).

Further research: O Jur 3d, Easements § 62.

LAW IN GENERAL

The extent of permissible uses under an easement is such as is reasonable, as determined by consideration of the terms of the conveyance, of the uses which have been made, and of the other circumstances. Am Jur 2d, Easements and Licenses § 72; CJS, Easements §§ 75, 86; Powell § 415; Restatement, Property §§ 477, 482; Tiffany § 802.

The servient owner may make such uses of the land as do not unreasonably interfere with the use authorized by the easement. CJS, Easements §§ 72, 91; Powell § 417; Restatement, Property §§ 481, 486; Tiffany § 811.

The dominant owner will be protected against interference with the use by the servient owner or by third persons. Either owner may maintain an action for damages and, if the remedy at law is inadequate, for injunction. Am Jur 2d, Easements and Licenses § 116; Am Law of Prop § 8.105; CJS, Easements § 103; Powell § 420; Restatement, Property § 511; Tiffany § 814.

No absolute right to park on a driveway easement exists in a joint owner of the easement, in a dominant owner, nor in a servient landowner, but each has a right to park thereon at such times and in such manner as not to interfere with its use by the other. 37 ALR2d 944.

The reasonableness of the use of an easement not expressly limited is the principal test in determining the propriety of both the purpose and the manner of the use. The dominant owner normally has no right under the grant to exclude the grantor or other persons having a like right. 3 ALR3d 1260.

10-13B Changes; Enlargement.

Prescription, see also 2-32B.

Use of an easement may enlarge to meet the use of the land. The easement would pass to each lot owner where a farm is allotted. Erie R.R. v. S. H. Kleinman Realty Co., 92 OS 96, 110 NE 527, 13 OLR 63, 95, 60 WLB 199, 240 (1915). A driveway established by general language may later be used for commercial purposes. Remington v. Fire Proof Warehouse Co., 17 CC(NS) 301, 32 CD 158 (1910).

Unless it appears that the incidental or additional use was hostile or under an adverse claim of right as to the one from whom the easement was obtained in the first place, or his successors in title, no enlargement or extension of the easement can be successfully asserted on the basis of prescription or adverse user. Pierce v. Cherry Valley Farms, 146 OS 400, 66 NE2d 639, 32 OO 448 (1946).

One common owner's expanded use of the private alley by reason of changed conditions and times was not unlawful. Another common owner is enjoined from occasional parking thereon. Mad River Securities v. Felman, 159 OS 512, 112 NE2d 646, 50 OO 429, 37 ALR2d 940 (1953).

Further research: O Jur 3d, Easements § 58.

LAW IN GENERAL

Changes in the use under an appurtenant easement are permitted to the extent that they result from the normal development of the dominant land. The use may not be extended for the benefit of other land. Each of the subsequent owners of separate parts of the dominant land are entitled to use of the easement. New uses of a prescriptive easement, which uses have continued for less than the period of prescription, are permitted when the inference is justified that effective objection would not have been made if the new uses had occurred during the prescriptive period. Am Law of Prop §§ 8.69, 8.74; CJS, Easements § 92; Powell § 418; Restatement, Property §§ 479, 484, 488; Tiffany § 809.

Whether a variation in the use of a prescriptive easement is permissible is usually determined by consideration of the use during the period of prescription, of whether the new use is substantial and material, and of whether the additional use is a change in kind or only a change in degree. 5 ALR3d 439.

A subsequent owner of a part of the dominant tenement generally has the right to use the appurtenant easement, even though his land does not abut upon the right-of-way. However, a number of cases hold that the right-of-way easement will not pass to subsequent owners of parts where the additional use materially burdens the servient estate. 10 ALR3d 960.

10-13C Removal of Obstructions.

Curbing and wheel blocks to delineate parking spaces within an easement constituted a continued trespass and injunction is an appropriate remedy. Goldberger v. Bexley Properties, 5 OS3d 82, 448 NE2d 1380 (1983).

Where a property owner unlawfully obstructs or interferes with the easement rights of an easement holder, the holder of the easement has the authority to remove the obstructions. Rueckel v. Texas Eastern Transmission Corp., 3 App3d 153, 444 NE2d 77 (1981).

LAW IN GENERAL

The dominant owner may remove a wrongful obstruction if he can do so without a breach of the peace. An unjustified obstruction is a private nuisance which the owner of the easement may abate. Notice to the owner of the land is sometimes made a condition precedent to the exercise of this right. Am Jur 2d, Easements and Licenses §§ 92, 122; CJS, Easements § 100; Powell § 420; Tiffany § 816.

10-13D Gates; Fences.

Partition fences, see 3-15B.

R.C. 4959.02 provides that a railroad shall construct and maintain a fence, sufficient to turn stock, along the line of its land. (As eff. 11-3-77.)

The owner of the servient estate may use the land for any purpose that does not interfere with the easement and may erect gates across it unless they would unreasonably interfere with its use. Gibbons v. Ebding, 70 OS 298, 71 NE 720, 2 OLR 73, 49 WLB 297 (1904); Pomeroy v. Buckeye Salt Co., 37 OS 520, 7 WLB 110 (1882).

Further research: O Jur 3d, Easements § 63.

LAW IN GENERAL

As a general rule, gates and fences may be maintained by the landowner if there is no unreasonable interference with the use of the right-of-way under the circumstances. The owner of the easement usually does not have such rights in the absence of express provision unless enclosure is necessary and incidental to enjoyment of the easement. CJS, Easements § 98; Tiffany § 812.

SECTION 10-14: LOCATION

10-14A   Rules.

Where the terms of a grant of a right-of-way are general and indefinite, its location and use by the grantee, acquiesced in by the grantor, will have the same legal effect as if it had been fully described by the terms of the grant. Warner v. Columbus & L. E. R.R., 39 OS 70, 9 WLB 215 (1883); Columbus & E. R.R. v. Williams, 53 OS 268, 41 NE 261, 33 WLB 349, 34 WLB 76 (1895).

The right to locate an easement in the first instance belongs to the owner of the servient estate provided he exercises such right in a reasonable manner. Harper v. Jones, 74 NE2d 397, 35 OO 524, 49 Abs 289 (C.P. 1946).

A grant of a right-of-way on and over a parcel of real estate described by metes and bounds does not necessarily create a right-of-way over all of such parcel but ordinarily creates only the right to a reasonably convenient and suitable way over that parcel. Alban v. R.K. Co., 15 OS2d 229, 239 NE2d 22, 44 OO2d 198 (1968).

Further research: O Jur 3d, Easements § 50; Am Jur 2d, Easements and Licenses § 64; 110 ALR 174; CJS, Easements § 79; Tiffany § 804.

10-14B   Change; Deviation.

Where a way of necessity or implied easement exists and the owner of the dominant estate seeks an injunction, the court may decree that the owner of the servient land may move such right-of-way so long as such new access shall be as reasonably convenient as the old. A. S. D. Securities, Inc. v. J. H. Bellows Co., 48 App 101, 192 NE 472, 1 OO 47, 15 Abs 483 (1933).

Where the location of an easement has been definitely determined by the owners of the dominant and servient estates, it cannot be changed by either owner without the consent of the other owner. Hollosy v. Gershkowitz, 88 App 198, 98 NE2d 314, 44 OO 221 (1950).

Further research: O Jur 3d, Easements § 52.

LAW IN GENERAL

The definite location of the easement upon the land cannot be thereafter changed by either party without the consent of the other party. 80 ALR2d 743; Tiffany § 806.

The owner of a right-of-way has no right to deviate therefrom and go upon the adjoining land when the way becomes impassable, except when obstructed by the owner of the servient estate. CJS, Easements § 85.

SECTION 10-15: REPAIRS AND IMPROVEMENTS

10-15A Rules.

Removal of chattels, see 10-12E.

Unless the owner of the servient estate is bound by covenant or prescription to repair, he is under no obligation to do so. National Exchange Bank v. Cunningham, 46 OS 575, 22 NE 924, 22 WLB 353 (1889).

The burden devolves upon the owner of the dominant estate to make whatever repairs are necessary for his use of the easement. Lagonda Nat. Bank v. Robnett, 147 NE2d 637, 77 Abs 3 (App. 1957).

Further research: O Jur 3d, Easements § 60.

LAW IN GENERAL

In the absence of provisions to the contrary, the owner of the easement has the privilege of repairing and improving the property in a reasonable manner, but neither owner is obliged to make repairs or improvements. However, the owner of the easement may be liable in damages for injury to the land or to third persons resulting from his failure to repair.

Neither the dominant owner nor the servient owner may make material alterations without the consent of the other, even when the change in the servitude is a benefit to the other. When an easement is owned in common, each of the common owners may make reasonable repairs.

Am Jur 2d, Easements and Licenses §§ 85, 87; CJS, Easements § 94; Powell § 415; Restatement, Property §§ 480, 485; Tiffany § 810.

It has been held that the servient owner can repair an easement of way and recover part of the cost from the dominant owner under the terms of the grant or where both owners derived benefits from the use of the road. 20 ALR3d 1026.

SECTION 10-16: EASEMENTS IN GROSS; PROFITS

10-16A Definition and Nature of Easements in Gross.

Assignability and succession, see 10-16E

A right-of-way in gross is a right personal to the grantee, and cannot be made assignable or inheritable by any words in the deed by which it was granted. Where the way is appendant or appurtenant to other lands, very different considerations arise. In such case the right-of-way passes with the dominant estate as an incident thereto. A right-of-way appendant cannot be converted into a way in gross, nor can a way in gross be turned into a way appendant. Boatman v. Lasley, 23 OS 614 (1873).

A television transmission cable is not an additional burden on the land under an easement for the purpose of transmitting electric or other power. Jolliff v. Hardin Cable Television Co., 26 OS2d 103, 269 NE2d 588, 55 OO2d 203 (1971).

Further research: O Jur 3d, Easements § 15.

LAW IN GENERAL

An easement is in gross when the benefit is not incident to the possession of land owned by the owner of the easement, or when the grantor did not intend it to be appurtenant. The use of such easement will be protected as a property right. An easement in gross is real property if its duration is indefinite or measured by a lifetime. If its duration is for a definite period of time, it is a chattel real. Am Law of Prop § 8.9; CJS, Easements § 4; Powell § 405; Restatement, Property §§ 454, 510; Tiffany §§ 758, 760.

10-16B Distinguished From Appurtenant Easements; Contiguity.

A right-of-way that does not terminate on the lot to which it is claimed to be incident is a way in gross, and not a way appendant or appurtenant. Metzger & Co. v. Holwick, 17 CC 605, 6 CD 794, 3 OD 662 (1895), affd. 57 OS 654, 50 NE 1131, 38 WLB 269 (1897).

An easement is presumed to be appurtenant, not in gross. Fostoria Elks Home Co. v. Pelton, 2 Abs 728 (App. 1924).

The circumstances surrounding the grant and the intention of the parties must be examined to ascertain whether an easement is appurtenant or in gross. DeShon v. Parker, 49 App2d 366, 361 NE2d 457, 3 OO3d 430 (1974).

Further research: Am Jur 2d, Easements and Licenses § 13; Tiffany §§ 759, 762.

10-16C Profits.

LAW IN GENERAL

A profit, also known as a profit a prendre, is a right to take the soil or the products thereof from the lands of another. It may be appurtenant to other land or be in gross. CJS, Easements § 3; Tiffany § 839.

Profits are one of the types of easements. The law of easements in gross usually applies as profits are ordinarily in gross, except that a profit in gross is in its nature assignable, devisable and inheritable. Restatement, Property § 450; Tiffany § 842.

The right to take water from the land is usually not regarded as a profit. An oil and gas lease, or any other right to take minerals from the land, is a profit unless an estate in the minerals is granted. Tiffany §§ 841, 846.

10-16D Concurrent Ownership.

LAW IN GENERAL

Although interests similar to estates in land may be created under an easement in gross, the right to divide between concurrent owners is determined by the terms and circumstances of the original creation of the easement. 130 ALR 1253; Restatement, Property §§ 493, 496.

10-16E Transfer.

A pipeline easement for the transportation of gas is assignable. Geffine v. Thompson, 76 App 64, 62 NE2d 590, 31 OO 384, 43 Abs 400 (1945).

An easement to a power company, "its successors, assigns, lessees, and tenants" for transmitting electric power may be sublet to a television cable company. Jolliff v. Hardin Cable Television Co., 26 OS2d 103, 269 NE2d 588, 55 OO2d 203 (1971).

LAW IN GENERAL

Commercial easements in gross are alienable as other interests in land. The assignability or succession of other easements in gross is determined by the terms and circumstances of their creation. The formal requirements for transfer of an easement in gross are the same as for an estate in land. Am Law of Prop § 8.75; Powell § 419; Restatement, Property §§ 489, 494; Tiffany § 761.

SECTION 10-17: LICENSES

10-17A Definition.

Oral permission to run sewer pipes across lots was not irrevocable. "License" is personal, nonassignable, conferred by parol and for purpose of doing certain act on land without conferring rights of possession or interest. Land cannot be permanently encumbered on private oral agreement. St. Michael's Russian Orthodox Greek Catholic Church v. Clark, 37 App 200, 174 NE 607, 8 Abs 573, 33 OLR 345 (1930).

In real property law, license is a permission to do some act or series of acts on the land of licensor, without having any permanent interests in it. Fairbanks v. Power Oil Co., 81 App 116, 77 NE2d 499, 36 OO 418 (1945).

A person who enters the premises of another at his invitation possesses a license to do so, but it is revocable. When the authority to remain is revoked, the continued presence of the licensee on the premises may become a trespass. Mosher v. Cook United, Inc., 62 OS2d 316, 405 NE2d 720, 16 OO3d 361 (1980).

Further research: O Jur 3d, Business and Occupations §§ 32, 33, 35, 36, 38.

LAW IN GENERAL

A license is an authority (other than by easement) granted, either by writing or parol, to a person to do an act on the land of another. It is said to be revocable at the will of the possessor of the land and to be an interest in land consisting of the privilege of limited use of land in the possession of another. Am Law of Prop § 8.111; Restatement, Property § 512; Tiffany § 829.

10-17B Construction and Effectiveness.

A written license is not an encumbrance. A bona fide purchaser may not rescind the contract of purchase for such alleged encumbrance. Wilkins v. Irvine, 33 OS 138, 3 WLB 772 (1877).

Written agreement giving plaintiff right to use driveway on adjoining premises, but not acknowledged, creates merely a license, revocable by the present owner. Kirk v. Conrad, 9 Abs 717 (App. 1931).

An agreement giving only permission to erect, change and remove signs is a license and creates no interest in the land. Although the licensee has been damaged, suit cannot be maintained against the state. Ohio Valley Advertising Corp. v. Linzell, 168 OS 259, 153 NE2d 773, 6 OO2d 420 (1958).

LAW IN GENERAL

A license is construed according to the terms of the authority granted by the landowner. No formalities are required for the grant.

A right which would otherwise be an easement is a license when it lacks one of the formal requirements of an easement or when it can be terminated at the will of the landowner. A right which does not comply with the statute of frauds or other formal requirement may become effective as an easement through application of the principles of part performance or other equitable doctrine.

Am Jur 2d, Easements and Licenses § 123; Am Law of Prop §§ 8.110, 8.115; CJS, Licenses § 79; Powell § 427; Restatement, Property § 514; Tiffany § 830.

10-17C Remedies.

The boundaries of a man's private domain cannot be crossed without permission. In law this permission is called a license. If the permission is lacking, the invasion of the property is a trespass, even though unaccompanied by damage. Lawful license to enter one's premises may be given (1) impliedly by the owner (2) expressly by the owner; (3) by law. Antonik v. Chamberlain, 81 App 465, 78 NE2d 752, 37 OO 305 (1947).

LAW IN GENERAL

A licensee will not be protected against interference with the use by third persons except to the extent he has the right of possession against such persons. A license coupled with an interest, or an expenditure for improvements, may create a limited right of possession. A possessor of land ordinarily has the right to eject trespassers. Am Law of Prop § 8.121; Restatement, Property § 521.

10-17D Assignment.

A license is generally not assignable unless made so expressly. Fairbanks v. Power Oil Co., 81 App 116, 77 NE2d 499, 36 OO 418 (1945).

LAW IN GENERAL

No formalities are required for the assignment. A license coupled with an interest in a chattel, or one appurtenant to other land, can be assigned only in connection with the transfer of such chattel or of such other land. Am Law of Prop § 8.122; Restatement, Property § 517; Tiffany § 832.

10-17E Extinguishment; Coupled with Interest.

Crops, see also Section 7-14.
Fixtures, see also Sections 13-11 and 13-13.
Timber, see also 7-12C.

A parol license is terminated by the death of one party. Fowler v. Delaplain, 79 OS 279, 87 NE 260, 6 OLR 605, 54 WLB 40 (1909).

At the expiration of a license for a term, the action of the licensee in continuing to exercise rights previously granted under a license agreement gives rise to a license at will by implication and does not result in the renewal of the original license for another term. Bewigged by Suzzi, Inc. v. Atlantic Dept. Stores, Inc., 49 App2d 65, 359 NE2d 721, 3 OO3d 125 (1976).

When the licensee has a license coupled with an interest he may remove his property within a reasonable time after the license is revoked. When incidental to a grant of minerals in place or of other things on the land, the license may be irrevocable and be regarded in the nature of an implied easement.

LAW IN GENERAL

A license can be surrendered at the will of the licensee. It can be generally be revoked at the will of the landowner, but he may be liable for damages caused by a wrongful revocation. A license will terminate in accordance with the mutual intention at the time of creation.

When a license coupled with an interest (that is, a license incidental to ownership of a chattel on the land) is revoked, the licensee has a reasonable time to remove his property.

It is usually held that a licensee who has made expenditures in reasonable reliance on a license similar to an easement is entitled, by way of estoppel, to continue the use so as to realize upon his expenditures.

Am Law of Prop §§ 8.114, 8.124; Restatement, Property § 519; Tiffany § 833.

SECTION 10-18: TRANSFER OF APPURTENANT EASEMENTS

10-18A Generally.

An easement annexed to the land passes by a grant of the land without being mentioned in the conveyance. Shields v. Titus, 46 OS 528, 22 NE 717, 22 WLB 299, 342 (1889).

An easement is an interest in real estate and can be conveyed only as is real estate under our statutes. Henson v. Stine, 74 App 221, 57 NE2d 785, 29 OO 342 (1943).

An easement by implication passed by deed without express reference being made therein to appurtenances. Clement v. Fishler, 28 App 392, 162 NE 706, 5 Abs 663 (1927).

The rule that the owner of the dominant estate cannot transfer to the owners of other property any right in the servient estate may not be circumvented by conveying a small portion of the dominant estate to an adjoining landowner. Ricelli v. Atkinson, 99 App 175, 132 NE2d 123, 58 OO 305 (1955).

Further research: O Jur 3d, Easements § 71.

LAW IN GENERAL

An appurtenant easement passes with any transfer of the dominant land unless there are provisions to the contrary in the instrument transferring the dominant land or in the instrument creating the easement. An easement cannot be separated from the land to which it is appurtenant, nor be converted into an easement in gross. Am Jur 2d, Easements and Licenses § 94; Am Law of Prop §§ 8.71, 8.73; CJS, Easements § 45; Powell § 418; Restatement, Property § 487; Tiffany §§ 761, 998.

SECTION 10-19: DURATION AND EXTINGUISHMENT

10-19A Termination of Purpose.

An easement is extinguished when its purpose no longer exists. Waibel v. Schleppi, 77 App 305, 62 NE2d 897, 33 OO 97, 45 Abs 481 (1945).

LAW IN GENERAL

An easement for a certain purpose ceases when the purpose becomes impossible of accomplishment, or when the purpose ceases, as upon the acquisition of land bordering on a highway by the owner of a way of necessity. CJS, Easements § 54; Powell § 422; Tiffany § 817.

10-19B Express Release.

Relinquishment of part of an easement does not require a deed. It seems clear, upon authority, that an easement may be surrendered or relinquished by parol, or may be abandoned. Fremont v. June, 8 CC 124, 4 CD 326, 1 OD 333 (1893).

The above decision may not be followed. The general rule is that the release of an easement requires the same formalities as a transfer of an interest in land. Am Law of Prop § 8.95; CJS, Easements § 61; Powell § 423; Restatement, Property § 500; Tiffany § 424.

10-19C Bona Fide Purchasers.

See also 1-34A.

An easement created by implication is extinguished when there is nothing in the appearance or condition of the servient premises to put the bona fide purchaser on notice. Keyler v. Eustis, 13 NP(NS) 601, 24 OD 555 (1913).

LAW IN GENERAL

An easement is extinguished when the servient land is purchased by a person without actual notice of its existence and there is no record or apparent use of the easement. This rule has been held not to apply to easements of necessity or to easements acquired by prescription. 174 ALR 1241; Powell § 424.

10-19D Merger.

Where there has been a merger by the unity of title to the dominant and servient estates and the owner thereof conveys the dominant estate to another, a former easement does not ordinarily pass unless revived by force of the grant itself or by such words of description as could establish the easement by a new grant. "Together with the appurtenances thereto belonging" will not serve to create an easement or new right. Rex v. Hartman, 16 Abs 573 (App. 1934); Bates v. Sherwood, 5 CC(NS) 63, 14 CD 146 (1902).

After a merger of title of the dominant and servient tenements, any prior easement ceases and is not revived by a subsequent severance of ownership of the two estates. Civilian Defense v. Egan-Ryan Undertaking Co., 153 NE2d 351, 78 Abs 168 (C.P. 1957), affd. 152 NE2d 160, 78 Abs 172 (1958).

Further research: O Jur 3d, Easements § 83.

LAW IN GENERAL

Merger extinguishes an easement when the fee title with right of possession of both tracts vests in one person. An easement is partially extinguished when the dominant owner becomes entitled, as owner of the servient land, to some for the uses authorized by the easement. When the dominant owner acquires part of the area of the servient land, the increased burden on the remaining servient land may be such as to extinguish the entire easement. The terminated rights or interests are not revived by a subsequent severance of the parcels, unless under such circumstances as would create the easements anew. Am Jur 2d, Easements and Licenses § 108; Am Law of Prop § 8.88; CJS, Easements § 57; Powell § 425; Restatement, Property § 499; Tiffany § 822.

10-19E   Abandonment; Misuser.

To constitute an abandonment of a right-of-way there must be nonuser together with an intention to abandon. Schenck v. Cleveland, C. C. & St. L. Ry., 11 App 164, 30 CC(NS) 580, 64 WLB 451 (1919).

Nonuser alone will not divest the right to an easement unless continued for twenty-one years with the defendants claiming adversely. Krieger v. Cassis, 9 Abs 326 (App. 1930).

Further research: O Jur 3d, Easements § 85.

LAW IN GENERAL

Abandonment will extinguish an easement. The abandonment need not extend for the prescriptive period. An easement is terminated by acts respecting the use which show an intention never to make the use again. Am Jur 2d, Easements and Licenses § 104; Am Law of Prop § 8.96; 25 ALR2d 1265; CJS, Easements § 58; Powell § 423; Restatement, Property § 504; Tiffany § 825.

Misuser or nonuser will not effect an extinguishment unless an intention to relinquish is shown by conduct respecting the use, as by erection of a permanent obstruction. Misuser does not cause an extinguishment by waiver or forfeiture. 16 ALR2d 609.

10-19F   Tax Sales.

No easement by prescription is created by use of a pathway for fourteen years before the land was forfeited to the state for nonpayment of taxes. Cookston v. Box, 109 App 531, 160 NE2d 327, 12 OO2d 150 (1959).

10-19G   Destruction or Removal of Buildings.

LAW IN GENERAL

An easement in a structure is generally terminated by the destruction of the structure unless the interest is found to have also attached to the servient soil. The easement does not revive upon rebuilding. In some cases the rule is not applied when a building is voluntarily removed. 154 ALR 82; CJS, Easements § 55; Powell § 422; Tiffany § 820.

10-19H   Adverse Possession.

LAW IN GENERAL

The laws of adverse possession and prescription apply to the extinguishment of easements. Adverse possession, sufficient to extinguish an easement, must be such as to give rise to a cause of action in favor of the dominant owner and be wholly inconsistent with the enjoyment of the use. Am Jur 2d, Easements and Licenses § 110; 25 ALR2d 1265.

10-19I   Other Causes of Termination.

The duration of the easement may be fixed by the terms of the instrument creating it; it may continue in operation forever, or until terminated by completion of the purpose or necessity for which the easement was created, or by a change in the use or character of the property involved. Siferd v. Stambor, 5 App2d 79, 214 NE2d 106, 34 OO2d 189 (1966).

LAW IN GENERAL

An easement may be extinguished by estoppel, prescription, or appropriation under eminent domain. Am Law of Prop § 8.99; CJS, Easements § 62; Powell § 424; Restatement, Property § 504; Tiffany § 826.

CHAPTER 11: ESTATES AND FUTURE INTERESTS

DIVISION 11-1: IN GENERAL

DIVISION 11-2: ESTATES IN FEE SIMPLE ABSOLUTE

SECTION 11-21: GENERALLY
    11-21A Definition and Nature
    11-21B Vesting

DIVISION 11-3: ESTATES IN FEE TAIL

SECTION 11-31: CREATION
    11-31A Definitions
    11-31B Terms of Creation
    11-31C Particular Types of Interests
    11-31D Statute

SECTION 11-32: INCIDENTS OF THE ESTATE
    11-32A Nature
    11-32B Waste
    11-32C Claims of Creditors
    11-32D Transfer
    11-32E Judicial Sales
    11-32F Dower

SECTION 11-33: TERMINATION OF THE ESTATE
    11-33A Reversionary Interests and Remainders
    11-33B Statutes
    11-33C Restraints on Alienation

SECTION 11-34: FEE SIMPLE CONDITIONAL
    11-34A Generally

DIVISION 11-4: ESTATES SUBJECT TO CONDITION SUBSEQUENT; RIGHTS OF REENTRY

SECTION 11-41: NATURE OF THE INTERESTS
    11-41A Definition
    11-41B Discharge of the Condition; Performance Impossible
    11-41C Effect of Unexercised Right
    11-41D Effect of Exercise of Right

SECTION 11-42: TERMS OF CREATION
    11-42A Generally
    11-42B Preferences in Construction
    11-42C Void Conditions

SECTION 11-43: TRANSFER OF RIGHTS OF REENTRY
    11-43A Descent and Devise
    11-43B Conveyances
    11-43C Easements

DIVISION 11-5: ESTATES ON SPECIAL LIMITATION; POSSIBILITIES OF REVERTER

SECTION 11-51: NATURE AND CREATION OF THE INTERESTS
    11-51A Definitions; Nature
    11-51B Prior to Defeasance
    11-51C Dower

SECTION 11-52: TRANSFER OF POSSIBILITIES OF REVERTER
    11-52A Generally

DIVISION 11-1: IN GENERAL

SECTION 11-11: INTRODUCTION; CONSTRUCTION GENERALLY

Construction of deeds generally, see Section 8-31.
Construction of wills generally, see Section 9-21.
Cotenancy and joint ownership, see Chapter 5.
Disentailing sale of fee, see Section 17-42.

11-11A Classification of Possessory Estates.

Estates in possession are commonly classified as estates of freehold and estates less than freehold.

The estates of freehold are (a) estate in fee simple absolute, (b) estate in fee tail, (c) estate in fee simple defeasible, which includes the estate subject to condition subsequent or to special limitation or to any executory limitation, and (d) estate for life. Excepting the estate for life, they are also known as estates of inheritance.

The estates less than freehold are (a) tenancy for years, (b) tenancy from period to period, (c) tenancy at will, and (d) tenancy by sufferance.

Further research: O Jur 3d, Estates § 4.

11-11B Classification of Future Interests.

A future interest has been defined as an existing interest in land or other thing in which the privilege of possession or enjoyment is future and not present.

Future interests may be classified as (a) right of reentry, being the power of terminating an estate subject to condition subsequent, (b) possibility of reverter, being the right of possession upon the termination of an estate on special limitation, (c) reversion, being the interest left in the transferor which is not subject to a condition precedent, (d) vested remainder, including remainder vested indefeasibly, remainder vested subject to open, and remainder vested subject to complete defeasance, and (e) other interests subject to condition precedent, including executory interest and contingent remainder.

> "The conclusions to which this whole discussion has led us are three: First, there may be created in Ohio any future interest in land that may be created at common law and any future interest that may be created by executory limitations, including executory devises and springing and shifting uses. Second, the nonexistence of the Statute of Uses in Ohio has not had the effect of limiting the creation of future interests by deed. Third, the only limitation on the creation of future interests in land in Ohio is . . . our so-called 'statute against perpetuities.'" Charles C. White, "The Ohio Law as to the Creation of Future Interests in Land," 1 Cin. L. R. 136.

Further research: Am Law of Prop § 4.1; Powell § 269; Restatement, Property §§ 153, 157.

11-11C   Vested and Contingent Future Interests.

Construction as to vesting, see Section 11-81.

LAW IN GENERAL

A vested future interest is one with no condition imposed upon the taking effect in possession except the termination of the preceding estate. Any other condition attached to such interest is a condition subsequent, as where the happening of an event may divest the interest. In other words, a future interest is vested if it will become possessory upon the termination of the preceding estate, whenever and however such termination may occur. An interest may be vested even though subject to defeasance. Reversions are vested future interests.

A contingent future interest is one which may become vested or possessory upon the fulfillment of a condition precedent, that is, upon the happening of an event which may never occur or which may occur at a time precluding vesting. Executory interests, rights of reentry, and possibilities of reverter are nonvested interests and usually are contingent.

Remainders may be either vested or contingent, depending on whether the annexed condition is construed as being a condition subsequent or a condition precedent.

Am Law of Prop §§ 4.4, 21.5; Simes and Smith § 65.

11-11D   General Rules of Interpretation.

See also cross-references at beginning of this section.

Term "heirs" in a will will be given its legal and technical meaning where no intention of testator to otherwise use it appears from the will, when interpreted in light of circumstances known at time. Billman v. Billman, 25 App 242, 158 NE 12, 5 Abs 390 (1927).

In the construction of a written trust, like a will, the whole instrument must be considered to ascertain the intention of the settlor. Lloyd v. McDiarmid, 1 O Supp 136, 9 OO 279, 24 Abs 556 (C.P. 1937); Warner & Swasey Co. v. Rusterholz, 41 F Supp 498, 22 OO 114 (1941).

LAW IN GENERAL

Construction is the process of giving precise meaning to language that is not clear and unequivocal. A rule of construction is a guide established to aid in ascertaining the intention of the transferor of a gift or the intention of the parties to other transactions. The intention of the transferor or of the parties determines the effect of a limitation except to the extent that such effect is modified or nullified by a positive rule of law, such as the rule against perpetuities.

Between possible constructions, that one will be preferred which is legally more effective. The public interest and the necessity of establishing a rule may be considered. Other general rules which are said to amount to presumptions are: a vested interest is preferred over a contingent interest; a testator is presumed to intend to dispose of all his estate without partial intestacy; preferences are recognized for keeping property among blood relatives and against disinheriting an heir; and the technical meaning of technical words is favored. The earlier clause of a deed or the later clause of a will is usually effective when the conflict is irreconcilable. An instrument may be so indefinite and uncertain as to be wholly or partially ineffective. The tendency of the law is toward interpreting instruments as a whole, rather than to stress one provision which is inconsistent with another provision.

Am Law of Prop § 21.3; Powell § 315; Restatement, Property § 214; Simes and Smith § 461.

11-11E   Arbitration.

R.C. 2711.01 provides: "A provision in any written contract, except as hereinafter provided, to settle by arbitration a controversy thereafter arising out of such contract, or out of the refusal to perform the whole or any part thereof, or any agreement in writing between two or more persons to submit to arbitration any controversy existing between them at the time of the agreement to submit, or thereafter arising, from a relationship then existing between them or which they simultaneously create shall be valid, irrevocable, and enforceable, save upon such grounds as exist at law or in equity for the revocation of any contract.

"Sections 2711.01 to 2711.15, inclusive, of the Revised Code shall not apply to controversies involving the title to or the possession of real estate, with the following exceptions:

"(A) Controversies involving the amount of increased or decreased valuation of the property at the termination of certain periods, as provided in a lease;

"(B) Controversies involving the amount of rentals due under any lease;

"(C) Controversies involving the determination of the value of improvements at the termination of any lease;

"(D) Controversies involving the appraisal of property values in connection with making or renewing any lease;

"(E) Controversies involving the boundaries of real estate." (As eff. 7-28-75.)

Defendant could not be compelled to arbitrate, except by order of the court. After submitting his answer and counterclaim to the arbitrator, he is estopped to deny the arbitrability of the dispute. Rosser v. Hochwalt, 12 App2d 129, 231 NE2d 334, 41 OO2d 196 (1967).

SECTION 11-12: WORDS OF INHERITANCE

11-12A Rule.

R.C. 5301.02 provides: "The use of terms of inheritance or succession are not necessary to create a fee simple estate, and every grant, conveyance, or mortgage of lands, tenements, or hereditaments shall convey or mortgage the entire interest which the grantor could lawfully grant, convey, or mortgage, unless it clearly appears by the deed, mortgage, or instrument that the grantor intended to convey or mortgage a less estate." (As eff. 10-1-53.)

A deed effective prior to June 13, 1925, without words of inheritance, passed only a life estate to the grantee. Ford v. Johnson, 41 OS 366, 11 WLB 168, 13 WLB 257 (1884); Embleton v. McMechen, 110 OS 18, 143 NE 177, 2 Abs 244, 22 OLR 29, 34 ALR 689 (1924).

Deed, given before passage of statute abrogating rule that "heirs" or other appropriate words of perpetuity are essential to pass fee simple title, held subject to such rule. The rule was subject to exceptions that words of perpetuity were unnecessary in a deed to a corporation aggregate, and that a deed to trustees without words of perpetuity conveyed title commensurate with the trust. Such words were not required in a special limitation. Schurch v. Harraman, 47 App 383, 191 NE 907, 15 Abs 581, 40 OLR 303 (1933).

11-12B Wills.

R.C. 2107.51 provides: "Every devise of lands, tenements, or hereditaments in a will shall convey all the estate of the devisor therein, unless it clearly appears by the will that the devisor intended to convey a less estate." (As eff. 10-1-53.)

11-12C Reservations; Exceptions.

Words of inheritance or perpetuity are essential to the effectiveness of a reservation to the grantor under a conveyance made before June 13, 1925. First New Jerusalem Church v. Singer, 68 App. 119, 34 NE2d 1007, 22 OO 217, 33 Abs 518 (1941).

Such words were never necessary for effective exceptions.

SECTION 11-13: RULE IN SHELLEY'S CASE

11-13A Generally.

R.C. 2107.49 provides: "When lands, tenements, or hereditaments are given by deed or will to a person for his life, and after his death to his heirs in fee, the conveyance shall vest an estate for life only in such first taker and a remainder in fee simple in his heirs. If the remainder is given to the heirs of the body of the life tenant, the conveyance shall vest an estate for life only in such first taker and a remainder in fee simple in the heirs of his body. The rule in Shelley's case is abolished by this section and shall not be given effect."

(As eff. 10-1-53.) The rule has not been effective as to wills since the year 1840.

Equitable estates will merge into an equitable fee simple in the first cestui que trust. Armstrong v. Zane, 12 Ohio 287 (1843).

As to instruments effective before the rule in Shelley's Case was abrogated, a deed or devise to A for life and then mediately or immediately to go to his heirs, A took an estate in fee simple. Brockschmidt v. Archer, 64 OS 502, 60 NE 623, 45 WLB 319, 46 WLB 4 (1901).

Further research: Modern status of the Rule in Shelley's Case, 99 ALR2d 1161.

LAW IN GENERAL

Under the rule, where a particular estate of freehold (usually a life estate) is conveyed or devised to a person with an estate in remainder to his heirs or to the heirs of his body, such person also takes the remainder in fee simple or fee tail. The rule operates to give the ancestor a fee simple or fee tail estate in such case.

The rule does not apply when a third estate intervenes between the life estate, or other particular estate, and the remainder; however, the heirs may be divested of the remainder if the requirements of the rule are met after the effective date of the instrument.

In order to come within the rule, both estates must be legal or both equitable; and, one estate being a remainder, both must be created by the same conveyance or devise.

The rule is a rule of law and not of construction, that is, it operates without regard to the intention of the grantor or testator. However, problems of construction do arise, such as the meaning of the words "children," or "heirs" in a will. This rule is distinct from the requirement of words of inheritance and from the rules concerning conveyances to the heirs of the grantor, known as the doctrine of worthier title.

Where the rule has been abolished by statute, "heirs" may be a word of purchase instead of a word of limitation, that is, then an intention that the heirs take as purchasers may be effective.

Am Law of Prop §§ 4.40, 21.40; Powell § 378; Restatement, Property § 312; Simes and Smith § 1541; Tiffany § 342.

SECTION 11-14: EXPECTANCIES

Conveyance, see 8-34H.

11-14A Definition.

LAW IN GENERAL

An expectancy is the interest which a person is likely to receive as heir or devisee on the death of another. It is neither an estate nor a future interest. The expectancy is extinguished by the death of such person before the death of the prospective testator or ancestor. CJS, Descent, etc. § 61; Simes and Smith §§ 2, 391.

11-14B Transfer; Claims of Creditors.

Estoppel by deed, see Section 8-34.

An assignment by an heir apparent of his expectancy in the estate of an ancestor is invalid and unenforceable in an action at law. After the death of the ancestor a court of equity will entertain jurisdiction of a suit to enforce specific performance of the contract. Hite v. Hite, 120 OS 253, 166 NE 193, 7 Abs 159, 28 OLR 514 (1929); Needles v. Needles, 7 OS 432 (1857); Hart v. Gregg, 32 OS 502, 3 WLB 281 (1877).

LAW IN GENERAL

By the weight of authority, the owner of an expectancy has the power to relinquish or transfer his interest for a fair consideration. An assignment of an expectancy fails when the assignor predeceases the ancestor. However, the release of an expectancy to the ancestor is usually binding upon the children of the releasing child if the ancestor is survived by another child. Creditors of the owner of an expectancy can subject the interest to their claims only if they are assignees for a fair consideration. Creditors of a transferee of an expectancy can subject the interest to their claims. Am Law of Prop § 14.12; CJS, Descent, etc. § 62; Powell § 382; Restatement, Property § 315; Simes and Smith § 394.

11-14C After-acquired Title.

A clause in a deed, releasing son's expectancy of inheritance from his mother, is invalid and does not operate to confer title, by estoppel or otherwise, upon the other heirs of the mother. Ferenbaugh v. Ferenbaugh, 104 OS 556, 136 NE 213, 20 OLR 82 (1922).

11-14D Bankruptcy.

All property which vests in a bankrupt within 180 days after bankruptcy by bequest, devise or inheritance passes to the trustee in bankruptcy. 11 U.S.C. § 541(a)(5)(A). See 17-3.

SECTION 11-15: MERGER

11-15A Generally.

Merger is the absorption of one estate in another, and takes place usually when a greater and a less estate coincide and meet in one and the same person without any intermediate estate, whereby the less is immediately merged or absorbed in the greater. To constitute a merger it is necessary that the two estates be in one and the same person, at one and the same time, and in one and the same right. Piper v. Lucey, 21 Abs 661 (App. 1936).

Equity will interpose to prevent a merger of an equitable and legal estate in order to work substantial justice. Waitman v. Emmons, 76 App 212, 61 NE2d 912, 31 OO 502, 43 Abs 121 (1945).

Further research: O Jur 3d, Estates § 136.

LAW IN GENERAL

Merger is the absorption of one estate in another when a greater and a less estate meet in the same person in the same right without any intermediate estate. Equitable principles are generally applied and merger prevented when it would be contrary to the intention of the parties or when injustice would result. Am Jur 2d, Estates § 286; CJS, Estates § 123.

11-15B   Fee Tail.

LAW IN GENERAL

The doctrine of merger does not apply so as to merge a fee tail and a fee simple. Tiffany § 47.

11-15C   Life Estates.

Drawing upon the testatrix's intention and substantial justice, the equitable life estate of her niece does not merge into the vested remainder which passed to the niece under the antilapse statute. Day v. Brooks, 10 Misc 273, 224 NE2d 557, 39 OO2d 441 (Prob. 1967).

LAW IN GENERAL

An estate for years will merge in an estate for life, and an estate for life will merge in a fee simple, when the two estates come into the same ownership. The rule is not applied when the estates are held in different rights, as when one is held in a fiduciary capacity. Merger will not occur if another estate intervenes between the particular estate and the reversion or remainder meeting in the same person. It will take place as to part of a parcel and as to an undivided interest. Tiffany § 70.

SECTION 11-16: FAILURE AND ACCELERATION OF INTERESTS

Illegal conditions, see 11-81O.

11-16A   Destructibility of Interests; Failure of Preceding Interests.

R.C. 2131.05 provides: "A remainder valid in its creation shall not be defeated by the determination of the precedent estate before the happening of the contingency on which the remainder was limited to take effect. Should such contingency afterwards happen, the remainder shall take effect in the same manner and to the same extent as if the precedent estate had continued to the same period." (As eff. 10-1-53.)

R.C. 2131.06 provides: "An expectant estate cannot be defeated or barred by any transfer or other act of the owner of the intermediate or precedent estate, nor by any destruction of such precedent estate by disseizen, forfeiture, surrender, merger, or otherwise; but an expectant estate may be defeated in any manner which the party creating such estate, in the creation thereof, has provided for or authorized. An expectant estate thus liable to be defeated shall not, on that ground, be adjudged void in its creation." (As eff. 10-1-53.)

Where a limitation, carved out of an estate by will prior to the statute, and falling within the denomination of a contingent remainder, has been defeated as a remainder by the lapse, or other failure, of the preceding estate, it may by construction, be allowed to take effect as an executory devise, in order to effectuate the intention of the testator. Thompson v. Hoop, 6 OS 480 (1856).

Further research: O Jur 3d, Estates § 136.

LAW IN GENERAL

At common law, a contingent remainder becomes invalid when it does not vest at or before the termination of a vested preceding freehold estate. This doctrine of destructibility by forfeiture or other premature termination of the preceding estate has been abrogated in most states.

An executory interest or a contingent remainder, which is subject to the contingency at the termination of the prior estate, generally continues in existence awaiting the fulfillment of the condition. However, the testator's intention may be construed to effect an immediate vesting of a remainder, which is contingent by its terms, when the prior estate terminates prematurely.

Am Jur 2d, Estates § 321; Am Law of Prop §§ 4.38, 4.59; CJS, Estates §§ 77, 91; Powell § 314; Restatement, Property § 229; Simes and Smith §§ 209, 795; Tiffany §§ 199, 386.

11-16B Failure of Succeeding Interests.

LAW IN GENERAL

The preceding interest is presumed to become indefeasible when the divesting interest is ineffective. A fee simple absolute is created when the limitation provides a fee on condition subsequent to be succeeded by an interest subject to a condition precedent and such succeeding interest is invalid at creation, unless a contrary intention is expressed by the grantor or testator. However, if the first fee is on special limitation it ends automatically at the happening of the event whether or not the gift over is valid. The failure, subsequent to creation, of an executory interest renders the preceding estate indefeasible, unless the conveyance or will otherwise provides. Am Law of Prop §§ 2.10, 2.47; Powell § 306; Restatement, Property § 229; Simes and Smith § 821; Tiffany §§ 199, 386.

11-16C   Acceleration; Sequestration.

The doctrine of acceleration rests upon the presumed intention of the testator and will be applied only when promotive of that intention. Stevens v. Stevens, 121 OS 490, 169 NE 570, 8 Abs 31, 30 OLR 598 (1929).

The widow's election to take under the law is equivalent to her death in acceleration of the enjoyment of the remainder. Davidson v. Miners & Mechanics Savings & Trust Co., 129 OS 418, 195 NE 845, 2 OO 404, 98 ALR 1318 (1935); Crabbe v. Lingo, 146 OS 489, 67 NE2d 1, 32 OO 561 (1946). See also R.C. 2107.39 at 9-27A.

The doctrine of acceleration of remainders will not be applied so as to defeat the testator's intention that the remaindermen in order to take must survive the life beneficiary where he renounces his interest. Ohio Nat. Bank of Columbus v. Adair, 54 OS2d 26, 374 NE2d 415, 8 OO3d 15 (1978).

Where remainder interests are accelerated by the renunciation of a life interest the rights of all subsequent beneficiaries are determined as though the life tenant had died at the time of renunciation. Central Nat. Bank of Cleveland v. Eells, 5 Misc 187, 215 NE2d 77, 33 OO2d 418 (Prob. 1965).

Further research: O Jur 3d, Estates § 116.

LAW IN GENERAL

Whether a succeeding interest will be accelerated to take effect and vest in possession upon the failure of the preceding interest is controlled by the intention of the grantor or testator. A prior interest may fail because of renunciation, merger, forfeiture or illegality. An interest is ordinarily accelerated when an earlier interest is invalid because in violation of a rule of law, such as the rule against perpetuities. Am Jur 2d, Estates § 305; Powell § 307; Restatement, Property § 230.

When an interest fails before the time contemplated by the testator, the succeeding interest is normally accelerated; such succeeding interest takes effect at once if it is an indefeasibly vested remainder; and a defeasible succeeding interest becomes indefeasible (usually including loss of its ability to open for new members of the class), unless contrary to the intention of the testator. A contingent remainder or other interest subject to a condition precedent is not accelerated unless it can be said that the testator intended a vesting in such case. The doctrine of acceleration will not be applied when it would work an injustice, but in such case the gift will be sequestered. Am Jur 2d, Estates § 311; CJS, Estates § 82; Powell § 308; Restatement, Property § 237; Tiffany §§ 337, 385.

When a devisee renounces an interest it will be sequestered and actual enjoyment or distribution will be postponed if such procedure would be equitable and would promote the testator's intention. However, the renunciation may change the testator's plan to such an extent that the entire disposition will be held ineffective. Am Jur 2d, Estates § 314; Am Law of Prop § 21.43; 36 ALR2d 291; Powell § 309; Restatement, Property § 231; Simes and Smith § 802; Tiffany § 339.

SECTION 11-17: RIGHTS ABOVE THE SURFACE; AVIATION

11-17A   Rule.

See also Division 3-1.

A cornice extending beyond the party wall and over the lot of an adjoining proprietor is a violation of the latter's property rights. Young v. Thedieck, 8 App 103, 28 CC(NS) 239, 29 CD 461 (1918).

LAW IN GENERAL

An old maxim of the law is that "he who owns the soil owns to the sky." A projection or suspension of tree branches, eaves, wires, etc. is a trespass or a nuisance and may be enjoined. Am Law of Prop § 28.4; Tiffany § 583.

11-17B   Aviation.

In order to warrant injunctive relief, it must be clearly established that a nuisance or appropriation must inevitably result from the construction and operation of the privately owned airport. Antonik v. Chamberlain, 81 App 465, 78 NE2d 752, 37 OO 305 (1947).

There exists a "taking" of private property for public use whenever air flights are so low and so frequent as to be a direct and immediate interference with enjoyment and use of the land. State ex rel. Royal v. Columbus, 3 OS2d 154, 209 NE2d 405, 32 OO2d 147 (1965). A four to three decision.

The city is the owner and lessor of the airport and must institute appropriation proceedings to determine compensation from frequent and low-level flights. State ex rel. Bower v. City of Columbus, 27 OS2d 7, 271 NE2d 860, 56 OO2d 4 (1971).

LAW IN GENERAL

The rule is much modified in recent law on account of the common flight of airplanes. It is held that the right of flight exists if exercised in a reasonable manner and in compliance with federal and state regulations. Where the manner of flight is found to be unjustifiable, it is held to be either a nuisance or a trespass. The modern tendency of the law is that the exclusive right of possession by the landowner of the airspace above is limited to purposes incident to the use and enjoyment of the surface, and that aviation rights do not prevent uses by the landowner for such purposes. Am Jur 2d, Aviation § 3; 25 ALR2d 1454; Tiffany § 584.

11-17C   Subjacent Support.

Condominium, see 5-24D.

LAW IN GENERAL

An estate in fee simple may exist in the upper floors only of a building. The owner has an easement for subjacent support. Tiffany § 626.

SECTION 11-18: REMEDIES OF AND AGAINST OWNERS OF FUTURE INTERESTS

Disentailing sale and investment, see Section 17-42.
Marketable Title Act, see Section 1-44.
Representation in judicial proceedings, see Section 17-22.

11-18A Claims of Creditors of Owners.

Where the owner of a defeasible fee made permanent improvements, and mortgaged his interest in the real estate; held that, after the defeasance, neither the land nor the improvements could be subjected, under the mortgage, to the payment of the mortgage debt. Taylor v. Foster, 22 OS 255 (1871).

A devise to one if he survives his mother is only a contingent estate, not subject to claims of the devisee's creditors. Crum v. Crum, 65 App 431, 30 NE2d 448, 19 OO 40, 31 Abs 397 (1940).

LAW IN GENERAL

Any future interest which the debtor has the power to transfer by conveyance inter vivos can be subjected to the claims of creditors by execution, creditor's bill, attachment or like procedures, except where limited by statute such as the Ohio statute referred to above. The right to sell may be denied when the interest is so uncertain that it cannot be fairly appraised. In an equity proceeding the sale may be postponed until the interest becomes possessory in order to prevent injustice to the debtor. A future interest can be subjected to the claims of creditors of the deceased owner if it could have been subjected during his lifetime by a judgment creditor, or if the interest became fully alienable by conveyance inter vivos on the death of the owner. Am Law of Prop § 4.78; Powell § 285; Restatement, Property § 166; Simes and Smith § 1921.

11-18B Remedies of Owners.

Actions against owners of right of present possession, see Section 11-19.

LAW IN GENERAL

An owner of a future interest may obtain relief against third persons by way of damages, quieting title, injunction or other equitable relief. Damages may be refused or sequestered when the interest is so uncertain that the amount of recovery cannot be fairly estimated. Am Law of Prop § 4.107; Powell § 297; Restatement, Property § 211; Simes and Smith § 1654.

11-18C Limitation of Actions.

Adverse possession, see Section 2-24.
Limitation of actions generally, see Division 16-4.

LAW IN GENERAL

The running of a statute of limitations is governed by the general principle that the period does not commence against the owner of a future interest until the interest becomes possessory. The rule as to the time of commencement generally applies to actions by the owner of a future interest against the holder of the possessory estate, at least if such owner did not have notice. Breach of a condition subsequent does not begin the period against the owner of a right of reentry until he elects to forfeit, although the right may be otherwise barred for failure to exercise it within a reasonable time. A statute of limitations ordinarily does not run against assertion of a future interest unless it commenced to run before the creation of such interest.

The statute does not run against actions to quiet title or in ejectment by the future interest holder. The period for recovery of damages begins to run against the owner of an indefeasibly vested remainder or reversion from the commission of the injury if he knew or should have known of the injury and could then have recovered damages. The period of prescription for an easement begins to run at the time the owner of the future interest has notice and also has a right to injunction or damages. When the statute runs against a trustee, it also normally runs against the beneficiaries of the trust.

Am Law of Prop § 4.113; 19 ALR2d 729; CJS, Estates § 97; Powell § 300; Restatement, Property § 222; Simes and Smith §§ 1667, 1964.

11-18D Declaratory Judgments.

See also Section 16-61.

LAW IN GENERAL

A proceeding for declaratory judgment is available for relief respecting future interests, subject to the discretion of the court under the particular circumstances. 174 ALR 880.

SECTION 11-19: WASTE

Meliorating waste or alteration, see 11-64A.

11-19A Definition and Nature.

The common-law rule as to waste does not prevail in Ohio. The question whether waste has been committed is to be determined largely in view of the particular facts in each case. Mohler v. Mohler, 23 Abs 138 (App. 1936). Further research: O Jur 2d, Waste § 3.

LAW IN GENERAL

Waste is any act by a holder of a limited interest in land, usually a tenant for life or for years, which diminishes the value of the premises to the damage of the reversioner or remainderman. Whether a particular act constitutes waste is said to depend upon the express or implied intention at the time of creating the interests. Trivial damage, or changing meadow to cultivated land, etc., is not waste. Customs of the community are considered in determining whether certain acts are waste. The obligations of the tenant may be modified by the terms of the creation of the estate, by an exercise of the police power, and by acts necessary for the preservation of the property. Am Law of Prop § 20.1; CJS, Estates §§ 43, 59; Powell § 636; Restatement, Property §§ 138, 141, 145; Tiffany § 630.

11-19B Permissive Waste; Voluntary Waste.

Life tenant is not required to reconstruct buildings destroyed by fire through no fault of the life tenant. Mohler v. Mohler, 23 Abs 138 (App. 1936).

Generally, it is the duty of the life tenant to make such repairs as are necessary to preserve the property, prevent waste, and where there is deterioration or decay, to restore the property to its original condition. Zywiczynski v. Zywiczynski, 82 App 96, 80 NE2d 807, 37 OO 397 (1947).

Further research: O Jur 2d, Waste § 12.

LAW IN GENERAL

Permissive waste is the damage to the remainderman or reversioner resulting from the tenant's failure to protect the premises, usually from the elements. Voluntary waste ordinarily involves some affirmative action.

In this country the tenant for life is liable for permissive waste and is required to keep the premises in a reasonable state of repair to the extent that issues and profits are available. He must make ordinary repairs but is not liable for damages caused by a stranger, by accident, or by extraordinary force of nature. Am Jur 2d, Life Tenants and Remaindermen § 259; Am Law of Prop §§ 2.18, 20.12; Restatement, Property §§ 139, 146; Simes and Smith § 1654; Tiffany § 640.

11-19C Estovers.

See also 11-19H.

LAW IN GENERAL

Estovers are the wood to which a tenant for life or for years is reasonably entitled for fuel used by himself and his servants, for fences, for agricultural structures, and for necessary improvements and repairs. Timber cut in improving the land belongs to the life tenant. Am Jur 2d, Life Tenants and Remaindermen § 136; Am Law of Prop § 20.4; 51 ALR2d 1374; Restatement, Property § 143; Tiffany § 635.

11-19D Ownership after Severance.

LAW IN GENERAL

Anything severed by waste belongs to the reversioner or remainderman, while the life tenant is the owner if severed lawfully. Tiffany § 650.

11-19E   Cotenancy.

See also Section 5-16.

LAW IN GENERAL

A cotenant is generally liable to the others under the rules as to waste except that injunction is commonly refused. In suits between cotenants, consideration is given to whether or not accounting can be compelled. Powell § 677; Tiffany § 651.

11-19F   Leaseholds; Mortgages; Contracts for Sale.

The law of waste generally is applied to estates less than freehold.

A mortgagee is entitled to protection against waste, at least when his security is impaired.

Each of the parties to a contract for sale is liable for waste injuring the other.

11-19G   Minerals, Oil and Gas.

The life tenant is entitled to the entire income from mines which were in operation at the testator's death. Brooks v. Hanna, 19 CC 216, 10 CD 480 (1899).

One acquiring a life estate in land before commencement of mining operations cannot operate for oil without committing enjoinable waste. Fourth & Central Trust Co. v. Woolley, 31 App 259, 165 NE 742, 28 OLR 497 (1928).

Further research: O Jur 2d, Waste § 11.

LAW IN GENERAL

The life tenant may not take minerals or earth from the land except to work mines and wells which were opened, but not entirely abandoned, before the tenancy commenced. He is entitled, under the same conditions, to the rents and royalties, not merely to the interest thereon. The beneficiaries of a trust are likewise entitled to the proceeds of minerals, oil or gas taken from mines previously opened. Am Jur 2d, Life Tenants and Remaindermen §§ 149-152; Am Law of Prop §§ 10.18, 20.6; 18 ALR2d 98; CJS, Waste § 8; Restatement, Property § 144; Tiffany § 633.

11-19H   Trees; Timber.

See also estovers, 11-19C.

Timber cut in improving the land belongs to the tenant for life, and not to the reversioner. Crockett v. Crockett, 2 OS 180 (1853).

Further research: O Jur 2d, Waste § 10.

LAW IN GENERAL

Cutting of trees to the extent of a reasonable use is held not to be waste. The test of good husbandry at the time of the use is commonly applied. The cutting of fruit trees or of trees for sale of the timber is usually waste. A life tenant may continue the cutting and sale of timber commenced before the creation of his estate. Am Law of Prop § 20.2; CJS, Waste § 9; Restatement, Property § 144; Tiffany § 634.

11-19I Other Acts Constituting Waste.

Removal by life tenant, see 11-64B.

The strict doctrine of the common law in regard to waste has never obtained in Ohio; hence, it is well settled that many things may be done by a tenant for life here, that if done in England would be waste; as, for example, the conversion of meadow into plowland, or woodland into farm. Crockett v. Crockett, 2 OS 180 (1853).

LAW IN GENERAL

Removal by the tenant of fixtures which have become part of the realty is waste. Hazardous activity, bad husbandry and other misuses by tenants have been held to be waste. Am Law of Prop § 20.7; CJS, Waste § 2.

11-19J Remedies.

R.C. 2103.07 provides: "A tenant in dower in real property who commits or suffers waste thereto will forfeit that part of the property to which such waste is committed or suffered to the person having the immediate estate in reversion or remainder and will be liable in damages to such person for the waste committed or suffered thereto." (As eff. 10-1-53.)

R.C. 2105.20 provides: "A tenant for life in real property who commits or suffers waste thereto shall forfeit that part of the property, to which such waste is committed or suffered, to the person having the immediate estate in reversion or remainder and such tenant will be liable in damages to such person for the waste committed or suffered thereto." (As eff. 10-1-53.)

The measure of damages for waste by a life tenant is the diminished value of the estate in remainder by reason of such waste. Kent v. Bentley, 10 CC 132, 6 CD 457, 3 OD 173 (1895).

The right to damages accrues at the time the waste is committed or suffered, and the right of action in favor of a remainderman is barred four years thereafter. Reams v. Henney, 88 App 409, 97 NE2d 37, 44 OO 196, 58 Abs 507 (1950).

Further research: O Jur 2d, Waste § 13.

LAW IN GENERAL

An action for damages or injunction, or both, is ordinarily available to the owner of a future interest. When the remainder is contingent or subject to a condition subsequent the owner thereof may not be entitled to damages but may be entitled to an injunction against unreasonable destruction. A tenant expressly not liable for waste may be likewise enjoined from unreasonable destruction. A tenant in fee tail will not be so restrained if he can cut off the future interest by a conveyance. Relief against the owner of a fee simple absolute by way of injunction against further waste, without award of damages, is granted to lien holders by the modern cases. Am Law of Prop §§ 4.101, 20.14; 144 ALR 769; CJS, Waste § 13; Powell § 641; Restatement, Property § 188; Simes and Smith § 1660; Tiffany §§ 631, 645, 649.

The damages recoverable by a landlord from his tenant are generally measured by the diminution in the value of the leased premises resulting from the waste. The cost of repairing the property or the value of the things removed or destroyed is frequently the measure in particular circumstances. 82 ALR2d 1106.

DIVISION 11-2: ESTATES IN FEE SIMPLE ABSOLUTE

SECTION 11-21: GENERALLY

11-21A Definition and Nature.

An estate in fee simple is the full and absolute estate in all that can be granted. Darling v. Hippel, 12 CD 754 (1897).
Further research: O Jur 3d, Estates § 5.

LAW IN GENERAL

A fee simple absolute is the largest estate in land known to the law. It is an estate having a potentially infinite duration and which is not limited to lineal heirs. The term "fee simple" is commonly used interchangeably with "fee simple absolute," although a fee simple may be defeasible or be subject to a special limitation, a condition subsequent or an executory limitation. A fee simple is characterized by freedom of alienation and of use by the tenant, although the use may not be such as to constitute a nuisance. Am Jur 2d, Estates §§ 9, 22; Powell § 179; Restatement, Property § 14; Tiffany §§ 27, 33.

11-21B Vesting.

Location of fee, see also 11-81L.

It is settled law by a host of authorities that the fee never stands in abeyance. It must and always does rest in someone. Maier v. Wyandt, 78 App 33, 69 NE2d 70, 33 OO 394 (1945).

LAW IN GENERAL

Only one estate in fee simple can exist in particular land. Some authorities say it may be only potentially existing, that is, it may be in abeyance. The question whether that is true is usually academic. The state of abeyance is odious in the law and the fee simple will be construed to be vested, if possible, even though subject to being divested. Am Jur 2d, Estates § 10.

DIVISION 11-3: ESTATES IN FEE TAIL

SECTION 11-31: CREATION

Definite and indefinite failure of issue, see 11-82F.

11-31A   Definitions.

Where lands are conveyed "to A, the heirs of his body, and assigns forever," the grantee takes a fee tail. By statute, the issue of A takes a fee simple. Pollock v. Speidel, 17 OS 439 (1867).

The statute to restrict entailment does not change the nature of the estate of the first donee in tail from an inheritable estate to an estate for life merely. Harkness v. Corning, 24 OS 416 (1873).

Further research: O Jur 3d, Estates § 27.

LAW IN GENERAL

A fee tail or estate tail is an estate of inheritance, the succession to which is confined to the heirs of the body of the owner. An estate tail general is created where the limitation is to a person and the heirs of his body generally. An estate tail special is limited to heirs of the body by a certain marriage. In an estate tail male or an estate tail female, devolution is restricted to the indicated sex even to remote heirs. CJS, Estates §§ 21, 23; Restatement, Property § 59; Tiffany § 36.

11-31B   Terms of Creation.

Where the devise is to S "and her issue and their heirs," held that S took an estate in fee tail. Harkness v. Corning, 24 OS 416 (1873).

Will providing for distribution after death of life tenants to their bodily heirs in fee simple held not to create an estate tail, in that words in fee simple are inconsistent with usual form of limitation in estate tail to bodily heirs. Pollock v. Brayton, 28 App 172, 162 NE 608, 6 Abs 616 (1924); McCrea v. McCrea, 5 App 351, 22 CC(NS) 433, 29 CD 623 (1915).

Where grantor conveyed certain premises to his wife for life, and to his son and to the heirs of his body, upon her death the son has an estate in fee tail therein. Miller v. Miller, 83 NE2d 254, 41 OO 233, 52 Abs 121 (C.P. 1948).

Further research: O Jur 3d, Estates § 28.

LAW IN GENERAL

Use of the term "heirs" is necessary in a deed creating an estate tail. The usual words "of his body" are not essential, even in a deed, if lineal descen-

419

dants are sufficiently indicated. However, a deed to a person "and his children" or "and his issue" does not create an estate tail. Tiffany §§ 38, 40, 42.

A devise to a person "and his children" is presumed to give the children interests as cotenants or as remaindermen, unless the will otherwise indicates. However, under the "rule in Wild's Case," the named devisee takes an estate tail if he has no children. Am Jur 2d, Estates §§ 281, 291, 292.

A devise to a person "and his issue" creates an estate tail unless a contrary intention is expressed. Use of "heirs" or other technical words are not necessary in a will. Tiffany § 340.

An estate tail may be created by a transfer to the first taker for life and remainder to the heirs of his body under the rule in Shelley's Case. Such estate may be created by a transfer in fee simple (or by a conveyance for life where the rule in Shelley's Case does not apply) with a gift over on indefinite failure of issue of the named grantee. Words of limitation will not be construed as creating a fee tail if the language is ambiguous or susceptible to construction. Am Jur 2d, Estates §§ 49, 50; Am Law of Prop § 2.14; Powell §§ 194, 197; Restatement, Property § 60; Tiffany § 44.

11-31C   Particular Types of Interests.

Estates tail are either general or special, depending on whether the limitation is to the donee and the heirs of his body generally or is restricted to certain heirs of his body, as for example, heirs of his body begotten of a certain wife. Dix v. Benzler, 32 Abs 599 (App. 1940).

LAW IN GENERAL

A fee tail may exist in an equitable interest or in a future interest, and the estate may be concurrently held by two or more persons. Terms for years and personal chattels cannot be entailed to heirs of the body. Restatement, Property § 63; Tiffany § 45.

11-31D   Statute.

See R.C. 2131.08.

SECTION 11-32: INCIDENTS OF THE ESTATE

11-32A   Nature.

Though the issue of the first donee in tail take by descent, yet the tenant in tail is not the source of their title; they take per forman doni, from the person who first created the estate, and are therefore not estopped by the deed of the tenant in tail. Pollock v. Speidel, 17 OS 439 (1867).

The common-law fee tail exists in Ohio and R.C. 2131.08, which converted estates tail into fees simple in the issue of the first donee in tail, did not change the nature of the estate in the first donee in tail from an inheritable estate to an estate for life, but merely restricted the entailment to the issue of such donee. Long v. Long, 45 OS2d 165, 343 NE2d 100, 74 OO2d 287 (1976).

Further research: O Jur 3d, Estates § 26.

LAW IN GENERAL

The heirs do not take by descent, but take as purchasers from the original donor. Therefore contracts and other acts of the present tenant do not bind subsequent tenants. The heirs of the body are ascertained from the common-law rules of descent notwithstanding statutory changes. CJS, Estates § 26; Powell § 196; Tiffany § 47.

11-32B Waste.

LAW IN GENERAL

The tenant is generally not liable for waste. He may be enjoined under some circumstances. See 11-19J.

11-32C Claims of Creditors.

LAW IN GENERAL

A creditor of a tenant in tail can subject to payment of the claim the interest which the tenant has the power to transfer. Restatement, Property § 83. See also 11-19J.

11-32D Transfer.

The conveyance of an estate tail in expectancy during the lifetime of the first donee in tail has no effect in law. Dungan v. Kline, 81 OS 371, 90 NE 938, 7 OLR 578, 55 WLB 21 (1910).

However, when made for a valuable consideration such conveyance is enforceable in equity as soon as the assigned expectancy has fallen into possession. Cook v. Hardin County Bank, 76 App. 203, 63 NE2d 686, 31 OO 498 (1945).

There remains in the grantor of a fee tail estate a reversion in fee simple expectant upon the failure of a stated condition, which reversion is a descendible, devisable and alienable estate, which, if otherwise undisposed of, passes upon the death of the grantor by descent to his heirs then living. Long v. Long, 45 OS2d 165, 343 NE2d 100, 74 OO2d 287 (1976).

Further research: O Jur 3d, Estates § 36.

LAW IN GENERAL

A fee tail may be conveyed by the owner subject to the entailment. It cannot be devised by the tenant in tail. Restatement, Property § 80.

11-32E   Judicial Sales.

Disentailment, see Section 17-42.

LAW IN GENERAL

The estate can be partitioned. The property can be disentailed by a judicial sale and reinvestment of the proceeds. Restatement, Property §§ 79, 82.

11-32F   Dower.

Under the law of Ohio, the surviving spouse of a tenant in tail has no dower interest in the entailed premises. Miller v. Miller, 83 NE2d 254, 41 OO 233, 52 Abs 121 (C.P. 1948).

SECTION 11-33: TERMINATION OF THE ESTATE

11-33A   Reversionary Interests and Remainders.

After the creation of a fee tail, the donor had a reversion expectant on the failure of issue before the fee tail could be converted into an absolute fee simple under the statute. Gibson v. McNeely, 11 OS 131 (1860).

LAW IN GENERAL

The interest remaining in the grantor is a reversion or possibility of reverter; or a remainder may be created by the same instrument, if it does not violate the rule against perpetuities. A fee tail is extinguished, the title usually reverting to the heirs of the original transferor, when lineal descendants of the tenant in tail become extinct. CJS, Estates § 27; Tiffany §§ 318, 323.

11-33B   Statutes.

Disentailment statutes, see Section 17-42.

LAW IN GENERAL

Statutes creating a right to defeat future interests do not apply to estates tail previously existing, but the rights of the issue of the tenant can be altered by statute. Restatement, Property § 86; Tiffany § 46.

11-33C   Restraints on Alienation.

LAW IN GENERAL

A restraint on alienation is not effective to abridge the right of a tenant in tail under a common recovery or fine. Restatement Second, Property (Donative Transfers) §§ 4.2, 4.3.

SECTION 11-34: FEE SIMPLE CONDITIONAL

11-34A   Generally.

LAW IN GENERAL

This estate is similar to a fee tail except that upon the birth of issue the donee can convey or encumber the property thereby binding the heirs. The interest remaining in the transferor or his heirs is known as a possibility of reverter. The estate was abolished in England in 1285 by the Statute De Donis and never existed in Ohio. Am Jur 2d, Estates § 38; Am Law of Prop § 2.11; Powell § 195; Restatement, Property § 68; Tiffany § 314.

DIVISION 11-4:   ESTATES SUBJECT TO CONDITION SUBSEQUENT; RIGHTS OF REENTRY

SECTION 11-41: NATURE OF THE INTERESTS

11-41A   Definition.

Upon the happening of the event which divests the son of the testator of his estate, the children of the son take the lands by devise from the testator in their own right and not in a representative capacity. In such case the lands pass to the heirs of the son free from the debts of the son to the estate of the testator. Rings v. Borton, 108 OS 280, 140 NE 515, 1 Abs 485, 21 OLR 150 (1923).

Further research: O Jur 3d, Estates § 14.

LAW IN GENERAL

An estate on condition subsequent is an estate which, by the terms of its creation, may be terminated by the transferor or his heirs before its normal expiration upon the happening of the specified contingency. An estate on special limitation is excluded; that is, the words of contingency must not be a part of the limitation creating the estate. Am Jur 2d, Estates §§ 155, 156; Am Law of Prop § 2.7; CJS, Deeds § 141; Powell § 188; Restatement, Property § 45; Tiffany § 187.

A right of reentry, also known as a right of entry or as a power of termination, is the future interest left in transferor or his heirs when an estate on condition subsequent is created. It is the power of the transferor or his heirs to terminate the estate transferred upon the happening of the specified contingency. It cannot be reserved to a stranger as it is the interest left untransferred on a conveyance or devise subject to a condition subsequent. A right of reentry is not a reversion, possibility of reversion, nor any vested interest in the land but is a power of termination of the estate subject to the condition. Am Jur 2d, Estates, §§ 189, 193; Am Law of Prop § 4.6; Powell § 271; Simes and Smith § 242.

11-41B Discharge of the Condition; Performance Impossible.

Failure of preceding or succeeding interest, see Section 11-16.

LAW IN GENERAL

The estate is freed from a condition which becomes impossible of performance for reasons not attributable to the owner of the estate. A condition calling for an unlawful act is void. Substantial compliance has also been held to discharge the condition. Am Law of Prop § 2.8; Simes and Smith § 2013; Tiffany §§ 195, 199.

The right of reentry may be barred by estoppel or waiver. One line of cases holds that a partial release or waiver in one instance will discharge the condition entirely if the condition is not continuing in character. If the transferor or his successor does not elect to forfeit the estate within a reasonable time after the condition occurs he will not later be permitted to do so. Am Law of Prop § 4.9; 39 ALR2d 1116; Simes and Smith § 258; Tiffany § 204.

11-41C Effect of Unexercised Right.

If the condition subsequent were broken, that did not ipso facto produce a reverter of the title. The estate continued in full force until the proper steps were taken to consummate the forfeiture. This could be done only by the grantor during his lifetime, and after his death by those in privity of blood with him. Walker Branch & Methodist Church v. Wesleyan Cemetery Ass'n, 11 CC 185, 5 CD 326 (1896). The omission to take any steps for seventeen years for the forfeiture of the title on the ground of a condition subsequently broken, constitutes a waiver of the right to insist upon forfeiture. Field v. Lake Shore & M. S. Ry., 3 CC(NS) 130, 13 CD 1 (1897). Failure to enforce forfeiture for five years held not a waiver. Bartholomew v. Rothrock, 20 Abs 513 (App. 1935).

Where the deed provided for reverting of the premises, equity will not compel performance of the conditions by injunction. New York Central R.R. v. Bucyrus, 126 OS 558, 186 NE 450, 38 OLR 478 (1933).

Further research: O Jur 3d, Estates § 83.

LAW IN GENERAL

Until the exercise of the right of reentry, the owner of the estate has the same rights and liabilities as though the condition did not exist, except that in rare cases the owner of the future interest may be entitled to protection against waste. Restatement, Property § 49.

An estate is not divested by breach of the condition until the right of reentry is exercised. Any act showing a claim to possession is equivalent to reentry and is sufficient under most of the modern decisions. Am Law of Prop § 2.9; Simes and Smith § 255.

11-41D Effect of Exercise of Right.

A court of equity will not lend its aid to enforce a forfeiture for breach of condition subsequent where the forfeiture seeks to compel the performance of a principal obligation payable by a definite sum, readily compensable in an action at law. Embleton v. McMechen, 110 OS 18, 143 NE 177, 2 Abs 244, 22 OLR 29, 34 ALR 689 (1924).

LAW IN GENERAL

Upon the exercise of the right of reentry, all interests created by the owner of the forfeited estate are divested. Dower attaches to the estate but does not survive the exercise of the right of reentry. Am Jur 2d, Dower and Curtesy §§ 75, 76; Am Law of Prop § 5.28; Powell § 215; Restatement, Property § 54; Simes and Smith § 265; Tiffany § 214.

In some cases forfeiture has been denied in equity when the breach of the condition was not willful and the breach could be adequately compensated by the payment of damages. Simes and Smith § 257; Tiffany §§ 203, 213, 215.

SECTION 11-42: TERMS OF CREATION

Condition precedent distinguished, see 11-81B.
Survival requirement, see Section 11-81.

11-42A Generally.

Life estate with power of disposal, 11-62D.

R.C. 2131.07 provides: "An estate in fee simple may be made defeasible upon the death of the holder thereof without having conveyed or devised the same, and the limitation over upon such event shall be a valid future interest. For the purpose of involuntary alienation, such a defeasible fee is a fee simple absolute." (As eff. 10-1-53.)

Where the deed provided that the premises be not used for any other purpose than the one specified, the title will not revest in the grantor or his heirs upon diversion to other uses. Ashland v. Greiner, 58 OS 67, 50 NE 99, 39 WLB 171, 296 (1898).

Will devising lots to testator's son in fee simple, and in case of his death leaving no issue, lots to go to grandson, vested estate in fee simple subject to be divested. O'Malley v. O'Malley, 20 App 279, 151 NE 795, 3 Abs 639, 23 OLR 408 (1925).

R.C. 2131.07 operates as to realty only. A provision in a will, "the balance of my estate, including the farm, I give to W. After she is through with the farm it is to go to the Masonic Home" creates a life estate with a vested remainder over in the Masonic Home. In re Knickel's Will, 185 NE2d 93, 89 Abs 135 (Prob. 1961).

LAW IN GENERAL

An estate on condition subsequent is created by a conveyance containing a phrase such as "upon the express condition," "provided that," or "but if" with a provision for reentry or termination of the estate by the grantor. A provision that if a certain event occurs the estate shall be null and void or shall revert, usually creates an estate on condition subsequent. However, the conveyance as a whole may show an intention to create an estate on special limitation. Where a clause for termination or reentry is absent, the weight of authority is that the condition is ineffective or that a covenant or encumbrance is created. A reservation of a right of reentry may be held to exist by necessary implication. Successive owners can create successive rights of reentry in themselves. Am Jur 2d, Estates § 139; Am Law of Prop §§ 2.8, 4.7; Powell § 188; Restatement, Property § 45; Simes and Smith §§ 244, 254; Tiffany § 190.

11-42B   Preferences in Construction.

Where the conveyance is to a grantee for certain uses but without a condition of reverter, it has been generally if not universally held that it amounts to a covenant as to the use, but does not involve a condition subsequent. May v. Board of Education, 12 App 456 (1920).

The rule of strict construction in favor of a covenant instead of a condition generally obtains and, where the language is not clear, all doubts are resolved in favor of the grantee for the purpose of avoiding a forfeiture. Church of God v. Glann, 93 App 337, 114 NE2d 98, 51 OO 90 (1952).

Where a fee simple title is conveyed subject to a provision in the deed requiring membership in a named organization without a penalty such as forfeiture, loss of possession, right of reentry or reverter for violation thereof, the provision will be construed as a covenant and not a condition. Wayne Lakes Park v. Warner, 104 App 167, 147 NE2d 269, 4 OO2d 235 (1957).

LAW IN GENERAL

Conditions are not favored in law. All ambiguities are construed in favor of the freer use of the land by the grantee or devisee. In construing a limitation, an estate on condition subsequent is preferred to a determinable fee and to an estate on condition precedent. A provision that the property shall be used for a certain purpose only does not in itself create a condition subsequent. 15 ALR2d 975; Simes and Smith § 248; Tiffany § 192.

The intention of the parties determines whether a condition or a covenant has been created. The expression "on condition" is not always conclusive against construction as a covenant. An instrument will be strictly construed in favor of a covenant. Am Law of Prop § 4.7.

11-42C   Void Conditions.

Discharge of the condition, see 11-41B.
Illegal conditions, see also 11-81O.
Miscellaneous restraints, see 9-21P.

The words "to be used as a parsonage" did not create an estate upon condition subsequent. First Presbyterian Church v. Tarr, 63 App 286, 26 NE2d 597, 17 OO 57 (1939).

LAW IN GENERAL

Conditions or restrictions which are contrary to public policy or which are inconsistent with the estate granted or devised are not enforced. A void condition subsequent generally leaves the gift absolute. Simes and Smith § 1520; Tiffany § 198.

SECTION 11-43: TRANSFER OF RIGHTS OF REENTRY

11-43A Descent and Devise.

R.C. 2131.04 provides: "Remainders, whether vested or contingent, executory interests, and other expectant estates are descendible, devisable, and alienable in the same manner as estates in possession." (As eff. 10-1-53.)

Possibilities of reverter and rights of entry were not alienable or devisable prior to 1932. Charles C. White, "Some Ohio Problems as to Future Interests in Land," 1 Cin. L. R. 36; Bartholomew v. Rothrock, 20 Abs 513 (App. 1935). It has been held that an attempt by the grantor to convey the right had the effect of extinguishing the condition. Walker Branch v. Wesleyan Cemetery Directors, 11 Dec Repr 809, 29 WLB 398 (1893). But future interests could always be released to the owner of the defeasible fee. Jeffers v. Lampson, 10 OS 101 (1859).

The words of the statute, "other expectant estates," include rights of reentry and possibilities of reverter. PCK Properties, Inc. v. Cuyahoga Falls, 112 App 492, 176 NE2d 441, 16 OO2d 378 (1960).

11-43B Conveyances.

The deed to the railway company of land to be used for railroad purposes with provision for reverter created a limited title to a right-of-way which ceased when its use was abandoned by the railway. The conveyance of the land by the same grantor (prior to the abandonment), containing an exception of the right and title of the railway company, left no interest remaining in him. In re Wyatt's Claim, 141 NE2d 308, 74 Abs 450 (App. 1955). The reasoning of the court seems to be based on a conveyance of the right of reentry which could not be done by the deed which was prior to the 1932 statute quoted in 11-43A. The judgment could have been properly based upon adverse possession.

Rights of reentry and possibilities of reverter were held to be alienable as expectant estates by PCK Properties, Inc. v. Cuyahoga Falls, 112 App 492, 176 NE2d 441, 16 OO2d 378 (1960). See 11-43A.

The possibility of reverter (right of reentry) in a dedicated street is presumed to be conveyed with the abutting land, unless a contrary intention is manifested, by a warranty deed describing the entire tract "excepting therefrom lands heretofore dedicated * * * for street purposes." Willis v. Hannah, 9 Misc 221, 224 NE2d 769, 38 OO2d 396 (C.P. 1966).

Further research: Am Jur 2d, Estates §§ 160, 190-192; Am Law of Prop § 4.68; 53 ALR2d 224; Powell § 282; Restatement, Property §§ 160 (Supp.), 161; Simes and Smith § 1862; Tiffany § 209.

11-43C Easements.

LAW IN GENERAL

The rule does not apply to prevent a subsequent purchaser of land burdened with an easement from terminating the easement for breach of a condition subsequent.

DIVISION 11-5: ESTATES ON SPECIAL LIMITATION; POSSIBILITIES OF REVERTER

SECTION 11-51: NATURE AND CREATION OF THE INTERESTS

11-51A Definitions; Nature.

Lands deeded to a board of education so long as used for school purposes revert automatically to the heirs of the grantor without an express condition of reverter. The board of education takes only a limited fee, terminating when the stipulated use ceases. May v. Board of Education, 12 App 456 (1920); Sperry v. Pond, 5 Ohio 387 (1832).

Where the habendum states "so long as said lot is held and used for church purposes" without any provision for forfeiture or reversion, such statement is not a condition or limitation of the grant and all the estate of the grantor was conveyed to the grantees. In re Copps Chapel Methodist Episcopal Church, 120 OS 309, 166 NE 218, 7 Abs 255, 29 OLR 72 (1929). See the dissenting opinion, disapproval in later cases, and other criticisms.

When a conveyance of land owned in fee simple is made to and accepted by a municipality in perpetuity for use as a park, and there is no provision for forfeiture or reversion, the entire estate of the grantor is divested, and the title of the municipality thereto is not a determinable fee but a fee simple. Miller v. Brookville, 152 OS 217, 89 NE2d 85, 40 OO 277, 15 ALR2d 967 (1949).

Where the habendum recites "so long as the same shall be used as a site for a school house and no longer" it clearly expressed an intention on the part of the original grantor to provide for a reverter and forfeiture. (Copps Chapel Case disapproved.) Board of Education v. Hollingsworth, 56 App 95, 10 NE2d 25, 9 OO 1, 23 Abs 81 (1936).

Deed to trustees of a named church "as long as used for church purposes" but with no stipulation for forfeiture or reversion, passed a fee determinable upon abandonment of such use, since clauses were limitations and not conditions subsequent. (Copps Chapel Case distinguished.) Schurch v. Harraman, 47 App 383, 191 NE 907, 15 Abs 581, 40 OLR 303 (1933); Burdette v. Jones, 72 NE2d 152, 34 OO 488, 47 Abs 593 (C.P. 1947).

Further research: O Jur 3d, Estates § 86.

LAW IN GENERAL

An estate on special limitation is an estate which, by the terms of its creation, automatically expires upon the happening of the specified contingency. Such an estate in fee is also known as a determinable fee. An estate on condition subsequent is excluded, that is, the words of contingency must be a part of the limitation creating the estate. The usual words are "so long as," "during," "until," etc. Am Jur 2d, Estates §§ 22, 23, 28; Am Law of Prop §§ 2.6, 4.13; Powell § 187; Restatement, Property § 44; Tiffany § 217.

A possibility of reverter is a future interest left in the grantor or in the testator's heirs which is subject to a condition precedent (that is, to the happening of the contingency) terminating the estate transferred. It exists with an estate on special limitation or a fee simple conditional; or it may arise upon the failure of an executory interest. The interest can be created only in the transferor or his heirs. Although it is not a vested interest it has the same effect as a reversion in automatically giving the transferor or his heirs the right to possession upon the termination of the determinable fee or particular estate. A right of reentry is distinguished from a possibility of reverter in that, under the former, the estate does not revert until entry is made or the power of termination is exercised. The possibility of reverter, being in the transferor, is not subject to the rule against perpetuities while the similar executory interest after a determinable fee is often void under that rule. Am Jur 2d, Estates § 182; Am Law of Prop §§ 4.12, 4.14; Powell § 278; Restatement, Property § 154; Simes and Smith § 281.

11-51B Prior to Defeasance.

LAW IN GENERAL

The owner of a determinable fee has the same rights and liabilities, subject to the defeasibility, as the owner of a fee simple absolute except that in very unusual circumstances he may be restrained from committing waste. Restatement, Property § 49; Tiffany § 220.

11-51C Dower.

LAW IN GENERAL

The right of dower attaches to a determinable fee but terminates upon the extinguishment of the estate to which it is incident. Am Jur 2d, Dower and Curtesy §§ 75, 76; Am Law of Prop § 5.28; Powell § 215; Restatement, Property § 54.

SECTION 11-52: TRANSFER OF POSSIBILITIES OF REVERTER

11-52A Generally.

Statute and citations, see Section 11-43.

LAW IN GENERAL

The owner of a possibility of reverter can usually transfer his interest by a conveyance inter vivos or by will. His interest passes under the statutes of descent if he dies intestate. Am Jur 2d, Estates §§ 184-186; Am Law of Prop § 4.70; 16 ALR2d 1246; Powell §§ 281, 284; Restatement, Property § 159; Simes and Smith § 1860; Tiffany § 314.

DIVISION 11-6: LIFE ESTATES

SECTION 11-61: INTRODUCTION.

11-61A Definition.

LAW IN GENERAL

A life estate is a freehold estate, the duration of which is measured by the life or lives of one or more persons. The estate is not terminable at any fixed period of time, although it may be defeasible except where the defeasibility is at the will of the grantor when the measure by life is inferred. It is not an estate of inheritance even when the estate continues upon the death of a tenant for the life of another. O Jur 3d, Estates § 39; Powell § 201; Restatement, Property § 18.

11-61B Classification.

Conventional life estates are created by acts of the parties; they are treated in this division. Legal life estates arise by operation of law and are (a) tenancy in tail after possibility of issue extinct, (b) dower, and (c) life estate by inheritance.

SECTION 11-62: CREATION

Cross remainders, see 11-73A.
Gifts over on "death" or "death without issue," see Section 11-82.

11-62A Terms of Creation.

Construction of deeds generally, see Section 8-31.
Construction of wills generally, see Section 9-21.
Words of inheritance, see Section 11-12.

A life tenancy devised to two persons is ordinarily enjoyed by the survivor in the whole property. See 11-73A. However, a vested gift of certain income for an ascertainable period to two persons passes, upon the death of either, to his estate as to his half interest. Central Trust Co. v. Bedinghaus, 8 Misc 183, 219 NE2d 243, 36 OO2d 99 (Prob. 1965).

LAW IN GENERAL

Language in a will or a deed sufficient to create a fee simple does not have that effect if other provisions clearly show a different intention; such as that the property shall pass to another on the death of the first named devisee. Simes and Smith § 497; Tiffany § 51.

The life of the survivor as the measure of the estate is favored in construing the intention of the testator when the lives of two or more persons determine the duration. The number of lives must not be so large as to make impracticable the determination of the duration. When the transferor owns a fee simple and makes a transfer to a person "for life," an estate for the life of the transferee is created. When the transferor owns a life estate, the attending circumstances will be considered in ascertaining his intention by a transfer "for life"; the entire estate of the transferor generally passes. Am Law of Prop § 2.15; Powell § 202; Restatement, Property §§ 107, 110.

11-62B By Implication.

Cross remainders, see 11-73A.
Remainders by implication, see 11-82E.

If a specified parcel of land be devised to A without further words indicating the estate so given, and the same land is devised "upon the death of A to B," A can hold only as tenant for life. Bierce v. Bierce, 41 OS 241, 12 WLB 191 (1884).

A devise of income from real estate during life is in effect a devise of a life estate in the realty. Boettcher v. Boettcher, 48 App 319, 193 NE 776, 1 OO 487, 17 Abs 17 (1934).

Further research: O Jur 3d, Estates § 45.

LAW IN GENERAL

An estate for life by implication is created in a designated person when a devise is to the heirs of testator, but such devise is postponed until death of the designated person. Am Jur 2d, Estates § 76; Am Law of Prop § 2.15; Powell § 203; Restatement, Property § 116.

11-62C Defeasible upon Marriage.

Restraints on marriage, see Section 14-16.

Where a testator devises to his wife all his real estate so long as she remains his widow, and the will provides that if she shall marry again then to any of certain other named persons, the widow takes a life estate, and the gift

431

over takes effect even though the tenant for life does not remarry. Fletcher v. Rynd, 18 App 136 (1920); Alexander v. Willis, 30 App 289, 165 NE 49 (1928). Further research: O Jur 3d, Estates § 48.

LAW IN GENERAL

A gift to a person until marriage, or so long as she remains a widow, is usually construed as creating a life estate subject to termination upon marriage. 73 ALR2d 484; Tiffany § 55.

11-62D   Power of Disposal Annexed.

Defeasible upon death without having conveyed, see 11-42A.
Power to sell for support, see 11-63G.

Where a devise in general terms is followed by a restricted power of disposal, a life estate by implication is created, even though there is no limitation over. Stableton v. Ellison, 21 OS 527 (1871).

The authorities in Ohio as well as most sister states are clearly against the theory of enlargement of a life estate in lands (to a fee) by the annexing of an unlimited power of sale. Fetter v. Rettig, 98 OS 428, 121 NE 696, 16 OLR 89, 401, 63 WLB 210, 482 (1918); Moore v. Blauser, 25 App 48, 156 NE 915, 5 Abs 72 (1926).

Devise for the use and benefit of another, with express power of sale and a gift over, creates a life estate with a vested remainder subject to be divested by exercise of the power of sale. Murphy v. Widows' Home & Asylum, 21 App 174, 151 NE 783, 4 Abs 251, 24 OLR 290 (1925).

The portion of the proceeds of sale not used for the express purposes provided in the will is held by the life tenant as a trustee for the benefit of the remaindermen. In re Graham's Estate, 98 NE2d 104, 44 OO 230, 65 Abs 161 (Prob. 1950).

"Because of the conflicting decisions it is impossible to lay down any positive rules for the construction of devises of the sort discussed herein. The best we can do is to say that the tendency of the Ohio courts seems to be as follows:

"If there be a general devise, with express power of sale, followed by a gift over of the corpus, the tendency of the Ohio courts is to construe the gift to the first taker as a life estate, and the gift over valid. [Baxter v. Bowyer, 19 OS 490 (1869).]

"If there be a general devise, with express power of sale, followed by a gift over of the residue, the tendency is to construe the gift to the first taker as a life estate, and the gift over valid. [Johnson v. Johnson, 51 OS 446, 38 NE 61, 31 WLB 370, 32 WLB 219 (1894); Tax Commission v. Oswald, 109 OS 36, 141 NE 678, 1 Abs 859, 21 OLR 329 (1923); Coyle v. Underwood, 88 NE2d 189, 41 OO 461, 55 Abs 257 (Prob. 1948).]

"If there be a general devise, with no power of disposal except such as is implied from the gift over of an undisposed-of residue, with a gift over of the residue, the tendency of the courts is to construe the gift to the first taker as a fee, or absolute interest, and the gift over void. [Watkins v. Price, 16 App 27, 21 OLR 260 (1921).]

"If there be a general devise, with no power express or implied, with a gift over of the corpus, the cases are so conflicting as to make it impossible to determine the tendency. As noted above the cases stand two supreme court cases and one nisi prius case in favor of life estates, to one nisi prius case and one court of appeals case in favor of a fee simple. [Howe v. Fuller, 19 Ohio 51 (1850); Robbins v. Smith, 72 OS 1, 73 NE 1051, 2 OLR 494, 50 WLB 94 (1905); Moeller v. Poland, 80 OS 418, 89 NE 100, 7 OLR 91, 54 WLB 239 (1909); Finlay Brewing Co. v. Dick, 1 NP(NS) 592, 13 OD 581, 48 WLB 618; Stophlet v. Stophlet, 22 App 327, 153 NE 867, 4 Abs 644 (1926).]

"It may further be said that where there is a power superadded to an apparent fee, or absolute interest, the tendency is to construe the power as a limited power and thus cut down the apparent fee to a life estate. But that where the power is implied as an incident to the estate granted, the tendency is to construe the general devise as a fee." Charles C. White, "Life Estate or Fee?", 1 Cin. L. R. 405. (Citations added.)

Further research: O Jur 3d, Estates § 51.

LAW IN GENERAL

A life estate is not converted into a fee by the mere annexation of a power of disposal, according to the great weight of authority. However, much diversity exists in the application of the rule in respect to whether the devise and power are express or implied, whether the power is absolute or qualified, and whether a gift over of the residue is made or not. Am Jur 2d, Estates § 78; Am Law of Prop § 2.15; Simes and Smith § 893; Tiffany § 56.

Where there is a general devise with an added power to dispose of in fee simple, the addition does not generally aid the validity of a subsequent limitation over to another. However, where the added power can be exercised only under restricted circumstances the general devise is usually construed to be a life estate. Powell § 204; Tiffany § 375.

SECTION 11-63: INCIDENTS OF THE ESTATE

Estovers, see 11-19C.
Merger, see Section 11-15.
Waste, see Section 11-19.

11-63A Alienation.

LAW IN GENERAL

The interest of a life tenant may be conveyed, leased, encumbered, or sold to pay his debts. Am Law of Prop § 2.17; CJS, Estates § 33; Powell § 208; Restatement, Property § 124; Tiffany §§ 59, 61.

11-63B Termination.

LAW IN GENERAL

A life estate may be terminated before its natural expiration by merger, by forfeiture, by adverse possession, or by the terms of its creation. The life tenant is under obligation to avoid causing or accelerating termination of a future interest in the land. CJS, Estates § 65; Powell § 211; Restatement, Property §§ 112, 135.

11-63C Crops.

After termination of tenancy, see 7-14A.
Executors and administrators, see 7-13A.

R.C. 2115.10 provides: "The emblements raised by labor, whether severed or not from the land of the deceased at the time of his death, are assets in the hands of the executor or administrator and shall be included in the inventory required by section 2115.02 of the Revised Code.

"The executor or administrator, or the person to whom he sells such emblements, at all reasonable times may enter upon the lands to cultivate, sever, and gather them." (As eff. 10-1-53.)

Further research: Am Law of Prop § 2.162; Powell § 207; Restatement, Property § 121; Tiffany § 67.

11-63D Quiet Enjoyment.

Remedies, see Sections 11-18, 11-19.

LAW IN GENERAL

The life tenant is entitled to the undisturbed possession of the land except that the owner of a future interest may act to protect his interest. The remainderman or reversioner has the right to enter in order to discover whether or not waste has been committed. The tenant has the right to all the issues and profits from the land during his tenancy. Am Law of Prop § 2.16; CJS, Estates § 34; Powell § 207; Restatement, Property §§ 117, 119; Thompson § 1898.

11-63E Measure of Damages.

LAW IN GENERAL

The measure of the damages which the life tenant may recover is the difference between the value of the life estate before and after the injury. He usually cannot recover for damages to the inheritance. Am Law of Prop § 2.16c; CJS, Estates § 67; Powell § 207; Restatement, Property § 118.

In a number of cases, the life tenant in possession has recovered damages from a stranger not only for injury to his own possessory interest but also to the reversion or remainder. 49 ALR2d 1119.

11-63F   Acquisition of Adverse Interest; Foreclosure.

Adverse possession, see 2-24A.

LAW IN GENERAL

The tenant for life acquires no interest adverse to the remainderman by purchase of the fee at a sale for a sum payable by the life tenant. If the sum is partly payable by the life tenant, he may have a right of redemption upon sale to another person. The remainderman has the right to contribute his share of the purchase price at foreclosure sale to the life tenant, or to the cost of an encumbrance or adverse title acquired by the life tenant. Either party is entitled to a lien on the interest of the other when he pays off an encumbrance on both interests. The life tenant or the remainderman may pay a mortgage debt and enforce the mortgage as assignee or subrogee in the amount for which the other is liable. Am Jur 2d, Life Tenants and Remaindermen §§ 275-277; Am Law of Prop § 222; 87 ALR 220; CJS, Estates § 35; Restatement, Property § 149; Simes and Smith § 1700; Tiffany § 68.

11-63G   Power to Sell for Support.

Power of disposal annexed, see 11-62D.

LAW IN GENERAL

The exercise of a power given to the life tenant to sell the remainder if necessary for his support is generally held to be within his discretion and to be a valid sale in the absence of fraud or bad faith. Many cases also hold that a life tenant has the entire estate if necessary for his maintenance where there is a gift over of "what remains" after the life estate. Am Jur 2d, Life Tenants and Remaindermen § 59.

11-63H   Payment of Current Charges; Valuation of Estate.

Special assessments, see 11-64D.

R.C. 2131.01 provides: "The American experience table of mortality is the basis of determining present values in probate matters." (As eff. 10-1-53.) For estate tax computation, see R.C. 5731.23.

Income should be charged with taxes on principal during the life tenancy and with current charges. Boggs v. Taylor, 29 OS 172, 1 WLB 378 (1876).

Mortality tables may be used in determining proportionate values as between life tenant and remaindermen. Whipple v. Ortlepp, 21 Abs 11 (App. 1935).

LAW IN GENERAL

The life tenant is obliged to pay interest on encumbrances, current taxes, periodic charges, and management expenses to the extent of income received or to the extent of the rental value if he occupies the premises. The remainderman may enforce this duty through appointment of a receiver, payment and recovery, or enforcement of his lien. The tenant is entitled to part of the proceeds of judicial sale of the property, proportionate to his expectancy of life as ascertained by using mortality tables. Am Law of Prop § 2.24; CJS, Estates § 47; Restatement, Property § 129; Simes and Smith § 1691; Tiffany § 63.

When the remainderman pays current charges, encumbrances on the land, or special assessments in order to protect his interest, he is entitled to a lien on the life estate. Am Law of Prop § 2.19; Restatement, Property § 131.

The proceeds of a voluntary sale by the life tenant and the remainderman without agreement as to the division will ordinarily be commuted to lump sums and paid to them. By the weight of authority at judicial sale of the fee the life tenant cannot demand, and cannot be required to accept, the lump sum instead of the interest. The present value of a life estate is the present value of an annuity equaling the annual net income or equaling the interest at the legal rate on the value of the property, for the life expectancy of the tenant as shown by mortality tables. In some of the cases consideration is taken of his circumstances and health. Am Jur 2d, Life Tenants and Remaindermen § 90; Am Law of Prop § 2.25; 102 ALR 978; CJS, Estates §§ 36, 53.

Disposition of condemnation proceeds is made by most courts between the life tenant and the remainderman by appointing a trustee to invest the proceeds and pay the income to the life tenant. Among other solutions, the fund is sometimes divided by use of mortality tables. 91 ALR2d 963.

11-63I Insurance.

A life tenant is not ordinarily bound to keep the premises insured for the benefit of the remainderman. In re Daring, 32 Abs 456 (App. 1940).

LAW IN GENERAL

When a policy of insurance protects both the owner of the life estate and the owner of the remainder, either may compel a practicable and reasonable restoration of the property. If neither owner causes such restoration, the life tenant is usually entitled to use of the policy proceeds during his tenancy. It has been held, however, that the life tenant is entitled to the value of his estate as computed with reference to mortality tables.

The life tenant is not obliged to provide insurance on the interest of the remainderman unless by the terms of a mortgage or of the creating instrument, or by other special requirement.

Under the majority rule, neither of the parties is entitled to the benefit of insurance obtained on the interest of the other, in the absence of a fiduciary relationship or other special circumstances.

Am Jur 2d, Life Tenants and Remaindermen §§ 158-161; Am Law of Prop § 2.23; 126 ALR 333; CJS, Estates § 46; Restatement, Property § 123; Simes and Smith § 1695; Tiffany § 65.

SECTION 11-64: IMPROVEMENTS; SPECIAL ASSESSMENTS

Repairs, see 11-19B.

11-64A Alterations; Meliorating Waste.

An act which results in improving instead of doing injury to the inheritance will not be enjoined. J. H. Bellows Co v. Covell, 28 App 277, 162 NE 621, 6 Abs 307 (1927).

LAW IN GENERAL

The life tenant does not have the right to make alterations in the premises to the damage of the remainderman. The doctrine of liability for material alterations increasing the value of the premises, known as meliorating waste, has been generally repudiated in this country. The tendency of the modern cases is to be liberal in permitting a tenant for life to make alterations. Am Jur 2d, Life Tenants and Remaindermen § 33; Am Law of Prop § 20.11; CJS, Waste § 7; Restatement, Property § 140; Simes and Smith § 1654; Tiffany § 630.

11-64B Fixtures.

LAW IN GENERAL

A chattel annexed by a life tenant may generally be removed by him or by his personal representative within a reasonable time after his death, provided it has not lost its identity or would not be destroyed by removal, and provided the removal would not cause lasting injury to the freehold. Am Law of Prop § 2.16.

11-64C Improvements.

A life tenant has no right to recover from the remainderman for improvements made during possession under the life estate. Stein v. White, 109 OS 578, 143 NE 124, 2 Abs 227, 22 OLR 11 (1924). And his tenant cannot remove the structures. Haflick v. Stober, 11 OS 482 (1860).

LAW IN GENERAL

The life tenant is entitled to contribution from the remainderman for the cost of his permanent improvement (a) when the improvement was commenced by a previous owner of the fee, if such completion was reasonable, or (b) when the life tenant was obliged by governmental authority to make the improvement. The remainder may be subjected to a lien in the amount its value was increased by an improvement, but not to exceed the amount chargeable under a special assessment for a like improvement. In some cases, the tenant has been granted relief under the occupying claimants acts or in equity as believing he was the owner in fee simple. Am Jur 2d, Life Tenants and

437

Remaindermen § 266; Restatement, Property § 127; Simes and Smith § 1699; Tiffany § 64.

11-64D Special Assessments.

R.C. 5573.12 provides that upon application of the life tenant, assessments for a township road may be apportioned between the owner of the life estate and the owner of the fee in proportion to the value of their respective estates. (As eff. 10-1-53.)

An equitable action may be maintained by a life tenant to compel a remainderman to contribute to the payment of assessments levied against farm property, in proportion to the benefit which accrues to his estate. The American experience table of mortality may be employed in arriving at the proportion of assessments payable by each estate. Whipple v. Ortlepp, 21 Abs 11 (App. 1935).

The cost of permanent improvements should be apportioned in the proportion which the value of the life estate bears to the value of the estate in remainder. Reibold v. Evans, 65 App 123, 29 NE2d 369, 18 OO 331, 31 Abs 285 (1940).

Further research: O Jur 3d, Estates § 65.

LAW IN GENERAL

When the remainderman pays all of a special assessment to protect his interest he is generally entitled to reimbursement from the life tenant (a) for the amount paid with interest if the life of the improvement does not exceed the reasonably expected duration of the life estate, or (b) for the part of the special assessment in the proportion of the present value of the life estate to the present value of a life estate having the duration of the life of the improvement, with interest. The life tenant is entitled to contribution upon payment by him when the improvement is permanent, in a like manner. The above method of apportionment is stated by the Restatement. Many cases approve apportionment in proportion to the value of each estate; the value of the life estate being ascertained through use of mortality tables, and the value of the remainder or reversion being the balance of the value of the entire fee. Am Jur 2d, Life Tenants and Remaindermen §§ 272-274; Am Law of Prop § 2.21; CJS, Estates §§ 45, 47; Restatement, Property § 133; Simes and Smith § 1698; Tiffany § 63.

Where an improvement is of a permanent nature the burden of the assessments therefor must be shared by the life tenant and the remainderman. If the improvement is of a temporary nature and will be primarily enjoyed by the life tenant, it has been held that he must pay the entire assessment. 10 ALR3d 1309.

SECTION 11-65: ESTATE FOR LIFE OF ANOTHER

11-65A Generally.

A tenant for life may convey his entire interest in such life estate to another. Howell v. Howell, 122 OS 543, 172 NE 528, 8 Abs 337, 32 OLR 76, 71 ALR 1182 (1930).

Further research: O Jur 3d, Estates § 40.

LAW IN GENERAL

An estate pur autre vie may be created by an express limitation or by transfer from a life tenant. It is regarded as a lesser estate than one for the life of the tenant and will therefore merge in the latter. If the limitation is for the life of the tenant and the life of another person, merger does not take place but, upon the death of the tenant, the estate will pass as an estate for the life of another. However, a limitation may create successive life estates or create a life estate in the survivor for the entire interest. Am Jur 2d, Estates § 2.

11-65B Devolution on Death of Tenant.

LAW IN GENERAL

According to the weight of authority, the unexpired estate on the death of a tenant pur autre vie passes by his will or, if he dies intestate as to the interest, passes to the executor or administrator.

Under some decisions the undevised residue passes to the heirs as special occupants in accordance with the common law as it existed until the enactment of the Statute of Frauds in 1677, or passes by decisions as real property under the statutes of descent. Other special occupants who will take the residue may be provided in the creation or transfer of the estate. An estate for life of another is not subject to dower as it is not an estate of inheritance.

Am Law of Prop § 2.26; Powell § 209; Restatement, Property §§ 128, 151; Tiffany § 60.

SECTION 11-66: TENANCY IN TAIL AFTER POSSIBILITY OF IS-SUE EXTINCT

11-66A Generally.

LAW IN GENERAL

This life tenancy arises in the original donee of an estate tail special when one of the parties to the specified marriage dies without issue. It differs from other life estates in that the tenant is not liable for ordinary waste. CJS, Estates § 28; Tiffany § 71.

DIVISION 11-7: REMAINDERS AND REVERSIONS IN GENERAL

SECTION 11-71: INTRODUCTION; DEFINITIONS

Creation by implication from gift over, see Section 11-82.
Rule in Shelley's Case, see Section 11-13.
Worthier title, see 8-31O and 9-21K.

11-71A Definitions.

Condition subsequent distinguished, see 11-81B.
Construction as to vesting, see Section 11-81.
Executory interests defined, see 11-83A.

Where the grantor devised only a life estate he and his heirs have a reversion. Bunnell v. Evans, 26 OS 409 (1875).

Estate in remainder is estate limited to take effect in possession immediately after expiration of prior estate created at same time by same instrument. Remainder is vested where there is present fixed right to future enjoyment. Remainder is contingent which comes into enjoyment or possession on happening of some uncertain event. Simpson v. Welsh, 44 App 115, 184 NE 242, 13 Abs 714 (1932).

LAW IN GENERAL

A "reversion" is any future interest left in a grantor, or in the successor in interest of a testator, which is not subject to a condition precedent. It arises by operation of law when an owner transfers a vested estate less than his own; for example, when a tenant in fee simple transfers an estate in fee tail, a life estate, or an estate for years. The term is also used to mean the returning of the right of possession to the transferor after the transferred estate has expired. A reversion is always vested, although it may be defeasible. A remainder, executory interest, right of reentry, or possibility of reverter is not a reversion. "Reversionary interest" is used as excluding a right of reentry, and as including a possibility of reverter which is equivalent to a reversion subject to a condition precedent. Am Law of Prop § 4.16; CJS, Estates § 105; Powell § 271; Restatement, Property § 154; Simes and Smith §§ 82, 92; Tiffany § 311a.

A "remainder" is any future interest, other than an executory interest, which can be created in a transferee. In other words, it is a future interest which may become an estate in possession in the transferee upon the expiration of all prior interests simultaneously created. It does not include a reversion, right of reentry, or possibility of reverter. Am Law of Prop § 4.26; Powell § 273; Restatement, Property § 156; Tiffany § 317.

A "vested remainder" is a remainder limited to one or more ascertained persons with no condition imposed upon the taking effect in possession other than the termination of the prior estate or estates. It can divest only an interest left in the transferor. Uncertainty may exist as to whether or not it will ever be enjoyed in possession as it may be defeasible or otherwise expire before becoming possessory. A vested remainder is characterized, while it exists, as being ready to take effect in possession whenever and however the preceding estate terminates. Difficulties often arise in determining whether a certain remainder is vested or contingent. Tiffany § 319.

A "contingent remainder" is a remainder subject to a condition precedent other than the termination, whenever and however it may occur, of all preceding estates. It may be a remainder created in favor of an unascertained person or persons. It is characterized by uncertainty in the gift itself or in who is to take, that is, the contingency may relate to either person or event. When no identifiable person can take the present interest if all prior rights to the present interest should presently terminate, the remainder is contingent. A remainder is contingent if an event, other than the possible termination of the prior estates, must happen before the remainder becomes a present estate. The interest becomes a vested remainder when the condition precedent is satisfied or the person to take is ascertained, the particular estate still existing. Powell § 278; Restatement, Property § 157; Tiffany §§ 320, 363.

A "condition precedent" is an event which must happen or be performed before the estate to which it is annexed can vest or be enlarged. The ultimate occurrence of the event may be either certain or uncertain, although, if certain, it must be possible for the occurrence to be at a time which precludes vesting. Executory interests and contingent remainders are future interests subject to conditions precedent. Tiffany §§ 320, 363.

11-71B Reversions and Remainders Distinguished.

LAW IN GENERAL

Reversions and remainders are chiefly distinguished by whether they are interests remaining in the transferor or interests created in a transferee, and whether arising by operation of law or by acts of the parties. An incidental difference is that a remainder is created at the same time as the estate in possession. The remedies available to a reversioner and to the owner of a vested remainder are ordinarily the same. Am Jur 2d, Life Tenants and Remaindermen § 22; Am Law of Prop §§ 4.16, 4.25, 4.39; CJS, Estates § 111; Simes and Smith § 108.

11-71C Destructibility of Remainders.

At common law it was necessary that a remainder be supported by a particular freehold estate and that enjoyment of the remainder begin immediately upon the normal termination of the particular estate. Where the rule has not been changed by statute, an interest of this nature can usually be sustained as a future use under a deed (even in states where the statute of uses is not in force) or as an executory devise.

441

Since 1931 the Ohio statute has provided that a remainder shall not be defeated by the determination of the precedent estate before the happening of the contingency on which the remainder was limited to take effect. It is also provided by statute that an expectant estate cannot be defeated by any act of the owner of the precedent estate nor by any destruction of such precedent estate. See 11-16A.

11-71D Classification of Remainders.

Contingent remainders, see Section 11-81.
Remainders vested subject to open, see Section 11-91.

Remainders may be classified as (a) vested indefeasibly, (b) vested subject to open, (c) vested subject to complete defeasance, and (d) subject to condition precedent, also known as contingent remainders.

Further research: Am Law of Prop § 4.32.

11-71E Remainders Vested Indefeasibly.

A remainder is vested indefeasibly when the fee simple will certainly be acquired and retained in possession by an ascertained person or through him by his grantees, heirs or devisees.

Further research: O Jur 3d, Estates § 97; Am Law of Prop § 4.33; Powell § 275; Restatement, Property § 157.

11-71F Remainders Vested Subject to Complete Defeasance.

See examples at the other divisions of this chapter.

By a devise "to the three children of T. L. W., providing they live to legal age," the devisees acquire a vested right immediately on the death of the testator, subject only to be divested in the event of death before they arrive at legal age. Foster v. Wick, 17 Ohio 250 (1848).

The devise of the remainder of the estate not consumed by the life tenant, with a power of sale in life tenant, creates a vested right in the remainder-men. Johnson v. Johnson, 51 OS 446, 38 NE 61, 31 WLB 370, 32 WLB 219 (1894).

A defeasible vested remainder is one which is subject to be divested by some future uncertain event. Miller v. Berk, 14 Abs 23 (App. 1933).

Where a testator devised real estate to one for and during her natural life and after her death to the heirs of her body, the reversion in fee descended to and vested in the residuary devisee or his heirs, subject to be divested in the event the devisee for life should die leaving heirs of her body surviving her. Welsh v. Weyrich, 123 NE2d 661, 68 Abs 584 (App. 1952).

Further research: O Jur 3d, Estates § 98.

LAW IN GENERAL

A remainder subject to complete defeasance may be defeated in a variety of ways, as by expiration before becoming possessory, by right of reentry, by

REMAINDERS AND REVERSIONS

possibility of reverter, by executory interest, or by exercise of a power. However, it can be accelerated on the failure of a prior interest while a contingent remainder cannot. Am Law of Prop § 4.35; Powell § 277; Restatement, Property § 231; Simes and Smith § 113.

A remainder is subject to defeasance rather than being contingent where the creator of an inter vivos trust provides a remainder but also reserves a right to revoke the trust, or gives to himself or another the power to consume or divert the property, 61 ALR2d 477.

SECTION 11-72: INCIDENTS OF REMAINDERS AND REVERSIONS

Adverse possession, see Section 2-24.
Life estates, see Division 11-6.

11-72A Transfer of the Interests.

Contingent remainders, see Section 11-84.
Statute, see 11-43A.

A vested defeasible remainder may be devised by the remainderman subject only to the same limitations and possibility of defeasance as were imposed upon the interest held by the testator. First Nat. Bank v. Tenney, 165 OS 513, 138 NE2d 15, 60 OO 481, 61 ALR2d 470 (1956).

Remainders, whether vested or contingent, executory interests, and other expectant estates are descendible, devisable and alienable in the same manner as estates in possession. R.C. 2131.04. Eastman v. Sohl, 66 App 383, 34 NE2d 291 (1940).

LAW IN GENERAL

The owner of a reversion or vested remainder can transfer or encumber his interest by a conveyance inter vivos. Such interests pass by devise when he dies testate or by descent when he dies intestate. Am Law of Prop § 4.74; CJS, Estates §§ 88, 90; Powell §§ 281, 283; Restatement, Property §§ 159, 162, 164; Simes and Smith § 1856; Tiffany §§ 313, 340.

11-72B Grant to Heirs of Grantor.

At common law the heirs do not take any estate under a conveyance for life which provides that the remaining estate shall go to the heirs of the grantor. See 8-310.

11-72C Dower.

Termination by executory limitation, see 11-83D.

LAW IN GENERAL

Dower does not attach, at common law nor under the ordinary statutes, when the deceased spouse was the owner of a reversion or remainder or of any other future interest. The rule does not apply to prevent the inchoate right of dower from attaching when the husband was the owner of a reversion or remainder following a term for years. Am Jur 2d, Dower and Curtesy § 79; Am Law of Prop § 5.16; Powell § 212; Simes and Smith § 1887; Tiffany § 501.

11-72D   Limitation of Actions.

Adverse possession, see Section 2-24.
Future interests generally, see 11-18C.

LAW IN GENERAL

The general rule is that laches, estoppel, or the statute of limitations will not begin to run against a remainderman until the termination of the particular estate. Am Jur 2d, Life Tenants and Remaindermen, § 14.

11-72E   Equitable Remainders.

LAW IN GENERAL

So-called "equitable remainders" are generally treated the same as remainders in legal estates. Tiffany § 335.

SECTION 11-73:   CROSS REMAINDERS; ALTERNATIVE REMAINDERS

One of survivors dying without issue, see 11-82G.
Survival requirement, see Section 11-81.
Survivorship deeds, see Section 8-16.

11-73A   Cross Remainders.

In a devise "to my four sons, or to the survivor of them, and their heirs and assigns, to be equally divided among them when the youngest attains the age of twenty-one years," cross remainders are not raised but each takes a fee. Cross remainders are not to be raised by implication, except between two only. Lawrence v. McArter, 10 Ohio 37 (1840).

Under a devise to two persons "for the term of their natural lives" with remainder to a third person, the survivor of the life tenants enjoys a life estate in the whole property. Enyeart v. Driver, 93 App 500, 113 NE2d 739, 51 OO 215 (1952).

Further research: O Jur 3d, Estates § 101.

LAW IN GENERAL

Cross remainders arise where remainders are limited after concurrent estates (usually life estates) to two or more persons so that at the death of each life tenant the remainder in his share passes to the survivors for life, with the reversioner or ultimate remainderman not let into sole possession until the termination of all the prior life estates. For example, under a conveyance to A,

B and C for their lives with cross remainders between them, upon the death of A the right of possession is in B and C, and upon the subsequent death of B the entire right of possession is in C.

Cross-remainder estates for life are created by implication in life tenants holding in common when a remainder is also limited to take effect on the death of the survivor of the life tenants. A few cases hold that, contrary to the weight of authority, cross remainders will not be raised by implication in a deed.

Am Jur 2d, Estates § 230; Am Law of Prop § 21.35; CJS, Estates § 74; Powell § 324; Restatement, Property § 115; Simes and Smith § 843; Tiffany § 334.

11-73B   Cross Executory Limitations.

LAW IN GENERAL

Cross executory limitations are treated as cross remainders except that they are not implied so as to divest an estate. Tiffany § 383.

11-73C   Alternative Remainders.

LAW IN GENERAL

Alternative remainders, also known as remainders on a contingency with a double aspect, exist when two or more contingent remainders are limited so that one becomes effective on the failure of the other or others. Such a remainder does not occur in cases where it is held that the first devisee has a vested remainder subject to being divested, and that the second devisee has an executory interest. The first-stated limitation is generally held to be vested subject to defeasance if its language would create a vested remainder in the absence of the second-stated limitation. Am Jur 2d, Estates §§ 216, 302, 303; CJS, Estates § 75; Powell § 350; Restatement, Property § 277; Simes and Smith § 149; Tiffany §§ 333, 382.

DIVISION 11-8: CONTINGENT REMAINDERS; EXECUTORY INTERESTS

SECTION 11-81: CONSTRUCTION AS TO VESTING; CONTINGENT REMAINDERS

Alternative remainders, see 11-73C.
Class gifts, see Section 11-91.
Construction generally, see 11-11D.
Destructibility, see 11-16A.
Failure and acceleration of interests, see Section 11-16.
Gifts over on death or death without issue, see Section 11-82.
Lapse statutes, see Section 9-26.
Statute on transfer, see 11-43A.

11-81A Rules as to Vesting.

LAW IN GENERAL

The primary rule is that the intention of the testator or grantor determines whether a remainder is vested or contingent. The determination is of practical importance principally because the owner of a contingent interest cannot alienate it so as to bind other persons in whom the interest subsequently vests. The distinction between vested and contingent also arises in other problems of taxation, partition, rule against perpetuities, destructibility, and alienability. Am Jur 2d, Estates § 215.

The law favors the vesting of estates at the earliest time consistent with the terms of their creation. A devise will vest at the death of the testator unless a contrary intent appears from the language of the will. A construction is preferred which will not create an estate on condition; and a condition subsequent is preferred over a condition precedent under the terms of its creation. Am Jur 2d, Estates § 252; CJS, Deeds § 141; Simes and Smith § 573; Tiffany §§ 324, 378.

The tendency of the courts is to hold a remainder vested subject to being divested where it cannot be held to be indefeasibly vested. However, a careful examination of the language used in any particular case is necessary in order to determine whether or not a condition precedent is created; for example, a remainder is vested subject to being divested where the remainder is devised to the children of the life tenant with a gift over to another of the interest of any child who does not survive the life tenant, while a remainder is contingent where the remainder is devised to the children of the life tenant who survive him. Am Jur 2d, Wills §§ 1363, 1367; CJS, Estates § 83; Simes and Smith § 132; Tiffany § 323.

11-81B   Vested and Contingent Remainders Distinguished.

Definitions, see 11-71A.

It is the uncertainty of the right of enjoyment, and not the uncertainty of its actual enjoyment, which renders a remainder contingent. Smith v. Block, 29 OS 488 (1876).

If the contingency is attached to the thing or right given, or to the person to take, the interest is contingent; if it is attached to the time when the thing or right is to be enjoyed, it is vested, the contingency referring merely to the payment or division. Richey v. Johnson, 30 OS 288, 2 WLB 150 (1876); Peck v. Chatfield, 24 App 176, 156 NE 459, 6 Abs 63 (1927).

No degree of uncertainty as to the remainderman ever enjoying the estate which is limited to him by way of remainder will render such remainder a contingent one, provided he has by such limitation a present absolute right to have the estate the instant the prior estate shall determine. The present capacity of taking effect in possession (if the possession were to become vacant) distinguishes a vested from a contingent remainder, and not the certainty that the possession will become vacant while the remainder continued. McCarthy v. Hansel, 4 App 425, 25 CC(NS) 283, 28 CD 608 (1915).

In cases of doubt or of ambiguity in the language employed in creating a remainder, a construction is favored that will make the remainder a vested one. Miller v. Berk, 14 Abs 23 (App. 1933); Stahl v. Mohr, 35 App 411, 172 NE 431 (1928).

A contingent remainder is one where the estate in remainder is limited either to an uncertain person, or upon the happening of an uncertain event, so that the particular estate may chance to be determined and the remainder never take effect. Piper v. Lucey, 21 Abs 661 (App. 1936).

If the condition on which the estate depends is precedent, the estate is contingent; if subsequent, it is vested subject to defeasance. A condition precedent is a condition upon the happening of which an estate will vest. A condition subsequent defeats an estate already vested. There are no technical words to distinguish between conditions precedent and conditions subsequent. No presumptions are indulged by law to create conditions precedent in a will. Winters Nat. Bank & Trust Co. v. Cullen, 58 NE2d 702, 41 Abs 417 (App. 1944).

The law favors the vesting of remainders and, in the absence of a clearly expressed intention of a testator to postpone the vesting of an estate to some future time, this rule will govern. Smith v. Weinkoff, 80 App 206, 75 NE2d 81, 35 OO 521 (1947). First Nat. Bank v. Tenney, 165 OS 513, 138 NE2d 15, 60 OO 481, 61 ALR2d 470 (1956).

When an interest is so limited that the right to possession or enjoyment is subject to a condition precedent other than the termination of prior interests, such interest is said to be contingent. Cleveland Trust Co. v. Mansfield, 71 NE2d 287, 34 OO 26 (C.P. 1945).

A remainder which is otherwise vested is nonetheless vested because it is liable to be divested by a subsequent event, nor is it made contingent by the fact that the interest of the remainderman may be divested by his death before the death of the life tenant. First-Central Trust Co. v. Claflin, 73 NE2d 388, 49 Abs 29 (C.P. 1947).

Further research: O Jur 3d, Estates § 102.

LAW IN GENERAL

A remainder or other future interest is vested if it may take effect in possession without the happening of any condition other than the termination of prior estates, whenever and however the termination may occur. An interest is contingent if any other condition must happen before the taking effect in possession. Am Jur 2d, Estates § 217.

A condition is a condition precedent if the act or event must necessarily precede the vesting, while it is a condition subsequent if the act or event may follow the vesting. A remainder to unascertained persons is contingent. Other rules for distinguishing vested and contingent remainders are: that a remainder is vested where the words of contingency are not incorporated into the gift to the remainderman but the words of contingency are in an added clause divesting the gift; and that the capacity of a remainder throughout its existence to take effect immediately in possession, however and whenever the particular estate terminates, renders it vested. Am Law of Prop § 4.36; CJS, Wills § 946; Tiffany § 194.

Uncertainty whether a remainder will ever vest in possession does not make it contingent; for example, a vested remainder for life may terminate before the expiration of the prior estate. A vested remainder may be uncertain as to the actual enjoyment of the deferred possession, while a contingent remainder is uncertain as to the right of future enjoyment. Am Jur 2d, Estates § 243; Simes and Smith § 165; Tiffany § 323.

Where the testator's intention as to vesting cannot be ascertained from the language of the will, the question is sometimes resolved by finding that the condition for support or services is a condition subsequent instead of precedent in view of the rule that the law favors vesting of estates. 25 ALR3d 762.

11-81C   Words of Futurity.

Even though such words as "when" and "after" are used in bestowing a remainder after a life estate, such words are generally considered to relate to the enjoyment of the estate rather than the time of its vesting in interest. First Nat. Bank v. Tenney, 165 OS 513, 138 NE2d 15, 60 OO 481, 61 ALR2d 470 (1956); Ohio Nat. Bank v. Boone, 139 OS 361, 40 NE2d 149, 22 OO 414, 44 ALR 1150 (1942).

A devise of real property to the widow of the testator for life "and upon her death said property and the title thereto shall vest in the name and title of my sons . . . absolutely and in fee simple" is a devise of vested remainders to the sons as of the death of the testator. Lane v. Lane, 116 App 100, 187 NE2d 71, 21 OO2d 375 (1961).

Under a will providing for distribution to persons named "or their issue . . . upon the termination of ten years after the death of my said wife," it was the intention of the testator, as shown by the entire language of the will, that no interest in his trust estate will vest until ten years after his wife's death. First Nat. Bank of Cincinnati v. Gaines, 15 Misc 109, 237 NE2d 182, 43 OO2d 101 (1967).

LAW IN GENERAL

A devise of a remainder to A is indefeasibly vested, prior to the termination of the preceding estate, when the will discloses an intention that such termination is the time fixed merely as the time of division or of the right to possession or when the will contains words importing a gift in the present with only the time of enjoyment postponed. However, where there are no words of present gift, an intention to create a contingent remainder may be judicially ascertained from consideration of the entire will. Am Jur 2d, Wills § 1380.

Words of postponement or futurity, when for the convenience of the estate or when to let in some other interest, are presumed to relate to the time of enjoyment rather than to the time of vesting. The remainder is contingent if the postponement enters into the substance of the gift, as when the gift depends upon a contingency which may not happen. An illustration of the tendency of courts not to construe a limitation as a condition precedent is that a devise to a person "on," "at," "from," or "after" the death of the life tenant refers to the time of taking possession and therefore creates a vested remainder, unless controlled by other provisions of the will. Am Jur 2d, Estates § 255; Am Law of Prop § 21.9; Simes and Smith § 585; Tiffany § 324.

11-81D   Words of Survivorship.

Antilapse statute, see 9-26A.
Divide and pay over, see 11-81I.

Where there is a clause of survivorship it prima facie refers to the time at which the property to be divided comes into enjoyment — that is to say, if there be no previous life estate, it means surviving at the death of the testator; if there be a previous life estate, then it means surviving at the termination of that life estate. No interest vested in a child of testator who died during his mother's life estate where the will directed equal division after the mother's death among the children or the survivors of them. Sinton v. Boyd, 19 OS 30 (1869).

A common instance of a remainder contingent because of uncertainty in the remainderman is presented by the limitation of a remainder to the heirs of a living person named, in which case the heirs cannot be ascertained until such person's death on the principle that there can be no heir to a living person. A gift to A for life with remainder to his children living at his death creates a contingent remainder (since the remaindermen cannot be ascertained till A's

449

death), as also does a gift to A for life and, after his death, to the children of B "if he leave any surviving him." Barlow v. Ostott, 25 CC(NS) 347, 35 CD 267 (1902); Lisle v. Miller, 21 CC(NS) 317, 25 CD 127 (1912); Welles v. Pape, 63 App 432, 27 NE2d 169, 17 OO 167, 31 Abs 102 (1940).

Further research: O Jur 3d, Estates § 109.

LAW IN GENERAL

As a general rule, survival only until the death of the testator is required for vesting of a gift if enjoyment in possession is not postponed; and the difficult problems of survival do not arise unless the vesting is or may be postponed, as on account of a preceding life estate. Simes and Smith § 135.

Words of survivorship are presumed to relate to the time of termination of the preceding estate instead of the time of testator's death, unless a different intent is manifested by the will. The remainder with a survival requirement is contingent during the existence of the preceding estate. However, in a number of instances particular language is held to manifest a different intent. A requirement of survival always defeats the gift to the named donee if he dies before the effective date of the instrument. A requirement of further survival does not exist merely because enjoyment of the gift is postponed to a subsequent date where the words of survivorship intend to refer to the effective date of the will or other instrument. It should be kept in mind that the provision for survival may be such that it will operate to divest the interest rather than to prevent vesting. Am Jur 2d, Estates § 266; Am Law of Prop § 21.10; 20 ALR2d 830; 57 ALR2d 202; CJS, Wills § 729; Simes and Smith § 575; Tiffany § 380.

11-81E   "Heirs"; "Children"; "Issue"; "Living."

Children and the like, see also Section 11-92.
Heirs and the like, see also Section 11-93.

In the absence of clear testamentary intent, remainders vest in interest and title at once upon testator's death in the persons then comprising the class described, but the right of possession should be postponed until the life estate has become extinguished. Everhard v. Brown, 75 App 451, 62 NE2d 901, 31 OO 268 (1945).

In a remainder "to the lawful heirs of my children who are of my blood" no interest vests in such heirs until the time of distribution where the determination of such heirs at such future time is necessary to effectuate the general plan of property remaining in the bloodline. Casey v. Gallagher, 11 OS2d 42, 227 NE2d 801, 40 OO2d 55 (1967).

Further research: O Jur 3d, Estates § 108.

LAW IN GENERAL

The interest generally does not vest until and unless the intended takers do survive where the limitation is to "heirs," "next of kin," etc., of a living person, nor where the limitation is to persons living at a specified time. Survival is usually not required for vesting where the takers are described as "children," "issue," or "descendants." However, where the taking is per stirpes many cases hold that vesting is deferred to the end of the postponement. The required time of survival is generally presumed to be the time of termination of preceding interests where the limitation is to persons "surviving" or "living" but the time is not specified. Am Law of Prop § 21.11; 57 ALR2d 103; Powell § 327; Restatement, Property § 249; Simes and Smith §§ 146, 578.

Under a provision in a will that children, etc., of a remainderman who dies before expiration of the precedent estate or the time fixed for distribution, shall take the share to which he would have been entitled, most of the cases find the primary remainder to be vested subject to being divested. 47 ALR2d 926.

Where the gift or limitation is to take immediate effect in possession or enjoyment the "heirs," "children" or "issue" to take are ascertained as of the time the instrument goes into effect, that is, under a will as of the death of the testator. 60 ALR2d 1399.

11-81F   "Or."

See also 9-26B.

The fact that the devise to the children is to them "or their heirs" does not make it contingent; the words "or their heirs" being regarded as words of limitation, and not as the substitution of a new class of beneficiaries, taking as purchasers from the testator. Bolton v. Ohio Nat. Bank, 50 OS 290, 33 NE 1115, 29 WLB 287, 329 (1893).

It is the well settled rule of construction that where two contingencies are specified, and are connected by the disjunctive "or," the word "or" may be construed "and," and that consequently the estate does not pass to the ulterior devisees unless both the specified events happen. The courts repeatedly refuse to construe "or" in its strict disjunctive sense, unless the entire tenor of the will demands such construction. Van Tilburg v. Martin, 120 OS 26, 165 NE 539, 7 Abs 159, 28 OLR 514 (1929).

LAW IN GENERAL

A limitation to a named person "or his children" or similar use of the word "or" usually does not vest the interest in the named person until and unless he survives the termination of the preceding interest. The interest vests in the children or other alternative takers on the failure of the named person to so survive. Am Jur 2d, Estates §§ 300, 301; Am Law of Prop § 21.24; Powell § 329; Restatement, Property §§ 27d, 27e, 37, 252; Simes and Smith § 149.

11-81G   Failure to Survive; Construction of Divesting Contingency.

LAW IN GENERAL

When there is a gift over on the failure of a taker to survive to a future time, the interest of such taker only is defeated on the expressed condition. A requirement that a taker survive under certain circumstances does not indicate an intention that he must survive under other circumstances. Am Law of Prop §§ 21.16, 21.23; Restatement, Property § 254.

The rule of construction in favor of vested interests is generally applied when the problem is interpretation as a defeasibly vested interest or as a contingent interest. When the condition is stated both as a condition precedent and as a divesting contingency, the prevailing view is that the gift will be construed as vested subject to divestiture, except where the condition inheres in the description of the takers. Am Law of Prop § 21.31; Restatement, Property § 253; Simes and Smith § 147.

11-81H Alternative Gift; Present Gift; Income.

Alternative remainders, see 11-73C.
Words of futurity, see 11-81C.

Where the will provides "I give and devise to my beloved wife the farm . . . during the time till the youngest child, Thomas Linton, shall be twenty-one years of age. . . . When the youngest child is twenty-one years of age, the real estate aforesaid, and such part of said personal property, or the proceeds thereof, as may then remain unconsumed and unexpended, to be equally divided amongst all my children then living, or their heirs," the estate vested in the children at the death of the testator, subject to the estate for years; and was not divested by the death of a child during the term, but his share descended to his heirs, who take the same by inheritance, and not as devised under the will. "A devise to one when he arrives at a given age, the intermediate estate being devised to another, vests on the death of the testator, and is not defeated by the death of the devisee before the specified age. The words of futurity importing contingency are not necessarily inconsistent with the immediate vesting of the estate, but may be regarded as merely postponing the possession." Linton v. Laycock, 33 OS 128, 3 WLB 491 (1877); Provident Savings Bank & Trust Co. v. Volhard, 54 App 327, 7 NE2d 234, 8 OO 56, 23 Abs 269 (1936).

LAW IN GENERAL

Absence of an alternative gift may be sufficient to show that survival was not intended as a precedent requirement. Language of a gift in the present may eliminate the necessity of survival for the effectiveness of the gift. A gift to B in the present is indicated by a gift to A for life and "then I give to B" or "upon A's death I give to B." By the weight of authority, survival to the designated age is required for vesting where the gift is "when" or "at" (etc.) attaining such age. The rule is that survival is not required when the gift is "payable" when or at attaining the designated age. Words indicating survival to a future time in order for an interest to vest are usually not given that effect if coupled with a gift to the devisee of income prior to that time. Am Law of Prop § 21.17; Powell § 331; Restatement, Property § 255; Simes and Smith §§ 149, 581.

11-81I Divide-and-Pay-Over Rule; Charge on Land.

Lien of charges, see 9-21N.

Where the will provides "after the death of said (life tenant), I direct my executors and trustees to pay the unconsumed portion . . . to my heirs share and share alike," the remainder vests at the death of the testator. Ohio Nat. Bank v. Boone, 139 OS 361, 40 NE2d 149, 22 OO 414, 144 ALR 1150 (1942). A four to three decision.

Further research: O Jur 3d, Estates § 115.

LAW IN GENERAL

Vesting is not prevented and survival is not required by words of gift consisting of a direction to "divide and pay over" at a stated future time, according to the great weight of authority. Some authorities hold that a gift is contingent when it is implied only from the direction to divide and pay over. Charging a legacy on land does not show that the legatee must survive to the time of distribution. Am Jur 2d, Estates §§ 258, 259; Am Law of Prop § 21.21; 16 ALR2d 1383; CJS, Wills § 934; Powell § 333; Restatement, Property §§ 260, 263; Simes and Smith §§ 151, 582.

11-81J Remainder Contingent but Survival Not Required.

LAW IN GENERAL

Survival is not made a condition precedent by the fact that the gift itself is subject to a condition precedent, according to the weight of authority. Thus, under a devise "to A for life and remainder to his issue, but if A dies without issue then to B and his heirs," B's interest is not defeated by his death before A's death without issue. Am Law of Prop § 21.25; Powell § 334; Restatement, Property § 261; Simes and Smith §§ 594, 777.

11-81K Ability to Have Children.

LAW IN GENERAL

The presumption that a man or woman is capable of having children can be rebutted and the impossibility of the birth of a person to whom a future interest is limited can be established, according to the weight of authority, especially in cases involving the distribution of an estate, specific performance of a land contract, termination of a trust, and fixing a tax liability. 146 ALR 802; 98 ALR2d 1285; Powell § 347; Restatement, Property § 274.

11-81L Location of Fee.

The fee simple title was in the testator until his death, and if it did not pass by his will to any devisee named therein, it either ceased to exist in anyone, or it passed by way of descent to his heirs at law. In our opinion, it descended to the heirs; subject, however, to be divested by force of the will. Gilpin v. Williams, 25 OS 283 (1874).

LAW IN GENERAL

The fee remains in the grantor or his heirs, or passes to the heirs of the testator, when a contingent remainder is created, according to the prevailing view. Am Jur 2d, Estates § 223; Tiffany § 332.

11-81M Power to Consume or Appoint.

Power of disposal annexed, see 11-62D.

LAW IN GENERAL

The existence of a power to consume or to appoint does not make a remainder contingent, but the remainder is defeated to the extent that the power is exercised. However, an executory interest is usually held invalid, when it is subsequent to a fee simple which includes a power to defeat the executory interest; for example, a future interest limited to arise if the devisee of the fee dies without having conveyed. Am Law of Prop § 21.31; Powell § 349; Restatement, Property § 276; Simes and Smith § 150.

11-81N Behavior Requirements.

Miscellaneous restraints, see 9-21P.

LAW IN GENERAL

When the gift of a future interest is subject to certain behavior of the donee, either an estate on condition subsequent or an estate on condition precedent is generally created, depending upon the intention of the grantor or testator. Am Law of Prop § 21.31; Powell § 348; Restatement, Property § 275; Simes and Smith § 1519.

11-81O Illegal Conditions; Impossibility of Performance.

Failure of interests, see Section 11-16.
Void conditions subsequent, see 11-42C.

A devise subject to a condition precedent, which at its inception is or subsequently becomes impossible of performance, fails and the property passes under the residuary clause or as intestate property. When a condition subsequent is impossible of performance, the devise is free of the condition. Neidler v. Donaldson, 9 Misc 208, 224 NE2d 404, 38 OO2d 360 (Prob. 1967).

LAW IN GENERAL

The authorities are conflicting as to the effect of illegality of a condition precedent. Considerable authority exists for each of the following inconsistent rules: (a) any condition precedent must be performed before the gift vests, (b) the illegality of a condition precedent renders the gift absolute, (c) the illegality of a condition precedent defeats the gift, and (d) the effect of illegality is a problem of construction for the purpose of giving effect to the testamentary intention insofar as consistent with public policy, with recourse to (c) if such intention cannot be ascertained. It is said that (d) should also be applied to illegal conditions subsequent. Am Law of Prop § 27.22; Simes and Smith § 1511.

Where a condition precedent is attached to a testamentary gift of real estate, and its performance is or becomes impossible, the devise generally fails. However, some cases hold that the devisee takes free of the condition where impossibility of his performance arose by the act of a third person. 39 ALR2d 522.

SECTION 11-82: GIFTS OVER ON "DEATH" OR "DEATH WITHOUT ISSUE"

Survival requirement generally, see Section 11-81.

11-82A Gift Over if General Devisee Dies.

A devise to A but "if he dies" or "in case of his death," or the like, refers to the time from which the will speaks, that is the time of testator's death. Renner v. Williams, 71 OS 340, 73 NE 221, 2 OLR 411, 50 WLB 41 (1905).

LAW IN GENERAL

A general devise to B with a further gift "if B dies" or "in the event of the death of B" does not ordinarily reduce B's estate from a fee simple to a life estate if he survives the testator; thus, a devise "to B and his heirs, but if B dies, then to C" or the like, means if B dies before the testator, in the absence of other language to the contrary. Am Law of Prop § 21.60; 51 ALR2d 205; Powell § 337; Restatement, Property § 263; Simes and Smith § 534; Tiffany § 368.

11-82B Gift Over when General Devisee Dies.

Words of futurity, see 11-81C.
Words of present gift, see 11-81H.

LAW IN GENERAL

When a general devise is to B with a gift over to C to be effective "at," "after" or "on" the death of B or "when B dies," it is generally held that B takes a life estate and that the remainder is vested in C. Am Jur 2d, Estates § 217.

455

11-82C Gifts Over on All Alternatives.

Alternative remainders, see 11-73C.

The devise to testator's children provided that if any of his children "shall die leaving issue," the share should go to the issue; if any "shall die leaving no issue," the share should go to the remaining children. Held: such clauses refer to the death of testator's children at any time. Ohio Nat. Bank v. Harris, 126 OS 360, 185 NE 532, 37 OLR 576 (1933).

LAW IN GENERAL

The gift over is said to be on all alternatives where there is a general devise to B accompanied by provisions that if he die with issue, to the issue, but if he die without issue, to C. When B survives the testator he takes a life estate in Ohio; in most states he takes a fee simple absolute. Powell § 203; Simes and Smith § 549; Tiffany § 53.

11-82D Gift Over if Remainderman Dies.

Where the will provides: "I give, devise and bequeath to my beloved wife for her sole use and benefit during the term of her natural life, all the residue of my estate, both real and personal and at her death I direct that the same shall be distributed equally share and share alike between my children, and if any of my children shall not then be living, then the share of such to their child or children, if there by any then living," deed from widow and children conveyed good title "subject only to the possible contingency that the death of any child prior to the death of the mother, [leaving issue living at the time of the death of the mother,] would operate to defeat the title to that part of the property which would otherwise have gone to the deceased child." Millison v. Drake, 123 OS 249, 174 NE 776, 9 Abs 446, 34 OLR 97 (1931).

Where the first taker is a life tenant, and the remainder is devised to his children, but if any of the children shall die and leave heirs, then to such heirs; held, that the estate vests an absolute fee simple at the death of the life tenant in the son of such a deceased child. The title of a child of the life tenant is divested when he dies before the life tenant. McCulloch v. Yost, 148 OS 675, 76 NE2d 707, 36 OO 274 (1947).

Further research: O Jur 3d, Decedents' Estates § 685.

LAW IN GENERAL

A conveyance or devise "to B for life, remainder to C and his heirs, but if C dies, then to D" or similar language, usually means if C dies before B, unless a different intent is otherwise manifested by the grantor or testator. Am Law of Prop § 21.59; 51 ALR2d 205; Powell § 338; Restatement, Property § 264; Tiffany § 369.

11-82E Gifts by Implication.

Life estates by implication, see 11-62B.

Lineal descendants have no estate by implication nor any interest against grantee of a devisee under a will providing for a gift over upon the death of the devisee without lineal descendants. Anderson v. United Realty Co., 79 OS 23, 86 NE 644, 6 OLR 516, 53 WLB 426 (1908).

A bequest to testatrix's son with a gift over for his children does not create a gift by implication for such children upon the renunciation by the son. Howland v. Stone Foundation, 17 Misc 179, 243 NE2d 892, 46 OO2d 253 (Prob. 1969).

Where the testator's intent is not otherwise determinable, there is a presumption that a gift of the income from property, without limitation as to time, and without an unconditional gift over of the principal, amounts to a gift of the principal. Cleveland Trust Co. v. Reed, 17 Misc 317, 244 NE2d 900, 46 OO2d 433 (Prob. 1969).

LAW IN GENERAL

A general devise to B with a gift over on the death of B without issue, does not cut down the estate of B to a life estate and give a remainder by implication to his issue; B has a defeasible fee. Simes and Smith § 532; Tiffany § 54.

A limitation "to B for life, and if B dies without issue, then to C" implies a remainder to the issue of B if any survive him. Am Law of Prop § 21.34; Powell §§ 323, 344; Restatement, Property § 272; Simes and Smith § 842.

A remainder or executory interest to children, issue, wife, or the like is often created by implication from a gift over on default of such persons. A gift to testator's child has also been held to be implied from a gift to another if the child should not be alive at the happening of the designated event. 22 ALR2d 177; Simes and Smith § 844.

11-82F Death without Issue; Definite and Indefinite Failure of Issue.

Alternative gift with or without issue, see 11-82C.

A testator devised his real estate to his widow and daughter and to the survivor of them, and directed that if both should die without issue, it should go to the wife's brother. The widow died leaving issue of a second marriage. Afterward the daughter died without issue. Held, that the surviving issue of the widow is entitled to the estate. Shaw v. Hoard, 18 OS 227 (1868).

Where the will gives the widow a life estate with power of sale and "after the death of my wife whatever property remains of my estate I will and bequeath as follows to [brothers]. At the time of this distribution, should either of my brothers above be deceased, without leaving issue — then such share shall go to the brother remaining or his issue," the gift over of what remains unconsumed is a vested remainder, subject to being divested as to any brother who dies without issue before the life tenant dies. Tax Commission v. Oswald, 109 OS 36, 141 NE 678, 1 Abs 859, 21 OLR 329 (1923); Min Young v. Min Young, 47 OS 501, 25 NE 168, 24 WLB 260 (1890).

Where there is a devise or bequest (without no preceding estate) to one coupled with a provision that if he die without issue such property shall go to another refers to the time of the death of the first taker, unless a contrary intention is clearly manifested. Briggs v. Hopkins, 103 OS 321, 132 NE 843, 19 OLR 371 (1921). In such case, the fee taken by the first devisee with no preceding life estate, is determinable only on the contingency of her dying without leaving such heirs living at the time of her death. Piatt v. Sinton, 37 OS 353, 6 WLB 717, 799 (1881); Niles v. Gray, 12 OS 320 (1861).

The entire will may show an intention to vest the fee simple in the first taker upon an event prior to the death of the first taker. Fetterman v. Bingham, 115 OS 35, 152 NE 10, 4 Abs 303, 24 OLR 412 (1926).

An indefinite failure of issue signifies a general failure of issue whenever it may happen. Woodlief v. Duckwall, 19 CC 564, 10 CD 686 (1900). Such failure is not important in Ohio law.

Where a testator devises a life estate in real property to his wife and, at her death to his son, but "should he die leaving no children," then to another, the quoted words refer to the death of the son without issue during the lifetime of his mother, and, where the son survives his mother, title to such property becomes absolute in him. Trumbo v. Trumbo, 106 App 382, 155 NE2d 62, 7 OO2d 112 (1957).

The devise is to testator's son and daughter, "and in case of the death of either without living issue then" to my living children, etc. The quoted language refers to the time of death of the son or daughter. An adopted child of one of such devisees is "living issue" within the meaning of such will. Cook v. Crabill, 110 App 45, 164 NE2d 425, 12 OO2d 220, 82 Abs 164 (1959).

The words "die without issue" means to die without issue surviving. Wagner v. Wagner, 3 O Supp 34, 3 OO 55 (C.P. 1934).

Further research: O Jur 3d, Decedents' Estates § 684.

LAW IN GENERAL

A person dies with issue although the birth is posthumous. A definite failure of issue means an absence of lineal descendants at the death of the first taker or at another fixed time. Such intention is generally presumed. A devise defeasible upon a definite failure of issue becomes absolute if the devisee has lineal descendants at the time fixed. A indefinite failure of issue means the extinction of the first taker's lineal descendants at any time in the future, as in a fee tail.

A conveyance or devise to B but if he dies without issue then to C, is construed by the weight of authority as referring to the death of the first taker B at any time; that is, B's estate is defeated if he is not survived by lineal descendants. In distinguishing this rule from the following, the vital fact must be kept in mind that here there is no preceding estate or other postponement of the gift to B.

When the devise over on death without issue is also subject to a withholding of control or to a defeasance for a stated period, and the period is likely to end before the death of the devisee, the time of death referred to is death before the end of such period.

A definite failure of issue at the termination of the particular estate is the presumed intent when a future interest is limited on death without issue, according to the prevailing rule; thus, when the conveyance or devise is "to B for life (or for years) and remainder to C but if C dies without issue then to D," the grant or gift to D does not take effect unless C dies without issue before the termination of the estate for life or for years. In such a case C's interest is indefeasible if he survives B.

Am Law of Prop § 21.49; CJS, Wills § 724; Powell § 339; Restatement, Property § 265; Simes and Smith § 527; Tiffany §§ 44, 373.

Both conditions must ordinarily be fulfilled before property can pass under a gift over upon death without issue and upon another contingency. 73 ALR2d 466.

11-82G One of Survivors Dying without Issue.

Cross remainders, see 11-73A.

Where the will provided that if any of the devisees "should die without issue, that the share or shares of such decedent or decedents shall be equally divided among the survivors of them"; held, that on the death, without issue, of a devisee who had succeeded to a portion of a share of a prior decedent, such portion was subject to the same contingency as the original share and passed to the survivor or survivors. Taylor v. Foster, 17 OS 166 (1867).

LAW IN GENERAL

A provision that the share of any of three or more takers who die without issue shall pass to the survivors does not apply to the interest accruing to a survivor when such survivor thereafter dies without issue; thus, under a devise "to B, C and D but if any die without issue his share shall pass to the survivors," when B dies first without issue his share passes to C and D but when C dies without issue survived by D the one-sixth interest which came to C from B passes to C's heirs or devisees. Powell § 345; Restatement, Property § 271; Simes and Smith § 547.

SECTION 11-83: EXECUTORY INTERESTS

Failure and acceleration of interests, see Section 11-16.
Survival requirement, see Section 11-81.

11-83A Definitions.

Other future interests, see 11-71A.

LAW IN GENERAL

An "executory interest" is any future interest, other than a remainder, which can be created in a transferee. In other words, it is a nonvested future interest created so that it will vest on the happening of a condition in a person other than the transferor or his heirs, and which divests a prior vested interest other than a fee simple before the normal expiration thereof, or which succeeds a determinable fee. Other characteristics of an executory interest are that it does not vest until the happening of the condition precedent which may or may not be certain to occur, and that it vests automatically without entry when the condition is fulfilled. Am Law of Prop § 4.53; CJS, Estates § 120; Powell § 279; Simes and Smith § 221.

A "springing use" extinguishes or modifies the interest left in the transferor. A "shifting use" defeats the interest simultaneously created in a third person. These uses are commonly called executory interests where they are legal interests. "Executory devise" is frequently used to designate an executory interest created by will. Simes and Smith § 30; Tiffany §§ 356, 359.

11-83B   Creation.

An estate in land may be created by will in Ohio that will not vest until the expiration of a definite period, or the happening of some event after the death of the testator, without the creation by will of an intervening estate upon which to rest it. Heath v. Cleveland, 114 OS 535, 151 NE 649, 4 Abs 256, 24 OLR 366 (1926).

Further research: O Jur 3d, Estates § 130.

LAW IN GENERAL

Executory interests are not required to take effect in possession at the expiration of a preceding estate. They also arise, even in some states where the statute of uses is not in force, in a person other than the grantor upon the happening of an event which terminates a preceding estate before it would normally expire.

Such interests may be created by deed, although they are usually created by will and known as executory devises. A deed cannot convey to an unascertained person, therefore executory interests do not arise under a conveyance inter vivos to a person and his heirs.

An executory limitation is ordinarily indestructible by premature termination of a preceding estate. Attempted executory limitations are frequently void for violation of the rule against perpetuities.

An executory interest may be valid while a condition subsequent on the same contingency would be void as against public policy.

Am Jur 2d, Estates § 333; Am Law of Prop § 4.54; CJS, Estates § 122; Simes and Smith § 222; Tiffany §§ 356, 358.

11-83C   Construction.

"The rule of law is also well established that where possible the contingent interest will be determined to be a contingent remainder rather than an executory devise. The nature and character of the estates are identical, but

460

the rules applicable to executory devises are only invoked when necessary to carry out the intention of the testator." Piper v. Lucey, 21 Abs 661 (App. 1936).

Further research: O Jur 3d, Estates § 131.

LAW IN GENERAL

Executory interests and contingent remainders are principally differentiated in that an executory interest can divest the preceding estate, and in that a contingent remainder is supported by a prior freehold estate. Whether a devise takes effect as an executory interest or as a remainder depends upon the circumstances at the death of the testator, a remainder being preferred if the devise can be effective as such. An executory interest may later become a contingent remainder. The converse is not true, that is, the destructibility of a contingent remainder cannot be avoided by regarding it as changed to an executory interest. Am Law of Prop § 21.39; Simes and Smith § 191; Tiffany §§ 361, 364.

11-83D Dower.

Dower does not attach to any future interest unless and until the deceased spouse comes into possession of the interest.

LAW IN GENERAL

A dower right ceases to exist when the estate from which it is derived is terminated during the husband's lifetime by an executory limitation. Where the limitation does not take effect until or after the husband's death there is a diversity of authority. The position of the Restatement that dower is extinguished is supported by slight case authority. Am Jur 2d, Dower and Curtesy §§ 61, 102; Am Law of Prop § 529; 25 ALR2d 333; Powell §§ 191, 215; Restatement, Property § 54; Tiffany § 510.

SECTION 11-84: TRANSFER OF THE INTERESTS

Judicial sales of future interests, see Section 17-42.

11-84A Alienation Inter Vivos.

See also Section 11-43.

R.C. 2131.04 provides: "Remainders, whether vested or contingent, executory interests, and other expectant estates are descendible, devisable, and alienable in the same manner as estates in possession." (As eff. 10-1-53.)

A future contingent interest in real estate, in the nature of a contingent remainder or executory devise, being an interest in land, known to the law, is transmissible by devise or deed. Thompson v. Hoop, 6 OS 480 (1856).

Where the will provides: "If my son C should die before the sale of said block, and before the division of the proceeds thereof" one-half of his interest shall go to his child or children and one-half to his brothers and sisters; held that the sale by C of his contingent interest and his death before the sale and division provided in the will, did not defeat the claim of the son of C. Parthe v. Parthe, 6 App 317, 26 CC(NS) 577, 28 CD 242 (1917).

Further research: O Jur 3d, Estates § 129; Am Jur 2d, Estates §§ 316, 317; Am Law of Prop § 4.67; CJS, Estates § 88; Powell § 283; Restatement, Property § 162; Simes and Smith § 1858; Tiffany §§ 341, 387.

11-84B   Devolution upon Death.

See also statute at 11-84A.

Where the devise was to a daughter for life, should she remain single "but in case of her marriage or death, then all of my lands or real estate to be equally divided between my then surviving children or their heirs": Held that a will (or conveyance) by another child of the testator passes nothing if such child dies before the life tenant. Gill v. Alcorn, 19 App 122 (1924).

Further research: Am Law of Prop § 4.74; Powell § 284; Restatement, Property § 164; Simes and Smith § 1883; Tiffany §§ 341, 388.

DIVISION 11-9:   CLASS GIFTS; PER STIRPES OR PER CAPITA

SECTION 11-91:   CLASS GIFTS GENERALLY

Survival requirement, see Section 11-81.

11-91A   Rules.

In the absence of clear and unambiguous indications of a contrary intention disclosed in a will, the members of a class are to be ascertained as of the death of the testator. Provident Savings Bank & Trust Co. v. Nash, 75 App 493, 62 NE2d 736, 31 OO 290 (1945).

Further research: O Jur 3d, Estates § 108.

LAW IN GENERAL

A remainder to a class, as a gift to children of life tenant, vests at testator's death in the living members of the class, subject to opening to admit members of the class afterward coming into being before the termination of the postponement. If there are no such children at testator's death the remainder is contingent until one of the class comes into being. Upon the death of a member of the class during the existence of the particular estate, his interest passes to his heirs or devisees. The remainder as a whole may be contingent under the ordinary principles of construction as to vesting. Am Jur 2d, Wills § 1408; 65 ALR2d 1408; CJS, Estates § 73; Powell § 276; Restatement, Property § 269; Tiffany § 325.

11-91B   Class Gifts Distinguished.

Where beneficiaries are described both by name and as a class, with nothing more to show the testator's intent, the gift is to individuals to which the class description is added by way of identification; the gift to such beneficiaries, who were nonrelatives and predeceased the testator, lapsed and passed into the residuary estate. Nolan v. Borger, 203 NE2d 274, 32 OO2d 255, 95 Abs 225 (Prob. 1963).

LAW IN GENERAL

A transfer is a class gift only where the testator or grantor intended to designate a group capable of future change in members; thus, a gift to "children," or the like, is presumed to be a class gift unless an intention to designate certain individuals is shown. Am Law of Prop § 22.4; 61 ALR2d 212; Powell § 352; Restatement, Property § 279; Simes and Smith § 611; Tiffany § 381.

A gift is one to a class if the number of persons to take is to be ascertained in the future. A class gift may assign amounts or portions to the present members of the class if the disposition contemplates that the persons who eventually take shall take amounts or portions sufficiently defined. 61 ALR2d 221.

11-91C   Increase and Decrease in Membership; Closing a Class.

When there is a member of the class in being at the time the limitation takes effect, and when a member of the class thereafter and before the termination of the particular estate comes into being, the remainder vests at once and will open to let in after-born members of the class if any such appear before the termination of the particular estate. Wiley v. Bricker, 21 CC 109, 11 CD 429 (1900).

Under will providing that on life beneficiary's death the fund should be equally divided between beneficiary's children, children living at testator's death took vested remainder, though designated class was subject to enlargement, and though children predeceased beneficiary. Simpson v. Welsh, 44 App 115, 184 NE 242, 13 Abs 714 (1932).

Further research: O Jur 3d, Decedents' Estates § 712.

LAW IN GENERAL

An immediate class gift passes to only those members in being at the date the will or deed becomes effective, subject to a contrary intention shown by the will. An exception to the rule is made when the immediate gift is an aggregate sum limited to a class of which none are yet in existence, in which case the sum is set aside for future distribution.

When the gift is a stated sum per capita and one of the class is in being at testator's death, the whole class gift will be defeated if failure to close the class would interfere with settlement of the estate.

When enjoyment of the gift is postponed the number of takers will increase to include those of the group in being at the time a class member is entitled to demand possession of his share. When one is admitted to a class his interest is not terminated by his death, unless by the terms of the limitation or by the rules of survival requirement. A grantor or testator may provide a substituted disposition on the elimination of a possible taker; or a lapse statute may be applicable.

Am Law of Prop § 22.39; 6 ALR2d 1342; CJS, Wills § 694; Powell § 362; Restatement, Property § 294; Simes and Smith § 634.

Most courts have applied the date of distribution as the time for ascertainment of the class where the members are described as heirs, descendants, family or the like. 33 ALR2d 244.

11-91D Life Tenant as Member.

LAW IN GENERAL

The life tenant may also be a member of the class. When he happens to be the sole member of the designated class, the circumstance is considered in ascertaining the intention of the grantor or testator. Am Jur 2d, Estates §§ 281, 291, 292.

11-91E Alienation.

Sale of interests of after-born members of the class, see Section 17-42.

LAW IN GENERAL

A remainder to a class may be transferred by the members in being, but a sale by them does not extinguish the interests of after-born members of the class. Tiffany § 340.

SECTION 11-92: GIFTS TO CHILDREN AND THE LIKE

Survival requirement, see Section 11-81.

11-92A To a Parent "and His Children"; To a Person and a Group.

Under a bequest to be divided among the children living of A and B, and C and D, share and share alike, provided they are living at testator's death, C and D share and share alike with the children living of A and B. Falor v. Slusser, 18 CC(NS) 309, 29 CD 513 (1910).

Under a will devising realty to a wife "and to her children," each takes an equal undivided portion as tenant in common. Clark v. Clark, 13 App 164, 31 CC(NS) 472 (1920).

The will created a fee tail estate where it gave a remainder to the testator's two sons and their children and where the sons had no children at the death of the testator. Hover v. Gardner, 2 Abs 135 (App. 1924).

Further research: O Jur 3d, Decedents' Estates § 692.

LAW IN GENERAL

A devise or conveyance "to B and his children" is usually a gift to a class composed of B and his children. This rule is in accord with the second resolution in Wild's Case. Children born after the effective date of the instrument are held to be excluded.

If B has no child at the effective date of the instrument, the limitation has been variously construed that B takes a life estate with a class gift to his children, that B takes the entire fee, or that B takes a fee tail. The last mentioned holding is known as the first resolution in Wild's Case.

When the gift is to a named person (other than a parent of the group) and a group, or to two or more groups, all are members of a single group according to the weight of authority.

Am Jur 2d, Estates § 69; Am Law of Prop § 22.12; 161 ALR 612; Powell § 355; Restatement, Property § 283; Simes and Smith § 691.

11-92B   To Children.

As a general rule, the use of the word "children" excludes descendants beyond those of the first degree but will be held to include issue whenever reason demands. Monroe v. Leckey, 142 NE2d 314, 4 OO2d 208, 75 Abs 560 (C.P. 1956).

A bequest "to the children of" a named person is a class gift, and does not include within the class a child who died before the execution of the will. Clark v. Cushing, 6 Misc 75, 213 NE2d 216, 34 OO2d 206 (Prob. 1966).

Further research: O Jur 3d, Decedents' Estates §§ 608, 611.

LAW IN GENERAL

A gift to children of a certain person is generally construed to be to issue of the first generation, born in lawful wedlock, of such person. This rule may be modified by statute, or by the intention of the transferor, to enlarge or restrict the number of takers. The circumstances are frequently held to preclude the application of the rule, as when grandchildren or illegitimate children are the only possible takers, or when the transferor is the adoptive parent, or when the transferor knew of the previous adoption by the named person. Am Law of Prop § 22.29; 14 ALR2d 1242; CJS, Wills § 652; Powell § 357; Restatement, Property § 285; Simes and Smith § 723.

11-92C   To Grandchildren, Brothers and the Like.

A devise to issue is a devise to lineal descendants in the absence of additional language showing an intention to devise to children only. Rieck v. Richards, 40 App 201, 178 NE 276, 10 Abs 264 (1931).

Where a testator has designated in his will that his estate descend to "my nieces and nephews," such designation means the children of his brothers and sisters and does not include the nieces and nephews of the testator's prior

465

deceased spouse. Frederick v. Hoffman, 7 App2d 27, 218 NE2d 478, 36 OO2d 88 (1966).

LAW IN GENERAL

The usual terms used in making a class gift which do not ordinarily require consideration of the statutes of descent are children, grandchildren, brothers, sisters, nephews, nieces, cousins, issue, descendants and family.

Gifts to grandchildren, brothers and sisters, nephews and nieces, or cousins are construed as gifts to children of the appropriate persons; for example, "to cousins of B" is regarded as meaning "to the children of the uncles and aunts of B." Collateral relatives of the half blood are included and relatives by affinity are excluded, as a rule.

Gifts to issue or descendants of a certain person are to offspring of any generation who are within the line of inheritance, as modified by a different intention.

The term family is presumed to mean the spouse and issue of the designated person in a majority of the cases.

Am Law of Prop § 22.35; CJS, Wills § 659; Powell § 359; Restatement, Property § 291; Simes and Smith § 726.

SECTION 11-93: GIFTS TO HEIRS AND THE LIKE

Deeds to heirs, see 8-32A.
Remainders, see 11-81E.
Survival requirement, see also Section 11-81.
Worthier title, see 8-31O and 9-21K.

11-93A Generally.

Where the devise is to son of testator "through his natural life and then to his heirs," and in another part of the will "heirs" is used in the sense of "children," the son took a life estate only and upon his death without issue, the estate reverted to the heirs of the testator. Bunnell v. Evans, 26 OS 409 (1875); Cultice v. Mills, 97 OS 112, 119 NE 200, 15 OLR 538, 63 WLB 18 (1918).

Heirs in its technical sense embraces those who take under the statute of descent and distribution. The widow of a son of testator is an heir where the will devises a life estate to the son and remainder to his heirs unless the will provides otherwise. Holt v. Miller, 133 OS 418, 14 NE2d 409, 11 OO 85 (1938).

The general rule is that "next of kin" denotes the person or persons nearest of kindred to the deceased who are most nearly related to deceased by blood. State ex rel. Weiss v. Feldman, 28 Abs 104 (App. 1938).

Further research: O Jur 3d, Decedents' Estates § 598.

LAW IN GENERAL

A gift "to the heirs of B" passes to the persons who would take the subject property under the statutes of descent applied as of the death of B, unless a

CLASS GIFTS; PER STIRPES OR PER CAPITA   11-94A

contrary intention is evidenced. When B dies before the testator an exception to the rule is ordinarily made and B's heirs are ascertained as of the time of testator's death.

"Heirs of the body of B" restricts the takers to lineal descendants of B, as in fee tail estates. "Next of kin" or "relatives" restricts the takers to those taking the personal property, according to the prevailing rule.

Under any of such descriptions the property passes at the death of the named ancestor and in the proportions required by the statutes of descent and distribution. A common example of a remainder which is contingent, because limited to unascertained persons, is where the limitation is to the heirs of a living person.

When the gift is to groups of such persons or to such an individual and group having a common ancestor, then the share of each person is as though the property descended from such ancestor, that is, per stirpes. When the two groups are heirs of husband and wife each group receives an equal share.

These rules do not apply when the court finds that a different intention was manifested by the testator. Use of words such as "then" or "remaining interest" are not sufficient to show a different intention.

Am Law of Prop § 22.56; 19 ALR2d 371; CJS, Wills § 671; Powell § 371; Restatement, Property § 305; Simes and Smith § 727; Tiffany § 321.

The words "relatives" or "relations" include persons related by consanguinity and exclude those related by affinity, or the words are restricted to heirs or next of kin under the statutes of descent and distribution. This rule is subordinate to ascertainment of a contrary intention of the testator. 5 ALR2d 715.

A class described as the grantor's or trust settlor's "heirs," "next of kin" or the like designated to take a future interest will, subject to a different intention being shown, have its members ascertained as of the death of the ancestor. 38 ALR2d 327.

SECTION 11-94: PER STIRPES OR PER CAPITA

11-94A Generally.

Intestate property, see also 9-11F.

Nephews and nieces take per capita; and a nephew or niece who died before the intestate, leaving children, such children take per stirpes the share of the deceased parent. Ewers v. Follin, 9 OS 327 (1859); Hasse v. Morison, 110 OS 153, 143 NE 551, 2 Abs 259, 22 OLR 49 (1924); Dutoit v. Doyle, 16 OS 400 (1865).

By reference to the statute we ascertain who are to take, and by the plain provisions of the will itself, we are told how they are to take, that is: "equally, share and share alike," per capita and not per stirpes. Mooney v. Purpus, 70 OS 57, 70 NE 894, 2 OLR 3, 49 WLB 189 (1904).

The testamentary direction "to distribute equally to my legal heirs" is equivalent to a direction to make distribution in accordance with the statutes providing for descent and distribution. Barr v. Denney, 79 OS 358, 87 NE 267, 6 OLR 616, 54 WLB 52 (1909).

"The term, 'per stirpes,' as used by a testator means simply that his devise or bequest is to be divided into as many equal shares as there are members of the root generation, counting both living and deceased members leaving lineal descendants with an equal share being distributed to each living member of such generation and the share of each deceased member of such generation being divided and subdivided, in turn, per stirpes, among his lineal descendants. The term, 'per capita,' as used by a testator means simply that his devise or bequest is to be divided into as many equal shares as there are surviving members of a certain generation or class of people . . . and the lineal descendants of any deceased member receiving nothing." Kraemer v. Hook, 168 OS 221, 152 NE2d 430, 6 OO2d 11 (1958).

Where testator devised real estate to the children of A and the children of B, all such children being grandchildren of testator, each of the grandchildren will take an equal share. Broermann v. Kessling, 6 App 7, 30 CD 103, 28 CC(NS) 321 (1914).

Where those entitled to share in an estate are nieces, nephews, grandnieces and grandnephews of the intestate, the nieces and nephews take equally, per capita, according to the total number of nieces and nephews whether surviving or not, and the grandnieces and grandnephews take per stirpes or by representation the shares of their deceased parents. Kincaid v. Cronin, 61 App 300, 22 NE2d 576, 15 OO 198, 28 Abs 475 (1939).

The general rule is that a devise to a class, such as "all my nephews" and the like, calls for a per capita distribution. Jones v. Lewis, 70 App 17, 44 NE2d 735, 24 OO 328 (1941).

In the absence of controlling context, courts of this state favor per stirpes, rather than per capita, connotation of the word "issue." Cleveland Trust Co. v. Mansfield, 71 NE2d 287, 34 OO 26 (C.P. 1945).

Under devise "in equal shares to the children of my deceased brother, _____, and to the children of my brother, _____, who survive me, share and share alike," all of such children take per capita as a class. The antilapse statute applies only to the children of the deceased brother. Cowgill v. Faulconer, 57 Misc 6, 385 NE2d 327, 8 OO3d 423 (1978).

"We submit that the weight of authority shows the law to be as follows: (a) In the absence of phraseology to the contrary, both in statutes of descent and distribution and in wills, the distribution is per capita when the takers are in equal degree of consanguinity to the decedent. The distribution is per stirpes when the takers are not equally related to the decedent. (b) The 'stirpes' or 'stocks' are determined from the number of nearest living relatives plus the number of stocks descended from deceased relatives in the same degree of kindred." Charles C. White, "Per Stirpes or Per Capita," 13 Cin. L. R. 298.

Further research: O Jur 3d, Decedents' Estates §§ 721, 722.

LAW IN GENERAL

Per stirpes or per capita indicates what fractional share of an estate is taken, not who shall take. Stirpes means literally roots or stocks, and per stirpes denotes that persons take by representation of their ancestors. Division per capita means that the individual takers have equal shares. The general presumption is that beneficiaries take per capita when the proportions are not specified, although the intention of the testator governs in all cases. Many cases hold under slight indication of intention that the division shall be per stirpes. Per stirpes is the presumed intent when the beneficiaries are in unequal degrees of relationship to their ancestor, particularly if relatives of the testator. Some evidence of a per stirpital intent is shown by use of "between," and of per capital intent by use of "among." The words "share and share alike" or "equally" import a division per capita, but are found in some particular cases to intend equality between those of nearest kinship. Am Jur 2d, Wills § 1449; 13 ALR2d 1023; 40 ALR2d 263; CJS, Wills § 707; Simes and Smith § 746.

The distribution to a class is generally per capita except (a) when a different intent is shown, (b) when a possible taker does not survive and his children are substituted, such children take per stirpes, (c) when the class is described as "issue" or "descendants" the shares of the takers are determined by the statutes of descent as of the date the members of the class are finally fixed, or (d) when the class is described as "family" the statutes of descent control with the modification that the spouse receives a primary share. A person with two descriptions in a per capita class gift takes only one share. Am Law of Prop § 21.13; Powell § 368; Restatement, Property § 300; Simes and Smith § 740.

CHAPTER 12: EXECUTORS AND ADMINISTRATORS

DIVISION 12-1: IN GENERAL

DIVISION 12-1: IN GENERAL

SECTION 12-11: GENERALLY

Equitable conversion, see Section 16-63.

12-11A Title and Rights; Rents.

R.C. 2113.311 provides that, upon application, the probate court may authorize the executor or administrator to assume the management and rental of real estate owned by the decedent. The executor or administrator may be authorized to collect rents; make certain disbursements; rent the property on a month-to-month basis, or, upon a court order, for a period not to exceed one year; or prosecute actions for forcible entry and detention. The authority shall terminate upon transfer to the heirs or devisees, upon sale, or upon application of executor or administrator, or for good cause shown upon application of an heir or devisee. (As eff. 11-9-59.)

An administrator conveys without covenants of warranty, and cannot render the estate liable by false representations as to the title or encumbrances. Dunlap v. Robinson, 12 OS 530 (1861).

The rents of the lands of an insolvent intestate, accruing between the death of the intestate and a sale of the lands for the payment of debts by the administrator, belong to the heir and not to the administrator. Overturf v. Dugan, 29 OS 230 (1876).

When executors with power of sale under the will enter into a contract of sale of lands of their decedent, the laws of Ohio are read into such contract and such executors are amenable to the same actions, suits and legal processes as other persons. State ex rel. Black v. White, 132 OS 58, 5 NE2d 163, 7 OO 165 (1936).

Title to personal property of a deceased person passes to his executor or administrator, pending the settlement of the estate, whether he dies testate or intestate. Winters Nat. Bank & Trust Co. v. Riffe, 2 OS2d 72, 206 NE2d 212, 31 OO2d 56 (1965).

As a general rule, the duties of the executor as such, are coextensive with the provisions of the will; and it is only in cases of unmistakable intention, or of inherent necessity, that a separate character will be assigned to him. In re Crawford's Estate, 21 CC 554, 11 CD 605 (1901).

An administrator has no claim or interest in the real estate of his decedent except the statutory right in land sale proceedings. Bickley v. Citizens Savings Bank & Trust Co., 34 NE2d 262, 5 OO 45, 20 Abs 363 (App. 1935).

When certain persons are named as executors and trustees under a will, they will not take as trustees until they have fully discharged their duties as executors and not until the trust property has been set apart as such. Before acting as trustees they should be appointed as such by the court. In re Emswiler's Estate, 38 NE2d 917, 24 OO 539, 36 Abs 8 (App. 1941).

Title to all personal property belonging to a decedent vests in his administrator upon the acceptance of the trust, but the administrator has no right in

472

joint and survivorship certificates of deposit. Hoover v. Hoover, 90 App 148, 104 NE2d 41, 47 OO 37 (1950).

LAW IN GENERAL

Title to personal property of the decedent vests in his personal representative, that is, in the executor or administrator upon his appointment. Title to real property passes to the heir or devisee, who may also be the personal representative, upon the decedent's death.

The right of the administrator in the realty is wholly statutory and includes the power to sell for payment of claims against the estate. The executor or administrator has no right to lease or to collect rent becoming due after decedent's death, and has no other interest in or control over the realty of his decedent except as provided by the will or by statute. The will may give the executor the right to rents by virtue of an equitable conversion as when a sale is directed. The consent of the heirs or devisees has been held to warrant the collection of rent by him as an agent or trustee. Am Law of Prop §§ 14.7, 14.30; CJS, Descent and Distribution § 69; CJS, Executors and Administrators § 252.

12-11B Appointment; Bond.

Residence and domicile, see also 9-28A.

R.C. 2109.02 provides: "Every fiduciary, before entering upon the execution of a trust, shall receive letters of appointment from a probate court having jurisdiction of the subject matter of the trust.

"The duties of a fiduciary shall be those required by law, and such additional duties as the court orders. Letters of appointment shall not issue until a fiduciary has executed a written acceptance of his duties, acknowledging that he is subject to removal for failure to perform his duties, and that he is subject to possible penalties for conversion of property he holds as a fiduciary. The written acceptance may be filed with the application for appointment.

"No act or transaction by a fiduciary is valid prior to the issuance of letters of appointment to him. This section does not prevent an executor named in a will, or an executor nominated pursuant to a power as described in section 2107.65 of the Revised Code, from paying funeral expenses, or prevent necessary acts for the preservation of the trust estate prior to the issuance of such letters." (As eff. 10-14-83.)

R.C. 2109.04 provides that unless otherwise provided by law, every fiduciary shall, prior to issuance of his letters, file in probate court a bond in not less than double the probable value of the personal estate and annual rentals. If the instrument creating the trust dispenses with bond, the court may require bond. A successor fiduciary shall give bond unless clearly relieved by the instrument. (As eff. 10-4-84.)

R.C. 2109.21 provides residence qualifications of fiduciary. (As eff. 10-14-83.)

R.C. 2109.26 provides for the appointment in probate court of a successor fiduciary. (As eff. 10-1-53.)

R.C. 2113.01 provides: "Upon the death of a resident of this state intestate, letters of administration of his estate shall be granted by the probate court of the county in which he was a resident at the time he died.

"If the will of any person is admitted to probate in this state, letters testamentary or of administration shall be granted by the probate court in which such will was admitted to probate." (As eff. 10-1-53.)

R.C. 2113.08 provides for publication of notice of appointment for three consecutive weeks. (As eff. 1-1-76.)

R.C. 2113.15 to 2113.17 provide that when there is delay in granting letters, the court may appoint a special administrator to collect and preserve the effects of the deceased. The time of limitation for suits against the estate shall begin to run from the granting of letters in the usual form. (As eff. 10-1-53.)

"Resident" is not synonymous with "domiciled." The appointment of an administrator in a county where decedent was resident is suspended by the probate of the will of such decedent in the county where he was domiciled. State ex rel. Overlander v. Brewer, 147 OS 386, 72 NE2d 84, 34 OO 338 (1947).

Further research: O Jur 3d, Decedents' Estates § 999.

LAW IN GENERAL

Appointment by the court is essential to the authority of the executor or administrator. When made the appointment relates back to the death of the decedent. Appointment of an executor or administrator is not necessary to the devolution of title to the devisees or heirs. However, it may be necessary in order to show the payment of succession taxes and other claims against the estate, or to establish the names of the heirs and other facts of inheritance.

12-11C Inventory.

Exceptions to inventory, see 16-17B.

R.C. 2115.01 et seq. provide for inventory by executor or administrator.

Standard of Title Examination

(Adopted by Ohio State Bar Association in 1952)

Problem 5.1A:
  Does omission of the real estate from the inventory and appraisement cast a cloud on the title?

Standard 5.1A:
  No, such omission standing alone does not affect marketability.

Further research: O Jur 3d, Decedents' Estates §§ 1362, 1363.

12-11D   Presumed Decedents; Absentees' Estates.

Presumption of death, see 9-11K.

R.C. 2113.81 provides that money or other property due from an estate to a nonresident of the United States may be held by a trustee or the county treasurer. (As eff. 10-6-55.)

R.C. 2119.01 to 2119.05 provide for trustees of the estates of absent persons. (As eff. 10-1-53.)

R.C. 2121.01 to 2121.09 provide that a person is presumed dead when he has disappeared and been continuously absent from his last domicile for five years without being heard from, or for less than that period if he was exposed to a specific peril of death at his disappearance, or when he was in the armed forces of United States (2121.01). Probate court proceedings for a decree are prescribed (2121.02). Qualification of witnesses is provided (2121.03). Court may decree that a presumption of death has been established; the date of death shall be for all purposes the date of such decree; the marriage of the decedent, if any, is dissolved by the decree (2121.04). Upon signing of the decree, administration may proceed and a three-year bond may be required conditioned upon the presumed decedent being alive (2121.05). If real estate passes upon the decree, the persons taking may sell or mortgage it free from any claim of the presumed decedent except during the three-year period unless a bond has been given for that period conditioned upon the presumed decedent being alive (2121.06). A three-year bond may be ordered before distribution of personal property but this section does not preclude a purchaser, transferee, or mortgagee from acquiring good title (2121.07). The court may vacate the decree within three years and all previous proceedings shall remain valid; the rights of recovery are provided to the presumed decedent from persons who received property under the original decree (2121.08). After vacation of the decree the presumed decedent may be substituted as plaintiff or defendant in all actions brought by or against the executor or administrator. (As eff. 9-30-74; R.C. 2121.06 and 2121.08 as eff. 11-1-77.)

So far as the administration of decedent's estate is concerned, the common-law rule has been modified by statute, and the presumption of death in the case of unexplained absence for the prescribed number of years arises as of the date of the decree of the probate court authorized by statute. In re McWilson's Estate, 155 OS 261, 98 NE2d 289, 44 OO 262 (1951).

In a proceeding to determine heirship, the provisions of the Presumed Decedents' Act (R.C. 2121.01 et seq.) are not applicable to presumptively fix the date of the death of one who if living would participate in the estate. Baker v. Myers, 160 OS 376, 116 NE2d 711, 52 OO 239 (1953).

A trustee for a missing person may maintain an action for equitable partition. His authority to act is not terminated with the expiration of seven years' absence of such missing person. In re Parrett, 86 App 162, 90 NE2d 425, 41 OO 20 (1949).

In an action for declaratory judgment to determine the distributive rights of a missing devisee, the probate court may fix the date of his death at any time between his disappearance and the decree. Freiberg v. Schloss, 112 NE2d 352, 50 OO 156, 65 Abs 331 (Prob. 1953).

The statute restricting distribution from an estate, R.C. 2113.81, to nonresidents of United States is invalid because it infringes upon the exclusive power of the federal government over foreign affairs. First Nat. Bank of Cincinnati v. Fishman, 16 Misc 185, 239 NE2d 270, 43 OO2d 384 (Prob. 1968).

Further research: O Jur 3d, Death §§ 6, 16.

12-11E Determination of Heirship; Distribution and Accounting.

Suits to construe wills, see 9-21Q.

R.C. 2109.30 provides for accounting by fiduciaries. (As eff. 10-4-84.)

R.C. 2109.32 provides for hearing on the account and that the final account of an executor or administrator shall not be approved until after four months since appointment and until the surviving spouse has filed an election to take under or against the will or the time therefor has expired. (As eff. 1-1-76.)

R.C. 2109.35 in part provides: "The vacation of an order settling an account, made after notice given in the manner provided in section 2109.32 or 2109.33 of the Revised Code, shall not affect the rights of a purchaser for value in good faith, a lessee for value in good faith, or an encumbrancer for value in good faith. . . ." (As eff. 10-1-53.)

R.C. 2123.01 to 2123.06 provide for determination of heirship. (As eff. 10-1-53.)

R.C. 2123.07 provides: "Any fiduciary may make a final distribution of an estate or take any other appropriate action respecting a trust, upon the determination set forth in section 2123.05 of the Revised Code, and shall thereupon, together with the surety, be discharged from liability arising from such determined interest, and the title to any property thereupon purchased from such fiduciary shall be free from such determined interest." (As eff. 10-1-53.)

Common pleas court has concurrent jurisdiction under Declaratory Judgment Act (R.C. 2721.01 et seq.) of determination of heirship. Kane v. Kane, 146 OS 686, 67 NE2d 783, 33 OO 166 (1946).

An order settling the final account, from which it appears that no allowance has been made to the widow for her year's support and no property set off to her as exempt, and that said estate has been fully settled, operates as a judgment at law or decree in equity adjudicating that the widow had no right to any distributive share, allowance for year's support, or to exempt property in the estate. Eckhart v. Wiles, 61 App 32, 22 NE2d 289, 15 OO 61 (1938).

Probate court has jurisdiction to adjudicate the rights of parties in specific items of property under these sections or under its general powers. Speidel v. Schaller, 73 App 141, 55 NE2d 346, 28 OO 252, 40 Abs 190 (1943).

Judgments of Probate Court cannot be attacked collaterally, except for fraud, and this applies to judgments approving the accounts of fiduciaries. Border v. Ohio Savings & Trust Co., 26 Misc 273, 267 NE2d 120, 55 OO2d 410 (C.P. 1970).

12-11F Completion of Improvements.

LAW IN GENERAL

The right or duty of the personal representative to pay out of the personal estate for decedent's contract for improvements has been both denied and affirmed in the cases so that a rule cannot be stated. 5 ALR2d 1250.

12-11G Conveyance to Administrator.

A deed to a person as administrator conveys the legal title in trust for the creditors and other beneficiaries of the estate. A purchaser from the administrator is bound to take notice of the trust. Matoon v. Clapp, 8 Ohio 248 (1837).

An administrator has no power to purchase real estate.

12-11H Relieving Estate from Administration.

Claims as liens, see 12-12B.

R.C. 2113.03 provides: "(A) Upon the application of any interested party, after notice of the filing of the application has been given to the surviving spouse and heirs at law in the manner and for the length of time the probate court directs, and after three weeks' notice to all interested parties by publication once each week in a newspaper of general circulation in the county, unless the notices are waived or found unnecessary, the court, when satisfied that the assets of an estate are twenty-five thousand dollars or less in value, and that creditors will not be prejudiced, may make an order relieving the estate from administration and directing delivery of personal property and transfer of real estate to the persons entitled to them.

"For the purposes of this section, the value of an estate that can reasonably be considered to approximate twenty-five thousand dollars or less, and that is not composed entirely of money, stocks, bonds, or other property the value of which is readily ascertainable, shall be determined by an appraiser selected by the applicant, subject to the approval of the court. The appraiser's valuation of the property shall be reported to the court in the application to relieve the estate from administration. The appraiser shall be paid in accordance with section 2115.06 of the Revised Code.

"For the purposes of this section, the amount of property to be delivered or transferred to the surviving spouse or minor children of the deceased as the allowance for support, shall be established in accordance with section 2117.20 of the Revised Code.

"When a delivery, sale, or transfer of personal property has been ordered from an estate that has been relieved from administration, the court may appoint a commissioner to execute all necessary instruments of conveyance. The commissioner shall receipt for the property, distribute the proceeds of the conveyance upon court order, and report to the court after distribution.

"When the decedent died testate, the will shall be presented for probate, and, if admitted to probate, the court may relieve the estate from administration and order distribution of the estate under the will.

"An order of the court relieving an estate from administration shall have the same effect as administration proceedings in freeing land in the hands of an innocent purchaser for value from possible claims of unsecured creditors.

"(B) An application to relieve an estate from administration shall be in writing and shall contain the following information:

"(1) The name, date of death, and place of residence at the time of death, of the decedent;

"(2) The name of the surviving spouse of the decedent, and the names, ages, and addresses of the persons entitled to the next estate of inheritance under the statutes of descent and distribution, and their respective degrees of relationship to the decedent and to the surviving spouse of the decedent;

"(3) A summary statement of the character and value of the property comprising the estate;

"(4) A list of all known creditors of the decedent, and the amount of their claims;

"(5) If the decedent died testate or intestate, a statement to that effect.

"(C) The application shall be in the following form, and this form shall be used exclusively by the probate courts in this state:

"Application for Release of Estate from Administration
Revised Code, Sec. 2113.03

No...... Doc...... Page...... Filed........ , 19 ....

Common Pleas Court, Probate Division, ...

County, Ohio

In the Matter of   )

   THE ESTATE OF   )   No. ....

.......................)   ...., 19....

           Deceased)

....says

that ....late a resident of the

.... of ....

.... County, Ohio, died .... on

                                  (testate or intestate)

the ..... day of ...., 19......., leaving

.... surviving spouse, and the following persons entitled to the next estate of inheritance under the statutes of descent and distribution whose names, ages, their respective degrees of relationship to the decedent, relationship to the surviving spouse of the decedent, and addresses are as follows:

Name	Age	Relationship to Decedent	Relationship to Surviving Spouse of Decedent	Address
....	....	....	....	....
....	....	....	....	....

   The applicant selects .... to act when required, as appraiser of the real and personal property of the decedent, the value of which is not readily ascertainable.

The following is a summary statement of the character and value of the property comprising the estate.

Appraiser's Report:

I certify that the foregoing is a true and correct appraisement of the property exhibited to me.

Dated ...., 19.... ....

Appraiser

RECAPITULATION OF ASSETS

Personal Property of the value of .... $ ....

Real Estate of the value of .... $ ....

Total Estate $ ....

That the debts owing by the decedent and to whom owing are as follows:

Name	Address	For What	Amount
....			
....			

The estate being $25,000 or less in amount, the applicant asks that the estate be relieved from administration and that delivery or transfer of the property be made to the following persons:

Name	Address	Property to be Delivered or Transferred
....		
....		
....		

Applicant

WAIVER

We the undersigned, surviving spouse and heirs at law of the above named decedent and interested parties in the above entitled action hereby waive service of notice in the above entitled action and consent to the delivery or transfer of the described property as prayed for above.

Dated this .... day of ...., 19....

....

....

....

....

....

ORDER RELIEVING ESTATE FROM ADMINISTRATION

The court finds that the decedent died on ....

...................., 19........, and that the entire estate of the decedent consists of assets having the value of $ ....

The court finds from the representations made that further notice is unnecessary, that the estate is within the provisions of section 2113.03 of the Revised Code, and that creditors will not be prejudiced by granting the order. It is therefore ordered and decreed that the estate be, and is hereby relieved from administration, and it is further ordered that the property of the estate be delivered and transferred to the following persons:

		Property to be Delivered
Name	Address	or Transferred
....	....	....
....	....	....
		.... ,
		Probate Judge."

(As eff. 10-20-87.)

Appointment of a commissioner to execute instruments of conveyance is a ministerial act and not essential to land title, although it may be necessary as to personal property such as stock certificates.

If the decedent left a will it must be admitted to probate even though no appointment of executor or administrator is necessary.

The statute now provides for admitting the will to probate and distributing the estate under the will. Therefore, where the decedent died testate since December 2, 1971 and the estate is relieved from administration, a certificate for transfer may be issued transferring real estate according to the terms of the will.

Prior to the 1976 revision of R.C. 2113.03, the statute contained no provision for transferring property exempted from administration or assigned as a year's allowance to the widow and children. The 1976 revision specified that the amount of property to be delivered to the surviving spouse and minor children as allowance for support (limited by R.C. 2117.20 to $5,000) "shall be established."

Further research: O Jur 3d, Decedents' Estates § 1957.

SECTION 12-12: CLAIMS AGAINST ESTATE

12-12A Payment Out of Personalty.

Abatement of devises and legacies, see 9-21M.

R.C. 2107.53 provides: "When part of the real estate of a testator descends to his heirs because it was not disposed of by his will, and his personal estate is insufficient to pay his debts, the undevised real estate shall be chargeable first with the debts, as far as it will go, in exoneration of the real estate that is devised, unless it appears from the will that a different arrangement of assets was made for the payment of such testator's debts, in which case such assets shall be applied for that purpose in conformity with the will." (As eff. 10-1-53.)

Even though a debt is secured by mortgage on real estate, if it is the personal debt of the intestate it is to be paid primarily out of the personal estate. Foreman v. Medina County Nat. Bank, 119 OS 17, 162 NE 42, 6 Abs 357, 26 OLR 461 (1928).

A devisee of a mortgaged estate cannot claim exoneration as against a pecuniary legatee. Tucker v. Lungren, 12 CC 622, 5 CD 577 (1896).

As against residuary clause in a will, property devised with mortgage on it, where there is provision that all debts be paid, passes free and clear and mortgage debt is chargeable to personal estate. Hart v. Hart, 6 Abs 580, 27 OLR 270 (App. 1928).

Further research: Am Law of Prop § 14.25; Tiffany § 1474.

LAW IN GENERAL

The decedent's residuary personal estate is primarily responsible for the exoneration of liens on his devised real estate. The common-law rule of exoneration is not applied at the expense of specific legatees nor applied to liens which are not for the decedent's personal obligation. 4 ALR2d 1023.

12-12B Claims as Liens.

Lien of legacies and charges, see 9-21N.
Relieving estate from administration, see 12-11H.

R.C. 2117.29 provides: "When the only debts of an estate remaining unpaid are secured by liens on property of the estate, the devisees, legatees, or heirs entitled to receive such property may be permitted to take the same subject to such liens, if all the lienholders consent and waive recourse to all the other assets of the estate in the event such property so taken is insufficient to pay the debts secured by such liens." (As eff. 1-10-61.)

R.C. 2117.36 provides: "No real estate of a deceased person which has been aliened or encumbered by the decedent's heirs prior to the issuing of letters testamentary or of administration shall be liable while in the hands of a bona fide purchaser for value or to the prejudice of a bona fide lessee or encumbrancer for value for debts of the deceased person unless letters testamentary or of administration are granted within four years from the date of death of such deceased person. No real estate of a deceased person which has been aliened or encumbered by the decedent's heirs or devisees after the issue of letters testamentary or of administration shall be liable while in the hands of a bona fide purchaser for value or to the prejudice of a bona fide lessee or encumbrancer for value for debts of a deceased person unless suit is brought to subject such real estate to the payment of such debts prior to the settlement of the executor's or administrator's final account or what purports to be his final account; provided that if such final account is not filed and settled within four years after the granting of letters testamentary or of administration, but excluding for the purposes hereof the time that any action is pending against the executors or administrators for the establishment or collection of any claim against the deceased, such real estate so aliened shall not be liable for the debts of the deceased unless suit is brought to subject such real estate thereto within such four-year period. The heir or devisee aliening such real estate shall be liable for the value thereof, with legal interest from the time of alienation, to the creditors of the deceased in the manner and within the limitations provided by law. This section does not enlarge or extend the right of the creditors of any deceased person against his real estate, or repeal any limitations contained in other sections of the Revised Code, or apply to mortgages or liens of record at the time of the death of such deceased person." (As eff. 10-1-53.)

Section 2117.36 refers to debts of the decedent and not debts or obligations created by law, such as year's allowance and moneys set off to the widow. Thornberry v. Freudiger, 28 Abs 142 (App. 1937).

The debts of decedent are a lien upon the real estate of which he died seized. Ruff v. Baker, 146 OS 456, 66 NE2d 540, 32 OO 537 (1946). At land sale such liens are transferred to the proceeds. In re Saviers' Estate, 23 Abs 166 (App. 1936); Cooper v. Cooper, 1 O Supp 267, 3 OO 431 (Prob. 1935).

The time that any action is pending against an executrix on a claim against her decedent extends to that extent the four-year period. Kohn v. Kohn, 67 App 404, 36 NE2d 1009, 21 OO 348 (1941).

Standard of Title Examination
(Adopted by Ohio State Bar Association in 1953; amended 1976)

Problem 5.2A:

Should objection be made to the title of a purchaser from the heirs on account of decedent's unpaid debts (a) where the estate has not been administered and more than four years have elapsed since decedent's death, or (b) where the final account has not been approved in the administration and more than four years have elapsed since the granting of letters without suit to subject the real estate having been commenced?

Standard 5.2A:

No.

Comment 5.2A:

The lien of (estate) inheritance tax is not barred by the four-year statute of limitations.

Further research: O Jur 3d, Decedents' Estates § 1614.

12-12C Presentation and Priority.

R.C. 2113.24 provides that the time during which the office of the executor or administrator is vacant shall be excluded in computing the period of limitation for presenting a claim or instituting a proceeding. (As eff. 10-1-53.)

R.C. 2117.06 provides that all claims, except contingent ones and except for personal property taxes, shall be presented within three months after appointment of the executor or administrator. (As eff. 6-22-84.)

R.C. 2117.07 provides for presentation, subject to statutory conditions, of claims after four months and that such claims shall not prevail against bona fide purchasers and other persons who have dealt with the executor or administrator in good faith; and that a claim not presented within four months is forever barred. (As eff. 1-1-76.)

R.C. 2117.10 provides: "The failure of the holder of a valid lien upon any of the assets of an estate to present his claim upon the indebtedness secured by such lien, as provided in Chapter 2117 of the Revised Code, shall not affect such lien if the same is evidenced by a document admitted to public record, or is evidenced by actual possession of the real or personal property which is subject to such lien." (As eff. 1-23-63.)

R.C. 2117.12 provides for commencement of suit on a claim within two months after it is rejected or becomes due. (As eff. 10-1-53.)

R.C. 2117.17 provides: "At any time after three months have elapsed since the date of the appointment of the executor or administrator, the probate court on its own motion may, and on motion of the executor or administrator shall, assign all claims against the estate that have been presented and any other known valid debts of the estate for hearing on a day certain. Forthwith upon such assignment, and in no case less than ten days before the date fixed for hearing or such longer period as the court may order, the executor or administrator shall cause written notice of the hearing to be served upon the following persons who have not waived the notice in writing or otherwise voluntarily entered their appearance:

"(A) If it appears that the estate is fully solvent, such notice shall be given to the surviving spouse and all other persons having an interest in the estate as devisees, legatees, heirs, and distributees.

"(B) If it appears probable that there will not be sufficient assets to pay all of the valid debts of the estate in full, then such notice also shall be given to all creditors and claimants whose claims have been rejected and whose rights have not been finally determined by judgment, reference, or lapse of time.

"The notice required by this section shall state that a hearing concerning the debts has been scheduled, shall set forth the time and place of the hearing, and shall state that the action of the executor or administrator in allowing and classifying claims will be confirmed at such hearing unless cause to the contrary is shown. The notice shall be served personally or by certified mail in the manner specified for service of notice of the rejection of a claim under section 2117.11 of the Revised Code. Proof of service of the notice to the satisfaction of the court, by affidavit or otherwise, and all waivers of service shall be filed in court at the time of the hearing. At any time before hearing, any interested person may file exceptions in writing to the allowance or classification of any specific claim. The court may cause or permit other interested persons to be served with notice and witnesses to be subpoenaed as may be required to present the issues fully.

"The court, upon hearing, shall determine whether the executor or administrator acted properly in allowing and classifying each claim and shall make an order confirming or disapproving such action.

"An order of the court disapproving the allowance of a claim shall have the same effect as a rejection of the claim on the date on which the claimant is served with notice of the court's order. Notice of the court's order shall be served personally or by certified mail in the manner specified for service of notice of the rejection of a claim under section 2117.11 of the Revised Code. An order of the court confirming the allowance or classification of a claim shall constitute a final order and shall have the same effect as a judgment at law or decree in equity, and shall be final as to all persons having notice of the hearing and as to claimants subsequently presenting their claims, though without notice of such hearing. In the absence of fraud, the allowance and classification of a claim and the subsequent payment of it in good faith shall not be subject to question upon exceptions to the executor's or administrator's accounts. The confirmation of a claim by the court shall not preclude the executor or administrator from thereafter rejecting the claim on discovery of error in his previous action or on requisition as provided in sections 2117.13 and 2117.14 of the Revised Code." (As eff. 10-14-83.)

R.C. 2117.25 provides the order in which debts are to be paid. (As eff. 8-26-77.)

R.C. 2117.28 provides that debts not due may, and on demand of the creditor shall, be paid if assets are available. (As eff. 10-1-53.)

R.C. 2117.37 to 2117.42 provide that upon accrual of a contingent claim, it be presented to executor or administrator as other claims or within two months after accrual, if account of final distribution has not been filed; procedure for collection of contingent claims against beneficiaries of estate.

The requirement of presentment within four months is mandatory and may not be waived by the executor or administrator. Prudential Ins. Co. v. Joyce Bldg. Realty Co., 143 OS 564, 56 NE2d 168, 28 OO 480 (1944).

If the claimant had actual notice of the decedent's death in sufficient time to present his claim within the statutory period, he may not be granted leave to file thereafter. Redifer Bus Co. v. Lumme, 171 OS 471, 172 NE2d 304, 14 OO2d 374 (1961).

A claim not presented within four months is barred unless it is reinstated as provided by statute. Beach v. Mizner, 131 OS 481, 3 NE2d 417, 6 OO 155 (1936).

If creditor under mortgage not due refuses to accept payment, the fiduciary shall set aside the amount due, and the mortgage may be canceled by order of the court. Meiser v. Kissinger, 11 O Supp 80, 26 OO 146, 38 Abs 253 (Prob. 1942).

A contingent claim is one where the liability depends upon some indefinite or uncertain future event which may never happen, and liability may never arise. Keifer v. Kissell, 83 App 133, 75 NE2d 692, 38 OO 224, 50 Abs 375 (1947).

The amount of fees to attorneys employed by executors or administrators may be either included in the settlement account to be allowed by the court or approved upon an application on notice to the interested parties. Compensation to counsel, if found to be reasonable, is a legitimate part of the expense of administration. Where the fiduciary acts as his own counsel, he is entitled, in addition to compensation for services as fiduciary, to compensation for his legal services. In re Haggerty's Estate, 128 NE2d 680, 70 Abs 463 (Prob. 1955).

Ohio statutory requirements of presentation to the executor and of commencing suit do not apply to claims of the United States. Baker v. Charles, 202 NE2d 646, 31 OO2d 310, 95 Abs 97 (Prob. 1963).

SECTION 12-13: RIGHTS OF SURVIVING SPOUSE

Descent, see Section 9-15.
Election not to take under will, see Section 9-27.
Husband and wife generally, see Chapter 14.

12-13A Foreign Estates.

R.C. 2117.23 provides a family allowance when a nonresident decedent leaves property in Ohio. (As eff. 1-1-76.)

LAW IN GENERAL

An award to the widow or children of a nonresident decedent under the laws of his domicile is not effective as to the title of lands in this state unless in accord with Ohio laws. 51 ALR2d 1026.

12-13B Quarantine; Right to Mansion House.

Homestead, see Section 14-42.

R.C. 2117.24 provides: "A surviving spouse may remain in the mansion house of the deceased consort free of charge for one year, except that such real estate may be sold within that time for payment of debts of the decedent, in which event such surviving spouse shall be compensated from the estate to the extent of the fair rental value for the unexpired term, such compensation to have the same priority in payment of debts of estates as the allowance made to the surviving spouse or children." (As eff. 5-26-76.)

The right of the widow to remain in the mansion house is not restricted to personally occupying the premises, but she may rent them. Conger v. Atwood, 28 OS 134, 1 WLB 275 (1875).

The right to remain in the mansion house under R.C. 2117.24 is not limited to a surviving spouse who was resident in it at the time of decedent's death. In re Estate of Johnson, 14 App3d 235, 470 NE2d 492 (1984).

An election to take under the will does not bar the right to remain in the mansion house unless the will otherwise directs as provided by R.C. 2107.42 (quoted at 9-27A).

Further research: O Jur 3d, Decedents' Estates § 1792.

12-13C Exemption from Administration.

Barred by final account, see 12-11E.
For comments on transfer of real estate to surviving spouse as exempt property, see 12-11H.

Prior to its repeal in 1976, R.C. 2115.13 created a claim exempting certain personal property of the decedent in favor of the surviving spouse or minor children. Until paid, the claim was a lien against the real property of the decedent.

An election to take under the will does not bar the right to claim property set off as exempt unless the will otherwise directs as provided by R.C. 2107.42 (quoted at 9-27A).

12-13D Family Allowance.

Barred by final account, see 12-11E.

R.C. 2117.20 provides: "If a person dies leaving a surviving spouse, or leaving minor children and no surviving spouse, the surviving spouse or the minor children shall be entitled to receive in money or property the sum of five thousand dollars as an allowance for support. The money or property set off as an allowance shall be considered estate assets. (As eff. 1-1-76.)

Prior to the 1976 amendment, R.C. 2117.20 provided for an allowance to a widow and children under eighteen years of age of a sufficient amount to support them for twelve months.

An election to take under the will does not bar the right to a year's allowance as provided by R.C. 2107.42 (quoted at 9-27A).

Further research: O Jur 3d, Decedents' Estates § 1802.

12-13E Taking at Appraised Value.

R.C. 2105.062 provides: "(A) The surviving spouse may elect to receive, as part of the surviving spouse's share of the intestate estate under section 2105.06 of the Revised Code, the entire interest of the decedent spouse in the mansion house. The interest of the decedent spouse in the mansion house is valued at the appraised value with the deduction of that portion of all liens on the mansion house, existing at the time of death and attributable to the decedent's interest in the mansion house.

"(B) The election pursuant to division (A) of this section shall be made at or before the time a final account is rendered.

"(C) If the spouse makes an election pursuant to division (A) of this section, the administrator or executor shall file, unless the election is one made under division (D) of this section, an application for a certificate of transfer as provided for in section 2113.61 of the Revised Code. The application also shall contain an inventory of the property that the spouse is entitled to receive under section 2105.06 of the Revised Code. If the value of the property the spouse is entitled to receive is equal to or greater than the value of the mansion house, the court shall issue the certificate of transfer.

"(D) The surviving spouse may make an election pursuant to division (A) of this section in an estate relieved from administration under section 2113.03 of the Revised Code. The election shall be made at the time of or prior to the entry of the order relieving the estate from administration. Either the spouse or the applicant for the order relieving the estate from administration shall file the application for certificate of transfer under division (C) of this section.

"(E) If the surviving spouse dies prior to making an election pursuant to division (A) of this section, the surviving spouse shall be conclusively presumed not to have made an election pursuant to that division. After the surviving spouse's death, no other person is authorized to make an election pursuant to that division on behalf of the estate of the surviving spouse.

"(F) As used in this section, the mansion house includes the decedent's title in the parcel of land on which the house is situated and, at the option of the surviving spouse, the decedent's title in the household goods contained within the house and the lots or farm land adjacent to the house and used in conjunction with it as the home of the decedent." (As eff. 12-17-86.)

R.C. 2113.38 provides: "A surviving spouse, even though acting as executor or administrator, may purchase the following property, if left by the decedent, and if not specifically devised or bequeathed:

"(A) The decedent's interest in the mansion house, including the decedent's title in the parcel of land on which such house is situated and lots or farm land adjacent to the house and used in conjunction with it as the home of the decedent, and the decedent's title in the household goods contained in the house, at the appraised value as fixed by the appraisers;

"(B) Securities listed on an approved stock exchange, as defined in division (E) of section 1707.02 of the Revised Code, at the market price at the time of purchase;

"(C) Any other real or personal property of the decedent not exceeding, with the decedent's interest in the mansion house and the decedent's title in the land used in conjunction with it, and the decedent's title in the household goods the spouse elects to purchase, one third of the gross appraised value of the estate, at the appraised value as fixed by the appraisers.

"A spouse desiring to exercise this right of purchase with respect to personal property shall file in the probate court an application setting forth an accurate description of the personal property, and the election of the spouse to purchase it at the appraised or market value, as the case may be. No notice is required for the court to hear the application, insofar as it appertains to household goods contained in the mansion house or securities listed on an approved stock exchange. If the application includes other personal property, the court shall cause a notice of the time and place of the hearing of the application with respect to such other personal property to be given to the executor or administrator, the heirs or beneficiaries interested in the estate, and to such other interested persons as the court determines.

"A spouse desiring to exercise this right of purchase with respect to an interest in real estate shall file in the court a petition containing an accurate description of the real estate, and naming as parties defendant the executor or administrator, the persons to whom the real estate passes by inheritance or residuary devise, and all mortgagees and other lienholders whose claims affect the real estate or any part of it. Spouses of parties defendant need not be made parties defendant. The petition shall set forth the election of the surviving spouse to purchase the interest in real estate at the appraised value, and shall contain a prayer accordingly. A summons shall thereupon be issued and served on the defendants, in the same manner as provided for service of summons in actions to sell real estate to pay debts. No hearing on the application or petition shall be held until the inventory is approved.

"On the hearing of the application or petition, the finding of the court shall be in favor of the surviving spouse, unless it appears that the appraisement was made as a result of collusion or fraud, or that it is so manifestly inadequate that a sale at that price would unconscionably prejudice the rights of the parties in interest or creditors. The action of the court shall not be held to prejudice the rights of lienholders.

"Upon a finding in favor of the surviving spouse, the court shall make an entry fixing the terms of payment to the executor or administrator for the property, having regard for the rights of creditors of the estate, and ordering the executor or administrator, or a commissioner who may be appointed and authorized for the purpose, to transfer and convey the property to the spouse upon compliance with the terms fixed by the court. If the court, having regard for the amount of property to be purchased, its appraised value, and the distribution to be made of the proceeds arising from the sale, finds that the original bond given by the executor or administrator is sufficient, the court may dispense with the giving of additional bonds. If the court finds that the original bond is insufficient, as a condition to transfer and conveyance, the court shall require the executor or administrator to execute an additional bond in an amount as the court may fix, with proper surety, conditioned and payable as provided in section 2127.27 of the Revised Code. This section does not prevent the court from ordering transfer and conveyance without bond in cases where the will of a testator provides that the executor need not give bond. The executor or administrator, or a commissioner, thereupon shall execute and deliver to the spouse a proper bill of sale or deed, as the case may be, for the property, and make a return to the court.

"The death of the surviving spouse prior to the filing of the court's entry fixing the terms of payment for property elected to be purchased shall nullify the election. The property, whether real or personal, thereafter shall be free of the right granted in this section.

"The application or petition provided for in this section shall not be filed prior to filing the inventory, nor later than one month after the approval of the inventory required by section 2115.02 of the Revised Code. Failure to file an application or petition within that time nullifies the election with respect to the property required to be included, and the property, whether real or personal, thereafter shall be free of the right granted in this section." (As eff. 12-17-86.)

Prior to September 3, 1935, no provision was made for any notice.

From September 3, 1935 to October 6, 1949, a citation instead of a summons was required to be served on the defendants.

Prior to August 22, 1941, it was not provided that lienholders be made parties defendant.

Prior to October 7, 1949, no provisions concerning bond were included.

Prior to October 7, 1949, the provision that spouses of parties defendant need not be made parties defendant was not included.

Prior to October 7, 1949, there were no provisions regarding the death of the surviving spouse during pendency of the proceeding, although the decision in the case of Jewell v. Chiles, 79 NE2d 710, 37 OO 33 (Prob. 1947) is in accord with the present statute.

Prior to October 7, 1949, there was no specific provision that the time for filing the petition was mandatory, but the time was held mandatory in Palmer v. Smith, 28 Abs 673 (App. 1939).

An order of court modifying the inventory (more than one month after it had been approved) as to certain personal property and year's allowance does not constitute a vacation of the previous approval so as to reinstate the right of election to purchase by the surviving spouse. In re Hrabnicky's Estate, 167 OS 507, 149 NE2d 909, 5 OO2d 181 (1958).

Surviving spouse is not entitled to so purchase other buildings on the same lot, not used in conjunction with the mansion house. In re Burgoon's Estate, 80 App 465, 76 NE2d 310, 36 OO 200 (1946).

The surviving spouse is entitled to purchase the mansion house at the appraised value and either deduct from the purchase price the amount of the mortgage or pay the full purchase price and require the fiduciary to pay the amount of the unpaid mortgage. McAdams v. Bolsinger, 129 NE2d 878, 57 OO 338, 71 Abs 531 (Prob. 1950).

A surviving spouse may purchase decedent's half interest in the 37-acre farm owned by them jointly, operated by them as a farm, and used as their residence. The entire premises make up the "farm home" and is not a commercial enterprise even though both husband and wife had outside employment. Young v. Young, 106 App 206, 154 NE2d 19, 6 OO2d 458 (1958).

When the election is made prior to the approval of the inventory, it satisfies the requirement of R.C. 2113.38. Strawser v. Stanton, 103 NE2d 797, 47 OO 255, 66 Abs 121 (C.P. 1952).

Where it appears to the probate court that it would be to the best interests of the ward to elect to purchase the mansion house at the appraised value, such court has the inherent power to permit and direct the guardian to make the election to so elect. Dorfmeier v. Dorfmeier, 123 NE2d 681, 69 Abs 15 (Prob. 1954).

If there is no other devise of any real property, a devise of "all my real property" is equivalent to a residuary devise and is not a specific devise. In re Witteman's Estate, 21 OS2d 3, 254 NE2d 345, 50 OO2d 2 (1969).

SECTION 12-14: LAND SALES

Attack upon sales, see Chapter 16.
Rights of purchasers generally, see Section 17-15.

12-14A Authority of Personal Representative.

Authority generally, see 12-11A.

R.C. 2127.30 provides for sale of real estate in which the ward or estate has an equitable interest only. (As eff. 10-1-53.)

An executor without power of sale under the will, has no capacity, before issuance of the order of sale, to contract for the sale of real property belonging to the estate. Binns v. Isabel, 72 App 222, 51 NE2d 501, 27 OO 87, 39 Abs 237 (1943).

Where an administrator contracted to sell land subject to approval of court prior to commencing land sale proceedings in the probate court and never obtained approval of sale to the contract purchaser, the purchaser cannot enforce the contract. Where the administrator then sells at a lower price than offered by the prospective purchaser only the heirs, and not the prospective purchaser, may object. Bilang v. Benson, 62 App2d 134, 405 NE2d 311, 16 OO3d 297 (1978).

Further research: O Jur 3d, Decedents' Estates § 1612.

12-14B Necessity and Form of Conveyance.

Official deeds, see 8-31Q.

LAW IN GENERAL

A conveyance from the executor or administrator of the property sold is essential to the title of the purchaser. A recital in the deed of the proceedings should be made but its omission does not invalidate the deed. Am Law of Prop § 13.6b.

12-14C Statutory Procedure.

Procedure in judicial sales generally, see Division 17-2.

R.C. 2127.15 provides: "All pleadings and proceedings in an action to obtain authority to sell the real estate of a decedent or a ward in the probate court shall be the same as in other civil actions, except as otherwise provided in sections 2127.01 to 2127.43 of the Revised Code." (As eff. 1-1-76.)

12-14D When Executor or Administrator Shall Sell.

Sale after four years, see 12-12B.
Undevised land sold first, see 12-12A.

R.C. 2127.01 provides: "All proceedings for the sale of lands by executors, administrators, and guardians shall be in accordance with section(s) 2127.01

to 2127.43, inclusive, of the Revised Code, except where the executor has testamentary power of sale, and in that case the executor may proceed under such sections or under the will. (As eff. 10-1-53.)

R.C. 2127.011 provides: "(A) In addition to the other methods provided by law or in the will and unless expressly prohibited by the will, an executor or administrator may sell at public or private sale, grant options to sell, exchange, re-exchange, or otherwise dispose of any parcel of real estate belonging to the estate at any time at prices and upon terms as are consistent with this section and may execute and deliver deeds and other instruments of conveyance if all of the following conditions are met:

"(1) The surviving spouse, all of the legatees and devisees in the case of testacy, and all of the heirs in the case of intestacy, give written consent to a power of sale for a particular parcel of real estate or to a power of sale for all the real estate belonging to the estate. Each consent to a power of sale provided for in this section shall be filed in the probate court.

"(2) Any sale under a power of sale authorized pursuant to this section shall be made at a price of at least eighty per cent of the appraised value, as set forth in an approved inventory.

"(3) No power of sale provided for in this section is effective if the surviving spouse, any legatee, devisee, or heir is a minor. No person may give the consent of the minor that is required by this section.

"(B) A surviving spouse who is the executor or administrator may sell real estate to himself pursuant to this section." (As eff. 5-26-76.)

R.C. 2127.02 provides: "As soon as an executor or administrator ascertains that the personal property in his hands is insufficient to pay all the debts of the deceased, together with the allowance to the surviving spouse and children, and the costs of administering the estate, he shall commence a civil action in the probate court for authority to sell the decedent's real estate." (As eff. 1-1-76.)

R.C. 2127.03 provides: "When by operation of law or the provisions of a will a legacy is effectual to charge real estate, and the personal property is insufficient to pay the legacy, together with all the debts, the allowance to the surviving spouse and children, and the costs of administering the estate, the executor or administrator with will annexed shall commence a civil action in the probate court for authority to sell the real estate so charged.

"If the executor, administrator, or administrator with the will annexed fails to commence the action mentioned in this section or section 2127.02 of the Revised Code, the probate court in which letters testamentary have been granted, upon its own motion or upon motion by a creditor or legatee, shall order the executor, administrator, or administrator with the will annexed to commence such an action, and proceed in the manner prescribed by sections 2127.04 to 2127.43 of the Revised Code." (As eff. 1-1-76.)

R.C. 2127.04 provides: "(A) With the consent of all persons entitled to share in an estate upon distribution, the executor, administrator, or administrator with the will annexed may, and upon the request of these persons shall, commence an action in the probate court for authority to sell any part or all of the decedent's real estate, even though not required to be sold to pay debts or legacies. A guardian may make such a request, or give consent, on behalf of his ward.

"(B) An executor, administrator, or administrator with the will annexed may commence an action in the probate court, on his own motion, to sell any part or all of the decedent's real estate, even though it is not required to be sold to pay debts or legacies. The court shall not issue an order of sale in the action unless one of the following categories applies:

"(1) At least fifty per cent of all the persons interested in the real estate proposed to be sold have consented to the sale; and, prior to the issuance of the order, no written objection is filed with the court by any person or persons who hold aggregate interests in the interest of the decedent in the real estate proposed to be sold, that total in excess of twenty-five per cent; and the court determines that the sale is in the best interest of the decedent's estate.

"(2) No person's interest in the interest of the decedent in the real estate proposed to be sold exceeds ten per cent; and, prior to the issuance of the order, no written objection is filed with the court by any person or persons who hold aggregate interests in the interest of the decedent in the real estate proposed to be sold, that total in excess of twenty-five per cent; and the court determines that the sale is in the best interest of the decedent's estate.

"(3) The real estate proposed to be sold escheats to the state under division (J) of section 2105.06 of the Revised Code.

"(C) Notwithstanding any provision of the Revised Code, an executor, administrator, or administrator with the will annexed shall commence an action in the probate court to sell any part or all of the decedent's real estate if any person who is entitled to inherit all or part of the real estate cannot be found after a due and diligent search. The court shall not issue an order of sale in the action unless the sale is in the best interest of the person who cannot be found and in the best interest of the decedent's estate.

"If a sale is ordered under this division, the costs of its administration shall be taken from the proceeds of the sale.

"(D) A surviving spouse who is an executor or administrator of the decedent spouse's estate is not disqualified, by reason of being executor or administrator, as a person to whom a parcel of real estate may be sold pursuant to this section." (As eff. 2-2-82.)

Lands of a decedent cannot be sold to pay the costs of administration alone. Carr v. Hull, 65 OS 394, 62 NE 439, 46 WLB 271, 47 WLB 91 (1901); In re Cregyer's Estate, 68 NE2d 96, 33 OO 335 (Prob. 1946).

Proceedings to subject lands to the payment of debts must be brought within six years from the discovery by the administrator that the personalty is insufficient to pay the debts. Ling v. Strome, 12 CC(NS) 161, 21 CD 569 (1909).

12-14E Successor Fiduciary.

R.C. 2127.06 provides: "If the fiduciary who brings an action under section(s) 2127.01 to 2127.43, inclusive, of the Revised Code, dies, resigns, or is removed, or his powers cease at any time before the real estate sold is conveyed, a successor fiduciary may be substituted as a party to the action and may convey land, whether sold before or after his appointment. He may also be required to give an additional bond." (As eff. 10-1-53.)

12-14F   Interests Subject to Sale.

R.C. 2127.07 provides: "Any interest in real estate, whether legal or equitable, which the deceased had a right to sell or dispose of at the time of his decease, or of which the ward was seized at the time the action was brought, including coal, iron ore, limestone, fireclay, or other mineral upon or under such real estate, or the right to mine them, may be sold by an executor, administrator, or guardian under sections 2127.01 to 2127.43, inclusive, of the Revised Code. This section does not give an executor or administrator with the will annexed authority to sell real estate for the payment of legacies, other than as charged by the testator or by operation of law. This section does not give a guardian authority to sell an equitable estate in real estate placed by deed of trust, beyond the power of the ward to sell, convey, or assign." (As eff. 10-1-53.)

12-14G   Fractional Interests.

Appraisement, see 12-14N.

R.C. 2127.08 provides: "When the interest of a decedent or ward in real estate is fractional and undivided, the action for authority to sell such real estate shall include only such undivided fractional interest, except that the executor, administrator, or guardian, or the owner of any other fractional interest, or any lien holder may, by pleading filed in the cause setting forth all interests in the property and liens thereon, require that the action include the entire interest in the property, and the owner of said interests and liens shall receive his respective share of the proceeds of sale after payment has been made of the expenses of sale including reasonable attorney fees for services in the case, which fees must be paid to the plaintiff's attorney unless the court awards some part thereof to other counsel for services in the case for the common benefit of all the parties, having regard to the interest of the parties, the benefit each may derive from the sale, and the equities of the case. The fees of the executor, administrator, or guardian shall be a charge only against such portion of the proceeds of sale as represents the interests of the decedent or ward." (As eff. 10-1-53.)

This section has been to the same effect since January 1, 1932 except as to fees.

Section 2127.08 is constitutional. Hatch v. Tipton, 131 OS 364, 2 NE2d 875, 6 OO 68 (1936).

Further research: O Jur 3d, Decedents' Estates § 1619.

12-14H   Venue; Filing of Transcript.

R.C. 2127.09 provides: "An action by an executor, administrator, or guardian to obtain authority to sell real estate shall be brought in the county in which he was appointed or in which the real estate subject to sale or any part thereof is situated. If the action is brought in a county other than that in which the real estate or a part thereof is situated, a certified transcript of the record of all proceedings had therein shall be filed with and recorded by the probate court of each county in which such real estate or any part thereof is situated." (As eff. 10-1-53.)

12-14I Petition; Process.

Service of process, see also Section 16-78.

R.C. 2127.10 provides: "An action to obtain authority to sell real estate shall be commenced by the executor, administrator, or guardian by filing a complaint with the probate court.

"The complaint shall contain a description of the real estate proposed to be sold and its value, as near as can be ascertained, a statement of the nature of the interest of the decedent or ward in the real estate, a recital of all mortgages and liens upon and adverse interests in the real estate, the facts showing the reason or necessity for the sale, and any additional facts necessary to constitute the cause of action under the section of the Revised Code on which the action is predicated." (As eff. 1-1-76.)

R.C. 2127.14 provides: "Service of summons, actual or constructive, in an action to sell the real estate of a decedent or a ward shall be had as in other civil actions, but if any competent person in interest enters appearance or consents in writing to the sale, service on such person shall not be necessary. If all parties consent in writing to the sale, an order therefor may issue forthwith." (As eff. 10-1-53.)

Further research: O Jur 3d, Decedents' Estates § 1654.

12-14J Summary Sale When under $3000.

R.C. 2127.11 provides: "When the actual market value of a decedent's or ward's real estate which is to be sold is less than three thousand dollars and the court so finds, it may by summary order authorize the sale and conveyance of the land at private sale, on such terms as it deems proper, and in such proceeding all requirements of sections 2127.01 to 2127.43 of the Revised Code, as to service of summons, appraisal, and additional bond shall be waived." (As eff. 1-1-76.)

Standard of Title Examination

(Adopted by Ohio State Bar Association in 1955)

Problem 5.4A:
   Should failure to give notice of any kind in summary land sale proceedings pursuant to R.C. 2127.11 render the title unmarketable?

Standard 5.4A:
   No.

Standard of Title Examination

(Adopted by Ohio State Bar Association in 1955)

Problem 5.4B:

Is a summary land sale valid when prosecuted under R.C. 2127.11 by a commissioner appointed by the court as provided by R.C. 2113.03 in estates under $1000?

Standard 5.4B:

No; only an executor or administrator is authorized to institute summary land sale proceedings.

12-14K Parties Defendant.

R.C. 2127.12 provides: "In an action by an executor or administrator to obtain authority to sell real estate the following persons shall be made parties defendant:

"(A) The surviving spouse;

"(B) The heirs, devisees, or persons entitled to the next estate of inheritance from the decedent in such real estate and having an interest therein, but their spouses need not be made parties defendant;

"(C) All mortgagees and other lienholders whose claims affect such real estate or any part thereof;

"(D) If the interest subject to sale is equitable, all persons holding legal title thereto or any part thereof and those who are entitled to the purchase money therefor, other than creditors;

"(E) If a fraudulent conveyance is sought to be set aside, all persons holding or claiming thereunder;

"(F) All other persons having an interest in such real estate." (As eff. 10-1-53.)

From January 1, 1932 to August 19, 1943 the words "but their spouses need not be made parties defendant" were not in the statute. Notice should be taken that the added clause does not apply to all persons who may be parties defendant; for example, the spouse of an owner of another fractional interest or the new spouse of the surviving spouse should be parties.

In action to sell real estate to pay debts, any person may be made a defendant who has or claims an interest in the land. Doan v. Biteley, 49 OS 588, 32 NE 600, 28 WLB 267, 344 (1892).

Holders of liens acquired upon the share of an heir after the death of the ancestor are necessary parties to the petition of the administrator to sell to pay debts. Keenan v. Wilson, 19 App 499 (1925).

Further research: O Jur 3d, Decedents' Estates § 1649.

12-14L Dower.

R.C. 2127.16 provides: "In a sale of real estate by an executor, administrator, or guardian, such real estate shall be sold free of all right and expectancy of dower therein, but out of the proceeds of the sale, in lieu of dower, the court shall allow to the person having any dower interest in the property such sum in money as is the just and reasonable value of such dower, unless the answer of such person waives such allowance." (As eff. 10-1-53.)

12-14M   Subject to Mortgage.

R.C. 2127.20 provides: "The probate court, with the consent of the mortgagee, may authorize the sale of lands subject to mortgage, but the giving of any such consent shall release the estate of the decedent or ward should a deficit later appear." (As eff. 10-5-61.)

12-14N   Appraisement.

See also 12-14O.

R.C. 2127.22 provides: "If an appraisement of the real estate is contained in the inventory required of an executor or administrator by section 2115.02 of the Revised Code, and of a guardian by section 2111.14 of the Revised Code, the probate court may order a sale in accordance with the appraisement, or order a new appraisement. If a new appraisement is not ordered, the value set forth in the inventory shall be the appraised value of the real estate. If the court orders a new appraisement, the value returned shall be the appraised value of the real estate.

"If the interest of the deceased or ward in the real estate is fractional and undivided, and if a party requests and the court orders the entire interest in the real estate to be sold, a new appraisement of the entire interest in the real estate shall be ordered.

"If the relief requested is granted and new appraisement is ordered, the court shall appoint one, or on request of the executor, administrator, or guardian, not exceeding three judicious and disinterested persons of the vicinity, not next of kin of the complainant, to appraise the real estate in whole and in parcels at its true value in money. Where the real estate lies in two or more counties the court may appoint appraisers in any or all of the counties in which the real estate or a part of it is situated." (As eff. 1-1-76.)

12-14O   The Sale.

R.C. 2109.45 provides that before a private sale is confirmed the probate court shall require the fiduciary to file an affidavit that the sale reported is the highest price he could get for the property. (As eff. 10-1-53.)

R.C. 2127.29 provides: "When the bond required by section 2127.27 of the Revised Code is filed and approved by the court, it shall order the sale of the real estate included in the complaint set forth in section 2127.10 of the Revised Code, or the part of the real estate it deems necessary for the interest of all parties concerned. If the complaint alleges that it is necessary to sell part of the real estate, and that by the partial sale the residue of the estate, or a specific part of it, would be greatly injured, the court, if it so finds, may order a sale of the whole estate." (As eff. 1-1-76.)

R.C. 2127.32 provides: "The real estate included in the court's order of sale, as provided in section 2127.29 of the Revised Code, shall be sold either in whole or in parcels at public auction at the door of the courthouse in the county in which the order of sale was granted, or at another place, as the court directs, and the order shall fix the place, day, and hour of sale. If it appears to be more for the interest of the ward or the estate to sell the real estate at private sale, the court may authorize the complainant to sell it either in whole or in parcels. If an order for private sale is issued, it shall be returned by the complainant. Upon motion and showing of a person interested in the proceeds of the sale, filed after thirty days from the date of the order, the court may require the complainant to return the order, if the premises have not been sold. Thereupon, the court may order the real estate to be sold at public sale.

"If upon showing of any person interested, the court finds that it will be to the interest of the ward or the estate, it may order a reappraisement and sale in parcels.

"If the sale is to be public, the executor, administrator, or guardian must .give notice of the time and place of the sale by advertisement at least three weeks successively in a newspaper published in the county where the lands are situated." (As eff. 10-7-77.)

R.C. 2127.33 provides: "Where the sale authorized by a court as provided in section 2127.32 of the Revised Code, is private, the real estate shall not be sold for less than the appraised value. When the sale is at public auction the real estate if improved shall not be sold for less than two-thirds of the appraised value, or if not improved, for less than one half of the appraised value. In private sales if no sale has been effected after one bona fide effort to sell under this section, or if in public sales the land remains unsold for want of bidders when offered pursuant to advertisement, the court may fix the price for which such real estate may be sold or may set aside the appraisement and order a new appraisement. If such new appraisement does not exceed five hundred dollars, and upon the first offer thereunder at public sale there are no bids, then upon the motion of any party interested the court may order the real estate to be readvertised and sold at public auction to the highest bidder." (As eff. 10-1-53.)

R.C. 2127.34 provides: "The order for the sale of real estate, granted by the probate court in an action by an executor, administrator, or guardian, shall prescribe the terms of the sale and payment of the purchase money either in whole or in part for cash or on deferred payments. In the sales by executors or administrators, deferred payments shall not exceed two years with interest." (As eff. 1-1-76.)

R.C. 2127.36 provides: "The order for the sale of real estate granted in an action by an executor, administrator, or guardian shall require that before the delivery of the deed the deferred installments of the purchase money be secured by mortgage on the real estate sold, and mortgage notes bearing interest at a rate approved by the probate court. If after the sale is made, and

497

before delivery of deed, the purchaser offers to pay the full amount of the purchase money in cash, the court may order that it be accepted, if for the best interest of the estate or the ward, and direct its distribution.

"The court in such an order may also direct the sale, without recourse, of any or all of the notes taken for deferred payments, if for the best interest of the estate or the ward, at not less than their face value with accrued interest, and direct the distribution of the proceeds." (As eff. 1-1-76.)

In a land sale by executors or administrators, the record must show an order of sale by the court or the sale is void. Goforth v. Longworth, 4 Ohio 129 (1829).

The court is without power to confirm the sale for part cash and balance in other property. Binns v. Isabel, 72 App 222, 51 NE2d 501, 27 OO 87, 39 Abs 237 (1943).

A private sale for less than the appraised value in a land sale proceeding is not subject to collateral attack. Pierson v. Merritt, 134 NE2d 591, 4 OO2d 425, 73 Abs 431 (C.P. 1956).

Further research: O Jur 3d, Decedents' Estates § 1662.

12-14P Homestead.

Statute, see 17-41B.

Upon the repeal of R.C. 2329.75, effective September 28, 1979, and R.C. 2127.26, effective March 23, 1981, the only remaining Ohio homestead exemption is provided by R.C. 2329.66, which states, in part: "Every person who is domiciled in this state may hold property exempt from execution, garnishment, attachment, or sale to satisfy a judgment or order, as follows: (1) The person's interest, not to exceed five thousand dollars, in one parcel or item of real or personal property that the person or a dependent of the person uses as a residence...." (As eff. 10-5-87.)

12-14Q Bond.

Bond of trust company, see 12-11B.

R.C. 2127.27 provides that upon approval of appraisement, the court shall order additional bond unless the court finds the original bond to be sufficient or the will provides that the executor shall not be required to give bond; if action is pending in another court, certificate from court of appointment shall be filed. (As eff. 10-1-53.) The Revised Code omits the provisions of G.C. 10510-31 designed to validate sales made between January 1, 1932 and October 7, 1949 even though no additional bond was given and whether or not dispensed with by court order.

R.C. 2127.31 provides for giving of bond to prevent the sale. (As eff. 1-1-76.)

12-14R Payment for Title Evidence and Commission.

R.C. 2127.28 provides: "The probate court may, after notice to all parties in interest, allow a real estate commission in an action to sell real estate by an executor, administrator, or guardian, but such allowance shall be passed upon by the court prior to the sale.

"The court may allow payment for certificate or abstract of title or policy of title insurance in connection with the sale of any land by an executor, administrator, or guardian." (As eff. 1-1-76.)

12-14S Confirmation and Distribution.

R.C. 2127.35 provides: "An executor, administrator, or guardian shall make return of his proceedings under the order for the sale of real estate granted by the probate court. The court, after careful examination, if satisfied that the sale has in all respects been legally made, shall confirm the sale and order the executor, administrator, or guardian to make a deed to the purchaser.

"The deed shall be received in all courts as prima-facie evidence that the executor, administrator, or guardian in all respects observed the direction of the court, and complied with the requirements of the law, and shall convey the interest in the real estate directed to be sold by the court, and shall vest title to the interest in the purchaser as if conveyed by the deceased in his lifetime, or by the ward free from disability, and by the owners of the remaining interests in the real estate." (As eff. 1-1-76.)

R.C. 2127.38 provides for distribution of the proceeds of sale to payment of costs and expenses (including reasonable attorney fees to be fixed by the court) and of taxes and assessments; in sales by an executor or administrator, the remaining proceeds shall be applied to legacies charged on the real estate and to claims and debts, and the surplus disposed of as real estate. (As eff. 9-21-82.)

Where the proceeds of a probate sale of real estate, the county treasurer being a party to the proceeding, were insufficient to pay the taxes and assessments, the court cannot order a release of the lien therefor. The unpaid portion remains a lien as in other judicial sales. Marini v. Roach, 54 App2d 114, 375 NE2d 808, 8 OO3d 212 (1976).

Further research: O Jur 3d, Decedents' Estates § 1714.

SECTION 12-15: ESTATES OF NONRESIDENT DECEDENTS

12-15A Foreign Administration.

Election by surviving spouse, see Section 9-27.
Probate and record of foreign wills, see 9-28C.

R.C. 2113.70 to 2113.75 provide procedure against executors or administrators appointed in any other state or country; and that they may commence and prosecute a proceeding in any court of this state as a nonresident is permitted to sue. (As eff. 10-1-53.)

R.C. 2129.02 provides: "When letters of administration or letters testamentary have been granted in any state other than this state, in any territory, or possession of the United States, or in any foreign country, as to the estate of a deceased resident of that state, territory, possession, or country, and when no ancillary administration proceedings have been commenced in this state, the person to whom the letters of appointment were granted may file an authenticated copy of them in the probate court of any county of this state in which is located real estate of the decedent. That court shall cause notice of the filing to be published for three consecutive weeks in a newspaper of general circulation in that county.

"The claim of any creditor of such a decedent shall be presented to such court within three months after the date of the filing or be forever barred as a possible lien upon the real estate of the decedent in this state. If, at the expiration of that three-month period, any such claim has been filed and remains unpaid after reasonable notice of the claim to the nonresident executor or administrator, ancillary administration proceedings as to the estate may be had forthwith." (As eff. 10-20-87.)

R.C. 2129.27 to 2129.30 provide that a trustee named in a foreign will may execute the trust upon giving bond, except that bond may not be required if so requested in the will; a testamentary trustee appointed by a foreign court may execute the trust upon giving bond and filing an authenticated record of his appointment; when necessary the probate court where the property affected by the testamentary trust is situated may appoint a trustee, who must give bond. (As eff. 10-1-53.)

Further research: O Jur 3d, Decedents' Estates § 1832.

LAW IN GENERAL

A domiciliary executor or administrator has no authority concerning real estate located in another state unless so provided by the statutes of such other state. A will probated in a foreign state likewise does not operate on the title to land except under statutory provisions of the state of the situs. Am Law of Prop § 14.45.

12-15B Ancillary Administration.

Election by surviving spouse, see 9-27B.

R.C. 2129.04 in part provides: "When a nonresident decedent leaves property in Ohio, ancillary administration proceedings may be had upon application of any interested person in any county in Ohio in which is located property of the decedent, or in which a debtor of such decedent resides." (As eff. 10-1-53.)

R.C. 2129.08 provides: "After an authenticated copy of the last will and testament of a nonresident decedent has been allowed and admitted to record as provided by sections 2129.01 to 2129.30 of the Revised Code, and after there has been filed in the probate court a complete exemplification of the record of the grant of the domiciliary letters of appointment and of such other records of the court of domiciliary administration as the court requires, the court shall appoint as the ancillary administrator the person named in such will as general executor or as executor of the Ohio estate of the decedent, provided that such person is a resident of Ohio, makes application, and qualifies in all other respects as required by law, except that if the testator in the will naming such executor orders or requests that bond be not given by him, bond shall not be required unless for sufficient reason the court requires it. If such decedent dies intestate or failed to designate in his will any person qualified to act as ancillary administrator, the court shall appoint in such capacity some suitable person resident of the county, who may be a creditor of the estate. An ancillary administrator acting as to the Ohio estate of a testate decedent may sell and convey the real and personal estate by virtue of the will as executors or administrators with the will annexed may do. No person shall be appointed ancillary administrator as to the Ohio estate of a nonresident presumed decedent except after sections 2121.01 to 2121.09 of the Revised Code, relative to the appointment of an ancillary administrator have been complied with." (As eff. 9-30-74.)

R.C. 2129.11 provides: "If no domiciliary administration has been commenced, the ancillary administrator shall proceed with the administration in Ohio as though the decedent had been a resident of Ohio at the time of his death." (As eff. 10-1-53.)

An allowance for property exempt from administration must be set off to a nonresident surviving spouse in the local estate of a nonresident decedent. In re Mitchell's Estate, 97 App 443, 127 NE2d 39, 56 OO 357, 51 ALR2d 1020 (1954).

Further research: O Jur 3d, Decedents' Estates § 1845.

12-15C   Records of Foreign County or State.

Foreign wills, see 9-28C.

R.C. 2127.09 in part provides: "If the action is brought in a county other than that in which the real estate or a part thereof is situated, a certified transcript of the record of all proceedings had therein shall be filed with and recorded by the probate court of each county in which such real estate or any part thereof is situated." (As eff. 10-1-53.)

When so recorded, further questions may be properly raised as to the facts of admission to probate, of proceedings to contest, of taxes or other unpaid claims against the estate, and as to whether or not the executor was in office at the date of the deed.

Standard of Title Examination

(As Amended by Ohio State Bar Association in 1971)

Problem 5.5A:

If administration proceedings in an Ohio estate are not admitted to record locally, should objection be made to the record title if such proceedings are not required to be so admitted to record by statute or the Civil Rules?

501

Standard 5.5A:
  Yes.

Comment 5.5A:
  Before title can be considered to be marketable of record, it is necessary to admit to record locally at least those portions of the foreign proceedings which are necessary to show that the title which was derived through such proceedings is at the time in question free from liens and defects resulting from or related to such proceedings.

CHAPTER 13: FIXTURES

DIVISION 13-1: IN GENERAL

DIVISION 13-1: IN GENERAL

SECTION 13-11: GENERALLY

Crops, see Chapter 7.
Life tenants, see Section 11-64.

13-11A Definition and Requirements.

A fixture is an article which was a chattel, but which, by being affixed to the realty, became accessory to it and parcel of it. Teaff v. Hewitt, 1 OS 511 (1853).

For a chattel to become a fixture requires the combined application of (1) actual annexation to the realty or something appurtenant thereto; (2) appropriation to the use or purpose of the realty; (3) the intention of the party making the annexation to make the article a permanent accession to the freehold. Zangerle v. Standard Oil Co., 144 OS 506, 60 NE2d 52, 30 OO 151 (1945); Zangerle v. Republic Steel Corp., 144 OS 529, 60 NE2d 170, 30 OO 160 (1945).

Further research: O Jur 3d, Fixtures § 1.

LAW IN GENERAL

A fixture is an article which was a chattel but, while retaining its identity, is so connected with the realty that it would ordinarily be considered a part thereof. An article normally becomes a part of the realty by the intention of the party owning and affixing it to make a permanent accession to the free-

503

hold. The intention cannot be a secret thought but must be ascertained from the following criterions. The tests for determining whether a chattel becomes real estate are (a) the manner of the annexation, (b) the nature of the article and its adaptation to the purposes for which the realty is used, and (c) the relationship of the parties. Am Jur 2d, Fixtures § 1; Am Law of Prop § 19.1; CJS, Fixtures § 1; Powell § 651; Tiffany § 606.

13-11B Annexation.

Slight attachment may be sufficient. As a general rule the chattel must be so attached that it loses its identity as such or that it cannot be removed without injury to itself or to the freehold. Zangerle v. Standard Oil Co., 144 OS 506, 60 NE2d 52, 30 OO 151 (1945); Zangerle v. Republic Steel Corp., 144 OS 529, 60 NE2d 170, 30 OO 160 (1945).

Held in this particular case that storm doors, windows and sash pass to the purchaser, although kept available in the garage; that lighting fixture would pass because included in "lighting" in the contract; that seller may remove and take detachable radiant heater, radiator covers not specially manufactured nor measured, mirrors attached after completion of the building by screws or brackets, bathroom accessories, curtain rods, door chimes, linoleum not attached, and medicine cabinet. Silverberg v. Kramer, 68 NE2d 835, 34 OO 145 (Mu. 1946).

A wall-to-wall carpet and pad attached to the unfinished floor of a house with staples and mechanically stretched and affixed with smoothing strips is a fixture annexed to the real estate. Merchants & Mechanics Federal Savings & Loan Ass'n v. Herald, 120 App 115, 201 NE2d 237, 28 OO2d 302 (1964).

Further research: O Jur 3d, Fixtures § 3.

LAW IN GENERAL

The annexation may be constructive: as a heavy addition held in place by gravity; as an article specially made for or an essential part of the particular real estate; or as a thing temporarily severed from the land. Chattels placed on the land with the intention of annexing them have been held realty. Whether or not a fixture can be removed without material injury to the freehold is an important factor in some situations. A chattel always becomes part of the realty when incorporated so as to lose its identity in the real estate. 109 ALR 1424.

13-11C Adaptation and Use.

Articles which have been annexed to the premises as accessory to it, whatever business may be carried on upon it, and not peculiarly for the benefit of a present business which may be of temporary duration, become subservient to the realty and acquire and retain legal character. Fortman v. Goepper, 14 OS 558 (1863).

If the articles which are annexed to realty become so absorbed within it, by virtue of their adaptability to the use of the realty, that their identity as personalty may be said to be destroyed, they become fixtures, regardless of the intention of the parties. First Federal Sav. & Loan Ass'n v. Smith, 6 Misc 68, 216 NE2d 396, 35 OO2d 167 (C.P. 1965).

Carpet which is installed by the owner of an apartment building where the floors are of concrete covered with a thin layer of rough plywood constitutes a fixture. Exchange Leasing Corp. v. Finster N. Aegen, Inc., 7 App2d 11, 218 NE2d 633, 36 OO2d 63 (1966).

Further research: O Jur 3d, Fixtures § 4.

LAW IN GENERAL

Adaptation or application to the use of the real estate will be considered in determining whether or not a chattel becomes realty. Articles placed on the land which do not increase its value or which merely serve a temporary purpose indicate an intention that they remain chattels. Items losing their identity in the realty become part thereof although affixed by mistake. See citations as 13-11A.

13-11D Relationship of Parties.

Improvements, see 13-11E.

The intention of the annexer must be determined from the nature of the article affixed; the relation and situation of the party making the annexation; the structure and mode of annexation; and the purpose or use for which the annexation has been made. Zangerle v. Standard Oil Co., 144 OS 506, 60 NE2d 52, 30 OO 151 (1945); Zangerle v. Republic Steel Corp., 144 OS 529, 60 NE2d 170, 30 OO 160 (1945).

LAW IN GENERAL

The relation between the parties is often conclusive. Fixtures annexed by a trespasser become part of the realty and cannot be removed by him. Controversies involving the relationship of the parties are frequently determined from whether the annexation was made by the owner of the fee or was made by the owner of a lesser estate. If annexed by a fee owner the presumption is that the fixture becomes real estate, especially as between vendor and purchaser. A licensee impliedly has the right to remove fixtures installed by him, subject to the obligation to repair any injury to the premises; however, the prevailing rule is that he is not protected against subsequent bona fide purchasers or mortgagees. The owner of the chattel must consent to its annexation in order to be deprived of his title unless the chattel loses its identity in the real estate. See citations at 13-11A.

13-11E Improvements; Encroachments.

Occupying claimants, see Section 16-62.

Generally, a building erected on the lands of another by his consent or license does not become a part of the realty, but remains the property of the person annexing it. Round v. Plating & Galvanizing Co., 5 O Supp 155, 17 OO 464, 31 Abs 477 (C.P. 1940): Wagner v. Cleveland & T. R.R., 22 OS 563 (1872).

LAW IN GENERAL

Chattels annexed by a person having no interest in the real estate with the consent of the landowner are presumed not to become realty in the absence of circumstances indicating a different intention of the parties. Improvements constructed on realty by a person having no interest in the land, without the consent of the landowner, become the property of the landowner. Occupying claimant statutes do not change this rule, but relief is frequently granted under them or in equity to a person making the improvement in good faith. The rules stated in this paragraph apply to structures which encroach on another's land through mistake as to boundary or location. Am Jur 2d, Improvements § 2; 130 ALR 1034; CJS, Improvements § 3; Powell § 658; Tiffany § 625.

13-11F Agreement as to Character.

As between the parties by agreement, the property may be made to preserve the character of personalty; yet, if the attachment is as a fixture, the agreement will be of no avail against a subsequent mortgagee of the realty without notice. Case Mfg. Co. v. Garven, 45 OS 289, 13 NE 493, 18 WLB 18 (1887); XXth Century Heating & Ventilating Co. v. Home Owners' Loan Corp., 56 App 188, 10 NE2d 229, 8 OO 237, 24 Abs 56 (1937).

Further research: O Jur 3d, Fixtures § 15.

13-11G Severance; Contracts for Sale.

Annexation, see 13-11B.

R.C. 1302.03 provides: "(A) A contract for the sale of minerals, or the like or a structure or its materials to be removed from realty is a contract for the sale of goods within sections 1302.01 to 1302.98, inclusive, of the Revised Code, if they are to be severed by the seller but until severance a purported present sale thereof which is not effective as a transfer of an interest in land is effective only as a contract to sell.

"(B) A contract for the sale apart from the land of growing crops or other things attached to realty and capable of severance without material harm thereto but not described in division (A) of this section or of timber to be cut is a contract for the sale of goods within sections 1302.01 to 1302.98, inclusive, of the Revised Code, whether the subject matter is to be severed by the buyer or by the seller even though it forms part of the realty at the time of contracting, and the parties can by identification effect a present sale before severance.

"(C) The provisions of this section are subject to any third party rights provided by section 5301.25 of the Revised Code relating to realty records, and the contract for sale may be executed and recorded as a document transferring an interest in land, as provided in section 5301.25 of the Revised Code, and shall then constitute notice to third parties of the buyer's rights under the contract for sale." (As eff. 1-1-79.)

The measure of damages for wrongful severance is the difference in the value of the property before and immediately after the injury occurred. Greif v. Kiewell, 18 CC(NS) 450, 33 CD 153 (1911).

LAW IN GENERAL

A fixture will resume its original character as a chattel if it is removed by the owner with the intention that the severance be permanent, provided the rights of other persons have not intervened. A constructive severance by agreement may likewise be upheld as between the parties to the agreement. Tiffany § 623.

13-11H Taxation; Condemnation.

The machinery and equipment are more properly accessory to the business carried on upon the realty than to the realty itself and therefore taxable as personal property and not as real property. Standard Oil Co. v. Zangerle, 144 OS 523, 60 NE2d 59, 30 OO 158 (1945).

LAW IN GENERAL

A majority of the cases hold that fixtures are taxable as real property, even when there is an undisclosed right of removal or an agreement for retention of title. It has been held that machinery is personal property. Am Law of Prop § 19.13; Powell § 660.

A similar rule is applied upon condemnation, to the effect that fixtures will pass and compensation be awarded as though they were part of the real estate. Am Law of Prop § 19.14.

13-11I Transfer upon Death.

Crops, see 7-13A.
Executors and administrators, see 12-11A.

LAW IN GENERAL

As between the heirs and the personal representative, fixtures normally pass to the heirs of the deceased landowner. Powell § 652.

SECTION 13-12: ENCUMBRANCES ON FIXTURES

13-12A Between the Parties.

Agreement, see 13-11F.

LAW IN GENERAL

A chattel mortgage or conditional sale is effective as to the annexed article between the parties by virtue of their agreement unless it has lost its identity in a realty or, in a few cases, unless removal would cause substantial damage. Tiffany § 612.

13-12B Prior and Subsequent Purchasers and Lien Holders.

Agreement, see 13-11F.
Contracts for sale, see 13-11G.

R.C. 1309.32 (priority of security interest in fixtures) provides, among other things: that goods are fixtures (that is, are real estate) when they become so under the general Ohio law on fixtures; that a "fixture filing" is the filing where a real estate mortgage would be recorded of a financing statement on the goods which are or are to become fixtures and conforming to the requirements of R.C. 1309.39(E) noted below; that a security interest may continue in goods which become fixtures but no security interest exists under this chapter in ordinary building materials incorporated into an improvement on land; that a purchase money security interest has priority over the conflicting interest of the real estate encumbrancer or owner if the financing statement is filed before the goods become fixtures or within ten days thereafter (which can result in the interest under a mortgage or deed being subordinated when a financing statement is subsequently filed within the ten days) and the debtor has an interest of record in the real estate *or is in possession thereof* (this gives priority to a lien on a replacement fixture over an existing mortgage); that a security interest in readily removable factory or office machines or readily removable replacements of domestic appliances that are consumer goods (such property is not a fixture), which interest has been perfected by any means before the property was installed in the real estate, has priority over the conflicting interest of an encumbrancer or owner in the real estate; that a construction mortgage, or a mortgage given to refinance it, has priority over a security interest under prescribed conditions; and that when the secured party has priority over all owners and encumbrancers of the real estate, he may, upon default, remove the collateral from the real estate under the given circumstances. (As eff. 1-1-79.)

R.C. 1309.38 (place of filing) provides, among other things, for the place of filing certain financing statements and that a filing in good faith in an improper place is effective against any person who has knowledge of the contents of such financing statement. (As eff. 1-1-84.)

R.C. 1309.39 (formal requisites) provides, among other things, that (E) a financing statement covering crops growing or to be grown or timber to be cut or minerals or the like including oil and gas, or a financing statement filed as a fixture filing must show that it covers this type of collateral, must recite that it is to be indexed in the real estate records of the county in which the real estate is situated, and the financing statement must contain a description of the real estate sufficient if it were contained in a mortgage of the real estate to give constructive notice of the mortgage. If the debtor does not have an interest of record in the real estate, the financing statement must show the name of a record owner or record lessee. (As eff. 3-15-82.)

R.C. 1309.40 (what constitutes filing; duration; lapsed filing; duties of officer) provides: "(A) Presentation for filing of a financing statement and tender of the filing fee or acceptance of the statement by the filing officer constitutes filing under sections 1309.01 to 1309.50 of the Revised Code.

"(B)(1) Except as provided in divisions (B)(2) and (F) of this section, a filed financing statement is effective for a period of five years from the date of filing. The effectiveness of a filed financing statement lapses on the expiration of the five-year period unless a continuation statement is filed prior to the lapse. If a security interest perfected by filing exists at the time insolvency proceedings are commenced by or against the debtor, the security interest remains perfected until termination of the insolvency proceedings and thereafter for a period of sixty days or until expiration of the five-year period, whichever occurs later. Upon lapse the security interest becomes unperfected, unless it is perfected without filing. If the security interest becomes unperfected upon lapse, it is deemed to have been unperfected as against a person who became a purchaser or lien creditor before lapse.

"(2) A filed financing statement which states that it relates to an obligation secured by both (a) a mortgage upon real estate filed for record within this state and (b) a security interest in collateral, whether or not such collateral includes or consists of goods which are or are to become fixtures situated upon such real estate, shall, if such financing statement states a maturity date of such obligation, or the final installment thereof, of more than five years, be fully effective until the maturity date set forth therein. Such financing statement shall also contain a reference to the recorder's file number of the mortgage upon real estate or to the volume and page of the mortgage record in which such mortgage is recorded.

"(C) A continuation statement may be filed by the secured party within six months prior to the expiration of the five-year period specified in division (B)(1) of this section, or within six months prior to the stated maturity date referred to in division (B)(2) of this section. Any such continuation statement must be signed by the secured party, identify the original statement by file number, and state that the original statement is still effective. A continuation statement signed by a person other than the secured party of record must be accompanied by a separate written statement of assignment signed by the secured party of record and complying with division (B) of section 1309.42 of the Revised Code, including payment of the required fee. Upon timely filing of

509

the continuation statement, the effectiveness of the original statement is continued for five years after the last date to which the filing was effective whereupon it lapses in the same manner as provided in division (B) of this section unless another continuation statement is filed prior to such lapse. Succeeding continuation statements may be filed in the same manner to continue the effectiveness of the original statement. The filing officer may remove a lapsed statement from the files and destroy it immediately if he has retained a microfilm or other photographic record, or in other cases one year after the lapse. The filing officer shall so arrange matters by physical annexation of financing statements to continuation statements or other related filings, or by other means, that if he physically destroys the financing statements of a period more than five years past, those which have been continued by a continuation statement or which are still effective under division (B)(2) or (F) of this section shall be retained.

"(D) Except as provided in division (G) of this section, a filing officer shall mark each statement with a consecutive file number and with the date and hour of filing and shall hold the statement or a microfilm or other photographic copy thereof for public inspection. In addition the filing officer shall index the statements according to the name of the debtor and shall note in the index the file number and the address of the debtor given in the statement. In addition to the indexing required in the previous sentence, statements covering crops growing or to be grown or timber to be cut or minerals or the like, including oil and gas, or accounts subject to division (E) of section 1309.03 of the Revised Code, or a financing statement filed as a fixture filing pursuant to section 1309.32 of the Revised Code shall also be indexed in the real estate mortgage records by the filing officer according to the name of the debtor or, if the financing statement shows the record owner or record lessee to be other than the debtor, than according to the name of the record owner or record lessee given in the statement. The fee to be charged for indexing financing statements in the real estate mortgage records shall be two dollars for each record owner or lessee listed in the statement, as provided in division (H) of section 317.32 of the Revised Code.

"(E) The fee for filing, indexing, and furnishing filing data for an original, amended, or a continuation statement on a form prescribed by the secretary of state or on any other form approved by the filing officer shall, when collected by the secretary of state, be nine dollars, and shall, when collected by the county recorder, be five dollars. The fee for filing, indexing, and furnishing filing data for an original, amended, or a continuation statement on a form neither prescribed by the secretary of state nor on any other form approved by the filing officer shall, when collected by the secretary of state, be eleven dollars, and shall, when collected by the county recorder, be seven dollars.

"(F) If the debtor is a transmitting utility and a filed financing statement so states, it is effective until a termination statement is filed. A real estate mortgage which is effective as a fixture filing under division (F) of section 1309.39 of the Revised Code remains effective as a fixture filing until the mortgage is released or satisfied of record or its effectiveness otherwise terminates as to the real estate.

"(G) If the person filing any original or amended financing statement, termination statement, statement of assignment, or statement of release, furnishes the filing officer a copy thereof, the filing officer shall upon request note upon the copy the file number and date and hour of the filing of the original and deliver or send the copy to such person.

"(H) Upon request of any person, the filing officer shall issue his certificate showing whether there is on file on the date and hour stated therein, any presently effective financing statement naming a particular debtor, owner, lessee, and any statement of assignment thereof and if there is, giving the date and hour of filing of each such statement and the names and addresses of each secured party therein. The fee for such a certificate shall, when collected by the secretary of state, be nine dollars plus one dollar for each financing statement and for each statement of assignment reported therein, and shall, when collected by the county recorder, be five dollars plus one dollar for each financing statement and for each statement of assignment reported therein. Upon request the filing officer shall furnish a copy of any filed financing statement or statement of assignment for a uniform fee of one dollar per page." (As eff. 1-1-85.)

R.C. 1701.66 provides that a mortgage from a railroad or public utility or a municipal corporation pursuant to Article XVIII, section 12, of the Ohio Constitution or the state, a county, or a municipal corporation, pursuant to Chapter 165 of the Revised Code, or a port authority pursuant to section 4582.06 of the Revised Code, need not otherwise be filed or refiled under the Uniform Commercial Code. (As eff. 7-9-82.)

If the financing statement purports to cover crops or fixtures and names an owner or lessee, whether or not such status is distinguishable, such name shall be indexed in the real estate mortgage index as the grantor. 1965 OAG 113.

Under the Ohio amendments to the Uniform Commercial Code, the holder of a security interest may have priority over parties acquiring interests in the real estate subsequent to both perfection of the security interest and affixation of the goods to the real estate. However, to obtain a valid lien against a subsequent lien holder or bona fide purchaser of the real estate, the financing statement covering crops or fixtures must be indexed in the real estate mortgage records in the name of the record owner or record lessee and must reasonably identify the real estate.

A security interest is invalid against a party who acquired his interest in the real estate prior to the time the security interest is perfected or to the time the goods are affixed, unless he consented or disclaimed.

SECTION 13-13: REMOVAL BY TENANT; TRADE FIXTURES

Life estates, see also Section 11-64.
Waste, see Section 11-19.

13-13A Generally.

A tenant under an oil and gas lease has the right to remove casing, etc., prior to the expiration of the lease as they are trade fixtures. Siler v. Globe Window Glass Co., 21 CC 284, 11 CD 784 (1900).

A tenant does not lose, as against a purchaser of the real estate, his right to remove articles, by entering into a new lease. Dunkel v. Hedges, 15 App 259 (1921).

Further research: O Jur 3d, Fixtures § 14.

LAW IN GENERAL

Improvements made by the tenant with the intention that they be permanently annexed to the realty are not removable by the tenant as against the landlord.

Fixtures which have been annexed by the tenant for a term, for the purposes of the particular business conducted on the land, do not belong to the landlord unless removal would cause permanent and substantial injury to the real estate. The rule applies not only to trade fixtures but to domestic and ornamental fixtures annexed by the tenant for his comfort or convenience, and usually also applies to agricultural fixtures or any other installation by a tenant. In a majority of the cases removable fixtures installed by a lessee are treated as personalty. The right to remove has been held to be lost by entering into a new lease.

Under some decisions the right of removal is extended to life tenants and tenants of other limited estates.

A subsequent purchaser or encumbrancer usually has notice of the right of removal, although he will prevail over the right if he was without notice and paid value.

Am Jur 2d, Fixtures §§ 3, 22, 23, 35, 36, 38-41, 57, 94, 107, 108; Am Law of Prop § 19.11; CJS, Fixtures § 33; Powell § 656; Tiffany § 616.

13-13B Substituted Fixtures.

LAW IN GENERAL

It is often held that the right of the tenant to remove does not attach to a new fixture substituted by him for a fixture annexed by the landlord. 110 ALR 490.

13-13C Time of Removal.

"The general rule is, that the tenant must remove fixtures put up by him before he quits the possession, on the expiration of his lease; if not removed during the term, they become the property of the landlord." Haflick v. Stober, 11 OS 482 (1860).

LAW IN GENERAL

The tenant must remove the fixtures to which he is entitled before he surrenders possession, as a rule. An exception to the rule, where the time of termination of the tenancy is not fixed, is that he has a reasonable time for removal after the termination. Am Law of Prop § 19.11; 6 ALR2d 322.

CHAPTER 14: HUSBAND AND WIFE

DIVISION 14-1: IN GENERAL

SECTION 14-11: INTRODUCTION; COMMON-LAW MARRIAGE
 14-11A Validity of Marriages
 14-11B Common-law Marriage

SECTION 14-12: SPOUSE'S RIGHTS DURING MARRIAGE
 14-12A Estate by the Marital Right

SECTION 14-13: DISABILITIES OF COVERTURE
 14-13A Rules
 14-13B Postnuptial Agreements between Spouses

SECTION 14-14: ANTENUPTIAL AGREEMENTS
 14-14A Rules

SECTION 14-15: SEPARATION AGREEMENTS
 14-15A Rules
 14-15B Law of Situs

SECTION 14-16: RESTRAINTS ON MARRIAGE
 14-16A Rules

SECTION 14-17: ANNULMENT OF MARRIAGE
 14-17A Equitable Actions
 14-17B Under Statutes

DIVISION 14-2: DOWER

SECTION 14-21: GENERALLY; NATURE AND REQUISITES
 14-21A Definitions; Rules
 14-21B Validity of Marriage
 14-21C Required Seisin of Husband
 14-21D Right of Redemption

SECTION 14-22: ESTATES AND INTERESTS SUBJECT TO DOWER
 14-22A Future Interests
 14-22B Trustees; Vendors under Contracts for Sale
 14-22C Equitable Interests; Vendees under Contracts for Sale
 14-22D Fraud of Dower
 14-22E Leaseholds
 14-22F Joint Ownership
 14-22G Equitable Conversion
 14-22H Exchange of Lands
 14-22I Dower out of Dower

SECTION 14-23: VALUATION AND ASSIGNMENT
 14-23A Statutes
 14-23B Manner of Assignment and Valuation
 14-23C Effect of Assignment; Consummate Dower
 14-23D Inchoate Dower
 14-23E Accounting
 14-23F Priorities; Mortgages and Other Liens

SECTION 14-24: EXTINGUISHMENT AND CONVEYANCE
 14-24A Effectiveness of Release or Transfer
 14-24B Express Release Required before 1925

516

DIVISION 14-1: IN GENERAL

SECTION 14-11: INTRODUCTION; COMMON-LAW MARRIAGE

Cotenancy, see Division 5-2.
Descent, see Section 9-15.
Election by surviving spouse, see Section 9-27.
Surviving spouse generally, see Section 12-13.

14-11A Validity of Marriages.

R.C. 3105.12 provides that proof of cohabitation, and reputation of the marriage of the parties, is competent evidence to prove such marriage, and within the discretion of the court, may be sufficient therefor. (As eff. 10-1-53.)

An action for a declaratory judgment can be maintained to determine marital status only, although plaintiff seeks no coercive relief. Smerda v. Smerda, 74 NE2d 751, 35 OO 472, 48 Abs 232 (C.P. 1947); Seabold v. Seabold, 84 App 83, 84 NE2d 521, 39 OO 112 (1948).

Without dissolution of a prior common-law marriage, a second marriage is void. In re Zemmick's Estate, 76 NE2d 902, 49 Abs 353 (App. 1946).

Further research: O Jur 3d, Family Law § 59.

14-11B Common-law Marriage.

An agreement to marry in praesenti, made by parties competent to contract, accompanied and followed by cohabitation as husband and wife, with the result that they are treated and reputed as husband and wife in the community in which they reside, constitutes a common-law marriage. Nestor v. Nestor, 15 OS3d 143, 472 NE2d 1091 (1984); Markley v. Hudson, 143 OS 163, 54 NE2d 304, 28 OO 81 (1944); Umbenhower v. Labus, 85 OS 238, 97 NE 832, 9 OLR 554, 57 WLB 37 (1912).

While such an agreement to marry in praesenti must be proved by clear and convincing evidence, it may be established by proof of the acts, declarations and conduct of the parties and their recognized status in the community in which they reside. Markley v. Hudson, 143 OS 163, 54 NE2d 304, 28 OO 81 (1944).

Existence of common-law marriage is to be determined by law of the state where it is consummated. Howard v. Central Nat. Bank, 21 App 74, 152 NE 784, 4 Abs 700 (1926).

Where a contract of common-law marriage was executed in another state not recognizing such marriage, upon removal to this state with continued cohabitation and all the relations of husband and wife, law will supply the imputation of renewal of their marriage agreement in praesenti. Knight v. Shields, 19 Abs 37 (App. 1935).

Conduct of the parties at the time of the marriage contract may be sufficient to establish a common-law marriage. Gatterdam v. Gatterdam, 86 App 29, 85 NE2d 526, 40 OO 459, 54 Abs 271 (1949).

A common-law marriage may be established in Ohio only when each of the following five essential elements is proved by clear and convincing evidence, namely: (1) An agreement of marriage per verba de praesenti, (2) made by parties competent to marry, (3) followed by cohabitation, (4) a holding out as husband and wife, (5) and a reputation as being husband and wife. In re Soeder's Estate, 7 App2d 271, 220 NE2d 547, 36 OO2d 404 (1966).

Further research: O Jur 3d, Family Law § 44.

SECTION 14-12: SPOUSE'S RIGHTS DURING MARRIAGE

14-12A   Estate by the Marital Right.

R.C. 3103.04 provides that neither husband nor wife has any interest in the property of the other except rights to support, dower and mansion house. (As eff. 10-1-53.)

Neither husband nor wife has any interest in the property of the other except the present right of support and rights given by statute to a surviving spouse. Mark v. Mark, 145 OS 301, 61 NE2d 595, 30 OO 534, 160 ALR 608 (1945).

Further research: O Jur 3d, Family Law § 101.

LAW IN GENERAL

At common law, a husband had a freehold estate in his wife's freehold estate which entitled him to all rents and profits during coverture; as to the wife's estates of inheritance, the husband's estate was terminated by the birth of issue as well as by the death of either or by dissolution of the marriage. Such rights did not extend to the equitable separate estate of the wife. These rights are known as the estate by the marital right. As a result of modern married women's acts, few vestiges of the estate remain in the law. The husband's rights after birth of issue are known as curtesy which is supplanted in Ohio by dower. Am Law of Prop § 4.50; Powell § 117; Tiffany § 484.

SECTION 14-13: DISABILITIES OF COVERTURE

14-13A   Rules.

R.C. 3103.07 provides: "A married person may take, hold, and dispose of property, real or personal, the same as if unmarried." (As eff. 10-1-53.)

R.C. 5301.04 provides: "A deed, mortgage, or lease of any interest of a married person in real property must be signed, attested, acknowledged, and certified as provided in section 5301.01 of the Revised Code." (As eff. 10-1-53.)

Further research: O Jur 3d, Family Law § 105.

LAW IN GENERAL

In legal contemplation under the common law, husband and wife are one person and that person is the husband. This unity places a wife under disability to deal with property without the consent of the husband, to contract, and to sue or be sued alone. The disabilities do not operate in full force as to equitable separate estates; a married woman may generally alienate such an estate unless restrained by the provisions of the instrument creating the separate estate. Legislation has removed or modified these restrictions until married women are emancipated from practically all of the common-law disabilities. Am Law of Prop §§ 5.68, 18.43; Powell §§ 118, 123; Tiffany § 1359.

14-13B Postnuptial Agreements between Spouses.

Separation agreements, see Section 14-15.

R.C. 3103.05 provides: "A husband or wife may enter into any engagement or transaction with the other, or with any other person, which either might if unmarried; subject, in transactions between themselves, to the general rules which control the actions of persons occupying confidential relations with each other." (As eff. 10-1-53.)

A husband and wife living together cannot alter their legal relations by a postnuptial agreement contracting away the property provisions which the law gave to each of them upon the death of the consort, including distributive share and dower rights. Du Bois v. Coen, 100 OS 17, 125 NE 121, 17 OLR 63, 66, 64 WLB 176 (1919).

Transactions between husband and wife must be fair and made without undue advantage, and they will be closely scrutinized to prevent unfair treatment of the wife. Hasselschwert v. Hasselschwert, 90 App 331, 106 NE2d 786, 47 OO 494 (1951).

Further research: O Jur 3d, Family Law § 813.

SECTION 14-14: ANTENUPTIAL AGREEMENTS

14-14A Rules.

The intended wife will be bound by voluntarily entering into the contract after full disclosure or with full knowledge. The burden is upon those claiming the validity of the contract to show full disclosure or full knowledge. Juhasz v. Juhasz, 134 OS 257, 16 NE2d 328, 12 OO 57, 117 ALR 993 (1938).

Such contract will not bar the claim of the wife unless the provisions in her favor have been fairly performed. Phillips v. Phillips, 14 OS 308 (1863); Whistler v. Allward, 57 App 147, 12 NE2d 299, 10 OO 197, 23 Abs 536 (1936).

A properly executed prenuptial agreement bars the widow from the statutory exemption, year's allowance, and privilege of administering the estate where the wording clearly shows that such a result was intended. Troha v. Sneller, 169 OS 397, 159 NE2d 899, 8 OO2d 435 (1959).

A written agreement executed after marriage by a husband and wife, reciting an oral antenuptial agreement, constitutes a sufficient memorandum to comply with the statute of frauds and is not a contract between husband and wife to alter their legal relations. In re Weber's Estate, 170 OS 567, 167 NE2d 98, 11 OO2d 415 (1960).

The statutory limitation of an action to set aside an antenuptial agreement does not apply to an agreement void for fraud in the making. Petrich v. Petrich, 97 NE2d 56, 44 OO 457, 58 Abs 566 (App. 1950). See R.C. 2131.03 at 14-15A.

Further research: O Jur 3d, Family Law § 758.

LAW IN GENERAL

Agreements between prospective spouses concerning their property rights are enforceable after the marriage in equity and under modern married women's acts. They are not otherwise enforceable at common law during the existence of the relation. Antenuptial agreements are voidable when not entered into voluntarily with adequate knowledge of the surrounding facts and with good faith by both parties. The parties are under a duty to make a fair disclosure of the property owned. Am Jur 2d, Husband and Wife § 283; Am Law of Prop § 539; 27 ALR2d 883; CJS, Husband and Wife § 80; Powell § 216; Tiffany § 527.

The right of the surviving spouse to take under the will of the other has been upheld in most of the cases notwithstanding an antenuptial or postnuptial agreement. 53 ALR2d 475.

SECTION 14-15: SEPARATION AGREEMENTS

14-15A Rules.

Revocation of will, see 9-24A.

R.C. 2131.03 provides: "Any antenuptial or separation agreement to which a decedent was a party is valid unless action to set it aside is begun within six months after the appointment of the executor or administrator of the estate of such decedent, or unless within such period the validity of such agreement is otherwise attacked." (As eff. 10-1-53.)

R.C. 3103.06 provides: "A husband and wife cannot, by any contract with each other, alter their legal relations, except that they may agree to an immediate separation and make provisions for the support of either of them and their children during the separation." (As eff. 10-1-53.)

Where a separation agreement provides that husband shall pay wife a named sum monthly during her life, a valid obligation is imposed upon his estate in case of his death before hers. Hassaurek v. Markbreit, 68 OS 554, 67 NE 1066, 1 OLR 150, 535, 48 WLB 581, 696 (1903).

Such agreement may be valid if the separation occurs pursuant thereto. Hoagland v. Hoagland, 113 OS 228, 148 NE 585, 3 Abs 387, 388, 23 OLR 322 (1925).

A decree of divorce, which is silent on the subject, does not of its own force terminate a separation agreement. Mendelson v. Mendelson, 123 OS 11, 173

NE 615, 8 Abs 754, 33 OLR 321 (1930); Tefft v. Tefft, 73 App 399, 54 NE2d 423, 29 OO 99 (1943).

Since no attack, which invoked the jurisdiction of a court to hear and determine the validity of the contract, was made within the six-month period, the contract must be deemed valid. Juhasz v. Juhasz, 134 OS 257, 16 NE2d 328, 12 OO 57, 117 ALR 993 (1938).

Prior agreement of separation is annulled by the resumption of the marital relation. Geesey v. Wakefield State Bank, 3 Abs 171 (App. 1924).

Such contract must be supported by proof that it was understood by the wife and was voluntarily signed by her, and its execution must be followed by an actual separation. Snyder v. Buckeye State Bldg. & Loan Co., 26 App 166, 160 NE 37, 6 Abs 203 (1927).

Where the court finds that a separation agreement is not "fair, just or reasonable" to the wife, it will set such agreement aside. Brewer v. Brewer, 84 App 35, 78 NE2d 919, 39 OO 89, 52 Abs 116 (1948).

In an action for divorce and alimony the court is without authority to modify or alter a separation agreement which is not the subject of any allegations in the pleadings. Nellis v. Nellis, 98 App 247, 129 NE2d 217, 57 OO 281 (1955).

Further research: O Jur 3d, Family Law § 762.

14-15B   Law of Situs.

Antenuptial and separation agreements which are not contrary to the policy of our laws will be enforced in this state. Scheferling v. Huffman, 4 OS 241 (1854).

LAW IN GENERAL

Separation and postnuptial agreements concerning land are ordinarily governed by the law of the situs. 18 ALR2d 760.

SECTION 14-16:   RESTRAINTS ON MARRIAGE

14-16A   Rules.

Miscellaneous restraints, see 9-21P.

By election of the widow, she took under the will alone, subject to the condition of losing the property by marrying again. And as she took all the property under the will, she lost all of it by her subsequent marriage. Luigart v. Ripley, 19 OS 24 (1869).

A condition in a will making the receipt of a legacy dependent on a separation of husband and wife is contrary to public policy and void, and the legatee takes the legacy absolutely. Moores v. Gwynne, 15 CC(NS) 31, 23 CD 463 (1911).

An item in a will which provides that devises and bequests made to nieces and nephews shall not be executed if any of them should marry outside of the

Protestant faith, is null and void as against public policy. Moses v. Zook, 18 Abs 373 (App. 1934).

A restraint against a second marriage is an exception to the general rule that a general restraint against marriage is against public policy and void. Where a restraint against marriage is limited in effect, its validity depends upon its reasonableness. Saslow v. Saslow, 104 App 157, 147 NE2d 262, 4 OO2d 230 (1957).

A conveyance by a mother to her daughter subject to a condition that the latter must reconvey to the former in case of the daughter's marriage, created a valid condition subsequent if the dominant motive of the grantor was to provide support for the daughter until such marriage. Winters v. Miller, 23 Misc 73, 261 NE2d 205, 52 OO2d 130 (C.P. 1970).

Gifts conditioned upon the beneficiary marrying within a particular religious class or faith are reasonable. Shapiro v. Union Nat. Bank, 39 Misc 28, 315 NE2d 825, 66 OO2d 268 (C.P. 1974).

LAW IN GENERAL

A provision making the acquisition or retention of a gift contingent upon the recipient not entering into any first marriage is invalid unless the intention is clearly to provide support until the marriage. Such provision is valid if only a particular first marriage is prohibited, except when a permitted marriage is not likely to occur. 122 ALR 22; Powell § 851; Restatement, Second, Property (Donative Transfers) § 6.1.

Valid restraints on remarriage of the recipient can be imposed by his or her spouse. Forfeiture provisions imposed by a person other than the spouse are invalid if found to be unreasonable. Powell § 853; Restatement, Property § 26.

A provision for forfeiture which encourages separation or divorce is invalid unless the intention is clearly to provide support in such event. Powell § 854; Restatement, Second, Property (Donative Transfers) § 7.1; Simes and Smith § 1515.

The above rules are not without dissent, many cases especially upholding restraints attached to gifts on special limitation until marriage.

Additional references: Am Jur 2d, Marriage §§ 168-183; Am Law of Prop § 27.12; Simes and Smith § 1514; Tiffany § 196.

SECTION 14-17: ANNULMENT OF MARRIAGE

See also Section 14-31.

14-17A Equitable Actions.

Divorce may be granted when "either party had a husband or wife living at the time of the marriage from which the divorce is sought." See R.C. 3105.01 at 14-31A.

A court of chancery, in the exercise of its ordinary powers, will entertain jurisdiction at the suit of the imbecile's guardian to declare the ward's marriage a nullity. Waymire v. Jetmore, 22 OS 271 (1872).

A guardian of an incompetent may maintain, by way of a cross-petition, without the consent of his ward, an action for annulment of a claimed marriage which the ward contracted during the period of the guardianship. Duncan v. Duncan, 88 App 243, 99 NE2d 510, 44 OO 453 (1950).

A court of equity may entertain a suit for annulment; and the divorce statutes should not be construed as being involved unless the facts require their use. Nyhuis v. Pierce, 114 NE2d 75, 65 Abs 73 (App. 1952).

An action for annulment of marriage is not one of the cases in which service by publication is allowed. Johnson v. Johnson, 16 O Supp 81, 31 OO 122 (C.P. 1945).

Further research: O Jur 3d, Family Law § 909.

LAW IN GENERAL

Courts of equity exercise jurisdiction to declare a purported marriage to be a nullity. Annulment is distinguished from divorce in that under the former the marriage is found (a) to be void from the beginning, or (b) to be invalid on account of facts existing at the time of the marriage making it voidable in equity. Jurisdiction is commonly exercised in the state of domicile by analogy to actions for divorce. Am Jur 2d, Annulment of Marriage § 1; CJS, Marriage §§ 48, 68.

14-17B   Under Statutes.

Revocation of will, see 9-24A.
Venue, see 14-31B.

R.C. 3105.31 provides: "A marriage may be annulled for any of the following causes existing at the time of the marriage:

"(A) That the party in whose behalf it is sought to have the marriage annulled was under the age at which persons may be joined in marriage as established by section 3101.01 of the Revised Code, unless after attaining such age such party cohabited with the other as husband or wife;

"(B) That the former husband or wife of either party was living and the marriage with such former husband or wife was then and still is in force;

"(C) That either party has been adjudicated to be mentally incompetent, unless such party after being restored to competency cohabited with the other as husband or wife;

"(D) That the consent of either party was obtained by fraud, unless such party afterwards, with full knowledge of the facts constituting the fraud, cohabited with the other as husband or wife;

"(E) That the consent to the marriage of either party was obtained by force, unless such party afterwards cohabited with the other as husband or wife;

"(F) That the marriage between the parties was never consummated although otherwise valid." (As eff. 9-24-63.)

R.C. 3105.32 provides time limitations within which an action must be commenced under each of the above divisions of section 3105.31. (As eff. 9-24-63.)

R.C. 3105.34 provides for restoration of former name of wife. (As eff. 10-25-78.)

DIVISION 14-2: DOWER

SECTION 14-21: GENERALLY; NATURE AND REQUISITES

14-21A Definitions; Rules.

R.C. 2103.02 provides: "A spouse who has not relinquished or been barred from it shall be endowed of an estate for life in one third of the real property of which the consort was seized as an estate of inheritance at any time during the marriage. Such dower interest shall terminate upon the death of the consort except:

"(A) To the extent that any such real property was conveyed by the deceased consort during the marriage, the surviving spouse not having relinquished or been barred from dower therein;

"(B) To the extent that any such real property during the marriage was encumbered by the deceased consort by mortgage, judgment, lien except tax lien, or otherwise, or aliened by involuntary sale, the surviving spouse not having relinquished or been barred from dower therein. If such real property was encumbered or aliened prior to decease, the dower interest of the surviving spouse therein shall be computed on the basis of the amount of the encumbrance at the time of the death of such consort or at the time of such alienation, but not upon an amount exceeding the sale price of such property.

"In lieu of such dower interest which terminates pursuant to this section, a surviving spouse shall be entitled to the distributive share provided by section 2105.06 of the Revised Code.

"Dower interest shall terminate upon the granting of an absolute divorce in favor of or against such spouse by a court of competent jurisdiction within or without this state.

"Wherever dower is referred to in Chapters 2101. to 2131., inclusive, of the Revised Code, it means the dower to which a spouse is entitled by this section." (As eff. 10-1-53.) From January 1, 1932 to September 1, 1935 this statute did not specifically provide for property aliened during the marriage by involuntary sale.

Vested or consummate dower is the interest of a surviving spouse in the lands in which the deceased spouse was seized of an estate of inheritance during the marriage; after assignment it has the attributes of a life estate. Contingent or inchoate dower is the dower right of one spouse during the lifetime of the other spouse. Goodman v. Gerstle, 158 OS 353, 109 NE2d 489, 49 OO 235 (1952).

The dower interest which survives to the surviving spouse under the present statute is given to protect his or her interest in real estate which the deceased consort aliened or permitted to be aliened during his or her lifetime. In re Freeman's Estate, 16 O Supp 6, 31 OO 232, 43 Abs 106 (Prob. 1944).

Further research: O Jur 3d, Family Law § 660.

LAW IN GENERAL

Dower at common law consists of the right of the widow to a life estate in one third of the real estate of which her husband was beneficially seized at any time during the marriage; the requisite estate of the husband being one which could pass by inheritance to the children of the marriage. Am Jur 2d, Dower § 1; Am Law of Prop § 5.1; CJS, Dower §§ 1, 42; Powell §§ 212, 217.

14-21B Validity of Marriage.

Proof of validity, see 14-11A.

LAW IN GENERAL

Dower does not arise unless there is a valid marriage according to the law of the place where the marriage took place. A voidable marriage which was not annulled is sufficient to support dower. Where common-law marriages are recognized they ordinarily support a claim to dower. Am Law of Prop § 5.7; CJS, Dower § 8; Tiffany § 488.

14-21C Required Seisin of Husband.

Particular applications of the requirements, see Section 14-22.

LAW IN GENERAL

The duration of the husband's seisin is immaterial except when it is said to be momentary or instantaneous, as when land is acquired and disposed of in the same transaction. Am Law of Prop §§ 5.10, 5.12.

14-21D Right of Redemption.

LAW IN GENERAL

The holder of an inchoate or of a consummate right of dower is entitled to redeem from a prior encumbrance. The general rule in equity is contribution, whether the encumbrance was paid by the surviving spouse or paid by an heir or assignee of the deceased spouse. Am Jur 2d, Dower § 95; Am Law of Prop § 5.24; CJS, Dower § 36; Tiffany § 500.

SECTION 14-22: ESTATES AND INTERESTS SUBJECT TO DOWER

Determinable fees, see 11-51C.
Estates subject to condition subsequent, see 11-51C.
Estates tail, see 11-32F.
Executory interests, see 11-83D.
Fraudulent conveyances, see 8-54D.
Mortgaged property, see 14-23F.
Partition, see 5-34H.
Partnerships, see Section 4-28.
Quarantine, see 12-13B.
Remainders and reversions, see 11-72C.

14-22A Future Interests.

Particular interests, see cross-references above.

In case of voluntary partition the weight of authority is to the effect that the right of dower upon the cotenant's share is remitted to the allotment to him, although dower is barred where the division is by judicial proceedings. Fleming v. Morningstar, 4 NP(NS) 405, 17 OD 430 (1904), affd. 72 OS 647 (1905). Further research: O Jur 3d, Family Law § 691.

LAW IN GENERAL

A present estate of inheritance during the marriage is a requisite of dower. A right of reentry, although condition broken, does not constitute such seisin as will support dower. 21 ALR 1073; CJS, Dower § 17.

14-22B Trustees; Vendors under Contracts for Sale.

A widow cannot have dower in lands of which her husband held the legal title in trust for others with no beneficial interest in himself. Derush v. Brown, 8 Ohio 412 (1838).

Where the trustee of a freehold estate acquires a substantial beneficial interest under the trust, there is a merger of the legal and equitable estates to the extent of the beneficial interest, and dower of the trustee's wife attaches to the merged estate. Ragland v. First Nat. Bank, 48 App 441, 194 NE 389, 2 OO 19, 17 Abs 104 (1934).

LAW IN GENERAL

Ownership without a beneficial interest does not support a claim to dower, as where the legal title is subject to a resulting or constructive trust. The interest of a trustee having the bare legal title is not subject to dower as where a grantee is a mere instrument for passing the title. Am Jur 2d, Dower § 25; Am Law of Prop § 5.11; CJS, Dower § 31; Thompson § 1918; Tiffany §§ 499, 508.

Dower does not attach, as against the equitable rights of the purchaser, where before marriage the vendor had entered into a valid contract to convey the land. 8 ALR3d 569.

14-22C   Equitable Interests; Vendees under Contracts for Sale.

To entitle a widow to dower, it is necessary that her husband should have had a legal estate of inheritance, in the premises in which dower is claimed, during the coverture. Miller v. Wilson, 15 Ohio 108 (1846); Rands v. Kendall, 15 Ohio 671 (1846).

Ohio follows the general rule that dower does not attach unless the deceased spouse held legal title. Therefore the spouse of a vendee under a contract for sale need not join in an assignment of the contract by the vendee.

LAW IN GENERAL

Equitable estates are not subject to dower at common law. In jurisdictions where there is no dower in equitable estates generally, the right does exist by the weight of authority in the interest of a vendee under an executory contract of purchase if the purchase price has been paid in full. Am Jur 2d, Dower § 86; Am Law of Prop §§ 5.23, 11.28; CJS, Dower § 29; Tiffany § 497.

14-22D   Fraud of Dower.

R.C. 2103.06 provides: "If a husband or wife gives up real property by collusion or fraud, or loses it by default, the widow or widower may recover dower therein." (As eff. 10-1-53.)

A conveyance without a valuable consideration and without the consent of the grantor's contemplated wife is a fraud on her marital rights, and she is entitled to dower at his death. Ward v. Ward, 63 OS 125, 57 NE 1095, 43 WLB 449, 44 WLB 205 (1900).

A conveyance of realty to children of a former marriage, without consideration other than love and affection, by a man engaged to be married, without disclosure to his intended wife whom he later married, does not defraud her of her right to dower. (Ward v. Ward, 63 OS 125, 57 NE 1095, 43 WLB 449, 44 WLB 205 (1900) overruled.) Perlberg v. Perlberg, 18 OS2d 55, 247 NE2d 306, 47 OO2d 167 (1969).

LAW IN GENERAL

Dower is not barred by a conveyance in fraud which is intended to bar dower even though made before the marriage. Am Law of Prop § 5.32; CJS, Dower §§ 32, 58; Tiffany § 506.

14-22E   Leaseholds.

The surviving spouse of the owner of an unexpired estate for years is not entitled to dower, except in perpetual and long-term leases.

14-22F Joint Ownership.

Partition, see 5-34H.

Joint tenancy is not recognized in Ohio. When the conveyance is to husband and wife, each has inchoate dower in the undivided half interest of the other. Further research: O Jur 3d, Family Law § 673.

14-22G Equitable Conversion.

No conversion of real estate into personalty can defeat the widow's dower without her consent. In re Davis, 21 CC 720, 12 CD 29 (1901), revd. on other grounds 68 OS 160, 67 NE 251 (1903).

LAW IN GENERAL

The doctrine of equitable conversion is sometimes applied so as to sustain dower or to defeat it. Tiffany § 491.

14-22H Exchange of Lands.

LAW IN GENERAL

When a husband exchanged land for an equal interest in other land, many cases hold that the widow is not entitled to dower in both parcels but she must make an election between the tracts. Am Law of Prop § 5.21; Tiffany § 494.

14-22I Dower out of Dower.

LAW IN GENERAL

There is no dower out of dower; thus, a decedent's widow is not entitled to dower out of the estate assigned to the widow of decedent's ancestor. For example, when a son inherits land subject to his mother's dower and dies before his mother, then his widow's dower is computed only to the two-thirds interest not subject to his mother's dower. Am Law of Prop § 5.13; CJS, Dower § 28; Tiffany § 502.

SECTION 14-23: VALUATION AND ASSIGNMENT

14-23A Statutes.

R.C. 5305.01 to 5305.17 provide for the assignment of dower. (As eff. 10-1-53.)

LAW IN GENERAL

Statutes ordinarily provide proceedings to compel the assignment of consummate dower in specific lands in order to ascertain and fix the rights of the surviving spouse. Such proceedings are usually not exclusive of the common-law remedies or of equitable relief. Am Law of Prop § 5.45; CJS, Dower § 79; Tiffany § 544.

14-23B Manner of Assignment and Valuation.

Widow is to be endowed according to the value at the time of the assignment, excluding increase of value from improvement, but including increased value from other extrinsic and general causes. Dunseth v. Bank of United States, 6 Ohio 76 (1833); Larrowe v. Beam, 10 Ohio 498 (1841).

LAW IN GENERAL

The surviving spouse is entitled to an assignment by metes and bounds of the equivalent of one third of the rents and profits as of the time of the assignment. The exception is that the surviving spouse is not entitled to the benefit of improvements made by a purchaser, the exception not applying to improvements made by the heirs. The assignment may be made by agreement, by the owner of the freehold, or by the one in possession, subject to statutory provisions. Am Jur 2d, Dower § 182; Am Law of Prop § 5.46; CJS, Dower § 82; Tiffany § 536.

14-23C Effect of Assignment; Consummate Dower.

A surviving spouse, having only a consummate dower right is not entitled to possession, rents, profits or right of entry until dower has been ascertained and set off. Huffman v. Huffman, 57 App 33, 11 NE2d 271, 10 OO 24, 25 Abs 5 (1937).

Unassigned dower consummate is transferable and the transferee may maintain an action against the owner of the fee to have the estate set off in possession or in a share of the net rent. Thoms v. Bissinger Candy Co., 77 App 339, 67 NE2d 734, 33 OO 191, 46 Abs 257 (1946).

LAW IN GENERAL

After assignment, the estate of the surviving spouse relates back to the time of death of the deceased spouse except that the right to an accounting may be limited. The interest acquired by the assignment is equivalent to a life estate with all its usual rights and liabilities. Before assignment the interest, even though vested and consummate, is a mere right of action without the right of possession; it is generally subject to creditor's bill but not to execution. Am Jur 2d, Dower §§ 6 to 8; Am Law of Prop §§ 5.43, 5.49; CJS, Dower §§ 67, 76, 110; Tiffany §§ 534, 550.

14-23D Inchoate Dower.

The contingent right of dower is property of substantial value and may be ascertained with reasonable certainty from established tables of mortality, aided by evidence respecting the state of health and constitutional vigor of the husband and wife respectively. Mandel v. McClave, 46 OS 407, 22 NE 290, 21 WLB 258, 22 WLB 267 (1889); Unger v. Leiter, 32 OS 210, 2 WLB 339 (1877).

LAW IN GENERAL

Annuity tables may be used by taking one third of the present value of an annuity for the life of the claimant, based on the proceeds of the property to which the contingent right of dower attaches, and deducting the value of a similar annuity for the life of the other spouse. Upon foreclosure during the husband's life he is generally held entitled to the surplus proceeds free from his wife's inchoate dower. Am Jur 2d, Dower § 76; 64 ALR 1053; CJS, Dower § 45; Tiffany § 533.

14-23E Accounting.

See also 14-23B and 14-23C.

While the dower right attaches upon the death of the deceased spouse, the surviving spouse is not entitled to anything by reason thereof until the same has been set off or otherwise ascertained in a proper action. Huffman v. Huffman, 57 App 33, 11 NE2d 271, 10 OO 24, 25 Abs 5 (1937).

14-23F Priorities; Mortgages and Other Liens.

Circuity of lien, see 1-31G.
Judicial sales, see also 17-21E.
Right of redemption, see 14-21D.

When a mortgage (excepting a purchase-money mortgage) is executed during the marriage, dower is computed on the entire proceeds. Payment of the dower interest is subject to satisfaction of the mortgage in which the spouse has released dower. Mandel v. McClave, 46 OS 407, 22 NE 290, 21 WLB 258, 22 WLB 267 (1889).

Where the mortgagor subsequently married and after foreclosure that was no surplus for the mortgagor, the spouse of mortgagor was not entitled to dower. Home Owners Loan Corp. v. Grant, 3 O Supp 24, 20 OO 116, 33 Abs 662 (C.P. 1938); Rands v. Kendall, 15 Ohio 671 (1846). The rule is the same as to an assumed mortgage. George v. George, 51 App 174, 200 NE 145, 4 OO 260, 20 Abs 448 (1924).

The wife's right of dower is barred by a sale to satisfy a judgment rendered against the husband before marriage. When there is a surplus after satisfaction of the superior lien, she is entitled to dower computed on the surplus. Phillips v. Keels, 4 CC 316, 2 CD 568 (1890).

Only those claiming through the mortgage instrument can defeat the wife's contingent right of dower. Sprague v. Law, 17 CC 735, 8 CD 428 (1898).

Where prior to marriage the owner of land has entered into a valid contract to convey the same, no right of dower attaches to his title therein; or at least it may be said that any right of dower attaching thereto is subject to the equitable rights of the purchaser. Rohn v. Leach, 1 Abs 700 (App. 1923).

The surviving spouse, standing in the relation of an heir at law with those who take under the statutes of descent and distribution, takes subject to decedent's debts. Disher v. Disher, 35 NE2d 582, 8 OO 203, 21 Abs 610 (App. 1936).

Where property is encumbered by judgments in which a spouse has not relinquished dower, and by mortgages over which such judgments have a priority, in which the spouse has relinquished dower, the dower interest must be paid to the mortgagees in their order of priority to the extent that the same is necessary to satisfy the mortgages, and such dower interest has a preference over the judgments. Geese v. Murphy, 3 O Supp 52, 8 OO 32, 24 Abs 189 (Prob. 1937).

Inchoate dower interest in a foreclosure action is computed on the surplus above the mortgage executed by the husband before the marriage. Central Trust Co. v. Gilardi, 186 NE2d 771, 21 OO2d 183 (C.P. 1962).

In the case of purchase-money mortgages (whether executed before or after marriage), in the case of mortgages made before marriage (whether or not condition be broken before marriage), and in the case of mortgages assumed by the spouse as part of the purchase price, the beneficial interest upon which dower is figured is the surplus over and above the mortgage. Charles C. White, "Ohio Theory of a Mortgage," 3 Cin. L. R. 405; Nicholas v. French, 83 OS 162, 93 NE 897, 8 OLR 521, 524, 56 WLB 5 (1910).

Further research: O Jur 3d, Family Law § 707.

LAW IN GENERAL

Unreleased dower is prior, as a rule, to all liens except those that attached to the property before the marriage or before acquisition by the husband, and except purchase-money mortgages. Liens are superior to dower if they attached before marriage or before acquisition by the deceased spouse. Dower is usually computed on the surplus above a purchase-money mortgage, above a mortgage given by a previous owner, above a mortgage made before marriage, or above a mortgage not expressly assumed by the husband's grantee. With the exceptions above noted, dower is ordinarily calculated on the entire interest of the deceased spouse. Am Law of Prop §§ 5.24, 5.31; 65 ALR 963; CJS, Dower § 36; Tiffany § 511.

SECTION 14-24: EXTINGUISHMENT AND CONVEYANCE

Divorce, see 14-31F.
Infants, see 15-11K and 15-11L.
Partition, see 5-34H.

14-24A   Effectiveness of Release or Transfer.

Antenuptial agreements, see Section 14-14.
Separation agreements, see Section 14-15.

R.C. 2103.03 and 2103.04 provide that a valid conveyance to a person in lieu of dower, to take effect on the death of grantor, if accepted by grantee, will bar dower. (As eff. 10-1-53.)

A release of dower is binding only as to the releasee and his privies. Ridgway v. Masting, 23 OS 294 (1872).

A husband or wife living together cannot alter their legal relations by contracting away the dower rights provided by law for each of them. Du Bois v. Coen, 100 OS 17, 125 NE 121, 17 OLR 63, 66, 64 WLB 176 (1919).

Further research: O Jur 3d, Family Law § 737.

LAW IN GENERAL

A release of dower in a deed, mortgage or lease is incidental to the conveyance and is generally inoperative if the conveyance is invalid. A mortgage or release is ordinarily effective only in favor of the person to whom made and those claiming under him. Am Law of Prop § 5.31; CJS, Dower § 66; Powell § 213; Tiffany § 515.

Inchoate dower cannot be conveyed to a third person or be released directly to the other spouse. It may be released by her sole deed to a previous grantee of the other spouse. Am Law of Prop § 5.34; Tiffany § 512.

14-24B   Express Release Required before 1925.

Curative act since 1925, see 8-31R.

Where a wife is named only in the clause describing parties and in the attesting clause of a deed, and no terms employed touching the wife's contingent dower, the wife is not barred, although she join in a formal execution of the deed. McFarland v. Febigers, 7 Ohio (pt. 1) 194 (1835); Cincinnati v. Newell, 7 OS 37 (1857); Foster v. Dennison, 9 Ohio 121 (1839).

14-24C   Defeasibility of Interest.

See also cross-references for Section 14-22.

LAW IN GENERAL

Dower is extinguished, as a general rule, when the deceased spouse's estate is terminated by enforcement of a superior lien, by assertion of title para-

532

mount, by exercise of a right of reentry, or by happening of the event under a special limitation. Escheat for lack of heirs does not affect dower. The inchoate right is unaffected by the husband's bankruptcy or by adverse possession during his lifetime. Am Law of Prop § 5.26; 25 ALR2d 333; Powell § 215; Tiffany § 510.

14-24D   Limitation of Actions.

Adverse possession, see 2-28A.

A vested dower interest in real estate is a personal right which must be asserted during the life of the owner and no right thereto survives unless an action to have it assigned is commenced during that life. Dick v. Bauman, 73 App 107, 55 NE2d 137, 28 OO 176 (1943).
Further research: CJS, Dower § 71; Tiffany § 548.

14-24E   Bar by Testamentary Provision.

Election by surviving spouse, see Section 9-27.

No decisions have been found, since the 1932 Probate Code, as to whether an election to take under the will bars dower in lands conveyed or encumbered by the deceased spouse without a release of dower. The statutes on election do not mention dower. At common law a widow takes both the testamentary gift and dower unless the will otherwise provides, although before 1932 the Ohio statute barred dower upon election to take under the will. Acceptance of a testamentary gift, specifically in lieu of dower, does bar dower. A testamentary provision barring dower is of no effect upon an election to take under the law.
Further research: O Jur 3d, Family Law § 768.

14-24F   Misconduct of Spouse.

R.C. 2103.05 provides: "A husband or wife who leaves the other and dwells in adultery will be barred from dower in the real property of the other, unless the offense is condoned by the injured consort." (As eff. 10-1-53.)

14-24G   Judicial Sales.

Bankruptcy, see Division 17-3.
Circular priority, see 1-31G.
Sale of dower, see 17-21E.
Valuation, see Section 14-23.

A widow's unassigned right of dower may be subjected by proceedings in equity to payment of a judgment against her. Boltz v. Stolz, 41 OS 540, 11 WLB 124, 326, 13 WLB 499 (1885).
A sale of land at the suit of a judgment creditor of the husband brought to marshal liens does not have the effect to bar or foreclose the inchoate dower of

the wife. Jewett v. Feldheiser, 68 OS 523, 67 NE 1072, 1 OLR 136, 509, 48 WLB 566, 688 (1903). Otherwise if the lien attached prior to marriage. Phillips v. Keels, 4 CC 316, 2 CD 568 (1890).

A mere inchoate right of dower cannot be reached by a creditor's bill. Geiselman v. Wise, 137 OS 93, 28 NE2d 199, 17 OO 430 (1940).

A spouse is entitled to payment of her dower interest prior to judgment creditors of the other spouse. Welbaum v. Baker, 19 Abs 23 (App. 1935).

Inchoate dower may be protected in a judicial sale by sequestering from the proceeds, pending determination of whether spouse of claimant held the land as trustee, an amount equal to the calculated value of such dower interest. Liberty Folder Co. v. Anderson, 86 App 399, 90 NE2d 409, 41 OO 521, 55 Abs 388 (1949).

Further research: O Jur 3d, Family Law § 746; CJS, Dower § 61.

14-24H Recitals.

Standard of Title Examination

(Adopted by Ohio State Bar Association in 1952)

Problem 3.6A:

After what lapse of time should the omission from a deed of a recital of grantor's marital status not be regarded as a defect?

Standard 3.6A:

The omission of such recital is not a defect when the deed has been of record for more than fifty years, in the absence of notice of subsequent facts indicating the contrary.

Standard of Title Examination

(Adopted by Ohio State Bar Association in 1953)

Problem 3.6B:

Should an objection be raised when the chain of title discloses that the grantor previously had a spouse who does not release dower?

Standard 3.6B:

Yes, unless omission of the release is satisfactorily explained.

Standard of Title Examination

(Adopted by Ohio State Bar Association in 1953)

Problem 3.6C:

Should a title objection be made where the deed recites that the grantor is divorced and the record of the divorce proceedings is not available for examination?

Standard 3.6C:

Yes.

Standard of Title Examination

(Adopted by Ohio State Bar Association in 1955)

Problem 3.6D:

Should the descriptive terms "single," "widow," and "widower" be considered a sufficient showing of marital status?

Standard 3.6D:

Yes.

Comment:

The descriptive term "relict" is not sufficient.

LAW IN GENERAL

A conveyance of land falsely reciting that the grantor is unmarried estops the grantor, his heirs and assigns, but does not affect the claim of the spouse.

It has been held that the absence of a statement as to marital status does not raise a presumption that the grantor is married or make the title unmarketable. However, it is customary to require such a recital or other evidence.

Since a purchaser is bound by the actual facts, it is common practice for title examiners to require evidence that inchoate dower has been barred by death or by divorce when the record discloses that an owner was married and that he later conveys as unmarried.

39 ALR2d 1082.

14-24I Barring Dower of Insane Persons.

Sale or release of dower by guardian, see 15-13G.

R.C. 5305.18 provides: "A person owning real property in this state, encumbered by the contingent or vested right of dower of an insane person, may apply, by petition to the court of common pleas of the county in which the real estate, or any part thereof, is situated, making defendants thereto such insane person, and the spouse and guardian, if such insane person has either or both, for leave to sell any part of such real property, discharged and unencumbered of such contingent or vested right of dower. The petition must set forth the insanity of the person, together with a description of the land proposed to be sold. Thereupon the court shall appoint a committee of six competent men, of whom at least three are physicians, who, under oath, shall inquire into the insanity of such person, and hear testimony to be produced by the spouse or guardian, or, if there is no such guardian, by a guardian ad litem to be appointed in the action. The committee shall make a report, in writing, of the result of its investigation, signed by its members." (As eff. 8-6-76.)

R.C. 5305.19 provides: "If the committee provided for in section 5305.18 of the Revised Code unanimously reports that the person having a contingent or vested right of dower, in its opinion, is permanently insane, the court of common pleas shall appoint three judicious freeholders to appraise the real estate described in the petition mentioned in said section, whether or not such real estate is in one or several counties. Such freeholders shall report in writing the value of each tract." (As eff. 10-1-53.)

R.C. 5305.20 provides: "When the report provided for in section 5305.19 of the Revised Code is filed, the court of common pleas may direct the petitioner, by a sufficient deed of conveyance, to convey to the insane person, to be held by such person in fee, such proportion of the real estate described in the petition as seems just, or the court may assign to such insane person, to be held by him during life, after the death of the spouse of such person, such proportion of the real estate described in the petition as seems just, for his support, or the court may order the petitioner to invest an amount by it fixed, in the stock of a company, or stocks created by the laws of this state, as the court designates, the profits, and dividends or distributions, arising from such investment to be applied to the support and maintenance of the insane person after the death of the spouse of such person. The petitioner, upon his compliance with the order of the court, may sell all the real property he is possessed of, described in the petition, free and unencumbered of the contingent or vested right of dower of such insane person." (As eff. 7-30-84.)

R.C. 5305.21 provides: "When the spouse of an insane person conveys real estate in this state, in which such person has a contingent or vested right of dower, and the insane person does not join the spouse in the conveyance, the spouse may apply by petition to the court of common pleas of the county in which the insane person resides, or, if such insane person resides out of the state, then in the county in which the real estate is situated, for leave to have part or all of such real estate so conveyed, released of the dower right therein. Such petition shall set forth the insanity of the insane person, and a description of the land proposed to be affected. The insane person, guardian, if there is one, and all persons in interest, shall be made defendants, and the action shall be proceeded with as prescribed in sections 5305.18 to 5305.20, inclusive, of the Revised Code, except that instead of ordering the petitioner to sell the real estate or to convey or assign to such insane person any part of it, the court shall direct the petitioner to make such investment as is provided in section 5305.20 of the Revised Code, or require him to secure the amount to the use of the insane person by mortgage or unencumbered real estate of at least double the value thereof. Upon compliance by the petitioner with the order made, the court shall enter a judgment releasing and discharging the real estate from the encumbrance of such right of dower, and adjudge the holder of the legal title, or other party liable, to pay to the petitioner any sum withheld or retained as indemnity against such dower right." (As eff. 10-1-53.)

14-24J Acquisition after Spouse Adjudged Insane.

R.C. 5305.22 provides: "Any real estate or interest therein coming to a person by purchase, inheritance, or otherwise, after the spouse of such person is adjudged insane, and is an inmate of a hospital for the insane in this state, or confined in the insane department of any epileptic hospital of this state, or any state of the United States, or is an inmate of a hospital for the insane, or confined in the insane department of any hospital of the United States, may be conveyed by such person while such insane spouse remains an inmate thereof, free and clear from any dower right or expectancy of such insane spouse. Dower shall not attach to any real estate so acquired and conveyed during the time described in this section in favor of such insane spouse. The indorsement upon the instrument of conveyance, by the superintendent of the hospital, that such spouse is an insane inmate thereof, stating when received therein and signed officially by him, shall be sufficient evidence of the fact that such spouse is such inmate. This indorsement shall be a part of the instrument of conveyance." (As eff. 10-1-53.)

From 1902 to June 25, 1941 this section did not provide for inmate of hospital of United States and did not contain the words "inheritance or otherwise."

DIVISION 14-3: DIVORCE AND ALIMONY

SECTION 14-31: DIVORCE GENERALLY

Annulment, see Section 14-17.

14-31A Law Governing; Grounds.

Revocation of will, see 9-24A.

R.C. 3105.01 provides: "The court of common pleas may grant divorces for the following causes:

"(A) Either party had a husband or wife living at the time of the marriage from which the divorce is sought;

"(B) Willful absence of the adverse party for one year;

"(C) Adultery;

"(D) Impotency;

"(E) Extreme cruelty;

"(F) Fraudulent contract;

"(G) Any gross neglect of duty;

"(H) Habitual drunkenness;

"(I) Imprisonment of the adverse party in a state or federal penal institution under sentence thereto at the time of filing the petition;

"(J) Procurement of a divorce without this state, by a husband or wife, by virtue of which the party who procured it is released from the obligations of the marriage, while such obligations remain binding upon the other party;

"(K) On the application of either party, when husband and wife have, without interruption for one year, lived separate and apart without cohabitation.

A plea of res judicata or of recrimination with respect to any provision of this section does not bar either party from obtaining a divorce on this ground." (As eff. 7-12-82.)

537

R.C. 3105.61 to 3105.65 provide for dissolution of marriage upon a petition signed by both spouses and containing a separation agreement. The hearing shall be not less than thirty nor more than ninety days after filing of the petition. A decree of dissolution has the same effect on property rights as a decree of divorce. The court retains jurisdiction to modify all matters of custody, child support, visitation, and alimony payments. (As eff. 9-23-74.)

This section authorizing the granting of a divorce where "either party had a husband or wife living at the time of the marriage from which the divorce is sought" provides an exclusive remedy in cases involving that situation. Eggleston v. Eggleston, 156 OS 422, 103 NE2d 395, 46 OO 351 (1952).

Further research: O Jur 3d, Family Law § 929.

LAW IN GENERAL

The status of a person is fixed by the law of the domicile. The law of the forum controls the validity of the divorce; the laws of another state are never applied in determining whether a cause of action exists. CJS, Divorce § 2.

14-31B Residence; Domicile.

Foreign decrees, see Section 14-33.
Residence and domicile generally, see 9-28A.

R.C. 3105.03 provides: "The plaintiff in actions for divorce and annulment shall have been a resident of the state at least six months immediately before filing the complaint. Actions for divorce and annulment shall be brought in the proper county for commencement of action pursuant to the civil rules. The court of common pleas shall hear and determine the case, whether the marriage took place, or the cause of divorce or annulment occurred, within or without the state.

"Actions for alimony shall be brought in the proper county for commencement of actions pursuant to Civil Rules." (As eff. 9-23-74.)

The use of the term "residence" in a divorce statute is generally deemed to import the requirement of domicile. While one can have only a single domicile, he may have several residences. To effect a change of domicile from one locality or state to another, there must be an actual abandonment of the first domicile, coupled with an intention not to return to it, and there must be a new domicile acquired by actual residence in another place or jurisdiction, with the intention of making the last-acquired residence a permanent home. Domicile once established continues until it is superseded by a new domicile, and the old domicile is not lost until a new one is acquired. Spires v. Spires, 214 NE2d 691, 35 OO2d 289 (C.P. 1966).

Further research: O Jur 3d, Family Law §§ 1047-1049.

LAW IN GENERAL

Courts generally do not have jurisdiction unless at least one of the parties has a domicile or residence within the state of the forum. The rule is that a statutory requirement of residence requires actual residence and also a legal domicile. Domicile is the place where a person lives or has his home with the intention of remaining indefinitely and to which, when absent, he intends to return. Am Jur 2d, Divorce, etc. § 246; 12 ALR2d 757; CJS, Divorce §§ 71, 81.

14-31C Equitable Jurisdiction.

Full equitable powers and jurisdiction as under R.C. 3105.20, repealed effective July 1, 1971 as being in conflict with Civil Rule 75(I), were restored on August 1, 1975, by enactment of R.C. 3105.011 shown at 14-32A.

In the exercise of its full equity powers under R.C. 3105.20, the trial court is authorized to adjudicate a complete dissolution of the marriage relationship, including a determination of the rights of the parties to alimony and to a division of property. Clark v. Clark, 165 OS 457, 136 NE2d 52, 60 OO 115 (1956).

Upon a petition for alimony only, the court is authorized to exercise its full equity powers and jurisdiction. Griste v. Griste, 171 OS 160, 167 NE2d 924, 12 OO2d 176 (1960).

14-31D Service of Process; Jurisdiction as to Property.

Alimony, see 14-32B.
Lis pendens, see 14-32D.
Modification of decree, see also 14-32E.
Separation agreements, see 14-15A.
Service generally, see 16-71F.

R.C. 3105.06 provides: "If the residence of a defendant in an action for divorce, annulment, or alimony is unknown, or if the defendant is not a resident of this state or is a resident of this state but absent from the state, notice of the pendency of the action shall be given by publication as provided by the Rules of Civil Procedure." (As eff. 6-7-79.)

Civil Rules 4(A) and 4(B) provide for issuance and form of summons. (As eff. 7-1-84.)

Civil Rule 4.5 provides alternative provisions for service in a foreign country. (As eff. 7-1-70.)

Civil Rule 75(J) provides: "No action for divorce, annulment or alimony may be heard and decided until the expiration of forty-two days after the service of process or twenty-eight days after the last publication of notice upon the complaint; nor shall any such action be heard and decided earlier than twenty-eight days after the service of a counterclaim, which under this rule may be designated a cross-complaint, unless the plaintiff files a written waiver of such twenty-eight day period." (As eff. 7-1-77.)

The statutes relating to service of process in divorce and alimony cases and to the six-week period after service apply to a cross-petition. Calvert v. Calvert, 130 OS 369, 199 NE 473, 4 OO 464 (1936).

An entry of appearance of itself does not give jurisdiction over the person of the defendant in a divorce case; but where in such a case personal service of process, though irregular, is neither quashed nor sought to be quashed and is followed by an entry of appearance, the court acquires personal jurisdiction. State ex rel. Engh v. Hoffman, 146 OS 193, 65 NE2d 59, 32 OO 170 (1946); Tucker v. Tucker, 143 OS 658, 56 NE2d 202, 28 OO 526 (1944).

The affidavit must show that defendant is not a resident of this state or that his residence is unknown. A divorce decree cannot be collaterally attacked where the record is silent as to whether the defendant was mailed a summons and a copy of the petition, and the journal states that the defendant was legally summoned. In re Lombard's Estate, 97 NE2d 87, 44 OO 357, 58 Abs 459 (App. 1950).

In a divorce proceeding between an Ohio plaintiff and a defendant whose last known residence was in a foreign country, service by publication in a Cleveland paper which does not contain defendant's last known address is defective and does not confer jurisdiction on the Ohio trial court to grant a default judgment. Demianczuk v. Demianczuk, 20 App 3d 244, 485 NE2d 785 (1984).

In an action for divorce and alimony with personal service, it is not essential for jurisdiction of the court to subject real estate to alimony that either the pleadings or published notice contain a description of the real estate. Dexter v. Taylor, 107 NE2d 402, 47 OO 398, 63 Abs 266 (App. 1951).

Where a divorce judgment contains provisions with respect to property rights in future or of an executory nature, the court entering the judgment impliedly reserves continuing jurisdiction to enforce compliance by entry of a judgment ancillary in nature upon a motion. Ellis v. Ellis, 94 App 339, 115 NE2d 180, 52 OO 14 (1953). Alimony, see 14-32E.

There is no legal requirement for new service of process in a divorce action because of the filing of an amended petition, particularly where the amended petition restated the same cause of action as contained in the original petition. Belcher v. Belcher, 161 NE2d 413, 81 Abs 232 (App. 1959).

Where, during the pendency of a divorce action in which certain real property of the parties is involved, a judgment is acquired against the defendant husband, a judgment lien cannot be perfected against such real property subsequently awarded the wife in the divorce decree. Foundation Savings & Loan Co. v. Rosenbaum, 113 App 501, 171 NE2d 359, 18 OO2d 101 (1960).

Lis pendens extends to real estate awarded to defendant whose pleadings did not describe the real estate but where it was described in the complaint. Bowles v. Middletown Collateral Loan Co., 328 NE2d 821, 71 OO2d 110 (1974).

A property settlement provision of a separation agreement, incorporated in a divorce decree or decree of dissolution, is enforceable by contempt proceedings. Harris v. Harris, 58 OS2d 303, 390 NE2d 789, 12 OO3d 291 (1979).

Further research: O Jur 3d, Family Law § 1040.

Standard of Title Examination

(Adopted by Ohio State Bar Association in 1971)

Problem 9.4A:

Should objection be made to a title derived through an uncontested divorce, alimony or annulment action when the certified mail return receipt or the sheriff's return of service in the action shows that summons was served on the defendant by delivering it to the plaintiff?

Standard 9.4A:

Yes.

Comment 9.4A:

In such an action under the circumstances described, proof that the defendant actually received the summons should be required. If furnished, such proof should be made a matter of record.

LAW IN GENERAL

Special provisions for service of summons must be strictly complied with. Where a nonresident is not served personally and does not appear, jurisdiction is limited to the status of the parties, as a general rule. When the service is constructive, exceptions to the rule are often made as to property within the jurisdiction of the court. CJS, Divorce § 78.

14-31E Personal Disabilities; Name.

Infants as parties, see 15-13A, 17-24B.
Service of process on minor, see 15-11I.

R.C. 3105.16 provides: "When a divorce is granted the court of common pleas shall, if the person so desires, restore any name that the person had before the marriage." (As eff. 10-25-78.)

A decree of divorce may be entered against an insane defendant for aggressions prior to the insanity. Benton v. Benton, 16 CC(NS) 121, 26 CD 613 (1909).

The court of common pleas is without jurisdiction to entertain an action for divorce instituted by a guardian on behalf of his ward, a mental incompetent. Jack v. Jack, 75 NE2d 484, 49 Abs 207 (App. 1947); Prather v. Prather, 4 O Supp 243, 1 OO 188, 33 Abs 336 (C.P. 1934).

LAW IN GENERAL

An action for divorce by a person under disability is prosecuted by a next friend or guardian; the action generally cannot be maintained in behalf of an insane person. In the absence of statute, a divorce will not be granted on the ground of insanity. 24 ALR2d 873.

14-31F Dower.

Foreign divorces, see Section 14-33.

R.C. 3105.10 in part provides: "(D) Upon the granting of a divorce, on a complaint or counterclaim, by force of the judgment, each party shall be barred of all right of dower in real estate situated within this state of which the other was seized at any time during coverture.

"(E) Upon the granting of a judgment for alimony, when by the force of the judgment real estate is granted to one party, the other party is barred of all right of dower in the real estate and the court may provide that each party shall be barred of all rights of dower in the real estate acquired by either party at any time subsequent to the judgment.

"'Dower' as used in this section has the meaning set forth in section 2103.02 of the Revised Code." (As eff. 8-1-75.)

Inchoate dower was barred by the enactment of G.C. 10502-1, effective January 1, 1932 (now R.C. 2103.02), where a divorce was granted to one of the spouses prior to that date even though the divorce decree expressly provided that the right of dower was not barred. Goodman v. Gerstle, 158 OS 353, 109 NE2d 489, 49 OO 235 (1952).

Words barring dower in decree of divorce are mere surplusage. Ball v. Ball, 47 App 547, 192 NE 364, 17 Abs 592, 40 OLR 407 (1933).

Further research: O Jur 3d, Family Law § 763.

LAW IN GENERAL

Dower is barred by a valid divorce even though the decree is made in another state or country. Am Law of Prop § 5.36; 168 ALR 793; CJS, Dower § 53.

14-31G Res Judicata.

Where one or both of the parties to a divorce action dies during appeal proceedings, revivor may be had. Porter v. Lerch, 129 OS 47, 193 NE 766, 1 OO 356 (1934).

The common pleas court has power to vacate a judgment of divorce rendered by it at a previous term for fraud practiced by the successful party in obtaining the judgment. Jelm v. Jelm, 155 OS 226, 98 NE2d 401, 44 OO 246, 22 ALR2d 1300 (1951).

The court of appeals has jurisdiction to reverse and set aside a decree of divorce when such decree has been granted in violation of the legal rights of a party. Martin v. Martin, 87 NE2d 499, 54 Abs 369 (App. 1949).

A court has no jurisdiction to modify a divorce judgment after term, except on the grounds enumerated and in the manner specified in R.C. 2325.01 et seq. Ellis v. Ellis, 94 App 339, 115 NE2d 180, 52 OO 14 (1953). See also 14-32E.

The provision of R.C. 3105.08 for an investigation is not a jurisdictional prerequisite to an order for maintenance of children or to a divorce decree. Rolls v. Rolls, 9 OS2d 59, 223 NE2d 604, 38 OO2d 159 (1967).

SECTION 14-32: ALIMONY GENERALLY

14-32A Definition; Jurisdiction in Equity; Grounds.

R.C. 3105.011 provides: "The court of common pleas including divisions of courts of domestic relations, has full equitable powers and jurisdiction appropriate to the determination of all domestic relations matters. This section is not a determination by the General Assembly that such equitable powers and jurisdictions do not exist with respect to any such matter." (As eff. 8-1-75.)

R.C. 3105.17 provides: "Either party to the marriage may file a complaint for divorce or for alimony, and when filed the other may file a counterclaim for divorce or for alimony. The court of common pleas may grant alimony on a complaint or counterclaim, regardless of whether the parties are living separately at the time the complaint or counterclaim is filed, for the following causes:

"(A) Adultery;

"(B) Any gross neglect of duty;

"(C) Abandonment without good cause;

"(D) Ill-treatment by the adverse party;

"(E) Habitual drunkenness;

"(F) Imprisonment of the adverse party in a state or federal penal institution under sentence thereto at the time of filing the petition." (As eff. 9-23-74.)

R.C. 3105.18 provides: "(A) In divorce, dissolution of marriage, or alimony proceedings, the court of common pleas may allow alimony it considers reasonable to either party.

"The alimony may be allowed in real or personal property, or both, or by decreeing a sum of money, payable either in gross or by installments, as the court considers equitable.

"(B) In determining whether alimony is necessary, and in determining the nature, amount, and manner of payment of alimony, the court shall consider all relevant factors, including, but not limited to the following:

"(1) The relative earning abilities of the parties;

"(2) The ages, and the physical and emotional conditions of the parties;

"(3) The retirement benefits of the parties;

"(4) The expectancies and inheritances of the parties;

"(5) The duration of the marriage;

"(6) The extent to which it would be inappropriate for a party, because he will be custodian of a minor child of the marriage, to seek employment outside the home;

"(7) The standard of living of the parties established during the marriage;

"(8) The relative extent of education of the parties;

"(9) The relative assets and liabilities of the parties;

"(10) The property brought to the marriage by either party;

"(11) The contribution of a spouse as homemaker.

"(C) In an action brought solely for an order for alimony under section 3105.17 of the Revised Code, any continuing order for periodic payments of money entered pursuant to this section is subject to further order of the court upon changed circumstances of either party.

"(D) If a continuing order for periodic payments of money as alimony is entered in a divorce or dissolution of marriage action that is determined on or after May 2, 1986, the court that enters the decree of divorce or dissolution of marriage does not have jurisdiction to modify the amount or terms of the alimony unless the court determines that the circumstances of either party have changed and unless one of the following applies:

"(1) In the case of a divorce, the decree or a separation agreement of the parties to the divorce that is incorporated into the decree contains a provision specifically authorizing the court to modify the amount or terms of alimony;

"(2) In the case of a dissolution of marriage, the separation agreement that is approved by the court and incorporated into the decree contains a provision specifically authorizing the court to modify the amount or terms of alimony.

"(E) Each order for alimony made or modified by a court on or after December 1, 1986, shall be accompanied by one or more orders described in division (D) or (H) of section 3113.21 of the Revised Code, whichever is appropriate under the requirements of that section, a statement requiring all parties to the order to notify the bureau of support in writing of their current mailing address, their current residence address, and of any changes in either address, and a notice that the requirement to notify the bureau of support of all changes in either address continues until further notice from the court.

"If any person required to pay alimony under an order made or modified by a court on or after December 1, 1986, is found in contempt of court for failure to make alimony payments under the order, the court that makes the finding shall, in addition to any other penalty or remedy imposed, assess all court costs arising out of the contempt proceeding against the person and require the person to pay any reasonable attorney's fees of any adverse party, as determined by the court, that arose in relation to the act of contempt." (As eff. 10-5-87.)

The repeal of R.C. 3105.20 repealed as in conflict with Civil Rule 75 (H) effective July 1, 1971, divests the domestic relations courts of equity jurisdiction to make divisions of property. Accordingly, the trial court is without authority to make a division of property unless it is pursuant to an alimony award under R.C. 3105.18. Soyk v. Soyk, 45 App2d 319, 345 NE2d 461, 74 OO2d 532 (1975). This decision applies only to decrees after July 1, 1971, and before August 1, 1975, the effective date of R.C. 3105.011 above.

When a divorce is granted on the ground that "either party had a husband or wife living at the time of the marriage from which the divorce is sought," the court has jurisdiction to grant alimony and other relief authorized by the statutes on divorce and alimony. Eggleston v. Eggleston, 156 OS 422, 103 NE2d 395, 46 OO 351 (1952).

Under R.C. 3105.17 and 3105.18, a court has the same power in awarding alimony only that it does in awarding alimony where a divorce is granted. Goetzel v. Goetzel, 169 OS 350, 159 NE2d 751, 8 OO2d 355 (1959).

Alimony, temporary and permanent, is an incident of a valid marriage only. Basile v. Basile, 86 App 535, 93 NE2d 564, 42 OO 205 (1948).

Where a marriage has been declared void from its very inception by way of an annulment, neither party has a right to an award of alimony. A petition for annulment should be addressed to the equity jurisdiction of the court. Short v. Short, 102 NE2d 719, 61 Abs 49 (App. 1951).

Under R.C. 3105.18 and 3105.20, the court of common pleas is given full equity powers to settle all property rights between husband and wife in a suit for alimony; and in a suit for alimony, such court may order a division of property. Morrison v. Morrison, 102 App 376, 143 NE2d 591, 2 OO2d 392 (1956).

Further research: O Jur 3d, Family Law §§ 971, 978, 983, 984, 1122.

14-32B Service of Process; Jurisdiction as to Property.

Process generally, see Section 16-71.
Standard of Title Examination on service of summons, see 14-31D.
Statutes applying to alimony with divorce, see Section 14-31.

In an action for divorce, where the petition contains a prayer for general relief, the court has jurisdiction to adjust and settle the nature and amount of alimony. Julier v. Julier, 62 OS 90, 56 NE 661, 43 WLB 104, 175 (1900); Rainsburg v. Rainsburg, 80 App 303, 75 NE2d 481, 36 OO 13 (1946).

Upon constructive service in an action for divorce, alimony and equitable relief, the court has power to award real estate of the defendant within the county to the plaintiff as alimony if the petition specifically describes the real estate. Reed v. Reed, 121 OS 188, 167 NE 684, 7 Abs 381, 29 OLR 399, 64 ALR 1384 (1929).

The 1951 amendment of R.C. 3105.18 eliminated the element of aggression as controlling the discretion of the trial court in awarding alimony to either husband or wife. Gage v. Gage, 164 OS 462, 136 NE2d 56, 60 OO 117 (1956).

"Although the award is without designation in the decree, it is apparent that the court acted under the provision that 'the husband shall be allowed such alimony out of the real and personal property of the wife as the court deems reasonable'" as the statute provided prior to August 28, 1951 when the divorce was for the aggression of the wife. Arbogast v. Arbogast, 165 OS 459, 136 NE2d 54, 60 OO 116 (1956).

A decree for alimony is a decree in personam and cannot be based upon constructive service. Stephenson v. Stephenson, 54 App 239, 6 NE2d 1005, 6 OO 559, 22 Abs 580 (1936).

Service by publication in a divorce action does not clothe the court with jurisdiction to decree payment of money, either by way of support of minor children or by way of alimony. Sutovich v. Sutovich, 120 App 473, 200 NE2d 716, 29 OO2d 371 (1964).

Further research: O Jur 3d, Family Law §§ 1059, 1060, 1071.

LAW IN GENERAL

A decree for alimony against a nonresident served only by publication is void except as to property within the jurisdiction of the court; neither can a personal judgment against a resident ordinarily be based on constructive service. Residence or domicile is immaterial where the parties appear or are personally served with process. Am Jur 2d, Divorce, etc. § 544.

The court may award property located in its jurisdiction as alimony, although the owner is a defendant served only by publication, if the action is in the nature of a proceeding in rem; description of the property in the petition with an appropriate prayer, injunction, seizure or receivership is generally required and sufficient to give the court jurisdiction. Am Jur 2d, Divorce, etc. § 546.

14-32C Action after Divorce.

Foreign divorce, see Section 14-33.

Where a wife obtains a divorce from her husband in this state without a decree for alimony, he being personally served with process, she cannot thereafter maintain a separate action for alimony. Weidman v. Weidman, 57 OS 101, 48 NE 506, 38 WLB 269, 304 (1897); Whitaker v. Whitaker, 52 App 223, 3 NE2d 667, 6 OO 316, 21 Abs 599 (1936).

A court has the power to approve an agreement made by the husband and wife adjusting alimony, and a consent decree cannot be collaterally attacked. Sponseller v. Sponseller, 110 OS 395, 144 NE 48, 2 Abs 372, 22 OLR 159 (1924).

Where the wife obtains a decree of divorce in an action based upon constructive service, such decree does not bar her right to have the question of alimony litigated in a subsequent action. Stephenson v. Stephenson, 54 App 239, 6 NE2d 1005, 6 OO 559, 22 Abs 580 (1936); Wick v. Wick, 58 App 72, 15 NE2d 780, 11 OO 463 (1938).

LAW IN GENERAL

As a rule, an action for alimony may be maintained after a valid divorce on constructive service. The allowance is usually refused, in the absence of reservation in the decree, if the court had jurisdiction in the divorce action of the person or property of the defendant; that is, the question of alimony is res judicata if it could have been litigated. Am Jur 2d, Divorce, etc. § 662; CJS, Divorce § 231.

14-32D As a Lien.

A decree for alimony, charged upon real estate, where the petition for divorce is general in its terms, binds the estate only from its rendition. Hamlin v. Bevans, 7 Ohio (pt. 1) 161 (1835).

A decree for alimony payable in installments is not a final judgment and is not a lien unless made so by the terms of the decree. Olin v. Hungerford, 10 Ohio 268 (1840); Gilbert v. Gilbert, 83 OS 265, 94 NE 421, 8 OLR 595, 56 WLB 65 (1911).

If the petition for divorce and alimony specifically describes certain real estate, the proceedings operate as a lis pendens. Tolerton v. Williard, 30 OS 579 (1876); Cook v. Mozer, 108 OS 30, 140 NE 590, 1 Abs 436, 845, 21 OLR 117 (1923).

A decree or judgment for alimony in gross was a lien on the real estate of the debtor and did not become dormant in five years. Lemert v. Lemert, 72 OS 364, 74 NE 194, 2 OLR 535, 3 OLR 20, 50 WLB 163 (1905); Peeke v. Fitzpatrick, 74 OS 396, 78 NE 519, 4 OLR 168, 51 WLB 239 (1906).

"In order to have a judgment lien, there must be a final judgment for the payment of a definite and certain amount of money which may be collected by execution on property of the judgment debtor. A judgment for periodic installments for an indefinite time can not create a lien on real property, in the absence of a provision in the judgment itself for a lien." Roach v. Roach, 164 OS 587, 132 NE2d 742, 59 OO 1, 59 ALR2d 685 (1956).

A lien for alimony installments decreed to be a charge on real estate is a superior lien to a subsequent judgment and levy although all of the alimony installments became payable after the intervening judgment and the judgment for the installments due were after the intervening judgment. McNealy v. Cochran, 59 App 254, 17 NE2d 670, 12 OO 525 (1937).

A judgment for the accumulated installments, under a decree not based upon an agreement of the parties, without notice or its equivalent to the party sought to be charged, is void. Collins v. Collins, 79 App 329, 73 NE2d 814, 35 OO 101 (1947).

A suit for divorce and alimony, where the petition does not seek a right against any specifically described property, is not lis pendens so as to give alimony priority over a judgment lien taken during the pendency of such petition. An amended petition does not relate back to the commencement of the action under this doctrine. Domino v. Domino, 99 NE2d 825, 45 OO 151, 60 Abs 484 (C.P. 1951).

Since August 29, 1935 "any judgment or decree" shall be a lien from the time there is filled a certificate of judgment as provided by R.C. 2329.02.

Further research: O Jur 3d, Family Law §§ 1152, 1153, 1215, 1217.

LAW IN GENERAL

Alimony may become a lien by order of the court, by specific statutory provision, or in the same manner as any other money judgment. An award of alimony in cash is normally enforced as any other money judgment. However, the lien does not terminate or become dormant by lapse of time if it arises by virtue of the order of the court, as distinguished from arising by virtue of being a money judgment. Am Jur 2d, Divorce, etc. § 739; CJS, Divorce § 268.

Unless a decree for periodical payments for support or alimony specifically states that it shall be a lien on property, none arises, in the absence of a statute to the contrary. 59 ALR2d 656.

14-32E Modification of Decree.

Civil Rule 75(I) prescribes the procedure for invoking the continuing jurisdiction of the court "by motion filed in the original action, notice of which shall be served in the manner provided for the service of process under Rule 4 through Rule 4.6." (As eff. 7-1-77.)

See Civil Rule 75(J) quoted at 14-31(D).

A court has no jurisdiction to reopen an alimony case and modify its former decree where the judgment awarding the original alimony is a final determination of the rights of the wife and there is nothing within the judgment entry to indicate any purpose of the court to maintain a continuing jurisdiction. Blake v. Blake, 20 Abs 3 (App. 1935); Law v. Law, 64 OS 369, 60 NE 560, 45 WLB 227, 364 (1901); Joshua v. Joshua, 87 NE2d 106, 53 Abs 561 (App. 1948).

Accrued alimony payments, although for support of children, are in the nature of judgments, and are not subject to modification unless the original entry so provides. McPherson v. McPherson, 153 OS 82, 90 NE2d 675, 41 OO 151 (1950).

An alimony decree based on an agreement between the parties is not subject to modification by a court after term in the absence of mistake, misrepresentation or fraud and in the absence of a reservation of jurisdiction with reference thereto. Newman v. Newman, 161 OS 247, 118 NE2d 649, 53 OO 135 (1954).

Notice of the motion to modify must comply with R.C. 2309.67 and 2309.69 to give the court jurisdiction. Reynolds v. Reynolds, 12 App 63, 31 CC(NS) 129 (1919); Vida v. Vida, 86 App 139, 90 NE2d 441, 41 OO 10 (1949).

The court may exercise its equitable jurisdiction in the enforcement of the decretal right to installments of alimony. Wolfe v. Wolfe, 124 NE2d 485, 55 OO 465, 70 Abs 22 (C.P. 1954).

Further research: O Jur 3d, Family Law §§ 1162, 1177, 1178, 1189.

14-32F Support of Children.

Modification of decree, see 14-32E.

R.C. 3105.21 provides: "(A) Upon satisfactory proof of the causes in the complaint for divorce, annulment, or alimony, the court of common pleas shall make an order for the disposition, care, and maintenance of the children of the marriage, as is in their best interests, and in accordance with section 3109.04 of the Revised Code.

"(B) Upon the failure of proof of the causes in the complaint, the court may make the order for the disposition, care, and maintenance of any dependent child of the marriage as is in the child's best interest, and in accordance with section 3109.04 of the Revised Code.

"(C) Each order for child support made or modified under this section on or after December 1, 1986, shall be accompanied by one or more orders described in division (D) or (H) of section 3113.21 of the Revised Code, whichever is appropriate under the requirements of that section, a statement requiring all parties to the order to notify the bureau of support in writing of their current mailing address, their current residence address, and of any changes in either address, and a notice that the requirement to notify the bureau of support of all changes in either address continues until further notice from the court. If any person required to pay child support under an order made under this section on or after April 15, 1985, or modified on or after December 1, 1986, is found in contempt of court for failure to make support payments under the order, the court that makes the finding shall, in addition to any other penalty or remedy imposed, assess all court costs arising out of the contempt proceeding against the person and require the person to pay any reasonable attorney's fees of any adverse party, as determined by the court, that arose in relation to the act of contempt." (As eff. 10-5-87.)

A decree of divorce which provides for the support of minor children, continues the jurisdiction of the court to increase the amount during the minority or a lesser period named in the decree without any express reservation in the decree. Corbett v. Corbett, 123 OS 76, 174 NE 10, 9 Abs 58, 33 OLR 357 (1930); McDonagh v. McDonagh, 4 App3d 207, 447 NE2d 758 (1982); Bean v. Bean, 14 App3d 358, 471 NE2d 785 (1983).

The decree may not be subsequently modified by the court so as to lessen the unconditionally fixed amount of support for minor child. Tullis v. Tullis, 138 OS 187, 34 NE2d 212, 20 OO 237 (1941).

In a divorce, alimony, custody, support and maintenance proceeding the court is without power to provide for the support of an adult child. Jurisdiction may be acquired in an equitable action, under a contract or when the child is insane. Miller v. Miller, 154 OS 530, 97 NE2d 213, 43 OO 496 (1951).

The court retains jurisdiction to modify a decree which requires a certain weekly payment for support of minor children "until further order of this court." Seitz v. Seitz, 156 OS 516, 103 NE2d 741, 46 OO 423 (1952).

Further research: O Jur 3d, Family Law § 1024.

14-32G   Effect of Death.

By virtue of the amendments of the statutes in 1951, a court granting a divorce may embody in the judgment an order for the payment of alimony in future installments, which order will be operative according to its terms against the estate to the party charged with such payments after his death. DeMilo v. Watson, 166 OS 433, 143 NE2d 707, 2 OO2d 433 (1957).

The estate of the husband is not liable for installment payments of alimony and support for the period after the death of the husband, unless the parties have so agreed and the agreement is approved by the court and is incorporated in the decree. Platt v. Davies, 82 App 182, 77 NE2d 486, 37 OO 533, 50 Abs 225 (1947).

The estate of a deceased father may be liable for payments for support of children in accordance with a separation agreement incorporated in a divorce decree. Silberman v. Brown, 72 NE2d 267, 34 OO 295, 48 Abs 97 (C.P. 1946).

R.C. 2107.33 (quoted at 9-24A) provides that where a testator is divorced after executing a will "any disposition or appointment of property made by the will to the former spouse or to a trust with powers created by or available to the former spouse, any provision in the will conferring a general or special power of appointment on the former spouse, and any nomination in the will of the former spouse as executor, trustee, or guardian, shall be revoked unless the will expressly provides otherwise." The statute is effective as to a will executed prior to its effective date and does not thereby violate the prohibition in Section 28, Article II of the Ohio Constitution against retroactive laws. Buehler v. Buehler, 67 App2d 7, 425 NE2d 905, 21 OO3d 330 (1979).

Further research: O Jur 3d, Family Law §§ 1167, 1169, 1206, 1209.

SECTION 14-33: FOREIGN DIVORCE AND ALIMONY DECREES

14-33A Validity of Divorces in Foreign States.

LAW IN GENERAL

A divorce decree is presumptively valid everywhere. The validity of a divorce granted in a sister state must be recognized to the extent it is valid in such state (a) if either party was domiciled in the state where the divorce was granted, or (b) if the defendant was personally served within the jurisdiction of the court or appeared and participated in the suit, although neither party was domiciled in such state. Participation is not required to consist of actual contest of the issue of domicile.

When the jurisdiction of the divorce court is based upon constructive service on a nonresident defendant who did not make an appearance, the divorce may be found invalid in the courts of another state on the ground that the plaintiff did not have a bona fide domicile in the state where the divorce was granted.

To summarize, a divorce in a foreign state may be impeached only when (a) neither party was a resident of the foreign state, and (b) the defendant was not personally served and did not enter an appearance in the suit.

Am Jur 2d, Divorce, etc. § 954; 1 ALR2d 1385; 28 ALR2d 1303, 1346; CJS, Divorce § 326.

Further research: O Jur 3d, Family Law §§ 1233-1235, 1248.

14-33B Divorce Decrees in Foreign Countries.

The court of Mexico had no jurisdiction to grant a divorce decree where the plaintiff never acquired a bona fide residence in that country, even though both parties appeared and consented to that court exercising jurisdiction. Bobala v. Bobala, 68 App 63, 33 NE2d 845, 20 OO 45, 33 Abs 440 (1940).

The rule that the judgment of a court of a foreign country is conclusive is uniformly qualified with the limitation that it has, in a given case, jurisdiction of the person and the subject matter, and in the absence thereof, the judgment is of no effect. In re Vanderborght, 91 NE2d 47, 57 Abs 143 (C.P. 1950).

Where important factual recitals in a foreign divorce decree are false, that decree is not entitled to comity and is not recognized. Yoder v. Yoder, 24 App2d 71, 263 NE2d 913, 53 OO2d 193 (1970).

Further research: O Jur 3d, Family Law §§ 1243, 1244, 1260, 1261.

LAW IN GENERAL

A divorce granted in a foreign country is valid here if both parties had a bona fide residence there; it is void if neither party was domiciled in the foreign country. When the plaintiff only had a domicile in the foreign country, whether or not recognition will be given to the foreign divorce depends upon the rules of comity under the facts in the particular case. A decree cannot directly affect the title to land in another country. Am Jur 2d, Divorce, etc. §§ 964, 965, 995; CJS, Divorce §§ 326 to 337.

A divorce granted in a foreign country by a court having jurisdiction is generally recognized under the rules of comity. The tests of jurisdiction are those of the domestic court and a divorce is normally not given effect if neither party had a domicile in that country. This principle is applied whether the decree was the mail-order type, or was upon constructive service, or was based on voluntary submission by both parties to the jurisdiction of the foreign court. Equitable doctrines are sometimes available to sustain the decree. 13 ALR3d 1419.

14-33C Foreign Alimony Decrees.

LAW IN GENERAL

An alimony decree does not operate on the title to land in another state. A decree for alimony rendered in another state by a court having jurisdiction of the parties and the subject matter will be enforced in personam by Ohio courts under the full faith and credit clause of the Constitution, provided the decree is final and is not subject to modification as to accrued amounts in the state where rendered. When the nonresident defendant did not enter his appearance and was served only by publication or by service outside the state, a foreign alimony decree (a) cannot operate as a personal judgment, (b) does not affect property rights in the state of the matrimonial domicile, and (c) is not conclusive in a subsequent suit for alimony. See citations for 14-33A.

Further research: O Jur 3d, Family Law §§ 1258, 1259.

14-33D Alimony before and after Foreign Divorce.

A valid divorce decree obtained in a foreign state against a nonresident defendant solely upon service by publication does not, as to a denial of alimony therein, operate extraterritorially and is not entitled to full faith and credit in the state of defendant's residence. Armstrong v. Armstrong, 162 OS

406, 123 NE2d 267, 55 OO 234 (1954), affd. 350 US 568, 100 L Ed 705, 76 Sup Ct 629, 60 OO 268, 73 Abs 514 (1956).

LAW IN GENERAL

The local court is free to hold that a prior alimony decree survives a foreign divorce obtained against a husband on constructive service, provided the husband did not participate in the divorce. If the husband's obligation would be terminated under the law of the state where the divorce was granted, that law will be given effect when the wife has been personally served or has participated in the divorce action. 28 ALR2d 1378; 49 ALR3d 1266.

14-33E Effect of Foreign Divorce on Title.

Where a divorce has been granted to a husband in a foreign court having no jurisdiction of the property rights of the parties, the divorced wife may file an action for divorce and alimony in a court having jurisdiction of the divorced husband and the property of the parties, and the court has jurisdiction to make a division of their property as though it had granted a divorce to the wife. Slapp v. Slapp, 143 OS 105, 54 NE2d 153, 28 OO 47 (1944).

Further research: 22 ALR2d 724.

14-33F Dower.

Effect of local divorce, see 14-31F.

LAW IN GENERAL

A valid foreign divorce has the same effect in barring dower as a valid local divorce. Am Jur 2d, Dower § 148.

DIVISION 14-4: HOMESTEAD

SECTION 14-41: GENERALLY

Statute, see 17-41B.

14-41A Nature.

Exemption laws should be liberally construed. Exceptions to a statutory exemption right should be strictly construed against the judgment creditor. Troutman v. Eichar, 64 App 415, 28 NE2d 953, 18 OO 183 (1940).

Further research: O Jur 3d, Exemptions §§ 4-8.

LAW IN GENERAL

Homestead rights are the exemptions to the head of a family of a residence from liability for debts or an exemption of a certain sum of money in lieu of homestead. Am Law of Prop § 5.75; Powell §§ 121, 263.

SECTION 14-42: PERSONS ENTITLED; CLAIMS EXCEPTED

14-42A Persons Entitled.

Quarantine, see 12-13B.

See R.C. 2329.66 quoted at 17-41B.

Where husband and wife are tenants in common and husband's interest is sold at judicial sale, the wife is entitled to homestead, and neither is entitled to allowance in lieu. Schumacher v. Ohio Savings & Trust Co., 121 OS 446, 169 NE 442, 7 Abs 735, 30 OLR 525 (1929).

A widow may claim exemptions only as to claims against her individually and not as to property owned by her husband during his lifetime. Dillman v. Warner, 54 App 170, 6 NE2d 757, 7 OO 492, 20 Abs 459 (1935).

A divorced person is not entitled to an exemption in lieu of homestead. Condon v. Condon, 5 O Supp 50, 19 OO 549, 33 Abs 474 (C.P. 1940).

Further research: O Jur 3d, Exemptions § 11.

14-42B Claims Excepted.

See R.C. 2329.661 quoted at 17-41B.
Further research: O Jur 3d, Exemptions §§ 43-47.

14-42C Time and Manner of Claiming Exemption.

In land sale proceedings, see 12-14P.

The exemption may be claimed by the debtor at any time before the sale. Frost v. Shaw, 3 OS 270 (1854).

The proper time to have homestead exempted from sale is when the sheriff is about to execute the writ. Sears v. Hanks, 14 OS 298 (1863).

Judgment debtor is entitled to assignment of homestead where real estate was so occupied after the judgment but before order of sale issued. Wildermuth v. Koenig, 41 OS 180, 11 WLB 324 (1884); Rodler v. Trovillo, 2 O Supp 233, 11 OO 512, 26 Abs 556 (C.P. 1938).

Further research: O Jur 3d, Exemptions §§ 53, 54.

SECTION 14-43: PROPERTY WHICH MAY BE EXEMPTED

14-43A Amount.

Statute, see 17-41B.

14-43B Actual Occupancy.

The property set off is relieved from being subject to payment of the judgment only while occupied by the debtor's family as a homestead. Kerns v. Linden, 3 CC(NS) 37, 13 CD 162 (1901).

14-43C Particular Types of Interests.

An owner of a life estate in lands occupied by him, who has conveyed his interest as security for a debt, is the owner of a homestead. Biddinger v. Pratt, 50 OS 719, 35 NE 795, 30 WLB 392, 31 WLB 5 (1893).

Exemptions are not confined to rights as against execution, but can be asserted against an order of attachment, an order of sale in equity, or any other writ. Radford v. Kachman, 27 App 86, 160 NE 875, 5 Abs 742 (1927).

A homestead may be claimed in land of which the party is in possession under a contract of purchase or any other equitable title. Radford v. Kachman, 27 App. 86, 160 NE 875, 5 Abs 742 (1927).

Where a judgment creditor asks that liens be marshaled and a mortgagee sets up a mortgage but does not ask foreclosure, the judgment debtor is not entitled to a homestead exemption but to the allowance in lieu thereof. Aikin Loan Co. v. Mustaine, 63 App 227, 26 NE2d 229, 16 OO 542, 30 Abs 532 (1939).

A judgment debtor may claim homestead exemptions in real estate owned by himself and his wife as tenants in common. New Martinsville Grocery Co. v. Hannibal Store Co., 65 App 50, 29 NE2d 226, 18 OO 276 (1940).

14-43D Proceeds of Sale; Money in Lieu of Homestead.

"But the exemption which the law gives in lieu of a homestead is an absolute exemption and whether it be taken in personal or real property, the judgment debtor acquires, in and to the property so exempt, when selected and taken, an absolute ownership with full power of disposition." Genell v. Hirons, 70 OS 309, 71 NE 709, 2 OLR 74, 49 WLB 298 (1904).

The right to demand an allowance in lieu of a homestead is to be determined at the time the surplus arising from the sale is finally disposed of. Niehaus v. Faul, 43 OS 63, 1 NE 87, 13 WLB 337 (1885); Russell v. Rexroad, 3 O Supp 316, 16 OO 209, 30 Abs 450 (Prob. 1939).

SECTION 14-44: TRANSFER AND ENCUMBRANCE OF EXEMPT PROPERTY

14-44A Rules.

A sale of lands by an executor to pay debts, subject to the homestead, and while the same is occupied as such homestead, is void. Wehrle v. Wehrle, 39 OS 365, 10 WLB 314 (1883).

A homestead exemption is a personal privilege which is not assignable. Schuler v. Miller, 45 OS 325, 13 NE 275 (1887).

In this case a 280-acre farm was sold under proceedings in bankruptcy after five acres thereof had been set off to the bankrupt as a homestead. Held that a homestead exemption is not a fee; that the bankruptcy court had jurisdiction in the matter of the construction and application of state laws; and that the referee in bankruptcy had jurisdiction to order the sale of the reversionary interest in the homestead which had previously been set off. Morgridge v. Converse, 150 OS 239, 81 NE2d 112, 37 OO 486 (1948).

14-44B   Judgment and Execution Liens.

Particular judgments, see 14-42B.

A homestead is subject to a judgment or execution lien, although not subject to sale, both before and after it is set off. Roig v. Schults, 42 OS 165 (1884).

A homestead does not become immune from levy and execution sale until after application and assignment and retains such immunity only so long as used as a homestead. Property in lieu of homestead becomes exempt only after it has been awarded. Gledhill v. Walker, 143 OS 381, 55 NE2d 647, 28 OO 339 (1944).

The question of exemption from execution against a lien created by a divorce decree, is res judicata. James v. James, 69 App 485, 44 NE2d 368, 24 OO 206, 37 Abs 66 (1942).

SECTION 14-45:   TERMINATION; WAIVER

14-45A   Rules.

The right to a homestead is personal and cannot be conveyed, and is lost by neglect to claim it, or by abandonment of the homestead. McComb v. Thompson, 42 OS 139, 11 WLB 250 (1884).

A stipulation in an executory contract, agreeing to waive the benefit of homestead exemption laws, is void as against the public policy. Dennis v. Smith, 125 OS 120, 180 NE 638, 11 Abs 510, 36 OLR 228 (1932). See also statute at 14-42B.

Fraudulent conveyance will be set aside although value of property was not in excess of mortgage plus $500 in lieu of homestead. Gledhill v. Walker, 143 OS 381, 55 NE2d 647, 28 OO 339 (1944).

LAW IN GENERAL

A homestead right exists only so long as the property is held as a homestead. It may continue as long as one of the family occupies the premises as a residence. The right to the exemption is terminated by abandonment when the removal has occurred without intention of returning. Fraud of the debtor or a fraudulent conveyance usually does not terminate the homestead right. Tiffany § 1339.

The right of homestead may be waived by a mortgage or by a failure to claim the right. The debtor is required to file his claim of exemption in the proceeding. Tiffany § 1341.

CHAPTER 15: INFANTS, INSANE PERSONS AND OTHER INCOMPETENTS

DIVISION 15-1: IN GENERAL

DIVISION 15-1: IN GENERAL

SECTION 15-11: INFANTS

Defense of incompetents in judicial proceedings, see Section 17-24.
Saving clauses in judicial proceedings, see 16-42B.

15-11A   Statutes; Time Disabilities Are Removed.

Statute on adverse possession, see 2-11A.
Statute on limitation of actions, see 16-42B.

R.C. 3109.01 provides: "All persons of the age of eighteen years or more, who are under no legal disability, are capable of contracting and are of full age for all purposes." (As eff. 1-1-74.)

From 1834 to July 19, 1923 females were of full age at eighteen years. Further research: O Jur 3d, Family Law §§ 140, 141.

LAW IN GENERAL

In common-law states a person becomes of age on the day before the twenty-first anniversary of his birth. Capacity concerning real estate is governed by the law of the state where the land is located. Am Jur 2d, Infants; CJS, Infants; Powell §§ 124, 150; Tiffany § 1362.

15-11B   Disaffirmance; Ratification.

Estoppel, see Section 16-69.
Limitation of actions, see Division 16-4.

Where an infant conveys land, mere lapse of time after he arrives at full age will not amount to a confirmation, unless after reaching age of majority. But lapse of time for a less period, in connection with other facts and circumstances, may amount to confirmation. The infant is not required to refund or offer to refund the purchase money before he disaffirms the contract. Cresinger v. Welch, 15 Ohio 156 (1846).

Where an infant executes a purchase-money mortgage to the vendor, he cannot, on the ground of infancy, avoid the mortgage without also avoiding the purchase. Curtiss v. McDougal, 26 OS 66 (1875).

Right to disaffirm a deed made during minority is not barred until twenty-one years after majority. Lanning v. Brown, 84 OS 385, 95 NE 921, 9 OLR 130, 56 WLB 230 (1911).

When an infant remainderman is not made a party to partition, his share is not affected, unless by some act or conduct, after reaching majority, such proceeding has been ratified. Hampshire County Trust Co. v. Stevenson, 114 OS 1, 150 NE 726, 4 Abs 73, 74, 24 OLR 135 (1926).

A deed of a minor may be ratified by him after arriving at full age by a letter to the other party containing language creating a clear implication of an intention to ratify. Schulman v. Villensky, 103 App 300, 143 NE2d 754, 3 OO2d 328 (1957).

A mortgage given by husband and wife, on property in both names and the wife being a minor, the proceeds of which go to the purchase price, is a valid mortgage which may be foreclosed. A deficiency judgment cannot be taken against the minor defendant. Kenwood Savings & Loan Ass'n v. Williams, 8 Misc 23, 220 NE2d 582, 37 OO2d 24 (C.P. 1966).

Further research: O Jur 3d, Family Law § 163.

15-11C   Estoppel; Bona Fide Purchaser.

LAW IN GENERAL

Under some decisions, an infant may be estopped to disaffirm a conveyance if he misrepresented his age or if he remained silent while a purchaser made improvements. A bond fide purchaser from the infant's grantee is usually not protected against avoidance by the infant. In general, a disaffirmance renders a contract void from the beginning. It has been held that an infant can recover rent only from the time of disaffirmance. See citations at 15-11A.

15-11D   Restoration of Consideration.

Waiver of service, see 16-72A.
See also cases at 15-11B.

Upon disaffirmance of a deed, an infant is required to restore the consideration he received if it was in his control when he attained majority. Curtiss v. McDougal, 26 OS 66 (1875).

15-11E   Conveyances.

A deed executed by a minor wife does not bar her right of dower. Hughes v. Watson, 10 Ohio 127 (1840). Sale or release of dower by guardian, see 15-13G.

A deed duly executed by a minor is not void, but voidable only. Card v. Patterson, 5 OS 319 (1855).

The validity of a deed is not affected by the infancy of the grantee. See 15-12A.

Further research: O Jur 3d, Family Law § 157.

15-11F   Wills.

A person over eighteen years of age can make a valid devise of land. See 9-23A.

15-11G   Powers; Trusts.

An infant may execute a power and where he purchased land for another, to whom he immediately conveys, the conveyance is not voidable. Sheldon v. Newton, 3 OS 494 (1854); Starr v. Wright, 20 OS 97 (1870).

LAW IN GENERAL

An infant does not ordinarily have capacity to act as trustee or other fiduciary. A conveyance by an infant is commonly held not to be voidable when it transfers only the bare legal title. It is generally held that an infant may exercise a power of attorney but not a power of appointment. Tiffany § 241.

15-11H Transfer of Right of Avoidance.

LAW IN GENERAL

If the infant dies before reaching majority his personal representatives may generally exercise his right of avoidance. An exception is that the right of an infant under a contract to purchase land passes to his heirs. Am Jur 2d, Infants §§ 60, 86, 94; CJS, Infants § 131.

A number of cases hold that a deed made by an infant during his disability may be avoided, during the same period that the infant could do so, by his heir or devisee or by a purchaser holding under a right derived from an infant grantor after he reached full age. 33 ALR 52.

15-11I Service of Process.

*For coverage of rules on process and its service, see Division 16-7.
Defense of incompetents, see Section 17-24.*

Civil Rule 8(H) (disclosure of minority or incompetency) provides: "Every pleading or motion made by or on behalf of a minor or an incompetent shall set forth such fact unless the fact of minority or incompetency has been disclosed in a prior pleading or motion in the same action or proceeding." (As eff. 7-1-70.)

See Civil Rule 4.2 (who may be served) quoted at 16-74A.

From September 5, 1967 to July 1, 1970 former R.C. 2703.132 provided that a minor defendant over eighteen years of age could be served as an adult in an action for divorce, annulment or alimony.

Where service is by publication, the proceedings will be binding against minors who have been made defendants. Morgan v. Burnet, 18 Ohio 535 (1849).

A defendant, improperly served with summons while a minor, may, after attaining his majority, cure such defect in service by voluntarily entering his appearance. The defense of the statute of limitations is barred by the general appearance. Russell v. Drake, 164 OS 520, 132 NE2d 467, 58 OO 387 (1956).

Where a summons is served upon an infant and thereafter a new summons with a later answer day is served upon the parents, jurisdiction is conferred over the person of the minor. Matthews v. Vandervoort, 18 App 174 (1923).

In a suit against a minor, jurisdiction can be acquired only by service of process in the manner provided by the statutes, and the minor cannot waive compliance with said statutes. Feigi v. Lopartkovich, 38 App 338, 176 NE 670, 9 Abs 69 (1930).

The defendant, by his course of conduct after he became of age, waived service of summons upon him as a minor and entered his appearance in the cause. Hobert v. Francis, 40 App 491, 178 NE 715, 10 Abs 346 (1931); Miller v. Smith, 18 Abs 286 (App. 1934); Haisman v. Crismar, 18 Abs 180 (App. 1934).

Service may be made upon a minor in a civil action by leaving a copy at his usual place of residence. 1930 OAG 2560; Hershner v. Deibig, 64 App 328, 28 NE2d 784, 18 OO 134, 31 Abs 308 (1939); Langan v. Kessinger, 23 Abs 392 (App. 1936).

The action did not abate by the defendant coming to majority during the pendency of the action. Shroyer v. Shroyer, 101 NE2d 298, 46 OO 136, 60 Abs 316 (App. 1950).

Service of process upon a minor defendant in a civil action is properly made by delivering a copy of the summons to the minor defendant personally, or by leaving a copy at his usual place of residence. Thomas v. Tehan, 16 OS2d 25, 242 NE2d 559, 45 OO2d 273 (1968). In this case the minor and his father were out of the country when the service was made.

The filing of an answer by the guardian ad litem does not waive any rights of the minor or dispense with service of summons upon the minor in the manner prescribed by statute. Farley v. Head, 11 Misc 255, 221 NE2d 849, 40 OO2d 105 (C.P. 1966).

Summary of service of process on minors:

1. If the minor is under sixteen years of age, (a) serve his guardian or serve any one of the following persons with whom he lives or resides: father, mother, or the individual having the care of such minor (in any of such cases service on the minor himself is not required), or (b) serve the minor himself when he neither has a guardian nor lives or resides with a parent or a person having his care, Civil Rule 4.2(2). (As eff. 7-1-71.)

2. If the minor is sixteen years of age or over, serve the minor only, Civil Rule 4.2(1). (As eff. 7-1-70.)

3. Service may be waived in writing by any of those who may be served except by a person over sixteen and under eighteen years of age, Civil Rules 4(D) and 73(G). (As eff. 7-1-75.)

Prior to January 1, 1974 a person under eighteen years of age could not waive service.

See also note below in this section.

Summary of service of process on other incompetents.

1. The guardian, if any, may always be served, Civil Rule 4.2(3). (As eff. 7-1-71.)

2. If no guardian has been appointed and the incompetent is not under confinement or committed, serve the incompetent, Civil Rule 4.2(3). (As eff. 7-1-71.)

3. If the incompetent is confined in a mental institution or is committed by court order to custody, the superintendent or similar official of the institution or the person having custody may be served, Civil Rule 4.2(5). (As eff. 7-1-71.)

4. Service may be waived in writing by any of those who may be served except by the incompetent, Civil Rules 4(D) and 73(G). (As eff. 7-1-75.)

Note: A minor or other incompetent shall be represented in the action by his guardian, guardian ad litem, or as otherwise provided by Civil Rule 17(B).

Service of notice in probate court without court intervention, see Civil Rules 73(E) and 73(F).

Further research: O Jur 3d, Family Law § 194.

15-11J Marketability.

Marketable title generally, see Section 1-43.

LAW IN GENERAL

Title is unmarketable when there is a reasonable doubt as to whether or not an infant's interest has been lawfully divested, or when a purchaser would be exposed to the hazard of litigation in behalf of an infant claiming an interest in the land. 24 ALR2d 1306.

15-11K Mortgages and Deeds from Veterans.

R.C. 3109.02 provides: "Any person who is eligible for a loan under the Servicemen's Readjustment Act of 1944, any amendments thereto or re-enactment thereof, the Veterans Readjustment Assistance Act of 1952, any amendments thereto or re-enactment thereof, the Act of September 2, 1958, Public Law 85-857, 72 Stat. 1105, any amendments thereto or re-enactment thereof, or the Veterans' Readjustment Benefits Act of 1966, any amendments thereto or re-enactments thereof, whether or not he or his spouse is a minor, may, in his name and without any order of court or the intervention of a guardian or trustee, execute any instruments, take title to real property, borrow money thereon, and do all other acts necessary to secure to him all rights and benefits under said acts, or any regulations thereunder, in as full and ample manner as if he and his spouse had attained the age of eighteen years. No person eligible for such loan, or his spouse, is, by reason only of such minority, incompetent to acquire title to property by contract or to borrow thereon; and no instrument made in connection with acquiring title to real estate or making such loan shall be voidable on the grounds of minority of such person or his spouse.

"Any person who has qualified under said acts or any regulations thereunder and has secured a loan and taken title to real property thereunder is capable of disposing of such property by deed or other conveyance, notwithstanding the fact that he or his spouse is a minor, and no such deed or other conveyance shall be voidable on the grounds of minority of such person or his spouse." (As eff. 1-1-74.)

The minor spouse of a serviceman executing a promissory note in payment of three unimproved lots, as a separate consideration from the consideration paid for the dwelling house, upon arriving at her majority, may disaffirm her liability on such note, where the loan under the Servicemen's Act was obtained only on the dwelling house. Lambright v. Heck, 86 App 456, 93 NE2d 45, 42 OO 64 (1949).

15-11L   Release of Dower.

A deed made by an infant is voidable and may be avoided by an action for dower. Hughes v. Watson, 10 Ohio 127 (1840).

R.C. 3109.08, which concerned minor's release of dower rights was repealed effective July 1, 1974.

SECTION 15-12:   INSANE   PERSONS;   OTHER   INCOMPETENTS GENERALLY

Defense of incompetents, see Section 17-24.
Disability saving clauses, see 16-42B.
Married women, see Section 14-13.

15-12A   Acquisition of Title.

A person under disability by reason of insanity may take property by deed where such deed imposes no obligation or burden on such grantee; and acceptance is presumed. Alexander v. Greenfield, 94 App 471, 109 NE2d 549, 52 OO 263, 63 Abs 293 (1951).

15-12B   Criterion of Capacity.

A deed will be declared void, where the evidence discloses that grantor lacked mental capacity to transact business or make deed. Where grantor has sufficient intellect to understand in a general way the nature, effect and immediate consequences of transaction, and he consents to it, it is valid and binding. Monroe v. Shrivers, 29 App 109, 162 NE 780, 6 Abs 709 (1927).

LAW IN GENERAL

An instrument will not be set aside on the ground of unsound mind, including complete intoxication, unless the person executing it lacked the mental capacity to comprehend in a general way the nature and effect of the transaction. Am Jur 2d, Incompetent Persons; CJS, Insane Persons; Powell § 126; Tiffany § 1370.

15-12C   Presumptions.

If it is proved that at a given time one was mentally incapacitated, the presumption arises that he continued to be so thereafter, and this presumption is rebuttable and removed on sufficient evidence. Lee v. Stephens, 50 NE2d 622, 38 Abs 431 (App. 1942); Kennedy v. Walcutt, 118 OS 442, 161 NE 336, 6 Abs 205, 26 OLR 215 (1928).

With respect to a transaction by a person prior to adjudication of insanity, no presumption of insanity at the time of such transaction arises, but evidence of such adjudication within a reasonable time thereafter may be considered along with direct evidence relating to competence. Shupp v. Farrar, 85 App 366, 88 NE2d 924, 40 OO 239 (1949).

A court of common pleas has authority to find that a person formerly adjudged incompetent is competent at a subsequent date. Vnerakraft, Inc. v. Arcaro, 110 App 62, 168 NE2d 623, 12 OO2d 229 (1959).

15-12D Lucid Interval.

An insane person may execute a deed during a lucid interval. Ford v. Bachman, 32 NE2d 511, 11 OO 475, 26 Abs 620 (App. 1938).

15-12E Acts as Void or Voidable.

A deed of conveyance made by a person of unsound mind is voidable only and not void. Lower v. Gardner, 22 CC(NS) 385, 33 CD 623 (1908).

A deed executed by an insane person is not void unless the person is so bereft of reason as to make him incapable of giving even an imperfect assent to the transaction. Fissel v. Gordon, 83 App 349, 83 NE2d 525, 38 OO 407, 54 Abs 223 (1948).

LAW IN GENERAL

The conveyances and contracts of an insane person are generally voidable, not void, if made before the appointment of a guardian. By the majority rule, the conveyances and contracts made by a lunatic after the appointment of a guardian for his estate are void. These rules are applied to mortgages. See citations at 15-12B.

15-12F Ratification.

Estoppel, see Section 16-69.

A voidable conveyance may be ratified by the grantor after his restoration to sanity or by his heirs after his death.

15-12G Subrogation.

See also Section 16-67.

LAW IN GENERAL

If the proceeds of the incompetent's mortgage are used to discharge a valid lien, the mortgagee may be entitled to relief by way of subrogation. 151 ALR 413.

15-12H   Service of Process.

For coverage of rules on process and its service, see Division 16-7.
Defense of incompetents, see Section 17-24.
Disclosure of incompetency, see 15-11I.
Summary of service, see 15-11I.

15-12I   Rescission Granted When.

Limitation of actions, see Section 16-42.

A contract made in such a state of intoxication as to deprive the party of his discretion and ordinary judgment, will be set aside in equity, although the other party had no agency in producing the intoxication. French v. French, 8 Ohio 214 (1837). The evidence should be clear and convincing. Coppolina v. Radice, 30 App 179, 164 NE 643, 6 Abs 669, 27 OLR 451 (1928).

LAW IN GENERAL

The right to avoid may be exercised within a reasonable time by the grantor upon the recovery of his sanity. The right passes to his guardian, heirs or personal representative. Equitable principles are taken into consideration in determining whether or not a deed will be set aside. Transactions by a person of unsound mind which are wholly executory may ordinarily be rescinded. Am Jur 2d, Incompetent Persons §§ 82, 83; CJS, Insane Persons, § 113.

Good faith does not prevent an order of cancellation if restitution of benefits received can be made. Rescission of the transaction is generally refused in favor of a person acting in entire good faith when the parties cannot be placed in status quo ante, when no adjudication of insanity or appointment of guardian has been made, and when no inequities would result. Am Jur 2d, Cancellation of Instruments §§ 4, 13.

15-12J   Bona Fide Purchaser from Grantee.

LAW IN GENERAL

The authorities are conflicting as to the rights of a bona fide purchaser who acquired title subsequent to the deed by a lunatic. Many decisions protect such a purchaser particularly when the deed was voidable, not void. See citations for 15-12B.

15-12K   Restoration of Sanity or Competency.

R.C. 2111.47 provides: "Upon reasonable notice to the guardian, to the ward and to the person on whose application the appointment was made, and upon satisfactory proof that the necessity for the guardianship no longer exists or that the letters of appointment were improperly issued, the probate court shall order that the guardianship of an incompetent terminate and shall make an appropriate entry upon the journal. Thereupon the guardianship shall cease, the accounts of the guardian shall be settled by the court, and the ward shall be restored to the full control of his property as before the appointment. Such entry terminating the guardianship of an insane person shall have the same effect as a determination by the court that such person is restored to sanity." (As eff. 10-25-61.)

R.C. 5122.21 provides: "(A) The head of a hospital shall as frequently as practicable examine or cause to be examined every patient and, whenever he determines that the conditions justifying involuntary hospitalization no longer obtain, shall, except as provided in division (C) of this section, discharge the patient not under indictment or conviction for crime and immediately make a report of the discharge to the division of mental health facilities and services. The head of the hospital may discharge a patient who is under indictment, sentence of imprisonment, or on probation or parole ten days after written notice of intent to discharge the patient has been given by personal service or certified mail, return receipt requested, to the court having criminal jurisdiction over the patient. Except when the patient was found not guilty by reason of insanity and his commitment is pursuant to section 2945.40 of the Revised Code, the head of the hospital has final authority to discharge a patient who is under indictment, sentence of imprisonment, or on probation or parole.

"(B) After a finding pursuant to section 5122.15 of the Revised Code that a person is a mentally ill person subject to hospitalization by court order, the head of the hospital to which the person is ordered or to which the person is transferred under section 5122.20 of the Revised Code, may, except as provided in division (C) of this section, grant a discharge without the consent or authorization of any court.

"Upon discharge, the head of the hospital shall notify the court that caused the judicial hospitalization of the discharge from the hospital.

"(C) Whenever the head of a hospital intends to discharge a person who was found incompetent to stand trial and whose commitment resulted from an affidavit filed pursuant to division (C) of section 2945.38 of the Revised Code, the head of the hospital shall give notice of the discharge to the prosecutor and the attorney general at least ten days prior to the date on which the person will be discharged. Whenever the head of the hospital intends to discharge a person who was found not guilty by reason of insanity and whose commitment was pursuant to section 2945.40 of the Revised Code, the head of the hospital shall not discharge the person until he has complied with division (F) of section 2945.40 of the Revised Code." (As eff. 4-9-81.)

R.C. 5122.36 provides: "If the legal residence of a person suffering from mental illness is in another county of the state, the necessary expense of his return shall be a proper charge against the county of residence. If an adjudication and order of hospitalization by the county of temporary residence is required, the regular probate court fees and expenses incident to the order of hospitalization, under this chapter, and any other expense incurred in his behalf, shall be charged to and paid by the county of his legal residence upon the approval and certificate of the probate judge thereof. A certified transcript of all proceedings had in the ordering court shall be sent to the probate court of the county of the residence of such person. The court shall enter and record such transcript. The certified transcript shall be prima-facie evidence of the residence of such person. When the residence of the person cannot be established as represented by the ordering court, the matter of residence shall be referred to the department of mental health for investigation and determination." (As eff. 7-1-80.)

R.C. 5122.38 provides: "Each individual now or formerly hospitalized pursuant to this chapter or former Chapter 5123. of the Revised Code, is entitled to an adjudication of competency or incompetency or termination of guardianship upon written request by any such individual, his guardian, or the head of the hospital to the probate court. The court, on its own motion, may initiate such a hearing.

"Upon filing of such application, or on the court's own motion, notice of the purpose, time, and place of the hearing shall be given to the person upon whose affidavit such adjudication was made, to the guardian of the applicant, and to his spouse at his residence, if such address is known.

"Upon hearing, if it is proven that such applicant is competent, the court shall so find and enter the finding on its journal. The adjudicating court shall send a transcript of the adjudication to the county of the patient's residence." (As eff. 10-10-63.)

> **Note:** Section 5122.38 applies generally to adjudications of competency or incompetency of persons now or formerly hospitalized, subject to the restriction, on the time of requesting a hearing, in section 5122.36 which applies only to persons indeterminately hospitalized. Section 2111.47 has general application where there is a guardian.

The Probate Court lacks exclusive jurisdiction as to decision on restoration to competence or sanity of a person charged with a felony and committed to Lima State Hospital by the Common Pleas Court "until restored to reason." In re Moser, 246 NE2d 626, 47 OO2d 420 (C.P. 1967).

SECTION 15-13: GUARDIAN AND WARD GENERALLY

15-13A Rules.

Effect of appointment on capacity of ward, see 15-12E.
Representation in court actions, see 17-24B.
Termination of guardianship, see 15-12K.

R.C. 2109.37 in part provides: "(C)(1) In addition to the investments allowed by this section, a guardian or trustee, with the approval of the court, may invest funds belonging to the trust in productive real estate located within the state, provided that neither the guardian nor the trustee nor any member of the family of either has any interest in such real estate or in the proceeds of the purchase price. The title to any real estate so purchased by a guardian must be taken in the name of the ward.

567

"(2) Notwithstanding the provisions of subdivision (C)(1) of this section, the court may permit the funds to be used to purchase or acquire a home for the ward or an interest in a home for the ward in which a member of the ward's family may have an interest." (As eff. 10-20-87.)

R.C. 2111.05 provides: "When the whole estate of a ward, or of several wards jointly, under the same guardianship, does not exceed ten thousand dollars in value, the guardian may apply to the probate court for an order to terminate the guardianship. Upon proof that it would be for the best interest of the ward to terminate the guardianship, the court may order the guardianship terminated, and direct the guardian, if the ward is a minor, to deposit the assets of the guardianship in a depository authorized to receive fiduciary funds, payable to the ward when he attains majority, or the court may authorize the delivery of the assets to the natural guardian of the minor, to the person by whom the minor is maintained, to the executive secretary of children services in the county, or to the minor himself.

"If the ward is an incompetent, and the court orders the guardianship terminated, the court may authorize the deposit of the assets of the guardianship in a depository authorized to receive fiduciary funds in the name of a suitable person to be designated by the court, or if the assets do not consist of money, the court may authorize delivery to a suitable person to be designated by the court. The person receiving the assets shall hold and dispose of them in the manner the court directs.

"If the court refuses to grant the application to terminate the guardianship, or if no such application is presented to the court, the guardian shall only be required to render account upon the termination of his guardianship, upon order of the probate court made upon its own motion, or upon the order of the court made on the motion of a person interested in the wards or their property, for good cause shown, and set forth upon the journal of the court.

"If the estate is ten thousand dollars or less and the ward is a minor, the court may, without the appointment of a guardian by the court, or the giving of bond, authorize the deposit in a depository authorized to receive fiduciary funds, payable to the guardian when appointed, or to the ward when he attains majority, or the court may authorize delivery to the natural guardian of the minor, to the person by whom the minor is maintained, to the executive secretary who is responsible for the administration of children services in the county, to the department of mental retardation and developmental disabilities or to the administrator of an agency under contract with the department for the provision of protective service under sections 5123.55 to 5123.59 of the Revised Code, or to the minor himself.

"If the whole estate of a person over eighteen years of age, who has been adjudged mentally ill or mentally retarded, does not exceed ten thousand dollars in value, the court may, without the appointment of a guardian by the court or the giving of bond, authorize the deposit of the estate in a depository authorized to receive fiduciary funds in the name of a suitable person to be designated by the court, or if the assets do not consist of money, the court may authorize delivery to a suitable person to be designated by the court. The person receiving the assets shall hold and dispose of them in the manner the court directs." (As eff. 7-1-80.)

R.C. 2111.17 provides that a guardian may sue as guardian and that pending actions shall not abate upon the termination of the guardianship. (As eff. 10-1-53.)

R.C. 2131.02 provides: "'Legal disability' as used in Chapters 2101., 2103., 2105., 2107., 2109., 2111., 2113., 2115., 2117., 2119., 2121., 2123., 2125., 2127., 2129., and 2131. of the Revised Code includes the following:

"(A) Persons under the age of eighteen years;

"(B) Persons of unsound mind;

"(C) Persons in captivity;

"(D) Persons under guardianship of the person and estate, or either." (As eff. 1-1-74.)

R.C. 5905.17 provides for purchase of real estate by a guardian appointed under Veterans' Guardianship Law. (As eff. 9-17-47.)

See Civil Rule 17(B) (minors or incompetent persons) shown at 17-24B.

Death of ward terminates all duties and powers upon the part of the guardian. Simpson v. Holmes, 106 OS 437, 140 NE 395, 1 Abs 73, 20 OLR 497 (1922).

Where a guardian has been appointed for the person and property of an incompetent, all actions in behalf of the ward must be conducted by his guardian and cannot be prosecuted by a next friend or trustee for the action. Murphy v. Murphy, 85 App 392, 87 NE2d 102, 40 OO 254, 54 Abs 116 (1948).

A person confined in the county jail under indictment for murder in the first degree is a person in captivity and consequently under a legal disability. In re Gogan's Estate, 108 NE2d 170, 63 Abs 69 (App. 1951).

The authority of the guardian to continue the proceeding to sell real estate ceased at the time of the death of the ward. Becker v. Becker, 125 NE2d 563, 69 Abs 414 (App. 1952).

The appointment of a next friend to bring an action for an infant is a matter of procedure rather than of jurisdiction, and the failure to appoint does not render an action void on that ground alone. Tanner v. Tanner, 16 App2d 101, 242 NE2d 585, 45 OO2d 278 (1968).

LAW IN GENERAL

A guardianship may be of the person or of the estate of a ward, or of both. The powers of a guardian of the person only are not considered here.

A collateral attack on the appointment of a guardian is usually not upheld unless the proceedings show on their face that the court was without jurisdiction. Am Jur 2d, Guardian and Ward § 50; CJS, Guardian and Ward § 35.

The powers of a guardian over the ward's real estate are limited to its management and preservation, except as otherwise provided by statute or as judicially sanctioned. A court will not ordinarily authorize a mortgage except under statutory provisions. The guardian is entitled to the possession and rents but may not, without the order of the court, make any leases or otherwise affect the title to the land beyond his tenure as guardian. Am Jur 2d, Guardian and Ward § 110; CJS, Guardian and Ward § 72.

15-13B   Appointment; Bond; Accounting.

Accounting, see 12-11E.

R.C. 2109.12 et seq. provide for bond of a guardian. (As eff. 10-4-84.)

R.C. 2111.02 et seq. provide for appointment of guardian upon three days' notice. (As eff. 10-14-83.)

R.C. 2111.09 provides when an executor or administrator may be appointed as guardian of a ward interested in the estate being administered. (As eff. 9-4-57.)

An order appointing a guardian made by a probate court in the exercise of its jurisdiction cannot be impeached collaterally. In re Clendenning, 145 OS 82, 60 NE2d 676, 30 OO 301 (1945).

A testamentary guardian of a minor is without authority to act until he has been appointed guardian by the probate court. Henicle v. Flack, 3 App 444, 23 CC(NS) 447 (1914).

The appointment of a guardian is void where made without statutory notice to the ward. In re Koenigshoff, 99 App 39, 119 NE2d 652, 69 Abs 121 (1954).

Further research: O Jur 3d, Guardian and Ward § 11.

15-13C   Nonresident Guardian or Ward.

R.C. 2111.37 to 2111.40 provide for appointment of a resident guardian of a nonresident ward with all the authority, as to property in this state, of a guardian of a resident ward. (As eff. 10-1-53.)

R.C. 2111.41 to 2111.44 provide for guardianship of a nonresident ward and that guardians appointed by foreign courts for nonresident wards may bring and maintain actions in the same manner and to the same extent that they could if appointed in this state, upon giving security for costs.

R.C. 2111.471 provides for transfer of jurisdiction when a ward removes to another county in this state. (As eff. 10-5-61.)

R.C. 2127.42 provides that wards living out of this state are entitled to the benefits of the Ohio statutes for sales of real estate by fiduciaries. (As eff. 1-1-76.)

15-13D   Land Contracts.

R.C. 2111.19 provides: "A guardian, whether appointed by a court in this state or elsewhere, may complete the contracts of his ward for the purchase or sale of real estate or any authorized contract relating to real estate entered into by a guardian who has died or been removed. Said guardian shall proceed in the manner provided by sections 2113.48 to 2113.50, inclusive, of the Revised Code." (As eff. 10-5-61.)

15-13E   Leases; Mortgages.

R.C. 2109.46 to 2109.48 provide for mortgage of ward's real estate by a guardian or other fiduciary. (As eff. 10-1-53.)

R.C. 2111.25 to 2111.32 provide for lease by guardian of ward's real estate. (As eff. 10-1-53.)

15-13F   Improvement of Real Estate.

R.C. 2111.33 to 2111.36 provide for improvement of ward's real estate by a guardian. (As eff. 10-25-61.)

15-13G   Sale or Release of Dower.

Acquisition of land after spouse is adjudged insane, see 14-24J.
Dower of insane persons barred in common pleas court, see 14-24I.

R.C. 2111.21 provides: "The guardian of a ward who has or is claimed to have a right of dower, or a contingent right to it, in lands or tenements of which the spouse of such ward was or is seized as an estate of inheritance, where the dower has not been assigned, may sell, compromise, or adjust such dower or may release such contingent right of dower in the event the spouse of such ward desires to mortgage such property upon such terms as such guardian deems for the interest of such ward and upon such terms as the probate court of the county in which the guardian was appointed approves, or if such guardian was appointed in a foreign state, upon such terms as the probate court of the county wherein the land is situated approves. After such approval, the guardian may execute and deliver all the necessary deeds, mortgages, releases, and agreements for the sale, compromise, assignment, or mortgage of such dower or contingent right to dower. As a basis for computing the value of an inchoate dower right in any sale, compromise, or adjustment pursuant to this section, the value of the lands or tenements may be considered to be the sale price or, if there is no sale, the appraised value. Such sale, compromise, adjustment, or mortgage may be made upon application and entry in the pending proceedings." (As eff. 10-1-53.)

From January 1, 1932 to September 22, 1947, the statute did not include the provision for release of contingent dower in event of a mortgage.

SECTION 15-14:   LAND SALES BY GUARDIANS

Attack upon sales, see Section 16-13.
Rights of purchasers, see Section 17-15.

15-14A   Generally.

For statutory provisions which also apply to sales by executors and administrators, see Section 12-14.

R.C. 2127.05 provides: "Whenever necessary for the education, support, or the payment of the just debts of the ward, or for the discharge of liens on the real estate of the ward, or wherever the real estate of the ward is suffering unavoidable waste, or a better investment of its value can be made, or whenever it appears that a sale of the real estate will be for the benefit of the ward or his children, the guardian of the person and estate or of the estate only of a minor, person unable to manage his property because of mental illness or deficiency, habitual drunkard, confined person, or other person under disability may commence a civil action in the probate court for authority to sell all or any part of the real estate of the ward. If it appears to the advantage of the ward to lay out all or any part of the land in town lots, application for such authority may also be made in the action.

"When the same person is guardian for two or more wards whose real estate is owned by them jointly or in common, the actions may be joined, and in one complaint the guardian may ask for the sale of the interest of all or any number of his wards in the real estate. If different persons are guardians of wards interested jointly or in common in the same real estate, they may join as parties plaintiff in the same action. On the hearing, in either case, the court may authorize the sale of the interest of one or more of the wards." (As eff. 1-1-76.)

R.C. 2127.13 provides: "In an action by a guardian to obtain authority to sell the real estate of his ward the following persons shall be made parties defendant:

"(A) The ward;

"(B) The spouse of the ward;

"(C) All persons entitled to the next estate of inheritance from the ward in such real estate who are known to reside in Ohio, but their spouses need not be made parties defendant;

"(D) All lienholders whose claims affect such real estate or any part thereof;

"(E) If the interest subject to such sale is equitable, all persons holding legal title thereto or any part thereof;

"(F) All other persons having an interest in such real estate, other than creditors." (As eff. 10-1-53.)

R.C. 2127.21 provides: "If a guardian's complaint in an action to obtain authority to sell real estate seeks to have land laid out in town lots, and the court finds it to the advantage of the ward, it shall authorize the survey and platting of the land as provided by law. Upon subsequent return of the survey and plat, the court, if it approves it, shall authorize the guardian on behalf of his ward to sign, seal, and acknowledge the plat in that behalf for record." (As eff. 1-1-76.)

There is no express provision authorizing platting of the land in an action by an executor or administrator, although a sale in parcels is authorized.

Further research: O Jur 3d, Guardian and Ward § 138.

SECTION 15-15: ALIENS

15-15A Rules.

Escheat, see Section 9-17.

R.C. 2105.16 provides: "No person who is capable of inheriting shall be deprived of the inheritance by reason of any of his ancestors having been aliens. Aliens may hold, possess, and enjoy lands, tenements, and hereditaments within this state, either by descent, devise, gift, or purchase, as fully as any citizen of the United States or of this state may do." (As eff. 10-1-53.)

R.C. 5301.254 provides that every nonresident alien who acquires any interest, whether in his name or in another name, in real estate in excess of three acres or having a market value of $100,000 or any interest in minerals or mining having a market value of over $50,000 shall file the prescribed information with the secretary of state within thirty days of the acquisition. (As eff. 3-19-79.)

R.C. 5301.99 provides that a violator of R.C. 5301.254 shall be fined not less than $5,000 or more than 1/4 of the market value of the property. (As eff. 3-19-79.)

Further research: O Jur 3d, Aliens and Citizens § 14.

LAW IN GENERAL

At common law, an alien cannot acquire land by operation of law; he can acquire it by purchase or devise and hold it until a forfeiture is enforced by the state. He generally may convey, mortgage, lease and, under some decisions, may devise an acquired interest. A transferee from an alien usually acquires an indefeasible interest if the transfer is made before escheat proceedings are instituted by the state.

The marriage of a female to an alien taking place after September 21, 1922 does not cause her to lose her citizenship in this country unless married to an alien ineligible to citizenship. The title to land is within the jurisdiction of the several states except as to enemy aliens and except as modified by treaties. Resident friendly aliens are under no disabilities in a majority of the states.

Am Jur 2d, Aliens §§ 13, 26; Am Law of Prop § 5.17; 79 ALR 1366; CJS, Aliens § 16; Powell § 100; Tiffany § 1377.

SECTION 15-16: CONVICTS; CIVIL DEATH

15-16A Generally.

Descent or devise to murderer, see 9-16B.

Ohio has no statutes on this topic except as to descent or devise to a murderer.

CHAPTER 16: JUDGMENTS

DIVISION 16-1: IN GENERAL

DIVISION 16-7: PROCESS AND ITS SERVICE

DIVISION 16-1: IN GENERAL

SECTION 16-11: JURISDICTION GENERALLY

Extraterritorial effect of judgments, see Section 16-21.
Nonresidents under long-arm statute, see 16-77B.
Parties, see Section 17-21.

16-11A Necessity of Jurisdiction.

Collateral attack, see Section 16-13.

Where the court has jurisdiction over the parties and the subject matter in a proceeding, the issuance of an order therein which is not within the powers conferred upon such court renders such order void. Morgridge v. Converse, 72 NE2d 295, 48 Abs 272 (App. 1947), revd. on other grounds 150 OS 239, 81 NE2d 112, 37 OO 486 (1948).

A judgment or decree made by a court without jurisdiction is void, not merely voidable. A sale or other proceeding based thereon is likewise without legal effect. The presumptions that a court acts with proper authority and that its proceedings are regular do not overcome a lack of jurisdiction appearing on the records, even as to purchasers for value without actual notice. Jurisdiction is both conferred and limited by constitution, statute or common law.

Further research: O Jur 3d, Judgments §§ 107, 108.

16-11B   Occasions of Lack of Jurisdiction.

When a general jurisdiction of the subject matter exists, but the statute has prescribed the mode and particular limits in which it must be exercised, it cannot be exercised in any other manner or upon any other terms. McCleary v. McClain, 2 OS 368 (1853).

Jurisdiction of the subject matter is always fixed and determined by law, while jurisdiction of the person may be fixed and determined by consent of the parties, failure to timely and properly object, and the like. Rogers v. State, 87 OS 308, 101 NE 143, 10 OLR 600, 58 WLB 58 (1913).

"Although a court may have jurisdiction of the parties and the subject-matter in an action it cannot transcend the power legally conferred on it." Russel v. Fourth Nat. Bank, 102 OS 248, 131 NE 726, 19 OLR 56, 66 WLB 217 (1921).

Jurisdiction of person may be waived, though jurisdiction of subject matter may not be waived. Dayton Morris Plan Bank v. Graham, 47 App 310, 191 NE 817, 16 Abs 689, 40 OLR 279 (1934).

A trial court has the power to determine its own jurisdiction only with regard to matters where proper facts are required to be established in certain instances before the court is, by law, given jurisdiction, but not to matters wherein the court is not, by the constitution or statutes, given jurisdiction. State ex rel. Bechtel v. McCabe, 60 App 233, 20 NE2d 381, 14 OO 100 (1938).

The most frequent occasions of lack of jurisdiction are: (a) lack of jurisdiction of the person arising from defects in service of summons or other process, or from omission of necessary parties defendant to the action, or from institution of the action by a person not authorized to maintain it; or (b) lack of jurisdiction of the subject matter arising from failure to observe statutory provisions conferring jurisdiction or limiting its exercise, or from insufficient description of the property, or from location of the property without the territorial jurisdiction of the court, or from absence of authority under statute or in equity for the court to decide the particular question or to grant the particular relief.

16-11C   Operation of Decrees in Equity; Transfer of Title.

Foreign judgments, see 16-21A.

Civil Rule 70 provides: "If a judgment directs a party to execute a conveyance of land, to transfer title or possession of personal property, to deliver deeds or other documents, or to perform any other specific act, and the party fails to comply within the time specified, the court may, where necessary, direct the act to be done at the cost of the disobedient party by some other person appointed by the court, and the act when so done has like effect as if done by the party. On application of the party entitled to performance, the clerk shall issue a writ of attachment against the property of the disobedient party to compel obedience to the judgment. The court may also in proper cases adjudge the party in contempt. If real or personal property is within this state, the court in lieu of directing a conveyance thereof may enter a judgment divesting the title of any party and vesting it in others, and such judgment has the effect of a conveyance executed in due form of law. When any order or judgment is for the delivery of possession, the party in whose favor it is entered is entitled to a writ of execution upon application to the clerk." (As eff. 7-1-70.)

A decree may enforce a trust or contract relating to land in another state; although it cannot operate to transfer the title, it is binding upon the parties. Burnley v. Stevenson, 24 OS 474 (1873).

Except as restricted by statute, the court of common pleas has such jurisdiction in equity as courts of chancery had at common law. Madden v. Shallenberger, 121 OS 401, 169 NE 450, 8 Abs 28, 30 OLR 569 (1929).

LAW IN GENERAL

Decrees of a court in equity operate only in personam except under statutes, such as those providing that the decree itself may operate as a conveyance. A transfer of title under such a statute is set aside by reversal of the decree if the transfer is made during the time an appeal may be filed or is pending. CJS, Equity § 613.

16-11D Venue.

Notice of pendency, see 17-12A.
Venue in probate court, see 16-78.

Civil Rule 3(B) (venue; where proper) provides comprehensively for a proper county where an action should be commenced and decided; subsection (5) states that proper venue lies in "A county in which the property, or any part thereof, is situated if the subject of the action is real property or tangible personal property." (As eff. 7-1-86.)

Civil Rule 3(C) specifies procedure relating to change of venue and provides when the action is brought in an improper county, it will be transferred to one of the proper counties if the defendant makes timely objection. (As eff. 7-1-86.)

Civil Rule 3(G) provides in part: "No order, judgment, or decree shall be void or subject to collateral attack solely on the ground that there was improper venue." (As eff. 7-1-86.)

R.C. 2323.07 in part provides: "When the mortgaged property is situated in more than one county, the court may order the sheriff or master of each county to make sale of the property in his county, or may direct one officer to sell the whole. When it consists of a single tract, the court may direct that it be sold as one tract or in separate parcels, and shall direct whether appraisers shall be selected for each county or one set for all; and whether publication of the sale shall be made in all the counties, or in one county only." (As eff. 10-1-53.)

An action for cancellation and discharge of a mechanic's lien is not properly brought in the county where the land is located if no defendant can be served with process in such county. Gustafson v. Buckley, 161 OS 160, 118 NE2d 403, 53 OO 71 (1954).

While the municipal court did not have territorial jurisdiction of the defendant, he submitted to such jurisdiction by seeking and being granted leave to plead. Schumacher v. Iron Fireman Mfg. Co., 102 App 347, 133 NE2d 801, 2 OO2d 376, 74 Abs 165 (1956).

Further research: O Jur 2d, Venue § 2.

16-11E   Construction of Decisions.

When a principle has been settled for many years, and has become a rule of property, and titles have been vested on the strength of it, such decisions will not be disturbed without the most urgent necessity. Kearny v. Buttles, 1 OS 362 (1853).

The syllabus of a decision of the Supreme Court of Ohio states the law of Ohio, but such pronouncement must be interpreted with reference to the facts upon which it is predicated and the questions presented to and considered by the court. When obiter creeps into a syllabus it must be so recognized and so considered. Williamson Heater Co. v. Radich, 128 OS 124, 190 NE 403, 40 OLR 646 (1934).

A court speaks through its journal. When a court's opinion and journal are in conflict, the latter controls and the former must be disregarded. Will v. McCoy, 135 OS 241, 20 NE2d 371, 14 OO 85 (1939).

SECTION 16-12:   RES JUDICATA

16-12A   Rules.

Material facts or questions which were in issue in a former suit and were there judicially determined by a court of competent jurisdiction are conclusively settled by the judgment therein so far as concerns the parties to that action and persons in privity with them and cannot be again litigated in any future action between the same parties or privies, and this applies not only to what was determined but also to every other question which might properly have been litigated in the case. Quinn v. State ex rel. Leroy, 118 OS 48, 160 NE 453, 6 Abs 77, 26 OLR 64 (1928); Babcock & Co. v. Camp, 12 OS 11 (1861).

A judgment is not conclusive on the parties in subsequent litigation unless they were adversary parties in the former suit. Koelsch v. Mixer, 52 OS 207, 39 NE 417, 32 WLB 419, 33 WLB 41 (1894).

The doctrine of res judicata is a branch of the law of estoppel and may be waived, and a failure or neglect to plead and prove a former adjudication constitutes a waiver. Clark v. Baranowski, 111 OS 436, 145 NE 760, 3 Abs 4, 22 OLR 645 (1924).

In an action upon a different cause of action from that involved in a prior action between the same parties, the judgment in such prior action will operate as an adjudication between the parties only as to points or questions actually litigated and determined, or which must necessarily have been determined in order to support that judgment, and not as to other matters which might have been litigated and determined. Taylor v. Monroe, 158 OS 266, 109 NE2d 271, 49 OO 118 (1952).

A determination that a land contract vendee is not entitled to specific performance but that the contract was still in force is not res judicata and does not bar a later suit by the vendee claiming a later breach of the land contract. Stowers v. Baron, 65 App2d 283, 418 NE2d 404, 19 OO3d 260 (1979).

Further research: O Jur 3d, Judgments §§ 400, 401.

LAW IN GENERAL

Res judicata is the doctrine that an existing final judgment, rendered on the merits and without fraud, by a court of competent jurisdiction is conclusive of the rights and facts in issue, as to the parties and their privies at all other actions in the same court or in any other court of concurrent jurisdiction. The rule operates against collateral attack but not against direct attack. The doctrine extends to matters which could properly have been determined in the former litigation under the same cause of action. The application of the doctrine may be precluded by estoppel, waiver or other equitable principle. Failure to plead the former judgment is generally regarded as a waiver. Am Jur 2d, Judgments § 1126; CJS, Judgments § 592.

SECTION 16-13: COLLATERAL ATTACK

Occasions of lack of jurisdiction, see 16-11B.
Service of process, see 16-74B.

16-13A Definition; Nature.

Res judicata, see Section 16-12.

Judgments of probate courts are protected against collateral attack to the same extent as judgments of other courts of record. State ex rel. Young v. Morrow, 131 OS 266, 2 NE2d 595, 5 OO 584 (1936).

The trial court primarily had jurisdiction to determine whether the wife had a right of action and that determination by the court, whether erroneous or not, cannot be collaterally attacked by her in another action. Straka v. Cleveland Ry. Co., 34 App 252, 170 NE 611 (1929).

Whenever the court's jurisdiction is dependent upon a certain state of facts the court has jurisdiction to inquire and determine whether such state of facts exists, and when the court's finding on the jurisdictional facts is supported by evidence its judgment cannot be questioned collaterally. Busse & Borgmann Co. v. Upchurch, 60 App 349, 21 NE2d 349, 12 OO 493, 27 Abs 575 (1938).

Laches does not operate to preclude the opening or vacating of a void judgment and it may be collaterally attacked. Morgridge v. Converse, 72 NE2d 295, 48 Abs 272 (App. 1947), revd. on other grounds 150 OS 239, 81 NE2d 112, 37 OO 486 (1948).

LAW IN GENERAL

A collateral attack is an attempt to defeat the operation of a judgment in a proceeding where some new right derived from or through the judgment is involved. A proceeding to enforce a judgment is collateral; therefore a defense therein of the invalidity of the judgment is a collateral attack. Any proceeding having an independent purpose involves a collateral attack if impeaching the judgment is essential to the success of the action. Apparent confusion is caused by the tendency of some courts to characterize certain direct attacks, which fail, as collateral attacks.

O Jur 3d, Judgments § 526; Am Jur 2d, Judgments § 346; CJS, Judgments § 401.

16-13B   Direct Attack Distinguished.

If the judgment or decree is void, the result or consequence is precisely as though no judgment or decree had ever been rendered or pronounced. If the judgment or decree be not void, but simply erroneous, it must be impeached directly and cannot be questioned collaterally. Boswell v. Sharp, 15 Ohio 447 (1846).

A direct attack on a judgment is one by which the judgment is directly assailed in some mode authorized by law; while a collateral attack is an attempt to defeat the operation of a judgment in a proceeding where some new right derived from or through the judgment is involved. Marshall v. Heckerman, 103 OS 559, 134 NE 449, 19 OLR 463 (1921).

Further research: O Jur 3d, Judgments §§ 525, 533, 536.

LAW IN GENERAL

A direct attack on a judgment is one by which the judgment is directly assailed in some mode authorized by law, such as an appeal. Direct attacks include suits to set aside or prevent enforcement of judgments on the ground of fraud in the procurement or on the ground of lack of jurisdiction. Courts are inclined to name any attacks as direct when the attacks have sufficient equities to constitute fraud. A void judgment may be attacked either directly or collaterally. See citations for 16-13A.

16-13C   Requirements for Successful Collateral Attack.

The finding of a court of general jurisdiction upon a subject matter properly before it shall not be collaterally impeached. Fowler v. Whiteman, 2 OS 270 (1853).

Where the court has jurisdiction of the parties and the subject matter, and its judgment is not beyond the authority of the court to enter, such judgment is not open to collateral attack. State ex rel. Hawke v. LeBlond, 108 OS 126, 140 NE 510, 1 Abs 453, 21 OLR 137 (1923).

Mere irregularities in the procurement do not render judgment void and thus subject to collateral attack; but such irregularities as are voidable can be relieved against only by proceedings in error. The only questions, therefore, that can be considered by this court in testing the soundness of the judgment in the partition case are whether the common pleas court in entering its decree had jurisdiction of the subject matter and jurisdiction of the parties. Huffer v. Prindle, 22 App 241, 153 NE 527, 5 Abs 40 (1926).

Further research: O Jur 3d, Judgments § 542.

LAW IN GENERAL

When the court has jurisdiction of the parties and the subject matter, and its judgment is not beyond the authority of the court to enter, the judgment is not subject to collateral attack.

Irregularities not going to the jurisdiction do not make a judgment open to collateral attack. If they render the judgment merely voidable, relief can be had by appeal proceedings.

Findings of the jurisdictional facts by a court of general jurisdiction cannot be collaterally impeached, as a rule, if such findings are not contradicted by the record. A judgment will be set aside in a collateral proceeding when the lack of jurisdiction is apparent on the record, but will ordinarily not be set aside when the record is silent as to the jurisdictional facts. See citations at 16-13A.

16-13D Attack on Service of Process.

Conclusiveness of return, see 16-74B.

Courts of common pleas being courts of general jurisdiction, as to them, the existence of jurisdiction will be presumed, their records being silent upon the subject, whenever an attempt is made to impeach their judgments collaterally. The records of that court will be taken as true if they contain the statement that service of process has been made upon the defendant. Morgan v. Burnet, 18 Ohio 535 (1849).

Where it affirmatively appears that minor defendants have not been served with process, a decree purporting to determine their rights is void. The return of the officer is the evidence to the court and to the world whether the party has been subjected to its process or not, whether he has been brought into court, whether jurisdiction is claimed to have been obtained over his person. If the process is returned served, it is proof of that fact. If the return is no service, it is proof equally explicit that no service has been made. This case differs from cases in which the record is silent on the subject of process or service. Moore v. Starks, 1 OS 369 (1853).

The finding of the court that the defendants are properly before the court cannot be collaterally attacked. Callen v. Ellison, 13 OS 446 (1862).

As between the parties and privies and others whose rights are necessarily dependent upon it, the return is conclusive until vacated or set aside by due course of law; but as to all other persons such return is prima facie. Phillips v. Elwell, 14 OS 240 (1863).

Defendants served by publication, on the ground that they were nonresidents of the state, will not be allowed, in a collateral proceeding, to prove that they were residents of the state. Hammond v. Davenport, 16 OS 177 (1865).

Where, in an action brought to foreclose a mortgage, an affidavit in due form to obtain service by publication is filed and publication had, a finding by the court that the defendant has been "duly served with notice of the pendency of said cause of action" is conclusive against said defendant in a collateral attack upon the judgment. Winemiller v. Laughlin, 51 OS 421, 38 NE 111, 31 WLB 370, 32 WLB 261 (1894); Fowler v. Whiteman, 2 OS 270 (1853).

In an action to enforce a personal judgment where the rights of third parties are not involved, defense of lack of service is in the nature of a direct attack, and it is competent to plead and prove that defendant was not served with process, although in contradiction to the record. Kingsborough v. Tousley, 56 OS 450, 47 NE 541, 37 WLB 402, 38 WLB 39 (1897); Conner v. Miller, 154 OS 313, 96 NE2d 13, 43 OO 212 (1950).

Where it does not otherwise affirmatively appear from the record, it will be presumed that a court of general jurisdiction regularly acquired and lawfully exercised its jurisdiction over the parties. Paulin v. Sparrow, 91 OS 279, 110 NE 528, 12 OLR 509, 574, 60 WLB 56, 77 (1915).

Even in an attack in the original action, the impeachment is collateral so far as it seeks to affect others than parties to the record. Moor v. Parsons, 98 OS 233, 120 NE 305, 16 OLR 35, 76, 63 WLB 171, 188 (1918).

Notice by publication and posting provided to a mortgagee of real property to inform him of the sale of the mortgage property for nonpayment of taxes does not meet the requirements of the due process clause of the fourteenth amendment if the mortgagee's name and address are reasonably ascertainable. Mennonite Board of Missions v. Adams, 462 U.S. 791, 103 SCt 2706, 77 LEd2d 180 (1983).

A decree and deed in a tax foreclosure suit may be set aside in a subsequent action in which it is alleged and proved that the decree is void for want of jurisdiction over the defendant's person because the summons was left at a place not in fact the defendant's "usual place of residence." Such a challenge is a direct attack on the decree and is not within the rule which forbids the collateral impeachment of judgments. Lenz v. Frank, 152 OS 153, 87 NE2d 578, 39 OO 451 (1949). Caveat: This decision limits the application of some of the court's earlier pronouncements shown above in this subsection. See dissenting opinion.

Where M, the mortgagor, had died but the sheriff's return showed residence service, and the heir demands a right to redeem, it was held "that as the record showed that M was served with process, the court of common pleas prima facie had jurisdiction and as the proceedings appeared to be regular on their face, its judgment could not be collaterally impeached, and the purchaser's title disturbed." Hentz v. Ward, 13 Dec Repr 615, 1 CSCR 387 (1871).

Where the record affirmatively shows that the law in regard to publication has not been complied with, the order of the court being to publish five weeks instead of six, all proceedings under the same are void. In re Cloud's Estate, 7 CC 67, 3 CD 666 (1891).

The return of a sheriff will not be set aside in a collateral proceeding, especially when the rights of an innocent purchaser at such sale have intervened. Korfer v. Katz, 14 NP(NS) 345, 31 OD 312 (1913).

Finding that service on minor defendants in former partition case was legal cannot be impeached on account of recital in petition in such partition (it also appearing from the decree) that such defendants had a father who should have been served instead of the custodian. Huffer v. Prindle, 22 App 241, 153 NE 527, 5 Abs 40 (1926).

Sheriff's return of service may be proved erroneous by direct attack. Sunday Creek Coal Co. v. West, 47 App 537, 192 NE 284, 17 Abs 558, 40 OLR 402 (1933).

The presumption, upon collateral attack, in favor of due service cannot prevail where it affirmatively appears from the record that the court never had jurisdiction of the person of the defendant. In re Frankenberg's Estate, 70 App 495, 47 NE2d 239, 25 OO 301 (1942).

Where court finds that service of process has been duly made, such finding is conclusive in the absence of an affirmative showing in a proper proceeding that no such service was had. Hinman v. Executive Committee, 71 App 76, 47 NE2d 820, 25 OO 49 (1942).

SECTION 16-14: APPEALS

16-14A   Rules; Reversal.

The Ohio Rules of Appellate Procedure, cited as "Appellate Rules" or "App. R. ____," became effective July 1, 1971 and constitute a major revision of procedure in the Courts of Appeal. All statutes are inoperative to the extent that they conflict with such rules.

Timely filing of notice of appeal is the only step essential to the validity of the appeal. App. R. 3(A). The notice shall be filed with the clerk of the trial court within thirty days of the entry of the judgment or order appealed from, or within ten days after a first notice was filed; a judgment or order is entered when it is filed with the clerk of the trial court for journalization; time for filing a notice is suspended by a motion for judgment notwithstanding the verdict or for new trial made and served within fourteen days after the judgment, and time for filing a notice extends for thirty days after the motion is denied or granted. App. R. 4(A). The court may not enlarge or reduce the time for filing the notice. App. R. 14(B).

Application for a stay of the judgment or order of a trial court pending appeal, or for approval of a supersedeas bond, must ordinarily be made in the first instance in the trial court; the motion for a stay in particular circumstances or for an order suspending, modifying, restoring or granting an injunction during the pendency of an appeal may be made to the court of appeals or to a judge thereof; bond may be required. App. R. 7(A).

R.C. 2101.42 provides: "From any final order, judgment, or decree of the probate court, an appeal on a question of law may be prosecuted to the court of appeals in the manner and within the time provided for the prosecution of such appeals from the court of common pleas to the court of appeals. For the purpose of prosecuting appeals on questions of law from the probate court, the probate court shall exercise judicial functions inferior only to the court of appeals and the supreme court." (G.C. 10501-56 as eff. 1-1-76.)

R.C. 2505.07 provides: "After the entry of a final order of an administrative officer, agency, board, department, tribunal, commission, or other instrumentality, the period of time within which the appeal shall be perfected, unless otherwise provided by law, is thirty days." (As eff. 3-17-87.)

R.C. 2505.09, 2505.11 and 2505.12 provide that no appeal shall operate as a stay of execution until a supersedeas bond is executed; except that a directed conveyance may be deposited, cash may be deposited, and that bond need not be given by certain fiduciaries, the government and public officers. (As eff. 3-17-87.)

R.C. 2701.19 provides: "When the party against whom a judgment is rendered appeals his cause, the lien of the opposite party on the real estate of the appellant that was created by the judgment, shall not be removed or vacated. The real estate shall be bound in the same manner as if the appeal had not been taken, until final determination of the cause." (As eff. 3-17-87.)

R.C. 2329.06 provides for the same result when an action is removed to the Supreme Court. (As eff. 10-1-53.)

R.C. 2329.45 provides: "If a judgment in satisfaction of which lands, or tenements are sold, is reversed, such reversal shall not defeat or affect the title of the purchaser. In such case restitution must be made by the judgment creditor of the money for which such lands or tenements were sold, with interest from the day of sale." (As eff. 10-1-53.)

Section 2329.45 does not protect a purchaser at foreclosure sale where the judgment, order of sale and confirmation are reversed and set aside. In this case there was no valid sale because there was no effective confirmation. McMahan v. Davis, 19 CC 242, 10 CD 467 (1899).

The title of a purchaser of real estate sold by an administrator to pay debts is not divested by a subsequent reversal of the order of sale. Irwin v. Jeffers, 3 OS 389 (1854).

An appeal perfected suspends all proceedings upon the judgment appealed from, and a sale of real estate will not be confirmed after the appeal is perfected. Bassett v. Daniels, 10 OS 617 (1858).

Where the mortgagee purchases under judicial proceedings and continues to own the premises until reversal, the mortgagor is entitled to his right of redemption. Hubbell v. Broadwell, 8 Ohio 120 (1837); McBain v. McBain, 15 OS 337 (1864).

The filing of a notice of appeal is the only jurisdictional step in an appeal from the common pleas court to the court of appeals. Damar Realty Co. v. Cleveland, 140 OS 432, 45 NE2d 209, 24 OO 435 (1942).

A lien holder, who fails to perfect an appeal within twenty days from a judgment determining priorities, cannot thereafter attack such judgment in an appeal from a subsequent judgment confirming such priorities. Queen City Savings & Loan Co. v. Foley, 170 OS 383, 165 NE2d 633, 11 OO2d 116 (1960).

Giving notice of appeal within twenty days after journal entry of the final order is jurisdictional and necessary to a consideration of the appeal. State ex rel. Arter v. Donnally, 85 NE2d 407, 53 Abs 127 (App. 1948).

Where there is a motion to dismiss an appeal on questions of law and fact because of failure to file an appeal bond and the time for such filing has expired, the cause will be retained for hearing on questions of law only. Home Owners Service Corp. v. Hadley, 86 App 340, 84 NE2d 314, 41 OO 377, 54 Abs 236 (1949).

Where a motion for new trial is not filed within ten days after the judgment entry, the notice of appeal must be filed within twenty days after the judgment entry. State ex rel. Davis v. Severt, 123 NE2d 669, 69 Abs 63 (App. 1950).

An appeal from probate court must be to court of appeals, instead of the court of common pleas, where oral testimony and other matters necessary to a bill of exceptions have been preserved by some means. In re Todd's Estate, 104 App 284, 148 NE2d 261, 4 OO2d 421 (1957).

Where a motion for new trial is filed within the statutory time, the time for perfecting an appeal to the court of appeals does not begin to run, and an appeal cannot be taken, until the entry of the order overruling or sustaining the motion for new trial. Kartorie v. San-Nor Oil Co., 119 App 507, 200 NE2d 691, 28 OO2d 129 (1963).

The court of appeals may award to the appellee reasonable expenses, including costs and attorney fees, when it determines that the appellant has taken a frivolous appeal. Arena Produce Co. v. McMillan, 27 App3d 384, 501 NE2d 679 (1986).

An application for rehearing has no legal effect on the operation of the judgment.

LAW IN GENERAL

A reversal of a decree of sale for irregularity or error will not divest the title of a stranger to the proceeding if he purchased the property in good faith before the appeal was taken. The rule does not apply when the appeal is based on lack of jurisdiction to make the sale. By the weight of authority, a sale to a party to the suit is invalidated by a reversal except where he has sold to a bona fide purchaser before the appeal was pending.

When the title is based upon a decree of court, as distinguished from a judicial sale, the above rules do not apply. In such a case, the title is unmarketable, and the action considered to be lis pendens, while there is a right to appeal or a pending appeal.

Am Jur 2d, Judicial Sales §§ 53-55, 57, 59, 62; Am Law of Prop § 18.64; 155 ALR 1252; CJS, Judicial Sales § 42.

SECTION 16-15: MODIFICATION AND VACATION

16-15A Within the Term of Court.

A court of general jurisdiction has control of its own orders and judgments during the term at which they were rendered, which control may be exercised, within the sphere of sound discretion, as an inherent right founded upon the common law. First Nat. Bank v. Smith, 102 OS 120, 130 NE 502, 18 OLR 535, 66 WLB 148 (1921); Niles v. Parks, 49 OS 370, 34 NE 735 (1892).

Where a trial court, in the proper discharge of its judicial functions, vacates a judgment previously entered, the legal status is the same as if the judgment had never existed. Tims v. Holland Furnace Co., 152 OS 469, 90 NE2d 376, 40 OO 487 (1950).

Further research: O Jur 3d, Judgments §§ 555-557.

16-15B Nunc Pro Tunc.

Where a party to an action dies after trial and submission to the court, the court may enter judgment nunc pro tunc as of the day of submission. In re Jarrett's Estate, 42 OS 199 (1884).

The court, in making a correction, may, by nunc pro tunc order, make it as of the term when the mistake was made, if there are no intervening rights or equities. Elliott v. Plattor, 43 OS 198, 1 NE 222, 13 WLB 516, 623 (1885).

Power to enter orders nunc pro tunc is restricted to placing on record evidence of judicial action which has been actually taken. Ruby v. Wolf, 39 App 144, 177 NE 240, 34 OLR 415 (1931); Reinbolt v. Reinbolt, 112 OS 526, 147 NE 808, 3 Abs 297, 23 OLR 242 (1925).

Since the intervening attachment creditors were preexisting creditors with knowledge, they obtained no priority as against the amended judgment. Webb v. Western Reserve Bond & Share Co., 115 OS 247, 153 NE 289, 4 Abs 394, 24 OLR 479, 48 ALR 1176 (1926).

To preserve the right of review, the date upon which a judgment nunc pro tunc is actually filed will control. Belden v. Stott, 150 OS 393, 83 NE2d 58, 38 OO 258 (1948).

After the term, the court may not by an order entered nunc pro tunc, enter an order it might have made or intended to make, but which in fact was not made, attempted, or directed to be made. Reynolds v. Reynolds, 12 App 63, 31 CC(NS) 129 (1919).

When a nunc pro tunc entry is made it relates back to the date when the judgment was actually rendered, but it will not be permitted to affect those who were not parties to the original suit. Johnson v. Harlan, 15 App 247, 32 CC(NS) 238 (1920).

A third person who did not act upon conditions then existing, nor pay value or otherwise change her condition upon faith in the court records, is not within the class of excepted persons not bound by a judgment nunc pro tunc. Snodgrass v. Snodgrass, 85 App 285, 88 NE2d 616, 40 OO 195 (1948).

Further research: O Jur 3d, Judgments § 83.

LAW IN GENERAL

A nunc pro tunc (now for then) entry is a journal entry made later of something previously done. It may be made at any time and relates back, as between the parties, to the time it should have been made. Intervening rights of third persons are not affected. Such entry can be made by a court only to correct its record, not to correct its judgment. CJS, Courts § 227; CJS, Judgments § 117.

16-15C   Direct Attack After Term.

R.C. 2325.03 provides: "The title to property which title is the subject of a final judgment or order sought to be vacated, modified, or set aside by any type of proceeding or attack and which title has, by, in consequence of, or in reliance upon the final judgment or order passed to a purchaser in good faith, shall not be affected by the proceeding or attack; nor shall the title to property that is sold before judgment under an attachment be affected by the proceeding or attack. 'Purchaser in good faith,' as used in this section, includes a purchaser at a duly confirmed judicial sale.

"This section does not apply if in the proceeding resulting in the judgment or order sought to be vacated, modified, or set aside, the person then holding the title in question was not lawfully served with process or notice, as required by the law or Civil Rules applicable to the proceeding." (As eff. 11-15-77.)

Civil Rule 60 provides procedure upon mistake, inadvertence, excusable neglect, new evidence, fraud, etc. (As eff. 7-1-70.)

Failure to defend, resulting in a default judgment, is not sufficient reason to permit granting relief after judgment under Civil Rule 60(B). To be entitled to such relief, a party must show (1) the existence of a meritorious defense, (2) entitlement to relief under one of the grounds set forth in the rule, and (3) that the motion is made within a reasonable time. Blasco v. Mislik, 69 OS2d 684, 433 NE2d 612 (1982); GTE Automatic Elec. v. ARC Indus., 47 OS2d 146, 351 NE2d 113 (1976).

The grounds for invoking Civil Rule 60(B) should be substantial. Caruso-Ciresi, Inc. v. Lohman, 5 OS3d 64, 448 NE2d 1365 (1963).

The statutes authorizing the vacation of judgments are subject to the provision that title of a purchaser in good faith shall not be affected by the proceedings to vacate. Stewart v. Kellough, 104 OS 347, 135 NE 608, 19 OLR 736 (1922).

A judgment void for lack of service, appearing on the record, may be vacated after term upon motion. Snyder v. Clough, 71 App 440, 50 NE2d 384, 26 OO 367 (1942).

A court is without power to vacate a judgment after term unless there is a strict compliance with the controlling statutory provisions. Grelle v. Humbel, 84 App 277, 81 NE2d 718, 39 OO 411, 53 Abs 159 (1948).

SECTION 16-16: CONSTRUCTION OF STATUTES

16-16A   Primary Rule.

R.C. 1.41 et seq. provides for the construction of statutes. (As eff. 1-3-72.)

When an estate in realty is once vested, the legislature, by subsequent enactment, is without power to set aside, enlarge or lessen the vested interest. Jackson v. Rutherford, 23 App 506, 155 NE 813, 4 Abs 628 (1926).

LAW IN GENERAL

The primary rule of construction is to ascertain the intention of the legislature. When the language of a statute is clear and unambiguous the court has no right to interpret it but only to apply it. Am Jur 2d, Statutes § 145; CJS, Statutes § 312.

16-16B   Inconsistencies Between Statutes.

R.C. 1.30 provides that any legislation with the stated purpose of correcting nonsubstantive errors in the Revised Code shall be substituted in a continuing way for the preceding statutory provision. (As eff. 12-23-86.)

Courts will not consider former legislation repealed by implication where the former and later acts may be harmonized by a reasonable construction so as to continue both in operation. Cott-Mohrman Co. v. Massillon Foundry & Mach. Co., 12 App 51, 31 CC(NS) 141 (1919).

A special statutory provision which applies to a specific subject matter constitutes an exception to a general statutory provision. Acme Engineering Co. v. Jones, 150 OS 423, 83 NE2d 202, 38 OO 294 (1948).

Statutes relating to the same subject matter should be construed in pari materia, although they were enacted in different sessions of the General Assembly. Warner v. Ohio Edison Co., 152 OS 303, 89 NE2d 463, 40 OO 355 (1949).

The primary purpose of the judiciary in the interpretation or construction of statutes is to give effect to the intention of the General Assembly. Henry v. Central Nat. Bank, 16 OS2d 16, 242 NE2d 342, 45 OO2d 262 (1968).

LAW IN GENERAL

When two or more statutes relate to the same matter they are generally considered in pari materia, that is, construed together and reconciled even though not enacted at the same time.

When they are not reconcilable, a presumption exists to a limited extent in favor of the later expression of the legislative intention.

When the legislative intention is not clear, a statute regulating a particular part of a subject is preferred over a statute regulating the subject generally.

Am Jur 2d, Statutes § 186; CJS, Statutes § 366.

16-16C   Change of Common Law.

A statute in derogation of the common law must be strictly construed and applied. Sabol v. Pekoc, 148 OS 545, 76 NE2d 84, 36 OO 182 (1947); Holthouse v. Akom, 79 NE2d 589, 37 OO 31, 51 Abs 176 (App. 1947).

LAW IN GENERAL

Statutes are frequently held to be declaratory of the common law and applied accordingly.

A common-law rule is not changed or abrogated by implication unless the rule is so repugnant to the statute that both cannot be enforced.

Am Jur 2d, Statutes § 185; CJS, Statutes § 363.

SECTION 16-17:   PROBATE AND OTHER COURTS OF LIMITED JURISDICTION

16-17A   Generally.

LAW IN GENERAL

Probate courts are primarily courts with jurisdiction of the administration of estates of deceased persons, infants, insane persons and other incompetents. They are creatures of local constitutions and statutes with the powers thereby given. Although they do not have inherent general equity jurisdiction, it is commonly held that they are courts of record and have all the authority of courts of general jurisdiction within the sphere of their constitutional or statutory jurisdiction. Other courts of limited jurisdiction, such as municipal or justice of the peace courts, are sometimes given statutory authority which can be exercised to effect the title to real estate. Am Jur 2d, Courts §§ 32, 104.

16-17B   Jurisdiction of Probate Court.

R.C. 2101.24 in part provides: "(A) Except as otherwise provided by law, the probate court has exclusive jurisdiction: ...

"(11) To construe wills;

"(12) To render declaratory judgments, including, but not limited to, those rendered pursuant to section 2107.084 of the Revised Code;

"(13) To direct and control the conduct of fiduciaries and settle their accounts;

"(14) To authorize the sale or lease of any estate created by will if the estate is held in trust on petition by trustee;

"(15) To terminate a testamentary trust in any case in which a court of equity may do so;

"(16) To hear and determine actions to contest the validity of wills;

"(17) To make a determination of the presumption of death of missing persons and to adjudicate the property rights and obligations of all parties affected thereby;

"(18) To hear and determine an action commenced pursuant to section 3107.41 of the Revised Code to obtain the release of information pertaining to the birth name of the adopted person and the identity of his biological parents and biologican siblings.

"(B) The probate court has concurrent jurisdiction with, and the same powers at law and in equity as, the general division of the court of common pleas to hear and determine actions involving inter vivos trusts.

"(C) The probate court has plenary power at law and in equity fully to dispose of any matter properly before the court, unless the power is expressly otherwise limited or denied by statute.

"(D) The jurisdiction acquired by a probate court over a matter or proceeding is exclusive of that of any other probate court, except when otherwise provided by law." (As eff. 3-13-86.)

R.C. 2101.35 provides: "Orders for the payment of money may be enforced as judgments in the court of common pleas. Such execution shall be directed to the sheriff, or, in the sheriff's absence or disability, to the coroner." (As eff. 10-1-53.)

R.C. 2101.36 to 2101.39 provide that a judge of the common pleas court or a judge appointed by the chief justice of the Supreme Court may act in the place of a probate judge who is disqualified or otherwise unable to act.

From 1904 until January 1, 1932 former G.C. 10494 (97 O.L. 113 and 108 O.L., pt. 1, 625) provided that the probate courts of Pickaway, Licking, Richland, Perry, Defiance, Henry, Fayette, and Coshocton have concurrent jurisdiction with the courts of common pleas in all proceedings in divorce, alimony, partition, and foreclosure of mortgages.

The decree of a probate court, involving the exercise of general jurisdiction of a court of equity, must be considered as void. Gilliland v. Sellers, 2 OS 223 (1853).

Probate courts are courts of record, having power to determine their own jurisdiction in proceedings not void ab initio. State ex rel. Young v. Morrow, 131 OS 266, 2 NE2d 595, 5 OO 584 (1936).

The power to entertain suits for specific performance is not included in the grants of equitable jurisdiction to probate courts. State ex rel. Black v. White, 132 OS 58, 5 NE2d 163, 7 OO 165 (1936).

The probate court may entertain an action of a declaratory judgment although the administration of the estate is then pending. Radaszewski v. Keating, 141 OS 489, 49 NE2d 167, 26 OO 75 (1943).

The jurisdiction of probate court in respect to vacation or modification of its judgments is not limited to statutory grounds only but includes equitable grounds. Abicht v. O'Donnell, 52 App 513, 3 NE2d 993, 6 OO 462, 22 Abs 82 (1936).

The probate court does not have jurisdiction upon exceptions to the inventory, to determine title to real or personal property that had been duly transferred and possession delivered by the decedent before her death. In re Brunskill's Estate, 63 App 529, 27 NE2d 492, 17 OO 265 (1940).

The grant of limited jurisdiction to the probate court does not oust the common pleas court from its original equity jurisdiction to declare void the judgments and orders of the probate court for lack of jurisdiction. Young v. Guella, 67 App 11, 35 NE2d 997, 21 OO 66 (1941).

The specific grant of power to the probate court does not confer upon such court general equity jurisdiction. Hooffstetter v. Adams, 67 App 21, 35 NE2d 896, 21 OO 70 (1941).

The probate court is without jurisdiction, in a proceeding to probate a will, to determine that the will was revoked by the divorce of the testator. In re Lester's Estate, 76 App 263, 64 NE2d 71, 31 OO 579 (1945).

In controlling the administration of a testamentary trust, the probate court has the power to determine the validity of a deed from the beneficiary of the trust where the validity is challenged on the ground of undue influence, mental incapacity or fraud. In re Stuckey's Will, 80 App 421, 73 NE2d 208, 36 OO 117 (1947).

The probate court is a court of limited, not general jurisdiction. Any grant of jurisdiction to it must be specific, and incidental and auxiliary powers are to be limited to such only as are necessary and proper to carry into effect the powers expressly granted. Flax v. Oppenheimer, 3 O Supp 212, 12 OO 48, 27 Abs 17 (C.P. 1938).

A declaratory judgment rendered by a Probate Court is void unless it concerns some subject matter within the jurisdiction of such court. State ex rel. Mayfield Heights v. Bartunek, 12 App2d 141, 231 NE2d 326, 41 OO2d 222 (1967).

The determination by Probate Court in the summary proceedings upon exceptions to the inventory that assets (even those transferred during the lifetime of the testatrix under a power of attorney) should be included in the estate makes the question of title res adjudicata except that such judgment may be attacked in a subsequent action by an interested person who was not a party to the proceeding. Cole v. Ottawa Home and Savings Assn., 18 OS2d 1, 246 NE2d 542, 47 OO2d 1 (1969).

The probate division of the Court of Common Pleas is without jurisdiction either to reform a deed executed prior to an owner's death or to order a series of conveyances to correct alleged defects in that deed. Oncu v. Bell, 49 App2d 109, 359 NE2d 712, 3 OO3d 175 (1976).

Further research: O Jur 3d, Courts and Judges § 344.

16-17C Municipal Court.

R.C. 1901.17 provides: "A municipal court shall have jurisdiction only in those cases where the amount claimed by any party, or the appraised value of the personal property sought to be recovered, does not exceed ten thousand dollars.

"Judgment may be rendered in excess of the jurisdictional amount, when the excess consists of interest, damages for the detention of personal property, or costs accrued after the commencement of the action.

"This section shall not limit the jurisdiction of a municipal court to appoint trustees to receive and distribute earnings in accordance with section 2329.70 of the Revised Code." (As eff. 5-1-74.)

R.C. 1901.18 provides: "(A) Subject to the monetary jurisdiction of municipal courts set forth in section 1901.17 of the Revised Code, a municipal court has original jurisdiction within its territory in all of the following actions and to perform all of the following functions:

"(1) In any civil action, of whatever nature or remedy, of which judges of county courts have jurisdiction;

"(2) In any action or proceeding at law for the recovery of money or personal property of which the court of common pleas has jurisdiction;

"(3) In any action at law based on contract, to determine, preserve, and enforce all legal and equitable rights involved in the contract, to decree an accounting, reformation, or cancellation of the contract, and to hear and determine all legal and equitable remedies necessary or proper for a complete determination of the rights of the parties to the contract;

"(4) In any action or proceeding for the sale of personal property under chattel mortgage, lien, encumbrance, or other charge, for the foreclosure and marshalling of liens thereon and the rendering of personal judgment therein;

"(5) In any action or proceeding to enforce the collection of its own judgments, or the judgments rendered by any court within the territory to which the municipal court has succeeded, and to subject the interest of a judgment debtor in personal property to satisfy judgments enforceable by the municipal court;

"(6) In any action or proceeding in the nature of interpleader;

"(7) In any action of replevin;

"(8) In any action of forcible entry and detainer;

"(9) In any action concerning the issuance and enforcement of temporary protection orders pursuant to section 2919.26 of the Revised Code;

"(10) In any action over which a housing division of a municipal court is given exclusive jurisdiction by section 1901.181 of the Revised Code, if the municipal court has a housing division;

"(11) In any action brought pursuant to division (I) of section 3733.11 of the Revised Code, if the residential premises that are the subject of the action are located within the territorial jurisdiction of the court.

"(B) The municipal court of Cleveland shall also have jurisdiction within its territory in all of the following actions and to perform all of the following functions:

"(1) In all actions and proceedings for the sale of real property under lien of a judgment of the municipal court, or a lien thereon for machinery, material, fuel furnished, or labor performed, irrespective of amount, and in such cases the court may proceed to foreclose and marshal all liens thereon, and all rights, vested or contingent therein, to appoint a receiver therefor, and to render personal judgment irrespective of amount in favor of any party;

"(2) In all actions for the foreclosure of a mortgage on real property given to secure the payment of money, the enforcement of a specific lien for money or other encumbrance or charge on real property when the amount claimed by the plaintiff does not exceed ten thousand dollars and the real property is situated within the territory, and in such cases the court may proceed to foreclose all liens thereon and all rights vested and contingent therein and proceed to render such judgments, and make such findings and orders, between the parties, in the same manner and to the same extent as in like cases in the court of common pleas;

"(3) In all actions for the recovery of real property situated within the territory to the same extent as courts of common pleas have jurisdiction;

"(4) In all actions for injunction to prevent or terminate violations of the ordinances and regulations of the city of Cleveland enacted or promulgated under the police power of the city of Cleveland, pursuant to Section 3 of Article XVIII, Ohio Constitution, over which the court of common pleas has or may have jurisdiction, and in such case the court may proceed to render such judgments and make such findings and orders in the same manner and to the same extent as in like cases in the court of common pleas." (As eff. 3-19-87.)

R.C. 1901.181 provides: "(A) Subject to section 1901.17 of the Revised Code, if a municipal court has a housing division, the housing division has exclusive jurisdiction in any civil action to enforce any local building, housing, air pollution, sanitation, health, fire, or safety code, ordinance, or regulation applicable to premises used or intended for use as a place of human habitation, buildings, structures, or any other real property subject to any such code, ordinance, or regulation, and in any civil action commenced pursuant to Chapter 1923. or 5321. or sections 5303.03 to 5303.07 of the Revised Code. Subject to section 1901.20 of the Revised Code, the housing division of a municipal court has exclusive jurisdiction in any criminal action for violation of any local building, housing, air pollution, sanitation, health, fire, or safety code, ordinance, or regulation applicable to premises used or intended for use as a place of human habitation, buildings, structures, or any other real property subject to any such code, ordinance, or regulation.

"(B) A counterclaim or cross-claim does not affect the jurisdiction of the housing division even if the subject matter of the counterclaim or cross-claim would not be within the jurisdiction of the housing division as authorized by this section if it were filed as an original action." (As eff. 4-2-80.)

R.C. 1901.19 provides: "(A) Subject to the monetary jurisdiction of municipal courts as set forth in section 1901.17 of the Revised Code, a municipal court and a housing division of a municipal court have jurisdiction within its territory in all of the following actions and to perform all of the following functions:

"(1) To compel attendance of witnesses in any pending action or proceeding in the same manner as the court of common pleas;

"(2) To issue executions on its own judgments;

"(3) In any legal or equitable action or proceeding, to enforce the collection of its own judgments;

"(4) In any civil action or proceeding at law in which the subject matter of the action or proceeding is located within the territory or when the defendant or some one of the defendants resides or is served with summons within the territory;

"(5) To issue and enforce any order of attachment;

"(6) In any action or proceeding in the nature of creditors' bills, and in aid of execution to subject the interest of a judgment debtor in personal property to the payment of a judgment of the court;

"(7) To issue and enforce temporary protection orders pursuant to section 2919.26 of the Revised Code.

"(B)(1) In any action for garnishment for personal earnings brought in a municipal court, the court has jurisdiction to serve process pursuant to section 2716.05 of the Revised Code upon a garnishee who resides in a county contiguous to that in which the court is located.

"(2) In any action for garnishment of property, other than personal earnings, brought in a municipal court under section 2716.11 of the Revised Code, the court has jurisdiction to serve process pursuant to section 2716.13 of the Revised Code upon a garnishee who resides in a county contiguous to that in which the court is located.

"(3) Whenever a motion for attachment is filed in a municipal court under section 2715.03 of the Revised Code, the court has jurisdiction to serve process pursuant to section 2715.091 [2715.09.1] of the Revised Code upon a garnishee who resides in a county contiguous to that in which the court is located.

"(C) The municipal court of Cleveland also has jurisdiction in all actions and proceedings in the nature of creditors' bills, and in aid of execution to subject the interests of a judgment debtor in real or personal property to the payment of a judgment of the municipal court. In such actions and proceedings, the court may proceed to marshal and foreclose all liens on the property irrespective of the amount of the lien, and all vested or contingent rights in the property." (As eff. 3-19-87.)

The Cleveland municipal court is the only one of the state's municipal courts which has jurisdiction for the sale of real property. Swarts v. Purdy, 2 Misc 176, 207 NE2d 806, 31 OO2d 437 (Mu. 1964).

Further research: O Jur 3d, Courts and Judges § 22.

16-17D County Courts.

R.C. 1907.011 provides for a county court in each county for all territory, if any, not within the territorial jurisdiction of any municipal court. (As eff. 6-17-57.)

R.C. 1907.05 provides "County courts have jurisdiction in civil actions in which the title to real estate may be drawn in question as follows:

"(A) In actions for trespass on real estate in which the damages demanded do not exceed three thousand dollars;

"(B) In actions to recover from the owner of adjoining land the equal proportion to the expense incurred in obtaining evidence in surveys to fix corners or settle boundary lines." (As eff. 3-1-87.)

R.C. 1907.04 provides: "County courts do not have jurisdiction of any civil action for any of the following purposes:

"(A) To recover damages for an assault or assault and battery;

"(B) For malicious prosecution;

"(C) Against county court judges, or other officers, for misconduct in office, except as provided in this chapter;

"(D) For slander or libel;

"(E) On contracts for real estate;

"(F) For the recovery of title to real estate, or in an action in which title to real estate may be drawn in question, except as provided in section 1907.05 of the Revised Code." (As eff. 3-1-87.)

Further research: O Jur 3d, Courts and Judges § 23.

DIVISION 16-2: CONFLICT BETWEEN COURTS; CONFLICT OF LAWS

SECTION 16-21: GENERALLY; FOREIGN JUDGMENTS

Federal courts, see Section 16-23.
Foreign divorces and alimony decrees, see Section 14-33.

16-21A Between States.

Operation of decrees in equity, see 16-11C.

The record of a judgment rendered in another state may be contradicted, as to the facts necessary to give the court jurisdiction; and if it be shown that such facts did not exist, the record will be a nullity, notwithstanding it may recite they did exist. Pennywit v. Foote, 27 OS 600, 1 WLB 242 (1875).

Courts of Indiana are powerless to authorize conveyance of interest in real estate in Ohio by guardian of insane person. Smith v. McKelvey, 28 App 361, 162 NE 722, 6 Abs 677 (1928).

The decree of a court of another state cannot, in and of itself, operate to transfer title to real estate in Ohio. Beebe v. Brownlee, 109 NE2d 528, 63 Abs 381 (App. 1952).

A judgment of a sister state's court is not subject to collateral attack in Ohio if the defendant submitted to the jurisdiction of the sister state's court by an appearance precluding collateral attack in such state. Litsinger Sign Co. v. American Sign Co., 11 OS2d 1, 227 NE2d 609, 40 OO2d 30 (1967).

LAW IN GENERAL

Title to real property is governed by the law of the state where the land is located. A decree of a state court never operates of its own force to transfer or directly affect the title to land located in another state. Although a foreign court may have jurisdiction of the person, its decree is not necessarily binding on the courts of the situs and is recognized only as a matter of comity; as in cases involving trusts or fraud, a foreign decree operates only in personam. A suit for specific performance is a good example of this rule. Am Law of Prop § 13.15; CJS, Judgments § 889.

SECTION 16-22: EXCLUSIVENESS OF JURISDICTION FIRST OBTAINED

16-22A   Rules.

Neither a state court nor a federal court may, by collateral suit, assume to deal with property rights or rights of action "constituting part of the estate within the exclusive jurisdiction and control of the courts of the other." When a court of competent jurisdiction has, by appropriate proceedings, taken property into its possession through its officers, the property is thereby withdrawn from the jurisdiction of all other courts. Roof v. Conway, 133 F2d 819, 26 OO 43 (1943).

As between federal and state courts, comity requires the court, which first obtains actual or constructive possession of the property in the exercise of its jurisdiction, be permitted to retain control of the property without interference from the other. Hickok v. Gulf Oil Corp., 265 F2d 798, 11 OO2d 308, 84 Abs 272 (1959).

Where mortgagee files petition for foreclosure after assignment for the benefit of creditors, the assignee subsequently filing an action to sell, the common pleas court has jurisdiction when the probate court cannot give a complete and adequate remedy at law. Williams v. Buckeye State Bldg. & Loan Co., 2 O Supp 149, 3 OO 398, 19 Abs 403 (Prob. 1935); Robinson v. Williams, 62 OS 401, 57 NE 55, 43 WLB 280, 359 (1900).

To maintain his action the mortgagee must allege and prove that sale by the assignee would not furnish full and adequate relief to the mortgagee. Madigan v. Dollar Bldg. & Loan Co., 49 App 69, 195 NE 250, 2 OO 236, 15 Abs 459 (1933).

As between a mortgagee seeking foreclosure in the common pleas court and an administrator seeking authority to sell land to pay debts in the probate court, the court which first acquired jurisdiction retains it to the exclusion of the other. Peoples Savings Ass'n v. Sanford, 59 App 294, 18 NE2d 126, 13 OO 86 (1938); Home Bldg. & Savings Co. v. Sanford, 59 App 302, 18 NE2d 127, 13 OO 90 (1938).

As between courts of concurrent and coextensive jurisdiction, the one whose power is first invoked by the institution of proper proceedings and the service of the required process acquires the right to adjudicate upon the whole issue and to settle the rights of the parties to the exclusion of all other tribunals. Miller v. Court of Common Pleas, 143 OS 68, 54 NE2d 130, 28 OO 19 (1944); John Weenink & Sons v. Court of Common Pleas, 150 OS 349, 82 NE2d 730, 38 OO 189 (1948).

The rule has no application where the conflict of jurisdiction is between a court of general jurisdiction and one whose limited powers are inadequate to afford full relief to the parties. State ex rel. McHenry v. Calhoun, 87 App 1, 93 NE2d 317, 42 OO 231, 57 Abs 12 (1950).

An order by common pleas court regarding rights of the parties in a divorce action is not a bar to an action in Cleveland municipal court to marshal liens and for foreclosure and sale. Swirsky v. Iwanyckyj, 11 OS2d 92, 228 NE2d 329, 40 OO2d 96 (1967).

Where actions have been filed in two courts of concurrent and coextensive jurisdiction the one in which service of process is first completed acquires exclusive jurisdiction. State ex rel. Balson v. Harnishfeger, 55 OS2d 38, 377 NE2d 750, 9 OO3d 21 (1978).

Further research: O Jur 3d, Courts and Judges § 321.

LAW IN GENERAL

By comity, the court which first acquires jurisdiction of specific property retains it for the purposes necessary to give effect to its judgment, to the exclusion of all courts of concurrent jurisdiction. The rule is not applied when complete and adequate relief is available only in the second suit. Both actions may be maintained when the judgment asked in the first action would not bar the relief sought in the second. The rule is usually applied in cases of conflicting and concurrent jurisdiction between state and federal courts, especially when the property is in the possession of a receiver. Am Jur 2d, Courts §§ 128, 134; CJS, Courts §§ 492, 522.

16-22B Partition and Probate Actions.

Where an action in partition has been instituted, following the death of a co-owner, and subsequent thereto the executor or administrator of such deceased co-owner institutes land sale proceedings to sell the entire interest, the latter supersedes and prevails over the former. Hatch v. Tipton, 131 OS 364, 2 NE2d 875, 6 OO 68 (1936).

A suit by the surviving spouse to purchase the mansion house filed after a partition suit will oust the common pleas court of its jurisdiction in partition, at least to the extent of the property properly included in the election to purchase. Strawser v. Stanton, 103 NE2d 797, 47 OO 255, 66 Abs 121 (C.P. 1952).

An action to partition devised land prevails over a purported sale by the executor under a testamentary power exercised during the pendency of the action if the action was commenced more than one year after his appointment. Kufel v. Chopcinski, 29 Misc 61, 278 NE2d 60, 58 OO2d 97 (C.P. 1971).

SECTION 16-23: UNITED STATES COURTS

Government as party defendant, see Section 17-23.

16-23A Application of State Law.

Except in matters governed by the Federal Constitution or by Acts of Congress, the law to be applied in any case is the law of the state; and whether the law of the state shall be declared by its legislature in a statute, or by its highest court in a decision, is not a matter of federal concern. Erie R.R. v. Tompkins, 304 US 64, 82 L Ed 1188, 58 Sup Ct 817, 114 ALR 1487 (1938).

A federal court having jurisdiction of a suit upon the basis of diversity of citizenship must follow the rules of the courts of the state in which it sits on common law as well as on statutory matters. Warner v. Republic Steel Corp., 103 FSupp 998, 48 OO 470, 64 Abs 391 (1952).

LAW IN GENERAL

Federal courts generally follow the applicable state law. 28 U.S.C. 1652 provides that laws of the several states shall be regarded as rules of decision where they apply except when federal law otherwise requires. In Erie R.R. v. Tompkins, the United States Supreme Court decided that, in cases based on diversity of citizenship, federal courts should follow the decisions of state appellate courts to the same extent as the state statutory law is followed. When a conflict between the laws of different states is involved, the doctrine of Erie R.R. v. Tompkins requires federal courts to follow the public policy and rules of the state in which they sit as to enforcement of rights arising in another state. 21 ALR2d 247.

As a general rule, federal courts follow the statutes and decisions of the state on questions incidental or preliminary to an ultimate federal question. However, there is considerable authority to the effect that they are not bound by state law, even as to collateral questions, if the controversy arose under the Constitution or statutes of the United States, except in those instances where the federal statutes expressly so require. 16 ALR2d 839.

16-23B Lis Pendens.

Lis pendens generally, see Section 17-12.

28 U.S.C. 1964 provides that an action pending in a United States district court is not constructive notice as it relates to real property in the state unless it is registered, recorded, docketed, or indexed according to the state law applying to both state and federal court actions. (As enacted 8-20-58.) This statute, together with Civil Rule 3(F)(1), shown at 17-12A, makes filing with the clerk of common pleas court necessary for lis pendens and constructive notice of an action in district court except in the county where such court sits.

The United States is bound by the doctrine of lis pendens in state courts insofar as federal tax liens are concerned in judicial sales. See 17-23A.

The state statutes relate to actions brought and judgments rendered in the state courts and not to those in courts of the United States. Steward v. Wheeling & L. E. R.R., 53 OS 151, 41 NE 247, 33 WLB 329, 34 WLB 56 (1895).

LAW IN GENERAL

The doctrine of lis pendens applies in federal courts, with some exceptions as to bankruptcy proceedings. In the absence of statute, a pending action is constructive notice, throughout the territory over which the court has jurisdiction, even though there may be no record in the county where the property is situated. No federal statute has been enacted concerning lis pendens. Am Law of Prop §§ 17.11, 18.84.

16-23C Res Judicata.

Res judicata generally, see Section 16-12.

Both the federal and state courts comply with the principles of res judicata as to the judgments of the other.

Further research: CJS, Judgments § 899.

16-23D Conflicting Jurisdiction of Bankruptcy Courts.

Bankruptcy generally, see 17-3.

On October 1, 1979, the Bankruptcy Reform Act of 1978 became effective. 11 U.S.C. § 101 et seq. On June 28, 1982, the United States Supreme Court, in Northern Pipeline Constr. Co. v. Marathon Pipe Line Co., 458 U.S. 50, 102 SCt 2858, 73 LEd2d 598, declared unconstitutional the broad grant of jurisdiction to the Bankruptcy Court contained in the 1978 Act. See U.S.C. § 1471.

Upon the filing of a petition seeking any form of bankruptcy relief, an automatic stay of all proceedings against the debtor becomes effective. 11 U.S.C. § 362.

Unless the automatic stay is released, the parties in any proceedings in any court other than the Bankruptcy Court must refrain from continuing proceedings against the property of the debtor. For example, a sheriff's sale may not proceed even though the judgment ordering the foreclosure was granted prior to the commencement of the bankruptcy case.

In Chapter 7 cases, relief from the stay is not enough to authorize the state court to continue proceedings. The control of the Bankruptcy Court is not interrupted unless the property has been abandoned by the Court. A listing in the schedules of property among the exemptions is not conclusive and should not be relied upon while the bankruptcy proceedings remain pending in the absence of abandonment.

Proceedings for liquidating the assets of a debtor are conducted under Chapter 7 of the Bankruptcy Code. Proceedings for the adjustments of debts of a municipality are conducted under Chapter 9. Business reorganizations are under Chapter 11. Proceedings for adjustment of debts of an individual with regular income are under Chapter 13.

Prior to October 1, 1979, the doctrine of lis pendens applied as between state court and bankruptcy proceedings, except that the Bankruptcy Court acquired jurisdiction over a receivership, trusteeship or insolvency proceeding which had been commenced in a state court prior to the bankruptcy. § 69(d) of the Bankruptcy Act of 1898.

The automatic stay does not prevent the filing and service of affidavits to perfect a mechanic's lien based on materials delivered or services performed before the commencement of the bankruptcy case. 11 U.S.C. § 546(h). Enforcement of the lien, however, is blocked by the stay.

DIVISION 16-3: ABATEMENT, REVIVAL AND SURVIVAL; DEATH OF PARTY

SECTION 16-31: ABATEMENT AND REVIVAL OF PENDING ACTIONS

Execution sale, see 17-41H.
Soldiers' and Sailors' Civil Relief Act, see Section 16-43.

16-31A Abatement Generally.

R.C. 2311.21 provides: "Unless otherwise provided, no action or proceeding pending in any court shall abate by the death of either or both of the parties thereto, except actions for libel, slander, malicious prosecution, for a nuisance, or against a judge of a county court for misconduct in office, which shall abate by the death of either party." (As eff. 1-1-58.)

Further research: O Jur 3d, Actions § 127.

LAW IN GENERAL

Abatement operates to merely suspend the action unless the cause of action abates entirely upon the death of a party as provided by R.C. 2311.21. It is ordinarily not necessary to commence a new suit upon the death of a party. Pendency of another action between the parties, incapacity of plaintiff to sue, and misjoinder or nonjoinder of parties are also common grounds of abatement. CJS, Abatement and Revival § 1.

16-31B Revival Generally.

Civil Rule 25 (substitution of parties) provides procedure upon the death, incompetency, transfer of interest or separation from office of a party and for suggestion on record by the attorney upon death or incompetency. (As eff. 7-1-70.)

Upon transfer by a plaintiff, during the pendency of an action, of all his interest therein, the transfer is no defense to the action. Lowry v. Anderson, 57 OS 179, 48 NE 810 (1897).

Notice to or consent of the defendant must be had of the revivor of the action against him. French v. Friesinger, 38 NE2d 90, 34 Abs 509 (App. 1941). But if the record is silent in the matter, jurisdiction will be presumed. Pokrandt v. Konorski, 17 CC(NS) 423, 32 CD 213 (1911).

Further research: O Jur 3d, Actions §§ 169, 172.

16-31C Death of Party.

Complete abatement, see 16-31A.
Execution sales, see 17-41H.
Revival generally, see 16-31B.

See Civil Rule 25 noted at 16-31B.

R.C. 2311.22 provides: "If the plaintiff in an action for dower dies before final judgment therein, the action may be revived in the name of the personal representative of such plaintiff for the purpose of recovering the value of such dower, from the beginning of the action to the decedent's death." (As eff. 10-1-53.)

R.C. 2311.33 provides: "An order to revive an action against the successor of a defendant, other than the executor or administrator, shall not be made without the consent of such successor, unless made within one year from the time it first could have been made." (As eff. 10-1-53.)

R.C. 2311.34 provides: "An order to revive an action in the name of the representative or successor of a plaintiff may be made forthwith, but shall not be made, of right, without the consent of the defendant, after the expiration of one year from the time it might first have been made. When the powers of the defendant have ceased, the order of revivor may be made in the period limited in section 2311.33 of the Revised Code." (As eff. 10-1-53.)

After jurisdiction is acquired, the court may proceed to the final disposition of the case and sale of the attached property, notwithstanding the death of the debtor before judgment. It is merely erroneous as to parties and privies and binding upon them until reversed in a direct proceeding. Cochran v. Loring, 17 Ohio 409 (1848).

The personal representative of the deceased plaintiff may be required to revive the action before an order of sale is issued. Moore v. Ogden, 35 OS 430, 5 WLB 107 (1880).

A judgment of reversal is effective notwithstanding the death of the appellant during the pendency of the proceedings. Williams v. Englebrecht, 38 OS 96 (1882).

The sheriff cannot be required to proceed with an order of sale issued after the death of the plaintiff, without revivor. Cist v. Beresford, 1 CC 32, 1 CD 19, 13 WLB 363 (1885).

Where a defendant, who has been properly served with summons, dies during the pendency of the action, and without revivor of the action, judgment is rendered against such deceased defendant, the judgment is not void, but may be reversed for error by a direct proceeding for that purpose. Bevitt v. Diehl, 12 OD 315 (1902).

It therefore appears that a judgment entered or order of sale issued without revivor, after death of either plaintiff or defendant, is erroneous but is not subject to collateral attack.

Further research: O Jur 3d, Actions § 148.

LAW IN GENERAL

When a pending suit involves real property, the heirs or devisees of the deceased owner should ordinarily be substituted as new parties. Am Jur 2d, Abatement and Revival § 120; CJS, Abatement and Revival §§ 164, 172.

The general rule is that the death of a party after judgment has been rendered does not abate the action, and that a judicial sale may proceed if the decree was before the death. It is usually held that a judgment, after death of a party over whom the court has jurisdiction, is not subject to collateral attack. Am Jur 2d, Abatement and Revival §§ 47, 48; CJS, Abatement and Revival § 114.

SECTION 16-32: SURVIVAL OF CAUSES OF ACTION

16-32A Statutes.

Complete abatement, see also 16-31A.

R.C. 2305.21 provides: "In addition to the causes of action which survive at common law, causes of action for mesne profits, or injuries to the person or property, or for deceit or fraud, also shall survive; and such actions may be brought notwithstanding the death of the person entitled or liable thereto." (As eff. 10-1-53.)

16-32B Generally.

Rescission, see also 8-51E.

If the grantor of a deed wrongfully obtained dies testate, such grantor's devisee who would have taken the property, and not the grantor's executor, is the proper person to institute proceedings for cancellation. Eysenback v. Reilly, 92 App 207, 109 NE2d 664, 49 OO 324 (1951).

Further research: O Jur 3d, Actions § 150.

DIVISION 16-4: LIMITATION OF ACTIONS

SECTION 16-41: GENERALLY

Adverse possession, see Chapter 2.
Future interests, see 11-18C.
Marketable Title Act, see Section 1-44.

16-41A Rules.

R.C. 2305.06 provides: "Except as provided in section 1302.98 of the Revised Code, an action upon a specialty or an agreement, contract, or promise in writing shall be brought within fifteen years after the cause thereof accrued." (As eff. 7-1-62.) Section 1302.98 concerns contracts for sale of personal property under the Uniform Commercial Code.

R.C. 2305.07 provides: "Except as provided in section 1302.98 of the Revised Code, an action upon a contract not in writing, express or implied, or upon a liability created by statute other than a forfeiture or penalty, shall be brought within six years after the cause thereof accrued." (As eff. 7-1-62.)

R.C. 2305.09 provides: "An action for any of the following causes shall be brought within four years after the cause thereof accrued:

"(A) For trespassing upon real property;

"(B) For the recovery of personal property, or for taking or detaining it;

"(C) For relief on the ground of fraud;

"(D) For an injury to the rights of the plaintiff not arising on contract nor enumerated in sections 2305.10 to 2305.12, inclusive, 2305.14 and 1304.29 of the Revised Code.

"If the action is for trespassing underground or injury to mines, or for the wrongful taking of personal property, the causes thereof shall not accrue until the wrongdoer is discovered; not if it is for fraud, until the fraud is discovered." (As eff. 7-1-62.)

R.C. 2305.11 in part provides: "An action for libel, slander, malicious prosecution, or false imprisonment, ... or an action upon a statute for a penalty or forfeiture, shall be commenced within one year after the cause of action accrued...." (As eff. 10-20-87.)

R.C. 2305.12 provides: "An action on the official bond, or undertaking of an officer, assignee, trustee, executor, administrator, or guardian, or on a bond or undertaking given in pursuance of statute, shall be brought within ten years after the cause thereof accrued." (As eff. 10-1-53.)

R.C. 2305.14 provides: "An action for relief not provided for in sections 2305.04 to 2305.131, inclusive, and section 1304.29 of the Revised Code, shall be brought within ten years after the cause thereof accrued. This section does not apply to an action on a judgment rendered in another state or territory." (As eff. 9-10-63.)

The statute of limitations must be pleaded in answer by way of defense. Lockwood v. Wildman, 13 Ohio 430 (1844).

A cause of action accrues, for the purpose of the statute of limitations, on the date of the promise when no date of repayment of the debt is specified. Johnston v. Thomas, 275 FSupp 32, 15 Misc 242 (1967).

Further research: O Jur 3d, Limitations and Laches § 18.

LAW IN GENERAL

Statutes of limitation go to the remedy and not to the right itself; therefore, a claim may be valid for some purposes although it will not be judicially enforced if the defense of the statute is pleaded. Adverse possession is an exception to the rule as it extinguishes the former right and title. Particular statutes which operate to extinguish obligations are also commonly called statutes of limitation. As a general rule, a lien may be enforced although recovery of the secured debt is barred. Am Jur 2d, Limitation of Actions §§ 23, 167; Am Law of Prop § 18.96; CJS, Limitation of Actions § 6.

The law of the forum, in the first instance, determines the time within which a cause of action may be enforced. However, the law of the forum includes its own conflict of laws rules. 67 ALR2d 216.

16-41B Extension and Revival.

Exceptions, see also Section 16-42.

R.C. 2305.08 provides: "If payment has been made upon any demand founded on a contract, or a written acknowledgment thereof, or a promise to pay it has been made and signed by the party to be charged, an action may be brought thereon within the time limited by sections 2305.06 and 2305.07 of the Revised Code, after such payment, acknowledgment, or promise." (As eff. 10-1-53.)

A payment by the assuming grantee does not toll the statute of limitations as to the mortgagor when the latter neither participates in nor has knowledge of such payment. Frost v. Johnson, 140 OS 315, 43 NE2d 277, 23 OO 538, 142 ALR 609 (1942).

Further research: O Jur 3d, Limitations and Laches § 172.

LAW IN GENERAL

The period of limitation is extended or revived by a new promise to pay, by an unqualified acknowledgment of the debt, or by part payment. Am Jur 2d, Limitation of Actions § 319; CJS, Limitation of Actions § 302.

16-41C Commencement of Action.

See also 16-75D.

Civil Rule 3(A) provides: "A civil action is commenced by filing a complaint with the court, if service is obtained within one year from such filing upon a named defendant, or upon an incorrectly named defendant whose name is later corrected pursuant to Rule 15(C), or upon a defendant identified by a fictitious name whose name is later corrected pursuant to Rule 15(D)." (As eff. 7-1-86.)

R.C. 2127.10, quoted at 12-14I, provides that a land sale under the probate code shall be commenced by filing a petition with the probate court. (As eff. 1-1-76.)

R.C. 2305.17 provides: "An action is commenced within the meaning of sections 2305.03 to 2305.22, inclusive, and sections 1302.98 and 1304.29 of the Revised Code, by filing a petition in the office of the clerk of the proper court together with a praecipe demanding that summons issue or an affidavit for service by publication, if service is obtained within one year." (As eff. 10-30-65.)

R.C. 2305.19 in part provides: "In an action commenced, or attempted to be commenced, if in due time a judgment for the plaintiff is reversed, or if the plaintiff fails otherwise than upon the merits, and the time limited for the commencement of such action at the date of reversal or failure has expired, the plaintiff, or, if he dies and the cause of action survives, his representatives may commence a new action within one year after such date. This provision applies to any claim asserted in any pleading by a defendant." Further provisions concern service of the process. (As eff. 10-1-53.)

It is well settled that when a substitution by amendment makes no change in the cause of action, the amendment relates back to the commencement of the suit and stops the running of the statute of limitations at that point. Second Nat. Bank v. American Bonding Co., 93 OS 362, 113 NE 221, 13 OLR 580, 61 WLB 51 (1916).

The time of commencing civil actions as to compliance with the statutes of limitations is prescribed by R.C. 2305.17. Crandall v. Irwin, 139 OS 253, 39 NE2d 608, 22 OO 273, 139 ALR 895 (1942).

Where, after the limitation period had expired, plaintiff amended his petition to designate the defendant a minor and he was properly served, the petition was timely filed. Byers v. Dobies, 193 NE2d 417, 27 OO2d 70, 93 Abs 114 (App. 1963).

Service upon one of the members of a class united in interest (one of legatees, not heirs), if made within the limitation period, commences the action as to all members of the class, and actual service of summons may be thereafter made at any time upon the remainder of the defendants of that class. Cook v. Sears, 9 App2d 197, 223 NE2d 613, 38 OO2d 209 (1967).

Further research: O Jur 3d, Limitations and Laches § 144.

SECTION 16-42: EXCEPTIONS TO AND SUSPENSION OF STATUTE

16-42A Against Governments.

Adverse possession, see 2-21A.

R.C. 2305.26 in part provides: "(A) An action by the state or an agency or political subdivision of the state to enforce a lien upon real or personal property created under and by virtue of sections 1901.21, 2505.13, 2937.25, 4123.76, 4123.78, 4141.23, 4509.60, 5719.04, 5733.18, 5735.03, and 5749.02 of the Revised Code shall be brought within six years from the date when the lien or notice of continuation of the lien has been filed in the office of the county recorder.

"(B) A notice of continuation of lien may be filed in the office of the county recorder within six months prior to the expiration of the six-year period following the original filing of the lien or the filing of the notice of continuation of the lien as specified in division (A) of this section. The notice must identify the original notice of lien and state that the original lien is still effective. Upon timely filing of a notice of continuation of lien, the effectiveness of the original lien is continued for six years after the last date on which the lien was effective, whereupon it lapses, unless another notice of continuation of lien is filed prior to the lapse. Succeeding notices of continuation of lien may be filed in the same manner to continue the effectiveness of the original lien." (C) and (D) provide the manner of filing and indexing a notice of continuation of lien. (As eff. 8-26-77.)

R.C. 2329.07 on the limitation on judgment liens in favor of the state is shown at 19-21I.

Where a statute does not expressly exempt a political subdivision, the exemption does not exist. State ex rel. Board of Education v. Gibson, 130 OS 318, 199 NE 185, 4 OO 352 (1935).

Where there is no applicable federal statute of limitations to an action by the federal government for money due under a contract, an applicable state statute cannot of itself bar the government's claim. United States v. Frank Killian Co., 269 F2d 491, 10 OO2d 40, 83 Abs 55 (1959).

Statutes of limitation do no run against the federal or state government unless a statute so provides.

Further research: O Jur 3d, Limitations and Laches § 196.

16-42B Personal Disabilities; Absence.

R.C. 2305.15 provides: "(A) When a cause of action accrues against a person, if he is out of the state, has absconded, or conceals himself, the period of limitation for the commencement of the action as provided in sections 2305.04 to 2305.14, 1302.98, and 1304.29 of the Revised Code does not begin to run until he comes into the state or while he is so absconded or concealed. After the cause of action accrues if he departs from the state, absconds, or conceals himself, the time of his absence or concealment shall not be computed as any part of a period within which the action must be brought.

"(B) When a person is imprisoned for the commission of any offense, the time of his imprisonment shall not be computed as any part of any period of limitation, as provided in section 2305.09, 2305.10, 2305.11, or 2305.14 of the Revised Code, within which any person must bring any action against the imprisoned person." (As eff. 7-9-86.)

R.C. 2305.16 provides: "Unless otherwise specially provided in sections 2305.04 to 2305.14, inclusive, and sections 1302.98 and 1304.29 of the Revised Code, if a person entitled to bring any action mentioned in such sections, unless for penalty or forfeiture, is, at the time the cause of action accrues, within the age of minority, of unsound mind, or imprisoned, such person may bring it within the respective times limited by such sections, after such disability is removed. When the interests of two or more parties are joint and inseparable, the disability of one shall inure to the benefit of all.

"After the cause of action accrues, if the person entitled to bring such action becomes of unsound mind and is adjudicated as such by a court of competent jurisdiction or is confined in an institution or hospital under a diagnosed condition or disease which renders him of unsound mind, the time during which he is of unsound mind and so adjudicated or so confined shall not be computed as any part of the period within which the action must be brought." (As eff. 10-30-65.)

R.C. 2323.21 provides: "It is not necessary to reserve in a judgment or order the right of a minor to show cause against it after attaining the age of majority; but in any case in which, but for this section, such reservation would have been proper, within one year after his majority, the minor may show cause against such order or judgment." (As eff. 10-1-53.)

The privilege given under the statute of limitations to a person under disability extends only to disabilities existing at the time when the right or cause of action first accrues. Cozzens v. Farnan, 30 OS 491, 2 WLB 258 (1876); Coventry v. Atherton, 9 Ohio 34 (1839). This rule was changed as of October 30, 1965 by the amendment of R.C. 2305.16 shown above.

The disability of absence is removed by death, and the heir, whether himself under disability or not, is barred unless he sues within the statutory period after the death of his ancestor. Whitney v. Webb, 10 Ohio 513 (1841).

The disability of absence from the state ceases from the time the actual presence of the person in the state begins, even though such presence be of short duration, and is not revived by his subsequent absence even during his infancy. Powell v. Koehler, 52 OS 103, 39 NE 195, 32 WLB 406, 33 WLB 20 (1894).

Where the interests of two defendants are joint and inseparable, and the rights of one are saved on account of his disability, such saving inures to the benefit of the other defendant. Sturges v. Longworth, 1 OS 544 (1853).

The title of a bona fide purchaser cannot be impeached by a minor upon a defense not going to the jurisdiction of the court nor appearing upon the face of the record in that case. Kellough v. Moses, 32 CC(NS) 49, 35 CD 685, 66 WLB 197 (1920), affd. 104 OS 347, 135 NE 608, 19 OLR 736 (1922).

The statute of limitations did not run against the action during the three months the defendant was out of the state visiting a relative in Florida. George v. Perrin, 221 FSupp 312, 25 OO2d 240 (1963).

The statute, R.C. 2305, does not toll the running of the statute of limitations where the defendant domestic corporation is continually amenable to process through service on the secretary of state under R.C. 1701.07 (H). Thompson v. Horvath, 10 OS2d 247, 227 NE2d 225, 39 OO2d 404 (1967).

"Where a defendant temporarily leaves the state after a cause of action accrues against him, he 'departs from the state' within the meaning of R.C. 2305.15, and the time of his absence is not computed as any part of a period within which an action may be brought." The absence in this case was at least twenty-five days and the period for commencing the suit was extended for that time. Wetzel v. Weyant, 41 OS2d 135, 323 NE2d 711, 70 OO2d 227 (1975).

Further research: O Jur 3d, Limitations and Laches § 112.

LAW IN GENERAL

Personal disabilities do not extend the period within which an action may be brought, unless by express statutory provision. Am Jur 2d, Limitation of Actions § 178.

When a statute of limitations begins to run it will not be suspended nor the period extended by a disability occurring thereafter except as provided by statute; thus, the disability of infancy is not available to an heir where the statute had commenced to run against the ancestor. Successive disabilities, whether of the same or different persons, do not postpone the statute. The statute will not commence to run until the removal of all the disabilities existing at the time the right of action accrues. As a general rule, rights are saved when they are joint but not saved when they are joint and several. CJS, Limitation of Actions § 218.

16-42C Death.

When the statute of limitations begins to run against the intestate in his lifetime, it will run to its completion without interruption by the death. Granger v. Granger, 6 Ohio 35 (1833).

Where one has a claim against an estate, it is incumbent upon him, if no administrator has been appointed, to procure the appointment of an administrator against whom he can proceed. Wrinkle v. Trabert, 174 OS 233, 188 NE2d 587, 22 OO2d 248 (1963).

Death may start the period of the statute by the elimination of personal disabilities.

Further research: O Jur 3d, Limitations and Laches § 104.

16-42D War.

As to alien enemies, the running of the statute of limitations is suspended by war. Industrial Commission v. Rotar, 124 OS 418, 179 NE 135, 10 Abs 736, 35 OLR 368 (1931).

The war ended August 14, 1945, for the purpose of this lease, despite the fact that actual treaties of peace have not been signed and ratified. Watkins v. Cohen, 91 NE2d 708, 56 Abs 202 (C.P. 1949).

16-42E Pending Actions.

In an action to foreclose and marshal liens, a judgment creditor will not lose his right to share in the proceeds by the fact that his judgment became dormant pending the action. Dempsey v. Bush, 18 OS 376 (1868).

LAW IN GENERAL

The running of the statute is interrupted during the pendency of an action as to the causes of action set forth in the petition and as to the defenses thereto. Limitations are also tolled by the pendency of an action preventing the enforcement of the right. Am Jur 2d, Limitation of Actions §§ 170, 200; CJS, Limitation of Actions §§ 247, 261.

16-42F Waiver; Estoppel.

The running of the statute of limitations may be suspended by the mutual agreement of the parties. Dietrick v. Noel, 42 OS 18, 11 WLB 134 (1884).

LAW IN GENERAL

Under the majority rule, an agreement waiving a statute of limitations is invalid as contrary to public policy if made at the creation of the obligation or if made when the liability arises. A subsequent contractual waiver is commonly upheld. 1 ALR2d 1445.

The doctrine of estoppel is applied to preclude a defendant from asserting the statute of limitation when the assertion would be inequitable. 24 ALR2d 1413.

16-42G   Trusts; Vendees.

R.C. 2305.22 provides: "Sections 2305.03 to 2305.21, inclusive, and sections 1302.98 and 1304.29 of the Revised Code, respecting lapse of time as a bar to suit, do not apply in the case of a continuing and subsisting trust, nor to an action by a vendee of real property, in possession thereof, to obtain a conveyance of it." (As eff. 7-1-62.)

To constitute a continuing or subsisting trust against which the statute of limitations will not run, it must be a direct trust of the kind belonging exclusively to the jurisdiction of a court of equity, and the question must arise between the trustee and the cestui que trust. Allen v. Deardoff, 14 App 16 (1921).

It is a general rule that whenever the right of action in a trustee, who is vested with the legal estate and is competent to sue, is barred by limitation, the right of the cestui que trust is also barred, whether the cestui que trust is sui juris or under disability during the period of limitation, in the absence of statute declaring otherwise. Rogers v. Schuller, 27 Abs 449 (App. 1938).

A trust created for the benefit of creditors is not one of those trusts as to which the statute of limitations does not run. Johnston v. Thomas, 275 FSupp 32, 15 Misc 242 (1967).

SECTION 16-43:   SOLDIERS' AND SAILORS' CIVIL RELIEF ACT OF 1940

16-43A   Default Judgments.

Section 200 of the Act (50 U.S.C. Appx. § 520 (1)) provides: "In any action or proceeding commenced in any court, if there shall be a default of any appearance by the defendant, the plaintiff, before entering judgment shall file in the court an affidavit setting forth facts showing that the defendant is not in military service. If unable to file such affidavit plaintiff shall in lieu thereof file an affidavit setting forth either that the defendant is in the military service or that plaintiff is not able to determine whether or not defendant is in such service. If an affidavit is not filed showing that the defendant is not in the military service, no judgment shall be entered without first securing an order of court directing such entry, and no such order shall be made if the defendant is in such service until after the court shall have appointed an attorney to represent defendant and protect his interest, and the court shall on application make such appointment. Unless it appears that the defendant is not in such service the court may require, as a condition before judgment is entered, that the plaintiff file a bond approved by the court conditioned to indemnify the defendant, if in military service, against any loss or damage that he may suffer by reason of any judgment should the judgment be thereafter set aside in whole or in part. And the court may make such other and further order or enter such judgment as in its opinion may be necessary to protect the rights of the defendant under this act." An unsworn statement may be filed instead of an affidavit. (As eff. 9-8-60.)

A proceeding to admit a will to probate is not an adversary proceeding and the Soldiers' and Sailors' Civil Relief Act has no application. Case v. Case, 124 NE2d 856, 55 OO 317, 70 Abs 2 (Prob. 1955).

16-43B Opening Judgments.

Section 200(4) of the Act (50 U.S.C. Appx. § 520 (4)) provides: "If any judgment shall be rendered in any action or proceeding governed by this section against any person in military service during the period of such service or within thirty days thereafter, and it appears that such person was prejudiced by reason of his military service in making his defense thereto, such judgment may, upon application, made by such person or his legal representative, not later than ninety days after the termination of such service, be opened by the court rendering the same and such defendant or his legal representative let in to defend; provided it is made to appear that the defendant has a meritorious or legal defense to the action or some part thereof. Vacating, setting aside, or reversing any judgment because of any of the provisions of this Act shall not impair any right or title acquired by any bona fide purchaser for value under such judgment." (As eff. 10-17-40.)

In Mims Bros. v. N.A. James, Inc., 174 SW2d 276 (Tex. Civ. App. 1943), it was held that a default judgment taken without affidavit or other requirements of the Act is not void but merely voidable at the instance of the serviceman on proper showing of prejudice or injury; that the Act was for the exclusive benefit of servicemen and others mentioned, and that they alone can take advantage of it and then only on showing that their interest has been deleteriously affected.

Where a default judgment is rendered without a filing of the affidavit required by the Soldiers' and Sailors' Civil Relief Act, the judgment is not void but merely voidable, subject to being vacated at the instance of the serviceman on (1) a showing that he has been prejudiced by reason of his military service in making his defense, (2) a showing of a meritorious or legal defense to the action which should be specially pleaded. Thompson v. Lowman, 108 App 453, 155 NE2d 258, 9 OO2d 407, 80 Abs 213 (1958).

16-43C Statutes of Limitation.

Section 205 of the Act (50 U.S.C. Appx. § 525) provides: "The period of military service shall not be included in computing any period now or hereafter to be limited by any law, regulation, or order for the bringing of any action or proceeding in any court, board, bureau, commission, department, or other agency of government by or against any person in military service or by or against his heirs, executors, administrators, or assigns, whether such cause of action or the right or privilege to institute such action or proceedings shall have accrued prior to or during the period of such service, nor shall any part of such period which occurs after the date of enactment of the Soldiers' and Sailors' Civil Relief Act Amendments of 1942 be included in computing any period now or hereafter provided by any law for the redemption of real property sold or forfeited to enforce any obligation, tax, or assessment." (As eff. 10-6-42.)

The period of military service is held to be excluded in determining the period limited by law for filing a suit on a mechanic's lien, as was held in Clark v. Mechanics' American Nat. Bank, 282 Fed 589 (1922).

These provisions are valid and they extend the period for bringing an action or proceeding under state statutes as well as under federal statutes. 36 ALR Fed 420.

16-43D Stay of Proceedings.

Section 201 of the Act (50 U.S.C. Appx. § 521) provides: "At any stage thereof any action or proceeding in any court in which a person in military service is involved, either as plaintiff or defendant, during the period of such service or within sixty days thereafter may, in the discretion of the court in which it is pending, on its own motion, and shall, on application to it by such person or some person on his behalf, be stayed as provided in this Act, unless, in the opinion of the court, the ability of plaintiff to prosecute the action or the defendant to conduct his defense is not materially affected by reason of his military service." (As eff. 10-17-40.)

Sections 203 and 204 of the Act (50 U.S.C. Appx. §§ 523 and 524) provide that the court may stay the action for the period of military service and three months thereafter, or any part thereof, subject to such terms as may be just, and may stay the execution of any judgment or attachment. (As eff. 10-17-40.)

16-43E Eviction.

Section 300 of the Act (50 U.S.C. Appx. § 530) provides that the court may stay eviction proceedings against dependents of a person in the armed forces for not longer than three months if the rent does not exceed $150 per month. (As eff. 3-3-66.)

16-43F Land Contracts.

Section 301 of the Act (50 U.S.C. Appx. § 531 as eff. 10-6-42) provides that a contract of purchase shall not be terminated nor possession be resumed except by action in court. Upon hearing the court may make such order as is equitable. 24 ALR2d 1074.

16-43G   Termination of Leases.

Section 304 of the Act (50 U.S.C. Appx. § 534) provides for termination by a serviceman of a lease in which he is lessee upon thirty days' notice. (As eff. 10-6-42.)

16-43H   Mortgages and Trust Deeds.

Section 206 of the Act (50 U.S.C. Appx. § 526) provides that interest is limited to six per centum, including all charges, when charged to a member of the armed forces on an obligation incurred by him prior to his entry into the service. (As eff. 10-6-42.)

Section 302 of the Act (50 U.S.C. Appx. § 532) provides that mortgages shall not be foreclosed or powers of sale exercised during the period of military service and not within three months thereafter upon obligations which originated prior to military service, unless upon such terms as the court shall deem equitable and shall previously order. (As eff. 6-23-52.)

16-43I   Termination of Act.

Notwithstanding Section 604 of the Act (50 U.S.C. Appx. § 584) it is provided by Section 14 of the Selective Service Act as amended September 27, 1950 (50 U.S.C. Appx. § 464) that the Soldiers' and Sailors' Civil Relief Act shall be applicable until repealed by subsequent act of Congress.

DIVISION 16-5:   TIME

SECTION 16-51:   COMPUTATION OF TIME

16-51A   Intention; Forfeiture.

The rule that fractions of a day are not generally considered in the legal computation of time is true only in a limited sense and, being a mere legal fiction, will yield to considerations of right and justice. Thrasher v. Kelly, 73 App 304, 55 NE2d 873, 28 OO 457, 40 Abs 309 (1943).

Further research: O Jur 2d, Time § 11.

LAW IN GENERAL

Courts construe a contractual provision as to time in accordance with the intention of the parties. The rules are applied so as to prevent a forfeiture if possible. Am Jur 2d, Time § 13.

16-51B   First Day and Last Day.

R.C. 1.14 provides: "The time within which an act is required by law to be done shall be computed by excluding the first and including the last day; except that when the last day falls on Sunday or a legal holiday, then the act may be done on the next succeeding day which is not Sunday or a legal holiday.

"When a public office in which an act, required by law, is to be performed is closed to the public for the entire day which constitutes the last day for doing such act or before its usual closing time on such day, then such act may be performed on the next succeeding day which is not a Sunday or a legal holiday as defined in this section.

"'Legal holiday' as used in this section means the following days:

"(A) The first day of January, known as New Year's day;

"(B) The third Monday in January, known as Martin Luther King day;

"(C) The third Monday in February, known as Washington-Lincoln day;

"(D) The day designated in the 'Act of September 18, 1975,' 89 Stat. 479, 5 U.S.C. 6103, as now or hereafter amended, for the commemoration of Memorial day;

"(E) The fourth day of July, known as Independence day;

"(F) The first Monday in September, known as Labor day;

"(G) The second Monday in October, known as Columbus day;

"(H) The eleventh day of November, known as Veterans' day;

"(I) The fourth Thursday in November, known as Thanksgiving day;

"(J) The twenty-fifth day of December, known as Christmas day;

"(K) Any day appointed and recommended by the governor of this state or the president of the United States as a holiday.

"If any day designated in this section as a legal holiday falls on Sunday, the next succeeding day is a legal holiday." (As eff. 3-14-85.)

Civil Rule 6(A) (time: computation) provides: "In computing any period of time prescribed or allowed by these rules, by the local rules of any court, by order of court, or by any applicable statute, the date of the act, event, or default from which the designated period of time begins to run shall not be included. The last day of the period so computed shall be included, unless it is a Saturday, a Sunday, or a legal holiday, in which even the period runs until the end of the next day which is not a Saturday, a Sunday, or a legal holiday. When the period of time prescribed or allowed is less than seven days, intermediate Saturdays, Sundays, and legal holidays shall be excluded in the computation.

"When a public office in which an act, required by law, rule, or order of court, is to be performed is closed to the public for the entire day which constitutes the last day for doing such an act, or before its usual closing time on such day, then such act may be performed on the next succeeding day which is not a Saturday, a Sunday, or a legal holiday." (As eff. 7-1-78.)

Where a statute requires that an act be performed a fixed number of days previous to a specified day, the last day should be excluded and the first day included in making the computation. State ex rel. Jones v. Board of Deputy State Supervisors & Inspectors, 93 OS 14, 112 NE 136, 13 OLR 394, 450, 60 WLB 419, 469 (1915).

The statute, R.C. 1.14, applies generally to all acts required or permitted by law to be done. Neiswander v. Brickner, 116 OS 249, 156 NE 138, 5 Abs 198, 25 OLR 278 (1927).

The statute, R.C. 1.14, applies to all computations of time except where the act to be done is *not less than* a fixed number of days before a day certain, or a fixed number of days after a day certain. Ohio Power Co. v. Davidson, 49 App 184, 195 NE 871, 2 OO 448, 19 Abs 35 (1934).

When the last day for filing in a public office falls on Saturday, the filing may be done on the following Monday. Van Meter v. Segal-Schadel Co., 5 OS2d 185, 214 NE2d 664, 34 OO2d 345 (1966).

Further research: O Jur 2d, Time § 15.

LAW IN GENERAL

The rule is that when time is computed from a certain day, the first day is excluded and the last day is included. The day on which the cause of action accrued is excluded from the period under statutes of limitation, according to the overwhelming weight of authority. 20 ALR2d 1249.

The rule that an infant becomes of age at the beginning of the day preceding the anniversary of his birth is an exception, in excluding one terminal day, to the general method of measuring time. 5 ALR2d 1143.

SECTION 16-52: SUNDAYS AND HOLIDAYS

16-52A   Rules.

See also statute at 16-51B.

Judicial acts performed on Sunday are not void. They may constitute an abuse of discretion so as to make the proceedings voidable and warrant a vacation thereof. State v. McElhinney, 88 App 431, 100 NE2d 273, 45 OO 225 (1950).

Further research: O Jur 2d, Sundays and Holidays § 2.

LAW IN GENERAL

Judicial acts performed on a Sunday are void at common law and are held invalid in most of the modern decisions. With that exception anything may be done on a Sunday or a holiday which may be done on any other day except as otherwise provided by statute. Holidays affect transactions only as set forth in the statutes establishing them and a judgment on such a day is generally valid. Am Jur 2d, Sundays and Holidays §§ 1, 3, 70, 72, 89; 85 ALR2d 595; CJS, Sunday § 41, CJS, Holidays § 1.

DIVISION 16-6:   PARTICULAR TYPES OF JUDGMENTS

SECTION 16-61:   DECLARATORY JUDGMENTS

16-61A   Generally.

R.C. 2721.02 provides: "Courts of record may declare rights, status, and other legal relations whether or not further relief is or could be claimed. No action or proceeding is open to objection on the ground that a declaratory judgment or decree is prayed for. The declaration may be either affirmative or negative in form and effect. Such declaration has the effect of a final judgment or decree." (As eff. 10-1-53.)

R.C. 2721.03 provides: "Any person interested under a deed, will, written contract, or other writing constituting a contract, or whose rights, status, or other legal relations are affected by a constitutional provision, statute, rule as defined in section 119.01 of the Revised Code, municipal ordinance, contract, or franchise, may have determined any question of construction or validity arising under such instrument, constitutional provision, statute, rule, ordinance, contract, or franchise and obtain a declaration of rights, status, or other legal relations thereunder.

"The testator of a will may have the validity of the will determined at any time during his lifetime pursuant to sections 2107.081 to 2107.085 of the Revised Code." (As eff. 1-1-79.)

R.C. 2721.04 provides: "A contract may be construed by a declaratory judgment either before or after there has been a breach thereof." (As eff. 10-1-53.)

R.C. 2721.05 provides: "Any person interested as or through an executor, administrator, trustee, guardian, or other fiduciary, creditor, devisee, legatee, heir, next of kin, or cestui que trust, in the administration of a trust, or of the estate of a decedent, an infant, lunatic, or insolvent, may have a declaration of rights or legal relations in respect thereto in any of the following cases:

"(A) To ascertain any class of creditors, devisees, legatees, heirs, next of kin, or others;

"(B) To direct the executors, administrators, trustees, or other fiduciaries to do or abstain from doing any particular act in their fiduciary capacity;

"(C) To determine any question arising in the administration of the estate or trust, including questions of construction of wills and other writings." (As eff. 10-1-53.)

Civil Rule 57 in part provides: "The existence of another adequate remedy does not preclude a judgment for declaratory relief in cases where it is appropriate." (As eff. 7-1-70.)

A court may refuse to render such a judgment or decree when no uncertainty or controversy would be terminated thereby. Walker v. Walker, 132 OS 137, 5 NE2d 405, 7 OO 237 (1936).

The jurisdiction to grant such a judgment is not limited by the terms of the statutes to those cases in which no alternative remedy is available either at law or in equity. Schaefer v. First Nat. Bank, 134 OS 511, 18 NE2d 263, 13 OO 129 (1938).

The act is applicable to petition for declaration of rights of parties after lease has expired and lessee has remained in possession. Coshocton Real Estate Co. v. Smith, 147 OS 45, 67 NE2d 904, 33 OO 241 (1946).

An owner is entitled to a declaratory judgment of rights in a claimed easement. Freiden v. Western Bank & Trust Co., 72 App 471, 50 NE2d 369, 27 OO 419, 38 Abs 241 (1943).

The power of a court to render a declaratory judgment by virtue of provisions of Uniform Declaratory Judgments Act does not empower the court to expand its jurisdiction over subject matter. Sherrets v. Tuscarawas Savings & Loan Co., 78 App 307, 70 NE2d 127, 34 OO 21 (1945).

Court should not entertain petition containing allegations out of which no cause of action could ever arise. Alf v. Hunsicker, 82 App 197, 80 NE2d 511, 37 OO 539, 51 Abs 50 (1947); Hammontree v. Hawley, 57 NE2d 319, 40 Abs 483 (App. 1943).

Further research: O Jur 3d, Declaratory Judgments, etc. § 1.

LAW IN GENERAL

Declaratory judgments are distinguished from other judgments in that they are not primarily for the purpose of obtaining some form of execution. They are for the purpose of adjudicating rights and legal relations without requiring prior acts which may violate legal obligations, so that delay or accrual of actual damages may be avoided by a party who is uncertain of his rights.

The authority for such judgments is statutory. Prior to such enactments the courts were accustomed to grant similar relief in actions to quiet title, to construe wills, and the like. Jurisdiction of courts is not expanded as to subject matter or otherwise changed except as expressly provided. Such statutes are primarily concerned with the adequacy of the remedy rather than with substantive rights. They are not designed to supplant other actions, but the existence of another adequate remedy does not oust the jurisdiction of the court.

Exercise of the jurisdiction is within the sound discretion of the court. Judgments will not be rendered when a mere advisory opinion is sought, when no actual controversy exists which could give rise to a cause of action, nor when the uncertainty would not be thereby terminated.

Declaratory judgment proceedings are frequently employed to determine status or property rights related thereto, and to construe and determine the validity of statutes, governmental regulations, wills, trusts, deeds, mortgages, leases, easements and contracts in general.

Am Jur 2d, Declaratory Judgments § 3.

SECTION 16-62: EJECTMENT; OCCUPYING CLAIMANTS

Cotenants, see Section 5-11.
Encroachments, see Section 3-11.
Ownership of improvements, see 13-11E.

16-62A Ejectment Generally.

R.C. 5303.03 provides: "In an action for the recovery of real property, it is sufficient if the plaintiff states in his petition that he has a legal estate therein and is entitled to the possession thereof, describing it with such certainty as to identify the property, and that the defendant unlawfully keeps him out of the possession. It is not necessary to state how the plaintiff's estate or ownership is derived." (As eff. 10-1-53.)

R.C. 5303.04 provides: "In an action for the recovery of real property, it is sufficient if in his answer the defendant denies generally the title alleged in the petition, or that he withholds the possession. If he denies the title only, possession by him shall be taken as admitted. When he does not defend for the whole premises, the answer shall describe the particular part for which defense is made. The defendant also may set forth in his answer other grounds of defense and counterclaim, as in any other form of action." (As eff. 10-1-53.)

R.C. 5303.05 provides: "In an action by a tenant in common of real property against a cotenant, the plaintiff must state, in addition to what is required in section 5303.03 of the Revised Code, that the defendant either denied the plaintiff's right, or did some act amounting to such denial." (As eff. 10-1-53.)

R.C. 5303.06 provides: "In an action for the recovery of real property, when the plaintiff shows a right to recover at the time the action was begun, but during its pendency his right has terminated, the verdict and judgment must be according to the fact, and the plaintiff may recover for the withholding of the property." (As eff. 10-1-53.)

A plaintiff in ejectment cannot recover on the weakness of defendant's title, but only on the strength of his own. Toledo, St. L. & Western Ry. v. Turney, 7 CC(NS) 370, 18 CD 110 (1904).

The jurisdiction of a court of equity cannot be invoked when the plaintiff has a plain, adequate remedy at law. If the defendant is in possession and claims title adverse to the plaintiff's title, then the plaintiff's remedy would be an action in ejectment to recover the lands, under R.C. 5303.03, in which action all questions of plaintiff's and defendant's titles, legal and equitable could be raised. Harlan v. Veidt, 6 App 45, 28 CC(NS) 401 (1915).

The legal defense is triable by jury and the equitable defense is triable by the court. Cossett v. Moore, 71 App 447, 49 NE2d 190, 26 OO 370, 38 Abs 96 (1942).

A question of title to real estate cannot be determined in an action for injunction, but must be determined in a court of law. Turnbull v. Xenia, 80 App 389, 69 NE2d 378, 36 OO 91, 47 Abs 482 (1946).

Pursuant to R.C. 5303.03 any question respecting title to land may be raised in an action in ejectment, and it is necessary that the plaintiff have a present legal title to such land. Horn v. Childers, 116 App 175, 187 NE2d 402, 22 OO2d 34 (1959).

A cause of action in ejectment is a separate and specific statutory remedy which is distinguished by statute and case law from the statutory remedy of forcible entry and detainer. A pending action for the latter remedy, which discloses a bona fide dispute involving the title, is not a bar to a subsequent action in ejectment. Bond v. Frost, 125 NE2d 379, 57 OO 360, 70 Abs 206 (C.P. 1955).

Further research: O Jur 3d, Ejectment, etc. §§ 1, 2.

LAW IN GENERAL

Ejectment is an action at law to recover possession and damages to the possession. The common-law procedure has been modified, or substitute action provided, in all states. Actions for the recovery of real property, for trespass to try title, and to determine adverse claims to real estate are in the nature of ejectment and are construed with reference to the rules in ejectment.

Title and ouster are the requisites to the right of action. The plaintiff must have a possessory title or a bona fide possession at the time of the ouster and also have the right to possession at the commencement of the action. He can recover only on the strength of his own title, not on the weakness of the defendant's. However, title by estoppel may be sufficient. Legal title in the plaintiff is ordinarily necessary. Equitable defenses are usually available either by express statutory provision or an account of the union of courts of law and of equity.

The ouster must be under claim or color of right; otherwise the entry is merely a trespass. A demand for possession is not ordinarily essential to the action unless there is privity between the parties. Damages are nominal unless proven. Damages for mesne profits or rental value can generally be recovered in the same action.

Am Jur 2d, Ejectment; CJS, Ejectment.

16-62B Recovery in Equity for Improvements.

If a vendor sells and conveys land by a correct description, but, by mutual mistake of the parties, without fraud on the part of the vendor, the vendee enters upon a wrong tract and makes improvement, he cannot sustain a bill in chancery to recover the value of his improvements. Shroll v. Klinker, 15 Ohio 152 (1846). Nor under the act for the relief of occupying claimants of lands. Waldron v. Woodcock, 15 Ohio 13 (1846).

"It is a familiar rule, which a court of equity always enforces, that if an owner of an estate stands by and suffers another, acting in good faith and without notice of his title, to place improvements thereon, which add permanent value to the estate, such improvements will constitute a lien thereon." Preston v. Brown, 35 OS 18, 28, 4 WLB 381 (1878).

Occupants who fail to set up a claim for improvements in an action by one claiming title paramount are barred by the adverse judgment in such action from thereafter recovering the value of their improvements. Raymond v. Ross, 40 OS 343, 11 WLB 60 (1883).

The owner of a lot, upon which another erects a house by mistake, will be required to elect whether he will permit removal of improvements, will pay for the improvements, or will accept compensation for a conveyance. Weingarten v. Hricka, 19 Abs 21 (App. 1934).

Even though not entitled to benefit of occupying claimants law, the occupying claimant will be entitled in equity to a lien for the increased value and taxes paid when the owner with notice remained silent. Sommers v. Gray, 31 Abs 26 (App. 1939).

LAW IN GENERAL

Courts of equity have general jurisdiction to grant relief to a person who has made permanent improvements on land in his possession in good faith under the mistaken belief that he was the owner. The true owner may be denied possession until he has paid compensation for the value of the improvement less the value of the use of the land. In some cases recovery has been allowed at the suit of the occupant. Recovery at law for the rents and profits is limited to the excess above the value of the improvements.

Estoppel may warrant equitable relief. Mistake may be under such circumstances as to justify the intervention of equity, especially in an action by the actual owner. Relief on the ground of mistake in the boundary is extended in some decisions to all instances of mutual mistake.

In proper cases, equity also may give the owner the option of compensating the occupant or receiving the value of the property without the improvement, may order a sale, may vest the title in common, or may charge the value of the improvement as a lien.

Am Law of Prop § 28.15; 57 ALR2d 263; Tiffany § 1565.

16-62C Occupying Claimants' Acts.

R.C. 5303.07 provides: "In an action for the recovery of real property the parties may avail themselves of the benefit of sections 5303.08 to 5303.17, inclusive, of the Revised Code." (As eff. 10-1-53.)

R.C. 5303.08 provides: "A person who, without fraud or collusion on his part, obtained title to and is in the quiet possession of lands or tenements, claiming to own them, shall not be evicted or turned out of possession by any person who sets up and proves an adverse and better title, until the occupying claimant, or his heirs, is paid the value of lasting improvements made by the occupying claimant on the land, or by the person under whom he holds, before the commencement of suit on the adverse claim by which such eviction may be effected, unless the occupying claimant refuses to pay to the party establishing a better title the value of the lands without such improvements, on demand by him or his heirs, when such occupying claimant holds:

"(A) Under a plain and connected title, in law or equity, derived from the records of a public office;

"(B) By deed, devise, descent, contract, bond, or agreement, from and under a person claiming a plain and connected title, in law or equity, derived from the records of a public office, or by deed authenticated and recorded;

"(C) Under sale on execution against a person claiming a plain and connected title, in law or equity, derived from the records of a public office, or by deed authenticated and recorded;

"(D) Under a sale for taxes authorized by the laws of this state;

"(E) Under a sale and conveyance made by executors, administrators, or guardians, or by any other person, in pursuance of an order or decree of court, where lands are directed to be sold." (As eff. 10-1-31.)

R.C. 5303.09 provides that an occupying claimant holding under a sale for taxes has sufficient title to demand the value of the improvements under section 5303.08. (As eff. 10-1-31.)

Occupying claimant is entitled to compensation for improvements made before his title commenced. Shaler v. Magin, 2 Ohio 235 (1826); Davis v. Powell, 13 Ohio 308 (1844).

The act extends to all cases where a party purchases in good faith and receives a deed, properly authenticated, which has been recorded, and under which he has held quiet possession and made valuable improvements, supposing himself to be the owner. Glick v. Gregg, 19 Ohio 57 (1850).

A person seeking the benefits of the occupying claimants law will not be presumed to know any defects or recitals that do not appear upon the muniments which are not necessary to establish his claim under that act. Thus, in a case like the present, he will not be presumed to know recitals in deeds prior to the deed to his grantor. Beardsley v. Chapman, 1 OS 118 (1853).

The provisions of the occupying claimants law are inapplicable in an action in equity to quiet title brought against one who has no other claim to the title than a deed from a third party who held no title of record at the time. Sommers v. Gray, 31 Abs 26 (App. 1939).

No allowance can be made under the statutes for improvements placed upon real estate by an occupying claimant if at the time the improvements were made the claimant knew that there were defects in the title under which he claimed. Berger v. Baker, 13 Abs 611 (App. 1933); Smith v. Vankirk, 76 NE2d 924, 49 Abs 372 (App. 1945).

Further research: O Jur 3d, Occupying Claimants §§ 1-3.

LAW IN GENERAL

Equitable and common-law actions have generally been supplanted by actions under occupying claimants acts, also known as betterment acts. They usually follow the equitable rules of making compensation to the occupant a condition of relief to the owner or of giving the owner the option of paying for the improvements or of receiving the value of the land without the improvements.

It is ordinarily required that the improvements had been made by an occupant in good faith under a possession which was adverse to the true owner and with color of title. Tenants, owners of life estates, licensees, trespassers and persons lacking the appearance of title do not come within the requirements of adverse possession and good faith. The authorities are not in accord as to the allowance for improvements made before color of title was acquired. The cases are also conflicting as to what circumstances of actual knowledge or constructive notice of a claim adverse to the occupant will constitute a lack of good faith.

Am Jur 2d, Improvements § 4; CJS, Improvements § 6.

Recovery by the occupant is limited to permanent improvements which increase the value of the land to the benefit of the owner. The measure of damages, both in equity and under the statutes, is the amount of the increased value of the property less the rental value of the land. Recovery is allowed for a wide variety of improvements. 24 ALR2d 11.

SECTION 16-63: EQUITABLE CONVERSION

16-63A Definition and Effect.

By equitable conversion is meant a change of property from real into personal or from personal into real, not actually taking place but presumed to exist only by construction or intendment of equity. Bonadio v. Bonadio, 30 NP(NS) 470 (C.P. 1933).

LAW IN GENERAL

Equitable conversion is the doctrine under which courts of equity consider land as money or money as land for the purpose of determining the interest of persons in certain property. The application of the doctrine may determine whether the property passes to the heir or to the administrator, whether certain assets are within a devise of land or a bequest of personalty, or whether dower attaches. Conversion may also be decisive in partition proceedings, in problems under the rule against perpetuities, and in questions of subjection to a judgment lien. Conversion does not affect the form of an action for the recovery of the property. Tiffany §§ 296, 299, 301.

Where there is a conflict of laws, the law of the state where the land is located governs whether or not the land has been converted to personalty. The law of the situs has also been applied in a few cases to disposition of property after determination of such conversion. 43 ALR2d 569.

16-63B Direction to Convert.

Reconversion, see 16-63J.

Where the direction is to sell "if necessary," a devisee may have partition if his share can be set off (subject to exercise of the power if necessary) without manifest injury to the others. Hoyt v. Day, 32 OS 101 (1877).

Where a particular estate in real property is created for life or a term of years, with directions that the property be sold on the termination of the particular estate and the proceeds distributed among certain named beneficiaries, the doctrine of equitable conversion obtains and the remainder will be treated as personal property, not as real estate. Planson v. Scott, 26 App 122, 158 NE 588, 5 Abs 388 (1927).

Where will directs executor to sell the real estate and bequeaths all the proceeds to his children, vests in children the naked legal title without right to partition (final account had not been filed). Hoffman v. Hoffman, 61 App 371, 22 NE2d 652, 15 OO 255, 29 Abs 345 (1939).

Further research: O Jur 3d, Conversion in Equity § 6.

LAW IN GENERAL

The doctrine is applied when the investment of money in land is directed, or when the sale of land is directed or necessarily implied, but the conversion has not actually taken place. Intent and equitable considerations govern the matter. A power to convert is not sufficient to constitute a conversion. An intention that there be a conversion must clearly appear. A discretion as to the time of sale does not prevent conversion. 124 ALR 1448; CJS, Conversion § 7; Tiffany § 297.

16-63C   Time of Conversion.

Where the will shows an intention that original form of property shall be changed, then conversion takes place, and if no contrary intention is apparent from the will, conversion takes effect from time of death of testator. Davison v. Hersman, 6 Abs 454 (App. 1928).

Further research: O Jur 3d, Conversion in Equity § 18.

LAW IN GENERAL

Conversion by will is effective from the death of the testator. Conversion by conveyance or contract is effective from the date of the execution and delivery. Both of these rules are subject to judicial interpretation of the intention of the testator or of the parties. The time of conversion is not deferred by a discretion as to the time of sale. The cases are not in harmony as to whether or not the conversion is postponed where the time of actual conversion is stated. CJS, Conversion §§ 12, 23; Tiffany § 300.

16-63D   Failure of Purpose; Surplus.

Where the purpose of the testator fails, equitable conversion does not occur and the property passes in its original form. Patton v. Patton, 39 OS 590, 10 WLB 450 (1883).

LAW IN GENERAL

Upon partial failure of the purpose of a conversion directed by a deed or contract, the grantor will take the surplus as converted even where the conversion has not actually occurred. If there is a complete failure of purpose, the grantor or his successor in interest takes the property in its original form. 144 ALR 1236; Tiffany § 304.

When the testator intended the conversion only for a certain purpose, the surplus, remaining after the purpose is accomplished, passes to the persons entitled to the property in its original character. However, although the surplus of land directed to be sold passes to the heirs as undisposed of, upon the death of an heir before possession his interest passes to his personal representative. Equitable conversion does not take place when the testator's intention is impossible of accomplishment or otherwise fails entirely, unless an intent clearly appears that conversion shall occur notwithstanding the failure. CJS, Conversion § 29; Tiffany § 302.

16-63E Incompetents; Trusts.

Reconversion, see 16-63J.

LAW IN GENERAL

Where necessary for the protection of incompetent persons or of beneficiaries of a trust, equity will regard property as retaining its original nature although it has actually been converted. Compensation for land of such persons appropriated under eminent domain is usually treated as land. Tiffany § 306.

16-63F Judicial Sales.

In order to work a conversion of land into money from the time of testator's death and prevent partition, there must be either (1) a positive direction to sell, (2) an absolute necessity to sell in order to execute the will, or (3) a blending of real and personal estate to create a fund which is bequeathed. Padley v. Jones, 20 App 203, 153 NE 185, 4 Abs 503 (1924).

LAW IN GENERAL

The surplus of the proceeds of a judicial sale usually goes to the persons who were entitled to the land. There is conversion as to matters happening after the proceeding is completed. Real property sold to pay debts is converted only to the extent necessary for that purpose. CJS, Conversion § 30.

The majority of the cases hold that equitable conversion of the realty into personalty dates from the judicial confirmation of the sale. 66 ALR2d 1266.

16-63G Contracts for Sale.

Interest of vendee under contract of purchase is equitable title to realty. Berndt v. Lusher, 40 App 172, 178 NE 14, 10 Abs 54 (1931). As long as contract remains in force. State ex rel. Morgan v. Stevenson, 39 App 335, 177 NE 247, 10 Abs 278, 616, 35 OLR 7 (1931).

The doctrine of equitable conversion does not apply to contracts for sale, by virtue of the statute, so as to constitute an ademption of a devise. Sells v. Needles, 69 NE2d 767, 34 OO 186, 47 Abs 427 (Prob. 1946).

Further research: O Jur 3d, Conversion in Equity § 10; Am Jur 2d, Equitable Conversion §§ 8, 11; CJS, Conversion § 9; Tiffany § 307.

16-63H Options.

The conversion of the realty into personalty will take place at the time of exercising the option to purchase contained in a perpetual lease and will not relate back to the time of the execution of the lease containing the option. Smith v. Loewenstein, 50 OS 346, 34 NE 159, 29 WLB 322, 355 (1893).

Where part of the leased land is appropriated for public use, the lease with an option to purchase is an interest in land and, when the option is later exercised, that interest, under the doctrine of equitable conversion, relates back to the original date of the lease and option. Twenty-three Tracts of Land, etc. v. United States, 177 F2d 967, 41 OO 137, 57 Abs 135 (1949); Cullen & Vaughn Co. v. Bender Co., 122 OS 82, 170 NE 633, 8 Abs 174, 31 OLR 308, 68 ALR 1332 (1930).

Further research: O Jur 3d, Conversion in Equity § 17.

LAW IN GENERAL

A majority of courts hold that the conversion does not relate back to the date of the option, and that the purchase price goes to the heir or devisee when an option is exercised after the death of the person granting the option. Land acquired by the exercise of an option after the death of the optionee generally passes to the executor or administrator. Am Jur 2d, Equitable Conversion §§ 12, 16; Am Law of Prop § 3.84; 172 ALR 438.

16-63I   Partnerships.

Uniform Partnership Act, see 4-28B.

16-63J   Reconversion; Election Against Conversion.

Where the purposes of a trust have been accomplished, the beneficiary may cause a reconversion by electing to take the land instead of the proceeds of a sale. Craig v. Jennings, 31 OS 84 (1876).

Where land is directed to be sold and proceeds paid to designated beneficiaries, they may elect to take the land itself and prevent the sale. Belle Center v. Board of Trustees, 99 OS 50, 122 NE 41, 16 OLR 395, 63 WLB 483 (1918).

Further research: O Jur 3d, Conversion in Equity § 19.

LAW IN GENERAL

Reconversion to the original character of the property will sometimes occur, as where a contract for sale is rescinded or is abandoned by the purchaser. Reconversion also takes place upon an election, before the actual conversion, to take the property in its existing character, if the trust purpose is not thereby defeated. Such election must be by all the owners of the beneficial interest, who must be sui juris. An intention to elect against conversion, as shown by a conveyance of the land for example, is sufficient to effect a reconversion. Authority to sell real estate for the purpose of division is terminated by a valid election, made before the sale, to take the real estate instead of the proceeds. Am Jur 2d, Equitable Conversion §§ 17, 20; 130 ALR 1379; CJS, Conversion § 51; Tiffany § 305.

SECTION 16-64: INJUNCTION

Decrees in equity, see also 16-11C.

16-64A Definition; Generally.

R.C. 2727.12 provides: "Upon being satisfied, by affidavit, of the breach of an injunction or restraining order, the court or judge who issued such injunction or order may issue an attachment against the guilty party who shall pay a fine of not more than two hundred dollars, for the use of the county, make immediate restitution to the party injured, and give further security to obey the injunction or restraining order. In default thereof, said party may be committed to close custody until he complies with such requirement, or is otherwise discharged." (As eff. 10-1-53.)

The jurisdiction of a court of equity cannot be invoked when the plaintiff has a plain, adequate remedy at law. The averments of the petition disclose a cause of action in ejectment. Harlan v. Veidt, 6 App 45, 28 CC(NS) 401 (1915).

Injunction is equitable in nature and subject to all the rules of courts of chancery. It is designed to guard against future injury. Cleveland v. Amalgamated Ass'n of Street Elec. Ry. & Motor Coach Employees, 84 App 43, 81 NE2d 310, 39 OO 93, 51 Abs 498 (1948).

LAW IN GENERAL

An injunction is an order, writ or process issued by a court of equity whereby a person is required to do or refrain from doing certain acts which are deemed inequitable. Failure to obey the injunction may be punished as contempt of court or may subject the disobeying party to the further order of the court. Am Jur 2d, Injunctions § 1; CJS, Injunctions § 2.

16-64B Persons Bound.

Civil Rule 65(C) (security) provides for a bond before a temporary restraining order or preliminary injunction is operative. (As eff. 7-1-70.)

Civil Rule 65(D) (form and scope of restraining order or injunction) provides for the form and for binding the parties, their officers, agents, servants, employees, attorneys and those persons in active concert or participation with them who receive actual notice of the order. (As eff. 7-1-70.)

A person not a party to an injunction suit may not be held guilty of contempt for violating the injunction unless he is shown to be identified with, or is an aider and abettor of, the party originally enjoined. Swetland v. Curry, 188 F2d 841, 45 OO 178, 61 Abs 377 (1951).

LAW IN GENERAL

Injunction is an equitable remedy and operates only in personam, not in rem. While the decree is enforceable against individuals and not against property, it is difficult to formulate a precise rule as to what persons are bound.

Parties to the suit, agents of the parties, persons represented by the parties, and all those in privity or acting in concert with the parties with bound from the time they have notice of the order. A decree may be enforced against any member of the class intended to be restrained who has notice. Persons without knowledge of the injunction are not bound although it purports to bind all persons. Am Jur 2d, Injunctions; CJS, Injunctions.

SECTION 16-65: QUIETING TITLE

16-65A Nature of Jurisdiction.

R.C. 5303.01 provides: "An action may be brought by a person in possession of real property, by himself or tenant, against any person who claims an interest therein adverse to him, for the purpose of determining such adverse interest. Such action may be brought also by a person out of possession, having, or claiming to have, an interest in remainder or reversion in real property, against any person who claims to have an interest therein, adverse to him, for the purpose of determining the interests of the parties therein.

"Whenever the state or any agency or political subdivision thereof has, or appears to have, an interest in real property adverse to the person in possession claiming the right thereto, the state or such agency or such political subdivision may be made a party in any action brought under this section.

"The clerk of the court shall cause to be recorded in the deed records of each county in which any part of the real property lies, a certified copy of the judgment or decree determining the interests of the parties. The usual fees of the clerk and recorder shall be taxed as part of the costs of the case." (As eff. 3-31-73.)

28 U.S.C. 2409(a) provides that quiet title actions, not based on adverse possession, may be brought in district courts against the United States. The statute does not apply to federal security interests, water rights, trust lands, restricted Indian lands nor to actions authorized by the enumerated statutes. The limitation of actions is twelve years. (As eff. 10-25-72.)

The judgment of the court is conclusive as to all questions within the issue, and which might have been litigated. Desnoyers v. Dennison, 19 CC 320, 10 CD 430 (1899).

Actions for quieting title have long been entertained by chancery, and have been held in this state to be equitable in character, and as such are appealable under our practice. Lust v. Farmers' Bank & Savings Co., 114 OS 312, 151 NE 189, 4 Abs 193, 24 OLR 312 (1926); W. C. McBride, Inc. v. Murphy, 111 OS 443, 145 NE 855, 3 Abs 4, 22 OLR 646 (1924).

"The present suit is simply an action to quiet title against a former decree of the same court in an action to quiet title ... while its decree was erroneous and subject to direct attack, it cannot now be collaterally attacked in this proceeding." Kinsinger v. Cummins, 42 App 468, 182 NE 524, 11 Abs 641 (1931).

Although the petition is indefinite in particulars and subject to motion to make certain, it states a good cause of action for quieting title. Long v. Olinger, 16 Abs 182 (App. 1933).

Title was properly quieted against a restrictive covenant in a deed where the neighborhood had so changed as to render enforcement inequitable. Olberding v. Smith, 34 NE2d 296, 34 Abs 84 (App. 1934).

Further research: O Jur 3d, Ejectment, etc. § 122.

LAW IN GENERAL

Jurisdiction to quiet title is inherent in courts of equity. A court of law is the proper forum for determination of disputed titles, and a court of equity will not assume jurisdiction unless some equitable ground is shown. Am Jur 2d, Quieting Title §§ 1, 2; CJS, Quieting Title § 10.

16-65B Future Interests.

Remainders and reversions, see also Section 2-24.

A party cannot maintain an action to quiet title against persons who claim no present or certain interest in the land. Collins v. Collins, 19 OS 468 (1869). But it is not necessary that the adverse claim of defendants should relate to or affect the right of present possession. Rhea v. Dick, 34 OS 420, 4 WLB 17, 57 (1878).

Title may be quieted against a claimed possibility of reverter where court finds that plaintiff has an indefeasible fee simple, although heirs of the grantor are not asserting that any act of forfeiture or any act creating a right of reversion has been committed. First New Jerusalem Church v. Singer, 68 App 119, 34 NE2d 1007, 22 OO 217, 33 Abs 518 (1941).

Until breach occurs, no right of reentry exists and the statute would start to run only upon the accrual of such right, a common example is a deed which provides that, upon violation of stated building and use restrictions, title shall revert to the grantor. No cause of action based upon the ground of adverse possession could exist until the statute had run its full course after violation occurred. So a decree quieting title upon any such ground would be worthless. William R. Kinney, 19 O. Bar 225.

No statute of limitations will run against dower as long as it is inchoate and therefore a court cannot, on a claim of adverse possession, quiet title against it. William R. Kinney, 19 O. Bar 225.

Further research: O Jur 3d, Ejectment, etc. §§ 211, 212.

LAW IN GENERAL

Claims to possibilities of reverter, to rights of reentry and to other contingent or future interests are adverse claims against which title may be quieted under the statutes, provided such claims are invalid. If such claims are valid, the statutes of limitations do not begin to run until a cause of action accrues. For example, title cannot be quieted against a valid possibility of reverter on the ground of adverse possession until the period has run after the happening of the contingency. CJS, Quieting Title § 39; Simes and Smith § 1741.

16-65C   Cloud on Title.

Where devisee is in possession of the lands devised, she may maintain an action to remove a cloud upon the title, although it involves the construction of the will. Darlington v. Compton, 20 CC 242, 11 CD 97 (1900).
Further research: O Jur 3d, Ejectment, etc. § 149.

LAW IN GENERAL

A cloud on the title which equity will remove is an invalid interest which appears to be valid and which casts a doubt on the record title, or is a claim which reasonably causes a fear that it may be asserted to the injury of the true owner. CJS, Quieting Title § 12.

16-65D   Title and Possession of Plaintiff.

Decree quieting title under which no possession was taken will not interrupt running of limitations as to a strip in possession of adjoining owner. Rosenstihl v. Cherry, 114 OS 401, 151 NE 642, 4 Abs 224, 24 OLR 352 (1926).
Where a person not in possession, in an action to quiet title, alleges that he is the owner in fee simple, the cause of action is not within the jurisdiction of a court of equity. Lichtenberger v. Milligan, 63 App 107, 25 NE2d 357, 16 OO 382 (1939).
An action may be brought by a person in possession of real estate against anyone that holds adverse interest to him without further characterization of title set forth in the petition. Jones v. Van Deboe Hager Co., 29 Abs 385 (App. 1939).
If neither party is an actual possession, constructive possession of the plaintiff will support the action, and a plaintiff as successor in title to the holders of a tax deed had prima facie title and constructive possession. Haban v. Suburban Home Mortgage Co., 57 NE2d 97, 40 Abs 78 (App. 1943).
Further research: O Jur 3d, Ejectment, etc. § 7.

LAW IN GENERAL

The plaintiff must have actual or constructive possession in addition to a title, as a general rule. However, in some cases a ground of equitable jurisdiction may be sufficient to support the right of action although the plaintiff is out of possession and does have the legal title. Am Jur 2d, Quieting Title § 36; CJS, Quieting Title § 27.

16-65E   Who May Maintain Action.

Where a will directs an executor to sell the real estate, he may maintain an action to quiet title and it is not necessary that the heirs of the testator be parties thereto. Mitchell v. Bridgeport, 8 App 51, 30 CC(NS) 358 (1917).
A trustee holding the legal title may maintain an action to quiet title. Dickerson v. Curtin, 80 App 486, 76 NE2d 619, 36 OO 249, 49 Abs 632 (1947).

631

A third party who is not relying upon any title sought to be established in the action will not be permitted to interplead and have his independent claim of title adjudicated therein. Dexter v. Taylor, 95 NE2d 790, 43 OO 236, 58 Abs 532 (C.P. 1950).

Further research: O Jur 3d, Ejectment, etc. § 167.

LAW IN GENERAL

It has been held that an action to quiet title may be maintained by an encumbrancer, cotenant, vendor, vendee, lessor, or a grantor, and may be maintained by the owner of an easement, standing timber, mineral right, water right, dower interest, future interest, or naked legal title. CJS, Quieting Title § 16.

SECTION 16-66: REFORMATION

Cancellation of instruments, see Section 8-51.

16-66A Definition; Generally.

R.C. 2719.01 to 2719.06 provide procedure whereby the courts of common pleas may give effect to instruments and proceedings according to the intention of the parties. (As eff. 10-1-53.)

Reformation cannot be granted to supply formalities required for the execution of an instrument. R.C. 2719.01 does not validate a defectively executed lease. Delfino v. Paul Davies Chevrolet, Inc., 2 OS2d 282, 209 NE2d 194, 31 OO2d 557 (1965).

Reformation is the remedy afforded, by courts possessing equitable jurisdiction, to the parties and the privies of parties to written instruments which import a legal obligation, to reform or rectify such instruments whenever they fail, through fraud or mutual mistake, to express the real agreement or intention of the parties. Greenfield v. Aetna Casualty & Surety Co., 75 App 122, 61 NE2d 226, 30 OO 427 (1944).

LAW IN GENERAL

Reformation is the remedy by which a written instrument importing a legal obligation is reformed by courts of equity to express the real agreement of the parties when the instrument fails in such expression because of mistake or inequitable conduct. Am Jur 2d, Reformation of Instruments; CJS, Reformation of Instruments.

16-66B Nature of Mistake.

Cancellation for mistake, see Section 8-52.

Where an instrument, by a mistake of the parties as to the legal effect of the terms used, fails to carry out their intention, relief may be afforded in equity.

A mistake of law may be corrected in equity. Evants v. Strode, 11 Ohio 480 (1842).

Where reformation of an instrument is sought on the ground of mistake, it is necessary that the mistake be mutual, which must be proved by clear and convincing evidence. Castle v. Daniels, 16 App3d 209, 475 NE2d 149 (1984).

When the deed cannot be reformed to conform to the intention of either party, the facts are ground for rescission, not reformation. Stewart v. Gordon, 60 OS 170, 53 NE 797, 41 WLB 287, 333 (1899).

No relief will be granted in the absence of clear and convincing evidence that a mistake of fact was made and that such mistake was mutual. Bellish v. C. I. T. Corp., 142 OS 36, 50 NE2d 147, 26 OO 234 (1943).

Mistake, warranting reformation of instrument must be mutual in absence of fraud, bad faith, or inequitable conduct. Mulby v. Dunham, 29 App 51, 162 NE 718, 6 Abs 171 (1927).

Where the parties make and accept a deed in fee simple with a contemporaneous agreement that such deed was to be regarded as a deed for a life estate only, there is no mutual mistake sufficiently shown to require reformation of such deed. Saum v. Orrill, 42 NE2d 925, 36 Abs 111 (App. 1942).

Equity favors carrying out the intent of the contracting parties and whenever a writing fails to conform such intent, equity will reform it to make it conform, unless there is some overruling equity. The deed will be reformed in this suit. Hartman v. Tillett, 86 App 20, 89 NE2d 613, 40 OO 456 (1948).

Further research: O Jur 3d, Cancellation and Reformation of Instruments § 73.

LAW IN GENERAL

The mistake must be mutual to warrant reformation against a person who paid a consideration, unless fraud or inequitable conduct is involved. Many decisions declare that reformation will not be decreed for a mistake of law only. However, circumstances are very frequently found, in the discretion of the court, to justify exercise of the equitable jurisdiction. Am Jur 2d, Reformation of Instruments § 13; CJS, Reformation of Instruments § 25.

16-66C   Inequitable Conduct.

There are numerous cases allowing the verbal stipulations to be proved and enforced and the written agreement to be reformed on the ground that the refusal to abide by the whole agreement constitutes a fraud which equity ought to prohibit. Thacker v. Matthews, 70 App 314, 43 NE2d 108, 25 OO 63, 36 Abs 145 (1942).

Further research: O Jur 3d, Cancellation and Reformation of Instruments § 72.

LAW IN GENERAL

Unconscionable conduct of a party authorizes relief on the ground of fraud. Misrepresentation of a fact, although not willful, upon which the other party relied to his injury may be sufficient ground for reformation. Am Jur 2d, Reformation of Instruments § 24; CJS, Reformation of Instruments § 29.

16-66D Effective Date.

The mortgage, as reformed, is not merged in the former decree of foreclosure; and as the original mistake of describing land not owned by the mortgagor infects all the subsequent proceedings, they are nugatory. Davenport v. Sovil, 6 OS 459 (1856).

A defective mortgage when reformed will not affect the lien of a judgment rendered between the dates of the execution and reformation. Van Thorniley v. Peters, 26 OS 471 (1875). For priority the judgments must attach prior to commencement of the suit to reform. Caldwell Bldg. & Loan Ass'n v. Bigley, 2 CC(NS) 297, 15 CD 431 (1903).

A mortgage, as between the mortgagee and a subsequent vendee who has taken the property, bona fide in payment of a preexisting debt, will take effect only from the time of correction. Clements v. Doerner, 40 OS 632, 11 WLB 204 (1884).

LAW IN GENERAL

Upon reformation the instrument is effective as reformed from the time of its original execution, except as the intervening rights of third persons. Am Jur 2d, Reformation of Instruments § 127; CJS, Reformation of Instruments § 92.

16-66E Consideration to Grantor.

A mistake of including land, for which no consideration was paid nor intended to be paid, can be corrected in equity even after confirmation and deed. Stites v. Wiedner, 35 OS 555, 5 WLB 276 (1880).

If conveyance represents gift as distinguished from sale, donor is entitled to reformation regardless of whether mistake was shared by donee. Where conveyance is not based on valuable or meritorious consideration, relief will not be given against donor. Lyon v. Balthis, 24 App 57, 155 NE 815, 5 Abs 796 (1926).

Further research: O Jur 3d, Cancellation and Reformation of Instruments § 69.

LAW IN GENERAL

Voluntary instruments executed without consideration will not, as a rule, be reformed as against the grantor. Exceptions to the rule are made in favor of charities and on equitable grounds, as when the grantee has made improvements has conveyed to a bona fide purchaser. Am Jur 2d, Reformation of Instruments § 42; CJS, Reformation of Instruments § 10.

16-66F Action by and against Whom.

A mistake in the attempted description will be corrected as against judgment creditors and purchasers with notice of the mistake. Strang v. Beach, 11 OS 283 (1860).

An action to reform on the ground of mistake may be commenced within ten years after the cause of action accrues. The time when the statute begins to run is not postponed to the discovery of the mistake, as it is to the discovery of the fraud. Bryant v. Swetland, 48 OS 194, 27 NE 100, 25 WLB 124, 257 (1891).

The plaintiff is entitled to a decree reforming the defectively executed lease to conform to the intention of the parties. Anthony Carlin Co. v. Burrows Bros. Co., 54 App 202, 6 NE2d 761, 7 OO 180, 22 Abs 495 (1936).

Possession of land is notice to a subsequent purchaser of the remaining portion of the tract so as to preclude his being an innocent purchaser, and the first grantee may have reformation of his deed as against the subsequent grantee. Klar v. Hoopingarner, 62 App 102, 23 NE2d 326, 15 OO 450 (1939).

Further research: O Jur 3d, Cancellation and Reformation of Instruments § 85.

LAW IN GENERAL

The action may generally be maintained by or against the original parties, or persons in privity with them. However, a decree will not be granted to the prejudice of bona fide purchasers, lien holders for a present consideration without notice, or other third parties whose rights intervene. 79 ALR2d 1186.

SECTION 16-67: SUBROGATION

16-67A Definition; Nature.

In Ohio the doctrine of subrogation is applied for the relief of one who in the discharge of his own liability pays an obligation upon which another is liable where circumstances of fraud or mistake of fact exist, provided such subrogation will not add to the burdens of the creditor. In re Braker, 127 F2d 652, 23 OO 483 (1942).

Any person, other than a volunteer, having an interest in property subject to encumbrance which may defeat or impair his title has a right to relieve the property by payment thereof and is thereby entitled to be subrogated to the rights of the encumbrances against the property. Jones v. Remley, 74 NE2d 109, 48 Abs 609 (App. 1947).

Further research: O Jur 3d, Contribution, Indemnity, and Subrogation §§ 1-3.

LAW IN GENERAL

Subrogation is the equitable doctrine under which one person is substituted for another with reference to a lawful claim or right. It usually arises by operation of law when a person having a liability or right in the matter pays a debt owed by another in such manner that he becomes entitled to the security for the discharged debt. The doctrine operates as an equitable assignment to transfer the debt and all incidental rights. "Conventional" subrogation is distinguished from "legal" subrogation by being based on an agreement of the parties. It does not arise unless with the express agreement of the debtor. Am Jur 2d, Subrogation § 90; Am Law of Prop § 16.145; Tiffany § 1506.

16-67B   Relief Granted When.

R.C. 2329.46 provides: "Upon the sale of property on execution, if the title of the purchaser is invalid by reason of a defect in the proceedings, he may be subrogated to the right of the creditor against the debtor to the extent of the money paid and applied to the debtor's benefit, and, to the same extent, may have a lien on the property sold, as against all persons, except bona fide purchasers without notice. This section does not require the creditor to refund the purchase money by reason of the invalidity of such sales.

"This section applies to sales by order of court, sales by executors, administrators, guardians, and assignees, and to sales for taxes." (As eff. 10-1-53.)

Where the purchase money is applied in satisfaction of the mortgage debt, equity will keep the mortgage security alive for the benefit of the purchaser. Joyce v. Dauntz, 55 OS 538, 45 NE 900, 36 WLB 345, 37 WLB 69 (1896).

Where creditor commenced suit before the subrogation transaction and obtained a judgment lien after the transaction and cancellation of the prior mortgage, the subrogee will have a lien prior to the judgment. Miller v. Scott, 23 App 50, 154 NE 358, 2 Abs 330, 21 OLR 593 (1924).

Where a person through misrepresentation or oversight, is induced to loan money to pay off existing mortgage liens on the assurance that he should have a first mortgage lien, such person is entitled to be subrogated to the canceled mortgages, where it places no greater burden on the intervening judgment lien holder. Union Trust Co. v. Lessovitz, 51 App 69, 199 NE 614, 4 OO 499, 10 Abs 171 (1931); Priddy v. Schmidt, 21 Abs 90 (App. 1935).

New mortgage has priority by subrogation, over second mortgage previously recorded, to the extent proceeds of such new mortgage were used to pay off the first mortgage. Harter Bank v. Cooper, 11 Abs 300, 35 OLR 657 (App. 1931).

In the absence of expressed intent and where the lien holder acts in ignorance of an intervening lien, it will be presumed that he did not intend to release his prior lien (although canceled of record) and equity will reinstate his priority. Union County Savings & Loan Ass'n v. King, 18 Abs 519 (App. 1934); Canton Morris Plan Bank v. Most, 44 App 180, 184 NE 765, 14 Abs 65 (1932).

A purchaser of property who takes it subject to a mortgage, but does not assume or agree to pay it, then later does pay it, is entitled to be protected against the subsequent judgment lien holder. Ehrman v. Bayer, 41 NE2d 900, 35 Abs 483 (App. 1940).

It would seem that one acting in good faith in making his payment, and under a reasonable belief that it is necessary for his protection, is entitled to subrogation, even though it turns out that he had no interest to protect. Reed v. Ramey, 82 App 171, 80 NE2d 250, 37 OO 529, 50 Abs 596 (1947).

In the absence of some prejudice resulting to the junior lienor from the change of owners, the rights of subrogation of the purchaser who paid the senior lien are not changed by the fact that the junior lien was of record and the purchaser was negligent in not discovering the existence of such lien. Hill v. Hurless, 4 O Supp 1, 5 OO 399 (C.P. 1936).

Generally, a person having an interest in an estate, who makes payment of debts due by decedent's estate becomes a creditor of the estate and is subrogated to the rights of the creditors or of the executor or administrator. In re Outhwaite's Estate, 94 NE2d 122, 42 OO 442, 58 Abs 97 (Prob. 1949).

When a mortgagee satisfies and cancels its mortgage after filing a later mortgage to itself, the mortgagee loses priority over intervening liens of which it was unaware either because of failure to recheck the title at the time of the cancellation or by reason of errors if the title had been rechecked. State of Ohio, Dept. of Taxation v. Jones, 61 OS2d 99, 399 NE2d 1215, 15 OO3d 132 (1980).

Further research: O Jur 3d, Contribution, Indemnity, and Subrogation §§ 2, 57.

LAW IN GENERAL

The doctrine is applied when a cotenant pays a debt so as to permit him to enforce contribution, when payment is required from a grantor who conveyed the land expressly subject to the mortgage, when the payor is obliged as surety to pay, when a junior lienor pays a prior lien, when the circumstances give rise to an equitable lien as where a lender pays an encumbrance with an agreement that he shall have a first lien, when one makes payment in the mistaken belief that he has an interest to protect, and when a person purchases at an invalid judicial sale. Mistake and fraud are common grounds for exercise of the jurisdiction. The relief may be granted even though the lien to which subrogation is allowed has been canceled of record. A lessee is generally entitled to the benefits of the doctrine. By the weight of authority, relief against intervening interests may be granted to a person who advances the money to discharge a prior lien in reliance upon getting a first lien, and to a grantee who assumes or takes subject to a first mortgage and discharges it without actual notice of subsequent liens. Am Jur 2d, Subrogation §§ 93, 103; Am Law of Prop §§ 16.146, 16.149; 1 ALR2d 286; CJS, Subrogation §§ 9, 38; Powell § 455; Tiffany §§ 1507, 1509.

16-67C Relief Denied When.

An action to be subrogated will be barred unless brought within ten years from the time the cause of action accrued. Zuellig v. Hemerlie, 60 OS 27, 53 NE 447, 41 WLB 206, 272 (1899); Neal v. Nash, 23 OS 483 (1872).

The equitable right of subrogation will not prevail against intervening bona fide purchasers without notice, or those occupying a like position. Amick v. Woodworth, 58 OS 86, 50 NE 437, 39 WLB 172, 338 (1898).

A purchaser under suit of a judgment creditor to marshal liens is not subrogated to the rights of a mortgagee where the mortgagee had not filed answer and cross-petition at the time the judgment is rendered and sale made. Jewett v. Feldheiser, 68 OS 523, 67 NE 1072, 1 OLR 136, 509 48 WLB 566, 688 (1903). (Obiter in syllabus.)

The doctrine of subrogation will not be applied to prefer one creditor over another where an inequitable result will be accomplished thereby. W. E. Wright Co. v. Parshall, 101 OS 517, 130 NE 942, 18 OLR 32, 156, 65 WLB 210, 317 (1920).

A mortgagee who cancels a mortgage which is paid from a new mortgage to the mortgagee, cannot assert subrogation to his original position against intervening mechanics lienors when the facts show no fraud or mistake and when the work was apparent before the mortgage was recorded. Zimpher v. Schwartz, 64 App 7, 27 NE2d 499, 17 OO 308, 31 Abs 84 (1940); Canton Morris Plan Bank v. Most, 44 App 180, 184 NE 765, 14 Abs 65 (1932).

In the absence of agreement or waiver of the creditor's rights, subrogation will not be permitted except upon payment of the entire claim of the creditor. Lauric v. Hockman, 6 Misc 223, 217 NE2d 721, 35 OO2d 389 (C.P. 1965).

LAW IN GENERAL

A mere stranger who voluntarily pays off a lien will be denied subrogation. A person who is primarily liable for the debt is not entitled to the relief. When part of the original debt remains unpaid, subrogation will ordinarily not be decreed in the absence of express agreement by the debtor. Subrogation is not allowed if it would prejudice the rights of intervening lien holders or of bona fide purchasers. The doctrine does not operate when enforcement would be inequitable for any reason. Am Law of Prop §§ 16.148, 16.151; CJS, Subrogation §§ 8, 10; Powell § 453; Tiffany § 1508.

SECTION 16-68: TRESPASS AND NUISANCE

Light and view, see Section 3-14.

16-68A Trespass.

One who invades the rights of adjoining owner, either by throwing missiles or by concussion, is guilty of trespass or a wrongful act in the nature of trespass, and may be enjoined. Heilman v. France Stone Co., 20 App 261, 151 NE 798, 3 Abs 243 (1925).

If an injury to real property is permanent, the measure of damages is the difference in values before and after the injury. If an injury is susceptible of repair, the measure of damages is the reasonable cost of restoration of the property plus a reasonable compensation for the loss of use, unless such cost of restoration exceeds the difference in values before and after the injury, in which case the difference in values becomes the measure. Cincinnati v. Wright, 2 NP(NS) 53, 14 OD 600 (1903); Upson Coal & Mining Co. v. Williams, 7 CC(NS) 293, 18 CD 388 (1905), affd. 75 OS 644, 80 NE 1134, 4 OLR 674, 52 WLB 84 (1907).

A "trespasser" may be defined as one who unauthorizedly goes upon the private premises of another without invitation or inducement, express or implied, but purely for his own purposes or convenience; and where no mutuality of interest exists between him and the owner or occupant. A trespasser is liable if his trespass was the proximate cause of the damage. Allstate Fire Ins. Co. v. Singler, 14 OS2d 27, 236 NE2d 79, 43 OO2d 43 (1968).

Exceptions are made to the general rule limiting recovery to the difference in market value. Where trees are destroyed by trespassers, the owner may be awarded as damages the fair cost of restoring his land to a reasonable approximation of its former condition. Thatcher v. Lane Constr. Co., 21 App2d 41, 254 NE2d 703, 50 OO2d 95 (1970).

Where a trespasser removes trees which were a woodland mix not particularly unique to the parcel and not rare or ornamental, the cost of restoration is not the proper measure of damages. Damages should be based on the difference in fair market value before and after removal of the trees. Kapcsos v. Hammond, 13 App3d 140, 468 NE2d 325 (1983).

Further research: O Jur 2d, Trespass § 2.

LAW IN GENERAL

Trespass to realty is an unlawful act committed with some degree of force to the damage of another person's property. Injury to the possession is the gist of a trespass. The intent with which the act is done is not material. Damages are the ordinary recovery in an action of trespass. CJS, Trespass § 105.

Trespass is also defined as an entry or encroachment which violates a possessory right in land. The right of the possessor of the surface extends underground and into the overlying air space. An intended invasion is actionable even though damages are nominal. Repeated or continuous invasion may constitute a nuisance. Entry incidental to an interest in the land or to recover chattels wrongfully held thereon is privileged. A social need may also justify intrusions on another's land. Am Law of Prop §§ 28.1, 28.19.

Injunction is a proper remedy to restrain repeated or continuing trespasses where the remedy at law is inadequate because of the nature of the injury, or because of the necessity of a multiplicity of actions to obtain redress at law. 60 ALR2d 316.

16-68B Nuisance Generally.

What amount of annoyance or inconvenience will constitute a nuisance, being a question of degree, dependent on varying circumstances, cannot be precisely defined. Columbus Gas Light & Coke Co. v. Freeland, 12 OS 392

(1861); Weishahn v. Kemper, 32 App 313, 167 NE 468, 6 Abs 467 (1928); Ohio Stock Food Co. v. Gintling, 22 App 82, 153 NE 341, 5 Abs 263 (1926).

Further research: O Jur 3d, Nuisances § 1.

LAW IN GENERAL

A nuisance has been defined as anything wrongfully done or permitted which injures or annoys another in the use and enjoyment of his legal rights. It is distinguished from trespass in that it ordinarily consists of the use of a person's own property, while the physical invasion of another's property is a trespass. To be actionable as a nuisance, the interference must be unreasonable and do substantial harm. A nuisance affecting the public in general is a public or common nuisance as distinguished from a private nuisance. What amount of annoyance or inconvenience will constitute a nuisance, being a question of degree and dependent on varying circumstances, cannot be precisely defined. Certain acts or conditions are frequently declared nuisances by statute. Am Law of Prop § 28.24; Powell § 704; Tiffany § 717.

16-68C Prescriptive Right.

Easements by prescription, see Section 2-12.

As an independent cause of action is constantly arising in the continuing public nuisance, the statute necessarily cannot affect the right of removal. Little Miami R.R. v. Commissioners, 31 OS 338, 3 WLB 84 (1877).

An action may be brought until the continued trespass or nuisance by adverse use ripens into and becomes a prescriptive right. Louisville Brick & Tile Co. v. Calmelat, 6 App 435, 28 CC(NS) 356, 30 CD 159 (1917); Little Miami R.R. v. Hambleton, 40 OS 496, 11 WLB 91 (1884).

Where the nuisance is a continuous one, the statute of limitation does not begin to run until it is discovered. McCrary v. Knight, 97 NE2d 559, 69 Abs 353 (C.P. 1951).

The right to maintain a private nuisance may be acquired by prescription. Prijatel v. Sifco Industries, Inc., 47 Misc 31, 353 NE2d 923, 1 OO3d 322 (1974).

LAW IN GENERAL

A right to maintain a public nuisance cannot be acquired by prescription. It is generally held that a prescriptive right to maintain a private nuisance may be acquired as against an individual although the conduct also constitutes a public nuisance. Am Jur 2d, Nuisances § 225; CJS, Nuisances § 90.

Where the injury is not a kind for which an action in trespass could not have been brought at common law, it has usually been held that a limitation statute using the word "trespass" is inapplicable. 15 ALR3d 1228.

16-68D Persons Liable for Nuisance.

Where the owner of real estate willfully suffers a nuisance to be created, or to be continued by another, on or adjacent to his premises, in prosecution of a business for his benefit, when he has the power to prevent or abate the nuisance, he would be liable for injury resulting therefrom to a third person. Clark v. Fry, 8 OS 358 (1858).

Further research: O Jur 3d, Nuisances § 16.

LAW IN GENERAL

Ownership of land in itself does not support liability, although a person may be liable without being negligent. Persons who create or continue a nuisance are liable for injuries to which their acts contributed. Those who join in the creation or maintenance may be jointly and severally liable. A person who permits the continuance of a nuisance existing before his ownership is not liable in damages until after he has been requested to remove it. Am Law of Prop § 28.30; Tiffany § 715.

16-68E   Remedies for Nuisance.

The operation of a stone quarry in a residential area, which causes serious distress in the every day living of nearby home owners, is a nuisance and will be enjoined. Adams v. Snouffer, 88 App 79, 87 NE2d 484, 44 OO 17, 55 Abs 14 (1949).

A court of equity will not enjoin something as a nuisance where the injury is not irreparable and there exists an adequate remedy at law. Harden Chevrolet Co. v. Pickaway Grain Co., 194 NE2d 177, 27 OO2d 144, 92 Abs 161 (C.P. 1961).

Private individuals have no right to an injunction to abate a public nuisance, that is, one which annoys a whole neighborhood or any considerable number of persons. Clabaugh v. Harris, 27 Misc 153, 273 NE2d 923, 56 OO2d 407 (C.P. 1971).

Further research: O Jur 3d, Nuisances § 25.

LAW IN GENERAL

The usual remedies are actions for damages or injunction, or both. A suit to enjoin a nuisance is generally held to be local in nature and to be properly brought in the county where the nuisance is located. A person suffering from a private nuisance may abate it, even by entering upon the land of another, if he can do so without causing a breach of the peace. A public nuisance must usually be abated by a proceeding brought in the name of the state. Am Law of Prop § 28.31; 7 ALR2d 481.

Contributory negligence is not a defense, as a general rule, in a nuisance action. However, where the gist of the action was defendant's negligence, rather than interference with the proper use of plaintiff's land, most courts have held that contributory negligence was a good defense. 73 ALR2d 1378.

16-68F   Measure of Damages from Nuisance.

Damages by trespassers, see 16-68A.

When the nuisance and injury are not of a permanent character, the measure of damage will not be limited to the decrease in rental value but will include inconvenience and discomfort suffered, the recovery being limited to actual damages. Mansfield v. Hunt, 19 CC 488, 10 CD 567 (1900); Graham & Wagner, Inc. v. Ridge, 41 App 288, 179 NE 693, 11 Abs 518 (1931).

The measure of damages for an injury to real property which is permanent in character is the difference in value immediately before and immediately after the injury. Klein v. Garrison, 91 App 418, 108 NE2d 381, 49 OO 25 (1951).

Further research: O Jur 3d, Nuisances § 66.

LAW IN GENERAL

The rule for measure of damages from a permanent nuisance is the depreciation in the market value of the property injured. The measure of damages from a temporary nuisance is the diminution in the rental of use value. However, recovery is sometimes awarded for diminution in the value of the use by a permanent nuisance. Am Law of Prop §§ 28.14, 28.33; 10 ALR2d 669.

16-68G Particular Nuisances and Trespasses.

A person making use of high power explosives will be liable for damages resulting therefrom, irrespective of the question of negligence. Louden v. Cincinnati, 90 OS 144, 106 NE 970, 11 OLR 518, 59 WLB 102 (1914).

LAW IN GENERAL

The manufacture, transportation or storage of explosives is often held to constitute a nuisance. The person responsible for such a nuisance is generally liable for all damages, irrespective of any negligence. In some cases, injury resulting from vibration or concussion caused by an explosion is held to create a liability on the ground of trespass; in other cases, negligence is held to be necessary when the only damage is from concussion. A person who causes a blast, throwing matter on the land of another, is generally liable as a trespasser. Am Jur 2d, Explosions, etc. §§ 32, 33, 41, 90; 20 ALR2d 1372; CJS, Explosives § 4.

Injunctions have been allowed or damages awarded in a considerable number of cases on the basis of quarries, gravel pits and the like as nuisances. 47 ALR2d 490.

The landowner may be found liable under the doctrine of attractive nuisance as formulated in Restatement of Torts, Section 339, when a trespassing child is injured by sliding on his land. The doctrine has been held inapplicable under some special circumstances. 19 ALR3d 184.

SECTION 16-69: ESTOPPEL; OTHER TYPES

After-acquired title, see Section 8-34.
Fiduciaries and agents, see 8-34I.

16-69A Estoppel Generally.

Estoppel by deed, see Section 8-34.

An estoppel is defined as a bar which precludes a person from denying the truth of a fact which has in contemplation of law become settled by the acts and proceedings of judicial officers or by the act of the party himself. Sanborn v. Sanborn, 106 OS 641, 140 NE 407, 1 Abs 102, 134, 880, 20 OLR 501, 530 (1922).

Further research: O Jur 3d, Estoppel, etc. § 81.

LAW IN GENERAL

Estoppel is a bar which precludes a person from denying the truth, or asserting the contrary, of a fact which has in contemplation of law become settled because of his own previous acts or because of judicial or legislative action. CJS, Estoppel § 1.

Estoppels are classified as (a) estoppel by record, which precludes denial of matters appearing on a judicial or legislative record, (b) estoppel by deed, and (c) equitable estoppel, which is also called estoppel in pais, estoppel by conduct and estoppel by representation. CJS, Estoppel §§ 2, 4.

16-69B Equitable Estoppel.

In order to create an equitable estoppel, the representations (whether consisting of words, acts, or omissions) must have been believed by the party claiming the benefit thereof and it must be shown that he relied thereon and was influenced and misled thereby. Joseph Turk Mfg. Co. v. Singer Steel Co., 111 F Supp 485, 52 OO 67, 67 Abs 38 (1951).

If one man knowingly, though he does it passively by looking on, suffers another to purchase and expend money on land, under an erroneous opinion of the title, without making known his claim, he shall not afterward be permitted to exercise his legal right against such person. Buckingham v. Smith, 10 Ohio 288 (1840).

To work an estoppel in pais, and forfeit title, the acts and declarations of the owner must, in general, be willful, that is, with knowledge of his rights, or with intention to deceive the other party. McAfferty v. Conover, 7 OS 99 (1857); Pennsylvania Co. v. Platt, 47 OS 366, 25 NE 1028, 23 WLB 385, 24 WLB 477 (1890).

Declarations made in good faith may be made under such circumstances as to operate by way of estoppel. Beardsley v. Foot, 14 OS 414 (1863).

Estoppel applies only to parties and privies, and does not extend to stranger to transaction. Lubric Oil Co. v. Drawe, 26 App 478, 160 NE 93, 6 Abs 404 (1927).

Subsequent grantees through a succession in the chain of title stand in the same position as the original grantee and are in privity with him. Bailey v. Stedronsky, 57 App 265, 13 NE2d 588, 10 OO 451, 26 Abs 274 (1936).

The doctrine is administered in the same manner, and in conformity with the same rules, by the courts of both law and equity. West v. Cleveland Ry., 58 NE2d 799, 41 Abs 554 (App. 1944).

LAW IN GENERAL

Equitable estoppel arises when a person is precluded by his conduct or representation from asserting rights against another person. The doctrine is ordinarily applied at law as well as in equity, being known as equitable estoppel because it arose in courts of equity. Equitable estoppel concludes the truth in order to prevent fraud. It operates as a shield, not as a sword, so that it prevails over other rules only to the extent necessary to accomplish justice.

Title is said to pass by equitable estoppel only when a clear case of fraudulent intent is established. The estoppel is insufficient for a marketable title as not being of record, unless established by decree.

An estoppel may operate against another estoppel, known as an estoppel on an estoppel, so that the two will neutralize each other, as when a person is barred from asserting a right which arose by virtue of an estoppel.

Parties to the transaction and their privies only are bound. Application of the doctrine against the state or its political subdivisions is usually refused. Strangers are not entitled to any of the benefits arising from an estoppel. Am Jur 2d, Estoppel and Waiver § 26; CJS, Estoppel § 59; Tiffany § 1235.

The doctrine is often applied where the owner remains silent, to the damage of a purchaser of the land, under circumstances establishing an obligation to speak. If the owner's interest is of record or if he is possession of the land, an estoppel will not arise unless his conduct amounts to active misrepresentation. 50 ALR 668.

The principles of equitable estoppel apply to mortgagees so that a mortgagee is generally estopped to contest his mortgagor's title so long as such title has not terminated. 11 ALR2d 1397.

16-69C   Ratification.

If an agent is not authorized in the manner and form required by statute to execute a lease for real property, knowledge of his principal that the tenant is in possession and paying rent is not in and of itself sufficient to work either a ratification or estoppel. Lithograph Bldg. Co. v. Watt, 96 OS 74, 117 NE 25, 15 OLR 82, 62 WLB 152 (1917).

The share of an infant not made a party in partition will remain undivested unless, upon reaching majority, such partition proceeding has been ratified. A ratification cannot be partial. Ratification means that one under no disability voluntarily adopts and gives sanction to some unauthorized act or defective proceeding which without his sanction would not be binding upon him. Hampshire County Trust Co. v. Stevenson, 114 OS 1, 150 NE 726, 4 Abs 73, 74, 24 OLR 135 (1926).

Where the deceased, during her lifetime, accepted the fruits of a tax foreclosure sale by accepting that part of the sale proceeds which exceeded taxes and court costs, the deceased's heirs, who were in the identical legal position of the deceased, were estopped to question the proceedings in the foreclosure actions. Clark v. Reissig, 164 F Supp 823, 7 OO2d 174, 80 Abs 295 (1958).

LAW IN GENERAL

Ratification validates an earlier act and requires an intention to approve. An ineffective instrument, which is not wholly void, may be made effective through the operation of the doctrine of ratification or of estoppel, as by joining in the subsequent execution of an instrument recognizing the former one. Such ineffective instrument takes effect from its date, except as to innocent third parties, when the facts bring either or both of the doctrines into operation. This result may occur through estoppel by deed as when a subsequent deed expressly corrects the former one. 7 ALR2d 294; CJS, Deeds § 66.

16-69D   Laches.

Delay in asserting a right does not of itself constitute laches, and in order to successfully invoke the equitable doctrine of laches it must be shown that the person for whose benefit the doctrine will operate has been materially prejudiced by the delay of the person asserting his claim. Smith v. Smith, 168 OS 447, 156 NE2d 113, 7 OO2d 276, 70 ALR2d 1241 (1959).

In an equitable action by an heir to set aside a sale of real estate by an administrator to his wife, the defense of laches is applicable to such heir who, with full knowledge of the sale of subsequent events, delays the filing of his action for seventeen years. Christman v. Christman, 171 OS 152, 168 NE2d 153, 12 OO2d 172 (1960).

Laches does not operate to preclude the opening or vacating of a void judgment for the reason that no amount of acquiescence can make it valid. Morgridge v. Converse, 72 NE2d 295, 48 Abs 272 (App. 1947), revd. on other grounds 150 OS 239, 81 NE2d 112, 37 OO 486 (1948).

Before granting summary judgment against a claimant, the court should permit the claimant to have a reasonable time for discovery of the facts. Tucker v. Webb Corp., 4 OS3d 121, 447 NE2d 100 (1983).

LAW IN GENERAL

Laches is undue delay in asserting a right. It may be sufficient to operate as an estoppel but is ordinarily not relied upon to establish marketability of title because the delay may be excusable for reasons not of record.

16-69E   Summary Judgment.

Civil Rule 56 provides that a party to a pending action may move, with or without supporting affidavits, for summary judgment upon all or part of the claim. Such a judgment shall be rendered forthwith if the instruments filed in the action show that there is no genuine issue as to any material fact and that the moving party is entitled to judgment as a matter of law. Such a judgment shall not be rendered unless reasonable minds can reach only a conclusion adverse to the party against whom the motion is made, such party being entitled to have the evidence or stipulation construed most strongly in his favor. (As eff. 7-1-76.)

The essence of a motion for summary judgment is that there is no bona fide factual issue between the parties, and one of the parties is entitled to judgment as a matter of law. Hagesfeld v. Campbell, 170 NE2d 514, 85 Abs 61 (App. 1960).

Before rendering a summary judgment, the court must be satisfied not only that there is no issue as to a material fact, but also that the moving party is entitled to a judgment as a matter of law. Washington County Farm Bureau Co-op. Ass'n v. B. & O. R.R., 31 App2d 84, 286 NE2d 287, 60 OO2d 174 (1972).

Further research: O Jur 2d, Summary Judgment § 2.

DIVISION 16-7: PROCESS AND ITS SERVICE

SECTION 16-71: GENERALLY

Associations, see 4-29A.
Corporations, see 4-11B.
Persons under disability, see 15-11I and 15-12H.
United States, see 17-23A.

16-71A Nature; Necessity.

Where there is no service of process; a court is without jurisdiction to render judgment and if a judgment is rendered it is void ab initio. Shaman v. Roberts, 87 App 328, 94 NE2d 630, 43 OO 50, 57 Abs 502 (1950).

Further research: O Jur 3d, Process § 2.

LAW IN GENERAL

The purpose of process is to give notice to the party addressed of a legal proceeding against him. Summons is the most common form. Process is regulated by civil rules prescribed by the Supreme Court of Ohio. Notice or waiver of notice is essential to the jurisdiction of the court. The exceptions are proceedings in rem which are very uncommon and in which no persons are made defendants. Knowledge of the suit is not sufficient, a proceeding being void as to a defendant who has not been served with process as provided by law and who has not waived service. Jurisdiction of the plaintiff is obtained by his commencement of the suit. Summons is not issued merely by preparation by the clerk of court; delivery by appropriate service of process being ordinarily required. Am Jur 2d, Process §§ 1, 2; CJS, Process §§ 1, 2.

16-71B   Presumptions.

Attack on service, see 16-13D.
Conclusiveness of return, see also 16-74B.

LAW IN GENERAL

Proper service is usually presumed in litigation concerning it, as to the judgments of a court of general jurisdiction, if the record is silent or does not show otherwise. However, silence of the record is ordinarily not sufficient for an acceptable title. Am Jur 2d, Process § 170; CJS, Process § 98.

16-71C   Amended Complaint; Cross-claim.

Divorce, see 14-32D.
Pleadings generally, see 17-21K.

Civil Rule 5(B) provides that service subsequent to the original complaint shall be upon an attorney of record unless service upon the party himself is ordered by the court. (As eff. 7-1-71.)

A judgment rendered for a new cause of action not embodied in the original pleading is wholly void in the absence of a new appearance or of new process. Brawner v. Welfare Finance Corp., 104 NE2d 203, 61 Abs 329 (App. 1950).

LAW IN GENERAL

New summons upon a cross-petition or upon an amendment to the petition is not essential to jurisdiction to grant the relief asked therein unless the cause of action is substantially changed or unless new relief is asked. Am Jur 2d, Process § 35; CJS, Process § 4.

16-71D   Fraud, Trickery or Force.

Service procured by fraud or equivalent misconduct is voidable, not void. The misconduct raises a question not of jurisdiction but of propriety of exercising jurisdiction. Albright v. Boyd, 85 OS 34, 96 NE 711, 9 OLR 367, 56 WLB 374 (1911); Pilcher v. Graham, 18 CC 5, 9 CD 825 (1899).

Personal service effected by fraud or trickery, or by forcibly entering a dwelling, will be set aside upon proper application to the court.

Further research: O Jur 3d, Process §§ 53, 54.

16-71E   Exemption from Service.

Collateral attack, see 16-13D.

Although a nonresident litigant or witness or other person may be immune from service of process, the judgment rendered is not thereby subject to collateral attack. The privilege is waived if not asserted promptly and properly.

Further research: O Jur 3d, Process § 36.

16-71F Personal and Constructive Service in General.

Personal judgment against a nonresident, see 16-77B.
Statutes on return, see 16-74A.

Personal service is to be made by delivering a copy of the summons, with the endorsements thereon, to the defendant personally. Sears v. Weimer, 143 OS 312, 55 NE2d 413, 28 OO 270 (1944). The service in question was by publication.

A summons left with a room clerk of a hotel, for a defendant who was at the time a resident of the hotel, does not constitute "residence service" as required by law or comply with the requirement of "leaving a copy thereof at his address." Ruckert v. Matil Realty Co., 40 NE2d 688, 35 Abs 324 (App. 1941).

A summons left at the usual place of residence of the defendant and not served personally upon him does not constitute personal service. Lyon v. Toriello, 116 NE2d 19, 66 Abs 100 (App. 1952).

Residence or domicile of person entering the armed forces remains the same throughout the period of his service unless he voluntarily selects a new domicile. Glassman v. Glassman, 75 App 47, 60 NE2d 716, 30 OO 352, 42 Abs 385 (1944); Commercial Motor Freight Lines Co. v. Monson, 17 O Supp 99, 32 OO 58 (C.P. 1945).

Whether residence service be called "substituted service" or what not, it is actual service and is just as efficacious as "personal service" so called. Charles C. White, "Service of Process and Related Subjects," a pamphlet published by Land Title Guarantee and Trust Company.

Further research: O Jur 3d, Process § 18.

LAW IN GENERAL

Service of process is divided into the two classes of (a) personal service, such as handing a copy to the defendant or his authorized agent, and (b) constructive service, also known as substituted service, such as publishing notice. Am Jur 2d, Process § 46; CJS, Process § 25.

Personal service ordinarily means delivery to the defendant in person. Under some statutes, leaving at the residence, or similar service as distinguished from publication, is equivalent to personal service, at least as to residents of the state. Am Jur 2d, Process § 41; 172 ALR 521; CJS, Process § 26.

Although constructive service may be the equivalent of personal service for some purposes, personal service or waiver is always essential to a personal judgment against a nonresident. By the weight of authority, a personal judgment based on service by publication cannot be obtained against even a resident of the state. Am Jur 2d, Process § 44; CJS, Process § 57.

Constructive service on nonresidents of the state is valid as to their property within the state. Nonresidents may be served personally when found within the state. Am Jur 2d, Process § 75; Am Law of Prop § 18.60.

Service of process must be personal in the absence of statutory authority for another method. Substituted service can be resorted to only when personal service is impracticable, and has been held insufficient when the defendant could have been found within the state. Am Jur 2d, Process § 66.

Strict compliance with the statutory procedure, ordinarily including the prior filing of an affidavit, is required for the validity of constructive service. Am Jur 2d, Process §§ 65, 68; CJS, Process § 43.

SECTION 16-72: WAIVER OR APPEARANCE

16-72A Generally.

Authority of attorney, see also 17-21K.

Civil Rule 4(D) provides: "Service of summons may be waived in writing by any person entitled thereto under Rule 4.2 who is at least eighteen years of age and not under disability." (As eff. 7-1-75). A minor sixteen years of age or older may be served alone but service cannot be waived by or for him. Prior to July 1, 1975 a person under twenty-one years of age could not waive service.

The absence of process is immaterial where the defendant files a demurrer. Evans v. Iles, 7 OS 234 (1857).

Where a party applied, by her attorney, and obtained leave to answer, she effected her appearance as a party to the suit. Brundage v. Biggs, 25 OS 652 (1874).

The appearance of a defendant in court for the sole purpose of objecting by motion, to the jurisdiction of the court over his person, is not a general appearance or a waiver. Smith v. Hoover, 39 OS 249, 10 WLB 164 (1883).

Where a motion is made by an attorney employed by the defendant for a dismissal of such cause "for the reason that the court in which the action was filed has no jurisdiction of the subject-matter involved," such motion enters a general appearance of the person of the defendant. Klein v. Lust, 110 OS 197, 143 NE 527, 2 Abs 275, 22 OLR 73 (1924).

Defendant was a proper party and having entered its appearance by answer it will be deemed to have waived any jurisdictional question of service of summons. Michigan Automobile Ins. Exchange v. Vaughan, 19 App 149, 2 Abs 55 (1923).

Where the answer is verified and filed by an attorney employed by the defendant, the filing of such pleading amounts to a waiver of irregularities in the service of summons and enters a general appearance of the person of the defendant in the action. First Federal Savings & Loan Assn. v. Shorts, 82 NE2d 426, 52 Abs 110 (App. 1947).

A voluntary general appearance of a party defendant is equivalent to service of summons and, where jurisdiction of the person is acquired, it cannot be withdrawn. Fayette County Agricultural Society v. Scott, 96 App 6, 121 NE2d 118, 54 OO 148 (1953).

LAW IN GENERAL

A general appearance by a defendant in the action confers jurisdiction of his person, and constitutes a waiver of summons or of any defects in the process.

The authority of an attorney to enter appearance for a defendant is presumed but may be rebutted. Am Jur 2d, Process §§ 161-163; Am Law of Prop § 18.60.

16-72B Acknowledgment of Service.

Civil Rule 4.1 on methods of service is shown at 16-74A and 16-76A. No provision is found regarding acknowledgment of service since 6-30-70.

LAW IN GENERAL

An acknowledgment of service within the territorial jurisdiction is equivalent to actual personal service. Outside the territorial jurisdiction of the court, by the weight of authority, an acknowledgment or acceptance of service is not effective as personal service. However, its terms may be such as to constitute a waiver or appearance. CJS, Process § 38.

SECTION 16-73: FORM AND CONTENTS OF PROCESS

16-73A Generally.

Civil Rule 4(B) (summons: form: copy of complaint) specifies the form of the summons and provides that a copy of the complaint shall be attached to each summons. (As eff. 7-1-73.)

Civil Rule 4.6(A) (limits of effective service) provides that all process may be served anywhere in this state. (As eff. 7-1-70.)

R.C. 311.07 requires the sheriff in any Ohio county to execute process issued from another state. (As eff. 9-3-86.)

The court may order a defective summons amended, without requiring such amended summons to be served, if it be shown that the party served will not be prejudiced thereby. State ex rel. Heck v. Sucher, 77 App 257, 65 NE2d 268, 32 OO 578 (1946).

When a summons is served on a defendant he is called upon to examine its total content and where the nature of the relief sought was not stated in the body of the summons but was endorsed on the back thereof, the summons was valid and it was prejudicial error to quash service of the summons for failure to state "the nature of the relief sought" as required by the former statute. Baldine v. Klee, 14 App2d 181, 237 NE2d 905, 43 OO2d 391 (1968), reversing 10 Misc 203, 224 NE2d 544, 39 OO2d 295 (C.P. 1965).

LAW IN GENERAL

Process which is irregular but in substantial compliance with the statute is voidable only; it may be amended and will confer jurisdiction unless directly attacked. When the process does not substantially comply with the statute it cannot be amended but the defect may be waived unless the form of process is prohibited. Am Jur 2d, Process § 7; CJS, Process § 114.

SECTION 16-74: RETURN AND ITS CONCLUSIVENESS

16-74A Definition; Statutes.

Corporations and associations, see 4-11B and 4-29A.
Incompetents, see 15-11I and 15-12H.
Personal and constructive service in general, see 16-71F.
United States, see 17-23A.

R.C. 311.22 provides: "The court or judge may, for good cause, appoint a person to serve a particular process or order, and such person shall have the same power to execute such process or order which the sheriff has. Such person may be appointed on the motion of the party who obtains the process or order, and the return must be verified by affidavit. He shall be entitled to the fees allowed to the sheriff for similar services." (As eff. 10-1-53.)

Civil Rule 4.1, in the introductory paragraph, provides: "All methods of service within this state, except service by publication as provided in Rule 4.4(A) are described herein. Methods of out-of-state service and for service in a foreign country are described in Rule 4.3 and Rule 4.5."

Civil Rule 4.1(1) (service by certified mail) is quoted, along with the pertinent Standard of Title Examination in 16-76A. See also Civil Rules 4.6(C), (D) quoted, below, in this section.

Civil Rule 4.1(2) (personal service) provides: "When the plaintiff files a written request with the clerk for personal service, service of process shall be made by that method.

"When the process issued from the supreme court, a court of appeals, a court of common pleas or a county court is to be served personally, the clerk of the court shall deliver the process and sufficient copies of the process and complaint, or other document to be served, to the sheriff of the county in which the party to be served resides or may be found. When process issues from the municipal court, delivery shall be to the bailiff of the court for service on all defendants who reside or may be found within the county or counties in which that court has territorial jurisdiction and to the sheriff of any other county in this state for service upon a defendant who resides in or may be found in that other county. In the alternative, process issuing from any of these courts may be delivered by the clerk to any person not less than eighteen years of age, who is not a party and who has been designated by order of the court to make service of process. Such person serving process shall locate the person to be served and shall tender a copy of the process and accompanying documents to the person to be served. When the copy of the process has been served, the person serving process shall endorse that fact on the process and return it to the clerk who shall make the appropriate entry on the appearance docket.

"When the person serving process is unable to serve a copy of the process within twenty-eight days, he shall endorse that fact and the reasons therefor on the process and return the process and copies to the clerk who shall make the appropriate entry on the appearance docket. In the event of failure of service, the clerk shall follow the notification procedure set forth in subsection

(1) of this rule. Failure to make service within the twenty-eight day period and failure to make proof of service do not affect the validity of the service." (As eff. 7-1-70.)

Civil Rule 4.1(3) (residence service) provides that service shall be effected, upon written request to the clerk, "by leaving a copy of the process and the complaint, or other document to be served, at the usual place of residence of the person to be served with some person of suitable age and discretion residing therein." The issuance and return shall be in the manner of personal service. The provisions upon failure to serve are as in the case of personal service. (As eff. 7-1-70.)

Civil Rule 4.2 (who may be served) provides: "Service of process, except service by publication as provided in Rule 4.4(A), pursuant to Rule 4 through Rule 4.6 shall be made as follows:

"(1) Upon an **individual**, other than a person under sixteen years of age or an incompetent person, by serving the individual;

"(2) Upon a person **under sixteen years** of age by serving either his guardian or any one of the following persons with whom he lives or resides: father, mother, or the individual having the care of such person; or by serving such person if he neither has a guardian nor lives or resides with a parent or a person having his care;

"(3) Upon an **incompetent** person by serving either the incompetent's guardian or the person designated in subdivision (5) of this rule, but if no guardian has been appointed and the incompetent is not under confinement or commitment, by serving the incompetent;

"(4) Upon an individual, **confined to a penal institution** of this state, by serving the individual, except that when the individual to be served is a person under sixteen years of age, the provisions of subdivision (2) of this rule shall be applicable;

"(5) Upon an **incompetent person who is confined** in any institution for the mentally ill or mentally deficient or committed by order of court to the custody of some other institution or person by serving the superintendent or similar official of the institution to which the incompetent is confined or committed or the person to whose custody the incompetent is committed;

"(6) Upon a **corporation** either domestic or foreign: by serving the agent authorized by appointment or by law to receive service of process; or by serving the corporation by certified mail at any of its usual places of business; or by serving an officer or a managing or general agent of the corporation;

"(7) Upon a **partnership,** a limited partnership, or a limited partnership association by serving the entity by certified mail at any of its usual places of business or by serving a partner, limited partner, or manager or member;

"(8) Upon an **unincorporated association** by serving it in its entity name by certified mail at any of its usual places of business or by serving an officer of the unincorporated association;

"(9) Upon a **professional association** by serving the association in its corporate name by certified mail at the place where the corporate offices are maintained or by serving a shareholder;

"(10) Upon this **state** or any one of its departments, offices and institutions as defined in Section 121.01(C), Revised Code, by serving the officer responsible for the administration of the department, office or institution or by serving the attorney general of this state;

"(11) Upon a **county** or upon any of its offices, agencies, districts, departments, institutions or administrative units, by serving the officer responsible for the administration of the office, agency, district, department, institution or unit or by serving the prosecuting attorney of the county;

"(12) Upon a **township** by serving one or more of the township trustees or the township clerk or by serving the prosecuting attorney of the county in which the township is located;

"(13) Upon a **municipal corporation** or upon any of its offices, departments, agencies, authorities, institutions or administrative units by serving the officer responsible for the administration of the office, department, agency, authority, institution or unit or by serving the city solicitor or comparable legal officer;

"(14) Upon **any governmental entity** not mentioned above by serving the person, officer, group or body responsible for the administration of that entity or by serving the appropriate legal officer, if any, representing the entity. Service upon any person who is a member of the 'group' or 'body' responsible for the administration of the entity shall be sufficient." (As eff. 7-1-71.)

Although service upon a person sixteen years of age or over may be upon him only, a defendant under twenty-one years of age must be represented in the action by his guardian or guardian ad litem except in an action for divorce, annulment or alimony if he is eighteen years of age or older. Civil Rule 4.2 governs service of summons in probate proceedings.

Civil Rule 4.6(C) (service refused) provides: "If service of process is refused, and the certified mail envelope is returned with an endorsement showing such refusal, or the return of the person serving process states that service of process has been refused, the clerk shall forthwith notify, by mail, the attorney of record or if there is no attorney of record, the party at whose instance process was issued. If the attorney, or serving party, after notification by the clerk, files with the clerk a written request for ordinary mail service, the clerk shall send by ordinary mail a copy of the summons and complaint or other document to be served to the defendant at the address set forth in the caption, or at the address set forth in written instructions furnished to the clerk. The mailing shall be evidenced by a certificate of mailing which shall be completed and filed by the clerk. Answer day shall be twenty-eight days after the date of mailing as evidenced by the certificate of mailing. The clerk shall endorse this answer date upon the summons which is sent by ordinary mail. Service shall be deemed complete when the fact of mailing is entered of record. Failure to claim certified mail service is not refusal of service within the meaning of this subdivision." (As eff. 7-1-71.)

Civil Rule 4.6(D) (service unclaimed) provides: "If a certified mail envelope is returned with an endorsement showing that the envelope was unclaimed, the clerk shall forthwith notify, by mail, the attorney of record or if there is no attorney of record, the party at whose instance process was issued. If the attorney, or serving party, after notification by the clerk, files with the clerk a written request for ordinary mail service, the clerk shall send by ordinary mail a copy of the summons and complaint or other document to be served to the defendant at the address set forth in the caption, or at the address set forth in written instructions furnished to the clerk. The mailing shall be evidenced by a certificate of mailing which shall be completed and filed by the clerk. Answer day shall be twenty-eight days after the date of mailing as evidenced by the certificate of mailing. The clerk shall endorse this answer date upon the summons which is sent by ordinary mail. Service shall be deemed complete when the fact of mailing is entered of record, provided that the ordinary mail envelope is not returned by the postal authorities with an endorsement showing failure of delivery. If the ordinary mail envelope is returned undelivered, the clerk shall forthwith notify the attorney, or serving party, by mail." (As eff. 7-1-71.)

It is necessary that the authority of the person appointed by the sheriff be endorsed upon the writ. Barry v. Hovey, 30 OS 344, 2 WLB 154 (1876).

A return is a written statement certifying the acts done concerning service of the process.

Further research: O Jur 3d, Process § 113.

16-74B   Conclusiveness.

Collateral attack, see Section 16-13.

When a return of service is regular on its face, there is a presumption in favor of valid service which stands until overcome by proof showing the contrary. Nickerson v. Nickerson, 85 App 372, 87 NE2d 915, 40 OO 241, 54 Abs 445 (1949).

Where process against a defendant appears on the face of the record to be regular, he may, nevertheless, show that it is defective. Where the process appears to be irregular on the face of the record, it may be shown that no defect, irregularity or deviation from statutory particulars has, in fact, occurred. Krabill v. Gibbs, 14 OS2d 1, 235 NE2d 514, 43 OO2d 1 (1968).

A motion to vacate a judgment on the ground that the attempted service of summons was not sufficient to obtain jurisdiction over the person of the defendant may be considered at any time. Ohio Casualty Ins. Co. v. Reese, 24 Misc 34, 259 NE2d 183, 52 OO2d 361 (Mun. Ct. 1970).

Service of process may be made at an individual business address pursuant to Civil Rule 4.1(1), but such service must comport with the requirements of due process. Where a person is served at a business address where he does not maintain an office, it does not comport with due process. Akron-Canton Regional Airport Authority v. Swinehart, 62 OS2d 403, 406 NE2d 811, 16 OO3d 436 (1980).

The judgment of a court of general jurisdiction will usually not be set aside on collateral attack where the record is silent as to service, especially if there is a finding by the court of due service. However, where there is a complete failure of actual service the courts often consider an attack to be in the nature of a direct attack; thus, where there is actually no service the court sometimes finds a lack of jurisdiction even when the attack is technically collateral. Although an officer is presumed to have performed his duties according to law, neither this presumption nor a general finding of regularity by the court will overcome the effect of defective service appearing on the record.

Further research: O Jur 3d, Process § 116.

16-74C   Amendment.

Civil Rule 4.6(B) provides that the court may at any time allow amendment of any process or proof of service. (As eff. 7-1-70.)

A court has authority to order the return amended in accordance with the facts either before or at any time after judgment. Paulin v. Sparrow, 91 OS 279, 110 NE 528, 12 OLR 509, 574, 60 WLB 56, 77 (1915). But not to the prejudice of third persons. Barry v. Hovey, 30 OS 344, 2 WLB 154 (1876).

Further research: O Jur 3d, Process § 14.

LAW IN GENERAL

The fact of service, not the return, gives jurisdiction. The court may permit the officer who made the return to amend it at any time to conform to the facts, if intervening rights are not thereby prejudiced. An amendment relates back to the time of the original return except as to the interests of third persons. Am Jur 2d, Process § 172; CJS, Process § 116.

16-74D   Service After Return Day.

See also Civil Rules 4.1(2) and 4.1(3) at 16-74A.

Although filed after return day, the sheriff's return is competent evidence and sufficient to show, in the absence of evidence to the contrary, that the defendant was legally and lawfully served with summons. Rhodes v. Valley Greyhound Lines, 98 App 187, 128 NE2d 824, 57 OO 232 (1954).

Service of summons on the day after it should have been returned does not render the service void but only voidable. Kunzelmann v. Duval, 61 App 360, 22 NE2d 632, 14 OO 519, 29 Abs 200 (1939).

SECTION 16-75:   SERVICE BY PUBLICATION

Divorce and alimony, see 14-31D and 14-32B.

16-75A   Generally.

Constructive service generally, see 16-71F.

R.C. 2703.14 provides: "Service may be made by publication in any of the following cases:

"(A) In an action for the recovery of real property or of an estate or interest therein, when the defendant is not a resident of this state or his place of residence cannot be ascertained;

"(B) In an action for the partition of real property, when the defendant is not a resident of this state or his place of residence cannot be ascertained;

"(C) In an action to foreclose a mortgage or to enforce a lien or other encumbrance or charge on real property, when the defendant is not a resident of this state or his place of residence cannot be ascertained;

"(D) In an action to compel the specific performance of a contract for the sale of real property, when the defendant is not a resident of this state or his place of residence cannot be ascertained;

"(E) In an action to establish or set aside a will, when the defendant is not a resident of this state or his place of residence cannot be ascertained;

"(F) In an action by an executor, administrator, guardian, or trustee seeking the direction of the court respecting the trust or property to be administered and the rights of the parties in interest, when the defendant is not a resident of this state or his place of residence cannot be ascertained;

"(G) In an action in which it is sought by a provisional remedy to take or to appropriate in any way property of the defendant, when the defendant is not a resident of this state or is a foreign corporation or his place of residence cannot be ascertained;

"(H) In an action against a corporation organized under the laws of this state, which has failed to elect officers or to appoint an agent upon whom service of summons can be made, and which has no place of doing business in this state;

"(I) In an action which relates to or the subject of which is real or personal property in this state, when the defendant has or claims a lien thereon, or an actual or contingent interest therein, or the relief demanded consists wholly or partly in excluding him from any interest therein, and such defendant is not a resident of this state or is a foreign corporation or his place of residence cannot be ascertained;

"(J) In an action against an executor, administrator, or guardian who has given bond as such in this state, but at the time of the commencement of the action is not a resident of this state or his place of residence cannot be ascertained;

"(K) In an action or proceeding for a new trial or other relief after judgment, or to impeach a judgment or order for fraud, or to obtain an order of satisfaction thereof, when the defendant is not a resident of this state or his place of residence cannot be ascertained;

"(L) In an action where the defendant, being a resident of this state, has departed from the county of his residence with intent to delay or defraud his creditors or to avoid the service of a summons, or keeps himself concealed with like intent." (As eff. 10-1-53.)

No valid judgment in personam can be rendered although service was made by publication. Oil Well Supply Co. v. Koen, 64 OS 422, 60 NE 603, 45 WLB 398 (1901).

Strict compliance with statutory provisions is essential to valid service.

A money judgment in an in personam action is in all respects valid where service has been duly made by publication under the Civil Rules. Rasmussen v. Vance, 34 Misc 87, 293 NE2d 114, 63 OO2d 400 (C.P. 1973).

Service of process by ordinary mail to the listed owner and by publication as to all others with an interest in or lien upon the title in an in rem tax foreclosure under R.C. 5721.18(B) was upheld as valid by the Ohio Supreme Court in In re Foreclosure of Liens, 62 OS2d 333, 405 NE2d 1030, 16 OO3d 393 (1980). The U.S. Supreme Court held that actual service on a mortgagee is essential to divest his interest in a tax foreclosure in Mennonite Board of Missions v. Adams, 462 U.S. 791, 103 SCt 2706, 77 LEd2d 180 (1983), and thereby invalidated procedures such as the Ohio in rem tax foreclosure under R.C. 5721.18(B).

Further research: O Jur 3d, Process § 62.

16-75B   Right of Bona Fide Purchaser.

Direct attack, see also 16-15C.

The right of a party served by publication to have the judgment opened and be let in to defend within five years is limited by the statutory provision that the title which has passed in consequence of the judgment to a bona fide purchaser shall not be affected. Moor v. Parsons, 98 OS 233, 120 NE 305, 16 OLR 35, 76, 63 WLB 171, 188 (1918).

LAW IN GENERAL

The common statutory provision that persons served by publication may attack the judgment within a specified time does not render a title unmarketable, according to the general rule, unless there is a reasonable prospect that a successful attack will be made. 9 ALR2d 710.

16-75C   Unknown Persons.

Unborn persons, see 17-22B.

Civil Rule 15(D) provides that where defendant's name is unknown, he may be designated by any name or description with an averment that the plaintiff could not discover the name. The summons must contain the words "name unknown" and must be served personally. When the name is discovered, an amendment of the pleading or proceeding must be made accordingly. (As eff. 7-1-70.)

R.C. 2703.24 provides: "When it appears by affidavit that the name and residence of a necessary party are unknown to the plaintiff, proceedings against him may be had without naming him; and the court shall make an order respecting the publication of notice, but the order shall require not less than six weeks' publication." (As eff. 10-4-55.) Between the year 1900 and this effective date, the statute provided only for unknown heirs and devisees.

An action against Mrs. Wm. Rogers, whose first name is unknown, fell within the purview of the former statute requiring personal service. No jurisdiction was acquired by residence service. Uihlein v. Gladieux, 74 OS 232, 78 NE 363, 4 OLR 59, 51 WLB 196 (1906). Such situations may now be brought within the purview of R.C. 2703.24 as amended effective October 4, 1955.

The real party in interest, when duly served under incorrect name must make a timely plea or the defect is waived and judgment conclusive. Maloney v. Callahan, 127 OS 387, 188 NE 656, 39 OLR 652 (1933).

Where petition is against and service by publication is on Isom Lam "or" his unknown heirs no jurisdiction is obtained as to either. "The attempt to obtain service by publication was a failure. It notified Isom Lamb, or his unknown heirs, whether the one or the others, no one can tell." Lamb v. Boyd, 4 CC 499, 2 CD 672 (1890).

A proceeding to quiet title against the "unknown heirs" of a former owner does not affect the title of heirs whose names and places of residence in Ohio, though known to plaintiff, are not named as parties and who have no actual notice thereof. Wilson v. Wilson, 11 CC(NS) 450, 21 CD 39 (1908).

The necessity of identifying the defendant so that personal service may be made is not dispensed with by Civil Rule 15(D). If he is not identified, the action is not commenced against anyone. Vocke v. Dayton, 36 App2d 139, 303 NE2d 892, 65 OO2d 159 (1973).

When it cannot be shown whether a named defendant is alive, his unknown heirs and devisees should also be made parties and served by publication.

Standard of Title Examination

(Adopted by Ohio State Bar Association in 1971)

Problem 9.2A:

Does Rule 15(D) require personal service in a case covered by R.C. 2703.24?

Standard 9.2A:

No.

16-75D Affidavit.

Civil Rule 4.4(A) (residence unknown) provides: "When the residence of a defendant is unknown, service shall be made by publication in actions where such service is authorized by law. Before service by publication can be made, an affidavit of a party or his counsel must be filed with the court. The affidavit shall aver that service of summons cannot be made because the residence of the defendant is unknown to the affiant and cannot with reasonable diligence be ascertained.

"Upon the filing of the affidavit the clerk shall cause service of notice to be made by publication in a newspaper of general circulation in the county in which the complaint is filed. If no newspaper is published in that county, then publication shall be in a newspaper published in an adjoining county. The publication shall contain the name and address of the court, the case number, the name of the first party on each side, and the name and last known address, if any, of the person or persons whose residence is unknown. The publication shall also contain a summary statement of the object of the complaint and demand for relief and shall notify the person to be served that he is required to answer within twenty-eight days after the last publication. The publication shall be published at least once a week for six successive weeks unless publication for a lesser number of weeks is specifically provided by law. Service shall be complete at the date of the last publication.

"After the last publication, the publisher or his agent shall file with the court an affidavit showing the fact of publication together with a copy of the notice of publication. The affidavit and copy of the notice shall constitute proof of service." (As eff. 7-1-71.)

Prior to adoption of the Civil Rules, where an affidavit for service by publication upon a nonresident did not recite that service of summons cannot be made on such nonresident in this state, the attempted service based on such affidavit was void and the court did not acquire jurisdiction over such person. Beachler v. Ford, 77 App 41, 60 NE2d 330, 32 OO 317, 42 Abs 609 (1945). Affidavit is insufficient if made merely an affiant's belief. Morton v. Davezac, 20 App 427, 152 NE 679, 3 Abs 637 (1925).

The date of the first publication will be considered to be the date service was obtained, if the publication is regularly made. The action was not barred by the statute of limitations. Dolan v. Fulkert, 30 App2d 165, 284 NE2d 179, 55 OO2d 277 (1972).

Where an attempt is made to serve a party by certified mail and the summons is returned indicating a failure of delivery, service by publication, pursuant to Civil Rule 4.4, is insufficient if the affidavit fails to assert any of the grounds listed in R.C. 2703.14, but merely states that the defendant's residence is unknown and cannot be ascertained. Brown v. Gonzales, 50 App2d 254, 362 NE2d 658, 4 OO3d 220 (1975).

Service by publication is defective but not invalid where the last known address of a defendant is not included in the published notice. Northland Dodge, Inc. v. Damachi, 56 App2d 262, 382 NE2d 779, 10 OO3d 273 (1978).

The affidavit for service by publication need not state that the action is one in which such service is authorized by law. Wilson v. Sinsabaugh, 61 App2d 224, 401 NE2d 454, 15 OO3d 365 (1978); note: this decision conflicts with Brown v. Gonzales, supra.

Concealment of a defendant, as that term is used in R.C. 2703.14, may be reasonably inferred from inability to locate that defendant after the exercise of "reasonable diligence." This inference is sufficient to support service by publication unless evidence is presented contradicting the inference. Brooks v. Rollins, 9 OS 3d 8, 457 NE2d 1158 (1984).

The affidavit should include the known residence of a defendant since it must be in the publication.

Further research: O Jur 3d, Process § 81.

16-75E   The Publication.

See Civil Rule 4.4(A) (residence unknown) shown at 16-75D.

Civil Rule 4.4(B) (residence known) provides: "If the residence of a defendant is known, and the action is one in which service by publication is authorized by law, service of process shall be effected by a method other than by publication as provided by:

"(1) Rule 4.1, if the defendant is a resident of this state,

"(2) Rule 4.3(B) if defendant is not a resident of this state, or

"(3) Rule 4.5, in the alternative, if service on defendant is to be effected in a foreign country.

"If service of process cannot be effected under the provisions of this subdivision or Rule 4.6(C) or Rule 4.6(D), service of process shall proceed by publication." (As eff. 7-1-71.)

If a second affidavit is necessary, we should presume in a collateral proceeding that it was made. Winemiller v. Laughlin, 51 OS 421, 38 NE 111, 31 WLB 370, 32 WLB 261 (1894). For article submitting that second affidavit is not necessary, see 34 OO 68.

Where it is apparent on the face of the record that a copy of the publication was not mailed to each defendant nor an entry made on the docket as to the mailing, the court is without jurisdiction and the judgment is void ab initio. A sale of real property pursuant to the judgment will be set aside as to a purchaser in good faith. Lincoln Tavern v. Snader, 165 OS 61, 133 NE2d 606, 59 OO 74 (1956).

The delivery to the clerk of the courts of a copy of the first publication of notice, twenty days after the publication, for mailing to the defendant, is not a sufficient compliance with R.C. 2703.16. Corbett v. Fowble, 145 NE2d 466, 76 Abs 158 (App. 1956).

The second affidavit under the former statute, where the residences of defendants are unknown, is mere evidence and the failure to file such an affidavit does not defeat the jurisdiction of the court. First Nat. City Bank v. Martin, 217 NE2d 55, 34 OO2d 215 (C.P. 1965).

Standard of Title Examination

(Adopted by Ohio State Bar Association in 1956; amended 1970)

Problem 6.1A:

Where the residence of the defendant is not known, must the "affidavit that the residence of the defendant is unknown and cannot with reasonable diligence be ascertained" be by a second instrument?

Standard 6.1A:

No, the original affidavit may include compliance with the requirement. Since July 1, 1970 the rule of this Standard has been adopted under Rule 4.4(A) of the Ohio Rules of Civil Procedure.

Standard of Title Examination

(Adopted by Ohio State Bar Association in 1971)

Problem 6.2A:

Where service is had by publication in an action relating to title to real property, must the publication identify the real property?

Standard 6.2A:

Yes.

Comment 6.2A:

Such was the requirement under R.C. Sec. 2703.17, which was replaced with similar language by Rule 4.4(A) of the Rules of Civil Procedure.

Further research: O Jur 3d, Process § 84.

SECTION 16-76: SERVICE BY MAIL

16-76A   Generally.

Constructive service generally, see 16-71F.

R.C. 1.02 in part provides that as used in the Revised Code, unless the context otherwise requires, "registered mail" includes certified mail and certified mail includes registered mail. (As eff. 1-3-72.)

Civil Rule 4.1(1) (service by certified mail) provides: "Evidenced by return receipt signed by any person service of any process shall be by certified mail unless otherwise permitted by these rules. The clerk shall place a copy of the process and complaint or other document to be served in an envelope. He shall address the envelope to the person to be served at the address set forth in the caption or at the address set forth in written instructions furnished to the clerk with instructions to forward. He shall affix adequate postage and place the sealed envelope in the United States mail as certified mail return receipt requested with instructions to the delivering postal employee to show to whom delivered, date of delivery, and address where delivered.

"The clerk shall forthwith enter the fact of mailing on the appearance docket and make a similar entry when the return receipt is received by him. If the envelope is returned with an endorsement showing failure of delivery, the clerk shall forthwith notify, by mail, the attorney of record or if there is no attorney of record, the party at whose instance process was issued. He shall enter the fact of notification on the appearance docket. The clerk shall file the return receipt or returned envelope in the records of the action.

"All postage shall be charged to costs. If the parties to be served by certified mail are numerous and the clerk determines there is insufficient security for costs, he may require the party requesting service to advance an amount estimated by the clerk to be sufficient to pay the postage." (As eff. 7-1-80.)

See also Civil Rules 4.6(C), (D) quoted at 16-74A.

The plaintiff has the burden to prove when it was denied that the address to which the summons was made, was the correct residence address of the defendant. Porter v. Toops, 62 NE2d 769, 44 Abs 329 (App. 1945).

Service by mail, properly made in compliance with statute, is complete from the time the notice or other paper to be served is deposited in the post office with the proper amount of postage, and the risk of failure of the mail is upon the party to whom the paper is addressed. McCoy v. Bureau of Unemployment Compensation, 81 App 158, 77 NE2d 76, 36 OO 463, 4 Abs 310 (1947).

Where the record shows that service was made in conformity with the statute, there is a presumption of valid service, but this presumption is rebuttable. Shaman v. Roberts, 87 App 328, 94 NE2d 630, 43 OO 50, 57 Abs 502 (1950).

Statutes providing for service of process have been held not to apply to service of notice and, in the absence of a statute providing otherwise, notice is not given until it is received by the one to be notified. Schutt v. Blankenship, 107 NE2d 218, 62 Abs 209 (App. 1951).

Certified mail service under the provisions of Civil Rule 4.1(1), where used to serve a defendant being sued as an individual, is valid only where such is delivered to the defendant or delivered to a person authorized by appointment or by law to receive service of process for such defendant. Southgate Shopping Center Corp. v. Jones, 49 App2d 358, 361 NE2d 460, 3 OO3d 426 (1975).

Service of process may be made at a person's business address, provided it is an address which he visits with sufficient regularity. Where service was made at a place which the person visited only two or three times a month and which was not his regular place of business, the service did not constitute due process of law. Akron-Canton Regional Airport Authority v. Swinehart, 62 OS2d 403, 406 NE2d 811, 16 OO3d 436 (1980).

Certified mail service is valid where delivered to a person other than the defendant at the defendant's address. Fancher v. Fancher, 8 App3d 79, 455 NE2d 1344 (1982). This decision conflicts with In re Estate of Jones, 1 App3d 70, 439 NE 2d 458 (1981).

Where service by certified mail is returned "unclaimed" and new service is sent by ordinary mail to the same address, the court will not presume that delivery was not forwarded to defendant's new address where defendant has not claimed that he did not receive service and presented no evidence upon the issue. J.R. Productions, Inc. v. Young, 3 App3d 407, 445 NE2d 740 (1982).

Service by mail must comply with the requirements that:

(a) Service by registered mail or otherwise be provided for by rule of the court and be in accord with such rule,

(b) Such mailing be not returned as undelivered,

(c) Return by clerk that summons was deposited in the mail and addressed to defendant at a given address, and

(d) Such address be the correct address of the party to be served (which usually cannot be determined from the record).

Standards of Title Examination

(Adopted by Ohio State Bar Association in 1971; amended 1972)

Caveat: See Appendix B (post).

9.1 Ohio Rules of Civil Procedure: Return Receipt under Rule 4.

Problem A:
Is it a requirement that the return receipt be signed by the addressee himself?

Standard A:
No.

Problem B:
When the return receipt is signed by someone other than the addressee, is it a requirement that the addressee's name appear on the return receipt as the post office form provides?

Standard B:
No.

Comment B:
However, in multiple-defendant cases, each return receipt should show data sufficient to enable the examiner to identify the addressee to whom the receipt pertains. If the name of the addressee does not appear on the receipt or is illegible, the examiner should attempt to identify the addressee by comparing the certified number, the address where delivered, the postmark or other data shown on the receipt with the clerk's records concerning the mailing and with the other return receipts in the file.

Problem C:
Is it a requirement that signatures on the return receipt be legible?

Standard C:
No.

Comment C:
The illegibility of a signature should be considered objectionable only when the identity of the signatory would be especially significant (as in Title Standard 9.4, for example) and such identity is not otherwise ascertainable from the record.

Problem D:
Is it a requirement that the return receipt bear the certified number?

Standard D:
No.

Comment D:
But see Comment B above.

Problem E:

Is it a requirement that the return receipt show: (1) to whom delivered, (2) the date of delivery, and (3) the address where delivered, as the post office form provides?

Standard E:

No.

Comment E:

The receipt should ordinarily be considered sufficient if it appears to show that delivery was made by the postal authorities either to the addressee or to another for the addressee, notwithstanding the fact that it is incompletely or improperly filled out.

Problem F:

Is it a requirement that the return receipt be a part of the file?

Standard F:

Yes.

Comment F:

If the receipt is missing from the file, the examiner, in an appropriate case, may wish to rely upon the docket entry made by the clerk in accordance with Rule 4.1 (1) or Rule 4.3(B) (1) with respect to the fact of notification.

Problem G:

When the return receipt is not signed by the addressee himself, is it necessary that inquiry be made concerning the identity of the recipient, his relationship to the addressee or his connection with the place of delivery?

Standard G:

No, unless there are other factors which would be sufficient to create a reasonable doubt in the mind of the examiner concerning the propriety of the delivery.

Comment G:

The fact that the record fails to reveal any apparent relationship between the recipient and the addressee or the place of delivery is not of itself sufficient ground for questioning the propriety of the delivery. In the absence of other circumstances which would create a reasonable doubt in the mind of the examiner, it should ordinarily be presumed that delivery was made by the postal authorities to an appropriate person at a proper address. If the circumstances as a whole are sufficient to create such a doubt, satisfactory proof of ultimate delivery to the addressee himself should be required. If furnished, such proof should be made a matter of record.

SECTION 16-77:   SERVICE OUTSIDE OF STATE; NONRESIDENTS

Constructive service generally, see 16-71F.
Service by publication, see Section 16-75.

16-77A   Generally.

Venue, see 16-77B.

Civil Rule 4.3 (out-of-state service), in subdivision (A), provides that service of process may be made outside the state upon a nonresident or upon a resident who is absent from the state, including a personal representative or any legal or commercial entity, on a claim arising from specified events including transacting any business in this state, certain marital obligations, and having an interest in, using, or possessing real property in this state. Subdivision (B) of the Rule provides that, when ordered by the court, service may be personal and may be made by any person over eighteen years of age who is not a party and who has been designated by order of court. Otherwise, service, evidenced by return receipt signed by any person, shall be by certified mail with provisions corresponding to such service in this state. Residence service cannot be made out of the state. If the envelope is returned showing failure of delivery, service is complete when the attorney or serving party, after notification by the clerk, files an affidavit setting forth facts indicating the reasonable diligence utilized to ascertain the whereabouts of the party to be served. (Service by such an affidavit is of doubtful constitutionality; service by publication or personal service is recommended when the envelope is returned showing failure of delivery. See Standard 9.5A below.) The issuance and return are otherwise the same as for service within the state. (As eff. 7-1-80.)

Civil Rule 4.5 (alternative provisions for service in a foreign country) lists alternative methods for service of summons and complaint in a foreign country when service is allowed outside the state by Rules 4.3 or 4.4. (As eff. 7-1-70.) Rule 4.4 is shown at 16-75D and 16-75E.

Standard of Title Examination

(Adopted by Ohio State Bar Association in 1971)

Problem 9.5A:

In an action affecting title to real property in which service by publication is authorized by law, when service of summons has been attempted on an alleged out-of-state defendant by certified mail but the envelope is returned with an endorsement showing failure of delivery, may service be completed by filing an affidavit of due diligence in accordance with Civil Rule 4.3(B)(1)?

Standard 9.5A:
   No.

Comment 9.5A:

In such an action under the circumstances described, service should be effected by some other authorized method, including service by publication if the whereabouts of the defendant proves to be unknown. (Civil Rule 4.4(B), effective July 1, 1971.)

LAW IN GENERAL

Delivery of a summons outside of the state where issued is substituted service and is the equivalent of service by publication. It is not equivalent to personal service, by the weight of authority, even as to residents of the state where the summons is issued. Personal service outside the state must be preceded by the same steps as other forms of constructive service unless the statute otherwise provides. Am Jur 2d, Process §§ 41, 48, 49, 70; CJS, Process §§ 32, 73.

16-77B Nonresidents.

Out-of-state service, see also 16-77A.

R.C. 2307.382 provides: "(A) A court may exercise personal jurisdiction over a person who acts directly or by an agent, as to a cause of action arising from the person's:

"(1) Transacting any business in this state;

"(2) Contracting to supply services or goods in this state;

"(3) Causing tortious injury by an act or omission in this state;

"(4) Causing tortious injury in this state by an act or omission outside this state if he regularly does or solicits business, or engages in any other persistent course of conduct, or derives substantial revenue from goods used or consumed or services rendered in this state;

"(5) Causing injury in this state to any person by breach of warranty expressly or impliedly made in the sale of goods outside this state when he might reasonably have expected such person to use, consume, or be affected by the goods in this state, provided that he also regularly does or solicits business, or engages in any other persistent course of conduct, or derives substantial revenue from goods used or consumed or services rendered in this state;

"(6) Causing tortious injury in this state to any person by an act outside this state committed with the purpose of injuring persons, when he might reasonably have expected that some person would be injured thereby in this state;

"(7) Causing tortious injury to any person by a criminal act, any element of which takes place in this state, which he commits or in the commission of which he is guilty of complicity;

"(8) Having an interest in, using, or possessing real property in this state;

"(9) Contracting to insure any person, property, or risk located within this state at the time of contracting.

"(B) When jurisdiction over a person is based solely upon this section, only a cause of action arising from acts enumerated in this section may be asserted against him." (As eff. 10-1-76.)

Note: The Ohio long-arm statute (R.C. 2307.382) provides for personal jurisdiction over nonresidents under a rule superseding the doctrine of Pennoyer v. Neff, 95 US 714, 24 L Ed 565 (1878). Such statutes in several states are a development of the decision in International Shoe Co. v. State of Washington, 326 US 310, 90 L Ed 95, 66 Sup Ct 154, 161 ALR2d 1027 (1945) in which Chief Justice Stone said that due process "requires only that in order to subject a defendant to a judgment in personam, if he be not present in the territory of the forum, he have certain minimum contacts with it such that the maintenance of the suit does not offend 'traditional notions of fair play and substantial justice.'"

R.C. 2703.29 provides: "When a plaintiff is not a resident of the state and a defendant files a cross petition, service of summons on the cross petition may be made upon such nonresident plaintiff by registered mail directed to the plaintiff at the address listed by plaintiff with the clerk of courts of the county in which the action is pending and the return of the sheriff shall be in accordance with section 2703.23 of the Revised Code.

"Thereafter continued prosecution of the case by the nonresident plaintiff shall be deemed a waiver of service of summons on the cross petition." (As eff. 7-23-65.)

Note: R.C. 2703.23 is repealed. See Civil Rule 4.1.

Civil Rule 3(B) (venue; where proper) provides comprehensively for a proper county where an action should be commenced and decided; subsection (7) states: "In actions described in Rule 4.3 (out-of-state service) [proper venue lies] in the county where the plaintiff resides." (As eff. 7-1-86.)

Where service on a Florida corporation was made by certified mail and personal jurisdiction was sought under the Ohio long-arm statute, and the corporation made no showing that it was not properly notified, service was properly made. Air Transport, Inc. v. Ransom Aircraft Sales & Brokerage, Inc., 61 OO2d 403, 333 FSupp 1106 (U.S. Dist. Ct. 1971).

Service of process was attempted through the Canadian postal service. No signed return card was received, but the Canadian postal authorities responded to an inquiry by stating: "subject register delivered on 20/7/77 to signature of recognized representative." This was held to be valid service of process. Fieno v. Beaton, 68 App2d 13, 426 NE2d 203, 22 OO3d 8 (1980).

SECTION 16-78: PROBATE COURT ACTIONS

16-78A Applicability of Civil Rules; Venue; Service of Summons; Service Subsequent to Original Pleadings.

Civil Rule 73 concerns the Probate Division of the Court of Common Pleas. Other Civil Rules referred to in Rule 73 are listed numerically in the Table of Rules of Civil Procedure.

Civil Rule 73(A) (applicability) provides: "These Rules of Civil Procedure shall apply to proceedings in the probate division of the court of common pleas as indicated in this rule. Additionally, all of the Rules of Civil Procedure though not specifically mentioned in this rule shall apply except to the extent that by their nature they would be clearly inapplicable." (As eff. 7-1-80.)

Civil Rule 73(B) (venue) provides: "Rule 3(B) shall not apply to proceedings in the probate division of the court of common pleas. Such proceeding shall be venued as provided by law except that proceedings which may, under Chapters 2101 through 2131, Revised Code, be venued in the general division or the probate division of the court of common pleas, shall be venued in the probate division of the appropriate court of common pleas.

"Proceedings which are improperly venued shall be transferred to a proper venue provided by law and this subdivision, and the court may assess costs including reasonable attorney fees, to the time of transfer against the party who commenced the action in an improper venue." (As eff. 7-1-80.)

Note: Civil Rule 3(B) is the general venue rule in common pleas court. See 16-77B. The second sentence of Rule 73(B), above, requires proceedings under the probate code to be venued in probate court notwithstanding statutory provisions for concurrent jurisdiction with common pleas court.

Civil Rule 73(C) (service of summons) provides: "Rules 4 through 4.6 shall apply in any proceeding in the probate division of the court of common pleas requiring service of summons." (As eff. 7-1-80.)

Civil Rule 73(D) (service and filing of pleadings and papers subsequent to original pleading) provides: "In proceedings requiring service of summons, Rule 5 shall apply to the service and filing of pleadings and papers subsequent to the original pleading." (As eff. 7-1-80.)

16-78B   Service of Notice.

Service generally, see 16-74A.

Civil Rule 73(E) (service of notice) provides: "In any proceeding where any type of notice other than service of summons is required by law or deemed necessary by the court and the statute providing for such notice neither directs nor authorizes the court to direct the manner of its service, such notice shall be given in writing and may be served by or on behalf of any interested party without court intervention by one of the following methods:

"(1) By delivering a copy thereof to the person to be served;

"(2) By leaving a copy thereof at the usual place of residence of such person;

"(3) By certified mail, addressed to such person at his usual place of residence with instructions to forward, return receipt requested, with instructions to the delivering postal employee to show to whom delivered, date of delivery, and address where delivered, provided that the certified mail envelope is not returned with an endorsement showing failure of delivery;

"(4) By ordinary mail after a certified mail envelope is returned with an endorsement showing that it was refused;

"(5) By ordinary mail after a certified mail envelope is returned with an endorsement showing that it was unclaimed, provided that the ordinary mail envelope is not returned by the postal authorities with an endorsement showing failure of delivery;

"(6) By publication once each week for three consecutive weeks in some newspaper of general circulation in the county when the name, usual place of residence, or existence of such person is unknown and cannot with reasonable diligence be ascertained: provided that before such publication may be utilized, the person giving notice shall file an affidavit which states that the name, usual place of residence, or existence of such person is unknown and cannot with reasonable diligence be ascertained;

"(7) By such other method as the court may direct.

"Rule 4.2 shall apply in determining who may be served and how particular persons or entities must be served." (As eff. 7-1-80.)

Civil Rule 73(F) (proof of service of notice; when service of notice complete) provides: "When service is made through the court, proof of service of notice shall be in the same manner as proof of service of summons.

"When service is made without court intervention, proof of service of notice shall be made by affidavit. When service is made by certified mail, the certified mail return receipt which shows delivery shall be attached to the affidavit. When service is made by ordinary mail, the prior returned certified mail envelope which shows that the mail was refused or unclaimed shall be attached to the affidavit.

"Service of notice by ordinary mail shall be complete when the fact of mailing is entered of record except as stated in subdivision (E) (5) of this rule. Service by publication shall be complete at the date of the last publication." (As eff. 7-1-80.)

Civil rule 73(G) (waiver of service of notice) provides: "Rule 4(D) shall apply in determining who may waive service of notice." (As eff. 7-1-80.)

16-78C   Absent Fiduciary.

R.C. 2109.03 provides that if the fiduciary is absent from the state, summonses, citations and notices may be served upon him by delivering duplicate copies thereof to his designated attorney. (As eff. 10-1-53.)

The statutory provision for service by delivering to the attorney is all-inclusive and is not limited or restricted to summonses in actions originating in the probate court. Meisner v. Flemion, 109 App 117, 164 NE2d 183, 10 OO2d 302 (1958).

Such service requires an affirmative allegation in the body of the petition that the fiduciary is absent from the state. A foreign address in the caption is not sufficient. Kaczenski v. Kaczenski, 169 NE2d 36, 83 Abs 469 (App. 1959).

16-78D   Forms.

Civil Rule 73(H) (forms used in probate practice) provides: "Forms used in proceedings in the probate division of the courts of common pleas shall be those prescribed in Rule 16 of the Rules of Superintendence for Courts of Common Pleas. Forms not prescribed in Rule 16 of the Rules of Superintendence for Courts of Common Pleas may be used as permitted by that rule.

"Blank forms reproduced for use in probate practice for any filing to which Rule 17 of the Rules of Superintendence for Courts of Common Pleas applies shall conform to the specifications set forth in that rule.

"No pleading, application, acknowledgment, certification, account, report, statement, allegation, or other matter filed in the probate division of the courts of common pleas shall be required to be executed under oath, and it is sufficient if it is made upon the signature alone of the person making it." (As eff. 7-1-80.)

CHAPTER 17: JUDICIAL SALES

DIVISION 17-1: IN GENERAL

DIVISION 17-2: PARTIES; PROCEDURE

672

DIVISION 17-1: IN GENERAL

SECTION 17-11: INTRODUCTION; FORECLOSURE OF MORT-GAGES GENERALLY

Executors and administrators, see Section 12-14.
Guardian and ward, see Section 15-14.
Partition, see Section 5-34.

17-11A   Definition; Nature.

A foreclosure action in which the mortgagee does not ask for a personal judgment is an equity case giving neither party the right to demand a jury. Acme Mortgage Co. v. Parker, 17 Abs 97 (App. 1934).

LAW IN GENERAL

A judicial sale is one made pursuant to a judgment or decree of a court having authority to order the sale. An execution sale is not a judicial sale although it has some characteristics of the latter. Am Jur 2d, Judicial Sales §§ 1, 2; CJS, Judicial Sales § 1.

17-11B   Methods of Enforcing Mortgages.

R.C. 1309.44 in part provides that if the security agreement covers both real and personal property, the secured party may proceed as to both in accordance with his rights and remedies in respect of the real property. (As eff. 10-16-80.)

Strict foreclosure is prohibited by R.C. 2323.07, which in part provides: "When a mortgage is foreclosed or a specific lien enforced, a sale of the property shall be ordered."

Where the foreclosure is barred by an adjudication that the fifteen-year statute of limitations had run, the mortgagee is not thereafter estopped from maintaining an action in ejectment. Taylor v. Quinn, 68 App 164, 39 NE2d 627, 22 OO 292 (1941). See also 17-11J.

LAW IN GENERAL

The usual method of enforcing a mortgage is by a suit in chancery for foreclosure of the equity of redemption and judicial sale of the land. The ordinary rules of judicial sales are applicable. Am Jur 2d, Mortgages § 552; CJS, Mortgages § 605.

Strict foreclosure is a barring of the equity of redemption by a decree in equity which fixes the amount due and the time within which the right to redeem may be exercised. It vests the absolute title in the mortgagee. It is still recognized and used in some states to clear title against a claimant of an equity of redemption who was omitted from a concluded foreclosure sale proceeding. Enforcement by entry or writ of entry after breach of the condition of the mortgage, and holding possession during the period allowed for redemption, is permitted in a few jurisdictions. Am Law of Prop § 16.179; Powell § 469; Tiffany § 1518.

17-11C Right of Redemption under Statutes.

Statutory redemption after foreclosure should be distinguished from the equity of redemption before foreclosure. Many states have statutes giving a right to redeem, for a limited time after foreclosure, to the former owner of the equity of redemption. Ohio has no statutory redemption after foreclosure.

17-11D Concurrent and Successive Actions.

Personal judgments, see Section 17-13.

A dismissal of the foreclosure proceedings on the merits is not a bar to a later suit on the note. Although if the debt is paid the lien is extinct, the converse is not true, and the debt may be justly due, although the land is never bound by the lien. Longworth v. Flagg, 10 Ohio 300 (1840).

When a creditor, whose debt is secured by mortgage, recovers judgment for the secured debt and causes the mortgaged premises to be sold on execution, the purchaser takes title free of the mortgage although the money made is not sufficient to satisfy the entire debt. Fosdick v. Risk, 15 Ohio 84 (1846).

The pendency of an action to have the amount found due on the note and for sale of the property described in the mortgage, but in which no personal judgment is demanded, is not a bar to another action on the note. Spence v. Union Central Life Ins. Co., 40 OS 517, 11 WLB 135 (1884).

Further research: O Jur 3d, Mortgages, etc. § 265; 122 ALR 485; Tiffany § 1486.

17-11E   Setoff and Counterclaim.

In an action by mortgagee against mortgagor upon a note and mortgage given for the purchase money of the premises, the mortgagor may set up a counterclaim for damages by reason of the fraud of the mortgagee in concealing material facts as to the situation and extent of the property. Pierce v. Tiersch, 40 OS 168, 10 WLB 178 (1883).

17-11F   Lien after Decree or Sale Thereon.

Lien on proceeds, see 17-28A.
Prior liens, see 17-21H.
Standards of title examination, see 1-43B.

An entry by the clerk of court of the cancellation on the record of the mortgage is not essential to remove the mortgage as a cloud upon the title when a proper foreclosure sale has been had. Walker v. Scott, 7 App 335, 29 CC(NS) 89 (1914).

The liens for debts of the decedent are transferred from the real estate to the proceeds of the sale by land sale proceedings. In re Saviers' Estate, 23 Abs 166 (App. 1936).

LAW IN GENERAL

The lien is not merged in the decree until sale of the property, according to the weight of authority. A lien is extinguished by the sale as to any unpaid balance due to the holder of the encumbrance being enforced, or due to subsequent lien holders who are parties to the action, unless the sale is to a person primarily liable for the debt. Am Jur 2d, Mortgages § 623; CJS, Mortgages § 700.

17-11G   Leases.

Effect of foreclosure, see 17-21C.

LAW IN GENERAL

The rights of a tenant under a lease are not affected by a subsequent mortgage. Where the mortgage is prior to the lease, the tenant's rights are not affected until foreclosure and sale unless the mortgagee has the right of possession. Tiffany § 1421.

17-11H   Attorney Fees.

A stipulation in a mortgage that a fee for services of plaintiff's attorney be paid out of the proceeds of foreclosure sale, is against public policy and void. Leavans v. Ohio Nat. Bank, 50 OS 591, 34 NE 1089, 30 WLB 307 (1893).

Further research: 17 ALR2d 288; CJS, Mortgages § 812.

17-11I Tender.

A tender of the debt during foreclosure generally operates to preclude further proceedings.

17-11J Limitation of Actions; Refiling Mortgage.

Statutes generally, see 16-41A.

R.C. 5301.30 provides: "The record of any mortgage which remains unsatisfied or unreleased of record for more than twenty-one years after the date of the mortgage or twenty-one years after the stated maturity date of the principal sum, if a stated date of maturity is provided in the mortgage, whichever is later, secured as shown in the record of such mortgage, does not give notice to or put on inquiry any person dealing with the land described in such mortgage that such mortgage debt remains unpaid or has been extended or renewed. As to subsequent bona fide purchasers, mortgagees, and other persons dealing with such land for value, the lien of such mortgage has expired. The mortgage creditor may at any time refile in the county recorder's office the mortgage or a sworn copy thereof for record, together with an affidavit stating the amount remaining due thereon and the due date thereof, whether or not such date has been extended. Subject to the rights of bona fide purchasers, mortgagees, and other persons dealing with such land for value, whose rights were acquired or vested between such expiration and refiling, such refiling is constructive notice of such mortgage only for a period of twenty-one years after such refiling, or for twenty-one years after the stated maturity of the debt, whichever is the longer period." (As eff. 7-26-63.) From 1925 to September 30, 1955 the statute did not require the maturity date to be stated in order to extend the period after twenty-one years from the date of the mortgage.

If the action by the mortgagee is in ejectment, the statutory bar of fifteen years on the note does not apply. The bar in such action is twenty-one years. Bradfield v. Hale, 67 OS 316, 65 NE 1008, 47 WLB 901, 48 WLB 129 (1902); Bruml v. Herold, 14 O Supp 123, 29 OO 146 (C.P. 1944). The heirs of the mortgagee, who was not in possession at his death, cannot maintain ejectment; the action to obtain possession must be brought by his executor or administrator. Stafford v. Collins, 16 Abs 621 (App. 1933).

A credit made within twenty-one years on the note does not toll the statute on the unrefiled mortgage and hence the action in ejectment based on the mortgage was barred twenty-one years after the due date of the note. Eastwood v. Capel, 164 OS 506, 132 NE2d 202, 58 OO 352 (1956).

The provisions of R.C. 5301.30 are for the protection of persons whose rights were acquired after expiration of the statutory period and have no application to a subsequent mortgagee who became a mortgagee before the twenty-one-year period referred to in the statute had run. Marshall v. Ebling, 70 App 145, 45 NE2d 318, 24 OO 477 (1942).

LAW IN GENERAL

Statutes of limitation do not apply to trust deeds in the nature of a mortgage, except as specifically provided, and the trustee may exercise his power of sale even though action on the debt has been barred. In a majority of the decisions, acts of the mortgagor which extend the period of limitation as to him will also extend it as to grantees and junior lienors, but acts of a grantee which keep the debt enforceable do not bind the mortgagor. Am Jur 2d, Mortgages § 602; Am Law of Prop § 16.163; Powell § 461; Tiffany §§ 1485, 1517.

SECTION 17-12: LIS PENDENS

United States courts, see 16-23B.

17-12A   Rules.

Statutes, see 17-12F.
Transfer of pending action, see 16-11D.

Civil Rule 3(F) (venue: notice of pending litigation; transfer of judgments) provides: "(1) When an action affecting the title to or possession of real property or tangible personal property is commenced in a county other than the county in which all of the real property or tangible personal property is situated, the plaintiff must cause a certified copy of the complaint to be filed with the clerk of the court of common pleas in each county or additional county in which the real property or tangible personal property affected by the action is situated. If the plaintiff fails to file such certified copy of the complaint, third persons will not be charged with notice of the pendency of the action.

"To the extent authorized by the laws of the United States, this subsection also applies to actions, other than proceedings in bankruptcy, affecting title to or possession of real property in this state commenced in a United States District Court whenever such real property is situated wholly or partly in a county other than the county in which the permanent records of such court are kept.

"(2) After final judgment, or upon dismissal of the action, the clerk of the court that issued the judgment shall transmit a certified copy of the judgment or dismissal to the clerk of the court of common pleas in each county or additional county in which real or tangible personal property affected by the action is situated.

"(3) When the clerk has transmitted a certified copy of the judgment to another county in accordance with subsection (2) above, and such judgment is later appealed, vacated or modified, the appellant or the party at whose instance the judgment was vacated or modified must cause a certified copy of the notice of appeal or order of vacation or modification to be filed with the clerk of the court of common pleas of each county or additional county in which the real property or tangible personal property is situated. Unless a certified copy of the notice of appeal or order of vacation or modification is so filed, third persons will not be charged with notice of the appeal, vacation or modification.

"(4) The clerk of the court receiving a certified copy filed or transmitted in accordance with the provisions of this subdivision shall number, index, docket and file it in the records of the receiving court. He shall index the first such certified copy he receives in connection with a particular action in the indices to the records of actions commenced in his own court, but he may number, docket and file it in either the regular records of his own court or in a separate set of records. When he subsequently receives a certified copy in connection with that same action, he need not index it, but he shall docket and file it in the same set of records under the same case number he previously assigned to the action.

"(5) When an action affecting title to registered land is commenced in a county other than the county in which all of such land is situated, any certified copy required or permitted by this subdivision shall be filed with or transmitted to the county recorder, rather than the clerk of the court of common pleas, of each county or additional county in which such land is situated." (As eff. 7-1-86.)

The federal statute making the above rule effective as to pending suits in United States district courts is shown at 16-23B.

Standard of Title Examination

(Adopted by Ohio State Bar Association in 1971)

Problem 9.3A:

Should objection to the record title be made if a certified copy of the proceedings are not filed with the certified copy of the judgment transmitted in accordance with Civil Rule 3(F)?

Standard 9.3A:
Yes.

The doctrine of lis pendens does not apply unless the court has acquired, in some manner, jurisdiction of the subject matter involved in the suit. Lis pendens does not operate until summons is served or waived or until publication is made. Benton v. Shafer, 47 OS 117, 24 NE 197, 23 WLB 174, 275 (1890).

The rule as to lis pendens is founded on its necessity to prevent alienation of property in dispute and to give effect to court proceedings, and does not rest on the theory of notice. Meck v. Clabaugh, 16 App 367, 32 CC(NS) 414, 35 CD 781, 21 OLR 344 (1922); Cook v. Mozer, 108 OS 30, 140 NE 590, 1 Abs 436, 845, 21 OLR 117 (1923).

An action for money only is not within the doctrine of lis pendens. Stone v. Equitable Mortgage Co., 25 App 382, 158 NE 275, 5 Abs 528 (1927).

Purchasers of realty during pendency of an action relating to such realty take subject to whatever judgment might be entered in the action. Fissel v. Gordon, 83 App 349, 83 NE2d 525, 38 OO 407, 54 Abs 223 (1948).

Lis pendens does not apply where no property is specifically identified in the pleadings. Domino v. Domino, 99 NE2d 825, 45 OO 151, 60 Abs 484 (C.P. 1951).

The rules of lis pendens generally do not apply against the state or federal government, as in eminent domain and in enforcement of a tax lien.

Further research: O Jur 3d, Lis Pendens § 1.

LAW IN GENERAL

Under the doctrine of lis pendens, whoever acquires, through a party to the suit, an interest in land involved in pending litigation takes it subject to any judgment which may be rendered in the suit. While pending, the suit is constructive notice of the claims of the litigants. Third persons who are not in privity with a party to the action are not bound. Am Law of Prop § 13.12; Tiffany § 1294.

The doctrine does not apply where the court lacks jurisdiction of the subject matter or of the person. It does not apply where no specific real property is affected, as when a money judgment only is sought even though the suit arises out of a matter involving particular real estate. CJS, Lis Pendens § 4.

17-12B   Action Commenced When.

Statutes, see 17-12F.

When notice of the pendency has been duly published, the suit is commenced and pending, and a subsequent disposition of the subject in dispute is a pendente lite purchase. Bennet v. Williams, 5 Ohio 461 (1832).

An action is not lis pendens as to the interest of a defendant until he has been duly served with process. Barry v. Hovey, 30 OS 344, 2 WLB 154 (1876).

17-12C   Previously Acquired Interests.

The doctrine of lis pendens does not apply to a party in interest under an unrecorded deed. When such deed is recorded, the record operates as constructive notice. Irvin v. Smith, 17 Ohio 226 (1848); Harris v. Paul, 37 App 206, 174 NE 615, 9 Abs 201, 33 OLR 586 (1930).

The doctrine of lis pendens does not cut off an interest in real property acquired by a mortgage filed four days before a summons is served but after filing of the complaint in a foreclosure. Pease Co. v. Huntington Nat. Bank, 24 App3d 227, 495 NE2d 45 (1985).

Further research: O Jur 3d, Lis Pendens § 20.

LAW IN GENERAL

A bona fide purchaser is protected under the recording laws as to interests not of record at the date of the decree. Prior interests placed on record after the commencement of the suit, and before the decree, are not barred according to a majority of the cases; that is, a purchaser at judicial sale takes subject to an interest acquired before the suit was begun if the interest is of record before the decree is entered. Am Law of Prop § 18.84; CJS, Lis Pendens § 44.

17-12D Sale to a Party to Action.

Bona fide purchaser, see 1-32F and 17-12C.
Appeals, see 16-14A.

17-12E Dismissal; Laches.

The benefit of the rule of lis pendens may be lost by such long continued inaction as amounts to gross negligence in the party prosecuting, when such inaction is to the prejudice of innocent persons. Fox v. Reeder, 28 OS 181, 1 WLB 307 (1875).

LAW IN GENERAL

The doctrine is not applied unless the suit has been prosecuted with due diligence under the circumstances. 8 ALR2d 986.

17-12F Statutes.

Rules of Civil Procedure, see 17-12A.

R.C. 2703.26 provides: "When summons has been served or publication made, the action is pending so as to charge third persons with notice of its pendency. While pending, no interest can be acquired by third persons in the subject of the action, as against the plaintiff's title." (As eff. 10-1-53.)

R.C. 2703.27 provides: "When a part of real property, the subject matter of an action, is situated in a county other than the one in which the action is brought, a certified copy of the judgment in such action must be recorded in the county recorder's office of such other county before it operates therein as notice so as to charge third persons, as provided in section 2703.26 of the Revised Code. It shall operate as such notice, without record, in the county where it is rendered. This section does not apply to actions or proceedings under any statute which does not require such record." (As eff. 10-1-53.)

SECTION 17-13: PERSONAL LIABILITY; DEFICIENCY JUDG-MENTS; MORATORIA

Necessity of personal service, see 16-71F.

17-13A Necessity of Personal Liability.

A mortgage can be valid although there is no personal liability which can be enforced against the mortgagor or his successors. Thus, it has been held that ejectment may be maintained where foreclosure has been barred by running of the statute of limitations against the note.

17-13B Action before, after or during Foreclosure.

Concurrent and successive remedies generally, see 17-11D.

Civil Rule 55 (default) provides for judgment when a party fails to defend. (As eff. 7-1-71.)

Action may be maintained or judgment recovered on the note prior to the sale of the mortgaged premises. Simon v. Union Trust Co., 126 OS 346, 185 NE 425, 37 OLR 561 (1933).

Whether or not the statute applies, the judgment was not void because prematurely entered, it could be no more than erroneous. State ex rel. Hughes v. Cramer, 138 OS 267, 34 NE2d 772, 20 OO 334 (1941).

A finding of the amount due on the note in a mortgage foreclosure is not a money judgment. Carr v. Home Owners Loan Corp., 148 OS 533, 76 NE2d 389, 36 OO 177 (1947).

A separate action after foreclosure may be maintained against an assuming grantee for the deficiency, and it is not necessary that he be made a party defendant to the foreclosure action unless he has some right, title or lien in the real estate. State ex rel. Squire v. Kofron, 58 App 65, 15 NE2d 783, 10 OO 332, 26 Abs 58 (1937). Contra: Union Savings & Loan Co. v. Kupetz, 37 App 371, 174 NE 806, 8 Abs 505, 32 OLR 511 (1930); Marion Development Co. v. Bruce, 39 App 253, 177 NE 471 (1931).

Foreclosure proceeding is no bar to concurrent or successive suit on purchase-money note secured by mortgage, unless note has been paid. Cooper v. Wagner, 45 App 516, 187 NE 368, 15 Abs 366, 39 OLR 205 (1933).

Further research: CJS, Mortgages §§ 342, 790; Powell § 452; Tiffany § 1554.

17-13C Deficiency Judgments.

Limitation on enforcement, see 17-13D.

A jury trial is demandable of right where the petition asks a money judgment for the amount due. Keller v. Wenzell, 23 OS 579 (1873); Crellin v. Armstrong, 32 NE2d 60, 7 OO 153, 21 Abs 295 (App. 1936).

The court may not condition the right of foreclosure upon the plaintiff waiving a deficiency judgment or other similar condition. Provident Bldg. & Loan Ass'n v. Pekarek, 52 App 492, 3 NE2d 983, 5 OO 40, 21 Abs 44 (1936).

The determination of the amount due on the debt in a foreclosure proceeding is not a money judgment. Citizens Loan & Savings Co. v. Stone, 1 App 2d 551, 206 NE2d 17, 30 OO2d 584 (1965).

Further research: O Jur 3d, Mortgages, etc. § 458.

LAW IN GENERAL

A mortgagee is entitled to a personal judgment for the deficiency between the proceeds of the sale applied to the debt and the full amount owed, subject to statutory restrictions.

The judgment is usually rendered in the foreclosure proceeding if prayed for and if personal service was had on the debtor. A jury trial to ascertain the amount due may generally not be demanded.

Am Jur 2d, Mortgages §§ 905, 908, 909; Am Law of Prop § 16.200; CJS, Mortgages § 774.

17-13D Moratoria Statutes.

Soldiers' and Sailors' Civil Relief Act, see Section 16-43.

R.C. 2329.08 provides: "Any judgment for money rendered in a court of record in this state upon any indebtedness which is secured or evidenced by a mortgage, or other instrument in the nature of a mortgage, on real property or any interest therein, upon which real property there has been located a dwelling or dwellings for not more than two families which has been used in whole or in part as a home or farm dwelling or which at any time was held as a homestead by the person who executed or assumed such mortgage or other instrument, or which has been held by such person as a homesite, shall be unenforceable as to any deficiency remaining due thereon, after the expiration of two years from the date of the confirmation of any judicial sale of such property completed subsequent to the rendition of such judgment. Any execution issued upon such judgment, or any action or proceeding in aid of execution, or in the nature thereof, or to marshal liens, commenced prior to the expiration of such two year period, shall not be affected by this section. This section does not affect any action or proceeding in the nature of a creditor's bill, commenced within such two year period, to subject the interest of the judgment debtor in any property owned at the date of such judgment and concealed with intent to hinder, delay, or defraud creditors.

"This section may be waived by an instrument in writing, executed by the judgment debtor within such two year period, but such waiver shall not be effective unless within such two year period, such waiver is filed in the office of the clerk of the court in which the judgment was rendered. Upon the filing of said waiver such clerk shall enter a memorial thereof on the docket in which the judgment was rendered." (As eff. 9-16-57.)

This section does not limit the enforceability of a judgment rendered after the property originally securing the indebtedness has become wholly unavailable by reason of its previous sale to satisfy a senior claim. The finding of the amount due does not constitute a judgment for money. Carr v. Home Owners Loan Corp., 148 OS 533, 543, 76 NE2d 389, 36 OO 177, 181 (1947).

A deficiency may exist before all the mortgaged real estate has been sold to satisfy the judgment. State ex rel. Squire v. Pejsa, 148 OS 1, 72 NE2d 374, 34 OO 447 (1947).

A judgment is unenforceable under R.C. 2329.08 against a mortgagor who did not occupy the premises subsequent to the mortgage if the premises were subsequently occupied as a home by the purchaser who assumed the mortgage. Kocsorak v. Cleveland Trust Co., 151 OS 212, 85 NE2d 96, 39 OO 36 (1949).

Mere intention to occupy premises at some indefinite future time is insufficient to establish a homestead. Mutual Bldg. & Investment Co. v. Efros, 152 OS 369, 89 NE2d 648, 40 OO 389 (1949).

The statute does not preclude enforcement of a deficiency judgment where a dwelling was located on the second floor and two storerooms on the first floor were used for business purposes. Glaros v. Cleveland Trust Co., 164 OS 511, 132 NE2d 220, 58 OO 382 (1956).

Issuance of a certificate of judgment does not toll this statute. Whalen v. Citizens Bldg. & Loan Co., 67 App 139, 36 NE2d 54, 21 OO 148 (1940).

An unmarried person may be entitled to the benefits of R.C. 2329.08. Mutual Bldg. & Investment Co. v. Efros, 75 NE2d 75, 48 Abs 633 (App. 1947).

Where the second mortgagee prayed for foreclosure and personal judgment, the statutory limitation is applicable even though the proceeds of the sale were insufficient for any payment to him. First Federal Savings & Loan Ass'n v. Sloan, 104 NE2d 459, 61 Abs 369 (App. 1951).

Section 2329.08 does not apply to endorsers. Shatelrow v. Brim, 14 O Supp 130, 29 OO 121 (C.P. 1944).

Further research: O Jur 3d, Mortgages, etc. §§ 465-467.

SECTION 17-14: MARSHALING SECURITIES; INVERSE ORDER OF ALIENATION

17-14A Marshaling Securities.

The rule of equity that where one has a lien upon two funds and another a subsequent lien upon one of them only, the former will be compelled first to exhaust the subject of his exclusive lien, cannot be invoked if the application of such rule would be inequitable. Langel v. Moore, 119 OS 299, 164 NE 118, 6 Abs 694, 695, 27 OLR 641 (1928).

The rule does not apply where two junior mortgagees have liens on separate lots. In such case the first mortgagee will be required to take his debts out of both lots, in proportion to the amount each will produce. Green v. Ramage, 18 Ohio 428 (1849).

An equity to marshal assets will be enforced against a judgment lien subsequently acquired, or against inferior equities. Union Central Life Ins. Co. v. Cherry, 39 App 298, 177 NE 486, 10 Abs 735 (1931).

To obtain relief under the doctrine of marshaling securities, both funds must belong to same debtor, and senior creditor must have lien on both funds. The remedy is not available if its application would prejudice the paramount encumbrancer. Parker v. Wheeler, 47 App 301, 191 NE 798, 16 Abs 266, 40 OLR 262 (1933); Peoples State Bank v. First Nat. Bank, 40 App 374, 178 NE 702, 10 Abs 505 (1931).

Further research: O Jur 3d, Creditors' Rights and Remedies § 912.

LAW IN GENERAL

When one person holds a prior lien on two tracts of land and another person holds a junior lien on one of the tracts, the senior lien holder will be required in equity to first exhaust the subject of his exclusive lien before resorting to the other tract, in order to protect the junior lien holder. If the senior lien holder obtains payment from the proceeds of the tract subject to both liens, the junior lien holder is subrogated to his rights in the other tract. This doctrine is extended to the benefit of others besides creditors but may not be invoked if its application would be inequitable to anyone. Am Jur 2d, Marshaling Assets § 1; Am Law of Prop § 16.154; CJS, Marshaling Assets and Securities § 1.

17-14B   Recourse in Inverse Order of Alienation.

As between successive purchasers of separate parcels, encumbered by a prior mortgage on the whole, a sale of the same to satisfy the mortgage will be made in the inverse order of alienation. Sternberger v. Hanna, 42 OS 305, 12 WLB 226 (1884); Commercial Bank of Lake Erie v. Western Reserve Bank, 11 Ohio 444 (1842).

Where the mortgagor leases part of the mortgaged premises with option to purchase and the mortgagee, with knowledge of the leases, releases the residue of the mortgaged premises, and where resort to the leased premises is necessary for satisfaction of the mortgage, then effect is given to the option. Broughton v. Mt. Healthy Flying Service, 104 App 479, 143 NE2d 597, 5 OO2d 224 (1957).

LAW IN GENERAL

When the owner transfers part of encumbered land without referring to the encumbrance, such part is not liable for the encumbrance if the residue is sufficient for the satisfaction thereof. A transferee of the residue stands in the place of the original owner. When the whole tract is transferred to different persons at different times, the parcel last transferred is subjected to the whole debt before resort is had to the parcel next previously transferred, and so on in the inverse order of alienation. A junior encumbrancer also has the right to invoke the benefit of this doctrine. An assumption of the lien, or a conveyance expressly subject to the lien, may cause the grantee of the first parcel sold to be primarily liable. 131 ALR 4; CJS, Mortgages § 429.

The doctrine is controlled by other equitable principles and by the intention of the parties. It is not applied (a) when the conveyances are simultaneous and similar, (b) when the subsequent grantee did not have notice of the prior conveyance, (c) when the conveyance is made expressly subject to the encumbrance, or (d) when it would work an injustice or would prejudice the paramount encumbrancer. When the parts are transferred at the same time by similar conveyances not referring to the encumbrance, the grantees are liable according to the proportionate value of their land.

If the paramount encumbrancer with notice of the first transfer releases the second parcel transferred, the value of the released parcel will be deducted from the amount enforceable against the first transferee. The required notice is not constructive notice arising from the record, but is actual notice or notice presumed from the circumstances.

Am Jur 2d, Marshaling Assets §§ 2, 5, 44, 47, 55; Am Law of Prop § 16.155; CJS, Mortgages § 430; Powell § 460; Tiffany § 1446.

SECTION 17-15: RIGHTS AND LIABILITIES OF PURCHASERS

17-15A Title Acquired When.

Effect of confirmation, see also 17-28A.

A sheriff's deed takes effect from the day of sale, so as to pass whatever interest the judgment debtor had in the lands sold at the time of the levy. Boyd v. Longworth, 11 Ohio 235 (1842).

The purchaser is entitled to intermediate rents and to crops planted after the date of the sale. Jashenosky v. Volrath, 59 OS 540, 53 NE 46, 41 WLB 97, 196 (1899); Parker v. Storts, 15 OS 351 (1864).

The title of a purchaser at judicial sale is fixed as of the date of the sale, and from that date the purchaser receives the benefits from the property and bears the burdens thereof. Schmidt v. Penn. Mut. Life Ins. Co., 25 Abs 652 (App. 1935).

LAW IN GENERAL

By the acceptance of his bid, the purchaser acquires a certain inchoate title which is protected by law. He acquires the full equitable title by the confirmation; and he acquires the legal title by the decree vesting it or by delivery of the deed. The title is held in trust for the purchaser from the time of sale, his subsequently acquired title relating back to the time of sale. Am Jur 2d, Judicial Sales § 201; Am Jur 2d, Mortgages § 780; Am Law of Prop §§ 16.189, 16.195; CJS, Judicial Sales § 38.

17-15B Interests Acquired.

Lien holders, see also 1-32F.
Senior liens, see 17-21H.

A purchaser under a judgment is entitled to stand in the place of the judgment creditor, and is invested with all his rights against the judgment debtor and those claiming under him. Barr v. Hatch, 3 Ohio 527 (1828).

A sheriff's deed, under judicial sale, passes all rights and interests of the mortgagee in the premises to the purchaser. Childs v. Childs, 10 OS 339 (1859); Frische v. Kramer, 16 Ohio 125 (1847).

Further research: O Jur 3d, Judicial Sales § 114; O Jur 3d, Mortgages, etc. § 444.

LAW IN GENERAL

All the interests of the parties to the proceeding who were properly before the court pass by the sale, unless otherwise ordered by the court. The purchaser acquires no other rights except, by virtue of being a bona fide purchaser, outstanding equities may be barred. Interests of which the purchaser had actual or constructive notice are not affected by the sale unless the owners were properly before the court. Tiffany § 1528.

17-15C   As Bona Fide Purchasers; Warranty.

Notice, see also 1-32F.

The rule of caveat emptor applies in all its rigor to purchasers at judicial sales. They take the property without warranty and subject to every lien which could be asserted against the creditor upon whose judgment the land is sold. Corwin v. Benham, 2 OS 36 (1853).

After payment of the purchase price, a purchaser at judicial sale occupies the general position of a bona fide purchaser. He is subject to the recording laws and is entitled to their protection.

Further research: O Jur 3d, Judicial Sales § 120.

LAW IN GENERAL

A considerable number of cases have held that the purchaser may be entitled to an abatement in price, or to rescission or avoidance of the sale for mistake or misrepresentation as to acreage or boundaries of the tract sold. 69 ALR2d 254.

17-15D   Liability for Purchase Price; Defects in Title.

Application of purchase price, see 17-28D.
Liability before confirmation, see 17-28B.

R.C. 2329.30 provides: "The court from which an execution or order of sale issues, upon notice and motion of the officer who makes the sale, or of an interested party, shall punish as for contempt any purchaser of real property who fails to pay the purchase money therefor." (As eff. 10-1-53.)

There is an essential difference between a sheriff's sale and a private sale, in this: The purchaser at the former purchases at his peril, and the purchase money goes to the creditor — not to the owner of the land; and if the title fails he loses his consideration. He has no recourse. The purchaser at private sale may look to his vendor for redress. If his title fails, he may sue and recover back the consideration paid. Oviatt v. Brown, 14 Ohio 285 (1846).

Where, under a decree in equity, real estate has been sold and, after confirmation of the sale, suit is brought against the purchaser to recover the purchase money, it is no defense to show that the purchaser was mistaken as to the character and quality of the property. "If, before the sale was confirmed by the court, the defendant had applied for relief, and had moved to set the sale aside, the court in its discretion, might have done so." Mechanics' Savings & Bldg. Loan Ass'n v. O'Conner, 29 OS 651, 656 (1876).

A purchaser at executor's land sale cannot recover back sufficient of the purchase price to compensate him for loss by reason of outstanding dower. Arnold v. Donaldson, 46 OS 73, 18 NE 540, 20 WLB 390, 431 (1888).

Where a party having a dower interest was not made party to foreclosure suit, purchaser could not be adjudged guilty of contempt for declining to take the property. Gale Realty Co. v. Cook, 32 App 22, 165 NE 744, 7 Abs 230, 29 OLR 74 (1929).

Judgment directing imprisonment until purchase price is paid held erroneous as without due process and amounting to imprisonment for debt. Bloomberg v. Roach, 43 App 178, 182 NE 891, 13 Abs 87 (1930).

LAW IN GENERAL

The liability of the purchaser after confirmation for the purchase price may be enforced by an action at law for the amount of the bid or for damages, or by charging him with the amount of the deficiency at a resale, or by proceedings in contempt, or by other summary process. The purchaser is required to make payment to the proper person. He is not bound to see to the application of the purchase price. Am Jur 2d, Judicial Sales § 318; CJS, Judicial Sales § 46.

Many cases hold that, after confirmation, the purchaser may not defend against payment of the purchase price except for fraud. However, relief is frequently granted, prior to payment of the purchase price, for defects in or liens on the title or for material damage to the property. 63 ALR 974.

17-15E   Invalid Sales.

Collateral attack, see Section 16-13.
Reversal, see Section 16-14.

A decree, if erroneous, cannot be questioned in resisting a sale upon execution under it. Title will pass under such an execution sale but not upon an execution sale under a void judgment. Douglass v. Massie, 16 Ohio 271 (1847); Piatt v. Piatt, 9 Ohio 37 (1839).

LAW IN GENERAL

When the sale is invalid, or is vacated, the purchaser is entitled to a return of the purchase money paid or is entitled to subrogation. Am Law of Prop § 14.27; 142 ALR 310; CJS, Judicial Sales § 67.

17-15F   Purchase by Officer.

Statute, see 17-26B.

A purchase of real estate at a judicial sale by one who served as an appraiser is not strictly void, but is voidable only. Terrill v. Auchauer, 14 OS 80 (1862).

Further research: O Jur 3d, Judicial Sales § 31.

LAW IN GENERAL

A purchase by the officer conducting the sale, or by any person inconsistent with his duties, is voidable only, even when the statute declares it to be void. Such a sale is ordinarily set aside as to such purchaser without proof of actual fraud but is not set aside as to a subsequent innocent purchaser for value. Am Law of Prop § 13.21; CJS, Judicial Sales § 14.

17-15G Purchase by Obligor.

Cotenants, see Section 5-12.
Life tenants, see 11-63F.

LAW IN GENERAL

A lien is revived or remains on the premises sold under some decisions in other states, when the purchaser has an obligation to pay the lien. Am Jur 2d, Judicial Sales §§ 268, 269; CJS, Judicial Sales § 40.

17-15H Right to Redeem.

No statutory right to redeem, see 17-11C.

17-15I Ratification and Estoppel.

See also Section 16-69.

A party who has received a part of the proceeds arising from a sale of property, is estopped from denying or disputing the legality of such sale. Merry v. Walker, 2 Dec Repr 308 (C.P. 1860).

LAW IN GENERAL

Acceptance or retention of his share of the proceeds by a party with full knowledge of his rights is usually held to be sufficient as a ratification, if the court had jurisdiction of the subject matter. 2 ALR2d 6; CJS, Judicial Sales § 26.

The conduct of a person may prevent him, under the general equitable principles of estoppel, from attacking the sale. Claimants may be estopped by acquiescence in the sale or by failure to assert their rights. Am Jur 2d, Judicial Sales §§ 368, 369, 371.

17-15J Writ of Possession.

A writ of possession can be used only against the parties to the suit, and cannot be used to disturb the possession of a stranger to such suit. Nunn v. Hutchison, 1 Abs 283 (App. 1922).

A purchaser in foreclosure is entitled to an equitable writ to put him in possession against the defendants or those who come into possession under the defendants during pendency of the suit. Tetterbach v. Meyer, 10 Dec Repr 212, 19 WLB 221 (C.P. 1888).

Further research: O Jur 3d, Mortgages, etc. § 454.

DIVISION 17-2: PARTIES; PROCEDURE

SECTION 17-21: PARTIES GENERALLY

Class suits, see Section 17-22.
Lis pendens, see Section 17-12.
Names of parties, see Section 1-27.

17-21A One of Joint Lien Holders as Plaintiff.

Civil Rule 19.1 (compulsory joinder) requires joinder not formerly required under Ohio procedure or the federal rules. (As eff. 7-1-70.)

17-21B Foreclosure upon One of Two Liens.

Res judicata, see 16-12A.

LAW IN GENERAL

When a party holds two liens upon the subject land and forecloses the senior one, without setting up the other, he is barred from asserting the junior lien. Am Jur 2d, Mortgages § 557.

17-21C Necessary Parties.

Leases, see also 17-11G.

Necessary parties are those without whom no decree at all can be effectively made determining the principal issues in the cause. Proper parties are those without whom a substantial decree may be made, but not a decree which shall completely settle all the questions which may be involved in the controversy and conclude the rights of all the persons who have any interest in the subject matter of the litigation. Schmidt v. Weather-Seal, Inc., 71 App 387, 50 NE2d 362, 26 OO 322 (1943).

One appearing in a representative capacity in a lawsuit is a different person from that same individual appearing on his own behalf. McKelvey v. McKelvey, 90 App 563, 107 NE2d 555, 48 OO 207 (1951).

The rights of a tenant under a lease of real estate previously mortgaged are not terminated by a foreclosure action upon the mortgage to which the tenant has not been made a party. The case of New York Life Ins. Co. v. Simplex Products Corp., 135 OS 501, 21 NE2d 585, 14 OO 396 (1939) holds that the purchaser at foreclosure sale acquires no rights against the mortgagor's lessee; the rule that foreclosure of a prior mortgage terminates a tenant's obligations under a lease made by the mortgagor after the lease, even though the tenant is not joined in the foreclosure action, is for the purpose of releasing the tenant from his obligations to a defaulting landlord and is an application of the rule that a covenant to pay rent is dependent upon the landlord's covenant of quiet enjoyment. Davis v. Boyajian, 11 Misc 97, 229 NE2d 116, 40 OO2d 344 (C.P. 1967).

Further research: O Jur 3d, Judicial Sales § 8.

LAW IN GENERAL

All persons who acquired interests in the land subsequent to the lien being enforced must be made parties in order to bar all rights of redemption. However, a minority of authorities hold that foreclosure terminating the interest of the mortgagor also extinguishes a lease made subsequent to the mortgage. Prior encumbrancers are necessary parties if the entire estate is to be sold unencumbered. All owners of the claim being enforced are necessary parties. 109 ALR 447; Tiffany § 1534.

17-21D Omission of Lien Holder or Owner.

Persons having liens upon land, not being made parties to the proceeding, will not be affected by a decree subjecting such lands to sale. Myers v. Hewitt, 16 Ohio 449 (1847).

Where a junior mortgagee is not made a party to the action for foreclosure, his rights remain unaffected and are not prejudiced by the foreclosure. Stewart v. Johnson, 30 OS 24, 2 WLB 64 (1876); Lumbermen's Mortgage Co. v. Stevens, 46 App 5, 187 NE 641, 12 Abs 553, 39 OLR 232 (1932).

It is error for the court to dismiss, without prejudice, a defendant lien holder, and order a sale of the property subject to his undetermined lien. Thatcher v. Dickinson, 3 CC 144, 2 CD 82 (1888).

"Failure to make a judgment lienholder a party defendant does not, in and of itself, deprive the court of jurisdiction to order a sale." Schmidt v. Weather-Seal, Inc., 71 App 387, 50 NE2d 362, 26 OO 322 (1943).

A proceeding in probate court to sell real estate to pay debts, without notice to an heir, is void as to that heir's interest and may be collaterally attacked by him. He may maintain an action in partition. Shackelford v. Alford, 119 App 63, 196 NE2d 609, 26 OO2d 152 (1963).

LAW IN GENERAL

When a lien holder is not joined, the proceeding is invalid and ineffective only as to such lien holder; that is, joinder is not necessary to the jurisdiction of the court. A purchaser at foreclosure may reforeclose against an omitted junior lien holder. The title of an owner of the land who is not a party is not affected, the purchaser at the judicial sale being merely subrogated to the rights of the parties. Am Law of Prop § 16.191; Tiffany § 1535.

17-21E Dower.

Partition, see 5-34H.
Priorities, see 14-23F.
Procedure, see also 14-24G.

R.C. 2103.041 provides: "In any action involving the judicial sale of real property for the purpose of satisfying the claims of creditors of an owner of an interest in the property, the spouse of the owner may be made a party to the action and the dower interest of the spouse, whether inchoate or otherwise, may be subjected to the sale without the consent of the spouse. The court shall determine the present value and priority of the dower interest, using the American Experience Table of Mortality as the basis for determining the value, and shall award the spouse a sum of money equal to the present value of the dower interest, to be paid out of the proceeds of the sale according to the priority of the interest. To the extent that the owner and his spouse are both liable for the indebtedness, the dower interest of the spouse is subordinate to the claims of their common creditors." (As eff. 11-16-77.)

R.C. 5305.15 to 5305.17 provide that answer may be filed by surviving spouse, or by guardian if insane, asking allowance in lieu of dower of money out of the proceeds of sale. The answer has the same effect as a deed of release to the purchaser of such estate of the dower interest of such spouse. (As eff. 10-1-53.)

A foreclosure, during the lifetime of the husband, to which the wife is not a party, does not bar her equity of redemption. McArthur v. Franklin, 15 OS 485 (1864).

Dower of spouse of owner is not barred where she is not a party to the suit. Where spouse of mortgagor did not execute the mortgage, her dower is not barred although she be a party to the suit but did not consent to the sale. Parmenter v. Binkley, 28 OS 32, 1 WLB 258 (1875).

Dower of wife is not barred in an action to marshal liens where mortgagee filed cross-petition asking for sale but no summons issues thereon for the wife. Kaufman v. Heckman, 13 CC(NS) 309, 22 CD 277, 282, 56 WLB 125 (1908).

Unassigned dower or dower inchoate is not subject to levy and execution. Answer by judgment debtors, holding inchoate right of dower, in proceedings to sell real estate in execution of judgment, consenting to sale, did not operate to transfer a lien to the purchase money (that is, to bar dower) since the creditor did not have a lien on the dower interest. The statutes apply to dower of a surviving spouse and not an inchoate dower. Good v. Crist, 23 App 484, 156 NE 146, 5 Abs 178 (1926).

Computation must be made separately on each tract and limited to the proceeds of such tract where the aggregate of the judgment liens on the tract exceeds the sale price. Dillman v. Warner, 54 App 170, 6 NE2d 757, 7 OO 492, 20 Abs 459 (1935).

Inchoate or consummate dower can be barred whether or not it is subordinate to the lien being enforced.

17-21F Personal Obligations.

Concurrent and successive actions, see 17-11D.

The holder may, in a single action, have judgment against all the makers of the note, and a sale of the mortgaged premises, although the mortgage is executed by only a part of the makers of the note. King v. Safford, 19 OS 587 (1869).

A mortgagor who has conveyed all his interest in the land, or any person who has only a personal liability on the mortgage obligation, is not a necessary party, unless for the purpose of obtaining a personal judgment against him.

17-21G   Executors and Administrators.

Mortgage not due, see 12-12C.

R.C. 2113.47 provides: "A mortgage belonging to an estate may be foreclosed by the executor or administrator." (As eff. 10-1-53.)

In proceedings to foreclose a mortgage after the death of the mortgagor, when no money judgment is demanded, the administrator of a deceased mortgagor is not a necessary party. McMahan v. Davis, 19 CC 242, 10 CD 467 (1899).

The administrator of mortgagor is not a necessary party, the sale price being less than the lien. Brownfield v. Home Owners Loan Corp., 49 NE2d 92, 38 Abs 30 (App. 1942).

An administratrix is not a proper party to an action involving real estate not needed to close the estate. Bracken v. Wagner, 134 NE2d 382, 3 OO2d 25, 74 Abs 85 (App. 1956). He should be made a party if a deficiency judgment is sought.

17-21H   Prior Lien Holders.

Claims not due in land sale proceedings, see 12-12C.
Statute on sale subject to prior liens, see R.C. 2329.20 at 17-25A.

It is prejudicial error to decree foreclosure of undue first mortgage, without consent, upon suit of subsequent lien holder; the proper practice is to grant foreclosure and sale subject to the first mortgage. Metropolitan Mortgage Co. v. Nugent Furniture Co., 40 App 302, 179 NE 362, 11 Abs 7 (1931).

A mortgagee is not entitled to an injunction preventing the sale of the mortgaged premises by the sheriff at the instance of inferior attachment lienors. Nevins v. McClure, 22 Abs 187 (App. 1936).

The holder of a senior mortgage not due may be made a party defendant for the purpose of ascertaining the amount owing on it or of contesting its validity.

LAW IN GENERAL

Holders of liens prior to the one being enforced cannot be compelled to accept payment from the proceeds of sale unless their liens have matured. A senior lien holder is not a necessary party to an action to sell subject to his lien. He may be omitted as a party, and the property sold subject to his lien, unless he consents to the sale in the suit by the junior lienor. Exception to these rules may be made by statute, as in land sales by an administrator to pay debts of the estate. If the owner of any superior claim is made a party, he should act to protect his interest against an adverse decree. Am Law of Prop § 16.190; CJS, Mortgages § 514; Powell § 463.

17-21I Unknown Persons.

See statutes at 16-75C.

Unknown persons are bound by a judgment upon strict compliance with the statutes.

17-21J Adverse Claimants.

LAW IN GENERAL

Many cases hold that adverse claimants are not proper parties to a proceeding for judicial sale. However, the joinder is frequently sustained on equitable grounds, such as being incidental to the primary jurisdiction. Am Law of Prop § 16.190; Tiffany § 1537.

17-21K Pleading Generally.

Authority of attorney as to waiver or appearance, see 16-72A.
Jurisdiction, see Section 16-11.

Civil Rule 11 (signing of pleadings) provides in part: "Except when otherwise specifically provided by these rules, pleadings need not be verified or accompanied by affidavit." (As eff. 7-1-70.) The only common exception to this rule is for a temporary restraining order.

Civil Rule 18 (joinder of claims and remedies) permits unrelated claims to be asserted as in Federal Rule 18(a). (As eff. 7-1-70.)

A cross-petitioner may proceed to secure satisfaction of his judgment lien after dismissal by the plaintiff. Central Hyde Park Savings & Loan Co. v. Feck, 77 App 343, 67 NE2d 44, 33 OO 203, 45 Abs 129 (1945).

When a petition is filed by regularly admitted members of the bar, a presumption arises that they were duly authorized to file it. State of Minnesota v. Karp, 84 App 51, 84 NE2d 76, 39 OO 96, 52 Abs 513 (1948).

The judgment of a court upon a subject of litigation within its jurisdiction, but not brought before it by any statement of claim of the parties is void as lacking due process. Boyle v. Public Adjustment & Constr. Co., 87 App 264, 93 NE2d 795, 42 OO 478, 57 Abs 129 (1950).

Even when judgment cannot be rendered on a cross-petition on a note and to foreclose the mortgage, the court is not precluded from awarding compensation thereon, in equity, for valuable improvements made with knowledge of the parties. Rittenour v. Smith, 107 App 119, 157 NE2d 367, 7 OO2d 493 (1958).

The filing of an amended petition is an abandonment of the pleading thus amended, and the pleading supersedes the original petition. The amount of damages prayed for cannot be increased by the amendment without new service being had. Miller v. Risman, 2 App 2d 306, 199 NE2d 897, 31 OO2d 354, 94 Abs 368 (1964).

An attorney who is without special authorization has no implied or apparent authority, solely by virtue of his general retainer, to compromise and settle his client's claim or cause of action. Ratification must follow knowledge of the facts. Morr v. Crouch, 19 OS2d 24, 249 NE2d 80, 48 OO2d 43 (1969).

Standard of Title Examination

(Adopted by Ohio State Bar Association in 1957)

Problem 7.1A:
 Does the omission or irregularity of a verification of a pleading render a title unmarketable which is based upon a subsequent decree in the case?

Standard 7.1A:
 No.

SECTION 17-22: REPRESENTATION OF INTERESTS

Attorneys at law, see 17-21K.
Process and its service, see Section 16-75.
Reinvestment of proceeds, see Section 17-42.
Unknown persons made defendants, see 16-75C.

17-22A Living Persons; Virtual Representation.

Members of a class may be bound by a judgment upon the doctrine of virtual representation, where there exists a community of interest between those to be bound and their representatives. The interest of those who are absent must be identical with those who are before the court. Winfrey v. Marks, 14 App2d 127, 237 NE2d 324, 43 OO2d 307 (1968). (Class suits in which one or more persons sue or defend for all, see Civil Rule 23.)

LAW IN GENERAL

As a general rule in the absence of statute, a living owner of a future interest who is not a party is bound by the proceeding provided (a) he was not a presumptive taker at the commencement of the action, (b) one or more of the presumptive takers, not acting hostilely to the represented interest, is a party, and (c) the limitation creating the interest is indefinite as to persons, such as to "heirs" or to "surviving spouse." A future appointee of a power is usually held to be represented by the donee of the power.

The rule is based on the principle that the interests so bound are sufficiently represented by the persons who are parties, and is known as the doctrine of virtual representation. The qualifications of the doctrine usually make it insufficient for a marketable title insofar as the claims of living persons are concerned. Representation of the owners of an interest which subsequently fails is immaterial.

Am Law of Prop §§ 4.86, 4.89; Powell § 295; Restatement, Property § 181; Simes and Smith § 1803.

17-22B Unborn Persons.

Unknown persons, see 16-75C.

R.C. 2307.131 provides: "If in any action it shall appear that any persons not yet born are or may become entitled to, or may upon coming into being claim to be entitled to, any future interest, legal or equitable, whether arising by way of remainder, reversion, possibility of reverter, executory devise, upon the happening of a condition subsequent, or otherwise, in any property, real or personal, involved in such suit, the court may, and upon the application of any party to the action shall, appoint some competent and disinterested person as trustee of the interest of such persons not yet born, to appear for and represent in such cause such future interest and to defend the suit for and on behalf of such persons not yet born; and any judgment or decree rendered in such suit shall be as binding and effectual for all purposes as though such persons were born and were parties to such suit. Such persons not yet born need not be served by publication.

"In case the beneficiary of any such future interest is a charitable trust, not in being, service shall be made upon the attorney general who shall represent such interest." (As eff. 10-4-55.) Prior to October 4, 1955 there was no statute as to representation of unborn persons.

A decree in a suit to which the first holder, a living person, is made a party will conclude the rights of after-born remaindermen. Bennett v. Fleming, 105 OS 352, 137 NE 900, 1 Abs 214, 20 OLR 166, 172 (1922).

None of the class of devisees named in the will as unborn were then in being. Held, that it was unnecessary to name these unborn devisees as parties to the action brought to disentail the property. Schneider v. Wolf, 120 OS 524, 166 NE 679, 7 Abs 335, 29 OLR 256 (1929).

The doctrine of virtual representation requires that the representative for unborn persons must have a similar or identical interest in the litigation. Remaindermen who had sold their interests could not represent unborn remaindermen. Benner & Co. v. Atlas Remainder, Inc., 20 Misc 59, 47 OO2d 466 (U.S. Dist. Ct. 1969).

LAW IN GENERAL

A child conceived but unborn is a living person for most purposes but not for the purpose of determining whether he is bound by a judicial proceeding. An unborn person is bound under the doctrine of virtual representation when he would have been bound if living; he is also bound under the doctrine when (a) a party to the action is a member of a class to which the unborn person may be admitted, or (b) a party has a vested estate of inheritance which is prior to the future interest of the unborn person, or (c) a party is the presumptive taker of an estate of inheritance and the unborn person may take in his stead, or (d) a party has a life estate with remainder to his unborn issue. It is required that such party not act hostilely to the interest of the unborn person, and that the decree not discriminate against such interest in favor of the party.

Am Law of Prop § 4.87; Powell § 296; Restatement, Property § 183.

17-22C Trusts.

Civil Rule 17(A) (real party in interest) provides for prosecution of actions in the name of the real party in interest or his representative. (As eff. 7-1-70.)

LAW IN GENERAL

A beneficiary of a trust, whether living or not, is not a necessary party where the trustee is a party, provided the latter is competent to represent the beneficiary under the law of trusts. Whether or not the trustee will be regarded as sufficiently representing the beneficiary is often a difficult problem; the solution is said to depend upon (a) the nature of the suit and (b) the character and extent of the trusteeship. Am Law of Prop § 8.45; 9 ALR2d 10; Restatement, Property §§ 181, 186; Simes and Smith § 1811; Tiffany § 243.

SECTION 17-23: GOVERNMENT AS PARTY DEFENDANT

17-23A United States.

28 U.S.C. § 1399 (Partition action involving United States) provides: "Any civil action by any tenant in common or joint tenant for the partition of lands, where the United States is one of the tenants in common or joint tenants, may be brought only in the judicial district where such lands are located or, if located in different districts in the same State, in any of such districts." (As eff. 6-25-48.)

28 U.S.C. § 1444 (Foreclosure action against United States) provides: "Any action brought under section 2410 of this title against the United States in any state court may be removed by the United States to the district court of the United States for the district and division in which the action is pending." (As eff. 5-24-49.)

28 U.S.C. § 2409 (Partition actions involving United States) provides that any action by any tenant in common, where the United States is one of such tenants and a defendant, shall proceed, and be determined, in the same manner as would a similar action between private persons. (As eff. 6-25-48.)

28 U.S.C. § 2410 (Joinder of United States in certain proceedings) provides: "(a) Under the conditions prescribed in this section and section 1444 [providing for removal by the United States to district court] of this title for the protection of the United States, the United States may be named a party in any civil action or suit in any district court, or in any state court having jurisdiction of the subject matter —

"(1) to quiet title to,

"(2) to foreclose a mortgage or other lien upon,

"(3) to partition,

"(4) to condemn, or

"(5) of interpleader or in the nature of interpleader with respect to,

real or personal property on which the United States has or claims a mortgage or other lien.

"(b) The complaint or pleading shall set forth with particularity the nature of the interest or lien of the United States. In actions or suits involving liens arising under the internal revenue laws the complaint or pleading shall include the name and address of the taxpayer whose liability created the lien and, if a notice of the tax lien was filed, the identity of the internal revenue office which filed the notice, and the date and place such notice of lien was filed. In actions in the state courts service upon the United States shall be made by serving the process of the court with a copy of the complaint upon the United States attorney for the district in which the action is brought or upon an assistant United States attorney or clerical employee designated by the United States attorney in writing filed with the clerk of the court in which the action is brought and by sending copies of the process and complaint, by registered mail, or by certified mail, to the Attorney General of the United States at Washington, District of Columbia. In such actions the United States may appear and answer, plead or demur within sixty days after such service or such further time as the court may allow.

"(c) A judgment or decree in such action or suit shall have the same effect respecting the discharge of the property from the mortgage or other lien held by the United States as may be provided with respect to such matters by the local law of the place where the court is situated. However, an action to foreclose a mortgage or other lien, naming the United States as a party under this section, must seek judicial sale. A sale to satisfy a lien inferior to one of the United States shall be made subject to and without disturbing the lien of the United States, unless the United States consents that the property may be sold free of its lien and the proceeds divided as the parties may be entitled. Where a sale of real estate is made to satisfy a lien prior to that of the United States, the United States shall have one year from the date of sale within which to redeem, except that with respect to a lien arising under the internal revenue laws the period shall be 120 days or the period allowable for redemption under state law, whichever is longer, and in any case in which, under the provisions of Section 505 of the Housing Act of 1950, as amended (12 U.S.C. 1701k), and subsection (d) of Section 1820 of Title 38 of the United States Code, the right to redeem does not arise, there shall be no right of redemption. In any case where the debt owing the United States is due, the United States may ask, by way of affirmative relief, for the foreclosure of its own lien and where property is sold to satisfy a first lien held by the United States, the United States may bid at the sale such sum, not exceeding the amount of its claim with expenses of sale, as may be directed by the head (or his delegate) of the department or agency of the United States which has charge of the administration of the laws in respect to which the claim of the United States arises.

"(d) In any case in which the United States redeems real property under this section or Section 7425 of the Internal Revenue Code of 1954, the amount to be paid for such property shall be the sum of —

"(1) the actual amount paid by the purchaser at such sale (which, in the case of a purchaser who is the holder of the lien being foreclosed, shall include the amount of the obligation secured by such lien to the extent satisfied by reason of such sale),

"(2) interest on the amount paid (as determined under paragraph (1)) at six per cent per annum from the date of such sale, and

"(3) the amount (if any) equal to the excess of (A) the expenses necessarily incurred in connection with such property, over (B) the income from such property plus (to the extent such property is used by the purchaser) a reasonable rental value of such property.

"(e) Whenever any person has a lien upon any real or personal property, duly recorded in the jurisdiction in which the property is located, and a junior lien, other than a tax lien, in favor of the United States attaches to such property, such person may make a written request to the officer charged with the administration of the laws in respect of which the lien of the United States arises, to have the same extinguished. If after appropriate investigation, it appears to such officer that the proceeds from the sale of the property would be insufficient to wholly or partly satisfy the lien of the United States, or that the claim of the United States has been satisfied or by lapse of time or otherwise has become unenforceable, such officer shall so report to the Comptroller General who may issue a certificate releasing the property from such lien." (As eff. 11-2-66.)

The amendment of 28 U.S.C. § 2410 by the Federal Tax Lien Act of 1966 was explained by the United States Attorneys of Columbus and Cleveland by a statement shown in "Ohio Bar" of January 23, 1967 as follows:

"Under 28 U.S.C., Section 2410, as enacted and previously amended, the United States has consented to be named a party defendant in any suit instituted in a federal or state court having jurisdiction of the subject matter for the purpose of quieting title to or foreclosing a mortgage or other lien upon real or personal property on which the United States has or claims a mortgage or other lien. As amended by Section 201 of the Federal Tax Lien Act of 1966, the Government's consent to be sued under Section 2410 has been broadened to include 'partition' actions, 'condemnation' actions, 'interpleader' actions and actions 'in the nature of interpleader.'

"Any pleading (whether or not designated as a complaint) which attempts to join the United States as a party in the types of actions named, where the action involved liens arising under the Internal Revenue Code, must set forth with particularity the nature of the interest or lien of the United States, i.e., (1) the name and address of the delinquent taxpayer, (2) if a notice of tax lien has been filed, the identity of the internal revenue office which filed the notice, and (3) the date and place such notice of lien was filed. Moreover, as in the past, service of process must be made upon the United States Attorney's office and a copy of the process and complaint must be sent to the Attorney

General of the United States by registered or certified mail. Unless these requirements are met, the pleading is defective as to the United States and is subject to a motion to dismiss. In such event, a judgment rendered in such a suit, or a judicial sale pursuant to such judgment, will not disturb the lien of the United States.

"A judgment or decree in any such action shall have the same effect respecting the discharge of the property from the mortgage or other lien held by the United States as may be provided with respect to such matters by the local law of the place where the court is situated. However, in a mortgage or lien foreclosure action, the property involved will be discharged from a junior federal mortgage or lien only if a judicial sale of the property is sought; in such situations, except where federal law precludes redemption, the United States may redeem real property sold within 120 days from the date of sale, or such longer period as may be allowed under local law."

28 U.S.C. § 2412 provides for the payment of costs and fees when United States is a party. (As eff. 9-3-82.)

INTERNAL REVENUE CODE PROVISIONS

26 U.S.C. § 7402(e) provides that an action to quiet title may be brought by United States in district court if the title it claims was derived from enforcement of a lien under the Internal Revenue Code. (As eff. 11-2-66.)

26 U.S.C. § 7424 (Intervention) provides: "If the United States is not a party to a civil action or suit, the United States may intervene in such action or suit to assert any lien arising under this title on the property which is the subject of such action or suit. The provisions of section 2410 of title 28 of the United States Code (except subsection (b)) and of section 1444 of title 28 of the United States Code shall apply in any case in which the United States intervenes as if the United States had originally been named a defendant in such action or suit. In any case in which the application of the United States to intervene is denied, the adjudication in such civil action or suit shall have no effect upon such lien." (As eff. 11-2-66.)

26 U.S.C. § 7425(a) (2) provides that doctrine of lis pendens is recognized as applicable to federal tax liens by stating that if notice of the lien has not been filed, at time the action is commenced, a judicial sale therein "shall have the same effect with respect to the discharge or divestment of such lien of the United States as may be provided with respect to such matters by the local law of the place where such property is situated." Provision is also made (subsection (d) (1)) for discharge of a federal tax lien upon a nonjudicial sale with the right of the government to redeem within 120 days after such a sale. (Lis pendens is still not operative against a junior federal mortgage or other nontax lien.) (As eff. 10-22-86.)

SECTION 17-24: DEFENSE OF INCOMPETENTS

Incompetents generally, see Chapter 15.

17-24A   Generally.

Service of process, see 15-11I and 15-12H.

See Civil Rule 17(B) (minors and incompetents) shown at 17-24B.

Civil Rule 25(B) (incompetency) provides for continuation of the action if a party is adjudged incompetent. (As eff. 7-1-70.)

17-24B   Guardians ad Litem.

Civil Rule 17(B) (minors or incompetent persons) provides: "Whenever a minor or incompetent person has a representative, such as a guardian or other like fiduciary, the representative may sue or defend on behalf of the minor or incompetent person. If a minor or incompetent person does not have a duly appointed representative he may sue by a next friend or defend by a guardian ad litem. When a minor or incompetent person is not otherwise represented in an action the court shall appoint a guardian ad litem or shall make such other order as it deems proper for the protection of such minor or incompetent person." (As eff. 7-1-85.)

Civil Rule 55(A) (entry of default judgment) provides, in part, that "no judgment by default shall be entered against a minor or an incompetent person unless represented in the action by a guardian or other such representative who has appeared therein." (As eff. 7-1-71.)

It is error for the court to decree against a lunatic without an answer from his guardian ad litem (trustee for suit). Sturges v. Longworth, 1 OS 544 (1853).

Where one appears and answers as guardian, and his answer is received and acted on by the court, the effect is the same as though he had been expressly appointed guardian ad litem, and appeared and answered as such. Rankin v. Kemp, 21 OS 651 (1871); Jelen v. Hine, 12 O Supp 12, 26 OO 191, 38 Abs 318 (C.P. 1943); Harvey v. Sampson, 50 NE2d 423, 38 Abs 375 (App. 1943).

A judgment rendered against an insane person, without the intervention of a trustee or guardian, is not void. It may be directly attacked. Johnson v. Pomeroy, 31 OS 247 (1877).

A judgment in an action against an infant who is sued personally without a guardian is not absolutely void, but is voidable only, if the record shows that a proper summons was issued and personal service was had upon the defendant, and cannot be collaterally attacked because a guardian ad litem was not appointed. Such a judgment is, however, open to direct attack, as by a proceeding to have it set aside; it will remain subject to review until a sufficient time shall have elapsed after the removal of the disability to bar such review. Nichols Bros. v. Koshinick, 19 CC(NS) 148, 32 CD 388 (1911); Long v. Mulford, 17 OS 484 (1867).

Appointment of guardian ad litem and filing of answer before service upon minor held nullities conferring no jurisdiction on the court. Carroll v. Employers Liability Assur. Corp., 47 App 146, 190 NE 590, 17 Abs 9, 40 OLR 132 (1933).

The defense of the ward under the designation of guardian ad litem instead of trustee for the suit could not prejudice the rights of the ward. Plessinger v. Bireley, 76 App 183, 62 NE2d 720, 31 OO 477, 43 Abs 631 (1945).

Adult codefendants of the minor may not invoke the failure to appoint a guardian for the suit to set the judgment aside as to them. Robinson v. Gatch, 85 App 484, 87 NE2d 904, 40 OO 345, 54 Abs 437 (1949).

The appointment of a guardian ad litem in a partition action after the sale has been confirmed but before distribution of the proceeds is not a defense of the minor under R.C. 2307.16. Beaver v. Bates, 109 App 164, 164 NE2d 429, 10 OO2d 386 (1958).

The duly appointed guardian can make defense for his ward in the guardian's land sale proceedings and no additional appointment of another person or of the guardian is necessary. Hasty v. Weller, 6 O Supp 71, 19 OO 304, 33 Abs 190 (Prob. 1940).

17-24C Statutes in Probate Code.

R.C. 2111.23 provides: "Whenever a ward, for whom a guardian of the estate or of the person and estate has been appointed, is interested in any suit or proceeding in the probate court, such guardian shall in all such suits or proceedings act as guardian ad litem for such ward, except as to suits or proceedings in which the guardian has an adverse interest. Whenever a minor or other person under legal disability, for whom no guardian of the estate or of the person and estate has been appointed, is interested in any suit or proceeding in such court, the court may appoint a guardian or a guardian ad litem. In a suit or proceeding in which the guardian has an adverse interest, the court shall appoint a guardian ad litem to represent such minor or other person under legal disability." (As eff. 10-16-53.)

From January 1, 1932 until October 16, 1953 this statute read "in which the guardian is personally interested" instead of "in which the guardian has an adverse interest."

SECTION 17-25: APPRAISEMENT

17-25A Generally.

Corporate property, see also 17-27C.

R.C. 2329.17 provides: "When execution is levied upon lands and tenements, the officer who makes the levy shall call an inquest of three disinterested freeholders, residents of the county where the lands taken in execution are situated, and administer to them an oath impartially to appraise the property so levied upon, upon actual view. They forthwith shall return to such officer, under their hands, an estimate of the real value of the property in money." (As eff. 10-1-53.)

R.C. 2329.20 provides: "No tract of land shall be sold for less than two thirds of the value returned in the inquest required by section 2329.17 of the Revised Code; except that in all cases where a junior mortgage or other junior lien is sought to be enforced against real estate by an order, judgment, or decree of court, subject to a prior lien thereon, and such prior lien, and the claims or obligations secured thereby, are unaffected by such order, judgment, or decree, the court making such order, judgment, or decree, may determine the minimum amount for which such real estate may be sold, such minimum amount to be not less than two thirds of the difference between the value of the real estate appraised as provided in such section, and the amount remaining unpaid on the claims or obligations secured by such prior lien." (As eff. 10-1-53.) It is very seldom practicable in execution sales for the court to make a finding of the unpaid amount of the prior liens.

R.C. 2329.22 provides: "Sections 2329.19 to 2329.21, inclusive, of the Revised Code do not affect the sale of lands by the state. All lands, the property of individuals, indebted to the state for debt, taxes, or in any other manner shall be sold without valuation for the discharge of such debt or taxes." (As eff. 10-1-53.)

R.C. 2329.25 provides: "If the property of a clerk of the court of common pleas, sheriff, coroner, county court judge, or constable, or of a collector of state, county, municipal corporation, or township taxes, is levied on, for or on account of money by him collected or received in his official capacity, the property so levied on shall be sold without valuation." (As eff. 1-1-58.)

R.C. 2329.52 in part provides: "When premises are ordered to be sold, if said premises, or a part thereof, remain unsold for want of bidders after having been once appraised, advertised, and offered for sale, the court from which the order of sale issued may, on motion of the plaintiff or defendant and from time to time until said premises are disposed of, order a new appraisement and sale or direct the amount for which said premises, or a part thereof, may be sold." (As eff. 10-1-53.)

Further research: O Jur 3d, Judicial Sales § 23; O Jur 3d, Mortgages, etc. §§ 403-405.

SECTION 17-26: NOTICE; TIME AND PLACE OF SALE

17-26A Notice of Sale.

R.C. 2329.23 and 2329.24 provide that advertisements for sale of lands in a city or village, in addition to a description, shall contain the street number. If no such number exists then the name of the street upon which located and the names of the intersecting streets immediately north and south or east and west. If for land outside a city or village, then to contain the name of the township. (As eff. 10-1-53.)

R.C. 2329.26 provides: "Lands and tenements taken in execution shall not be sold until the officer taking them gives public notice of the time and place of sale, for at least thirty days before the day of sale, by advertisement in a newspaper printed and of general circulation in the county. The court ordering sale may, in the order of sale, designate the newspaper in which such notice shall be published." (As eff. 10-7-77.)

R.C. 2329.27 provides that it is sufficient to publish the advertisement for three consecutive weeks. (As eff. 9-27-76.)

Where a public sale was ordered by the court, held and confirmed, and the purchaser received his deed, such sale will not be set aside on appeal on the ground that twenty-eight days provided in G.C. 10510-38 (final paragraph, R.C. 2127.32) had not elapsed from the first publication of notice to the date of sale. Richcreek v. Clark, 64 App 305, 28 NE2d 670, 18 OO 118 (1939).

Further research: O Jur 3d, Judicial Sales § 48.

17-26B   Time and Place of Sale.

Purchase by officer, see also 17-15F.

R.C. 2329.39 provides: "Sale of lands or tenements under execution or order of sale must be held in the county in which they are situated and at the courthouse, unless otherwise ordered by the court. Purchase of real and personal property, by the officer making the sale thereof, or by an appraiser of such property, shall be fraudulent and void." (As eff. 10-1-53.)

Further research: O Jur 3d, Judicial Sales § 59.

SECTION 17-27:   BIDS; TERMS OF SALE; RETURN

17-27A   Bids Generally.

Liability for purchase price, see 17-15D.
Resale ordered, see 17-28B.

The contract of purchase is made with the officer as representing all the interests involved in the suit. He and the purchaser are the only parties to the contract; and he alone can maintain an action for breach of the contract. Galpin v. Lamb, 29 OS 529, 2 WLB 43 (1876).

A judicial sale of real estate will not be set aside for inadequacy of price, unless the inadequacy is so great as to shock the conscience, or unless there are additional circumstances against its fairness. Dairymen's Co-op. Sales Co. v. Frederick Dairy, Inc., 17 Abs 690 (App. 1934).

Further research: O Jur 3d, Judicial Sales § 74.

LAW IN GENERAL

An offer may be withdrawn by the bidder before it is accepted, or a sale may be adjourned by the officer but a right to neither withdrawal nor adjournment exists after a bid has been accepted. Am Jur 2d, Judicial Sales §§ 141, 142; CJS, Judicial Sales § 22.

17-27B Assignment of Bid.

Bid at judicial sale is proper subject of assignment, and rights thereunder are capable of passing to assignee. Watson v. Watson, 24 App 45, 156 NE 241 (1927).

17-27C Terms of Sale.

R.C. 1701.77 provides: "Property of any description, and any interest therein, of a corporation, domestic or foreign, may be sold under the judgment or decree of a court, as provided in the Revised Code with respect to similar property of natural persons, at public or private sale, in such manner, at such time and place, on such notice by publication or otherwise, and on such terms, as the court adjudging or decreeing such sale deems equitable and proper, but it shall not be necessary to appraise such property or to advertise the sale thereof otherwise than as the court adjudges or decrees." (As eff. 10-11-55.)

R.C. 2329.52 in part provides: "The court may order that the premises be sold as follows: One third cash in hand, one third in nine months from the day of sale, and the remaining one third in eighteen months from the day of sale, the deferred payments to draw interest at six per cent and be secured by a mortgage on the premises." (As eff. 10-1-53.)

Further research: O Jur 3d, Judicial Sales § 65.

17-27D Sale in Parcels.

Property in more than one county, see 16-11D.

R.C. 2323.07 in part provides: "When the real property to be sold is in one or more tracts, the court may order the officer who makes the sale to subdivide, appraise, and sell them in parcels, or sell any one of the tracts as a whole." (As eff. 10-1-53.)

Sheriffs, guardians, and administrators, making public sale of lands, may divide a tract levied upon and appraised entire, and sell it in parcels, being responsible for abuse of discretion. Stall v. Macalester, 9 Ohio 19 (1839).

Further research: O Jur 3d, Judicial Sales § 61.

17-27E Return of Order of Sale.

R.C. 2329.28 provides: "The sheriff shall indorse on the writ of execution his proceedings thereon, and the clerk of the court of common pleas, upon the return thereof, immediately shall record all such indorsements at length, in the execution docket, or other docket provided for that purpose. That record shall be a part of the record of the court of common pleas." (As eff. 10-1-51.)

Further research: O Jur 3d, Mortgages, etc. § 429.

SECTION 17-28: CONFIRMATION AND OTHER ORDERS OF COURT

17-28A Necessity and Effect of Confirmation.

Collateral attack, see Section 16-13.
Occasions of lack of jurisdiction, see 16-11B.
Official deeds, see 8-31Q.

R.C. 2329.31 provides that if the court finds that the sale was made in conformity with law, it shall direct the clerk to make such journal entry and the officer to make a deed to the purchaser. (As eff. 10-1-53.)

The title does not pass to the purchaser, the sheriff has no authority to make a deed to the purchaser, and the purchaser is not entitled to the possession of the land, until the court has judicially determined that the sale has been legally made, and has confirmed the sale and ordered the sheriff to make a deed. Bassett v. Daniels, 10 OS 617, 619 (1858); Curtis v. Norton, 1 Ohio 278 (1824).

Mere irregularities are cured by the order of confirmation. Mayer v. Wick, 15 OS 548, 552 (1864).

A deed for real estate executed by an officer of the court pursuant to its order confirming a judicial sale takes effect by relation back on the day of sale and vests in the purchaser the right to intermediate rents. Jashenosky v. Volrath, 59 OS 540, 53 NE 46, 41 WLB 97, 196 (1899).

A judicial sale of property at public auction to an innocent purchaser and confirmation thereof may not be set aside in the absence of fraud, irregularity or bad faith. Kavas v. Barry, 167 NE2d 674, 14 OO2d 276, 83 Abs 554 (App. 1960).

The mortgagor's right to redeem exists and may be exercised as an absolute right until confirmation of the sale. Where the only valid lien was redeemed by payment prior to the sale, it is error thereafter to confirm such sale. Citizens Loan & Savings Co. v. Stone, 1 App2d 551, 206 NE2d 17, 30 OO2d 584 (1965).

Further research: O Jur 3d, Enforcement and Execution of Judgments §§ 253-256; O Jur 3d, Judicial Sales § 80; O Jur 3d, Mortgages, etc. §§ 430, 431.

LAW IN GENERAL

Confirmation is conclusive of the rights of the parties and of the purchaser to the extent that the sale cannot thereafter be collaterally attacked for irregularities. It cures all defects except those materially affecting the validity of the sale. Lack of jurisdiction is not cured as the entire proceeding is void in such case. CJS, Judicial Sales § 29.

The claims of the parties are transferred from the land to the proceeds by a judicial sale, with the right to distribution in the order of their priority. Tiffany § 1529.

17-28B   Refusal of Confirmation; Ordering Resale.

Liability for purchase price after confirmation, see 17-15D.

If before the sale was confirmed by the court, the defendant had moved to set the sale aside, the court in its discretion might have done so. Mechanics' Savings & Bldg. Loan Ass'n v. O'Conner, 29 OS 651, 656 (1876).

The court should either confirm or set aside the sale, but should not modify its terms. Ohio Life Ins. & Trust Co. v. Goodin, 10 OS 557 (1860).

Where the judgment debtor pays the judgment in full, after a sheriff's sale of his lands to satisfy it, it is error for the court thereafter to confirm such sale against the debtor's objection. Reed v. Radigan, 42 OS 292, 12 WLB 226 (1884).

The confirmation of the sale rests in the sound discretion of the trial court. Laub v. Warren Guarantee Title & Mortgage Co., 54 App 457, 8 NE2d 258, 8 OO 220, 23 Abs 514 (1936).

In the absence of any legal ground for withholding confirmation, it is the duty of the court to confirm the sale and upon confirmation the purchaser is vested with an equitable title which merges into legal title upon delivery of the deed. Central Nat. Bank v. Ely, 44 NE2d 822, 37 Abs 18 (App. 1942).

In a proceeding to set aside a judicial sale, the purchasers are not parties in interest before confirmation, but after such confirmation they become necessary parties. Ozias v. Renner, 78 App 166, 64 NE2d 325, 33 OO 504, 44 Abs 415 (1945).

A judicial sale of real estate will not be set aside for inadequacy of price, unless the inadequacy is so great as to shock the conscience, or unless there be additional circumstances against its fairness. Myers v. Duibley, 94 App 228, 236, 114 NE2d 832, 51 OO 393 (1952).

"Generally, a judicial sale can be set aside after confirmation only upon a showing of gross inadequacy of price, but the court may refuse to confirm a sale upon a showing of substantial inadequacy of price." German Village Products, Inc. v. Miller, 32 App2d 288, 290 NE2d 855, 61 OO2d 350 (1972).

The court may refuse to confirm a sheriff's sale in foreclosure where the motion to set aside the sale is filed on the day of the sale, and the court determines in its own discretion that to confirm the sale would be inequitable and unfair. Michigan Mortgage Corp. v. Oakley, 68 App2d 83, 426 NE2d 1195, 22 OO3d 76 (1980).

Further research: O Jur 3d, Judicial Sales § 90.

LAW IN GENERAL

The purchaser at the sale has a right to confirmation in the absence of fraud, misconduct or other circumstance which would make approval inequitable. Lapse of time does not extinguish the right to confirmation. Defective title, mistake without negligence of the complainant, and destruction of the property have been held sufficient to justify refusal of confirmation. The refusal extinguishes the liability of the purchaser. Am Jur 2d, Judicial Sales §§ 181, 182; CJS, Judicial Sales § 28.

Ordering a resale is within the sound discretion of a court of equity. Am Jur 2d, Judicial Sales § 178; CJS, Judicial Sales § 28.

17-28C   Order to Sell.

Return of order, see 17-27E.

A decree for sale does not become dormant, and a plea of laches on account of a delay of fifteen years in applying for confirmation does not lie in the mouth of the debtor who raises no question except the delay in the confirmation. Walters v. Homberg, 3 App 326, 19 CC(NS) 514, 25 CD 337, 60 WLB 57 (1914); Beaumont v. Herrick, 24 OS 445 (1873).

Further research: O Jur 3d, Mortgages, etc. § 397.

LAW IN GENERAL

An order or decree prior to the sale is essential to a valid judicial sale. The omission cannot be later supplied, and the proceeding is not validated by a confirmation. However, issuance of the order may be presumed. Am Jur 2d, Judicial Sales §§ 38, 40; CJS, Judicial Sales § 8.

17-28D   Distribution.

Official deeds, see 8-31Q.

R.C. 311.17 provides fees of sheriff for service and return of writs and for "poundage on all moneys actually made and paid to the sheriff on execution, decree, or sale of real estate, one per cent." (As eff. 12-26-84.)

R.C. 2109.57 provides for the appointment by probate court of a trustee to collect and manage the unpaid part of the proceeds of the property sold in any action pending in any court of record, if any person entitled is unknown or is a nonresident and not presented in the action. (As eff. 10-1-53.)

Interest on a judgment can be properly computed only to the day of the judicial sale. Schmidt v. Penn. Mut. Life Ins. Co., 25 Abs 652 (App. 1935).

When the property is sold to the second mortgagee for an amount insufficient to pay his claim in full, the sheriff is not entitled to any poundage. Union Joint Stock Land Bank v. Selden, 64 App 182, 28 NE2d 567, 18 OO2d 28 (1939).

In partition, the sheriff is not entitled to poundage when one of the parties elects to take at the appraised value. 1950 OAG 2613.

LAW IN GENERAL

The proceeds of the sale take the place of the land when the title of the parties is divested by the confirmation. The money is distributed in accordance with an order of the court commonly included in the decree of confirmation. The purchaser is under no obligation concerning the proper application of the purchase price. Tiffany §§ 1528, 1529.

DIVISION 17-3: BANKRUPTCY

SECTION 17-31: GENERALLY

Conflicting jurisdiction of state courts, see 16-23D.

17-31A Effect of Discharge.

11 U.S.C. § 727(b) provides in part that "except as provided in Sec. 523, a discharge discharges the debtor from all debts that arose before the date of the order for relief" under chapter 7.

There is no difference in the law or procedure after adjudication in bankruptcy between voluntary and involuntary proceedings.

LAW IN GENERAL

Unless the court orders otherwise, any property scheduled and otherwise administered at the time of the closing of a case is abandoned to the debtor. 11 U.S.C. § 554.

The trustee may avoid any transfer of an interest of the debtor made within ninety days before filing the petition which is deemed preferential and may avoid a preferential transfer made up to one year before the filing of the petition if the creditor was an insider. 11 U.S.C. § 547.

The trustee may avoid any transfer of an interest of the debtor in property, or any obligation incurred by the debtor, made or incurred within one year before the date of filing of the petition, if the debtor made such transfer or incurred such obligation for less than reasonable value. 11 U.S.C. § 548.

A discharge of a debtor under chapter 13 may be granted after completion by debtor of all payments under the plan, and it thereby discharges the debtor from all debts provided for by the plan or disallowed under Sec. 502 with a few exceptions. 11 U.S.C. § 1328.

17-31B Revocation of Discharge.

LAW IN GENERAL

On request of the trustee or a creditor, and after notice and a hearing, the court shall revoke a discharge if the discharge was obtained through fraud of the debtor and the requesting party did not know of the fraud before the discharge was granted; or if the debtor acquired property that is property of the estate and fraudulently failed to report the acquisition; or the debtor refused to obey a lawful order of the court. 11 U.S.C. § 727(d).

The request for revocation of a discharge must be made within one year after the discharge is granted, or in some cases within one year after the case is closed. 11 U.S.C. § 727(e).

17-31C   After-acquired Property.

LAW IN GENERAL

Any interest in property acquired by the debtor within 180 days after date of filing the petition, by bequest, devise, or inheritance, or as a result of a property settlement agreement with debtor spouse, or as beneficiary or a life insurance policy or death benefit plan is an asset of the estate. 11 U.S.C. § 541(2).

17-31D   Provable Debts.

LAW IN GENERAL

A claim in bankruptcy means: "(A) right to payment whether or not such right is reduced to judgment, liquidated, unliquidated, fixed, contingent, matured, unmatured, disputed, undisputed, legal, equitable, secured, or unsecured; or

"(B) right to an equitable remedy for breach of performance if such breach gives rise to a right to payment, whether or not such equitable remedy is reduced to judgment, fixed, contingent, matured, unmatured, disputed, undisputed, secured, or unsecured." 11 U.S.C. § 101(4).

17-31E   Excepted Debts.

LAW IN GENERAL

A debtor is not discharged from a debt for a tax or customs duty; for a debt to the extent obtained by false pretenses, false representation or fraud, for a debt for consumer debts to a single creditor aggregating more than $500 for luxury goods or services incurred within forty days before the order for relief, or cash advances of consumer credit aggregating more than $1,000 obtained within 20 days of the order for relief; or for a debt neither listed nor scheduled unless the creditor had notice or actual knowledge of the case in time to file the claim; or for a claim based on fraud or defalcation while acting in a fiduciary capacity, or embezzlement or larceny; or for a claim for alimony or child support or maintenance and support; or for willful or malicious injury; or for a fine, penalty or forfeiture; or for an education loan made, insured or guaranteed by a governmental unit or nonprofit institution; or for liability resulting from driving while intoxicated. 11 U.S.C. § 523.

A discharge does not discharge an individual debtor from any debt for money, property, services or refinancing of credit to the extent obtained by a false pretense, a false representation, or actual fraud. 11 U.S.C. § 523(a)(2)(A).

17-31F   Lease and Executory Contracts.

LAW IN GENERAL

The trustee, subject to the court's approval, may assume or reject any executory contract or unexpired lease of the debtor. 11 U.S.C. § 365(2).

If an executory contract or unexpired lease is in default, the trustee may not assume it without curing the default, providing adequate assurance that the trustee will cure the default and also providing adequate assurance of future performance under the contract or lease. 11 U.S.C. § 365.

DIVISION 17-4: OTHER CLASSES OF PROCEEDINGS

SECTION 17-41: EXECUTION SALE

Exemptions, see Division 14-4.

17-41A Nature; General Rules.

R.C. 2327.01 provides: "An execution is a process of a court, issued by its clerk, and directed to the sheriff of the county. Executions may be issued to the sheriffs of different counties at the same time." (As eff. 10-1-53.)

"A writ of execution as distinguished from a mere levy on real property is a civil proceeding for the enforcement of a judgment against such property." Lash v. Mann, 141 OS 577, 49 NE2d 689, 26 OO 158 (1943).

Further research: O Jur 3d, Enforcement and Execution of Judgments § 215.

LAW IN GENERAL

An execution is a writ issued for the enforcement of a judgment. A judgment creditor has the right to cause a writ of execution to issue. Enforcement of the writ proceeds without the direct action of the court until application for confirmation or other judicial action is made by either party. The writ and the statute are the sheriff's authority to sell the property, not an order of court as in a judicial sale. No title is acquired at an execution sale based on a void judgment. Am Law of Prop § 13.2; Tiffany § 1241.

17-41B Interests Subject to Execution Sale.

Homestead, see 14-44B.
Survivorship deeds, see 8-16A.

R.C. 2329.66 provides: "(A) Every person who is domiciled in this state may hold property exempt from execution, garnishment, attachment, or sale to satisfy a judgment or order, as follows:

"(1) The person's interest, not to exceed five thousand dollars, in one parcel or item of real or personal property that the person or a dependent of the person uses as a residence;

"(2) The person's interest, not to exceed one thousand dollars, in one motor vehicle;

"(3) The person's interest, not to exceed two hundred dollars in any particular item, in wearing apparel, beds, and bedding, and the person's interest, not to exceed three hundred dollars in each item, in one cooking unit and one refrigerator or other food preservation unit;

"(4)(a) The person's interest, not to exceed four hundred dollars, in cash on hand, money due and payable, money to become due within ninety days, tax refunds, and money on deposit with a bank, building and loan association, savings and loan association, credit union, public utility, landlord, or other person. This division applies only in bankruptcy proceedings. This exemption may include the portion of personal earnings that is not exempt under division (A)(13) of this section.

"(b) Subject to division (A)(4)(d) of this section, the person's interest, not to exceed two hundred dollars in any particular item, in household furnishings, household goods, appliances, books, animals, crops, musical instruments, firearms, and hunting and fishing equipment, that are held primarily for the personal, family, or household use of the person.

"(c) Subject to division (A)(4)(d) of this section, the person's interest in one or more items of jewelry, not to exceed four hundred dollars in one item of jewelry and not to exceed two hundred dollars in every other item of jewelry.

"(d) Divisions (A)(4)(b) and (4)(c) of this section do not include items of personal property listed in division (A)(3) of this section.

"If the person does not claim an exemption under division (A)(1) of this section, the total exemption claimed under division (A)(4)(b) of this section shall be added to the total exemption claimed under division (A)(4)(c) of this section and the total shall not exceed two thousand dollars. If the person claims an exemption under division (A)(1) of this section, the total exemption claimed under division (A)(4)(b) of this section shall be added to the total exemption claimed under division (A)(4)(c) of this section and the total shall not exceed one thousand five hundred dollars.

"(5) The person's interest, not to exceed an aggregate of seven hundred fifty dollars, in all implements, professional books, or tools of his profession, trade, or business, including agriculture;

"(6)(a) The person's interest in a beneficiary fund set apart, appropriated, or paid by a benevolent association or society, as exempted by section 2329.63 of the Revised Code;

"(b) The person's interest in contracts of life or endowment insurance or annuities, as exempted by section 3911.10 of the Revised Code;

"(c) The person's interest in a policy of group insurance or the proceeds of such a policy, as exempted by section 3917.05 of the Revised Code;

"(d) The person's interest in money, benefits, charity, relief, or aid to be paid, provided, or rendered by a fraternal benefit society, as exempted by section 3921.18 of the Revised Code;

"(e) The person's interest in the portion of benefits under policies of sickness and accident insurance and in lump sum payments for dismemberment and other losses insured under such policies, as exempted by section 3923.19 of the Revised Code.

"(7) The person's professionally prescribed or medically necessary health aids;

711

"(8) The person's interest in a burial lot, including, but not limited to, exemptions under section 517.09 or 1721.07 of the Revised Code;

"(9) The person's interest in:

"(a) Moneys paid or payable for living maintenance or rights, as exempted by section 3304.19 of the Revised Code;

"(b) Workers' compensation, as exempted by section 4123.67 of the Revised Code;

"(c) Unemployment compensation benefits, as exempted by section 4141.32 of the Revised Code;

"(d) Aid to dependent children payments, as exempted by section 5107.12 of the Revised Code;

"(e) General assistance payments, as exempted by section 5113.01 of the Revised Code.

"(10)(a) Except in cases in which the person was convicted of or pleaded guilty to a violation of section 2921.41 of the Revised Code and in which an order for the withholding of restitution from such payments was issued under division (C)(2)(b) of that section, and only to the extent provided in the order, and except as provided in section 3113.21 of the Revised Code the person's right to a pension, benefit, annuity, or retirement allowance and to accumulated contributions, as exempted by sections 145.56, 146.13, 742.47, 3307.71, 3309.66, or 5505.22 of the Revised Code, and the person's right to benefits from the policemen and firemen's death benefit fund;

"(b) Except as provided in section 3113.21 of the Revised Code, the person's right to receive a payment under any pension, annuity, or similar plan or contract, not including a payment from a stock bonus or profit sharing plan or a payment included in division (A)(6)(b) or (10)(a) of this section, on account of illness, disability, death, age, or length of service, to the extent reasonably necessary for the support of the person and any of his dependents, except if all the following apply:

"(i) The plan or contract was established by or under the auspices of an insider that employed the person at the time his rights under the plan or contract arose;

"(ii) The payment is on account of age or length of service;

"(iii) The plan or contract is not qualified under the 'Internal Revenue Code of 1986,' 100 Stat. 2085, 26 U.S.C. 1, as amended.

"(c) Except for any portion of the assets that were deposited for the purpose of evading the payment of any debt, the person's right in the assets held in, or to receive any payment under, any individual retirement account, individual retirement annuity, or Keogh or "H.R. 10" plan that provides benefits by reason of illness, disability, death, or age, to the extent reasonably necessary for the support of the person and any of his dependents;

"(11) The person's right to receive alimony, child support, an allowance, or maintenance to the extent reasonably necessary for the support of the person and any of his dependents;

"(12) The person's right to receive, or moneys received during the preceding twelve calendar months from any of the following:

"(a) An award of reparations under sections 2743.51 to 2743.72 of the Revised Code, to the extent exempted by division (D) of section 2743.66 of the Revised Code;

"(b) A payment on account of the wrongful death of an individual of whom the person was a dependent on the date of the individual's death, to the extent reasonably necessary for the support of the person and any of his dependents;

"(c) A payment not to exceed five thousand dollars, on account of personal bodily injury, not including pain and suffering or compensation for actual pecuniary loss, of the person or an individual for whom the person is a dependent;

"(d) A payment in compensation for loss of future earnings of the person or an individual of whom the person is or was a dependent, to the extent reasonably necessary for the support of the debtor and any of his dependents.

"(13) Except as provided in section 3113.21 of the Revised Code, personal earnings of the person owed to him for services rendered within thirty days before the issuing of an attachment or other process, the rendition of a judgment, or the making of an order, under which the attempt may be made to subject such earnings to the payment of a debt, damage, fine, or amercement, in an amount equal to the greater of the following amounts:

"(a) If paid weekly, thirty times the current federal minimum hourly wage; if paid biweekly, sixty times the current federal minimum hourly wage; if paid semi-monthly, sixty-five times the current federal minimum hourly wage; or if paid monthly, one hundred thirty times the current federal minimum hourly wage which is in effect at the time the earnings are payable, as prescribed by the 'Fair Labor Standards Act of 1938,' 52 Stat. 1060, 29 U.S.C. 206(a)(1), as amended;

"(b) Seventy-five per cent of the disposable earnings owed to the person.

"(14) The person's right in specific partnership property, as exempted by division (B)(3) of section 1775.24 of the Revised Code;

"(15) A seal and official register of a notary public, as exempted by section 147.04 of the Revised Code.

"(16) Any other property that is specifically exempted from execution, attachment, garnishment, or sale by federal statutes other than the 'Bankruptcy Reform Act of 1978,' 92 Stat. 2549, 11 U.S.C. 101, as amended.

"(17) The person's interest, not to exceed four hundred dollars, in any property, except that this division applies only in bankruptcy proceedings.

"(B) As used in this section:

"(1) 'Disposable earnings' means net earnings after the garnishee has made deductions required by law, excluding the deductions ordered pursuant to section 3113.21 of the Revised Code.

"(2) 'Insider' means:

"(a) If the person who claims an exemption is an individual, a relative of the individual, a relative of a general partner of the individual, a partnership in which the individual is a general partner, a general partner of the individual, or a corporation of which the individual is a director, officer, or in control;

713

"(b) If the person who claims an exemption is a corporation, a director or officer of the corporation; a person in control of the corporation; a partnership in which the corporation is a general partner; a general partner of the corporation; or a relative of a general partner, director, officer, or person in control of the corporation;

"(c) If the person who claims an exemption is a partnership, a general partner in the partnership; a general partner of the partnership; a person in control of the partnership; a partnership in which the partnership is a general partner; or a relative in, a general partner of, or a person in control of the partnership;

"(d) An entity or person to which or whom any of the following apply:

"(i) The entity directly or indirectly owns, controls, or holds with power to vote, twenty per cent or more of the outstanding voting securities of the person who claims an exemption, unless the entity holds the securities in a fiduciary or agency capacity without sole discretionary power to vote the securities or holds the securities solely to secure to debt and the entity has not in fact exercised the power to vote;

"(ii) The entity is a corporation, twenty per cent or more of whose outstanding voting securities are directly or indirectly owned, controlled, or held with power to vote, by the person who claims an exemption, or by an entity to which division (B)(2)(d)(i) of this section applies;

"(iii) A person whose business is operated under a lease or operating agreement by the person who claims an exemption, or a person substantially all of whose business is operated under an operating agreement with the person who claims an exemption;

"(iv) The entity operates the business or all or substantially all of the property of the person who claims an exemption under a lease or operating agreement.

"(e) An insider, as otherwise defined in this section, of a person or entity to which division (B)(2)(d)(i), (ii), (iii), or (iv) of this section applies, as if the person or entity were a person who claims an exemption;

"(f) A managing agent of the person who claims an exemption.

"(C) For purposes of this section, 'interest' shall be determined:

"(1) In bankruptcy proceedings, as of the date a petition is filed with the bankruptcy court commencing a case under Title 11 of the United States Code;

"(2) In all cases other than bankruptcy proceedings, as of the date of an appraisal, if necessary under section 2329.68 of the Revised Code, or the issuance of a writ of execution.

"An interest, as determined under division (C)(1) or (2) of this section, shall not include the amount of any lien otherwise valid pursuant to section 2329.661 of the Revised Code." (As eff. 10-5-87.)

R.C. 2329.661 provides: "(A) Division (A)(1) of section 2329.66 of the Revised Code does not:

"(1) Extend to a judgment rendered on a mortgage executed or security interest given on real or personal property by a debtor or to a claim for less than four hundred dollars for manual work or labor;

"(2) Impair the lien, by mortgage or otherwise, of the vendor for the purchase money of real or personal property that the debtor or a dependent of the debtor uses as a residence, the lien of a mechanic or other person, under a statute of this state, for materials furnished or labor performed in the erection of a dwelling house on real property, or a lien for the payment of taxes due on real property;

"(3) Affect or invalidate any mortgage on any real property, or any lien created by such a mortgage.

"(B) No promise, agreement, or contract shall be made or entered into that would waive the exemption laws of this state, and every promise, agreement, or contract insofar as it seeks to waive the exemption laws of this state is void.

"(C) Section 2329.66 of the Revised Code does not affect or invalidate any sale, contract of sale, conditional sale, security interest, or pledge of any personal property, or any lien created thereby." (As eff. 9-28-79.)

R.C. 2329.662 provides: "Pursuant to the 'Bankruptcy Reform Act of 1978,' 92 Stat. 2549, 11 U.S.C. 522(b)(1), this state specifically does not authorize debtors who are domiciled in this state to exempt the property specified in the 'Bankruptcy Reform Act of 1978,' 92 Stat. 2549, 11 U.S.C. 522(d)." (As eff. 9-28-79.) This section was to have been repealed effective January 1, 1986, but the section repealing it was itself repealed so R.C. 2329.662 continues in effect. Comment by Ohio Legislative Service Commission, dated 12-19-85.

Property subject to judgment or execution lien, including vested legal estates and leaseholds renewable forever, are subject to sale in execution. Equitable or contingent interests, dower, and after-acquired property are not subject to lien or sale as appears at 19-21B.

17-41C Public Service Corporations.

Enforcement, see 4-13A.

LAW IN GENERAL

Property of a public service corporation which is essential to the exercise of its franchise is ordinarily not subject to execution. Am Jur 2d, Executions § 203; CJS, Executions § 35.

17-41D Municipalities and Other Subdivisions.

LAW IN GENERAL

As a general rule, the property of municipal corporations, and other political subdivisions and state agencies may be seized on execution if owned in a proprietary capacity; the property of such owners being exempt if held in a public or governmental capacity. Am Jur 2d, Executions §§ 195, 197, 198; CJS, Executions § 35.

17-41E   Procedure.

See also Sections 17-25 to 17-27.
Advertisement, see 17-26A.
Appraisement and prior lien, see 17-25A.
Confirmation, see 17-28A.
Order of sale, see 17-27E, 17-28C.

R.C. 2329.09 in part provides: "The writ of execution against the property of a judgment debtor issuing from a court of record shall command the officer to whom it is directed to levy on the goods and chattels of the debtor. If no goods or chattels can be found, the officer shall levy on the lands and tenements of the debtor. If the court rendering the judgment or decree so orders, real estate may be sold under execution as follows: one third cash on the day of sale, one third in one year, one third in two years thereafter, with interest on deferred payments, to be secured by mortgage on the premises so sold." (As eff. 10-1-53.)

R.C. 2329.51 provides: "When real estate taken on execution and appraised, advertised, and offered for sale is unsold for want of bidders, the court from which the execution issued, on motion of the plaintiff, shall set aside such appraisement and order a new appraisement to be made, or shall set aside the levy and appraisement and award a new execution to issue. When such real estate or a part of it has been two times appraised and thereafter advertised and offered for sale, and is unsold for want of bidders, the court may direct the amount for which it shall be sold." (As eff. 10-1-53.)

Where several executions are levied upon the same lands and sale made under one, the surplus money in the hands of the sheriff may be appropriated to the others, if application be made in season. Douglass v. McCoy, 5 Ohio 522 (1832).

In selling a mortgagor's interest in the mortgaged premises upon execution, the valuation must be of the entire estate. The valuers may not make an estimate of the value and deduct the encumbrance. Baird v. Kirtland, 8 Ohio 21 (1837).

Section 2329.51 has no application to an action to foreclose a mortgage. Kentucky Joint Stock Land Bank v. Hellriegel, 59 App 467, 18 NE2d 620, 13 OO 224 (1937).

If the judgment itself is valid and unsatisfied at the time of sale, and if the sale is confirmed by the court, the sale will ordinarily not be set aside for irregularities in the sheriff's proceedings or for omissions from the record.

The ordinary basic steps taken in an execution sale are: (1) precipe for writ of execution filed by judgment creditor's attorney, (2) writ issued by the clerk of court and description of real estate delivered to the sheriff, (3) writ returned by the sheriff, levied on the real estate described, (4) precipe for order of sale filed by plaintiff's attorney, (5) order of sale issued by the clerk, (6) appraisement conducted by the sheriff, (7) advertisement of sale upon order of the sheriff, (8) proof of publication filed by newspaper, (9) sale made and writ returned by the sheriff, (10) sale confirmed, deed and distribution ordered by the court, and (11) deed of sheriff delivered to the purchaser.

Further research: O Jur 3d, Enforcement and Execution of Judgments § 229.

17-41F The Conveyance.

Official deeds, see 8-31Q.

The sheriff's deed is part of the execution procedure and is necessary to the purchaser's title. When the deed is delivered, the title conveyed relates back to the date of sale.

Further research: O Jur 3d, Enforcement and Execution of Judgments § 267.

17-41G Reversal or Vacation.

Appeal, see 16-14A.
Vacation, see also Section 16-15.

A vacation or reversal of a judgment, which is erroneous or voidable but not void, generally does not affect the title acquired at execution sale on such judgment by a person not a party to the judgment, if the title was acquired before the vacation or reversal.

Further research: O Jur 3d, Enforcement and Execution of Judgments § 369.

17-41H Death of a Party.

Abatement and revival generally, see Section 16-31.

Execution levied, without revivor, after the death of defendant, upon judgment rendered and execution issued in his lifetime, is void. Massie v. Long, 2 Ohio 287 (1826).

An execution or an order of sale once begun, is not abated by the death of the plaintiff. Craig v. Fox, 16 Ohio 563 (1847).

Real estate levied on during the life of the judgment debtor may be sold under the levy after his death without first making his representative party to the judgment. Bigelow v. Renker, 25 OS 542 (1874).

Further research: O Jur 3d, Enforcement and Execution of Judgments § 49.

17-41I Title of Purchaser.

Lien holders, see 1-32F.
Rights of purchasers, see Section 17-15.

LAW IN GENERAL

An execution purchaser for value without actual notice ordinarily acquires the title free from equities and instruments not of record at the date of the sale, in like manner as does a bona fide purchaser at judicial sale. Legal estates outstanding of record in third persons before the lien attached are not affected by the sale in any case. The rights of holders of prior encumbrances usually remain unchanged. The law of judicial sales is followed when applicable. Am Jur 2d, Executions §§ 433, 443; Am Law of Prop § 17.30.

SECTION 17-42: DISENTAILING SALE OF FUTURE INTERESTS

Representation of parties, see Section 17-22.

17-42A   Generally.

R.C. 5303.21 provides: "(A) In an action by the tenant in tail or for life, or in an action by the grantee or devisee of a qualified or conditional fee, or of any other qualified, conditional, or determinable interest, or in an action by a person claiming under such tenant, grantee, or devisee, or in an action by the trustee or beneficiaries, if the estate is held in trust, courts of common pleas may, subject to division (B) of this section, authorize the sale of any estate, whether it was created by will, deed, or contract, or came by descent, when satisfied that such sale would be for the benefit of the person holding the first and present estate, interest, or use, and do no substantial injury to the heirs in tail, or others in expectancy, succession, reversion, or remainder. This division does not extend to estates in dower.

"(B) If an estate is held in trust and if the trustee is authorized by the trust instrument to sell real property, a court of common pleas shall not authorize the sale of the estate pursuant to division (A) of this section unless the trustee consents to the sale." (As eff. 10-14-83.)

R.C. 5303.211 provides: "Where the estate sought to be sold or leased is held in trust under the jurisdiction of a probate court, an action may be brought by the trustee in the probate court of the county in which he was appointed or in which the estate subject to sale or lease or any part thereof is situated; and the sale or lease of such estate may be authorized by such court which shall have the same jurisdiction and power as is provided for courts of common pleas in sections 5303.21 to 5303.31, inclusive, of the Revised Code.

"If the action is brought in a county other than that in which the estate or a part thereof is situated, a certified transcript of the record of all proceedings had therein shall be filed with and recorded by the probate court of each county in which such estate or any part thereof is situated." (As eff. 8-10-65.)

R.C. 5303.22 to 5303.31 provide judicial procedure; that net income be paid to person or persons who would be entitled to the use or income of the estate were it unsold; that guardians, in the place of their wards, may assent to the sale; that court may direct that such estate be leased.

A sale made in an action in partition which in all respects complies with these sections disentails the property. Schneider v. Wolf, 120 OS 524, 166 NE 679, 7 Abs 335, 29 OLR 256 (1929).

Under these statutes only parties in being are necessary parties because the sale does not eliminate the contingent interests but merely removes them from the real estate, the proceeds of the sale being held in trust for the possible future beneficiaries. Voss v. Voss, 129 NE2d 322, 57 OO 246, 71 Abs 577 (C.P. 1955).

Under authority of R.C. 5303.21 et seq., real estate held in trust may be sold upon petition of the trustee even though the will creating the trust directed that the trustee should hold the subject asset as long as permitted by law. First Nat. Bank of Minneapolis v. Wilder, 8 Misc 43, 219 NE2d 254, 37 OO2d 57 (Prob. 1966).

Where both life tenants enjoy excellent health, the value of their shares is determined under the statutory 6% formula and the mortality table at R.C. 2131.01 for the age of the younger life tenant, with the resulting percentage distributed equally between such life tenants. The balance should be placed in trust and accumulated until the death of the surviving life tenant, and then distributed among the remaindermen. Henderson v. Henderson, 15 Misc 276, 237 NE2d 336, 44 OO2d 463 (C.P. 1968).

Further research: O Jur 3d, Estates, etc. § 138.

SECTION 17-43: ASSIGNMENT FOR BENEFIT OF CREDITORS

17-43A   Generally.

R.C. 1313.01 to 1313.52 and 1313.56 to 1313.59, as amended, provide that assignee shall file assignment and bond in probate court; assignment is effective from delivery to probate judge; court may remove assignee and appoint trustee; notice of appointment must be published for three successive weeks; exempt property may be excluded; notice of sale shall be published for four consecutive weeks; sale shall not be for less than two-thirds of the appraised value but may be reappraised; private sale may be ordered; court shall confirm the sale; husband or wife may file answer to have sale free of contingent dower and to allow him or her its value out of the proceeds; sale shall be free of dower when wife has joined in mortgage or when a purchase-money mortgage; sale may be in common pleas court.

The inchoate right of dower of the spouse of assignor can be extinguished only where the property is subject to prior mortgage or upon answer and waiver by wife. Dwyer v. Garlough, 31 OS 158 (1877).

The rights of the assignee in the property assigned are no greater than those of the debtor prior to the assignment. Hodgson v. Barrett, 33 OS 63, 3 WLB 442 (1877).

The legal title to the land is in the assignee by virtue of the instrument of assignment. Schuler v. Miller, 45 OS 325, 13 NE 275, 18 WLB 254, 316 (1887).

A deed of assignment is effective from the time it is filed in the probate court. It need not be recorded in the office of the county recorder except as to land located in a county other than that of the residence of the assignor. Eggleston v. Harrison, 61 OS 397, 55 NE 993, 43 WLB 27, 62 (1900).

An assignment for benefit of creditors cannot be set aside by the trustee in bankruptcy unless made within four months prior to the filing of the bankruptcy petition.

Further research: O Jur 3d, Creditors' Rights and Remedies § 37.

LAW IN GENERAL

An assignment for the benefit of creditors is a conveyance by a debtor to an assignee of all his property, except that exempt from execution, for the purpose of paying his debts. The assignee holds the legal title in trust for the creditors. The property is beyond the control of the assignor and beyond the immediate reach of the creditors. The matter is controlled by statutes which prescribe the procedure for sale of the real estate. The proceeding does not relieve the debtor from the legal obligation to pay his debts in full. These statutes are not now in common use but proceedings thereunder are valid so long as they do not conflict with bankruptcy proceedings. Am Jur 2d, Assignments for Benefit of Creditors §§ 1, 4, 6; Am Law of Prop § 18.65; CJS, Assignments for Benefit of Creditors § 2.

SECTION 17-44: RECEIVERS

Bankruptcy, see Division 17-3.
Concurrent and conflicting jurisdiction, see Division 16-2.
Statutory liquidators, see 4-22B.

17-44A Definition.

The appointment of a receiver is an extraordinary provisional remedy of ancillary character, regulated by statutory provision and allowable only in cases pending for some other purpose. Hoiles v. Watkins, 117 OS 165, 157 NE 557, 5 Abs 419, 423, 25 OLR 385, 61 ALR 1203 (1927).

A receiver is a person appointed by a court to take into his custody, control and management the property of another person pending judicial action concerning it.

Further research: O Jur 3d, Receivers § 1.

17-44B Jurisdiction.

R.C. 2333.22 and 2333.23 provide in proceedings in aid of execution that the judge may appoint a receiver of the property of the judgment debtor; a receiver, other than the sheriff, must take an oath and give bond. (As eff. 10-1-53.)

R.C. 2333.24 provides: "If it appears that the judgment debtor has an interest in real estate, in the county in which proceedings under sections 2333.09 to 2333.27, inclusive, of the Revised Code, are had, as mortgagor, mortgagee, or otherwise, and his interest can be ascertained as between himself and the person holding the legal estate, or the person having a lien on or interest in the property, without controversy as to the interest of the person holding such estate, or interest therein, or lien thereon, the receiver appointed pursuant to section 2333.22 of the Revised Code may be ordered to sell and convey such real estate, or the interest of the debtor therein. The sale shall be conducted as is provided for the sale of real estate upon execution, and the proceedings of sale before the execution of the deed shall be approved by the court in which the judgment was rendered, or the transcript filed." (As eff. 10-1-53.)

R.C. 2735.01 provides that a receiver may be appointed by the Supreme Court, the court of appeals, the common pleas court or probate court in causes pending in such courts in specified cases and in all other cases in which receivers have been appointed by the usages of equity. (As eff. 10-1-53.)

R.C. 2735.02 provides: "No party, attorney, or person interested in an action shall be appointed receiver therein except by consent of the parties. No person except a resident of this state shall be appointed or act as receiver of a railroad or other corporation within this state." (As eff. 10-1-53.)

R.C. 2735.03 provides that the receiver must be sworn and furnish bond in such sum as the court directs. (As eff. 10-1-53.)

R.C. 2735.04 provides: "Under the control of the court which appointed him, as provided in section 2735.01 of the Revised Code, a receiver may bring and defend actions in his own name as receiver, take and keep possession of property, receive rents, collect, compound for, and compromise demands, make transfers, and generally do such acts respecting the property as the court authorizes." (As eff. 10-1-53.)

A receiver may be appointed without notice upon proper averment and finding of probable irreparable loss, if notice be thereafter given. Eaton Loan & Home Aid Co. v. Wespiser, 20 Abs 690 (App. 1935).

Every presumption attends the validity and regularity of the order appointing a receiver. Tonti v. Tonti, 118 NE2d 200, 66 Abs 356 (App. 1951).

A receiver in a foreclosure action is not a receiver of property not described in the petition and hence such property is not subject to the jurisdiction of the appointing court. New Waterford Bank v. Goodwin, 116 App 161, 187 NE2d 389, 22 OO2d 15 (1961).

The appointment of a receiver is justified to collect rents, accruing after filing a certificate of judgment, where it is shown that the value of the land probably will not be sufficient to satisfy the judgment lien on forced sale, and receivership is ancillary to the final relief sought. Wood v. Galpert, 1 App2d 202, 204 NE2d 384, 30 OO2d 242 (1965).

Ohio courts lack authority to appoint a receiver until after notice has been given to all parties and a hearing held, unless the plaintiff establishes that the time taken to give such notice will result in irreparable loss to the plaintiff. Real Estate Capital Corp. v. Thunder Corp., 31 Misc 169, 278 NE2d 838, 60 OO2d 342 (C.P. 1972).

Further research: O Jur 3d, Receivers §§ 82, 83.

LAW IN GENERAL

Apart from statute, courts of equity have jurisdiction to the exclusion of courts of law in the appointment of receivers. The power is ordinarily exercised to prevent fraud or to preserve the subject property from material injury or destruction.

The court may authorize the receiver to borrow necessary funds by issuing receiver's certificates creating a lien prior to previously existing liens.

A receiver may be appointed for the protection of a mortgagee when waste is threatened or when the security is inadequate and the personal liability is insufficient, even though the rents and profits are not pledged. Receivership may be refused even though authorized by the mortgagee. A receiver to sequester the rents and profits will not be appointed, as a general rule, unless it is shown that the security will probably be insufficient to discharge the debt and that the persons liable are insolvent.

CJS, Mortgages § 657; CJS, Receivers § 3; Powell §§ 465, 492; Tiffany § 1420.

17-44C   Effect of Receivership.

Creditor did not acquire a preference by levy of execution after receivership action was brought but the court may permit the levy to enable the judgment creditor to secure any rights which the levy would give if the receivership action should not be maintained. Coe v. Columbus, P. & Q. & I. R.R., 10 OS 372, 404 (1859).

The receiver obtains authority by the act of the court, not having the title, but standing as the ministerial officer of the court. Cheney v. Maumee Cycle Co., 64 OS 205, 214, 60 NE 207, 45 WLB 175, 281 (1901).

A judgment may be obtained against one whose property is then in the hands of a receiver, but levy upon or sale of property while in the possession of the receiver cannot be made without leave of the court appointing the receiver. Croy v. Marshall, 3 CC 489, 2 CD 280 (1888).

If expenditures for proposed repairs are unusual or substantial, the receiver should apply to the court for authority to make them, and notice should be given to interested parties. American Savings Bank Co. v. Union Trust Co., 124 OS 126, 177 NE 199, 10 Abs 124, 34 OLR 501, 79 ALR 160 (1931).

Further research: O Jur 3d, Receivers §§ 93, 94.

LAW IN GENERAL

A receiver is an officer of the court. His appointment does not operate to divest the title of the owners. He is entitled to the possession and control of the property subject to the orders of the court appointing him. The right of the receiver normally relates back to the date of the order appointing him. CJS, Mortgages § 667; CJS, Receivers §§ 103, 115.

The possession of the receiver cannot be interfered with unless with the consent of the appointing court. A sale on execution without such consent does not affect the right to possession. Liens acquired before the appointment are not divested thereby, although the right to enforce them is suspended or modified by the receivership. Liens cannot be acquired after the appointment to the prejudice of other creditors entitled to distribution in the receivership. CJS, Receivers § 128.

17-44D Foreign and Ancillary Receivers.

As a matter of comity the courts of one state may recognize a receiver appointed in another state or country, but are not bound to do so. State ex rel. Haavind v. Crabbe, 114 OS 504, 151 NE 755, 4 Abs 177, 178, 256, 258, 24 OLR 299, 366 (1926).

Further research: O Jur 3d, Receivers § 215.

LAW IN GENERAL

Neither a court nor the receiver appointed by it has authority over land outside the court's territorial jurisdiction. An ancillary receiver may be appointed by the domestic court in aid of the foreign receiver. CJS, Receivers § 391.

17-44E Duration of Receivership.

A receivership established during the lifetime of decedent with assets in custodia legis is not terminated by his death or appointment of executor. Ford v. Fulton, 19 Abs 314 (App. 1935).

Receivership is not terminated by filing of the receiver's final account, but only by order of the court. Hoover-Bond Co. v. Sun-Glow Industries, Inc., 57 App 246, 13 NE2d 368, 10 OO 424, 22 Abs 63 (1936).

Further research: O Jur 3d, Receivers §§ 203, 204, 208-210.

LAW IN GENERAL

Unless expressly appointed for a specified period, the tenure of a receiver is indefinite and may be terminated only by court order. The receivership is not ended by the death of the receiver. CJS, Receivers §§ 92, 97.

17-44F Sales.

Receiver in aid of execution, see 17-44B.

The court fixing the time that the sale was to be advertised at two weeks, it is not necessary that the sale be advertised as is provided for sale of real estate on execution. Dunbar v. American Casket Co., 19 CC 585, 10 CD 684 (1900).

Sale for less than two-thirds of appraised value in advertisement of sale, held not to invalidate sale where sale was confirmed. Bloomberg v. Roach, 43 App 178, 182 NE 891, 13 Abs 87 (1930).

Further research: O Jur 3d, Receivers §§ 113-115.

LAW IN GENERAL

A sale by a receiver is not required to comply with the general statutory provisions for judicial sales. It is essential that the court appoint a receiver of the property in a suit where it has equitable jurisdiction, that the sale be made under the authority of the court, and that the sale be confirmed. No particular notice of sale is required in the absence of special statutory provision. However, the property remains subject to liens if no notice is given to lien holders and they are in no way parties. Am Jur 2d, Receivers § 397; Am Law of Prop § 18.65; CJS, Receivers § 220.

SECTION 17-45: CREDITOR'S BILL

17-45A Generally.

Future interests, see also 11-18A.

R.C. 2333.01 provides: "When a judgment debtor does not have sufficient personal or real property subject to levy on execution to satisfy the judgment, any equitable interest which he has in real estate as mortgagor, mortgagee, or otherwise ... shall be subject to the payment of the judgment by action." (As eff. 10-1-53.)

The action by creditor's bill is one in equity by which a judgment creditor seeks to subject to the payment of his existing judgment an interest of the judgment debtor that cannot be reached on execution. Union Properties, Inc. v. Patterson, 143 OS 192, 54 NE2d 668, 28 OO 111 (1944).

A suit in the nature of a creditor's bill may be brought in the court of common pleas of a county where property in which the debtor has equitable interests is situated. The judgment debtor may be served with summons in another county of which he is resident. Dwelle v. Hinde, 18 CC 618, 8 CD 177 (1897).

The lien of proceedings under R.C. 2333.01 dates from the date of service of summons. Citizens Savings & Trust Co. v. Palmer, 23 CC(NS) 349, 34 CD 290 (1912).

Equitable interest may be sold where the judgment debtor defendant has no personal or real property subject to execution but is entitled to balance after payment of an undetermined amount to a defendant who holds the legal title. Womack v. Eversman, 67 App 287, 37 NE2d 678, 21 OO 260, 33 Abs 630 (1941).

A creditor's bill is in the nature of an equitable execution. It is ordinarily a suit in equity brought by a judgment creditor to subject property of the debtor which cannot be reached under an execution.

McDERMOTT'S
OHIO REAL
PROPERTY
LAW AND PRACTICE

FOURTH EDITION

VOLUME 1

1995 CUMULATIVE
SUPPLEMENT

by

ROBERT M. CURRY

MICHIE
Law Publishers
CHARLOTTESVILLE, VIRGINIA

Place in pocket of bound volume
and recycle previous supplement.

TABLE OF CONTENTS

Volume 1

CHAPTER 1: ABSTRACTS AND RECORDS OF TITLE

DIVISION 1-1: ABSTRACTS AND OTHER EVIDENCES OF TITLE

TABLE OF CONTENTS

TABLE OF CONTENTS

DIVISION 4-2: PARTICULAR TYPES OF ORGANIZATIONS

CHAPTER 5: COTENANCY AND JOINT OWNERSHIP

DIVISION 5-2: PARTICULAR CLASSES OF INTERESTS

DIVISION 5-3: PARTITION

CHAPTER 6: COVENANTS AND RESTRICTIONS

DIVISION 6-3: RESTRICTIONS AS TO USE

CHAPTER 7: CROPS AND OTHER GROWING THINGS

DIVISION 7-1: IN GENERAL

CHAPTER 8: DEEDS

DIVISION 8-1: IN GENERAL

TABLE OF CONTENTS

DIVISION 8-2: ACKNOWLEDGMENT

DIVISION 8-4: ESCROW

DIVISION 8-5: CANCELLATION OR RESCISSION

CHAPTER 9: DESCENT AND WILLS

DIVISION 9-1: DESCENT

TABLE OF CONTENTS

CHAPTER 11: ESTATES AND FUTURE INTERESTS

DIVISION 11-1: IN GENERAL

DIVISION 11-4: ESTATES SUBJECT TO CONDITION SUBSEQUENT; RIGHTS OF REENTRY

DIVISION 11-8: CONTINGENT REMAINDERS; EXECUTORY INTERESTS

DIVISION 11-9: CLASS GIFTS; PER STIRPES OR PER CAPITA

TABLE OF CONTENTS

CHAPTER 12: EXECUTORS AND ADMINISTRATORS

DIVISION 12-1: IN GENERAL

CHAPTER 13: FIXTURES

DIVISION 13-1: IN GENERAL

CHAPTER 14: HUSBAND AND WIFE

DIVISION 14-1: IN GENERAL

DIVISION 14-3: DIVORCE AND ALIMONY

CHAPTER 15: INFANTS, INSANE PERSONS AND OTHER INCOMPETENTS

DIVISION 15-1: IN GENERAL

TABLE OF CONTENTS

CHAPTER 16: JUDGMENTS

DIVISION 16-1: IN GENERAL

DIVISION 16-2: CONFLICT BETWEEN COURTS; CONFLICT OF LAWS

DIVISION 16-4: LIMITATION OF ACTIONS

TABLE OF CONTENTS

TABLE OF CONTENTS

CHAPTER 17: JUDICIAL SALES

DIVISION 17-1: IN GENERAL

DIVISION 17-2: PARTIES; PROCEDURE

DIVISION 17-3: BANKRUPTCY

TABLE OF CONTENTS

VOLUME 1

CHAPTER 1: ABSTRACTS AND RECORDS OF TITLE

DIVISION 1-1: ABSTRACTS AND OTHER EVIDENCES OF TITLE

DIVISION 1-2: RECORDS AND RECORDING LAWS

DIVISION 1-3: NOTICE; PRIORITIES

DIVISION 1-1: ABSTRACTS AND OTHER EVIDENCES OF TITLE

SECTION 1-12: CERTIFICATES OF TITLE

1-12B Contents.

Standard of Title Examination 2.3 amended January 18, 1991, as follows:

2.3 EXAMINATION — FORM

[Adopted by OSBA Nov. 1, 1952; Amended May 8, 1969]

Problem A:

What should a report on title contain?

Standard A:

The certificate or opinion should include:

(1) The period of time of the examination.

(2) That the opinion is based on an abstract of title or is based on an examination of the public records of _____ County, Ohio, as disclosed by the public indexes relating to the premises.

(3) That the opinion or certificate does not purport to cover the following: (a) Matters not of record, (b) Rights of persons in possession, (c) Questions which a correct survey or inspection of the premises would disclose, (d) Rights to file

mechanic's liens, (e) Special taxes and assessments not shown by the county treasurer's records, (f) Zoning and other governmental regulations, (g) Liens asserted by the United States and State of Ohio, their agencies and officers under the Ohio Solid and Hazardous Waste and Disposal Act and Federal Super Fund Amendments, and under Racketeering Influence and Corrupt Organization acts and receivership liens, unless the lien is filed in the public records of the county in which the property is located.

(4) An opinion or certification that the _____ title is vested in _____ by instrument of record, recorded in _____ Records, Volume _____ , Page _____ .

(5) That the title is marketable and free from encumbrances except those matters set forth.

(6) Clear and concise language setting forth the defects and encumbrances.

The following basic form is suggested:

The undersigned hereby certifies that he has made a thorough examination of the records of _____ County, Ohio, as disclosed by the public indexes in accordance with the Ohio Marketable Title Act, relating to the premises hereinafter described as Item 1.

[NOTE: The 1969 amendment by OSBA substituted the words "in accordance with the Ohio Marketable Title Act" for "covering the period from _____ , 19____ to the date hereof" in the above paragraph. However, although not formally adopted by OSBA, the phrase "Since _____ ," should be inserted before "as disclosed by" according to a memorandum in the Ohio Bar of July 30, 1979.]

This certificate does not purport to cover matters not of record in said County, including rights of persons in possession, questions which a correct survey or inspection would disclose, rights to file mechanics' liens, special taxes and assessments not shown by the county treasurer's records, or zoning and other governmental regulations.

The undersigned hereby certifies that in his opinion, based upon said records, the fee simple title to said premises is vested in _____ by a _____ from _____ , dated _____ filed for record _____ at ____ M., and recorded at volume _____ , page _____ of the deed records; and that, as appears from said county records, the title is marketable and free from encumbrances except and subject to the matters set forth herein at Items 2 to ____ , inclusive.

Dated at _____ , Ohio this _____ day of _____ , 19____ .

_____
Attorney at Law

3

DIVISION 1-2: RECORDS AND RECORDING LAWS

SECTION 1-21: INTRODUCTION; RECORDING ACTS GENERALLY

1-21A Theory of the Recording Acts.

R.C. 5301.23 amended to provide that all mortgages presented for record shall contain the then-current mailing address of the mortgagee. Omission of the address or inclusion of an incorrect address shall not affect the validity of instrument. (As eff. 1-1-94.)

1-21B Effect of Recording.

Further research: O Jur 3d, Records and Recording § 64.

1-21C Records as Evidence.

Further research: O Jur 3d, Records and Recording § 5.

1-21E Place and Manner of Recording.

Further research: O Jur 3d, Records and Recording §§ 55-57.

SECTION 1-23: CUSTODY AND USE OF RECORDS.

1-23A Rights to Inspect and Use.

R.C. 149.43(1) amended to include, in the definition of "public record," records containing information that is confidential under Section 4112.05 of the Revised Code (as eff. 7-1-93), and DNA records stored in the DNA database pursuant to section 109.573 of the Revised Code. (As eff. 8-30-95.)

Further research: O Jur 3d, Records and Recording §§ 15, 20, 33.

SECTION 1-24: PARTICULAR TYPES OF INSTRUMENTS AND RECORDS

1-24A Entitled to Record.

R.C. 317.08 amended to provide: "Except as provided in division (F) of this section, the county recorder shall keep five separate sets of records as follows:

"(A) A record of deeds, in which shall be recorded all deeds and other instruments of writing for the absolute and unconditional sale or conveyance of lands, tenements, and hereditaments; all notices, as provided for in sections 5301.47 to 5301.56 of the Revised Code; all judgments or decrees in actions brought under section 5303.01 of the Revised Code; all declarations and bylaws as provided for in Chapter 5311 of the Revised Code; affidavits as provided for in section 5301.252 of the Revised Code; all certificates as provided for in section 5311.17 of the Revised Code; all articles dedicating archaeological preserves accepted by the director of the Ohio historical society under section 149.52 of the Revised Code; all articles dedicating nature preserves accepted by the director of natural resources under section 1517.05 of the Revised Code; all agreements for the registration of lands as archaeological or historical landmarks under sections 149.51 or 149.55 of the Revised Code; all conveyances of conservation easements under section 5301.68 of the Revised Code; all instruments or orders described in division (B)(1)(c)(ii) of section 5301.56 of the Revised Code; and all memoranda of trust, as described in division (A) of section 5301.255 of the Revised Code, that describe specific real property;

"(B) A record of mortgages, in which shall be recorded all of the following:

"(1) All mortgages, including amendments, supplements, modifications, and extensions of mortgages, or other instruments of writing by which lands, tenements, or hereditaments are or may be mortgaged or otherwise conditionally sold, conveyed, affected, or encumbered;

"(2) All executory installment contracts for the sale of land executed after September 29, 1961, that by their terms are not required to be fully performed by one or more of the parties to them within one year of the date of the contracts;

"(3) All options to purchase real estate, including supplements, modifications, and amendments of the options, but no option of that nature shall be recorded if it does not state a specific day and year of expiration of its validity.

"(C) A record of powers of attorney, including all memoranda of trust, as described in division (A) of section 5301.255 of the Revised Code, that do not describe specific real property;

"(D) A record of plats, in which shall be recorded all plats and maps of town lots, of the subdivision of town lots, and of other divisions or surveys of lands, any centerline survey of a highway located within the county, the plat of which shall be furnished by the director of transportation or county engineer, and all drawings as provided for in Chapter 5311. of the Revised Code;

"(E) A record of leases, in which shall be recorded all leases, memoranda of leases, and supplements, modifications, and amendments of leases and memoranda of leases.

"All instruments or memoranda of instruments entitled to record shall be recorded in the proper record in the order in which they are presented for record. The recorder may index, keep, and record in one volume unemployment compensation liens, internal revenue tax liens and other liens in favor of the United States as described in division (A) of section 317.09 of the Revised Code, personal tax liens, mechanic's liens, agricultural product liens, notices of liens, certificates of satisfaction or partial release of estate tax liens, discharges of recognizances, excise and franchise tax liens on corporations, and liens provided for in sections 1513.33, 1513.370, 5111.021 and 5311.18 of the Revised Code.

"The recording of an option to purchase real estate, including any supplement, modification, and amendment of the option, under this section shall serve as notice to any purchaser of an interest in the real estate covered by the option only during the period of the validity of the option as stated in the option.

"(F) In lieu of keeping the five separate sets of records required in divisions (A) to (E) of this section and the records required in division (G) of this section, a county recorder may record all the instruments required to be recorded by this section in two separate sets of record books. One set shall be called the 'official records' and shall contain the instruments listed in divisions (A), (B), (C), (E), and (G) of this section. The second set of records shall contain the instruments listed in division (D) of this section.

"(G) Except as provided in division (F) of this section, the county recorder shall keep a separate set of records containing all corrupt activity lien notices filed with the recorder pursuant to § 2923.36 of the Revised Code." (As eff. 10-10-91 and 8-10-94.)

R.C. 317.09 was also amended to provide for the filing of environmental liens in the "federal tax and other federal lien index" to be maintained by the county recorder. (As eff. 10-10-91 and 7-1-93.)

R.C. 2323.261 amended without material change as to the statement in the Parent Volume. (As eff. 1-1-93.)

1-24D Indexes.

R.C. 317.20 provides: "When, in the opinion of the board of county commissioners sectional indexes are needed, and it so directs, in addition to the alphabetical indexes provided for in section 317.18 of the Revised Code, the board may provide for making, in books prepared for that purpose, sectional indexes to the records of all real estate in the county, beginning with some designated year and continuing through such period of years as it specified, by placing under the heads of the original surveyed sections or surveys, or parts of a section or survey, squares, subdivisions, or the permanent parcel numbers provided for under section 319.28 of the Revised Code, or lots, on the left-hand page, or on the upper portion of such page of the index books, the following:

"(A) The name of the grantor;

"(B) Next to the right, the name of the grantee;

"(C) The number and page of the record where the instrument is found recorded;

"(D) The character of the instrument, to be followed by a pertinent description of the property conveyed by the deed, lease, or assignment of lease;

"(E) On the opposite page, or on the lower portion of the same page, beginning at the bottom, in like manner, all the mortgages, liens, notices as provided for in sections 5301.51, 5301.52, and 5301.56 of the Revised Code, or other encumbrances affecting such real estate.

"The compensation for the services rendered under this section shall be paid from the general revenue fund of the county, and no additional levy shall be made in consequence of such services. If the board decides to have such sectional index made, it shall advertise for three consecutive weeks in one newspaper of general circulation in the county for sealed proposals to do such work as provided in this section, shall let the work to the lowest and best bidder, and shall require him to give bond for the faithful performance of the contract, in such sums as the board fixes, and such work shall be done to the acceptance of the auditor of state upon allowance by such board. The board may reject any and all bids for the work, provided that no more than five cents shall be paid for each entry of each tract or lot of land.

"When brought up and completed, the county recorder shall keep up the indexes described in this section." (As eff. 3-22-89.)

SECTION 1-25: ERRORS OF RECORDING OFFICER

1-25B Correction of Records.

Further research: O Jur 3d, Records and Recording § 7.

SECTION 1-26: LOST OR DESTROYED RECORDS

1-26B Authorized Destruction.

R.C. 149.38 amended without material change as to the statement in the Parent Volume. (As eff. 8-19-92.)

R.C. 2101.141 amended to provide that vouchers or other evidence of expenditures and distributions stated in an account may be ordered destroyed five years after the account has been approved or settled. Inventories, schedules of debts, accounts, pleadings, wills, trusts, bonds and other papers filed in the probate court (excluding vouchers) may be ordered destroyed after being microfilmed. If any of those instruments are not micro-filmed, their destruction may be ordered after twenty-one years from the closing or termination of the matter. (As eff. 9-26-90.)

SECTION 1-27: NAMES; VARIANCE IN NAME

1-27A Notice.

See discussion of National Packaging Corp. v. Belmont at 1-27C below.

1-27C Idem Sonans.

The doctrine of idem sonans, which means "sounding the same," has been held inapplicable to names misspelled in a judgment lien index. The court refused to apply the doctrine to preserve the rights of a judgment lienholder who was excluded from foreclosure proceedings due to a misspelling of the judgment debtor's surname ("Bolen" instead of "Bolan") on the recorded certificate of judgment. National Packaging Corp. v. Belmont, 47 Ohio App. 3d 86, 547 N.E.2d 373 (1988).

1-27G Change of Name.

R.C. 1701.81 amended in connection with Ohio's adoption of laws concerning limited liability companies, but without material change as to the statement in the Parent Volume. (As eff. 10-8-92 and 7-1-94.)

R.C. 1701.82 amended in connection with Ohio's adoption of laws concerning limited liability companies, but without material change as to the statement in the Parent Volume. (As eff. 7-1-94.)

R.C. 1701.73 amended without material change as to the statement in the Parent Volume. (As eff. 7-1-94.)

SECTION 1-28: SLANDER OF TITLE; DISPARAGEMENT OF PROPERTY

1-28A General Rules.

An assignee's recording of a mortgage for which it knew or should have known the funds had not been disbursed to the homeowners was done in reckless disregard of the rights of the homeowners and constituted slander of title. The plaintiffs may recover for any special pecuniary losses incurred by them. Childers v. Commerce Mtg. Invs., 63 Ohio App. 3d 389, 579 N.E.2d 219 (1989).

DIVISION 1-3: NOTICE; PRIORITIES

SECTION 1-31: CONSTRUCTIVE NOTICE AND PRIORITIES GENERALLY

1-31C The Chain of Title.

Standard of Title Examination 3.13 amended January 18, 1991, as follows:

3.13 CONVEYANCES — DEED FROM STRANGER

Problem A:

Is a cloud on the title created by a deed or encumbrance from a stranger to the record title?

Standard A:

A stray deed or other interloping instrument does not create a cloud on the title unless its recitals or other known circumstances are sufficient to put a purchaser on inquiry. Other known circumstances should include the

passage of time and consideration of the Ohio Marketable Title Act (R.C. 5301.47 et seq.).

Comment A:

The examiner must consider the possible application of the Ohio Marketable Title Act (R.C. 5301.47 et seq.), under which a stray deed can become the "root of title" to a competing chain of record title that is superior to the chain of transactions being searched.

Gas company's purported easement recorded outside of chain of title due to an erroneous property description does not constitute constructive notice and is not enforceable against the property owner. Columbia Gas Transmission Corp. v. Bennett, 71 Ohio App. 3d 307, 594 N.E.2d 1 (1990), mot. granted, 59 Ohio St. 3d 708, 571 N.E.2d 133, later proceeding, 61 Ohio St. 3d 1411, 574 N.E.2d 1075 (1991), appeal dismissed, 63 Ohio St. 3d 1207, 588 N.E.2d 126, mot. granted, 63 Ohio St. 3d 1465, 590 N.E.2d 1265 (1992).

Further research: O Jur 3d, Records and Recording § 65.

Where an instrument erroneously identifies the property burdened by an easement and that erroneous description causes the instrument to be recorded outside the chain of title through no fault of the recorder, a subsequent bona fide purchaser cannot as a matter of law be charged with constructive notice of the easement. Columbia Gas Transmission Corp. v. Bennett, 71 Ohio App. 3d 307, 594 N.E.2d 1 (1990), mot. granted, 59 Ohio St. 3d 708, 571 N.E.2d 133, later proceeding, 61 Ohio St. 3d 1411, 574 N.E.2d 1075 (1991), appeal dismissed, 63 Ohio St. 3d 1207, 588 N.E.2d 126 (1992), mot. granted, 63 Ohio St. 3d 1465, 590 N.E.2d 1265 (1992).

1-31F Recitals.

Further research: O Jur 3d, Records and Recording § 66.

SECTION 1-32: BONA FIDE PURCHASER

1-32C Necessity of Legal Title.

Further research: O Jur 3d, Real Property Sales and Exchanges § 216.

SECTION 1-33: ACTUAL NOTICE GENERALLY; POSSESSION

1-33A Rules.

Further research: O Jur 3d, Real Property Sales and Exchanges § 219.

SECTION 1-34: EASEMENTS; TRUSTS; EQUITIES; OTHER INTERESTS

1-34A Easements.

Where an instrument erroneously identifies the property burdened by an easement and that erroneous description causes the instrument to be recorded outside the chain of title through no fault of the recorder, a subsequent bona fide purchaser cannot as a matter of law be charged with constructive notice of the easement. Columbia Gas Transmission Corp. v. Bennett, 71 Ohio App. 3d 307, 594 N.E.2d 1 (1990), mot. granted, 59 Ohio St. 3d 708, 571 N.E.2d 133, later proceeding, 61 Ohio St. 3d 1411, 574 N.E.2d 1075 (1991), appeal dismissed, 63 Ohio St. 3d 1207, 588 N.E.2d 126, mot. granted, 63 Ohio St. 3d 1465, 590 N.E.2d 1265 (1992).

DIVISION 1-4: EXAMINATION IN GENERAL

SECTION 1-42: LEGAL LIABILITY

1-42C Limitation of Actions.

R.C. 2305.07 amended to provide an additional exception to the 15 year statute of limitations with respect to matters arising under Section 126.301 of the Revised Code. R.C. 126.301 provides that any action against the State of Ohio or an agency thereof to make any distribution or other payment, except for unclaimed funds, shall be brought within five years after the cause of action has accrued. (As eff. 7-1-93.)

R.C. 2305.11 amended without material change as to the statement in the Parent Volume. (As eff. 4-16-93.)

SECTION 1-43: MARKETABLE TITLE

1-43A Rules.

An objection to title must have some substantive merit in order to defeat a claim for specific performance of a contract for the sale of real estate made by a vendor charged with producing "good and marketable" title. An improperly recorded memorandum of lease intended to provide notice of a lease that has lapsed by its own terms, or has been canceled for breach of its conditions, does not constitute a defect sufficiently substantive to warrant a purchaser's refusal to perform. G/GM Real Estate Corp. v. Susse Chalet Motor Lodge of Ohio, Inc., 61 Ohio St. 3d 375, 575 N.E.2d 141 (1991).

Further research: O Jur 3d, Real Property Sales and Exchanges §§ 74-81.

1-43B Liens.

Further research: O Jur 3d, Real Property Sales and Exchanges §§ 86, 87, 247.

1-43C Restrictions.

A deed which incorporates by reference previously created use restrictions, preserves those restrictions under R.C. 5301.49 if the reference specifically identifies the recorded title transaction which created them. Blakely v. Capitan, 34 Ohio App. 3d 46, 516 N.E.2d 248 (1986).

Further research: O Jur 3d, Real Property Sales and Exchanges § 93.

SECTION 1-44: MARKETABLE TITLE ACT

1-44A Generally.

R.C. 5301.51 amended without material change as to the statement in the Parent Volume. (As eff. 5-31-86.)

R.C. 5301.52 provides: "(A) To be effective and entitled to recording, the notice referred to in section 5301.51 of the Revised Code shall satisfy all of the following:

"(1) Be in the form of an affidavit;

"(2) State the nature of the claim to be preserved and the names and addresses of the persons for whose benefit the notice is being filed;

"(3) Contain an accurate and full description of all land affected by the notice, which description shall be set forth in particular terms and not by general inclusions except that if the claim is founded upon a recorded instrument, the description in the notice may be the same as that contained in such recorded instrument;

"(4) State the name of each record owner of the land affected by the notice, at the time of its recording, together with the recording information of the instrument by which each record owner acquired title to the land;

"(5) Be made by any person who has knowledge of the relevant facts or is competent to testify concerning them in court.

"(B) The notice shall be filed for record in the office of the recorder of the county or counties where the land described in it is situated. The recorder of each county shall accept all such notices presented to him which describe land situated in the county in which he serves, shall enter and record them in the deed records of that county, and shall index each notice in the grantee deed index under the names of the claimants appearing in that notice and in the grantor deed index under the names of the record owners appearing in that notice. Such notices also shall be indexed under the description of the real estate involved in a book set apart for that purpose to be known as the "Notice Index." Each recorder may charge the same fees for the recording of such notices as are charged for recording deeds.

"(C) A notice prepared, executed, and recorded in conformity with the requirements of this section, or a certified copy of it, shall be accepted as evidence of the facts stated insofar as they affect title to the land affected by that notice.

"(D) Any person who knowingly makes any false statement in a notice executed under this section is guilty of perjury under section 2921.11 of the Revised Code." (As eff. 5-31-88.)

Under the Marketable Title Act, a stray or wild recorded deed may be the basis for marketable record title. When the Marketable Title Act does not extinguish either party's claim to the property, the act is no longer applicable and the parties' interests must be determined as though the act were not in effect. Minnich v. Guernsey S & L Co., 36 Ohio App. 3d 54, 521 N.E.2d 489 (1987).

A court decree that use restrictions on real property are enforceable is a title transaction within the meaning of R.C. 5301.47(F), and a deed which incorporates by reference previously created use restrictions preserves those restrictions under R.C. 5301.49 if the reference specifically identifies the recorded title transaction which created them. Blakely v. Capitan, 34 Ohio App. 3d 46, 516 N.E.2d 248 (1986).

R.C. 5301.53 amended without material change as to the statement in the Parent Volume. (As eff. 3-22-89.)

R.C. 5301.56 provides for mineral interests in realty. (As eff. 3-22-89.)

An express easement that existed prior to the root of title and has not been properly preserved pursuant to the Marketable Title Act may still be valid if the express easement can be considered an easement by prescription in accordance with R.C. 5301.49(C). However, the easement by prescription can also be lost through the doctrines of estoppel and laches if it is not properly enforced. Zimmerman v. Cindle, 48 Ohio App. 3d 164, 548 N.E.2d 1315 (1988).

SECTION 1-45: STANDARDS OF TITLE EXAMINATION

1-45A Generally.

Standard of Title Examination 4.9 adopted effective November 9, 1991, as follows:

4.9 ENCUMBRANCES — CURRENT AGRICULTURAL USE VALUATION

Problem A:

Is the title examiner under a duty to report that the land has been certified for Current Agricultural Use Valuation for reduced taxation?

Standard A:

Yes.

Comment A:

Pursuant to R.C. 5713.31 et seq., so long as the owner of farm land annually renews the qualifications for reduction in taxation, no lien arises. However, in any year that the land loses its agricultural tax status, there arises a charge levied upon such land in an amount equal to the tax savings during the four preceding tax years. This lien continues upon the title of a subsequent owner. There is no limitation upon the duration of the lien.

DIVISION 1-5: REGISTRATION OF TITLES

SECTION 1-51: THE SYSTEM

1-51A In General.

R.C. 5309.31-.54 establish a procedure by which the county commissioners of a county may abolish the land registration system in that county. These statutes also prescribe the effect of abolition on previously registered land. (As eff. 2-28-91.)

R.C. 5309.06, R.C. 5309.29 and R.C. 5309.92 amended to conform to the new statutes concerning the election by a county to abolish the land registration system. (As eff. 2-28-91.)

CHAPTER 2: ADVERSE POSSESSION

DIVISION 2-1: IN GENERAL

SECTION 2-11: INTRODUCTION; NATURE OF THE TITLE AND RIGHTS ACQUIRED

2-11A Statutes; Generally.

R.C. 2305.04 amended to delete imprisonment as a basis for tolling the statute of limitations. (As eff. 1-13-91.)

SECTION 2-12: PRESCRIPTION

2-12B Requirements.

In order to establish an easement by prescription, the adverse element must be demonstrated. Where the owner of the servient estate claims that use was permissive and meets the burden of proving that the use was permissive, an easement by prescription does not arise. McCune v. Brandon, 85 Ohio App. 3d 697, 621 N.E.2d 434, mot. overruled, 67 Ohio St. 3d 1455, 619 N.E.2d 423 (1993).

To establish a prescriptive easement for a storm sewer, the "open and notorious" elements are not satisfied merely because the original owner must have known of and seen the city's storm sewer being put in beneath the residence. Rather, the city has the burden of proving that the prescriptive elements were continuously present for 21 years. Nice v. Marysville, 82 Ohio App.3d 109, 611 N.E.2d 468 (1992).

A person claiming a prescriptive easement does not have the burden of proving that the use of the easement was without the property owner's permission. Pence v. Darst, 62 Ohio App. 3d 32, 574 N.E.2d 548 (1989).

DIVISION 2-2: BY AND AGAINST WHOM INTEREST IS ACQUIRED

SECTION 2-21: GOVERNMENT; HIGHWAYS AND STREETS

2-21B Subdivisions of the State.

To establish a prescriptive easement for a storm sewer, the "open and notorious" elements are not satisfied merely because the original owner must have known of and seen the city's storm sewer being put in beneath the residence. Rather, the city has the burden of proving that the prescriptive elements were continuously present for 21 years. Nice v. Marysville, 82 Ohio App.3d 109, 611 N.E.2d 468 (1992).

Land titled in a county and supporting the county's bridge falls within the general rule that the state and its political subdivisions cannot be deprived of its streets and highways by adverse possession. 1540 Columbus Corp. v. Cuyahoga County, 68 Ohio App. 3d 713, 589 N.E.2d 467 (1990).

DIVISION 2-3: NATURE OF THE REQUIRED POSSESSION

SECTION 2-31: PERIOD; CONTINUITY; TACKING

2-31A Period.

Claimant, acting in the mistaken belief that the land in question was part of an adjoining parcel he was in the process of acquiring, began development activities on the disputed land. These activities — taking down trees and shrubbery, filling in stump holes, grading and putting drain tile on the land — were sufficient to begin the statutory period, as the owner's permission to enter extended only to the adjoining land. Raymond v. Cary, 63

Ohio App. 3d 342, 578 N.E.2d 865, mot. overruled, 46 Ohio St. 3d 705, 545 N.E.2d 1284 (1989).

SECTION 2-32: AS HOSTILE AND UNDER CLAIM OF RIGHT; CHANGE IN USE

2-32A Rule; Permission.

Claimant, acting in the mistaken belief that the land in question was part of an adjoining parcel he was in the process of acquiring, began development activities on the disputed land. These activities — taking down trees and shrubbery, filling in stump holes, grading and putting drain tile on the land — were sufficient to begin the statutory period, as the owner's permission to enter extended only to the adjoining land. Raymond v. Cary, 63 Ohio App. 3d 342, 578 N.E.2d 865, mot. overruled, 46 Ohio St. 3d 705, 545 N.E.2d 1284 (1989).

CHAPTER 3: BOUNDARIES AND DESCRIPTIONS

DIVISION 3-1: IN GENERAL

SECTION 3-14: LIGHT, AIR AND VIEW

3-14B Spite Fences.

Construction of fences with the city's approval, although apparently in violation of city ordinances, did not rise to the level of extreme and outrageous conduct so as to state a claim for intentional infliction of emotional distress. Furthermore, assuming that the violation of the city ordinances constituted tortious conduct, summary judgment was proper where the plaintiffs failed to show any evidence that they had been damaged. Cherney v. Amherst, 66 Ohio App. 3d 411, 584 N.E.2d 84 (1991).

SECTION 3-15: FENCES

3-15B Partition Fences.

R.C. 971.02 amended to provide: "The owners of adjoining lands shall build, keep up, and maintain in good repair, in equal shares, all partition fences between them, unless otherwise agreed upon by them in writing and witnessed by two persons. The fact that any land or tract of land is wholly unenclosed or is not used, adapted, or intended by its owner for use for agricultural purposes shall not excuse the owner thereof from the obligations imposed by this chapter on him as an adjoining owner. This chapter does not apply to the enclosure of lots in municipal corporations, or of adjoining lands both of which are laid out into lots outside municipal corporations, or affect sections 4959.02 to 4959.06 of the Revised Code, relating to fences required to be constructed by persons or corporations owning, controlling, or managing a railroad." (As eff. 6-29-88.)

DIVISION 3-2: CONSTRUCTION OF DESCRIPTIONS

SECTION 3-21: GENERALLY

3-21B Reformation.

Where clear and convincing evidence is offered at trial to demonstrate that both the grantors and grantees were mistaken as to what was being conveyed by the description contained in the deed, reformation of the deed is appropriate. Mason v. Swartz, 76 Ohio App. 3d 43, 600 N.E.2d 1121 (1991).

3-21H Monuments; Adjoiners.

If the monuments placed by the original surveyor cannot be ascertained, the second survey may turn to the courses, distances, and still-existent monuments to determine the boundaries. The trial court was justified in concluding that the original monuments were not located because the surveyors found iron pipe and not iron pins, and most of the iron pipes were not located where the original survey indicated the placement of iron pins. Yuhasz v. Mrdenovich, 82 Ohio App.3d 490, 612 N.E.2d 763 (1992).

A public street or road or the boundary line of other property may be used as a monument. Sanders v. Webb, 85 Ohio App.3d 674, 621 N.E.2d 420, mot. overruled, 67 Ohio St.3d 1455, 619 N.E.2d 423 (1993).

SECTION 3-22: DEFICIENCY OR SURPLUS; MORE OR LESS

3-22A More or Less.

Further research: O Jur 3d, Real Property Sales and Exchanges § 42.

SECTION 3-23: WATERS AND WATERCOURSES

3-23E Watercourse Between States.

Further research: O Jur 3d, State of Ohio § 7.

SECTION 3-26: SURVEYS

3-26A Rules.

The primary purpose of construction is to follow the footsteps of the surveyor on the ground (citing McDermott's). The trial court was justified in concluding that, relying on old plats and surveys, the section line changed direction so as to lie along the centerline of Salem Cave Road in the disputed area. Sanders v. Webb, 85 Ohio App.3d 674, mot. overruled, 67 Ohio St.3d 1455, 619 N.E.2d 423 (1993).

DIVISION 3-3: ESTABLISHMENT OF BOUNDARIES

SECTION 3-31: AGREEMENT OF PARTIES

3-31A Rules.

R.C. 2711.01 amended to provide as follows:

"(A) A provision in any written contract, except as provided in division (B) of this section, to settle by arbitration a controversy that subsequently arises out of the contract, or out of the refusal to perform the whole or any part of the contract, or any agreement in writing between two or more persons to submit to arbitration any controversy existing between them at the time of the agreement to submit, or arising after the agreement to submit, from a relationship then existing between them or that they simultaneously create, shall be valid, irrevocable, and enforceable, except upon grounds that exist at law or in equity for the revocation of any contract.

"(B)(1) Sections 2711.01 to 2711.16 of the Revised Code do not apply to controversies involving the title to or the possession of real estate with the following exceptions:

"(a) Controversies involving the amount of increased or decreased valuation of the property at the termination of certain periods, as provided in a lease;

"(b) Controversies involving the amount of rentals due under any lease;

"(c) Controversies involving the determination of the value of improvements at the termination of any lease;

"(d) Controversies involving the appraisal of property values in connection with making or renewing any lease;

"(e) Controversies involving the boundaries of real estate.

"(2) Sections 2711.01 to 2711.16 of the Revised Code do not apply to controversies involving international commercial arbitration or conciliation that are subject to Chapter 2712. of the Revised Code." (As eff. 10-23-91.)

CHAPTER 4: CORPORATIONS AND ASSOCIATIONS

DIVISION 4-1: IN GENERAL

DIVISION 4-1: IN GENERAL

SECTION 4-11: INTRODUCTION

4-11B   Service of Process.

R.C. 1701.07 amended to provide as follows:

"(A) Every corporation shall have and maintain an agent, sometimes referred to as the "statutory agent," upon whom any process, notice, or demand required or permitted by statute to be served upon a corporation may be served. The agent may be a natural person who is a resident of this state or may be a domestic corporation or a foreign corporation holding a license as such under the laws of this state that is authorized by its articles of incorporation to act as such agent and that has a business address in this state.

"(B) The secretary of state shall not accept original articles for filing unless there is filed with the articles a written appointment of an agent that is signed by the incorporators of the corporation or a majority of them and a written acceptance of the appointment that is signed by the agent. In all other cases, the corporation shall appoint the agent and shall file in the office of the secretary of state a written appointment of the agent that is signed by any authorized officer of the corporation and a written acceptance of the appointment that is either the original acceptance signed by the agent or a photocopy or similar reproduction of the original acceptance signed by the agent.

"(C) The written appointment of an agent shall set forth the name and address in this state of the agent, including the street and number or other particular description, and shall otherwise be in such form as the secretary of state prescribes. The secretary of state shall keep a record of the names of corporations, and the names and addresses of their respective agents.

"(D) If any agent dies, removes from the state, or resigns, the corporation shall forthwith appoint another agent and file with the secretary of state a written appointment of the agent.

"(E) If the agent changes his or its address from that appearing upon the record in the office of the secretary of state, the corporation shall forthwith file with the secretary of state a written statement setting forth the new address.

"(F) An agent may resign by filing with the secretary of state a written notice to that effect that is signed by the agent and by sending a copy of the notice to the corporation at the current or last known address of its principal office on or prior to the date the notice is filed with the secretary of state. The notice shall set forth the name of the corporation, the name and current address of the agent, the current or last known address, including the street and number or other particular description, of the corporation's principal office, the resignation of the agent, and a statement that a copy of the notice has been sent to the corporation within the time and in the manner prescribed by this division. Upon the expiration of thirty days after the filing, the authority of the agent shall terminate.

"(G) A corporation may revoke the appointment of an agent by filing with the secretary of state a written appointment of another agent and a statement that the appointment of the former agent is revoked.

"(H) Any process, notice, or demand required or permitted by statute to be served upon a corporation may be served upon the corporation by delivering a copy of it to its agent, if a natural person, or by delivering a copy of it at the address of its agent in this state, as the address appears upon the record in the office of the secretary of state. If (1) the agent cannot be found, or (2) the agent no longer has that address, or (3) the corporation has failed to maintain an agent shall have filed with the secretary of state an affidavit stating that one of the foregoing conditions exists and stating the most recent address of the corporation which the party after diligent search has been able to ascertain, then service of process, notice, or demand upon the secretary of state, as the agent of the corporation, may be initiated by delivering to him or at his office quadruplicate copies of such process, notice, or demand and by paying to him a fee of five dollars. The secretary of state shall forthwith give notice of the delivery to the corporation at its principal office as shown upon the record in this office and at any different address shown on its last franchise tax report filed in this state, or to the corporation at any different address set forth in the above mentioned affidavit, and shall forward to the corporation at said addresses, by certified mail, with request for return receipt, a copy of the process, notice, or demand; and thereupon service upon the corporation shall be deemed to have been made.

''(I) The secretary of state shall keep a record of each process, notice, and demand delivered to him or at his office under this section or any other law of this state that authorizes service upon him and shall record the time of the delivery and his action thereafter with respect thereto.

''(J) This section does not limit or affect the right to serve any process, notice, or demand upon a corporation in any other manner permitted by law.

''(K) Every corporation shall state in each annual report filed by it with the department of taxation the name and address of its statutory agent.

''(L) Except when an original appointment of an agent is filed with the original articles, a written appointment of an agent or a written statement filed by a corporation with the secretary of state shall be signed by any authorized officer of the corporation or by the incorporators of the corporation or a majority of them if no directors have been elected.

''(M) For filing a written appointment of an agent other than one filed with original articles, and for filing a statement of change of address of an agent, the secretary of state shall charge and collect a fee of three dollars.

''(N) Upon the failure of a corporation to appoint another agent or to file a statement of change of address of an agent, the secretary of state shall give notice thereof by certified mail to the corporation at the address set forth in the notice of resignation or on the last franchise tax return filed in this state by the corporation. Unless the default is cured within thirty days after the mailing by the secretary of state of the notice or within any further period of time that the secretary of state grants, upon the expiration of that period of time from the date of the mailing, the articles of the corporation shall be canceled without further notice or action by the secretary of state. The secretary of state shall make a notation of the cancellation on his records.

''A corporation whose articles have been canceled may be reinstated by filing an application for reinstatement and the required appointment of agent or required statement, and by paying a filing fee of ten dollars. The rights, privileges, and franchises of a corporation whose articles have been reinstated are subject to section 1701.922 of the Revised Code. The secretary of state shall furnish the tax commissioner a monthly list of all corporations canceled and reinstated under this division.

"(O) This section does not apply to banks, trust companies, insurance companies, or any corporation defined under the laws of this state as a public utility for taxation purposes." (As eff. 10-8-92 and 7-1-94.)

SECTION 4-12: CORPORATE POWER TO ACQUIRE AND HOLD

4-12A Generally.

R.C. 1701.13 amended without material change as to the statement in the Parent Volume. (As eff. 4-11-90 and 7-1-94.)

SECTION 4-13: CORPORATE POWER TO SELL, CONVEY AND ENCUMBER

4-13A Limitations on the Power; Capacity.

R.C. 1701.85 provides for relief of a dissenting shareholder of a domestic corporation. (As eff. 4-19-88 and 7-1-94.)

R.C. 1701.13 amended without material change as to the statement in the Parent Volume. (As eff. 4-11-90 and 7-1-94.)

R.C. 1701.76 amended without material change as to the statement in the Parent Volume. (As eff. 4-11-90.)

4-13B Authority to Exercise Power.

R.C. 1701.59 amended to provide: "(A) Except where the law, the articles, or the regulations require action to be authorized or taken by shareholders, all of the authority of a corporation shall be exercised by or under the direction of its directors. For their own government, the directors may adopt bylaws that are not inconsistent with the articles or the regulations. The selection of a time frame for the achievement of corporate goals shall be the responsibility of the directors.

"(B) A director shall perform his duties as a director, including his duties as a member of any committee of the directors upon which he may serve, in good faith, in a manner he reasonably believes to be in or not opposed to the best interests of the corporation, and with the care that an ordinarily prudent person in a like position would use under similar circumstances. In performing his duties, a director is entitled to rely on information, opinions, reports, or statements, including financial statements and other financial data, that are prepared or presented by:

"(1) One or more directors, officers, or employees of the corporation who the director reasonably believes are reliable and competent to the matters prepared or presented;

"(2) Counsel, public accountants, or other persons as to matters that the director reasonably believes are within the person's professional or expert competence;

"(3) A committee of the directors upon which he does not serve, duly established in accordance with a provision of the articles or the regulations, as to matters within its designated authority, which committee the director reasonably believes to merit confidence.

"(C) For purposes of division (B) of this section:

"(1) A director shall not be found to have violated his duties under division (B) of this section unless it is proved by clear and convincing evidence that the director has not acted in good faith, in a manner he reasonably believes to be in or not opposed to the best interests of the corporation, or with the care that an ordinarily prudent person in a like position would use under similar circumstances, in any action brought against a director, including actions involving or affecting any of the following:

"(a) A change or potential change in control of the corporation, including a determination to resist a change or potential change in control made pursuant to division (F)(7) of section 1701.13 of the Revised Code;

"(b) A termination or potential termination of his service to the corporation as a director;

"(c) His service in any other position or relationship with the corporation.

"(2) A director shall not be considered to be acting in good faith if he has knowledge concerning the matter in question that would cause reliance on information, opinions, reports, or statements that are prepared or presented by the persons described in division (B)(1) to (3) of this section to be unwarranted.

"(3) Nothing contained in this division limits relief available under section 1701.60 of the Revised Code.

"(D) A director shall be liable in damages for any action he takes or fails to take as a director only if it is proved by clear and convincing evidence in a court of competent jurisdiction that his action or failure to act involved an act or omission undertaken with deliberate intent to cause injury to the corporation or undertaken with reckless disregard for the best interests as of the corporation. Nothing contained in this division affects the liability of directors under section 1701.60 of the Revised Code. This division does not apply if, and only to the extent that, at the time of a director's act or omission that is the subject of complaint, the articles or the regulations of the corporation state by specific reference to this division that the provisions of this division do not apply to the corporation.

"(E) For purposes of this section, a director, in determining what he reasonably believes to be in the best interests of the corporation, shall consider the interests of the corporation's shareholders and, in his discretion, may consider any of the following:

"(1) The interests of the corporation's employees, suppliers, creditors, and customers;

"(2) The economy of the state and nation;

"(3) Community and societal considerations;

"(4) The long-term as well as short-term interests of the corporation and its shareholders, including the possibility that these interests may be best served by the continued independence of the corporation.

"(F) Nothing contained in division (C) or (D) of this section affects the duties of either of the following:

"(1) A director who acts in any capacity other than his capacity as a director;

"(2) A director of a corporation that does not have issued and outstanding shares that are listed on a national securities exchange or are regularly quoted in an over-the-counter market by one or more members of a national or affiliated securities association, who votes for or assents to any action taken by the directors of the corporation that, in connection with a change in control of the corporation, directly results in the holder or holders of a majority of the outstanding shares of the corporation receiving a greater consideration for their shares than other shareholders." (As eff. 4-11-90.)

DIVISION 4-2: PARTICULAR TYPES OF ORGANIZATIONS

SECTION 4-21: NONPROFIT CORPORATIONS

4-21A Statutory Regulations.

R.C. 1702.30 in part provides: "(A) Except where the law, the articles, or the regulations require that action be otherwise authorized or taken, all of the authority of a corporation shall be exercised by or under the direction of its trustees. For their own government, the trustees may adopt bylaws that are not inconsistent with the articles or regulations." (As eff. 3-29-88 and 7-1-94.)

R.C. 1702.06 amended without material change as to the statement in the Parent Volume. (As eff. 10-8-92 and 7-1-94.)

R.C. 1702.60 provides that upon reinstatement of a corporation whose articles of incorporation have been cancelled, all real and personal property rights and credits and all contracts and other rights of the corporation existing at the time its articles of incorporation were cancelled shall be fully vested in the corporation as if the articles had not been cancelled. (As eff. 7-1-94.)

SECTION 4-22: DISSOLVED CORPORATIONS

4-22A Rules.

R.C. 1701.88 amended to provide: "(A) When a corporation is dissolved voluntarily, when the articles of incorporation have been canceled, or when the period of existence of the corporation specified in its articles has expired, the corporation shall cease to carry on business and shall do only such acts as are required to wind up its affairs, or to obtain reinstatement of the articles in accordance with sections 1701.07, 1701.921, 1785.06 or 5733.22 of the Revised Code, or are permitted upon reinstatement by division (C) of section 1701.922 of the Revised Code, and for such purposes it shall continue as a corporation.'' (As eff. 7-1-94.)

R.C. 5727.54 amended without material change as to the statement in the Parent Volume. (As eff. 12-31-89.)

R.C. 5733.22 amended without material change as to the statement in the Parent Volume. (As eff. 7-1-93 and 7-1-94.)

SECTION 4-25: BANKS AND LOAN ASSOCIATIONS

4-25B As Mortgagees.

R.C. 1321.52 amended without material change as to the statement in the Parent Volume. (As eff. 10-2-89.)

SECTION 4-26: RELIGIOUS SOCIETIES; BENEVOLENT ASSOCIATIONS

4-26A Rules.

A court may look beyond deeds and articles of incorporation to church constitutions and similar documents to determine a property dispute between a national church and a local church, upon determining that a hierarchical relationship existed. Minutes of the national church organization did not create an express trust in favor of the national church with respect to the real property owned by the local church, and a constructive trust would not be imposed where the funds to purchase the property came only from the local church. Southern Ohio State Exec. Offices of Church of God v. Fairborn Church of God, 61 Ohio App. 3d 526, 573 N.E.2d 172, mot. overruled, 45 Ohio St. 3d 708, 544 N.E.2d 695, cert. denied, 493 U.S. 1072 (1990).

Further research: O Jur 3d, Religious Organizations §§ 42, 45.

4-26B Sale or Encumbrance.

Further research: O Jur 3d, Religious Organizations §§ 50-54.

SECTION 4-28: PARTNERSHIPS

4-28A Generally.

R.C. 1336.08 repealed by the adoption of the Ohio Uniform Fraudulent Transfer Act. See discussion at 8-54 below.

Individuals who were both limited partners of a limited partnership and agents or employees of the corporations that were the general partners of the limited partnership are personally liable to a third party performing work for the limited partnership where (1) the individuals exceeded their roles as limited partners; and (2) they failed to establish that they had authority to act on behalf of the corporations, and that they had properly told the person performing the work about their status as agents of the corporations. Hommel v. Micco, 76 Ohio App. 3d 690, 602 N.E.2d 1259 (1991).

R.C. 1775.61-63 provide for the creation of registered partnerships having limited liability — the partnership version of a limited liability company. (As eff. 7-1-94.)

Second paragraph of R.C. 1777.02 amended to provide:

"The certificate shall be signed by the partners and acknowledged by some officer authorized to take acknowledgements of deeds, except that in the case of a joint stock company or a commercial partnership, whose capital stock is represented by shares or certificates of stock transferable on the books of the concern and whose business is conducted by a board of directors and by officers, the president, secretary, or cashier of such company or partnership may sign and acknowledge the certificate, giving in it the names of all the persons interested as partners or shareholders in such company or partnership, and except that a domestic or foreign limited partnership that is formed under or registered pursuant to Chapter 1782 of the Revised Code need not file a certificate pursuant to this section."

Third paragraph of R.C. 1777.02 amended to change the word "without" to "outside." (As eff. 7-1-94.)

R.C. 1782.21 amended without material change as to the statement in the Parent Volume. (As eff. 7-1-94.)

4-28B Uniform Partnership Act.

R.C. 1775.24 amended to provide: "(A) A partner is co-owner with his partners of specific partnership property, holding as a tenant in partnership.

"(B) The incidents of this tenancy are such that:

"(1) A partner, subject to this chapter, and to any agreement between the partners, has an equal right with his partners to possess specific partnership property for partnership purposes; but he has no right to possess the property for any other purpose without the consent of his partners.

"(2) A partner's right in specific partnership property is not assignable except in connection with the assignment of rights of all the partners in the same property.

"(3) A partner's right in specific partnership property is not subject to attachment or execution, except on a claim against the partnership. When partnership property is attached for a partnership debt, the partners, or any of them, or the representatives of a deceased partner, cannot claim any right under exemption laws.

"(4) On the death of a partner, his right in specific partnership property vests in the surviving partners, unless he was the last surviving partner, in which case his right in the property vests in his legal representative. The surviving partners have, or the legal representative of the last surviving partner has, no right to possess the partnership property for any but a partnership purpose. This division is subject to the procedures set forth in Chapter 1779 of the Revised Code.

"(5) A partner's right in specific partnership property is not subject to dower, any statutory interest of a surviving spouse, heirs, or next of kin, or any allowance to a surviving spouse, minor children, or both a surviving spouse and minor children, including, but not limited to, the allowance for support under section 2106.13 of the Revised Code." (As eff. 5-31-90.)

In accord with R.C. 2329.09, partners are not primarily liable for the contractual obligations incurred by their partnership. A creditor in proceedings in execution of a judgment against the partnership must first exhaust partnership property before resorting to the personal assets of partners under R.C. 1775.14(B). At common law, as well as pursuant to R.C. 1775.14(B), general partners are jointly liable, rather than jointly and severally liable, for partnership contractual debts in the absence of an agreement among themselves to the contrary. Wayne Smith Constr. Co. v. Wolman, Duberstein & Thompson, 65 Ohio St. 3d 383, 604 N.E.2d 157, reh'g denied, 65 Ohio St. 3d 1482, 604 N.E.2d 758 (1992).

SECTION 4-29: OTHER ORGANIZATIONS

4-29C   Title Insurance Companies.

The requirement that a title insurance company deposit $50,000 of bonds with the superintendent of insurance was deleted from R.C. 3929.01 but added to R.C. 3953.06. (As eff. 8-8-91.) The option to deposit $100,000 in securities in another state remains under R.C. 3929.07.

4-29F   Limited Liability Companies.

R.C. 1705.01-58, effective July 1, 1994, provide for the creation and governance of limited liability companies. A "limited liability company" is a hybrid form of entity that combines features of both a partnership and a corporation. Like a corporation, the limited liability company shields its owners (referred to as "members") from liability for the company's obligations. R.C. 1705.48. However, for federal tax purposes, a properly constituted limited liability company will be treated as a pass-through entity, similar to a partnership.

A limited liability company is formed by filing articles of organization with the Ohio Secretary of State and paying the mandatory filing fee. R.C. 1705.04. The name of the company must include the words "Limited Liability Company," without abbreviation, or one of the following abbreviations: "Limited," "Ltd," or "Ltd." R.C. 1705.05(A). Title transactions involving a limited liability company (acquisition of ownership, etc.) should not occur before the entity is officially formed. Once formed, a limited liability company has fairly general powers, including the power to acquire, lease, hold, use, encumber, sell, exchange, transfer and dispose of property. R.C. 1705.03.

The affairs of the limited liability company are governed by the "Operating Agreement" (similar to a partnership agreement) among its members. R.C. 1705.01(J). Unless otherwise provided in the Operating Agreement, management of the limited liability company is vested in all members in proportion to their capital. R.C. 1705.24. The Operating Agreement may provide for the appointment of managers (who may or may not be members) to conduct the business of the limited liability company. R.C. 1705.25. Although a third party dealing with a member or manager may, unless it has knowledge to the contrary, rely upon the authority of that member or manager to bind the company in the ordinary course of its business (R.C. 1705.25), lenders, title insurers and others dealing with limited liability companies are well-advised to require documentation evidencing the authority of any member or manager purporting to act on behalf of the company.

Like a partnership, a limited liability company may be dissolved upon the occurrence of certain events such as the expiration of the term of the Operating Agreement or withdrawal of a member. R.C. 1705.43(A). Upon dissolution, the entity must be wound up and liquidated unless all of the remaining members, or such lesser number as is provided in the Operating Agreement, agree to continue the business of the limited liability company. Id.; R.C. 1705.44.

Ohio law also recognizes a new entity referred to as a "registered partnership having limited liability." R.C. 1775.61. In a partnership with this status, each partner is not jointly and severally liable for partnership acts or omissions caused by another partner or an employee, agent or representative of the partnership. R.C. 1775.14(A). However, each partner is liable for his own actions or omissions, and those of any partners, employees, agents or representatives under his direct supervision or control. Id. A registered partnership having limited liability is formed by filing a registration application with the Ohio Secretary of State and paying the filing fee. R.C. 1775.61. The name of the entity must include the words "registered partnership having limited liability" or the abbreviation "P.L.L." R.C. 1775.62.

CHAPTER 5: COTENANCY AND JOINT OWNERSHIP

DIVISION 5-2: PARTICULAR CLASSES OF INTERESTS

SECTION 5-24: OTHER INTERESTS

5-24D Condominiums and Cooperatives.

Under R.C. 5311, while the owner of a condominium unit has exclusive ownership of and responsibility for his unit (R.C. 5311.03(B)), the owner's freedom of action is of necessity limited by the fact that the unit is one of many units. River Terrace Condo. Ass'n v. Lewis, 33 Ohio App. 3d 52, 514 N.E.2d 732 (1986).

Condominium declarations established pursuant to Ohio's Condominium Act must be strictly construed since the condominium concept depends upon reasonable use and occupancy rules and restrictions. Thus, individual unit owners cannot be permitted to disrupt the integrity of the common scheme through their desire for changes. Georgetown Arms Condo. v. Super, 33 Ohio App. 3d 132, 514 N.E.2d 899 (1986).

Provisions contained within a declaration of condominium ownership and/or condominium bylaws requiring a defaulting unit owner to be responsible for payment of attorneys fees incurred by the unit owners' association in either a collection action or foreclosure action against the defaulting unit owner for unpaid common assessments are enforceable and not void or against public policy so long as the fees sounded fair, just and reasonable as determined by the trial court upon full consideration of all the circumstances of the case. Nottingdale Homeowners Ass'n v. Darby, 33 Ohio St. 3d 32, 514 N.E.2d 702 (1987).

An amendment to a condominium declaration prohibiting unit owners from leasing their units is not per se unenforceable against owners who acquired their condominium units prior to the adoption of that amendment. Rather, the amendment must be evaluated under a "reasonableness" test in light of the surrounding circumstances. Worthinglen Condo. Unit Owners' Ass'n v. Brown, 57 Ohio App. 3d 73, 566 N.E.2d 1275 (1989).

Language in a condominium declaration prohibiting "anything placed on the outside walls of the building" is sufficiently definite to preclude installation of a screen door, and the unit owners' association's decision to reject application for a front exterior screen door, as part of the uniform enforcement of the prohibition, is not arbitrary or capricious. Sprunk v. Creekwood Condo. Unit Owners' Ass'n, 60 Ohio App. 3d 52, 573 N.E.2d 197, cert. denied, 47 Ohio St. 3d 712, 548 N.E.2d 244 (1989).

A provision in a condominium declaration prohibiting structures on the common areas of the condominium applies to ham radio antennas. Applying the test for reasonableness articulated in River Terrace Condominium Ass'n. v. Lewis, this restriction was found to be reasonable. Monday Villas Prop. Owners Ass'n v. Barbe, 75 Ohio App. 3d 167, 598 N.E.2d 1291 (1991).

Condominium developers do not have a fiduciary duty to the condominium owners' association. If the developer has failed to make proper disclosure of material facts, R.C. 5311.26 imposes strict liability; in such case, a plaintiff does not have to prove the elements of common-law fraud. Once the inadequate disclosure is proven, liability attaches and plaintiff must then prove damages under R.C. 5311.27. A corporate veil will not be pierced where a developer, on behalf of unit owners' association, entered into an unfair lease of a portion of the condominium property with an entity controlled by the developer. Belvedere Condominium Unit Owners' Ass'n v. R. E. Roark Cos., Inc., 67 Ohio St. 3d 274, 617 N.E.2d 1075 (1993).

A negligence claim against the builder-developer of a condominium was barred by the statute of limitations when three instances of underlayment failure were discovered more than four years before the action was brought. Gardens of Bay Landings Condominiums v. Flair Builders, Inc., 96 Ohio App. 3d 353 (1994), dismissed, mot. overruled, 71 Ohio St. 3d 1444, 644 N.E.2d 406 (1995).

In an action for foreclosure of a lien for condominium assessments, the condominium association has a statutory right, pursuant to R.C. 5311.18, to the appointment of a receiver to collect a reasonable rental from the owners of the unit. Jamestown Village Condominium Owners Ass'n v. Market Media Resources, Inc., 96 Ohio App. 3d 678 (1994).

Restriction in condominium declaration that prohibited parking trucks in the common areas was reasonable and enforceable against the owner of a pickup truck. Bluffs of Wildwood Condominium Homeowners' Ass'n, Inc. v. Dinkel, 96 Ohio App. 3d 278, appeal overruled, 71 Ohio St. 3d 1421, 642 N.E.2d 386 (1994).

Claims against a developer for violation of the condominium disclosure statute accrued when the disclosure statements were given to purchasers, not when the defects were discovered. Such claims may be asserted only by the condominium association (where the claims relate to the common areas and facilities) and by purchasers in privity with the developer, and are subject to the six-year statute of limitations provided in R.C. 2305.07. Separate claims for fraudulent concealment were barred by the "as is" clauses and warranty limitations contained in the purchase contracts with the unit purchasers. Arbor Village Condominium Ass'n v. Arbor Village, Ltd., 95 Ohio App. 3d 499, appeal overruled, 71 Ohio St. 3d 1406, 641 N.E.2d 204 (1994).

DIVISION 5-3: PARTITION

SECTION 5-34: JUDICIAL PROCEDURE

5-34A Equity Jurisdiction; Statutes.

Where the commissioners failed to understand and complete their statutory duties, and did not attempt to divide the property because they thought that they could not do so on a perfectly equitable basis, the commissioners' determination that the property could not be partitioned without manifest injury to its value was erroneous. In addition, when making a determination that the property cannot be divided without manifest injury to its value, the commissioners must make factual findings to support their conclusion. The commissioners' report must contain sufficient information to enable a trial judge to render his own decision; the responsibilities of the commissioners are analogous to those of referees. McGill v. Roush, 87 Ohio App. 3d 66, 621 N.E.2d 865 (1993).

5-34C Owelty; Equalization Shares.

Ohio law favors the partition of property over the sale of property. R.C. 5307.06 does not require the commissioners to achieve perfect equity. It is up to the trial court, not the commissioners, to produce true equity and partition. Owelty is an important tool for a trial court to produce "perfect" equity from a "most equitable partition" by commissioners. McGill v. Roush, 87 Ohio App. 3d 66, 621 N.E.2d 865 (1993).

The presumption that two co-owners hold equal interests may be rebutted by showing unequal contributions toward the purchase price, and on that showing a presumption arises that the parties intended to share the property in proportion to their contributions. Bryan v. Looker, 94 Ohio App. 3d 228 (1994), appeal after remand, 1995 Ohio App. LEXIS 712 (Ohio Ct. App., Allen County Feb. 21, 1995), appeal dismissed, 72 Ohio St. 3d 1551, 650 N.E.2d 1370 (1995).

5-34F Fiduciaries as Parties.

R.C. 2127.41 amended without material change as to the statement in the Parent Volume. (As eff. 5-31-90.)

5-34G Liens.

R.C. 5721.26 amended without change as to the statement in the Parent Volume. (As eff. 6-24-88.)

CHAPTER 6: COVENANTS AND RESTRICTIONS

DIVISION 6-3: RESTRICTIONS AS TO USE

SECTION 6-31: GENERALLY; CREATION AND CONSTRUCTION

6-31D Rule of Interpretation.

Where a restrictive covenant governing the use of residential property is ambiguous, the ambiguity will be strictly construed against placing limitations on the contested use, so that all doubts should be resolved against a possible construction of the covenant which would increase the restriction upon the use of the real estate. Aurora Shores Homeowners' Ass'n v. Hardy, 37 Ohio App. 3d 169, 525 N.E.2d 26 (1987).

An unrecorded land use restriction is not enforceable against the bona fide purchaser for value unless the purchaser has actual notice of the restriction. Although actual notice in some instances may be inferred, it may not be imputed to the purchaser on the basis of familiarity with the deed restriction recorded in another county or on the basis of the purchaser's awareness of the bare existence of the document containing the restrictions. Emrick v. Multicon Bldrs., Inc., 57 Ohio St. 3d 107, 566 N.E.2d 1189 (1991).

Where a restrictive covenant makes no distinction between satellite dishes and ordinary antennas, and the satellite dish installed by the homeowner complies with the express requirements of the antenna restrictions, the restriction is not violated. Because antennas were dealt with explicitly in a separate restriction, antennas would be construed as an exception to another restriction requiring approval of "structures" attached to the exterior of the building, especially in the absence of evidence that the prohibition on structures had been uniformly applied to antennas as well. Woodcreek Ass'n v. Bengle, 73 Ohio App. 3d 506, 597 N.E.2d 1153 (1991).

SECTION 6-32: PARTICULAR APPLICATIONS

6-32B Racial Restrictions; Discrimination.

R.C. 4112.02 amended to prohibit discrimination in housing accommodations on the basis of familial status, to prohibit additional forms of housing discrimination against handicapped persons, and to give parties to a housing discrimination civil action the right to a jury trial. The word "age" was deleted from the statute as it pertains to discrimination in housing accommodations. (As eff. 5-31-90 (as to "age")) and as eff. 6-30-92.)

6-32E Residential Purposes.

Construction of a shelter house for social gatherings violates a restriction that the premises shall be used "solely and exclusively for single family residential purposes." The claim is not barred by laches merely because minor violations had occurred in the past; the construction of the shelter house changed the character and frequency of the violations. Dean v. Nugent Canal Yacht Club, Inc., 66 Ohio App. 3d 471, 585 N.E.2d 554, mot. overruled, 53 Ohio St. 3d 705, 558 N.E.2d 61, appeal after reward, 1991 Ohio App. LEXIS 5916 (Ohio Ct. App., Ottawa County 1991).

Joining lots in an oil and gas drilling unit violates restrictive covenants providing that the lots were to be used "solely for private residence and agricultural purposes," even though no actual drilling would be conducted on the restricted lots. Devendorf v. Akbar Petr. Corp., 62 Ohio App. 3d 842, 577 N.E.2d 707 (1989).

A single residence restriction in a deed may no longer be enforceable when there is clear and convincing evidence that there has been a substantial change in the character of the neighborhood; that enforcement of the restriction would not restore the neighborhood to its residential character; and that enforcement of the covenant would appear to impose a great hardship on the party seeking to avoid the restriction with minimal benefit to the party seeking to enforce it. Nutis v. Schottenstein Trustees, 41 Ohio App. 3d 63, 534 N.E.2d 380 (1987).

Restrictive covenant stating that "All lots in this tract shall be known and described as residential lots. No structures shall be erected, altered, placed or permitted to remain on the residential building plot other than one detached single family dwelling ..." does not prohibit the conversion of the residence on the lot into a real estate sales office. Northwest Civic Group v. Bernstein, 91 Ohio App.3d 18, 631 N.E.2d 671 (1993).

6-32F Consent to Construction.

A restriction requiring prior approval of building plans is enforceable, even absent specific guidelines to indicate criteria for approval, if actual or constructive notice of the restriction exists, and (1) the restriction is used to enforce a "general plan or scheme" of development; or (2) some other restriction or guideline exists to act in conjunction with the prior approval restriction to give an overall limiting effect to the absolute discretion of those empowered with granting or denying the general approval; or (3) the restriction itself contains some limit on the scope of approval. Berry v. Paisley, 66 Ohio App. 3d 77, 583 N.E.2d 430, cause dismissed, 52 Ohio St. 3d 712, 557 N.E.2d 1220 (1990).

6-32H Other Applications.

Construction of a bay window and a storage area and deck on a boathouse violates a restriction requiring approval of other owners of exterior alterations or additions. The restriction is enforceable even absent specific guidelines to indicate criteria for approval if the owner has actual or constructive notice of the restriction and (1) the restriction is used to enforce a "general plan or scheme" of development; or (2) some other restriction or guideline exists to act in conjunction with the prior approval restriction to give an overall limiting effect to the absolute discretion of those empowered with granting or denying the general approval; or (3) the restriction itself contains some limit on the scope of approval. Berry v. Paisley, 66 Ohio App. 3d 77, 583 N.E.2d 430, cause dismissed, 52 Ohio St. 3d 712, 557 N.E.2d 1220 (1990).

A pole-mounted satellite dish violated a restriction stating that "no pole ... whether for use in connection with radio, television, electric light or any purpose, shall be erected ... upon any lot ... without the consent to the Developer." However, while removal of the pole could be mandated, the trial court had no basis for refusing to permit installation of the satellite dish on an alternative mounting. Woodstream Dev. Co. v. Payak, 93 Ohio App. 3d 25, appeal dismissed, 69 Ohio St. 3d 1439, 632 N.E.2d 522 (1994).

SECTION 6-33: RUNNING OF BURDENS; OBLIGATIONS OF PURCHASER

6-33A Subsequent Owners.

Restrictions placed against a single parcel of land for the benefit of the adjoining property are valid and enforceable notwithstanding the lack of a "general scheme." The restricted land was not part of a "tract" development;

therefore, evidence of a "general scheme" is not required. LuMac Dev. Corp. v. Buck Point Ltd. P'ship, 61 Ohio App. 3d 558, 573 N.E.2d 681 (1988).

A land restriction can be enforced against one who takes the estate with notice of the restriction, even though the restriction or covenant does not purport to bind subsequent assignees. Hi-Lo Oil Co. v. McCollum, 38 Ohio App. 3d 12, 526 N.E.2d 90 (1987).

An unrecorded land use restriction is not enforceable against the bona fide purchaser for value unless the purchaser has actual notice of the restriction. Although actual notice in some instances may be inferred, it may not be imputed to the purchaser on the basis of familiarity with the deed restriction recorded in another county or on the basis of the purchaser's awareness of the bare existence of the document containing the restrictions. Emrick v. Multicon Bldrs., Inc., 57 Ohio St. 3d 107, 566 N.E.2d 1189 (1991).

SECTION 6-34: RUNNING OF BENEFITS; ENFORCEMENT BY PURCHASER

6-34A Enforcement by Subsequent Owners.

The owner of one property in a development may enforce a restrictive covenant against another property owner in the development only if the covenant is for their mutual benefit and protection, e.g., there is a uniform plan of development; otherwise, there is a lack of standing. Nutis v. Schottenstein Trustees, 41 Ohio App. 3d 63, 534 N.E.2d 380 (1987).

6-34B Notice.

An unrecorded land use restriction is not enforceable against the bona fide purchaser for value unless the purchaser has actual notice of the restriction. Although actual notice in some instances may be inferred, it may not be imputed to the purchaser on the basis of familiarity with the deed restriction recorded in another county or on the basis of the purchaser's awareness of the bare existence of the document containing the restrictions. Emrick v. Multicon Bldrs., Inc., 57 Ohio St. 3d 107, 566 N.E.2d 1189 (1991).

SECTION 6-35: REMEDIES; MODIFICATION; EXTINGUISHMENT

6-35A Matters Terminating Right to Enforcement.

A single residence restriction in a deed may no longer be enforceable when there is clear and convincing evidence that there has been a substantial change in the character of the neighborhood; that enforcement of the restriction would not restore the neighborhood to its residential character; and that enforcement of the covenant would appear to impose a great hardship on the party seeking to avoid the restriction with minimal benefit to the party seeking to enforce it. Nutis v. Schottenstein Trustees, 41 Ohio App. 3d 63, 534 N.E.2d 380 (1987).

6-35G Tax Sales.

R.C. 5721.19 amended without material change as to the statement in the Parent Volume. (As eff. 1-8-93 and 5-25-94.)

R.C. 5723.12 amended without material change as to the statement in the Parent Volume. (As eff. 5-25-94.)

CHAPTER 7: CROPS AND OTHER GROWING THINGS

DIVISION 7-1: IN GENERAL

SECTION 7-16:   AGRICULTURAL PRODUCT LIENS

DIVISION 7-1: IN GENERAL

SECTION 7-16: AGRICULTURAL PRODUCT LIENS

7-16A Definitions.

R.C. 1311.55(A) provides as follows: "As used in this section:

"(1) 'Agricultural product' means all fruit and vegetable crops, meat and meat products, milk and dairy products, poultry and poultry products, wool, and all seeds harvested by a producer for sale, except that it does not include any grain crop that is subject to the fee that the director of agriculture may require to be remitted under section 926.16 of the Revised Code.

"(2) 'Agricultural product handling' means engaging in or participating in the business of buying, selling, exchanging, or negotiating or soliciting a purchase, sale, resale, exchange or transfer of an agricultural product.

"(3) 'Agricultural product handler' or 'handler' means any person who is engaged in the business of agricultural product handling, except that a person who sells only those agricultural products that he has produced, or buys agricultural products for his own use, is not an agricultural product handler.

"(4) 'Agricultural producer' or 'producer' means any person who grows, raises or produces an agricultural product on land that he owns or leases.

"(5) 'Proceeds' has the same meaning as in division (A) of section 1309.25 of the Revised Code." (As eff. 10-30-90.)

7-16B Establishment of Right to Lien.

R.C. 1311.55(B) provides: "An agricultural producer who delivers an agricultural product under an express or implied contract to an agricultural product handler, or an agricultural product handler who delivers an agricultural product under an express or implied contract to another agricultural contract handler, has a lien to secure the payment for all of the agricultural product delivered under that contract. The lien attaches to the product, whether in a raw or processed condition, while in the possession of the agricultural product handler, and to the proceeds of the sale of the agricultural product. The lien attaches from the date of delivery of the agricultural product to the handler, or if there is a series of deliveries under the contract, from the date of the first delivery. The lien is contingent until the producer or handler complies with section 1311.56 of the Revised Code [dealing with perfection of the lien by filing the affidavit described in 7-16C below].'' (As eff. 10-30-90.)

R.C. 1311.55(C) provides: ''The lien on an agricultural product covers the contract price agreed upon, or when there is no agreed price at the time of delivery, the value of the agricultural product as determined by the 'market news service' of the Ohio department of agriculture on the date the agricultural producer or handler files the affidavit permitted under section 1311.56 of the Revised Code.'' (As eff. 10-30-90.)

R.C. 1311.55(D) provides that ''Any waiver by a producer or handler of his right to an agricultural product lien is void as being contrary to public policy.'' (As eff. 10-30-90.)

7-16C Perfection of Lien by Affidavit.

Form of affidavit, Form 1705

Pursuant to R.C. 1311.56 (as eff. 10-30-90), the agricultural producer or handler may perfect his lien by recording an affidavit in the office of the county recorder in the county where the agricultural product was delivered to the agricultural product handler. The affidavit should include: (1) the date of delivery, or first delivery if there was a series of deliveries under the contract, (2) the name of the agricultural product handler to whom the agricultural product was delivered, and (3) the amount owed by the lien claimant by the handler, or, if there was no agreed price at the time of delivery or first delivery, a description of the pricing method which the lien claimant and handler agreed to utilize in their contract. In the latter cases, and for informational purposes only, the lien claimant should include in the affidavit an estimate of the amount owed him by the handler, based upon current market conditions. The affidavit may be verified before any person authorized to administer oaths, including an attorney for the agricultural product handler, lien claimant, or an interested other party.

7-16D Priority of Perfected Lien; Duration of Lien.

R.C. 1311.57(A) provides: ''An agricultural producer or handler who perfects his lien within 60 days after the date of delivery, or first delivery if there was a series of deliveries under the contract, of the agricultural product has priority over all liens, claims, or encumbrances except wage and salary claims of workers who have no ownership interest in the business of the agricultural product handler, warehouseman's liens as provided in section 1307.14 of the Revised Code, and amounts owed by the lienholder to the handler that are subject to set off, and except that secured creditors who have security interests under Chapter 1309. of the Revised Code have priority over liens perfected by agri-cultural handlers pursuant to section 1311.56 of the Revised Code. If several liens are obtained by several persons on the same agricultural product, the person who perfects his lien first has priority over all other agricultural product lienholders.

''A producer or handler who does not perfect his lien within the time period defined in this division has the status of an unsecured general creditor.'' (As eff. 4-16-93.)

R.C. 1311.57(B) provides that the agricultural product lien remains in effect for two years after the recording of the affidavit and throughout any insolvency proceedings involving the agricultural product handler named in the affidavit. (As eff. 10-30-90.)

CHAPTER 8: DEEDS

DIVISION 8-1: IN GENERAL

SECTION 8-11: INTRODUCTION; FORM AND EXECUTION
8-11B   Effect of Defects
8-11D   Statutory Deed Forms

SECTION 8-13: EXCEPTION AND RESERVATION; DATE; SIGNATURE
8-13A   Exception and Reservation Generally

SECTION 8-14: SEAL; WITNESSES
8-14B   Witnesses

SECTION 8-16: SURVIVORSHIP DEEDS; "OR"
8-16B   Form
8-16D   Simultaneous Deaths
8-16E   Estate by Entireties

SECTION 8-18: EXECUTION REQUIREMENTS IN EACH STATE
8-18A   Foreign Execution

DIVISION 8-2 ACKNOWLEDGMENT

SECTION 8-21: GENERALLY
8-21A   Definition; Statute

SECTION 8-23: WHO MAY TAKE
8-23A   Statutes
8-23H   Armed Forces

SECTION 8-24: TIME AND PLACE OF TAKING
8-24C   Venue

DIVISION 8-4 ESCROW

SECTION 8-45: STATUS AND LIABILITIES OF DEPOSITARY
8-45B   Conflict with Agreement

DIVISION 8-5 CANCELLATION OR RESCISSION

SECTION 8-52: MISTAKE
8-52A   Rules

SECTION 8-53: FRAUD; DURESS AND UNDUE INFLUENCE
8-53B   Duress; Undue Influence

SECTION 8-54: FRAUDULENT TRANSFERS
8-54A   Fraudulent Transfers as Against Present and Future Creditors
8-54B   Fraudulent Transfers as Against Present Creditors

DIVISION 8-1: IN GENERAL

SECTION 8-11: INTRODUCTION; FORM AND EXECUTION

8-11B Effect of Defects.

When the grantors signed a deed outside the presence of both the witnesses and did not appear before the notary public who certified the acknowledgment, the grantees received at most an equitable interest in the property. Basil v. Vincello, 50 Ohio St. 3d 185, 553 N.E.2d 602, reh'g denied, 51 Ohio St. 3d 705, 555 N.E.2d 322 (1990).

8-11D Statutory Deed Forms.

R.C. 5302.01 amended to include the forms set forth in R.C. 5302.17. (As eff. 5-31-88.)

R.C. 5302.02 amended to include rules and definitions contained in R.C. 5302.17-.21 (As eff. 5-31-88.)

SECTION 8-13: EXCEPTION AND RESERVATION; DATE; SIGNATURE.

8-13A Exception and Reservation Generally.

A deed conveying land but "excepting and reserving ... a roadway" creates only an easement across the property conveyed. Although generally the terms "excepting" and "reserving" mean different things — the grantor retaining title to the excepted part, but reserving only an easement or some benefit in the case of a reservation — the two terms are often employed indiscriminately. In case of doubt, the conveyance is to be construed against the grantor. Campbell v. Johnson, 87 Ohio App. 3d 543, 622 N.E.2d 717, mot. overruled, 67 Ohio St. 3d 1471, 619 N.E.2d 1028 (1993).

SECTION 8-14: SEAL; WITNESSES

8-14B Witnesses.

R.C. 5301.01 amended to provide as follows: "A deed, mortgage, land contract as referred to in division (B)(2) of section 317.08 of the Revised Code, or lease of any interest in real property and a memorandum of trust as described in division (A) of section 5301.255 of the Revised Code shall be signed by the grantor, mortgagor, vendor, or lessor in the case of a deed, mortgage, land contract, or lease or shall be signed by the settlor and the trustee in the case of a memorandum of trust. This signing shall be acknowledged by the grantor, mortgagor, vendor or lessor, or by the settlor and trustee, in the presence of two witnesses, who shall attest the signing and subscribe their name to the attestation. The signing shall be acknowledged by the grantor, mortgagor, vendor, or lessor, or by the settlor and trustee, before a judge or clerk of court of record in this state, or a county auditor, county engineer, notary public or mayor, who shall certify the acknowledgment and subscribe his name to the certificate of the acknowledgment.'' (As eff. 8-10-94.)

SECTION 8-16: SURVIVORSHIP DEEDS; "OR"

8-16B Form.

R.C. 5302.17 amended to provide as follows:

''A deed conveying any interest in real property to two or more persons, and in substance following the form set forth in this section, when duly executed in accordance with Chapter 5301 of the Revised Code, creates a survivorship tenancy in the grantees, and upon the death of any of the grantees, vests the interest of the decedent in the survivor, survivors, or his or their separate heirs and assigns.''

''SURVIVORSHIP DEED''

_____(marital status), of _____ County, for valuable consideration paid, grant(s), (covenants, if any), to _____ _____ (marital status) and _____, (marital status) for their joint lives, remainder to the survivor of them, whose tax-mailing addresses are _____, the following real property:
(description of land or interest therein and encumbrances, reservations, and exceptions, if any)
Prior Instrument Reference: _____, wife (husband) of the grantor, releases all rights of dower therein.
Witness _____ hand this day of _____.''
(Execution in accordance with Chapter 5301. of the Revised Code)''

''Any persons who are the sole owners of real property, prior to April 4, 1985, as tenants with a right of survivorship under the common or statutory law of this state or as tenants in common, may create in themselves and in any other person or persons a survivorship tenancy in the real property by executing a deed as provided in this section conveying their entire, separate interests in the real property to themselves and to the other person or persons.
''Except as otherwise provided in this section, when a person holding real property as a survivorship tenant dies, the transfer of the interest of the decedent

may be recorded by presenting to the county auditor and filing with the county recorder either a certificate of transfer as provided in section 2113.61 of the Revised Code, or an affidavit accompanied by a certified copy of a death certificate. The affidavit shall recite the names of the other survivorship tenant or tenants, the address of the other survivorship tenant or tenants, the date of death of the decedent, and a description of the real property. The county recorder shall make index reference to any certificate or affidavit so filed in the record of deeds. When a person holding real property as a survivorship tenant dies and the title to the property is registered pursuant to Chapter 5309. of the Revised Code, the procedure for the transfer of the interest of the decedent shall be pursuant to section 5309.081 of the Revised Code.'' (As eff. 8-19-92.)

8-16D Simultaneous Deaths.

Where the actual time of deaths of joint and survivorship tenants cannot be determined (husband shot wife, then shot himself), title to the property passes as if they had been tenants in common pursuant to R.C. 5302.20. The presumption of order of death statute, R.C. 2105.21, has no applicability. Furthermore, since the husband was not convicted, or found guilty by reason of insanity, of aggravated murder, murder or voluntary manslaughter, R.C. 2105.19, which prevents persons from benefiting by the death of another, does not apply. In re Estate of Price, 62 Ohio Misc. 2d 26, 587 N.E.2d 995 (Adams Cty. C.P. 1990).

8-16E Estate by Entireties.

Creditors of a debtor in a Chapter 7 Bankruptcy cannot reach the debtor's interest in real property under a tenancy by the entireties created prior to the amendment to the Ohio survivorship statute. In re William L. Cline, 167 Bankruptcy Reptr. 592 (U.S. Bankruptcy Ct. S.D. Ohio, W.D. 1994).

A deed executed while former 5302.17 was in effect which conveys title to ''husband and wife for their joint lives, remainder to the survivor of them,'' creates an estate by the entireties only when the word ''entireties'' is included in either the title or text of the deed. Central Benefits Mut. Ins. Co. v. RIS Administrators Agency, Inc., 70 Ohio St. 3d 68 (1994).

SECTION 8-18: EXECUTION REQUIREMENTS IN EACH STATE

8-18A Foreign Execution.

R.C. 5301.05 repealed. (As eff. 5-31-88.)

DIVISION 8-2: ACKNOWLEDGMENT

SECTION 8-21: GENERALLY

8-21A Definition; Statute.

R.C. 5301.01 amended as set forth in 8-14B of this supplement. (As eff. 8-10-94.)

SECTION 8-23: WHO MAY TAKE

8-23A Statutes.

R.C. 147.01 amended to provide as follows:

"(A) The governor may appoint and commission as notaries public as many persons who meet the qualifications of division (B) of this section as he considers necessary.

"(B) In order for a person to qualify to be appointed and commissioned as a notary public, the person must satisfy both of the following:

"(1) The person has attained the age of eighteen years.

"(2) One of the following applies:

"(a) The person is a citizen of this state who is not an attorney admitted to the practice of law.

"(b) The person is a citizen of this state who is an attorney admitted to the practice of law in this state by the Ohio Supreme Court.

"(c) The person is not a citizen of this state, is an attorney admitted to the practice of law in this state by the Ohio Supreme Court, and
has his principal place of business or his primary practice in this state.

"(C) A notary public shall be appointed and commissioned as a notary public for the state. The governor may revoke a commission issued to a notary public upon presentation of satisfactory evidence of official misconduct or incapacity." (As eff. 5-20-92.)

R.C. 5301.01 amended without material change as to the statement in the Parent Volume. (As eff. 8-10-94.)

8-23H Armed Forces.

R.C. 147.38 repealed. (As eff. 5-31-88.) See discussion of the Uniform Recognition of Acknowledgments Act at 8-26A in the Parent Volume.

SECTION 8-24: TIME AND PLACE OF TAKING

8-24C Venue.

R.C. 1907.18 amended without material change as to the statement in the Parent Volume. (As eff. 11-5-92.)

DIVISION 8-4: ESCROW

SECTION 8-45: STATUS AND LIABILITIES OF DEPOSITARY

8-45B Conflict with Agreement

Where a purchase agreement provided that the purchaser would take subject to real estate taxes and assessments not yet due and payable, the escrow agent acted improperly when it prorated the real estate taxes and charged the sellers for a portion of the taxes not yet due and payable. Farkas v. Chicago Title Ins. Co., 71 Ohio App. 3d 633, 594 N.E.2d 1140 (1991).

DIVISION 8-5: CANCELLATION OR RESCISSION

SECTION 8-52: MISTAKE

8-52A Rules.

Where clear and convincing evidence is offered at trial to demonstrate that both the grantors and grantees were mistaken as to what was being conveyed by the description contained in the deed, reformation of the deed is appropriate. Mason v. Swartz, 76 Ohio App. 3d 43, 600 N.E.2d 1121 (1991).

In order to maintain an action for reformation of a deed on the ground of mistake, the plaintiff bears the burden to prove a mutual mistake occurred by clear and convincing evidence. Where the plaintiff fails to read the deed and fails to require that the deed contain the conditions she intended to attach, the mistake is a unilateral mistake. Henkle v. Henkle, 75 Ohio App. 3d 732, 600 N.E.2d 791 (1991).

SECTION 8-53: FRAUD; DURESS AND UNDUE INFLUENCE

8-53B Duress; Undue Influence.

A party seeking recission and cancellation of a deed because of undue influence has the burden of proof by clear and convincing evidence. In order to sustain an allegation of undue influence, a plaintiff must prove: (1) that the testator was "susceptible;" (2) that another person had the opportunity to exert the influence; (3) that improper influence was exerted or attempted; and (4) that the influence had the desired effect. Equity will impose a constructive trust where there is some ground such as fraud, duress, undue influence or mistake.

However, where the evidence fails to show that the grantee exerted such influence over the grantor that her will was overborne, no relief will be granted. Henkle v. Henkle, 75 Ohio App. 3d 732, 600 N.E.2d 791 (1991).

SECTION 8-54: FRAUDULENT TRANSFERS

Note: Effective September 28, 1990, the Uniform Fraudulent Transfer Act, R.C. 1336.01-.11, was enacted in Ohio. Former R.C. 1336.01-.11 were repealed in their entirety. The following materials supersede former Section 8-54 of the Parent Volume.

8-54A Fraudulent Transfers as Against Present and Future Creditors.

R.C. 1336.04 (as eff. 10-28-90) provides that certain transfers made or obligations incurred by a debtor are fraudulent as against present and future creditors of the debtor.

Under R.C. 1336.04(A)(1), transfers made or obligations incurred "with actual intent to hinder, delay or defraud any creditor of the debtor" are declared fraudulent.

Under R.C. 1336.04(B), in determining "actual intent," consideration may be given to all relevant factors, including the following:

"(1) Whether the transfer or obligation was to an insider;

"(2) Whether the debtor retained possession or control of the property transferred after the transfer;

"(3) Whether the transfer or obligation was disclosed or concealed;

"(4) Whether before the transfer was made or the obligation was incurred, the debtor has been sued or threatened with suit;

"(5) Whether the transfer was substantially all of the assets of the debtor;

"(6) Whether the debtor absconded;

"(7) Whether the debtor removed or concealed assets;

"(8) Whether the value of the consideration received by the debtor was reasonably equivalent to the value of the asset transferred or the amount of the obligation incurred;

"(9) Whether the debtor was insolvent or became insolvent shortly after the transfer was paid or the obligation was incurred;

"(10) Whether the transfer occurred shortly before or shortly after a substantial debt was incurred;

"(11) Whether the debtor transferred the essential assets of the business to a lienholder who transferred the assets to an insider of the debtor."

Under R.C. 1326.04(A)(2), transfers made or obligations incurred without receiving "reasonably equivalent value" (see definition in 8-54C below) are declared fraudulent in either of the following circumstances:

"(a) The debtor was engaged or was about to engage in a business or transaction for which the remaining assets of the debtor were unreasonably small in relation to the business or transaction;

"(b) The debtor intended to incur, or believed or reasonably should have believed that he would incur, debts beyond his ability to pay as they became due."

Whether or not conveyances were fraudulent must be determined under the requirements of R.C. Chapter 1336 as it existed at the time of the conveyances. The 1990 amendments to the Chapter will be applied prospectively only. Fifth Third Bank of Columbus v. McCloud, 90 Ohio App. 3d 196, 628 N.E.2d 131 (1993).

COMMENT

R.C. 1336.04 establishes two distinct categories of fraudulent transfers. Under division (A)(1) of the statute, transfers are fraudulent if they are made with an actual intent to defraud, as evidenced by the "badges of fraud" enumerated in the statute or otherwise. Under division (A)(2) of the statute, transfers are considered fraudulent regardless of the debtor's intent when (a) the debtor does not receive reasonably equivalent value and (b) the transaction leaves the debtor in a position where his assets are unreasonably small or he knows or should know that he will be unable to pay his debts as they become due.

8-54B Fraudulent Transfers as Against Present Creditors.

R.C. 1336.05 (as eff. 9-28-90) establishes two additional types of fraudulent transfers as against present (but not future) creditors of the debtor.

Under R.C. 1336.05(A), a transfer made or obligation incurred is fraudulent as against an existing creditor (one whose claim arose before the transfer was made or the obligation was incurred) if "the debtor made the transfer or incurred obligation without receiving reasonably equivalent value ... and the debtor was insolvent at that time or the debtor became insolvent as a result of the transfer or obligation."

Under R.C. 1336.05(B), a transfer made or obligation incurred is fraudulent as against an existing creditor if "the transfer was made or the obligation was incurred with respect to an insider for an antecedent debt, the debtor was insolvent at that time, and the insider had reasonable cause to believe that the debtor was insolvent."

COMMENT

To prove a fraudulent transfer under division (A) of R.C. 1336.05, the creditor must show that the debtor did not receive "reasonably equivalent value" and was "insolvent" (or rendered insolvent). These terms are defined in 8-54C below.

Fraudulent transfers under division (B) of R.C. 1336.05 require proof that (1) the transfer was made or obligation incurred with respect to an "insider," (2) for an antecedent debt, (3) at a time when the debtor was "insolvent," and (4) the insider had reasonable cause to believe that the debtor was insolvent. The definitions of "insider" and "insolvent" are set forth in 8-54C below.

8-54C Definitions.

For purposes of the Ohio Uniform Fraudulent Transfer Act:

A "claim" is broadly defined to include "a right to payment, whether or not the right is reduced to judgment, liquidated, unliquidated, fixed, contingent, matured, unmatured, disputed, undisputed, legal, equitable, secured, or unsecured." R.C. 1336.01(C) (as eff. 9-28-90).

"Creditor" means "a person who has a claim." R.C. 1336.01(D) (as eff. 9-28-90).

"Insider" includes: (a) In the case of an individual, relatives of the debtor or of any general partner of the debtor; a partnership of which the debtor is a general partner and all other general partners of that partnership; and a corporation of which the debtor is a director, officer, or person in control; (b) with regard to corporate debtors, "insiders" include directors; officers; persons in control; partnerships in which the debtor is a general partner and all other general partners of that partnership; and relatives of a general partner, director, officer or person in control of the debtor; (c) with regard to partnerships, "insiders" include general partners in the debtor; relatives of a general partner in, a general partner of, or a person in control of the debtor; another partnership in which the debtor is a general partner, and all other general partners of that partnership; and a person in control of the debtor; (d) in all cases (individuals, corporations, and partnerships), "insiders" also include any "affiliates" or insiders of affiliates (as if the affiliate were the debtor). In addition, a managing agent of the debtor is an "insider." R.C. 1336.01(G) (as eff. 9-28-90).

For purposes of the "insider" definition, a "relative" is a spouse or an individual related by consanguinity within the third degree to either the person in question or his spouse. R.C. 1336.01(K) (as eff. 9-28-90). "Affiliate" is defined in detail in R.C. 1336.01(A) (as eff. 9-28-90), and generally includes a person who directly or indirectly owns, controls, or holds 20% or more of the voting interests in the debtor; a corporation of which the debtor owns, controls or holds a 20% or greater voting interest; a person whose business is operated by the debtor, or substantially all of whose assets are controlled by the debtor; and a person who operates the business of the debtor or controls substantially all of the debtor's assets.

"Insolvent" is defined in R.C. 1336.02(A) (as eff. 9-28-90), which provides: "(1) A debtor is insolvent if the sum of the debts of the debtor is greater than all of the assets of the debtor at a fair valuation. (2) A debtor who generally is not paying his debts as they become due is presumed to be insolvent." The statute provides an exception for partnerships by requiring that the value of the non-partnership assets of the general partners, after deducting their nonpartnership debts, be added to the calculation. R.C. 1336.02(B) (as eff. 9-28-90).

"Reasonably equivalent value" is not specifically defined in the Ohio Uniform Fraudulent Transfer Act. However, R.C. 1336.03(A) (as eff. 9-28-90) states that "value" may be given if "property is transferred or an antecedent debt is secured or satisfied, but value does not include an unperformed promise made otherwise than in the ordinary course of the business of the promisor to furnish support to the debtor or another person." Furthermore, pursuant to R.C. 1336.03(B) (as eff. 9-28-90), "reasonably equivalent value" is deemed given if a person acquires the debtor's interest "pursuant to a regularly conducted, noncollusive foreclosure sale or execution of power of sale ... upon default under a mortgage, deed of trust, or security agreement."

"Transfer" means "every direct or indirect, absolute or conditional, and voluntary or involuntary method of disposing of or parting with an asset or an interest in an asset, and includes payment of money, release, lease, and creation of a lien or other encumbrance." R.C. 1336.01(C) (as eff. 9-28-90).

8-54D Remedies of Creditors.

Subject to the exceptions and limitations described in 8-54E and 8-54F below, a creditor seeking redress for a fraudulent transfer may obtain one of the following:

"(1) Avoidance of the transfer or obligation to the extent necessary to satisfy the claim of the creditor;

"(2) An attachment or garnishment against the asset transferred or other property of the transferee in accordance with Chapters 2715 and 2716 of the Revised Code;

"(3) Subject to the applicable principles of equity and in accordance with the Rules of Civil Procedure, any of the following:

"(a) an injunction against further disposition by the debtor or a transferee, or both, of the asset transferred or of other property;

"(b) appointment of a receiver to take charge of the asset transferred or of other property of the transferee;

"(c) any other relief that the circumstances may require." R.C. 1336.07(A) (as eff 9-28-90).

In addition, if the creditor has obtained a judgment on a claim against the debtor, the creditor may, if the court so orders, levy execution on the fraudulently transferred asset or its proceeds in accordance with Chapter 2339 of the Revised Code. R.C. 1336.07(B) (as eff. 9-28-90).

The Ohio Uniform Fraudulent Transfer Act does not preclude other consistent remedies or claims for relief. R.C. 1336.10 (as eff. 9-28-90) provides that "Unless displaced by this chapter, the principles of law and equity, including, but not limited to, the law merchant and the law relating to principal and agent, estoppel, laches, fraud, misrepresentation, duress, coercion, mistake, insolvency, or other validating or invalidating cause, supplement the provisions of this chapter."

8-54E Exceptions; Good Faith Purchasers.

R.C. 1336.08 (as eff. 9-28-90) provides for certain exceptions to, and limitations upon, the Ohio Uniform Fraudulent Transfer Act. These exceptions and limitations operate primarily for the benefit of good faith transferees.

R.C. 1336.08(A) provides that a transfer or obligation is not fraudulent under R.C. 1336.04(A)(1) (actual intent to defraud) as against "a person who took in good faith and for a reasonably equivalent value or against any subsequent transferee or obligee." This exception protects a good faith purchaser for reasonably equivalent value regardless of the debtor's actual intent to defraud creditors. Subsequent transferees are similarly protected.

R.C. 1336.08(B) applies to all fraudulent transfers under the Ohio Uniform Fraudulent Transfers Act, and limits the recovery that a creditor may make against a transferee of an asset in a fraudulent transfer. The creditor may recover judgment "for the value of the asset transferred ... or the amount necessary to satisfy the claim of the creditor, whichever is less." The value of the asset is based upon the value at the time of the transfer, subject to adjustment "as the equities may require." The creditor's judgment may be entered against either "the first transferee ... or any subsequent transferee other than a good faith transferee who took for value or from any subsequent transferee." It should be noted that the protection afforded to the second transferee applies only if the second transferee took in good faith for "value" — but not necessarily "reasonably equivalent value." The third transferee is protected if he is a good faith transferee, regardless of whether he gave value for the asset.

R.C. 1336.08(C) also applies to all fraudulent transfers under the Act, and establishes certain rights for the benefit of good faith transferees. If a transfer is made or an obligation is incurred that constitutes a fraudulent transfer, but the transferee or obligee took in good faith (as might occur, for example, when value is given but not reasonably equivalent value), the good faith transferee is entitled, *to the extent of the value given to the debtor for the transfer or obligation*, to any of the following: "(1) a lien on or right to retain any interest in the asset transferred; (2) enforcement of any obligation incurred; (3) a reduction in the amount of the liability on the judgment."

R.C. 1336.08(D) creates an exception applicable to fraudulent transfers other than those under R.C. 1336.04(A)(1) (actual intent to defraud). The exception covers transfers resulting from either: "(1) termination of a lease upon default by the debtor when the termination is pursuant to the lease and applicable law; (2) enforcement of a security interest in compliance with section 1309.44 of the Revised Code." This exception might, for example, allow an insider to enforce a security interest through the normal legal means.

Finally, R.C. 1336.08(E) creates an exception applicable only to fraudulent transfers under R.C. 1336.05(B) (i.e., transfers with respect to insiders, for an antecedent debt, when the debtor was insolvent and the insider had reasonable cause to believe that the debtor was insolvent). The exception applies: "(1) to the extent the insider gave new value ... after the transfer was made, unless the new value was secured by a valid lien; (2) if made in the ordinary course of business or financial affairs of the debtor and insider; (3) if made pursuant to a good faith effort to rehabilitate the debtor and the transfer secured the present value given for that purpose as well as an antecedent debt of the debtor."

COMMENT

The Ohio Uniform Fraudulent Transfer Act creates four categories of fraudulent transfers: (1) transfers involving actual intent to defraud (R.C. 1336.04(A)(1)); (2) transfers for less than reasonably equivalent value when the debtor is left in a position where his assets are unreasonably small or he will be unable to pay his debts as they become due (R.C. 1336.04(A)(2)); (3) transfers for less than reasonably equivalent value when the debtor is insolvent or is rendered insolvent by the transfer (R.C. 1336.05(A)); and (4) transfers with respect to insiders for an antecedent debt when the debtor was insolvent. The fraudulent transfers under (1) and (2) apply to both existing and future creditors, while those under (3) and (4) apply only to existing creditors.

The five exceptions created by R.C. 1336.08 apply to the four categories of fraudulent transfers as follows:

R.C. 1336.08(A) — the exception as to good faith transferees for reasonably equivalent value — applies to (1) only.

R.C. 1336.08(B) — the limitations on recovery against transferees in a fraudulent transfer — applies to (1), (2), (3), and (4).

R.C. 1336.08(C) — protecting the rights of good faith transferees to the extent of value given — applies to (1), (2), (3), and (4).

R.C. 1336.08(D) — the right to enforce a lease default or security interest — applies to (1) only.

R.C. 1336.08(E) — rehabilitation efforts by insiders — applies to (4) only.

8-54F   Time Limitations.

R.C. 1336.09 (as eff. 9-28-90) establishes time limitations for asserting claims based upon fraudulent transfers. The right to assert a claim is extinguished unless an action is brought within one of the following:

"(A) If the transfer or obligation is fraudulent under division (A)(1) of section 1336.04 of the Revised Code [actual intent to defraud], within four years after the transfer was made or the obligation was incurred or, if later, within one year after the transfer or obligation was or reasonably could have been discovered by the claimant;

"(B) If the transfer or obligation is fraudulent under division (A)(2) of section 1336.04 [transfers for less than reasonably equivalent value if the debtor's remaining assets will be unreasonably small or the debtor will be unable to pay his debts as they become due] or division (A) of section 1336.05 of the Revised Code [transfers for less than reasonably equivalent value when the debtor is insolvent or is rendered insolvent by the transfer], within four years after the transfer was made or the obligation was incurred;

"(C) If the transfer or obligation is fraudulent under division (B) of section 1336.05 of the Revised Code [transfers with respect to an insider for an antecedent debt when the debtor was insolvent and the insider had reasonable cause to believe that the debtor was insolvent], within one year after the transfer was made or the obligation was incurred."

CHAPTER 9: DESCENT AND WILLS

DIVISION 9-1: DESCENT

DIVISION 9-2: WILLS

DIVISION 9-1: DESCENT

SECTION 9-11: GENERALLY

9-11B Statute.

R.C. 2105.061 provides: "Except any real property that a surviving spouse elects to receive under section 2106.10 of the Revised Code, the title to real property in an intestate estate shall descend and pass in parcenary to those persons entitled to it under division (B) or (C) of section 2105.06 of the Revised Code, subject to the monetary charge of the surviving spouse. The administrator or executor shall file an application for a certificate of transfer as provided in section 2113.61 of the Revised Code, which shall include a statement of the amount of money that remains due and payable to the surviving spouse as found by the probate court. The certificate of transfer ordered by the probate court shall recite that the title to the real property described in the certificate is subject to the monetary charge in favor of the surviving spouse, and shall recite the value in dollars of the charge on the title to the real property included in the certificate." (As eff. 5-31-90.)

R.C. 2105.063 has been renumbered as R.C. 2106.11 and provides: "Subject to the right of the surviving spouse to elect to receive the decedent's interest in the mansion house pursuant to section 2106.10 of the Revised Code, the specific monetary share payable to a surviving spouse under division (B) or (C) of section 2105.06 of the Revised Code shall be paid out of the tangible and intangible personal property in the intestate estate to the extent that the personal property is available for distribution. The personal property distributed to the surviving spouse, other than cash, shall be valued at the appraised value.

"Before tangible and intangible personal property is transferred to the surviving spouse in payment or part payment of the specific monetary share, the adminis-trator or executor shall file an application that includes an inventory of the personal property intended to be distributed in kind to the surviving spouse, together with a statement of the appraised value of each item of personal property included. The court shall examine the application and make a finding of the amount of personal property to be distributed to the surviving spouse, and shall order that the personal property be distributed to the surviving spouse. The court concurrently shall make a finding of the amount of money that remains due and payable to the surviving spouse in satisfaction of the specific monetary share to which the surviving spouse is entitled under division (B) or (C) of section 2105.06 of the Revised Code. Any amount that remains due and payable shall be a charge on the title to any real property in the estate but the charge does not bear interest. This charge may be conveyed or released in the same manner as any other interest in real estate and may be enforced by foreclosure or any other appropriate remedy.'' (As eff. 5-31-90.)

9-11L Death Within Thirty Days; Presumed Order of Death.

Where the actual time of deaths of joint and survivorship tenants cannot be determined (husband shot wife, then shot himself), title to the property passes as if they had been tenants in common pursuant to R.C. 5302.20. The presumption of order of death statute, R.C. 2105.21, has no applicability. Furthermore, since the husband was not convicted or found guilty by reason of insanity, of aggravated murder, murder or voluntary manslaughter, R.C. 2105.19, which prevents persons from benefiting by the death of another, does not apply. In re Estate of Price, 62 Ohio Misc. 2d 26, 587 N.E.2d 995 (Adams Cty. C.P. 1990).

SECTION 9-12: ADVANCEMENTS

9-12A Definitions.

Decedent's transfer of property to spouse immediately before his death was not an ''advancement'' against the statutory share the spouse elected to take against the decedent's will. R.C. 2105.051 permits the value of an advancement to be counted against an intestate share only if it is (1) declared to be an advancement in a contemporaneous writing by the decedent or (2) acknowledged in writing by the heir to be an advancement. These methods of proof are exclusive. King v. King, 82 Ohio App. 3d 747, 613 N.E.2d 251 (1992).

SECTION 9-13: ADOPTED CHILDREN

9-13B Inheritance Through Adoptive Parent.

Provisions of an inter vivos trust are governed by the law existing at the time of its creation, absent a contrary intent within the instrument itself. A trust created in 1944, providing for the distribution of trust assets to the settlor's ''living children and to the living children of each deceased grandchild,'' will be construed in accordance with the ''stranger to the adoption rule'' then in effect to include only the settlor's natural children and grandchildren, thereby excluding the settlor's legally adopted grandchildren. R.C. 3107.15, effective January 1, 1977, will be applied prospectively only to those documents, statutes and instruments, whether executed before or after an adoption is decreed, which do not expressly exclude the adopted person from the laws' or instruments' operation and effect. Ohio Citizens Bank v. Mills, 45 Ohio St. 3d 153, 543 N.E.2d 1206 (1989).

9-13G Statute and Chart.

R.C. 3107.15, effective January 1, 1977, will be applied prospectively only to those documents, statutes, and instruments, whether executed before or after an adoption is decreed, which do not expressly exclude the adopted person from the laws' or instruments' operation and effect. Ohio Citizens Bank v. Mills, 45 Ohio St. 3d 153, 543 N.E.2d 1206 (1989).

SECTION 9-14: ILLEGITIMATE CHILDREN

9-14A Rule.

R.C. 2105.18 amended to provide:

"(A) The natural father, natural mother, or other custodian or guardian of a child, a child support enforcement agency, or a hospital staff person pursuant to section 3727.17 of the Revised Code, in person or by mail, may file an acknowledgment of paternity in the probate court of the county in which the natural father, natural mother, or other guardian or custodian of the child resides, in the county in which the child resides, or the county in which the child was born, acknow-ledging that the child is the child of the natural father who signed the acknowledgment. The acknowledgment of paternity shall state that the natural father who signs the acknowledgment of paternity acknowledges that he is the natural father of the named child and that he assumes the parental duty of support of that child. The acknowledgment of paternity shall be signed by the natural father and the natural mother in the presence of two competent and disinterested witnesses who are eighteen years of age or older and by the two witnesses. If an acknowledgment of paternity is completed and filed in accordance with this section and if the acknowledgment is accompanied by the appropriate fee prescribed in section 2101.16 of the Revised Code, the probate court shall enter the acknowledg-ment upon its journal. Thereafter, the child is the child of the man who signed the acknowledgment of paternity, as though born to him in lawful wedlock, and, if the mother is unmarried, the man who signed the acknowledg-ment of paternity, the parents of the man who signed the acknowledgment of paternity, any relative of the man who signed the acknowledgment of paternity, the parent of the mother, and any relative of the mother may file a complaint pursuant to section 3109.12 of the Revised Code requesting the granting under that section of reasonable companionship or visitation rights with respect to the child.

"(B) After a probate court enters an acknowledgment upon its journal pursuant to division (A) of this section, the man who signed the acknowledgment of paternity is the father of the child and assumes the parental duty of support. Notwithstanding section 3109.01 of the Revised Code, the parental duty of support of the father to the child shall continue beyond the age of majority as long as the child attends on a full-time basis any recognized and accredited high school. The duty of support of the father shall continue during seasonal vacation periods. After the probate court enters the acknowledgment upon its journal, the mother or other custodian or guardian of the child may file a complaint pursuant to section 2151.231 of the Revised Code in the court of common pleas of the county in which the child or the guardian or legal custodian of the child resides requesting the court to order the father to pay an amount for the support of the child, may contact the child support enforcement agency for assistance in obtaining the order, or may request an administrative officer of a child support enforcement agency to issue an administrative order for the payment of child support pursuant to division (D) of section 3111.20 of the Revised Code.'' (As eff. 4-16-92.)

An illegitimate child of the testator has standing to bring a will contest action where the parent-child relationship has been established at law before the testator's death. However, where the testator, with knowledge of the existence of an illegitimate child, makes specific bequests to his other children but makes no mention of the illegitimate child, it is presumed that the testator intended to disinherit the child. Birman v. Sproat, 47 Ohio App. 3d 65, 546 N.E.2d 1354 (1988).

DIVISION 9-2: WILLS

SECTION 9-21: GENERALLY; RULES OF INTERPRETATION

9-21C Intention of the Testator.

The court may consider extrinsic evidence to determine the testator's intention only when the language used in the will creates doubt as to the meaning of the will. Oliver v. Bank One, Dayton, N.A., 60 Ohio St. 3d 32, 573 N.E.2d 55 (1991).

9-21Q Suits to Construe Wills.

R.C. 2107.40 has been renumbered as R.C. 2106.03 and provides: ''Within the times described in division (E) of section 2106.01 of the Revised Code for making an election, the surviving spouse may file a complaint in the probate court, making all persons interested in the will defendants, that requests a construction of the will in favor of the surviving spouse and for the court to render a judgment to that effect.'' (As eff. 5-31-90.)

A probate court does not have jurisdiction to render a declaratory judgment as to the validity or enforceability of a contract providing for a division of the testator's estate different from that provided in the will. Such contracts are not directly related to the administration of the testator's estate. Zuendel v. Zuendel, 63 Ohio St. 3d 733, 590 N.E.2d 1260 (1992).

SECTION 9-23: TESTAMENTARY CAPACITY; UNDUE INFLUENCE

9-23B Undue Influence.

A presumption of undue influence, rebuttable by a preponderance of the evidence, arises when (a) the relationship of attorney and client exists between a testator and an attorney, (b) the attorney is named as a beneficiary in the will, (c) the attorney/beneficiary is not related by blood or marriage to the testator, and (d) the attorney/beneficiary actively participates in the preparation of the will. Krischbaum v. Dillon, 58 Ohio St. 3d 58, 567 N.E.2d 1291 (1991).

The rule that the anti-lapse statute, R.C. 2107.52, applies only to "relatives" who are related by consanguinity, excluding those related by affinity, was reaffirmed in Oliver v. Bank One, Dayton, N.A., 60 Ohio St. 3d 32, 573 N.E.2d 55 (1991).

SECTION 9-24: REVOCATION; ALTERATIONS; ADEMPTION

9-24G Ademption.

Ademption is a bequest or devise of specific property where the property is not in the testator's estate at his death. As a general rule, however, the doctrine of ademption does not apply to a general legacy (of cash, for example) or to a demonstrative legacy (where, for example, a cash legacy is to be paid from a particular source but the source is not in the testator's estate at the time of death). Therefore, a $15,000 distribution will not be considered adeemed, even though the will provided that the $15,000 was to have been paid by other legatees who were to receive certain real estate that was not owned by the testator at the time of his death. Estate of Parks v. Hodge, 87 Ohio App. 3d 831, 623 N.E.2d 227 (1993).

SECTION 9-26: LAPSED AND VOID GIFTS

9-26A Generally.

R.C. 2107.52 amended to provide as follows:

"(A) As used in this section, 'relative' means an individual who is related to a testator by consanguinity and an heir at law designated pursuant to section 2105.15 of the Revised Code.

"(B) Unless a contrary intention is manifested in the will, if a devise of real property or a bequest of personal property is made to a relative of a testator and the relative was dead at the time the will was made or dies after that time, leaving issue surviving the testator, those issue shall take by representation the devised or bequeathed property as the devisee or legatee would have done if he had survived the testator. If the testator devised or bequeathed a residuary estate or the entire estate after debts, other general or specific devises and bequests, or an interest less than a fee or absolute ownership to that devisee or legatee and relatives of the testator and if that devisee or legatee leaves no issue, the estate devised or bequeathed shall vest in the other devisees or legatees surviving the testator in such proportions as the testamentary share of each devisee or legatee in the devised or bequeathed property bears to the total of the shares of all the surviving devisees or legatees, unless a different disposition is made or required by the will." (As eff. 10-8-92.)

R.C. 2107.63 amended to provide as follows:

"A testator may by will devise, bequeath, or appoint real or personal property or any interest in real or personal property to a trustee of a trust that is evidenced by a written instrument signed by the testator or any other settlor either before or on the same date of the execution of the will of the testator that is identified in the will, and that has been signed, or is signed at any time after the execution of the testator's will, by the trustee or trustees identified in the will or their successors or by any other person lawfully serving, by court appointment or otherwise, as a trustee.

"The property or interest so devised, bequeathed, or appointed to the trustee shall become a part of the trust estate, shall be subject to the jurisdiction of the court having jurisdiction of the trust, and shall be administered in accordance with the terms and provisions of the instrument creating the trust, including, unless the will specifically provides otherwise, any amendments or modifications of the trust made in writing before, concurrently with, or after the making of the will and prior to the death of the testator. The termination of the trust, or its entire revocation prior to the testator's death, shall invalidate the devise, bequest, or appointment to the trustee.

"This section shall not affect any of the rights accorded to a surviving spouse under section 2106.01 of the Revised Code. This section applies, and shall be construed as applying, to the wills of decedents who die on or after the effective date of this amendment, regardless of the date of the execution of their wills." (As eff. 10-8-92.)

9-26D Adopted Children; Other Particular Classes.

Provisions of an inter vivos trust are governed by the law existing at the time of its creation, absent a contrary intent within the instrument itself. A trust created in 1944, providing for the distribution of trust assets to the settlor's "living children and to the living children of each deceased grandchild," will be construed in accordance with the "stranger to the adoption rule" then in effect to include only the settlor's natural children and grandchildren, thereby excluding the settlor's legally adopted grandchildren. R.C. 3107.15, effective January 1, 1977, will be applied prospectively only to those documents, statutes and instruments, whether executed before or after an adoption is decreed, which do not expressly exclude the adopted person from the laws' or instruments' operation and effect. Ohio Citizens Bank v. Mills, 45 Ohio St. 3d 153, 543 N.E.2d 1206 (1989).

As noted in *Mills*, the "stranger to the adoption" rule remained applicable to inter vivos trusts until R.C. 3107.13, the predecessor of the current R.C. 3107.15, became effective January 26, 1972. (The last vestiges of the rule were eliminated in the current version of R.C. 3107.15, effective January 1, 1977.) However, with regard to wills, including testamentary trusts created under wills, the "stranger to the adoption" rule had already been abolished by the statutory changes which became effective August 28, 1951. This key distinction between inter vivos trusts and testamentary trusts was explained in Central Trust Co. v. Smith, 50 Ohio St. 3d 133, 553 N.E.2d 265 (1990).

Under a testamentary trust in favor of the testator's grandchildren, the class of testamentary beneficiaries had not closed at the time a grandchild was adopted because no mandatory distribution was required under the trust instrument prior to the adoption. A previous court-ordered distribution of funds to the biological grandchildren does not constitute a mandatory distribution. Bank One, Youngstown, N.A. v. Heltzel, 76 Ohio App. 3d 524, 602 N.E.2d 412, (1991), mot. overruled, 63 Ohio St. 3d 1458, 590 N.E.2d 753 (1992).

Foster children not named in will lack the direct, immediate and legally ascertainable pecuniary interest in the testator's estate as would allow them to contest the will. The law of "equitable adoption" has not been extended to the law of inheritance. York v. Nunley, 80 Ohio App. 3d 697, 610 N.E.2d 576 (1992).

SECTION 9-27: ELECTION BY SURVIVING SPOUSE

9-27A Statutes.

R.C. 2107.39 has been renumbered as R.C. 2106.01 and amended to provide:
"(A) After the probate of a will and the filing of the inventory and the appraisement, the probate court shall issue a citation to the surviving spouse, if any is living at the time of the issuance of the citation, to elect whether to take under the will or under section 2105.06 of the Revised Code.

"(B) If the surviving spouse elects to take under section 2105.06 of the Revised Code and if the value of the property that the surviving spouse is entitled to receive is equal to or greater than the value of the decedent's interest in the mansion house as determined under section 2106.10 of the Revised Code, the surviving spouse also is entitled to make an election pursuant to division (A) of section 2106.10 of the Revised Code.

"(C) If the surviving spouse elects to take under section 2105.06 of the Revised Code, the surviving spouse shall take not to exceed one-half of the net estate, unless two or more of the decedent's children or their lineal descendants survive, in which case the surviving spouse shall take not to exceed one-third of the net estate.

"For purposes of this division, the net estate shall be determined before payment of federal estate tax, estate taxes under Chapter 5731. of the Revised Code, or any other tax that is subject to apportionment under section 2113.86 or 2113.861 of the Revised Code.

"(D) Unless the will expressly provides that in case of an election under division (A) of this section there shall be no acceleration of remainder or other interests bequeathed or devised by the will, the balance of the net estate shall be disposed of as though the surviving spouse had predeceased the testator. If there is a disposition by a will to an inter vivos trust that was created by the testator, if under the terms of the trust the surviving spouse is entitled to any interest in the trust or is granted any power or nomination with respect to the trust, and if the surviving spouse makes an election to take under section 2105.06 of the Revised Code, then, unless the trust instrument provides otherwise, the surviving spouse is deemed for purposes of the trust to have predeceased the testator, and there shall be an acceleration of remainder or other interests in all property bequeathed or devised to the trust by the will, in all property held by the trustee at the time of the death of the decedent, and in all property that comes into the hand of the trustee by reason of the death of the decedent.

"(E) The election of a surviving spouse to take under a will or under section 2105.06 of the Revised Code may be made at any time after the death of the decedent, but shall be made not later than one month from the service of the citation to elect. On a motion filed before the expiration of the one-month period, and for good cause shown, the court may allow further time for the making of the election. If no action is taken by the surviving spouse before the expiration of the one-month period, it is conclusively presumed that the surviving spouse elects to take under the will. The election shall be entered on the journal of the court.

"When proceedings for advice or to contest the validity of a will are begun within the time allowed by this division for making the election, the election may be made within three months after the final disposition of the proceedings, if the will is not set aside.

"(F) When a surviving spouse succeeds to the entire estate of the testator, having been named the sole devisee and legatee, it shall be presumed that the spouse elects to take under the will of the testator. No citation shall be issued to the surviving spouse as provided in division (A) of this section, and no election shall be required, unless the surviving spouse manifests a contrary intention." (As eff. 5-31-90.)

R.C. 2107.41 has been renumbered as R.C. 2106.04 and amended to provide: "If the surviving spouse dies before probate of the will, or, having survived the probate, thereafter either fails to make the election provided by section 2106.01 of the Revised Code or dies without having made an election within the times described in division (E) of that section, the surviving spouse shall be conclusively presumed to have elected to take under the will, and the surviving spouse and the heirs, devisees, and legatees of the surviving spouse, and those claiming through or under them, shall be bound by the conclusive presumption, and persons may deal with the property of the decedent accordingly; provided that, if applicable, the provisions of section 2105.21 of the Revised Code shall prevail over the provisions relating to the right of election of a surviving spouse." (As eff. 5-31-90.)

R.C. 2107.42 has been renumbered as R.C. 2106.05 and amended to provide: "If a surviving spouse elects to take under the will, the surviving spouse shall be barred of all right to an intestate share of the property passing under the will and shall take under the will alone, unless it plainly appears from the will that the provision for the surviving spouse was intended to be in addition to an intestate share. An election to take under the will does not bar the right of the surviving spouse to an intestate share of that portion of the estate as to which the decedent dies intestate. Unless the will expressly otherwise directs, an election to take under the will does not bar the right of the surviving spouse to remain in the mansion house, and does not bar the right of the surviving spouse to receive the allowance for the support provided by section 2106.13 of the Revised Code." (As eff. 5-31-90.)

R.C. 2107.43 has been renumbered as R.C. 2106.06 and amended to provide: "The election of a surviving spouse to take under section 2105.06 of the Revised Code and thereby refusing to take under the will shall be made in person before the probate judge, or a deputy clerk who has been appointed to act as a referee, except as provided in sectionsection 2106.07 and 2106.08 of the Revised Code.

"When the election is made in person before the judge or referee, the judge or referee shall explain the will, the rights under the will, and the rights, by law, in the event of a refusal to take under the will." (As eff. 5-31-90.)

R.C. 2129.07 amended to provide that when a copy of a will probated in a foreign country has been duly admitted to record in an Ohio county in which there is any estate upon which the will may operate, and when no ancillary administration proceedings have been had or are being had in this state, sectionsection 2106.01 to 2106.08 of the Revised Code, relating to the election of a surviving spouse, shall apply the same as in the case of resident decedents, except that an election under section 2106.01 of the Revised Code shall not be made subject to division (E) of that section, but instead shall be made at any time after the death of a decedent but not later than six months after the recording of the copy of the will. (As eff. 5-31-90.)

SECTION 9-28: PROBATE; CONTEST

9-28A Probate Generally.

R.C. 2107.18 amended to provide: "The probate court shall admit a will to probate if it appears from the face of the will, or if the probate court requires, in its discretion, the testimony of the witnesses to a will and it appears from that testimony that the execution of the will complies with the law in force at the time of the execution of the will in the jurisdiction in which it was executed, or with the law in force in this state at the time of the death of the testator, or with the law in force in the jurisdiction in which the testator was domiciled at the time of his death.

"The probate court shall admit a will to probate when there has been a prior judgment by a probate court declaring that the will is valid, rendered pursuant to section 2107.084 of the Revised Code, if the will has not been removed from the possession of the probate judge and has not been modified or revoked under division (C) or (D) of section 2107.084 of the Revised Code." (As eff. 5-31-90.) This section amended in response to the dicta in Palazzi v. Estate of Gardner, 32 Ohio St. 3d 169, 512 N.E.2d 971 (1987).

9-28C Foreign Wills.

R.C. 2129.07 amended without material change as to the statement in the Parent Volume. (As eff. 5-31-90.)

9-28D After-discovered Wills; Bona Fide Purchasers.

R.C. 2107.22 amended to provide for probate of a later will and for revocation of the earlier one upon giving notice to persons interested in the earlier will and to those persons required to be notified under R.C. 2107.19. (As eff. 5-31-90.) See R.C. 2107.19 quoted at 9-28F below. This section amended in response to the dicta in Palazzi v. Estate of Gardner, 32 Ohio St. 3d 169, 512 N.E.2d 971 (1987).

Where an after-discovered will was admitted to probate after the estate was closed, and as a result, the surviving spouse would receive only a one-half interest rather than the entire interest in the decedent's real estate, the probate court did not error in permitting the spouse to purchase the real estate and receive credit for taxes previously paid and the surviving spouse's year's allowance. The admission of the will after the final administration cannot restart the time for presentation of charges against the estate, particularly when the creditors had actual notice of the decedent's death. In re Estate of Hudson, 82 Ohio App. 3d 422, 612 N.E.2d 506 (1993).

9-28E   Contest.

R.C. 2107.76 amended to provide: "No person who has received or waived the right to receive the notice of the admission of a will to probate required by section 2107.19 of the Revised Code may commence an action permitted by section 2107.71 of the Revised Code to contest the validity of the will more than four months after filing of the certificate described in division (A)(3) of section 2107.19 of the Revised Code certifying the giving of that notice to or the waiving of that notice by that person. No other person may commence an action permitted by section 2107.71 of the Revised Code to contest the validity of the will more than four months after the initial filing of a certificate described in division (A)(3) of section 2107.19 of the Revised Code. A person under legal disability nevertheless may commence an action permitted by section 2107.71 of the Revised Code to contest the validity of the will within four months after the disability is removed, but the rights saved shall not affect the rights of a purchaser, lessee, or encumbrancer for value in good faith, and shall not impose any liability upon a fiduciary who has acted in good faith, or upon a person delivering or transferring property to any other person under authority of a will, whether or not the purchaser, lessee, encumbrancer, fiduciary, or other person had actual or constructive notice of the legal disability." (As eff. 6-23-94.)

Foster children not named in will lack the direct, immediate and legally ascertainable pecuniary interest in the testator's estate as would allow them to contest the will. The law of "equitable adoption" has not been extended to the law of inheritance. York v. Nunley, 80 Ohio App. 3d 697, 610 N.E.2d 576 (1992).

9-28F   Notice of Application to Probate.

R.C. 2107.13 repealed (as eff. 5-31-90) in response to the dicta in Palazzi v. Estate of Gardner, 32 Ohio St. 3d 169, 512 N.E.2d 971 (1987).

R.C. 2107.19 provides: "(A)(1) Subject to divisions (A)(2) and (B) of this section, when a will has been admitted to probate, the fiduciary for the estate or another person specified in division (A)(4) of this section promptly shall give a notice as described in this division and in the manner provided by Civil Rule 73(E) to the surviving spouse of the testator, to all persons who would be entitled to inherit from the testator under Chapter 2105. of the Revised Code if he had died intestate, and to all legatees and devisees named in the will. The notice shall mention the probate of the will and, if a particular person being given the notice is a legatee or devisee named in the will, shall state that the person is named in the will as a beneficiary. A copy of the will admitted to probate is not required to be given with the notice.

"(2) A person entitled to be given the notice described in division (A)(1) of this section may waive the right by filing a written waiver of the right to receive the notice in the probate court. The person may file the waiver of the right to receive the notice at any time prior to or after the will has been admitted to probate.

"(3) The fact that the notice described in division (A)(1) of this section has been given, subject to division (B) of this section, to all persons described in division (A)(1) of this section who have not waived their right to receive the notice, and, if applicable, the fact that certain persons described in that division have waived their right to receive the notice in accordance with division (A)(2) of this section, shall be evidenced by a certificate that shall be filed in the probate court in accordance with division (A)(4) of this section.

"(4) The notice of the admission of the will to probate required by division (A)(1) of this section and the certificate of giving notice or waiver of notice required by division (A)(3) of this section shall be given or filed by fiduciary for the estate or by the applicant for the admission of the will to probate, the applicant for a release from administration, any other interested person, or the attorney for the fiduciary or for any of the preceding persons.

"(B) The fiduciary or another person specified in division (A)(4) of this section is not required to give a notice pursuant to division (A)(1) of this section to persons who have been notified of the application for probate of the will or of a contest as to jurisdiction, or to persons whose names or places of residence are unknown and cannot with reasonable diligence be ascertained, and a person authorized by division (A)(4) of this section to give notice shall file in the probate court a certificate to that effect." (As eff. 6-23-94.)

Chapter 10: EASEMENTS

DIVISION 10-1: IN GENERAL

SECTION 10-11: INTRODUCTION; CREATION GENERALLY

10-11A Definition.

A perpetual easement and right-of-way for public highway use and road purposes, including limitation of access, is an easement rather than an interest in fee simple. The easement may be perpetual and exclusive, yet it differs from a fee in that the holder of the easement: (1) has no estate in land; (2) can make use of the land only for a limited purpose; (3) cannot control the freehold itself; and (4) once the holder of the easement abandons his prescribed use, the property reverts to the fee holders. Smith v. Gilbraith, 75 Ohio App. 3d 428, 599 N.E.2d 798, mot. overruled, 62 Ohio St. 3d 1484, 581 N.E.2d 1390 (1991).

10-11F Manner of Creation.

By a single instrument of conveyance, there may be created an estate in land in one person and an easement in another. Zurn Indus. v. Lawyers Title Ins., 33 Ohio App. 3d 59, 514 N.E.2d 447 (1986).

10-11G Reservations; Exceptions.

Prior to the enactment of GC8510-1 (1925), which eliminated the need for words of inheritance or perpetuity in conveyances, deed reservations without such words did not pass to heirs or successors any interest of the grantor. Thus, a clause in an 1880 deed reserving a roadway to the grantor, which clause was not accompanied by words of inheritance, prevents the grantor's successors in interest from successfully establishing their claim to an easement by reservation in the land of the grantee's successors in interest. Ewing v. McClanahan, 33 Ohio App. 3d 46, 514 N.E.2d 444 (1986).

SECTION 10-12: EASEMENTS BY IMPLICATION; WAYS OF NECESSITY

10-12B Requirements.

Township's actions in maintaining and repairing a cul-de-sac at the end of a dedicated street were insufficient to create an easement by estoppel. Since a governmental entity is chargeable with knowledge of the ownership of its streets, and has the alternative of eminent domain available to it, alleged easements by estoppel will be construed narrowly against the governmental entity. Passive acquiescence by the landowner will not suffice. Maloney v. Patterson, 63 Ohio App. 3d 405, 579 N.E.2d 230, mot. overruled, 46 Ohio St. 3d 705, 545 N.E.2d 1284 (1989).

An implied easement arising from an existing use need not be shown to be strictly necessary to use of the dominant estate, as is the case with an implied easement by necessity, but only reasonably necessary to the beneficial enjoyment of the dominant estate. Martin v. Sheehy, 33 Ohio App. 3d 332, 515 N.E.2d 1000 (1986).

SECTION 10-13: PERMISSIBLE USES; OBSTRUCTION

10-13A Rules.

Where the grant of access in an easement to a power company for maintenance and control of power lines and towers is indefinite, global, and allows access over the entire dominant property, a court of equity has jurisdiction to monitor the competing interests of the dominant and servient estates and grant appropriate relief to both interests. In exercising this equity jurisdiction, the court may only be reversed upon a showing of abuse of discretion. Ohio Power Co. v. Bauer, 60 Ohio App. 3d 57, 573 N.E.2d 780 (1989).

An easement which does not specify any certain width or area is subject to a court's determination as to the necessary and reasonable width that may be enforced. The necessary and reasonable width for a 12-inch high pressure gas line is 25 feet each side of the line. Columbia Gas Transmission Corp. v. Adams, 68 Ohio Misc. 2d 29 (1994).

10-13B Changes; Enlargement.

A roadway easement granted as an easement appurtenant to a 77.7-acre tract cannot be extended by the owner to any other property unless so provided in the instrument. A plan by the Ohio Department of Natural Resources to use the easement to conduct forest management on 4,842 adjacent acres of land would be an unreasonable increase and a burden to the servient estate. State ex rel. Fisher v. McNutt, 73 Ohio App. 3d 403, 597 N.E.2d 539 (1992).

SECTION 10-14: LOCATION

10-14A Rules.

Where an easement for maintenance and control of power lines and towers is indefinite, global, and allows access over the entire dominant property, an equity court has jurisdiction to monitor the competing interests. The court may impose equitable restrictions on both parties as a condition of granting the equitable relief requested by the parties. Ohio Power Co. v. Bauer, 60 Ohio App. 3d 57, 573 N.E.2d 780 (1989).

An easement which does not specify any certain width or area is subject to a court's determination as to the necessary and reasonable width that may be enforced. The necessary and reasonable width for a 12-inch high pressure gas line is 25 feet each side of the line. Columbia Gas Transmission Corp. v. Adams, 68 Ohio Misc. 2d 29 (1994).

SECTION 10-16: EASEMENTS IN GROSS; PROFITS

10-16A Definition and Nature of Easements in Gross.

The transmission of television signals through coaxial cable constitutes a use similar to the transmission of electric energy through a power line, and the stringing of coaxial cable by a cable television company along an easement owned by an electric company constitutes no additional burden to the owner of the servient estate. Centel Cable T.V. Co. v. Cook, 58 Ohio St. 3d 8, 567 N.E.2d 1010, cert. denied, 111 S. Ct. 2883 (1991).

10-16E Transfer.

Where (1) an easement in gross is intended to be apportionable, (2) the apportioned use is similar to the use granted in the easement, and (3) the apportioned use places no additional burden on the property, the holder of the easement in gross may apportion and partially assign its easement to the other user. If the easement is silent as to apportionability, the right to apportion may be inferred when the holder of the easement possesses the exclusive use of the easement (e.g., the landowner is prohibited from constructing buildings or structures within the limits of the easement), and the right to apportion increases the easement's value to the holder of the easement. Centel Cable T.V. Co. v. Cook, 58 Ohio St. 3d 8, 567 N.E.2d 1010, cert. denied, 111 S. Ct. 2883 (1991) (authorizing apportionment of an electric power easement to allow transmission of television signals through a coaxial cable placed along the power line).

SECTION 10-19: DURATION AND EXTINGUISHMENT

10-19E Abandonment; Misuser.

Although nonuse of an easement obtained by prescription does not, by itself, amount to an abandonment, where the holders of the subservient estate have made substantial changes and improvements to the disputed land, the holders of the dominant estate may not "sit" on their rights but must take positive and timely action or risk loss of the easement through the doctrines of estoppel and laches. Zimmerman v. Cindle, 48 Ohio App. 3d 164, 548 N.E.2d 1315 (1988).

10-19I Other Causes of Termination.

The Ohio Marketable Title Act may also operate to bar or extinguish an easement unless the easement is "clearly observable by physical evidence of its use." R.C. 5301.53 (as eff. 9-30-74). An easement by prescription is not "clearly observable" if the easement is no longer discernible when the holders of the subservient estate purchase the property. Zimmerman v. Cindle, 48 Ohio App. 3d 164, 548 N.E.2d 1315 (1988).

CHAPTER 11: ESTATES AND FUTURE INTERESTS

DIVISION 11-1: IN GENERAL

SECTION 11-11: INTRODUCTION; CONSTRUCTION GENERALLY

11-11E Arbitration.

R.C. 2711.01 amended as quoted at 3-31A above. (As eff. 10-23-91.)

SECTION 11-13: RULE IN SHELLEY'S CASE

11-13A Generally.

R.C. 2107.49, which abolishes the Rule in Shelley's Case, will not be applied retroactively to trusts created before the rule was abolished in 1941. With regard to conveyances prior to 1941, the Rule in Shelley's Case will be applied to both real and personal property. Society Nat'l Bank v. Jacobson, 54 Ohio St. 3d 15, 560 N.E.2d 217, reh'g denied, 54 Ohio St. 3d 709, 563 N.E.2d 302 (1990).

SECTION 11-15: MERGER

11-15A Generally.

The question of whether there is a merger of a leasehold interest with a fee estate, when both interests meet in the same person, is a question of fact, depending upon the intention of the parties and whether equity will be served by ruling that both the leasehold and real property interests should merge. Colopy v. Wilson, 48 Ohio App. 3d 148, 548 N.E.2d 1322 (1989).

SECTION 11-19: WASTE

11-19A Definition and Nature.

Further research: O Jur 3d, Waste §§ 1-4, 19.

11-19B Permissive Waste; Voluntary Waste.

Further research: O Jur 3d, Waste §§ 10, 11.

11-19G Minerals, Oil and Gas.

Further research: O Jur 3d, Waste § 9.

11-19H Trees; Timber.

Further research: O Jur 3d, Waste § 8.

11-19J Remedies.

Further research: O Jur 3d, Waste §§ 12, 18.

DIVISION 11-4: ESTATES SUBJECT TO CONDITION SUBSEQUENT; RIGHTS OF REENTRY

SECTION 11-42: TERMS OF CREATION

11-42A Generally.

A conveyance "upon the express condition that said property shall be used for the purpose of ... railway tracks" is sufficient to create a qualified fee, and where the language appears in the granting clause, a clause of re-entry or forfeiture is not necessary since such language declares a condition and imports a forfeiture. Upon breach of the condition subsequent, the existing estate is destroyed and title to the premises revests as before the conveyance, provided that the holder of the reversionary interest takes the proper steps to consummate forfeiture. A reversionary interest, however, is not an interest that attaches to land, but rather is the residue of an estate that is left in the grantor. Upon termination of a qualified fee, the land conveyed reverts to a person and not the other land. For the adjoining property owners to prevail, they must show that they have acquired the reversionary interest by some other conveyance. Walker v. Lucas County Bd. of Comm'rs, 73 Ohio App. 3d 617, 598 N.E.2d 101 (1991).

DIVISION 11-8: CONTINGENT REMAINDERS; EXECUTORY INTERESTS

SECTION 11-81: CONSTRUCTION AS TO VESTING; CONTINGENT REMAINDERS

11-81A Rules as to Vesting.

An inter vivos trust which, on the death of the grantor, allocates substantially all the trust assets to a marital deduction trust with the entire income payable to the surviving spouse, and which grants an unlimited testamentary power of appointment to the surviving spouse with the remainder over to the children of the grantor, creates in the remaindermen a vested interest subject to defeasance by the exercise of the power of appointment. Papiernik v. Papiernik, 45 Ohio St. 3d 337, 544 N.E.2d 664 (1989).

11-81M Power to Consume or Appoint.

See Papiernik v. Papiernik, 45 Ohio St. 3d 337, 544 N.E.2d 664 (1989), discussed at 11-81A above.

DIVISION 11-9: CLASS GIFTS; PER STIRPES OR PER CAPITA

SECTION 11-91: CLASS GIFTS GENERALLY

11-91C Increase and Decrease in Membership; Closing a Class.

A class in a testamentary trust does not necessarily close at the death of the testator, but remains open to enlargement, if the language of the instrument, interpreted in light of applicable laws and all pertinent circumstances of the execution of the instrument, shows that to be the intent of the testator. In general, if a testamentary gift to a class has no time specified for distribution, the death of the testator will fix the time for distribution, and close the class at the time of death of the testator. However, where a reasonable interpretation of the instrument would permit the class to remain open, and the gift is a present bequest to be distributed at a later determinable date (in this case, when the oldest child reaches the age of twenty-five), the class may be enlarged until the time of the first mandatory distribution. Thus, additional grandchildren born after the death of the testator could become members of the class. Until the class is to close at the time of the first mandatory distribution, the children take a vested interest in the trust subject to adjustment upon the birth (or adoption) of another class member. Central Trust Co. v. Smith, 50 Ohio St. 3d 133, 553 N.E.2d 265 (1990).

CHAPTER 12: EXECUTORS AND ADMINISTRATORS

DIVISION 12-1: IN GENERAL

DIVISION 12-1: IN GENERAL

SECTION 12-11: GENERALLY

12-11A Title and Rights; Rents.

A fiduciary who is also the sole beneficiary of an estate, who requests a bank to release certificates of deposit prior to the fiduciary's formal appointment as executrix, cannot require the bank to pay the funds again because of its alleged violation of the statute invalidating the prior transaction. The bank is entitled to liability protection based on its reliance on the conduct of the apparent fiduciary, and the doctrine of "relation back" validates the executrix's actions performed prior to a formal appointment. North Akron Sav. & Loan Ass'n v. Rondy, 68 Ohio App. 3d 518, 589 N.E.2d 82 (1990).

12-11B Appointment; Bond.

R.C. 2109.022 provides: "(A) As used in this section, 'fiduciary' means a trustee under any testamentary or other trust, an executor or administrator, or any other person who is acting in a fiduciary capacity for any person, trust, or estate.

"(B) When an instrument under which a fiduciary acts reserves to the grantor, or vests in an advisory or investment committee or in one or more other persons, including one or more fiduciaries, to the exclusion of the fiduciary or of one or more of several fiduciaries, any power, including, but not limited to, the authority to direct the acquisition, disposition, or retention of any investment or the power to authorize any act that an excluded fiduciary may propose, any excluded fiduciary is not liable, either individually or as a fiduciary, for either of the following:

"(1) Any loss that results from compliance with an authorized direction of the grantor, committee, person, or persons;

"(2) Any loss that results from a failure to take any action proposed by an excluded fiduciary that requires a prior authorization of the grantor, committee, person, or persons if that excluded fiduciary timely sought but failed to obtain that authorization.

"(C) Any excluded fiduciary as described in division (B) of this section is relieved from any obligation to perform investment reviews and make recommendations with respect to any investments to the extent the grantor, an advisory or investment committee, or one or more other persons have authority to direct the acquisition, disposition, or retention of any investment.

"(D) This section does not apply to the extent that the instrument under which an excluded fiduciary as described in division (B) of this section acts contains provisions that are inconsistent with this section." (As eff. 3-22-89.)

R.C. 2109.04 amended without material change as to the statement in the Parent Volume. (As eff. 9-10-91.)

R.C. 2109.21 amended without change as to statement in the Parent Volume. (As eff. 5-31-90.)

R.C. 2113.08 repealed. (As eff. 5-31-90.)

12-11D Presumed Decedents; Absentees' Estates.

R.C. 2110.03 amended without material change as to the statement in the Parent Volume. (As eff. 1-1-91.)

12-11E Determination of Heirship; Distribution and Accounting.

R.C. 2109.30 amended to provide for certificates of termination without a partial or final account when the sole legatee, devisee or heir is also the executor or administrator and all debts and claims against the estate have been paid. (As eff. 10-8-92 and 6-23-94.)

R.C. 2109.32 amended to provide that the final account shall not be approved until three months have passed since the death of the decedent and the surviving spouse has filed an election to take under or against the will, or the time for making the election has expired. (As eff. 10-8-92 and 6-23-94.)

R.C. 2109.35 amended without material change as to the statement in the Parent Volume. (As eff. 10-8-92 and 6-23-94.)

12-11H Relieving Estate from Administration.

R.C. 2113.03 amended to provide:

"(A) Subject to division (D) of this section, an estate may be released from administration under division (B) of this section if either of the following applies:

"(1) The value of the assets of the estate is thirty-five thousand dollars or less.

"(2) The value of the assets of the estate is eighty-five thousand dollars or less and either of the following applies:

"(a) The decedent devised and bequeathed in a valid will all of the assets of his estate to a person who is named in the will as his spouse, and the decedent is survived by that person.

"(b) The decedent is survived by a spouse whose marriage to the decedent was solemnized in a manner consistent with Chapter 3101 of the Revised Code or with a similar law of another state of nation, the decedent died without a valid will, and the decedent's surviving spouse is entitled to receive all of the assets of his estate under section 2105.06 of the Revised Code or by the operation of that section and division (B)(1) or (2) of section 2106.13 of the Revised Code.

"(B) Upon the application of any interested party, after notice of the filing of the application has been given to the surviving spouse and heirs at law in the manner and for the length of time the probate court directs, and after notice to all interested parties by publication in a newspaper of general circulation in the county, unless the notices are waived or found unnecessary, the court, when satisfied that division (A)(1) or (2) of this section is satisfied, may enter an order relieving the estate from administration and directing delivery of personal property and transfer of real estate to the persons entitled to the personal property or real estate.

"For the purpose of this division, the value of an estate that reasonably can be considered to be in an amount specified in division (A)(1) or (2) of this section and that is not composed entirely of money, stocks, bonds, or other property the value of which is readily ascertainable, shall be determined by an appraiser selected by the applicant, subject to the approval of the court. The appraiser's valuation of the property shall be reported to the court in the application to relieve the estate from administration. The appraiser shall be paid in accordance with section 2115.06 of the Revised Code.

"For the purposes of this division, the amount of property to be delivered or transferred to the surviving spouse, minor children, or both of the decedent as the allowance for support shall be established in accordance with section 2106.13 of the Revised Code."

"When a delivery, sale, or transfer of personal property has been ordered from an estate that has been relieved from administration, the court may appoint a commissioner to execute all necessary instruments of conveyance. The commissioner shall receipt for the property, distribute the proceeds of the conveyance upon court order, and report to the court after distribution.

"When the decedent died testate, the will shall be presented for probate, and, if admitted to probate, the court may relieve the estate from administration and order distribution of the estate under the will.

"An order of the court relieving an estate from administration shall have the same effect as administration proceedings in freeing land in the hands of an innocent purchaser for value from possible claims of unsecured creditors.

"(C) Any delivery of personal property or transfer of real estate pursuant to an order relieving an estate from administration is made subject to the limitations pertaining to the claims of creditors set forth in divisions (B) and (C) of section 2117.07 of the Revised Code.

"(D) The release of an estate from administration under this section does not affect any duty of any person to file an estate tax return and certificate under division (A) of section 5731.21 of the Revised Code and does not affect the duties of a probate court set forth in that division." (As eff. 9-14-93 and 11-9-94.)

Substitute for next to last paragraph of this section in the Parent Volume:

Prior to the 1976 revision of R.C. 2113.03, the statute contained no provision for transferring property exempted from administration or assigned as a year's allowance to the widow and children. The 1976 revision specified that the amount of property to be delivered to the surviving spouse and minor children as allowance for support "shall be established."

SECTION 12-12: CLAIMS AGAINST ESTATE

12-12B Claims against Estate.

Standard of Title Examination 5.2 amended May 15, 1991, as follows:

5.2 PROBATE COURT PROCEEDINGS — DEBTS
AFTER FOUR YEARS

[Adopted by OSBA May 21, 1953; Amended to insert "estate" in 1976]
Problem A:

Should objection be made to the title of a purchaser from the heirs on account of decedent's unpaid debts (a) where the estate has not been administered and more than four years have elapsed since decedent's death, or (b) where the final account has not been approved in the administration and more than four years have elapsed since the granting of letters without suit to subject the real estate having been commenced?

Standard A:

No.

Comment A:

The rule of this standard is set forth in R.C. 2117.36. The lien of estate (inheritance) tax is not barred by the four-year statute of limitations.

Advisory note:

This standard has been referred to the Title Standards Committee of the Real Property Section for study and possible revision to conform with the recent amendments to R.C. 2117.06.

12-12C Presentation and Priority.

R.C. 2117.06(B) provides that all claims, except those with different time periods pursuant to R.C. 2125.02, 2305.09, 2305.10, 2305.11 or 2305.12 (See R.C. 2117.06(G)) "shall be presented within one year after the death of the decedent, whether or not the estate is released from administration or an executor or administrator is appointed during that one-year period" and R.C. 2117.06(C) provides: "(C) A claim that is not presented within one year after the death of the decedent shall be forever barred as to all parties, including, but not limited to, devisees, legatees, and distributees. No payment shall be made on the claim and no action shall be maintained on the claim, except as otherwise provided in sections 2117.37 to 2117.42 of the Revised Code, with reference to contingent claims." (As eff. 5-31-90.)

Former R.C. 2117.07 repealed. (As eff. 5-31-90.) See R.C. 2117.06(C) above regarding barring of claims. New R.C. 2117.07 provides a mechanism for the executor or administrator to accelerate the bar under section 2117.06 by giving thirty days' written notice to potential claimants.

The first sentence of R.C. 2117.17 amended to provide: "The probate court on its own motion may, and on motion of the executor or administrator shall, assign all claims against the estate that have been presented and any other known valid debts of the estate for hearing on a day certain." (As eff. 5-31-90.)

R.C. 2117.25 amended without material change as to the statement in the Parent Volume. (As eff. 5-31-90.)

R.C. 2117.37-.42 amended to provide that upon accrual of a contingent claim, it be presented to the executor or administrator before the expiration of one year after the date of death of the decedent, or before the expiration of two months after the cause of action accrues, whichever is later, except in the case of contingent claims. (As eff. 5-31-90.)

Real estate broker's right to a commission was a contingent claim against the estate of the decedent. The claim accrued when the decedent's lessee exercised its option to purchase. Because the claim was not presented within the statutory period (six months under the statute in effect at that time), it was barred, even though the broker did not discover that the sale occurred until two years later. Priestman v. Elder, 97 Ohio App. 3d 86 (1994).

SECTION 12-13: RIGHTS OF SURVIVING SPOUSE

12-13A Foreign Estates.

R.C. 2117.23 repealed. (As eff. 5-31-90.)

12-13B Quarantine; Right to Mansion House.

R.C. 2117.24 renumbered as R.C. 2106.15 and amended to provide: "A surviving spouse may remain in the mansion house free of charge for one year, except that such real property may be sold within that time for the payment of debts of the decedent. If the real property is so sold, the surviving spouse shall be compensated from the estate to the extent of the fair rental value for the unexpired term, such compensation to have the same priority in payment of debts of estates as the allowance for support made to the surviving spouse, minor children, or surviving spouse and minor children of the decedent under section 2106.13 of the Revised Code." (As eff. 5-31-90.)

R.C. 2107.42 renumbered as R.C. 2106.05 and amended as quoted at 9-27A above. (As eff. 5-31-90.)

12-13C Exemption from Administration.

R.C. 2107.42 renumbered as R.C. 2106.05 and amended as quoted at 9-27A above. (As eff. 5-31-90.)

12-13D Family Allowance.

R.C. 2117.20 renumbered as R.C. 2106.13 and amended to provide: "(A) If a person dies leaving a surviving spouse and no minor children, leaving a surviving spouse and minor children, or leaving minor children and no surviving spouse, the surviving spouse, minor children, or both shall be entitled to receive, subject to division (B) of this section, in money or property the sum of twenty-five thousand dollars as an allowance for support. The money or property set off as an allowance shall be considered estate assets.

"(B) The probate court shall order the distribution of the allowance for support described in division (A) of this section as follows:

"(1) If the person died leaving a surviving spouse and no minor children, one hundred percent to the surviving spouse;

"(2) If the person died leaving a surviving spouse and minor children, and if all of the minor children are the children of the surviving spouse, one hundred percent to the surviving spouse;

"(3) If the person died leaving a surviving spouse and minor children, and if not all of the minor children are children of the surviving spouse, in equitable shares, as fixed by the probate court in accordance with this division, to the surviving spouse and the minor children who are not the children of the surviving spouse. In determining equitable shares under this division, the probate court shall do all of the following:

"(a) Consider the respective needs of the surviving spouse, the minor children who are the children of the surviving spouse, and the minor children who are not children of the surviving spouse;

"(b) Allocate to the surviving spouse, the share that is equitable in light of the needs of the surviving spouse and the minor children who are children of the surviving spouse;

"(c) Allocate to the minor children who are not children of the surviving spouse, the share that is equitable in light of the needs of those minor children.

"(4) If the person died leaving minor children and no surviving spouse, in equitable shares, as fixed by the probate court in accordance with this division, to the minor children. In determining equitable shares under this division, the probate court shall consider the respective needs of the minor children and allocate to each minor child the share that is equitable in light of his needs." (As eff. 5-31-90.)

R.C. 2107.42 has been renumbered as R.C. 2106.05 and amended as quoted at 9-27A above. (As eff. 5-31-90.)

Where an after-discovered will was probated after the estate was closed, and the surviving spouse received only a one-half interest in the real estate rather than the entire interest, the probate court did not error in allowing the spouse to purchase the real estate, permitting the year's allowance to apply as a credit against the purchase price, and refusing to reopen the administration of the estate. In re Estate of Hudson, 82 Ohio App. 3d 422, 612 N.E.2d 506 (1993).

12-13E Taking at Appraised Value.

R.C. 2105.062 renumbered as R.C. 2106.10; division (A) has been amended to provide: "(A) A surviving spouse may elect to receive, as part of the surviving spouse's share of an intestate estate under section 2105.06 of the Revised Code, the entire interest of the decedent spouse in the mansion house. The interest of the decedent spouse in the mansion house shall be valued at the appraised value with the deduction of that portion of all liens on the mansion house, existing at the time of death and attributable to the decedent's interest in the mansion house." (As eff. 5-31-90.)

R.C. 2113.38 renumbered as R.C. 2106.16 and amended to provide: "A surviving spouse, even though acting as executor or administrator, may purchase the following property, if left by the decedent, and if not specifically devised or bequeathed:

"(A) The decedent's interest in the mansion house, including the decedent's title in the parcel of land on which such house is situated and lots or farm land adjacent to the house and used in conjunction with it as the home of the decedent, and the decedent's title in the household goods contained in the house, at the appraised value as fixed by the appraisers;

"(B) Any other real or personal property of the decedent not exceeding, with the decedent's interest in the mansion house and the decedent's title in the land used in conjunction with it, and the decedent's title in the household goods the spouse elects to purchase, one-third of the gross appraised value of the estate, at the appraised value as fixed by the appraisers.

"A spouse desiring to exercise this right of purchase with respect to personal property shall file in the probate court an application setting forth an accurate description of the personal property, and the election of the spouse to purchase it at the appraised value. No notice is required for the court to hear the application, insofar as it appertains to household goods contained in the mansion house. If the application includes other personal property, the court shall cause a notice of the time and place of the hearing of the application with respect to such other personal property to be given to the executor or administrator, the heirs or beneficiaries interested in the estate, and to such other interested persons as the court determines.

"A spouse desiring to exercise this right of purchase with respect to an interest in real property shall file in the court a petition containing an accurate description of the real property, and naming as parties defendant the executor or administrator, the persons to whom the real property passes by inheritance or residuary devise, and all mortgagees and other lienholders whose claims affect the real property or any part of it. Spouses of parties defendant need not be made parties defendant. The petition shall set forth the election of the surviving spouse to purchase the interest in real property at the appraised value, and shall contain a prayer accordingly. A summons upon that petition shall be issued and served on the defendants, in the same manner as provided for service of summons in actions to sell real property to pay debts.

"No hearing on the application or petition shall be held until the inventory is approved. On the hearing of the application or petition, the finding of the court shall be in favor of the surviving spouse, unless it appears that the appraisement was made as a result of collusion or fraud, or that it is so manifestly inadequate that a sale at that price would unconscionably prejudice the rights of the parties in interest or creditors. The action of the court shall not be held to prejudice the rights of lienholders.

"Upon a finding in favor of the surviving spouse, the court shall make an entry fixing the terms of payment to the executor or administrator for the property, having regard for the rights of creditors of the estate, and ordering the executor or administrator, or a commissioner who may be appointed and authorized for the purpose, to transfer and convey the property to the spouse upon compliance with the terms fixed by the court. If the court, having regard for the amount of property to be purchased, its appraised value, and the distribution to be made of the proceeds arising from the sale, finds that the original bond given by the executor or administrator is sufficient, the court may dispense with the giving of additional bonds. If the court finds that the original bond is insufficient, as a condition to transfer and conveyance, the court shall require the executor or administrator to execute an additional bond in an amount as the court may fix, with proper surety, conditioned and payable as provided in section 2127.27 of the Revised Code. This section does not prevent the court from ordering transfer and conveyance without bond in cases where the will of a testator provides that the executor need not give bond. The executor or administrator, or a commissioner, then shall execute and deliver to the surviving spouse a proper bill of sale or deed, as the case may be, for the property, and make a return to the court.

"The death of the surviving spouse prior to the filing of the court's entry fixing the terms of payment for property elected to be purchased shall nullify the election. The real or personal property then shall be free of the right granted in this section.

"The application or petition provided for in this section shall not be filed prior to filing the inventory, nor later than one month after the approval of the inventory required by section 2115.02 of the Revised Code. Failure to file an application or petition within that time nullifies the election with respect to the property required to be included, and the real or personal property then shall be free of the right granted in this section." (As eff. 5-31-90.)

SECTION 12-14: LAND SALES

12-14D When Executor or Administrator Shall Sell.

R.C. 2127.02 amended to provide: "As soon as an executor or administrator ascertains that the personal property in his hands is insufficient to pay all the debts of the decedent, together with the allowance for support to the surviving spouse, minor children, or surviving spouse and minor children of the decedent as provided in section 2106.13 of the Revised Code, and the costs of administering the estate, he shall commence a civil action in the probate court for authority to sell the decedent's real property." (As eff. 5-31-90.)

R.C. 2127.03 amended to provide: "When by operation of law or the provisions of a will, a legacy is effectual to charge real property, and the personal property is insufficient to pay the legacy, together with all the debts, the allowance to the surviving spouse, minor children, or surviving spouse and minor children as provided in section 2106.13 of the Revised Code, and the costs of administering the estate, the executor, administrator, or administrator with the will annexed shall commence a civil action in the probate court for authority to sell the real property so charged.

"If the executor, administrator, or administrator with the will annexed fails to commence the action mentioned in this section or section 2127.02 of the Revised Code, the probate court in which letters testamentary have been granted, upon its own motion or upon motion by a creditor or legatee, shall order the executor, administrator, or administrator with the will annexed to commence such an action, and proceed in the manner prescribed in this chapter." (As eff. 5-31-90.)

12-14J Summary Sale When under $3000.

Problem 5.4B of the Standards of Title Examination was revised January 18, 1991, to conform with an earlier amendment to R.C. 2127.11 which increased the authority for summary land sales from a value of less than $1000 to a value of less than $3000.

12-14K Parties Defendant.

R.C. 2127.12 amended to change "fraudulent conveyance" to "fraudulent transfer" and to make other non-substantive changes. (As eff. 9-28-90.)

12-14O The Sale.

R.C. 2109.45 amended without material change as to the statement in the Parent Volume, except that the fiduciary is required to file a "statement" rather than an affidavit. (As eff. 10-8-92.)

12-14P Homestead.

R.C. 2329.66 amended as set forth in 17-41B of this Supplement. (As eff. 11-5-92, 1-14-93, 12-31-93 and 7-1-94.)

12-14Q Bond.

R.C. 2127.31 amended without material change as to the statement in the Parent Volume. (As eff. 5-31-90.)

SECTION 12-15: ESTATES OF NONRESIDENT DECEDENTS

12-15A Foreign Administration.

R.C. 2129.02 amended to provide: "When letters of administration or letters testamentary have been granted in any state other than this state, in any territory or possession of the United States, or in any foreign country, as to the estate of a deceased resident of that state, territory, possession, or country, and when no ancillary administration proceedings have been commenced in this state, the person to whom the letters of appointment were granted may file an authenticated copy of them in the probate court of any county of this state in which is located real estate of decedent.

"The claim of any creditor of such a decedent shall be subject to section 2117.06 of the Revised Code. The person filing such letters in the probate court may accelerate the bar against claims against the estate established by that section, by giving written notice to a potential claimant that identifies the decedent by name, states the date of the death of the decedent, identifies the court, states its mailing address, and informs the potential claimant that any claims he may have against the estate are required to be presented to the court within the earlier of thirty days after receipt of the notice by the potential claimant or one year after the date of the death of the decedent. A claim of that potential claimant that is not presented to the court within the earlier of thirty days after receipt of the notice by the potential claimant or one year after the date of the death of the decedent is forever barred as a possible lien upon the real estate of the decedent in this state. If, at the expiration of that period, any such claim has been filed and remains unpaid after reasonable notice of the claim to the nonresident executor or administrator, ancillary administration proceedings as to the estate may be had forthwith." (As eff. 5-31-90.)

12-15B Ancillary Administration.

R.C. 2129.08 amended to provide: "(A) After an authenticated copy of the will of a nonresident decedent has been allowed and admitted to record as provided in this chapter, and after there has been filed in the probate court a complete exemplification of the record of the grant of the domiciliary letters of appointment and of any other records of the court of domiciliary administration that the court requires, the court shall appoint as the ancillary administrator the person named in the will, or nominated in accordance with any power of nomination conferred in the will, as general executor of the decedent's estate or as executor of the portion of the decedent's estate located in this state, provided that the person makes application and qualifies under division (B)(2) of section 2109.21 of the Revised Code and in all other respects as required by law. If the testator in the will naming or providing for the nomination of that executor orders or requests that bond not be given by him, bond shall not be required unless, for sufficient reason, the court requires it.

"(B) If a nonresident decedent died intestate, or failed to designate in his will any person qualified to act as ancillary administrator or to confer in the will a power to nominate a person as an executor as described in division (A) of this section, or if the will of a nonresident decedent conferred such a power but no person qualified to act as ancillary administrator was nominated, the court shall appoint in such capacity some suitable person who is a resident of the county including, but not limited to, a creditor of the estate.

"(C) An ancillary administrator, acting as to the estate of a testate decedent that is located in this state, may sell and convey the real and personal property by virtue of the will as executors or administrators with the will annexed may do.

"(D) No person shall be appointed as an ancillary administrator of the estate of a nonresident presumed decedent that is located in this state, except after Chapter 2121 of the Revised Code, relative to the appointment of an ancillary administrator, has been complied with." (As eff. 5-31-90.)

CHAPTER 13: FIXTURES

DIVISION 13-1: IN GENERAL

SECTION 13-11: GENERALLY

13-11A Definition and Requirements.

Heat pump located outside of residence constitutes a "fixture" under the three tests established by *Teaff v. Hewitt*. Household Fin. Corp. v. BancOhio, 62 Ohio App. 3d 691, 577 N.E.2d 405 (1989).

Where jewelry cases were installed by a prior tenant, attached to the real estate and appropriated to the use of the real estate, the cases became real estate fixtures rather than trade fixtures, particularly in the absence of some indicia or proof that the jewelry cases were sold or transferred from the prior tenant to the current tenant. York v. George Framm Enterprises, Inc., 62 Ohio Misc. 2d 752, 610 N.E.2d 655 (Cleve. Mun. Ct. 1992).

Five-ton air conditioning unit installed by restaurant tenant is a fixture that is indispensable to the operation of the property and is, therefore, not subject to repossession by tenant's creditor. While ceiling fans and track lighting are not fixtures and may be removed, any damage to the property caused by that removal must be repaired by the creditor. Rose v. Marlowe's Cafe, Inc., 68 Ohio Misc. 2d 9 (1994).

13-11B Annexation.

Connection of heat pump to house with wires and tubes is sufficient to constitute annexation to the real estate. Household Fin. Corp. v. BancOhio, 62 Ohio App. 3d 691, 577 N.E.2d 405 (1989).

13-11H Taxation; Condemnation.

In the context of an appropriation, additional factors to be considered in determining whether an item is a fixture include the degree of difficulty and the extent of any economic loss involved in removing it from the realty, as well as the damage to the severed property which removal would cause. In this context, railway cars on public display as museum pieces which were of such a large and/or firmly affixed nature that there was an intent that they would become a permanent part of the museum's real property, could be considered fixtures. State ex rel. Fisher v. Waterfront Elec. Ry., Inc., 63 Ohio Misc. 2d 507, 635 N.E.2d 81 (Lucas Cty. C.P. 1993).

SECTION 13-12: ENCUMBRANCES ON FIXTURES

13-12B Prior and Subsequent Purchasers and Lien Holders.

R.C. 1309.40(E) and 1309.40(H) amended to read as follows:

"(E) The fee for filing, indexing and furnishing filing data for an original, amended, or a continuation statement on a form prescribed by the secretary of state or on any other form approved by the filing officer shall be nine dollars. The fee for filing, indexing, and furnishing filing data for an original, amended, or a continuation statement on a form neither prescribed by the secretary of state nor on any other form approved by the filing officer shall be eleven dollars.

"(H) Upon request of any person, the filing officer shall issue his certificate showing whether there is on file on the date and hour stated therein, any presently effective financing statement naming a particular debtor, owner, lessee, and any statement of assignment thereof and if there is, giving the date and hour of filing of each such statement and the names and addresses of each secured party therein. The fee for such a certificate shall be nine dollars plus one dollar for each financing statement and for each statement of assignment reported therein. Upon request the filing officer shall furnish a copy of the filed financing statement or statement of assignment for a uniform fee of one dollar per page." (As eff. 7-1-93.)

Although a heat pump can be characterized as a "consumer good," R.C. 1309.21 requires a fixture filing to preserve the priority of a purchase money security interest therein. Where the holder of the security interest has failed to record its security interest by executing a fixture filing, an action for repossession will fail as against a mortgagee that has acquired the property through foreclosure. Household Fin. Corp. v. BancOhio, 62 Ohio App. 3d 691, 577 N.E.2d 405 (1989).

CHAPTER 14: HUSBAND AND WIFE

DIVISION 14-1: IN GENERAL

SECTION 14-11: INTRODUCTION; COMMON-LAW MARRIAGE

14-11A Validity of Marriages.

R.C. 3105.12 amended to prohibit common-law marriages under Ohio law. Common-law marriages occurring prior to the effective date of the amendment (October 10, 1991) remain valid. (As eff. 10-10-91.)

SECTION 14-14: ANTENUPTIAL AGREEMENTS

14-14A Rules.

R.C. 2131.03 renumbered as R.C. 2106.22 and amended as quoted at 14-15A below. (As eff. 5-31-90.)

When an antenuptial agreement provides for an inequitable distribution, the burden is on the one claiming the validity of the contract to show that the other party entered into it with full knowledge or disclosure of the assets of the proponent. However, the burden of proving fraud, duress, coercion, or over-reaching remains with the party challenging the agreement. Fletcher v. Fletcher, 68 Ohio St. 3d 464, 628 N.E.2d 1343 (1994).

SECTION 14-15: SEPARATION AGREEMENTS

14-15A Rules.

R.C. 2131.03 renumbered as R.C. 2106.22 and amended to provide: "Any antenuptial or separation agreement to which a decedent was a party is valid unless an action to set it aside is commenced within four months after the appointment of the executor or administrator of the estate of the decedent, or unless, within the four-month period, the validity of the agreement otherwise is attacked." (As eff. 5-31-90.)

SECTION 14-17: ANNULMENT OF MARRIAGE

14-17A   Equitable Actions.

R.C. 3105.01 amended as quoted at 14-31A below. (As eff. 1-1-91 and 10-6-94.)

DIVISION 14-3: DIVORCE AND ALIMONY

SECTION 14-31: DIVORCE GENERALLY

14-31A Law Governing; Grounds.

R.C. 3105.01 amended to provide: "The court of common pleas may grant divorces for the following causes:

"(A) Either party had a husband or wife living at the time of the marriage from which the divorce is sought;

"(B) Willful absence of the adverse party for one year;

"(C) Adultery;

"(D) Extreme cruelty;

"(E) Fraudulent contract;

"(F) Any gross neglect of duty;

"(G) Habitual drunkenness;

"(H) Imprisonment of the adverse party in a state or federal correctional institution at the time of filing the complaint;

"(I) Procurement of a divorce outside this state, by a husband or wife, by virtue of which the party who procured it is released from the obligations of the marriage, while those obligations remain binding upon the other party;

"(J) On the application of either party, when husband and wife have, without interruption for one year, lived separate and apart without cohabitation;

"(K) Incompatibility, unless denied by either party.

"A plea of res judicata or of recrimination with respect to any provision of this section does not bar either party from obtaining a divorce on this ground." (As eff. 1-1-91 and 10-6-94.)

R.C. 3105.61-.65 amended without change as to the statement in the Parent Volume. (As eff. 6-13-90.)

R.C. 3105.63 and R.C. 3105.65 further amended without material change as to the statement in the Parent Volume. (As eff. 1-1-91, 4-11-91 and 11-5-92.)

14-31B Residence; Domicile.

R.C. 3105.03 amended to change "civil rules" to "Rules of Civil Procedure" and to change "alimony" to "legal separation." (As eff. 1-1-91.)

14-31D Service of Process; Jurisdiction as to Property.

Civil Rule 75(J) amended to provide as follows: "No action for divorce, annulment, or legal separation may be heard and decided until the expiration of 42 days after the service of process or 28 days after the last publication of notice of the complaint, and no action for divorce, annulment, or legal separation shall be heard and decided earlier than 28 days after the service of a counterclaim, which under this rule may be designated a cross-complaint, unless the plaintiff files a written waiver of the 28-day period." (As eff. 7-1-91.)

14-31F Dower.

R.C. 3105.10 amended without change as to the portion quoted in the Parent Volume, except to change "alimony" to "legal separation." (As eff. 1-1-91.)

SECTION 14-32: ALIMONY GENERALLY

14-32A Definition; Jurisdiction in Equity; Grounds.

R.C. 3105.17 amended to provide: "(A) Either party to the marriage may file a complaint for divorce or for legal separation, and when filed the other may file a counterclaim for divorce or for legal separation. The court of common pleas may grant divorces for the causes set forth in section 3105.01 of the Revised Code. The court of common pleas may grant legal separation on a complaint or counterclaim, regardless of whether the parties are living separately at the time the complaint or counterclaim is filed, for the following causes:

"(1) Either party had a husband or wife living at the time of the marriage from which legal separation is sought;

"(2) Willful absence of the adverse party for one year;

"(3) Adultery;

"(4) Extreme cruelty;

"(5) Fraudulent contract;

"(6) Any gross neglect of duty;

"(7) Habitual drunkenness;

"(8) Imprisonment of the adverse party in a state or federal correctional institution at the time of filing the complaint;

"(9) On the application of either party, when husband and wife have, without interruption for one year, lived separate and apart without cohabitation;

"(10) Incompatibility, unless denied by either party.

"(B) The filing of a complaint or counterclaim for legal separation or the granting of a decree of legal separation under this section does not bar either party from filing a complaint or counterclaim for a divorce or annulment or obtaining a divorce or annulment." (As eff. 1-1-91 and 10-6-94.)

R.C. 3105.171 provides as follows: "(A) As used in this section:

"(1) 'Distributive award' means any payment or payments, in real or personal property, that are payable in a lump sum or over time, in fixed amounts, that are made from separate property or income, and that are not made from marital property and do not constitute payments of spousal support, as defined in section 3105.18 of the Revised Code.

"(2) 'During the marriage' means whichever of the following is applicable:

"(a) Except as provided in division (A)(2)(b) of this section, the period of time from the date of the marriage through the date of the final hearing in an action for divorce or in an action for legal separation;

"(b) If the court determines that the use of either or both of the dates specified in division (A)(2)(a) of this section would be inequitable, the court may select dates that it considers equitable in determining marital property. If the court selects dates that it considers equitable in determining marital property, 'during the marriage' means the period of time between those dates selected and specified by the court.

"(3)(a) 'Marital property' means, subject to division (A)(3)(b) of this section, all of the following:

"(i) All real and personal property that currently is owned by either or both of the spouses, including, but not limited to, the retirement benefits of the spouses, and that was acquired by either or both of the spouses during the marriage;

"(ii) All interest that either or both of the spouses currently has in any real or personal property, including, but not limited to, the retirement benefits of the spouses, and that was acquired by either or both of the spouses during the marriage;

"(iii) Except as otherwise provided in this section, all income and appreciation on separate property, due to the labor, monetary, or in-kind contribution of either or both of the spouses that occurred during the marriage;

"(iv) A participant account, as defined in Section 145.71 of the Revised Code, of either of the spouses, to the extent of the following: the monies that have been deferred by a continuing member or participating employee, as defined in that section, and that have been transmitted to the Ohio public employees deferred compensation board during the marriage and any income that is derived from the investment of those monies during the marriage; the monies that have been deferred by an officer or employee of a municipal corporation and that have been transmitted to the governing board, administrator, depository, or trustee of the deferred compensation program of the municipal corporation during the marriage and any income that is derived from the investment of those monies during the marriage; or the monies that have been deferred by an officer or employee of a government unit, as defined in section 145.74 of the Revised Code, and that have been transmitted to the governing board, as defined in that section, during the marriage and any income that is derived from the investment of those monies during the marriage.

"(b) 'Marital property' does not include any separate property.

"(4) 'Passive income' means income acquired other than as a result of the labor, monetary, or in-kind contribution of either spouse.

"(5) 'Personal property' includes both tangible and intangible personal property.

"(6)(a) 'Separate property' means all real and personal property and any interest in real or personal property and any interest in real or personal property that is found by the court to be any of the following:

"(i) An inheritance by one spouse by bequest, devise, or descent during the course of the marriage;

"(ii) Any real or personal property or interest in real or personal property that was acquired by one spouse prior to the date of the marriage;

"(iii) Passive income and appreciation acquired from separate property by one spouse during the marriage;

"(iv) Any real or personal property or interest in real or personal property acquired by one spouse after a decree of legal separation issued under section 3105.17 of the Revised Code;

"(v) Any real or personal property or interest in real or personal property that is excluded by a valid antenuptial agreement;

"(vi) Compensation to a spouse for the spouse's personal injury, except for a loss of marital earnings and compensation for expenses paid from marital assets;

"(vii) Any gift of any real or personal property or of an interest in real or personal property that is made after the date of the marriage and that is proven by clear and convincing evidence to have been given to only one spouse.

"(b) The commingling of separate property with other property of any type does not destroy the identity of the separate property as separate property, except when the separate property is not traceable.

"(B) In divorce proceedings, the court shall, and in legal separation proceedings upon the request of either spouse, the court may, determine what constitutes marital property and what constitutes separate property. In either case, upon making such a determination, the court shall divide the marital and separate property equitably between the spouses, in accordance with this section. For purposes of this section, the court has jurisdiction over all property in which one or both spouses have an interest.

"(C)(1) Except as provided in this division or division (E) of this section, the division of marital property shall be equal. If an equal division of marital property would be inequitable, the court shall not divide the marital property equally but instead shall divide it between the spouses in the manner the court determines equitable. In making a division of marital property, the court shall consider all relevant factors, including those set forth in division (F) of this section.

"(2) Each spouse shall be considered to have contributed equally to the production and acquisition of marital property.

"(3) The court shall provide for an equitable division of marital property under this section prior to making any award of spousal support to either spouse under section 3105.18 of the Revised Code, and without regard to any spousal support so awarded.

"(4) If the marital property includes a participant account, as defined in section 145.71 of the Revised Code, the court shall not order the division or disbursement of the monies and income described in division (A)(3)(a)(iv) of this section to occur in a manner that is inconsistent with the law, rules, or plan governing the deferred compensation program involved or prior to the time the spouse in whose name the participant account is maintained commences receipt of the monies and income credited to the account in accordance with that law, rules, and plan.

"(D) Except as otherwise provided in division (E) of this section or by another provision of this section, the court shall disburse a spouse's separate property to that spouse. If a court does not disburse a spouse's separate property to that spouse, the court shall make written findings of fact that explain the factors that it considered in making its determination that the spouse's separate property should not be disbursed to that spouse.

"(E)(1) The court may make a distributive award to facilitate, effectuate, or supplement a division of marital property. The court may require any distributive award to be secured by a lien on the payor's specific marital property or separate property.

"(2) The court may make a distributive award in lieu of a division of marital property in order to achieve equity between the spouses, if the court determines that a division of the marital property in kind or in money would be impractical or burdensome.

"(3) If a spouse has engaged in financial misconduct, including, but not limited to, the dissipation, destruction, concealment, or fraudulent disposition of assets, the court may compensate the offended spouse with a distributive award or with a greater award of marital property.

"(F) In making a division of marital property and in determining whether to make and the amount of any distributive award under this section, the court shall consider all of the following factors:

"(1) The duration of the marriage;

"(2) The assets and liabilities of the spouses;

"(3) The desirability of awarding the family home, or the right to reside in the family home for reasonable periods of time, to the spouse with custody of the children of the marriage;

"(4) The liquidity of the property to be distributed;

"(5) The economic desirability of retaining intact an asset or an interest in an asset;

"(6) The tax consequences of the property division upon the respective awards to be made to each spouse;

"(7) The costs of sale, if it is necessary that an asset be sold to effectuate an equitable distribution of property;

"(8) Any division or disbursement of property made in a separation agreement that was voluntarily entered into by the spouses;

"(9) Any other factor that the court expressly finds to be relevant and equitable.

"(G) In any order for the division or disbursement of property or a distributive award made pursuant to this section, the court shall make written findings of fact that support the determination that the marital property has been equitably divided and shall specify the dates it used in determining the meaning of 'during the marriage.'

"(H) Except as otherwise provided in this section, the holding of title to property by one spouse individually or by both spouses in a form of co-ownership does not determine whether the property is marital property or separate property.

"(I) A division or disbursement of property or a distributive award made under this section is not subject to future modification by the court.

"(J) The court may issue any orders under this section that it determines equitable, including, but not limited to, either of the following types of orders:

"(1) An order granting a spouse the right to use the marital dwelling or any other marital property or separate property for any reasonable period of time;

"(2) An order requiring the sale or encumbrancing of any real or personal property, with the proceeds from the sale and the funds from any loan secured by the encumbrance to be applied as determined by the court." (As eff. 11-5-92.)

R.C. 3105.18 amended to provide: "(A) As used in this section, 'spousal support' means any payment or payments to be made to a spouse or former spouse, or to a third party for the benefit of a spouse or a former spouse, that is both for sustenance and for support of the spouse or former spouse. 'Spousal support' does not include any payment made to a spouse or former spouse, or to a third party for the benefit of a spouse or former spouse, that is made as part of a division or distribution of property or a distributive award under section 3105.171 of the Revised Code.

"(B) In divorce and legal separation proceedings, upon the request of either party and after the court determines the division or disbursement of property under section 3105.171 of the Revised Code, the court of common pleas may award reasonable spousal support to either party. During the pendency of any divorce, or legal separation proceeding, the court may award reasonable temporary spousal support to either party.

"An award of spousal support may be allowed in real or personal property, or both, or by decreeing a sum of money, payable either in gross or by installments, from future income or otherwise, as the court considers equitable.

"Any award of spousal support made under this section shall terminate upon the death of either party, unless the order containing the award expressly provides otherwise.

"(C)(1) In determining whether spousal support is appropriate and reasonable, and in determining the nature, amount, and terms of payment, and duration of spousal support, which is payable either in gross or in installments, the court shall consider all of the following factors:

"(a) The income of the parties, from all sources, including, but not limited to, income derived from property divided, disbursed, or distributed under section 3105.171 of the Revised Code;

"(b) The relative earning abilities of the parties;

"(c) The ages and the physical, mental, and emotional conditions of the parties;

"(d) The retirement benefits of the parties;

"(e) The duration of the marriage;

"(f) The extent to which it would be inappropriate for a party, because he will be custodian of a minor child of the marriage, to seek employment outside the home;

"(g) The standard of living of the parties established during the marriage;

"(h) The relative extent of education of the parties;

104

"(i) The relative assets and liabilities of the parties, including but not limited to any court-ordered payments by the parties;

"(j) The contribution of each party to the education, training, or earning ability of the other party, including, but not limited to, any party's contribution to the acquisition of a professional degree of the other party;

"(k) The time and expense necessary for the spouse who is seeking spousal support to acquire education, training, or job experience so that the spouse will be qualified to obtain appropriate employment, provided the education, training or job experience, and employment is, in fact, sought;

"(l) The tax consequences, for each party, of an award of spousal support;

"(m) The lost income production capacity of either party that resulted from that party's marital responsibilities;

"(n) Any other factor that the court expressly finds to be relevant and equitable.

"(2) In determining whether spousal support is reasonable and in determining the amount and terms of payment of spousal support, each party shall be considered to have contributed equally to the production of marital income.

"(D) In an action brought solely for an order for legal separation under section 3105.17 of the Revised Code, any continuing order for periodic payments of money entered pursuant to this section is subject to further order of the court upon changed circumstances of either party.

"(E) If a continuing order for periodic payments of money as alimony is entered in a divorce or dissolution of marriage action that is determined on or after May 2, 1986, and before January 1, 1991, or if a continuing order for periodic payments of money as spousal support is entered in a divorce or dissolution of marriage action that is determined on or after January 1, 1991, the court that enters the decree of divorce or dissolution of marriage does not have jurisdiction to modify the amount or terms of the alimony or spousal support unless the court determines that the circumstances of either party have changed and unless one of the following applies:

"(1) In the case of a divorce, the decree or separation agreement of the parties to the divorce that is incorporated into the decree contains a provision specifically authorizing the court to modify the amount or terms of alimony or spousal support.

"(2) In the case of a dissolution of marriage, the separation agreement that is approved by the court and incorporated into the decree contains a provision specifically authorizing the court to modify the amount or terms of alimony or spousal support.

"(F) For purposes of divisions (D) and (E) of this section, a change in the circumstances of a party includes, but is not limited to, any increase or involuntary decrease in the party's wages, salary, bonuses, living expenses, or medical expenses.

"(G) Each order for alimony made or modified by a court on or after December 31, 1993, shall include as part of the order a general provision, as described in division (A)(1) of section 3113.21 of the Revised Code, requiring the withholding or deduction of wages or assets of the obligor under the order as described division (D) of section 3113.21 of the Revised Code or another type of appropriate requirement as described in division (D)(6), (D)(7), or (H) of that section, to ensure that withholding or deduction from the wages or assets of the obligor is available from the commencement of the support order for collection of the support and of any arrearages that occur; a statement requiring all parties to the order to notify the child support enforcement agency in writing of their current mailing address, their current residence address, and of any changes in either address; and a notice that the requirement to notify the agency of all changes in either address continues until further notice from the court.

"If any person required to pay alimony under an order made or modified by a court on or after December 1, 1986, and before January 1, 1991, or any person required to pay spousal support under an order made or modified by a court on or after January 1, 1991, is found in contempt of court for failure to make alimony or spousal support payments under the order, the court that makes the finding, in addition to any other penalty or remedy imposed, shall assess all court costs arising out of the contempt proceeding against the person and shall require the person to pay any reasonable attorney's fees of any adverse party, as determined by the court, that arose in relation to the act of contempt.

"(H) In divorce or legal separation proceedings, the court may award reasonable attorney's fees to either party at any stage of the proceedings, including, but not limited to, any appeal, any proceeding arising from a motion to modify a prior order or decree, and any proceeding to enforce a prior order or decree, if it determines that the other party has the ability to pay the attorney's fees that the court awards. When the court determines whether to award reasonable attorney's fees to any party pursuant to this division, it shall determine whether either party will be prevented from fully litigating his rights and adequately protecting his interests if it does not award reasonable attorney's fees." (As eff. 1-1-91, 4-11-91 and 12-31-93.)

14-32B   Service of Process; Jurisdiction as to Property.

An indigent plaintiff in a divorce action may require the appropriate public officials to effect service by publication without prepayment by the indigent plaintiff of the costs of publication. Blevins v. Mowrey, 45 Ohio St. 3d 20, 543 N.E.2d 99 (1989).

14-32C   Action after Divorce.

In general, the amendments to R.C. 3105.17 and R.C. 3105.18, and the enactment of R.C. 3105.171, quoted at 14-32A above, modified the domestic relations law of Ohio to provide for spousal support and the division of marital property and separate property, instead of for alimony. (As eff. 1-1-91.)

14-32D   As a Lien.

R.C. 3105.06 amended to change "alimony" to "legal separation." (As eff. 1-1-91.)

A judgment of divorce, incorporating a separation agreement by which one spouse deeds her interest in the marital residence to the other spouse in return for a note and mortgage, does not constitute a lien on such property where the judgment has not been properly recorded in the county recorder's office pursuant to R.C. 2329.02. Vickroy v. Vickroy, 44 Ohio App. 3d 210, 542 N.E.2d 700 (1988).

In general, the amendments to R.C. 3105.17 and R.C. 3105.18, and the enactment of R.C. 3105.171, quoted at 14-32A above, modified the domestic relations law of Ohio to provide for spousal support and the division of marital property and separate property, instead of for alimony. (As eff. 1-1-91.)

14-32E   Modification of Decree.

In general, the amendments to R.C. 3105.17 and R.C. 3105.18, and the enactment of R.C. 3105.171, quoted at 14-32A above, modified the domestic relations law of Ohio to provide for spousal support and the division of marital property and separate property, instead of for alimony. (As eff. 1-1-91.)

Civil Rule 75(I) amended without material change as to the statement in the Parent Volume. (As eff. 7-1-94.)

14-32F   Support of Children.

R.C. 3105.21 amended to provide as follows:

"(A) Upon satisfactory proof of the causes in the complaint for divorce, annulment, or legal separation, the court of common pleas shall make an order for the disposition, care, and maintenance of the children of the marriage, as is in their best interests, and in accordance with section 3109.04 of the Revised Code.

"(B) Upon the failure of proof of the causes in the complaint, the court may make the order for the disposition, care, and maintenance of any dependent child of the marriage as is in the child's best interest, and in accordance with section 3109.04 of the Revised Code.

"(C) Each order for child support made or modified under this section on or after December 1, 1986, shall be accompanied by one or more orders described in division (D) or (H) of section 3113.21 of the Revised Code, whichever is appropriate under the requirements of that section, a statement requiring all parties to the order to notify the child support enforcement agency in writing of their current mailing address, their current residence address, and any changes in either address, and a notice that the requirement to notify the agency of all changes in either address continues until further notice from the court. Any court of common pleas that makes or modifies an order for child support under this section on or after April 12, 1990, shall comply with sections 3113.21 to 3113.219 of the Revised Code. If any person required to pay child support under an order made under this section on or after April 15, 1985, or modified on or after December 1, 1986, is found in contempt of court for failure to make support payments under the order, the court that makes the finding, in addition to any other penalty or remedy imposed, shall assess all court costs arising out of the contempt proceeding against the person and require the person to pay any reasonable attorney's fees of any adverse party, as determined by the court, that arose in relation to the act of contempt.

"(D) Notwithstanding section 3109.01 of the Revised Code, if a court issues a child support order under this section, the order shall remain in effect beyond the child's eighteenth birthday as long as the child continuously attends on a full-time basis any recognized and accredited high school. Any parent ordered to pay support under a child support order issued under this section shall continue to pay support under the order, including during seasonal vacation periods, until the order terminates." (As eff. 4-16-92).

CHAPTER 15: INFANTS, INSANE PERSONS AND OTHER INCOMPETENTS

DIVISION 15-1: IN GENERAL

DIVISION 15-1: IN GENERAL

SECTION 15-12: INSANE PERSONS; OTHER INCOMPETENTS GENERALLY

15-12B Criterion of Capacity.

In matters which do not conflict with a guardian's authority, an adjudication of incompetency is only prima facie evidence of the ward's incapacity. Actions by ward in changing the beneficiaries on her bank accounts was not contrary to her guardian's authority. Such actions will be upheld when the evidence is sufficient to overcome the rebuttable presumption of incompetency. Witt v. Ward, 60 Ohio App. 3d 21, 573 N.E.2d 201, cert. denied, 43 Ohio St. 3d 712, 541 N.E.2d 78 (1989).

15-12C Presumptions.

See discussion of Witt v. Ward at 15-12B above.

15-12D Lucid Interval.

See discussion of Witt v. Ward at 15-12B above.

15-12K Restoration of Sanity or Competency.

R.C. 5122.21 amended to provide: "(A) The chief clinical officer shall as frequently as practicable, and at least once every thirty days, examine or cause to be examined every patient and, whenever he determines that the conditions justifying involuntary hospitalization or commitment no longer obtain, shall, except as provided in division (C) of this section, discharge the patient not under indictment or conviction for crime and immediately make a report of the discharge to the department of mental health. The chief clinical officer may discharge a patient who is under indictment, sentence of imprisonment, or on probation or parole ten days after written notice of intent to discharge the patient has been given by personal service or certified mail, return receipt requested, to the court having criminal jurisdiction over the patient. Except when the patient was found not guilty by reason of insanity and his commitment is pursuant to section 2945.40 of the Revised Code, the chief clinical officer has final authority to discharge a patient who is under indictment, sentence of imprisonment, or on probation or parole.

"(B) After a finding pursuant to section 5122.15 of the Revised Code that a person is a mentally ill person subject to hospitalization by court order, the chief clinical officer of the hospital or agency to which the person is ordered or to which the person is transferred under section 5122.20 of the Revised Code, may, except as provided in division (C) of this section, grant a discharge without the consent or authorization of any court.

"Upon discharge, the chief clinical officer shall notify the court that caused the judicial hospitalization of the discharge from the hospital.

"(C) Whenever the chief clinical officer intends to discharge a person who was found incompetent to stand trial and whose commitment resulted from an affidavit filed pursuant to division (C) of section 2945.38 of the Revised Code, the chief clinical officer shall give notice of the discharge to the prosecutor and the attorney the board designated, if any, at least ten days prior to the date on which the person will be discharged. Whenever the chief clinical officer intends to discharge a person who was found not guilty by reason of insanity and whose commitment was pursuant to section 2945.40 of the Revised Code, the chief clinical officer shall not discharge the person until he has complied with division (F) of section 2945.40 of the Revised Code." (As eff. 7-1-89.)

R.C. 5122.38 provides: "Each individual now or formerly hospitalized pursuant to this chapter or former Chapter 5123 of the Revised Code, is entitled to an adjudication of competency or incompetency or termination of guardianship upon written request by any such individual, his guardian, or the chief clinical officer to the probate court. The court, on its own motion, may initiate such a hearing.

"Upon filing of such application, or on the court's own motion, notice of the purpose, time, and place of the hearing shall be given to the person upon whose affidavit such adjudication was made, to the guardian of the applicant, and to his spouse at his residence, if such address is known.

"Upon hearing, if it is proven that such applicant is competent, the court shall so find and enter the finding on its journal. The adjudicating court shall send a transcript of the adjudication to the county of the patient's residence." (As eff. 7-1-89.)

SECTION 15-13: GUARDIAN AND WARD GENERALLY

15-13A Rules.

R.C. 2109.37 amended without change as to the statement in the Parent Volume. (As eff. 3-22-89, 10-6-92 and 10-6-94.)

The first paragraph of R.C. 2111.05 amended to change designation of "executive secretary" to "executive director."

The third and fourth paragraphs of R.C. 2111.05 amended to provide:

"If the court refuses to grant the application to terminate the guardianship, or if no such application is presented to the court, the guardian only shall be required to render account upon the termination of his guardianship, upon order of the probate court made upon its own motion, or upon the order of the court made on the motion of a person interested in the wards or their property, for good cause shown, and set forth upon the journal of the court.

"If the estate is ten thousand dollars or less and the ward is a minor, the court, without the appointment of a guardian by the court, or the giving of bond, may authorize the deposit in a depository authorized to receive fiduciary funds, payable to the guardian when appointed, or to the ward when he attains majority, or the court may authorize delivery to the natural guardian of the minor, to the person by whom the minor is maintained, to the executive director who is responsible for the administration of children services in the county, or to the minor himself." (As eff. 9-10-91.)

Guardians do not have the authority to change the names of beneficiaries of p.o.d. and joint and survivorship accounts, giving one guardian a personal interest in the accounts, when such a change does not relate to managing or preserving the ward's estate and when it is not in the best interest of the ward. Witt v. Ward, 60 Ohio App. 3d 21, 573 N.E.2d 201, cert. denied, 43 Ohio St. 3d 712, 541 N.E.2d 78 (1989).

15-13B Appointment; Bond; Accounting.

R.C. 2109.12 amended without material change as to the statement in the Parent Volume. (As eff. 10-8-92.)

R.C. 2111.02 et seq., amended to provide, in part, for appointment of guardian upon seven days' notice. (As eff. 1-1-90.)

R.C. 2111.091, effective March 6, 1992, provides:

"No attorney who represents any person other than himself who is appointed as a guardian under this chapter or under any other provision of the Revised Code shall do either of the following:

"(A) Act as a person with co-responsibility for any guardianship asset for which the guardian he represents is responsible;

"(B) Be a cosignatory on any financial account related to the guardianship, including any checking account, savings account, or other banking or trust account." (As eff. 3-6-92.)

15-13E Leases; Mortgages.

R.C. 2109.47 amended without material change as to the statement in the Parent Volume. (As eff. 10-8-92.)

15-13F Improvement of Real Estate.

R.C. 2111.36 amended without material change as to the statement in the Parent Volume. (As eff. 10-8-92.)

CHAPTER 16: JUDGMENTS

DIVISION 16-1: IN GENERAL

SECTION 16-11:   JURISDICTION GENERALLY
16-11D   Venue

SECTION 16-12:   RES JUDICATA
16-12A   Rules

SECTION 16-14:   APPEALS
16-14A   Rules; Reversal

SECTION 16-15:   MODIFICATION AND VACATION
16-15C   Direct Attack After Term

SECTION 16-17:   PROBATE AND OTHER COURTS OF LIMITED JURISDICTION
16-17B   Jurisdiction of Probate Court
16-17C   Municipal Court
16-17D   County Courts

DIVISION 16-2 CONFLICT BETWEEN COURTS; CONFLICT OF LAWS

SECTION 16-21:   GENERALLY; FOREIGN JUDGMENTS
16-21A   Between States

SECTION 16-22:   EXCLUSIVENESS OF JURISDICTION FIRST OBTAINED
16-22A   Rules

SECTION 16-23:   UNITED STATES COURTS
16-23D   Conflicting Jurisdiction of Bankruptcy Courts

DIVISION 16-4: LIMITATION OF ACTIONS

SECTION 16-41:   GENERALLY
16-41A   Rules
16-41C   Commencement of Action

SECTION 16-42:   EXCEPTIONS TO AND SUSPENSION OF STATUTE
16-42B   Personal Disabilities; Absence
16-42G   Trusts; Vendees

SECTION 16-43:   SOLDIERS' AND SAILORS' CIVIL RELIEF ACT OF 1940
16-43C   Statutes of Limitation
16-43E   Eviction
16-43F   Land Contracts
16-43G   Termination of Leases
16-43H   Mortgages and Trust Deeds

113

DIVISION 16-1: IN GENERAL

SECTION 16-11: JURISDICTION GENERALLY

16-11D Venue.

Civil Rule 3(G) amended to provide, in part: "No order, judgment, or decree shall be void or subject to collateral attack solely on the ground that there was improper venue; however, nothing here shall affect the right to appeal an error of court concerning venue.'' (As eff. 7-1-91.)

Further research: O Jur 3d, Venue §§ 1, 3.

SECTION 16-12: RES JUDICATA

16-12A Rules.

Generally, a change in decisional law which might arguably reverse the outcome in a prior civil action does not bar the application of the doctrine of res judicata. Since the doctrine of res judicata serves important public and private interests, exceptions to the doctrine's application should be narrowly construed. National Amusements, Inc. v. Springdale, 53 Ohio St. 3d 60, 558 N.E.2d 1178, reh'g denied, 54 Ohio St. 3d 710, 561 N.E.2d 945 (1990), and cert. denied, 111 S. Ct. 1075 (1991) (a prior action upholding the validity of a cinema tax cannot be relitigated solely because a subsequent U.S. Supreme Court case struck down a similar tax on First Amendment grounds).

A declaratory judgment action to determine the validity of a condominium association's right of first refusal does not operate as res judicata to bar a subsequent action to foreclose a lien for unpaid assessments. Jamestown Village Condominium Owners Ass'n v. Market Media Research, Inc., 96 Ohio App. 3d 678 (1994), appeal dismissed, 71 Ohio St. 3d 1444, 644 N.E.2d 406 (1995).

SECTION 16-14: APPEALS

16-14A Rules; Reversal.

Where a plaintiff obtained judgment on an account and a judgment for attorney fees, but the award of attorney fees was reversed on appeal, the reversal had the effect of vacating the judgment lien as to the attorney fees. Therefore, as of the date foreclosure was ordered, plaintiff did not hold a valid judgment lien as to the attorney fee award, even though the judgment for attorney fees was awarded again on remand. The plaintiff may reassert its judgment lien as a result of the decision on remand, but the priority of that lien will have to be redetermined. Merrill Lynch, Pierce, Fenner & Smith, Inc. v. Stark, 75 Ohio App. 3d 611, 600 N.E.2d 354, appeal after remand, 1991 Ohio App. LEXIS 4228 (Ohio Ct. App., Cuyahoga County Aug. 29, 1991), review pending, 62 Ohio St. 3d. 1502, 583 N.E.2d 973, mot. denied, 65 Ohio St. 3d 1469, 603 N.E.2d 250, aff'd, 65 Ohio St. 3d 312, 603 N.E.2d 997, mot. overruled, 62 Ohio St. 3d 1494, 583 N.E.2d 966 (1992).

Judgment for foreclosure is not a final, appealable order when other claims of the lender against the borrowers for fraud and for money damages on the borrowers' note have not been disposed of by the trial court. Federal Home Loan Mtg. Corp. v. Wuest, 64 Ohio App. 3d 513, 582 N.E.2d 7 (1989).

SECTION 16-15: MODIFICATION AND VACATION

16-15C Direct Attack After Term.

The existence of a valid defense would constitute sufficient grounds for relief from a cognovit judgment. However, plaintiff's acceptance of a late payment will not be sufficient to permit vacation of the judgment, where the late payment was only inadvertently accepted and was thereafter refunded. Society Nat'l Bank v. Val Halla Athletic Club & Rec. Ctr., Inc., 63 Ohio App. 3d 413, 579 N.E.2d 234, mot. overruled, 45 Ohio St. 3d 715 (1989).

SECTION 16-17: PROBATE AND OTHER COURTS OF LIMITED JURISDICTION

16-17B Jurisdiction of Probate Court.

R.C. 2101.24 amended to provide in part:

"(A)(1) Except as otherwise provided by law, the probate court has exclusive jurisdiction:

...

"(j) To construe wills;

"(k) To render declaratory judgments, including, but not limited to, those rendered pursuant to section 2107.084 of the Revised Code;

"(l) To direct and control the conduct of fiduciaries and settle their accounts;

"(m) To authorize the sale or lease of any estate created by will if the estate is held in trust, on petition by the trustee;

"(n) To terminate a testamentary trust in any case in which a court of equity may do so;

"(o) To hear and determine actions to contest the validity of wills;

"(p) To make a determination of the presumption of death of missing persons and to adjudicate the property rights and obligations of all parties affected by the presumption;

"(q) To hear and determine an action commenced pursuant to section 3107.41 of the Revised Code to obtain the release of information pertaining to the birth name of the adopted person and the identity of his biological parents and biological siblings;

"(r) To act for and issue orders regarding wards pursuant to section 2111.50 of the Revised Code;

"(s) To hear and determine actions against sureties on the bonds of fiduciaries appointed by the probate court;

"(t) To hear and determine actions involving informed consent for medication of persons hospitalized pursuant to section 5122.141 or 5122.15 of the Revised Code;

"(u) To hear and determine actions relating to durable powers of attorney for health care as described in division (D) of section 1337.16 of the Revised Code;

"(v) To hear and determine actions commenced by objecting individuals, in accordance with section 2133.05 of the Revised Code;

"(w) To hear and determine complaints that pertain to the use or continuation, or the withholding or withdrawal, of life-sustaining treatment in connection with certain patients allegedly in a terminal condition or in a permanently unconscious state pursuant to division (E) of section 2133.08 of the Revised Code, in accordance with that division;

"(x) To hear and determine applications that pertain to the withholding or withdrawal of nutrition and hydration from certain patients allegedly in a permanently unconscious state pursuant to section 2133.09 of the Revised Code, in accordance with that section;

"(y) To hear and determine applications of attending physicians in accordance with division (B) of section 2133.15 of the Revised Code;

"(z) To hear and determine actions relative to the use or continuation of comfort care in connection with certain principals under durable powers of attorney for health care, declarants under declarations, or patients in accordance with division (E) of either section 1337.16 or 2133.12 of the Revised Code.

"(2) In addition to the exclusive jurisdiction conferred upon the probate court by division (A)(1) of this section, the probate court shall have exclusive jurisdiction over a particular subject matter if both of the following apply:

"(a) Another section of the Revised Code expressly confers jurisdiction over that subject matter upon the probate court;

"(b) No section of the Revised Code expressly confers jurisdiction over that subject matter upon any other court or agency.

"(B)(1) The probate court has concurrent jurisdiction with, and the same powers at law and in equity as, the general division of the court of common pleas to issue writs and orders, and to hear and determine actions as follows:

"(a) If jurisdiction relative to a particular subject matter is stated to be concurrent in a section of the Revised Code or has been construed by judicial decision to be concurrent, any action that involves that subject matter;

"(b) Any action that involves an inter vivos trust; a trust created pursuant to section 1339.51 of the Revised Code; a charitable trust or foundation; subject to divisions (A)(1)(u) and (z) of this section, a power of attorney, including, but not limited to, a durable power of attorney; the medical treatment of a competent adult; or a writ of habeas corpus.

"(2) Any action that involves a concurrent jurisdiction subject matter and that is before the probate court may be transferred by the probate court, on its order, to the general division of the court of common pleas.

"(C) The probate court has plenary power at law and in equity to dispose fully of any matter that is properly before the court, unless the power is expressly otherwise limited or denied by a section of the Revised Code.

"(D) The jurisdiction acquired by a probate court over a matter or proceeding is exclusive of that of any other probate court, except when otherwise provided by law." (As eff. 4-16-93.)

A probate court does not have jurisdiction to render a declaratory judgment as to the validity or enforceability of a contract entered into by an executor and certain beneficiaries of a will providing for a division of the estate different from that provided in the will. Such contracts are not directly related to the administration of the testator's estate. Zuendel v. Zuendel, 63 Ohio St. 3d 733, 590 N.E.2d 1260 (1992).

16-17C Municipal Court.

R.C. 1901.18 provides: "(A) Except as otherwise provided in this division or section 1901.181 of the Revised Code, subject to the monetary jurisdiction of municipal courts as set forth in section 1901.17 of the Revised Code, a municipal court has original jurisdiction within its territory in all of the following actions and to perform all of the following functions:

"(1) In any civil action, of whatever nature or remedy, of which judges of county courts have jurisdiction;

"(2) In any action or proceeding at law for the recovery of money or personal property of which the court of common pleas has jurisdiction;

"(3) In any action at law based on contract, to determine, preserve, and enforce all legal and equitable rights involved in the contract, to decree an accounting, reformation, or cancellation of the contract, and to hear and determine all legal and equitable remedies necessary or proper for a complete determination of the rights of the parties to the contract;

"(4) In any action or proceeding for the sale of personal property under chattel mortgage, lien, encumbrance, or other charge, for the foreclosure and marshalling of liens on such personal property and, for the rendering of personal judgment in the action or proceeding;

"(5) In any action or proceeding to enforce the collection of its own judgments, or the judgments rendered by any court within the territory to which the muni-cipal court has succeeded, and to subject the interest of a judgment debtor in personal property to satisfy judgments enforceable by the municipal court;

"(6) In any action or proceeding in the nature of interpleader;

"(7) In any action of replevin;

"(8) In any action of forcible entry and detainer;

"(9) In any action concerning the issuance and enforcement of temporary protection orders pursuant to section 2919.26 of the Revised Code or anti-stalking protection orders pursuant to section 2903.213 of the Revised Code;

"(10) If the municipal court has a housing or environmental division, in any action over which the division is given exclusive jurisdiction by section 1901.181 of the Revised Code, provided that, except as specified in division (C) of that section, no judge of the court other than the judge of the division shall hear or determine any action over which the division has jurisdiction;

"(11) In any action brought pursuant to division (I) of section 3733.11 of the Revised Code, if the residential premises that are the subject of the action are located within the territorial jurisdiction of the court;

"(12) In any civil action as described in division (B)(1) of section 3767.41 of the Revised Code that relates to a public nuisance, and, to the extent any provision of this chapter conflicts or is inconsistent with a provision of that section, the provision of that section shall control in the civil action.

"(B) The municipal court of Cleveland also shall have jurisdiction within its territory in all of the following actions and to perform all of the following functions:

"(1) In all actions and proceedings for the sale of real property under lien of a judgment of the municipal court, or a lien for machinery, material, fuel furnished, or labor performed, irrespective of amount, and in such cases the court may proceed to foreclose and marshal all liens, and all vested or contingent rights, to appoint a receiver, and to render personal judgment irrespective of amount in favor of any party;

"(2) In all actions for the foreclosure of a mortgage on real property given to secure the payment of money, the enforcement of a specific lien for money or other encumbrance or charge on real property when the amount claimed by the plaintiff does not exceed ten thousand dollars and the real property is situated within the territory, and in such cases the court may proceed to foreclose all liens and all vested and contingent rights, and proceed to render such judgments, and make such findings and orders, between the parties, in the same manner and to the same extent as in like cases in the court of common pleas;

"(3) In all actions for the recovery of real property situated within the territory to the same extent as courts of common pleas have jurisdiction;

"(4) In all actions for injunction to prevent or terminate violations of the ordinances and regulations of the city of Cleveland enacted or promulgated under the police power of the city of Cleveland, pursuant to Section 3 of Article XVIII, Ohio Constitution, over which the court of common pleas has or may have jurisdiction, and in such case the court may proceed to render such judgments and make such findings and orders in the same manner and to the same extent as in like cases in the court of common pleas." (As eff. 11-5-92.)

R.C. 1901.181 amended to provide: "(A)(1) Except as otherwise provided in this division, and division (A)(2) of this section and subject to section 1901.17 of the Revised Code and to division (C) of this section, if a municipal court has a housing or environmental division, the division has exclusive jurisdiction within the territory of the court in any civil action to enforce any local building, housing, air pollution, sanitation, health, fire, zoning, or safety code, ordinance, or regulation applicable to premises used or intended for use as a place of human habitation, buildings, structures, or any other real property subject to any such code, ordinance, or regulation, and, except in the environmental division of the Franklin County municipal court, in any civil action commenced pursuant to Chapter 1923 or 5321 or sections 5303.03 to 5303.07 of the Revised Code. Except as otherwise provided in division (A)(2) of this section and subject to section 1901.20 of the Revised Code and to division (C) of this section, the housing or environmental division of a municipal court has exclusive jurisdiction within the territory of the court in any criminal action for a violation of any local building, housing, air pollution, sanitation, health, fire, zoning, or safety code, ordinance, or regulation applicable to premises used or intended for use as a place of human habitation, buildings, structures, or any other real property subject to any such code, ordinance, or regulation. Except as otherwise provided in division (A)(2) of this section and subject to division (C) of this section, the housing or environmental division of a municipal court also has exclusive jurisdiction within the territory of the court in any civil action as described in division (B)(1) of section 3767.41 of the Revised Code that relates to a public nuisance. To the extent any provision of this chapter conflicts or is inconsistent with a provision of section 3767.41 of the Revised Code, the provision of that section shall control in a civil action described in division (B)(1) of that section.

"(2) If a municipal court has an environmental division, if the mayor of any municipal corporation within the territory of the municipal court conducts a mayor's court, and if any action described in division (A)(1) of this section as being within the jurisdiction of the environmental division otherwise is within the jurisdiction of the mayor's court, as set forth in section 1905.01 of the Revised Code, the jurisdiction of the environmental division over the action is concurrent with the jurisdiction of that mayor's court over the action.

"(B) A counterclaim or cross-claim does not affect the jurisdiction of the housing or environmental division even if the subject matter of the counterclaim or cross-claim would not be within the jurisdiction of the housing division as authorized by this section if it were filed as an original action.

"(C)(1) If the judge of the environmental division of the Franklin county municipal court is on vacation, sick, or absent, recuses himself, or otherwise is unavailable, the administrative judge of the court, in accordance with the Rules of Superintendence for Municipal Courts and County Courts, shall assign another judge or judges of the court to handle any action or proceeding or, if necessary, all actions and proceedings of the division during the time that its judge is unavailable.

"(2) The Franklin county municipal court may adopt, by rule, procedures for other judges of the court to handle particular proceedings arising out of actions within the jurisdiction of the environmental division of the court when the judge of that division is unable for any reason to handle a particular proceeding at the time, or within the time period, necessary for a timely or appropriate disposition of the proceeding. Upon the adoption of and in accordance with those rules, any judge of the court may handle any proceeding that arises out of an action within the jurisdiction of the environmental division of the court." (As eff. 3-24-92.)

R.C. 1901.19 provides: "(A) Subject to the monetary jurisdiction of municipal courts as set forth in section 1901.17 of the Revised Code, a municipal court and a housing division of a municipal court have jurisdiction within its territory in all of the following actions and to perform all of the following functions:

"(1) To compel attendance of witnesses in any pending action or proceeding in the same manner as the court of common pleas;

"(2) To issue executions on its own judgments;

"(3) In any legal or equitable action or proceeding, to enforce the collection of its own judgments;

"(4) In any civil action or proceeding at law in which the subject matter of the action or proceeding is located within the territory or when the defendant or some one of the defendants resides or is served with summons within the territory;

"(5) To issue and enforce any order of attachment;

"(6) In any action or proceeding in the nature of creditors' bills, and in aid of execution to subject the interest of a judgment debtor in personal property to the payment of the judgment of the court;

"(7) To issue and enforce temporary protection orders pursuant to section 2919.26 of the Revised Code and anti-stalking protection orders pursuant to section 2903.213 of the Revised Code.

"(B) Subject to the limitation set forth in this division, a municipal court or a housing division of a municipal court has jurisdiction outside its territory in a proceeding in aid of execution to subject to the payment of the judgment the interest in personal property of a judgment debtor under a judgment rendered by the court or housing division. The jurisdiction provided under this division includes the county or counties in which the territory of the court in question is situated and any county that is contiguous to that in which the court is located. A court or a housing division that has jurisdiction under this division outside its territory in a proceeding in aid of execution has the same powers, duties, and functions relative to such a proceeding that it has relative to proceedings in aid of execution over which it has jurisdiction other than under this division.

"(C)(1) In any action for garnishment of personal earnings brought in a municipal court, the court has jurisdiction to serve process pursuant to section 2716.05 of the Revised Code upon a garnishee who resides in a county contiguous to that in which the court is located.

"(2) In any action for garnishment of property, other than personal earnings, brought in a municipal court under section 2716.11 of the Revised Code, the court has jurisdiction to serve process pursuant to section 2716.13 of the Revised Code upon a garnishee who resides in a county contiguous to that in which the court is located.

"(3) Whenever a motion for attachment is filed in a municipal court under section 2715.03 of the Revised Code, the court has jurisdiction to serve process pursuant to section 2715.091 of the Revised Code upon a garnishee who resides in a county contiguous to that in which the court is located.

"(D) The municipal court of Cleveland also has jurisdiction in all actions and proceedings in the nature of creditors' bills, and in aid of execution to subject to the interests of a judgment debtor in real or personal property to the payment of a judgment of the municipal court. In such actions and proceedings, the court may proceed to marshal and foreclose all liens on the property irrespective of the amount of the lien, and all vested or contingent rights in the property." (As eff. 11-5-92.)

The Housing Division of the Cleveland Municipal Court lacks subject matter jurisdiction in a case alleging violation of a variance from zoning ordinance. Cleveland v. Sun Oil Co., 62 Ohio App. 3d 732, 577 N.E.2d 431 (1989).

16-17D County Courts.

R.C. 1907.011 amended to give county courts bordering on the Ohio River concurrent jurisdiction on the river with adjacent courts or with Kentucky or West Virginia courts. (As eff. 5-20-92 and 1-17-93.)

DIVISION 16-2: CONFLICT BETWEEN COURTS; CONFLICT OF LAWS

SECTION 16-21: GENERALLY; FOREIGN JUDGMENTS

16-21A Between States.

Mortgagee obtained judgments in Pennsylvania and foreclosed mortgages on Pennsylvania property. Mortgagee then filed foreign judgments in Ohio and sought foreclosure against Ohio real estate. Although the Pennsylvania judgments were entitled to full faith and credit, the foreclosure action in Ohio must be stayed pending the determination of the Pennsylvania court of the deficiency judgment pursuant to Pennsylvania's deficiency statute. Because further enforcement of the Pennsylvania judgments could not be had in Pennsylvania until the determination of the deficiency, enforcement of the judgments filed in Ohio must similarly be stayed until the determination is made. Phenix Fed. Sav. & Loan Ass'n, F.A. v. Ticzon, 68 Ohio App. 3d 268, 588 N.E.2d 222 (1990).

SECTION 16-22: EXCLUSIVENESS OF JURISDICTION FIRST OB-TAINED

16-22A Rules.

Lessee sought to enforce a purchase option by filing suit in Mercer County. In a prior action, in which lessee was not a party, the Franklin County Court of Common Pleas entered a declaratory judgment instructing the lessee to whom it should make its lease payments and the Franklin County Court retained jurisdiction over the matter. The Supreme Court determined that Mercer County had jurisdiction over the litigation involving the purchase option because the property in issue was located in Mercer County; the prior action in Franklin County concerned only distribution of lease payments; lessee was never a party to the Franklin County action; and the issue of the validity of the purchase option under the lease could not be litigated without the lessee as a party. Knowlton Co. v. Knowlton, 63 Ohio St. 3d 677, 590 N.E.2d 1219 (1992).

Pendency of federal action against mortgage company for its alleged violation of Federal Bank Holding Company Act did not prevent trial court from exercising jurisdiction over mortgage foreclosure action. Huntington Mortgage Co. v. Shanker, 92 Ohio App. 3d 144, 634 N.E.2d 641 (1993), dismissed, mot. overruled, 68 Ohio St. 3d 1434, 625 N.E.2d 622 (1994).

SECTION 16-23: UNITED STATES COURTS

16-23D Conflicting Jurisdiction of Bankruptcy Courts.

The reference to 11 U.S.C § 546(h) in the Parent Volume should be to 11 U.S.C. § 546(b).

DIVISION 16-4: LIMITATION OF ACTIONS

SECTION 16-41: GENERALLY

16-41A Rules.

R.C. 2305.06 amended to provide: "Except as provided in sections 126.301 and 1302.98 of the Revised Code, an action upon a specialty or an agreement, contract, or promise in writing shall be brought within fifteen years after the cause thereof accrued." (As eff. 7-1-93.) The reference to R.C. 126.301 pertains to claims made against the State of Ohio or agencies thereof.

R.C. 2305.07 amended to provide: "Except as provided in section 126.301 and 1302.98 of the Revised Code, an action upon a contract not in writing, express or implied, or upon a liability created by statute other than a forfeiture or penalty, shall be brought within six years after the cause thereof accrued." (As eff. 7-1-93.) Again, the reference to R.C. 126.031 deals with claims against the State of Ohio or agencies thereof.

R.C. 2305.09 and 2305.14 amended to delete the reference to R.C. 1304.29 and to substitute, in its place, a reference to R.C. 1304.35. (As eff. 8-19-94.)

Claims against a developer for violation of the condominium disclosure statute accrued when the disclosure statements were given to purchasers, not when the defects were discovered. Such claims may be asserted only by the condominium association (with respect to defects in the common areas and facilities) and by purchasers in privity with the developer, and are subject to the six-year statute of limitations provided in R.C. 2305.07. Arbor Village Condominium Owners Ass'n v. Arbor Village, Ltd., 95 Ohio App. 3d 499, appeal overruled, 71 Ohio St. 3d 1406, 641 N.E.2d 204 (1994).

A negligence claim against the builder-developer of a condominium was barred by the four-year statute of limitations when three instances of underlayment failure were discovered more than four years before the action was brought. Gardens of Bay Landing Condominiums v. Flair Builders, Inc., 96 Ohio App. 3d 353 (1994).

An action based upon the faulty manufacturing of brick which becomes incorporated into real estate, and is therefore real property, is a product liability action for injury to real property and, hence, is subject to the four-year statute of limitations under R.C. 2305.09. Plaintiffs' contention that although they first noticed fragments of brick in 1982, they were not fully aware that the bricks were defective until 1985, was sufficient to create a material issue of fact as to the accrual of the claim. Aglinsky v. Cleveland Bldrs. Supply Co., 68 Ohio App. 3d 810, 589 N.E.2d 1365 (1990).

R.C. 2305.11 amended without change as to the statement in the Parent Volume. (As eff. 4-16-93.)

A pressurized hot water system designed and constructed as part of a can manufacturing plant constitutes an "improvement to real property." Accordingly, an injured worker's action against an architect or engineer is barred by the ten year statute of repose contained in R.C. 2305.131. Sette v. Benham, Blair & Affiliates, 70 Ohio App. 3d 651, 591 N.E.2d 871 (1991), mot. overruled, 61 Ohio St. 3d 1426, 575 N.E.2d 215 (1991).

16-41C Commencement of Action.

R.C. 2305.17 amended to delete the reference to R.C. 1304.29 and to substitute a reference to R.C. 1304.35. (As eff. 8-19-94.)

SECTION 16-42: EXCEPTIONS TO AND SUSPENSION OF STATUTE

16-42B Personal Disabilities; Absence.

R.C. 2305.15 amended to delete the reference to R.C. 1304.29 and to substitute a reference to R.C. 1304.35. (As eff. 8-19-94.)

R.C. 2305.16 amended to delete imprisonment as a disability and to substitute R.C. 1304.35 for a former reference to R.C. 1304.29. Minor, non-substantive changes also made. (As eff. 7-13-90 and 8-19-94.)

16-42G Trusts; Vendees.

R.C. 2305.22 amended to delete the reference to R.C. 1304.29 and to substitute a reference to R.C. 1304.35. (As eff. 8-19-94.)

SECTION 16-43: SOLDIERS' AND SAILORS' CIVIL RELIEF ACT OF 1940

16-43C Statutes of Limitation.

50 U.S.C. Appx. § 525 has been amended to substitute "October 6, 1942" for "the date of enactment of the Soldiers' and Sailors' Civil Relief Act Amendments of 1942." (As eff. 3-18-91.)

16-43E Eviction.

50 U.S.C. Appx. § 530 has been amended to provide that a court may stay eviction proceedings against dependents of a person in the armed forces if the rent does not exceed $1,200 per month. (As eff. 3-18-91.)

16-43F Land Contracts.

50 U.S.C. Appx. § 531 has been amended without material change as to the statement in the Parent Volume. (As eff. 3-18-91.)

16-43G Termination of Leases.

50 U.S.C. Appx. § 534 has been amended without material change as to the statement in the Parent Volume. (As eff. 3-18-91.)

16-43H Mortgages and Trust Deeds.

50 U.S.C. Appx. §§ 526 and 532 have been amended without material change as to the statements in the Parent Volume. (As eff. 3-18-91.)

DIVISION 16-5: TIME

SECTION 16-51: COMPUTATION OF TIME

16-51A Intention; Forfeiture.

Further research: O Jur 3d, Time § 11.

16-51B First Day and Last Day.

Further research: O Jur 3d, Time §§ 17, 18, 20.

SECTION 16-52: SUNDAYS AND HOLIDAYS

16-52A Rules.

Further research: O Jur 3d, Sundays and Holidays §§ 1, 2.

DIVISION 16-6: PARTICULAR TYPES OF JUDGMENTS

SECTION 16-61: DECLARATORY JUDGMENTS

16-61A Generally.

R.C. 2721.03 amended to provide as follows:

"Any person interested under a deed, will, written contract, or other writing constituting a contract, or whose rights, status, or other legal relations are affected by a constitutional provision, statute, rule as defined in section 119.01 of the Revised Code, municipal ordinance, township resolution, contract, or franchise, may have determined any question of construction or validity arising under such instrument, constitutional provision, statute, rule, ordinance, resolution, contract, or franchise and obtain a declaration of rights, status, or other legal relations thereunder.

"The testator of a will may have the validity of the will determined at any time during his lifetime pursuant to sections 2107.081 to 2107.085 of the Revised Code." (As eff. 9-17-91.)

While the Ohio Environmental Protection Agency has a duty to investigate violations, this does not mean that it must conduct on-site testing at the request of a landowner. Where the OEPA has declined to test the property, and has merely reserved the right to conduct future investigations, there is no justiciable controversy that would allow the owner to seek a declaratory judgement that his property is in compliance with the environmental laws. State ex rel. Bolin v. Ohio Environmental Protection Agency, 82 Ohio App. 3d 410, 612 N.E.2d 477 (1992), mot. overruled, 66 Ohio St. 3d 1405, 605 N.E.2d 1262 (1993).

A landowner is not required to exhaust administrative remedies before seeking a declaratory judgment that the current zoning of its property is unconstitutional. Perrico Property Systems v. Independence, 96 Ohio App. 3d 134, appeal dismissed, 71 Ohio St. 3d 1423, 642 N.E.2d 388 (1994).

SECTION 16-65: QUIETING TITLE

16-65C Cloud on Title.

Where the holder of a judgment files a creditor's bill seeking to charge the debtor's beneficial interest in real estate held in trust with the payment of the judgment debt, the creditor does not create a cloud on title by filing an affidavit pursuant to R.C. 5301.252 attesting to the fact that the title to the property may be affected by the creditor's bill. The filing of the affidavit creates no interest in the subject real property or encumbrance on the title. As such, the filing of the affidavit does not support a cause of action to quiet title. Catawba West, Inc. v. Domo, 75 Ohio App. 3d 80, 598 N.E.2d 883 (1991).

SECTION 16-66: REFORMATION

16-66A Definition; Generally.

To reform a deed, a court must find by clear and convincing evidence that the parties were mutually mistaken regarding the contents of the deed. The deed conveying property to James D. Harvey and Son, a partnership consisting of two individuals and their spouses, was properly reformed when it was shown that the spouses were never partners in the partnership. Harvey v. Harvey, 91 Ohio App. 3d 404, 632 N.E.2d 956 (1993).

SECTION 16-68: TRESPASS AND NUISANCE

16-68A Trespass.

Where a person enters a property as an invitee (newspaper carrier), but exceeds the limits of the invitation (crossing through another portion of the property), his status has changed from invitee to licensee. He does not thereby become a trespasser, at least in the absence of entering upon some clearly delimited part of the premises upon which his entry is not permitted. Dayton v. McLaughlin, 50 Ohio App. 3d 69, 552 N.E.2d 965 (1988).

Where property owner failed to show that seven sugar maple trees inadvertently cut by his neighbor had particular value to him, other than as a portion of his woods, replacement or restoration cost of the trees was an inappropriate measure of damages. Schuyler v. Miller, 70 Ohio App. 3d 290, 590 N.E.2d 1358 (1990).

Further research: O Jur 3d, Trespass §§ 1, 2, 35, 36.

A genuine issue of material fact exists as to whether a landowner acted willfully and wantonly in failing to warn known trespassers by stringing or maintaining an unmarked cable in such a manner that there was a great probability that harm would result. Seeholzer v. Kellstone, Inc., 80 Ohio App. 3d 726, 604 N.E.2d 169, mot. overruled, 65 Ohio St. 3d 1478, 604 N.E.2d 169 (1992).

For an invasion of property to constitute a trespass, there must be physical damage to the real property. Odors emanating from a facility, or mere diminution of value, are insufficient to state a trespass claim. Brown v. Scioto Cty. Bd. of Commissioners, 87 Ohio App. 3d 704, 622 N.E.2d 1153 (1993).

The measure of damages for the improper removal of trees from land of another is either the stumpage value of the trees or the diminution in value of the real estate, whichever the plaintiff selects as the damage award. Where the removal was reckless, the plaintiff is entitled to treble damages pursuant to R.C. 901.99. Miller v. Jordan, 87 Ohio App. 3d 819, 623 N.E.2d 219 (1993).

16-68B Nuisance Generally.

The fact that a junkyard operation constitutes a nonconforming use under the zoning laws does not prevent the city from enforcing other ordinances, enacted under the city's police powers, declaring junkyards a nuisance if they are not entirely enclosed by a fence. Grove City v. Weethee, 71 Ohio App. 3d 405, 594 N.E.2d 63 (1991).

The operation of a sewage disposal plant cannot be a common-law public nuisance or an absolute nuisance. However, where a lawful act is so negligently or carelessly done as to have created an unreasonable risk of harm which in due course results in injury to another, a qualified nuisance premised upon negligence may arise. Where the evidence indicates that the sewage plant was in "deplorable condition," with numerous Ohio EPA violations, and that the plaintiffs lost a prospective purchaser, suffered nausea and were unable to fully use their property, a genuine issue of material fact arose as to whether the defendants' conduct constituted a qualified private nuisance. Brown v. Scioto Cty. Bd. of Commissioners, 87 Ohio App. 3d 704, 622 N.E.2d 1153 (1993).

Adjoining landowners who are specially damaged have standing to bring an injunction action for the removal of a building that encroaches on a public street. However, the injunction will not be issued without application of equitable principles. Where the encroachment was not deliberate or willful, and the remedy of removal far exceeds the damages of those who are damaged by the encroachment, and the latter damages are not irreparable, an injunction should not issue.

Miller v. West Carollton, 91 Ohio App. 3d 291, 632 N.E.2d 582 (1993), dismissed, mot. overruled, 69 Ohio St. 3d 1043, 629 N.E.2d 1365 (1994).

A duly licensed and duly regulated sanitary landfill cannot be held liable to adjoining landowners on the basis of absolute nuisance. Instead, to be found liable for maintaining a nuisance, negligence must be established. State ex rel. Schoener v. Hamilton Cty. Bd. of Commissioners, 84 Ohio App. 3d 794, 619 N.E.2d 2 (1992), appeal dismissed, 66 Ohio St. 3d 1502, 613 N.E.2d 648 (1993).

Landlord's violation of a city ordinance mandating that an obstructed drain be cleaned was not negligence per se or an absolute nuisance. A claim based on qualified nuisance also could not be maintained because the tenant had the obligation to clean the drain and a "landlord out of position and control" cannot be held liable for the tenant's negligence under common-law. Ogle v. Kelly, 90 Ohio App. 3d 392, 629 N.E.2d 495 (1993), mot. overruled, 68 Ohio St. 3d 1448, 626 N.E.2d 689 (1994).

Question whether a landfill is an absolute nuisance, i.e., whether collecting and keeping the waste items was inherently dangerous and/or likely to do mischief, is a matter of fact to be determined by a jury. Collova v. Matousek, 85 Ohio App. 3d 440, 620 N.E.2d 104, mot. overruled, 67 Ohio St. 3d 1410, 615 N.E.2d 1044 (1993).

There is no right to a jury trial in a nuisance abatement action brought under R.C. Chapter 3767 (involving chronic felony drug law violations on a parcel of property). State ex rel. Miller v. Anthony, 72 Ohio St. 3d 132 (1995).

16-68E Remedies for Nuisance.

Adjoining landowners who are specially damaged have standing to bring an injunction action for the removal of a building that encroaches on a public street. However, the injunction will not be issued without application of equitable principles. Where the encroachment was not deliberate or willful, and the remedy of removal far exceeds the damages of those who are damaged by the encroachment, and the latter damages are not irreparable, an injunction should not issue. Miller v. West Carollton, 91 Ohio App. 3d 291, 632 N.E.2d 582 (1993), dismissed, mot. overruled, 69 Ohio St. 3d 1043, 629 N.E.2d 1365 (1994).

SECTION 16-69: ESTOPPEL; OTHER TYPES

16-69E Summary Judgment.

Further research: O Jur 3d, Summary Judgment §§ 2-4, 40-42.

DIVISION 16-7: PROCESS AND ITS SERVICE

SECTION 16-71: GENERALLY

16-71C Amended Complaint; Cross-Claim.

Civil Rule 5(B) amended without material change as to the statement in the Parent Volume. (As eff. 7-1-94.)

SECTION 16-75: SERVICE BY PUBLICATION

16-75A Generally.

R.C. 2703.14(A), R.C. 2703.14(E), R.C. 2703.14 (H), R.C. 2703.14(I), R.C. 2703.14(K) and R.C. 2703.14(L) amended to provide that service by publication may be made in the following cases:

"(A) In an action for the recovery of real property or of an estate or interest in real property, when the defendant is not a resident of this state or his place of residence cannot be ascertained;

...

"(E) In connection with giving notice of the admission of a will to probate, when the place of residence of a defendant or other person entitled to notice is not known and cannot with reasonable diligence be ascertained;

...

"(H) In an action against a corporation organized under the laws of this state that has failed to elect officers or to appoint an agent upon whom service of summons can be made and that has no place of doing business in this state;

...

"(I) In an action that relates to or the subject of which is real or personal property in this state, when the defendant has or claims a lien on the property, or an actual or contingent interest in the property, or the relief demanded consists wholly or partly in excluding him from any interest in the property, and the defendant is not a resident of this state or is a foreign corporation or his place of residence cannot be ascertained;

...

"(J) In an action against an executor, administrator, or guardian who has given bond in that capacity in this state but who, at the time of commencement of the action, is not a resident of this state or his place of residence cannot be ascertained;

...

"(L) In an action where the defendant, being a resident of this state, has departed from the county of his residence with intent to delay or defraud his creditors or to avoid the service of a summons, or keeps himself concealed with like intent.'' (As eff. 5-31-90 and 6-23-94.)

16-75D Affidavit.

Civil Rule 4.4(A) amended to provide as follows:

''(1) Except in an action governed by division (A)(2) of this rule, if the residence of a defendant is unknown, service shall be made by publication in actions where such service is authorized by law. Before service by publication can be made, an affidavit of a party or his counsel shall be filed with the court. The affidavit shall aver that service of summons cannot be made because the residence of the defendant is unknown to the affiant, all of the efforts made on behalf of the party to ascertain the residence of the defendant, and that the residence cannot be ascertained with reasonable diligence.

''Upon the filing of the affidavit, the clerk shall cause service of notice to be made by publication in a newspaper of general circulation in the county in which the complaint is filed. If no newspaper is published in that county, then publication shall be in a newspaper published in an adjoining county. The publication shall contain the name and address of the court, the case number, the name of the first party on each side, and the name and last known address, if any, of the person or persons whose residence is unknown. The publication also shall contain a summary statement of the object of the complaint and demand for relief, and shall notify the person to be served that he or she is required to answer within twenty-eight days after the publication. The publication shall be published at least once a week for six successive weeks unless publication for a lesser number of weeks is specifically provided by law. Service shall be complete at the date of the last publication.

''(2) In a divorce, annulment, or legal separation action, if the plaintiff is proceeding *in forma pauperis* and if the residence of the defendant is unknown, service by publication shall be made by posting and mail. Before service by posting and mail can be made, an affidavit of a party or the party's counsel shall be filed with the court. The affidavit shall contain the same averments required by division (A)(2) of this rule and, in addition, shall set forth the defendant's last known address.

''Upon the filing of the affidavit, the clerk shall cause service of notice to be made by posting in a conspicuous place in the courthouse or courthouses in which the general and domestic relations divisions of the court of common pleas for the county are located and in two additional public places in the county that have been designated by local rule for the posting of notices pursuant to this rule. The notice shall contain the same information required by division (A)(2) of this rule to be contained in a newspaper publication. The notice shall be posted in the required locations for six successive weeks.

"The clerk shall also cause the complaint and summons to be mailed by ordinary mail, address correction requested, to the defendant's last known address. The clerk shall obtain a certificate of mailing from the United States Postal Service. If the clerk is notified of a corrected or forwarding address of the defendant within the six-week period that notice is posted pursuant to division (A)(2) of this rule, the clerk shall cause the complaint and summons to be mailed to the corrected or forwarding address. The clerk shall note the name, address, and date of each mailing in the docket.

"After the last week of posting, the clerk shall note on the docket where and when notice was posted. Service shall be complete upon entry of posting." (As eff. 7-1-91.)

16-75E The Publication.

Standards of Title Examination 6.1 and 6.2 amended May 15, 1991, and January 18, 1991, respectively, as follows:

6.1 PROCESS — SERVICE BY PUBLICATION WHEN NAME AND ADDRESS OF DEFENDANT ARE UNKNOWN

[Adopted by OSBA Nov. 17, 1956; Comment A added Nov. 21, 1970]

Problem A:
Where both the name and residence of a Defendant are unknown to the Plaintiff, must the Plaintiff seek a Court order respecting the publication of notice in addition to the affidavit required in Civil Rule 4.4?

Standard A:
Yes, Rule 4.4(a) of the Ohio Rules of Civil Procedure did not overrule R.C. Sec. 2703.24, which requires that, when it appears by affidavit that the name and residence of a necessary party are unknown to the Plaintiff, the Court shall make an order respecting the publication of notice.

6.2 SERVICE BY PUBLICATION — NECESSITY TO IDENTIFY REAL PROPERTY
[Adopted by OSBA NOV. 13, 1971]

Problem A:
Where service is had by publication in an action relating to title to real property, must the publication identify the real property?

Standard A:
Yes.

Comment A:

Neither Rule 4.4(a) of the Ohio Rules of Civil Procedure nor former R.C. section 2703.17 specifies that the publication contain a description of the real property to be subjected to the action. To "identify" the real property does not make it mandatory for the party to set forth entire metes and bounds description. Other methods of identification may be used, and it is suggested that reference to inter-sections, roads and streets, official municipal street numbers or county designated house numbers, county auditor's permanent parcel numbers, or other like descriptions would be sufficient.

SECTION 16-77: SERVICE OUTSIDE OF STATE; NONRESIDENTS

16-77A Generally.

Civil Rule 4.3(A) amended without material change as to the statement in the Parent Volume. (As eff. 7-1-91.)

16-77B Nonresidents.

R.C. 2307.382 provides: "(A) A court may exercise personal jurisdiction over a person who acts directly or by an agent, as to a cause of action arising from the person's:

"(1) Transacting any business in this state;

"(2) Contracting to supply services or goods in this state;

"(3) Causing tortious injury by an act or omission in this state;

"(4) Causing tortious injury in this state by an act or omission outside this state if he regularly does or solicits business, or engages in any other persistent course of conduct, or derives substantial revenue from goods used or consumed or services rendered in this state;

"(5) Causing injury in this state to any person by breach of warranty expressly or impliedly made in the sale of goods outside this state when he might reasonably have expected such person to use, consume, or be affected by the goods in this state, provided that he also regularly does or solicits business, or engages in any other persistent course of conduct, or derives substantial revenue from goods used or consumed or services rendered in this state;

"(6) Causing tortious injury in this state to any person by an act outside this state committed with the purpose of injuring persons, when he might reasonably have expected that some person would be injured thereby in this state;

"(7) Causing tortious injury to any person by a criminal act, any element of which takes place in this state, which he commits or in the commission of which he is guilty of complicity.

"(8) Having an interest in, using, or possessing real property in this state;

"(9) Contracting to insure any person, property, or risk located within this state at the time of contracting.

''(B) For purposes of this section, a person who enters into an agreement, as a principal, with a sales representative for the solicitation of orders in this state is transacting business in this state. As used in this division, 'principal' and 'sales representative' have the same meanings as in section 1335.11 of the Revised Code.

''(C) When jurisdiction over a person is based solely upon this section, only a cause of action arising from acts enumerated in this section may be asserted against him.'' (As eff. 9-9-88.)

A commercial lessee based in Georgia, negotiating with an Ohio-based lessor for space located in Kentucky, is ''transacting business'' for purposes of personal jurisdiction in Ohio when the lessee negotiates, and through the course of dealing becomes obligated, to make payments to its lessor in Ohio. Kentucky Oaks Mall Co. v. Mitchell's Formal Wear, Inc., 53 Ohio St. 3d 73, 559 N.E.2d 477 (1990), cert. denied, 111 S. Ct. 1619 (1991).

CHAPTER 17: JUDICIAL SALES

DIVISION 17-1: IN GENERAL

SECTION 17-11:   INTRODUCTION; FORECLOSURE OF MORTGAGES GENERALLY
17-11B   Methods of Enforcing Mortgages
17-11C   Right of Redemption Under Statutes
17-11D   Concurrent and Successive Actions
17-11E   Setoff and Counterclaim
17-11G   Leases

SECTION 17-12:   LIS PENDENS
17-12A   Rules

SECTION 17-13:   PERSONAL LIABILITY; DEFICIENCY JUDGMENTS; MORATORIA
17-13B   Action Before, After or During Foreclosure

SECTION 17-15:   RIGHTS AND LIABILITIES OF PURCHASERS
17-15A   Title Acquired When
17-15D   Liability for Purchase Price; Defects in Title

DIVISION 17-2: PARTIES; PROCEDURE

SECTION 17-21:   PARTIES GENERALLY
17-21C   Necessary Parties
17-21D   Omission of Lien Holder or Owner
17-21K   Pleading Generally

SECTION 17-23:   GOVERNMENT AS PARTY DEFENDANT
17-23A   United States

SECTION 17-26:   NOTICE; TIME AND PLACE OF SALE
17-26A   Notice of Sale

SECTION 17-28:   CONFIRMATION AND OTHER ORDERS OF COURT
17-28A   Necessity and Effect of Confirmation
17-28B   Refusal of Confirmation; Ordering Resale

DIVISION 17-3: BANKRUPTCY

SECTION 17-31:   GENERALLY
17-31A   Effect of Discharge
17-31C   After-acquired Property
17-31D   Provable Debts
17-31E   Excepted Debts
17-31F   Lease and Executory Contracts

DIVISION 17-4: OTHER CLASSES OF PROCEEDINGS

SECTION 17-41:   EXECUTION SALE
17-41B   Interests Subject to Execution Sale
17-41E   Procedure
17-41G   Reversal or Vacation

DIVISION 17-1: IN GENERAL

SECTION 17-11: INTRODUCTION; FORECLOSURE OF MORTGAGES GENERALLY

17-11B Methods of Enforcing Mortgages.

R.C. 1309.44 amended without material change as to the statement in the Parent Volume. (As eff. 7-1-92.)

17-11C Right of Redemption Under Statutes.

R.C. 2329.33 provides: "In sales of real estate on execution or order of sale, at any time before the confirmation thereof, the debtor may redeem it from sale by depositing in the hands of the Clerk of the Court of Common Pleas to which such execution or order is returnable, the amount of the judgment or decree upon which such lands were sold, with all costs, including poundage, and interest at the rate of eight percent per annum on the purchase money from the day of sale to the time of such deposit, except where the judgment creditor is the purchaser, the interest at such rate on the excess above his claim. The Court of Common Pleas thereupon shall make an order setting aside such sale, and apply the deposit to the payment of such judgment or decree and costs, and award such interest to the purchaser, who shall receive from the officer making the sale the purchase money paid by him and the interest from the clerk." (As eff. 10-1-53.)

A surety bond, standing alone, cannot satisfy the deposit requirements of R.C. 2329.33. Posting of such bond will not effect a redemption of the property. Women's Sav. Bank v. Pappedakes, 38 Ohio St. 3d 143, 527 N.E.2d 792, reh'g denied, 39 Ohio St. 3d 707, 534 N.E.2d 92 (1988).

After real property has been sold by the sheriff at a foreclosure sale, but before confirmation thereof by the trial court, the judgment debtor may redeem its property by depositing sufficient funds with the clerk of courts. Toledo Trust Co. v. Yakumithis Enter. Inc., 35 Ohio App. 3d 31, 519 N.E.2d 425 (1987).

17-11D Concurrent and Successive Actions.

A borrower's action in federal court asserting violations of the Bank Holding Company Act, breach of contract, fraud, estoppel and negligence does not preclude the state courts from exercising jurisdiction over a mortgage foreclosure action brought by the lender. Huntington Mortgage Co. v. Shanker, 92 Ohio App. 3d 144 (1993), appeal overruled, 68 Ohio St. 3d 1434, 625 N.E.2d 622 (1994).

17-11E Setoff and Counterclaim.

A creditor must be in possession of the collateral in order to be responsible for its unjustified impairment. In addition, a guarantor may not avoid liability where the guaranty agreement expressly waives the right to any defense on account of impairment of collateral. Buckeye Fed. Sav. & Loan Ass'n v. Guirlinger, 62 Ohio St. 3d 312, 581 N.E.2d 1352 (1991).

17-11G Leases.

Foreclosure of senior mortgage terminates the right of possession of a lessee who also had an unrecorded executory contract to purchase the property. Lessee was not a necessary party to the foreclosure action. A vendee, however, is a necessary party. Where the mortgagee-purchaser had notice of the equitable rights of the vendee under the executory contract, those rights are not cut off by the foreclosure. Accordingly, the equity of redemption of the vendee survives and remains a burden on the title. Hembree v. Mid-America Fed. Sav. & Loan Ass'n, 64 Ohio App. 3d 144, 580 N.E.2d 1103 (1989).

SECTION 17-12: LIS PENDENS

17-12A Rules.

In a mortgage foreclosure action, all persons acquiring an interest in the property after service and during pendency of the suit are bound by the decree and the sale thereunder. In addition, while the foreclosure motion is pending, no other action may be commenced concerning the property. AVCO Fin. Servs. Loan, Inc. v. Hale, 36 Ohio App. 3d 65, 520 N.E.2d 1378 (1987).

In order for the doctrine of lis pendens to apply, the property described in the complaint must be directly affected by the judgment in the pending suit. Where the plaintiffs were allegedly "squeezed out" of a joint venture interested in acquiring and developing certain real property, their complaint based on claims of breach of fiduciary duty, fraud, breach of contract, negligent misrepresentations, promissory estoppel, unjust enrichment and constructive trust, was insufficient to invoke the doctrine. The property itself was not the essence of the complaint; rather, the real estate essentially constituted a lost business opportunity. Even if the doctrine were held to apply by virtue of the claim for constructive trust, lis pendens does not create a substantive right and is subject to equitable principles. Katz v. Banning, 84 Ohio App. 3d 543, 617 N.E.2d 729, appeal dismissed, 66 Ohio St. 3d 1448, 609 N.E.2d 563 (1993).

SECTION 17-13: PERSONAL LIABILITY; DEFICIENCY JUDGMENTS; MORATORIA

17-13B Action Before, After or During Foreclosure.

A creditor must be in possession of the collateral in order to be responsible for its unjustified impairment. In addition, a guarantor may not avoid liability where the guaranty agreement expressly waives the right to any defense on account of impairment of collateral. Buckeye Fed. Sav. & Loan Ass'n v. Guirlinger, 62 Ohio St. 3d 312, 581 N.E.2d 1352 (1991).

SECTION 17-15: RIGHTS AND LIABILITIES OF PURCHASERS

17-15A Title Acquired When.

Purchasers at a foreclosure sale have no vested interest in the property prior to confirmation of the sale by the trial court. As a result, the purchasers have no standing to appeal when the trial court denies confirmation (due to debtors' exercise of the right of redemption under R.C. 2329.33). Ohio Sav. Bank v. Ambrose, 56 Ohio St. 3d 53, 563 N.E.2d 1388 (1990).

17-15D Liability for Purchase Price; Defects in Title.

When the successful bidder at a foreclosure sale defaults and is made a party to the action, and the property is sold at a second sale for a lower price, the first purchaser can be held liable for the deficiency only if he was advised that the second sale was at his risk. Notice must be given that he will be held responsible for any deficiency. First Nat'l Bank of Southeastern Ohio v. Gaydoc, 68 Ohio Misc. 2d 36 (1994).

DIVISION 17-2: PARTIES; PROCEDURE

SECTION 17-21: PARTIES GENERALLY

17-21C Necessary Parties.

Foreclosure of senior mortgage terminates the right of possession of a lessee who also had an unrecorded executory contract to purchase the property. Lessee was not a necessary party to the foreclosure action. A vendee, however, is a necessary party. Where the mortgagee-purchaser had notice of the equitable rights of the vendee under the executory contract, those rights are not cut off by the foreclosure. Accordingly, the equity of redemption of the vendee survives and remains a burden on the title. Hembree v. Mid-America Fed. Sav. & Loan Ass'n, 64 Ohio App. 3d 144, 580 N.E.2d 1103 (1989).

17-21D Omission of Lien Holder or Owner.

Foreclosure of senior mortgage terminates the right of possession of a lessee who also had an unrecorded executory contract to purchase the property. Lessee was not a necessary party to the foreclosure action. A vendee, however, is a necessary party. Where the mortgagee-purchaser had notice of the equitable rights of the vendee under the executory contract, those rights are not cut off by the foreclosure. Accordingly, the equity of redemption of the vendee survives and remains a burden on the title. Hembree v. Mid-America Fed. Sav. & Loan Ass'n, 64 Ohio App. 3d 144, 580 N.E.2d 1103 (1989).

The holder of the senior mortgage is not a necessary party to a foreclosure action by a junior lienholder. However, the trial court abused its discretion in ordering the release and satisfaction of the senior mortgagee's interest in the property, where the senior mortgagee was not a party to the action. Society Bank & Trust Co. v. Zigterman, 82 Ohio App. 3d 124, 611 N.E.2d 477 (1992).

17-21K Pleading Generally.

Civil Rule 11 amended without material change as to the statement in the Parent Volume. (As eff. 7-1-94.)

SECTION 17-23: GOVERNMENT AS PARTY DEFENDANT

17-23A United States.

28 U.S.C. § 2410(c) amended to add the following sentence at the end of the subsection: "In any case where the United States is a bidder at the judicial sale, it may credit the amount determined to be due it against the amount it bids at such sales." (As eff. 11-29-90.)

SECTION 17-26: NOTICE; TIME AND PLACE OF SALE

17-26A Notice of Sale.

In Record Pub'g Co. v. Kainrad, 49 Ohio St. 3d 296, 551 N.E.2d 1286 (1990), the Ohio Supreme Court held that: (1) a legal newspaper, published once each week, is not a "daily" law journal for purposes of R.C. 2701.09; (2) if a county has a daily law journal, the judges of the courts of record in that county (excluding the judges of the court of appeals) are required to designate that journal as the place where all court calendars will be published; (3) if a county does not have a daily law journal, the judges of the courts of record have the inherent power to designate where their own calendars will be published; (4) the judges of the courts of record do not have the authority to designate a specific publication to be the exclusive carrier of all legal notices; and (5) to be a "newspaper of general circulation," a publication must meet all of the requirements of R.C. 7.12, including the requirement that the publication be a type to which the general public resorts for news of passing events.

The Ohio Supreme Court's holding in *Record Publishing* was later clarified in Court Press Index, Inc. v. Deters, 56 Ohio St. 3d 140, 565 N.E.2d 532 (1990). Construing an exception in the wording of R.C. 2701.09, the court held that a daily law journal designated as the official publisher of court calendars automatically qualifies as a "newspaper of general circulation" under R.C. 7.12. *Record Publishing* was distinguished because even though the publication in question was the official publisher of court calendars, it was not a *daily* law journal, and therefore not within the exception created by R.C. 2701.09.

A further clarification was made in Daily Reporter v. Franklin Cty. Ct. of Common Pleas, 56 Ohio St. 3d 145, 565 N.E.2d 536 (1990). In *Daily Reporter,* the publication was a daily law journal and was the designated publisher of court calendars, therefore qualifying as a "newspaper of general circulation" under the exception described in *Court Press Index.* Nevertheless, the Franklin County Court of Common Pleas had designated a different newspaper for the publication of notices of foreclosure sales. The Supreme Court held that R.C. 2329.26, which permits a court to designate the newspaper in which notices of sale are to be published, prevails over and is an exception to the general requirements of R.C. 7.12. Thus, while R.C. 7.12 will not permit the local courts to designate a single newspaper as the exclusive publisher of *all* legal notices, R.C. 2329.26 will allow the courts to establish an exclusive publisher of *judicial sale notices.*

Notice only by publication to a party to a foreclosure sale or to a person having an interest therein is insufficient to satisfy due process when the address of that party or interested person is known or easily ascertainable. In this action, the property was sold at public auction to Jerry Maxwell, but Maxwell failed to produce the purchase price. Maxwell was given notice of the time, date and location of a second sheriff's sale, but the property did not sell at the second sale. A third sale was held, but no specific notice of the time, date and location of sale was given to Maxwell; the only notice was the publication of the sale. In a subsequent attempt to enforce the forfeiture of the deposit made by Maxwell at the initial sale, the court held that Maxwell was deprived of due process. Central Trust Co. v. Jensen, 67 Ohio St. 3d 140, 662 N.E.2d 1171 (1993).

SECTION 17-28: CONFIRMATION AND OTHER ORDERS OF COURT

17-28A Necessity and Effect of Confirmation.

Confirmation of judicial sale properly vacated where mortgagors filed petition in bankruptcy after judicial sale but prior to the entry of confirmation. However, vacation of the sheriff's sale was not required because purchaser-mortgagee can seek relief through the bankruptcy court. Huntington Nat'l Bank v. Muraco, 70 Ohio App. 3d 96, 590 N.E.2d 420 (1990).

17-28B Refusal of Confirmation; Ordering Resale.

Purchasers at a foreclosure sale have no vested interest in the property prior to confirmation of the sale by the trial court. As a result, the purchasers have no standing to appeal when the trial court denies confirmation (due to debtors' exercise of the right of redemption under R.C. 2329.33). Ohio Sav. Bank v. Ambrose, 56 Ohio St. 3d 53, 563 N.E.2d 1388 (1990).

DIVISION 17-3: BANKRUPTCY

SECTION 17-31: GENERALLY

17-31A Effect of Discharge.

The first sentence under "Law in General," page 708 in the Parent Volume, should be corrected to read as follows (adding the word "not"): "Unless the court orders otherwise, any property scheduled and not otherwise administered at the time of the closing of a case is abandoned to the debtor."
11 U.S.C. § 554.

17-31C After-acquired Property.

When the debtors failed to obtain confirmation of their proposed reorganization plan, and the bankruptcy was dismissed, federal law no longer controlled. Accordingly, state law determines the rights and duties of debtors and creditors relating to the after-acquired property (crops planted after the filing of the bankruptcy). Production Credit Ass'n. v. Hedges, 87 Ohio App. 3d 207, 621 N.E.2d 1360 (1993), mot. overruled, 67 Ohio St. 3d 1467, 619 N.E.2d 701 (1993).

17-31D Provable Debts.

11 U.S.C. § 101(4) renumbered as § 101(5) but otherwise unchanged as to the material quoted in the Parent Volume. (As eff. 10-22-94.)

17-31E Excepted Debts.

11 U.S.C. § 523 has been amended to provide that the debtor is not discharged from a debt for tax or customs duty; for a debt to the extent it was obtained by false pretenses, false representation or fraud; for a debt for consumer debts to a single creditor aggregating more than $1,000 for luxury goods or services incurred within sixty days before the order for relief, or cash advances of consumer credit aggregating more than $1,000 obtained within 60 days of the order for relief; or for a debt neither listed nor scheduled unless the creditor has notice or actual knowledge of the case in time to file the claim; or for a claim

based on fraud or defalcation while acting in a fiduciary capacity, or embezzlement or larceny; or for a claim for alimony or child support or maintenance and support or otherwise incurred in connection with a separation agreement or divorce decree (with some limitations); or for willful or malicious injury; or for a fine, penalty or forfeiture; or for an educational benefit overpayment or loan made, insured or guaranteed by a governmental unit or nonprofit institution or for an obligation to repay funds received as an educa-tional benefit, scholarship or stipend; or for death or personal injury resulting from driving while intoxicated; or for a debt arising from fraud or defalcation while acting in a fiduciary capacity with respect to any depository institution or insured credit union; or for malicious or reckless failure to fulfill any commit-ment by the debtor to a Federal depository institution's regulatory agency to maintain the capital of an insured depository institution; or from a debt incurred for payment of federal taxes; or for condominium or similar membership institution fees incurred after filing bankruptcy but before surrendering the property. (As eff. 11-29-90 and 10-22-94.)

17-31F Lease and Executory Contracts.

The reference in the Parent Volume to 11 U.S.C. § 365(2) should be to 11 U.S.C. § 365(a).

DIVISION 17-4: OTHER CLASSES OF PROCEEDINGS

SECTION 17-41: EXECUTION SALE

17-41B Interests Subject to Execution Sale.

R.C. 2329.66 amended to provide as follows:

"(A) Every person who is domiciled in this state may hold property exempt from execution, garnishment, attachment, or sale to satisfy a judgment or order, as follows:

"(1)(a) In the case of a judgment or order regarding money owed for health care services rendered or health care supplies provided to the person or a dependent of the person, one parcel or item of real or personal property that the person or a dependent of the person uses as a residence. Division (A)(1)(a) of this section does not preclude, affect, or invalidate the creation under this chapter of a judgment lien upon the executed property but only delays the enforcement of the lien until the property is sold or otherwise transferred by the owner or in accordance with other applicable laws to a person or entity other than the surviving spouse or surviving minor children of the judgment debtor. Every person who is domiciled in this state may hold exempt from a judgment lien created pursuant to division (A)(1)(a) of this section his interest, not to exceed five thousand dollars, in the exempted property.

"(b) In the case of all other judgments and orders, the person's interest, not to exceed five thousand dollars, in one parcel or item of real or personal property that the person or a dependent of the person uses as a residence.

"(2)(a) In the case of a judgment or order regarding money owed for health care services rendered or health care supplies provided to the person or a dependent of the person, one motor vehicle;

"(b) In the case of all other judgments and orders, the person's interest, not to exceed one thousand dollars, in one motor vehicle.

"(3) The person's interest, not to exceed two hundred dollars in any particular item, in wearing apparel, beds, and bedding, and the person's interest, not to exceed three hundred dollars in each item, in one cooking unit and one refrigerator or other food preservation unit;

"(4)(a) The person's interest, not to exceed four hundred dollars, in cash on hand, money due and payable, money to become due within ninety days, tax refunds, and money on deposit with a bank, savings and loan association, credit union, public utility, landlord, or other person. This division applies only in bankruptcy proceedings. This exemption may include the portion of personal earnings that is not exempt under division (A)(13) of this section.

"(b) Subject to division (A)(4)(d) of this section, the person's interest, not to exceed two hundred dollars in any particular item, in household furnishings, household goods, appliances, books, animals, crops, musical instruments, firearms, and hunting and fishing equipment, that are held primarily for the personal, family, or household use of the person.

"(c) Subject to division (A)(4)(d) of this section, the person's interest in one or more items of jewelry, not to exceed four hundred dollars in one item of jewelry and not to exceed two hundred dollars in every other item of jewelry.

"(d) Divisions (A)(4)(b) and (c) of this section do not include items of personal property listed in division (A)(3) of this section.

"If the person does not claim an exemption under division (A)(1) of this section, the total exemption claimed under division (A)(4)(b) of this section shall be added to the total exemption claimed under division (A)(4)(c) of this section, and the total shall not exceed two thousand dollars. If the person claims an exemption under division (A)(2) of this section, the total exception claimed under division (A)(4)(b) of this section shall be added to the total exemption claimed under division (A)(4)(c) of this section, and the total shall not exceed one thousand five hundred dollars.

"(5) The person's interest, not to exceed an aggregate of seven hundred fifty dollars, in all implements, professional books, or tools of his profession, trade, or business, including agriculture;

"(6)(a) The person's interest in a beneficiary fund set apart, appropriated, or paid by a benevolent association or society, as exempted by section 2329.63 of the Revised Code;

143

"(b) The person's interest in contracts of life or endowment insurance or annuities, as exempted by section 3911.10 of the Revised Code;

"(c) The person's interest in a policy of group insurance or the proceeds of a policy of group insurance, as exempted by section 3917.05 of the Revised Code.

"(d) The person's interest in money, benefits, charity, relief, or aid to be paid, provided, or rendered by a fraternal benefit society, as exempted by section 3921.18 of the Revised Code;

"(e) The person's interest in the portion of benefits under policies of sickness and accident insurance and in lump sum payments for dismemberment and other losses insured under those policies, as exempted by section 3923.19 of the Revised Code.

"(7) The person's professionally prescribed or medically necessary health aids;

"(8) The person's interest in a burial lot, including, but not limited to, exemptions under section 517.09 or section 1721.07 of the Revised Code;

"(9) The person's interest in the following:

"(a) Moneys paid or payable for living maintenance or rights, as exempted by section 3304.19 of the Revised Code;

"(b) Worker's compensation, as exempted by section 4123.67 of the Revised Code;

"(c) Unemployment compensation benefits, as exempted by section 4141.32 of the Revised Code.

"(d) Aid to dependent children payments, as exempted by section 5107.12 of the Revised Code.

"(e) General assistance payments, as exempted by section 5113.03 of the Revised Code.

"(f) Disability assistance payments, as exempted by section 5115.07 of the Revised Code.

"(10)(a) Except in cases in which the person was convicted of or pleaded guilty to a violation of section 2921.41 of the Revised Code and in which an order for the withholding of restitution from payments was issued under division (C)(2)(b) of that section, and only to the extent provided in the order, and except as provided in sections 3105.171, 3105.63, 3111.23 and 3113.21 of the Revised Code, the person's right to a pension, benefit, annuity, retirement allowance, or accumulated contributions, the person's right to a participant account in any deferred compensation program offered by the Ohio public employees deferred compensation board, a government unit, or a municipal corporation, or the person's other accrued or accruing rights, as exempted by sections 145.56, 145.75, 146.13, 742.47, 3307.71, 3309.66, or 5505.22 of the Revised Code, and the person's right to benefits from the policemen and firemen's death benefit fund;

"(b) Except as provided in sections 3111.23 and 3113.21 of the Revised Code, the person's right to receive a payment under any pension, annuity, or similar

144

plan or contract, not including a payment from a stock bonus or profit-sharing plan or a payment included in division (A)(6)(b) or (10)(a) of this section, on account of illness, disability, death, age, or length of service, to the extent reasonably necessary for the support of the person and any of his dependents, except if all the following apply:

"(i) The plan or contract was established by or under the auspices of an insider that employed the person at the time his rights under the plan or contract arose.

"(ii) The payment is on account of age or length of service.

"(iii) The plan or contract is not qualified under the "Internal Revenue Code of 1986," 100 Stat. 2085, 26 U.S.C. 1, as amended.

"(c) Except for any portion of the assets that were deposited for the purpose of evading the payment of any debt and except as provided in sections 3111.23 and 3113.21 of the Revised Code, the person's right in the assets held in, or to receive any payment under, any individual retirement account, individual retirement annuity, or Keogh or "H.R. 10" plan that provides benefits by reason of illness, disability, death, or age, to the extent reasonably necessary for the support of the person and any of his dependents.

"(11) The person's right to receive spousal support, child support, an allowance, or other maintenance to the extent reasonably necessary for the support of the person and any of his dependents;

"(12) The person's right to receive, or moneys received during the preceding twelve calendar months from, any of the following:

"(a) An award of reparations under sections 2743.51 to 2743.72 of the Revised Code, to the extent exempted by division (D) of section 2743.66 of the Revised Code;

"(b) A payment on account of the wrongful death of an individual of whom the person was a dependent on the date of the individual's death, to the extent reasonably necessary for the support of the person and any of his dependents;

"(c) A payment, not to exceed five thousand dollars, on account of personal bodily injury, not including pain and suffering or compensation for actual pecuniary loss, of the person or an individual for whom the person is a dependent;

"(d) A payment in compensation for loss of future earnings of the person or an individual of whom the person is or was a dependent, to the extent reasonably necessary for the support of the debtor and any of his dependents.

"(13) Except as provided in sections 3111.23 and 3113.21 of the Revised Code, personal earnings of the person owed to him for services rendered within thirty days before the issuing of an attachment of other process, the rendition of a judgment, or the making of an order, under which the attempt may be made to subject those earnings to the payment of a debt, damage, fine, or amercement, in an amount equal to:

"(a) In the case of a judgment or order regarding money owed for health care services rendered or health care supplies provided to the person or a dependent of the person, the greater of the following amounts:

"(i) If paid weekly, thirty times the current federal minimum hourly wage; if paid biweekly, sixty times the current federal minimum hourly wage; if paid semimonthly, sixty-five times the current federal minimum hourly wage; or if paid monthly, one hundred thirty times the current federal minimum hourly wage that is in effect at the time the earnings are payable, as prescribed by the "Fair Labor Standards Act of 1938," 52 Stat. 1060, 29 U.S.C. 206(a)(1), as amended;

"(ii) Eighty-eight per cent of the disposable earnings owed to the person.

"(b) In the case of all other judgments and orders, the greater of the following amounts:

"(i) The amount specified in division (A)(13)(a)(i) of this section;

"(ii) Seventy-five per cent of the disposable earnings owed to the person.

"(14) The person's right in specific partnership property, as exempted by division (B)(3) of section 1775.24 of the Revised Code;

"(15) A seal and official register of a notary public, as exempted by section 147.04 of the Revised Code;

"(16) The person's interest in a tuition credit or a payment under section 3334.09 of the Revised Code pursuant to a tuition credit contract, as exempted by section 3334.15 of the Revised Code.

"(17) Any other property that is specifically exempted from execution, attachment, garnishment, or sale by federal statutes other than the "Bankruptcy Reform Act of 1978," 92 Stat. 2549, 11 U.S.C.A. 101, as amended;

"(18) The person's interest, not to exceed four hundred dollars, in any property, except that this division applies only in bankruptcy proceedings.

"(B) As used in this section:

"(1) "Disposable earnings" means net earnings after the garnishee has made deductions required by law, excluding the deductions ordered pursuant to section 3111.23 or section 3113.21 of the Revised Code.

"(2) "Insider" means:

"(a) If the person who claims an exemption is an individual, a relative of the individual, a relative of a general partner of the individual, a partnership in which the individual is a general partner, a general partner of the individual, or a corporation of which the individual is a director, officer, or in control;

"(b) If the person who claims an exemption is a corporation, a director or officer of the corporation; a person in control of the corporation; a partnership in which the corporation is a general partner; a general partner of the corporation; or a relative of a general partner, director, officer, or person in control of the corporation;

"(c) If the person who claims an exemption is a partnership, a general partner in the partnership; a general partner of the partnership; a person in control of the partnership; a partnership in which the partnership is a general partner; or a relative in, a general partner of, or a person in control of the partnership;

"(d) An entity or person to which or whom any of the following apply:

"(i) The entity directly or indirectly owns, controls, or holds with power to vote, twenty per cent or more of the outstanding voting securities of the person who claims an exemption, unless the entity holds the securities in a fiduciary or agency capacity without sole discretionary power to vote the securities or holds the securities solely to secure to debt and the entity has not in fact exercised the power to vote.

"(ii) The entity is a corporation, twenty per cent or more ob whose outstanding voting securities are directly or indirectly owned, controlled, or held with power to vote, by the person who claims an exemption, or by an entity to which division (B)(2)(d)(i) of this section applies.

"(iii) A person whose business is operated under a lease or operating agreement by the person who claims an exemption, or a person substantially all of whose business is operated under an operating agreement with the person who claims an exemption.

"(iv) The entity operates the business or all or substantially all of the property of the person who claims an exemption under a lease or operating agreement.

"(e) An insider, as otherwise defined in this section, of a person or entity to which division (B)(2)(d)(i), (ii), (iii), or (iv) of this section applies, as if the person or entity were a person who claims an exemption.

"(f) A managing agent of the person who claims an exemption.

"(3) "Participant account" has the same meaning as in section 145.71 of the Revised Code.

"(4) "Government unit" has the same meaning as in section 145.74 of the Revised Code.

"(C) For purposes of this section, "interest" shall be determined as follows:

"(1) In bankruptcy proceedings, as of the date a petition is filed with the bankruptcy court commencing a case under Title 11 of the United States Code;

"(2) In all cases other than bankruptcy proceedings, as of the date of an appraisal, if necessary under section 2329.68 of the Revised Code, or the issuance of a writ of execution.

"An interest, as determined under division (C)(1) or (2) of this section, shall not include the amount of any lien otherwise valid pursuant to section 2329.661 of the Revised Code." (As eff. 12-31-93 and 7-1-94.)

17-41E Procedure.

R.C. 2329.091 provides the procedure for the clerk of courts to serve a notice and hearing request form on the judgment debtor, and for a hearing to be held if timely requested by the debtor. (As eff. 8-19-94.)

A law enforcement officer who levies execution on the property owned by a person other than the judgment debtor named in the writ may be held responsible for the damages suffered by the innocent third person as a consequence of the wrongful levy. Bethel v. Dunipace, 57 Ohio App. 3d 89, 566 N.E.2d 1252 (1988).

17-41G Reversal or Vacation.

Where a plaintiff obtained judgment on an account and a judgment for attorney fees, but the award of attorney fees was reversed on appeal, the reversal had the effect of vacating the judgment lien as to the attorney fees. Therefore, as of the date foreclosure was ordered, plaintiff did not hold a valid judgment lien as to the attorney fee award, even though the judgment for attorney fees was awarded again on remand. The plaintiff may reassert its judgment lien as a result of the decision on remand, but the priority of that lien will have to be redetermined. Merrill Lynch, Pierce, Fenner & Smith, Inc. v. Stark, 75 Ohio App. 3d 611, 600 N.E.2d 354, appeal after remand, 1991 Ohio App. LEXIS 4228 (Ohio Ct. App., Cuyahoga County Aug. 29, 1991), review pending, 62 Ohio St. 3d 1502, 583 N.E.2d 973, mot. denied, 65 Ohio St. 3d 1469, 603 N.E.2d 250, aff'd, 65 Ohio St. 3d 312, 603 N.E.2d 997, mot. overruled, 62 Ohio St. 3d 1494, 583 N.E.2d 966 (1992).

SECTION 17-44: RECEIVERS

17-44B Jurisdiction.

A provision in the mortgage agreement whereby the mortgagor waives his entitlement to notice of the appointment of a receiver for the mortgaged property is valid and enforceable. Manufacturers Life Ins. Co. v. Patterson, 51 Ohio App. 3d 99, 554 N.E.2d 134, appeal dismissed, 39 Ohio St. 3d 726, 534 N.E.2d 361 (1988).

When a court-appointed receiver is in control of the property, a mortgagee cannot be held liable for negligently failing to prevent deterioration of the property because the mortgagee does not maintain control over the property, the receiver is not the agent of mortgagee, and the mortgaeee has no duty to protect collateral in the receiver's possession. In re Greenleaf Apartments, Ltd., 158 Bankruptcy Reptr. 456 (U.S. Bankruptcy Ct. S.D. Ohio E.D. 1993).